Unequal Sisters

"This remarkable collection of essays challenges traditional conceptions of womanhood. Ruiz has selected highly readable interpretations of women's historical experiences as they emerge from a wide array of perspectives, including women's political standpoints, their ethnic and racial situations, sexual preferences, and class positions. Taken together the essays signal a new direction in the history of women."
—Alice Kessler-Harris, author of *Gendering Labor History*

"With over a dozen new essays, the fourth edition of *Unequal Sisters* is perhaps the strongest yet in terms of depth, breadth, and diversity of analysis. It is an exciting, vital mix of now-classic statements and cutting-edge work that brilliantly illuminates the complexities of ethnicity, race, class, region, gender, and sexuality. The anthology is undoubtedly among the very best in the field."
—Michele Mitchell, author of *Righteous Propagation: African Americans and the Politics of Racial Destiny after Reconstruction*

"This remarkable collection showcases the multiple ways in which women of color make history for themselves and others within and beyond U.S. borders. New studies combined with classic feminist writings make it an indispensable tool for advancing an inclusive women's history."
— Shirley Hune, co-author of *Asian/Pacific Islander American Women: A Historical Anthology*

"Grounded in the exploration of gender, race, class, and generational differences, this new edition of *Unequal Sisters* proves, yet again, that the field of Women's History continues to be at the forefront of our collective desire to understand the ways that women's complex pasts remain deeply relevant for all those who struggle for equality and a just society today. Without a doubt, this book is essential reading for all!"
—Suzanne Oboler, author of *Latinos and Citizenship: The Dilemma of Belonging*

With its broad, multicultural approach, *Unequal Sisters* revolutionized the field when it was first published in 1990. This fourth edition brings together essays from the previous three editions, along with new perspectives and voices, including some of the most innovative work published since the last edition. With fifteen new essays, *Unequal Sisters* continues to emphasize feminist perspectives on race, ethnicity, region, and sexuality, while placing U.S. women's history in its global context. The book also includes completely revised and updated bibliographies on women of color. A groundbreaking volume, now revised to include the best of recent scholarship, *Unequal Sisters* is an illuminating guide to a more accurate and inclusive history of women in the United States today.

Vicki L. Ruiz is Professor of History and Chicano/Latino Studies at the University of California, Irvine and Interim Dean, School of Humanities. Past president of the Organization of American Historians and the Berkshire Conference of Women's Historians, she is currently president of the American Studies Association. She is the author or editor of many works in women's history, including *American Dreaming, Global Realities* (with Donna R. Gabaccia) and *Latinas in the United States: A Historical Encyclopedia* (with Virginia Sánchez Korrol).

Ellen Carol DuBois is Professor of History at UCLA. She has published extensively on the U.S. woman suffrage movement and is the co-author, with Lynn Dumenil, of *Through Women's Eyes: An American History with Documents*.

Unequal Sisters

An Inclusive Reader in U.S. Women's History

Fourth Edition

Edited by

Vicki L. Ruiz
with Ellen Carol DuBois

Routledge
Taylor & Francis Group

NEW YORK AND LONDON

First published 1990 by Routledge
Second edition published 1994
Third edition published 2000
This edition published 2008
by Routledge
270 Madison Ave, New York, NY 10016

Simultaneously published in the UK
by Routledge
2 Park Square, Milton Park, Abingdon, Oxon OX14 4RN

Routledge is an imprint of the Taylor & Francis Group, an informa business

© 2008 Taylor & Francis

Typeset in Minion by RefineCatch limited, Bungay, Suffolk
Printed and bound in the United States of America on acid-free paper by
Sheridan Books, Inc., MI

Library of Congress Cataloging in Publication Data
Unequal sisters : an inclusive reader in U.S. women's history / edited by Vicki L. Ruiz with
    Ellen Carol DuBois.—4th ed.
        p. cm.
    Includes bibliographical references and index.
        ISBN 978–0–415–95840–0 (hardcover : alk. paper)—ISBN 978–0–415–95841–7 (pbk. : alk.
paper)   1. Women—United States—History—Cross-cultural studies.   2. Sex role—United
States—History—Cross-cultural studies.   3. Minority women—United States—History.
4. African American women—History.   I. Ruíz, Vicki.   II. DuBois, Ellen Carol, 1947—
    HQ1410.U54 2008
    305.48′800973—dc22
    2007025704

ISBN10: 0–415–95840–7 (hbk)
ISBN10: 0–415–95841–5 (pbk)

ISBN13: 978–0–415–95840–0 (hbk)
ISBN13: 978–0–415–95841–7 (pbk)

It has become commonplace to say how we approach the past has everything to do with where we are located in the present. The historian has to stand someplace to generate her questions of the past. But investigating the past is also connected to what we want from the future . . .

Ellen Carol DuBois from her intellectual autobiography, *The Last Suffragist.*

Contents

Acknowledgments

On one level, it seems incredible that twenty years ago Ellen Carol DuBois and I met at the Wingspread Conference on Graduate Training in U.S. Women's History hosted by Gerda Lerner and Kitty Sklar. *Unequal Sisters* had its genesis in a contentious session on "difference" in which I was the facilitator and Ellen, the note-taker. I thank Ellen for her piercing intellect, friendship, and collaboration. Through our work together, I have become a more astute historian and academic.

On another level, I find great satisfaction as a witness to the florescence of a more inclusive and ever-dynamic U.S. women's history. Almost three decades have passed since Estelle Freedman's very first dissertation group and I certainly didn't realize then that the incredible synergy of Antonia Castañeda, Dorothy Sue Cobble, Gayle Gullett, Gary Sue Goodman, Gail Hershatter, Emily Honig, and Joanne Meyerowitz would carry me throughout my career. And to my brilliant friend for thirty years, Valerie J. Matsumoto whose wise counsel and wicked humor continue to sustain me. I am grateful for her willingness to read my work, often at a moment's notice. Her incisive comments strengthened the introduction to this volume.

I gratefully acknowledge all past and present contributors to *Unequal Sisters*—your scholarship signifies the dramatic shifts in how we conceptualize and teach U.S. women's history. I also owe a debt to the ten anonymous reviewers whose feedback has significantly shaped the contours of this present volume—thank you for your frank criticism and constructive suggestions. Routledge editor Kimberly Guinta has been a wonderful advocate for the volume. I appreciate her patience and professionalism at every stage and I thank her assistants Brendan O'Neill and Matthew Kopel. At the production stage special thanks to Siân Findlay and Richard Willis. In addition, Nick Bravo provided vital research assistance at crucial stages of this project. There is a new "face" to *Unequal Sisters* by the acclaimed Chicano artist Malaquias Montoya. I am grateful to Malaquias and Lezlie Salkowitz-Montoya for permission to reprint this evocative image. Mil gracias!

I thank the wonderful community of feminist historians and graduate students at UC Irvine and my colleagues in Chicano/Latino Studies—Lisa García-Bedolla, Deborah Vargas, Cynthia Feliciano, and Ana Rosas. Graduate students, past and present, have made me a better scholar, teacher, and mentor. I would like to acknowledge the following Ph.D. candidates at UCI: Margie Brown-Coronel, Veronica Castillo-Muñoz, Casey Christensen, Julie Cohen, Ryan Kray, Jennifer Thigpen, and Tracy Sachtjen (now hurry up and finish your dissertations). To my "sister" Virginia who always has a plan and to Victor with love and appreciation.

Vicki L. Ruiz
September 16, 2007

Introduction to the Fourth Edition

Vicki L. Ruiz

We hope, in this volume and in the future scholarship it may encourage, to contribute to a reconcep-
tualization of American women's history, as a series of dialectical relations among and across races
and classes of women, representing diverse cultures and unequal power. This sentence signifies the
shared vision of *Unequal Sisters*, now its fourth edition. Seventeen years ago, Ellen Carol DuBois
and I were unprepared, but elated, by the reception the first volume received. Glowing reviews,
some with titles like "Sisterhood Is Problematic" and "History Emerging," indicated that we had
tapped into a desire for a U.S. women's history that reached West as well as East, interrogating
"difference" beyond a black/white paradigm. In an article on teaching, Eileen Boris generously
mentioned that *Unequal Sisters* "has relieved my students from living in the reserve room . . .[1]"
Ideas that seemed so edgy in 1990 (e.g. multiple voices) have become common place, perhaps
complacently so. In retrospect, the first edition did mark a significant shift in the field and its
impact remains gratifying and humbling.

Several junior colleagues at UC Irvine on separate occasions informed me that they had read
Unequal Sisters as undergraduates. Such revelations brought me back to my own college days at
Florida State where in 1976 I enrolled in a U.S. women's history course. Nancy Cott's *Root of
Bitterness* and Eleanor Flexner's *Century of Struggle* became my treasures.[2] Because of the
devoted mentorship I received from the course instructor Jean Gould Hales (now Bryant), I
entered graduate school at Stanford. During my senior year, she charted my progress, offering
encouragement, counsel, and much needed constructive criticism. I can state with certainty that
my life would have been very different (as a high school teacher in Florida) had it not been for
that one class and that one professor. I also pursued classes in Black Studies offered by Leanor
Boulin Johnson, then a newly-minted Ph.D. in sociology, an African American from Pasadena
teaching in the South. I became a fixture (well, maybe a nuisance) during her office hours, as she
thoughtfully took an interest, even lending me readings in Chicano Studies.

The intersectionality of race, class, and gender has always meant more than an intellectual
enterprise. Indeed, memory looms large in historical consciousness, individual and collective.
Feminist tracings of memories and silences and of daily and extraordinary experiences animate
this reader. The chapters that follow convey astute, often provocative, insights about the past
without losing the emotion and agency of those who lived it. Before turning to a definition of
inclusive, it seems appropriate to revisit the three models of American women's history as
outlined in the first edition.

From the first edition

Most of the early work on U.S. women's history paid little attention to race, and assumed instead a universal women's experience, defined in contrast to "men's" history. While a stark focus on the difference between the male and female past helped to legitimize women's history, the past it explored was usually only that of middle-class white women. In this uniracial model, the universal man of American history was replaced with the universal woman.

For instance, much of nineteenth-century women's history scholarship rests on the assumption that women's lives were lived in a separate domestic women's "sphere," on which basis they were able to claim a kind of social power distinct from that of men. This concept grew out of the historical experience of white, leisured women. And despite historians' earnest efforts to include less privileged women—notably female slaves and immigrant wives—the narrative line of women's history could not help but marginalize them. These other histories came across either as exotic or deviant, providing no clue to the larger history of American womanhood. In this uniracial model, race and gender cannot be brought into the same theoretical field. White women appear "raceless," their historical experiences determined solely by gender. By contrast, the distinct historical experiences of women of color, to the degree that they are acknowledged, are credited solely to race. This uniracial framework leads women's historians, eager to expand their range, right into the trap of "women-and-minorities," a formula that accentuates rather than remedies the invisibility of women of color.

While the notion of a universal female past focuses on power relations between men and women, scholarship has begun to appear that explores power relations *between women*—of different races, classes, and cultures. Slave owner and slave, mistress and maid, reformer and immigrant, and social worker and client are some of the many relationships of inequality that run through women's history. When focused on questions of race, we term this sort of approach "biracial." Scholarship in this biracial mode benefits from a paradigm for examining power, not only between men and women, but also within women's history itself. This biracial approach shatters the notion of a universal sisterhood. Simply stated, it permits feminist historians to discard celebration for confrontation, and allows them to explore the dynamics through which women have oppressed other women.

While the biracial approach has effectively broken through the notion of a universal female experience, it has its limits. The framework itself leads the historian to focus her examination on the relation between a powerful group, almost always white women, and minority women, the varieties of whose experiences are too often obscured. In other words, the historical emphasis is on white power, and women of color have to compete for the role of "other." The historical testimonies of women of color thus tend to be compacted into a single voice. The biracial framework has helped create a situation in which the demand for greater understanding of race can be reduced to a black-and-white analysis—literally and figuratively.

Much of the uniracial framework in women's history is closely associated with the Northeast; the biracial model has its own regional bias, and seems best to describe the Southeast. For the possibilities of describing a richer palette for painting women's history, we turn to the West. Western women's historians are taking the lead in moving beyond biracialism, if only because the historical experiences of the region require a multifaceted approach. Given the confluence of many cultures and races in this region—Native American, Mexican, Asian, black, and Anglo—grappling with race at all requires a framework that has more than two positions. Nor is white history always center stage. Even the term "the West" reflects only one of several historical perspectives; the Anglo "West" is also the Mexican "North," the Native American "homeland," and the Asian "East." Nor are the possibilities for such an approach limited to one region. Even in areas that seem racially homogeneous or in which the struggle between two races understandably preoccupies historians, there are other peoples and positions to consider.

To describe this third framework, the one we seek to elaborate in *Unequal Sisters*, we use the term *multicultural*. We choose the term *multicultural* over *multiracial* because we seek to focus on the interplay of many races and cultures, because we acknowledge that not all white women's histories can be categorized under one label, and because we seek to suggest that the term *race* needs to be theorized rather than assumed. As a framework for women's history, a multicultural approach poses a variety of challenges to scholarship. Many groups of women, rarely explored or incorporated into women's history, await further study. There are distinctions to note and comparisons to be made among different groups of women with respect to family life, forms of work, definitions of womanhood, sources of power, and bonds among women. The various forms of white domination must be examined for their impact on women's history: the dispossession of Mexican land after 1848; the genocide and relocation of Native Americans; the legal exclusion of Asian Americans. Even slavery takes on multiple meanings for women's history through a multicultural lens. Finally, a multicultural approach to women's history invites the study of cultural contact and transformation, so important in understanding the development of family patterns, child-rearing practices, sexuality, and other cultural arenas crucial to women's history concerns.

In U.S. history, race has coincided closely with class. The segmentation of people of color into lower-echelon industrial, service, and agricultural jobs has served to blunt their opportunities for economic mobility. The multicultural framework allows for an analysis that takes class into account not as a separate entity, but as an intertwined component of both race and gender. The history of women cannot be studied without considering both race and class. Many of the essays in this volume provide insight into the structural and ideological components of class as it interplays with race and gender in the formations of women's consciousness.

At the risk of overreaching, it does seem that a multicultural approach, one in which many pasts can be explored simultaneously, may be the only way to organize a genuinely national, truly inclusive history of women.

Yes, the last sentence is audaciously naïve. Multiculturalism has admittedly become "a bit dated, a battered lightening rod of contested meanings."[3] More to the point, transgendered and transnational lives do not fit within a nationality-based frame. A more supple descriptor seems in order, to encompass more fully the multivalent dimensions of a U.S. women's history in the twenty-first century.

I use the term *inclusive* as this elastic, purposefully amorphous, adjective to take into account the array of historical actors, methodologies, perspectives, and possibilities featured in this volume. The discipline of history at a basic level is inclusive given the diversity of evidence on which historians draw. As Donna R. Gabaccia succinctly explains: "Historians cannot create their own data to answer their research questions. They can only pose questions about which surviving newspapers, books, government records, autobiographies, letters, diaries, statistics, graphic images, and material culture (to name just a few possibilities) provide information . . ."[4] Through a process of sifting, interpreting, and with a dash of serendipity, historians seek to make sense of the past, to understand historical actors within the possibilities and constraints of their time and circumstance.

Sometimes sources talk back to the scholar. Oral interviews, whether conducted by the author or housed in the archive, convey vibrant personalizations of the past, creating immediate, even intimate, connections between narrators and readers. "The right to remember" (to quote renowned writer Cherríe Moraga) is a political act, one that counters an erasure from the historical record.[5]

Remembering the narratives of women of color has been the cornerstone to every edition of *Unequal Sisters*. The fourth edition is no exception. Most of the chapters (well over thirty) address the ways in which women of color have made history in their own lives and in the lives of others. Their discursive webs of political, social, economic, and cultural relations provide a fuller recounting of U.S. history. Featuring fifteen new chapters, twelve of which were published after 2000 and eight since 2004, this edition seeks to strike a balance between classic feminist works that pursued such subjects as the claiming of public space within the nation-state to more recent pieces preoccupied with the claiming of citizenship across transnational borders. I encourage readers to engage the essays, to scour the notes, identifying the archival and ethnographic scaffolding of the scholarly argument. The chapters are organized chronologically and thematically. The ten sign posts that follow alert readers to the linkages across specific sets of texts. They present a few starting points for comparison, conversation, and debate.

Situating Stories. A theoretical mapping of "difference" connects the first three essays. Synthesizing a sizeable historiography, Estelle B. Freedman interrogates the impact of race and sexuality in the evolution of American feminism. For Nan Alamilla Boyd, the hidden scripts of lesbian and transgendered identities call for more permeable constructs of gender as a category of analysis. Tessie Liu underscores the importance of race and racial metaphors in "defining hierarchies and constituting boundaries of privilege." What is the difference between power and empowerment? Can one separate out race, class, and sexuality in deciphering gendered relations of power?

Of Slavery and Servitude. These four chapters focus on the centrality of gender in understanding a past predicated on bonded labor. James F. Brooks and Miroslava Chávez-García examine the contours of American Indian servitude in the Southwest; Brooks through a sweeping study of Indian-Hispanic relations in New Mexico, and Chávez-García through a single California murder case. With fresh insights on chattel slavery in the South, Jennifer Morgan and Stephanie M. H. Camp poignantly reconstruct the daily lives of enslaved African women. In particular, how does Jennifer Morgan complicate our understanding of "resistance" and "agency?" Did constellations of choice exist for women held in bondage across race and region?

Spheres of Influence. While much has been written about the separate spheres for nineteenth-century men and women (usually privileged and white), the following three essays disrupt the familiar narrative of home-bound women and public men. Jeanne Boydston clearly delineates the impact of industrialization on working-class women as they sought to sustain their families combining traditional household labor with participation in the informal economy. In contrast, Alice Fahs notes the gendered dimensions of literary production and memory, a female sensibility within a northern public imagination while Elsa Barkley Brown emphasizes the vital political activism among African American women in the South during Reconstruction. In what ways could women transcend conventions of domesticity and for what ends?

Class Acts and Color Lines. These three works lend insight into what Paige Raibmon refers to as "the practice of everyday colonialism," whether learning Latin at a Cherokee school, selling baskets to tourists, or engaging in racial uplift. Devon Mihesuah brings out the embedded contradictions of class and color at the Cherokee Female Seminary while Paige Raibmon focuses on how native peoples of the Pacific Northwest confronted inequality at every turn. Comparing black and white social reformers, Linda Gordon interprets the intricate class dynamics among African American women arguing that "there was less distance between helper and helped" than between EuroAmerican social workers and European immigrants. In what ways have race and class acted upon each other in shaping women's relations with one another?

Public Rights/Private Spheres. The following five chapters complicate our understanding of women's rights. Judy Yung teases out the transnational connections between women in China and in U.S. Chinatowns. Ellen Carol DuBois profiles Harriot Stanton Blatch, who helped forge a more militant suffrage movement, while Evelyn Brooks Higginbotham demonstrates how the Nineteenth Amendment strengthened African American women's political presence. Legal constructions of race have shaped the American social fabric and Peggy Pascoe cogently explains the strands of modern racial ideologies through gendered judgments. Centering on the social constructions of sexuality, Joanne J. Meyerowitz recounts the lives of young women who found shelter, love, and privacy in Chicago's rooming house district. What are the tools or frames scholars use to uncover the contours of historical agency, especially regarding intimacy?

Cultural Coalescence. In what ways have gender, generation, and sexuality mattered within immigrant families? Donna R. Gabaccia and I counter a standard "one size fits all" narrative of assimilation, taking into account "how the many pluralities—the very specific historical, economic, regional, and cultural contexts of immigrant lives—encourage interaction, connection, and a sense of belonging." One could argue that a quest to belong pervades the American consumerscape. Indeed, Kathy Peiss reveals the beauty industry's aggressive marketing of physical perfection as a key to women's well-being and popularity. Valerie J. Matsumoto and I explore how racial/ethnic adolescents during the 1930s embraced U.S. popular culture as means to achieve personal autonomy.

Cartographies of Community. As the following essays point out, "community" has infinite definitions; it can refer to a physical place, a group of like-minded individuals, or even a metaphorical imaginary. Virginia Sánchez Korrol features several religious women who, in the process of founding of a Catholic settlement house and an evangelical church, built community among Puerto Ricans in New York. Annelise Orleck recounts how "housewife activists" of the Depression created a national consumers' network while Devra Weber chronicles community through trade unions in her essay on *mexicana* farmworkers. Evelyn Nakano Glenn offers a macro-level analysis of racial/ethnic women's labor. In her words: "Race and gender emerge as socially constructed, interlocking systems that shape the material conditions, identities, and consciousness of all women."

Memory and History. Unequal Sisters considers the dialectic between reminiscence and reticence as well as the process by which the past becomes memory and then memory becomes history. The southern writer and anti-racist reformer Katherine DuPre Lumpkin becomes a haunting presence as Jacquelyn Dowd Hall unravels in unexpected ways "the power of 'open secrets.' " Similarly, Judy Tzu-Chun Wu breathes life into her biography of Dr. Margaret Chung, a woman who invented and reinvented herself in her quest for influence and acceptance. Drawing on oral histories, Sherrie Tucker presents glimpses into the daily lives of women jazz musicians, with both black and white women crossing the color line for an opportunity to play. By what means do feminist biographers gain access to and reveal the secrets of their subjects, especially sexual orientation?

Politics of Representation. The suburban housewife remains the dominant motif of the 1950s. Daniel Horowitz argues that Betty Friedan "did not write *The Feminine Mystique* simply because she was an unhappy housewife," but was influenced by her past as a union journalist. Women unable to conceive found no place to hide from the domestic ideal, as Elaine Tyler May demonstrates in her account of women and infertility. Conversely, Laila Haidrarali conveys the lives of African American women who were professional models, literally posed as glamorous workers and housewives. Of course, the fifties signaled a burgeoning civil rights movement and Cynthia Griggs Fleming profiles Ruby Doris Smith Robinson, a young southern leader who combined family and social justice. Indeed, how have women negotiated idealized femininities?

Sin Fronteras. A transnational turn in U.S. women's history offers fresh directions for future scholarship. The final three chapters are not triumphal codas marking women's progress, but compelling narratives of rupture and loss, leavened with hopeful calls for collective action. Catherine Ceniza Choy recounts a trans-pacific vision of social justice among Filipina activists in the United States while Alicia Schmidt Camacho illuminates "how women's testimonies reveal a distinct female imaginary operating in the border space, one that moves with ambivalence and caution through competing claims of family, class, and nation in the transnational arena." Lara Deeb infuses a hint of optimism in her essay on Islamic and secular feminists in Lebanon and their Arab American counterparts.

Beyond the lens of her research, Deeb powerfully conveys the *ánimo* (or spirit) necessary for transnational feminist coalitions:

> Building alliances within our communities sometimes comes down to language, sometimes it amounts to listening to what is being said in the spaces around and between the words; above all, it is about appreciating the complementarity of the various social, political, and economic justices in which we are all engaged on a daily basis.

Unequal Sisters seeks to promote critical dialogues beyond the classroom. As feminist intellectuals, our obligations do not end at the campus parking lot. Or as Valerie J. Matsumoto eloquently stated: "Perhaps scholars should be reminded that we, no less than those we study, are actors in history, making choices that affect the lives of others."[6]

Notes

1. Philomena Mariani, "Sisterhood is Problematic: Living in a Sex Divided," *The Village Voice*, August 21, 1990: 69; Beverly Chico, "History Emerging," *The Bloomsbury Review* (April/May 1991); Eileen Boris, "Developments in the Teaching of U.S. Women's History," *Perspectives* (April 1996): 26.
2. Nancy F. Cott, *Root of Bitterness: Documents of the Social History of American Women* (New York: Dutton, 1972); Eleanor Flexner, *Century of Struggle: The Women's Rights Movement in the United States* (New York: Atheneum, 1972).
3. Eileen Boris, Susan J. Kleinberg, and Vicki L. Ruiz, "Introduction," in *The Practice of U.S. Women's History: Dialogues, Narratives, and Intersections* (New Brunswick, N.J. Rutgers University Press, 2007).
4. Donna R. Gabaccia, "Today's Immigration Policy Debates: Do We Need a Little History?," *Migration Information Source*, a web publication of Migration Policy Institute (November 2006) http://www.migrationinformation.org/Feature/display.cfm?id=488
5. "Keynote Lecture: Cherríe Moraga," UCI Gender Education Series (February 22, 2007). Note: The struggle against invisibility may seem like an old issue, but it persists. A recent best-selling text in U.S. women's history elides the historical presence of Latinas and Asian American women. See Gail Collins, *America's Women: Four Hundred Years of Dolls, Drudges, Helpmates, and Heroines* (New York: William Morrow, 2003).
6. Valerie J. Matsumoto, *Farming the Home Place: A Japanese American Community in California, 1919–1982* (Ithaca: Cornell University Press, 1993), 224.

1

Race and the Politics of Identity in U.S. Feminism

Estelle B. Freedman

The investigation of the rights of slaves has led me to a better understanding of my own.

— ANGELINA GRIMKÉ, UNITED STATES, 1838

Feminism is the political theory and practice that struggles to free all women. . . . Anything less than this vision of total freedom is not feminism, but merely female self-aggrandizement.

— BARBARA SMITH, UNITED STATES, 1979

In the spring of 1920 a group of African American women met to discuss how they could integrate white organizations. In the words of Lugenia Burns Hope, black women wanted to "stand side by side with women of the white race and work for full emancipation of all women." For such interracial cooperation to take place in the United States at this time would be highly unusual. American society divided the world into black and white, whether in neighborhoods, schools, churches, or cemeteries. So did the U.S. women's movement, despite its founding by antislavery activists. For a generation African American women had tried unsuccessfully to gain white women's support for their efforts to end racial hatred and its most virulent act, the murder of innocent blacks by lynching. Now a small opening appeared. A group of southern white women (YWCA) invited four distinguished African American women to speak to their conference in Memphis, Tennessee, in October 1920.

On the last day of the Memphis conference, North Carolina educator Charlotte Hawkins Brown reached across a wide chasm of racial distrust to deliver a talk that gave white women a firsthand account of the daily insults borne by African Americans. On the train ride to Memphis, Brown revealed, a dozen white men had forced her to leave her seat in the overnight sleeping car and ride in the segregated day coach for blacks only. Humiliated and angry, she told the audience that "the thing that grieved me most is that there were women in the car and there wasn't a dissenting voice." She asked the white women that day to put themselves in her place, to "just be colored for a few minutes." In closing her speech about the terrors of lynching and the daily insults to black womanhood, Brown reminded her white, Christian audience that "in the final analysis" they would all reach out a hand to the same God, "but I know that the dear Lord will not receive it if you are crushing me beneath your feet."[1]

In her speech that day Charlotte Hawkins Brown illustrated two critical themes in women's history: the power of personal testimony to reach across social boundaries and the role of

1

women of color in expanding the feminist agenda. By revealing her experience of both racial insult and racial pride, Brown forced white women to think outside their own experience, to reconceptualize womanhood as a more complicated entity, and to build a politics of coalition across the racial divide. Their dialogue provided an opportunity to "pivot the center," that is, to learn from the experience of others how to question the dominant culture.[2] By doing so, women's movements can incorporate difference, not merely for the sake of inclusion or diversity but also to change their fundamental goals for social justice.

Questioning the dominant meaning of womanhood can occur in any culture where racial or class divisions complicate feminism. The particularly troubled history of race relations in the United States has compelled women's movements to grapple with the complexities of women's identities. Race became central to national politics during the same period that feminism called for women's rights. While similar issues arose in Europe, until well into the twentieth century race remained largely at the distance of empire. In the United States, in contrast, the colonized lived among the colonizers. In a nation that simultaneously championed freedom, exterminated native people, and enslaved Africans, it is not surprising that issues of race would become so central to women's movements.

Beginning in the 1830s and continuing to the present, the crucible of race has forced U.S. feminists into a dialogue about difference and dominance. In each wave of the movement, women of color have insisted upon pivoting the center so that feminism addresses the needs of all women. During the first wave, when American laws enforced white dominance over blacks, African American women led the way in formulating this critique. After the 1960s, when the U.S. population had become more diverse, women who identified as Chicana, Native American, or Asian American, as well as lesbian or disabled, insisted on the significance of their experiences to second-wave feminism. The repeated process of naming difference, organizing separately, and building political coalitions has ultimately strengthened feminism in the United States by extending its critique of inequality to all women and recognizing its historical connection to all movements for social justice.

Race and Feminism, 1830–1930

The rejection of inherited privilege that nurtured European feminisms also called into question other social hierarchies such as those of age, class, and religion, but none more vigorously than those based on the concept of race. In the era of democratic revolutions, when republican political ideas justified self-rule, racial slavery represented a stark contradiction to both the liberal principle of unfettered individualism and the socialist principle of worker control over production. Yet the expansion of capitalism that enriched democratic nations rested in part on enslavement. While the Spanish seized land and labor in Mexico and Peru, the Dutch, English, and other Europeans transported twelve million African men and women to the Americas between 1500 and 1800 to raise sugar cane, cotton, and tobacco. The profits earned by slave traders, slave owners, and merchants helped finance the industrial revolution in England and the United States.

The very notion of race seemed to mark the slaves subordinate status. Popular beliefs in a biological, as well as theological, basis for racial hierarchy justified both slavery and colonialism. Scientists who investigated brain size and structure relegated both women and "lower races," such as Africans, to the bottom rungs of the human hierarchy. In North America theories of white (northern and western European) racial superiority also justified the appropriation of land inhabited by Native Americans and Mexicans and fostered hostility toward immigrants from Ireland, Asia, and southern or eastern Europe.

For white feminists, race presented a particularly vexing dilemma. Just as the principle of natural rights could exclude women on biological grounds of natural sex, the concept of natural race excluded Africans, Asians, and other non-Europeans as less fully human than Europeans.

White feminists could claim race privilege by insisting that they were more intelligent and deserving of rights than other demeaned groups, but doing so both negated the idea of a common womanhood and reinforced the subordination of African, Asian, Native American, and Mexican women as well as men. Would claims of universal womanhood extend to these racial others? Did the identity "woman" include all women, or only those entitled to rights based on their race or class? Just how profoundly would feminists challenge social hierarchies?

The Antislavery Movement and Women's Rights

The political birthplace of feminism in the United States was the antislavery movement. After independence, northern states gradually eliminated slave labor but the South increasingly relied upon it. Slavery politicized northern women for several reasons. Some white women opposed the system because the dispersal of slave families and the rape of female slaves offended their ideals of womanhood. Both religious principles and beliefs in female moral authority inspired them to form dozens of Female Anti-Slavery societies in the 1830s. Through pamphlets and talks they exhorted women to exercise their indirect political influence by praying to convert Americans to antislavery. Women gathered the bulk of the signatures asking legislators to abolish slavery. Taking direct action, northern women who supported the Underground Railroad hung special quilts on their clotheslines to mark safe houses for fugitives from slavery.

Yet opposition to slavery did not necessarily translate into a belief in racial equality. Some antislavery societies admitted only white women. In response, northern free black women formed their own groups and became activists on three fronts: to free the slaves, to end the race barrier within the female antislavery movement, and to gain rights as women. Their personal testimony about race initiated the dialogue on the complexities of womanhood. In 1837, for example, Sarah Forten circulated a poem at the first Anti-Slavery Convention of American Women asking white women to abandon their own race prejudice and in the name of sisterhood welcome all women to a common Christian cause. The convention admitted black women and called for the racial integration of churches.

In the free black community, women activists faced other obstacles. When Maria Stewart spoke in public against slavery, she was effectively ostracized by other northern free blacks who objected to her unwomanly behavior. "What if I am a woman[?]" she asked in 1833. "Is not the God of ancient times the God of these modern days[?]" Citing biblical and historical women, from Deborah and Mary Magdalene to medieval nuns, Stewart justified her right to speak out politically, whatever her race or sex. Although she withdrew from public speaking under pressure, in her farewell address she chastised African American reformers: "Let us no longer talk of prejudice till prejudice becomes extinct at home. Let us no longer talk of opposition till we cease to oppose our own."[3]

White women's determination to speak out against slavery initiated a crisis over women's rights in the abolition movement. Two southern white women, Sarah and Angelina Grimké, forced the issue. Raised in a southern, slaveholding family, the sisters converted to the Quaker faith and rejected slavery as a moral sin. They attempted to subvert the institution by illegally teaching their slaves to read. The Grimké sisters' views were so unpopular that they left the South for Philadelphia, where they joined the Female Anti-Slavery Society. At first they urged women to use their influence to extend natural rights to blacks. "Try to persuade your husband, father, brothers and sons that slavery is a crime against God and man," Angelina Grimké urged in *An Appeal to the Christian Women of the Southern States* (1836). But when she spoke out in public to audiences of men and women, she shared the fate of Maria Stewart. Northern white clergy condemned her for disobediently stepping outside the female sphere. "How monstrous, how anti-Christian is the doctrine that woman is dependent on man!" she responded. "The investigation of the rights of slaves has led me to a better understanding of my own."[4]

In the process of opposing slavery the Grimké sisters recognized the broader implications of political rights. In 1838, a decade before the Seneca Falls convention, they published *Letters on the Equality of the Sexes*, which analyzed women's inferior status, refuted biblical injunctions against women's activism, and rejected female subservience to men. Abolition, Angelina Grimké recognized, had "opened the way for the discussion of other rights, and the ultimate result will most certainly be the breaking of *every* yoke, the letting the oppressed of every grade and description go free."[5] Most abolitionists did not want to dilute their movement by adding women's rights, however. Only a handful of male allies, such as William Lloyd Garrison, protested when organizers of the 1840 World Anti-Slavery Convention in London refused to seat female delegates. Two of those women, Lucretia Mott and Elizabeth Cady Stanton, pledged to respond one day. With the support of abolitionists such as former slave Frederick Douglass, they organized the first women's rights convention in 1848.

Free African American women stood at the intersection of abolitionism and women's rights. Most concentrated on antislavery. A few, such as former slave and itinerant preacher Sojourner Truth, testified from their own experience that race and gender were inseparable. At one of the women's rights conventions held throughout the northern states in the 1850s, Truth defied clergymen who claimed that women needed to be supported and protected by men. "I have as much muscle as any man, and can do as much work as any man," she told the crowd. "I have plowed and reaped and husked and chopped and mowed, and can any man do more than that?"[6] Years later the white feminist Matilda Joselyn Gage reconstructed Truth's speech with a rhetorical flourish that became legendary: "Nobody ever helps me into carriages, or over mud puddles, or gives me any best place! And ain't I a woman?"[7] Apocryphal as the precise phrases may be, Sojourner Truth's message echoed for generations, reminding feminists that middle-class white women's experiences do not encompass the full range of women's subordination. By listening to other voices the movement could refute the argument that women should be satisfied with the privileges that only a few enjoy.

After the Civil War and the emancipation of slaves, the U.S. women's movement split over a constitutional amendment to enfranchise former slaves that did not include woman suffrage. When Frederick Douglass proclaimed, "This is the Negro's hour," Sojourner Truth, then eighty years old, predicted that "if colored men get their rights, and not colored women theirs, you see the colored men will be masters over the women, and it will be just as bad as it was before." But Truth recognized that she was "about the only colored woman that goes about to speak of the rights of the colored women."[8] In 1869 Douglass, along with Lucy Stone and others, supported the black suffrage amendment through the American Woman Suffrage Association (AWSA). Elizabeth Cady Stanton and her colleague Susan B. Anthony formed the National Woman Suffrage Association (NWSA) to press for black and woman suffrage. In 1870 the Fifteenth Amendment to the U.S. Constitution enfranchised black males only. The breach among black and women's rights advocates remained bitter.

Suffrage and Segregation

Over the next generation the U.S. women's movement reflected the increasingly racist national political climate. Jim Crow policies of segregation spread through the southern states, enforced by the white supremacist Ku Klux Klan (KKK), which terrorized blacks through vigilante violence and murder by lynch mobs. Northern support for reform diminished, while the economic and political plight of former slaves deteriorated. From the 1890s onward southern states found ways to disfranchise black male voters, depriving them of the power to challenge discriminatory practices.

The women's rights movement, blocked in its campaign for the vote, ignored these growing racial injustices. Some suffragists even tried to bolster their unpopular cause by exploiting racial stereotypes directed at both African Americans and the masses of Catholic and Jewish immigrants arriving from Europe. If ignorant black and immigrant men could vote, they argued, why not educated white women? They were not alone in their rhetorical tactic. In South Africa as well, English and Afrikaner women's suffrage associations were arguing that white women needed to vote to counter the political power of black Africans. In the United States, suffrage organizations agreed to exclude black women from leadership at conventions or visibility at demonstrations, partly to accommodate their southern members. The maternalist white women's club movement segregated African American women. The YWCA had separate African American (as well as Chinese American) branches. Only rare exceptions, such as white missionary teachers in the South, worked in a common cause across race, united by a belief in "woman's work for woman."[9]

Once again, African American women struggled on several fronts: for suffrage, to improve conditions for their race, and to achieve equality with white women. Black women wanted the vote not only for themselves but also as a way to represent their race in those northern states where blacks could exercise the franchise. Mary Church Terrell rejoiced "not only in the prospective enfranchisement of my sex but in the emancipation of my race."[10] In addition, middle-class African Americans tried to uplift former slaves through education and temperance. To avoid the condescension of white women, they formed separate black chapters of the maternalist Woman's Christian Temperance Union (WCTU). They also risked their lives to oppose racial discrimination. In the 1880s, for example, Memphis newspaper editor and former slave Ida B. Wells was run out of town when she tried to expose the trumped-up charges of rape used to justify the lynching of innocent African American men by white mobs. Wells turned to northern black women for support and inspired the first African American women's clubs. By 1909 the National Association of Colored Women had established branches in twenty states. Locals concentrated on community self-help by establishing day care facilities, hospitals, and mothers groups. They also turned their attention to the most pressing problem facing African Americans, lynching.

The black women's clubs attempted to dispel several myths about race and sexuality. Racial stereotypes cast all black women as sexually immoral and available to men, a legacy of black women's vulnerability to assault during slavery. As Anna Julia Cooper pointed out in the 1890s, American prejudice "cynically assumes 'A Negro woman cannot be a lady.' "[11] White women's reluctance to work with black women rested in part on this supposed moral divide between white female purity and black female depravity. Organized black womanhood insisted that women of their race were as chaste as white women and equally offended by unwanted sexual advances. Few white women's clubs took heed of this message. Along with excluding African Americans they ignored the call to help abolish lynching. When Wells called for support in her campaign, the leader of the influential WCTU, Frances Willard, failed to speak out and even seemed to condone lynching as necessary to protect white women's virtue.

Ignoring the voices of African American women did not advance the white women's movement. In 1890, when AWSA and NWSA united as the National American Woman Suffrage Association (NAWSA), to appease southern members they permitted chapters to exclude African American women. But this strategy won little support for suffrage in the South. Only northern state legislatures, and few of them, granted the vote to women. As the suffrage movement finally gathered momentum after 1910, African American women participated but did not feel welcome. The huge suffrage parades placed them at the back, but with the help of some white allies the black women literally forced their way into the mainstream of the marches. After Congress finally passed the suffrage amendment in 1919, only one southern state joined those ratifying the measure. Although the law now extended the vote to both black and white women after ratification in 1920, Jim Crow legislation effectively disenfranchised most black women, along with black men, in southern states.

Whose Equal Rights?

In the aftermath of suffrage, white women's racial attitudes ranged from intolerance to neglect to engagement. At one extreme, the resurgent Ku Klux Klan established a Women's KKK, which in 1924 claimed a membership of a quarter million. More typical was the dismissal of race by younger radicals such as Alice Paul, the charismatic leader of the self-identified feminists, who had helped revive the U.S. suffrage movement. Borrowing the militant tactics of the British suffragettes, they had chained themselves to the White House fence and survived hunger strikes in jail. In 1923 these militant feminists, now called the National Woman's Party, introduced the Equal Rights Amendment (ERA) to the U.S. Constitution to mandate that "equality of rights under the law shall not be denied or abridged by the United States or any state on account of sex." With a single focus on sex, however, they refused to discuss racial injustice, even when African American women raised the subject at their meetings.

This refusal to acknowledge racism recurred in the anti-Semitism of the women's movement. Like African Americans, Jewish women had formed their own clubs in response to exclusion from white Christian organizations. Although Jewish women supported suffrage more often than other groups, the suffrage movement had ignored their cultural life when it scheduled conventions and parades on the Jewish sabbath. Historian Elinor Lerner refers to these acts as "anti-Semitism by neglect."[12] After suffrage, Jewish women called on their Christian allies to protest anti-Semitism at home and in the growing Nazi movement in Germany in the 1920s and 1930s. The National Council of Jewish Women sought political support for amending restrictive immigration laws that prevented persecuted Jews from emigrating to the United States. They also hoped that the National Consumers League would join a boycott of German-made goods. Just as the National Woman's Party did not consider lynching a "woman's issue," most women reformers did not see anti-Semitism as part of their agenda. Former NAWSA president Carrie Chapman Catt did circulate a petition among non-Jewish feminists calling for an end to the persecution of German Jews, but neither the boycott nor the efforts to lift immigration quotas won feminist support.

Despite the legacy of racism and neglect, some postsuffrage activists began to sow the seeds of interracial cooperation. In 1924 the League of Women Voters, which had formed after suffrage to help educate women for politics, established a Committee on Negro Problems. The YWCA had begun to hold interracial conferences in 1915; in the 1920s its college branches confronted the organization's policy of segregated facilities. Charlotte Brown's 1920 Memphis speech contributed to this incipient interracial cooperation. By the 1930s the antilynching movement gained Women's Trade Union League, the Women's Joint Congressional Committee (which was the major women's lobbying group in Washington), and the YWCA, which in the 1940s fully integrated and adopted the goals of racial equality and civil rights for minorities.

In the 1930s white southerner Jessie Daniel Ames responded to pleas by black churchwomen by spearheading the Association of Southern Women for the Prevention of Lynching (ASWPL). The members decided to take responsibility for preventing or exposing the murders carried out by men who claimed to be protecting the purity of white womanhood when they lynched alleged black male rapists. Echoing the earlier ideas of Ida B. Wells, Ames recognized the deep connections between race and gender subordination. Ames reported that after reviewing the history of lynching, the ASWPL resolved "no longer to remain silent in the face of this crime done in their name."[13] By rejecting the pedestal of sexual protection, the ASWPL undermined the hold of white supremacy. The group collected forty thousand signatures from southern white women pledged to stop lynching in their localities.

After 1930, both interracial and interfaith cooperation found a foothold within the U.S. women's movement. First Lady Eleanor Roosevelt's gradual rejection of the racism and anti-Semitism she had learned growing up foreshadowed a later trend. The tentative connections made across race and religious lines would nurture the rebirth of feminism in the 1960s. As in the past, African American women in particular provided a critical perspective for white women, alerting them to the integral connections between race and gender. By articulating their personal experience of race, African American women contributed the knowledge that enfranchisement alone could not ensure equality; that the female pedestal was a myth; that sexual stereotypes, whether of purity or immorality, exerted forceful social controls; that power relations always rested upon both race and gender hierarchies; that alliance across race and gender could challenge these hierarchies; and that dignified resistance in the face of seeming powerlessness could be a mighty weapon for change.

Racial Justice, 1930–1970: Seedbed for Second-Wave Feminism

Viewed from the perspectives of race, class, and gender, the U.S. women's movement experienced significant growing pains in the decades after the suffrage victory. During the 1930s women organized as consumers, pacifists, professionals, and workers. The radical wing of the American labor movement spoke to the needs of working-class women, such as Mexican American cannery and field workers. In 1939, for example, labor organizer Luisa Moreno called on the Congress of Spanish-Speaking Peoples to form a women's committee to support the "education of the Mexican woman" and equality in wages and civil rights.[14] Women mobilized to support the war effort in the 1940s, and they did not necessarily demobilize afterward. With more women working for wages, female union membership expanded. A new generation of labor feminists revived socialist feminist goals and initiated a campaign for "equal pay for equal work." Above all, a movement for racial justice insisted that white supremacy had no place in the postwar democratic world. When the U.S. Supreme Court struck down the legality of public school segregation in 1954, it ushered in a revolution in race relations in which women played a central role.

Ella Baker, an organizer for the Southern Christian Leadership Conference (SCLC) and a founder of the Student Non-Violent Coordinating Committee (SNCC), recalled that "the movement of the 50s and 60s was carried largely by women, since it came out of church groups."[15] African American churchwomen fed, housed, clothed, and prayed for the black and white civil rights workers who mobilized throughout the South. They also helped organize and lead the movement. College professor Jo Ann Gibson Robinson and the Women's Political Council of Montgomery, Alabama, instigated and sustained the inspirational bus boycott of 1955–56 after Rosa Parks refused to move to the back of the bus. In 1964 former sharecropper Fannie Lou Hamer took the cause of black political representation to the floor of the Democratic National Convention to demand seating of popularly chosen black delegates. College students such as Anne Moody and Diane Nash bravely demonstrated at lunch counters, participated in the racially integrated Freedom Rides, and went to jail for challenging segregation.

The politics of racial justice directly inspired a revival of feminism from two political perspectives, one liberal and one radical. The Civil Rights Act of 1964 outlawed racial discrimination but also banned sex discrimination, partly at the urging of lobbyists from the aging National Woman's Party. The act established the Equal Employment Opportunity Commission (EEOC) to hear complaints about discrimination based on either race or gender. When the EEOC failed to respond to sex discrimination complaints, feminists decided they needed a political lobby akin to the National Association for the Advancement of Colored People. In 1966 three hundred charter members signed on to the National Organization for Women (NOW). They included black civil rights lawyer Pauli Murray, union leaders, professional women and men, and white feminists like Betty Friedan, whose 1963 book *The Feminine Mystique* had touched a nerve among educated suburban white women. The organization pledged "to bring women into full participation in the mainstream of American society, now, assuming all the privileges and responsibilities thereof in truly equal partnership with men."[16]

This liberal branch of the second wave of U.S. feminism emphasized antidiscrimination law, supporting court cases to achieve equal pay and promotion for women workers at all levels. The feminist magazine *Ms.*, founded in 1972 by journalist Gloria Steinem, promoted these and other goals in its pages. Along with the National Women's Political Caucus, NOW encouraged the election of women to public office. It also rallied behind the ERA, which Congress passed in 1972. Although the amendment failed to be ratified by enough states to become law, the equal-rights strategy ultimately prevailed. Legislation such as the Women's Educational Equity Act and the Equal Credit Opportunity Act (1974) banned discrimination in schools and lending, and the EEOC filed suits on behalf of workers who complained of sex discrimination in hiring, training, and promotion.

Though predominantly white, the ranks of liberal feminists included politically active women of color such as Shirley Chisholm, Patsy Mink, and Aileen Hernandez, a former labor organizer who in 1971 became NOW's second president. The National Black Feminist Organization reached out to African American women to embrace liberal feminism. One of its founders, Eleanor Holmes Norton, recognized that "every problem raised by white feminists has a disproportionately heavy impact on blacks." She also knew that the white feminist movement would "only take on the color line if we who are black join it."[17]

The second, radical wing of the feminist revival grew out of both the civil rights and student movements of the 1960s. During the voter registration and community organizing drives in the southern states, young white female volunteers met strong black women activists. "For the first time," one young white woman stated, "I had role models I could really respect."[18] Working with black leaders such as Ella Baker or Septima Clark taught these white students about women's potential for activism and leadership.

Radicalized in New Left organizations such as SNCC, idealistic activists soon objected to the limitations placed on them as women. Like Maria Stewart and Sarah and Angelina Grimké more than a century earlier, they hoped to be full participants in the quest for racial justice. When men in the movement relegated them to serving coffee, cooking, and having sex, these young women applied their political analysis to gender. Ruby Doris Smith Robinson, a black activist, inspired Casey Hayden and Mary King to write a position paper on women in the movement. The contradiction of sexual subordination in a liberation movement also inspired protest from women in Students for a Democratic Society (SDS). "Having learned from the Movement to think radically about the personal worth and abilities of people whose role in society had gone unchallenged before," they wrote in 1965, "a lot of women in the movement have begun trying to apply those lessons to their relations with men."[19]

Neither white nor black men responded with much enthusiasm, and some blatantly ridiculed women for raising these issues. The rhetoric escalated. In 1967 SDS women prepared the Women's Manifesto, which compared women to Third World people—colonized by white males. They called on SDS to work for communal child care, rights to birth control and abortion, and equality within the home. "[W]e demand that our brothers recognize that they must deal with their own problems of male chauvinism in their personal, social and political relationships," they wrote.[20]

Women's Liberation

Radical women began to extend the politics of self-determination to gender. Just as a call for Black Power purged whites from some interracial organizations and separate movements formed to empower Chicanos and Native Americans, some feminists articulated separatist politics. These radical, or cultural, feminists considered gender the most important aspect of all liberation struggles. To Shulamith Firestone, for example, injustices of class and race would end only when women achieved equality. Not surprisingly, the majority of those who adopted this strategy were white and middle-class.

Breaking away from the male-dominated New Left, the women's liberation movement created a network of predominantly white, women-only organizations. In Chicago, New York, Berkeley, Boston, and smaller cities, radical feminists formed groups such as the Redstockings, the Feminists, the Furies, and Radical Women. In private consciousness-raising sessions members revealed their personal struggles as women, including stories of rape, unwanted pregnancies, lesbian desires, illegal abortions, and the dilemmas of child care and housework. In mimeographed pamphlets they insisted that "the personal is political," rejecting the ideological division of public and private spheres that dismissed women's claims of injustice as merely personal. Power, these feminists realized, operated within and through personal relations, including sexuality and the family. In addition, they questioned the liberal feminist goal of integrating women into male power structures. "We in this segment of the movement," Bonnie Kreps explained in 1968, "do not believe that the oppression of women will be ended by giving them a bigger piece of the pie as Betty Friedan would have it. We believe that the pie itself is rotten."[21]

Through direct action, radical feminists challenged cherished beliefs about women's place. They gained publicity for women's liberation when they demonstrated against the Miss America pageant, occupied the offices of the *Ladies Home Journal*, and held speak-outs about once-unmentionable topics such as abortion, rape, and prostitution. They created woman-only spaces to heal from the daily wounds of patriarchy. To replace the demeaning images of women in the media they celebrated a positive "women's culture" through alternative bookstores, publishing firms, coffeehouses, record companies, concerts, spiritual retreats, exhibit spaces, and back-to-the-land cooperatives and communes.

Explorations of sexuality contributed to a new politics of identity. Second-wave radical feminists shared with first-wave moral reformers a critique of men's sexual exploitation of women. But they differed in their exploration of an explicitly sexual bond among women as an alternative to heterosexual relations. A group called Radicalesbians drew connections between the rejection of male dominance and the assertion of sexual love for other women. Their 1970 essay "The Woman-identified Woman" began by defining a lesbian as "the rage of all women condensed to the point of explosion." Because women's "self-hate and the lack of real self are rooted in our male-given identity," they reasoned, "only women can give to each other a new sense of self."[22] By embracing lesbianism as a positive identity, they rejected the stigma of mental illness that had previously been attached to love between women.

While not all radical feminists became lesbians, the message of putting women first pervaded separatist organizing. Much of the women's culture of the 1970s was largely lesbian culture, and lesbians provided a great deal of the woman power to run feminist bookstores, concerts, and conferences. In response to attempts to exclude or closet them in mainstream feminist organizations, lesbians formed separate consciousness-raising groups and caucuses. In essays, songs, and art they expressed their alternative experience of sexuality and insisted on its legitimacy. Along with the fledgling gay liberation movement, lesbian feminists helped forge an influential concept of sexual identity.

The Limits of Sisterhood and the Complexities of Identity, 1970–2000

Both liberal and radical feminists hoped to achieve gender solidarity through the politics of identity. Poet Robin Morgan called the anthology of feminist essays she edited in 1970 *Sisterhood Is Powerful*. As women of color pointed out from the beginning of the movement, sisterhood was also complicated. Many women of color felt excluded from a theory that elevated gender at the expense of race or class identity. By making white women's experience their standard, both liberal and radical feminists overlooked the perspectives of women of color. For example, when Betty Friedan called for liberating women from the home through employment, women of color who had always worked knew that joining the men of their race on the job meant they would still encounter discrimination. Or when the radical feminist theologian Mary Daly spoke about reclaiming women's spirituality through rituals honoring the goddess, African American poet Audre Lorde asked, "What color is your goddess?" A white female deity matched the white male deity, ignoring the heritage of African spirituality. Separatist politics troubled other women of color. For many Chicanas, the extended family represented both economic and cultural survival. "When a family is involved in a human rights movement, as is the Mexican-American family," Enriqueta Longeaux y Vásquez wrote in 1972, "there is little room for a woman's liberation movement alone."[23] Other women of color echoed the pervasive homophobia of the society when they rejected radical feminism because of its inclusion of lesbians.

Despite these tensions, women of color in the United States clearly recognized that gender as well as race affected their lives. A 1972 poll showed that two-thirds of black women, compared to only one-third of white women, were sympathetic to the women's movement. A 1976 survey of Chicana students found agreement with the goals of feminism as well as the view that the white women's movement was elitist and too focused on men as the oppressors. Many women of color longed for a more inclusive feminism. Former SNCC worker Elizabeth Martinez recalled that after the assassination of Martin Luther King Jr. in 1968 she realized "that if the struggle against sexism did not see itself as profoundly entwined with the fight against racism, I was gone." At the same time, though, she "looked hard at the sexism in the [Chicano] *movimiento*, and knew a Chicana feminism needed to be born."[24]

Women of color who shared feminist goals faced dual obstacles, from their own communities and from women's movements. Black nationalists, for example, urged women to align with racial rather than sexual politics, primarily by supporting men through women's roles as wives and mothers. Asian American feminists were criticized as traitors to their race for threatening ethnic identity, just as Chicana feminists risked being labeled "*vendidas*," or sellouts, in the Chicano movement, especially if they accepted lesbianism. Yet when women of color did join the women's movement, they encountered overt and subtle racial bias. Given their small numbers, they often felt the discomfort of being treated as tokens, expected to represent their race but not to bring their own issues to the table. "Inclusion without influence," Lynet Uttal called it, or as Bernice Johnson Reagon explained, "You don't really want Black folks, you are just looking for yourself with a little color in it."[25]

The title of one collection of African American women's writing captured well the quandary of exclusion: *All the Women Are White, All the Blacks Are Men, but Some of Us Are Brave* (1982). In response to this dilemma, women of color initiated a redefinition of identity politics. They refused the pressures from both men of color who would subsume women's issues and white women who would subsume race issues. As Pauli Murray poignantly explained her "equal stake" in women's liberation and black liberation: "I have one foot in each camp and cannot split myself apart."[26] When the Chicano movement called on the women of La Raza (the race) to reject feminism, Adelaida del Castillo insisted that "true freedom for our people can come about only if prefaced by the equality of individuals within La Raza."[27]

Just as women had separated from men within the New Left, women of color established their own groups. One of these, the Combahee River Collective, issued a "black feminist state-ment" in 1974 that pledged to "struggle together with black men against racism while we also struggle with black men about sexism."[28] Asian American Women United, Women of All Red Nations, and the National Black Women's Health Project served specific groups. Women from a variety of racial backgrounds formed Kitchen Table/Women of Color Press to present diverse women's stories. In 1981 they published an influential anthology, *This Bridge Called My Back:*

Writings by Radical Women of Color (1981), edited by Chicana feminists Cherríe Moraga and Gloria Anzaldúa, which opened a cultural space for further explorations of multiple personal identities.

The theme of bridging different female identities recurred in other personal writing that expanded beyond the historically dominant categories of black and white. Jewish and Asian American feminists wrote passionately about the two worlds they bridged. Lesbians insisted on the inclusion of sexuality as another component of identity. Disabled women called for access to feminist events and acknowledgment of their sexual and reproductive capacities. Latinas explored how language represented both a link to family and community and a potential barrier to understanding across ethnicities. In *Borderlands/La Frontera: The New Mestiza* (1987) Gloria Anzaldúa captured well the empowering effect of articulating a mixed, or mestizo, identity: "I will have my voice: Indian, Spanish, white. I will have my serpent's tongue—my woman's voice, my sexual voice, my poet's voice. I will overcome the tradition of silence."[29]

Of all these identity groups, women of color stood at a particularly critical intersection. Frustrated by racial exclusion in the women's movement and tired of being asked to educate white women, writers such as Moraga asked, "How can we—this time—not use our bodies to be thrown over a river of tormented history to bridge the gap?"[30] Only if white women took race into account would the burden be shared. Indeed, the work of radical women of color profoundly affected white feminists. Combahee River Collective member Barbara Smith, who led antiracism workshops for white women in Boston, felt that white feminists had to "take responsibility for their racism," and she believed they were learning to do so. As she told a predominantly white audience at the National Women's Studies Association meeting in 1979, "The reason racism is a feminist issue is easily explained by the inherent definition of feminism." In Smith's view, the struggle to free *all* women had to include "women of color, working-class women, poor women, disabled women, Jewish women, lesbians, old women—as well as white, economically privileged, heterosexual women. Anything less than this vision of total freedom is not feminism, but merely female self-aggrandizement."[31]

White women contributed to the redefinition of feminism that made alliance across races, religions, and sexual identities a possibility. By recognizing cultural difference, including their own fragmented identities, many rejected the primacy of gender that characterized early radical feminism. By acknowledging their own racism, they also began to question whiteness as a source of privilege. As Ruth Frankenberg put it in 1993, "Racism shapes white people's lives and identities in a way that is inseparable from other facets of daily life."[32] Recognizing white privilege did not have to be a source of immobilizing guilt; rather it could be a productive step toward applying that privilege to combating racism. Realizing that racial categories had been historically constructed—that whiteness, like any color, could change its meaning—opened an effort to "unlearn" the internalized racism that affected all women. As Gloria Yamato cautioned white women, "Work on racism for your sake, not 'their' sake."[33]

The intense conversations on identity and privilege encouraged some U.S. feminists to form coalitions across lines of race, ethnicity, gender, and sexuality. So did the political conservatism of the 1980s, which put feminists on the defensive. Whether addressing reproductive rights, the AIDS crisis, or welfare reform, feminists from diverse backgrounds built cross-cultural political support, sometimes painfully but also productively. Bernice Johnson Reagon captured the importance of this effort in a speech she gave at a women-only music festival. Separatism, she recognized, offered a safe space for groups who felt threatened by the outside world—lesbians, for example, or minorities—but it could be reactionary as well as healing. In the real world, she explained, "There is nowhere you can go and only be with people who are like you." Reagon challenged women to move from that safe space of separatism into the streets to engage in the difficult work of coalition politics.[34] Thus white women learned to protest race discrimination, heterosexual women of color to support lesbian rights, and feminist men to defend women's reproductive rights. Facing common opposition and learning to trust across difference, though never an easy task, helped sustain grassroots feminism in the face of opposition.

The Future of Identity Politics

For two centuries, women of color in the United States have stood in the vanguard of redefining feminism to ask not only what difference gender makes but how also women experience gender differently because of their access to or lack of social privilege. In defining a "multiracial feminism," social scientists Maxine Baca Zinn and Bonnie Thornton Dill point to the importance of going "beyond a mere recognition of diversity and difference among women to examine structures of domination." Sociologist Patricia Hill Collins refers to these structures as a "matrix of domination" in which gender is but one source of power, always connected to other forms. To recognize that matrix, to pivot the center, feminists have turned repeatedly to the lived experiences of women from diverse backgrounds.[35]

In the past two decades, some feminists have questioned whether the categories of gender and race continue to matter. For one, recognizing the multiplicity of identities within us reveals the limits of single labels. We need long strings of adjectives to locate our complex selves by race, religion, sexuality, physical ability, ethnicity, and the like. In addition, postmodern critics point out that Enlightenment ideas about fixed race and sex rest upon biological definitions that have often been used to restrict the rights of women and minorities. To Donna Haraway, who calls all identities "fabricated hybrids," our consciousness of gender, race, or class "is an achievement forced on us by the terrible historical experiences of . . . patriarchy, colonialism, and capitalism."[36] If so, refusing to be categorized by race or gender can become an act of political resistance. Claiming interracial or transgendered identities, for example, shakes up our beliefs about fixed biological categories. In her influential book *Gender Trouble* (1990), philosopher Judith Butler proposed that playing with the way we "perform" gender can also disrupt the category. In this view, exaggerated parodies of clothing and speech styles, such as the performances of drag queens or drag kings, could undermine the constraints of gender.

In contrast to those who emphasize the reactionary implications of our inherited categories, feminist critics such as Chela Sandoval and Paula Moya want to retain identity politics but refine them as well. Sandoval has insisted that identities are not necessarily imposed on us but that we may self-consciously choose among them, switching at times from an emphasis on our gender to an emphasis on our race or sexuality. Such "differential consciousness," she argues, can help forge political alliances among women. Paula Moya takes the argument further by calling for what she terms a "realist" account of identity. Since the social facts of race and gender continue to affect our personal experiences, to deny these categories overlooks "the fact that some people are more oppressed than others." Only by acknowledging this structural reality can we undermine it.[37]

The lived realities of race and sex remain as powerful in contemporary U.S. society as in the past. What has changed, however, is the political meaning of these categories. Instead of dismissing race, feminists have learned to confront its effects on all women. The acknowledgment of racial injustice has led to further explorations of personal identities that now empower many groups once relegated to the margins of women's movements. Listening to personal testimony has contributed to the feminist goal of extending the rights of women to all. The poet Audre Lorde recognized the importance of this historical process when she wrote that "those of us who have been forged in crucibles of difference—those of us who are poor, who are lesbians, who are Black, who are older," know that survival means "learning how to take our differences and make them strengths."[38] Nowhere would this lesson prove more challenging than when Western feminism reached beyond its cultural base and confronted gender inequality in the global arena.

Notes

1. Charlotte Hawkins Brown, October 8, 1920, in *Black Women in White America: A Documentary History*, ed. Gerda Lerner (New York: Vintage Books, 1973), 467–72.
2. Elsa Barkley Brown, "African-American Women's Quilting: A Framework for Conceptualizing and Teaching African-American Women's History," *Signs* 14:4 (1989), 922. Brown credits Bettina Aptheker with this phrase (*Tapestries of Life: Women's Work, Women's Consciousness and the Meaning of Daily Life* [Amherst: University of Massachusetts Press, 1989]); it is also adopted by Patricia Hill Collins, *Black Feminist Thought: Knowledge, Consciousness, and the Politics of Empowerment* (Boston: Unwin Hyman, 1990), 236–37.
3. "Mrs. Stewart's Farewell Address to Her Friends in the City of Boston. Delivered September 21, 1833," excerpted in Lerner *Black Women in White America*: 565–66.
4. Angelina Grimké to Catharine Beecher, Letter XII in Alice S. Rossi, *The Feminist Papers: From Adams to de Beauvoir* (New York: Columbia University Press, 1973), 320.
5. Quoted in Gerda Lerner, *The Grimké Sisters from South Carolina: Pioneers for Woman's Rights and Abolition* (New York: Schocken Books, 1971), 187.
6. Quoted in Nell Painter, *Sojourner Truth: A Life, a Symbol* (New York: W. W. Norton, 1996), 125.
7. "The Akron Convention," in *History of Woman Suffrage*, eds. Elizabeth Cady Stanton, Susan B. Anthony, and Matilda Joslyn Gage, reprinted in Rossi, *Feminist Papers*, 428.
8. Convention of the American Equal Rights Association, New York City, 1867, excerpted in Lerner, *Black Women in White America: A Documentary History*, 568.
9. Higginbotham, *Righteous Discontent: The Women's Movement in the Black Baptist Church, 1880–1920* (Cambridge: Harvard University Press, 1993), 91–105.
10. Quoted in Bettina Aptheker, *Women's Legacy: Essays on Race, Sex, and Class in American History* (Amherst: University of Massachusetts Press, 1982) 65.
11. Anna Julia Cooper, *A Voice From the South, by a Black Woman of the South* (Xenia, OH.; Aldine Printing House, 1892; repr., New York: Oxford University Press, 1988), 32.
12. Elinor Lerner, "American Feminism and the Jewish Question, 1890–1940," in *Anti-Semitism in American History*, ed. David Gerber (Urbana: University of Illinois Press, 1986), 305–28.
13. Quoted in Jacquelyn Dowd Hall, *Revolt Against Chivalry: Jessie Daniel Ames and the Women's Campaign Against Lynching* (New York: Columbia University Press, 1979), 164.
14. Moreno quoted in Vicki L. Ruiz, *From Out of the Shadows: Mexican Women in Twentieth-Century America* (New York: Oxford University Press, 1998), 101.
15. Baker quoted in Karen Anderson, *Changing Woman: A History of Racial Ethnic Women in Modern America* (New York: Oxford University Press, 1996), 211.
16. NOW mission statement in Miriam Schneir, *Feminism in Our Time* (New York: Vintage Books, 1994), 96.
17. Quoted in Susan Hartmann, *The Other Feminists: Activists in the Liberal Establishment* (New Haven: Yale University Press, 1998), 191.
18. Dorothy Dawson Burlage, quoted in Sara Evans, *Personal Politics: The Roots of Women's Liberation in the Civil Rights Movement and the New Left* (New York: Knopf, 1979), 51.
19. Casey Hayden and Mary King, "Sex and Caste," November 18, 1965, reprinted in Evans, *Personal Politics*, 236.
20. "Liberation of Women: New Left Notes, July 10, 1967," reprinted in Evans, *Personal Politics*, 241.
21. Kreps, "Radical Feminism I," in *Radical Feminism*, eds. Anne Koedt, Ellen Levine, and Anita Rapone (New York: Quadrangle Books, 1973), 239.
22. Ibid., 245.
23. Enriqueta Longeaux y Vásquez, "The Woman of La Raza," in *Chicana Feminist Thought: The Basic Historical Writings*, ed. Alma García (New York: Routledge, 1997), 31.
24. Elizabeth (Betita) Martinez, "History Makes Us, We Make History," in *The Feminist Memoir Project: Voices from Women's Liberation*, eds. Rachel Blau Duplessis and Ann Snitow (New York: Crown Publishing, 1998), 118–20.
25. Lynet Uttal, "Inclusion Without Influence: The Continuing Tokenism of Women of Color," in Gloria Anzaldúa, ed., *Making Face, Making Soul/Haciendo Caras: Creative and Critical Perspectives by Women of Color* (San Francisco: Aunt Lute Foundation, 1990), 42; Bernice Johnson Reagon, "Coalition Politics: Turning the Century," in *Homegirls: A Black Feminist Anthology*, ed. Barbara Smith (Brooklyn: Kitchen Table/Women of Color Press, 1983), 359.
26. Quoted in Hartmann, *The Other Feminists*, 205.
27. Del Castillo quoted in Ramón A. Gutiérrez, "Community, Patriarchy, and Individualism. The Politics of Chicano History and the Dream of Equality." in Vicki L. Ruiz and Ellen Carol DuBois,

Unequal Sisters: A Multicultural Reader in U.S. Women's History (New York: Routledge, 2000), 3d ed., 591.

28. Combahee River Collective, "Black Feminist Statement," in *Capitalist Patriarchy and Socialist Feminism*, Zillah Eisenstein, ed. (New York: Monthly Review Press, 1979), 366.

29. "How to Tame a Wild Tongue," in Gloria Anzaldúa, *Borderlands/La Frontera: The New Mestiza* (San Francisco: Spinsters/Aunt Lute, 1987), 59.

30. Cherríe Moraga, "Preface," *This Bridge Called My Back: Writings by Radical Women of Color* (Watertown, Mass.: Persephone Press, 1981; repr., New York: Kitchen Table/Women of Color Press, 1983), xv.

31. Smith, "Racism and Women's Studies," in *The Truth That Never Hurts* (New Brunswick, N.J.: Rutgers University Press, 1998), 96.

32. Ruth Frankenberg, *White Women, Race Matters: The Social Construction of Whiteness* (Minneapolis: University of Minnesota Press, 1993), 6.

33. Gloria Yamato, "Something About the Subject Makes It Hard to Name," in Anzaldúa, *Haciendo Caras*, 23–24.

34. Reagon, "Coalition Politics," 359.

35. Maxine Baca Zinn and Bonnie Thornton Dill, "Theorizing Difference from Multiracial Feminism," *Feminist Studies* 22:2 (1996), 321; Collins, *Black Feminist Thought*, 326; Barkley Brown, "African American Women," 921.

36. Donna Haraway, "A Cyborg Manifesto: Science, Technology, and Socialist-Feminism in the Late Twentieth Century," in *Simians, Cyborgs, and Women* (New York: Routledge, 1991), 150, 155.

37. Chela Sandoval, "U.S. Third World Feminism: The Theory and Method of Oppositional Consciousness in the Postmodern World," *Genders* 10 (spring 1991), 1–24; Paula M. L. Moya, "Postmodernism, 'Realism' and the Politics of Identity: Cherríe Moraga and Chicana Feminism," in *Feminist Genealogies, Colonial Legacies, Democratic Futures*, eds. M. Jacqui Alexander and Chandra Talpade Mohanty (New York: Routledge, 1997), 125–50.

38. Audre Lorde, "The Master's Tools Will Never Dismantle the Master's House," *Sister Outsider* (Freedom, Calif.: Crossing Press, 1984), 112.

2

Bodies in Motion
Lesbian and Transsexual Histories

Nan Alamilla Boyd

Here on the gender borders at the close of the twentieth century, with the faltering of phallocratic hegemony and the bumptious appearance of heteroglossic origin accounts, we find the epistemologies of white male medical practice, the rage of radical feminist theories and the chaos of lived gendered experience meeting on the battle field of the transsexual body: a hotly contested site of cultural inscription, a meaning machine for the production of ideal type.
—Sandy Stone, "The Empire Strikes Back: A Posttranssexual Manifesto"

My point of departure is that nationality . . . nationness, as well as nationalism, are cultural artifacts of a particular kind. To understand them properly we need to consider carefully how they have come into historical being, in what ways their meanings have changed over time, and why, today, they command such profound emotional legitimacy.
—Benedict Anderson, *Imagined Communities*

This essay concerns the relationship between bodies and nations, and more specifically, transsexual bodies and lesbian nations.[1] It explores how visible, intelligible, and legible bodies come to reflect, define, and regulate the nation as a boundaried political geography.[2] I suggest that the naturalized body is not simply a duped or docile subject; nor is it free to determine its own form.[3] Rather, the body remains a highly politicized, unstable, and symbolic structure, intimately connected to the state, and as a result, it reflects both nationalism and resistant social movements.

In many ways, the connection between nationalism's history and the body's relationship to the state remains obscure.[4] However, as Michel Foucault explains, while divinely ordained monarchies crumbled in the face of late nineteenth-century West European republicanism and the concomitant rise of state nationalism, state-sanctioned punishments (law) helped transform the body into a political anatomy.[5] Not only did the materiality of the body gain meaning as it became *subject to* new laws and regulations, but paradoxically the body became the *subject of* the state as a (perhaps interchangeable) physical representation of republican ideology.[6] In other words, the body begins to imagine itself meaningfully autonomous and individual only in relation to the collective: the republican state. Thus, the body's subjectivity—its social and political agency—remains linked to its physicality, to the social meaning of human corporeality. In this way, through the nineteenth century, as *individuals* began to participate more dynamically in the body politic, the body through its social and political gestures, indeed its social and political embodiments, began to participate more efficiently in its own regulation and prohibitions.

While the body becomes self-regulating as respectable or heteronormal, for example, in order to affirm an empowered relationship to the state, the body's intelligibility incorporates it within the nation. The nation, as Benedict Anderson argues, functions as "an imagined political community," a community that will never completely know itself—it will never know all its constituents—but it learns to recognize its members (even sight unseen) as part of a limited, boundaried, and sovereign entity, "a deep, horizontal comradeship."[7] The nation functions differently than the state in that the state emerged as the political invention of the Age of Revolution and Enlightenment, as a political geography sovereign through its own efforts and imaginings rather than its God-ordained nobility or territorial sweep. The nation, however, emerged as the state's cultural artifact and constant companion. The nation and nationalism, if Anderson's arguments are correct, claim cultural legitimacy for the state insofar as nationalism replaced religious and dynastic symbols with a secular semiotics of political representation.[8] However, as this essay will demonstrate, while nationalisms reflect, reinforce, and reinvigorate the state, contemporary social and political movements also invoke the language of nationalism in order to resist and restructure the state. In other words, while late eighteenth-century revolutionary movements engineered the hegemony of the modern nation/state in order to resist monarchial and/or colonial tyranny, contemporary resistant movements (anticolonial, socialist, antiracist, queer) often imagine themselves within a cultural system—nationalism— that reinscribes the foundations of state capitalism.

These notes help us understand the body's relationship to both the nation (nationalism) and the state (law), particularly since some bodies matter more than others. Bodies that inhabit or enact naturalized states of being remain culturally intelligible, socially valuable, and as a result, gain and retain the privilege of citizenship and its associated rights and protections. Bodies that matter, as Judith Butler argues, are worth protecting, saving, grieving.[9] Some bodies, however, are less intelligible or unintelligible and are not instrumental or valuable to the state; in fact, these bodies undermine in many different ways the recognition or comradeship central to nationalism's purpose. It makes no difference if these bodies die or if no one grieves them because, as Butler explains, abject bodies—bodies transgressive of borders and boundaries—do not matter. They do not function intelligibly as matter, and they do not have value. How then does the materiality or morphology of the body influence its social value, its political purchase? Do abject or queer bodies retain inchoate or inherently resistant positions vis-à-vis the state? Is it necessary to transition (or pass) from abject to intelligible in order to function within the state (or in order to resist a state-sanctioned, rights-based economy of value)? How do bodies that do not matter become bodies that matter?

Despite twentieth-century antihumanist and anti-essentialist gestures away from the body, the material body continues to influence contemporary social and political movements. For instance, as queers begin to visibly take up public space and imagine themselves part of a larger political community, they often do so around a system of meanings that transforms bodies into specific, cohesive, and authentic identities. Gay men, lesbians, bisexuals, and transsexuals, as increasingly viable subjects in relation to the state, police their own borders, regulating the social territories they inhabit, including their bodies, in an effort to secure and protect limited political entitlements. For example, in June 1994 the Human Rights Campaign Fund (HRCF), a U.S. gay and lesbian lobbying organization, brought antidiscrimination legislation to Congress through several key representatives. If adopted, this legislative package, known as ENDA (the Employment Non-Discrimination Act), would protect lesbians, bisexuals, and gay men in the United States from "job discrimination or special treatment on the basis of sexual orientation."[10] In an effort to speedily secure the bill, however, HRCF refused to use language that would also protect the transgendered from job discrimination.[11] When confronted by transgender activists who argued that ENDA failed to protect the "visibly queer," HRCF countered that trans-inclusive language would set back the legislative process and could cost ENDA twenty to thirty potential congressional votes.[12] In other words, in order to forge a relationship with the state, particularly around legal protections, the lesbian and gay nation regulates its borders and disciplines its body to project an intelligible picture of itself, one with clear boundaries around not just the sexual identity of its constituents but the unambiguous gender (and genital status) of those who might be protected by this legislation. With this move, the queer body becomes coherent and self-regulating in relation to the state, not queer at all, in fact.[13] It becomes, instead, disciplined and intelligible within a state-sanctioned language about appropriately gendered "lesbian," "gay," and perhaps "bisexual" bodies. While the struggle over queer antidiscrimination legislation continues, other theaters of struggle showcase the ambivalent relationship between subject and state, body and nation.[14]

The Theater of Historical Recuperation

History, as this story unfolds, is a battleground, an intellectual territory that serves political purposes, and lesbian, feminist, and transgender communities share a common but sometimes hostile relationship to overlapping historical geographies. In contemporary lesbian history, butch drag or female-to-male cross-dressing has signaled the presence of lesbians. Indeed, in a working-class context, butch iconography was lesbian iconography, and masculine gender codes when worn on an anatomically female body stood in for or advertised lesbian desire and sexuality.[15] However, because of the historical relationship between butchness and lesbian sexuality, lesbian histories often conflate "cross-dressing" (anatomical females sporting masculine appearance for the purpose of advertising lesbian sexuality) with "passing" (anatomical females donning masculine appearance for the purpose of being perceived as men).[16] Lesbian history, for example, particularly in its earlier phase, often documented the history of passing women as a method for bringing lesbians into history because these individuals (when "discovered" to be women) were the most visible and publicly accessible historical subjects.[17] However, transsexuals and transgender community historians and activists take a different approach to the historical recuperation of female-to-male cross-dressers. They argue that anatomical females who passed as men in public might just as easily be recuperated as transgendered men than passing women or cross-dressing lesbians in that their perceived gender identity was male rather than female. In this way, lesbian and transgender communities construct a usable past around the recuperation of many of the same historical figures.[18]

The slide show *She Even Chewed Tobacco*, for example, discusses cross-dressing and passing women in U.S. Western history. Created in 1979, it introduces the character Babe Bean, a "passing woman" who lived in Stockton, California, from 1897–98, and places Bean within a narrative about women's history that suggests that passing women functioned as a cultural precursor to contemporary butch lesbians.[19] The slide show's introductory segment states that in the nineteenth century, "a small but significant group of American women rejected the limitations of the female sphere and claimed the privileges enjoyed by men. They worked for men's wages, courted and married the women they loved and even voted. They did so by adopting men's clothing, hiding their female identities from most of the world and passing as men." *She Even Chewed Tobacco* uses passing women as liminal characters to highlight the gulf between male privilege and female oppression. It positions them within a late-1970s feminist discourse that stresses labor equity, suffrage rights, and lesbian love. Moreover, it tells a Horatio Alger-esque story, embedding a nationalist trope of success within feminist discourse: successful cross-dressing produced women who, as citizens, could vote. In this way *She Even Chewed Tobacco* gives nineteenth-century female-to-male cross-dressers a history as women within the rubric of contemporary lesbian and feminist concerns. No mention is made of cross-gender identity, and the only conclusion one might make about the lives of passing women is that if they lived at a time when they could enjoy economic freedom, political rights, or sexual love for women as a woman, they would not choose to masquerade as men. Indeed, it is this concept of masquerade that underscores the argument that nineteenth- and twentieth-century female-to-male cross-dressers were really women and, in fact, probably lesbians.

Babe Bean is a complicated historical figure, however, because for a short period of time Bean straddled the boundary between man and woman. In August 1897, Bean was arrested in Stockton, California, for cross-dressing. After the arrest s/he stayed in Stockton for approximately a year and became something of a local celebrity. Bean continued to dress entirely in men's clothing, lived alone on a houseboat, and attended meetings at the local Bachelor's Club. However, Bean communicated only through writing and refused to speak aloud, which shrouded the truth of her/his sex. In other words, even though Bean admitted to having a female body, her/his self-presentation was so consistently masculine that some of the citizens of Stockton remained unconvinced of Bean's sex. "The mystery is still unsolved as to whether 'Babe' Bean is a boy or girl, a man or a woman," one news article reported, dubbing Bean "the mysterious girl-boy, man-woman."[20]

In 1898, Bean left Stockton for San Francisco and joined the U.S. military, serving in the Philippines during the Spanish-American War. Bean returned to San Francisco after the war, his arms covered with elaborate tattoos, and he adopted the name Jack Garland. At this time in San Francisco, 1903, cross-dressing was made illegal by city ordinance. And although Garland spent the rest of his life in San Francisco, working as a male nurse and a free-lance social worker, he was not arrested again. However, when Jack Garland died in 1936, after almost forty years of living as a man, his "true sex" was revealed to be female. Jack Garland was born in 1869, daughter of José Marcos Mugarrieta, San Francisco's first Mexican consul, and Eliza Alice Garland.

The late Lou Sullivan, a female-to-male (FTM) transsexual and also an active member of San Francisco's Gay and Lesbian Historical Society (GLHS), published a biography of Jack Garland in 1990 entitled *From Female to Male: The Life of Jack Bee Garland*, which retextualizes Babe Bean's life as the life of Jack Garland. Sullivan states in his introduction that "Jack Garland demonstrated, through his lifelong adherence to his male identity, that his reasons for living as a man were more complex than just his dissatisfaction with the way society expected women to dress. [Jack Garland] was a female-to-male transsexual."[21] Furthermore, while many histories of female-to-male cross-dressers tell the story of how passing women were able to pursue the women they loved under the protective cover of male dress and, perhaps, male identity, this was not the case for Jack Garland. Garland preferred the company of men. Sullivan notes that "he dressed and lived as a man in order to be a man among men," which further unhinges any direct connection between cross-gender behavior and sexuality. In the memoirs he left behind, Jack Garland states that "Many have thought it strange that I do not care to mingle with women of my own age, and seem partial to men's company. Well, is it not natural that I should prefer the companionship of men? I am never happy nor contented unless with a few of 'the boys.' "[22]

While Sullivan rewrites lesbian history to produce a history of visible transsexuals, one cannot overlook Garland's racial, class, and national passings. The turn of the century was a period of intense racial, ethnic, and national consolidation which marked the rise of Anglo-Saxonism, the production of a nationalist discourse of U.S. exceptionalism, and intensified U.S. colonization. Garland's gender certainly did not exist independent of these circumstances. For instance, Garland chose Anglo names for himself, which signals a movement toward white-ethnic or Anglo-American identifications. Moreover, while his silence in Stockton masked, most obviously, the feminine tenor of his voice, it also hid any Spanish language affects that would have destabilized his ethnic and national crossings. Also, for the last decades of his life, Garland wandered the streets of San Francisco and lived in poverty. Here, gender remains inseparable from class—while Garland's maleness allowed for late-night street wandering and urban rescue work, the very public and class-specific nature of his activities reinforced his gender. Finally, Garland's participation in the Spanish-American War and his service to the U.S. military wrapped a cloak of nationalist allegiance around his political subjectivity, highlighting both his masculinity and Americanness. Clearly, the story of Babe Bean/Jack Garland exceeds a singularly recuperative narrative.

Billy Tipton, the jazz pianist and saxophonist whose so called true sex was revealed when he died in Spokane in 1989, provides another example of a historical subject claimed by both lesbian/feminist and transgendered communities. Like Jack Garland, Billy Tipton lived his adult life as a man, over fifty years. Born in Kansas City, Missouri, in 1914, at the age of eighteen he applied for a social security card under his brother's name, Billy, and hit the road as a musician. He formed the Billy Tipton Trio in 1954, recorded two albums, and toured the West until he settled in Spokane in the 1960s. Through these years, Tipton married several times but, according to his lovers, never revealed his female anatomy. Betty Cox, Tipton's lover from 1946–53, claims that Tipton must have used "sexual devices" when making love: "I know it sounds incredible, but I'm a normal healthy woman who enjoys her man . . . [a]nd if that little Billy was alive today, well, I'd still enjoy him."[23] On the other hand, Kitty Oakes, Tipton's third wife, claims that they didn't have sex during their eighteen-year marriage. She notes that Tipton had been injured in an auto accident, explaining "—there was an attraction between us, but it wasn't sexual."[24] Over the course of their relationship, Tipton and Oakes adopted and parented three sons.

Tipton did not have surgery or openly identify as a transsexual; instead, he represented himself, even to his closest friends and family, as a man. Clearly, Billy Tipton's gender identity was male. Still, critics and enthusiasts have recuperated Tipton as an example of the kind of extreme measures women must undergo to pursue equitable economic opportunities. "[Tipton] apparently began appearing as a man to improve her chances of success as a musician," one reporter noted.[25] Jason Cromwell, a sociologist specializing in female-to-male transsexual identities, refutes this idea. "You don't die from a treatable medical condition if you are simply a woman living as a man so you can take advantage of male privileges."[26] (Tipton died of an untreated bleeding ulcer.) A print graphic published in several transgender community newsletters and magazines takes this idea one step further. It positions a simple "trivial pursuit" question in the center of the page with statements swirling around it; the question reads: "Billy Tipton was a (choose one): a. woman, b. lesbian, c. crossdresser, d. man." A check is placed next to answer d, indicating that the correct answer is that Tipton was a man. Statements protectively encircling the ad read:

> Billy Tipton was a jazz musician. When he died, in 1989, television and newspaper sources proclaimed him to have been a woman who had lived as a man in order to be a jazz musician. "He gave up everything," they said. They were wrong. He didn't give up anything, for he wasn't a woman. The gay community was quick to proclaim Billy as a lesbian. They were wrong, too. Billy wasn't a lesbian, either. Billy was married, with three adopted sons. His family did not know of his female anatomy, but they knew something the newspaper and television and gay press didn't—that Billy Tipton was a man.

In smaller print, in the bottom right corner, a more provocative statement reads, "Billy Tipton was transsexual. . . . His life was not an imposture, and the notion that he was anything less than a man is a denial of everything that he was. Hands off! He's one of ours!"[27] Like Jack Garland, the recuperation of Billy Tipton's life exceeds a simple narrative about women's economic opportunities or lesbian sexual identity. Instead, without denying labor inequity or lesbian history, Tipton's life evidences the uneasy fit between unintelligible bodies and contemporary (recuperative) historical practice.

More recently, Brandon Teena, a twenty-one-year-old who, despite his female body, lived as a man and dated women, was murdered on December 31, 1993, in Humboldt, Nebraska. Three months earlier he had moved from his hometown, Lincoln, to Falls City, where, it was noted, he was "popular with the girls." After a misdemeanor arrest, however, police revealed his anatomical sex to the local press, who published it. This information angered two men, who disrobed Brandon Teena at a Christmas Eve party ostensibly to prove to his girlfriend that he was "actually a female." Early the next morning, on December 25, 1993, Brandon Teena was abducted, beaten, and raped by the same two men; they "threatened to silence her permanently" if he went to the police. A week later, after Brandon Teena filed charges, the same two men murdered him and two of his friends.[28]

The murders attracted a great deal of national attention, particularly after Brandon Teena's family asserted that the murders would not have occurred had the rape and battery been prosecuted by the local police.[29] Meanwhile, in the gay press, coverage of Brandon Teena's death evolved into a discussion about lesbian and gay civil rights. Pat Phelen of Citizens for Equal Protection, Nebraska's gay and lesbian rights organization, stated that "this incident underscores the need for the state to pass laws protecting the rights of Gays and those perceived as Gay."[30] The National Gay and Lesbian Task Force (NGLTF), San Francisco's Citizens United against Violence (CUAV), and New York City's Anti-Violence Project (AVP) similarly asserted that Brandon Teena's death exemplified the worst kind of violence against women and lesbians:

> Brandon Teena was raped and then murdered for being a woman who broke the rules: she presented herself as a man, dated the prettiest girl in town, and was not sexually involved with men. . . . For all these transgressions, as a woman and as a lesbian, she was murdered.[31]

Because gay press coverage of the events leading to Brandon Teena's death pointedly represented him as lesbian or female, these articles obscure his transgendered identity, erasing its specificity.

For example, Donna Minkowitz's *Village Voice* coverage of Brandon Teena's murder evades a direct analysis of transgender experience in order to buttress lesbian visibility and political subjectivity. While Minkowitz notes repeatedly that Brandon did not identify as a lesbian and that he talked frequently to his lovers and friends about being transsexual, Minkowitz nevertheless identifies Brandon Teena as a confused but sexy cross-dressing butch lesbian:

> From photos of the wonder-boychic playing pool, kissing babes, and lifting a straight male neighbor high up in the air to impress party goers . . . Brandon looks to be the handsomest butch item in history—not just good looking, but arrogant, audacious, cocky—everything they, and I, look for in lovers.[32]

Minkowitz's article ultimately functions as a cautionary tale about violence against lesbians, but it doubles back on itself in a gesture of "blame the victim." Minkowitz's article explains that if Brandon had only found someone to talk to about "her" latent homosexuality, to counsel "her" through "her" intense self-hatred as a lesbian, "she" would not have gotten so embroiled in the pattern of deceit that sealed "her" fate. As the final lines of Minkowitz's article explain, "The frustration she had felt for so long had finally frustrated others, and the fury she could not express was ultimately expressed on her. By men."[33]

Minkowitz's narrative places the facts of Brandon Teena's life, indeed his own statements about himself, within a lesbian and gay paradigm that stresses visibility, pride, and coming out of the closet. Minkowitz understands Brandon Teena's insistence that he was not a lesbian to be the words of an unrealized, homophobic young woman who, had she greater access to social services, might have adjusted to lesbian life.[34] In this light, as Jordy Jones argues in an article for *FTM*, a newsletter produced by and for female-to-male transsexuals, "Brandon Teena was not killed because *she* was a Lesbian, *he* was transgendered. This is neither more or less horrific than if he had been killed for lesbianism, but it is different." Jones continues that "If the queer community makes of Brandon a martyr to a cause, so be it. But if he is to be canonized in any way, it should be done in such a way that respects his right to self-definition."[35] Self-definition is often difficult to pin down where no written sources point to a transsexual or transgendered identity per se, but through his survivors, Brandon Teena speaks clearly. Brandon Teena's mother notes that he never identified as a lesbian but instead wanted to be a man. And his girlfriends, who identified as heterosexual, understood him, if they had knowledge about his genital status, as a preoperative transsexual. Lana Tisdel remembered, "He said he was born female, is a female, but wants to be a male," and another girlfriend recalled that Brandon Teena, "was a woman outside but felt like a man, and . . . was going to have an operation."[36]

Self-definition is central to the recuperation and, perhaps, appropriation of historical figures for presentist means. But gender cannot continue to function as a slippery subset of sexuality, as evidence for a history of sexual outlaws that obliterates the possibility of gender outlaws and erases transgender history and experience. As Jason Cromwell notes in an article on Billy Tipton,

> I know that as an FTM many within our community would like to claim Billy as one of our own. We have so few role models, even though history is filled with females who lived and passed as men. Billy did not have surgery to alter his sex, and he certainly lived during a time when it was available. However, this is true for many FTMs, because the results are not very good and quite costly. Billy left no written explanation for the actions of his life. He left us instead with a life lived for over 50 years as a man. Does his life as a man have no meaning?[37]

What is the meaning, then, of cross-gender behavior and identity? What are the facts of gender when, upon the death of an anatomical female who lived his entire adult life as a man, his so called true identity is revealed to be female and his sexuality is recuperated as lesbian? What is the material substance that determines the truth of one's gendered or sexual identity: written articulation, daily practice, or, finally, genitalia?[38] Clearly, in the last instance in these cases, hospital beds and autopsies—genitals remain the material fact of gender for many historians, and when gender (which often doubles back as biological sex) determines sexual identity, historical recuperation becomes a tricky political contest indeed. Yet these touchy and not so new questions about the materiality of gender are rarely addressed except by transsexuals and, not surprisingly, in lesbian S/M literature, where a discourse about the body remains central to community life. It is here that a relationship between lesbian and transsexual communities is more articulately fleshed out.

The Theater of Social Space

In the first issue of *Venus Infers*, a magazine for lesbian sadomasochists, Pat Califia poses the question, "Who is my sister?" and outlines some controversies that were raised at the 1992 Powersurge Conference, a conference for leather-dykes that had as its goal the creation of "lesbian only space." The Powersurge Conference was located in Seattle, hosted by the Outer Limits, a Seattle-based women's leather and S/M group. Its program advised that a "lesbian is a WOMAN who considers herself to be a lesbian." Furthermore, it cautioned that the conference organizers would not "be the gender police," so participants should respect this policy, noting that "Because gender lines are bending and fading in these changing times we also have a further clarification for attendance . . .: If you can not slam your dick in a drawer and walk away, then the Amazon Feast and the Dungeon parties are not available to you." However, despite the graphic imagery, two floating signifiers ("lesbian" and "WOMAN") refused to contain themselves during the conference, and the admission policy generated for Powersurge 2 in 1993 changed its tone, specifying that the conference "is open to and welcomes women born women leatherdykes (chromosomal [XX] females only)."[39]

Like the admission policies generated by the Michigan Womyn's Music Festival and the 1991 National Lesbian Conference in Atlanta, which banned "non-genetic women," the 1993 Powersurge Conference policy was generated in response to the participation of transsexuals. However, as Califia observes, this policy excluded lesbian-identified male-to-female transsexuals while it continued to include ex-lesbian female-to-male transsexuals, despite their male appearance and identity, because they remain "chromosomally correct" according to the 1993 admission policy. This raises some peculiar questions about the relationship between bodies and nations—questions that have indeed generated some creative responses (like chromosomal admission tests).[40]

Califia's article stresses the pressing need to address the conflicted relationship between ex-lesbian FTMs, lesbian-identified MTFs, and leatherdykes. Califia articulates her discomfort with continued FTM participation at lesbian (leather) events, particularly while lesbian-identified MTF transsexuals have been excluded. While maintaining the right to self-determination (including the right to identify as a male-to-female transsexual lesbian *or* a female-to-male transsexual lesbian), Califia nevertheless encourages FTMs to take responsibility for their chosen gender. She states that "If someone is taking male hormones, letting their facial hair grow, has taken a male name, changed their legal documents to say they are male, and expects to be addressed by a male name and male pronouns, I can't really visualize that person as being a lesbian."[41] She notes her discomfort as she watches a roomful of lesbians listen respectfully to FTM "leatherdykes" describe how they want to "cut off their tits," while MTF leatherdykes who "love their tits" are not allowed to participate in Powersurge. Thus, on the one hand, while Califia argues that the material that informs gender springs from a number of life experiences and choices (legal identity, hormonal therapy, facial hair, etc.), she concludes that the relationship one determines with her or his physical body ultimately underscores the social fact of gender. In other words, Califia argues that a line between genders does exist, and male-identified individuals, despite their chromosomes, socialization, or genital status, cannot be lesbians. FTMs must place themselves on a continuum that realistically and by choice pulls them into the category "man"—and out of "women only" spaces. So, while the precise boundary between genders remains unclear, the regulatory function of gender boundaries remains uncontested.

Controversies surrounding the Michigan Womyn's Music Festival's entrance policies frame these questions from a different angle. This festival, which has been in existence for twenty years, is a weeklong event where thousands of women gather in a Michigan forest to camp, socialize, attend workshops, and enjoy an impressive line-up of mostly lesbian musicians. Until 1991 the festival had no explicit policy with regard to the attendance of transsexuals (or exactly who "womyn" are), but in 1991 Nancy Jean Burkholder was expelled from the festival after one day of attendance because she was suspected of being a transsexual. Burkholder was not the first transsexual woman to enter the festival. In fact, she had attended the year before, but for some reason in August 1991, security tightened, and Burkholder was expelled because even though this policy remained absent from 1991 festival literature, a security guard asserted that "transsexuals were not permitted to attend the festival."[42] Before she left, however, Chris, the security guard and contact person for the producers, asked Burkholder whether she had had a sex change operation. Burkholder said Chris could look at her genitals, but Burkholder maintained that her surgical history was her own business.[43] This information signals the ambiguity of the festival's policy. Burkholder was being ejected, but was it because of her genital status, her surgical history, her consciousness, or her chromosomes? Chris stated that the festival had a "no transsexuals" policy, and while this may be true, her curiosity about Burkholder's surgical history suggests that morphology may, indeed, have something to do with gender, or in this case with "womyn."

As a result of these events, the 1992 Michigan Womyn's Music Festival's literature got clearer about its policies, stating that the festival was open to "womyn-born-womyn" only. Although no transsexuals were expelled from this festival even though there were several in attendance, the 1993 festival saw the expulsion of four MTF transsexual lesbians and the birth of "Camp Trans," a quasi-refugee colony that pitched tent just outside the entrance to the festival. From this venue transsexuals and friends continued to distribute literature about the festival's exclusionary policy in an attempt to gauge whether the producers' policies matched those of the festivalgoers. Through the next year, the protesters pressured the festival producers, Lisa Vogel and Barbara Price, to state explicitly that their "womyn-born-womyn only" policy really meant that the festival was open to non-transsexual women only, which would raise the stakes not only to the level of explicit discrimination but closer to the body where one might measure one's transsexualness against surgical or hormonal intervention. However, the festival producers refused to change their "womyn-born-womyn" policy and in August 1994 "Camp Trans, for humyn born humyns" reseated itself, hosting a wealth of extracurricular activities, again just outside the entrance of the festival.

In 1994, however, the scab fell off the uneasy peace between S/M and non-S/M dykes as Tribe-8, a raucous band of musicians, performed amid controversy about their ostensibly violent lyrics and stage presence. At the same time, the Lesbian Avengers gathered momentum inside the festival in defense of excluded (transsexual) Lesbian Avengers on the outside. On the sixth day of the festival, after a group of protesters walked to the front gate and challenged the festival's entrance policy with a variety of differently sexed and gendered bodies, the producers agreed to allow transsexuals to enter the festival but still under the rubric of "womyn-born-womyn."[44] This constituted a victory for the protesters in that the meaning of gender was placed within the realm of self-definition, but questions of morphology continued to plague the policing of borders as it remained unclear whether non- or pre-operative MTF transsexuals might enter the festival or whether FTMs at any stage remained within the rubric of "womyn-born-womyn." In other words, how much or in what ways did the body constitute consciousness? Could consciousness exist irrelevant to the body's contours? Could individuals with penises be "womyn-born-womyn"? Might individuals with vaginas be men?

At this point, the compromise/victory engineered at the 1994 Michigan Womyn's Music Festival sounds a lot like Califia's fluid boundary whereby in the end, despite your body hair, legal identity, genital status, or surgical history, you place yourself as a result of your consciousness at any particular point in time on a bipolar gender continuum that admits the existence of a boundary between men and women, male and female. You decide for yourself what you are and whether or not you can, in good faith, enter a gender-bound social space. Even with this fluid and self-determining approach to the meaning and function of gender difference, gender remains foundational to the articulation and function of community. Bodies take on social meaning in relation to, for instance, the lesbian nation only if they can fix themselves in time and space as one gender or another. Despite mutating morphology, or the potentially revolutionary transformation of the body in response to oppressive gender constructs, the ability to articulate oneself intelligibly as one gender or another remains central to the function of community, social identity, political formation, and ultimately the forging of a relationship to the state in the name of separatism or civil rights protections.

Discussion

In order to pose an alternative and more provocative perspective, one that does not necessarily reinscribe a boundary between male and female, I return to Powersurge's "slam your dick in a drawer" policy. This policy provides an example of a community that encourages gender play as an integral part of its practice but simultaneously struggles to maintain some kind of anatomy-based exclusionary policy around which the dyke part of the term "leatherdyke" continues to make sense. In this case the problem is not male-identification, self-definition, or surgical history but the function of the penis itself. In other words, dykes may have any variety of chromosomal configurations, shifting gender identifications, and most certainly ambiguous bodies, but Powersurge leatherdykes by definition cannot have functioning or particularly sensitive penises—or penises large enough to slam in a drawer. This policy, which remained in effect even though Powersurge 1995 dropped its "women-born-women" requirements, seems to be something of an innovative and practical solution to a theoretical conundrum (although it certainly raises a whole different set of problems). In many ways the "slam-your-dick-in-a-drawer" policy leaves a traditional sex/gender system behind in that sexuality (or dykeness) remains independent of gender and birth bodies. Dykeness has nothing to do with gender, is not something you are born with, nor is it a product of socialization or self-definition. Dykeness becomes a brute manifestation of one aspect of the body rather than an expression of genetic female same-gender or even cross-gender sexuality. Certainly, dykeness in this instance resonates loudly as lack, but because it is read from the body's immediate material form, gender's relationship to sexuality is erased and gender is innovatively excused from the picture.

Along a similar line, in a roundtable discussion, a number of FTMs challenge a sex/gender system that leaves no room for lesbians who are men or men who retain a lesbian history. Mike, for example, reveals that "I never really identified as female, but I identified as a lesbian for a while." He continues,

> Being a dyke gave me options. I knew I wasn't straight; I tried it, and it didn't work. I wanted to be with women. But the more I was out in the lesbian community, and the more I was out into S/M, the more I came to realize that, hey, I didn't fit there either, exactly. For me, it's not about being a man or being a woman, cuz there is some fluidity in there. I identify primarily as male, but I still have roots with the women's community that I don't want severed. I'm thankful that I was socialized female.[45]

Sky, another FTM, similarly unsettles an intuitively clear relationship between gender and sexual identity: "My emotional affinities are still very clearly with queer women. I'm forty years old, and I've been involved with dykes for more than half of my life. I'm not going to give that up . . . the dyke community is home."[46] According to these statements, Mike and Sky's lived practice as women (or lesbians) had become a historical anchor and the material fact of gender (or sexuality) despite their male bodies and male gender identities.[47] These statements suggest a paradigm in which sexual identity has social meaning beyond or outside gender, so that men might, at times, be lesbians—and women, gay men.[48]

These reconfigurations do not necessarily provide evidence for a third sex or third gender, nor do they indicate a postmodern proliferation of genders and sexualities. Instead, the tension between transsexual bodies and lesbian nations suggests a site where sex and gender no longer combine to flesh out culturally intelligible bodies. As Max Valerio argues, "Transsexuals are freaks, outsiders and outlaws in this world. We have lived the unthinkable. Are privy to information and experiences that most people have little conception of. This is our power, our damning glory."[49] Valerio's statement calls attention to the specificity of transsexual experience. He, along with sociologist Henry Rubin and literary critic Jay Prosser, argues that it is the materiality (the daily practice) of transsexual embodiment that confounds and displaces bipolar gender and sexual nationalism.[50] These observations resonate in response to gender and queer theory's appropriation of transsexual bodies as potentially revolutionary cultural artifacts.[51] They also resonate in response to a (lesbian) feminist critique and condemnation of transsexuality.

Most famously, Janice Raymond has argued that MTF transsexuals are dangerous to women and by extension lesbians because they not only colonize femaleness through embodiment, but they provide material for a medical-psychiatric empire to resolve a contemporary gender identity crisis by trading one set of gendered stereotypes for another. Raymond argues that through MTF transsexuals, doctors invade women's social spaces (as well as their bodies) and market the future of gender.[52] Bernice Hausman, in a more recent book, makes a similar claim. She argues that the contemporary concept of gender, as distinct from biological sex, is relatively new and emerged as a psychiatric response to medical technologies employed through the mid-twentieth century to "solve" the problem of intersexuality (or hermaphroditism). With the birth of new technologies such as endocrinology and plastic surgery, doctors found that they could reshape the genitals of an intersexed individual, usually a child, into something less ambiguous. The idea of a core gender identity grew out of these practices because some surgically altered individuals continued to express themselves as the "wrong" gender despite hormonal and surgical intervention. Gender, some psychiatrists reasoned, seemed to be fixed within the body rather than the product of socialization or an immediate expression of morphology. More surprisingly, the body's exterior began to seem more plastic than its interior. However, in Hausman's narrative, the agents of these inimical social changes shift from doctors to transsexuals in that through the late 1950s, as a response to the celebrity of Christine Jorgenson, transsexuals began to use the language of core gender identity to demand genital reconstruction. Thus, through the development and gradual acceptance of sex reassignment surgery as the appropriate medical intervention or cure for "gender dysphoria," transsexuals helped stabilize and naturalize the relatively new concept of gender identity. So while Hausman charts new territory in the history of medicine and its impact on feminist theory, she ultimately (like Raymond) blames transsexuals for normalizing, naturalizing, and codifying a bipolar gender system, fixing biological women into a feminine frame.[53]

As this essay illustrates, however, the meaning of gendered bodies, particularly transgendered bodies, remains complicated by and dependent on the territories (nations) bodies inhabit. Transsexuals do not fix gender in time and space, nor do they always already undermine its insipid naturalization. Rather, in the examples cited above, transsexual bodies reconfigure historical narrative and reterritorialize social space. Contrary to Raymond and Hausman's assertions, these actions upset a fixed relationship between sex, gender, and sexuality. In fact, while this essay does not intend to disrupt or deny the value of separatist practice, it illustrates (through the lens of lesbian nationalism) the function of intelligible bodies to the body politic. It argues that the body politic (the nation) exists for intelligible bodies, and despite anti-essentialist gestures to the contrary, contemporary sex/gender politics often document the absolutely desperate reiteration of bipolar gender as a foundation for sexual nationalism. Finally, this essay poses the specter of the outlaw (particularly as it takes the form of unruly, unreadable, inconsistent, but nevertheless material bodies) and suggests that outlaw bodies sharpen a boundary not between men and women, male and female, or even transsexual and non, but between abject and intelligible. This distinction evidences the possibility that while most bodies, even transgendered bodies, fit neatly or fold back into the body politic as readable, comprehensible, and intelligible, some retain or reclaim a fleeting moment of social and cultural unintelligibility, inhabiting a queer space, I would argue, outside, beyond, invisible to, and perhaps, as a result, in confrontation with the state.

Notes

The author thanks CLAGS, the Center for Lesbian and Gay Studies, for the generous Rockefeller Fellowship that made the production of this essay possible. Thanks also go to Michael Du Plessis, Elizabeth Freeman, Ben Singer, and especially Alex Harris for insight and support through the writing process.

1. While it is important to distinguish between the terms "transsexual" and "transgender," particularly since access to medical technologies and state entitlements (i.e., change of name, alteration of birth certificate) are often dependent on a medical diagnosis of "transsexualism," this essay uses these terms somewhat interchangeably in order to broaden the category transsexual. For instance, if the term "transsexual" is used to signify a body that has entered into a formal relationship with doctors and the state with regard to "sex reassignment" (with the stated goal of eventually completing "the surgery"—a nonsense term with regard to female-to-male transsexuals who experience a series of surgeries, if any), many pre- and nonoperative transsexuals, particularly female-to-males, fall out of the category "transsexual" and can only be understood as "transgendered." For diagnostic categories, see the American Psychiatric Association's *Diagnostic and Statistical Manual of Mental Disorders*, 4th ed. (1994); for a more comprehensive discussion of the term "transgender" and its relationship to transsexuality, see Susan Stryker, "My Words to Victor Frankenstein above the Village of Chamounix," *GLQ* 1:3 (1994) 251–52; for more information about FTM surgeries, see James Green, "Getting Real about FTM Surgery," *Chrysalis: The Journal of Transgressive Gender Identities* 2:2 (1995) 27–32.

2. As this essay will explore further, the concept of nationalism ("the nation") refers to both the creation and reiteration of world political and economic borders (i.e., the post-World War II consolidation of the nation-state as the legitimate international political form, most obviously visible in the creation of the United Nations) *and* the contemporary emergence and articulation of resistant, deterritorialized, subcultural, and political movements. While Black Nationalism functions as the most resilient form of state-resistant nationalisms in the United States, more recently one can speak of the Lesbian Nation, the Queer Nation, and the Transgender Nation. See Michael Warner's introduction and Lauren Berlant and Elizabeth Freeman, "Queer Nationality," in *Fear of a Queer Planet*, ed. Michael Warner (Minneapolis: Minnesota University Press, 1993); Eve Kosofsky Sedgwick, "Nationalisms and Sexualities in the Age of Wilde," in *Nationalisms and Sexualities*, ed. Andrew Parker, Mary Russo, Doris Sommer, and Patricia Yaeger (New York: Routledge, 1992); David Evans, *Sexual Citizenship* (New York: Routledge, 1994), particularly his chapter "Trans-Citizenship: Transvestism and Transsexualism."

3. For more on the naturalized body, see Michel Foucault, *Discipline and Punish: The Birth of the Prison* (New York: Vintage, 1979), particularly "Docile Bodies," 136–69.

4. See George Mosse, *Nationalism and Sexuality* (New York: Howard Fertig, 1985) for an account of the rise of state nationalism through the construction of sexually respectable bodies.

5. Foucault, *Discipline and Punish*.

6. See Elizabeth Grosz, *Volatile Bodies: Toward a Corporeal Feminism* (Bloomington: Indiana University Press, 1994); Robyn Wiegman, *American Anatomies: Theorizing Race and Gender* (Durham: Duke University Press, 1995); Thomas Laqueur, *Making Sex: Body and Gender from the Greeks to Freud* (Cambridge: Harvard University Press, 1990); Anne Fausto-Sterling, *Myths of Gender: Biological Theories about Women and Men* (New York: Basic Books, 1985); *Representations* 14 (spring 1986), particularly Catherine Gallagher, "The Body Versus the Social Body in the Works of Thomas Malthus and Henry Mayhew," 83–106. See also Jennifer Terry and Jacqueline Urla, eds., *Deviant Bodies* (Bloomington: Indiana University Press, 1995); Judith Halberstam and Ira Livingston, eds., *Posthuman Bodies* (Bloomington: Indiana University Press, 1995).

7. Benedict Anderson, *Imagined Communities* (New York: Verso, 1991), 5–7.

8. Anderson argues that "print culture" and "print capitalism," particularly the publication and distribution of the popular novel and newspaper, weakened and ultimately replaced historically sacred symbols. *Imagined Communities*, 9–46.

9. Judith Butler, *Bodies That Matter: On the Discursive Limits of "Sex"* (New York: Routledge, 1993), 16.

10. Doug Hattaway, "The Employment Non-Discrimination Act," *HRCF Quarterly* (summer 1995): 6–7.

11. "Trans Community Protests Human Rights Campaign Fund," *AEGIS News* (June 1995): 11.

12. "HRCF Kicks Transfolk Out of National Anti-Discrimination Bill!" *TNT: Transsexual News Telegraph* 5 (summer 1995): 8; Susie Day, "ENDA Discrimination," *Lesbian & Gay New York*, Sept. 17, 1995, 9.

13. Here I stress Michael Warner's use of the term "queer" as an identity that functions to both disrupt the minoritizing logic of toleration and assert a critique of heteronormalcy. See introduction to *Fear of a Queer Planet*, ed. Warner, vii–xxxi.

14. As Foucault notes, in the age of Enlightenment "there will be hundreds of tiny theaters of punishment" where specific territories or functional sites, like HRCF's Employment Non-Discrimination Act, aid the production of disciplined bodies. Michel Foucault, *Discipline and Punish: The Birth of the Prison* (New York: Vintage, 1979), 113.

15. Joan Nestle, *A Restricted Country* (Ithaca, N.Y.: Firebrand, 1987); Joan Nestle, ed., *The Persistent Desire: A Femme-Butch Reader* (Boston: Alyson, 1992); Elizabeth Lapovsky Kennedy and Madeline D. Davis, *Boots of Leather, Slippers of Gold: The History of a Lesbian Community* (New York: Routledge, 1993).

16. Judith Halberstam provides a historical account of lesbian masculinities in "Female Masculinities:

Tommies, Tribades and Inverts," and "Lesbian Masculinity or Even Stone Butches Get the Blues" (unpublished manuscripts).

17. Esther Newton problematizes the slippage between masculinity and lesbianism in "The Mythic Mannish Lesbian: Radclyff Hall and the New Woman," *Signs* 9:4 (1984): 557–75. Nestle's and Kennedy and Davis's recent work (cited above) also clarify the distinction between passing women and butch lesbians by articulating in rich detail the function of butch gender codes as a component of lesbian desire and representation.

18. Jason Cromwell, "Default Assumptions, or The Billy Tipton Phenomenon," *FTM* 28 (July 1994): 4–5; Susan Stryker, "Local Transsexual History," *TNT: Transsexual News Telegraph* 5 (summer–autumn 1995): 14–15.

19. Originally produced by the San Francisco Lesbian and Gay History Project (1979), *She Even Chewed Tobacco* is currently distributed in video form by Women Make Movies. See " 'She Even Chewed Tobacco': A Pictorial Narrative of Passing Women in America," in *Hidden from History: Reclaiming the Gay and Lesbian Past*, eds. Martin Duberman, Martha Vicinus, and George Chauncey, Jr. (New York: Penguin, 1989).

20. Louis Sullivan, *From Female to Male: The Life of Jack Bee Garland* (Boston: Alyson Press, 1990), 31.

21. Sullivan, *From Female to Male*, 3.

22. Sullivan, *From Female to Male*, 4.

23. Betty Cox, quoted by Cindy Kirshman in "The Tragic Masquerade of Billy Tipton," *Windy City Times*, March 1, 1990, 17.

24. Doug Clark, "Billy Tiptop: An Improvised Life," *Seattle Spokesman Review*, January 21, 1990. See also Cindy Kirshman, "The Tragic Masquerade"; Ann Japenga, "A Jazz Pianist's Ultimate Improvisation," *Los Angeles Times*, February 13, 1989.

25. Linda Lee, "Women Posing as Men Pursued Better Opportunities," *Seattle Post Intelligence: What's Happening*, September 10, 1989, 11. While the initial flurry of mainstream press coverage echos this analysis (see "Musician's Death at 74 Reveals He Was a Woman," *New York Times*, February 2, 1989; "Autopsy: Musician Was a Woman," *Newsday*, February 2, 1989), follow-up articles argued that Tipton's sexual or gender identity had more to do with his cross-dressing than his desire to succeed as a musician. See Kirshman, "The Tragic Masquerade"; Clark, "Billy Tipton: An Improvised Life"; and Japenga, "A Jazz Pianist's Ultimate Improvisation."

26. Jason Cromwell, "Default Assumptions, or The Billy Tipton Phenomenon," 4–5.

27. "Billy Tipton Was a (Choose One):" *TNT: Transsexual News Telegraph* 1 (summer 1993): 22. A smaller version of this "advertisement" also appeared in *Engender* 2 (July 1993).

28. "2 Men Held in Slaying of 3 at Humboldt," *Omaha World-Herald*, January 2, 1994; "Rape Report Tied to Killings: Family Says Slaying Were Preventable," *Lincoln Journal-Star*, January 4, 1994; "Woman Who Posed as a Man Is Found Slain with 2 Others," *New York Times*, January 4, 1994; "Her Fatal Deception?" *New York Newsday*, January 5, 1994; "Charade Revealed Prior to Killings," *Des Moines Register*, January 9, 1994; "Questions in Triple Homicide," San Francisco Chronicle, March 17, 1994.

29. "Rape Report Tied to Killings."

30. Kristina Campbell, "Transsexual, Two Others Murdered in Nebraska," *The Washington Blade*, January 14, 1994, 19; Mindy Ridgway, "Queers Have No Right to Life—In Nebraska," *San Francisco Bay Times*, January 13, 1994, 7.

31. Terry A. Moroney, letter to Anthony Marro, editor, *New York Newsday*, January 5, 1994. See also AVP press release, "Anti-Violence Project Calls for Bias Classification in Nebraska Lesbian Murder," January 5, 1994.

32. Donna Minkowitz, "Love Hurts," *Village Voice*, April 19, 1994.

33. Minkowitz, "Love Hurts."

34. In fact, Minkowitz is so sure Brandon Teena was a lesbian that she wonders why Brandon Teena moved from Lincoln, a city with a visible gay community, to Falls City, an even more remote Nebraska town, rather than San Francisco or Denver, "the gay mecca of choice for corn belters." Clearly, Minkowitz can not see the events of Brandon Teena's life and death outside a gay lens. Perhaps Brandon Teena wanted to evade *misrecognition* as a lesbian and as a result chose a city with heightened gender codes so to more effectively live as a man.

35. Jordy Jones, "FTM Crossdresser Murdered," *FTM* 26 (Feb. 1994): 3.

36. Campbell, "Transsexual, Two Others Murdered in Nebraska," 19; "Charade Revealed Prior to Killings," 4B; "Her Fatal Deception?" See also Denise Noe, "Why Was Brandon Teena Murdered?" *Chrysalis* 2:2 (1995): 50.

37. Cromwell, "Default Assumptions, or The Billy Tipton Phenomenon," 5.

38. See Grosz, *Volatile Bodies*, for a discussion of the materiality of subjectivity.

39. Pat Califia, "Who Is My Sister: Powersurge and the Limits of Our Community," *Venus Infers* 1:1 (summer 1993): 4–5.

40. Renee Richards, for example, was asked (but refused) to submit to a Barr body test in which cells from the inside of the cheek are examined to reveal chromosomal distributions. See Bernice Hausman, *Changing Sex: Transsexualism, Technology, and the Idea of Gender* (Durham: Duke University Press, 1995), 12.

41. Califia, "Who Is My Sister," 6.

42. Nancy Jean Burkholder, "A Kinder, Gentler Festival?" *TransSisters* 2 (November–December 1993): 4.

43. Burkholder, "Kinder, Gentler Festival?" 4.

44. Davina Anne Gabriel, "Mission to Michigan III: Barbarians at the Gates," *TransSisters* 7 (winter 1995): 14–32; Riki Anne Wilchins, "The Menace in Michigan," *Gendertrash* 3 (winter 1995): 17–19.

45. "FTM/Female-to-Male: An Interview with Mike, Eric, Billy, Sky, and Shadow," in *Dagger: On Butch Women*, ed. Lily Burana, Roxxie, and Linnea Due (Pittsburgh: Cleis Press, 1994), 155.

46. Sky, in "FTM/Female-to-Male," 158.

47. On the other hand, Henry Rubin argues in a study of FTM identity formation that FTMs often consolidate their gender identities around a vehement disidentification from butch lesbians. Henry Samuel Rubin, "Transformations: Emerging Female to Male Transsexual Identities" (Ph.D. diss. Brandeis University, 1996). See also Ben Singer, "Velveteen Realness" (paper delivered at the CLAGS Trans/Forming Knowledge Conference, May 2, 1996).

48. C. Jacob Hale, "Dyke Leatherboys and Their Daddies: How to Have Sex without Men or Women," paper delivered at the Berkshire Conference on the History of Women, June 8, 1996).

49. Max Wolf Valerio, "Legislating Freedom," review of *The Apartheid of Sex* by Martine Rothblatt, *TNT: Transsexual News Telegraph* 5 (summer–autumn 1995): 26.

50. Henry Samule Rubin, "Transformations: Emerging Female to Male Transsexual Identities"; Jay Prosser, "No Place Like Home: The Transgendered Narrative of Leslie Feinberg's *Stone Butch Blues*," *Modern Fiction Studies* 41 (fall–winter 1995).

51. For an overview of feminist and queer theory's approach to transsexual identities, see Kathleen Chapman and Michael du Plessis, " 'Don't Call Me *Girl*': Feminist Theory, Lesbian Theory, and Transsexual Identities" in *Cross Purposes: Lesbian Studies, Feminist Studies, and the Limits of Alliance*, Dana Heller, ed. (Bloomington: Indiana University Press, 1997); and Ki Namaste, " 'Tragic Misreadings': Queer Theory's Erasure of Transgender Subjectivity," in *Queer Studies: A Lesbian, Gay, Bisexual, and Transgender Anthology*, Brett Beemyn and Mickey Eliason, eds. (New York: New York University Press, 1996).

52. Janice G. Raymond, *The Transsexual Empire: The Making of the She-Male* (Boston: Beacon, 1979).

53. Hausman, *Changing Sex*.

3

Teaching the Differences among Women from a Historical Perspective
Rethinking Race and Gender as Social Categories

Tessie Liu

During the week-long Southwestern Institute on Research on Women seminar in 1989 on teaching women's studies from an international perspective, I experienced several epiphanic moments when a number of my research and teaching preoccupations melded and came into sharper focus. What follows is a progress report on my ruminations on this subject in the years since the seminar. In particular, I would like to share the conceptual inversions and reexamination of received categories through which this problem has led me.

What has emerged from this journey is a clearer vision that feminist scholars not only must talk about diversity, but also must better understand how the differences among women are constituted historically in identifiable social processes. In this paper, I explore the importance of race as an analytical tool for investigating and understanding the differences among women. To do so, we must recognize that race is a *gendered* social category. By exploring the connections between race oppression and sex oppression, specifically how the former is predicated on the latter, we will also gain new insights into the relationship between gender and class.

Epiphanal moments, in many ways, occur only when one is primed for them. The lectures and workshops in the seminar addressed questions with which I had been grappling throughout the academic year. My first set of concerns came out of a graduate course in comparative women's history that I taught at the University of Arizona with a colleague who specializes in Latin American history and women's history. Through the semester, students and instructors asked one another what we were trying to achieve by looking at women's experiences comparatively. Beyond our confidence that appreciating diversity would enrich us personally, as well as stimulate in us new questions to pose to our own areas of specialization, we raised many more questions than those for which we found definitive answers. One set of questions, in particular, troubled me. Throughout the semester, I wondered about the relationship between the kinds of comparisons in which we were engaged and feminist theory more generally. Were we looking for some kind of underlying sameness behind all the variations in women's experiences? Was our ultimate goal to build a unified theory of gender that would explain all the differences among women? Much later, I realized that my questions centered on the status of diversity in feminist theory and politics. Especially troubling to me was the lack of discussion on such questions as these: How do feminists explain the differences among women? Are there contradictions between the focus on differences and the claim to a universal sisterhood among women? How can these tensions be resolved?

The second set of concerns that I brought to this week-long workshop came out of ongoing discussions with my colleagues in the History Department over how to restructure and teach

Western civilization if we were to live up to our mandate to incorporate race, class, and gender.[1] Both sets of concerns address the problems of teaching cultural diversity. In this paper, I point out that the intellectual issues raised by adopting a more cross-cultural or international perspective in women's studies parallel the emotional and conceptual hurdles that my colleagues and I encountered in our attempts to integrate race, class, and gender into courses in Western civilization. Further, I suggest that the rethinking required to restructure such courses can be instructive to feminist scholars in offering an opportunity to reassess our own understanding of the relationships among race, class, and gender in feminist analysis.

The mandate to incorporate race, gender, and class into the western civilization curriculum originated as a political move. But even those of us who pushed for this integration did not have a clear idea of the fundamental intellectual changes entailed. We were initially motivated by the wish to establish diversity. This task is most easily accomplished thematically: that is, every so often we add a lecture on women, on African Americans, on Native Americans, and so on, aiming for a multicultural representation. Although it marked a good-faith beginning, this approach is particularly problematic in the context of courses such as those on Western civilization. This attempt to introduce diversity merely sprinkles color on a white background, as Abena Busia commented in her lecture to the summer institute. One unintended but very serious effect of merely adding women, other cultures, or even discussions of class conflict and colonialism without challenging the basic structure of the idea of Western civilization is that non-Europeans, all women, the poor, and all intersecting subsets of these identities appear in the story only as victims and losers.

One problem I had not anticipated was the capacity of my students, who are primarily white and middle-class, for sympathy and yet distance. To put this more starkly: To many students, they themselves embody the universal norm. In their heart of hearts, they believe that *white* establishes not merely skin color but the norm from which blacks, browns, yellows, and reds deviate. They condemn racism, which they believe is a problem out there between racists and the people they attack. Analogously, many male students accept the reality of sexism, feel bad about it for women, but think that they are not touched by it. Even though they sympathize, for these students poverty, racism, and even sexism are still other people's problems. Teaching them, I learned an important lesson about the politics of inclusion: For those who have been left out of the story of Western civilization, it is perfectly possible to be integrated and still remain marginal.

Teaching students to appreciate cultural differences with the aim of promoting tolerance may not be a bad goal in itself, but the mode of discourse surrounding tolerance does not challenge the basically Eurocentric worldview enshrined in Western-civilization courses. At best, tolerance teaches us to accept differences; at worst, it teaches the necessity of accepting what we fear or dislike. In fact, it often encourages an ethnocentric understanding of differences because this form of comparison does not break down the divisions between "us" and "them," between "self/subject" and "other." Most of all, it encourages us to realize that we are implicated in these differences—that our own identities are constituted relationally within them.

Maintaining the divide between "us" and "them," I suspect, is one way of distancing the uncomfortable reality of unequal power relations, which come to the fore once we include those previously excluded. Classically, Western-civilization courses eschew such discussions of power. The purpose of such courses, structured by very Hegelian notions of the march of progress, is to present world history as the inevitable ascent of Europeans. The noted Islamicist Marshall Hodgson aptly described this as the "torch theory of civilization": The torch was first lit in Mesopotamia, passed on to Greece and then to Rome, and carried to northern Europe; ultimately, it came to rest on the North American continent during and after World War II.[2] In this story, Europeans and their descendants bear the torch. The privileged subject is white and male, usually a member of the ruling elite, and the multiple social relationships that sustain his privilege are rarely, if ever, examined.

In light of these complexities, the basic problem in reforming Western-civilization courses changed. Our new problem was how to decenter the privileged white male (and sometimes female) subject—the "I"—in the story of Western civilization, which, not coincidentally, corresponds closely to the subjectivity students have been socialized to develop in relation to the world. We could not possibly modify or reform this strong underlying message with a sprinkle of diversity. The Euro- (andro-)centric viewpoint is embedded in categories of analysis, in notions of historical significance, in beliefs about who the important actors are, and in the causal logic of the story. We cannot integrate race, class, and gender without completely restructuring a course: critiquing foundations, developing new categories, telling a new story. The critical part of the decentering, however, is the painful process of self-examination. Needless to say, the intellectual and emotional hurdles of such a project must not be underestimated. We are teaching against the grain.

African American feminists in the United States have long argued that the historically privileged white male is paralleled in American feminist discourse by the white female subject. The problem is perhaps most explicitly and succinctly articulated in the title *All the Women Are White, All the Blacks Are Men, but Some of Us Are Brave: Black Women's Studies*.[3] Introducing and more fully representing women in all their diversity, although a good-faith beginning, is not sufficient in itself to correct the problems. The problem for Black women, as just one example, lies not just in their initial invisibility, but also in the manner in which they enter the mainstream. The real possibility of black (and other nonwhite) women being brought in as second-class citizens forces us to consider how we as feminists account for and explain the differences among women. What is the status of these differences in feminist theory and politics, especially with respect to the claims of universal sisterhood?

To illustrate the depth of these unresolved problems, let me refer to our discussions on sameness and difference throughout the week-long institute. My personal history is relevant in explaining my reactions. I am an immigrant born in Taiwan to parents who were political refugees from China; my education, however, is completely Western. My feminist consciousness was formed in the context of elite educational institutions, and my specialization is European history. Not surprisingly, I have lived with the contradictions of being simultaneously an insider and an outsider all of my life. The task of explaining why I do not fit anyone's categories is a burden I long ago accepted. All the same, the week's discussions on sameness and difference stirred within me the undercurrents of unresolved issues and brought into clearer focus how much this problem pervades feminist politics.

The first note of disquiet came on the first day when someone in my discussion group used the term "women of color." A Palestinian woman, two Chicanas, and I looked at each other and winked knowingly. All of a sudden we were others, strangers to each other but placed in the same group. We were all at this conference as feminist scholars, as insiders to the movement, yet suddenly we became outsiders because we had this special affiliation. This concept of diversity (however well meant) begs the question: Where is the feminist standpoint in theorizing about the differences among women? Who is the feminist self and, to borrow from Aihwa Ong, "who is the feminist other?"[4] In the previous paragraph, I deliberately used *difference* in the singular rather than *differences* in the plural because I believe that there is an important distinction. *Difference* has become a crucial concept in feminist theory, yet in this context we are tempted to ask, "Different from what or whom?" As "women of color," we were classed together, in spite of our obvious diversity, simply because we are not white. However well-intentioned such acts of inclusion are, they raise the question: Who is doing the comparing? Unless there is an Archimedean point outside social ties from which one could neutrally compare, as feminist scholars we must recognize that all discussions of differences and sameness are themselves inseparable from the power relations in which we live.[5] In this sense, I maintain, there is no true international or cross-cultural perspective. We can view the world only from where we stand.

Failure to recognize this fundamental limitation leads to the kind of ethnocentrism hidden in works such as Robin Morgan's 1984 anthology *Sisterhood Is Global*. Without doubt, Morgan's anthology is an impressive achievement. Covering seventy countries, it provides a wealth of information on women's lives and their legal, economic, and political status. As reviewers Hackstaff and Pierce (1985) point out, however, the implicit argument that women everywhere are fundamentally and similarly oppressed is extremely problematic. In *Sisterhood Is Global*, differences are treated as local variations on a universal theme. As a result, *why* women's experiences differ so radically is never seriously examined. Moreover, the reviewers point out a Western bias implicit in the uncritical and unself-conscious use of crucial terms such as *feminism, individual rights*, and *choice*, which retain definitions developed by Western feminists from industrialized countries, however inappropriate such working definitions may be in other cultural and social contexts. The problem is not only that women in other cultures define *feminism* or *self* in distinct ways that Morgan should have acknowledged. More fundamentally, an unproblematic assumption of common sisterhood overlooks the social reality within which texts such as *Sisterhood Is Global* are created. Morgan's vision of global feminism does not question the relative power and advantages from which feminists in North America and Western Europe claim the authority to speak in the name of others on the oppression of all women.[6]

This curious result—a catalogue of difference in which the relations among those who are different play no role—is symptomatic of a more general problem with what might be called a cross-cultural perspective. The classic anthropological use of *culture* understands the values, beliefs, and politics of various groups and societies as concrete realizations within the compass of human possibility. In an intellectual move with obvious benefits for liberal politics, difference is made a raw fact, irreducible to any hierarchical orderings of evolution or mental progress. A cross-cultural perspective rests on the notion of a transcendental or universal humanness, an essential similarity that makes it possible to understand the beliefs and behavior of others, however strange.[7]

This is a political vision with clear and obvious benefits. In the hands of members of a society that enjoys advantages of wealth and power over those with different cultures, however, it conceals more than it reveals. By not focusing on the unequal distribution of power permeates relations between groups, the liberal humanist discourse elides the necessary discussion of power. To assert that the differences among women conceal an essential sisterhood is not enough; this quick achievement of solidarity comes at the expense of a real examination of the nature of the connections that actually do exist, by virtue of the fact that we occupy different positions in a world inadequately described as a congeries of reified, discrete cultures.[8] Instead, we must understand difference in social structural terms, in terms of interests, privileges, and deprivation. Only then can we see the work required to make sisterhood more than a rhetorical assertion of common substance. The crucial alternative analytical framework, I argue, entails exploring how diverse women's experiences are constituted reciprocally within relations of power.

On these highly charged issues within feminist politics, Charlotte Bunch, our first speaker at the seminar, brought an important perspective on thinking about the differences among women, arguing that we must take differences as the starting point, as the feminist standpoint. In the process of exploring diversity, Bunch assured the audience, the similarities in women's experiences will emerge. For Bunch, however, difference is not opposed to sameness. Rather, recognizing the differences among women should lead us to ask how our different lives and experiences are connected. In contrast to Morgan, Bunch argues that sisterhood is not a natural category, stemming from an organic community. Rather, an international (or cross-cultural or cross-class) sisterhood is constructed out of common political strategies. In this sense, the possibility of sisterhood begins with the recognition that, despite the vast differences that could divide us, our fates are linked and that very connectedness necessitates common action and common solutions. The fact of difference, however, means that a common cause needs to be constructed; it cannot simply be asserted.[9]

Bunch's perspective is wholly consistent with the general goal of understanding differences across cultures. Yet I think that she asks us to investigate and appreciate diversity not just for its own sake, but also for its strategic importance to feminist politics. The goal of studying women's conditions across regions and cultures is not to demonstrate the sameness of women's oppression, but to understand the connections among the different ways in which women are oppressed (and, perhaps, to understand the connection between some women's privileges and others' deprivations). Because the connectedness of experience allows us to formulate strategies for common action, our study of differences must focus on how differences are constituted relationally. As a historian, I interpret these remarks through the possible contributions of my discipline. Methodologically, social history has much to add to the goal of understanding differences relationally. By situating experience as part of specific social processes, social history understands experience as the result of particular actions and actors, actions that establish connections among people and among groups.

In terms of understanding connections, the lessons I have drawn from revising the curriculum for courses on Western civilization are particularly instructive. Moreover, once we change the content of the course from the story of European ascendency to a critical history of European dominance, the global scale and time frame of the modern half of the course (post-1500) offer a framework for thinking through and empirically studying how the differences among women were relationally constituted.[10] This framework is important, I believe, because differences in the world that we have inherited are not neutral facts. The diversity of lived experiences that we encounter today within a single society and among societies around the globe cannot be abstracted from the legacy of colonization, forced contact, expropriation, and continuing inequalities. Of course, the cultures of subjugated peoples cannot be reduced to the fact of their domination alone, any more than the culture of colonizers can be reduced to conquest. Yet no analysis of cultural diversity can be complete without study of the forces that have so fundamentally shaped experience.

In the remainder of this paper, I offer the broad outlines of a conceptual inversion entailed in remaking courses in Western civilization to serve our goal of understanding the differences among women. At present, although within women's studies we speak often of race, class, and gender as aspects of experience, we continue to organize our courses around gender as the important analytical category. This focus is both understandable and logical because, after all, our subject is women. Yet I would like to suggest the usefulness of organizing courses around the concept of race. By understanding how race is a *gendered* social category, we can more systematically address the structural underpinnings of why women's experiences differ so radically and how these differences are relationally constituted.

In order to place race at the center of feminist inquiry, we need first to rethink how we conceptualize race as an analytical category. We tend to think that race is a relevant social category only when we encounter racism as a social phenomenon, in the form of bigotry, for example. Scholars have tried to understand racial hatred by analyzing characteristics such as skin color, skull size, and intelligence, which racist ideology deems important, and much of this scholarship has consisted of testing and refuting racial categories. As a result, scholars have let the ideologues of racism set the agenda for discussions of racism within the academy. Although this work is important, I think the scope is too narrow. I would like to suggest that it is fruitful to inquire into the social metaphors that allow racial thinking, that is, the kind of logic or type of reasoning about human relationships that allows racists to believe in the reality of their categories. In other words, we need to move beyond the belief that racial thinking is purely an outgrowth of (irrational) prejudices, because such a belief in fact exoticizes racism, in the sense that it makes racism incomprehensible to those who do not share the hatred. Rather, as I will specify below, the more radical position holds that race is a widespread principle of social organization.

Once we ask what kind of reasoning about the nature of human relationships allows racists to believe in the reality of their categories, we find racial metaphors in benign situations as well as under conditions of discrimination, overt hatred, and genocide. In other words, even those of us who do not hate on the basis of skin color must realize that racial thinking is disturbingly close to many of the acceptable ways that we conceptualize social relationships. In this sense, placing race at the intellectual center of courses such as those in Western civilization is decentering, for it attempts to break established habits of categorizing in terms of "self" and "other." My ideas on this subject, I should add, are still in the formative stages. I have sketched with broad strokes very complex and nuanced social situations in the hope of capturing simple patterns that have been overlooked. In making bold and overly schematic generalizations, I also hope to provoke opposition and controversy as one way to assess the usefulness of these ideas for further inquiry.

Let me begin with several dictionary definitions of race that I found quite surprising and illuminating. Under the first definition in the *Oxford English Dictionary*, we find *race* as "a group of persons, animals, or plants connected by common descent or origin." As illustrations, the dictionary lists "the offspring or posterity of a person; a set of children or descendants; breeding, the production of offspring; (rarely): a generation." In a second set of usages, it defines *race* as "a limited group descended from a common ancestor, a house, family, kindred." We find as examples "a tribe, nation, or people, regarded as common stock; a group of several tribes or peoples regarded as forming a distinct ethnic stock; one of the great divisions of mankind, having certain peculiarities in common." The last is qualified by this comment: "This term is often used imprecisely; even among anthropologists there is no generally accepted classification or terminology." These definitions are then followed by explanations of the meaning of *race* when applied to animals, plants, and so forth.

It is clear from the first two sets of usages that ideas about descent, blood ties, or common substance are basic to the notion of race. What struck me, in particular, was the second set of synonyms for *race: house, family, kindred*. Louis Flandrin made the reverse discovery when he looked up *famille* in a French dictionary, *Petit Robert*. *Famille* refers to "the entirety of persons mutually connected by marriage or filiation" or "the succession of individuals who descend from one another," that is to say, "a line," "a race," "a dynasty." Only secondarily does *Petit Robert* define family in the way we usually mean, as "related persons living under one roof," "more specifically, the father, the mother, the children." These dictionary definitions, taken all together, suggest that race as a social category is intimately linked to one of the basic ways in which human beings have organized society, that is, by kinship. As Flandrin points out, etymologically, at least in England and France, *race* as a kinship term, usually to denote the patronymic or family name—called literally "the name of the race," *le nom de race*—predated our current usage of the term, which denotes distinct large populations.[11]

Although the specific referent in notions of race is kinship, in order to understand the significance of racial thinking, we need to move beyond these neutral dictionary distinctions. When kinship becomes the key element in a stratified social order, as in dynastic politics or caste systems, the concept of race becomes important. Thus, European society, before actual contact with peoples of different skin tones and different cultures and customs, was organized by racial principles. The operating definition of race was based not on external physical characteristics but on blood ties—or, more precisely, some common substance passed on by fathers. In early modern Europe, when patriarchal rule and patrilineal descent predominated, political power, social station, and economic entitlements were closely bound to blood ties and lineage. Thus race also encapsulated the notion of class. But class in this society was an accident of birth: either according to birth order (determining which rights and privileges the child inherited) or, more generally, according to the family into which one was born (noble or common, propertied or not). The privileges or stigmas of birth, in this system, were as indelible and as discriminatory as any racial system based on skin color or some other trait. The notion of legitimate and illegitimate birth indicates that blood ties did not extend to all who shared genetic material, but only those with a culturally defined "common substance" passed on by fathers.

Understanding race as an element of social organization directs our attention to forms of stratification. The centrality of reproduction, especially in the transmission of common substance through heterosexual relations and ultimately through birth as the differentiating mark of social entitlements, for example, allows us to see the gendered dimensions of the concept of race. For societies organized by racial principles, reproductive politics are closely linked to establishing the boundaries of lineages. In a male-dominated system, regulating social relationships through racial metaphors necessitates control over women. The reproduction of the system entails not only regulating the sexuality of women in one's own group, but also differentiating between women according to legitimate access and prohibition. Considered in these terms, race as a social category functions through controlling sexuality and sexual behavior.

To borrow from Benedict Anderson's insights about the nature of nationalism, racial thinking, as a principle of social organization, is a way to imagine communities.[12] Basic to the notion of race is that an indelible common substance unites the people who possess it in a special community. It is significant that the community described with racial metaphors is always limited; the intent is to exclude in the process of including. Metaphors of common substance simultaneously articulate the quality of relationship among the members of a group and specify who belongs and who does not, asserting a natural, organic solidarity among people whose relations are described as indelible and nonvoluntary. Thus it is not accidental that racial thinking borrows its language from biology, particularly from a systemic vision of the natural world wherein hierarchies, differences, and even struggles are described as functional to the survival and health of the whole.

These core concepts in racial thinking are powerful and flexible. Racial metaphors are rife in other forms of community building. By analogy, kinship terms —*family, brotherhood, sisterhood,* each with its own specific meanings—are often invoked to create a sense of group affiliation; they can be applied to small communities mobilized for political action or to an entire society, in the sense of the body politic. Most notably, such metaphors are central to nationalist movements and nation building, wherein common language and culture are often linked to blood and soil. The invocation of common substance and frequent use of kinship terms to describe the relationships among members of the political community emphasize the indelible and nonvoluntary quality of the ties and deemphasize conflict and opposing interests. The familiarity of racial metaphors, however, should not lead us to overgeneralize the phenomenon. Racial metaphors are used to build particular kinds of communities, with a special brand of internal politics on which I will later elaborate, but we must remember that forms of community building exist that do not draw on racial metaphors. For example, there are communities, even families, conceived as voluntary associations built on common values and commitment to common goals, not on indelible ties.

The power and flexibility of racial metaphors lie, I think, in the malleability of notions of common substance. In the colonial societies that Europeans and their descendants created around the world, the older notion of race articulating a lineage-based system of entitlements and privileges was expanded and became the organizing concept through which Europeans attempted to rule subjugated populations. Only in this context of colonization did skin color become the mark of common substance and the differentiating feature between colonizers and the colonized, and, in many cases, between freedom and enslavement. Of course, the qualities designated as superior had power only because of the military force and other forms of coercion that reinforced the political and social privileges accompanying them.

Although colonial societies in the Americas, Africa, and Asia differed greatly in the taxonomy of racial categories and in the degree to which they tolerated sexual unions between colonizers and colonized, and thus had different miscegenation laws and roles for *mestizos*, the underlying problem of creating a hierarchal system of differentiation was similar. As Ann Stoler notes,

> Colonial authority was constructed on two powerful, but false premises. The first was the notion that Europeans in the colonies made up an easily identifiable and discrete biological and social entity; a "natural" community of class interests, racial attributes, political and social affinities and superior culture. The second was the related notion that the boundaries separating colonizer from colonized were thus self-evident and easily drawn.[13]

As scholars of colonial societies are quick to point out, neither premise reflected colonial realities. The rulers, divided by conflicting economic and political goals, differed even on which methods would best safeguard European (or white) rule. Yet colonial rule itself was contingent on the colonists' ability to construct and enforce legal and social classifications for who was white and who was native, who counted as European and by what degree, which progeny were legitimate and which were not.

Because racial distinctions claim that common substance is biologically transmitted, race as a social reality focuses particular attention on all women as reproducers of human life (as well as the social life of the group) and at the same time necessarily separates them into distinct groups with special but different burdens. To the degree that colonial authority was based on racial distinctions, then, one could argue that colonial authority itself was fundamentally structured in gendered terms. Although in reality there may have been many types of prohibited unions and contested relationships, "ultimately," as Stoler points out, "inclusion or exclusion required regulating the sexual, conjugal and domestic life of both Europeans in the colonies and their colonized subjects," especially in a racially based slaveholding society such as the American South, where the children of a slave woman were slaves and the children of a free woman were free. Under this juridical system, regulating who had sexual access to which group of women involved economic decisions as well.[14]

In colonial societies as different as Dutch Indonesia, British Nigeria, and the American plantation South, we find bifurcated visions of womanhood.[15] Women of European descent became the guardians of civilization. Thus, the Victorian cult of domesticity in the colonial world must be seen in the context of demarcations between groups. Because the structure of colonial race privileges focused particularly on limiting access to European status, the elevation of white women as civilization's guardians also confined them within narrow spheres. As the reproducers of the ruling elite, they established through their daily actions the boundaries of their group identity; hence their behavior came under group scrutiny.

By contrast, the images and treatment of colonized women resulted from more complex projections. On one hand, colonized women were not viewed as women at all in the European sense; they were spared neither harsh labor nor harsh punishment. On the other hand, as the reproducers of the labor force, colonized women were valued as one might value a prize broodmare. Equally, men of European descent eroticized colonized women as exotic, socially prohibited, but available and subjugated sexual objects. In this case, prohibition and availability are intimately connected to desire. Because such unions were socially invisible, the progeny from the union could be denied. Sex, under these conditions, became a personal rather than community or racial matter. In other words, in sexual unions with women from a socially prohibited category, men could step outside the normal restrictions and obligations imposed on sexual activity by shirking responsibility for their progeny.[16]

The same bifurcated images of women appear in European societies as the result of similar processes of creating hierarchy and class distinctions. Students of European history are not used to thinking about race as a relevant category for societies on European soil; these historians, including historians of women, much more readily accept class as the fundamental divide. Yet despite the presence of more democratically oriented notions of meritocracy in industrial society and the dissemination of Enlightenment notions of contractual policy, we should not underestimate the degree to which older (lineage-based) racial thinking rooted in kinship and family alliances remained basic to the accumulation and concentration of capital in propertied families. Racial metaphors (concerns over purity of stock and preservation of social boundaries) pervaded the rationale behind marriage alliances and inheritance. The European upper classes literally thought of themselves as a race apart from the common rabble. Belief in the reality of these social distinctions constructed around biological metaphors pervaded bourgeois imagination and social fears. Respectability centered on domestic virtues defended by the upper-class woman, the angel of the hearth. Just as the bourgeoisie championed its own vision of domestic order as a model for civic order, they feared the disorder and contagion of the working class.

This fear is evident in perceptions of nineteenth-century elite social reformers, particularly on such seemingly neutral subjects as social hygiene. In their studies of English and French attempts to control venereal diseases, historians Judith Walkowitz and Jill Harsin have shown that regulation focused particularly on policing female prostitutes and not their male clients. As Walkowitz has demonstrated for the port cities of England, forcing working-class women who occasionally stepped out with sailors to register on police blotters as prostitutes created a distinct outcast group, in a sense professionalizing these women while at the same time isolating them from their working-class neighbors. The ideological assumptions behind such police actions were more explicitly articulated in the French case. As Harsin shows, police regulations explicitly considered street prostitutes, called *les filles publiques* or public women, the source of contagion. Although ostensibly the problem concerned public health and the spread of venereal disease, the solutions reveal that elite social reformers such as Parent du Chatelet saw poor working-class women not only as the source of disease, but as infectants of civic order, as sources of social disorder.[17]

The improbability that impoverished street prostitutes could threaten civic order demonstrates the power of the biological metaphors that linked questions of physical health metaphorically to the health of the society (of the body politic). The perception of danger bespeaks how the French upper-class imagination represented working-class women. As the dialectical opposite of the pure and chaste bourgeois angel of the hearth, poor women of the streets symbolized dirt and sexual animality. Whether these perceptions accurately reflected real circumstances is immaterial. It is more important for us to see that elite reformers and the police acted as if their perceptions were true, putting into practice elaborate controls that had material effects on the lives of working-class women and, indirectly, on those of upper-class women as well. The perception of danger and disorder rests on the prior social reasoning that I have identified as racial metaphors.

The previous analysis of the relationship between prostitution and public health demonstrates both the malleability and the power of racial thinking to structure the terms of political debates and actions. In recent European history we can find many other examples where racial metaphors provide the basic vocabulary for political discourse. In the latter half of the nineteenth century the imperatives of competition for empire in a world already carved up by Europeans filtered back into European domestic politics in the form of anxiety over population decline and public health. In the eyes of the state, responsibility for the fitness of the nation rested on women's reproductive capacity, their place in the economy, and their role as mothers in protecting the welfare of children (the future soldiers for the empire).[18] Debates over the "woman question," in the form of feminist demands for greater equality within marriage and for political, economic, and reproductive rights, were debated in the context of colonial politics and concerns over the vitality of the master European races. Competition among European nations for colonial empire and their anxieties about themselves as colonizers set the terms for curtailing women's demands for greater freedom of action and autonomy. Antifeminist projects such as economically restrictive protective legislation, bans on birth control, and pronatalist policies went hand in hand with the campaign against women's suffrage.

In the twentieth century, within the European heartland, German National Socialists took these shared assumptions about the relation between national fitness and women's activities to their terrifying extreme. As Gisela Bock's study of women's reproductive rights in Nazi Germany indicates, obsession with race purity and population strength led to a policy of compulsory motherhood with the criminalization of abortion for Aryan women of the superior race and forced sterilization for the inferior races as part of their ultimate extermination.[19] This study of the differential effects of racial policy on women's reproductive rights shocks us into recognizing that the division of women into breeders and nonbreeders is wholly consistent with the logic of racial thinking, whether we encounter such divisions in European dynastic politics or as part of the effort to establish boundaries between the colonizers and the colonized. The most disturbing aspect of racial thinking is that it is *not* limited to the terrifying circumstances of genocide for some and compulsory motherhood for others. It is, in many respects, its very banality that should trouble us.

This brief survey of the common use and implications of what I have called racial metaphors in colonial contexts as well as in the home countries of colonizers, while hardly satisfactory in terms of detail, has at minimum, I hope, suggested an interesting point of departure for rethinking the connections among gender, race, and class. As Bock's study shows us, racism and sexism are not just analogous forms of oppression; institutionalized racism is a form of sexism. One form of oppression is predicated on the other. Racism is a kind of sexism that does not treat all women as the same, but drives wedges between us on the basis of our daily experiences, our assigned functions within the social order, and our perceived interests and mobilization. Although women everywhere have struggled against prescriptive images and have fought for greater autonomy and control, it should not be surprising that, given their different positions within the system and the vastly different material conditions of their lives, women have fashioned different notions of self, have had different grievances against their circumstances, and have often developed different strategies.

Thinking about differences in the ways that I have suggested in this paper requires overcoming very strong emotional and intellectual barriers. We are all products of societies that have taught us to hate others or, worse, to be indifferent to their suffering and blind to our own privileges and to those who labor to provide them. The historical legacy of these differences makes common bonds difficult to conceive. That which divides us may also connect us, but will not easily unite us. Still, if sisterhood beyond the boundaries of class, race, ethnicity, and nation is a meaningful goal, we must try to develop common strategies for change. As a first step, we can become aware that some of the most fundamental differences arise from our distinct locations within a social system that underprivileges all women, but in different ways. To bridge these differences, we must, as Peggy Pascoe has urged, take a candid took at the shameful side, recognizing that we cannot bury the past or wipe the slate completely clean.[20] We can only strive for empathy and mutual understanding. Some of us face the painful process of reexamining our definitions of "self" and "other," and of challenging the categories of analysis and conceptions of historical development that support our intimate vision of ourselves in the world. Others face the equally painful task of letting go of anger, not enough to forget it entirely, but enough to admit the possibility of common futures and joint strategies for transformation.

We cannot fully capture and understand the kinds of differences between women based on race and class by such phrases as "diversity of experiences." By focusing on race as an analytical category in accounting for the differences among women, we are in fact studying race as a principle of social organization and racial metaphors as part of the process of defining hierarchies and constituting boundaries of privilege. The core notion of common substance transmitted through heterosexual intercourse and birth underscores the gendered nature of the concept of race. In a male-dominated society, this concept focuses particular attention on women's activities, on reproductive politics, and, more generally, on control over sexuality and sexual behavior. Understanding this process allows us to see how much the identities of different groups of women in the same society are implicated in one another. Although their experiences of oppression differ dramatically, these differences are nonetheless relationally constituted in identifiable social processes.

Notes

This paper has benefited enormously from Ken Dauber's intellectual support and careful readings. I would also like to thank Karen Anderson, Jan Monk, Amy Newhall, and Pat Seavey for their insights and editorial suggestions.

1. Since 1987 all students earning the Bachelor of Arts and Sciences degree at the University of Arizona have been required to take one course, selected from a designated list, that focuses on gender, class, race, or ethnicity.

2. Marshall Hodgson, "The Interrelations of Societies in History," *Comparative Studies in Society and History* 5 (1963): 227–50.

3. Gloria T. Hull, Patricia Bell Scott, and Barbara Smith, *All the Women Are White, All the Blacks Are Men, but Some of Us Are Brave: Black Women's Studies* (Old Westbury, NY: Feminist Press, 1982).

4. Aihwa Ong, "Colonialism and Modernity: Feminist Representations of Women in Non-Western Societies," *Inscriptions (Journal of the Group for the Study of Discourse in Colonialism)* 3–4 (1988): 79–93.

5. Myra Jehlen, "Archimedes and the Paradox of Feminist Criticism," in Nannerl Keohane, Michelle Rosaldo, and Barbara Gelpi, eds., *Feminist Theory: A Critique of Ideology* (Chicago: University of Chicago Press, 1982); Chandra Talpade Mohanty, "Under Western Eyes: Feminist Scholarship and Colonial Discourses," *Boundaries* 2, 12–13 (1984): 333–58.

6. Karla Hackstaff and Jennifer Pierce, "Is Sisterhood Global?" *Berkeley Journal of Sociology* 30 (1985): 189–204, reviewing Robin Morgan, *Sisterhood Is Global* (New York: Anchor Press/Doubleday, 1984). See also Ong, "Colonialism and Modernity," and Mohanty, "Under Western Eyes."

7. James Clifford, "On Ethnographic Allegory," in James Clifford and George Marcus, eds., *Writing Culture: The Poetics and Politics of Ethnography* (Berkeley: University of California Press, 1986).

8. For a critique of this view of culture, see Peter Worsley, "Marxism and Culture: The Missing Concept," *Dialectical Anthropology* 6 (1981): 103–23; James Clifford, *The Predicament of Culture: Twentieth Century Ethnography, Literature, and Art* (Cambridge, Mass.: Harvard University Press, 1988).

9. Charlotte Bunch, "Bringing the Global Home," in Charlotte Bunch, ed., *Passionate Politics* (New York: St. Martin's, 1987).

10. Although I am vulnerable, in this move, to the charge that even in the posture of critique, I still privilege a Western perspective, I do so as a politically conscious first step. With regard to my earlier concerns with some of the problems of cross-cultural comparison, a focus on colonialism forces us to keep in the center of our vision the relationship between differences and power.

11. Jean-Louis Flandrin, *Families in Former Times: Kinship, Household, and Sexuality in Early Modern France*, trans. Richard Southern (Cambridge: Cambridge University Press, 1979).

12. Benedict Anderson, *Imagined Communities: Reflections on the Origin and Spread of Nationalism* (London: Verso, 1983).

13. Ann L. Stoler, "Making Empire Respectable: The Politics of Race and Sexual Morality in Twentieth Century Colonial Cultures," *American Ethnologist* 16 (1989): 635.

14. Ibid.

15. For Indonesia, see Jean Taylor, *The World of Batavia* (Madison: University of Wisconsin Press, 1983); for Nigeria, see Helen Callaway, *Gender, Culture, and Empire: European Women in Colonial Nigeria* (London: Macmillan, 1987); for the American South, see Elizabeth Fox-Genovese, *Within the Plantation Household: The Black and White Women of the Old South* (Chapel Hill: University of North Carolina Press, 1988).

16. I am indebted to Ken Dauber for this insight. For European parallels in relationships between upper-class men and working-class women, see Lenore Davidoff, "Class and Gender in Victorian England," in Judith L. Newton, Mary P. Ryan, and Judith R. Walkowitz, eds., *Sex and Class in Women's History* (London: Routledge and Kegan Paul, 1983).

17. Judith Walkowitz, *Prostitution and Victorian Society: Women, Class, and the State* (Cambridge: Cambridge University Press, 1980); Jill Harsin, *Policing Prostitution in Nineteenth Century Paris* (Princeton: Princeton University Press, 1985). For interesting parallels, see Luise White, "Prostitution, Identity, and Class Consciousness in Nairobi during World War II," *Signs* 11 (1986): 255–73, and "A Colonial State and an African Petty Bourgeoisie: Prostitution, Property and Class Struggle in Nairobi, 1930–1940," in Frederick Cooper, ed., *Struggle for the City: Migrant Labor, Capital, and the State in Urban Africa* (Beverly Hills, Calif.: Sage, 1983); see also Donna J. Guy, "White Slavery, Public Health, and the Socialist Position on Legalized Prostitution in Argentina, 1913–1936," *Latin American Research Review* 23, 3 (1988): 60–80.

18. Anna Davin, "Imperialism and Motherhood," *History Workshop* 5 (1978): 9–56.

19. Gisela Bock, "Racism and Sexism in Nazi Germany: Motherhood, Compulsory Sterilization, and the State," in Renate Bridenthal, Atina Grossman, and Marion Kaplan, eds., *When Biology Became Destiny: Women in Weimar and Nazi Germany* (New York: Monthly Review Press, 1984).

20. I refer to Pascoe's talk at the Western History Conference in Santa Fe, New Mexico, 1989. See also Pascoe, "At the Crossroads of Culture," *Women's Review of Books* 7, 5 (1990): 22–23.

4

"This Evil Extends Especially to the Feminine Sex"
Negotiating Captivity in the New Mexico Borderlands, 1700–1846

James F. Brooks

Late in the summer of 1760, a large Comanche raiding party besieged the fortified home of Pablo Villalpando in the village of Ranchos de Taos, New Mexico. After a daylong fight, the Comanches breached the walls and killed most of the male defenders. They then seized fifty-seven women and children, among whom was twenty-one-year-old María Rosa Villalpando, Pablo's second daughter, and carried them into captivity on the Great Plains. María's young husband, Juan José Xacques, was slain in the assault, but her infant son, José Juliano Xacques, somehow escaped both death and captivity.

The Comanches apparently traded María shortly thereafter to the Pawnees, for by 1767 she lived in a Pawnee village on the Platte River and had borne another son, who would come to be known as Antoine. In that year, the French trader and co-founder of St. Louis, Jean Salé dit Leroie, visited the Pawnees and began cohabiting with María. About one year later, she bore Salé a son, whom they named Lambert. Perhaps this arrangement suited Salé's trading goals, for it wasn't until 1770 that he ended María's Indian captivity and brought her to St. Louis, where they married.

Jean and María (now Marie Rose Salé) had three more children, when, for unknown reasons, Jean returned to France, where he remained the rest of his life. María stayed in St. Louis to become the matriarch of an increasingly prominent family. Her New Mexican son, José Juliano, would visit her there, although we will see that the reunion proved bitter-sweet. María finally died at the home of her daughter, Hélène, in 1830, at well over ninety years of age. For María Rosa Villalpando, captivity yielded a painful, yet paradoxically successful, passage across cultures into security and longevity.[1]

Long understood as a volatile and complex multiethnic borderland, greater New Mexico presents an intriguing problem to scholars of Indian-Euroamerican relations. Despite the reality of Spanish colonialism and the notable success of the Pueblo Revolt (1680–93), the region remained a "nondominant frontier" in which neither colonial New Mexicans nor the numerically superior indigenous peoples proved able (or willing) to dominate or eject the other completely.[2] This article takes one step toward a deeper understanding of the question, by exploring the role captive women like María Rosa played in promoting conflict and accommodation between colonial Spanish (and later Mexican) society and the indigenous people of greater New Mexico. During the Spanish and Mexican periods (c. 1600–1847), thousands of Indian and hundreds of Spanish women and children "crossed cultures" through the workings of a captive-exchange system that knit diverse communities into vital, and violent, webs of interdependence. These captives, whether of Spanish origin, or Native Americans "ransomed" by the Spanish at *rescates* (trade fairs), seem crucial to a "borderlands political economy" that utilized human beings in far-reaching social and economic exchange.[3]

Developing in the wake of Spanish slave raids and Indian reprisals, over time this commerce in captives provided the basis for a gradual convergence of cultural interests and identities at the village level, emerging in "borderlands communities of interest" by the middle years of the nineteenth century. Seen as both the most valuable "commodities" in intersocietal trade *and* as key transcultural actors in their own right, captive women and children participated in a terrifying, yet at times fortuitous, colonial dialectic between exploitation and negotiation. Until now, their histories have lain in the shadows of borderlands historiography.[4] Although firsthand accounts are rare, and other evidence must be used with caution, an examination of their experience may contribute to our understanding of colonial processes in New Mexico and elsewhere in North America.

Whatever the large-scale antagonisms between Spanish colonists and Native Americans, problems of day-to-day survival required methods of cross-cultural negotiation. Prolonged, intensive interaction between New Mexican *pobladores* (village settlers) and nomadic or pastoral Indian societies required some mutually intelligible symbols through which cultural values, interests, and needs could be defined. Horses, guns, and animal hides spring immediately to mind as customary symbols of exchange, but women and children proved even more valuable (and valorized) as agents (and objects) of cultural negotiations. In New Mexico, as elsewhere in North America, the "exchange of women" through systems of captivity, adoption, and marriage seem to have provided European and Native men with mutually understood symbols of power with which to bridge cultural barriers.[5]

Rival men had seized captives and exchanged women long before European colonialism in North America. The exogamous exchange of women between "precapitalist" societies appears to represent a phenomenon by which mutual obligations of reciprocity are established between kindreds, bands, and societies, serving both to reinforce male dominance and to extend the reproductive (social and biological) vigor of communities.[6] This article approaches the issue from a variety of sources and perspectives. Combining Spanish archival research with some of the classics of North American Indian ethnology, and viewing both through the lens of feminist critiques and extensions, I suggest that the capture and integration of women and children represented the most violent expression along a continuum of such exchange traditions. The patriarchal subordination of women and children, it has been argued, served as a foundation upon which other structures of power and inequality were erected. Gerda Lerner contends that the assertion of male control over captive women's sexual and reproductive services provided a model for patriarchal owner-ship of women in "monogamous" marriages by which patrilineal bloodlines remained "pure." From this sense of proprietorship grew other notions of property, including the enslavement of human beings as chattels.[7]

In New Spain, under the *Recopilación* of 1680 (a compendium of laws governing colonial/Indian relations), Spanish subjects had been encouraged to redeem indigenous captives from their captors, baptize them into the Catholic faith, and acculturate them as new "detribalized" colonial subjects.[8] These redemptions occurred in roughly two forms—either through formal "ransoming" at annual trade fairs (*ferias* or *rescates*) or small-scale bartering (*cambalaches*) in local villages or at trading places on the Great Plains. Trade fairs at Taos, Pecos, and Picuris Pueblos had long fostered the exchange of bison meat for corn, beans, and squash between Plains Indians and the Río Grande Pueblos and had probably included some exchanges of people as well.[9]

These seasonal events continued after the Spanish reconquest of New Mexico in 1692–96. Throughout the eighteenth century, Spanish church and secular authorities vied to gain control of this trade, variously blaming each other or local *alcaldes* (village mayors) for "the saddest of this commerce." In 1761 Fray Pedro Serrano chided Spanish governors, who "when the fleet was in" scrambled to gather as many horses, axes, hoes, wedges, picks, bridles, and knives in order to "gorge themselves" on the "great multitude of both sexes offered for sale."[10] Fifteen years later, Fray Anatasio Domínguez reported that the Comanches brought to Taos for sale "pagan Indians, of both sexes, whom they capture from other nations." The going rate of exchange, which held quite steady until the mid-nineteenth century, was "two good horses and some trifles" for an "Indian girl twelve to twenty years old." Male captive boys usually brought a "she mule" or one horse and a "poor bridle . . . garnished with red rags." The general atmosphere, according to Domínguez, resembled a "second hand market in Mexico, the way people mill about."[11]

After 1800 these formal *rescates* decline, replaced with smaller, more frequent on-the-spot bartering. This seems due to several factors-Plains Indians wishing to avoid possible exposure to Euroamerican disease, a desire on the part of New Mexican villagers to escape taxation of their Indian trade, and a geographical expansion of the borderlands economy. By the 1850s local traders like José Lucero and Powler Sandoval would purchase Mexican captives from Comanches at Plains outposts like "Quitaque" in Floyd County, Texas, giving, for example, "one mare, one rifle, one shirt, one pair of drawers, thirty small packages of powder, some bullets, and one buffalo robe" in exchange for ten-year-old Teodoro Martel of Saltillo, Mexico.[12]

Judging from extant New Mexican parochial registers, between 1700 and 1850, nearly 3,000 members of nomadic or pastoral Indian groups entered New Mexican society as *indios de rescate* (ransomed Indians), *indios genízaros* ("slaves"), *criados* (servants), or *huerfanos* (orphans), primarily through the artifice of "ransom" by colonial purchasers.[13] Ostensibly, the cost of ransom would be retired by ten to twenty years of service to the redeemers, after which time these individuals would become *vecinos* (tithes-paying citizens). In practice, these people appear to have experienced their bondage on a continuum that ranged from near-slavery to familial incorporation, an issue that will be addressed at length in this article.

Ransomed captives comprised an important component in colonial society, averaging about 10 to 15 percent of the colonial population, and especially in peripheral villages, where they may have represented as much as 40 percent of the "Spanish" residents.[14] Girls and boys under the age of fifteen composed approximately two thirds of these captives, and about two-thirds of all captives were women "of serviceable age" or prepubescent girls.[15]

This commerce in women and children proved more than a one way traffic, however. Throughout the period under consideration, nomadic groups like Comanches and Navajos made regular raids on the scattered *poblaciones* (settlements), at times seizing as many as fifty women and children.[16] In 1780, Spanish authorities estimated that the *Naciones del Norte* (Plains tribes of the northern frontier) alone held more than 150 Spanish citizens captive, and by 1830 the figure for the Comanches alone may have exceeded 500.[17] Among the Navajos, as late as 1883

Table 4.1   Baptisms of Selected Non-Pueblo Indians, 1700–1850

Tribe	1700–1750	1750–1800	1800–1850	Total
Apaches	632	260	87	979
Pawnees	18	2	3	23
Aas (Crows)	8	62	20	80
Kiowas	17	18	32	67
Comanches	14	179	33	226
Utes	11	63	551	625
Navajos	211	124	422	757
Total	911	708	1,148	2,757

Adapted from David M. Brugge, *Navajos in the Catholic Church Records of New Mexico, 1694–1875* (Tsaile, Ariz: Navajo Community College Press, 1985), 22–23.

U.S. Indian agent Dennis M. Riordan estimated that there were "300 slaves in the hands of the tribe," many of whom were "Mexicans captured in infancy"[18] Like their Indian counterparts, these women and children found themselves most often incorporated into their host society through indigenous systems of adoption. As fictive kin, they too experienced a range of treatment. It is impossible to arrive at precise numbers of New Mexican captives in Indian societies, their representation becomes increasingly significant in a discussion of the workings of the captive system and the personal experience of captives themselves.

The captive-exchange system appears overwhelmingly complex when examined through particular cases, but certain overall patterns seem consistent. First, captive taking and trading represented the most violent and exploitative component of a long-term pattern of militarized socioeconomic exchange between Indian and Spanish societies. Second, it seems that New Mexican captives and *indios de rescate* generally remained in their "host" societies throughout their life-times. Third, female captives often established families within the host society, and their descendants usually became full culture-group members. Male captives, on the other hand, suffered either a quick retributive death or, if young, grew to become semiautonomous auxiliary warriors within their new society. Finally, it appears that many captives found ways to transcend their subordinate status by exercising skills developed during their "cross-cultural" experience. In doing so, they negotiated profound changes in the cultural identity of the societies within which they resided, changes which continue to reverberate in the borderlands today.

The Captive Experience

Torn from their natal societies in "slave" raids, treated like *piezas* ("coins," a common term in New Spain for slaves, both Indian and African) in a volatile system of intercultural exchange, and finally the "property" of strangers, captive and ransomed women seem unlikely subjects as historical actors. But the experiences recounted henceforth show these women and children negotiating narrow fields of agency with noteworthy skill. From positions of virtual powerlessness, captive women learned quickly the range of movement allowed by the host culture, especially in regard to adoption and *compadrazgo* (god-parenthood) practices.[19] This first phase of integration gave them "kin" to whom they could turn for protection and guidance. But this security remained limited, and many faced coercive conjugal relationships, if not outright sexual exploitation by their new masters.

Whether of Spanish or Indian origin, two factors are essential to our understanding of the captive experience in greater New Mexico and perhaps to similar cases in other periods and regions. First, captives' status and treatment within the host society would establish the structural constraints (culturally specific customs and laws governing rights and obligations) within which individuals might pursue their goals.[20] Second, sheer luck and the individual captive's personal resources determined much of her actual lived experience, ranging from terror and exploitation to a few remarkable cases of deft negotiation and good fortune, into which María Rosa Villalpando's story certainly falls. Overall, the interplay of structural constraints, contingency, and skills can be seen in most captives' lives. Another captive woman, Juana Hurtado Galván, proved so adept at the cross-cultural enterprise that her story exemplifies successful adaptation.

Early in the summer of 1680, shortly before the conflagrations of the Pueblo Revolt, a band of *Apaches del Nabajo* ("Navajos") swept down upon the *rancho* of Captain Andrés Hurtado and took captive his seven-year-old daughter, Juana.[21] For the next twelve years, her life among the Navajos lies concealed, a blank in the historical record that can only be reconstructed by inference and imagination. But those years of captivity seem to hold the key to understanding much of Juana's subsequent life, a long and controversial career that ended in 1753. When she died, Juana owned her own *rancho* with three houses and managed extensive herds and flocks. Her illegitimate son, Juan Galván, served as the *teniente* (assistant magistrate) of the Zia district.[22] Nativity had given Juana linkages to both Spanish and Pueblo society, and in her captivity she developed linguistic and kinship ties with the Navajos. Throughout her life, her experience as a captive woman would afford her special negotiating skills with which she pursued security for her lineage.

Juana's mother had come from the Pueblo of Zia, probably as a *criada* (domestic servant) of Captain Hurtado, but we know little more about her life.[23] No doubt sexually used by Hurtado, the daughter she bore in 1673 was just one among hundreds of such *coyotas* (children of mixed Spanish/Indian parentage) resulting from the Spanish colonization of New Mexico. The mother's connection with Zia Pueblo, however, remained central to her daughter's story. After Juana's half-brother, Martín, a soldier in the Spanish *reconquista* of 1692, ransomed Juana from captivity, the young woman petitioned for and received a private *merced* (land grant) at the northwest corner of the Zia Pueblo lands, near the village known today as San Ysidro.[24] This *rancho* proved a key locus of trade among Navajos, Pueblos, and Spanish villagers for the next half-century and was the source of Juana's wealth and influence.[25]

Although restored to colonial society, Juana never severed connections with her onetime captors. Frequent visits by Navajos to her *rancho* suggest that she had experienced adoption into a Navajo clan. She may even have married in captivity, as she never formalized any future conjugal relationship. Kinship aside, her trilingual skills and cultural intermediacy facilitated economic exchanges between potential enemies. Her affinity with Navajos remained so close that Fray Miguel de Menchero commended her usefulness in assisting proselytization efforts: "They had kept her for so long [that] the Indians of said Nation make friendly visits to her, and in this way the father of the said mission has been able to instruct some of them."[26]

Juana's conduct, however, also attracted criticism from church authorities. Throughout her life, she persisted in maintaining a long-term liaison with a married man of Zia, presumably named Galván. By 1727, this relationship had resulted in four children and charges of scandalous behavior leveled against her by Franciscan *padres*. When authorities sought to place Juana in stocks, however, the people of Zia "threatened that the whole pueblo would move to the mesa tops, rather than have her mistreated."[27] Like the Navajos, the people of Zia apparently saw tangible benefits in the presence of this kinswoman on their borders. Defining kinship more broadly than did the Spanish, they seemed willing to provoke conflict in defense of their relationship with someone who provided a bridge across three cultures. As she drew upon her qualities and talents as a negotiator, Juana "La Galvana" utilized her experience as a captive to carve out an intermediate niche in the complex power relations of colonial New Mexico.

Juana's intermediacy was accentuated by her mixed-blood status, and her paternal linkage to a Spanish *encomendero* (holder of tributary rights to Indian labor) probably allowed her the opportunity to occupy a privileged niche compared with many captives. Because one aide of the captive system originates in indigenous, precontact exogamous exchange traditions, we need to look at gender and social hierarchies within Native American societies to begin to understand the structural constraints that Juana and other captives might have experienced. Although they display variation, women's and captives' status within Indian societies of the borderlands (Navajo, Apache, Ute, and Comanche) may be generally described as subordinate to men and holders of the "cultural franchise" but enhanced by traditions of matrilineality and social mobility.[28]

Navajo patterns of gender and social hierarchies show a blending of southern Athabascan systems and cultural adaptations to Spanish colonialism near their homelands. Navajo women owned the flocks of sheep and wove the textiles that formed the core of their pastoral economy. Matrilineal descent, therefore, conferred important productive resources as well as kin-reckoning through women. Navajo men, however, prevailed in "public" decisions involving warfare and diplomacy.[29]

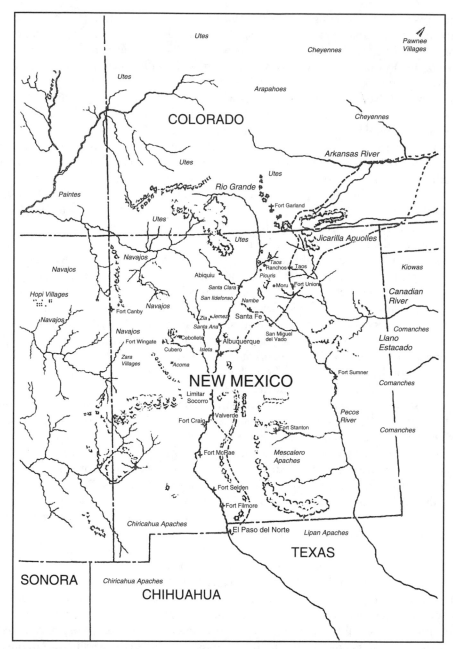

Figure 4.1. New Mexico, circa 1847

Captives taken in warfare with other tribes or raids on Spanish settlements again experienced a range of treatment. If not killed in vengeance satisfaction, the captive invariably suffered a period of harsh and terrifying ritual abuse. This "taming" process probably formed the first phase in adoption ritual.[30] After "taming," most captives became inducted into the clan of their captor, or the "rich man" who purchased them from the successful warrior. Once a clan member, it seems few barriers stood in the way of social advancement. The New Mexican captive Nakai Na'ddis Saal, raised in a clan on Black Mesa, "became a singer of the Nightway," an important Navajo ceremony. The Sonoran captive Jesus Arviso, taken by Chiricahua Apaches in 1850 as a boy and traded to the Navajo Kla Clan, served as the principal interpreter for his host society throughout the Fort Sumner "Long Walk" era. Marrying into the Nanasht'ezhii Clan, he chose to remain a Navajo, welcoming a congressional delegation to Fort Defiance in 1919 and living at Cubero until his death in 1932.[31]

Captive women usually became clan members and married exogamously. Even if not inducted into clan membership, their children by Navajo men were considered members of the father's clan.[32] Although we can only speculate, these clan and kin affiliations probably provided Juana Hurtado with the networks that allowed her to act as an intermediary between Zia Pueblo and Spanish society. Indeed, Juana seems noteworthy among captives for having chosen to return to her birthright, for some sources indicate that most captives, when "set free . . . immediately took the shortest trail back to the hogans of their masters."[33]

Captives seem to have fared less well among the Jicarilla Apaches, a semisedentary people who practiced a seasonal economy that balanced hunting and collecting with extensive horticulture. Apache women, however, benefited from matrilineality and ownership of fields and crops which "were planted, weeded, and harvested by the joint labors of the entire family." This gender-integrated labor diverged when men hunted or raided and women engaged in the life-cycle labor of family reproduction. Although subordinate to men, women made important ritual contributions to the success of hunters: "a man and his wife pray together and smoke ceremonially before the husband leaves for the hunt. After his departure the woman continues a series of ritual duties." Similarly, before men departed for warfare or raiding, "a woman [was] chosen to represent each man to serve as proxy in group decisions, [and she] obeyed many restrictions in matters of dress, food, and behavior to ensure his safe return."[34]

Warfare among the Jicarillas often involved the seizure of captives, either for vengeance satisfaction or cultural integration. Adult male captives "were tied to posts and slain by women with lances," but captive women and children found themselves incorporated into the band. A captive woman "could not be molested until she had been brought back and a ceremony . . . performed over her," probably some form of adoption that established her subordination within the Apachean levirate. Even with this adoption, captive women "were not considered fit wives. They were sexually used, and sent from camp to camp to do the heavy work. Their children by Apache men, however, were recognized as Jicarilla" and "accepted into Apache life."[35] We shall see that this second-generation integration appears nearly universal among the indigenous groups in question and provides another constraining structure in captive women's decisions to remain within the host society even when offered their "freedom."

These patterns of gender and social subordination, mitigated by adoption and generational enfranchisement, are reiterated in an examination of Comanche society. Drawing largely upon ethnographic data gathered in the 1930s, Jane Fishburne Collier has argued that women's status in prereservation (c. 1875) Comanche society, as reflected through the dynamics of bride-wealth marriage, "may best be understood in the context of relations between men."[36] Certainly, the Comanches seem to represent the most noteworthy case of Plains Indian individualism and status competition between men, where wifestealing often served as an intraband expression of a general cultural pattern. One of Collier's sources (E. Adamson Hoebel), pointed out, however, that although "before the law, [the] Comanche woman was a quasi-chattel," social custom allowed women a considerable degree of choice in extralegal activity.[37]

Surprisingly, first Hoebel then Collier overlooked evidence of women-centered status competition, a stretching of patriarchal structural constraints. In one-half of the marital disputes Hoebel recorded, women had left their husbands for other men, often joining their lovers on war parties. In one case, the couple stayed away from the band for two years, and when they returned, the woman had fifteen horses in her personal string.[38] Women could also obtain horses (next to captives the most prestigious "commodity" in Comanche society) through the institution of the "Shakedown Dance," whereby successful raiders were shamed into giving a part of their herd to young, unmarried women.[39] Status and prestige also accrued to women through the matrilineal transfer of medicine powers, as in the case of Sanapia, a Comanche Eagle Doctor.[40] These examples suggest that within male-defined cultural limitations, Comanche women exploited opportunities for competitive mobility and status enhancement. Captives, although initially lower in status, appear to have negotiated similar avenues toward social mobility.

No other Plains society engaged in captive raiding as vigorously as did the Comanches. This seems a result of both individual status competition and the need to replace a population ravaged by warfare and epidemic disease.[41] Comanche society offered several social locations into which captives could be integrated, ranging from chattels to kinsmen and women.[42] Ralph Linton suggests that the prestige value of captives reflected their "importance in the social and economic life of the tribe. Mostly Mexican, they tended the horse herds and practiced most of the specialized industries such as gun repairing and saddle-making." The honored position of center-pole cutter in the Comanche Sun Dance went either to a "virtuous Comanche woman, a virtuous captive woman, [or] a captive man who had a number of war-deeds to his credit."[43] Among the Kiowas, a Plains people closely allied with the Comanches after 1805, captives like Loki-Mokeen, a Mexican mulatto, could become officers of the Sun Dance and protectors of the sacred *Taimé* Bundle.[44] Andrés Martínez, called by the Kiowa "Andali," was seized from his family's pastures near Las Vegas, New Mexico, and grew to adulthood as a Kiowa warrior. In 1889 he converted to Methodism and told his story to the Reverend J. J. Methven.[45] Similarly, the "captive-friend" who fought alongside his Comanche warrior-brother, appears prominently as a type in Hoebel's ethnography.[46]

Captive women often found themselves under the protection of Comanche women. Rosita Rodrigues, writing in 1846, reported she "remained a prisoner among the Comanche Indians about one year, during which time I was obliged to work very hard, but was not otherwise badly treated as I became the property of an old squaw who became much attached to me."[47] Similarly, Sarah Ann Horn, taken captive in 1837, reported that she was taken in "by an old widow woman . . . a merciful exception to the general character of these merciless beings." Although she was "set to work to dress buffalo hides," she did not suffer sexual abuse.[48] It appears that at least some captive women were informally adopted by older women, by which action they received the protection of the Comanche incest taboo.[49] By extension, it bears consideration that in some cases, Comanche women may have identified and acted upon interests counter to those of Comanche men, protecting captive women either for their value as "chore sisters" or through basic empathy.

Rodrigues and Horn are among the very few women who, when repatriated, wrote of their experiences among the Comanche. Most captive women seem to have remained with their captors, marrying and establishing families in the host society.[50] Rodrigues herself left a son behind among the Comanche, reporting that she "heard from him a short time ago—he is well and hearty but he is pure Indian now."[51] Josiah Gregg noted the presence of Mexican women among the Comanche when he began traveling the Santa Fe Trail in the 1830s. He remarked with surprise that some of these "preferred remaining with [their captors], rather than encounter the horrible ordeal of ill-natured remarks on being restored to civilized life." One woman refused to return even after the offer of $1,000 for her ransom. She sent word that the Comanche "had disfigured her by tatooing; that she was married, and perhaps *enceinte* (pregnant), and she would be more unhappy returning . . . under these circumstances than remaining where she was."[52]

These women had good reason to fear social opprobrium if they returned to Spanish society. When authorities introduced an alms-gathering plan in 1780 to raise funds for the ransom of Spanish captives, Teodoro de Croix declared with alarm that "this evil [captivity] extends especially . . . to the feminine sex . . . on account of the lascivious vice of sensuality in which they are now afforded the greatest liberty to indulge themselves."[53] This may have been a rhetorical flourish to heighten interest in the plan, but it suggests that the conjugal arrangements of Comanche women might entail certain attractions to captive Spanish women as well.

Spanish concerns about the influence of Indian lifeways on their subjects went beyond anxieties about the behavior of "their" women in captivity. The simple fact that thousands of Indian captives and their descendants now resided in "Spanish" society stimulated a growing polemic of caste-conscious distancing by elite *españoles* vis-à-vis the culturally mixed people in the border villages. Elite anxieties were provoked by evidence that border villagers often exhibited behavior and pursued interests more in tune with their Indian neighbors than those contained in policy directives from Santa Fe or Mexico City. Gradual movement toward "borderlands communities of interest" linking New Mexican villagers with contiguous Indian groups emerged as one consequence of the presence of captive Indian women in colonial New Mexico.

Recently, Ramón Gutiérrez addressed one aspect of this cultural complexity, arguing that eighteenth-century New Mexico developed as a "timocracy," where "differences between aristocrats and landed peasants were of degree rather than kind. Spaniards, whatever their estate, were men of honor in comparison to the vanquished Indians." Gutiérrez contends that the *genízaro* (slave) caste, formed from the mass of *indios de rescate* obtained by the Spanish through ransom, constituted a "dishonored" status against which all Spanish, regardless of economic position, could define their *calidad* (rank).[54]

Although Gutiérrez offers strong evidence for this honor/dishonor distinction among elite *españoles*, his use of prescriptive sources generated by these elites tends to leave on-the-ground relations between *mestizo pobladores* (mixed descent settlers) and their *genízaro* neighbors somewhat obscure. As we will see, by the end of the eighteenth century, Spanish ecclesiastics and administrators spoke of their colonial villagers in terms usually associated with *los indios bárbaros*, often referring to them as "indolent," "rude," "independent," and "lewd." Captive exchange lay at the heart of this blurring of cultural boundaries.

New Mexico appears similar to other colonial borderlands, where patterns of cultural accommodation appear ongoing beneath longer-term themes of cultural conflict, and the exigencies of day-to-day survival promoted periods of relatively peaceful coexistence.[55] Always uncertain, and often punctuated by violent exchanges, relations between village-level New Mexicans and their nomadic-pastoral Indian neighbors may be viewed in like terms, but with heightened focus on exchanges of women and children as central objects and agents of intercultural negotiation. Locally constructed communities of interest were designed to foster mutual exchanges (economic and cultural) with a minimal loss of life. By late in the eighteenth century particular aspects of these relations received higher recognition in formal negotiations surrounding Spanish, Comanche, Ute, and Navajo peace treaties. The movement toward local mixed-cultural communities, however, distanced the village people of New Mexico from their colonial administrators, a trend that would lead to internal conflict by the nineteenth century.

Foreshadowing this turmoil, in 1794 Don Fernando de la Concha complained to incoming Governor Don Fernando Chacón that the village people of the province seemed "indolent": "They love distance which makes them independent; and if they recognize the advantages of union, they pretend not to understand them, in order to adopt the liberty and slovenliness they see . . . in their neighbors, the wild Indians."[56] Concern on the part of Spanish administrators had increased throughout the preceding decades. In 1776 Antonio de Bonilla had found the "settlements of the Spaniards . . . scattered and badly defended," protecting neither themselves nor "contributing to the defense of the province."[57] Two years later, Fray Juan Augustín de Morfi attributed this situation to the fact that the "*pobladores* liked to live apart, far from the prying eyes of neighbors and the restraining influence of authorities," where they could "commit with impunity all manner of immoral and criminal acts, and . . . were not ashamed to go about nude so that lewdness was seen here more than in the brutes."[58]

Like Morfi, Concha felt that social intercourse with the *Indios bárbaros* lay at the heart of this problem. Life in the villages, he told his successor, had become so distanced from colonial control that he recommended "the removal of more than two thousand [villagers]," whose "bad upbringing results from . . . the proximity and trade of the barbarous tribes." This trade appears to have become increasingly a part of the borderlands economy in New Mexico and one which villagers sought to conceal from colonial control. Concha complained that the villagers, "under a simulated appearance of ignorance or rusticity . . . conceal the most refined malice."[59]

A decade later, Chacón would note that the villagers were "little dedicated to farming," surviving instead on a vigorous trade with nomadic Indians. In exchange for the settlers' manufactured goods and agricultural products, nomads like the Comanches gave them "Indian captives of both sexes, mules, moccasins, colts, mustangs, all kinds of hides and buffalo meat."[60] As the Bourbon Reforms brought efforts to incorporate New Mexico within the economic sphere of New Spain, especially in a developing sheep and textile industry, the informal economic autonomy of villagers seemed a barrier to progress.[61]

Tensions between administrators in Santa Fe and their backcountry subjects exploded in August 1837. The villagers of Rio Arriba descended upon the *villa* and seized the government, executing Governor Albino Pérez in the process.[62] Infuriated by rumors of direct taxation under Santa Ana's centralizing Constitution of 1835, which threatened to interfere with their autonomous indigenous trade, the rebels identified themselves "with the savage tribes . . . making the same cause and their same interests."[63] Mexico restored central authority by 1838, but communities of interest between New Mexican villagers and their Native neighbors persisted. In 1847 the villages again rose in rebellion, this time against the American military government of occupation. Pueblo Indians and New Mexican allies killed Governor Charles Bent in Taos, while Manuel Cortés of Mora joined with Apache and Cheyenne allies to raid U.S. military and commercial supply lines on the eastern frontier.[64] This ability to build strategic linkages across cultural boundaries was a consequence of long experience in economic and human exchange.

The seeds of these linkages were both cultural and biological, which we see revealed in a village-level intermingling of status groups. In Ranchos de Taos, for example, the Spanish census of 1750 reported nine Spanish households of fifty-seven persons, six *coyote* households of fifty-five persons, and eight *genízaro* households of twenty-five persons. Even the Spanish households showed a blurring of caste category; the house of Antonio Atiensa included his *coyota* wife, María Romero; their *castizo* (*español* and *coyota*) son, Domingo Romero; and the widow, Juana, with her daughter, Manuela, no doubt *criadas*. Similarly, the house of Juan Rosalio Villalpando, an important *español*, included his wife, Maria Valdes, and their six children, all of whom are termed *coyote*, suggesting that Maria may have been an *india de rescate*. Pablo Francisco Villalpando's household, from which María Rosa would be seized ten years later, contained three female and two male *servientes*, two of whom carry the family name. Mixing may have crossed class as well as caste lines in some village families.[65]

The fact that the census arranged households by caste category reveals a conscious concern about caste status on the part of Spanish administrators, but the data also demonstrate how informally these categories might be arranged at the village level. Census findings from a cluster of Plazas at Belén show a somewhat different, yet consistent, pattern. In 1790 the third Plaza, "Nuestra Señora de los Dolores de los Genízaros," contained thirty-three households, all designated as *genízaro*, a strong indication that in some cases true communities developed among some *indios de rescate*. But the adjacent second Plaza of Jarales held thirty Spanish, twelve *mestizo*, four *coyote*, and two *genízaro* households. The marriage patterns from these communities reveal little caste-anxious endogamy; of the twenty-eight unions, only one is *español-española*. Six marriages involved *genízaro-genízara*, and five *mestizo-mestiza*. The remaining sixteen show a crossing of caste lines. In most of these, hypogamy seems the rule, with women marrying men of "lower" status. Children of these unions, for example, *gení-zaro-coyotu*, follow the father's status and are later enumerated as *genízaros*.[66]

By the late eighteenth century, however, this designation for children born of captive Indian women may not have carried only the "dishonored" quality that Gutiérrez proposes. Instead, it may indicate a movement toward identity formation on the part of the *genízaros*. As early as 1744, sources report that *genízaro* men played an important role as military auxiliaries for the Spanish.[67] By 1780, a group of thirty-three *genízaros* negotiated with Spanish authorities from a position of some power, threatening that if their lands in the Barrio de Analco in Santa Fe were not protected, they might go "in search of relief to our lands and nation."[68] Governor Joaquin del Real Alencaster organized an official *Tropa de Genízaros* (militia troop) in 1808 to patrol the eastern frontier of New Mexico, in response to Zebulon Pike's adventurism of the previous year.[69] And in 1837, following the Rio Arriba rebellion noted earlier, the revolutionary government elected José Gonzales, a *cibolero* (bison hunter) from Taos who may have been a *genízaro*, as their new governor.[70] As subordinate, yet militarily skilled members of New Mexican society, *genízaro* men found themselves valued in a colony always in need of men-at-arms. Once established on the outer marches of the province, they managed to assert an intermediate negotiatory identity.

Initially little more than pawns in a distinctive "slave trade," captive Indian women and children established families within New Mexican society whose members eventually owned land, served in the military, and even led major rebellions. In their cases, maternity provided avenues of agency, especially as they manipulated structural constraints to establish increasing security for their offspring and, consequently, for themselves.

Two such constraints applied particularly to women in colonial New Mexico: marriage and *compadrazgo* (godparent) relations. For Spanish women, and mixed-blood or captive women who had internalized their conversion to Christianity, the dictates of the Catholic Church structured their agency within marriage. Gutiérrez has shown how caste-endogamous marriages served to "purify" the bloodlines of New Mexico's ruling elite.[71] The gender hierarchy of the church also firmly established women's subordination as dependants under the patriarchal authority of husbands and the church, with preservation of family honor through legitimate offspring their principal social role. Unlike women in the English colonies, however, Spanish women maintained separate property throughout their marriage(s) and could bequeath their estates independent of their husbands' wills.[72]

Spanish women's "property" often included *indias de rescate*, who found themselves transferred to daughters as servants, or "emancipated" with the condition that they continue to "watch over and assist my daughter as if she were her mother."[73] Others received clear title to parcels of land "in appreciation of years of service to me without salary."[74] When José Riano contested the will of Gregoria Gongora in 1739, he explicitly excepted from the disputed property "a piece of land for the *india* who raised my youngest and other children."[75]

Although these cases suggest a familial quality to the relations between Spanish and Indian women, few masters or mistresses actually formalized this quality in godparent relations. Of the 3,294 "slave" baptisms in New Mexico between 1693 and 1849, only 14 percent feature "owners" as *padrinos* (god-parents), and the vast majority (65 percent) show "no apparent relationship," simply members of the local Spanish community. Gutiérrez argues that these figures reflect the internal contradictions between the benign character of *compadrazgo* and exploitative character of master-slave relations.[76]

An alternative explanation, and one more in keeping with the argument herein, might see these baptismal data as representative of mutually supportive relationships between the New Mexicans and *indios de rescate*, a variation upon traditions of adoption that we have seen as ubiquitous in nomadic and pastoral Indian society. Frances S. Quintana argues that in New Mexico, *compadrazgo* relations show two patterns, an "old world" tradition that "intensified existing kin relationships" among colonial elites, and a "new world" innovation that "helped to stabilize relationships between native Indian populations and Spanish and *mestizo* groups."[77]

In addition to the baptisms of *indios de rescate* noted above, during the same period we see the baptism of 1,984 "illegitimate" children born of the women of the *genízaro* caste. In fact, Gutiérrez has recorded only twenty church-sanctioned marriages among members of this group and suggests that this reveals the continuing control of masters over the sexual services of "slave" women.[78] Certain of his cases support Gutiérrez's conclusion, but we should also recognize that refusal to "consecrate" a conjugal union also served as an act of resistance among both Pueblo and nomadic Indian groups.[79] At Zia Pueblo, and among the Navajo, a refusal to name the parents of "illegitimate" children continually frustrated Spanish authorities.[80] It seems reasonable to conclude here a mixed pattern of sexual exploitation of *indias de rescate* by Spanish masters, and a collective strategy of identity maintenance that, by refusing Catholic structures, retained the offspring of those and voluntary unions with Indian men as members of the cultural community.

Although conceived in grossly unequal relationships, the children who resulted from unions with captors often served to strengthen the status of captive women. As full culture-group members of either Indian or *genízaro* communities, these daughters and sons provided social access and security to their mothers. As Marietta Morrissey has found for slave women in the Caribbean, concubinage with dominant men often involved a painful balancing of shame and hope. If they acceded to sexual relations with masters, their children were born free, and in a position to assist in the dream of manumission.[81] In some cases as well, real bonds of affection and respect developed between sugar planters and slave women, a factor that seems likely in some of the New Mexican examples.

Although the creation of kinship seems the primary avenue by which captive women sought security and identity, we may also discern other facets of their lives from within the historical record. In addition to the life-cycle labor of family reproduction, these women engaged in subsistence and market production. The eighteenth and nineteenth centuries saw dramatic shifts in the status and work of Plains Indian women as peoples like the Comanches, Kiowas, and Cheyennes began participating in the European fur and hide trade. With the horse and gun, one Indian man could procure fifty to sixty buffalo hides per season, twice as many as one Indian woman could tan for use or exchange. An increase in polygamy, and raiding for captive women, served to counteract this labor shortage.[82] The captivity narratives quoted earlier make it clear that captive women were "set to work to tan hides" almost immediately. The appearance of polygamous households probably made this work more efficient, for "cowives" might process hides while the "first-wife" performed higher-status production and distribution like cooking, clothing manufacture, and ceremonial activities.

Indias de rescate appear most often as household servants, but to consider their work entirely "domestic" is probably misleading. Because both Apache and Navajo captive women came from societies in which women were the principal horticulturists, they may have found themselves gardening and even tending flocks in New Mexican villages. We are only beginning to develop an understanding of women's economic life in colonial New Mexico, but Angelina F. Veyna's work with women's wills suggests that both Spanish and Indian women may have been more involved in farming than previously thought. The fact that women owned *rejas* (ploughshares) and willed them not to their sons but to their daughters suggests either a farming orientation or a means of attracting potential husbands.[83]

Navajo and Apache women held captive in New Mexican households also worked as weavers, both of basketry and textiles. H.P. Mera has described the nineteenth-century "Slave Blanket" as a crossover style between Navajo and New Mexican techniques, using New Mexican yarns and designs, but produced on the distinctive upright looms of Navajo women.[84] These early New Mexican *serapes* became important trade items at *rescates*, given in exchange for buffalo hides and dried pemmican. Although today in villages like Chimayo, men weave the distinctive Rio Grande blankets, this seems the result of a concerted effort early in the nineteenth century to develop a commercial textile industry.[85]

Captive women and children played important roles in one last area, that of Spanish-Indian diplomacy. Their cross-cultural experience made them valuable as interpreters, translators, and envoys for Spanish military leaders. By 1750 the Comanche had obtained French guns, and Governor Vélez declared that unless a peace were negotiated they might prove "the ruin of this province." In order to communicate with several Comanche hostages held in Santa Fe, Vélez utilized the interpretive services of a Kiowa woman who had been captured by the Comanche, lost to the Utes in a raid, then purchased as a *criada* by Antonio Martín. This negotiation resulted in a temporary truce, sealed by the exchange of several prisoners.[86]

When the peace collapsed in 1760, captive women again served in a diplomatic capacity, this time as emissaries. Unable to find the appropriate Comanche leaders with whom to bargain, Vélez "dispatched six Comanche women prisoners as ambassadors to their nation." Within a month, four of the women had returned, along with nine Comanche captains, and another truce was affirmed by the return to the Comanche of "thirty-one women and children, among whom, fortunately, were their relatives."[87] Similarly, when Governor Juan Bautista de Anza and Ecuer-acapa (Leather Jacket) negotiated the Spanish-Comanche Peace of 1786, which lasted until 1846, they sealed their agreement by exchanging a Comanche boy, "José Chiquito," for Alejandro Martín, "eleven years a captive among the band of Captain Tosapoy."[88]

Negotiating Captivity in the New Mexican Borderlands

Often deemed invisible commodities in the "slave trade" of the Spanish borderlands, the captive women and children discussed here emerge as human actors engaged in a deeply ambivalent dialectic between exploitation and negotiation. Their stories begin in a moment of abject powerlessness, where subordination serves as a substitute for violent death. But from that moment forward, we see them taking tentative steps toward autonomy and security. Captive women worked within the limits set by their captors, yet through the creation of kinship, their daily labors, and their diplomatic usefulness, they managed to carve out a future for themselves and their lineages. Although fewer in number, captive boys became men who utilized their military skills to attain status and limited autonomy.

Beginning with an indigenous tradition of captive taking, and intensified by Spanish military and economic exploitation, the captive-exchange system developed as one important component of a borderlands political economy that produced conflict *and* coexistence. Maria Mies has conceptualized the inter-linkage of men's militarism and the forcible exchange of women as a universal "predatory mode of appropriation," a paradigm for "all exploitative relations between human beings."[89] In New Mexico, Spanish and Indian men found that even more than horses, guns, or hides, their counterparts valued women and children; and they established some nominal agreement that these would serve as objects and agents of intersocietal exchange. Conflict and accommodation patterns, therefore, between these rival societies may represent attempts by differing forms of patriarchal power to achieve external economic and military objectives while reinforcing the stability of internal social and gender hierarchies.

Of course, the social consequences of exchanging women and children across ethnic boundaries proved difficult to contain, and both New Mexicans and their Indian neighbors found customary relations unsettled by cultural hybridity. In time, the mixed-blood descendants of captive women and children exhibited new collective interests that influenced their choice of cultural identification. The collective interests of second- (and subsequent-) generation descendants blurred the boundaries between New Mexican villagers and their Indian neighbors. Plains Indian societies became increasingly militarized and market oriented during this period, and New Mexican villagers increasingly mobile. By the 1830s, New Mexican *cibo-leros* (bison hunters) and *comancheros* (traders and raiders) appeared regularly in travel accounts.[90] Plains Indian societies displayed new forms of collective action, and villagers rose in radically democratic rebellions.

Despite the exploitative quality of the captive-exchange system, its victims found ways to exercise agency and achieve some measure of security and comfort for themselves and their descendants. Within the structural constraints considered here, there lay some opportunity, especially when captives found it possible to use newly acquired cross-cultural skills to their advantage. For example, Juana Hurtado received the support of the Zias and Navajos in her role as cultural center-person. A Crow woman might be sold at a *rescate* by some Comanches, escape to find her way homeward, and end up leading a French trading expedition back to New Mexico.[91] A Pawnee woman in Santa Fe could discover that her master had settled land upon her in his will, for the consideration that she continue to serve as *criada* to his son.[92] Finally, María Rosa Villalpando of Taos, whose story opened this article, found herself traded to the Pawnee, married there, then remarried to become the "matriarch" of a French fur-trading enterprise in St. Louis. Her New Mexican son, José Juliano, visited her there in 1802 and attempted to establish a claim as her heir. Perhaps conflicting maternal sentiments forced María into a hard choice—she paid José Juliano 200 pesos to relinquish his claim and sent him packing. José Juliano took a long route home, for in 1809 New Mexican authorities contacted Spanish administrators in San Antonio, Texas, and suggested José be forcibly sent home, for he had a wife and children "without support" in the village of Ojo Caliente.[93]

Although the American conquest of 1846–48 resulted in the erosion of shared values and interests between New Mexicans and southwestern Indians, vestiges of the borderlands communities of interest still survive. Miguel Montoya, historian of the village of Mora, defines the historical identity of his neighbors in this way: "We were Spanish by law, but Indian by thought-world and custom. We respected *los viejos* (the elders), who looked after our spiritual health. We have relatives in the Pueblos, and out there, in Oklahoma (pointing east, to the reservations of the Comanches, Kiowas, and Southern Cheyenne)."[94]

Notes

This article has been modified for publication in *Feminist Studies*. The original version will appear in Elizabeth Jameson and Susan Armitage, eds., *Writing the Range: Race, Class, and Culture in the Women's West* (Norman: University of Oklahoma Press, 1997). I wish to thank the editors and publishers of that volume for graciously agreeing to allow this version to be published here. I also gratefully acknowledge the financial support of the Center for Research on Women and Gender at the University of California, Davis, and the Phillips Fund for Research on Native American Ethnohistory of the American Philosophical Society, toward the creation of this article. I thank as well faculty and student colleagues at the University of California at Davis whose criticism has contributed to its refinement, including Vicki L. Ruiz, Susan Mann, and Cynthia Brantely. This version has benefited from questions posed by Natalie Alexia Lopez, great-granddaughter of the captive Jesus Arviso; the insightful criticisms offered by the anonymous reviewers of *Feminist Studies*, and from Rebecca Anne Allahyari, who guided me through its many revisions.

1. Jack B. Tykal, "Taos to St. Louis: The Journey of María Rosa Villalpando," *New Mexico Historical Review* (April 1990); 161–74.
2. Frances Swadesh (Quintana) first proposed the "nondominant frontier" concept in her "Structure of Hispanic-Indian Relations in New Mexico," in *The Survival of Spanish American Villages*, ed. Paul M. Kutsche (Colorado Springs: Colorado College Press, 1979), 53–61. For a recent synthesis of the Spanish Borderlands that reflects similar thinking, see David J. Weber, *The Spanish Frontier in North America* (New Haven: Yale University Press, 1991).
3. As used here, "borderlands political economy" indicates that despite profound and continuing cultural differences in the region, Native Americans and New Mexicans came to *share* some common understandings of the production and distribution of wealth, as conditioned by the social relations of power.

4. Treatments of "slavery" in New Mexico are L.R. Bailey's *The Indian Slave Trade in the Southwest* (Los Angeles: Westernlore Press, 1966), which contains no analysis of gender differentiation or captivity among Indian groups; David M. Brugge's *Navajos in the Catholic Church Records of New Mexico, 1694–1875* (Tsaile: Navajo Community College Press, 1985), an important piece of documentary research upon which this essay relies heavily but which does not attempt a unifying analytical framework; and the recent work of Ramón Gutiérrez, *When Jesus Came, the Corn Mothers Went Away: Marriage, Sexuality, and Power in New Mexico, 1500–1846* (Stanford: Stanford University Press, 1991), whose analysis relies on an exploitation paradigm drawn from chattel slavery in the southern United States. Gutiérrez does not consider the experience of Spanish captives in Indian societies.

5. For an in-depth treatment of this question of the meaning of the exchange of women, see the author's Ph.D. dissertation, "Captives and Cousins: Violence, Kinship, and Community in the New Mexico Borderlands, 1680–1880" (University of California, Davis, 1995).

6. Friedrich Engels, *The Origin of the Family, Private Property, and the State* (1884; rpt., New York: Pathfinder Press, 1972); Gerda Lerner, *The Creation of Patriarchy* (New York: Oxford University Press, 1986); Claude Levi-Strauss, *The Elementary Structures of Kinship* (1949; rpt., Boston: Beacon Press, 1969); Gayle Rubin, "The Traffic in Women: Notes on the 'Political Economy' of Sex" in *Toward an Anthropology of Women*, ed. Rayna R[app] Reiter (New York: Monthly Review Press, 1975); Verena Martínez-Alier, *Marriage, Class, and Colour in Nineteenth-Century Cuba.* (Cambridge: Cambridge University Press, 1974); Jane Fishburne Collier, *Marriage and Inequality in Classless Societies* (Stanford: Stanford University Press, 1988).

7. Lerner; Martínez-Alier applies this argument to nineteenth-century Cuba. Claude Meillassoux makes the case for the patrimony-to-property transition in his synthesis of indigenous/domestic African slave systems in *The Anthropology of Slavery: The Womb of Iron and Gold* (Chicago: University of Chicago Press, 1991).

8. While reiterating the ban on Indian slavery first set forth in 1542, the *Recopilación* reinforced the "just war" doctrine, whereby hostile Indians might be enslaved if taken in conflict. *Indios de rescate* (ransomed Indians), on the other hand, were "saved" from slavery among their captors and owed their redeemers loyalty and service. See Silvio Zavala, *Los Esclavos Indios en Nueva España* (Mexico City: El Colegio Nacional, 1967), for a complete treatment of these policies.

9. For theoretical and empirical cases, see the essays in Katherine Spielmann, ed., *Farmers, Hunters, and Colonists: Interaction between the Southwest and the Southern Plains* (Tucson: University of Arizona Press, 1991).

10. Report of the Reverend Father Provincial, Fray Pedro Serrano . . . to the Marquis de Cruillas . . . 1761, in *Historical Documents Relating to New Mexico, Nueva Vizcaya, and Approaches Thereto, to 1773*, trans. and ed. Charles Wilson Hackett (Washington, D.C.: Carnegie Institution of Washington, 1937), 486–87.

11. Fray Anatasio Domínguez, *The Missions of New Mexico, 1776*, ed. and trans., Eleanor B. Adams and Fray Angélico-Chávez (Albuquerque: University of New Mexico Press, 1956), 252. See also "Las Ferias hispano-indias del Nuevo Mexico," in *La España Illustrada en el Lejano Oeste*, ed. Armando Represa (Valladolid: Junta de Castilla y León, Consejeria de Cultura y Bienestan Social, 1990), 119–25.

12. James S. Calhoun to Commissioner Brown, 31 Mar. 1850, in *The Official Correspondence of James S. Calhoun, Indian Agent at Santa Fe*, ed. Annie Heloise Abel (Washington, D.C.: Government Printing Office, 1915), 181–83. For the archaeology of *comanchero* sites on the Plains, see Frances Levine, "Economic Perspectives on the Comanchero Trade," in *Farmers, Hunters, and Colonists*, 155–69.

13. Because only about 75 percent of baptismal registers still exist, the actual figures are probably somewhat higher. Brugge, 2; for breakdown by tribal derivation and date, see 22–23.

14. "Analysis of the Spanish Colonial Census of 1750," Eleanor Olmsted, comp., New Mexico State Records Center, indicates a rural village population of 1,052, of whom 447 are recorded as having some Indian blood. In the "urban" areas of Santa Fe and Albuquerque, a total population of 2,757 contains only 400 individuals similarly designated. For a more detailed demographic analysis, see Brooks, chap. 2.

15. Brugge (116), estimates a sixty-to-forty female-male ratio for the Navajo captives he has studied. Working again with the Spanish Colonial Census of 1750, where individuals are designated either by proper name, or by a gendered noun (*criada/o, genízara/o, india/o*), I find that women total 153 of 282 individuals, or 54 percent. Because some bondwomen, for example, are designated simply "cinco indias criadas y ocho coyotitas" (*Spanish Archives of New Mexico* [hereafter *SANM*], New Mexico State Records Center, Santa Fe, series 1, roll 4, frame 1175), we cannot determine a precise gender breakdown. Nineteenth-century figures demonstrate continuity: Lafayette Head's 1865 census of Indian captives held in Costilla and Conejos Counties, Colorado Territory, shows women numbering 99 of 148 captives (67 percent), with children under age fifteen 96 of those 148 (65 percent) *National*

Archives, New Mexico Superintendency, microcopy 234, roll 553. Microfilms in the Center for the Study of the Southwest, Fort Lewis College, Durango, Colorado. In 1770, Don Augustín Flores de Vargara donated "for the sermon of the day" at the Chapel of San Miguel in Santa Fe "one Indian girl of serviceable age valued at 80 pesos." See "Certified copy of the Expenditures made by Captain Don Augustín Flores de Vargara for the Chapel of Glorious San Miguel . . .," Crawford Buel Collection, New Mexico States Records Center, Santa Fe.

16. In 1760, a Comanche band attacked what is now Ranchos de Taos and carried fifty-seven women and children into captivity. See "Bishop Tamarón's Visitation of New Mexico, 1760," in *Historical Society of New Mexico Publications in History,* vol. 15, ed. and trans. Eleanor B. Adams (Albuquerque: National Historical Society of New Mexico, 1954), 58. See also a raid on Abiquiu in 1747, where twenty-three women and children were carried off: "An Account of Conditions in New Mexico, written by Fray Juan Sanz de Lezuan, in the year 1760," in *Historical Documents,* vol. 3, 477.

17. "*Bando* of Don Phelipe de Neve, Governor and Commander-General of the Interior Provinces of New Spain, May 8, 1784," Bexar Archives, University of Texas, Austin. For the 1830s' estimate, see Jean Luis Berlandier in *The Indians of Texas in 1830,* ed. John C. Ewers (Washington, D.C.: Smithsonian Institution Press, 1969), 119. The 1933 Comanche Ethnographic Field School in Oklahoma estimated that 70 percent of Comanche society at that time were mixed-bloods, of primarily Mexican-Comanche descent; see E. Adamson Hoebel, "The Political Organization and Law-Ways of the Comanche Indians," *Memoirs of the American Anthropological Association,* 54 (Menasha, Wis.: American Anthropological Association, 1940).

18. Dennis M. Riordan to Commissioner, 14 Aug. 1883, *Annual Report of the Commissioner of Indian Affairs for the Year 1883* (U.S. Department of the Interior, Washington, D.C.); it should be noted that here, twenty years after the Emancipation Proclamation, U.S. officials were still attempting to extinguish Indian "slavery" in New Mexico.

19. The best discussion of origins and functions of *compadrazgo* relations remains that of Sidney W. Mintz and Eric R. Wolf, "An Analysis of Ritual Co-Parenthood (*Compadrazgo*)" in *Southwest Journal of Anthropology* 6, no. 4 (1950); 341–68. In New Mexico, important new work is being done by Sandra Jaramillo Macias; see her "Bound by Family: Women and Cultural Change in Territorial Taos" (paper presented at the Carson Foundation, 30 July 1994, Taos, New Mexico), and "The Myth of High Skirts and Loose Blouses: Intercultural Marriage in the Mexican Period" (paper presented at the thirty-fifth Annual Conference of the Western History Association, 12 Oct. 1995, Denver).

20. My thinking on culturally specific structural constraints was inspired by Nancy Folbre, who in her work on the organization of social reproduction, defines "structures of constraint" as "sets of assets, rules, norms, and preferences that shape the interests and identities of individuals or social groups." In doing so, they "define the limits and rewards to individual choice." This conceptualization allows us to recognize the *simultaneity* of exploitation and agency, a key element in this essay. Nancy Folbre, *Who Pays for the Kids? Gender and the Structures of Constraint* (New York: Routledge, 1993).

21. See Fray Angélico Chávez, *Origins of New Mexico Families* (1954; rpt., Santa Fe: Museum of New Mexico Press, 1992), 49–50, for reference to Hurtado's *encomienda* holdings, including Santa Ana Pueblo.

22. "Inventory and settlement of the estate of Juana Galvana, *genízara* of Zia Pueblo, 1753," *SANM* 1, no. 193. I thank Frances Swadesh Quintana for suggesting Juana Hurtado as a case study in captivity and for sharing her notes with me. Her essay, "They Settled by Little Bubbling Springs," *El Palacio* 84 (autumn 1978): 19–49, treats the history of the Santísima Trinidad Grant at *Los Ojitos Hervidores.*

23. *SANM* 2, no. 367, reel 6, frames 1010–23.

24. The journal of Don Diego de Vargas records Martín ransoming Juana at the Zuni Pueblo of Halona, along with her fourteen-year-old daughter María Naranjo, as well as a younger daughter and a son "about three years-old." This raises some confusion as to Juana's age at her capture in 1680 and suggests that at least one, and probably two, of her children were born to her during her captivity. As we will see, if true, this would have given Juana and her "Navajo" children membership in a Navajo clan and may help explain her long-term good relations with Navajos in the years to come. See J. Manuel Espinosa, trans. and ed., *First Expedition of Vargas into New Mexico, 1692* (Albuquerque: University of New Mexico Press, 1940), 237.

25. *Archdiocesan Archives of Santa Fe* (hereafter *AASF*), Burials, reel 43, frame 371, New Mexico State Records; see also *SANM* 2, no. 406.

26. "Declaration of Fray Miguel de Menchero, Santa Barbara, May 10, 1744," in *Historical Documents,* vol. 3, 404–5.

27. Abandonment of the Pueblo for defensible mesa-top positions often preceded Pueblo-Spanish conflict. See Swadesh, "They Settled. . . ." See *SANM* 2, no. 345, for details of the incident. For a treatment in broader historical context, see Swadesh.

28. See Morris E. Opler, "The Kinship Systems of the Southern Athabascan-Speaking Tribes," *American Anthropologist*, n.s., (1936): 622–33, and "Cause and Effect in Apachean Agriculture, Division of Labor, Residence Patterns, and Girl's Puberty Rites," *American Anthropologist* 74 (1972); 1133–46; also Harold E. Driver's reply to Opler ibid., 1147–51; Jane Fishburne Collier.

29. See W.W. Hill, "Some Navaho Culture Changes during Two Centuries, with a Translation of the Early Eighteenth-Century Rabal Manuscript," in *Smithsonian Miscellaneous Collections* 100 (1939): 395–415. For Navajo kinship and marriage systems, see David F. Aberle, "Navaha," in *Matrilineal Kinship*, ed. David M. Schneider and Kathleen Gough (Berkeley: University of California Press, 1961), 96–201; and Gary Witherspoon, *Navajo Kinship and Marriage* (Chicago: University of Chicago Press, 1975).

30. For Navajo warfare, and raiding/assimilation patterns for captives and livestock, see W.W. Hill, "Navaho Warfare," *Yale University Publications in Anthropology*, no. 5 (1936): 3–19. See Arnold Van Gennep, *The Rites of Passage* (1909; rpt., Chicago: University of Chicago Press, 1960), for a treatment of the cross-cultural attributes of integration rituals.

31. Brugge, 138, citing a conversation with Bruce Yazzi, a son of Nakai Na'dis Saal. See appendix B, 175; David M. Brugge, "Story of Interpreter for Treaty of 1868. . . .," *Navajo Times*, 21 Aug. 1968, 22B.

32. Ibid., 139. This seems an anomaly in the matrilineal reckoning of kin by Navajo clans, but given the nonkin status of an unadopted captive, it would be the only method of integrating her progeny.

33. "Agent Bowman to the Commissioner of Indian Affairs, 3 Sept. 1884," in *Annual Report of the Commissioners of Indian Affairs for the Year 1884*, quoted with extensive corroborative evidence in Brugge, 142.

34. Morris E, Opler, "A Summary of Jicarilla Apache Culture," *American Anthropologist*, n.s., 38 (1936): 206, 208, 209.

35. Ibid., 213. This information, gathered by Opler in the 1930s, may reflect an intensification of social stratification following the American conquest of the 1850s,

36. Collier, 23.

37. See Adamson Hoebel, 49ff.

38. Hoebel, 51, 62. Absconding cases accounted for twenty-two of the forty-five marital disputes recorded by Hoebel.

39. See Ernest Wallace and E. Adamson Hoebel, *The Comanche: Lords of the Southern Plains* (Norman: University of Oklahoma Press, 1952), 72.

40. David E. Jones, *Sanapia: Comanche Medicine Woman* (1972; rpt., Prospect Heights, Ill.: Waveland Press, 1984). Sanapia received her medicine powers through her mother and maternal uncle, consistent with the Shoshonean levirate. They became fully developed only after she experienced menopause.

41. Stanley Noyes, Los *Comanches: The Horse People* (Albuquerque: University of New Mexico Press, 1993); Brooks, 133–35; also Dan Flores, "Bison Ecology and Bison Diplomacy: The Southern Plains from 1800–1850," *Journal of American History* 78 (September 1991): 465–85.

42. Wallace and Hoebel, 241–42.

43. Ralph Linton, "The Comanche Sun Dance," *American Anthropologist*, n.s,, 37 (1935): 420–28.

44. For Loki-Mokeen's story, and others, see Maurice Boyd, "The Southern Plains: Captives and Warfare," in *Kiowa Voices: Myths, Legends, and Folktales* (Fort Worth: Texas Christian University Press, 1983), 2: 155–82.

45. For Andrés Martínez life story, see James F. Brooks, ed., *Andele: The Mexican-Kiowa Captive* (1899; rpt., Albuquerque: University of New Mexico Press, 1996).

46. Hoebel, 68.

47. Rosita Rodrigues to Don Miguel Rodrigues, 13 Jan. 1846, Bexar Archives, Barker History Center, University of Texas, Austin.

48. "A Narrative of the Captivity of Mrs. Horn and Her Two Children" (St. Louis, 1839), reprinted in C.C. Rister, *Comanche Bondage* (Glendale, Calif.: Arthur H. Clarke Co., 1955), 157.

49. On the incest taboo, see Hoebel, 108, I am indebted to Tressa L. Berman for suggesting the association between captive women's low incidence of sexual abuse and the adoptive incest taboo. For similar examples among other Indian groups, see James Axtell, "The White Indians of Colonial America," *William and Mary Quarterly* 32 (January 1975): 55–88.

50. Cynthia Ann Parker, the mother of Quanah Parker, the last Comanche war chief, is the most famous example of women who remained with their captors. See Margaret Schmidt Hacker, *Cynthia Ann Parker* (El Paso: Texas Western Press, University of Texas at El Paso, 1990). Parker lived thirty-four years among the Comanche and died "of heartbreak" shortly after her "rescue."

51. Rodrigues letter.

52. Josiah Gregg, *The Commerce of the Prairies*, ed. Milo Milton Quaife (1844; rpt., Lincoln: University of Nebraska Press, 1967), 208.

53. "*Expediente* of de Croix, June 6, 1780; Bonilla's Certification of June 15, 1780," Bexar Archives.

54. Gutiérrez, 190, 206. *The genízaros* remain the center of scholarly debate around their true status in New Mexican society, focusing on whether they constituted a caste category, defined from without, or if in time they developed as an "ethnogenetic" identity group. See Tibo Chavez, chap. 10, "The *Genízaro" El Rio Abajo* (Albuquerque: Pampa Print Shop, n.d.); Fray Angélico Chávez, *"Genízaros,"* in *The Handbook of North American Indians* (Washington, D.C.: Smithsonian Institution, 1980), 198–200; Robert Archibald, "Acculturation and Assimilation in Colonial New Mexico," *New Mexico Historical Review* 53 (July 1978): 205–17; Steven M. Horvath, "The *Genízaro* of Eighteenth-Century New Mexico: A Re-Examination," *Discovery* (Santa Fe: School of American Research, 1977), 25–40; Russel M. Magnaghi, "Plains Indiana in New Mexico: The *Genízaro* Experience," *Great Plains Quarterly* 10 (spring 1990): 86–95.

55. See Richard White's *Middle Ground: Indians, Empires, and Republics in the Great Lakes Region, 1640–1815* (New York: Cambridge University Press, 1991); Gregory Evans Dowd, *A Spirited Resistance: The North American Indian Struggle for Unity, 1745–1815* (Baltimore: Johns Hopkins University Press, 1991); and Daniel H. Usner Jr., *Indians, Settlers, and Slaves in a Frontier Exchange Economy: The Lower Mississippi Valley before 1763* (Chapel Hill: University of North Carolina Press, 1992), for new, sometimes divergent, conceptualizations of these relationships. Other authors preceded White and Dowd in stressing the importance of intermarriage in patterns of accommodation, principally Sylvia Van Kirk in her *Many Tender Ties: Women in Fur Trade Society in Western Canada,, 1670–1870* (Norman: University of Oklahoma Press, 1980); and Jennifer S.H. Brown in *Strangers in Blood: Fur Trade Company Families in Indian Country* (Vancouver: University of British Columbia Press, 1980).

56. Donald E. Worcester, trans., "Don Fernando de la Concha to Lieutenant Colonel Don Fernando Chacón, Advice on Governing New Mexico, 1794," *New Mexico Historical Review* 24 (1949): 236–54, quotation on 250.

57. Alfred B. Thomas, ed. and trans., "Antonio de Bonilla and the Spanish Plans for the Defense of New Mexico, 1777–1778," in Alfred B. Thomas, *New Spain and the West* (Lancaster, Penn.: Lancaster Press, 1932), 1: 196.

58. Fray Juan Augustín de Morfi, "Desórdenes que se advierten en el Nuevo Mexico, 1780," *Archivo Generate del Nacion* (Mexico City), Historia, 25: 288.

59. "Don Fernando de la Concha to Lieutenant Colonel Don Fernando Chacón," 251.

60. Marc Simmons, ed. and trans., "The Chacón Economic Report of 1803," *New Mexico Historical Review* 60 (1985): 81–83, quotations on 83, 87.

61. The economic "modernization" of New Mexico has usually been attributed to the influence of the St. Louis-Santa Fe-Chíhuahua trade that began in 1821. For a much earlier emergence, see Ross H. Frank, "From Settler to Citizen: Economic Development and Cultural Change in Late Colonial New Mexico, 1750–1820" (Ph.D. diss., University of California, Berkeley, 1992); for this aspect in the sheep commerce, see John O. Baxter, *Las Carneradas: Sheep Trade in New Mexico, 1700–1860* (Albuquerque: University of New Mexico Press, 1987).

62. Janet Lecompte has collected and interpreted most of the primary source material on this revolt, in *Rebellion in Rio Arriba, 1837* (Albuquerque: University of New Mexico Press, 1985). Her class-conflict interpretation stressed tensions between *ricos* and *pobres* and neglects to consider the cultural issues at work.

63. Governor Manuel Armijo, "Diario del Gobierno de la Republica Mexicans," Nov. 30, 1837, translated ibid., 139.

64. For the extensiveness of the 1847 "Taos" Revolt, see U.S. Senate, 56th Congress, 1st sess., Document No. 442 (1900), *Insurrection against the Military Government in New Mexico and California, 1847 and 1848*; Michael McNierney, ed. and trans., *Taos 1847: The Revolt in Contemporary Accounts* (Boulder: Johnson Publishing Co., 1980); James W. Goodrich, "Revolt at Mora, 1847," *New Mexico Historical Review* 47 (1972): 49–60.

65. See the Spanish Colonial Census of 1750, Eleanor Olmsted comp., New Mexico State Records Center, 47, 48.

66. See Horvath.

67. Fray Miguel de Menchero claimed in 1744 that the "*genízaro* Indians . . . engage in agriculture and are under obligation to go out and explore the country in pursuit of the enemy, which they are doing with great bravery and zeal." See Declaration of Menchero, in *Historical Documents*, 3: 401.

68. See "Appeal of Bentura Bustamante, Lieutenant of Genízaro Indians," *SANM* 1, no. 1229, roll 6, frames 323–35, 20 June 1780.

69. "Jose Manrique, draft of a Report for Nemesio Salcedo y Salcedo, Nov. 26, 1808," Pinart Collection, Bancroft Library, University of California, Berkeley.

70. Locompte, 36–40, n. 54.

71. Gutiérrez, chap. 7–9.

72. Angelina F. Veyna, "*Hago, dispongo, y ordeno mi testamento*: Reflections of Colonial New Mexican Women" (paper presented at the Annual Meetings of the Western History Association, October 1991, Austin, Texas).

73. *SANM* 1, no. 344, cited in ibid.

74. "Testament of Don Santiago Roibal, 1762," fragment in New Mexico State Records Center, Santa Fe.

75. *SANM* 2, no. 427, roll 7, frames 1023–25.

76. Gutiérrez, 182.

77. Frances S. Quintans, *Pobladores: Hispanic Americans of the Ute Frontier* (Aztec, N.M., 1991 [originally published as *Los Primeros Pobladores: Hispanic Americans of the Ute Frontier* (South Bend: University of Notre Dame Press, 1974)], 206–10.

78. Gutiérrez, 252.

79. As early as 1714, Spanish authorities ordered "married" couples in the Rio Grande Pueblos to establish neolocal households, rather than residing with their parents, a clear attempt to break matrilocal residence patterns and assert colonial control over the institution of marriage. See *SANM* 2, reel 4, frame 1014, as an example.

80. Swadesh, 44.

81. Marietta Morrissey, *Slave Women in the New World: Gender Stratification in the Caribbean* (Lawrence; University of Kansas Press, 1989), 13–15. See also Barbara Bush, *Slave Women in Caribbean Society, 1650–1838* (Bloomington: Indiana University Press, 1990). The ambiguous benefits of maternity to women held captive in patrilineal societies is borne out by looking at women under indigenous African systems of captivity and slavery. Among the Margi of Nigeria, for example, social integration of captive-descended children could result in the elevation of mothers, if those children achieved social prominence in trade or warfare. See James H. Vaughan, "*Mafakur*: A Limbic Institution of the Margi," in *Slavery in Africa*, ed. Suzanne Miers and Igor Kopytoff (Wisconsin: University of Wisconsin Press, 1977), 85–102.

82. Alan M. Klein, "The Political Economy of Gender: A Nineteenth-Century Plains Indian Case Study," in *The Hidden Half: Studies of Plains Indian Women*, ed. Patricia Albers and Beatrice Medicine (Lanham, Md.: University Press of America, 1983), 143–74; for a study of the bison economy, see Flores, 465–85.

83. Veyna, 9. Veyna also notes that "when tools were distributed to the settlers of Santa Cruz de la Cañada in 1712, only women were allotted *rejas*."

84. H.P. Mera, *The Slave Blanket*, General Series Bulletin No. 5 (Santa Fe: New Mexico Laboratory of Anthropology, 1938).

85. See Lansing Bloom, "Early Weaving in New Mexico," *New Mexico Historical Review* 2 (1927): 228–38; Baxter, 60. See also Suzanne Baizerman, "Textile Traditions and Tourist Art: Hispanic Weaving in New Mexico" (Ph.D. diss., University of Minnesota, St. Paul, 1987), esp. 76–79; 130–31.

86. General Campaign: Report of Governor Vélez Cachupín to Conde de Revilla Gigedo, Nov. 27, 1751," in Alfred B. Thomas, *The Plains Indians and New Mexico, 1751–1778* (Norman: University of Oklahoma Press, 1940), 74. "Juan José Lobato to Vélez, August 28, 1752," ibid., 114–15.

87. "Report of Governor Vélez to Marqués de Cruillas, 1762," ibid., 152–53.

88. "Abstract of Report Offered by de Anza, as Written by Pedro Garrido y Durran, Chihuahua, December 21, 1786," in Alfred B. Thomas, *Forgotten. Frontiers: A Study of the Spanish Indian Policy of Don Juan Bautista de Anza, Governor of New Mexico, 1777–1787* (Norman: University of Oklahoma Press, 1932), 296; Elizabeth A. John, *Storms Brewed in Other Men's Worlds* (Lincoln: University of Nebraska Press, 1975), 732.

89. Maria Mies, "Social Origins of the Sexual Division of Labor," in *Women: The Last Colony*, ed. Maria Mies, Veronika Bennholdt-Thomsen, Claudia van Werlhof (London: Zed Books, 1988), 67–95, 87.

90. See Gregg, 86, 208, 219.

91. The French traders Jean Chapuis and Luis Fueilli were guided to Santa Fe in 1752 by "an Indian woman of the Aa tribe, who had fled to the house of her master [in Santa Fe] four months before and was following the road to her country." See "Vélez to Revilla Gigedo, Sept. 18, 1752," in Thomas, *Plains Indians and New Mexico*, 109.

92. See *SANM* 1, no. 657, "Demanda puesta por Lucia Ortega contra Roque Lovato sobre una Donacion—Ano del 1769," New Mexico State Records Center.

93. See Tykal; "Report of Governor Vélez to Marqués de Cruillas," in Thomas, *The Plains Indians*, 151. Vélez had asked the Comanche leader Nimiricante of the whereabouts of the women and children seized at Ranchos de Taos in 1760, Nimiricante replied that "they might have died, or been traded to the French and Jumanos." For José Juliano's problems in San Antonio, see Salcedo to Manrique, 27 July 1809, *SANM* 2, no. 2239.

94. Author's field notes, 17 Aug. 1990.

5

"Deluders and Seducers of Each Other"
Gender and the Changing Nature of Resistance

Jennifer L. Morgan

Women's experience of racial slavery at the hands of English colonizers suggests that the language of resistance and accommodation is always already insufficient. The dichotomies that emerge are uncomfortable. Women who became mothers enriched their captors' estates while simultaneously creating the communities that would foster profoundly complicated opposition to and compliance with American racial domination. Women who did not become mothers mourned the loss of their birthright or celebrated this blow to slaveowners' domination. "Resistance" and "accommodation" are static poles at opposite sides of a spectrum whose intent is to capture the wide range of responses to repression but whose effect, I would argue, is quite the opposite. Resorting to a binary view, even if one does so in service of illustrating the range of responses that run along the line between two points, suggests an ability to clearly delineate the meaning of various behaviors and does so while suggesting that there is consensus about the terms in play. Is there agreement about the interpretation of behavior under an oppressive regime? While we know that social behaviors are transformed under slavery, to presume that an unwillingness to follow orders, for instance, can be clearly interpreted is to presume too much.

It is a truism that the enslaved resisted their enslavement; to imagine otherwise is to reduce men, women, and children to the machine-like laborer who existed solely in the racial imaginary of slaveowners and their descendants. Refusing to separate "resistance" from the larger social-historical study of the African American past avoids the creation of an artificial divide through otherwise integrated aspects of daily life.[1] It allows for a fluid understanding of oppositionality in which the political is not segregated from the social or cultural, the unwillingness to conform to slaveowners' demands for efficiency is connected to the debilitating effects of forced hard labor on the body and the spirit, and the insurgent value of a trickster tale is not isolated from the experiential pleasure of a story told as the body and mind recover after a day of toil. The pleasure taken in the tale is inextricable from and dependent on its mutinous quality.

Nonetheless, an assumption that all behaviors under slavery were resistant culminates in precisely the same imaginary automaton. For in the vacuum of perpetual resistance, there is no pain, no suffering, no wounds. Perhaps no better evidence of this conflict in interpretive frames exists than childbirth in a system that both relied upon and devalued it. It is to that end that centering or isolating enslaved women's acts of political and economic autonomy is appropriate in a study that has explored the multiplicities of enslaved women's reproductive lives, lives that refuse easy categories of compliance or resistance. A reductive view of reproduction does not move us beyond binaries. If we see childbirth as nothing more than an opportunity to illustrate the ability of enslaved women to release a wellspring of motherlove onto benighted children whom they would sacrifice everything to save, we do no more than reinscribe ideologies of maternal caregivers grounded in outdated notions of separate spheres, the feminized emotional, and the dichotomies of public/private.[2] An examination of the complicated rewriting of mother-hood that occurs in the context of New World slavery offers instead a narrative of shifting meaning and reconceived foundations as the private, domestic, and noneconomic woman's womb becomes the site of venture capitalism. This chapter explores enslaved women's urge to contest enslavement both inside and outside their identities as mothers.

Efforts to Control

A cursory glance at colonial slave laws pinpoints the perception slaveowners had of the enslaved: they were a different, dangerously plentiful, and rebellious sort of property.[3] The contradiction at the heart of slavery—the claim on the part of slaveowners that the men and women they enslaved were not fully human—is explicated in the compulsory need to prevent the physical mobility and urge toward social intimacy is at the heart of human community. Colonial slave codes were universally concerned with regulating the movements of the enslaved, a concern rooted in both the pragmatics of social control and in the ideological nexus of human beings who were both real and chattel property.[4] In one of the earliest slave laws in Barbados, legislators determined in 1672 that the enslaved were real estate rather than chattel. This juridical identity meant little in the context of lived experience, but it does highlight the vexing problem of movement for slaveowners determined to tie the enslaved to the land ("to the intent that the Heir and Widow . . . may not have bare Land, without Negroes to manure the same") as inanimate objects whose value mimicked that of a house or barn.[5] In crafting legislation to "Better order and Govern" enslaved women and men, slaveowners consistently addressed the issue of mobility in the opening clauses of comprehensive slave codes. Virginia slaveowners highlighted the "pretense of feasts and burials" as the cause of the "frequent meetings" among the enslaved that needed to be curtailed.[6] Slaveowners in Barbados in 1688 found it "absolutely necessary to the safety of this place, that all due care be taken to restrain the wanderings and meetings of Negroes and other Slaves at all times, more especially on Saturday nights, Sundays and other Holidays." Antiguan slaveowners in 1697 adopted the Barbadian code largely unchanged and thus also focused primarily on controlling mobility. The second clause of the Carolina act, the one that immediately followed the definition of who exactly was enslaveable, said that no one "shall give their Negroes and other slaves leave, on Sundays hollidays or any other time to go out of their plantation."[7]

For decades, Englishmen in the Americas had struggled with the consequences of disparate population growth; settlers on Association Island abandoned the colony when "the great num-ber of Negroes" outnumbered them two to one.[8] John Drax expressed alarm at the rising rate of white emigration from Barbados and warned that this weakened state rendered the island's white population increasingly vulnerable to the "first Attempt." He suggested the creation of a manufacturing base on the island to replace costly imports and to "find Imployment for many of your poor [who] would continue not [to] goe off because they know not how to subsist in Barbados." To protect against the encroachment of slave artisans, the proposed jobs must be exclusive—"in this trade nor in any other [may] there be any Negroes employed except Artificers belonging to the sugar work."[9] As Carolina legislators would half a century later, Barbadian legislators blamed skilled slave labor and land consolidation for displacing the aspirations of poor working whites whose mobility led to white elite vulnerability.

On the other hand, as enslaved African men moved through the ranks of gang laborers and filled the positions of artisans, they too acquired mobility. Growing numbers of African blacksmiths, dockworkers, coopers, and haberdashers moved about the island, in and out of Bridgetown, making money for their owners and making connections for themselves.

Unsuccessful efforts to curb white reliance on African artisans did not mitigate the considerable economic gains for whites that owned them. In retaliation against owners who allowed this, the Assembly proposed taxes on "every Negro where there is no sugar works." In his letter, Drax allowed for African artisans at sugar works only so long as their owners did not contribute to the problem of slave mobility by hiring them out.[10]

The concern around mobility poses interesting questions about gender and movement. As we have seen, enslaved women had little access to artisan positions. Domestic services like laundering, cooking, and cleaning would be open only to a minority of women. Undeniably slaveowners primarily targeted enslaved men for their unregulated wanderings, but occasionally women too enjoyed the freedom to walk to a neighboring plantation or into Bridgetown to meet with friends and family—on Sundays perhaps, or on days like the first of June 1671, when all work, drinking, or entertaining ceased in order to commemorate the end of a period of "grievous sickness and pestintiall distempor."[11] But gender circumscribed mobility as it did work. Men were more likely to become mobile communicators outside the small plantation communities on which women provided the bulk of the field labor. However, women created the need for those lines of communication as, through their bodies, they created ties of consanguinity.

In the context of a community increasingly defined as creole—in other words, one in which connection and intimacy were made visible by the birth of children—the attempt to control and curtail movement was, in many ways, both futile and intuitive. Connections among the enslaved were evidenced by childbirth itself, by the shift from African to European languages, by run-aways aided and sequestered by friends and family, and by the ability and desire to plan and carry out revolts. Colonial legislators vainly passed laws disallowing communication among the enslaved on its most fundamental level. In Barbados, they prohibited the enslaved from "using or keeping of Drums, Horns, or other loud Instruments which may call [them] together, or give sign or notice to one another of their wicked designs and purposes." Similar legislation on the mainland focused on the ability to gather independently: In Carolina, "great numbers of slaves which do not dwell in Charlestown, on Sundays and holidays resort thither, to drink, querrell, fight, curse and swear . . . in great companies together, which may give them an opportunity of executing any wicked designs and purposes."[12] In order to prevent such gatherings, legislators turned to slaveowners, threatening them with fines for allowing those they enslaved off their property without legitimate reason and proper permission; control could not be wrested from the Sunday gatherers, so slaveowners were the logical target of frustrated legislators. Still, whether gathering in Charlestown, calling one another to clandestine meetings in Barbados's secluded groves, or attending feasts and funerals in Virginia, enslaved women and men traveled well outside the confines of rural plantations. As they moved from place to place, they carried with them the assumption that movement was their right; freedom of movement did not crumble in the face of regulatory attempts to limit it. The gathering of African peoples in private and in public places formed an essential part of their lives in the colonies.

If slave laws illuminate the extent to which enslaved men and women were moving all around the colonies, they also reflect another kind of movement as well, that of a slaveowning class's sense of racial identity. Slaveowners' legislation reflected a racial consciousness that developed over time, borne out in the owners' efforts to isolate themselves from those that they enslaved. In Barbados, as the planter class purchased more slaves, the legislative records of the island's council and assembly reflect growing anxiety about ethnic and religious differences among white colonists. In July 1661, for example, worry over English outmigration to other colonies led the council to request "three thousand Christian servants at the half yearly, [for] if wee are so supply'd then Jamaica or the Neighboring Collonys may probably bee furnish'd with a suitable number of freemen from us."[13] This desire for English settlers, which often manifested itself in pleas to the metropôle to send white women to the colonies, cannot be conflated at this stage with a straightforward desire for "whites" to offset "blacks." Longstanding ethno-religious differences and conflicts confounded the logic of racial slavery. Thus, at the same time, the council ordered lists, by parish, of "siditious troublesome or dangerous" Irish, and prohibited all Irishmen residing in Barbados from commanding "any shallop or boats belonging to or in this Island."[14] During the same session, the council compiled "Reasons against the being and sort of the Quakers within this Island"—a list of grievances arising from Quaker refusal to serve in the military as well as from their "dayly" proselytizing.[15] And, of course, endemic inter-European rivalries further complicated any simplistic notion of "whiteness" or common cause. Later that year, the council ordered guns and powder and an island-wide mobilization in anticipation of an attack from the Spanish.[16] During the 1666 war with the Dutch, which not incidentally coincided with a period of rising white emigration from the island, fear of external attack led to the arming of enslaved men. On this occasion, the need to defend against a foreign invasion was stronger than the fear that armed slaves would rebel.[17] Carolina legislators also felt themselves beleaguered by "outsiders" who encroached upon the safety and security of the colony. Their fears were justified. Hostilities with neighboring Native Americans alarmed and concerned Carolina's white settlers. Colonial policy exacerbated wars among Indians to guarantee favorable trading conditions for Carolina colonists dependent on the Native American trade.[18] Deerskin figured prominently alongside the foodstuffs and naval stores that served as Carolina's economic mainstays, and, in their efforts to ensure constant access to Native American trading goods, colonial officials pursued policies that led to open rebellion between English settlers and a Creek-Yamasee alliance in 1715, the Yamasee War, and placed white Carolinians squarely in the middle of a large regional Indian slave trade.[19]

For much of the first decades of settlement, then, white Carolinians, like slaveowners in Barbados, focused attention on external sources of aggression such as the dangers posed by the Spanish and Native Americans. But an inevitable polarization took place when, in the wake of staple monoculture exports, rapid black population growth transformed southern and Caribbean English colonies one by one into slave societies. Growing numbers of Africans intensified the sense of isolation experienced by slaveowning settlers up and down the Atlantic, who misinterpreted the extent of their marginality.[20]

While population growth at this stage occurred as a result of the slave trade, the transformation of Africans into Afro-Americans drew the attention of slaveowners in search of evidence of their own mastery. As William Willoughby searched for viable methods of social control, he felt that only "different tongues and Animosities in their own Countrey have . . . kept them from Insurrection," suggesting that the process of acculturation was a source of danger because it mitigated linguistic and cultural distances and thus gave voice to latent discontent. Willoughby believed he possessed the skills to discern the loyal from the mutinous and claimed credit for maintaining peace among "Creolian" slaves, who were now able to plot together on the basis of the trust he had in some island-born men, "as are best approved of for their Fidelities and Abilities," to advise him.[21] Elsewhere colonial Assemblies similarly looked to "worthy" black women and men to protect them. In 1706, for example, Carolina came under attack by combined French and Spanish forces. In his report of the event, Governor Johnson described the lurking presence of warships at Charlestown harbor and gratefully noted that "notice [was] brought by a Negro that ye Enemy had been on shoar." Fear, self-interest, or loyalty motivated the unnamed black man to raise the alarm. His ability to assess and report on the immanent danger of foreign ships speaks to the presence of acculturated women and men like himself who were versed in the boundaries of the colony and the rewards of "loyalty" to the colonial authorities.[22] Four years later, Thomas Nairne reported on the practice of arming enslaved men in the colony's militias; Carolina legislators acted on their confidence that they maintained control over the colony when they handed a gun to a man who expected "his Freedom, [if] in the Time of an Invasion [he] kills an Enemy."[23] As Willoughby had in Barbados, slaveowning legislators saw the cooperation of enslaved militiamen and loyal informants as evidence of their own ability to maintain order and evoke responsibility among black men.

Such individuals held an essential place in the slaveowners' arsenal as they searched for a way to neutralize the volatile population they lived among, if only symbolically. Writing to the Board of Trade in 1730, William Chapman argued against the imposition of taxes on "the Blacks[.] We represent to your Lordships that this is in Effect a Duty on the British manufacturers, the Blacks being the produce thereof."[24] This attempt to erase human and social origins spoke to the economic and symbolic necessity of a neutralized enslaved labor force. Faced with an increasingly African-born population, the writer located them as men and women who were remarkable for the color of their skin rather than their place of origin. Like all imports, once in the colony they would become part of the colony—in essence, creole—but until then the "Blacks" were nothing but British products.[25] The conflict between slaveowning legislators' desire to see the enslaved as passive, undifferentiated, controllable brutes and their experience with men and women whose agency demanded something different continued—particularly over the behavior of "acculturated" men and women. To balance their dependence on enslaved laborers with their awareness of the coercion inherent in the slave system must have been quite a task for colonial slaveowners.

Even before Willoughby turned to creole men for counsel, efforts to control and regulate were explicitly embedded in the reproducing bodies of enslaved women. Women's role in protecting the colonies was perhaps more complicated. Enslaved women's sexual identity cut two ways: it could pacify black men's aggression or give rise to creole laborers who were sometimes a source of peace and sometimes a source of danger. The relationship between ethnicity and rebellion warranted incessant analysis among Caribbean slaveowners. Elsewhere in the British West Indies, Antiguan slaveowners would be violently reminded of the potential for creole rebellion in 1737. At the same time, Willoughby's conviction that danger lay in acculturation would be tested by the wave of rebellions and revolts led by ethnic Africans that crisscrossed the eighteenth-century Caribbean. Primarily led by men, these revolts were undergirded by women who hosted gatherings, carried information, and ran away to join maroon communities—sometimes with children in tow. Faced with a recurring influx of ethnic Africans and the undeniable evidence of their unhappiness, many slaveowners turned a hopeful eye toward the large numbers of island-born creoles.[26]

A century and a half before Barbadian slaveowners embraced the abolition of the slave trade on the grounds that Africans posed a dangerous and, in their colony, unnecessary evil, they had already begun to articulate their assumption that it was Africanity rather than enslavement that caused defiance. As often was the case, pragmatic slaveowners contradicted legislative efforts to control. In 1663 the Barbados Assembly considered "An Act recommending the christening of Negroe children"; some fifty years later, slaveowners in Carolina would do the same.[27] But neither Barbadian nor Carolinian planters embraced efforts to instruct the children of enslaved women in Christian rituals. Planters' reluctance to provide religious instruction for the enslaved dated back to the mid-seventeenth century.[28] Evocations of Christianity had a minimal effect on the daily lives of the enslaved population, but they carried weight for legislators, who continued to hollowly exhort that "all Negroe slaves and servants remaining in the said colony shall be Instructed in the Principles of the . . . [Christian] Religion And that such who shall arrive at a competent knowledge therein be admitted to the Sacrament of Baptism."[29] Despite the refusal of slaveowners to allow the few available clergy regular access to the enslaved, the laws reflect the relationship between control, reproduction, and creolization. Christianity intersected with creolization. By symbolically transforming island-born children into God-fearing Christians, legislators must have presumed a formula for creating "worthy" creoles. There was also an unspoken assumption about enslaved women in these laws: enslaved women's reproductive power was both available and in use for the purpose of removing the perceived dangers of Africanity in the form of ethnically based rebellion.

Despite their willingness to draw on notions of black loyalty to the English flag, slaveowners were increasingly forced to understand the riptide of discontent under the surface. It was, perhaps, with this in mind that the Barbados council proclaimed in 1667 that acts and other important information must now be "published" in Bridgetown "by sound of Trumpett" in lieu of drums.[30] More than twenty years earlier, Richard Ligon commented on enslaved drummers' skills in invoking "pleasure to the most curious eares."[31] In 1661, Felix Spoeri chronicled night-long religious ceremonies among the enslaved that "consist[ed] of particular dances, [and] drumming on a hollow tree trunk over which an animal skin is stretched."[32] Whether or not it was pleasurable to European ears, drumming evoked Africa. By replacing the agitation of drumming with the thoroughly European, not to mention military, tones of the trumpet, white Barbadians calmed their nerves and more easily monitored networks of communication among the enslaved.

Despite the clearly articulated interest of Carolina's first settlers in opening the colony to slavery from its inception, slaveowners understood the black population as a source of consider-able danger and with petulance and violence sought to subjugate them. In 1691, the colonial legislators wrote of the need to "prevent the Mischeives which (as the Number of Slaves Shall Increase) Too much Liberty may occasion," thereby fusing the issue of mobility and population growth in one neat sentence. The code included provisions for fining slaveowners who did not employ sufficient numbers of whites on their plantations and at their cattlepens.[33] In August 1720, when Carolina's legislators calculated the colony's population at 9,000 whites and 12,000 blacks, they complained that the "Pitch and Tar Trade prodigiously Increasing ha[s] occasioned ye Inhabitants to buy Blacks to the great Indangering [of] the Province."[34] The Board of Trade responded with admonitions that "no body . . . may have more Negroes than ten to a white man."[35] Although Carolina planters ignored this proposed proportion of black to white, in the face of an always growing black population, they responded to slave resistance quickly and violently. When slaveowners discovered a plot on the part of a group of enslaved men that spring, the men involved ran south in an attempt to reach safety in Florida. Their attempts to entreat the assistance of Creek Indian guides failed, and upon their capture, legislators ordered their execution by hanging and fire.[36]

Informants and Litigants

As the realities of forced labor propelled both enslaved laborers and slaveowning legislators into implicit or explicit efforts to reposition power in the colonies, enslaved women could not have been unaware of the conversations about creole children's propensity for accommodation and violence. It is no wonder that slaveowners perceived enslaved women as vehicles for increasing the distance between themselves and the dangerous lurkings of an Africanity exemplified by the rhythmic resonance of drums and counter-weighted by slave children reciting the Lord's Prayer. But by the middle of the 1670s, enslaved men on the island had developed communication links that sustained an island-wide response to enslavement. In 1675, Barbadian slaveowners uncovered a full-scale insurrectionary plot to overthrow the plantation regime and establish an Ashanti- or Akan-style government and society in its place.[37] The belief on the part of the rebels that ethnic identity could be sustained and reproduced outside Africa is an important corollary to the desire of slaveowners to categorize the children of Africans as morally and culturally distinct from their parents. As news of the revolt came to light after three years of planning, members of the assembly mitigated their ignorance of such proximate rage by rallying the image of black conjugality. According to the Commissioners investigating the conspiracy, the revolt plans were so clandestine that "even . . . [the conspirators'] own wives" remained unaware of them.

However, ultimately, a woman became aware of the plans and used information about the impending revolt for her own end. Days before its intended inception, Fortuna, enslaved on the Hall plantation in St. Peters, revealed the plot and brought the conspiracy to a halt. Once slaveowning legislators quashed the conspiracy, they freed Fortuna "in Recompense of her Eminent Service to the Good of this country in Discovering the Intended plotted Rebellion of the negroes."[38] Little else is known about Fortuna, least of all her motivation for providing information that sent over 100 men to jail and seventeen to the gallows. It may have been that Fortuna's act testifies to the divide between ethnic Africans and creoles. It is significant that the insurrectionists were "almost exclusively Coromantee," and Fortuna's willingness to separate her fate from theirs certainly reflected a deep perceptual chasm between herself and them.[39]

While for the most part enslaved men were those who used occupational mobility to their advantage, Fortuna took the opportunity to seize her own mobility upon the heels of men's plans for freedom. Her reasons for doing so may have been utterly selfish or they may have grown out of a desire to protect and provide for members of her own family. Fortuna's gender, her occupational location, and the presence or absence of her kin all shaped the priorities that propelled her into the assembly chambers and from there to her freedom. But the action that so clearly set her aside from Coromantee men did not necessarily connect her to creole women. On the same day the assembly freed Fortuna, they paid Marroa, another Negro woman, twenty shillings for her "Diligent attending the Assembly."[40] The small sum and the language suggest that she waited upon the assemblymen, perhaps cleaning the meeting hall. Her silence, in light of her artisan's mobility and proximity to powerful white men, stands in sharp contrast to Fortuna's revelation, suggesting the multiplicities of women's responses to the terms of their enslavement, race, gender, and location.

Enslaved women threw their weight against the confines of their enslavement in many different ways. The tactics with which enslaved women expressed their anger, grief, and desperation about enslavement were obviously not strictly embodied—in other words, it was not just about regulating their fertility or raising children. While occupational diversity was outside most women's experience, some were able to use their occupational category to expand the boundaries of their lives. In 1734, members of the Court of Common Pleas in Carolina heard a "plea of tresspass" brought by "Phillis a Free Negroe Woman." Phillis brought suit against Samuel Fox (probably a working white man, as he signed the register only with his mark) for his failure to pay her wages for her work "nurs[ing] and tend[ing his] Infant Child." She had cared for and lodged this child for a full year and brought Fox to court when he refused her payment of the promised 2.8 pounds sterling.[41] The court found in her favor, and Fox registered his promise to pay the money.

Phillis was one of the "Negroes in Trade" that local merchants had recently petitioned the assembly to control. Although she barely fits the definition of an artisan or skilled worker, as a black woman who utilized the legal mechanisms of the colony with aplomb, she did, of course, pose a threat. It was at about the same time that Phillis appeared in court that white artisans organized a petition asking the Assembly to ban the use of enslaved persons as skilled workers. The petitioning traders surely did not think of a woman such as Phillis as on a par with the carpenters, blacksmiths, coopers, and sawyers who threatened their livelihoods. But black female litigants during the slavery period used the courts to reduce their own powerlessness and to oppose white gender stereotypes about them.[42] Perhaps the traders understood that. Their petition grew out of a moment in which the visibility of black men's access to the trades—and its destabilizing consequences for working whites—was highlighted by the anomaly of a black woman's successful use of the courts against one of their own.[43]

Phillis's presence in court could not have failed to command attention from the multitude of participants who lined the halls or milled about outside waiting for their turn before the judges. Did residents of Charlestown gossip about her audacity that February, or did the fact that Samuel Fox was not a man of means minimize attention to the case? In either instance, the behavior of black women in the city of Charlestown certainly warranted attention from legislators interested in social control. Through their work as marketers and sellers of goods, some women managed to move outside the plantation orbit just as enslaved men did through their work as artisans or craftsmen. While selling the produce from their provision grounds, these women moved from plantations into town, creating and cementing relationships as they went. Late in the eighteenth century a *South Carolina Gazette* columnist would accuse black market women of working in tandem with one another to "exclu[de] . . . every white person" from purchasing foodstuff at reasonable rates.[44] By that time, forms of autonomy in the hands of black women had become a daily reality for black and white residents of Charlestown. In hindsight, some Carolinians came to understand the original legislators' attempts to curtail the market-driven wanderings of African women and men, yet many others would have celebrated their failure to do so.[45] The presence of market women in Charlestown and throughout the English colonies was a constant reminder of the ineffectual nature of legislation in the face of pragmatic desires for consumer goods and the tenacious efforts of black women to protect this space of autonomy and mobility.

The particular place of enslaved women occupied a complicated position. In March 1743, legislators rewarded the enslaved woman Sabina for informing them of "the Design of several negroes to desert to St. Augustine."[46] Only she could assess whether the reward from the lieutenant governor sufficiently compensated for causing the capture and execution of one of the deserters. Her information should have shown the legislators that "the Designs" of the enslaved increased exponentially with their ability to navigate Carolina, an ability that accompanied acculturation. Indeed when a Spanish ship, flying a "Flag of Truce" lingered too long in Charlestown harbor, legislators feared that the Spaniards would be apprised of weaknesses in the colony's defense by "conversing with our slaves": men and women able to assess and inform upon the colony's weaknesses.[47]

The weaknesses of the colonies were, of course, myriad. They were made manifest not only in the ability of creole women and men to navigate the cultural terrain of the colony but also in the very process by which those men and women came into being. In January 1746, Kate drew the attention of the legislators. Committed to jail the previous June, Kate had languished there ever since. Without providing any other information, the legislators noted that Kate had murdered "a Negro Child" belonging to a man other than the one who owned her. Kate "had been reputed Mad for twelve months before she committed the said murder" and had confessed "with every Circumstance" to the crime.[48] Both the unknown causes of her madness and the circumstances that led her to murder a child whose relationship to her is unclear are buried beneath legislative debate over who should shoulder the cost of her imprisonment. One wonders about Kate and her family, whether her "madness" was in fact predicated by the sale of her own child to another plantation, and whether it was thus her own child she killed as a result. The legislators gave little further thought to her beyond her financial cost to them, perhaps knowing that to do so would bring them closer than they wished to the violence and, indeed, madness that lurked among the "increasing" women who constituted their labor force and their wealth. They maintained a distance from women and men whose actions, individual and collective, threatened to disrupt the orderly business of export production.

Runaways

While conflict with the Spanish and neighboring Native Americans displaced by English settlers demanded considerable attention from Carolina legislators, the problem of black resistance constantly caused alarm. In 1687, two women, one of whom carried a nursing infant girl, and eight men escaped Carolina by boat to St. Augustine, Florida, and thus formed the first group of escaped slaves from Carolina whose flight is recorded in the colonial records. The women were not named, but we know that the mother was wife to Mingo and that the three of them were enslaved together by Samuel De Bordieu. Their escape was a desperate one: Mingo had allegedly killed someone in the process. These men and women converted to Catholicism, married, and found work in Spanish Florida, the women as domestics in the home of the Spanish governor. When approached, Governor Quiroga refused to return the runaways to their English enslavers, although he offered to pay for them in the future and, in a gesture certain to have reeked of sarcastic taunting to English settlers who claimed to be ready to execute an enslaved person for repeated petty theft, said he would be willing to prosecute Mingo should the charges against him be substantiated.[49] In 1696, Don La Redno Del Torres St. Callas, governor of St. Augustine, had both "negroes and negroes women" in his custody and was loath to return them.[50] A decade after the 1706 attack, Carolina officials began listing annual accounts of "Negro and Indian Slaves taken . . . and carried to St. Augustine," and losses to individual planters near the southern boundary ranged from one to thirty enslaved workers "taken and carried" per year.[51] Hardly unwilling captives, black Carolinians continuously headed south. They understood that Spanish authorities would free them upon their arrival, and they needed little additional enticement to cross the border into Spanish Florida.[52]

Slaveowners anxiously looked for ways to mitigate the economic and moral threat of runaways to their enterprise. In the summer of 1721, legislators congratulated one another when Harry—for reasons unknown to us and to them—returned to Carolina from St. Augustine, having fled to escape enslavement at the hands of the widow Perry. Once he was back in Carolina, the governor recommended rewarding him for the information he provided and, of course, for his "faithfulness."[53] As the decade unfolded, the assembly was far more likely to involve itself in the inevitability of runaways than in the unlikely event of their return. Harry's return, apparently on his own initiative, stands as an anomaly in the complex narrative of enslaved workers "enticed," "captured," and "runaway" to St. Augustine.

Although formal negotiations between the two colonies' governments took place throughout the 1720s and 1730s about the question of escaped black women and men, rarely did those negotiations occasion return.[54] Slaveowners petitioned the assembly for monetary compensation for the loss of killed, absconded, or executed slaves. The assembly debated each request while railing against Spanish "theft" of enslaved men and women, sending a ship to St. Augustine late in 1722 to demand the return of seven runaway slaves.[55] Twenty years later, the problem had increased tenfold. In November 1738, at least seventy enslaved women and men found their way to St. Augustine, occasioning a series of unsuccessful international negotiations for their return to South Carolina.[56]

Less than a year after Harry's return, an enslaved woman similarly brought attention to herself from the colonial assembly. Flora found the terms of her enslavement so unbearable that she braved the wilderness that lay between her and St. Augustine to head there with her child, to the dismay of both her owner and the legislators.[57] Flora's flight—abetted through networks of communication between black people—appears less of an anomaly than Harry's. She chose to run in the context of a network of information, possibly propelled by the reality that her child's future would be entirely out of her hands if she did not. She escaped only a week after a Spanish expedition, which included a free black man, arrived in Charlestown. The unnamed man had the temerity to speak with the enslaved in Charlestown, a liberty that enraged the assemblymen. The legislators "believe[d] he can have no other view then to Entice them from their Masters," indeed, to "carry off" enslaved women and men from Charlestown.[58] The assembly's frustration with those who would not accept the confines that slaveowners wanted to impose upon them is palpable: "We think it very Improper that the Negroe that is come with [the Spanish] should . . . talk with the Town slaves[.]" It is significant that this posture of indignation was absent during discussions of the women who headed toward St. Augustine.

Slaveowners regularly used the language of seduction as they fumed against those responsible for the absence of their slaves. In the 1688 version of the Barbadian slave code, legislators disallowed slaveowners "of the Hebrew Nation residing in any Sea-Port Town" to enslave more than one male, "be he man or boy"—thereby suggesting both a diminished manliness on the part of Jewish settlers who were unable to control masculine Africans as well as a feminine passivity on the part of enslaved women who could be owned in any number without apparent danger.[59] But that language did not distinguish between the mutinous behavior of men and women. Where one might expect to find a degree of self-righteous and sexualized hubris around Spanish "enticement" or "use" of African women, the legislators discussed women's absences with a straightforwardness that suggests that they did not see women's resistance as either unexpected or differentiated from that of their brethren. Feminized enslaved men *and* women were "enticed" away to St. Augustine by masculine Spaniards or "decoyed" away by manly Indians.[60] Slaveowners negotiated the enterprise of control through language that relegated both black women and men to the mutable and weak—the feminine.

Enslaved women who were so defined upset the balance of the slaveowners' equation with decisions couched in the immediacy of their lives. Perhaps Flora listened carefully to what the English-speaking black man in Charlestown had to say. Could he have directed her way south, telling her of natural landmarks to assure that she maintained the proper course, convincing her that the hardship of the journey would be mitigated by the relative freedom that awaited her? Whether she decided to escape before or are after his arrival in Charlestown, she would have found a kind of familiarity if she and her child arrived in Florida. There were other women from Charlestown already there. The very day her owner reported her absence, another Carolina slaveowner reported news of his own. Two enslaved negro women, Abigail and Dinah, and one enslaved Indian woman named Peggy who ran from him, had been located "in the hands of the Spaniards at St. Augustine."[61] For these mothers with small children, Spanish Florida figured as a powerful site of emotional and physical safety. Presumably, Abigail and Dinah welcomed Flora and her child with joy and relief. If Flora arrived safely, their common bonds of experience at the hands of Carolina slaveowners would facilitate a mighty connection.

Ties of affection between mothers, children, and other adults transformed other mothers into runaways as well. In the summer of 1732, Delia ran away from James Searles with the child she still nursed. Delia had not been enslaved in the colony long enough to perfect her English, but she had lived in Carolina long enough to make some strong and important connections to other enslaved persons. One of these was Clarinda, another woman from the Searles plantation. Clarinda spoke "very good English," already had been enslaved by at least one other owner, and cared enough for Delia to link her fate to a woman whose child hampered both their mobility. Delia or Clarinda either retained boat-handling skills from her past or had the gumption to assume that navigating a twenty-five-foot long, three-foot wide canoe as a vehicle of escape could not be that difficult.[62] In addition to their mutual willingness to brave the waters, they also appear mutually willing to share the burden of Delia's child. The dangers of escape multiplied with the presence of a dependent baby. Clarinda's travel with the child implied a connection to Delia and her baby as well. For these two women, mothering constituted not an individual but a collective responsibility. And, indeed, it may have been the child itself who provided the impetus for these African women, at different levels of acculturation and acclimatization, to join one another in the attempt to leave behind their enslavement.

Delia's and Clarinda's bid for freedom did not occur in isolation. Between 1732 and 1739, slaveowners placed 195 advertisements in the *South Carolina Gazette* for runaway slaves (see Table 5.1).[63] Male runaways outnumbered female runaways three to one—191 men to 61 women. These numbers, however, obscure the impact of female runaways, since flight did not always involve a single person. Men were far more likely than women to escape collectively. In one-fourth of all reported instances, men ran together. But women almost always fled alone. Delia's and Clarinda's choice to tie their fates to one another was unusual; they are the only pair of women reported fleeing together in this period. There are two other instances of women in

Table 5.1 Runaways in South Carolina, 1732–50

	1732–39	1740–50
Advertisements	195	299
Male runaways	191	287
Male maroonage	139	231
Female runaways	61	91
Female maroonage	57	86
Women with children	7	21
African women	4	4
Mustee women	10	1
Women "well known" or "this country borne"	3	13

Source: Lathan A. Windley, ed., *Runaway Slave Advertisements: A Documentary History from the 1730s to 1790s* (Westport, Conn.: Greenwood Press, 1983).

groups, both of which involve both women and men. In 1732, Amoretta and Sarah, "being very clever Negroes," banded with Jack, Hercules, and Monday to escape from William Webb's plantation (shortly after being relocated from another plantation) by canoe. This group is one of two reported in which men and women ran together. Barbary, pregnant, and her husband Pompey in January 1739 were the other.[64] Ultimately, women constituted 57 of 196 instances of *petit maronage* (29 percent), and 61 of 252 individual runaways (24 percent).

The confines of slavery became so unbearable for some women that 11 percent of them, like Delia and Clarinda, willingly shouldered the risks of running with a child.[65] For these women, the intensity of their desire to protect themselves and their children is self-evident. Certainly Jeney exhibited extraordinary tenacity when she left her new owner, in the wake of her former owner's death (a common precondition for the decision to run) and "carried with her three children."[66] Were all the children hers? The language of the advertisements does not make that clear. Nonetheless, Jeney's emotional ties to the children, biologically or fictively hers, overrode her desire to expedite an individual escape.

Although most women ran alone, they likely ran toward friends or family. Only 6.5 percent (4 of 61) were described as having been born in Africa: these women might not as yet have forged familial or community bonds. Slaveowners called 16 percent (10 of 61) of the women "Mustee," indicating their ties to more than one ethnic community in the colony. Advertisers either listed the remainder as "Carolina born" or indicated, through other descriptive language, that they were fully integrated into the Carolina community. For example, "Sabina . . . speaks good English and is Daughter to a Negro woman named Tulah."[67] While few mothers took the extreme step of escape with dependent children, most women's escape was facilitated by their membership in families or communities from whom they could expect succor. For women who parented under slavery, children could both propel them to run and compel them to stay. Despite the hopes of slaveowners in the pacifying power of black women, family could act both as a pacifier and as an instigator of action. In the face of a labor force that always contained women, slaveowners had to struggle to maintain an image of black women as a source of calmness and a tool for the control of unrest.

Revolts

White Barbadians responded in ways to be expected in the immediate aftermath of the 1675 conspiracy. As planters discovered, tried, and executed those involved, they directed violence at the slave community that reverberated far beyond those directly involved in the attempted uprising. Legislators ordered at least thirty-five men executed after investigating the conspiracy,

They caused eleven of the conspirators to be beheaded and dragged their decapitated corpses through the streets of Speightstown.[68] The legislative measures that were taken to more carefully control and rigorously punish those who planned to revolt resulted in whippings and executions of "rebellious Negroes" throughout the next decade. Legislators housed the accused in Speightstown during their interrogation and dutifully reimbursed the owners of the executed men.[69] They passed laws to "Restrayne the too frequent wanderings and meetings of Negroes and to Punish such Crimes, Insolencys and Outrages as shall be Committed By them."[70] Desperate to explain this conspiracy, the slaveowners looked to forces outside the island and to outsiders in their midst. The council and assembly forbade the importation of "Indian slaves" from the "Adjacent collonyes" into Barbados. These Native Americans were styled "a People of too Subtill Bloody and Dangerous nature and Inclination to be remained."[71] They soundly condemned Quakers for bringing the enslaved into their Meetings "under pretense of converting . . . them to the Christian beliefe" and passed laws to forbid or "restrayne" that activity.[72] A few years later, the Jewish community, always highly taxed by the council and assembly, came under censure for its dealings with the enslaved; in 1679, the island's legislators passed "An Act to Restrayne the Jews from keeping and trading with Negroes." In 1683, when rumor spread of another rebellion, legislators had the five enslaved persons whose "threatening language" prompted the scare whipped and one executed by fire.[73]

The 1675 conspiracy had been an attempt to reproduce an old "home"—to bring ethnic African political and cultural institutions to Barbados.[74] The failure of the conspiracy may well have been contingent on similar attempts to reproduce "home" in the bodies of lovers and children. For some years preceding the 1675 conspiracy, the tanner James Lydiatt enslaved Isabella and her husband Toney in Speightstown. Lydiatt owned only Isabella, Toney, and their children. Given Lydiatt's profession Toney was, no doubt, accustomed to an artisan's autonomy and responsibility. After the conspiracy of 1675 officials held the conspirators in a private home in Speightstown for "Examination."[75] Nearby, Isabella and Toney may have harbored mixed feelings as the aftermath of the attempted revolt unfolded. If they sympathized with the rebels, they knew that their own security and that of their three children, Betty, Laurence, and Sabara, dictated maintaining distance from the conspirators. Perhaps they even felt some sense of relief that their family had survived the wave of executions and repression that followed the conspiracy's betrayal. In September 1676, however, the death of James Lydiatt shattered Isabella's family as much as the executions of the previous year shattered the conspirators' families. In order to satisfy Lydiatt's debts, his executors "disposed of" all five. In so doing, they destroyed the stability of the "home" Tony and Isabella had previously found in one another, just as certainly as stopping the insurrection destroyed the hopes for "home" harbored by others enslaved on Barbados.[76]

Four years after the 1675 conspiracy, William Bullard gave voice to what must have been a common sentiment by stipulating in his will that "if any of my negroes after my decease should prove refractory unruly and incorrigible than I allow my [wife Grace] to make sale of such negroe or negroes."[77] The conspiracy and its aftermath made clear the reality that "Refractory" and "incorrigible" behavior could signal dangers beneath the surface of even faithful servants. The fear that any black person could end up involved in organized violence must have reminded Barbadian planters that the familial connections upon which the edifice of "loyal creole slave" was constructed presupposed connections of greater importance to enslaved men and women than "loyalties" to planters—and could not be so easily harnessed.

For those men and women who found themselves negotiating intimacies alongside the demands of enslavement, the outcome was not inevitable. The irregular rhythms of birth, slaveowners' plans for women's increase, and the proportion of women listed as mothers did not alter perceptibly during the course of the fifteen years before and after the conspiracy. However, in the two years immediately following 1675, the number of recorded births among enslaved women dropped. Shortly afterward, by 1682, children appeared in wills five times as often as they had in 1676 and 1677, and by the end of 1684, between 14 and 42 percent of slaveowners wills identified enslaved children (see Table 5.2). It seems plausible that women responded to the sudden and increasingly dangerous climate of retaliatory violence by not bearing children until after the immediate crisis had passed. It is equally possible that in the aftermath of the conspiracy, slaveowners neglected to record children. The vision of blacks as violent rebels may have temporarily obliterated the other image—blacks as mothers and fathers. Either scenario would not have boded well for those enslaved women and men—parents and partners—caught in the turmoil of slaveowners' escalating perception of the enslaved as potential rebels.

In 1692 the contradiction of parenting and childbirth under slavery erupted when Afro-Barbadian creoles planned a slave revolt.[78] These men and women (of the fifty-one executed rebels, four were women) were the children of mothers who had struggled to maintain familial integrity in the face of a society wholly invested in slave labor. As slaveowners grew increasingly confident about their ability to control (and discern loyalty among) the enslaved population, they relied on growing numbers of creole black men to serve in the island's militia, effectively believing in their own ability to discern the safe from the dangerous. In turn, the organizers of the 1692 revolt relied on black militiamen as informants, turning the notion of safety on its head.[79] The island's legislators quickly moved past their sense of betrayal at the hands of "trusted men" and used the rebels' island birth against them. Legislators reported to the crown that the 1692 rebels lacked the brutal follow-through of Africans, that as creoles they were ineffective rebels. Slaveowners diminished the fear generated by island-born rebels by labeling the conspirators both transparent and effete.[80] If we remember the connection between creole slaves and reproducing women, we see an appropriation of women's bodies as symbolic tools of social

Table 5.2 Women and Children in Slaveowners' Wills, Barbados, 1670–84 (percentages in parentheses)

	1670	1671	1672	1673	1674
Total wills	55	89	57	63	87
With slaves	28	16	28	28	28
With women	14 (50)*	10 (62)*	18 (64)*	14 (63)*	21 (75)*
With children	8 (57)**	3 (33)**	2 (11)**	5 (35)**	5 (24)**
With parents	3 (21)**	3 (33)**	2 (11)**	5 (35)**	4 (19)**
Using "increase"	3 (21)**	3 (33)**	3 (16)**	1 (7)**	3 (14)

	1675	1676	1677	1678	1679
Total wills	67	61	51	77	94
With slaves	15	21	20	29	32
With women	9 (60)*	15 (71)*	16 (80)*	18 (62)*	19 (59)*
With children	2 (22)**	1 (5)**	—	4 (22)**	5 (26)**
With parents	2 (22)**	1 (5)**	—	2 (11)**	4 (21)**
Using "increase"	2 (22)**	3 (15)**	3 (19)**	4 (22)**	7 (21)**

	1680	1681	1682	1683	1684
Total wills	94	102	73	62	84
With slaves	37	39	34	32	43
With women	21 (57)*	27 (69)*	24 (70)*	28 (87)*	29 (67)*
With children	3 (14)**	7 (19)**	10 (42)**	6 (21)**	8 (27)**
With parents	1 (5)**	—	9 (37)**	5 (18)**	8 (27)**
Using "increase"	4 (19)**	4 (15)**	3 (11)**	1 (3)**	6 (21)**

* Percentage of women in wills in which slaves appear. **Percentage in wills in which women appear.

Source: Recopied Will Books, Series RB6, Barbados Archives, Cave Hill, St Michaels.

control in the language of the 1692 legislative report. The women who bore these rebels became evidence of safety and thus served a purpose for slaveowners at odds with the future women imagined for their children. The rebels may well have embodied their mothers' longing to wrest a future from the hands of slaveowners through the birth of children destined to rise up and out of slavery. But slaveowners took a great risk as they attempted to reduce the symbolic, as well as the real, threat of the enslaved. By mobilizing black mothers into their rhetorical arsenal of control, slaveowners created a precarious mental barrier between themselves and an undifferentiated violent black populace.

In the end, the symbolic meaning of these imaginary "safe" black mothers and their even safer children had its own meaning among the enslaved. Aside from a plot discovered in 1701, the conspirators of 1692 orchestrated the last recorded Barbadian revolt attempt until 1816. Hilary Beckles argues that there were so few eighteenth-century slave revolts in Barbados because white society became more militarized; the prospect of revolt was more dangerous for the enslaved in eighteenth-century Barbados than it had been in the seventeenth century.[81] I would suggest, however, that one must also consider the growth of family ties to explain the gap between revolt attempts. Enslaved men and women in eighteenth-century Barbados lived in communities increasingly marked by the birth and death of children and by the development of familial ties. Perhaps the presence of their own families magnified the potential dangers of violent resistance to slavery.

The 1692 conspirators sought to take control of the society they created. Unlike their precursors in 1675, they did not intend to recreate African political or cultural institutions on New World soil. Rather, they intended the revolt to guarantee their freedom and prosperity as Afro-Barbadians. We can only assume that the impulse to do so was reinforced by the presence of their mothers and fathers, their own children, and the children of the men and women around them. These creole sons and daughters both embodied life's possible parameters in a slave society, and made smaller the range of reasonable risks. The presence of children offered proof of enslaved men and women's humanity regardless of the dehumanizing process of enslavement or radical attempts to break free of it. As family members, or as those who lived among families, potential rebels might refocus their attention on actions that did not endanger lives. Meetings in town, unauthorized movement, or clandestine relationships all would become part of daily attempts to navigate the confines of enslavement without putting parents, siblings, or children into mortal danger.[82]

On February 26, 1734, word reached the Carolina Assembly that "several Large Companies of Negroes [have been] Meeting very Lately at Different Places." According to the assemblymen, "frequent Robberys Insolencys and unrestrained Libertys of most Slaves at this Time" were fomented and cultivated at these meetings. Fearful of an insurrectionary plot, the assembly identified ten individuals who were enslaved by various planters in the countryside, and brought them to Charlestown for interrogation. Among them was "Mr. Godin's Washer Wench." The freedom of movement she commanded (she frequently "was sent" into Charlestown) might have been comparable to that enjoyed by Phillis, the woman who sued for wages due in the Carolina Court of Common Pleas that year. Perhaps Phillis and the washerwoman knew one another. According to the assembly, the enslaved involved in the plot had "constant communication with one another" as they met and talked both in Charlestown and on outlying plantations.[83] Phillis, Flora and her child, the washerwoman, and others like them took their place alongside their male counterparts in ways that raised no *particular* alarm for the legislators. This silence on the matter of women's resistance suggests a ubiquity that historians have overlooked.

White elites in South Carolina, both in the government and on the plantations, understood their labor system as one that depended upon the growth of the slave population through both imports and childbirth. The wider concerns of balancing a growing enslaved population with mechanisms of control brought slaveowners to a heightened awareness of the interplay between acculturation, population growth, and social control. In the aftermath of the Stono Rebellion of 1739—the largest slave revolt in eighteenth-century mainland America—the Assembly enacted prohibitive duties on imported slaves, essentially stopping the importation of enslaved men and women from Africa and the Caribbean for the next decade.[84]

In enacting these taxes on African slaves, assemblymen did not fear a depletion of the enslaved population. While the halt to African imports indicated that slaveowners understood the African trade as a source of unrest in the colony, the 1740 Negro Act also reflects slaveowners' understanding of the dangers of acculturation among black men and women. As Leon Higginbotham has argued, the language of the 1740 act was not concerned with protecting white colonists from "wild and savage" Africans (as the 1712 act was) but rather with keeping black South Carolinians in "due subjection and obedience." This shift in language is significant both as Higginbotham notes—a move from protection to maintaining profit—and as a reflection of the consequences of reproduction and acculturation.[85] In the preamble to the 1740 Negro Act passed in the aftermath of the Stono Rebellion, childbirth continued to be intrinsic to the definition of enslavement:

> All negroes . . . mulattoes and mustizoes who now are, or shall hereafter be, in this Province, and all their issue and offspring, born or to be born, shall be . . . absolute slaves.[86]

The 1740 Negro Act went on to explicitly wrench any and all personal liberties from black men and women.[87] The writers of the 1740 Negro Act prohibited a wide range of activity such as buying and selling merchandise, keeping canoes or raising livestock, gathering or traveling in groups on roadways, renting houses or living quarters, or being taught to write—all the potential activities of acculturated or creole men and women. In addition, the act provides evidence that the legislators understood that enslaved women and men, through reproduction and through family formation, already created and reinforced their acculturated identities.

Ten years after the Stono Rebellion of 1739, legislators reviewed and revised Carolina's 1740 Negro Acts. One Act stated that a slave who "delude[d] or entice[d]" others to run away should be put to death. However it also noted that

> doubts have already, and may hereafter arise, where a number of Slaves are actually found proceeding out of the Province, either in Boats, Canoes or otherwise, and no Evidence appearing who amongst them was the Deluder or Seducer or Provider of the said Boats, Canoes, Ammunition, and so forth.[88]

To clarify the situation, legislators declared that all men or women found in the above situation "shall be presumed to be reciprocally Deluders and Seducers of each other," and all put to death. The language "deluders and seducers of each other" did not take into account the possibility that none of the enslaved were deluded and ignored the reality that all had seduced the legislators. It could hardly have been otherwise. The legislators were men long accustomed to the linguistic oxymorons the dialectics of "femininity" and female laborers, production and reproduction, the black majority and white supremacy necessitated. To preserve the many fictions about slavery they had created, slaveowning legislators had to see those who threw their collective weight against the boundaries of enslavement as victims of seduction.

Women were careful observers of the colonial landscape and responded to moments of unrest as did enslaved men. The proportion of women who appeared in runaway advertisements placed after the Stono Rebellion did not substantially change. Women constituted 24 percent of the total advertised runaway slaves between 1740 and 1749; in the decade prior to the Stono Rebellion they accounted for 31 percent (see Table 5.2 above). The substantial change occurs in the number of women who ran either while pregnant or with their children, in the later years, more women who escaped slavery did so with their children. In the 1740s, 23 percent of all female runaways ran with one or more children. Nancy ran "with her child" some time in late 1740. Though her owner William Stone hazarded no guess about her destination, her flight no doubt responded to individual circumstances that were made more unbearable by the presence of her vulnerable child.[89] Most women who ran with children did so alone, although presumably they ran toward someone. Pompey buttressed her desire to escape the bonds of enslavement with the support of a man who may have been the father of her children. She and her two children ran away with "an Angola Negro Man," and their flight illustrates the ties of kin and affinity forged both particularly between creole and ethnic Africans and generally, as both were "very well known in Town and Goose Creek."[90]

Unlike the women who ran away prior to the Stono Rebellion, many of Pompey's cohort ran with others and those who did ran with men.[91] Partnerships formed in slavery between men and women were evidenced not only in the lists of slaveowners' property but also in the decisions those men and women made about how to resist their enslavement. In September 1747, a slaveowner placed the following ad in the *South Carolina Gazette*:

> Runaway . . . on the 11 of July last a Negro Fellow named Mingo, about 40 years old, and his wife Quane, a sensible wench about 20, with her child a Boy about 3 years old, all this Country born: Also Cudjoe a sensible Coromantee Negro Fellow about 45 years old, stutters, and his wife Dinah an Ebo wench that speaks very good English, with her two Children a Boy about 8 years old, and a Girl of about 18 months.[92]

Quane and Dinah may have had little in the way of a common past—one was born in slavery and the other was transported to it—but that was not an obstacle to their shared present. Certainly their mutual experience of motherhood played an essential role in their decisions to run away with their partners. Perhaps Dinah, as the older of the two, advised Quane on parenting, reminded her of a lost African past, or convinced her that eight years of attempting to parent under slavery provided reason enough for flight.

The ethnic modifiers; the ages of Mingo, Quane, Cudjo, Dinah, and the children; Cudjo's stutter; Dinah's proficiency in English; and the simple fact that ties existed between the four adults strong enough to bridge barriers of ethnicity and individualism in this collective bid for freedom are all glimpses of personhood that are for the most part impossible to obtain from slaveowners' probate records. Dinah's children reflect the fact that some women born in Africa were among those to whom slaveowners successfully looked for reproductive value. Dinah's experience also suggests that parenting became part of the arsenal of survival and resistance for some African women in slavery. On a more general level, Dinah and her children suggest a possible shift in the effect that childbearing had on women. Proportionally two times more mothers with children were advertised as running away after the Stono Rebellion than before. (As shown above in Table 5.1, the proportional number of enslaved children inventoried in the aftermath of the Stono Rebellion dropped slightly, although the willingness or ability of slaveowners to recognize parental ties between women and children rose.) Had the regime of the plantation become more unbearable? Had the prospect of raising a child in slavery become less tolerable? Or did the emotional toll of forced separation propel more women to run with their children rather than face the terms of a slaveowner's will?

The 1739 Rebellion in Carolina was evidence of the consolidating power of the institution of slavery vis-à-vis African ethnicity and ethnic identity. The embargo on African imports changed little in terms of the economic landscape of the colony—rice and indigo production remained the same—and slaveowners did not manifest concerns that the institution of slavery would be damaged by lack of African imports. Just as Angolan men carried out the largest mainland slave rebellion in colonial American history and forced Carolina legislators to fundamentally interrogate the dangers of "africanity," so women at various stages of the creolization process emerged from the records in startling ways.

In early 1749 Kate, Susannah, and Sue became embroiled in an intricate and tangled conspiracy. Conspiracies are vexing pieces of history because they equally reflect an always simmering rage of discontent on the part of the enslaved and an always present quicksand of hysteria on the part of the slaveowners. The conspiracy of 1749 is particularly confusing to sort out because it ultimately seems to come down to the desire of a slaveowner to keep an enslaved woman by his side through an elaborate scheme to reward her with freedom for informing about a plot that perhaps never existed. In 1748, Joe, an enslaved man owned by James Akins, was accused of having burned down a barn on Akins's property some three years earlier. Justice was swift and brutal. He was publicly hanged, and Kate, who was also owned by Akins and was implicated in Joe's crime, was ordered sold from the colony—her proximity to such irreverent violence apparently was reason enough to warrant her banishment. Shortly afterward, it was revealed that Joe and a large group of other enslaved women and men in the area had been involved in a conspiracy to revolt and flee the colony and that in the aftermath of his death his cohorts planned to avenge his execution by staging the revolt on the one-year anniversary of his hanging. Akins had not followed the orders of the court, and Kate remained on his plantation when she and Susannah, who had been married to Joe, allegedly informed Akins about the plot, causing him to bring it to the attention of the authorities.[93]

The events that followed generated eighty pages of testimony in the South Carolina council journal as over 100 enslaved persons and sixteen free whites were accused of, provided testimony of, denied, and recanted evidence of a widespread plan to revolt that involved men and women enslaved on close to two dozen plantations in four parishes along the Cooper River. The conspiracy is remarkable for many reasons—its extent, the temporary imprisonment of whites on the basis of black testimony, and the lack of punishments in its aftermath—but what is most remarkable about it is the central role women played in its evolution and disclosure. While only nine of the 104 named conspirators were women, three of its four primary architects were Kate, Susannah, and Sue. Moreover, it is likely that Kate's relationship with James Akins and his unwillingness to banish a woman his neighbors claimed he cared for more than "his own Wife and Children" set the entire crisis in motion.[94]

On January 23, 1749, James Akins, having allegedly been informed of the plot by Kate and Susannah, brought Agrippa into town to make a confession before the magistrate to a plot forged in the Summer of 1748 by himself, three women, and six other men to escape the colony after "coming to Town [to] set the Town and Magazine afire."[95] While on their way to harvest oyster shells, Agrippa and the other men and women passed an evening in the home of Pompey, a driver on the Vanderdussen plantation, and his unnamed wife. While they ate and played music, the plan took shape. White boatmen and cobblers and others became implicated, accused of inciting and aiding the conspirators. Upon hearing Agrippa's story, Governor Glen immediately called for some fifteen enslaved men to be brought to Charlestown to be interrogated, and Akins similarly brought Susannah into Charlestown to confirm Agrippa's testimony. Within days, twenty-one enslaved and seven free white men were charged in the conspiracy, the militia was ordered on guard, and Governor Glen requested the assistance of the Royal Navy to keep watch because of fear that the revolt had not been contained.

The conspiracy, whether it was real or not, speaks volumes about the rhythm of slave life in colonial South Carolina. The men and women involved, who made their plans while undertaking legitimate business for their slaveowners, traveled among twenty-four plantations that stretched over hundreds of acres. Their testimony spoke of their day-to-day activities; they piloted boats and gathered in one another's homes for meals and barbeques and weddings. Their activities reveal a community in which boundaries between fieldworker and artisan or driver were quite fluid and in which talk of resistance if not actual acts of revolt—was ubiquitous.

Moreover, the pages of the testimony suggest that slaveowners responded to enslaved women's presence in Carolina in ways that reveal contours of gendered ideology. Atkins testified that Kate and Susannah were trustworthy; they had initially informed on Susannah's husband, Joe. Akins used Joe's alleged arson and execution to legitimize Kate and Sue's testimony; as he did so he charged that Joe had threatened both of them with physical violence for their loyalty to whites. Akins claimed that Kate and Sue came to him for protection after Joe threatened them with rape and violence.

> Joe had some time before asked them if they would leave this Province and go off with him and with others that would go off and that Will and George soon after asked the same two Wenches if they liked what Joe had proposed to them some time before . . . to which they answered that they did not and that. . . . the said two wenches in formed [Akins] that the said Joe had greatly threatened them for telling what they did and said if they told any more of that matter . . . he *would do all the mischief he could and knock their Brains out* and then go off.[96]

Akins also understood that Susannah, as Joe's wife, commanded a kind of testimonial authority. Whether free or enslaved, Susannah had lost her husband to his criminal refusal to accept his position as a slave. Her willingness to inform upon his accomplices positioned her well; Akins would have seen her loyalty to him and to the slaveowning community as heightened by the personal pain she had suffered as a result of her husband's execution.

In addition to Kate and Sue and Susannah's involvement in the plot, there are many women, beginning with Pompey's wife, who, while unnamed and unindicted, existed at the center of the community of slaves who so provoked the colonial authorities that winter. Toney, for example, had learned of the plans for revolt on the occasion of his wedding when he "had invited George and Joe on his Toneys going to take a wife who had been Georges Wife before."[97] This woman who had married George and then Toney is not named, but her identity as a conduit of community and evidence of a kind of marital flexibility among this population cannot be overstated. Both she and Pompey's wife suggest that in this county, where men only slightly outnumbered women, perhaps their relative absence from the records of this and other revolt attempts has more to do with the eyes and ears of magistrates and less to do with an intentional withdrawal of enslaved women from the conversations about resistance and revolt that clearly permeated the landscape. These women were wives and mothers. Susannah, for example, drew on her role as a mother when she sent her young son out as a lookout—presumably a welcome if nerve-wracking break from his usual task of watching over his younger siblings—when Akins unexpectedly came to the woods around the plantation.[98] And indeed, when Susannah finally recanted her testimony, she referred to her identity as a wife, claiming that "she had been in a sort of Prison ever since Joes Death and chained for days together."[99] She said that Akins had followed her around for days, apparently relentlessly "talking to her about white Peoples being about the Plantation and Enticing the Negroes to runaway,"

> she said she did not know what thing that Kate told her she had stood out as long as she could but her Master had made her say it that she is now convinced that if she continues to say as she formerly did these People that she had accused must suffer innocently . . . and that she believes Kate was the first beginner of it.[100]

Kate never retracted her story. Despite being "very solemnly pressed to consider what she was about," she maintained the veracity of the conspiracy on the part of both the enslaved and white men she had implicated. The governor declared the whole thing a "forgery" and both women, along with Robin and Sue, were ordered sent to the Workhouse immediately and to then be "sent off this Province." Akins "assured his Excellency [that] he would readily and chearfully" do so, and the whole affair came to an official close on February 7, 1749. Upon his death ten years later, James Akins's inventory included a woman named Kate, hinting that perhaps Akins had again avoided dispossessing himself of a woman whom his neighbors and family suspected had become far too intimate with her owner.[101] It appears that Robin, Susannah, and Sue suffered the intended banishment, as they do not reappear in the Carolina inventories. Susannah's "prison" had been transported, though if her sentiments were genuine, she was at least saved the anguish of implicating the innocents with whom she had made a home. Kate, on the other hand, must have constructed an entirely new prison—one in which she exchanged the ties of community for the isolation of her owners' affection.

The 1749 Carolina conspiracy explicitly reveals something that is implicit for the entire colonial period. Women lived and worked alongside enslaved men and in that capacity they resisted and accommodated to enslavement in ways that both were inflected by gendered conventions of mothering and femininity and resituated the meaning of motherhood, resistance, and political authority. Kate's proximity to Akins's emotional machinations is unusual, but her interpretive stance is perhaps less so. She watched the landscape for an opportunity to grab hold of some autonomy and did so in the context of a community defined by ties of work, friendship, marriage, sex, love, jealousy, and betrayal. The messiness of it all speaks volumes about what it meant to navigate the colonies as an enslaved woman.

Notes

1. For example, Neither Ira Berlin nor Philip Morgan devotes specific attention to resistance, although Morgan notes the omission and writes "the major triumph [of the enslaved] was the creation of an coherent culture—the subject of this book and *the* most significant act of resistance in its own right." Philip D. Morgan, *Slave Counterpoint: Black Culture in the Eighteenth-Century Chesapeake and Low-country* (Chapel Hill: University of North Carolina Press, 1998), xxii; Ira Berlin, *Many Thousands Gone: The First Two Centuries of Slavery in North America* (Cambridge, Mass.: Harvard University Press, 1998).

2. Patricia Hill Collins, "Shifting the Center: Race, Class, and Feminist Theorizing About Motherhood," in *Representations of Motherhood*, ed. Donna Bassin et al. (New Haven, Conn.: Yale University Press, 1994), 58.

3. David Barry Gaspar, "With a Rod of Iron: Barbados Slave Laws as a Model for Jamaica, South Carolina, and Antigua, 1661–97," in *Crossing Boundaries: Comparative History of Black People in Diaspora*, ed. Darlene Clark Hine and Jacqueline McLeod (Bloomington: Indiana University Press, 1999), 347.

4. Sidney Mintz and Richard Price point to this central contradiction in racial slavery in *An Anthropological Approach to the Afro-American Past: A Caribbean Perspective* (Philadelphia: Institute for the Study of Human Issues, 1976). See also Winthrop Jordan, *White over Black: American Attitudes Toward the Negro, 1550–1812* (Chapel Hill: University of North Carolina Press, 1968), 106.

5. By 1672, a secondary act allowing slaves to be removed from the land for the payment of Debts concludes that "Negroes shall be taken and deemed Real Estate, to all other intents and purposes whatsoever, except what before excepted." "An Act declaring the Negro-Slaves of this Island to be Real Estates," 1668, and "A declarative Act upon the Act making Negroes Real Estate," 1672, in *Acts Passed in the Island of Barbados, 1643–1762*, ed. Richard Hall (London, 1764), 64, 93. This vacillation about the legal identity of the enslaved is at the heart of English laws, which were primarily concerned with the fact that the enslaved were "a special kind of property," as opposed to the Spanish conviction that the enslaved were an "inferior kind of subject." See Elsa Goveia, "West Indian Slave Laws of the Eighteenth Century," in *Caribbean Slave Society and Economy*, ed. Hilary McD. Beckles and Verene Shepard (New York: New Press, 1991), 350.

6. Leon Higginbotham, *In the Matter of Color: Race and the American Legal Process, the Colonial Period* (New York: Oxford University Press, 1978), 39.

7. "An Act for the Governing of Negroes," 1688, in Hall, *Acts Passed*, 112; Gaspar "With a Rod of Iron," 358; and "An Act for the Better Ordering . . . of Negroes," 1696, in *Statutes at Large of South Carolina*, ed. David J. McCord (Columbia, S.C.: A.S. Johnston, 1840), 353. See also Kathleen Brown, *Good Wives, Nasty Wenches, and Anxious Patriarchs; Gender, Race, and Power in Colonial Virginia* (Chapel Hill: University of North Carolina Press, 1996), 154.

8. Alison Games, " 'The Sanctuarye of our Rebell Negroes': The Atlantic Context of Local Resistance on Providence Island, 1630–41," *Slavery and Abolition* 19 (December 1998): 12.

9. Col. John Drax to Barbados Assembly, December 14, 1670, CO31/2: 15, PRO.

10. Journal of Assembly, April 20, 1671, CO31/2: 24, PRO.

11. Journal of Assembly, May 17, 1671, CO31/1: 190, PRO.

12. Clause 7 in "An Act for the Better Ordering . . . of Negroes," in McCord, ed., *Statutes*, 353; and clause 2 in "An Act for the Governing of Negroes" in Hall, ed., *Acts Passed*, 112.

13. Journal of the Proceedings of the Governor and Council of Barbados, [1661], CO31/1: 49, PRO. See also the discussion on attracting white female servants and settlers in Chapter 3 above.

14. Journal of Council, July 11, 1660, CO31/1:10–11, PRO.

15. Journal of Council, July 27, 1660, CO31/1:13, PRO.

16. Journal of Council, June 11, 1660, CO31/1:1–6, PRO.

17. See Jerome Handler, "Freedmen and Slaves in the Barbados Militia," *Journal of Caribbean History* 19 (May 1984): 6, 20.

18. For discussions of the development of trade between Indians and colonists, see Joel Martin, "Southeastern Indians and the English Trade in Skins and Slaves," in *The Forgotten Centuries: Indians and Europeans in the American South 1512–1704*, ed. Charles Hudson and Carmen Chaves Tesser (Athens: University of Georgia Press, 1994), especially 310–13; and James H. Merrell, " 'Our Bond of Peace': Patterns of Intercultural Exchange in the Carolina Piedmont, 1650–1750," in *Powhatan's Mantle: Indians in the Colonial Southeast*, ed. Peter H. Wood, Gregory Waselkov, and M. Thomas Hatley (Lincoln: University of Nebraska Press, 1989), esp. 202–27.

19. Joel Martin suggests that a link exists between renegotiated relationships with Native Americans and the white colonists' impulse to direct their needs for slave labor primarily toward the West Indies and West Africa. Martin, "Southeastern Indians," 308, 323; see also M. Thomas Hatley, *The Dividing Paths: Cherokees and South Carolinians Through the Era of Revolution* (New York: Oxford University Press, 1993), 33–34.

20. By 1668, fostered by a heightened awareness of his minority status, Lord William Willoughby believed the Barbados black population to be "upwards of fourty thousand," although modern estimates are half that. Richard S. Dunn, *Sugar and Slaves: The Rise of the Planter Class in the English West Indies, 1624–1713* (Chapel Hill: University of North Carolina Press, 1972), 75–76. Dunn estimates a population of 20,000 whites and 20,000 blacks in 1660.

21. William Willoughby to Lords of His Majesties Council, 9 July 1668 CO29/1: 115, PRO.

22. An Account of the Invasion of South Carolina in the Month of August, 1706, Secretary of State Correspondence, 1699–1724, CO5/382: 20–22, PRO.

23. [Thomas Nairne], *A Letter from South Carolina* (London, 1710), in *Selling a New World: Two Colonial South Carolina Promotional Pamphlets*, ed. Jack Greene (Columbia: University of South Carolina Press, 1989), 52.

24. William Chapman to Board of Trade, March 25, 1730, CO5/361: 88.

25. Chapman's maneuver should be contrasted with the proclivity of South Carolina slaveowners to exploit the multiple ethnicities of newly arrived Africans as a way to differentiate, to order, and to maintain a sense of mastery over the always-growing black population. See Daniel Littlefield, *Rice and Slaves: Ethnicity and the Slave Trade in Colonial South Carolina* (Baton Rouge: Louisiana University Press, 1981), 3–32. Michael Mullin suggests that slaveowners evoked Africans' particular ethnicity only during times in which the white population felt threatened. In this regard, it is useful to point to Carolinians' enduring use of ethnic nomenclature as an indication of consistent unease among Carolina slaveholders. Michael Mullin, *Africa in America: Slave Acculturation and Resistance in the American South and the British Caribbean, 1736–1831* (Urbana: University of Illinois Press, 1994), 14.

26. Jerome Handler and Frederick Lange, *Plantation Slavery in Barbados: An Archaeological and Historical Investigation* (Cambridge, Mass.: Harvard University Press, 1978), 167–68. For the Antiguan conspiracy, see David Barry Gaspar, *Bondmen and Rebels: A Study of Master-Slave Relations in Antigua with Implications for Colonial British America* (Baltimore: Johns Hopkins University Press, 1985).

27. Journal of Council, November 23, 1663, CO31/1: 82, PRO.

28. Richard Ligon, *A True and Exact History of the Island of Barbados* (London, 1657), 49–50.

29. Entry Book, February 4, 1667, CO29/1: 65, PRO.

30. Journal of Council, [1667], CO31/1: 183, PRO; and Journal of Council [1661], CO31/1: 43, PRO.

31. Ligon, *True and Exact History of the Island of Barbados*, 48.

32. Alexander Gunkel and Jerome Handler, "A Swiss Medical Doctor's Description of Barbados in 1661: The Account of Felix Christian Spoeri," *Journal of the Barbados Museum and Historical Society* 33 (1969): 7; see also John Thorton, *Africa and Africans in the Making of the Atlantic World, 1400–1680*

(Cambridge: Cambridge University Press, 1992), 224–30 for his overview of African percussive music in American slave societies.

33. Clauses 1 and 22, "An Act for the Better Ordering . . . of Negroes," 1696, in McCord, ed., *Statutes*.

34. Josiah Boone to Board of Trade, August 23, 1720, Board of Trade Correspondence, 1720–21, C05/358: 14, PRO.

35. Board of Trade to Carolina Assembly, October 27, 1720, CO5/358: 47, PRO.

36. Josiah Boone, June 24, 1720, CO5/358: 7, PRO.

37. Anon., *Great Newes from the Barbados or a True and Faithful ACCOUNT of the Grand Conspiracy of the Negroes against the English* (London, 1676), 9. For a discussion of the intended rebellion see Hilary McD. Beckles, *Black Rebellion in Barbados: The Struggle Against Slavery, 1627–1838* (Barbados: Caribbean Research and Publications Inc., 1987), 37–41.

38. Journal of Assembly, November 25, 1675, CO31/2: 201, PRO.

39. Beckles, *Black Rebellion in Barbados*, 37. "Coromantee" referred to men and women from the Gold Coast, a region that supplied almost 20 percent of enslaved men and women in the 1680s. Handler and Lange, *Plantation Slavery in Barbados*, 22.

40. Journal of Assembly, November 25, 1675, CO31/2: 201, PRO.

41. Phillis a Free Negro Woman v. Samuel Fox, February court, 1734, p. 3, Judgment Book 1733/3–34/5, Records of the Court of Common Pleas, SCDAH.

42. Mindie Lazarus-Black, *Legitimate Acts and Illegal Encounters: Law and Society in Antigua and Barbuda* (Washington, D.C.: Smithsonian Institute Press, 1994), 52. For more on free black women's use of the courts in the Carolinas, see Kirsten Fischer, *Suspect Relations: Sex, Race, and Resistance in Colonial North Carolina* (Ithaca, N.Y.: Cornell University Press, 2002), 122–30.

43. Only two months after Phillis's court appearance, the assembly responded to the traders' petition, a document they had received some time earlier. April 9, 1734. Journal of Assembly, 1734: 126–38, SCDAH.

44. "The Stranger," *South Carolina Gazette*, September 24, 1774, quoted in Philip D. Morgan, "Black Life in Eighteenth-Century Charleston," *Perspectives in American History* New Series 1 (Cambridge: Cambridge University Press, 1984), 203.

45. Later, in clause 28 of the Carolina slave code, the lawmakers attempted to curtail the practice of allowing "slaves to do what and go whither they will and work where they please, upon condition that [they pay] their aforesaid masters so much money as . . . is agreed upon." This too was doubtless unsuccessful. McCord, ed., *Statutes*, 363.

46. Commons Journal, 3 March 1743, in Easterby, *Colonial Records*, 3: 264.

47. Commons Journal, 26 January 1745, in Easterby, *Colonial Records*, 4: 317.

48. Commons Journal, 15 January 1746, in Easterby, *Colonial Records*, 5: 43.

49. Jane Landers, *Black Society in Spanish Florida* (Urbana: University of Illinois Press, 1999), 24–25, n. 95; John J. TePaske, "The Fugitive Slave: Intercolonial Rivalry and Spanish Slave Policy, 1687–1764," in *Eighteenth-Century Florida and Its Borderlands*, ed. Samuel Proctor (Gainesville: University Presses of Florida, 1975), 3. For a discussion of freedom under the Spanish, see Jane Landers, "Gracia Real de Santa Theresa de Mose: A Free Black Town in Spanish Colonial Florida," *The American Historical Review* 95 (1990): 9–30.

50. Don La Redno to John Archdale, 1696, St. Augustine, in John Archdale Papers, Duke University Manuscript Department, Perkins Library, Durham, N.C.

51. "A List of Negroes and Indian Slaves Taken in the Year 1715," CO5/382: 102, PRO.

52. Not until 1733 would Spanish policy be explicitly focused on enticing the enslaved from Carolina. That year Philip V issued a *cedula* granting freedom to all runaways. He "hoped that the new policy would stimulate the mass exodus of slaves from Carolina." TePaske, "Fugitive Slave," 6.

53. Governor Nicholson to Assembly, August 11, 1721, CO5/425: 45, PRO.

54. In 1721, for example, Don Antonio Rexidor demanded the return of "three Slaves that were properly my own" from Carolina. Governor Nicholson maintained their justifiable capture, stating "that two of them did belong to Mr. John Smiley . . . taken from him by the Yamasee Indians and retaken again by our Indians." Antonio Rexidor to Governor Nicholson, received March 19, 1721, CO5/358: 325, PRO; and Governor Nicholson to Governor Marquis, March 19, 1721, CO5/358: 344, PRO.

55. Journal of Assembly, December 12, 1722, CO5/425: 377, PRO.

56. Commons Journal, January 19, 1739, and May 31, 1739, in Easterby ed., *Colonial Records*, 1: 596, 708.

57. Journal of Assembly, March 3, 1722, CO5/425: 285.

58. Assembly to Governor Nicholson, February 28, 1721, CO5/425: 281, PRO.

59. Clause 17, "An Act for the Governing of Negroes."

60. See, for example, Proclamation, January 5, 1722, CO5/425: 244; and Memorial of Robert Johnson, November 21, 1722, CO5/425: 368.

61. Petition of Robert Wilkinson, March 3, 1721, CO5/425: 285, PRO.

62. Clarinda and Delia's cooperative effort are evidence of a community among women of the sort that Deborah Gray White identifies in the antebellum period in *A'rn't I a Woman? Female Slaves in the Plantation South* (New York: W.W. Norton, 1985). Given the evidence of prolonged lactation, it is possible that Delia's child was as old as two years. "Delia and Clarinda," *South Carolina Gazette*, June 10–17, 1732, in *Runaway Slave Advertisements: A Documentary History from the 1730s to 1790s*, ed. Lathan A. Windley (Westport, Conn.: Greenwood Press, 1983), 3. Their comfort with the task of navigating the canoe may hint at their ethnic identity. Men and women from the Upper Guinea Coast were well accustomed to traveling by canoe.

63. The *Gazette* began its print run in 1732. Lathan Windley collects these ads, as cited above. For discussions of runaways that use the *Gazette* ads, see Peter H. Wood, *Black Majority: Negroes in Colonial South Carolina, from 1670 Through the Stono Rebellion* (New York: W.W. Norton, 1974), 239–68; Philip D. Morgan, "Colonial South Carolina Runaways: Their Significance for Slave Culture," *Slavery and Abolition* 6 (December 1985): 57–78; Daniel E. Meaders, "South Carolina Fugitives as Viewed Through Local Colonial Newspapers with Emphasis on Runaway Notices 1732–1801," *Journal of Negro History* 40 (1975): 288–319. For a study of a later period in South Carolina history, see Michael P. Johnson, "Runaway Slaves and the Slave Communities in South Carolina, 1799–1880," *William and Mary Quarterly* 3rd ser. 38 (July 1981): 418–41.

64. See Windley, ed., *Runaway Slave Advertisements*, 2, 36.

65. Philip Morgan cites the preponderance of women who ran away with children as evidence of "strong kin ties" and notes that while slaveowners suggested that one-third of male runaways left to "visit" family, they believed that over four fifths of all female runaways ran to members of their families. Morgan, "Colonial South Carolina Runaways," 67, and n.38. Morgan finds that during the fifty-year period 1732–82, 11 percent of all female runaways ran with children. Morgan, *Slave Counterpoint*, 542, n.72.

66. "Jeney," *South Carolina Gazette*, 5 July 1735, in Windley ed., *Runaway Slave Advertisements*, 16.

67. "Sabina," *South Carolina Gazette*, 26 June 1736, in Windley ed., *Runaway Slave Advertisements*, 22.

68. Anon., *Great Newes from the Barbados*, 12.

69. Journal of Assembly, March 21, 1676, CO31/2: 207, April 20, 1676 CO31/2: 220, PRO.

70. Journal of Assembly, July 7, 1675, CO31/2: 185, PRO.

71. Journal of Assembly, June 13, 1676, CO31/2: 223, PRO. Even before the insurrection conspiracy, Governor Atkins speculated on the danger of Indians in the mainland. He suggested that those whites who left Barbados for other colonies regretted doing so when faced with "great prejudice from the Indians whose defection and numbers dayly increase . . . so most of the plantations on the continent . . . have received much damage by them." For Atkins, the fault lay with settlers who believed that prayers could redeem the Native American. Governor Atkins to Board of Plantations, February 3, 1675, Entry of Papers, CO29/2: 55–56, PRO.

72. Journal of Assembly, March 21, 1676 and April 18, 1676, CO31/2: 207, 216, PRO.

73. Vincent Harlow, *A History of Barbados, 1625–1685* (Oxford: Clarendon Press, 1926; reprint New York: Negro Universities Press, 1969), 326–27; and Hilary McD. Beckles, *Black Rebellion in Barbados: The Struggle Against Slavery, 1627–1838* (Barbados: Caribbean Research and Publications Inc., 1987), 40–41. Journal of Assembly, November 27, 1679, CO31/2: 370, PRO.

74. See Eugene Genovese, *From Rebellion to Revolution: Afro-American Slave Revolts in the Making of the New World* (New York: Vintage Press, 1981), for a discussion of the different forms slave revolts took. Genovese argues that not until the Haitian Revolution were slave revolts "modern" in outlook. The 1675 attempt in Barbados, because of the desire to reestablish old African ways of life in Barbados, was part of a "restorative" tradition. I would suggest that a more nuanced understanding of what it means to attempt to transplant old forms onto new soil is called for. See, for example, Gaspar, *Bondmen and Rebels*, Chapters 8 and 11.

75. Journal of Assembly, April 20,1675, CO31/2: 220, PRO.

76. Will of James Lydiatt, September 16, 1676, RB6/13: 365, BA.

77. Will of William Bullard, January 11, 1679, RB6/13: 555, BA.

78. Beckles, *Black Rebellion in Barbados*, 43, table 8; and Edward Littleton to The Committee of Plantations, September 7, 1692, Board of Trade Correspondence, CO28/1: 174, PRO.

79. See Dunn, *Sugar and Slaves*, 256–58; Beckles, *Black Rebellion in Barbados*, 43–48; Gary A. Puckrein, *Little England: Plantation Society and Anglo-Barbadian Politics, 1627–1700* (New York: New York University Press, 1984), 164–65; and Michael Craton, *Testing the Chains: Resistance and Slavery in the British West Indies* (Ithaca, N.Y.: Cornell University Press, 1982), 111–14.

80. Craton, *Testing the Chains*, 110–11.

81. See Beccldes, *Black Rebellion in Barbados*, 43–48.

82. Thomas Holt's 1995 presidential address to the American Historical Association is a reminder of the power of the everyday as the girder of racial and racist systems. While not directly concerned with the institution of slavery, Holt's essay evokes a more nuanced approach to the power of the mundane to shape one's identity in, and response to, slavery. I would argue that the birth of children, itself a marker of persistence and duration, contributed to the importance of everyday resistance over revolt or large-scale conspiracy. Thomas Holt, "Marking: Race, Race-Making, and the Writing of History," *American Historical Review* 100 (February 1995): 1–20. The classic work on day to day resistance remains Raymond A. Bauer and Alice H. Bauer, "Day to Day Resistance to Slavery," *Journal of Negro History* 27 (October 1942): 388–419. For more contemporary discussions of women and resistance to slavery, see Barbara Bush, " 'The Family Tree Is Not Cut': Women and Cultural Resistance in Slave Family Life in the British Caribbean," and Elizabeth Fox-Genovese, "Strategies and Forms of Resistance: Focus on Slave Women in the United States," both in *In Resistance: Studies in African, Caribbean, and Afro-American History*, ed. Gary Y. Okihiro (Amherst: University of Massachusetts Press, 1986), 117–32 and 143–65 respectively. For a position that centers women's resistance in family, see Mary Ellison, "Resistance to Oppression: Black Women's Response to Slavery in the United States," *Slavery and Abolition* 4 (May 1983): 56–63.

83. February 26, 1734, Journal of Assembly, 1734: 32, SCDAH. In the face of insurrection, slaveowners once again looked to external enemies of the state on which to place the blame. "Amidst our other perilous circumstances, we are subject to Many intestine Dangers from the great number of Negroes that are now amongst us," they complained. They lived surrounded by real and imagined slave insurrections that, in 1734, were apparently fomented by the French, who might "instigate them by artfully giving them an Expectation of freedom." Assembly to King George 11, April 9, 1734, Board of Trade Correspondence 1733–38, CO5/363: 101, PRO. The report contains detailed concern about the encroachment of the French to the west of the colony, and their interference with the Indian trade.

84. For analysis of the rebellion and its aftermath, see Wood, *Black Majority*, chap. 12, "The Stono Rebellion and its Consequences," 308–26; see also John K. Thornton, "African Dimensions of the Stono Rebellion," *American Historical Review* 96 (October 1991): 1101–13.

85. Higginbotham, *In the Matter of Color*, 168.

86. "An Act for the Better Ordering and Governing Negroes and Other Slaves in This Province," 1740, *Statutes at Large of South Carolina*, ed. David J. McCord (Columbia: A.S. Johnston, 1840).

87. Wood writes "now the noose was being tightened"; *Black Majority*, 324.

88. Commons Journal, 17 May 1749, in Easterby, *Colonial Records*, 9: 120.

89. "Nancy," *South Carolina Gazette*, December 4, 1740, in Windley, *Runaway Slave Advertisements*, 43.

90. "Pompey," *South Carolina Gazette*, February 9, 1740, in Windley, *Runaway Slave Advertisements*, 40.

91. "Nanny and Clarinda, *South Carolina Gazette*, August 12, 1745, in Windley, *Runaway Slave Advertisements*, 65.

92. "Mingo and Quane," *South Carolina Gazette*, September 14, 1747, in Windley, *Runaway Slave Advertisements*, 79.

93. Philip D. Morgan and George D. Terry, "Slavery in Microcosm: A Conspiracy Scare in Colonial South Carolina," *Southern Studies* 21 (1982): 121–45. My discussion of the conspiracy draws from this article and transcripts of the council journal prepared by Robert Olwell. Morgan and Terry's article is the only in-depth discussion of the conspiracy, and while they initially discuss women's role in the testimony, their primary focus is elsewhere. I am deeply grateful to Robert Olwell for his generous and collegial gesture of making his transcripts available to myself and other scholars of early South Carolina during a seminar sponsored by the Program in the Carolina Lowcountry and the Atlantic World, Department of History, College of Charleston, February, 1999.

94. Morgan and Terry, "Slavery in Microcosm," 123, 126–27. Dr. William Bruce, a planter in St. Thomas and St. Dennis parish, made the allegation about James Akins's relationship with Kate.

95. Robert Olwell, " 'To Speak the Real Truth': Investigating a Slave Conspiracy in Colonial South Carolina," a document prepared from "A Journal of the Proceedings of His Majestys Honorable Council of South Carolina, From the 20th day of December 1748 To the 16th Day of December 1749," by James Bullock C[lerk of the] C[ouncil], 47 and 50; from a microfilm at the Library of Congress, originals held at SCDAH and PRO.

96. Journal of Council, 176, emphasis mine. I believe that the use of the term mischief suggests sexual violence of which neither Akins nor the women wanted to speak.

97. "To Speak the Real Truth," 78.

98. "To Speak the Real Truth," 129–30.

99. "To Speak the Real Truth," 162.

100. "To Speak the Real Truth," 163.

101. Morgan and Terry, "Slavery in Microcosm," 125, n.12.

6

The Pleasures of Resistance
Enslaved Women and Body Politics in the Plantation South, 1830–1861

Stephanie M. H. Camp

As a young woman, Nancy Williams joined other enslaved people and "cou'tin' couples" who would "slip 'way" to an "ole cabin" a few miles from the Virginia plantation where she lived. Deep in the woods, away from slaveholding eyes, they held secret parties, where they amused themselves dancing, performing music, drinking alcohol, and courting. A religious woman in her old age, Williams admitted only reluctantly to her interviewer that she had enjoyed the secular pleasures of dressing up and going to these outlaw dances. "Dem de day's when me'n de devil was runnin roun in de depths o' hell. No, don' even wanna talk 'bout it," she said. However, Williams ultimately agreed to discuss the outlaw parties she had attended, reasoning. "Guess I didn' know no better den," and remembering with fondness that, after all, "[d]em dances was somepin."[1]

Musicians played fiddles, tambourines, banjos, and "two sets o' [cow] bones" for the dancers. Williams was a gifted and enthusiastic dancer: she would get "out dere in de middle o' de flo' jes' a-dancin': me an Jennie, an' de devil Dancin' wid a glass o' water on my head an' three boys a hettin' on me." Williams often won this contest by dancing the longest while balancing the glass of water on her head without spilling a drop. She "[j]es' danced ole Jennie down." Like the other women in attendance, Williams took pride in her outfits at these illicit parties, and she went to great trouble to make them. She adorned one dress with ruffles and dyed others yellow or red. Her yellow dress even had matching yellow shoes; they were ill-fitting, as many bond-people's wooden brogans were, and "sho' did hurt me," but, animated by her own beautiful self-presentation, "dat ain' stop me fom dancin'." By illuminating a part of everyday life that bondpeople kept very hidden. Nancy Williams's account of attending outlaw slave parties helps uncover one part of the story of enslaved women's lives: the role that the body played in slaveholders' endeavors to control their labor force and in black resistance to bondage in the nineteenth-century plantation South. Despite planters' tremendous effort to prevent such escape, enslaved women and men sporadically "slip[ped] 'way" to take pleasure in their own bodies.[2]

At the heart of the process of enslavement was a geographical impulse to locate bondpeople in plantation space. Winthrop D. Jordan found that it was confinement, "[m]ore than any other single quality," that differentiated slavery from servitude in the early years of American slavery's formation. Not only a power or labor relation, "[e]nslavement was captivity." Accordingly, black mobility appears to have been the target of more official and planter regulations than other aspects of slave behavior.[3] Slaveholders strove to create controlled and controlling landscapes that would determine the uses to which enslaved people put their bodies. But body politics in the Old

South were not dictated by a monologue as slaveholders wished. To the contrary, slave owners' attempts to control black movement—and, indeed, most aspects of black bodily experience—created a terrain on which bondpeople would contest slaveholding power.

Bondpeople, who had their own plans for their bodies, violated the boundaries of space and time that were intended to demarcate and consolidate planters' patriarchal power over plantation households. Their alternative negotiation and mapping of plantation space might best be called, in Anne Godlewska and Neil Smith's phrase, a "rival geography." Enslaved people's rival geography was not a fixed spatial formation, for it included quarters, outbuildings, woods, swamps, and neighboring farms as opportunity granted them. Where slaveholders' mapping of the plantation was defined by rigid places for its residents, the rival geography was characterized by motion: the secret movement of bodies, objects, and information within and around plantation space. Together, but differently, women and men took flight to the very woods and swamps that planters intended to be the borders of the plantation's "geography of containment."[4] There they held clandestine and illegal parties. These parties were sporadic affairs, contingent as they were upon opportunity (itself informed by the season), availability of resources, and no doubt on the emotional climate within local black communities and between enslaved people and their owners. This article studies the personal and political meanings of bodily pleasure made and experienced at these parties, focusing on the activities of women, for whom dress was an especially important dimension of their enjoyment of slave communities' secret and secular institution.

No mere safety valve, bondpeople's rival geography demands to be understood in multiple ways. To a degree, black mappings and uses of southern space were the result and expression of the dialogic of power relations between owner and owned—part of day-to-day plantation relations characterized by a paternalistic combination of hegemonic cultural control and violent discipline. To a larger extent, however, the paternalist framework fails to sufficiently explain everyday slave resistance. The paternalist model offers an apt theory of plantation management but a fundamentally incomplete perspective on plantation, and particularly black, life. Viewing resistance other than organized rebellion or running away as only partial or even as cooptative distracts us from interesting and important possibilities for understanding black politics during slavery, such as the hidden, everyday acts that help to form overt resistance. The tendency to draw a sharp line between material and political issues on the one hand and aesthetic, spiritual, and intimate (emotionally and physically) issues on the other also limits our understanding of human lives in the past, especially women's lives.[5]

Evidence is spare, but it comes to us consistently from the upper South and the lower South in slaveholders' diaries and journals, in state legislative records, in nineteenth-century autobiographies, and in twentieth-century interviews of the formerly enslaved.[6] Many recent studies on American slavery focus on a subregion, a crop, or a county. This trend has deepened our understanding of the variations of work and culture in American slavery, has furthered our sense of important differences among enslaved people and has added texture and detail to our picture of day-to-day life in bondage. At the same time, studying slavery as a regional system—a system of domination, of profit, of racial formation—remains a valuable practice, as recent innovative and informative works on the slave past have also demonstrated.[7] Throughout the antebellum period and across the plantation South, enslaved people took flight to nearby woods and swamps for the secret parties they occasionally held at night for themselves.[8]

This article pieces together the story and politics of these illicit parties, arguing that these celebrations and the bodily pleasures that accompanied them occupied the wide terrain of political struggle between consent and open, organized rebellion.[9] The bondpeople who participated in activities in the rival geography expressed, enjoyed, and used their somatic selves in terms other than those of their relationship to their owners. They took pleasure in their bodies, competed with other enslaved people with them, and contested their owners' power over them. Bondpeople's everyday somatic politics had more than symbolic value: they resulted in temporal and material gains for enslaved people and in some loss of labor for slaveholders. If bond-people's uses of their bodies and their time were contingent upon the season, the ignorance of their owners, and the ability to find a safe location (and they were), these uses nonetheless also undermined slaveholders' claims to their bodies and their time. Everyday resistance to pass-laws and plantation rules was an endemic problem in the rural South, one that had real and sub-versive effects on slaveholding mastery and on plantation productivity—both of which rested on elite white spatial and temporal control of enslaved bodies.

The body, as French historian Dorinda Outram has written, is at once the most personal, intimate thing that people possess and the most public. The body, then, provides a "basic political resource" in struggles between dominant and subordinate classes. Second-wave femin-ists put it like this: the personal is political. Earlier, C. L. R. James, Grace C. Lee, and Pierre Chaulieu had already argued that "ordinary . . . people . . . are rebelling every day in ways of their own invention" in order to "regain control over their own conditions of life and their relations with one another"; oftentimes "their struggles are on a small personal scale." Enslaved people's everyday battles for regaining control—albeit temporally limited—took place on this very personal terrain.[10]

Enslaved people possessed multiple social bodies.[11] Inhabitants of a premodern society, they were made to suffer domination largely through the body in the form of exploitation, physical punishment, and captivity. Theorists of colonialism have analyzed the effects of somatic suffer-ing in other, analogous contexts. Describing the consequences of European colonialism on twentieth-century Africans' somatic experiences, Frantz Fanon wrote:

> [I]n the white world the man of color encounters difficulties in the development of his bodily schema. Consciousness of the body is solely a negating activity. It is a third-person consciousness. The body is surrounded by an atmosphere of certain uncertainty.

Caught in the white gaze, Fanon argued, blacks were "sealed in that crushing objecthood." Under colonialism, experiences of the body were "negating activit[ies]," in which identification with the colonizer resulted in degrees of self-hatred and humiliation. Students of American slavery will find much with which to agree in Fanon's analysis of black bodily experience. Violence, brutal and brutalizing labor, diseased environments (particularly in South Carolina's rice swamps), and the auction block were basic characteristics of life in slavery. Indeed, these characteristics were, in combination with elite white confinement of the black body, the essence of bondage.[12]

However, brutality did not constitute the whole of black bodily experience. For people, like bondpeople and women as a group, who have experienced oppression through the body, the body becomes an important site not only of suffering but also (and therefore) of resistance, enjoyment, and potentially, transcendence. Studying the body through a framework of contain-ment and transgression grants us access to new perspectives on resistance and the workings of gender difference within enslaved plantation communities. Thinking about the black body in space allows us to think about it materially and to watch as the prime implement of labor in the Old South moved in ways inconsistent with the rigors of agricultural production. And atten-tion to the body also facilitates thinking about issues beyond the material, such as the roles of movement and pleasure in the culture of opposition developed by enslaved people. A somatic approach, such as the one employed here, risks objectifying people, but the point is the opposite: to demonstrate how enslaved people claimed, animated, politicized, personalized, and enjoyed their bodies—flesh that was regarded by much of American society as no more than biddable property.

Most of all, attention to uses and experiences of the body is mandatory for those interested in the lives of women in slavery, for it was women's actual and imagined reproductive labor and their unique forms of bodily suffering (notably sexual exploitation) that most distinguished their lives from men's. Feminist scholars have shown that to study women's lives requires posing different questions of our sources, using new methods to interpret them, and fundamentally changing how we think about politics.[13] Historians of enslaved women have revealed the falseness of the dichotomy between the material/political and the personal, in large measure by showing how the body, so deeply personal, is also a political arena. Their work has demonstrated the extent to which women's bodies were unique sites of domination under slavery: yet, this scholarship has also shown that enslaved and formerly enslaved women used their bodies as sites of resistance.[14] Women employed their bodies in a wide variety of ways, form seizing control over the visual representation of their physical selves in narrative and photographic forms (both of which were in enormous demand among nineteenth-century northerners) to abortion.[15] In addition to the body's reproductive and sexual capacities and its representations, however, enslaved women's bodily pleasure was a resource in resistance to slavery. These diverse uses of the body are a fruitful site for investigating the origins of and women's role in bondpeople's political culture.

Recent scholarship has shown that perceptions of the proper uses of the black body, especially the female body, were central, materially and symbolically, to the formation of slaveholding mastery. As the English became entrenched in the slave trade in the second half of the seventeenth century, their preexisting ideas of Africans concretized into constructions of blackness and representations of bodily difference that justified the economically expedient turn to bound black labor. Jennifer L. Morgan has demonstrated that these constructions relied in large part upon sixteenth- and seventeenth-century male travelers' representations of African women's bodies as inherently laboring ones—as female drudges that stood in stark distinction to the idealized idle and dependent English woman. Male travelers to Africa in the earliest years of contact remarked on what they saw as African women's sexual deviance: the women lived in "common" (polygamously) with men, and they bared much of their bodies, most remarkably their breasts, with "no shame." Europeans depicted African women's breasts ("dugs") as large and droopy, "like the udder of a goate" as one traveler put it. Animal-like, African women's exposed dugs struck male observers as evidence of Africa's savagery and inferiority. To European eyes African women's reproductive bodies also demonstrated physical strength: they gave birth "withoute payne," suggesting that "the women here [Guinea] are of a cruder nature and stronger posture than the Females in our Lands in Europe." Confirming this conclusion was the fact that African women commonly worked in agriculture. Unencumbered by the delicacy that prevented the ideal English woman from such arduous work. African women were seen as naturally fit for demanding agricultural and reproductive labor.[16]

Englishmen began to encode these ideas of proto-racial difference based on perceptions of African women's laboring bodies into law in Virginia in 1643. Kathleen M. Brown has shown that in that year free African women were declared tithables (meaning their labor could be taxed), along with all free white men and male heads of households. Because white women were viewed as dependents—as "good wives" who performed household, not agricultural, labor—they remained untaxed. The very different treatment of African and English women, based on conceptions of their capacity to work in the fields, articulated very different projections of the roles each would play in the life of the colony. Two years later African men also became tithables and thus fell within the legal construction of African bodies as inherently laboring ones. Buttressed by ideas of Africans as savages, which themselves relied heavily on representations of African women's sexual and reproductive bodies. English lawmakers could, by 1670, force those servants who had arrived in Virginia "by shipping" (Africans) to serve lifelong terms of servitude, while those who had "come by land" (Indians) served limited terms. This law, combined with an earlier 1667 law banning the manumission of converted Christians, helped to crystallize the racial form of the emergent slave economy.[17] In the context of slavery, issues of representation of the black body, especially the female black body, and material expropriation could not be separated.

Enslaved people, then, possessed at least three bodies. The first served as a site of domination; it was the body acted upon by slave holders. Early constructions of African and black women's bodies and sexuality played a central role in rationalizing the African slave trade and gave license to sexual violence against enslaved women. Colonial and antebellum slaveholders believed that strict control of the black body, in particular its movement in space and time, was key to their enslavement of black people. By the late antebellum years planters were working energetically to master such black bodily minutiae as nourishment, ingestion of alcohol, and even dress, all as part of their paternalist management strategies. In the Old South the slave body, most intensely the female body, served as the "bio-text" on which slaveholders inscribed their authority.[18]

The second body was the subjective experience of this process. It was the body lived in moments and spaces of control and force, of terror and suffering. This was the colonized body that, in Fanon's terms, the person "of color" experienced "in the white world," where "consciousness of the body is solely a negating activity." Within the "white world"—within planters' controlled and controlling landscapes, vulnerable to sale, sexual and nonsexual violence, disease, and exploitative labor—enslaved bodies were, surely, "surrounded by an atmosphere of certain uncertainty."[19]

And yet, within and around the plantation, enslaved people's bodies were a hotly contested terrain of struggle. Again and again, enslaved people violated plantation boundaries of space and time; in the spaces they created, runaway partygoers celebrated their bodies and did what they could to reclaim them from planter control and view. This reclaimed body, this outlawed body, was the bondperson's third body: the body as site of pleasure and resistance. For enslaved women, whose bodies were so central to the history of black bondage, the third body was significant in two ways. First, their third body was a source of pleasure, pride, and self-expression. The enormous amount of energy, time, and care that some bondwomen put into such indulgences as making and wearing fancy dresses and attending illicit parties indicates how important such activities were to them. Pleasure was its own reward for those experiencing it, and it must be a part of our understanding of the lives of people in the past, even people who had little of it. Second, bondwomen's third body was a political site; it was an important symbolic and material resource in the plantation South, and its control was fiercely contested between owner and owned. Just as exploitation, containment, and punishment of the body were political acts, so too was enjoyment of the body. Far from accommodating bondage, or acting as a safety valve within it, everyday somatic politics acted in opposition to slavery's symbolic systems and its economic imperatives.

By the nineteenth century the centerpiece of the theory of mastery that elites laid out in law books and in plantation journals was a geography of containment that aimed to control slave mobility in space and in time. In his detailed memoir of life in bondage, Charles Ball summarized what he called the "principles of restraint" that governed black movement. "No slave dare leave" the plantation to which she or he belonged, he said, not even for "a single mile," or a "single hour, by night or by day," except by "exposing himself to the danger of being taken up and flogged."[20] At stake was nothing less than the good functioning of the plantation itself. One slave management manual instructed its readers that "no business of any kind can be successfully conducted without the aid of system and rule." In pursuit of "system and rule," the manual prescribed two core "maxims": first, "that there must be a time for everything and everything done in its time"; and second, that there must be "a rule for everything and everything done according to rule."[21]

Together, lawmakers and planters made up the rules governing spatial and temporal order. Bondpeople everywhere were forbidden by law to leave their owners' property without passes. Responsibility for enforcing the laws was shared unequally by non-elite whites, who most often manned slave patrols to police rural and urban areas, and slaveholders, who also did their best to enforce compliance with the law by insisting that the people they owned leave only with written permission. Even when planters did grant permission to travel off the plantation, they specified the spatial and temporal boundaries of a pass's tenure by writing the bondperson's destination and the pass's expiration date.[22] Enslaved women experienced the limits of the plantation's geography of containment in especially intense ways. Because most of the work that took bondpeople off the plantation was reserved for men, and because slaveholders almost always granted visiting privileges to the husband in an abroad marriage, women left farms and estates much less frequently than men did. Women were thus fixed even more firmly than men within plantation boundaries.[23]

Recognizing the potential for trouble nevertheless, slaveholders focused much of their managerial energy on regulating black movement in the nighttime. Almost all enslaved people were forbidden to leave the plantation at all in the evenings, and some were prohibited from even stirring from their quarters. In December 1846 Mississippi planter William Ethelbert Ervin codified his ideal of slave behavior by setting to paper the rules that were to govern his human property. Total control over his bondpeople's bodies was central to Ervin's conception of the master-slave relationship, as it was for so many other slaveholders; out of the four fundamental rules on Ervin's estate, two sought to control slave mobility. First, he indicated that plantation borders marked not only the edges of his estate but also hemmed in his bondpeople: No one was to "leave the place without leaf of absence." Second, within those spatial borders, he added temporal limits that bound enslaved people's movement even more: "at nine o'clock every night the Horne must be blown Which is the signal for each to retire to his or her house and there to remain until morning." Doing his best to guarantee a rested and orderly workforce, Ervin directed his overseers to check on people in the quarters, and if anyone was found "out of their places," they would be "delt with" "according to discretion." Most often, transgressors of boundaries of space and time were dealt with violently. Only so long as, in the words of one former bondwoman, "slaves stayed in deir places," were they not "whipped or put in chains."[24]

The nineteenth-century plantation system was a symbol for larger social relations, though, and the importance of rules of containment went beyond plantation efficiency and issues of production: the need for rules struck at the core of what it meant to be a master in the antebellum years. Seeking to restrain black bodies even further, some planters used plantation frolics as a paternalist mechanism of social control. Plantation parties, which carefully doled out joy on Saturday nights and on holidays, were intended to seem benevolent and to inspire respect, gratitude, deference, and importantly, obedience. As North Carolinian Midge Burnett noted sardonically, his owner held plantation frolics on holidays and gave bondpeople Christmas trees in December and an Easter egg hunt in the spring—all "ca[u]se Marse William intended ter make us a civilized bunch of blacks."[25]

Most of all, these sponsored frolics were supposed to control black pleasure by giving it periodic, approved release. Paternalist slaveholders accomplished this goal by attending and surveilling the parties. Indeed, the most important component of paternalistic plantation parties was the legitimating presence of the master. It was common for whites to "set around and watch," while bondpeople would "dance and sing."[26] Though sanctioning black pleasure, the slaveholders' gaze oversaw and contained that pleasure, ensuring that it would not become dangerous. For example, to make certain that the alcohol, music, dancing, "sundrie articles," and "treat[s]" he provided his bondpeople at holiday time served the dual purpose of giving limited expression to and restraining their bodily pleasure in time as well as space, John Nevitt made sure to "s[i]t up untill 2 oclock in the morning to keep order with them."[27] Both the former slave Henry Bibb and the former slaveholder Robert Criswell remembered the surveillance role that the slaveholders' presence played at plantation frolics, and both illustrated the constrictive effects of that gaze in their memoirs of antebellum plantation life (see Illustrations 6.1 and 6.2).

Illustration 6.1. *The Sabbath among the Slaves.* This illustration shows plantation festivities as Henry Bibb, a man who had been enslaved, remembered them. Enslaved people dance, play music, lounge, tussle, and drink, while four elite whites on the left watch, amused. The plantation patriarch, to the right of the center, distributes alcohol to a respectful bondman who has gratefully removed his hat and bows slightly. Note the very obvious presence of a fence on the right, as well as the wall of four white onlookers on the left. Together, these barriers contain and control this scene of black pleasure. From Henry Bibb, *Narrative of the life and Adventures of Henry Bibb, an American Slave* (New York, 1849), 21. *Reproduced by permission of the Library Company of Philadelphia.*

Illustration 6.2. *The Festival.* This illustrated memory, from a former slaveholder's autobiography, represents the centrality of white surveillance at plantation parties. Here, the planter and his family watch from a platform in a nearby tree. From Robert Criswell, *"Uncle Tom's Cabin" Contrasted with Buckingham Hall, the Planter's Home* (New York, 1852), 113. *Reproduced by permission of the Library Company of Philadelphia.*

Alcohol proved an important lubricant for production at plantation affairs. Neal Upson watched adults set a rhythm for their work of shucking a season's corn harvest by singing. As they sang and shucked, "de little brown jug was passed 'round." The "little brown jug" of alcohol gave the workers just enough liquor to warm their muscles and their spirits to the enterprise at hand: "When it [the jug] had gone de rounds a time or two, it was a sight to see how fast dem Niggers could keep time to dat singin'. Dey could do all sorts of double time den when dey had swigged enough liquor." Similarly, Bill Heard's owner provided "[p]lenty of corn liquor" to his bondpeople at corn shuckings in order to speed up the work. "[Y]ou know dat stuff is sho to make a Nigger hustle," Heard remembered. "Evvy time a red ear of corn was found dat meant a extra drink of liquor for de Nigger dat found it."[28] Even as planters attempted to master black bodily movement and pleasure in these ways, however, some enslaved people were not satisfied with official parties. They sought out secret and secular gatherings of their own making.

Bondwomen and men who worked in the gang system, the predominant form of work organization in the Old South, worked hard all day, almost every day of the year, with breaks only on Sundays and some holidays. "Dey wucks us from daylight till dark, an' sometimes we jist gits one meal a day," Charlie Crump said of his slavery experience.[29] Bondpeople in South Carolina and parts of Georgia who worked under the task system did not necessarily have to wait for the evening to end their toil, but they, like bondpeople employed in gang labor, were prohibited from leaving their home farms without a pass. Even bad weather meant only a change in routine—respite only from field labor but not from plantation maintenance chores. As they worked, bondpeople, in the words of one folk song sung by women textile workers in Virginia, kept their "eye on de sun," watching it cross the sky as the day wore long. Because "trouble don' las' always," they anticipated the end of the work day and on occasion planned illicit parties in the woods.[30]

Speaking for enslaved people everywhere, Charlie Crump recounted that "we ain't 'lowed ter go nowhar at night. . . ." "[D]at is," he added, "it dey knowed it." In violation of the planters' boundaries of space and time, Crump and many of the young people he knew who had worked "from daylight till dark" left at night. At the risk of terrible punishment, blacks "from all ober de neighborhood [would] gang up an' have fun anyhow. . . ." Similarly, Midge Burnett and his friends knew that "[d]e patterollers 'ud watch all de paths leadin' frum de plantation" to prevent bondpeople from running away. What the patrollers did not know, however, was that "dar wus a number of little paths what run through de woods dat nobody ain't watched ca[u]se dey ain't knowed dat de paths wus dar." Many partygoers traveled to their covert events through just such paths.[31]

"Yes, mam, they had dances all right," Georgian Jefferson Franklin Henry remembered. "That's how they got mixed up with paterollers. Negroes would go off to dances and stay out all night. . . ."[32] Since secrecy demanded a high level of planning, the outlaw gatherings were often prepared well in advance. Austin Steward and his neighbors and friends in rural Virginia were well aware of the laws and rules that forbade enslaved people from leaving "the plantation to which they belong, without a written pass." Nonetheless, they occasionally left their plantations to visit family, to worship, and sometimes, to hold parties. One spring the enslaved people on a nearby estate held an Easter frolic with the permission of their owner. But word of this legitimate "grand dance" quickly spread to "a large number of slaves on other plantations" who intended to attend the party whether or not they could obtain official passes.[33]

Meanwhile, the hosts began preparations. Reappropriation was the main way of obtaining the goods they needed. "[T]hey *took*, without saying, 'by your leave, Sir,'" the food and drink they wanted, Steward wrote, "reasoning among themselves, as slaves often do, that it can not be *stealing*, because 'it belongs to massa, and so do *we*, and we only use one part of his property to benefit another,'" The women took the ingredients and moved their owners' culinary property "from one location to another"—a relocation that made an enormous difference in the purposes of both the frolic and the food. With the ingredients in hand, women hid themselves in "valleys," swamps, and other "by-places" in order to cook in secret during the nights. "[N]ight after night" this went on: women prepared dishes late into the night, then "in the morning" headed back to their cabins, "carefully destroy[ing] everything likely to detect them" on their way. At the same time, the "knowing ones" continued to plan the celebration, encouraging each other's high spirits "with many a wink and nod."[34]

Finally, the appointed night arrived. A little after 10 P.M., the music began when an "old fiddler struck up some favorite tune," and people danced until midnight, when it was time to feast. The food was "well cooked," and the wine was "excellent," Steward reported. But he recalled more than the events; he went to the trouble of recording the affect of the moment. Steward had noted that planters believed that enslaved people hobbled through life "with no hope of release this side of the grave, and as far as the cruel oppressor is concerned, shut out from hope beyond it." Yet, despite—or perhaps in part because of—their abject poverty and the humiliations and cruelties of bondage, here at the party, "Every dusky face was lighted up, and every eye sparkled with joy. However ill fed they might have been, here, for once, there was plenty. Suffering and toil was forgotten, and they all seemed with one accord to give themselves up to the intoxication of pleasurable amusement." In the context of enslavement, such exhilarating pleasure gotten by illicit use of the body must be understood as important and meaningful enjoyment, as personal expression, and as oppositional engagement of the body.[35]

But there were limits to alternative uses of the body for the enslaved. Late in the night the fiddler suddenly stopped playing and adopted "a listening attitude." Everyone became quiet, "listening for the cause of the alarm." The dreaded call came to them when their lookout shouted, "*patrol!*" and perhaps ran away from the party, a common technique to throw off patrols. If the lookout at this party did so, he was unsuccessful, for the slave patrol, whose job it was to ensure that enslaved people (in Steward's words) "know their place" and stay in it, found the party and broke it up. Many people had run away immediately after the call came, but others, including Steward, had only managed to hide themselves and overheard the patrolmen talking.[36]

Two of the patrolmen debated the wisdom of a few white men attempting to disband a meeting of so many bondpeople. One hesitated to push the matter, arguing that they might "resist." After all, "they have been indulging their appetites, and we cannot tell what they may attempt to do." His colleague mocked his apprehension and wondered if he was really "so chicken-hearted as to suppose those d—d cowardly niggers are going to get up an insurrection?" The first patrolman defensively clarified that he only worried the partygoers "may forget themselves at this late hour." This patrolman's concerns were based on the realities at hand. In these woods, on the figurative if not the literal margins of the host plantation, there was a black majority. This particular black majority was made up of those who already had proven their lack of deference to white authority and their willingness to defy rules. While unprepared and perhaps unwilling to "get up an insurrection," they just might have been capable of "forgetting themselves" by challenging white authority to an incalculable extent. Indeed, in a sense they already had forgotten themselves, having abandoned "their place" in the plantation spatial and temporal order—and the "self" they had to be there—in favor of their own space and their own place.[37]

The party that Austin Steward remembered illustrates what was generally true: that the most important part of preparing a night meeting was evading slave patrols. In addition to doing their best to keep their own movements stealthy, bondpeople carefully monitored patrol activity. Inverting the dominant ideal of plantation surveillance, household, skilled, and personal bondpeople watched their surveillants and sometimes learned of a patrol's plan to be in the area. These bondpeople would pass the word along in the code, "dey bugs in de wheat," meaning the scheduled party had been found out. Sometimes the party was canceled; when it was not, some bondpeople would avoid the party completely, while others would attend anyway, alert and ready to leap out of windows and sprint out of sight when the patrol arrived. Revelers also protected their space by constructing borders of their own. They stretched vines across the paths to trip patrolmen and then horses, and they posted lookouts at key locations along the periphery.[38]

Young people also gathered in spaces outside of their owners' view. Very often they met, like Nancy Williams and the people she knew, in unoccupied cabins in the woods. At other times they simply came together in the open air. Occasionally, on very large plantations where outbuildings could be quite a distance from the slaveholder's house, they would meet in barns or in the quarters. Male musicians performed for their friends and neighbors, playing fiddles, banjos, and tambourines. They also made their instruments; for instance, the popular "quill" was created in places where sugar was grown from ten or so cane stems cut to different lengths, with a hole drilled in the top of each, bound together to make a flute. Musicians also improvised instruments out of reeds and handsaws to perform the melody and created the percussion with spoons, bones, pans, and buckets to play songs like "Turkey in the Straw" and other popular tunes.[39]

When no musicians were available, and even when they were, outlaw partygoers made music with their voices, singing lyrics sure to amuse. According to Dosia Harris, one went "somepin' lak dis":

> Oh' Miss Liza. Miss Liza Jane!
> Axed Miss Liza to marry me
> Guess what she said?
> She wouldn't marry me,
> If de last Nigger was dead.[40]

Dancers also sang, perhaps gloatingly, of their subterfuge:

> Buffalo, gals can't you come out tonight.
> Come out tonight, an' dance by the light of de moon?[41]

As morning approached, those who had caroused the night away warned each other of the approach of day and the danger of violating that temporal boundary (which located them properly at work): "Run nigger run, pattyrollers ketch you, run nigger run, it's breakin' days."[42] A variant elaborated:

> Run nigger run, de patterrollers ketch you—
> Run nigger run, fer hits almos' day.
> De nigger run; de nigger flew; de nigger los'
> His big old shoe.[43]

Dance tunes contained political meanings as well as entertainment value. The self-deprecating song about the rejected lover is one example: Liza Jane, the object of affection, is called by a title, "Miss," a sign of respect that whites denied bondpeople. Other songs were bolder. Mississippian Mollie Williams danced to and sang the following song, which was inflected by the spirit of resistance nurtured at outlaw parties:

> Run tell Coleman.
> Run tell everbody
> Dat de niggers is arisin'![44]

Together, women and men performed a variety of period dances. Many formerly enslaved people described the dances of their youth as proper and respectable (without the "man an woman squeezed up close to one another," as Mrs. Fannie Berry put it). When she was young, Liza Mention danced "de cardrille (quadrille)[,] de virginia reel, and de 16-hand cortillion." Mention insisted, "Dances in dem days warn't dese here huggin' kind of dances lak dey has now."[45] Instead, bondpeople chose physically expressive, but still respectable, dances like "pigeon wings"(flapping the arms like a bird and wiggling the legs, while "holdin yo' neck stiff like a bird do"), "gwine to de east, an' gwine to de west" (leaning in to kiss one's dance partner on each cheek but "widout wrappin' no arms roun' like de young folks do today"), "callin' de figgers" (following the fiddler's challenging calls), and "hack-back" (in which couples stood facing one another and "trotted back and forth"). Other dances included "set de flo'" (partners began by bowing to each other at the waist, with hands on the waist, then the dancers tap-danced, patting the floor firmly, "jus' like dey was puttin' it in place"), "dancin' on de spot" (the same as "set de flo'" except that dancers had to remain within the circumference of a circle drawn in the ground), "wringin' and twistin'" (the early basis of the "twist"), the "buzzard lope," "snake hips," and the "breakdown."[46]

Competition was a common form of amusement at outlaw dances, one that sometimes forged camaraderie among equals. To win a dance competition required the combination of expertly executing complex dance moves while maintaining an outward demeanor of "control and coolness," dance historian Katrina Hazzard-Gordon has written. For example, Nancy Williams competed with another woman, Jennie, to see who could dance most deftly and with the most mastery of their bodies. To make the challenge even greater, the two women danced with glasses of water on their heads; the winner was she who maintained her cool, making the performance of the dances look easy. Dance competition allowed some women to demonstrate the strength and agility of their bodies, as compared with men's, whose physical power was usually recognized as greater. Jane Smith Hill Harmon "allus could dance" and enjoyed, even as an old woman, "cut[ting] fancy steps now sometimes when I feels good." Her talent was awe-inspiring, and she regularly competed with men. "[O]ne night when I wuz young," she related to her interviewer, "I danced down seben big strong mens, dey thought dey wuz sumpin'! Huh, I danced eb'ry one down!" Dance competition could provide women moments of relief from black gender hierarchies as well as from slaveholding control.[47]

Such an issue as violence between women and men at secret parties is difficult to access in the sources. We know that enslaved families, like free ones, were home to resentment, betrayal, anger, and other disappointments of family life. Brenda F. Stevenson and Christopher Morris have shown that physical and verbal abuse between spouses was a part of life in the quarters in Virginia and in Mississippi.[48] For a single example, James Cornelius, who had been enslaved in Mississippi, openly told his interviewer about the time he hit his wife in the postbellum years. During their marriage ceremony, Cornelius had interrupted the preacher to make his wife promise never to accuse him of lying. She promised, and Cornelius reciprocated; he pronounced the exchange " 'a bargain' an' den de preacher went on wid de weddin'." A few years later his wife was suspicious about his whereabouts one evening, and when his excuse failed to convince her, she told him, "that's a lie." Cornelius responded in the manner he viewed as appropriate: "right den I raised my han' an' let her have it right by de side of de head, an' she niver called me a liar ag'in. No ma'm, dat is somethin' I won't stand for." While rates of domestic violence may have changed in the transition from slavery to freedom, incidents such as this one were certainly not new. Moreover, Cornelius learned of his manly prerogative to violently maintain the rules of his marriage from multiple sources, and a major influence on his conception of domestic life must have been his own (enslaved) family.[49] Violence was also a common aspect of drinking culture among both whites and blacks. It is therefore difficult to imagine that violence, as a part of life in the quarters and a part of drinking culture, did not occur between men, between women, and between men and women at outlawed parties. In particular, men's drinking must have created some difficulties for bondwomen. But violence was not solely a male form of expression.

Sometimes slave parties gave space for the continuation of rivalries between women who were not always, or even often, motivated by feelings of honorable competition between equals. Women's competition could turn viciously bitter and have tragic results. For instance, when two women, Rita and Retta, misunderstood "Aunt" Vira's laughter at a party as directed at them, they poisoned both Vira and her infant. [50]

While women and men danced together, outlaw parties were also characterized by gender differences in ideas of pleasure. Women, more than men, reclaimed their bodies through dressing up; and men, more than women, enjoyed drinking alcohol. Dress was a contested terrain: planters attempted to use it for disciplinary purposes, and women utilized it for purposes inconsistent with the social demands and economic imperatives of slave society. Under cover of night, women headed for secret frolics dressed in their best fancy dress, marking on their bodies the difference between the time that belonged to the master and the time that was their own.[51]

While at work, when their bodies were in the service of their owners, bondpeople looked, according to one observer, "very ragged and slovenly." Planters imprinted slave status on black bodies by vesting bondpeople in clothing of the poorest quality, made of fabric reserved for those of their station. In the summer enslaved people wore uncolored cotton or tow, a material made from rough, unprocessed flax. Many women's dresses were straight, shapeless, and stintingly cut, sometimes directly on the body to avoid wasting fabric. Charity McAllister's clothes were "poor. One-piece dress made o' carpet stuff, part of de time." Others were cut fuller, tapered at the waist, and most dresses were long. Almost all bondpeople's clothes were homemade, not store-bought, and those who wore them appreciated the difference. Fannie Dunn disagreed with her mother's assessment of conditions under slavery in North Carolina on the basis of the clothes she was forced to wear: "My mother said dat we all fared good, but of course we wore handmade clothes an' wooden bottomed shoes."[52]

Some planters, as part of their system of rule, annually or biannually distributed clothes with dramatic flair in order to represent themselves as the benevolent source of care and sustenance and thereby instill loyalty in their bondpeople. Many other plantations were characterized more by slaveholder neglect and avarice than by paternalistic management systems; on such farms slave owners gave little thought to enslaved people's physical conditions. Year after year, for example, Roswell King, Pierce Butler's Georgia overseer, pleaded with Butler, who lived in Philadelphia, to provide his bondpeople with clothing. King subscribed to the paternalist school's combination of cruel violence, stern order, and benevolent encouragement of disciplined behavior, but he could not find an ally in Butler. "Do you recollect," King wrote Butler on one occasion, "that you have not given your Negroes Summer clothing but twice in fifteen years past[?]" Old, torn, shredded, and dirty clothing certainly saved costs for slave owners, but it also had social effects. Poor quality clothing reflected and reified slaves' status and played a role in their subjugation. Harriet Jacobs wrote bitterly in her 1861 narrative of life as a bondwoman that the "linsey-woolsey dress given me every winter" by her mistress was "one of the badges of slavery."[53]

Another "badge of slavery" was the mitigation of gender distinctions that some experienced, effected by the grueling work routines, that many women followed during much of their lives. With a mixture of pride and bitterness, Anne Clark recalled that during her life in bondage she had worked like a man. She "ploughed, hoed, split rails. I done the hardest work ever a man ever did." "Women worked in de field same as de men. Some of dem plowed jes' like de men and boys," George Fleming remembered. Fleming claimed that the women he knew even resembled men in the fields; he "[c]ouldn't tell 'em apart in de field, as dey wore pantalets or breeches."[54]

Conversely, when bondpeople, especially women, dressed themselves for their own occasions, they went to a great deal of trouble to create and wear clothes of quality and, importantly, style. When possible, women exchanged homespun goods, produce from their gardens, and pelts with white itinerant traders for good-quality or decorative cloth, beads, and buttons. In South

Carolina the slaves' independent economy enabled women to purchase cloth, clothing, and dye. But even in Virginia, Frederick Law Olmsted noticed that some women were able to "purchase clothing for themselves" and, on their own time, to "look very smart." Enslaved women located near ports or major waterways were probably able to barter with black boat-workers, who carried on a lively trade with the plantation bondpeople they encountered in their travels.[55] Most women, however, procured fancy dress—when they could at all—simply by eking out time at night to make it, from beginning to end: they grew and processed the cotton, cultivated and gathered the roots and berries for the dye, wove the cloth, and sewed textiles into garments.

When they dressed up and when they refused to perform the regular nightly toil demanded of them in order to make fancy dress, enslaved women indicated that some Saturday nights, Sundays, holidays, and occasionally weeknights were their own. Women, whose bodies were subject to sexual exploitation, dangerous and potentially heartbreaking reproductive labor, and physically demanding agricultural labor, tried not to miss the opportunity to reclaim them from the brink of degradation at the hands of their masters. As much as women's bodies were sources of suffering and sites of planter domination, women also worked hard to make their bodies spaces of personal expression, pleasure, and resistance.

Fancy dress offered a challenge to status-enforcing clothing because dressing up was heterodox behavior. Pierre Bourdieu defines *doxa* as the "naturalization" of the social order accomplished through a number of social and symbolic mechanisms, including assumptions by dominant classes about the "uses" and presentation of the body. Within the reigning doxa, the black body was vested in slave dress, dress that enforced and naturalized its status. Enslaved women sporadically engaged in heterodox behavior—behavior that was conscious of the doxa, exposed its arbitrariness, and challenged it. When they adorned their bodies in fancy dress, rather than in the degrading rough and plain clothing, rags, or livery that slaveholders dressed them in, they challenged the axiomatic (doxic) quality of their enslaved status. In particular, women fashioned new identities that highlighted their femininity and creativity.[56]

Finally, women's heterodox style—expressed as they transgressed the plantation's boundaries of space and time—allowed them to take pleasure in their bodies while simultaneously denying that their bodies had exclusively fiduciary value and that the sole "[use] of the body" was to labor for their owners.[57] Indeed, the very act of slipping out of plantation boundaries to attend parties withheld labor, in that by failing to rest properly for the next day's chores, enslaved people worked less efficiently, much to the outrage of their owners. In the Old South, issues of representation of the black body and material expropriation could not be separated from one another.

When women adorned themselves in fancy dress of their own creation, they distanced themselves from what it felt like to wear slaves' low-status clothing. "Aunt" Adeline was, as her mother had been, an accomplished dyer. On one occasion she wore a dress that she would never forget "as long as I live. It was a hickory stripe dress they made for me, with brass buttons at the wrist bands." She was "so proud of that dress"; with her identity refashioned by it, she "felt so dressed up in it, I just strutted!" The heterodox aspects of fancy dress can also be detected in some of the reactions to the young women who dressed up. One time, the young Amelia walked out of her house on her way to church in the hoopskirt she adored. To her mortification, the other children "laugh[ed] at me" and accused her of "playin' lady"—of affecting a status beyond her own, to which she had no right. She was so hurt by their mockery of her status transgression, now seen as presumption, that she took off the offending skirt "and hide it in de wood." Enslaved people, young or adult, did not uniformly appreciate disrespect for the Old South's racial etiquette.[58]

In addition to the symbolic value dress held for plantation blacks and whites, clothing held more tangible meanings as well. The production, distribution, and uses of King Cotton—and cotton products such as clothing—were very material issues in the slave South. Textile production complicated the plantation's temporal order along gender lines: the nighttime was less neatly "off" time for bondwomen than it was for men. While women and men could both quit working for their owners at sunset, many women began a second shift of labor at night, and sometimes on Saturdays or Sundays, working for their families. At these times women performed reproductive labor, such as cooking, cleaning, gardening, washing and candle and soap-making, in their homes. Henry James Trentham saw women plowing during the day, working hard to "carry dat row an' keep up wid de men," then quit at sunset "an den do dere cookin' at night." Moreover, in their "off" time and during the winters, women were responsible for some to all of the production of textiles for plantation residents, black and white. Only on the very largest plantations was some of this work concentrated in the hands of women specialists.[59]

Most enslaved women, then, worked grueling first and second shifts. Their second shift of labor, however, also presented an opportunity, one they exploited, to devote a bit of their time to heterodox activity. Women spent some of their evenings turning the plain, uncolored tow denim, hemp, burlap, and cotton they had spun into decorative cloth. Morris Sheppard remembered his mother's handiwork: "Everything was stripedy 'cause old Mammy liked to make it fancy." Catharine Slim's mother, a talented weaver, wove stripes of red, white, and blue as well as flowers into the cloth she sewed into dresses for her daughter. Women dyed the coarse material allotted them with colors that they liked. Nancy Williams's dedication to style was unusual, but it remains instructive. "Clo'es chile? I had plenty clo'es dem days," she claimed. "Had dress all colors. How I get 'em? Jes' change dey colors. Took my white dress out to de polk berry bush an' jes' a-dyed it red, den dyed my shoes red. Took ole barn paint an' paint some mo' shoes yaller to match my yaller dress." Women set the colors fast in their cloth with saline solutions, vinegar and water, or "chamber lye" (urine). They hung the cloth on lines to dry and from there sewed the fabric into garments. Women also traded the products of their night time labor—their crafts such as quilts and baskets, the produce of their gardens, the eggs they collected, the berries they picked in the woods, and the skins of animals they hunted—for calico and fine or decorative cloth, as well as for ornamental objects.[60]

Once they had the cloth, enslaved women went to great effort to make themselves something more than the cheap, straight-cut dresses they were rationed. When possible, women cut their "dress-up" dresses generously so as to cover the length of the body and to sweep dramatically and elegantly. Some women accentuated the fullness of their skills by crisply starching them. Annie Wallace remembered that when her mother went "out at night to a party some of the colored folks was havin'," she would starch her skirts with "hominy water. . . . They were starched so stiff that every time you stopped they would pop real loud." Wallace's mother instructed her children to listen carefully for her return, in case the party was broken up by the arrival of Virginia's rural patrols, "And when we heared them petticoats apoppin' as she run down the path, we'd open the door wide and she would get away from the patteroll."[61]

Other women liked to draw attention to their skirts with hoops they made from grapevines or tree limbs. Though Salena Taswell's owner "would not let the servants wear hoops," she and the other household bondwomen sometimes swiped "the old ones that they threw away." Secretly, they "would go around with them on when they were gone and couldn't see us." Hoopskirts came into fashion during the early 1850s, coinciding with the emergence of the cult of domesticity, and stayed in style until the pressures of the Civil War made them both impractical and expensive. Among the elite women who wore them, however, hoopskirts symbolized "Victorian ideals of domesticity and . . . of a separate woman's sphere," as Drew Gilpin Faust has suggested. The style flaunted high levels of consumption and idleness (the skirts made physical labor tricky), and consistent with Victorian ideals of respectable womanhood, the hoopskirt hid the body. No doubt bondwomen's skirts were smaller than their owners', whose skirts could measure up to five feet in diameter. Nonetheless, Camilla Jackson told her interviewer that hoopskirts "were the fad in those days" among black as well as white women, one that enabled bondwomen to appropriate a symbol of leisure and femininity (and freedom) and denaturalize their slave status. "In dem days de women wore hoops. . . . De white folks dun it an' so did the slave wimen," Ebenezer Brown said.[62]

Yet black women's style did not simply mimic slaveholding women's fashions. It was enslaved women's use of accessories that most accentuated their originality. Topping off many women's outfits were head wraps or hairstyles done just so. Nineteenth-century bondwomen made the head wrap into a unique expressive form. Some women wore their favorite head wraps to outlaw parties, and many others removed the wrap to display the hairstyles—cornrows, plaits, and straightened hair—they had prepared. Women could straighten or relax their curls by wrapping sections of their hair in string, twine, or bits of cloth, then covering it during the week to hide the wrappings and to keep their hair clean and protected from the sun. On special occasions such women removed the head wrap and the strings, and their hair fell down straightened or in looser curls. Although accessories were more difficult to obtain, they were not overlooked. Some women made straw hats from "wheat straw which was dried out." They also made buttons and ornaments for their clothing out of "li'l round pieces of gourds" covered with cloth and from "cows and rams horns."[63]

Shoes posed a special problem for women engaged in the work of refashioning their bodily identities. Many bondpeople wore no shoes at all during the warm months and received wooden brogans against the cold only once a year. On some farms women received footwear even more infrequently. Perhaps because even their agricultural labor was denigrated as "women's work" and therefore considered easier work, some women received no shoes at all. W. L. Bost was appalled at the hardships women faced, especially their inadequate dress in cold weather: "They never had enough clothes on to keep a cat warm. The women never wore anything but a thin dress and a petticoat and one underwear. I've seen the ice balls hangin' on to the bottom of their dresses as they ran along, jes like sheep in a pasture 'fore they are sheared. They never wore shoes."[64]

Women's creation and appropriation of cloth and clothing helped them to express their personalities and their senses of style, but their uses of clothing also raised material issues. Women's alternative uses of dress laid claim to the product of their labor: they seized the cotton that they had raised and harvested, and they used it for their own purposes. "How I get 'em?" Nancy Williams seemed pleased with her interviewer's question and eager to tell of her ingenuity. Perhaps exaggerating, Williams said she had "plenty" of clothes during her life in bondage, though not due to any generosity from her owner. In addition to dyeing the plain cloth she was allotted, Williams reappropriated what she needed. Williams, for example, "[h]ad done stole de paint" to make yellow shoes to go with a yellow dress she wore to an illicit dance.[65]

Similarly, Mary Wyatt's Virginia owner had a dress that Wyatt adored. "Lawdy, I used to take dat dress when she warn't nowhere roun' an' hole it up against me an' 'magine myself wearin it." One Christmas season Wyatt decided to wear the dress to a plantation frolie. "[D]e debbil got in me good," she admitted. "Got dat gown out de house 'neath my petticoat tied rounst me an' wore it to de dance." Donning the fancy dress of her mistress, Wyatt shed the most outward markers of her slave status and adopted instead a symbol of freedom. Like other women who reappropriated their owners' clothing, when Mary Wyatt stole her owner's dress she committed not only a symbolic transgression of place, by "'magin[ing]" herself in a dress that was made of a design and material reserved for the free white women who could afford it, but also an act of material consequence. She reclaimed the product of her own labor. Women like her had picked the cotton, processed it, and made it into a dress; the institution of slavery made the dress her owner's, but Mary Wyatt made it hers. In Wyatt's case the act of reappropriation was brief. She returned the dress, putting it "back in place de nex' day." But even as the terror that gripped her while she stole and wore the dress indicates the power of her owners, her act also reveals the strength of her commitment to wearing the dress and suggests something of its importance to Wyatt.[66]

Bondwomen took tremendous risks in procuring and wearing fancy dress to plantation frolics and outlawed slave parties, and the potential extent of this personal endangerment is also a measure of the significance of the otherwise seemingly trivial concerns of dress and style. By dressing up to go to outlaw parties, bondwomen flagrantly violated the somatics of plantation social hierarchy as well as plantation boundaries of space and time. Then fancy dress heightened their risk because their conspicuousness exposed all of them (especially household bondwomen) to detection. The degree of danger involved in dressing up and running away for an evening and women's willingness to take the chance suggest just how urgent it was to some to extricate themselves from their proper places. Frances Miller, a slaveholding woman, encountered such determination as she endeavored to impose a "system of management" within her Virginia household. She rose at 4:30 every morning, in advance of her bondpeople, to wake them and prod them to work, not at all shying away from physical violence when their "insubordination" proved too much for her. Miller dedicated herself, in what she described as a "herculean" manner, to "always righting things up." Thanks to the "open rebellion, impudence and unfaithfulness of domestics," things seemed "never righted" in her household.[67]

Among the most egregious acts of "unfaithfulness" and "insubordination" that Miller witnessed in her household was the determination of her unruly bondwoman, Rose, to sneak away at night to a party. On her way to bed one night, Miller encountered Rose on her way out of the house, "dressed up as I supposed for a night's jaunt." Caught, Rose thought on her feet and, thrusting the candle that she held to light her passage toward Miller, asked Miller to carry it back for her. Miller had been hardened by Rose's long history of disobedience, however, and was not distracted from the issue at hand. When Miller sarcastically "asked her why she did not do it herself," Rose claimed that "she was going to wash." Rose's explanation for still being awake and heading out, when, according to the late hour, she ought to have been in bed in her room, was not convincing. Miller could tell by the way Rose was "dressed so spry" that she was not at all going to wash and so "did not believe her." Instead, she reminded Rose of her curfew and of where she ought to be, telling her "it was bedtime and she must go directly upstairs." Rose "refused" and remained determined to go out to "wash." Rose's plans were thwarted only after Miller "shut the door and locked it." With no key Rose had no way out. Angered that she would now miss the party, Rose insulted Miller, telling her "that I was the most contrary old thing that she ever saw."[68]

As punishment for attempting to disobey the household's boundaries of space and time, as well as for her effrontery, Miller promised to flog Rose, prompting Rose to assert that she "would not submit to any such thing and that she would go to the woods first." Rose, however, did not carry out her threat. Perhaps because she was so disappointed about having been prevented from going out, Rose "yielded with less difficulty than usual" to the bondman William's "switches." Miller succeeded in stopping Rose from leaving the household, but the whole incident left Miller "sorely grieved—sorely." She was frustrated "that the necessity had existed" to whip Rose. Rose's transgression of place mandated, to Miller's mind, the deployment of violence, which contradicted Miller's ideal of a mastery so effective as not to warrant its explicit use in the first place.[69]

Black women's and men's absentee nightly pleasures, such as sneaking off to parties to stay up late dancing and drinking, compromised slaveholding authority and plantation productivity. Julia Larken noted that her owner "never laked for nobody to be late in de mornin'," presumably because of the disorder and the inefficiency that tardiness caused. Nonetheless, lateness and fatigue were not unusual. When enslaved people stayed up late into the night worshiping, for example, they would be "sho tired" the next day. Charlie Tye Smith recalled that, no matter how late they had been up the night before, bondpeople "had better turn out at four o'clock when ole Marse blowed the horn!" They dragged themselves through the motions of their chores all morning and at lunchtime collapsed in the field. Those who had not attended the religious meeting looked upon a field "strowed with Niggers asleep in the cotton rows" until the midday break ended, and they all resumed work.[70]

And so it was after illicit parties, Jefferson Franklin Henry remembered how other bond-people, but not he, "would go off to dances and stay out all night; it would be wuk time when they got back. . . ." These revelers valiantly "tried to keep right on gwine," but they were worn out: "the Good Lord soon cut 'em down." These mornings-after did not inhibit future parties, however, nor did the Christian objections of other blacks make an impact: "You couldn't talk to folks that tried to git by with things lak that," Henry regretted. "[T]hey warn't gwine to do no diffunt, nohow."[71]

An extraordinary document survives that articulates for us not the "success" of slave resist-ance using the body but, given the extent to which the body was a point of conflict between slaves and their owners, what meanings the latter group ascribed to that conflict. In the mid-1840s slaveholders in the Edgefield and Barnwell Districts of South Carolina formed the Savannah River Anti-Slave Traffick Association to put a stop to disorderly house owners' practice of selling alcohol to bondpeople and published their regulations. Slave drinking, and the theft and black marketing that bondpeople engaged in to obtain liquor and other goods from obliging non-elite whites, resulted in what the Savannah River group deemed "very considerable losses." Bondwomen and men—like association member James Henry Hammond's own Urana—appropriated property from slave owners by breaking into "dwelling houses, barns, stables, smoke houses, [etc,]" with "false keys which abound among our negroes," or by "pick[ing] with instruments at which they have become very skilful" at crafting and using. Moreover, the neigh-bors complained that their crops were also vulnerable to appropriation: "Not content with plundering from Barns, our standing crops are beginning to suffer depredation." Thanks to these various activities, the Savannah River neighbors thought they had noticed their profits decline. "Often when a Farmer has expected to sell largely, he finds himself compelled to use the most stringent economy to make his provisions meet his own wants, and sometimes has actually to buy."[72]

Slaves' trading, stealing, and drinking were not the only "evils" worrying these South Carolina planters. Equally vexatious was the practice of "prowling" off to "night meetings." Because of the "too great negligence of slave owners in maintaining wholesome discipline," every night, or so it seemed, bondpeople could be found sneaking "abroad to night meetings." The association claimed that "hundreds of negroes it may be said without exaggeration are every night, and at all hours of the night, prowling about the country," stealing, trading, drinking, and meeting, almost certainly for secular affairs.[73]

The association weighed heavily the financial loss its members believed that they incurred when enslaved people were too hungover and tired to work well. "The negroes themselves are seriously impaired in physical qualities," it noted. The association's regulations further detailed that "their nightly expeditions are followed by days of languor." Seeing their "owners, and especially their overseers, as unjust and unfeeling oppressors," bondpeople, it seemed to these South Carolinians, responded with insubordination and work characterized by "sullenness [and] discontent."[74]

The Savannah River neighbors were mobilized to action by what they saw as a second pernicious effect of black nightly "prowling." In addition to the damage nightly pleasures had on productivity and the theft associated with such parties, association members complained of the resulting corrosion of slaveholding mastery. Black "minds are fatally corrupted" by these night-time activities, these South Carolinians believed. In the revisionist history that the association wrote, bondpeople were "beginning to" dissent from the paternalist contract that supposedly governed planters' estates. "Formerly Slaves were essentially members of the family to which they belonged, and a reciprocal interest and attachment existing between them, their relations were simple, agreeable, easily maintained, and mutually beneficial," the association contended. It seemed that the freedom bondpeople tasted at night compromised their willingness to be deferential and obedient during the day. The association complained of the "difficulty in managing" the bondpeople since night activity appeared to encourage many bondpeople to see their "Masters" as their "natural enemies." This perspective facilitated more disorderly behavior, and the members of the Savannah River organization were forced to admit to one another that they were having trouble "preserving proper subordination of our slaves."[75]

The apocalyptic end was clear to the Savannah River residents; in alarmist tones they predicted the end of slavery as they knew it if such unruliness continued. Reappropriating the "fruits of their own labors," working only with "sullenness [and] discontent," and skeptical of the authority of their masters, bondpeople in their neighborhood were creating "[s]uch a state of things [that] must speedily put an end to agriculture or to negro slavery." Engaging in these small, outlawed activities, the association argued, the "negro ceases to be a moral being, holding a position in the framework of society, and becomes a serpent gnawing at its vitals or a demon ready with knife and torch to demolish its foundations."[76]

Drinking and dancing at night rather than resting for the next day's work could not and did not bring down the house of slavery. Nonetheless, the histrionics of the Savannah River Anti-Slave Traffick Association are more than amusing; they are revealing. When engaged in these activities, enslaved people ceased, their owners thought, to hold a proper "position in the framework of society" because they disregarded slaveholders' control over their bodies. Stealing time and space for themselves and for members of their communities, those who attended secular parties acted on the assumption that their bodies were more than inherently and solely implements of agricultural production. While many planters desired and struggled for a smooth-running, paternalistic machine, some bondpeople created, among other things, a gendered culture of pleasure that "gnawed" at the fundamentals—the "vitals"—of slaveholding schemes for domination of the black body, a body that slaveholders had (ideally) located in a particular "position in the framework of society."

In a context where control and degradation of the black body were essential to the creation of slave-owning mastery—symbolically, socially, and materially—bondwomen's and men's nighttime pleasures insulted slaveholders' feelings of authority. Mastery demanded respect for spatial and temporal boundaries, but bondpeople sometimes transgressed these borders and forged spaces for themselves. While slave-owners' drive for production required rested slave bodies, bondpeople periodically reserved their energies for the night and exhausted themselves at play. Perhaps most important of all, enslaved women and men struggled against planters' inclination to confine them, in order to create the space and time to celebrate and enjoy their bodies as important personal and political entities in the plantation South.

Notes

1. Charles L. Perdue Jr., Thomas E. Barden, and Robert K. Phillips, eds., *Weevils in the Wheat: Interviews with Virgina Ex-Slaves* (Charlottesville, 1976), 316. Williams was fourteen years old when the Civil War began. Before slavery ended, however, she had reached young adulthood; she told her interviewer that she had "growd up" when she left the slaveholding house for field work. At about the same time, she "start[ed] dis cou'tin'." Like many, but not all, formerly enslaved interviewees in the 1930s, Williams had more than a child's memories of bondage. She offers, as do other interviewees, the remembrances of young adulthood.

   For generous insights and careful criticisms I am indebted to Drew Gilpin Faust, Houston Baker, Edward E. Baptist, Douglas R. Egerton, Farah Jasmine Griffin, Lani Guinier, Diannah Jackson Leigh, Nell Painter, Uta G. Poiger, Carroll Smith-Rosenberg, Lynn M. Thomas, and the Brown Bag Seminar of the McNeil Center for Early American Studies. I am also grateful to the *Journal of Southern History*'s anonymous reviewers for tough and inspiring comments. Many thanks to the Organization of American Historians, the Virginia Historical Society, the Library Company of Philadelphia, the Departments of History at the University of Pennsylvania and Vassar College, and the MacBride Faculty Fund and the Walter Chapin Simpson Center for the Humanities at the University of Washington for support of research and writing.

2. *Ibid.*

3. Withrop D. Jordon, *White Over Black: American Attitudes Toward the Negro, 1550–1812* (Chapel Hill, 1968), 55–56 (quotations), 107; Philip J. Schwarz, *Twice Condemned: Slaves and the Criminal Laws of Virginia, 1705–1865* (Baton Rouge, 1988), 2; Ira Berlin, *Many Thousands Gone: The First Two Centuries of Slavery in North America* (Cambridge, Mass., and London, 1998), 113. For more on the social geography of the colonial and antebellum South see Rhys Isaac, *The Transformation of Virginia, 1740–1790* (Chapel Hill and London, 1982), 11–57; Stephanie McCurry, *Masters of Small Worlds: Yeomen Households, Gender Relations, and the Political Culture of the Antebellam South Carolina Low Country* (New York and Oxford, 1995), 10–15; and David Goldfield, *Region, Race, and Cities: Interpreting the Urban South* (Baton Rouge and London, 1997), 69–86, 103–44.

4. Anne Godlewska and Neil Smith cited in Matthew Sparke, "Mapped Bodies and Disembodied Maps: (Dis)placing Cartographic Struggle in Colonial Canada," in Heidi J. Nast and Steve Pile, eds., *Places Through the Body* (London and New York, 1998), 305. John Michael Vlach discusses the "black system of place definition," its emphasis on movement, and its rejection of fixity in *Back of the Big House: The Architecture of Plantation Slavery* (Chapel Hill and London, 1993), 13–17 (quotation on p.14). The phrase "geography of containment" is Houston Baker's, from his response to Michael Hanchard, "Temporality, Transnationalism, and Afro-Modernity" (paper presented to the "Reshaping Afro-American Studies" Seminar at the Center for the Study of Black Literature and Culture, University of Pennsylvania, March 27, 1997).

5. Ulrich B, Phillips, *American Negro Slavery: A Survey of the Supply, Employment and Control of Negro Labor as Determined by the Plantation Regime* (New York, 1918; Baton Rouge, 1966), 327; Eugene D. Genovese, *Roll, Jordon, Roll: The World the Slaves Made* (New York, 1972), 3–7. Genovese's paternalism thesis has been the subject of intensive debate since the publication of his monumental *Roll, Jordon Roll.* Among the many questions at issue is the extent to which enslaved people could resist bondage and the importance of such resistance. Some historians have agreed that paternalist, slaveholding hegemony determined the shape of every feature of black life and, further, that the lives of bondpeople must be understood primarily in terms of their exploitation and oppression by slaveholders. Slaveholding power, in this view, flattened the possibility of meaningful oppositional activity, except for running away and organized rebellion: everyday forms of resistance "qualify at best as prepolitical and at worst as apolitical," Fox-Genovese, *Roll, Jordon, Roll,* 3, 6, 7, 22, 90–91, 125, 143–44, 284, 598 (quotation). See also Elizabeth Fox-Genovese, *Within the Plantation Household: Black and White Women of the Old South* (Chapel Hill and London, 1988), 30, 49–50, 319; Bertram Wyatt-Brown, "The Mask of Obedience: Male Slave Psychology in the Old South," *American Historical Review,* 93 (December 1988), 1228–52; and William Dusinberre, *Them Dark Days: Slavery in the American Rice Swamps* (New York and Oxford, 1996), 235, 248, 265, 270–71, 273. The focus on hegemony overestimates the extent of consent at the expense of the determining role of force. Other historians in the traditional debate have placed black communities, their struggles, and their sufferings at the center of bondpeople's lives—not slaveholders and their hegemonic aspirations. This article builds on this tradition, which includes Herbert Aptheker, *American Negro Slave Revolts* (New York, 1943); George P. Rawick, *From Sundown to Sunup: The Making of the Black Community* (Westport, Conn., 1972); John W. Blassingame, *The Slave Community: Plantation Life in the Antebellum South* (rev. ed.; New York and Oxford, 1979); Lawrance W. Levine, *Black Culture and Black Conciousness: Afro-American Folk Thought from Slavery to Freedon* (New York, 1977); Charles Joyner, *Down by the Riverside: A South Carolina Slave Community* (Urbana and Chicago, 1984); Rogar D. Abrahams, *Singing the Master: The Emergence of African American Culture in the Plantation South* (New York, 1992); Douglas R. Egerton, *Gabriel's Rebellion: The Virginia Slave Conspiracies of 1800 and 1802* (Chapel Hill and London, 1993); Shane White and Graham White, *Stylin': African American Expressive Culture from Its Beginnings to the Zoot Suit* (Ithaca, N.Y., 1998); and Douglas R. Egerton, *He Shall Go Out Free: The Lives of Denmark Vesey* (Madison, Wisc., 1999). This article departs from this literature and this debate, however, in its focus on women, gender difference and conflict, and culture politics, as well as in its attention not to lore or religion (that is, to the intellectual and moral history of enslaved communities) or to organized rebellion, but to values embodied in the everyday physical use of space, to political belief put into movement.

6. All of these sources present difficulties, and alone none tells all we might want to know. For all of the difficulties of plantation records and legal sources, however, historians of slavery tend to focus their methodological critiques on the interviews of ex-bondpeople. The criticisms contend that the interviews collected by the Works Progress Administration (WPA) were conducted decades after emancipation, after too much had transpired in the lives of the informants to make their recollections creditable. Many the interviews were also done by whites, further warping the information respondents gave. I do

not dispute the problems inherent in the WPA interviews but I do not conclude from these difficulties that the source is unworkable. This article gathers material from a range of sources—including black and white, contemporaneous and subsequent, and written and oral sources—building a story out of their agreements and common accounts, as well as from the insights offered by their differences. These sources also explain the periodization of this article. Because the WPA interviews refer, mostly, to the last decades of slavery and because black autobiographies proliferated in the same period, this article focuses on the years between 1830 and the beginning of the Civil War.

7. Thomas D. Morris, *Southern Slavery and the Law 1619–1860* (Chapel Hill and London, 1996); Christopher Morris, "The Articulation of Two Worlds: The Master–Slave Relationship Reconsidered," *Journal of American History*, 85 (December 1998), 982–1007; Walter Johnson, *Soul by Soul: Life Inside the Antebellum Slave Market* (Cambridge, Mass., and London, 1999). For all of the important differences caused by farm size, crop, type of work, and subregion, American slavery was, above all, a system of economic exploitation and racial subjugation that, when studied in a broad geographic range, reveals strong continuities as well as differences. We have much to learn about the interplay of local and individual experiences of enslavement, about slavery as a system, and about resistance to it as a practice with patterns and trends. In particular, the fragmentary nature of the evidence on a topic such as women's everyday forms of resistance demands a broad geographic sweep.

8. Bondpeople living on farms, in neighborhoods, and in states with small numbers of other enslaved people (like Florida or Delaware) would certainly have enjoyed far less frequent illegal parties, if they managed to organize any at all. There would have been differences between the upper South and the lower South, but the scarcity of sources precludes knowing for certain. It is possible to note, however, that while it might appear that illicit movement would have been more common in the upper South because of its proximity to the free North, the evidence does not support this hypothesis. Bondpeople in the lower South were also able to form an active rival geography and to organize and attend their own secret parties. Indeed, these forms of movement may have taken on special importance in the lower South precisely because bondpeople had little chance of escaping as fugitives. In particular South Carolina's black majority no doubt enjoyed greater discretion and autonomy when having parties. But enslaved South Carolinians were not the only ones to know life as a black majority: in 1850 about half (50.6 percent) of all bondpeople in the South lived on farms that had at least twenty enslaved people (with a significant minority of 13.1 percent living on holdings with fifty to a hundred enslaved people). Lewis Cecil Gray, *History of Agriculture in the Southern United States to 1860* (2 vols.; Washington, D.C., 1933), I, 530. Locally, then, many enslaved people inhabited communities among and near enough others to make independent socializing viable.

9. For the theory of everyday forms of resistance that undergirds the approach taken here, which sees day-to-day resistance as neither a safety valve, nor as revolutionary, but as a form at political struggle before and behind open political organization, see James C. Scott, *Weapons of the Weak: Everyday Forms of Peasant Resistance* (New Haven, 1985), esp. xv–xvi, 35–36, 285–303, 317; and Scott, *Domination and the Arts of Resistance: Hidden Transcripts* (New Haven and London, 1990), esp. 66, 178, 184–88. Historians who have skillfully employed Scott's theories to study U.S. slave resistance include Alex Lichtenstein, " 'That Disposition to Theft With Which They Have Been Branded': Moral Economy, Slave Management, and the Law," *Journal of Social History*, 21 (Spring 1988), 413–40: and Marvin L. Michael Kay and Lorin Lee Cary, *Slavery in North Carolina, 1748–1775* (Chapel Hill and London, 1995). Critics of Scott's work include Rosalind O'Hanlon, "Recovering the Subject: *Subaltern Studies* and Histories of Resistance in Colonial South Asia," *Modern Asian Studies*, 22 (February 1988), 189–224; and Sherry B. Ortner, "Resistance and the Problem of Ethnographic Refusal," *Comparative Studies in Society and History*, 37 (January 1995), 173–93.

10. Dorinda Outram, *The Body and the French Revolution: Sex, Class and Political Culture* (New Haven and London, 1989), 1; C. L. R. James, Grace C. Lee and Pierre Chaulieu, *Facing Reality* (Detroit, Mich., 1974), 5; Scott, *Weapons of the Weak*, 289–99; Dagmar Herzog and Uta Poiger have demonstrated that German feminist analyses connecting the personal and the political grew out of broader German New Left efforts to do the same. American and German feminist movements in the 1970s may have popularized the concept and applied it in especially liberatory ways to women's lives, but they did not invent it. See Dagmar Herzog, " 'Pleasure, Sex, and Politics Belong Together': Post-Holocaust Memory and the Sexual Revolution in West Germany," *Critical Inquiry*, 24 (Winter 1998), 393–444; Uta G. Poiger, *Jazz, Rock, and Rebels: Cold War Politics and American Culture in a Divided Germany* (Berkeley, Los Angeles and London 2000), 219, 269 n. 32.

11. This discussion is informed by the work of anthropologists and philosophers who have posited the body as an important terrain of conquest and as a site for the reproduction of the social order. They have also detailed what, following Mary Douglas's account of "two bodies," may be called a second body: the social imprint on the body that shapes and limits the experience of the body. See Frantz

Fanon, *Black Skin, White Masks,* trans. Charles Lam Markmann (New York, 1967) 109–40; Mary Douglas, *National Symbols: Explorations in Cosmology* (New York, 1970), chap. 5; and Michel Foucault, *Discipline and Punish: The Birth of the Prison,* trans. Alan Sheridan (New York, 1977). Recent scholarship has demonstrated that the black body has been more than a site of racial subjugation and suffering. Historians of black bodily joy include Robin D. G. Kelley, *Race Rebels: Culture, Politics, and the Black Working Class* (New York, 1994); Tera W. Hunter, *To 'Joy My Freedom: Southern Black Women's Lives and Labor After the Civil War* (Cambridge, Mass., and London, 1997); Helen Bradley Foster, *"New Raiments of Self": African American Clothing in the Antebellum South* (New York and Oxford, 1997); and White and White, *Stylin'.*

12. Fanon, *Black Skin, White Masks,* 110–11. There are at least two criticisms to be made of Fanon's point here. First, Fanon equates the experience of "being black" with domination allowing for no experience of "blackness" that is something other than oppressive or "othering." Fanon also goes too far in arguing for a space outside of ideology. Resistance is not created outside of hegemonic ideologies and other forms of domination but is constituted within them. Domination not only calls forth resistance, it also establishes the terrain over which struggle ensues. Slaveholders, who understood the importance of regulating the body to social control, identified the black body as a site of domination. Enslaved people responded by rendering their bodies a site of political struggle and enjoyment. This is no neat teleology, for everyday forms of resistance were not the mere shaping or measure of repression (though they were that, as well), as critics of everyday politics would have it. Everyday resistance also reveals the formation of genuine black subjectivities and the expression of human agency. These objections notwithstanding, Fanon's suggestion that in spaces away from the white gaze, colonial subjects may experience some freedom from domination is instructive. See also Ann Farnsworth-Alvear, "Orthodox Virginity/Heterodox Memories: Understanding Women's Stories of Mill Discipline in Medellin, Columbia," *Signs,* 23 (Autumn 1997), 71–101; and Scott, *Weapons of the Weak,* 299.

13. Mary Douglas, *Purity and Danger: An Analysis of Concepts of Pollution and Taboo* (London and Boston, 1966); Douglas *Natural Symbols*; Carolyn Kay Steedman, *Landscape for a Good Women: A Story of Two Lives* (New Brunswick, N.J., 1987); Joan Wallach Scott, *Gender and the Politics of History* (New York, 1988); Elizabeth Faue, *Community of Suffering and Struggle: Women, Men and the Labor Movement in Minneapolis, 1915–1945* (Chapel Hill and London, 1991); Evelyn Brooks Higginbotham, "African-American Women's History and the Metalanguage of Race," *Signs,* 17 (Winter 1992), 251–74.

14. For work on the somatics of bondwomen's enslavement see Darlene Clark Hine and Kate Wittenstein, "Female Slave Resistance: The Economics of Sex," in Filomena Chioma Steady, ed., *The Black Woman Cross-Culturally* (Cambridge, Mass., 1981); Deborah Gray White, *Ar'n't I a Woman? Female Slaves in the Plantation South* (New York and London, 1985); Stephanie J. Shaw, "Mothering Under Slavery in the Antebellum South," in Evelyn Nakano Glenn, Grace Chang, and Linda Rennie Forcey, eds., *Mothering: Ideology, Experience, and Agency* (New York and London, 1994), 237–58; Nell Irvin Painter, *Sojourner Truth: A Life, A Symbol* (New York and London, 1996); and Leslie A. Schwalm, *A Hard Fight for We: Women's Transition from Slavery to Freedom in South Carolina* (Urbana and Chicago, 1997). Many southern women's historians are also blurring the dichotomy between the personal and creative, and the political and material. See, for example, Elsa Barkley Brown, "Negotiating and Transforming the Public Sphere: African American Political Life in the Transition for Slavery to Freedom," *Public Culture,* 7 (Fall 1994), 107–46; Kathleen M. Brown, *Good Wives, Nasty Wenches, and Anxious Patriarchs: Gender, Race, and Power in Colonial Virginia* (Chapel Hill and London, 1996); Hunter, *To Joy My Freedom*; Jacquelyn Dowd Hall, "'You Must Remember This': Autobiography as Social Critique," *Journal of American History,* 85 (September 1998), 439–65. Paul Gilroy's work also informs the discussion here. See "One Nation under a Groove: The Cultural Politics of 'Race' and Racism in Britain," in David Theo Goldberg, ed., *Anatomy of Racism* (Minneapolis, 1990), 274.

15. White abolitionists used graphic representations of the exploited, abused, or degraded enslaved body to garner support for the antislavery cause. See Phillip Lapsansky, "Graphic Discord: Abolitionist and Antiabolitionist Images," in Jean Fagan Yellin and John C. Van Horne, eds., *The Abolitionist Sisterhood: Women's Political Culture in Antebellum America* (Ithaca, N.Y., and London, 1994), 201–30; and Elizabeth B. Clark, "'The Sacred Rights of the Weak': Pain, Sympathy, and the Culture of Individual Rights in Antebellum America," *Journal of American History,* 82 (September 1995), 463–93. Scholars of nineteenth-century slave narratives have demonstrated that black writers—especially women—used rhetorical strategies to draw attention away from their bodies, in order to emphasize their political voices rather than titillate white audiences. See Anthony G. Barthelemy, "Introduction," in Henry Louis Gates, Jr. ed., *Collected Black Women's Narratives* (New York 1988), xxix–xlviii; Carla L. Peterson, *"Doers of the Word": African-American Women Speakers and Writers in the North (1830–1880)* (New York and Oxford, 1995), esp. 22; and Jeannine DeLombard, "'Eye-Witness to the Cruelty': Southern

Violence and Northern Testimony in Frederick Douglass's 1845 *Narrative*," *American Literature*, 73 (June 2001), 245–75.

16. Jennifer L. Morgan, " 'Some Could Suckle Over Their Shoulder': Male Travelers, Female Bodies and the Gendering of Racial Ideology, 1500–1770," *William and Mary Quarterly*, 3d ser., 54 (January 1997), 167–92, esp. 179 (first quotation), 170 (second quotation), 184 (third and sixth quotations), 181 (fourth quotation), and 171 (fifth quotation).

17. Brown, *Good Wives, Nasty Wenches, and Anxious Patriarchs*, 116–19, 125, 135–36 (quotations on p. 136). For more on notions of racial difference and their relation to the expansion of the African slave trade and American slavery, see Edmund S. Morgan, *American Slavery, American Freedom: The Ordeal of Colonial Virginia* (New York, 1975), 295–337; Jordan,*White Over Black*; Alden T. Vaughn, "The Origins Debate: Slavery and Racism in Seventeenth Century Virginia," *Virginia Magazine of History and Biography*, 97 (July 1989), 311–54; and Peter Kolchin, *American Slavery, 1619–1877* (New York, 1993), 11–12, 17.

18. "Bio-text" is John O'Neill's phrase, from *The Communicative Body: Studies in Communicative Philosophy, Politics, and Sociology* (Evanston, Ill., 1898), 3.

19. Fanon, *Black Skin, White Masks*, 110–11.

20. "Charles Ball, *Slavery in the United States: A Narrative of the Life and Adventures of Charles Ball* (Lewistown, Pa., 1836: reprint, Detroit, Mich., 1970), 125.

21. The manual's instructions are printed on the inside cover of the Richard Eppes diary, 1858, Eppes Family Papers (Virginia Historical Society, Richmond, Va.; hereinafter cited as VHS). Mark M. Smith demonstrates the increasing importance of time discipline to plantation production during the antebellum period in the following works, "Time, Slavery, and Plantation Capitalism in the Ante-bellum American South," *Past and Present*, 150 (February 1996), 142–68; "Old South Time in Comparative Perspective," *American Historical Review*, 101 (December 1996), 142–69; and in his brilliant *Mastered by the Clock: Time, Slavery and Freedom on the American South* (Chapel Hill and London, 1997).

22. For a single example, Virginia slaveholder John Bassett wrote a pass for an enslaved person named Edward: "Edward is sent to Rich[mon]d. To remain till Monday next [.] Feby 25th 1826, John Basset." The note at the bottom at the pass confirmed Edward's movements: "I have recd five Dollars by your Boy Edward [.] R [.] Brooks." Section 17, Basset Family Papers (VHS). More passes can be found in Section 4. Hundley Family Papers (VHS): and Sections 5, 42 and 86, Spragins Family Papers (VHS). On slave patrols see Gladys-Marie Fry, *Night Riders to Black Folk History* (Knoxville, 1975); and Sally E. Hadden, *Slave Patrols: Law and Violence in Virginia and the Carolinas* (Cambridge, Mass., and London, 2001).

23. White, *Ar'n't I a Woman?* 75; see also the passes cited at note 22. Women occasionally were able to procure (legal) passes and leave the plantation, usually in perform labor. For example, enslaved women on the Hunter Family's Virginia estate obtained written permission to take their cloth to a dressmaker, Box 10, Mary Evelina (Dandridge) Hunter Papers, in Hunter Family Papers (VHS).

24. December 31, 1846, entry, William Ethelbert Ervin Diaries #247-z (Wilson Library, Southern Historical Collection, University of North Carolina at Chapel Hill; hereinafter cited as SHC); George P. Rawick, ed., *The American Slave: A Composite Autobiography* (19 vols.: Westport, Conn., 1972), XIII, Pt. 3, p. 128. Andrew Boone recalled, "If you wus out widout a pass dey would shore git you. De paterollers shore looked after you. Dey would come to de house at night to see who wus there. If you wus out of place, dey would wear you out," Rawick, ed., *American Slave*, XIV, 134.

25. Rawick, ed., *American Slave*, XIV, 157 (quotation). See also Genovese, *Roll, Jordan, Roll*, 3–7, 570, 577–80, 584. Roger D. Abrahams has shown how bondpeople sometimes turned paternalistic events like corn shuckings into rituals of their own meaning. Abrahams, *Singing the Master*, 83, 106.

26. Rawick, ed., *American Slave*, XVI, 23. Some WPA informants reported that attending plantation frolics was an activity reserved for white men. For instance, George Fleming said, "White ladies didn't go to de frolics, but some of de white men did." George P. Rawick, ed., *The American Slave: A Composite Autobiography*, supplemental series 1 (12 vols., Westport, Conn., 1977), XI, 128; hereinafter cited as *American Slave*, supp. ser. 1.

27. December 27, 1828, entry (first and third quotations), John Nevett Diary #543 (SHC). "Treat[s]" are mentioned in the December 25, 1827, December 25, 1829, and December 27, 1830, entries.

28. Rawick, ed., *American Slave*, XIII, Pt. 4, p. 68 (Neal Upson), and XII, Pt. 2, p. 142 (Bill Heard).

29. Rawick, ed., *American Slave*, XIV, 213.

30. The lyrics, as Bob Ellis remembered them, were "Keep yo' eye on de sun / See how she run / Don't let her catch you with your work undone, / I'm a trouble, I'm a trouble, /Trouble don' las' always." Perdue et al., eds., *Weevils in the Wheat*, 88. For another section see *ibid.*, 309.

31. Rawick, ed., *American Slave*, XIV, 213 (Charlie Crump), 156 (Midge Burnett)

32. Rawick, ed., *American Slave*, XII, Pt. 2, p. 188.

33. Austin Steward, *Twenty-Two Years a Slave, and Forty Years a Freeman*, intro. by Jane H. Pease and William H. Pease (Reading, Mass., and other cities, 1969), 19–22 (first quotation on p. 19: second and third quotations on p. 20). Steward's autobiography was originally published in 1857.

34. *Ibid.*, 20.

35. *Ibid.*, 15 (fourth quotation), 21 (first, second, third, and fifth quotations).

36. *Ibid.*, 20–24 (first, second, and third quotations on p. 22; fourth quotation on p. 20).

37. *Ibid.*, 23–24 (first quotation on p. 23; subsequent quotations on p. 24).

38. Hadden, *Slave Patrols*, 109; Fry, *Nightriders in Black Folk History*, 93: Perdue et al., eds., *Weevils in the Wheat*, 93, 297 (quotation); Rawick, ed., *American Slave*, XIII, Pt. 4, p. 80, XIV, Pt. 1, p. 213, and XVI [Maryland], 49–50.

39. Perdue et al., eds., *Weevils in the Wheat*, 316; Rawick, ed., *American Slave*, XIII, Pt. 4, p. 306, XV, Pt. 2, p. 132, and XIII, Pt. 4, pp. 40, 64 and 124: Rawick, ed., *American Slave*, supp. ser. 1. XI. 128.

40. Rawick, ed., *American Slave*, XII, Pt. 2, p. 110.

41. Rawick, ed., *American Slave*, VII [Mississippi], 161

42. *Ibid.*, 126.

43. *Ibid.*, 162.

44. *Ibid.*, 161.

45. Perdue et al., eds., *Weevils in the Wheat*, 49–50 (Fannie Berry); Rawick ed., *American Slave*, XIII, Pt. 3, p. 124 (Liza Mention).

46. The "pigeon wings," "gwine to de east, an' gwine to de west," "callin de figgers," "set de flo'," and "dancin' on de spot" are described in Perdue et al., eds., *Weevils in the Wheat*, 49–50; the "hack-back" is described in Rawick, ed., *American Slave*, supp. ser. 1, XI, 127–28; and the remaining dances are described in Katrina Hazzard-Gordon, *Jookin': The Rise of Social Dance Formations in African American Culture* (Philadelphia, 1990), 19.

47. Hazzard-Gordon, *Jookin'*, 20; Perdue et al., eds., *Weevils in the Wheat*, 316 (Nancy Williams); Rawick, ed., *American Slave*, XII, Pt. 2, p. 99 (Jane Smith Hall Harmon).

48. Brenda E. Stevenson, *Life in Black and White: Family and Community in the Slave South* (New York and Oxford, 1996), 23, 255: Christopher Morris, *Becoming Southern: The Evolution of a Way of Life, Warren County and Vicksburg, Mississippi, 1770 1860* (New York and London, 1995), 63.

49. Rawick, ed., *American Slave*, VII [Mississippi], 30. Domestic violence was a source of both comedy and moral judgment in the folk song "Old Dan Tucker," in which Tucker, "a mighty mean man" who "beat his wife wid a fryin' pan," ends up passed out drunk in a "red hot" fire. Dora Franks remembered singing this song with other enslaved youth in Mississippi, *ibid.*, 53.

50. Rawick, ed., *American Slave*, XIII, Pt. 4, p. 104.

51. For more on black style under slavery see Patricia K Hunt, "The Struggle to Achieve Individual Expression Through Clothing and Adornment: African American Women Under and After Slavery," in Patricia Morton, ed., *Discovering the Women in Slavery: Emancipating Perspectives on the American Past* (Athens, Ga., and London, 1996), 227–40; Foster, "New Raiments of Self"; and White and White, *Stylin'*.

52. Frederick Law Olmsted, *The Cotton Kingdom: A Traveller's Observations on Cotton and Slavery in the American Slave States . . .*, ed. Arthur M. Schlesinger Sr. (1953; reprint, New York, 1984), 82 (first quotation); Rawick, ed., *American Slave*, XII, Pt. 1, p. 4, XV, 62 (Charity McAllister), and XIV, 272 (Fannie Dunn).

53. Drew Gilpin Faust, *James Henry Hammond and the Old South: A Design for Mastery* (Baton Rouge and London, 1982), 100–103; Genovese, *Roll, Jordan, Roll*, 5–7; Roswell King to Pierce Butler, December 7, 1812, April 20, 1816, and July 6, 1817 (first quotation), Folder 9, Box 3, Butler Family Papers (Historical Society of Pennsylvania, Philadelphia, Pa.); Harriet A. Jacobs, *Incidents in the Life of Slave Girl, Written by Herself*, ed. Jean Fagan Yellin (Cambridge, Mass., and London, 1987), 11.

54. Rawick. ed., *American Slave*, IV, p. 223 (Anne Clark); Rawick, ed., *American Slave*, supp. ser. 1, XI, 130 (George Fleming). See also George P. Rawick, ed., *The American Slave: A Composite Autobiography*, supplemental series 2 (10 vols.; Westport, Conn., 1979), VIII, 2990. As enslaved women's historians have pointed out, this "masculinization" of bondwomen at work was never complete, and rarely did it define enslaved women's gender identities. At work in their specialized labor, their gender-segregated or gender-specific agricultural labor, and the reproductive labor they performed for their families, enslaved women constructed then own meanings and expressions of womanhood. See White, *Ar'n't I a Woman*; Jacqueline Jones, *Labor of Love, Labor of Sorrow: Black Women, Work, and the Family from Slavery to the Present* (New York, 1985); and Schwalm, *A Hard Fight for We*.

55. Joyner, *Down by the Riverside*, 74; Foster, "New Raiments of Self," 111–12; Schwalm, *A Hard Fight for We*, 60: Rawick, ed., *American Slave*, XIII, Pt. 3, pp. 2, 186: Olmsted, *Cotton Kingdom*. 82, Thomas C. Buchanan, "The Slave Mississippi; African-American Steamboat Workers, Networks of Resistance,

and the Commercial World of the Western Rivers, 1811–1880" (Ph.D. dissertation, Carnegie Mellon University, 1998), 175–84.

56. Pierre Bourdieu, *Outline of a Theory of Practice*, trans. Richard Nice (Cambridge, Eng., and other cities, 1977), 164–71 (quotations on pp. 164–65).

57. *Ibid.*, 165.

58. Rawick, ed., *American Slave*, XIII, Pt. 4, pp. 212 (Adeline), 220 (Amelia).

59. Rawick, ed., *American Slave*, XIII, Pt. 3, p. 72 and XV, 364 (Henry James Trentham); *Aunt Sally; or, The Cross the Way Freedom: A Narrative of the Slave-Life and Purchase of the Mother of Rev. Isaac Williams, of Detroit, Michigan* (Cincinnatti, Ohio, 1858), 47; Octavia V. Rogers Albert, *The House of Bondage; or Charlotte Brooks and Other Slaves* (New York, 1890; reprint, New York and Oxford, 1988), 64. See also Rawick, ed., *American Slave*, XIII, Pt. 4, p. 80, XIII, Pt. 4, p. 183, XV, 129, and XV, 179; and Foster, "*New Raiments of Self*," 104.

60. Foster, "*New Raiments of Self*," 112, 114 (Morris Sheppard). Appendix III; Perdue et al., eds., *Weevils in the Wheat*, 316–17 (Nancy Williams quotation on p. 316); Rawick, ed., *American Slave*, XI, 52–53, and XIV, 184. Omsted, *Cotton Kingdom*, 82.

61. Perdue et al., eds., *Weevils in the Wheat*, 294.

62. Rawick, ed., *American Slave*, XVII, 306 (Salena Taswell); Drew Gilpin Faust, *Mothers of Invention: Women of the Slaveholding South in the American Civil War* (Chapel Hill and London, 1996), 223; Rawick, ed., *American Slave*, XII, Pt. 2, p. 297 (Camilla Jackson); Rawick, ed., *American Slave*, supp. ser. 1, VI, 249 (Ebenezer Brown). Robert Shepherd similarly said, "De white ladies had nice silk dresses to wear to church. Slave 'omans had new calico dresses what dey wore wid hoopskirts dey made out of grapevines." Rawick, ed., *American Slave*, XIII, Pt. 3, p. 253.

63. Shane White and Graham White, "Slave Hair and African American Culture in the Eighteenth and Nineteenth Centuries," *Journal of Southern History*, 61 (February 1995), 70–71; Rawick, ed., *American Slave*, supp. ser. 1, XI, 57 (first quotation); Foster, "*New Raiments of Self*", 115, 252 (second and third quotations).

64. See the cothing distribution lists, 1802, in Jane Frances Walker Page, Commonplace Book (VHS); "List of negroes who received clothes," April 1846, November 1846, Vol. VI, George J. Kollock Plantation Journals #407 (SHC); Foster, "*New Raiments of Self*", 243–44; and Rawick, ed., *American Slave*, XIV, 139 (W. L. Bost).

65. Perdue et al., eds., *Weevils in the Wheat*, 316. For more on women's use of clothing to exhibit their "individuality," See Hunt, "Struggle to Achieve Individual Expression through Clothing and Adornment," 227–40.

66. Perdue et al., eds., *Weevils in the Wheat*, 333.

67. Frances (Scott) Miller diary, July 3, 1858 (first, second, third, and fifth quotations), and July 5, 1858 (fourth and sixth quotations), in Section 10, Armistead, Blanton, and Wallace Family Papers (VHS).

68. *Ibid.*, February 7, 1857.

69. *Ibid.*

70. Rawick, ed., *Americal Slave*, XIII, Pt. 3, pp. 39 (Julia Larken), 276 (Charlie Tye Smith).

71. Rawick, ed., *Americal Slave*, XII, Pt. 2, pp. 188–89. Fatigue, and its effects on plantation production, was a problem after paternalist frolics as well. Some slaveholders accounted for exhaustion and allowed some time the day following frolics for naps. For example, Addie Vinson remembered how after a dance given by her owner, "Niggers dat had done danced half de night would be so sleepy when de bugle sounded dey wouldn't have time to cook breakfast. Den 'bout de middle of de mawnin' dey would complain 'bout bein' so weak and hongry dat de overseer would fetch 'em in and have 'em fed. He let 'em rest 'bout a hour and a half; den he marched 'em back to de field and wuked 'em til slap black dark," Rawick, ed., *American Slave*, XIII, Pt. 4, p. 109.

72. *Preamble and Regulations of the Savannah River Anti-Slave Traffick Association* (adopted November 21, 1846), 3 (first quotation), 4 (subsequent quotations). For Hammond's complaints about drinking and theft among the enslaved population at Silver Bluff, see James Henry Hammond, plantation records for Silver Bluff, October 16, 1835 (South Carolina Library, University of South Carolina, Columbia, S.C.), on microfilm in Kenneth M. Stampp, ed., *Records of Ante-Bellum Southern Plantations from the Revolution through the Civil War*, ser. A, pt. 1, reel 1.

73. *Preamble and Regulations of the Savannah River Anti-Slave Traffick Association*, 3 (first and fourth quotations), 4 (second and sixth quotations), 5, 8 (third and fifth quotations).

74. *Ibid.* 3 (fourth quotation), 5 (first, second, and third quotations). Slaveholders' fears about the effects of slave drinking were not strictly racial in nature; elites attempted to curb poor white drinking as well. Many antebellum Americans believed that regular or excessive drinking impinged upon a person's productivity and stimulated flashes of anger. One newspaper editorialist, for example, opined that "in proportion as men become drunkards, they cease to be useful to themselves, to their families, or to

society. . . . When a common laborer becomes a drunkard, his family is soon reduced to the utmost need. The more he drinks the less he works, and the greater are his expenditures." Furthermore, the journalist warned, "An early effect of habitual drinking . . . is IRASCIBILITY OF TEMPER." Natchez (Miss.) *Southern Galaxy*, July 17, 1828, p. 1. There were, nonetheless, racial aspects to slaveholders' extreme concern regarding slave drinking. Decreased productivity in a working white man only indirectly cost others; the worker "ceas[ed] to be useful" to "society" generally. But an enslaved person's decreased productivity directly cost her or his owner. Moreover, alcohol, when inbibed by a black body, was widely believed to unleash black impulses—that is, innate African savagery and violence—otherwise repressed under slavery's ostensible civilizing influence. Denise Herd, "The Paradox of Temperance: Blacks and the Alcohol Question in Nineteenth-Century America," in Susanna Barrows and Robin Room, eds., *Drinking: Behavior and Belief in Modern History* (Berkeley, Los Angeles, and London, 1991), 354–75.

75. *Preamble and Regulations of the Savannah River Anti-Slave Traffick Association*, 4 (first quotation), 5 (second quotation), 3 (subsequent quotations). Everywhere in the slave South that blacks traded for and drank alcohol, slaveholders worried, as the Savannah River neighbors did, about the integrity of their property rights and the stability of slave "subordination." Kentucky's Supreme Court tellingly worried in 1845 that trading liquor to bondpeople would "tempt them to petty larcenies, by way of procuring the means necessary to buy." Equally important, access to alcohol threatened to "lead them to dissipation, insubordination and vice, and obstruct the good government, well being and harmony of society". Many white southerners, even those in the cities, would have concurred with the Savannah River Anti-Slave Traffick Association that black marketing and drinking gave bondpeople ideas inappropriate to their station and inspired behavior threatening to those who sought to maintain black "subordination". For example, in 1846 one Charleston jury pronounced that "the unrestrained intercourse and indulgence of familiarities between the black and white . . . are destructive of the respect and subserviency which our laws recognize as due from the one to the other and which form an essential feature in our institutions." Just a few years later, in 1851, another Charleston jury argued that slave liquor-trafficking brought "the negro slave in such familiar contact with the white man, as to . . . invite the assertion of equality, or draw from him exhibitions of presumption and insubordination," *Smith v. Commonwealth*, 6 B. Mon. (Ky.) 22 (September 1815); Charleston juries quoted in Richard C. Wade, *Slavery in the Cities: The South, 1820–1860* (New York and Oxford, 1964), 157.

76. *Preamble and Regulations of the Savannah River Anti-Slave Traffick Association*, 3 (second quotation), 4 (third quotation), 5 (first and fourth quotations).

7

Race, Culture, and Justice in Mexican Los Angeles

Miroslava Chávez-García

For nearly 300 years beginning in the early sixteenth century, Spain controlled a vast portion of the Americas. Whereas British colonists in North America typically eschewed social relationships with Native Americans, Spaniards intermarried widely, creating a diverse mestizo population. Despite the greater levels of social and cultural assimilation, however, Indian and mestizo communities in New Spain increasingly fought against Spanish colonial leaders and policies. Between 1808 and the mid-1820s, revolutionary discontent spread throughout the region, resulting in a declaration of Mexican independence in 1821.

California, the northernmost Spanish province, escaped almost all of the revolution's turmoil and bloodshed, and for the most part its peoples and leaders embraced the new Mexican government when word of the events first reached the region in 1822. The same social tensions that had launched the Mexican revolution were very much present in California, however, as its population encompassed tremendous social diversity. Among the region's peoples were numerous Native American, mulatto, mestizo, and Spanish communities as well as an increasing stream of American immigrants. At times these groups interacted peacefully, but violence and conflict often appeared. In this essay, Miroslava Chávez-García, a historian at the University of California, Davis, takes us into the Mexican pueblo of Los Angeles to shed light on how Mexican and Indian women related both interpersonally and within the legal system. Professor Chávez-García's analysis of the murder trial of Guadalupe Trujillo exposes how Californians struggled to make sense of shifting and competing interpretations of racial, ethnic, and state identity within the confines of Mexican law.

At approximately eleven in the morning on February 15, 1843, Guadalupe Trujillo and her Indian servant, Ysabel, quarreled over domestic chores. Trujillo and Ysabel, along with other members of the family, resided at Mission San Gabriel, fifteen miles from Los Angeles, a *pueblo* (town) of no more than 2,300 inhabitants. Their verbal argument quickly became heated and led to a physical altercation, prompting Trujillo to grab a large kitchen knife. After a brief struggle, the knife slashed Ysabel's throat and she fell to the floor, gasping for air. Within minutes, she died of her wound. By three o'clock that afternoon, the local justice of the peace had notified Judge Manuel Dominguez and a local doctor about the tragedy. Upon arriving, they found Ysabel's lifeless body covered by a blanket on the floor of the room. They removed the blanket and closely examined her body, identifying the severity of the wound that Trujillo had inflicted. Multiple smaller lacerations, they noted, flanked the main cut, which measured 2 inches deep and 8 in length and severed the artery. The doctor told the judge that the perpetrator had used "repetition and force."

Judge Dominguez's initial inquiry into the incident found no dispute about the central fact: Guadalupe Trujillo had stabbed Ysabel, her Indian servant. Trujillo told the judge that she had killed Ysabel for no other reason than self-defense. Following that initial investigation, the judge ordered a trial to determine if Trujillo had killed Ysabel in self-defense or if she, in fact, had premeditated a murder. Under Mexican law, judges and not juries determined the fate of defendants in capital crimes, and the law made capital crimes against Indians punishable by imprisonment. Throughout the trial, the prosecution as well as other witnesses challenged Trujillo's assertion of self-defense, with the prosecution arguing that Trujillo, not Ysabel, had instigated the fight. Trujillo, the prosecution contended, had grown tired of Ysabel's insolence and finally committed "premeditated murder."[1]

Trujillo's crime, while extreme, was not an aberration in the community. The court records from which this case is taken reveal that Mexican women such as Trujillo perpetrated crimes against members of their community, which included the so-called *gente de razón* (literally, people of reason) as well as their cultural and racial "other," California Indians, and that they were regularly prosecuted for their excesses. These cases also indicate that contentious social and family relations existed among women of different socioeconomic, cultural, and racial groups. Women from landowning families or those whose husbands were prominent political leaders had links to the power structure that their impoverished counterparts did not possess. Moreover, some Mexican women had access to economic, political, and social power that Native American women rarely achieved. Native women's entrance into the Hispanic world—where they learned to speak the Spanish language, worship in the Catholic faith, and follow Spanish cultural and gender prescriptions—did not ordinarily lead Mexican and Indian women to forge ties of sisterhood across cultural and socioeconomic lines. As the court trial would reveal, Trujillo and Ysabel's longtime relationship reflected such unequal and strained relations.[2]

Hierarchical relations between Indians and Mexicans, regardless of gender or social class, dated to the founding of Los Angeles in 1781. Though the population of the *pueblo* came originally from the lower strata of Mexican society and had racially mixed backgrounds of native, African, and Spanish ancestry, the settlers and their descendants distinguished themselves culturally and, later, ethnically from the *gentiles* (unbaptized California Indians) residing in villages and from the *neófitos* (neophytes, or baptized California Indians) living at the missions. That identity—*gente de razón*—also forged a cultural and social bond among them as they downplayed (and forgot) their own mixed heritages and saw themselves as *españoles* and eventually *californios*. They also distanced themselves socially from Indians—males and females, *gentiles* and *neófitos*—by relying on them almost exclusively as laborers in the *pueblo* and at nearby Mission San Gabriel. The *pobladores* (settlers) hired Gabrieleño men, women, and children (Indians living in or near Mission San Gabriel) from nearby villages and, later, *gentiles* from other *rancherías* and *neófitos* from the local mission, not only for the public projects but also for plowing, planting, harvesting, and tending to livestock. In return, *pobladores* paid them, their village chiefs, or the mission friars in kind, usually foodstuffs, blankets, small trinkets, or hides. Later, residents turned to locally brewed alcohol (*aguardiente*) as compensation, a practice, though outlawed in 1812, that led to drunkenness, violence, and other adverse social consequences for the Indians.[3]

Following secularization in the 1830s, when the Mexican government ended the mission system, neophytes left the missions and several hundred drifted into the *pueblo* and replaced the *gentiles* as the main source of labor. When the economy failed to accommodate the oversupply of workers who then became a "nuisance" to the *gente de razón*, city leaders enacted vagrancy ordinances in the late 1830s and 1840s. Those Indians unable to pay the fines found themselves performing forced labor on public works or being auctioned off to others. The result of captivity was often slavery in all but name.[4]

The social and cultural position of Indians vis-à-vis the *gente de razón* in Los Angeles provides the context in which to analyze the murder trial of Guadalupe Trujillo. It also allows us to examine how relations of power, based on gender, social status, and cultural and racial identity, structured and informed social and family relations between Trujillo and Ysabel. Only recently have scholars begun to probe the complex interactions between Mexicans and Native Americans, men and women, in California. These studies demonstrate that violence (including rape), labor (work patterns), fictive kinship links (created through marriage and baptism), family ties (established through intermarriage), and reciprocity (mutual obligations) shaped and character-ized bonds between Mexican and native peoples.[5] Though significant to our understanding of Mexican–Indian relations, these studies have largely ignored how the legal system—law and justice in the community—handled cross-cultural relationships that turned sour and, ultimately, led to deadly consequences. The documentation available for this trial also allows us to examine the subtleties and details of the incident surrounding Ysabel's death, providing an opportunity to understand how and why her relationship with Trujillo became strained and led to violence. The testimony discloses that their longtime relationship was tolerant at best and hostile at worst. As we will see, the judge had the sole responsibility for determining if Trujillo, as Ysabel's master and social better, had abused her power over the Indian woman. The evidence will enable us to explore closely the immediate circumstances that caused the women to see each other as adversaries and that drove Trujillo to kill Ysabel.

The trial will also allow us to explore not only how *angeleños* dealt with crime, but also how the local court viewed Trujillo's and Ysabel's relations and roles in the larger society. Every-one familiar with the incident agreed that Trujillo had committed a crime when she killed Ysabel, but disagreed as to the reason for and the severity of the crime. The arguments that the defense and the prosecution presented, while in opposition, disclose that both sides attempted to prove the victimization of their respective clients by invoking their cultural identities and social ranks and by drawing on *gente de razón* values that ascribed the role of master to Mexicans and servant to Indians. Trujillo, most residents agreed, was Ysabel's social better but, as the judge's ruling would demonstrate, Trujillo's socioeconomic status and cultural identity did not bar her from community standards of law and justice. The testimony of key witnesses, the counsels' arguments, and the judge's decision provide clues as to the ways in which the local community viewed cross-cultural social relations between the two Mexican and Native American women.[6]

Guadalupe Trujillo, the woman at the center of the controversy and trial, was not a native of Los Angeles or California. She and her family—which included a husband, a young daughter, and their servant, Ysabel—had originally migrated from their hometown of Abiqui, New Mexico, to the San Gabriel–Los Angeles region sometime after 1839. Their relocation was part of a larger trend of migration from New Mexico to California fueled initially, in the early 1830s, by Euro-American traders who went in search of new markets, goods, and livestock, and later by New Mexican families who removed themselves permanently in search of new opportunities.[7] In Abiqui, a small town of no more than 2,000 inhabitants, Trujillo and her family belonged to the lower-middle class, as they were neither members of the nobility nor *genizaros* nor detribalized Indians, as was Ysabel. When they arrived in Los Angeles, a *pueblo* that served as the nucleus of several dozen outlying *ranchos* (privately held large tracts of land for grazing livestock) and *rancherías* (Indian villages), the family had little economic means with which to acquire or maintain their own property, forcing them to rent a room at the mission and the father to work as a laborer for local proprietors, likely *rancheros* (*rancho* owners). In Mexican Los Angeles, land-based pursuits—livestock raising and agriculture—not only fueled the economy but also struc-tured a hierarchical social class system in which *rancho* holders (most of them former military men) and their families belonged to the elite, while those with smaller holdings, usually within the limits of the *pueblo*, belonged to the middle level of society. Those without any means of support, usually recent arrivals such as the Trujillos and former mission Indians, were among the lowest rank in the region.[8]

Ysabel held a lowly and subordinate position as a servant and an orphaned Navajo who had arrived in Trujillo's largely mestizo household at infancy. Her lack of a surname and of a genealogical tie to others in the community indicated that she was not only a *criada*, or servant, but also a *genizara*. In New Mexico, *genizaros* were captured Indians, most often Navajo and Apache, whom Spanish raiders sold or exchanged for payments in cash or in kind. As spoils of war and as captives, they were pressed into domestic service at a young age. In a society that marked captured slaves and the vanquished as dishonored and disgraced, Ysabel, like other *genizaros*, represented a group of individuals who were viewed as intruders and outsiders. *Genizaros* occupied the lowest social rank and were forced to "perform the community's most menial and degrading tasks."[9]

After Trujillo and her household migrated to Mexican Alta California, Ysabel's role as a servant and a slave who lacked honor, status, or privileges remained the same. Despite the fact that officials in colonial Mexico had outlawed slavery, New Mexicans and *angeleños* allowed this practice to continue by using captured Indians as domestics. In the San Gabriel–Los Angeles region, Indian raiders (sometimes native peoples of different tribes) regularly brought to town Yuma children and young women taken from the Colorado River region and put them to labor in the homes and *ranchos* of local residents. In Ysabel's case, she was, for all intents and purposes, a slave until her death, though the court records fail to disclose the reality of her perpetual servitude. How and why her social and family relations with Trujillo turned bitter and culminated in her death is an issue the criminal court addressed.

Guadalupe Trujillo's murder trial opened with the testimony of Juan Pérez, the manager of Mission San Gabriel.[10] Pérez recalled that on February 15, 1843, after he had returned from his early morning duties, he saw Trujillo with her daughter in the kitchen, and proceeded to his room. Soon thereafter, an Indian child came to him saying, "She's calling you." "Who is calling me?" he asked. "Ysabel," the child insisted. He turned and at that moment saw Ysabel on the floor, seriously injured, and he went to her aid.

"What have you done?" he asked Trujillo.

"Ysabel has insulted me on numerous occasions and this time I could no longer contain myself," Trujillo responded.

"Couldn't you have used a stick and punished her that way?" asked Pérez.

"[I] called to . . . Ysabel," she answered, "and told her to go and wash clothes, as she had yet to complete her chores. Ysabel, who was outside, . . . refused . . . so I pushed her in [the mission]. She then grabbed my rebozo and shirt and tore them." Once inside, "I asked Ysabel, 'Why do you refuse to do what I say? Since you haven't cooked the meal, why don't you go and complete the wash?' " In defiance, Ysabel declared, "I don't want to, I don't want to be with you any longer, I want to go wherever I wish. . . . Why is it that the Indian women of the mission work less than I do and [they] have skirts made of *indianilla* [a fine cloth]?" Ysabel's comments, as noted by Trujillo, reveal that the servant believed her master doled out unfair treatment as compared to the treatment received by other Indian women, who seemingly enjoyed more freedoms.

At that instant, Trujillo claimed, Ysabel grabbed a large kitchen knife. "What are you going to do with that knife?" demanded Trujillo. "You'll see," Ysabel responded. As Ysabel approached Trujillo with the knife Trujillo took advantage of an opportunity to wrestle the weapon from her. Ysabel then grabbed Trujillo by the hair. In an attempt to force Ysabel to loosen her hold, Trujillo put the knife at her throat, but when that move failed, Trujillo felt she had no other option than to stab Ysabel repeatedly.[11]

The manager's narrative, based on what Trujillo had recounted to him, supported Trujillo's claim that she had killed Ysabel in self-defense. Understandably, his testimony painted a picture of Ysabel as the aggressive and unmindful Indian servant who launched a surprise attack on the unsuspecting Trujillo, who clearly had no choice but to defend herself.

Bernardo Guirado, a worker at the mission, also testified about what he saw and heard following Ysabel's murder. Of all the testimonies in the trial, his proved the most damaging to Trujillo's claim of self-defense. The mission employee told the court what he had witnessed firsthand. He stated that on the fifteenth, he had arrived at the mission at about eleven in the morning in the company of the priest. As they entered, they saw Ysabel on the floor, lifeless. At that moment, he saw the manager of the mission, Juan Pérez—the first witness—enter the room. Guirado heard him declare that Trujillo was responsible for Ysabel's murder. To this comment, Guadalupe Trujillo responded, "It has been done. . . . If [I didn't] defend myself, the *india* would have killed me. And also, at the time she launched her attack against me, with the knife in hand, I managed to take hold of it and to remove it from her grasp."[12]

Guirado then informed the judge about details he knew concerning the incident that he had learned secondhand. (In the Mexican court system and Spanish civil law, hearsay was acceptable as testimony.) Francisco Villa, another field worker at the mission, told him about a rumor concerning Ysabel's death. Villa had overheard the story as it circulated among Indian workers at the mission. According to the rumor, the fight had begun when Ysabel slandered Trujillo's honor. Slurs against one's honor, observes historian Ramón Gutiérrez, constituted "the fiercest fighting words" that could be uttered.[13] The Indians also claimed that Trujillo had used the weight of her body to pin Ysabel to the floor and used her knee to hold Ysabel down while she called to her young daughter to bring her a knife from the kitchen cupboard. Guirado continued his testimony by recounting what another field worker at the mission, Tiburcio López, had informed him about the incident. While standing near an open window at the mission to light a cigarette, López told Guirado, he had overheard Ysabel exclaim in fear, "*No me mates hermana Guadalupe*" (Don't kill me, sister Guadalupe). As he turned to see the source of this cry, he witnessed Trujillo stabbing Ysabel in the neck. "What are you doing?" he yelled to Trujillo. "Go to hell," she retorted. López told Guirado that the scene had so startled him that he left the two women, rather than intervene in the scuffle or assist the victim.[14]

Guirado's testimony indicated that Ysabel's insolence had provoked the fight, thus refuting the idea that Trujillo had premeditated the murder. However, the hearsay evidence he presented on behalf of the Indians, Villa and López, not only placed blame on Trujillo for Ysabel's death but also suggested that Trujillo had callously murdered Ysabel, adding credence to the prosecution's contention that Trujillo had used more than self-defensive measures in killing Ysabel. In other words, Trujillo had planned the murder.

In addition to the manager's and field workers' testimony, Tiburcio López and Francisco Villa furnished their own accounts to the court. López supported Guirado's story that he had heard sounds of a fight coming through an open window of the mission. However, he had not heard Ysabel cry, "Don't kill me, sister Guadalupe." Instead, he claimed to hear Trujillo yell, "Is there not a Christian of God to save me?" Francisco Villa's statements before the judge also raised doubts about Guirado's testimony. Villa denied hearing or knowing anything about the incident. He admitted hearing talk among the Indians but, as he told the judge, he had no interest in their conversations. He only knew that Ysabel had died.[15]

Next, Antonio Arce, a transient from Loreto, Baja California, testified. "About eleven in the morning," he stated, "I went out to light a cigarette with the flame coming from a fire in front of Trujillo's home. At that moment," he continued, "I saw Trujillo come out, looking devastated, and she said to me, 'What do you say, Don Antonio, about what has happened to me with this *india*?' " Arce asked her to explain herself. "Look for yourself, look for yourself," she repeated, and then asked him to find the priest. Arce said that he then noticed blood on her hand and "calculated that a tragedy [*desgracia*] had occurred." He immediately went to get the priest and at that moment the padre arrived with Bernardo Guirado, the witness who had testified earlier. Arce's testimony, while insightful, provided no further clues as to motives behind the murder. The lack of an eyewitness other than Trujillo, who would testify last, only helped to obfuscate the facts surrounding the case and perhaps supported the defense's stance of self-defense.[16]

At the behest of Guadalupe Trujillo's husband, Antonio José Quintana, two former New Mexicans—Santiago Chacon and Miguel García—testified that Ysabel had lived a scandalous life in New Mexico. Quintana wanted the men to tell the court that Ysabel had committed an infanticide in New Mexico so as to tarnish her maternal instincts, humanity, and loyalty, traits that the court and the *gente de razón* at large expected of a woman and a servant. When the court interrogated the two men, they confirmed Quintana's allegations. Quintana also had another witness—Juan Pérez—inform the court that he knew of Ysabel's covert plan to leave the household. A fourth and final witness, Antonio Valenzuela, confirmed the assertion that Ysabel had been seduced by another man who had plotted to take her from San Gabriel. Clearly, Quintana's ploy was to characterize her as a depraved Indian woman and to remind the court of her lowly social position. The New Mexicans' testimony gave Trujillo's defense more ammunition on which to draw in their portrayal of Ysabel as the aggressive Indian servant who had stepped out of line when she challenged her master's orders.[17]

Finally, Guadalupe Trujillo, the only available eyewitness, testified on her own behalf. She claimed that Ysabel had become quite quarrelsome during the past few months. On the morning of the incident, Ysabel had refused to complete her domestic chores and announced, "I am leaving the household." Trujillo had immediately retorted, "You are not free to go anywhere because I have raised you since you were a child." "I am, too, free," Ysabel countered. Trujillo had then used physical force to get Ysabel to obey. Ysabel grabbed a knife from the kitchen and threatened to use it. Alarmed, Trujillo asked, "What are you doing with that knife?" "You'll see," Ysabel responded. Trujillo tried to take the knife away, and in the ensuing struggle the knife lodged itself in Ysabel's body. Trujillo called to her young daughter to find help. Trujillo told the judge she could not remember the details of the incident because she had become quite upset by what had transpired.

Trujillo sought to dispel any notion that her relationship with Ysabel had been stormy until the incident itself. She described their relations in language that drew upon a discourse of sisterhood and family unity. "I have always seen [Ysabel] as a sister," she told the judge, ". . . and I feel deeply for what I did. She was my father's orphan . . . and he gave her to me so that we would recognize each other as sisters."

The judge expressed skepticism.[18] "What do you have to say about causing the death of a woman whom you considered as a sister?"

"I killed her in *defensa propia* (self-defense) and without prior thought," she replied.

"How is it you killed her in self-defense? You took the knife away from the deceased and so wasn't the death unnecessary?"

"I took the knife away from her with the intent to throw it away, but I struck her, and I don't know," Trujillo explained.

"How do you not know how you struck her? The wound was such that it was done intentionally."

Trujillo tried to explain that Ysabel had her by the hair and she could not see what was happening, but the judge persisted.

"What do you have to say about using an illegal weapon in the act?" he asked.

"[I] didn't have it in the first place, the one who used it was [Ysabel], [I] took it from her to throw it away," she responded.

"Did you knowingly provoke the situation when you pushed Ysabel?"

"[I] didn't provoke her; what I wanted to do was to get her inside in order to reprimand her in another way," she explained.

"If you had wanted to correct her in another way, why not wait for your husband to do so; he could have used more prudence."

"[I intended] to correct Ysabel, as a mother does a daughter."

While Trujillo had previously informed the court that she had "always seen [Ysabel] as a sister," implying equality, now she characterized their relationship as hierarchical and unequal. Trujillo's conflicting testimony makes it unclear how they saw their roles in the household and in the larger community. Did they see each other as sisters, as Trujillo testified? Or did they perceive their arrangement as a parent–child relationship? While the case records never make clear how they viewed each other, the evidence reveals that their relations were anything but equal.[19]

The judge's interrogation of Trujillo's motives and actions suggests that he considered it improper for her to take the initiative to reprimand Ysabel. Customarily, the head of the household—the patriarch—held the power to govern and to correct members of the family, including any household servants, when they stepped out of line. In the judge's view, Trujillo had violated not only her role as the master but also her gender role in the family. In other words, she had temporarily usurped her husband's position as the family's head and had abused that power.

With the conclusion of the testimony, the prosecution, representing the people of Mexican Alta California, headed by José del Carmen Lugo, and the defense, headed by Vicente Sánchez, presented their arguments. In all likelihood, the trial took place in the home of a private citizen who rented it to the authorities for official affairs, as Los Angeles did not have a courthouse. The prosecutor, Lugo, began by boldly asserting, "On the fifteenth [February 1843], D[oñ]a Guadalupe Trujillo committed a scandalous murder of the unfortunate Indian woman from New Mexico, named Ysabel. It is true," he acknowledged, "that no witnesses appeared to justify the antecedents of such an attempt, but we must determine what occurred from those who manifest their declarations: the prisoner attempts to evade her crime frivolously, despite the existence of a notable contradiction in the [testimony]. Certainly, [s]he who uses vengeance does not do it without forethought but with premeditation." The prosecution declared that "persuasive evidence exists [of Trujillo's deceit and disdain of Ysabel] to prove that Trujillo had a motive to kill Ysabel," and did so at the moment when no one was present. The plea of self-defense, he concluded, was implausible. For her crime, he asked the court to "sentence her to two years of harsh imprisonment." Crimes against Mexicans undoubtedly brought harsher punishment.[20]

The defense attorney, Vicente Sánchez, responded to prosecutor Lugo by arguing that Ysabel had attacked Trujillo with ferocity. Trujillo had merely defended herself, he declared, "as is natural with any living being." She had not committed a scandalous crime but rather a simple homicide, done without prior thought. The defense reminded the court of the testimony of one of the witnesses, Tiburcio López, in which he heard Trujillo exclaim, "Is there not a Christian of God to save me?"—a declaration demonstrating that Trujillo had no choice but to defend herself. He also recalled for the court the word "*impensadamente*" (unintentionally), which Trujillo used to describe how she had killed Ysabel. The defense concluded by emphasizing the obvious—that Trujillo was a "woman of honor and family," a member of the *gente de razón* in the community. He did not have to remind anyone that Ysabel, as an Indian, was not among the *gente de razón*. To be Indian or, more precisely, a *genizara*, a domestic servant pressed into service, was to be without honor, family, or power.[21]

In his rebuttal, prosecutor Lugo directly challenged the defense's "attempt to excuse the severity of [Trujillo's] crime with the statement that she [is] an honorable woman with family." To argue that "she did not commit a crime" because of her position in the community, declared the prosecution, "insults the public." Lugo reminded the court that no member of the community, regardless of his or her social class, ethnicity, or gender, was above the law and justice. The judge agreed, ruling that Trujillo deserved a lengthier sentence than that suggested by the prosecution. On June 1, 1843, after weighing the evidence, he issued the following judgment: "In the criminal case against Guadalupe Trujillo . . . I sentence [Trujillo] to three years . . . in [the presidio of] Sonoma, or where the Superior Tribunal shall determine." While the judge ruled that Trujillo was at fault for killing Ysabel, he did not state whether he believed that she had killed Ysabel in self-defense or had premeditated the murder. Nevertheless, his decision to banish Trujillo to a sparsely populated and remote presidio northeast of Monterey reveals that he did not tolerate her actions. The sentence of banishment, which a contemporary noted was viewed as "equal to a sentence of death," served as a warning to any *gente de razón*, men as well as women, who contemplated taking such measures against their Indian servants.[22]

The judge's decision then passed to the Superior Tribunal of Monterey, an appellate body made up of three members who reviewed capital cases tried in the local courts throughout Mexican Alta California. The tribunal agreed with the Los Angeles local court that Trujillo had committed a crime but disagreed with the sentence that had been given to her. "It has been proven that Guadalupe Trujillo killed her *criada*, and for such an act she deserves punishment; but as the [punishment] should fit the crime and as the crime Trujillo committed was a homicide done in self-defense . . . [we] revoke the sentence of three years of seclusion." Instead of sending Trujillo to Sonoma for three years, the tribunal ordered her to the port of San Diego for one year, allowing her to remain in *pueblo* and in proximity to her family in the San Gabriel–Los Angeles region. While it did not completely excuse her actions, the tribunal officially upheld the claim that Ysabel had instigated the fight and that Trujillo had defended herself.[23]

The tribunal's decision also reveals that it did not share the Los Angeles court's views about Mexican and Indian women's social and family relations. While the local judge believed that Trujillo's transgression of acceptable master–servant standards of behavior deserved three years of banishment, the Superior Tribunal believed otherwise. In the tribunal's view, killing an Indian servant who had attacked a woman *de razón* did not merit such punishment. Nor did the tribunal see the malevolence in Trujillo's actions that was detected by the local court. Put simply, the tribunal overruled the local judge's findings and underlined his attempt to carry out justice, as he interpreted and applied that concept.

The local court's standards were further undermined when Guadalupe Trujillo was set free, though by whom or in what court is unknown, and allowed to return to Los Angeles less than a year after the tribunal's sentence. By the middle of 1844, she was living with her husband, Quintana, and daughter, María, within the *pueblo*'s limits. Apparently, the murder trial and conviction did little harm to their social mobility in the *pueblo*. Within six years, in 1850, the Trujillo-Quintana family had managed to acquire farmland valued at 2,000 pesos, and likely had become self-sufficient farmers. María, now seventeen, had also obtained her own level of social status, as she had married a local farmer from New Mexico who owned land, though worth only half that of the Trujillo-Quintana household. Thus, the family had managed to walk away from the incident relatively unharmed and rebuild their lives, while Ysabel had no doubt been forgotten.[24]

The murder trial of Guadalupe Trujillo has allowed us to explore an instance in which social and family relations between Mexicans and Indians became strained, and to examine the court's institutional role in the conflict in a larger cultural context. As we have seen, Trujillo's and Ysabel's social relations reflected a hierarchical and unequal distribution of power among women in the community. Despite commonalities of gender and patriarchal oppression, differences of socioeconomic status and cultural and racial identity relegated Ysabel, the Indian servant and "slave," to labor for Trujillo. Indeed, as Trujillo and Ysabel's soured relations indicate, women's material reality and cultural and racial identity drew a sharp distinction between Mexicans and Native Americans in the nineteenth century. Indian women labored for the *gente de razón*, and while the latter considered domestic servants as part of the larger household, the servants did not have the same privileges that their social betters enjoyed. The court case made these adversarial roles and relations clear.

The murder trial also reveals that Mexicans, men or women, regardless of social class, were not above the law even when their adversaries were Indian servants. In this case, the court's purpose was clear: to enforce the law and impart justice in the community, in spite of social, class, cultural, or racial considerations. Notwithstanding the local court's conflict with the appellate body and, ultimately, Trujillo's relatively light sentence, the Los Angeles judge's ruling served as a warning to all that such actions as Trujillo's would not be tolerated. To what extent the outcome of this case had an impact on social relations in Mexican Los Angeles is unclear. What is clear is that Mexican–Indian relationships were hierarchical and yet sometimes contested.

Notes

A grant from the Institute of American Cultures, University of California, Los Angeles, made the research for this paper possible. I thank Norris Hundley, Judith Ann Giesberg, Clark Davis and David Igler for their comments and suggestions.

1. Guadalupe Trujillo's trial is found in the *Alcalde Court Records, 1830–1850*, 9 vols. (hereafter cited as *ACR*) 1:1014–31. The collection is held at the Seaver Center for Western History, Natural History Museum of Los Angeles County. The initial proceedings of the case are found in ibid., 1014–22.
2. On the term *gente de razón*, see George Harwood Phillips, "Indians in Los Angeles, 1781–1875: Economic Integration, Social Disintegration," *Pacific Historical Review* 49 (August 1980): 430; and Gloria E. Miranda, "Racial and Cultural Dimensions of Gente de Razón Status in Spanish and Mexican California," *Southern California Quarterly* 70 (Fall 1988): 265–78.
3. Antonio Ríos-Bustamante and Pedro Castillo, *An Illustrated History of Mexican Los Angeles, 1781–1985* (Los Angeles, 1986), 24–25, 33; Lisbeth Haas, *Conquests and Historical Identities in California, 1769–1936* (Berkeley, 1995), 9–44; Douglas Monroy, *Thrown among Strangers: The Making of Mexican Culture in Frontier California* (Berkeley, 1990), 18–50; David J. Weber, *The Spanish Frontier in North America* (New Haven, 1992), 307; William Mason, "Indian and Mexican Cultural Exchange in the Los Angeles Area, 1781–1834," *Aztlán* 15, no. 1 (Spring 1984): 123–25; Mason, *The Census of 1790: A Demographic History of Colonial California* (Novato, CA, 1998); Miranda, "Racial and Cultural Dimensions of Gente de Razón," 265–78; and Thomas W. Temple, trans. and ed., "Documents Pertaining to the Founding of Los Angeles: Supplies for the Pobladores," *Historical Society of Southern California Quarterly* 15 (1931): 121–34.
4. The sources consulted for the discussion of Gabrieleños include William McCawley, *The First Angelinos: The Gabrielino Indians of Los Angeles* (Banning, CA, 1996); A. L. Kroeber, "Elements of Culture in Native California," in R. F. Heizer and M. A. Whipple, comps. and eds., *The California Indians* (Berkeley, 1965), 1–67; Sherburne F. Cook, *The Conflict between the California Indians and White Civilization* (Berkeley, 1976); and Phillips, "Indians in Los Angeles, 1781–1875," 427–51.
5. See Suggested Readings.
6. This analysis of Mexican and Native American women's relations builds on the work of Antonia I. Castañeda, including "Presidarias y Pobladoras: Spanish-Mexican Women in Frontier Monterey, Alta California, 1770–1821" (Ph.D. diss., Stanford University, 1990); and "Sexual Violence in the Politics and Policies of Conquest: Amerindian Women and the Spanish Conquest of Alta California," in Adela da la Torre and Beatríz M. Pesquera, eds. (Berkeley, 1993), 15–33. Some of the ideas developed in this essay are drawn from Karen Halttunen, " 'Domestic Differences': Competing Narratives of Womanhood in the Murder Trial of Lucretia Chapman," in Shirley Samuels, ed., *The Culture of Sentiment: Race, Gender, and Sentimentality in Nineteenth-Century America* (New York, 1992), 43; Richard Wightman Fox, "Intimacy on Trial: Cultural Meanings of the Beecher-Tilton Affair," 103–34, in Fox and T. J. Jackson Lears, eds., *The Power of Culture: Critical Essays in American History* (Chicago, 1993).
7. Hubert H. Bancroft, *History of California* (San Francisco, 1886), 3:395; ibid., 4:276–78.
8. For more information about Trujillo and her family, see "Padrón 1844," *Los Angeles City Archives*, 3:666–801, City of Los Angeles, Records Management Division, C. Erwin Piper Technical Bldg., Los Angeles, California. See also Warren A. Beck and Ynez D. Haase, *Historical Atlas of New Mexico* (Norman, OK, 1979), 20.
9. Ramón Gutiérrez, *When Jesus Came, the Corn Mothers Went Away: Marriage, Sexuality, and Power in New Mexico, 1500–1846* (Stanford, 1991), 149–56, 176–94.
10. Mission San Gabriel was secularized in 1833.
11. *ACR*, 1:1024–31.
12. Ibid., 1026.
13. Gutiérrez, *When Jesus Came, the Corn Mothers Went Away*, 205–6.
14. *ACR*, 1.1032 36.
15. Ibid., 1046–57.

16. Ibid., 1037–41.
17. Ibid., 1058–68.
18. Ibid., 1068–76.
19. Ibid., 1085–90.
20. Ibid., 1093–95.
21. Gutiérrez, *When Jesus Came, the Corn Mothers Went Away*, 205; *ACR*, 1:1099–1103.
22. Quote cited in *The Los Angeles Prefecture Records*, Los Angeles City Archives, Los Angeles, California, book l, part 1:112, 533, 613 (1841). See also *ACR*, 1:1108–9.
23. *ACR*, 1110–13.
24. See "Padrón 1844"; and Maurice H. Newmark and Marco R. Newmark, eds., *Census of the City and County of Los Angeles, California, for the Year 1850* (Los Angeles, 1929), 94.

8

To Earn Her Daily Bread
Housework and Antebellum Working-Class Subsistence

Jeanne Boydston

In 1845, in a volume entitled *The Sanitary Condition of the Laboring Population of New York*, former city health inspector John H. Griscom published his observations on the health of New York City's working poor. He sketched a bleak scene. Forced into crowded, tinder-box tenements that lacked adequate light or ventilation, and subjected daily to the waste that leached in from streets, outhouses, and animal yards, the laboring classes seemed to Griscom bound for extinction.[1]

Middle-class reformers such as Griscom tended to raise these specters as a way of deploring the alleged sloth and intemperance of the poor, rather than as a means of examining the economy that created the poverty.[2] Nevertheless, the conditions they so vividly documented have remained a subject of special interest to American historians, for these were the transitional generations—the households that lived the lurching transformations toward wage dependency. By the late 1870s, the number of people working solely for wages in manufacturing, construction, and transportation alone was almost equivalent to the size of the entire population in 1790.[3] The strategies that enabled working-class households to survive the intervening period tell us much, not only about the making of the American working classes, but, equally important, about the making of American industrial capitalism itself.

Historians have generally described the coming of industrialization in terms of changes in paid work. The transformation has been framed as one from a community of comparatively independent producers to a class of wage workers, forced for their survival to sell labor as a commodity on the capitalist market. This approach defines the problem of antebellum working-class subsistence as a question of pay. Wages are taken to correspond to "means of support" along the lines of Paul Faler's conclusion that by 1830 Lynn shoemakers "were full time wage earners with no important means of support other than . . . their income from shoemaking."[4]

Certainly, this emphasis reflects the way in which paid workers themselves formulated the problem of household survival. When the Philadelphia cordwainers complained in 1805 that the "pittance of subsistence" they received in wages was inadequate to provide "a fair and just support for our families," they expressed a conflation of "subsistence" and "wages" that was common among antebellum wage earners.[5] The clearest and most consistent statement of that conflation was in the growing insistence upon a "family wage." The "family wage," a wage for husbands high enough to eliminate the need for daughters and wives to work for pay, was based on an assumption that cash income constituted the entirety of the family subsistence: a "family wage" to the male head would, workingmen insisted, permit the mechanic to provide "a livelihood for himself and [his family]" from his "earnings" alone.[6]

Nevertheless, recent work in American social history suggests that this strict equation of wages with "means of support" does not accurately describe the range of strategies through which the nineteenth-century working classes pieced together their livelihoods. Christine Stansell has pointed to the importance of casual labor—"peddling, scavenging, and the shadier arts of theft and prostitution"—in "making ends meet" in the households of the laboring poor in mid-nineteenth-century New York City.[7] Judith E. Smith has noted the dense networks of resource sharing (including the sharing of food) that existed among immigrant families in turn-of-the-century Providence, Rhode Island.[8] Examining the grassroots politics of socialism in early-twentieth-century New York City, Dana Frank has demonstrated the power of housewives, in their work as shoppers, to force down food prices through community-based boycotts.[9] Each of these studies offers a vision of a survival economy based not solely on the cash income of waged labor, but on a far larger and more intricate fabric of resources.

In this essay, I will argue that the antebellum working classes did indeed rely for their subsistence upon means of support other than their wages. Among the key economic resources of antebellum working-class households was housework itself—the unwaged (although not always unremunerated) labor that wives performed within their own families. Working-class women understood their obligations as mothers and wives to extend from such unpaid labor as child rearing, cooking, and cleaning to such casualized forms of cash earning as taking in boarders and vending. In the course of this work, their labor represented a substantial economic benefit—both to their families and to the employers who paid their husbands' wages. Within the household, wives' labor produced as much as half of the family subsistence. Beyond the household, the value of housework accrued to the owners of mills and factories and shops, who were able to pay "subsistence" wages at levels that in fact represented only a fraction of the real price of workers' survival.

The distinctive value of housewives' labor lies largely unrecognized in the traditional Marxist analysis that has informed so much of the study of working-class history. This results from the way in which Marx formulated the concept of "means of subsistence." Marx defined "subsistence" as "the labour time necessary for the production [and reproduction] of labour power"—that is, the labor time required to ensure the survival of the wage earner both from day to day and from generation to generation.[10] But Marx assumed that the working class bought its entire subsistence on the market, with cash. In his discussion of the sale of labor power, for example, he identified "the means of subsistence" as "articles" that "must be bought or paid for," some "every day, others every week, others every quarter and so on."[11] He mentioned food, fuel, clothing, and furniture as examples. Having thus conceptually limited "subsistence" to what had to be purchased with income, Marx made a parallel limitation of the concept of "necessary labour-time" to labor time that earned money.

Limiting the definition of subsistence to that which had to be purchased with cash was a convenience for Marx, whose focus was on the potential of money to obscure inequalities in the buying and selling of labor. He reasoned that the price of labor, the wage, represented very different values to the worker and to the capitalist. The worker received the cost of subsistence; the capitalist purchased all that labor could produce in a given period of time. As the capitalist was able to increase the value labor produced over the cost of keeping labor alive, he gained for himself a "surplus value" that was the origin of new capital. Formulated in this way, the cash exchange—money, with its "inherent" "possibility . . . of a quantitative incongruity between price and magnitude of value"—became key to Marx's analysis.[12]

Marx was not entirely consistent in this formulation, however. One sometimes glimpses in *Capital* his own acknowledgment of the limitations of his analysis. His original definition of the value of labor power as "the labour-time necessary for the production, and consequently also the reproduction" of labor in no way excludes the labor time required to search the docks or borrow food in a period of shortage, for example.[13] At one point, moreover, he defined "subsistence" as the variety of resources "physically indispensable" to survival.[14] This definition might well include the labor of processing food into a digestible state, of nursing the sick back to health, and of tending small children—all of this routine in the labor of working-class housework. Finally, in his analysis of surplus value, Marx acknowledged that the wage might not always represent the value of subsistence. The capitalist could increase his margin of surplus value "by pushing the wage of the worker down below the value of his labour-power"—that is, below subsistence level.[15] This was not a mere hypothetical possibility for Marx, who acknowledged "the important part which this method plays in practice." But he found himself "excluded from considering it here by our assumption that all commodities, including labour-power, are bought and sold at their full value."[16]

Housework, however, was not bought and sold at its full value. Indeed, it was not bought and sold at all, but rather was exchanged directly for subsistence, in the manner of barter, within the family. Nonetheless, the cooking and cleaning, scavenging and borrowing, nursing and mending and child rearing that made up housework was clearly necessary to produce a husband's labor power. In other words, it was constituent in the total labor time represented by the commodity—labor power—the husband would sell on the market. At one point in his discussion of money, Marx noted that the *quantitative* contradiction expressed by the price could also become a *qualitative* one—that "a thing can, formally speaking, have a price without having a value."[17] The history of housework had left this labor in just the opposite position: It had a value without having a price. This distinguished housework from the forms of labor Marx was examining, but it did not exclude it from the process through which the surplus value of industrial capitalism was realized.

Indeed, for the northwestern United States at least, evidence suggests that the denial of the economic worth of housework was a historical process integral to the development of industrial capitalism.[18] The Europeans who settled the region in the seventeenth century appear to have recognized the economic contribution of wives' work. A largely subsistence-oriented people, New England Puritans defined the household as the "economical society" and understood that family survival required the wife's work in the garden, the barnyard, and the larder as much as it required the husband's work in the fields and meadows and barn.[19] Court records bear testimony to the perceived importance of wives' labor, in the form of actions to overturn a husband's will when magistrates concluded that the wife's share did not accurately reflect her "diligence and industry" in "the getting of the Estate."[20]

At the same time, colonial society contained the ideological foundations for later denial of the economic worth of wives' labor. As ministers reminded women, husbands—not wives—were the public representatives of the household: "Our Ribs were not ordained to be our Rulers."[21] Wives' subordination was embedded in the English common law that the Puritans brought with them to New England. As *feme covert*, a wife's legal identity was subsumed under that of her husband, who was recognized as the owner of her labor time, the products of that labor time, and any cash realized from the sale of either the labor or its products. However much individual males acknowledged individual wives' economic worth, the tradition of law identified that worth with the husband. Thus, Marx's assumption throughout *Capital* that the "possessor" of labor power and "the person whose labour-power it is" were one and the same person was historically inaccurate for housework in America from the beginning of English settlement.[22]

Mediated early on by the local nature of economic activity, wives' coverture became a more critical factor in the history of housework during the eighteenth century. Over the course of that century, the elaboration of cash markets and the growing competition among males for wages and property served to enhance the importance of money as a primary socially recognized index of economic worth. In public discussions of the economy, that is to say, industriousness was increasingly associated with moneymaking, while work that did not bring cash payment came scarcely to be recognized as work at all. This changing perception applied even to discussions of farming, still a largely subsistence-oriented activity. As Jared Eliot contended, the absence of a cash market "tends to enervate and abate the Vigor and Zeal" of the farmer and "renders him Indolent."[23] Working for the most part without prospect of payment, and unable to lay legal claim to payment even when it was made, the prototype of the free worker who labored outside of the cash marketplace was the wife.

This is not to say that wives never sold their labor, or the products of their labor, directly for cash.[24] But wives' formal relationship to the market remained ambiguous at best—as men's was not. Over the course of the eighteenth century, as the importance of cash markets increased, the absence of a formal relationship with those markets rendered women *as a group* less visible as participants in and contributors to the economy. Remunerated or not, their labor was conceptually subsumed under the labor of the person who owned it, their husbands. Laurel Thatcher Ulrich has suggested that by the mid-eighteenth century, the husband who would acknowledge the individuality of his wife's paid labor (as distinct from his own claim as head of household) was a rare exception.[25]

The growing equation of cash with economic value created for women palpable contradictions between experience and ideology. At a time when even the comparatively prosperous Esther Edwards Burr numbered among her labors cooking, cleaning, baking, seeing to her family's provision of vegetables, fruits, beverages, and dairy products, whitewashing walls, spinning, raising two children, covering chair bottoms, and making, remaking, and mending clothes,[26] colonial newspapers taunted that wives "want[ed] sense, and every kind of duty" and spent their time "more trifling than a baby."[27] From merely "owning" the family labor pool, husbands had now been ideologically identified as the *whole* of the family labor pool.

But the growing cultural invisibility of the economic value of the wife's labor in the family was not limited to the well-off. Indeed, by the end of the eighteenth century, the material conditions of survival in poor households provided a solid foundation, within the experience of working-class families themselves, for this new conception of the relation of men's paid labor or household support. As Ruth Schwartz Cowan has argued, one of the first effects of the coming of industrialization was the removal of men's labor from the household.[28] As poorer families could no longer provide land to their sons and as the growing power of masters and retailing middlemen undercut the traditional lines of advancement for journeymen in the trades, men experienced a dislocation in their ability to provide their share of the household maintenance. Under economic siege in the provision of their traditional portion of the family's subsistence, working-class men responded by conflating that part with the whole of the family economy. Certainly this conflation was made easier by the general and growing invisibility of the economic value of housework among the middle classes. But working-class men appear to have first expressed the conflation in the course of attempting to articulate and protest changes in the nature and status of their own labor. Like the Philadelphia cordwainers, early-nineteenth-century journeymen hatters complained that the erosion of the apprenticeship system was preventing them from "gain[ing] an honest livelihood for themselves and families," and the seamen who gathered at New York's City Hall to protest the Embargo Act in 1808 sought "wages which may enable them to support their families."[29]

Similarly, it was in this context that the demand for the family wage was forged; as Martha May has observed, workingmen recognized that under existing conditions, "the working-class family would be unable to maintain a tolerable standard of living or retain its customs and traditions."[30] But in the context of a society in which men's "ownership" of the family labor time had already been transformed into a perception that men were the only laborers in the family economy, the "family wage" ideal worked to reinforce the invisibility of the wife's contribution. As workingmen searched for a language through which to express concretely the brutalization of the paid workplace and the deterioration of their standard of living, the "family wage" ideal incorporated an ideal of female domesticity, including a distinction between women's household activities and economic labor. Workingmen's newspapers contrasted the "odious, cruel, unjust and tyrannical system" of the factory to the rejuvenative powers of the home.[31] *The Northern Star and Freeman's Advocate* agreed: "It is in the calm and quiet retreat of domestic life that relaxation from toil is obtained."[32] Early trade unionist William Sylvis waxed sentimental about the charm of women's mission:

> To guide the tottering footsteps of tender infancy in the paths of rectitude and virtue, to smooth down the wrinkles of our perverse nature, to weep over our shortcomings, and make us glad in the days of our adversity, to counsel, and console us in our declining years.[33]

In working-class as well as middle-class representations, counsel, comfort, and consolation had become the products of women's labor in the home.

Behind the rhetoric of female domesticity, however, antebellum working-class wives continued to engage in a complex array of subsistence-producing labor. They worked primarily as unpaid laborers in the family, where their work was of two general types. On the first level, wives (as well as children) were responsible for finding ways to increase the household provisions without spending cash. The most common form of this labor was scavenging—for food, for discarded clothing, for household implements, and for fuel. On the outskirts of cities and in smaller communities, wives and daughters collected bullrushes (which could be used to make chair bottoms), cattails (which could be used to stuff mattresses), and broom straw.[34] In the cities, women of the laboring poor haunted docks and wharves in search of damaged goods, and examined the refuse of the streets and marketplaces for food, cloth, or furniture that would be useful to their families.

Often carried out as an entirely legal enterprise, in practice the work of scavenging sometimes shaded into theft, another of the strategies through which families of the laboring poor added to their larders.[35] Throughout the antebellum period, both black and white women appeared in court to face charges of the theft of common and basic household implements: washtubs, frying pans, kettles, clothing, and other items that seem destined not for resale but for immediate consumption. When Mary Brennan stole a $3 pair of shoes from Percy S. White in 1841, "[s]he assigned her great destitution as the sole cause of the theft."[36]

Among more prosperous working-class families, shopping, household manufacturing, and gardening also functioned as means of avoiding cash outlays. Food bought in quantity was cheaper; grown in a garden, it was virtually free.[37] While the labor of gardening was often shared among family members, by the antebellum period marketing (which men had often done in earlier times) was women's work. In addition, some women continued to manufacture their own candles and make their own soap, and most women manufactured mattresses, pillows, linen, curtains, and clothing, and repaired furniture and garments.

Working-class wives worked not only to avoid spending money altogether, but also to reduce the size of necessary expenditures. Important for both of these ends was the maintenance of friendly contacts with neighbors, to whom one might turn for goods or services either as a regular supplement to one's own belongings or in periods of emergency. New to a building, neighborhood, or community, a woman depended upon her peers for information on the cheapest places to shop, the grocers least likely to cheat on weights and prices, and the likely spots for scavenging. Amicable relations with one's neighbors could yield someone to sit with a sick child or a friend from whom to borrow a pot or a few pieces of coal. In the event of fire, women often found that it was neighboring females who "exerted themselves in removing goods and furniture, and also in passing water" through the bucket brigade.[38] A history of friendly relations motivated one woman "to [go] herself to Whitehall after a load [of wood provided as public support], and   to see it delivered" when her neighbor's family was in danger of going without heat.[39]

Scarcity created tensions between cooperation and competition that required careful calculation. Boston's Mary Pepper complained that a neighbor had her run in as a drunk for no other reason than to get her evicted: "An its all along of your wanting my little place becaise ye cant pay the rent for your own," she charged.[40] Pepper was a single mother, responsible for the entirety of the household economy. Perhaps she had not had time to develop the bonds of mutual aid and obligation that might have prompted her neighbors to protect rather than complain of her. On the other hand, perhaps no amount of friendliness could have overridden a neighbor's need for her apartment. Indeed, Pepper herself may have acquired it by similar means.

Working-class wives also provided the bulk of the labor necessary to transform raw materials into items that the family could consume. That is to say, they hauled coal and wood, laid fires, and cooked the raw cornmeal, beans, onions, potatoes, and occasional meat that comprised the mainstay of working-class diets. Among working-class households able to afford cloth, wives made many of the family's garments and linens. Where clothing was scavenged and/or handed down, wives did the mending, the lengthening, the letting out and taking in. They lugged water into the dwelling—or else they carried laundry out—so that the family clothing could be washed. They carried the garbage from the building—or, more convenient and less backbreaking, sometimes simply threw it out of a window onto the streets.

Poverty simplified this labor. Since there was seldom enough money to buy food ahead or in large quantities, poorer wives spent relatively less time than middle-class wives in either food preparation or preservation. A table, a chair, some blankets and rags for mattresses, a cooking pot, and a few utensils might well constitute the sum of the household furnishings, requiring little of the general upkeep that occupied so much of the time of wives in wealthier families or even in more prosperous working-class households. Among the working poor, providing warmth, food, and clothing took precedence over providing a scrubbed and scoured environment. Moreover, exacting standards of cleanliness were to little avail in city tenant houses in which there were no outlets for the soot and fumes of cooking and into which water might run "at every storm."[41]

It was not uncommon for working-class wives also to be responsible for bringing some cash into the household economy. The regularity of this labor varied from household to household, depending not only on the size but also on the reliability of the husband's wage packet. Facing systemic economic hardship, married black women were more likely to undertake regular outside work as cooks, nurses, washerwomen, and maids. (Among whites, paid domestic service was commonly limited to single women.) Both black and white married women became seamstresses. Both sometimes became street vendors. If they lacked the 25-cents-a-day fee to rent a market stall, then from sidewalks and carts they hawked roots and herbs they had dug themselves, or fruits, vegetables, candy, eggs, peanuts, coffee, or chocolate.[42] Some women collected rags to sell to paper manufacturers, "poking into the gutters after rags before the stars go to bed."[43] If their husbands had employment building canals and railroads, wives sometimes took jobs for a season as cooks and laundresses for the entire work camp.[44]

But much of the cash earning of working-class wives was even less visible than these examples suggest. Virtually every wife whose husband worked in close proximity to the household (be he a tailor or a tavern keeper) was expected to contribute labor as his assistant. In this capacity, her portion of the labor was seldom distinguished by a separate wage or fees paid directly in her name. Rather, her work was subsumed under her husband's pay, or absorbed into an enterprise identified as exclusively his. For example, it was only in the course of a criminal prosecution in 1841 that it became clear on the record that John Cronin's wife "generally tended the junk shop" that bore his name.[45] Equally invisible was the cash that women earned by taking boarders into the household. In this instance, they exchanged their labor as cooks and maids, and sometimes as washerwomen and seamstresses, for a payment to the household. Virtually indistinguishable in nature from the labor they performed for free for their families, and enmeshed in that work in the course of the daily routine, boarding could nonetheless add as much as $3 or $4 a week to the household budget.

Through all of this, wives also took primary responsibility for nursing elderly or sick household members and for child rearing. In the conditions of the nineteenth-century city, the latter was a responsibility that brought special anxieties. The dangers of the city to children were legion—fires, horses running out of control, unmarked wells, unfenced piers, and disease, as well as temptations to theft and prostitution as means of making some money. In families where the household economy required that the mother or children go out to work, or that the mother focus her attention on needlework, for example, within the household, close supervision was impossible. This is not to suggest, as did the middle-class reformers of the period, that these parents were negligent. Within the demand for the family wage, and for working-class female domesticity, was a demand for a household in which children could be protected and better cared for. Wage-earning men longed for the day when "our wives, no longer doomed to servile labor, will be . . . the instructors of our children."[46]

The distinction between "paid labor" and "housework" implied in working-class men's yearning for the domestic ideal persisted in later-nineteenth-century analyses of women's unpaid labor and was eventually replicated in *Capital*. Because wives' work was largely unpaid, and because husbands came to the marketplace as the "possessors" of their wives' labor, Marx did not address the role of housework in the labor exchange that led to surplus value. Neither did he attend to the dynamics that permitted the husband to lay claim, in the price of his own labor, to the value of his wife's work.

The exchange value of housework is elusive, but it is not impossible to calculate. Some of it was directly paid, even when done by a wife in the context of her family duties—vending and needlework, for example. But even that labor for which wives were *not* paid when they worked in the context of their own families *was* paid when performed in the context of someone else's family, that is, as domestic service. The equivalence was direct, for in the antebellum period paid domestic service and unpaid housework were the same labor, often performed by the same woman, only in different locations and in different parts of her workday or workweek. Since paid domestic servants were customarily provided with room and board in addition to their wages, moreover, their earnings represented a price over and above food, shelter, and warmth, or, understood as an equivalent for housework, over and above the wife's basic maintenance.

In northeastern cities in 1860, cooks (who frequently also did the laundry) earned between $3 and $4 a week. Seamstresses averaged $2.50 a week, and maids made about the same amount. On the market, caring for children was at the lower end of the pay scale, commanding perhaps $2 a week. Taken at an average, this puts the price of a wife's basic housework at about $3 a week—or $150 a year—excluding the value of her own maintenance.[47]

To this should be added the value of goods a wife might make available within the family for free or at a reduced cost. Among poorer households, this was the labor of scavenging. A rag rug found among the refuse was worth 50 cents, an old coat several dollars. Flour for a week, scooped from a broken barrel on the docks, could save the household almost $1 in cash outlay.[48] When Mary Brennan stole the pair of shoes, she avoided a $3 expenditure (or would have, had she been successful). In these ways, a wife with a good eye and a quick hand might easily save her family $1 a week—or $50 or so over the course of the year.

Not all working-class wives scavenged. In households with more cash, wives were likely to spend that labor time in other forms of purchase-avoidance work. By shopping carefully, buying in bulk, and drying or salting extra food, a wife could save 10 to 50 percent on the family food budget, or about $1 a week on an income of $250 a year.[49] Wives who kept kitchen gardens could, at the very least, produce and preserve potatoes worth 25 cents a week, or some $10 to $15 a year.[50]

But there was also the cash that working-class wives brought into the household—in the form of needlework, vending, taking in boarders, running a grocery or a tavern from her kitchen, or working unpaid in her husband's trade. A boarder might pay $4 a week into the family economy. Subtracting $1.50 for food and rent, the wife's labor time represented $2.50 of that sum, or $130 a year.[51] Needlewomen averaged about $2 a week, or $100 a year.[52] Calculated on the basis of a "helper" in a trade, the wife's time working in her husband's occupation (for example, alongside her shoemaker husband for the equivalent of a day a week) was worth some $20 a year.[53]

The particular labor performed by a given woman depended on the size and resources of her household. In this way, housework remained entirely embedded within the family. Yet we can estimate a general market price of housework by combining the values of the individual activities that made it up: perhaps $150 for cooking, cleaning, laundry, and child rearing, even in poor households another $50 or so saved through scavenging and wise shopping, another $50 or so in cash brought directly into the household. This would set the price of a wife's labor time among the laboring poor at roughly $250 a year beyond maintenance, or in the neighborhood of $400 a year when the price of a single woman's maintenance purchased on the market (about $170 a year) is included. In households with more income, where the wife could focus her labor on saving money and on taking in a full-time boarder, that price might reach over $500 annually, or between $600 and $700 including maintenance.

The shift in the nature of and increase in the value of wives' work as a husband's income increased seems not to have been entirely lost on males, who advised young men that if they meant to get ahead, they should "get married."[54] This difference by income may also further explain the intersection of gender and economic interests that informed working-men's ideal of female domesticity. Women's wages were low—kept that way in part by the rhetoric surrounding the family wage ideal. Given this, a wife working without pay at home may have been more valuable to the family maintenance than a wife working for pay inside or outside the home. Similarly, the low levels of women's wages meant that few women could hope to earn the $170 a year necessary to purchase their maintenance on the market. This was true even for women in industrial work. While a full-time seamstress who earned $2.50 a week and was employed year-round would earn only $130 a year, an Irishwoman with ten years' seniority in the Hamilton mills earned only about $2.90 a week in 1860, or about $150 a year.[55]

Because of her need for access to cash, the wife's dependence on a wage earner within the family was particularly acute. She was not the only member benefiting from the amalgamation of labors that the household represented, however. A single adult male living in New York City in 1860 could scarcely hope to get by on less than $250 a year: $4 a week for room and board ($208 a year) and perhaps $15 a year for minimal clothing meant an outlay of almost $225 before laundry, medicines, and other occasional expenses.[56] Many working-class men did not earn $225 a year, and for them access to the domestic labor of a wife might be the critical variable in achieving maintenance. Even men who did earn this amount might find a clear advantage in marrying, for a wife saved money considerably over and above the cost she added for her own maintenance.

Historians have frequently analyzed the working-class family as a collectivity, run according to a communal ethic. But by both law and custom the marital exchange was not an even one. Finally the husband owned not only the value of his own labor time, but the value of his wife's as well—as expressed, for example, in cash or cooked food, manufactured or mended clothing, scavenged dishes or food, and children raised to an age at which they, too, could contribute to the household economy. There is no evidence that working-class males were prepared to give up the prerogatives of manhood. To the contrary, as we have seen, the rhetoric of the family wage suggests that they were engaged in a historical process of strengthening those claims.

Perhaps it would seem absurd to quibble over who owned the poverty or near-poverty that so often characterized working-class households. There were things to be owned, however, and ownership could prove the determining factor of subsistence or destitution if the household broke up. First, the husband possessed his own maintenance and any improvements in it that became possible as a result of the labor of his wife and children. He also owned whatever furnishings the family had accumulated. Although a table, a chair, clothing, bedding, and a few dishes seem (and were) scant enough property, they were the stuff of which life-and-death transactions were made in the laboring classes; pawned overnight, for example, clothes were important "currency" to cover the rent until payday. The husband also owned the children his wife raised; their wages (when they reached their mid-teens) might amount to several hundred dollars a year—almost as much as his own. Even while they were quite young, children might be helpful in scavenging fuel and food.

To be sure, wives commonly benefited from some or all of these sources of value, and both personal and community norms tended to restrain husbands from taking full advantage of their positions. Not only the affectional bonds of the family, but the expanding cultural emphasis on the husband as the "protector" and "provider" may have helped mediate emotionally the structural inequities of the household.

At the same time, community norms did not prevent the expression of individual self-interest in marriage, and the stresses of material hardship were as likely to rend as to create mutualities of concern. The frequency of incidents in which a wife had her husband arrested for battery and then "discharged at her request" suggests a complex, and less than romantic, dynamic of dependence in antebellum families. The continuing development of cash exchange networks throughout the antebellum period and the relegation of barter largely to domestic transactions had heightened that dynamic. A man could wear dirty clothes or look for cheaper accommodations or eat less to reduce his cash outlay, even if these choices might prove destructive in the long run. But the mariner's wife who stood with her four children on New York's docks, begging her husband for half of his wages, was in a far more extreme position of dependency. Her husband preferred to remain on board ship—with his wages.[57]

Husbands were not the only ones to benefit from the economic value of housework and from its invisibility. Employers were enabled by the presence of this sizeable but uncounted labor in the home to pay both men and women wages that were, in fact, below the level of subsistence. At a time when the level of capital accumulation in the Northeast remained precariously low and when, as a result, most new mills did not survive ten years, the margin of profit available from sub-subsistence wages was crucial.

Occasionally mill owners acknowledged that the wages they paid did not cover maintenance. One agent admitted:

> I regard my work-people just as I regard my machinery. So long as they can do my work *for what I choose to pay them*, I keep them, getting out of them all I can. . . . [H]ow they fare outside my walls I don't know, nor do I consider it my business to know. They must look out for themselves.[58]

More often, however, both capitalists and the political economists who rose in their defense maintained that they did indeed care about their workers, and that the wages they paid represented the true value of the labor they received, including the value of producing that labor. In 1825, for example, John McVickar caused to be reprinted in the United States the *Encyclopaedia Britannica* discussion of political economy, which asserted that "the cost of producing artificers, or labourers, regulates the wages they obtain."[59] Eleven years later, in *Public and Private Economy*, Theodore Sedgwick carried this optimism about the relationship of wages to subsistence one step further—at the same time revealing the dangerous uses to which the belief that wages represented subsistence could be put. Since "a little, a very little only" was required to maintain labor, Sedgwick argued, even at current levels of payment "in the factories of New England, very large numbers [of workers] may annually lay up half their wages; many much more."[60] Presumably wages not only covered but exceeded the value of maintenance. The other shoe would fall, again and again, as employers used the fact of working-class survival to justify further cuts in wages. The value of unpaid housework in mediating those cuts would remain invisible.

Although there is no evidence that capitalists consciously thought of it in this way, it was clearly in the interests of capital for housework to remain invisible. Following the lines of Marx's analysis, some scholars have concluded that, since it was unwaged, housework could not have created surplus value—that there must be a discrete exchange of money for that process to occur. Marx recognized, though, that the nature of the individual transaction was less important than its part in the general movement of capital. In the case of housework, which Marx did not examine, it was the very unwaged character of the labor that made it so profitable to capital. Traded first to the husband for partial subsistence, it then existed in the husband's labor as an element of subsistence made available to capital for free. Indeed, housework had achieved just the reverse of the qualitative contradiction Marx predicted: It had a value without having a price. Excluding the cash that working-class wives brought into the household, housework added several hundred dollars a year to the value of working-class subsistence—several hundred dollars that the employer did not have to pay as a part of the wage packet. Had the labor of housework been counted, wages would have soared to roughly twice their present levels. And as factory and mill owners knew well, "profits must vary inversely as wages, that is, they must fall as wages rise, and rise as wages fall."[61]

It is important to recognize that employers were able to appropriate the value of housework in part because the people they were paying *also* appropriated it. Paid workers protested many things during the antebellum period—long hours, pay cuts, production speedups—but there is no evidence that they objected to the fiction that wages were meant to cover the full value of household maintenance. Indeed, to have questioned that premise would have been to question the very structure of the gender system and of the family as socially constituted in the history of the northeastern United States. In this way, capital's claim to the surplus value of the wife's labor existed through and was dependent upon the husband's claim to that same value. So long as husbands understood their status as men (and so as heads of households) to depend upon the belief that they were the primary, if not the sole, "providers" of the family, the value of housework would remain unacknowledged by—and profitable to—their employers.

The history of industrialization in the United States and elsewhere has been written largely as a history of paid work. Housework, where it has been included at all, has been fitted into the historical scheme merely as an ancillary factor: Family life felt the shock waves of industrialization, but the epicenter of the quake was elsewhere, in the realm of "productive" labor. Marx himself drew the distinction between "productive" and "reproductive" work. He realized, however, as historians since have tended to forget, that the lines between these spheres were artificial: "[E]very social process of production is at the same time a process of reproduction."[62] The case of women's unpaid labor in the antebellum northeastern United States suggests that the opposite is also accurate. Only when we make the changing conditions and relations of housework integral parts of the narrative of economic and social transformation will our telling of the story become complete.

Notes

I would like to thank Betsy Blackmar, Carol Karlsen, Lori Ginzberg, Ileen DeVault, Nancy F. Cott, and the Columbia Seminar on Working-Class History for their helpful criticisms of various drafts of this article. I am also grateful to Rutgers University for its support, through the Henry Rutgers Research Fellowship.

1. John H. Griscom, *The Sanitary Condition of the Laboring Population of New York* (New York: Arno Press, 1970 [1845]).
2. For discussions of the attitudes of middle-class reformers toward the poor in the antebellum period, see Carroll Smith-Rosenberg, *Religion and the Rise of the American City: The New York City Mission Movement, 1812–1870* (Ithaca: Cornell University Press, 1971), and Paul Boyer, *Urban Masses and Moral Order in America, 1820–1920* (Cambridge: Harvard University Press, 1978). For a contemporary example, in addition to Griscom's, see Charles Loring Brace, *The Dangerous Classes of New York, and Twenty Years' Work, among Them* (New York: WynKoop and Hallenbeck, 1872).
3. U.S. Bureau of the Census, *Historical Statistics of the United States, Part I* (Washington, D.C.: United States Government Printing Office, 1975), Series A 6–8, 8, and Series D 167–181, 139.
4. Paul G. Faler, *Mechanics and Manufacturers in the Early Industrial Revolution: Lynn, Massachusetts, 1780–1860* (Albany: State University of New York Press, 1981), 84.
5. "The Address to the Working Shoemakers of the City of Philadelphia to the Public," as quoted in John Commons et al., *History of Labor in the United States* (New York: Macmillan Company, 1918), 1:141–42.
6. As quoted in Martha May, "Bread before Roses: American Workingmen, Labor Unions and the Family Wage," in Ruth Milkman, ed., *Women, Work and Protest: A Century of U.S. Women's Labor History* (Boston: Routledge and Kegan Paul, 1985), 3.
7. Christine Stansell, "Women, Children, and the Uses of the Streets: Class and Gender Conflict in New York City, 1850–1869," *Feminist Studies* 8, 2 (1982): 312–13.
8. Judith E. Smith, "Our Own Kind: Family and Community Networks in Providence," *Radical History Review* 17 (spring 1978): 99–120.
9. Dana Frank, "Housewives, Socialists, and the Politics of Food: The 1917 New York Cost-of-Living Protests," *Feminist Studies* 11, 2 (1985): 255–85.
10. Karl Marx, *Capital*, trans. Ben Fowkes (New York: Vintage Books, 1977), 1:274.
11. Ibid., 1:276.
12. Ibid., 1:196.
13. Ibid., 1:274.
14. Ibid., 1:277.
15. Ibid., 1:431.
16. Ibid., 1:431.
17. Ibid., 1:197.
18. For a more detailed discussion of the transformation of housework as an aspect of industrialization, see Jeanne Boydston, "Home and Work: The Industrialization of Housework in the Northeastern United States from the Colonial Period to the Civil War" (Ph. D. diss., Yale University, 1984).
19. For example, William Perkins gave his 1631 sermon on "oeconomie" the subtitle "Or, Household-Government: A Short Survey of the Right Manner of Erecting and Ordering a Family."
20. William Brigham, *The Compact with the Charter and Laws of the Colony of New Plymouth* (Boston: Dutton and Wentworth, 1836), 281.
21. William Seeker, "*A Wedding Ring for the Finger . . .*" (Boston: Samuel Green, 1690), n.p.
22. See, for example, Marx's discussion of the sale of labor power in *Capital*, 1:271.
23. Jared Eliot, *Essays upon Field Husbandry in New England and Other Papers, 1748–1762*, eds. Harry J. Carman and Rexford G. Tugwell (New York, 1942), as quoted in Richard L. Bushman, *From Puritan to Yankee: Character and the Social Order in Connecticut, 1690–1765* (New York: W. W. Norton and Company, 1967), 26–27.
24. See, for example, Laurel Thatcher Ulrich, " 'A Friendly Neighbor': Social Dimensions of Daily Work in Northern Colonial New England," *Feminist Studies* 6,2 (1980): 392–405; and Joan M. Jensen, "Cloth, Butter and Boarders: Women's Household Production for the Market," *The Review of Radical Political Economics* 12,2 (1980): 14–24.
25. Ulrich, " 'A Friendly Neighbor,' " 394–95.
26. Carol F. Karlsen and Laurie Crumpacker, eds., *The Journal of Esther Edwards Burr, 1754–1757* (New Haven: Yale University Press, 1984).
27. "A-La-Mode, for the Year 1756," *Boston Evening Post*, Supplement, 8 March 1756; "By the Ranger," *Boston Evening Post*, 16 October 1758.
28. Ruth Schwartz Cowan, *More Work for Mother: The Ironies of Household Technology from the Open Hearth to the Microwave* (New York: Basic Books, 1983), 63–67.
29. *American State Papers, 1789–1815*, vol. 2, *Finance* (Washington: Gales and Seaton, 1832), 257; George Daitman, "Labor and the 'Welfare State' in Early New York," *Labor History* 4 (fall 1963): 252.
30. May, "Bread before Roses," 4.
31. *The Man*, 13 May 1835, as quoted in Commons, *History of Labor*, 388.

32. *The Northern Star and Freeman's Advocate*, January 2, 1843.
33. James C. Sylvis, ed., *Life, Speeches, Labors, and Essays of William H. Sylvis* (Philadelphia: Claxton, Remsen, and Haffelfinger, 1872), 120.
34. Susan May Strasser, *Never Done: A History of American Housework* (New York: Pantheon, 1982), 18.
35. For an excellent discussion of the uses of theft as an economic tool among the antebellum laboring poor, see Stansell, "Women, Children, and the Uses of the Streets."
36. For examples, see the *New York Tribune*, 12, 14, 19, and 20 April 1841, and 17 May 1841. The quotation is from 20 April 1841.
37. See below, n. 48.
38. *Boston Evening Transcript*, 20 September 1830.
39. Ezra Stiles Ely, *Visits of Mercy*, 6th ed. (Philadelphia: S. F. Bradford, 1829), 1:88.
40. *Boston Evening Transcript*, 27 July 1830.
41. Griscom, *Sanitary Condition*, 9.
42. See, for example, Solon Robinson, *Hot Corn: Life Scenes in New York Illustrated* (New York: Dewitt and Davenport, 1854), 31; and Thomas F. DeVoe, *The Market Book, Containing a Historical Account of the Public Markets in the Cities of New York, Boston, Philadelphia and Brooklyn* (New York: Burt Franklin, 1862), 370.
43. Robinson, *Hot Corn*, 198.
44. DeVoe, *The Market Book*, 463; Robert Ernst, *Immigrant Life in New York City, 1825–1863* (New York: King's Crown Press, 1949), 66.
45. *New York Tribune*, 22 April 1841.
46. William English, as quoted in Martha May, "Bread before Roses," 5.
47. Wages are from Edger W. Martin, *The Standard of Living in 1860: American Consumption Levels on the Eve of the Civil War* (Chicago: University of Chicago Press, 1942), 177, and Faye E. Dudden, *Serving Women: Household Service in Nineteenth-Century America* (Middletown, Conn.: Wesleyan University Press, 1983), p.149.
48. This is calculated on the basis of an average weekly budget for a working-class family of five, as itemized in the *New York Tribune* in 1851. According to that budget, flour could be bought in bulk at $5 a barrel, a barrel lasting a family of five about eight weeks. Since the *Tribune* budget assumes a family with an annual income over $500 (and therefore able to benefit from the savings of buying in bulk), I have increased the cost by 30 percent. See Norman Ware, *The Industrial Worker, 1840–1860: The Reaction of American Industrial Society to the Advance of the Industrial Revolution* (New York: Quadrangle/The New York Times Book Company, 1974), 33. On savings from buying in bulk, see Griscom, *Sanitary Conditions*, 8. Other cash values are found in Martin, *Standard of Living*, 122, and in Richard Osborn Cummings, *The American and His Food: A History of Food Habits in the United States* (Chicago: University of Chicago Press, 1941), 75.
49. See above, n. 48.
50. Based on figures provided in Ware, *The Industrial Worker*, 33.
51. Martin, *Standard of Living*, 168.
52. Martin, *Standard of Living*, 177.
53. This calculation is based on wages in Carroll D. Wright, *Comparative Wages, Prices, and Cost of Living* (Boston: Wright and Potter Printing Company, 1889), 47, 55. It provides a very conservative index for wives' work; wives frequently had skills far beyond the "helper" level.
54. Grant Thorburn, *Sketches from the Note-book of Lurie Todd* (New York: D. Fanshaw, 1847), 12. Thorburn recommended marriage as a sensible economic decision for young men earning as little as $500 a year—more than males of the laboring poor, but within the range of better-paid workingmen.
55. Thomas Dublin, *Women at Work: The Transformation of Work and Community in Lowell, Massachusetts, 1826–1860* (New York: Columbia University Press, 1979), Table 11.12.
56. See Martin, *Standard of Living*, 168, for the average weekly cost of room and board for a single, adult male living in New York City.
57. Ely, *Visits of Mercy*, 194.
58. Quoted in Ware, *The Industrial Worker*, 77. Emphasis mine.
59. John McVickar, *Outlines of Political Economy* (New York: Wilder and Campbell, 1825), 107.
60. Theodore Sedgwick, *Public and Private Economy* (New York: Harper and Brothers, 1836), 30, 225.
61. McVickar, *Outlines*, 144.
62. Marx, *Capital*, 1:711.

9

The Feminized Civil War

Gender, Northern Popular Literature, and the Memory of War, 1861–1900

Alice Fahs

"What do women know about war?" asked Fleta in the popular Northern story paper the *Flag of Our Union* in January 1865. "What do they *not* know," she answered: "What drop in all the bitter cup have they not tasted?—what ball strikes home on the battle-field that strikes not hearts at the hearthstone as well?" Women knew about war, she argued, "who steadily crush back the blinding tears, and whisper through white, brave lips, 'Go,' " or "who wait in vain for the letter that never comes—who search, with sinking hearts, and eyes dark with anguish, the fearful battlelists." Chastising those who would ask such a question, she concluded, "let the desolate homes, the broken hearts, and the low wail of agony that God hears on his throne, make answer!"[1]

For the anonymous author Fleta, the Civil War occurred not just on the battle-front but also on the Northern home front, where a woman's war of sacrifice and suffering complemented a man's war of fighting. Her impassioned claim to women's knowledge of the war was part of a wide-ranging popular wartime literature that explored white women's domestic war experiences, imagining them as a source of self-knowledge, an education in patriotism, an initiation into the values of work, the occasion for romance, and, increasingly, the cause of unbearable anguish. The feminized Civil War of this article's title refers both to literature featuring women heroines on the Northern home front and to the domestic wartime concerns that such literature highlighted. Written by both men and women, and part of a wartime literature that marked the gender of both men and women, feminized literature often appeared side by side with masculinized literature exploring men's experiences of the war in a popular periodical such as *Harper's Weekly*.[2] Just as battlefield reports, war stories, and personal narratives concentrated on men's experiences of war, an extensive feminized war literature, including stories, essays, poems, articles, novels, broadsides, and cartoons, portrayed women's domestic war experiences as a vital part of the conflict.

Such literature reveals gendered dimensions of wartime culture that have often been invisible to scholars who have concentrated on elites, canonical writers, and Northern intellectuals in writing the cultural history of the war in the North. Not only did feminized war literature insist on the importance of women's contributions to the war effort, but increasingly it argued that women's homefront sufferings were equal to, or even greater than, those of men in battle. White women may have been largely shut out from the combat experience on which men later based their claims to the war's meanings and to national citizenship. Yet in popular literature women's domestic war experiences authorized a claim to participation not only in the war but also in the "imagined community" of the nation.[3]

Inspired by works that identify popular cultural forms as complex expressions of ideology and those that examine women's Civil War experiences, this article argues that popular culture was an important location for representing and exploring the gendered implications of the war. To make this argument, it draws upon nine major popular periodicals that encompass a wide spectrum of Northern wartime publishing. They include two national illustrated weeklies (*Harper's Weekly* and *Frank Leslie's Illustrated Newspaper*); three general-interest family magazines (the *Atlantic Monthly, Harper's New Monthly Magazine,* and the *Continental Monthly*); one of the "cheap" story papers that featured weekly fiction (the *Flag of Our Union*); a religious journal (the *Independent*); and two women's magazines (*Peterson's* and *Arthur's Home Magazine*). Together, they provide a constellation of cultural positions from high to low in the Northern literary marketplace, emphasizing the wide distribution of the feminized literary war.[4]

A closer look at one journal underscores the prevalence of wartime fictions presenting women's experiences of war. *Harper's Weekly* was one of the most popular publications during the war, advertising as early as June 15, 1861, that it had sold 115,000 copies of its previous number. In 1862 the *Weekly* published 46 war stories; of these, 30 featured Northern heroines on the home front, while the 16 remaining stories included first-person accounts of war campaigns by male narrators, stories featuring Southern heroines, and adventurous border stories set in Kentucky and Tennessee. In 1863 the *Weekly* published 41 war stories, with 26 of these featuring Northern heroines on the home front; in 1864 the *Weekly* published 59 war stories, with 34 of these feminized. In short, in this period a preponderance of the *Weekly's* war fiction featured feminized themes.[5]

The literary marketplace did much to create this distinctive woman's war, and this article draws upon recent works in the history of print culture to connect market processes with expressions of gendered nationalism. At the outset of the war the Northern literary marketplace was strikingly feminized in several ways. The dominant form of fiction was the domestic novel, with its simultaneous celebration of women's domestic power and exploration of women's domestic problems and concerns. A substantial female readership provided an audience for such domestic novels and magazine fiction. Midcentury publishing practices, with an emphasis on personal author-publisher relationships and benevolent paternalism, facilitated publication by women authors. Not surprisingly, during the war the literary marketplace supported an outpouring of popular literature portraying women's domestic participation in the war.[6]

While a study of that literature reveals much about the creation of a woman's war, it also has much to tell us about the changing postbellum memory of the war. At the close of the war, the popular literary memory of women's domestic participation in it seemed secure. Indeed, in the late 1860s a stream of novels and omnibus volumes explored Northern women's contributions to the war. Although popular literary interest in the war waned generally during the 1870s, representations of a Northern women's domestic war continued to appear, though less frequently.

But memories of wars are far from static or permanent, and in the 1880s and 1890s major shifts in popular literary representations of the war occurred. The war was reinvented as numerous groups "reclaimed a past of their own creation," to use Tony Horwitz's phrase. Foremost among them was the Grand Army of the Republic (GAR), whose dramatic growth in the 1880s and 1890s fueled publications that stressed the military experience of the war. A masculinized culture of Civil War remembrance focused on the conflict as a war of white "brotherhood," as Theodore Roosevelt put it in 1901, contributing to a nationalizing project of sectional reconciliation that stressed the shared heroism and bravery of white soldiers of "the blue and the gray." At the same time, interest in a woman's war moved south, as novelists and memoirists focused on southern slaveholding women's antebellum and war experiences, contributing to highly racialized "plantation" literature that bathed slavery in a nostalgic glow.[7]

Representations of Northern white women's war experiences became more and more infrequent. A study of six major late-nineteenth-century popular magazines—*Century, Harper's Monthly, McClure's, Ladies' Home Journal, Harper's Weekly*, and the *Atlantic Monthly*—reveals few portrayals of a Northern women's war. While numerous articles and illustrations in popular magazines depicted military aspects of the war, the Northern women's home front war so avidly discussed during the war appeared only sporadically in articles or fiction. If the Civil War in the North had been both a man's and a woman's war in popular literature, it was now increasingly redefined as a man's war only.

This late-nineteenth-century decline of a Northern women's war in popular literature forces us to reconsider the memory of the Civil War in American culture. Although it is often assumed that in the North an understanding of the war that highlighted male heroism and glory dominated popular interpretation of the war during the conflict itself, such masculinization occurred primarily in the 1880s and 1890s, when ideas of what constituted the experience of war narrowed to campaigns and battles. Ironically, the popular memory of the Civil War still follows the contours of late-nineteenth-century masculinized culture. Stephen Crane's 1895 *Red Badge of Courage*, for instance, is still often celebrated as the first realistic depiction of the war. Yet it can be argued that Crane's novel was a new invention of an all-masculine world of war that said far more about the changing social, cultural, and literary climate of the 1890s than about the so-called real war of the 1860s.[8]

Today, as James McPherson has commented, "the huge Civil War constituency . . . outside the ranks of professional historians and the halls of academe" remains interested "mainly if not exclusively in campaigns and battles." A recovery of the feminized Civil War teaches us that this was not always so. Literature exploring Northern women's war experiences was central to popular culture of the war during and immediately after the conflict. Such literature reveals that popular memories of the Civil War were once far wider-ranging and more inclusive than in much of the twentieth century.[9]

Within weeks of the start of war stories and vignettes stressing the vital role of women in the war effort began to appear in newspapers and popular magazines. Articles, illustrations, and stories commented on the importance of women's labor in preparing and packing provisions, sewing uniforms and havelocks (cloth pieces to attach to caps to protect soldiers from the sun), or knitting socks and mittens. The frontispiece of the June 29, 1861, *Harper's Weekly* was an engraving of women "making havelocks for the volunteers." In a poem titled "Stockings and Mittens," the *Weekly* evoked "a thousand needles" that "glisten with the loving of remembering eyes." *Arthur's Home Magazine* commended an "army of the knitters" in militarized language that linked battlefront and home front.[10]

Other writings praised women for supporting men's enlistment, often drawing parallels to the actions of revolutionary mothers. As *Arthur's Home Magazine* commented in November 1861, "our American mother has mused wonderingly over that heroism of Revolutionary times which armed the son, and sent him forth, to fight in the battles of his country. Admiration filled her heart—there was something saintly in the words, 'Our Revolutionary Mothers.' But, she did not feel strong enough for a like trial." Now women were learning to be like their revolutionary forebears: "There are few homes from which has not gone out a son, and few of these in which a reluctant heart is left behind. Our mothers are equal to their high duty, and strong enough for any sacrifice their country, in this hour of its trial, may demand." The *New York Times* approvingly reported an "incident" in a New York store in which "a matronly lady," after helping her son, a "fine youth of about nineteen years," buy his military equipment, remarked, " 'This, my son, is all that I can do. I have given you up to serve your country, and may God go with you! It is all a mother can do,' " Not only was the mother's remark made with "evident emotion," but "tearful eyes followed this patriotic mother and her son, as they departed from the place."[11]

Such emblematic portrayals revealed that at the outset of the war the ideology of republican motherhood shaped images of women's participation in the war. In early wartime feminized literature, women's appropriate role was to sacrifice their sons for the sake of country. But such literature revealed more about the culture of which it was a part than its propagandistic aims might suggest. As Mary Poovey has commented, texts "always produce meanings in excess of what seems to be" their "explicit design." Many of the "excess meanings" of wartime feminized literature involved a distinctive, sentimentalized patriotism.[12]

The "evident emotion" and "tearful eyes" mentioned in the *New York Times* vignette remind us that the Civil War took place within a sentimental culture that valued the expression of feeling and regarded women as the emotive center of the nation. In feminized war literature women's emotions, especially their tears, were often portrayed as giving appropriate value to men's actions, marking the transition of men from the private to the public realm—from home to the service of their country. Virginia F. Townsend's November 1861 war sketches, "Home Pictures of the Times," highlighted the tearful patriotism of women from several walks of life as they learned to sacrifice their men to the war. In one sketch, a mother, "poor and old," put her "feeble arms" around her only son, and "the sobs shook her gray hair." Yet at the son's urgings—"Come now, mother, give me a real, hearty, cheerful good bye"—she "swallowed down her sobs, and drawing down the sunburnt face to her lips, she said, with a tremulous smile, 'God bless you, my precious boy!'"[13]

Such sentimentalized patriotism highlighted the idea that women, especially mothers, personalized the nation, that they linked the private and the public realms. Indeed no sight was "more expressive," affirmed Samuel Osgood in *Harper's Monthly* in 1863, than

> the good mother seated at the window from which floats the household flag, and watching intently the passing regiment, and waving her handkerchief to some friend or kinsman. . . . The sight of her and her daughters brings the whole country nearer to us, and the great continent seems to rise before us in living personality, and to speak with her voice, and to glow with our affections. The nation seems to live in the person of its queen.[14]

For departing soldiers women and home were the most effective connection to the flag and nation. While there was a

> reverence for our flag amounting almost to worship; yet without some human face or word to go with it, the flag is a very insufficient incentive, and the good soldier feels its power far more when he receives the silken banner at the hands of some fair woman. . . . In some way every soldier is enabled to interpret his country by some such personal association, and so give it a place in his fancy and affections, as well as in his reason and conscience.[15]

Women's perceived ability to personalize the flag and therefore the nation also underlay the popularity of John Greenleaf Whittier's 1863 *Atlantic Monthly* ballad "Barbara Frietchie." Based on an apocryphal incident, "Barbara Frietchie" told of an old woman in Frederick, Maryland, who defied Stonewall Jackson by flying the Union flag from her window even after his troops had shot and "rent the banner with seam and gash":

> She leaned far out on the window-sill,
> And shook it forth with a royal will.
> "Shoot, if you must, this old gray head,
> But spare your country's flag," she said.

"Barbara Frietchie" was widely copied in newspapers throughout the North, made into a popular song, and the subject of numerous illustrations.[16]

That women personalized the nation for men was affirmed in a strikingly maternalist literature. Popular poetry imagined mothers as having authority over their sons' enlistment in the war, as in *Harper's Weekly's* March 1862 "Mother, May I Go?," by Horatio Alger Jr.:

> I am eager, anxious, longing to resist my country's foe:
> Shall I go, my dearest mother? tell me, mother, shall I go?

Many popular songs affirmed soldiers' continuing connections to their mothers even when on the battlefield. The popular song "Just Before the Battle, Mother," imagined a soldier's thoughts turning to his mother the night before a battle:

> Just before the battle, Mother,
> I am thinking most of you,
> While upon the field we're watching,
> With the enemy in view
> . . . .
> Farewell, Mother, you may never
> Press me to your heart again;
> But O, you'll not forget me, Mother,
> If I'm number'd with the slain.[17]

From early in the war numerous popular songs imagined a soldier's dying thoughts turning to his mother, including Charles Carroll Sawyer's "Who Will Care For Mother Now?" ("Soon with angels I'll be marching,/With bright laurels on my brow,/I have for my country fallen,/Who will care for mother now?"); and "The Dying Volunteer." A vast home front literature gendered the war by insisting that soldiers' true value could only be made known through their personal connections to women, especially their mothers.[18]

Younger women, too, were important in encouraging men's patriotism, although their role was often imagined as more astringent than nurturing. Prescriptive enlistment fables, poems, songs, and cartoons portrayed young women renouncing and chastising men who refused to enlist, often demonstrating their own earnestness and heroism as they revealed men's cowardice. T. S. Arthur's "Blue Yarn Stockings," published in the December 1861 *Harper's Monthly*, featured a heroine who "drank in with every breath the spirit of heroism and self-sacrifice." When a suitor laughed at her knitting socks for the soldiers, she showed him the door: "If you are not sufficiently inspired with love of country to lift an arm in her defense," Katie Maxwell told her admirer before dismissing him, "don't, I pray you, hinder, with light words even, the feeble service that a weak woman's hands may render. I am not a man, and can not, therefore, fight for liberty and good government; but what I am able to do I am doing from a state of mind that is hurt by levity." Likewise, Kate Sutherland's "The Laggard Recruit," published in *Arthur's Home Magazine* in January 1862, featured two young heroines who shamed an admirer for not enlisting: "If we ladies cannot fight for our country, we can at least organize ourselves into a band of recruiting sergeants, and bring in the lukewarm and the laggards. The test of favor now is courage. Men who stay at home, court our smiles in vain."[19]

Much feminized war literature, whether featuring republican mothers or their daughters, thus imagined women as encouraging, expressing, and valorizing men's patriotism. Robert Westbrook has argued that during World War II the figure of the pinup girl personified "what men were fighting for," part of "the cultural construction of women as objects of obligation" in order to persuade men to fight. Similarly, during the Civil War the figures of the patriotic mother and her daughter became a way of imagining personal obligation to the state.[20]

Figure 9.1. "Shoot, if you must, this old gray head, But spare your country's flag," she said. John Greenleaf Whittier's 1863 poem "Barbara Frietchie," first printed in the *Atlantic Monthly*, was widely popular throughout the North as an emblematic portrayal of women's patriotism. From L. P. Brockett and Mary C. Vaughan, *Woman's Work in the Civil War: A Record of Heroism, Patriotism, and Patience*, 1868. *Courtesy of the University of Michigan's "Making of America" project.*

SCENE, FIFTH AVENUE.

HE. "Ah! Dearest ADDIE! I've succeeded. I've got a Substitute!"
SHE. "Have you? What a curious coincidence! And *I* have found one FOR YOU!"

Figure 9.2. "Scene, Fifth Avenue," *Harper's Weekly*, August 30, 1862. During the war, many pro-enlistment cartoons prescribed women's appropriate wartime roles. *Reproduced with permission of the Library Company of Philadelphia.*

But not all Civil War literature representing the experiences of women construed women simply as vehicles for male patriotism. Differing feminized understandings of the war existed within popular literature, and some works concentrated on the wartime home front experiences of women themselves, finding in them a major drama of the war. Not that such homefront stories eschewed patriotism. Many plots revolved around women's need to learn to sacrifice their men for country, subordinating their own needs to the larger needs of the nation. Yet such stories focused on women's feelings and emotional struggles as a valid, indeed central, story of the war. They were sustained by a literary marketplace in which fiction exploring women's concerns had been a major form of cultural production before the war. Like that antebellum fiction, war literature representing women's experiences drew upon the intertwined languages of sentimentalism and melodrama, with their central assumption that both ordinary and extra-ordinary events were charged with intense emotionality and significance. As Peter Brooks has written, the pervasive nineteenth-century "melodramatic mode" insisted on the "dramatics and excitement discovered within the real," including the emotions of everyday life.[21]

Certainly, magazine fiction focused intently on women's feelings and emotional struggles as an important story of the war. *Harper's Weekly's* October 1861 "Red, White, and Blue" featured a young heroine who reacted with bitter anger when her fiancé told her he had enlisted. "You love your own glory better than you love me!" she accused. Breaking off her engagement, Caroline underwent a "wild, inward war," nursing "an insane sense of wrong, born of her defective education as a woman—of her ignorance." But after her lover's departure for the front, she began changing her reading habits: "on her table now, in place of romances," she put "newspapers and books pertaining to the various struggles for liberty in other countries, and all manner of patriotic addresses." She was "learning a new lesson. It filled her soul with sorrow and perplexity, but it elevated and enlarged it." After she had a patriotic epiphany in church, then waited in agony to hear whether her beloved had survived a battle, her education was complete: when he returned to her, she simply told him, "I was wrong, and you were right; but I sinned through ignorance. Life has wider meanings to me now. This war has been my education." Indeed, she now "put mere personal ends away and flung her sympathies into the common cause."[22]

The idea that war was educational for women dominated numerous similar stories in which women learned that they must sacrifice their personal interests for the sake of the nation. Yet this overt, didactic patriotic lesson was only one lesson of such fiction, which also taught that women's emotions and personal experiences were a central aspect of the conflict and that their sacrifices for the nation might even secure a personal love interest. Some stories depicted women's granting or withholding of love as a life-and-death matter, representing women as having enormous power over men's well-being, whether in battle or in hospital. In "Jessie Underhill's Thanksgiving," published in the December 1862 *Harper's Weekly*, the hero lay "sick, wounded, dying, as I thought"—until hearing that the woman he thought had rejected him loved him. "It was like a draught of immortality, an elixir of life to me," he told her later. "I grew better under the very eyes of the surgeon, who had told me I was a doomed man." The withholding of a woman's love had the opposite effect in "A Leaf from a Summer," published in November 1862. In that story a soldier faced an amputation hopefully because he had a letter from his beloved "next to his heart"; afterward, contrary to the surgeon's expectations, he "began to rally." But after he received a letter telling him that his shallow lover had changed her mind and would not "marry a cripple," the hour quickly came "when they lowered him into the earth, and fired their volleys over him." "His enemy had struck him unarmed and unaware." As such stories revealed, the war only intensified a long-standing literary connection between love and war: Not only was women's love vital to success in war; love itself equaled war in its power to kill men.[23]

By early 1864 war romances had become a staple not just of *Harper's Weekly*—the *Weekly* published 56 in 1862 and 1863—but of other monthlies and story papers. At least one magazine had had enough: In January the new journal the *Round Table* condemned the "so called 'Romances of the War' so much in vogue among magazines and 'story papers' during the two sorry years just past." Such romances, the *Round Table* acerbically commented, had "but one thread of a plot to hang the incidents upon." They began with a heroine initially objecting to a lover's enlistment, "weeping 'bitter tears' upon his coat collar and murmuring—always murmuring—'I cannot spare you *now!*' " After his enlistment there followed news of a battle, in which the hero was "reported killed, or there would be no little wholesome agony to depict." Finally, he miraculously returned so that the plot ended "with a wedding on the part of the couple, and a yawn on the part of the reader." "This tissue of flimsy plot, dreary platitude, and sickly sentiment," the *Round Table* complained, "floods the market of to-day, and gives us a healthy fear of opening most of the popular magazines."[24]

Wartime magazines and story papers continued to publish women's literature, which had been an important part of antebellum culture, with war romances sustained and even nourished by the conflict. Such war romances indicated women's important position in the imagined war—a position far more varied and complex than the *Round Table* critic acknowledged. Not all feminized war stories recounted miraculous returns or hospital-bed weddings. Some began to insist that a central meaning of the war was women's domestic suffering, the price they paid for personalizing the nation for men. In doing so, they constructed a form of citizenship for women that drew heavily upon mid-nineteenth-century American Protestantism, with its promise of salvation through suffering.[25]

Such suffering took several forms. Many writers made it clear that the unbearable passivity of women's role, in which the chief war work allowed them was intense feeling, itself caused enormous suffering. In an editorial titled "Soldiers' Wives," in the November 1862 *New York Ledger*, Fanny Fern (Sara Parton) commented on "what an immense amount of heroism among this class passes unnoticed, or is taken as a matter of course." Writing of the wife of the poor soldier, "who in giving her husband to her country, has given everything," Fern imagined her "as the lagging weeks of suspense creep on, and she stands bravely at her post, keeping want and starvation at bay; imagination busy among the heaps of dead and wounded." When "the history of this war shall be written," Fern concluded, "let the historian, what else soever he may forget, forget not to chronicle this sublime valor of the hearth-stone all over our struggling land."[26]

Many Northern women agreed that women's agonized waiting was a form of wartime valor. Indeed, there was a striking congruence on this point between feminized war stories and some Northern women's letters, which shared a similar sensibility and even style of language. As Elizabeth Boynton of Crawfordsville, Indiana, wrote to her soldier lover in August 1862, "I sometimes think it must seem almost like mockery to you when we talk of *appreciating* the sacrifices you make—We, who are sitting quietly at home."

> True, dear Will, we may not know of, no, not even *dream* of the *horrors* of war, but—oh, we do *know* what *weary waiting* is we *do know* what it is say to our *loved* ones, "go," and with calm brow & cheerful voice, cheer them on to victory, then return to *our lonely, desolate* homes to *wait*—and when I see the pale faces around me I think that perhaps Columbia's sons know not what gifts we lay at the alter of freedom.[27]

Feminized war literature consciously highlighted the "gifts" that women laid on the "alter of freedom." Many stories set up a moral economy in which women's suffering was seen as at least equal to, if not greater than, that of men. The narrator of Louise Chandler Moulton's 1863 "One of Many" claimed that women's domestic suffering, related to the passivity of their wartime role, was greater than the wartime suffering, of men: "Honor to the brave who fight and conquer, or fight and fall! But is theirs the hardest fate? Do not those suffer more who can not lose in action their fear and anguish?—who must count slow hours, shudder at tidings of onward movements, live on fragments of newspapers?"[28]

Other writers set up explicit reciprocities of suffering, between soldiers and those they left behind. If war demanded the ultimate sacrifice—life—from men, then much popular literature argued that it also demanded the same sacrifice from women. A much-repeated trope during the war was that every bullet killed or wounded twice, once on the home front. As the narrator of "One of Many" commented, "is it not true that every bullet shoots double, and the shot which flies farthest makes the sorest wound?" In the anonymous "My Absent Soldier," which appeared in *Harper's Weekly* in May 1862, the narrator imagined that if her husband were killed,

> I could not bear such anguish, love,
>   For all that I could do;
> I know my widowed heart would break,
>   And *I* should perish too!

Likewise in Julia Eugenia Mott's poem "Within a Year," when "the fatal tidings came" of a lover's death, the heroine also died: "she heard it, mutely, and fell forward prone/Upon the floor—so white and deathly still,/With features rigid as the sculptured stone."[29]

The ideas that a soldier's death (or even the possibility of his death) also killed a woman and that a soldier's wound also wounded a woman were treated, not as metaphors, but as literal truths in much popular literature during the war. If, as Elaine Scarry has argued, the wounding and destruction of bodies is a central goal of war, it is also central to claims of participation in war. Certainly, during the Civil War many writers claimed that wounds and their accompanying suffering connected the sufferer to the higher meanings of the war, whether political or religious. The poem "Our Wounded," published in the October 1862 *Continental Monthly*, invoked the "sublimity of suffering":

> Wounded! O sweet-lipped word! for on the page
> Of this strange history, all these scars shall be
> The hieroglyphics of a valiant age,
> Deep writ in freedom's blood-red mystery.

For men it was through wounds, with blood as ink, that the history of the war would be written.[30]

A feminized war literature reversed this formula: Through writing about the war women's own wartime wounds could be claimed. And war killed and wounded women on the home front, this literature argued, even if the injuries were invisible or the causes of death misunderstood. The July 1862 *Harper's Weekly* story "Wounded" presented a husband and wife's discussion of this point. Reading from the newspaper, the husband reported "six hundred and forty-three wounded" in the latest battle; his wife responded, "If that were all!" and when her husband expressed puzzlement, explained, "A great many more were wounded—a great many more." From "every battle-field," she continued, "go swift-winged messengers that kill or wound at a thousand miles instead of a thousand paces; bullets invisible to mortal eyes, that pierce loving hearts. Of the dead and wounded from these we have no report. They are casualties not spoken of by our commanding generals."[31]

A male character in the story elaborated on the gendered difference in wounds, saying that men's "wounds, so ghastly to the eyes, often get no deeper than the flesh and bone. The pain is short, and nature comes quickly to the work of cure with all her healing energies. We suffer for awhile, and then it is over." Women's wounds were more serious and longer lasting, with only a slow healing, and "often through abscess and ulceration. The larger number never entirely recover."[32]

"Our wounded!" the story concluded. "If you would find them all you must look beyond the hospitals."

> They are not every one bearded and in male attire. There sat beside you, in the car just now, a woman. You scarcely noticed her. She left at the corner below. There was not much life in her face; her steps, as they rested on the pavement, were slow. She has been wounded, and is dying. . . . Do you see a face at the window? "In the marblefront house." Yes. "It is sad enough, what in-looking eyes!" Wounded!

Here was a different sort of face than that of the patriotic mother at the window portrayed by Samuel Osgood. Yet that sad face too personalized the nation, the story concluded, and must not be forgotten.[33]

That women's wounds—represented as deeper than those of men—were at the emotional center of the nation was a point made pictorially by Winslow Homer in his June 14, 1862, illustration for *Harper's Weekly* "News from the War." Homer pictured war news in a variety of settings, including soldiers communally reading *Harper's Weekly*; soldiers eagerly reaching for the *Herald* as it was tossed from a newspaper train; a "special artist" from a paper sketching two soldiers; and a soldier delivering news for the staff on horseback. At the still center of all this activity, the point of repose that drew and kept the eye's attention, was a solitary woman seated at her parlor table, bent in agony over a letter held in her left hand. This illustration, simply titled "Wounded," told two stories: not only had she received news of the wounding of a beloved, but she too was now wounded. The icons of domesticity surrounding her—her workbasket on the parlor table, a birdcage in a corner, an ivy vine—only underlined the message that war had invaded Northern homes.[34]

In late 1862 and 1863, as the war became more brutal, more harrowing, Antietam and Fredericksburg began to figure in feminized war stories, registering upon women's consciousness in the dreaded word "killed" in a newspaper. At the same time, some stories began to suggest solutions to a desperate new dilemma: as women did not in fact die when their men died, what should they do with the rest of their lives? In the next few years, solutions emerged in feminized literature involving both an embrace of work outside the home and a newly expansive view of domesticity.

A turn to work concluded Louise Chandler Moulton's July 1863 "One of Many," in which the heroine's beloved died of wounds received at Antietam. After his death, "Margery Dane found her work," the narrator commented. "She is a nurse in a hospital." "I think she will live while her country has need of her, and then she will not be sorry to go to her love and her rest." Striking about this conclusion was that it imagined Margery's life after the loss of a lover, after the loss of domesticity as she had known it. Indeed, it was the death of her lover, and therefore of home as she had imagined it, that triggered her finding "her work."[35]

The connection between the death of a beloved and the turn to work by a middle-class woman also underlay Rose Terry's "A Woman," published in the *Atlantic Monthly* in December 1862. In that story a childish bride, criticized by another character in the story as a "giggling, silly little creature" and a "perfect gosling!" learned to be a "true woman" after the death of her husband in battle. She reassured the narrator that she was not going to die: "If I could, I wouldn't, Sue; for poor father and mother want me, and so will the soldiers by-and-by." Soon "she got admission to the hospitals" and "worked here like a sprite; nothing daunted or disgusted her." By the end of the story she was recognized as a "true heroine" as well as a "true woman."[36] War had allowed her to fulfill her womanhood, even while decimating her home.

As these stories revealed, by late 1862 and 1863 an increasing number of popular articles, illustrations, and stories approved women's nursing, which had been controversial earlier in the war. A two-page illustration titled "Our Women and the War" in the September 6, 1862, issue of *Harper's Weekly* exemplified this shift in opinion: The *Weekly* explained that its picture, featuring two vignettes of nurses, showed "what women may do toward relieving the sorrows and pains of the soldier": "This war of ours has developed scores of Florence Nightingales, whose names no one knows, but whose reward, in the soldier's gratitude and Heaven's approval, is the highest guerdon woman can ever win." Though approving of nursing—indeed, an October 1862 *Harper's Weekly* cartoon now made fun of women too frivolous to nurse—the *Weekly* also suggested that women nurses should be anonymous, with names "no one knows." In contrast, much feminized popular war literature—including, most famously, Louisa May Alcott's 1863 *Hospital Sketches*— placed nurses center stage in the war. Many of these writings made clear that nursing allowed women to be as heroic as soldiers. As the protagonist of Virginia F. Townsend's August 1862 "Hospital Nurse" said, "if I die in this work—why, I shall only follow the noble company of men and women who have sacrificed their lives for their country." The nurse in Bella Z. Spencer's July 1864 "One of the Noble" had just heard of the death of her husband in battle, yet "with a heroism worthy of immortality she carried relief to the suffering, ignoring the suffering in her own heart." When she died, the narrator commented that "America has received no purer or nobler sacrifice than that of her young, unselfish life."[37]

Much popular war literature connected women's wartime suffering, especially the "darkening" of their homes, and their turn to work in order to reconstitute a shattered domesticity. Harriet Beecher Stowe addressed that connection in "The Chimney Corner," published in the *Atlantic Monthly* in January 1865. She "had planned," she wrote to a friend in November 1864, "an article gay & sprightly wholly domestic but as I began & sketched the pleasant home & quiet fireside an irresistable impulse *wrote for me* what followed an offering of sympathy to the suffering & agonized, whose homes have forever been darkened."[38]

Stowe passionately addressed the women whose husbands, sons, or lovers had been killed in the war:

What can we say to you, in those many, many homes where the light has gone out forever? . . . The battle cry goes on, but for you it is passed by! the victory comes, but, oh, never more to bring him back to you! your offering to this great cause has been made, and been taken; you have thrown into it *all* your living, even all that you had, and from henceforth your house is left unto you desolate!

"But is there no consolation?" Stowe asked. In answer, she offered the twin consolations of patriotism and Christianity. "There remains to you a treasure," she told the bereaved mother, "the power to say, 'He died for his country.' In all the good that comes of this anguish you shall have a right and share by virtue of this sacrifice." Equally she offered the consolation of a Christianity that affirmed the "treasures" that "come through sorrow, and sorrow alone."[39]

Recognizing, however, that such consolation did not tell women what to do with the rest of their lives, Stowe urged bereaved women, after a period of suffering she recognized as "natural and inevitable," to seek out benevolent work: "We need but name the service of hospitals, the care and education of the freedmen," and, especially, work among the soldiers. "Ah, we have known mothers bereft of sons in this war, who have seemed at once to open wide their hearts, and to become mothers to every brave soldier in the field. They have lived only to work,—and in place of one lost, their sons have been counted by thousands."[40]

Women had been extensively involved in benevolent work before the war, but it had been imagined as an addition to domesticity, not a substitute for it. Now Stowe made clear that through benevolent work women might construct a new domesticity to replace family homes shattered by war: "In such associations . . . how many of the stricken and bereaved women of our country might find at once a home and an object in life!" If in the wake of war women could no longer be republican mothers in their own homes, they could transfer their domestic concerns to the larger sphere of national benevolence.[41]

As the home became increasingly associated with grief, loss, and the absence of men, several authors offered new religious versions of home that abandoned the project of domesticity in this world but promised the comforts of home in the next. The young writer Elizabeth Stuart Phelps, whose own fiancé was killed in the war, began late in the war to write a novel that imagined a new "heavenly home" as a solace to mourning women. In her 1896 memoirs, Phelps remembered that during the two years when she wrote the 1868 *The Gates Ajar*, "the country was dark with sorrowing women. The regiments came home, but the mourners went about the streets." The "drawn faces of bereaved wife, mother, sister, and widowed girl showed piteously everywhere." It was these bereaved women who inspired Phelps: She did not think "so much about the suffering of men" but instead "would have spoken" to the women—"the helpless, outnumbering, unconsulted women; they whom war trampled down, without a choice or protest; the patient, limited, domestic women, who thought little, but loved much, and loving, had lost all."[42]

It seemed to Phelps that "even the best and kindest forms of our prevailing beliefs had nothing to say to an afflicted woman that could help her much." After all, "creeds and commentaries and sermons were made by men," and "what tenderest of men knows how to comfort his own daughter when her heart is broken?" Doctrines were "chains of rusty iron, eating into raw hearts," while "the prayer of the preacher was not much better; it sounded like the language of an unknown race to a despairing girl."[43]

Reacting against what she perceived as an unfeeling, masculinist religion, Phelps created a new feminized theology in which she imagined a new heavenly domesticity. Phelps rejected the idea that heaven was "indefinite," a place "where the glory of God was to crowd out all individuality and all human joy from His most individual and human creatures." She instead sketched a domestic heaven where human loves "could outlive the shock of death" and the beloved forms of home could be recreated in spiritual form. A young woman whose brother Roy had been killed in battle was comforted by her aunt Phoebe, herself widowed: "Do I think you will see him again? You might as well ask me if I thought God made you and made Roy, and gave you to each other. See him! Why of course you will see him as you saw him here." By the end of the novel Phoebe, dying, looked forward to the comforts of heaven, including the home that her husband, John, might "be making ready for her coming." Indeed, Phoebe's last words made clear to readers that her vision of heaven had been realized: "It was quite dark when she turned her face at last towards the window. 'John!' she said,—'why, John!' " A major best seller, *The Gates Ajar* attested to the suffering that was an agonizing legacy of the war for many Northern women.[44]

The Gates Ajar was part of a postwar "literature of memory" that reinterpreted Northern women's imagined relationship to the Civil War. Between 1865 and 1900 the relationship shifted dramatically. Between 1865 and 1873, remembering and celebrating Northern women's war experiences and contributions to the war effort continued to be an important cultural project, with feminized war poems, stories, novels, and paintings produced. In 1866, for instance, the foremost female genre painter of the nineteenth century, Lilly Martin Spencer, codified the impact of the war on women in her *War Spirit at Home*. Spencer's painting portrayed a mother, with a baby on her lap, reading news of the July 4, 1863, victory at Vicksburg in the *New York Times*. While her other children made a game of war by parading gleefully around her, she was absorbed in scanning the newspaper, her intent stillness emphasizing that war was no child's play for women.[45]

Two 1867 omnibus volumes, Mary C. Vaughan's and Linus P. Brockett's *Woman's Work in the Civil War: A Record of Heroism, Patriotism and Patience* and Frank Moore's *Women of the War; Their Heroism and Self-Sacrifice*, celebrated women's contributions to the war effort with profiles of women who had been nurses, Sanitary Commission or aid society workers, and even soldiers. "The histories of wars are records of the achievements of men, for the most part," Moore commented, but "it has been different in our Conflict for the Union." Asking a correspondent for contributions to his compendium, Moore observed that the "labors, sacrifices, self denial and in some instances the sufferings and the Death even of women" in the war effort were "quite as worthy of grateful and perpetual memorial as the gallantry of our soldiers."[46]

In the immediate postwar period novels, too, portrayed Northern women's experiences of the war. Most famously, Louisa May Alcott's 1868 *Little Women* created a feminized world of war on the home front, focusing on the privations and emotional struggles of women. A nostalgic paean to domesticity written for girls, *Little Women* contrasted with Alcott's self-consciously "adult" novel of the same period, the 1873 *Work: A Story of Experience*, which featured a heroine whose husband died in the war. Rather than looking toward a "heavenly home," Christie Devon devoted herself to the cause of working women, creating a loving community of women that reconstituted the sense of domesticity shattered by the war. Underlining a theme articulated in feminized literature late in the war, *Work* celebrated work as the foundation of value in Christie's life: "in labor, and the efforts and experiences that grew out of it, I have found independence, education, happiness, and religion," she affirmed at the end of the novel.[47]

Figure 9.3. *The War Spirit at Home. Celebrating the Victory at Vicksburg* by Lilly M. Spencer, oil, 1866. The giddy children in Spencer's painting provide a sharp contrast to the still figure of the woman reading about Vicksburg. *Courtesy The Newark Museum/Art Resource, N. Y.*

In contrast to the the late 1860s and early 1870s, when a continuing stream of war-related publications appeared in the literary marketplace, in the mid- to late 1870s, interest in all aspects of the war waned dramatically. *Harper's Weekly*, which had published well over 100 Civil War stories during and immediately after the war, and which continued to advertise a readership of over 100,000, published only 2 Civil War stories in the 1870s, a sentimental story of a Northern veteran and a romance involving a Northern officer and a Confederate girl. As the Sanitary Commission leader Mary Livermore remembered, in the postwar period people "turned with relief to the employments of peaceful life, eager to forget the fearful years of battle and carnage." James Henry Harper of Harper and Brothers noted that "the public was tired of reading about the war, which had been the all-absorbing subject for four years, and other important topics now demanded their attention." Indeed, the pages of *Harper's Weekly* were filled with articles about war in Europe, Tammany Hall scandals, and the reconstruction of black life in the South.[48]

Still, a vestigial woman's war persisted in *Harper's Weekly* in occasional illustrations for Decoration Day (later Memorial Day) during the 1870s. In 1870, 1872, 1878, and 1879, full-page illustrations portrayed women putting flowers on soldiers' graves, hanging a wreath on a soldier's portrait, and reliving "sad memories" in an ornate parlor scene reminiscent of Winslow Homer's wartime "Wounded." Such illustrations linked women to the Decoration Day commemoration of the war, even if they made women static icons for the remembrance of men rather than exploring women's war experiences.[49]

The postwar *Harper's Weekly* provided a direct link with the popular culture that held sway during the war, but in the 1880s and 1890s new popular magazines not only achieved greater circulation than the *Weekly* but also signaled significant shifts in popular interest in, and memories of, the war. Foremost among them was the *Century* magazine, begun in 1881, which published its famous Battles and Leaders of the Civil War series from November 1884 until November 1887. The series, envisioned as articles "by the men who directed the battles of the Civil War," including generals Ulysses S. Grant, George McClellan, Pierre G. T. Beauregard, and James Longstreet, was an immediate hit with readers. By the second year of the series, monthly circulation of the magazine "had increased from 127,000 to 225,000," almost double the circulation of *Harper's Weekly*. The series soon expanded to cover a wide range of topics related to the war, including several reminiscences by Southern white women. But only Julia Ward Howe's series "Songs of the War" might have been expected to jog readers' memories that Northern women's war experiences had once been richly represented in the popular literature of war.[50]

The popularity of the *Century* series both resulted from and contributed to revived interest in the war in the mid-1880s, as the series helped redefine the war as one of "battles and leaders." A resurgence of interest was also indicated by the stunning growth of the GAR. Membership in this Civil War veterans' organization rose dramatically: from 30,000 in 1878 to 146,000 in 1883, 233,000 in 1884, and 320,000 in 1887. It reached a high-water mark at 428,000 members in 1890. Increasingly, the GAR dominated memorialization of the war throughout the North, especially in parades of veterans in annual Decoration Day or, later, Memorial Day ceremonies. Local posts of the GAR also sponsored the publication of numerous regimental histories in this period. Organizing itself on a military model with camping, drilling, and parading in uniforms as major activities, the GAR signaled a military revival that also addressed the generational concerns of veterans: It "licensed veterans to employ their positive memories of the war in compensation for the insufficiencies of their civilian lives."[51]

Under the influence of this emphasis on veterans, the iconography of Decoration Day in popular magazine literature began to shift. In the late 1880s *Harper's Weekly's* Decoration Day illustrations no longer represented women as the bearers of the war's memory. Its full-page 1891 Decoration Day illustration instead reflected the realities of GAR ceremonies by showing aged veterans decorating the graves of their fallen comrades. Sentimental illustrations and poems depicting aging veterans also characterized the *Weekly's* portrayal of Decoration Day in 1892 and 1893. Especially in the late 1880s and the 1890s, a new veteran-oriented war literature contributed to the political and cultural project of national reconciliation and reunion by asserting that the central meaning of the war was the shared bravery of Union and Confederate veterans. As the *Century* magazine commented in an 1889 article "Soldiers' Memorial Services," "upon the common ground of honoring the brave, the Union and Confederate veterans unite to offer tribute to departed valor." Likewise, *Harper's Weekly's* 1888 Decoration Day illustration portayed a wounded Yankee and Confederate, both ordinary soldiers, embracing on a monument inscribed "To the Nation's Dead Heroes"; the *Weekly's* 1896 Decoration Day illustration showed "The Blue and the Gray" chatting amicably "at Appomattox after General Lee's Surrender." The culmination of this Memorial Day emphasis on reunion among veterans came in the *Weekly's* poem "Memorial Day: May 30, 1899," which linked the Civil War and Spanish-American War by claiming that

> On Santiago summits we unite
> The grizzled foes of Chickamauga's day;
> The hatreds of a Shiloh sink from sight
> Beneath the waters of Manila Bay.

Theodore Roosevelt elaborated on this theme in a 1901 address, "Brotherhood and the Heroic Virtues," delivered before a Vermont veterans' reunion. "At the opening of this new century,"

Roosevelt said, "all of us, the children of a reunited country, have a right to glory in the countless deeds of valor done alike by the men of the North and the men of the South." Such tribute was hardly racially innocent, as David Blight and Kirk Savage, among others, have pointed out. The memory of the Civil War as shared bravery was used to underwrite ideas of the nation as a whites-only brotherhood, ideas that received stunning fictional expression in Thomas Dixon's 1905 novel, *The Clansman*, and in D. W. Griffith's 1915 film based on the novel, *Birth of a Nation*.[52]

The idea of the war as a whites-only brotherhood masculinized the memory of the war in popular literature. During the war and the immediate postwar period, sacrifice for the nation as a central meaning of the war had been available to both men and women, as feminized war literature revealed. In the 1880s and 1890s, however, commentators and writers increasingly attached the idea of Civil War sacrifice for the nation to men only, gendering the memory of the war in a new way.

In major popular magazines during the 1880s and 1890s, sentimental stories of veterans clearly outnumbered stories of a woman's war. In addition to its many Civil War articles and reminiscences of battle experience, the *Century* published 5 sentimental stories of veterans from 1887 to 1900. Contributions by Thomas Nelson Page and Joel Chandler Harris revealed that stories of Confederate veterans had now found a place within a literary marketplace that stressed reunion and reconciliation. In the same period, Northern women's experiences of the war were represented in the magazine by 2 stories, and no articles. Likewise, from its founding in 1893 until 1900, the popular general-interest magazine *McClure's* published, in addition to many articles on the military aspects of the Civil War, 9 war stories, including works by Stephen Crane and Harris. Only one of these, the 1897 "A Recent Confederate Victory," focused on a Northern woman, portraying a Kansas woman who, having lost her lover in the war, later adopted the orphaned son of a despised Confederate soldier.[53]

The rise in popularity of *McClure's* during the 1890s reveals a crucial change in representations of the war, as the popular literary emphasis on officers and generals common in the 1880s gave way to an emphasis on common soldiers. The circulation of *McClure's*, begun in 1893, eclipsed that of the *Century* during the 1890s, reaching 250,000 by 1896 and 370,000 by 1900, which put it "in the forefront of American magazines" of the period. Between 1893 and 1900 *McClure's* published some 60 articles and reminiscences on the Civil War, including series on Abraham Lincoln and Ulysses S. Grant as well as Charles A. Dana's "Reminiscences of Men and Events of the Civil War." Among the articles was a striking collection of veterans' memoirs, such as James B. Wilson's "An Actual Experience under Fire," and Ira Seymour's "The Song of the Rappahannock. The Real Experience in Battle of a Young Soldier in the Army of the Potomac."[54]

As the titles suggested, a new emphasis on the "real" or "actual" experience of battle marked the evolving Civil War literature of the 1890s, part of a new cult of experience that permeated American culture and that was marked as a masculinist ethos, most often excluding women. As Gerald Linderman has written, "participation in war became an important mark of merit. Honor attached itself less to courageous or cowardly conduct, battles won or lost, causes preserved or destroyed than to one's simple presence in the war." Thus it is no accident that Stephen Crane's best-selling 1895 novel *The Red Badge of Courage*, which traced the horrific and confusing battle experiences of Henry Fleming at Chancellorsville, was widely embraced as a realistic account of the war. Ironically, Crane himself, born in 1871, not only had not experienced the war first-hand, but drew on the *Century's* Battles and Leaders of the Civil War series for the historical underpinnings of his work.[55]

Significantly, Crane's novel ended with the assertion that his protagonist had drawn from his battle experiences, "a quiet manhood, non-assertive but of sturdy and strong blood." Henry Fleming "was a man," the novel repeated within the same paragraph. Numerous writers in the 1890s returned to the Civil War to find the underpinnings of a robust new masculine identity, one that often abandoned earlier attributes of manhood such as self-restraint and "civilized cultivation" in favor of "unrestrained nature" and "athletic virility." At the end of the decade, writers appealed to such interpretations of the Civil War to justify and glorify participation in the Spanish-American War. In his 1899 essay "The Strenuous Life," for instance, Theodore Roosevelt defended American imperialism by invoking an imagined Civil War past, including the "iron in the blood of our fathers, the men who upheld the wisdom of Lincoln, and bore the sword or rifle in the armies of Grant!"[56]

The new masculinization of the memory of the war dovetailed with the rise of literary realism, reflecting and reinforcing a newly masculinized literary marketplace. The cult of experience and of a strenuous life permeated realist literature at the turn of the century, from the works of Crane to those of Jack London and Frank Norris. Such writings often deliberately repudiated Victorian "feminized" writing. Many writers and editors, including some New Women writers, affirmed the new masculinist ethos of realism, sometimes explicitly disavowing earlier sentimental and domestic norms. Willa Cather, for instance, expressed disgust with women who had "scorn for the healthy commonplace." "I have not much faith in women in fiction," she wrote in 1895. "When a woman writes a story of adventure, a stout sea tale, a manly battle yarn, then I will begin to hope for something great from them, not before."[57]

Popular women's literature of the 1890s did not, however, turn to the production of "manly battle yarns." Nor did domestic, sentimental popular literature disappear from the literary marketplace, despite the critical ascendancy of realism. One of the most popular magazines of the 1880s and 1890s was the intensely domestic *Ladies' Home Journal*, begun in 1883. Subscriptions rose from 25,000 in 1884 to some 700,000 in 1892, remaining "in that neighborhood" for the rest of the decade. Yet though the *Journal* included sentimental stories of women's lives in every issue, only once between 1883 and 1900 did it publish a short story, the 1889 "Leshia," that mentioned the Civil War. In contrast, in the late 1890s the *Journal* ran numerous features on the Revolution, often glamorizing it through articles on fancy dress balls, George and Martha Washington's marriage, and other topics that imagined a distant, romantic, and fashionable past. The Northern women's Civil War, with its legacy of suffering, apparently did not inspire such romance.[58]

In the late 1890s the *Journal*, like other publications of the era, turned to the romance of the antebellum and Civil War South in nostalgic plantation poems and a reminiscence of Robert E. Lee. The imagined place of the South in the war literature of the 1880s and 1890s underlines how the new Civil War literature was racialized around ideas of whiteness. As literary representations of Northern women's domestic experiences of the war became rare, many Southern white women found in their domestic experiences of the war a powerful expression of a new sense of identity, and many published reminiscences of antebellum and wartime life. At the same time, as Nina Silber has pointed out, "countless novels and plays" contributed to the project of national reconciliation by portraying a "southern bride's submission to her northern husband," codifying an image of southern subservience to the conquering North.[59]

Writers both male and female expressed an increasing nostalgia for slaveholding society and slavery itself. During the 1880s and 1890s, plantation stories by Page, Harris, Maurice Thompson, and others became a staple of national magazines, inventing a world in which the relations between slave and master, or ex-slave and planter, were affectionate and untroubled. New war fictions by Thompson, Page, Constance Fenimore Woolson, Constance Cary Harrison, and Virginia Boyle Frazer, among others, featured white Southern heroines—an imaginative process that would ultimately culminate in Margaret Mitchell's creation of Scarlett O'Hara, still seen by many as the consummate Civil War heroine. There is great irony here: If Southern white women lost the war, as Drew Faust has argued, at the turn of the century they won the popular battle for its memory.[60]

The Northern women's war did not disappear entirely from the literary marketplace in the 1880s and 1890s. Several women who had been nurses and aid workers during the war published reminiscences, most prominent among them being Mary Livermore, who had been head of the Western Sanitary Commission during the war. Yet in her 1887 *My Story of the War*, Livermore criticized the new direction Civil War reminiscences were taking. "The public has listened eagerly to the stories of the great battles of the war of the rebellion," she said. But two important stories of the war had not been told, in her view. There was "a paucity of histories of the private soldier." And the story of Northern women was missing. "Who has fully narrated the consecrated and organized work of women?" she asked rhetorically. Women had "strengthened the sinews of the nation with their unflagging enthusiasm, and bridged over the chasm between civil and military life." Despite this stated need for women's war stories, Livermore's publisher was apparently nervous enough about publishing a woman's war memoirs to include "numerous illustrations of Northern and Southern battle flags in order to enhance sales."[61]

In the 1880s and 1890s Northern women's war experiences became marginal in the literary marketplace. Between 1880 and 1890, for instance, *Harper's Weekly* published 8 Civil War stories with Southern heroines, but only 2 with Northern heroines. Between 1880 and 1900, *Harper's Monthly* published 9 man's war stories, 11 nostalgic plantation stories, and 4 reconciliation stories featuring Northern men and Southern women, but only 2 war stories—set during the war or considering its legacy—with Northern heroines. Between 1893 and 1900 *McClure's* published 9 war stories and some 60 war articles, but only 1 story with a Northern heroine. Between the end of its Battles and Leaders series in 1887 and 1900, the *Century* published over 60 articles on the war, 9 plantation stories, 5 man's war stories, an article titled "Southern Womanhood As Affected by the War" as well as "A Woman's Reminiscences during the Siege of Vicksburg," but only 2 stories—and no articles—featuring Northern heroines. The *Ladies' Home Journal* published only 1 Northern woman's war story between 1885 and 1900.[62]

Significantly, several stories featuring Northern heroines protested against the rewriting of the war to exclude Northern women's experiences. In his 1889 "An Echo of Antietam," a *Century* story concentrating on the sufferings of a woman on the home front that might have been written during the conflict itself, Edward Bellamy commented that "many pictures of battles have been painted, but no true one yet, for the pictures contain only men. The women are unaccountably left out."

> We ought to see not alone the opposing lines of battle writhing and twisting in a death embrace, the batteries smoking and flaming, the hurricanes of cavalry, but innumerable women also, spectral forms of mothers, wives, sweethearts clinging about the necks of the advancing soldiers, vainly trying to shield them with their bosoms, extending supplicating hands to the foe, raising eyes of anguish to heaven.[63]

Elizabeth Stuart Phelps not only asked that her readers remember women's suffering and sacrifice in the war but also made special claims for women's memories of the conflict. Her 1887 *Harper's Monthly* story "Annie Laurie" portrayed a heroine who for twenty-one years had remained faithful to a lover who "fell in the terrible charge at Chancellorsville, and was not seen by comrade or friend again." She had "often prayed for a man's power of forgetting," but "knew that she would not have felt she was half a woman if she could forget." "Her story was the story of her country. Twenty-one, almost twenty-two years ago, Annie Laurie was one of those who 'gave their happiness instead.' He gave his life; she knew it was the easier portion; she never said so, lest she should seem to undervalue his share of their sacrifice or overvalue hers."[64] Here Phelps offered a gendered theory of memory, arguing that women's memories of the war were both more harrowing and longer lasting than those of men.

Phelps did more than offer a gendered plea for the memory of the war in her late war fictions: She undermined heroic stereotypes of veterans and ultimately challenged the veteran-dominated culture of remembrance itself. The lost hero eventually returned to Annie Laurie, but he was a "pitiful figure, wan with misery, ragged, with a scared face," "shattered," a "wreck." After the "wounds, fever, and hardships" he had suffered, he had experienced a "loss of identity" and had spent the years since the war in hospitals. In this story it was the Civil War veteran who lost his memory of the war, while a woman steadfastly maintained hers.[65]

But it was Phelps's story *Comrades*, published in the year of her death, 1911, that presented the most compelling arguments both for a gendered memory of the war and for Northern women's right publicly to commemorate that memory. In this story Patience, the tellingly named wife of an aging and infirm veteran, initially "did not join" the annual Decoration Day procession in which he was the sole remaining marcher. She chose instead "to walk abreast of it, at the side, as near as possible, without offense to the ceremonies, to the solitary figure of her husband." But the story made clear that it was her moment, not her husband's: "everything blossomed for her, and rested in her, and yearned toward her. The emotion of the day and of the hour seemed incarnate in her. She embodied in her strong and sweet personality all that blundering man has wrought on tormented woman by the savagery of war." She "remembered what she had suffered," the "slow news after slaughtering battles," "the rack of the imagination," and "inquisition of the nerve—pangs that no man-soldier of them all could understand. 'It comes on women—war,' she thought." And when her husband staggered, she went to him, "quietly grasped him by the arm, and fell into step beside him."

" 'What'll folks say?' cried the old soldier, in real anguish."

" 'They'll say I'm where I belong. Reuben! Reuben! I've *earned the right to*.' "[66]

Though Northern women had "earned the right" to the memory of the war, that memory was rarely expressed in the popular literary marketplace of the late nineteenth century. The memory of Northern women's war-borne suffering did not prove a lasting legacy of the conflict. The gendered popular literary nationalism that had held sway during and immediately after the war, which had included Northern women in the imagined community of the nation, gave way to a more exclusionary and restrictive nationalism defined not only by race but also by gender. Thus it is no accident that no ideological legacy comparable to republican motherhood emerged from the Civil War to represent the experiences of Northern women, for popular memory took a different path after the Civil War than in the wake of the Revolution. If the emergent women's culture of the antebellum period had encouraged an author such as Elizabeth Ellet to celebrate revolutionary women, the emergent masculinized and racialized culture of the late nineteenth century increasingly foreclosed the association of Northern women and African Americans with participation in the war.

That foreclosure is important, for just as the Civil War was a defining event in our national history, so too have memories of the Civil War helped define membership in the nation. The popular culture of memory that has surrounded the war has tended to remember it primarily as a white masculinist conflict, rather than a cataclysmic event that rent and remade the fabric of life for all Americans. The popular Civil War that emerged in the 1880s and 1890s belonged primarily to white men and to Southern white women, a late-nineteenth-century reinvention of the war. In the twentieth century the masculinization of the war's memory that was filtered through the new precepts of literary realism achieved not just ascendancy but an astonishing longevity when realism became a canonical part of American literary culture. "There was no real literature of our Civil War," Ernest Hemingway said in 1942, "until Stephen Crane wrote 'The Red Badge of Courage.' " Today, Crane's novel continues to be taught in high schools as a means of understanding the "real" Civil War. The great irony is that the most popular literary treatments of the Northern war were crystallized in the 1890s.[67]

A larger point here is that our memories of the Civil War have been profoundly shaped by the literary marketplace, including those cultural and social processes that have reified racialized and masculinized literary memories of the war. In the 1880s and 1890s, popular literary versions of the war co-existed with "unpopular" versions, those apparently supported by only a small audience. As Natalie Zemon Davis has pointed out, "mainstreams have their margins," and an examination of "unpopular" forms of culture may well lead us to recover voices that have been submerged or masked.[68]

In Northern memories of the Civil War, the "unpopular" has been the feminized Civil War. Indeed, it is ironic that in the wealth of new studies on women and the war, relatively little attention has been paid to Northern women. Rather than being an accidental phenomenon, this may well be a development sustained by a mode of thought set in motion over a century ago.

Notes

I am grateful to David Nord for his expert editorial guidance, to Drew Gilpin Faust and the anonymous reviewers for the *Journal of American History* for their astute and helpful comments, and to Susan Armeny, Scott Stephan, and Peter A. Kraemer for their help with preparation of this article. A version of this essay was presented at the annual meeting of the American Historical Association in January 1998, and I appreciate the helpful comments of Stuart McConnell, Matthew Gallman, and Amy Kinsel. I would also like to thank Bob Moeller, Joan Waugh, and Charles Chubb for their thoughtful assistance on several drafts of this essay. I benefitted from the helpful comments of Lynn Mally, Judith Jackson Fossett, David Blight, Bob Bonner, Jon Wiener, Anne Walthall, and Patrick Kelly, and, on an early version of this essay, from the comments of Nina Silber, Thomas Bender, Susan Ware, Eliza McFeely, Lyde Sizer, Susan Schoelwer, and Michael O'Malley. Finally, I appreciate the generous support of the American Antiquarian Society, the Duke University Library, and the Huntington Library.

1. Fleta, "Woman and War," *Flag of Our Union*, Jan. 28, 1865, p. 59.
2. The outpouring of popular wartime literature on martial themes also included histories, juveniles, humor, "songsters" (songbooks), poetry, and sensational novels. A few sensational novels, published as pamphlets, also portrayed female heroines. However, these heroines were almost always Unionist Southerners who lived in the border states or in the Confederacy itself, and such novels are beyond the scope of this article.
3. The foremost cultural history of the war is George M. Fredrickson, *The Inner Civil War: Northern Intellectuals and the Crisis of the Union* (New York, 1965). The standard literary histories of the war remain Daniel Aaron, *The Unwritten War* (New York, 1973); and Edmund Wilson, *Patriotic Gore: Studies in the Literature of the American Civil War* (New York, 1962). Benedict Anderson, *Imagined Communities: Reflections on the Origin and Spread of Nationalism* (London, 1983).
4. The best recent anthology of Civil War literature is Louis P. Masur, ed., *"The Real War Will Never Get in the Books": Selections from Writers during the Civil War* (New York, 1993). New studies on popular culture include Eric Lott, *Love and Theft: Blackface Minstrelsy and the American Working Class* (New York, 1993); and George Lipsitz, *Time Passages: Collective Memory and American Popular Culture* (Minneapolis, 1990). For the popular culture of the war, see Kathleen Diffley, *Where My Heart Is Turning Ever: Civil War Stories and Constitutional Reform, 1861–1876* (Athens, Ga., 1992); Timothy Sweet, *Traces of War: Poetry, Photography, and the Crisis of the Union* (Baltimore, 1990); Jim Cullen, *The Civil War in Popular Culture: A Reusable Past* (Washington, 1995); and Joyce Appleby, "Reconciliation and the Northern Novelist," *Civil War History*, 10 (June 1964), 117–29. Foremost among new studies discussing women's experiences of the war is Drew Gilpin Faust, *Mothers of Invention: Women of the Slaveholding South in the American Civil War* (Chapel Hill, 1997). See also LeeAnn Whites, *The Civil War as a Crisis in Gender: Augusta, Georgia, 1860–1890* (Athens, Ga., 1995); Elizabeth Young, "A Wound of One's Own: Louisa May Alcott's Civil War Fiction," *American Quarterly*, 48 (Sept. 1996), 439–74; Catherine Clinton and Nina Silber, eds., *Divided Houses: Gender and the Civil War* (New York, 1992); Nina Silber, *The Romance of Reunion: Northerners and the South, 1865–1900* (Chapel Hill, 1993); Lyde Cullen Sizer, " 'A Revolution in Woman Herself': Northern Women Writers and the American Civil War, 1850–1872" (Ph.D. diss., Brown University, 1994); Ann Douglas Wood, "The War within a War: Women Nurses in the Union Army," *Civil War History*, 18 (Sept. 1972), 197–212; and Elizabeth Leonard, *Yankee Women: Gender Battles in the Civil War* (New York, 1994). See also Sylvia G. L. Dannett, ed., *Noble Women of the North* (New York, 1959); Marjorie Barstow Greenbie, *Lincoln's*

Daughters of Mercy (New York, 1944); Mary Elizabeth Massey, *Bonnet Brigades* (New York, 1966); and Agatha Young, *The Women and the Crisis: Women of the North in the Civil War* (New York, 1959). Wartime circulation figures can be approximated for several publications reviewed for this essay in addition to *Harper's Weekly. Harper's New Monthly Magazine* claimed an average circulation of 110,000 for the war period; *Frank Leslie's Illustrated Newspaper* 164,000 in 1860, but only 50,000 by 1865; the *Independent* 35,000 in 1861 and 75,000 in 1863; the *Atlantic Monthly* 32,000 in 1863. See Frank Luther Mott, *A History of American Magazines* (5 vols., Cambridge, 1930–1957), II, 11, 10, 371, 372, 505.

5. *Harper's Weekly*, June 15, 1861, p. 369.
6. In its conception of the literary marketplace this study is dependent on work on the history of American print culture, including Cathy Davidson, *Revolution and the Word: The Rise of the Novel in America* (New York, 1986); Cathy Davidson, ed., *Reading in America: Literature & Social History* (Baltimore, 1989); Ezra Greenspan, *Walt Whitman and the American Reader* (Cambridge, Mass., 1990); Robert Gross, *Printing, Politics, and the People: The 1989 James Russell Wiggins Lecture in the History of the Book in American Culture at the American Antiquarian Society* (Worcester, 1989); David D. Hall, *Worlds of Wonder, Days of Judgment: Popular Religious Belief in Early New England* (Cambridge, Mass., 1990); Mary Kelley, *Private Woman, Public Stage: Literary Domesticity in Nineteenth-Century America* (New York, 1984); Susan Coultrap-McQuin, *Doing Literary Business: American Women Writers in the Nineteenth Century* (Chapel Hill, 1990); David Nord, *The Evangelical Origins of Mass Media in America, 1815–1835* (Columbia, S.C., 1984); Janice Radway, *Reading the Romance: Women, Patriarchy, and Popular Literature* (Chapel Hill, 1984); Ellery Sedgwick, *The Atlantic Monthly, 1857–1909* (Amherst, 1994); Michael Warner, *The Letters of the Republic: Publication and the Public Sphere in Eighteenth-Century America* (Cambridge, Mass., 1990); and Christopher P. Wilson, *The Labor of Words: Literary Professionalism in the Progressive Era* (Athens, Ga., 1985). On the domestic novel, see especially Nina Baym, *Woman's Fiction: A Guide to Novels by and about Women in America, 1820–1870* (Ithaca, 1978); and Jane Tompkins, *Sensational Designs: The Cultural Work of American Fiction, 1790–1860* (New York, 1985). On the practices of the mid-nineteenth-century literary marketplace that encouraged participation by women authors, see Coultrap-McQuin, *Doing Literary Business*; and Kelley, *Private Woman, Public Stage.*
7. Tony Horwitz, *Confederates in the Attic: Dispatches from the Unfinished Civil War* (New York, 1998), 101. Theodore Roosevelt, *The Strenuous Life* (New York, 1901), 263–78. On late-nineteenth-century plantation mythology, see Eric J. Sundquist, *To Wake the Nations: Race in the Making of American Literature* (Cambridge, Mass., 1993).
8. On Crane's realism and realism more generally, see Christopher P. Wilson, "Stephen Crane and the Police," *American Quarterly*, 48 (June 1996), 273–315; and Amy Kaplan, *The Social Construction of American Realism* (Chicago, 1988).
9. James M. McPherson, "Foreword," in *Divided Houses*, ed. Clinton and Silber, xiv.
10. "Stockings and Mittens," *Harper's Weekly*, Jan. 11, 1862, p. 30; "The Army of the Knitters." *Arthur's Home Magazine*, 19 (Jan. 1862), 61.
11. "The Mothers of To-Day," *Arthur's Home Magazine*, 18 (Nov. 1861), 263. The *New York Times* anecdote was reprinted in "Rumors and Incidents," *The Rebellion Record: A Diary of American Events, with Documents, Narratives, Illustrative Incidents, Poetry etc.*, ed. Frank Moore (11 vols., New York, 1861–1868), I, 55. For antebellum women writers' views of the Revolution, see Nina Baym, *American Women Writers and the Work of History, 1790–1860* (New Brunswick, 1995); and Linda K. Kerber, " 'History Can Do It No Justice': Women and the Reinterpretation of the American Revolution," in *Women in the Age of the American Revolution*, ed. Ronald Hoffman and Peter J. Albert (Charlottesville, 1989), 3–42.
12. On republican motherhood, see Linda K. Kerber, *Women of the Republic: Intellect and Ideology in Revolutionary America* (Chapel Hill, 1980). On the antebellum culture of domesticity that supported the ideology of republican motherhood, see Nancy Cott, *The Bonds of Womanhood: "Woman's Sphere" in New England, 1780–1835* (New Haven, 1977); Ann Douglas, *The Feminization of American Culture* (New York, 1977); Kelley, *Private Woman, Public Stage*; and Karen Halttunen, *Confidence Men and Painted Women: A Study of Middle-Class Culture in America, 1830–1870* (New Haven, 1982). Mary Poovey, *Uneven Developments: The Ideological Work of Gender in Mid-Victorian England* (Chicago, 1988), 16.
13. The idea that women were at the emotive center of the nation had been widely established in antebellum literature, the most prominent example of sentimental literary nationhood being Harriet Beecher Stowe, *Uncle Tom's Cabin* (New York, 1851). For emphasis on the vital role of patriotic mothers and "home-sentiment," see Elizabeth Ellet, *The Women of the American Revolution* (New York, 1848), 13–14. On Ellet's career, see Baym, *American Women Writers and the Work of History*; and Kerber, " 'History Can Do It No Justice.' " On nineteenth-century-sentimental culture, see Douglas, *Feminization of*

American Culture; Halttunen, *Confidence Men and Painted Women*; Barton Levi St. Armand, *Emily Dickinson and Her Culture: The Soul's Society* (New York, 1984); and Tompkins, *Sensational Designs*. Virginia F. Townsend, "Home Pictures of the Times," *Arthur's Home Magazine*, 18 (Nov. 1861), 235, 237. See also such popular songs as Mrs. Cornelia D. Rogers, *Ah! He Kissed Me When He Left Me* (Chicago, 1863), Sheet Music Collection (Special Collections Library, Duke University, Durham, N.C.). Soldiers' own accounts of partings often matched these literary versions in stressing the tears of women. See Will Colton's account of his departure in J. Matthew Gallman, *Mastering Wartime: A Social History of Philadelphia during the Civil War* (Cambridge, Mass., 1990), 63.

14. Samuel Osgood, "The Home and the Flag," *Harper's New Monthly Magazine*, 26 (April 1863), 664.

15. *Ibid.*

16. John Greenleaf Whittier initially steadfastly asserted the veracity of the story upon which his ballad was based, but after the war he backpedaled. See Samuel T. Pickard, *Life and Letters of John Greenleaf Whittier* (2 vols., Cambridge, Mass., 1894), II, 454–59. John Greenleaf Whittier, "Barbara Frietchie," *Atlantic Monthly*, 12 (Oct. 1863), 495–97.

17. Horatio Alger Jr., "Mother, Can I Go?," *Harper's Weekly*, March 22, 1862, p. 187. For his follow-up verse, see Horatio Alger Jr., "He Has Gone and I Have Sent Him," *ibid.*, Nov. 1, 1862, p. 694. Alger "often wrote his Civil War verse from the point of view of a woman, usually a mother or a sweetheart pining for a young soldier gone to war," his biographers have noted. See Gary Scharnhorst and Jack Bales, *The Lost Life of Horatio Alger Jr.* (Bloomington, 1985), 56. George F. Root, *Just Before the Battle, Mother* (Chicago, 1863). Sheet Music Collection.

18. Charles Carroll Sawyer, *Who Will Care for Mother Now?* (Brooklyn, 1863). Sheet Music Collection; *The Dying Volunteer* (New Orleans, 1865), *ibid*; Edward Clark, *The Dying Soldier or Kiss me good night Mother* (Boston, 1861), *ibid*; J. C. Johnson, *Is That Mother Bending O'er Me* (Boston, 1863), *ibid.*; Henry C. Work, *Our Captain's Last Words* (Chicago, 1861), *ibid.*; A. B. Chandler, *I've Fallen in the Battle* (New Orleans, 1864), *ibid.*; Ednor Rossiter, *I Loved That Dear Old Flag the Best* (Philadelphia, 1863), *ibid.*; Thomas Manahan, *Bear this gently to my Mother* (New York, 1864), *ibid.*

19. T. S. Arthur, "Blue Yarn Stockings," *Harper's New Monthly Magazine*, 24 (Dec. 1861), 112; Kate Sutherland, "The Laggard Recruit," *Arthur's Home Magazine*, 19 (Jan. 1862), 11. Other prescriptive enlistment fables featuring young women include Mary E. Dodge, "Netty's Touch-Stone," *Harper's New Monthly Magazine*, 28 (March 1864), 517; "The Conscript's Appeal," *Harper's Weekly*, Nov. 7, 1863, p. 710; and "The Narrow Escape," *ibid.*, Oct. 25, 1862, p. 686.

20. Robert B. Westbrook, " 'I Want a Girl, Just Like the Girl That Married Harry James': American Women and the Problem of Political Obligation in World War II," *American Quarterly*, 42 (Dec. 1990), 587–614, esp. 588–89.

21. Melodramas and sentimental literature often involved different styles of plot, with sentimental literature more interiorized, often set within domestic spaces, while melodramas involved more dramatic exteriorized action and settings. However, as *Uncle Tom's Cabin* shows, melodrama and sentimental literature blended into one another, drawing upon similar structures of feeling. Peter Brooks, *The Melodramatic Imagination: Balzac, Henry James, and the Mode of Excess* (1976; New Haven, 1995), 13, 205.

22. "Red, White, and Blue." *Harper's Weekly*. Oct. 19, 1861. pp. 666–67.

23. On the idea that war was an education for women, see also Mary C. Vaughan, "Wounded at Donelson," *New York Ledger*, Nov. 29, 1862, p. 2: "Recaptured," *Harper's Weekly*, Feb. 14, 1863, p. 103; "Blue Belle," *ibid.*, Aug. 20, 1864, p. 542; "Leap Year," *ibid.*, April 23, 1864, p. 266; "Devereux Date, Private," *ibid.*, Sept. 13, 1862, p. 587; and "Fighting and Waiting," *ibid.*, Jan. 10, 1863, pp. 22–23. "Jessie Underhill's Thanksgiving," *ibid.*, Dec. 6, 1862, p. 775; "A Leaf from a Summer," *ibid.*, Nov. 8, 1862, p. 718. For another example of love being treated as a life-and-death matter, see "The Blue Flowers," *ibid.*, Sept. 5, 1863, p. 566.

24. "Romances of the War," *Round Table*, Jan. 9, 1864, p. 59.

25. St. Armand, *Emily Dickinson and Her Culture*, esp. 111.

26. Fanny Fern, "Soldiers' Wives," *New York Ledger*, Nov. 8, 1862, p. 4. Literature sympathetic to the economic plight of soldiers' families drew upon a long literary tradition in which the only working-class women imagined positively were pale, genteel, passive victims; they were sharply distinguished from their "disorderly" sisters. See Christine Stansell, *City of Women* (New York, 1986).

27. Elizabeth Boynton to Will Harbert, Aug. 11, 1862, Elizabeth Boynton Harbert Papers (Huntington Library, San Marino, Calif.).

28. Louise Chandler Moulton, "One of Many," *Atlantic Monthly*, 27 (July 1863), 120. For stories concentrating on women's equal or greater suffering and sacrifice, see "Milly Graham's Rose Bush," *Harper's Weekly*, May 14, 1864, p. 311; "May Flowers" *ibid.*, May 28, 1864, p. 343; and "My Contribution," *ibid.*, June 14, 1862, p. 374. Many women writers made a point of quoting the following stanzas from

Elizabeth Barrett Browning's 1861 poem "Parting Lovers:" "Heroic males the country bears; / But daughters give up more than sons; / Flags wave, drums beat, and unawares / You flash your souls out with the guns / And take your heaven at once! / But we—we empty heart and home / Of life's life, love!" *Poems by Elizabeth Barrett Browning* (4 vols., New York, 1862), IV, 181. For a sampling of quotations of this poem in wartime fiction, see "One of Our Heroes," *Harper's Weekly*, July 5, 1862, p. 427; Catherine Earnshaw, "Loyal," *Flag of Our Union*, Jan. 28, 1865, p. 58; and Elizabeth Stuart Phelps, "A Sacrifice Consumed," *Harper's New Monthly Magazine.* 27 (Jan. 1864), 240.

29. Moulton, "One of Many," 120, 121. For a variation on this theme, see "Women and War," *Flag of Our Union*, Jan. 28, 1865, p. 59. "My Absent Soldier," *Harper's Weekly*, May 31, 1862, p. 343; Julia Eugenia Mott, "Within a Year," *Peterson's Magazine*, 41 (July 1862), 29. See also Almena C. S. Allard, "The Soldier's Dying Wife," *Arthur's Home Magazine*, 20 (Sept. 1862), 174; and "The Soldier's Mother," *Frank Leslie's Illustrated Newspaper*, April 26, 1862, p. 414.

30. Elaine Scarry, *The Body in Pain: The Making and Unmaking of the World* (New York, 1985); "Our Wounded," *Continental Monthly*, 2 (Oct. 1862), 465. On the popular embrace of violence during the war, see Charles Royster, *The Destructive War: William Tecumseh Sherman, Stonewall Jackson, and the Americans* (New York, 1991), esp. 232–95.

31. "Wounded," *Harper's Weekly*, July 12, 1862, p. 442. On the idea of claiming the wounds of war, see Young, "Wound of One's Own."

32. "Wounded," 442.

33. *Ibid.*

34. Winslow Homer, "News from the War," *Harper's Weekly.* June 14, 1862, pp. 376–77.

35. Moulton, "One of Many," 121.

36. Rose Terry, "A Woman," *Atlantic Monthly*, 10 (Dec. 1862), 696, 706, 707. See also Louisa May Alcott, "Love and Loyalty," *United States Service Magazine*, 2 (July, Aug., Sept., Nov., Dec., 1864), 58–64, 166–72, 273–80, 469–75, 543–51; and "Love's Sacrifice and Its Recompense," *Harper's Weekly*, March 5, 1864, p. 155.

37. On Civil War nursing, sec Jane E. Schultz, "The Inhospitable Hospital: Gender and Professionalism in Civil War Medicine," *Signs*, 17 (Winter 1992), 363–92; Kristie Ross, "Arranging a Doll's House: Refined Women as Union Nurses," in *Divided Houses*, ed. Clinton and Silber, 97–113; Leonard, *Yankee Women*; Sizer, " 'Revolution in Woman Herself' "; and Wood, "War Within a War:" "Our Women and the War," *Harper's Weekly*, Sept. 6, 1862, p. 570. For a fascinating analysis of *Hospital Sketches*, see Young, "Wound of One's Own." Virginia F. Townsend, "Hospital Nurse," *Arthur's Home Magazine*, 20 (Aug. 1862), 122; Bella Z. Spencer, "One of the Noble," *Harper's New Monthly Magazine*, 29 (July 1864), 205, 206. See also "Missing," *Harper's Weekly*, Oct. 18, 1862, pp. 662–63.

38. Harriet Beecher Stowe to Annie Adams Fields, Nov. 29, 1864, in *Fields of the Atlantic Monthly*, ed. James C. Austin (San Marino, 1953), 281.

39. Mrs. H. B. Stowe, "The Chimney-Corner," *Atlantic Monthly*, 15 (Jan. 1865), 109–10, 112.

40. *Ibid.*, 113, 114.

41. On women's antebellum benevolence, see Lori D. Ginzberg, *Women and the Work of Benevolence* (New Haven, 1990), esp., 16. Stowe, "Chimney-Corner," 113, 114. On the idea of transferring domestic concerns to the larger sphere of the nation, see Paula Baker, "The Domestication of Politics: Women and American Political Society, 1780–1920," *American Historical Review*, 89 (June 1984), 620–47.

42. Elizabeth Stuart Phelps, *Chapters from a Life* (Boston, 1896), 96–98. See Christine Stansell, "Elizabeth Stuart Phelps: A Study in Female Rebellion," *Massachusetts Review*, 13 (Winter–Spring 1972), 239–56. For stories and novels asking readers to remember women's war sacrifices, see also A. W. Crocker, "Part of the Price," *Harper's New Monthly Magazine*, 28 (March 1864), 553; *Ruth: A Song in the Desert* (Boston, 1864); and Elizabeth Stuart Phelps, "A Sacrifice Consumed," *Harper's New Monthly Magazine*, 27 (Jan. 1864), 236.

43. Phelps, *Chapters from a Life*, 98.

44. *Ibid.*, 47; Elizabeth Stuart Phelps, *The Gates Ajar* (1868; Cambridge, Mass., 1964), 130, 134–35, 38, 155.,161. *The Gates Ajar* reportedly sold 81,000 copies by the turn of the century. See Carol Farley Kessler, *Elizabeth Stuart Phelps* (Boston, 1982), 30.

45. The phrase "literature of memory" is Eric Sundquist's. See Eric Sundquist, "Realism and Regionalism," in *Columbia Literary History of the United States*, ed. Emory Elliott (New York, 1988), 508. See Robin-Bolton Smith, *The Joys of Sentiment: Lilly Martin Spencer, 1822–1902* (Washington, 1973). My thanks to Joan Waugh for pointing out this painting. For examples of postwar literature that reiterated the theme that war destroyed lives on the home front, see Henry Wadsworth Longfellow, "Killed at the Ford," *Atlantic Monthly*, 17 (April 1866), 479. Sarah Emma Edmonds, *Nurse and Spy in the Union Army: Comprising the Adventures and Experiences of a Woman in Hospitals, Camps, and Battle-fields* (Hartford, 1865); and Bella Z. Spencer, *Tried and True* (Springfield, Mass., 1866). In 1868 several novels appeared

in addition to *The Gates Ajar*, including Louisa May Alcott, *Little Women, or, Meg, Jo, Beth, and Amy* (Boston, 1868); and Mary J. Holmes, *Rose Mather, a Tale of the War* (New York, 1868). Several nurses also published accounts of their experiences in the war, including Anna Morris Ellis Holstein, *Three Years in the Field Hospitals of the Army of the Potomac* (Philadelphia, 1867); Jane Hoge, *The Boys in Blue* (New York, 1867); and Sophronia Bucklin, *In Hospital and Camp* (Philadelphia, 1868).

46. Mary C. Vaughan and Linus Brockett, *Woman's Work in the Civil War: A Record of Heroism, Patriotism and Patience* (Philadelphia, 1867); Frank Moore, *Women of the War; Their Heroism and Self-Sacrifice* (Hartford, 1867), iii. Frank Moore to John A. Andrew, Jan. 18, 1866, Frank Moore Papers (Special Collections Library, Duke University).

47. Louisa May Alcott, *Work: A Story of Experience*, ed. Joy S. Kasson (1873; New York, 1994), 343.

48. See Justin M'Carthy, " 'The Divine Emilye,' " *Harper's Weekly*, May 17, 1873; and "An Old Soldier," *ibid.*, July 3, 1875. On the waning of war-related fiction in *Harper's Weekly*, see Diffley, *Where My Heart Is Turning Ever*, xxvi. Mary Livermore, *My Story of the War: A Woman's Narrative of Four Years Personal Experience As Nurse in the Union Army, and in Relief Work at Home, in Hospitals, Camps, and at the Front, during the War of the Rebellion* (Hartford, 1887), 7; James Henry Harper, *The House of Harper: A Century of Publishing in Franklin Square* (New York, 1912), 243.

49. "In Memory of Our Dead Heroes, the Floral Tribute to the Nation's Dead," *Harper's Weekly*, June 4, 1870, p. 364; "In Memoriam—Decoration Day, 1872," *ibid.*, June 8, 1872, p. 441; "Decoration Day," *ibid.*, June 8, 1878, p. 449; "Sad Memories—Decoration Day," *ibid.*, June 7, 1879, p. 437.

50. The Century was a continuation of *Scribner's Monthly*. For publishing details of the *Century*, see Mott, *History of American Magazines*, III, 457-80. L. Frank Tooker, *The Joys and Tribulations of an Editor* (New York, 1923), 45, 46.

51. Gerald Linderman, *Embattled Courage: The Experience of Combat in the American Civil War* (New York, 1987), 275–76, 280. On the Grand Army of the Republic (GAR) see Stuart McConnell, *Glorious Contentment: The Grand Army of the Republic, 1865–1900* (Chapel Hill, 1992). Older histories of the GAR include Robert Beath, *History of the Grand Army of the Republic* (New York, 1889); and Mary R. Dearing, *Veterans in Politics: The Story of the G.A.R.* (Baton Rouge, 1952). In the North, women organized on the local level to aid veterans but had difficulty being accepted by the national GAR. See proceedings from the annual conventions of the Woman's Relief Corps, an auxiliary to the GAR, for example: *Report of the National Organization, Woman's Relief Corps . . . 1883, and Proceedings of the Second Annual National Convention, Woman's Relief Corps, . . . 1884* (Boston, 1903); and *Journal of the Seventh Annual Convention of the Woman's Relief Corps, Auxiliary to the Grand Army of the Republic . . . , 1889* (Boston, 1889).

52. See "Camp Echoes," *Harper's Weekly*, May 28, 1892, pp. 511, 512; "A Ballad of May," *ibid.*, May 27, 1893, p. 498; "Soldiers' Memorial Services," *Century*, 38 (May 1889), 156; "Decoration Day," *Harper's Weekly*, June 2, 1888, pp. 400–401; "The Blue and the Gray at Appomattox, After General Lee's Surrender, April 9, 1865," *ibid.*, May 30, 1896, 540–41; and "Memorial Day: May 30, 1899," *ibid.*, May 27, 1899, p. 528. Roosevelt, *Strenuous Life*, 266; David W. Blight, "Frederick Douglass and the Memory of the Civil War," *Journal of American History*, 75 (March 1989), 1162. See also David W. Blight, *Frederick Douglass' Civil War: Keeping Faith in Jubilee* (Baton Rouge, 1989). Kirk Savage, *Standing Soldiers, Kneeling Slaves: Race, War, and Monument in Nineteenth-Century America* (Princeton, 1997).

53. See Joel Chandler Harris, "A Conscript's Christmas," *Century*, 41 (Dec. 1890), 284–99; George Parsons Lathrop, "Marthy Virginia's Hand," *ibid.*, 282–83; Thomas Nelson Page, "A Gray Jacket," *ibid.*, 44 (May 1892), 27–33; William Henry Shelton, "Uncle Obadiah's Uncle Billy," *ibid.*, 46 (June 1893), 307–12; and Harry Stillwell Edwards, "Captain Jerry," *ibid.*, 47 (Jan. 1894), 478–80. The two *Century* stories of a woman's war were Edward Bellamy, "An Echo of Antietam," *ibid.*, 38 (July 1889), 374–81; and Frank Pope Humphrey, "A Comedy of War," *ibid.*, 52 (July 1896), 454–60. For *McClure's*, see Joel Chandler Harris, "A Comedy of War," *McClure's*, 1 (June 1893), 69–82; Stephen Crane, "The Little Regiment," *ibid.*, 7 (June 1896), 12–22; Stephen Crane, "The Veteran," *ibid.*, (Aug. 1896), 222–24; Robert W. Chambers, "The Pickets," *ibid.*, (Oct. 1896), 437–40; Octave Thanet, "An Old Grand Army Man," *ibid.*, 11 (June 1898), 162–69; Ray Stannard Baker, "Uncle Luther Dowell's Wooden Leg," *ibid.*, 11 (May 1898), 40–46; Marshall Putnam Thompson, "The Disbandment of the Army of Northern Virginia," *ibid.*, 12 (Nov. 1898), 79–81; and Henri Bronson and Viola Roseboro', "In Missouri," *ibid.*, 13 (May 1899), 68–73. The sole *McClure's* story with a Northern (or at least Union-affiliated) heroine was William Allen White, "A Recent Confederate Victory," *ibid.*, 9 (June 1897), 701–8.

54. Mott, *History of American Magazines*. IV, 591, 596. James B. Wilson, "An Actual Experience Under Fire," *McClure's*, 2 (April 1894), 486–88; Ira Seymour, "The Song of the Rappahannock. The Real Experience in Battle of a Young Soldier in the Army of the Potomac," *ibid.*, 8 (Feb. 1897), 314–20; Captain Musgrove Davis, "Some Personal Experiences in the War," *ibid.*, 9 (June 1897), 661–62.

55. On the new emphasis on battle experience, see John Pettegrew, " 'The Soldier's Faith': Turn-of-the-Century Memory of the Civil War and the Emergence of Modern American Nationalism," *Journal of Contemporary History*, 31 (Jan. 1996), 49–73. For a useful distinction between the rhetoric in Memorial Day addresses, with its emphasis on moral duty to country, and popular literature, with its emphasis on "real" experience, see *ibid.*, 55–56. Linderman, *Embattled Courage*, 277. On the new "cult of experience," see Wilson, *Labor of Words*, 92, 93. Stephen Crane, *The Red Badge of Courage* (1895; New York, 1983). On Crane's use of the 1880s *Century* series "Battles and Leaders of the Civil War" rather than accounts published during the war for the factual underpinnings of *The Red Badge of Courage*, see Eric J. Sundquist, "The Country of the Blue," in *American Realism: New Essays*, ed. Eric J. Sundquist (Baltimore, 1982), 4.

56. Crane, *Red Badge of Courage*, 130; Wilson, *Labor of Words*, 92, 93; Theodore Roosevelt, "The Strenuous Life," in Fredrickson, *Inner Civil War*, 225. Fredrickson's chapter "The Moral Equivalent of War" remains a compelling discussion of the changing uses of the memory of the Civil War in the late nineteenth century. Theodore Roosevelt, *An Autobiography* (New York, 1913), 275.

57. On the newly masculinized literary marketplace, see especially Wilson, *Labor of Words*. On the discomfort of some older "sentimental" writers, including Elizabeth Stuart Phelps, in that marketplace, see Coultrap-McQuin, *Doing Literary Business*. Willa Cather quoted in Sharon O'Brien, "Combat Envy and Survivor Guilt: Willa Cather's 'Manly Battle Yarn,' " in *Arms and the Woman: War, Gender, and Literary Representation*, ed. Helen M. Cooper et al. (Chapel Hill, 1989), 184. On the New Women writers, including Kate Chopin, Charlotte Perkins Gilman, and Willa Cather, see Cecelia Tichi, "Women Writers and the New Woman," in *Columbia Literary History of the United States*, ed. Elliott, 589–606.

58. Mott, *History of American Magazines*, III, 537–39; Kate Tannet Wood, "Leshia," *Ladies' Home Journal*, 6 (June, July 1889), 1–2. For examples of the romanticization of the Revolution and early national period, see Mrs. Burton Harrison, "With Washington in the Minuet," *ibid.*, 15 (Feb. 1898), 1–2; and William Perrine, "When Washington Was Married," *ibid.*, 16 (July 1899), 2.

59. For examples of the romanticization of the "Old South" in *Ladies' Home Journal*, see Francis Lynde, "The Graves in the Old Breastworks: A Memorial Day Story of Old Alabama," *Ladies' Home Journal*, 15 (June 1898), 8; Paul Laurence Dunbar, "Dat Christmas on de Ol' Plantation," *ibid.*, 16 (Dec. 1898), 9; and "The Anecdotal Side of Robert E. Lee," *ibid.* (Nov. 1899), 3. A partial listing of Southern white women's diaries and reminiscences includes Eliza Frances Andrews, *The War-Time Journal of a Georgia Girl* (New York, 1908); Myrta Lockeet Avary, *A Virginia Girl in the Civil War* (New York, 1903); Fannie A. Beers, *Memories: A Record of Personal Experience and Adventure during Four Years of War* (Philadelphia, 1888); Virginia Clay-Clopton, *A Belle of the Fifties: Memoirs of Mrs. Clay, of Alabama* (New York, 1905); Mary Ann Harris Gay, *Life in Dixie during the War* (Atlanta, 1892); Parthenia Antoinette Hague, *A Blockaded Family: Life in Southern Alabama during the Civil War* (Boston, 1888); Mrs. Burton Harrison, *Recollections Grave and Gay* (New York, 1911); Mrs. Irby Morgan, *How It Was; Four Years among the Rebels* (Nashville, 1892); Mrs. Roger A. Pryor, *Reminiscences of Peace and War* (New York, 1905); Elizabeth Saxon, *A Southern Woman's War Time Reminiscences* (Memphis, 1905); and Louise Wigfall Wright, *A Southern Girl in 61* (New York, 1905). See also omnibus volumes such as Mrs. Thomas Taylor et al., eds., *South Carolina Women in the Confederacy* (2 vols., Columbia, S.C., 1903); and *News and Courier, "Our Women in the War": The Lives They Lived, the Deaths They Died* (Charleston, S.C., 1885). Nina Silber, "The Northern Myth of the Rebel Girl," in *Women of the American South: A Multicultural Reader*, ed. Christie Anne Farnham (New York, 1997), 130; and Silber, *Romance of Reunion*.

60. A partial listing of the extensive fiction of the war by Southern white women includes Emma Lyon Bryan, *1860–1865; A Romance of the Valley of Virginia* (Harrisonburg, 1892); Mollie E. Moore Davis, *In War Times at La Rose Blanche* (Boston, 1888); Virginia Boyle Frazer, *Brokenburne. A Southern Auntie's War Tale* (New York, 1897); Mrs. Burton Harrison, *Flower de Hundred; The Story of a Virginia Plantation* (New York, 1890); Mrs. Burton Harrison, *The Carlyles: A Story of the Fall of the Confederacy* (New York, 1905); Mrs. Burton Harrison, *Belhaven Tales; Crow's Nest; Una and King David* (New York, 1892); Mary Johnston, *The Long Roll* (Boston, 1911); Grace King, *Tales of a Time and Place* (New York, 1892); Mary Noailles Murfree, *The Storm Centre* (New York, 1905); and Molly Elliott Seawell, *The Victory* (1906). For helpful listings of Civil War fiction in the late nineteenth century, see Rebecca Washington Smith, "The Civil War and Its Aftermath in American Fiction, 1861–1899" (Ph.D. diss., University of Chicago, 1937); Robert A. Lively, *Fiction Fights the Civil War: An Unfinished Chapter in the Literary History of the American People* (Chapel Hill, 1957); and Albert J. Menendez, *Civil War Novels: An Annotated Bibliography* (New York, 1986). On Southern-oriented war literature, see Silber, *Romance of Reunion*; and Jay B. Hubbell, *The South in American Literature, 1607–1900* (Durham, 1954), esp. 695–740. For a partial bibliography of postwar war novels, see Menendez, *Civil War Novels*. Several

African American writers published reminiscences and fiction about the Civil War in this period, including Susie King Taylor and Frances Ellen Watkins Harper. On Harper's *Iola Leroy* and African American writing in the late nineteenth century, see Dickson D. Bruce Jr., *Black American Writing from the Nadir: The Evolution of a Literary Tradition, 1877–1915* (Baton Rouge, 1989). Drew Gilpin Faust, "Altars of Sacrifice: Confederate Women and the Narratives of War," *Journal of American History*, 76 (March 1990), 1200–28. There are many similarities between Northern and Southern wartime literature representing a women's war, especially an insistence on the value of women's sacrifice for the nation. Representations of Northern women's war experiences, however, rarely expressed the loss of faith in the ideology of sacrifice that Faust has found in those of Southern women's experiences late in the war.

61. Livermore, *My Story of the War*, 8–9. For other memoirs by Northern nurses published in this period, see Amanda Akin Stearns, *The Lady Nurse of Ward E* (New York, 1909); Annie Wittenmyer, *Under the Guns: A Woman's Reminiscences of the Civil War* (Boston, 1895); Katherine Prescott Wormeley, *The Other Side of the War* (Boston, 1889); and Mary G. Holland, *Our Army Nurses* (Boston, 1895). A few Northern women published reminiscences of the war, including Septima M. Collis, *A Woman's War Record* (New York, 1889). Nina Silber, "Introduction," in Mary Livermore, *My Story of the War* (1887; New York, 1995), xii.

62. Wilbur Fisk Tillett, "Southern Womanhood as Affected by the War," *Century*, 43 (Nov. 1891), 9–16; and Lida Lord Reed, "A Woman's Experiences during the Siege of Vicksburg," *ibid.*, 61 (April 1901), 922–28.

63. Edward Bellamy, "An Echo of Antietam," *ibid.*, 38 (July 1889), 379. The most concerted protests against the rewriting of the war in the 1880s and 1890s came from African Americans. See Blight, *Frederick Douglass' Civil War.*

64. Elizabeth Stuart Phelps, "Annie Laurie," *Harper's New Monthly Magazine*, 76 (Dec. 1887), 127, 126. See also Elizabeth Stuart Phelps, "The Oath of Allegiance," *Atlantic Monthly*, 73 (April 1894), 465–76.

65. Phelps, "Annie Laurie," 135–37.

66. Elizabeth Stuart Phelps, *Comrades* (New York, 1911), 38, 39–40, 13.

67. Hemingway quoted in Aaron, *Unwritten War*, 210.

68. Natalie Zemon Davis, "Toward Mixtures and Margins," *American Historical Review*, 97 (Dec. 1992), 1415.

10

To Catch the Vision of Freedom
Reconstructing Southern Black Women's Political History, 1865–1880

Elsa Barkley Brown

After emancipation, African American women, as part of black communities throughout the South, struggled to define on their own terms the meaning of freedom. Much of the literature on Reconstruction-era African American women's political history has focused on the debates at the national level over the Fifteenth Amendment, which revolved around the question of whether the enfranchisement of African American men or the enfranchisement of women should take precedence.[1] Such discussions, explicitly or not, contribute to a political framework that assumes democratic political struggles in the late-nineteenth-century United States were waged in pursuit of constitutional guarantees of full personhood and citizenship. A careful investigation of the actions of African American women between 1865 and 1880, however, leads one to question that framework. Historians seeking to reconstruct the post-Civil War political history of African American women have first to determine whether the conceptualizations of republican representative government and liberal democracy, which are the parameters of such a discussion, are the most appropriate ones for understanding southern black women's search for freedom—even political freedom—following the Civil War.

The family and the concept of community as family offered the unifying thread that bound African Americans together in the postslavery world. The efforts to reunite family and to establish ways of providing for all community members occupied much of freed people's time and attention. In their June 1865 petition to President Andrew Johnson, black men and women in Richmond, Virginia, for example, took note of the considerable efforts many had undergone in the two months since emancipation to reunite "long estranged and affectionate families." It was probably in recognition of the hope inherent in emancipation's possibility of family units existing physically together that the city's African Baptist churches replaced the prewar seating patterns, which had placed men and women separately, with families sitting together.[2]

Family members provided a variety of support—physical, economic, emotional, and psychological. Camilla Jones cared for her husband and two children and for the home and son of her widowed brother, who lived in a separate apartment in the same tenement. Rachel and Abraham Johnson, who had no children, shared their home with Mary Jones, Rachel's widowed sister, and her three children. While the thirty-four-year-old widow Catherine Green went to work in a tobacco factory, her thirty-five-year-old single sister, Laura Gaines, cared for Catherine's son and took in washing to add to the family income. Elderly parents moved in with children, as did Mariah Morton, who lived in the 1870s with her two daughters, one a widow as well and the other single. Parents opened bank accounts for their children, even those who were adult, away from home, married, and employed. And children who left Richmond to search for work elsewhere provided for the money in their savings accounts to be used by other relatives, if needed, during their absence.[3] In all these ways African American women and men testified to the notion of family members as having a mutual and continuing responsibility to help each other and to prepare for hard times.

This sense of shared responsibility extended past blood ties to include in-laws and even fictive kin. Thus Eliza Winston, a sixty-year-old washerwoman, took in a fourteen-year-old girl, saw to it that she was able to attend school rather than seek employment, and made her the beneficiary of her savings account. Those who had a place to live made room in their homes for those with whom they had labored as "fellow servants" during slavery. Unmarried or widowed mothers moved in with other single mothers in order to provide mutual support.[4]

Churches and secret societies, based on similar ideas of collective consciousness and collective responsibility, served to extend and reaffirm notions of family throughout the black community. Not only in their houses but also in their meeting halls and places of worship, they were brothers and sisters caring for each other. The institutionalization of this notion of family cemented the community. Community/family members recognized that the understanding of collective responsibility had to be maintained from generation to generation. Such maintenance was in part the function of the juvenile branches of the mutual benefit associations, as articulated by the statement of purpose of the Children's Rosebud Fountains, Grand Fountain United Order of True Reformers:

> Teaching them ... to assist each other in sickness, sorrow and afflictions and in the struggles of life; teaching them that one's happiness greatly depends upon the others. . . . Teach them to live united. . . . The children of different families will know how to . . . talk, plot and plan for one another's peace and happiness in the journey of life.
>
> Teach them to . . . bear each other's burdens . . . to so bind and tie their love and affections together that one's sorrow may be the other's sorrow, one's distress be the other's distress, one's penny the other's penny.[5]

The institutions that ex-slaves developed give testament to the fact that their vision of freedom was not merely an individual one or, as historian Thomas C. Holt has put it, "that autonomy was not simply personal" but "embraced familial and community relationships as well." While Fanny Jackson, a student at the Lincoln Institute in Richmond in 1867, might declare, "I am highly animated to think that slavery is dead, and I am my own woman," the vision of autonomy which she then articulated embraced her husband, her children, and her community at large.[6] African Americans throughout the South in the post-Civil War period emphatically articulated their understanding that freedom and autonomy could not be independently achieved. In 1865 women in Richmond who attempted to support themselves and their families through domestic work noted the impossibility of paying the "rents asked for houses and rooms," given "the prices paid for our labor." They feared that many would be led "into temptation" out of economic necessity.[7] Mutual benefit societies and churches sought to provide some relief; a number of single black women banded together in homes and in secret societies. Despite these efforts, their worst fears were realized and an unknown number of black women were reduced to prostitution in order to feed, shelter, and clothe themselves and their loved ones. Ann Lipscomb, a single mother who worked, when possible, as a seamstress, was one such woman. Yet in 1872 when she joined with other single mothers to organize the Mutual Benevolent Society, they elected her president and entrusted their bank account to her.[8] Thus they quite emphatically demonstrated the notion of collective autonomy; they understood that none of them would be free until and unless Ann Lipscomb was also free. Their fates were intimately tied together; individual freedom could be achieved only through collective autonomy.

This understanding of autonomy was shared by those who had been slave and those who had been free.[9] In fact, the whole process of emancipation may have, at least momentarily, reaffirmed the common bonds of ex-slave and previously free, for, despite their individual freedom in law, "freedom" in actuality did not come to free black men and women until the emancipation of slaves. Thus their own personal experiences confirmed for previously free men and women as well as ex-slaves the limitations of personal autonomy and affirmed the idea of collective autonomy.[10]

The vision of social relations that Ann Lipscomb and her fellow black Richmonders articulated was not the traditional nineteenth-century notion of possessive individualism whereby society is merely an aggregation of individuals, each of whom is ultimately responsible for herself or himself.[11] In this individual autonomy, "whether one eats or starves depends solely on one's individual will and capacities." According to liberal ideology, it is the self-regulating impersonality of contractual relations that makes social relations just.[12] Such a notion of freedom and social responsibility was diametrically opposed to the one that undergirded black institutional developments in Richmond and elsewhere in the post-Civil War period, where the community and each individual in the community were ultimately responsible for every other person. Whether one eats or starves in this setting depends on the available resources within the community as a whole. Individuals must each do their part and are free to make decisions about their lives, but ultimately it is the resources of the whole that determine the fate of the individual. This vision of social responsibility was expressed in the Richmond Humane Society's September 1865 proposal that the approximately eighteen thousand black Baptists and Methodists in the city contribute twenty cents each to a coffer of $3,600 that could be the basis for providing relief for the poor in the community.[13] Black Richmonders were proud of their communal consciousness. In their 1865 petition to President Johnson they asserted that "none of our people are in the alms-house and when we were slaves, the aged and infirm who were turned away from the homes of hard masters, who had been enriched by their toil, our benevolent societies supported while they lived, and buried them when they died." Because of this assumption of communal responsibility, they proudly proclaimed, "comparatively few of us found it necessary to ask for Government rations, which have been so bountifully bestowed upon the unrepentant Rebels of Richmond."[14]

It is a striking example of the different vision held by white Freedmen's Bureau officials throughout the South that they regarded this ethos of mutuality as one of the negative traits that had to be curtailed in the process of preparing freedpeople for life in a liberal democratic society. One South Carolina bureau agent, John De Forest, lamented the tendency among freedpeople to assume obligations to "a horde of lazy relatives and neighbors, thus losing a precious opportunity to get ahead on their own." A case in point was Aunt Judy, who, though supporting herself and her children on her meager income as a laundress, had "benevolently taken in, and was nursing, a sick woman of her own race . . . The thoughtless charity of this penniless Negress in receiving another poverty-stricken creature under her roof was characteristic of the freedmen. However selfish, and even dishonest, they might be, they were extravagant in giving."[15] As historian Jacqueline Jones has pointed out, De Forest's notion that the willingness to share constituted a "thoughtless" act was a product of assumptions "that a 'rational' economic being would labor only to enhance her own material welfare."[16] The different vision of African American women, and of freedpeople in general, posed a persistent problem for northern white men and women, who consistently sought to reeducate and assimilate freedpeople to the requirements of the free labor ideology by introducing a different cultural worldview as a means of imposing a different economic and political worldview as well.

Recent historical explorations of the transition from slavery to freedom have provided substantial evidence that the economic vision of many African American women and men differed fundamentally from that imposed even by freedpeople's most supportive white allies. Northern white men and women assumed that ex-slaves would, in the postwar world, form a disciplined working class. Ex-slaves, in large part, shared a different economic vision.[17] They were "always on the move," searching for family, denying their labor to "dishonest or oppressive employers," and asserting their independence through their mobility. Rather than staying in place, working as much as possible for as high a wage as possible, and thus possibly accumulating a greater array of material goods, a large number of freedpeople sought not to maximize income but to minimize the amount of "time spent at work on other people's behalf." Domestic workers who moved from employer to employer, thus exasperating white women who despaired of ever finding reliable—that is, stable, permanent—servants, showed elements of this pattern.[18] Black men and women throughout the South, whether laboring on small farms or plantations or in homes or factories, generally made economic decisions based on family priorities rather than individual aspirations. For many men and women, higher wages served as an incentive not to more work but to less, for they allowed one to obtain the basic necessities in shorter periods of time and thus eliminate the need for long-term employment under someone else's control. Such behavior appeared lazy or irrational to those who assumed freedpeople should adopt naturally those habits of thrift, diligence, and acquisitiveness that were a cornerstone of free labor ideology.[19]

In a larger society that assumed economic behavior to be a reflection of innate human characteristics rather than socially defined ones, freedwomen's behavior, like freedmen's, left them subject to a variety of assumptions about their inherent "nature," in light of their obvious nonconformity to what was presented as normal human behavior. Racist ideology was thus fed ex-slaves' adoption of a different economic worldview than that which was increasingly becoming the norm in the late-nineteenth-century United States. So deeply embedded are these assumptions that historians, too, have often assumed the imperative of a free wage labor system to be the equivalent of normal behavior and thus either have berated ex-slaves for not voluntarily adopting these modes of behavior at emancipation or, more sympathetically, have tried to defend ex-slaves against charges of being lazy by arguing that they did follow this norm but racist white people just did not admit it. As the works of historians Barbara Fields and Thomas Holt point out, both of these sets of interpretations stem from a framework much like that adopted by post-Civil War white northerners.[20] Rather than accepting ex-slaves' behavior as evidence of a different and equally valid consciousness that refutes our socially defined assumptions about innate economic behavior, both interpretations assume an absolute norm and then proceed to demonstrate how well ex-slaves either did or did not measure up. While the purpose of one may be proving the inferiority of African Americans, and of the other rescuing ex-slaves from such declarations of inferiority, both begin with the same externally imposed parameters and thus miss the ex-slaves' experiences altogether.

The ex-slaves' economic worldview developed from different criteria than those of the larger white society. The worldview that defined the black community's notions of the function of labor equally defined its image of freedom and the approach to secure it. It is this worldview from which all social, political, and economic institutions took shape. If an understanding of the different worldviews from which African Americans and Euro-Americans operated in the post-Civil War South is necessary to analyze work, family, and community behavior, then a similar understanding is also fundamental to an analysis of the political position of African American women in this same time period. Relatively little has been written about southern black women's participation in Reconstruction-era politics; what has been cited has often been descriptive and anecdotal. The few efforts at analysis have failed to consider the possibility of a radically different political worldview in the African American community. For example, Jacqueline Jones notes the fundamental difference in Aunt Judy's "ethos of mutuality" and John De Forest's "possessive individualism" as it pertained to Aunt Judy's economic behavior, but she then fails to adopt a similar logic in her political analysis. Instead, she falls back on notions of republican representative government that stem from the same theory of possessive individualism she has rejected as inappropriate to her economic analysis. Thus Jones "searches in vain for any mention of women delegates in accounts of formal black political conventions . . . local and state gatherings during which men formulated and articulated their vision of a just postwar society." Jones does note that "freedwomen sometimes spoke up forcefully at meetings devoted to specific community issues." But she concludes that "black men . . . like other groups in nineteenth century America . . . believed that males alone were responsible for—and capable of—the serious business of politicking." Freedwomen, Jones tells us, "remained outside the formal political process" and thus occupied "in this respect . . . a similarly inferior position" as white women.[21] Jones's analysis assumes a universal meaning to the fact that men—black and white—were able to cast a vote and women—black and white—were not. She thus invests the meaning in the act of voting itself rather than in the relations in which that act is embedded. As this essay will demonstrate, just what, in any given case, voting or not voting means has to be investigated and determined, not presumed. Having looked for and not found women delegates, women officeholders, or women otherwise exercising a *legal* franchise—all the important political liberties in a republican representative government—Jones misses what she does see: women participating in democracy in a most fundamental way. Jones's perspective rests on a common contemporary assumption, drawn from nineteenth-century political ideology, that the key political right, and responsibility, is the exercise of a legally granted franchise. The obsession in African American women's political history with questions of legal enfranchisement thus stems from this larger preconception.[22]

A thorough effort to uncover evidence of southern black women's political behavior during the latter half of the nineteenth century is vitally needed. In addition, there is a need to develop an interpretative framework consistent with the alternative economic, institutional, and cultural worldview of freedpeople. The following analysis is based on my ongoing research on Richmond, Virginia, and on published materials on the postwar years in other areas of the South.[23]

The Reconstruction Act of 1867 required all the former Confederate states, except Tennessee, to hold constitutional conventions. Black men were enfranchised for the delegate selection and ratification ballots. In Virginia, Republican ward clubs elected delegates to the party's state convention, where a platform was to be adopted. On 1 August, the day the Republican state convention opened in Richmond, thousands of African American men, women, and children absented themselves from their employment and joined the delegates at the convention site, the First African Baptist Church. Tobacco factories, lacking a major portion of their workers, were forced to close for the day. This pattern persisted whenever a major issue came before the state and city Republican conventions held during the summer and fall of 1867 or the state constitutional convention that convened in Richmond from December 1867 to March 1868. A *New York Times* reporter estimated that "the entire colored population of Richmond" attended the October 1867 local Republican convention, where delegates to the state constitutional convention were nominated. Noting that female domestic servants composed a large portion of those in attendance, the correspondent reported: "[A]s is usual on such occasions, families which employ servants were forced to cook their own dinners, or content themselves with a cold lunch. Not only had Sambo gone to the Convention, but Dinah was there also."[24]

It is important to note that these men and women did not absent themselves from work just to be onlookers at the proceedings. Rather, they intended to be active participants. They assumed as equal a right to be present and participate as the delegates themselves, a fact they made abundantly clear at the August 1867 Republican state convention. Having begun to arrive four hours before the opening session, African American women and men had filled the meeting place long before the delegates arrived. Having shown up to speak for themselves, they did not assume delegates had priority—in discussion or in seating. Disgusted at the scene, as well as unable to find seats, the conservative white Republican delegates removed to the Capitol Square to convene an outdoor session. That was quite acceptable to the several thousand additional

African American men and women who, unable to squeeze into the church, were now able to participate in the important discussions and to vote down the proposals of the conservative faction.[25]

Black Richmonders were also active participants throughout the state constitutional convention. A *New York Times* reporter commented on the tendency for the galleries to be crowded "with the 'unprivileged,' and altogether black." At issue was not just these men's and women's presence but also their behavior. White women, for example, certainly on occasion sat in the convention's gallery as visitors silently observing the proceedings; these African Americans, however, participated from the gallery, loudly engaging in the debates. At points of heated controversy, black delegates turned to the crowds as they made their addresses on the convention floor, obviously soliciting and relying upon mass participation. Outside the convention hours, mass meetings were held to discuss and vote on the major issue. At these gatherings vote was either by voice or by rising, and men, women, and children voted. These meetings were not mock assemblies; they were important gatherings at which the community made plans for freedom. The most radical black Republican faction argued that the major convention issues should actually be settled at these mass meetings with delegates merely casting the community's vote on the convention floor. Though this did not occur, black delegates were no doubt influenced by the mass meetings in the community and the African American presence in the galleries, both of which included women.[26]

Black Richmonders were, in fact, operating in two political arenas— an internal one and an external one. Though these arenas were related, each proceeded from different assumptions, had different purposes, and therefore operated according to different rules. Within the internal political process women were enfranchised and participated in all public forums —the parades, rallies, mass meetings, and conventions themselves.[27] Richmond is not atypical in this regard.[28]

It was the state constitutional convention, however, that would decide African American women's and men's status in the political process external to the African American community. When the Virginia convention began its deliberations regarding the franchise, Thomas Bayne, a black delegate from Norfolk, argued the inherent link between freedom and suffrage and contended that those who opposed universal suffrage were actually opposing the freedom of African American people:

> If the negro was out of the question, I think it would be admitted that it [suffrage] was a God-given right. . . . [T]he State of Virginia [has] no rights to give to the black man . . . How can any man assume to give me a right. . . . I want this Convention to understand that the right of suffrage and the right of liberty cannot be separated. . . . When one ceases, the other ceases. . . . No sooner did separation take place between these rights, than the strong began to oppress and predominate over the weak. . . . I repeat it as the sincere conviction of my heart, that this is an inherent right, this right of suffrage. . . . If you tell a man that this right is a privilege that you have to confer upon him, he will want to know where you got it. . . . If it is a right that men can confer, that power of the right to confer is because of their strength. . . . When we have the right to exercise this right of suffrage . . . the weak can stand up in their manhood and in their knowledge that it is God-given, and bear down all opposition.[29]

In rejoinder, E. L. Gibson, a conservative white delegate, enunciated several principles of republican representative government. Contending that "a man might be free and still not have the right to vote," Gibson explained the fallacy of assuming that this civil right was an inherent corollary to freedom: If the right were inherent, then it would belong to both sexes and to all from "the first moment of existence" and to foreigners immediately. This was "an absurdity too egregious to be contemplated."[30] And yet this "absurd" notion of political rights was in practice in the Richmond black community, where males and females voted without regard to age and the thousands of rural migrants who came into Richmond were subject to no waiting period but immediately possessed the full rights of the community.[31] What was absurd to Gibson and most white men—Republican or Democrat—was obviously quite rational to many black Richmonders. Two different conceptions of freedom and public participation in the political process were in place.

Gibson's arguments relied on several assumptions that were by then basic to U.S. democracy.[32] First were the ideas that freedom and political liberty were not synonymous and that people could be free without having political liberty. In fact, not all free people were entitled to political liberty because some persons were not capable, that is, not "fit" to exercise political liberty. Thus only those persons who had acquired the manners and morals that enabled them to exercise their freedom responsibly and properly were entitled to political liberty. A certain uniformity was expected; persons who had not yet learned to regulate their lives appropriately—to be thrifty, industrious, and diligent—were not yet capable of responsibly exercising this liberty. Those not capable of political liberty would rely on those capable of it to protect their freedom.[33]

Although Gibson did not specifically articulate this next point, the logic of his assumptions leads to the conclusion that even those with political liberty—as indicated by the right of suffrage—were not equally capable of political decision making. Thus the majority of the people, including the majority of those with suffrage, were expected to leave political decision making to those more qualified. Such political assumptions required that an individual, having once achieved freedom, hand over to others the responsibilities and rights of preserving her or his freedom. In fact, late-nineteenth-century assumptions concerning republican representative government required that the majority of people be passive in their exercise of freedom for the proper operation of democracy. Suffrage granted people not the right to participate in political decision making but the right to participate in choosing political decision makers. Having become accustomed to this political process by now, we often act as if the two are synonymous. Freedpeople knew they were not.

In a frequently noted observation on women in Reconstruction-era politics, Elizabeth Botume, a northern white teacher in Beaufort, South Carolina, made clear that the political view many white northerners tried to impose was consistent with a particular economic view, too:

> Most of the field-work was done by the women and girls; their lords and masters were much interrupted in agricultural pursuits by their political and religious duties. When the days of "*conventions*" came, the men were rarely at home; but the women kept steadily at work in the fields. As we drove around, we saw them patiently "cleaning up their ground," "listing," "chopping down the old cotton stalks and hoeing them under," gathering "sedge" and "trash" from the riverside, which they carried in baskets on their heads, and spread over the land. And later, hoeing the crops and gathering them in.
>
> We could not help wishing that since so much of the work was done by the colored women,—raising the provisions for their families, besides making and selling their own cotton, they might also hold some of the offices held by the men. I am confident they would despatch business if allowed to go to the polls; instead of listening and hanging around all day, discussing matters of which they knew so little, they would exclaim,—
>
> "Let me vote and go; I've got work to do."[34]

Botume's analysis hinged on several assumptions: that adoption of habits of thrift and diligence were the factors that qualified one for suffrage; that voting equaled political participation; and that "listening and hanging around all day, discussing matters," were not important forms of political participation. Botume, like so many northern allies, thought free black people were to earn the rights of freedom by adopting the proper habits of responsibility and industry. Her lament was that these African American women, who had been "reconstructed" in that sense, were not rewarded by the franchise.[35] Central to her complaint about African American women's disfranchisement is her exasperation at African American men's assumption that political rights included the right to participate in political discussions (and thereby political decision making). She believed these industrious women, having come to exercise their proper economic role, would also adopt their appropriate role in the political system and would properly exercise the suffrage. They would vote and get on back to work rather than hang around engaging in political issues that, she thought, neither they nor the men had capacity to understand. Botume would leave it to others more capable to make the important political decisions. Thus even the slight support southern black women mustered among white northerners for their enfranchisement came in a context that would have preferred to leave them far less active in the political process than they had been in the most immediate post-Civil War days.

The history of African American women's political involvement in South Carolina and elsewhere leaves one dubious about Botume's predictions regarding how black women would exercise the franchise. Nevertheless, Botume's observations do point to the fact that in the end only men obtained the legal franchise. The impact of this decision is neither inconsequential nor fully definitive. African American women were by law excluded from the political arena external to their community. Yet this does not mean that they were not active in that arena—witness Richmond women's participation in the Republican and the constitutional conventions.

Southern black men and women debated the issue of woman suffrage in both the external and internal political arenas, with varying results. Delegates to the South Carolina convention, 56 percent of whom were black, adopted a constitution that included "male" as a qualification for voting, despite a stirring argument for woman suffrage from William J. Whipper, a black delegate from Beaufort. Nevertheless, a significant proportion of South Carolina's Reconstruction-era black elected officials favored woman suffrage or were at least open to a serious discussion of the issue. It was the South Carolina House of Representatives, which was 61 percent black, that allowed Louisa Rollin to speak on the floor of the assembly in support of woman suffrage in March 1869. Several black male representatives argued in favor of the proposal then and again two years later, when Lottie Rollin led a woman suffrage rally at the state capital. In March 1872 Beverly Nash, a state senator, and Whipper, then a state representative, joined with other delegates to propose a woman suffrage amendment to the state constitution. Alonzo J. Ransier, U.S. congressman from South Carolina and later the state's first black lieutenant governor, presented his argument on the floor of the U.S. House of Representatives in 1874: "[U]ntil [women as well as men have the right to vote] the government of the United States cannot be said to rest upon the 'consent of the governed.' " According to historian Rosalyn Terborg-Penn, Ransier, who was president of the South Carolina Woman's Rights Association, was widely supported by his black South Carolinian colleagues. In fact, six of the eight black men who represented South Carolina in the U.S. Congress during the Reconstruction era supported woman suffrage.[36]

The question of woman suffrage was a subject of discussion in other southern legislative chambers as well. It was often raised by white men to demonstrate the absurdity of black delegates' argument for the inherent right of suffrage. Black delegates, even when they rejected woman suffrage, were far more likely to treat it as a matter for serious discussion. If not expressing support, which they often did, black delegates were far more likely to express at least ambivalence rather than firm conviction of the absurdity of female electorates. Thomas Bayne, the Virginia delegate who so articulately delineated the argument for suffrage as an inherent right, presents one of the more complex cases. Unsupported by white Republicans in his assertion of inherent right and jeered by Gibson and other white conservative delegates, Bayne retorted,

> In speaking of the right to women to vote, I thought it an inherent right, and that women were wrongfully deprived of it. While I do not say that this is my opinion, yet I would simply say, in answer to that, that woman's right is a right to stay home. It is woman's right to raise and bear children, and to train them for their future duties in life. When she does that she is performing high duties which God himself has imposed upon her, in order that those children may carry out and exercise this very God-given right.[37]

Thus Bayne followed the logic of his "inherent right" argument, rejected his opponents' belief that woman suffrage was an absurdity, and conceded that as an inherent right "women were wrongfully deprived of it." He then, however, proceeded to what on the surface appears a very traditional statement of women's roles as confined to the domestic arena. But, by stating domestic roles as "rights," given the context of Reconstruction labor relations, he perhaps implies that his quarrel was not with those who supported woman suffrage but with those who would deny black women the right to domestic duties by obligating them to labor outside the home. Bayne did not, for example, say that a woman's right to stay home was her only right, nor did he suggest that training children was her highest duty or only duty. Historian Michael Hucles has pointed out that Bayne himself, in a discussion of his own terminology, said he often used the word *men* to stand for all human beings, male and female, thus affirming the possibility that his arguments for suffrage were intended as statements regarding universal suffrage, as in fact they were taken by Gibson and other white conservatives and radicals. Until more detailed research is done, determining Bayne's true meaning is well-nigh impossible. He does, however, clarify the problems with simplistic gender analyses of black male and female behavior in a time period when all economic, political, and social relations were in a state of redefinition. Black women and men had to redefine their relationships within the context of their own worldview and the realities of late-nineteenth-century U.S. society. Bayne may well have found himself confronted with the ambiguities inherent in such a situation, and his own position may be as contradictory as it sounds. Alternatively, he may have been stating quite clearly two distinct and contradictory rights of black women—rights in what historians would call both the public and private spheres—thus making clear the artificiality of the distinctions that historians make.[38] Whatever Bayne's particular position, it is clear that serious discussion of woman suffrage in southern legislative chambers during the Reconstruction era seemed to depend upon a strong African American representation.

The debate over woman suffrage occurred in the internal arena as well, with varying results. In Nansemond County, Virginia, a mass meeting held that women should get the legal franchise; in Richmond, while a number of participants in a mass meeting held for female suffrage, the majority opinion swung against it.[39] But the meaning of that decision was not as straightforward as it may seem. The debate as to whether women should be given the vote in the external political arena occurred in internal political arena mass meetings where women participated and voted not just before and during *but also after* the negative decision regarding legal enfranchisement. This mass meeting's decision maintained the status quo in the external community; ironically enough, the status quo in the internal community was maintained as well—women continued to have a vote. Both African American men and women clearly operated within two distinct political systems. Eventually the external system would have its effect and the debate over women's enfranchisement would come to be more fully related to the internal political system. When this occurred, it had ramifications far into internal community institutions as well. Thus African American women sitting in Richmond's First African Baptist Church in the 1880s had to fight for the right to vote in church meetings and were in the 1890s even asked to defend their presence at these meetings.[40]

Focusing on formal disfranchisement, however, obscures the larger story. The economic and political circumstances of African Americans underwent significant change in the years following emancipation. We may imagine that the political frameworks thus significantly changed as well. Black women's vision of freedom and democracy, like that of black people as a whole, may never have been that expansive again. Yet we must be alert to the persistence of old patterns along with the adoption of new. In the changing political frameworks one might expect to find a continuing thread of women's political participation even at the same time as one finds them more and more fundamentally excluded from both the external and the internal political process.

In Richmond and throughout the South exclusion from legal enfranchisement did not prevent African American women from affecting the vote and the political decisions. They organized political societies such as the Rising Daughters of Liberty, which actively engaged in political campaigns by educating the community on the issues, raising funds for candidates, and getting out the vote. Coal miners' wives living outside Manchester, Virginia, played a similar role through the United Daughters of Liberty. Mississippi freedwomen placed themselves in potentially dangerous positions by wearing Republican campaign buttons during the 1868 election. In some instances the women walked "all the way to town, as many as twenty or thirty miles," to "buy, beg, or borrow one, and thus equipped return and wear it openly in defiance of . . . master, mistress, or overseer" and sometimes of husband as well. Domestic servants also risked job and perhaps personal injury by wearing their buttons to work. "To refuse, neglect, or lack the courage to wear that badge . . . amounted almost to a voluntary return to slavery," according to many freedwomen and freedmen.[41]

Black women initially took an active role in the South Carolina political meetings. Those disfranchised women whom Botume imagined would vote and go home, not involving themselves in political discussion, displayed a particular insistence on continued *public* political activity. The assumptions that underlay these women's activities are instructive. Laura Towne, a northern white teacher, tells us it was the white Republicans who first announced to the freedpeople that "women and children ought to stay at home on such occasions." Yet it does not appear to be merely the presence of females that disturbed these white men, for they quickly made it clear that Towne, of course, was welcome. Their announcement was meant to exclude "outsiders who were making some noise." Probably because of protests or disregard of the exclusion notice, the white Republicans modified their initial ban to state that "the *females* can come or not as they choose, . . . but the meeting is for men voters." It was clearly the women's failure to take the position of passive observers that was being censured.[42] Some black men took their cue, one even using the occasion to prompt women to " 'stay at home and cut grass,' that is, hoe the corn and cotton fields—clear them of grass!" while the men were at the political meetings.[43]

Even though they were excluded from further participation in the Republican meetings by the late 1860s, African American women in South Carolina, Louisiana, and elsewhere were still attending the meetings in the 1870s.[44] Although women were never elected delegates, it does appear that occasionally women were sent to the political meetings on behalf of their community. Lucy McMillan, a South Carolina widow, reported that her attendance at a political meeting was the result of community pressure: "They all kept at me to go. I went home and they quizzed me to hear what was said, and I told them as far as my senses allowed me."[45]

Women's presence at the meetings was often anything but passive. In the violent political atmosphere of the last years of Reconstruction, they had an especially important—and dangerous—role. While the men participated in the meeting, the women guarded the guns—thus serving in part as the protectors of the meeting. This was not a symbolic or safe role in a time when "men are shot at, hunted down, trapped and held till certain meetings are over, and intimidated in every possible way." During the violent times of late Reconstruction, African American women in South Carolina were reported "in arms, carrying axes or hatchets in their hands hanging down at their sides, their aprons or dresses half-concealing the weapons." One clergyman, contending African Americans could defend themselves if necessary, noted that "80,000 black men in the State . . . can use Winchesters and 200,000 black women . . . can light a torch and use a knife." At times women as well as men actually took up arms. In 1878 Robert Smalls, attacked by redshirts* while attempting to address a Republican meeting in Gillison-ville, sought refuge and later reported that "every colored man and woman seized whatever was at hand—guns, axes, hoes, etc., and ran to the rescue." Some of these women probably had double incentive, as the redshirts had "slap[ped] the faces of the colored women coming to the meeting."[46]

African American women took the political events to heart and took dramatic steps to make their political sentiments known. They also expressed their outrage when the political tide turned against their interests. Alabama women reportedly "were converted to Radicalism long before the men and almost invariably used their influence strongly for the purpose of the League." South Carolina Democrats believed African American women to be "the head and fount of the opposition." Thomas Holt has suggested that the South Carolina black woman's "reputation for political partisanship was . . . enhanced by her frequent appearance at the head of angry Charleston mobs, like the one which wreaked havoc on the German merchants after the Republican defeat in the municipal elections of 1871."[47]

African American women in South Carolina and elsewhere understood themselves to have a vital stake in African American men's franchise. The fact that only men had been granted the vote did not mean that only men should exercise that vote. Women reportedly initiated sanctions against men who voted Democratic. One South Carolina witness reported that "no mens were to go to the polls unless their wives were right alongside of them; some had hickory sticks; some had nails—four nails drive in the shape of a cross—and dare their husbands to vote any other than the Republican ticket." In the highly charged political atmosphere of the late 1870s it was no small matter for these women to show up at the election site carrying weapons. Armed Democrats patrolled the polling areas, and Republicans were often "driven from the polls with knives and clubs. Some of them were badly wounded."[48] We might wonder whether the weapons the women carried were for use on their husbands or on the Democratic opponents, but in either case these women very publicly declared their stake in their husband's vote.

Black Republican politicians throughout the South took women's participation seriously and publicly encouraged them to abstain from sexual relations with any man who voted Democratic. Some women left their Democratic husbands. Engaged women were encouraged to postpone the wedding until after the election, when they could obtain assurance that their future husband was not a Democrat. In Alabama women banded together in political clubs to enforce these sanctions collectively. Some politicians also endorsed women's use of weapons to influence their husbands' vote.[49] It is likely that, rather than initiating these actions on the part of African American women, Republican legislators merely recognized and endorsed actions initiated by the women themselves. These examples all suggest that African American women and men understood the vote as a collective possession, not an individual one, and furthermore that African American women, unable to cast a separate vote, viewed African American men's vote as equally theirs. Their belief that the franchise should be cast in the best interest of both was not the nineteenth-century patriarchal notion that men voted on behalf of their wives and children. By the latter assumption, women had no individual wills; rather, men operated in women's best interest because women were assumed to have no right of input. African American women assumed the political rights that came with being a member of the community, even though they were not granted the political rights they thought should come with being citizens of the state.

---

* Rifle clubs organized to intimidate black voters and secure Wade Hamptom's election as governor in 1876; sometimes used to describe any armed white supremacist group in late 1870s South Carolina.

The whole sense of the ballot as collectively owned is most eloquently presented by Violet Keeling, a tobacco worker who testified in February 1884 before a Senate committee investigating the violence in the previous year's elections in Danville, Virginia. Assenting in her husband's decision not to vote in that election for fear he might be killed, she made it clear that she would not, however, assent in his or anyone else's voting Democratic: "[A]s for my part, if I hear of a colored man voting the Democratic ticket I stay, as far from him as I can; I don't have nothing in the world to do with him. . . . No, sir; I don't 'tallow him to come in my house." Asked why she should "have such a dislike to a colored man that votes the Democratic ticket," she replied:

> I think that if the race of colored people that has got no friends nohow, and if they don't hang together they won't have none while one party is going one way and another the other. I don't wish to see a colored man sell himself when he can do without. Of course we all have to live, and I always like to have a man live even if he works for 25 cents a day, but I don't want to see him sell himself away. . . . I think if a colored man votes the Democratic ticket he has always sold himself. . . . If I knew a colored man that voted the Democratic ticket to come to my house, I would tell him to go somewhere else and visit.

Asked "suppose your husband should go and vote a Democratic ticket," she responded: "I would just picke up my clothes and go to my father's, if I had a father, or would go to work for 25 cents a day."[50]

Violet Keeling clearly articulated the notion that a black man could not exercise his vote only in his own behalf. If he sold his vote, he sold hers. The whole issue of the ostracism of black Democrats reveals very clearly the assumptions regarding suffrage that were operative throughout African American communities. Black Democrats were subject to the severest exclusion: disciplined within or quite often expelled from their churches, kicked out of mutual benefit societies, not allowed to work alongside others in the fields or accepted in leadership positions at work or in the community. Ministers were dismissed from their churches or had their licenses to preach revoked; teachers who voted Democratic found themselves without pupils. Democrats' children were not allowed in schools. And, perhaps the most severe sanction of all, black Democrats found themselves unaided at the time of a family member's death. Women participated in all of these actions as well as in the mobs that jeered, jostled, and sometimes beat black Democrats or rescued those who were arrested for such behavior. In fact, women were often reported to be the leaders of such mob involvements.[51] One historian noted that "the average negro . . . believed it was a crime 'to vote against their race.' "[52]

From the perspective of liberal democratic political ideology, these activities might be perceived as "unconscionable" "interference with the [individual voter's] expression of . . . political preference."[53] But African Americans in the post-Civil War South understood quite clearly that the actions of one member of the community affected, and in this instance endangered, all others in that community. Thus they understood there was no such thing as an individual action or a "possessive individual," owing nothing to society. This understanding was most clearly put by Robert Gleed, a Mississippi state senator, in his 1871 testimony before the U.S. Senate:

> [I]t is traitorous in these men to acquiesce with a party who says we have no rights in the community in common with other citizens. . . . They [black Democrats] have the right [to vote Democratic] just like Benedict Arnold had a right to trade off the army just like he did; but that does not make it justice and equity because he did.[54]

The issue, as Gleed and many black men and women understood it, was not autonomy but responsibility. It was that sense of suffrage as a collective possession, not an individual one, that was the foundation of much of women's political activities.[55]

Sarah Nash, Nancy Hodges, and the other female hucksters who gathered in Portsmouth, Virginia, in May 1866 "to consult each other and talk our troubles over" made that collective possession clear. Nash and Hodges, along with seven other women "representing many hundreds" of others "who huckster for a living," signed a petition to General O. O. Howard complaining about the unfair taxation policies that were driving them out of business, about their husbands' and children's loss of jobs, and about the general "obbitrary power" controlling them in many matters regarding which they had "never been consulted." These women were speaking, however, not of whether each individually had voice and representation but of whether their community had a voice. Thus they noted that "their husbands, though called upon to pay a head tax of ($4.00) four dollars, have no voice in making city, State or national government."[56] This is not to suggest that African American women did not desire the vote or that they did not often disagree with the actions taken by some black men. One should, however, be careful about imposing presentist notions of gender equality on these women. Clearly for them the question was not an abstract notion of individual gender equality but rather one of community. That such a vision might over time lead to a patriarchal conception of gender roles is not a reason to dismiss the equity of its inception.

Women's presence at the polls was not just a negative sanction; it was also a positive expression of the degree to which they understood the men's franchise to be a new political opportunity for themselves as well as their children. They reinforced this idea of black men's voting as a new freedom that they had all achieved by turning the occasion into a public festival and celebration, bringing lemonade and ginger cakes and spending the day at the polls. Of course, the principal reason for the group presence at the polls was protection. The tendency for "crowds" of freedmen to go to the polls together was seen by their white contemporaries and by some historians as evidence that they were forced to vote the Republican ticket or that they did not take seriously the franchise but instead saw election day as an opportunity for a picnic or other entertainment. Henderson Hamilton Donald, for example, noting that freedmen "always voted in companies," found this behavior "odd and sometimes amusing." Yet his own description suggests the real meaning: "When distances were great, crowds of them under leaders went to the polling places a day in advance and *camped out like soldiers on the march*."[57] Women and children often went along, their presence reflecting their excitement about the franchise but also their understanding of the dangers involved in voting. Women may have gone for additional protection of the voters, like those women in South Carolina who carried weapons, or to avoid potential danger to those left alone in the countryside while the men were gone. But, in any case, the necessity for a group presence at the polls reinforced the sense of collective enfranchisement. What may have been chiefly for protection was turned into festivity as women participated in a symbolic reversal of the meaning of the group presence.

African American women throughout the South in the Reconstruction era assumed *publicly* the right to be active participants in the political process long after they had been formally removed—and they did so, in part, through their husbands. They operated out of an assumption that his vote was theirs. Unlike many northern white middle-class women, southern black women in the immediate post-Civil War era did not base their political participation in justifications of superior female morality or public motherhood. They did not need to; their own cultural, economic, and political traditions provided rationale enough—"autonomy was not simply personal."

One of the ramifications of liberal democratic political theory is that our notion of politics is severely circumscribed. In a context where only certain persons have the rights and abilities to participate fully, the *formal* political process takes on an exclusivity and sanctity all its own. Historians operating from this perspective often ascribe the totality of politics to the formal political arena. With this assumption, Jacqueline Jones asserts that "the vitality of the political process, tainted though it was by virulent racial prejudice and violence, provided black men with a public forum distinct from the private sphere inhabited by their womenfolk."[58] But these women's actions were fundamentally *political*. That African American women did not operate inside the formal political process does not negate the intensely political character of their actions. These actions represented a continuous significant political participation on their part. Black women, therefore, were hardly confined (even without the franchise or elective office) to a private sphere.[59] They were certainly not confined to any less bloody sphere.[60]

African American women understood "that freedom meant above all the right to participate in the process of creating it."[61] Being denied this right in the external political arena and having this right increasingly circumscribed in the internal arena as well, these women created their own political expression, thus inventing the power their freedom required. Their actions were not merely a grievance against their own lack of political rights or lack of rights of the black community but, more important, a critique of the absence of freedom and democracy, as they understood it, in the society at large. By their actions and assumptions they challenged the fundamental assumptions of the U.S. political process itself.

Citizenship entails constitutionally granted political rights and privileges that make one a full-fledged and active member of the body politic. Thus one must be granted the right to be active in the political process. But these women operated out of a notion of community, wherein all—men, women, and children; freeborn and formerly slave; native and migrant—had inherent rights and responsibilities requiring no higher authority than their commitment to each other. Their sense of community, related to the collective character of their notion of freedom, had foundation in their understanding that freedom, in reality, would accrue to each of them individually only when it was acquired by all of them collectively. It was this very sense of community rather than citizenship, of peoplehood rather than personhood, that was the basis for their activities. In other words, it was their vision of freedom that granted them the right to assume the political responsibilities that neither the state nor some members of their own community acknowledged to be theirs.

It is clear that to understand southern black women's political history in the post-Civil War era requires that we develop alternative political definitions to those defined by liberal demo cratic thought. Even the terminology by which we understand African American women's political struggle must be rethought, for we currently have no language in which to express the concepts that these women understood. The significance of this may be difficult to contemplate—both for black women historically and for our notions of how far we have progressed today. For understanding African American women's involvement in the political process in the post-Civil War era, even without the franchise, requires us at least to consider the possibility that when black women, such as those in Richmond, obtained the legal franchise in the 1920s they may actually have been far less involved in the political decision-making process than were their unenfranchised foremothers in the immediate post-Civil War period.[62]

Ultimately northern and southern white men may have denied African American women the freedom fully to shape their own lives in the post-Civil War era. But we, trapped in our own mental prisons, have denied them their freedom as well, insisting instead that they accept our very limited and pessimistic vision of human possibilities. There is an enormous amount of work yet to be done on southern black women's political history in the last four decades of the nineteenth century. Just as African American women, as part of black communities throughout the South, struggled in the post-Civil War era to catch, that is, to make real, their vision of freedom, we, as historians, must now struggle to catch, that is, to understand, their vision of freedom. In the process we need not only to refine our base of information but also to reconstruct our frameworks, creating new ones that allow us to interpret these women's lives in ways that do justice to their vision of freedom.

Notes

This essay had its origins in my students' questions and insights as we explored definitions of freedom in African American Studies 100 and History 202 at Emory University, 1986–87. Their excitement about the ideas and their willingness to challenge not only my assumptions but their own deeply held convictions were inspirational as well as informative. Earlier versions of this essay were presented at the "Afro-American Women and the Vote, 1837 to 1965" conference, University of Massachusetts at Amherst, 14 November 1987, where I benefited from the comments of Ena Farley; the Social History Seminar, Newberry Library, Chicago, Illinois, 16 October 1991; and the workshop on "Historical Perspectives on Race and Racial Ideologies" Postemancipation Studies Project, Center for Afroamerican and African Studies, University of Michigan, 22 November 1991. I would like to thank Thea Arnold, Jacquelyn Dowd Hall, Nancy Hewitt, Thomas C. Holt, Lillian Jones, Dee Dee Joyce, Joseph Reidy, Leslie S. Rowland, Rebecca Scott, David Thelen, and Dale Tomich for their careful readings and critiques of this essay.

1. See, for example, Angela Davis, *Women, Race, and Class* (New York: Random House, 1981), 70–86; Paula Giddings, *When and Where I Enter: The Impact of Black Women on Race and Sex in America* (New York: William Morrow, 1984), 64–71; Rosalyn Terborg-Penn, "Afro-Americans in the Struggle for Woman Suffrage" (Ph.D. diss., Howard University, 1977), ch. 2; Bettina Aptheker, "Abolitionism, Woman's Rights, and the Battle over the Fifteenth Amendment," in *Woman's Legacy: Essays on Race, Sex, and Class in American History* (Amherst: University of Massachusetts Press, 1982).

2. *New York Tribune*, 17 June 1865; Peter Randolph, *From Slave Cabin to Pulpit* (Boston: Earle, 1893). For discussions of freedpeople's efforts to reunite families throughout the South, see Robert H. Abzug, "The Black Family during Reconstruction;" in Nathan I. Huggins, Martin Kilson, and Daniel M. Fox, eds., *Key Issues in the Afro-American Experience*, vol. 2, *Since 1865* (New York: Harcourt Brace Jovanovich, 1971), 32–34; Ira Berlin, Steven F. Miller, and Leslie S. Rowland, "Afro-American Families in Transition from Slavery to Freedom," *Radical History Review* 42 (1988): 89–121; Eric Foner, *Reconstruction: America's Unfinished Revolution, 1863–1877* (New York: Harper and Row, 1988), 82–85; Leon F. Litwack, *Been in the Storm So Long: The Aftermath of Slavery* (New York: Random House, 1979), 229–47; Peter J. Rachleff, *Black Labor in the South: Richmond, Virginia, 1865–1890* (Philadelphia: Temple University Press, 1984), 15–16.

3. Using the records of the Freedman's Savings and Trust Company and the manuscript census, Peter J. Rachleff has done an extensive job of re-creating this family network (*Black Labor in the South*, 15–23).

4. Rachleff, *Black Labor in the South*, 17, 22, 26; *Freedmen's Record* 2, 3 (March 1866): 53.

5. W. P. Burrell and D. E. Johnson Sr., *Twenty-five Years History of the Grand Fountain of the United Order of True Reformers, 1881–1905* (Richmond: Grand Fountain, United Order of True Reformers, 1909), 76–77.

6. Thomas C. Holt, " 'An Empire over the Mind': Emancipation, Race, and Ideology in the British West Indies and the American South," in J. Morgan Kousser and James McPherson, eds., *Region, Race, and Reconstruction: Essays in Honor of C. Vann Woodward* (New York: Oxford University Press, 1982), 299; Fanny Jackson to Friends of the North, 22 March 1867, in *Freedmen's Record* 3, 6 (June 1867): 106. See also David Montgomery, *The American Civil War and the Meanings of Freedom: An Inaugural Lecture Delivered before the University of Oxford on 24 February 1987* (Oxford: Clarendon Press, 1987), 11–13: "[T]he former slaves' own conception of freedom . . . was above all a collective vision, rooted in generations of common experience in the United States. . . . The point is not simply that former slaves lacked experience in bourgeois ways but rather that they did not define either freedom or property in the same individualistic and market-oriented terms that their northern liberators employed."

7. Rachleff, *Black Labor in the South*, 37–38.

8. Ibid., 26–27.

9. Locating the origins of this collective worldview is beyond the scope of this essay, but several works are suggestive of both African origins and the degree to which this democratic ethos was a response to the necessities of life for black people—slave or free—in a slave society. On the African origins of one of the primary institutional expressions of this collective worldview, see Betty M. Kuyk, "The African Derivation of Black Fraternal Orders in the United States," *Comparative Studies in Society and History* 25 (October 1983): 559–92. Lawrence Levine offers evidence of a collective worldview, African in origin but transformed to meet the needs of life under slavery and freedom; see *Black Culture and Black Consciousness: Afro-American Folk Thought from Slavery to Freedom* (New York: Oxford University Press, 1977). One of the most striking evidences of the democratic ethos under slavery comes to us from a study of children at play. David K. Wiggins tells us that slave children played no games that eliminated players: The rules they devised for their various games of dodge ball and tag prevented the removal of any participants. When one of the main fears of daily life was being removed from the

community—sold or hired out—slaves chose not to duplicate that fear in their own social structure. Slave children attempted to provide some security by ensuring that none of them would be excluded from participating and thus through their play reinforced the basic communal values of the slave community. See "The Play of Slave Children in the Plantation Communities of the Old South, 1820–1860," in N. Ray Hiner and Joseph M. Hawes, eds., *Growing Up in America: Childhood in Historical Perspective* (Urbana: University of Illinois Press, 1985), 181–82. See also Thomas L. Webber, *Deep like the Rivers: Education in the Slave Quarter Community, 1831–1865* (New York: W. W. Norton, 1978), esp. 63–70, 144, 224–44; Herbert G. Gutman, *The Black Family in Slavery and Freedom, 1750–1925* (New York: Pantheon Books, 1976), esp. ch. 5; Ira Berlin, *Slaves without Masters: The Free Negro in the Antebellum South* (New York: Pantheon Books, 1974), ch. 9.

10. My effort in this essay is to distinguish the collective vision of these African Americans from the individualistic vision of the government officials, businessmen, missionaries, and teachers who developed and implemented Reconstruction policies. This is not to suggest that there was a monolithic "black" versus a monolithic "white" vision of freedom. Northern white industrial workers and southern white yeoman farmers also often expressed a collectivist vision and understood the individualistic assumptions of free labor ideology in a market economy as detrimental to their collective (and individual) self-interest (Montgomery, *American Civil War*). Contemporary U.S. historians' own socialization often leads them to assume individualism as natural human behavior and thus to assume that collective identity is the "peculiarity" that needs explaining, when in fact collective identity has been the foundation of many people's understanding of self. "Throughout most of human history the antithesis of slavery has not been autonomy but belonging; defining freedom as individual autonomy is a phenomenon of the modern era" (Thomas C. Holt, "Of Human Progress and Intellectual Apostasy," *Reviews in American History* 15 [March 1987]: 58).

11. C. B. Macpherson, *The Political Theory of Possessive Individualism: Hobbes and Locke* (Oxford: Oxford University Press, 1962).

12. Holt, " 'An Empire over the Mind,' " 287.

13. John Thomas O'Brien Jr., "From Bondage to Citizenship: The Richmond Black Community, 1865–1867" (Ph.D. diss., University of Rochester, 1974), 78, 174–75, 277–78. For a discussion of institutional developments in Richmond's black community as an outgrowth of this collective consciousness and its attendant understandings of social responsibility, see Rachleff, *Black Labor in the South*. For similar discussions regarding other southern black communities in the post-Civil War era, see Edward Magdol, *A Right to the Land: Essays on the Freedmen's Community* (Westport, Conn.: Greenwood Press, 1977); Herbert G. Gutman, "Schools for Freedom: The Post-Emancipation Origins of Afro-American Education," in Herbert G. Gutman, *Power & Culture: Essays on the American Working Class*, ed. Ira Berlin (New York: Pantheon Books, 1987), 260–97.

14. *New York Tribune*, 17 June 1865.

15. John William De Forest, *A Union Officer in the Reconstruction* (Hamden, Conn.: Archon Books, 1968 [1948]), 97–99. For an extended discussion of the ways in which this ethos of mutuality shaped a variety of freedpeople's communities, see Magdol, *Right to the Land*. Habits of mutuality are not exclusive to persons of African descent. For similar discussions of European and Euro-American working-class and rural communities, see, for example, E. P. Thompson, *The Making of the English Working Class* (London: Victor Gollancz, 1963); Jacquelyn Dowd Hall, James Leloudis, Robert Korstad, Mary Murphy, LuAnn Jones, and Christopher B. Daly, *Like a Family: The Making of a Southern Cotton Mill World* (Chapel Hill: University of North Carolina Press, 1987); Steven Hahn, *The Roots of Southern Populism: Yeoman Farmers and the Transformation of the Georgia Upcountry, 1850–1890* (New York: Oxford University Press, 1983).

16. Jacqueline Jones, *Labor of Love, Labor of Sorrow: Black Women, Work, and the Family from Slavery to the Present* (New York: Basic Books, 1985), 65–66. Assumptions of individual autonomy permeate the conceptual frameworks that shape much contemporary discussion of African American women's economic conditions as well. Consider, for example, analyses of women's wages that treat the closing gap between the earnings of full-time black and white female employees as evidence of increasing economic parity among women. Such analyses extract women from their families and communities, assuming they are "possessive individuals" whose well-being and status are determined solely by their individual resources. Yet in reality the economic base and status of black and white full-time wage-earning women are markedly different, since the majority of these white women live in households in which there are two full-time wage earners and the majority of these black women live in households in which they are the only full-time wage earners. A critique of such analyses was presented by Linda Burnham, "Struggling to Make the Turn: Black Women and the Transition to a Post-Industrial Society," at the Schomburg Center for Research in Black Culture Symposium "Survival and Resistance: Black Women in the Americas," 9 June 1989.

17. Gerald David Jaynes, *Branches without Roots: Genesis of the Black Working Class in the American South, 1862–1882* (New York: Oxford University Press, 1986); Barbara Jeanne Fields, *Slavery and Freedom on the Middle Ground: Maryland during the Nineteenth Century* (New Haven: Yale University Press, 1985); Holt, " 'An Empire over the Mind,' " 283–314; Julie Saville, "A Measure of Freedom: From Slave to Wage Laborer in South Carolina, 1860–1868" (Ph.D. diss., Yale University, 1986); Ira Berlin, Steven Hahn, Steven F. Miller, Joseph P. Reidy, and Leslie S. Rowland, "The Terrain of Freedom: The Struggle over the Meaning of Free Labor in the U.S. South," *History Workshop Journal* 22 (autumn 1986): 108–30; Armstead L. Robinson, " 'Worser dan Jeff Davis': The Coming of Free Labor during the Civil War, 1861–1865," in Thavolia Glymph and John J. Kushma, ed., *Essays on the Postbellum Southern Economy* (Arlington: University of Texas, 1985), 11–47; Harold D. Woodman, "The Reconstruction of the Cotton Plantation in the New South," in Glymph and Kushma, eds., *Postbellum Southern Economy*, 95–119; Lawrence N. Powell, *New Masters: Northern Planters during the Civil War and Reconstruction* (New Haven: Yale University Press, 1980), esp. ch. 6.

18. Fields, *Slavery and Freedom*, 157–65.

19. Ibid., 157–66; Saville, "Measure of Freedom"; Holt, " 'An Empire over the Mind.' "

20. Fields, *Slavery and Freedom*, 165–66; Holt, " 'An Empire over the Mind.' "

21. Jones, *Labor of Love*, 66–67.

22. For studies of black women's struggle for legal enfranchisement, see note 1 above; see also Beverly Lynn Guy-Sheftall, "Books, Brooms, Bibles and Ballots: Black Women and the Public Sphere," in *"Daughters of Sorrow": Attitudes toward Black Women, 1880–1920* (Brooklyn, N.Y.: Carlson Publishing, 1990).

23. This analysis is necessarily generalized. Further research will no doubt reveal important distinctions in black women's political activism across regions within the South, within states, and between rural and urban areas.

24. *Richmond Dispatch*, 1, 2 August, 30 September, 9 October 1867; *New York Times*, 1, 2, 6 August, 15, 18 October 1867. My discussion of these events follows closely Rachleff, *Black Labor in the South*, 45–46. See also Richard L. Morton, *The Negro in Virginia Politics*, 1865–1902, Publications of the University of Virginia Phelps-Stokes Fellowship Papers, no. 4 (Charlottesville: University of Virginia Press, 1919), 40–43. Similar reports issued from other areas throughout the South, causing one chronicler to report that "the Southern ballot-box" was as much "the vexation of housekeepers" as it was of farmers, businessmen, statesmen, or others: "Elections were preceded by political meetings, often incendiary in character, which all one's servants must attend." Election day itself could also be a problem. As one Tennessean reported in 1867, "Negro women went [to the polls], too; my wife was her own cook and chambermaid" (Myrta Lockett Avary, *Dixie after the War: An Exposition of Social Conditions Existing in the South, during the Twelve Years Succeeding the Fall of Richmond* [1906 New York: Negro Universities Press, 1969], 282–84). For similar occurrences in Florida, see Susan Bradford Eppes, *Through Some Eventful Years* (Gainesville: University of Florida Press, 1968 [1926]), 282–86.

25. *Richmond Dispatch*, 1, 2 August 1867; *New York Times*, 2, 6 August 1867; see also Rachleff, *Black Labor in the South*, 45; Morton, *Negro in Virginia Politics*, 40–43.

26. The October 1867 city Republican ward meetings and nominating convention adopted the practice common in the black community's mass meetings: a voice or standing vote that enfranchised men, women, and children. See, for example, the 8 October Second Ward meeting for delegate selection: "All who favored Mr. Washburne were first requested to rise, and forty were found on the floor, including women." *Richmond Dispatch*, 30 September, 9 October 1867, 2, 4, 14, 23, 24 January, 15, 25 February, 3, 8, 25 April 1868; *New York Times*, 6 August, 15, 18 October 1867, 11 January 1868; Rachleff, *Black Labor in the South*, 45–49; Avary, *Dixie after the War*, 229–31, 254.

Throughout the state of Virginia, the internal community political gatherings adopted measures by a voice or standing vote that could often enfranchise not only women but children as well. See, for example, the minutes of the mass meeting of colored citizens of Elizabeth City County, Virginia, 5 December 1865: "When upon this motion the entire audience rose to their feet and remained standing some time"; Brig. Gen. S. Brown to Brig. Gen. B. C. Card, Washington, D.C., 19 December 1865, "Negroes, Employment of," Consolidated Correspondence File, ser. 225, Central Records, Records of the Office of the Quartermaster General, Record Group 92, National Archives, Washington, D.C. [Y–719]. (Bracketed numbers refer to file numbers of documents in the Freedmen and Southern Society Project, University of Maryland. I thank Leslie S. Rowland, project director, for facilitating my access to these files.)

The issue of children's participation is an interesting one, suggestive of the means by which personal experience rather than societal norms shaped ex-slaves' vision of politics. A similarly telling example was in the initial proposal of the African National Congress that the new South African constitution set the voting age at fourteen, a testament to the young people, such as those in Soweto, who experienced the ravages of apartheid and whose fight against it helped bring about the political negotiations to secure African political rights and self-determination.

27. Compare southern black women's active participation in formal politics—internal and external—in the first decades after the Civil War to Michael McGerr's assessment that nineteenth-century "women were allowed in to the male political realm only to play typical feminine roles—to cook, sew, and cheer for men and to symbolize virtue and beauty. Men denied women the central experiences of the popular style: not only the ballot but also the experience of mass mobilization." McGerr's analysis fails to acknowledge the racial basis of his study, that is, that it is an assessment of white women's political participation. Michael McGerr, "Political Style and Women's Power, 1830–1930," *Journal of American History* 77 (December 1990): 864–85, esp. 867. My analysis also differs substantially from Mary P. Ryan, *Women in Public: Between Banners and Ballots, 1825–1880* (Baltimore: Johns Hopkins University Press, 1990). Ryan gives only cursory attention to African Americans but finds black women's political expression in the Civil War and Reconstruction eras restricted "with particular severity" and "buried beneath the surface of the public sphere"; see esp. 146–47, 156.

28. For women's participation in political parades in Louisville, Kentucky, Mobile, Alabama, and Charleston, South Carolina, see Gutman, *Black Family in Slavery and Freedom*, 380; *Liberatora*, 21 July 1865, and *New York Daily Tribune*, 4 April 1865, both reprinted in Dorothy Sterling, ed., *The Trouble They Seen: Black People Tell the Story of Reconstruction* (Garden City, N.Y.: Doubleday, 1976), 2–4. In other areas of Virginia besides Richmond, and in South Carolina, Louisiana, and Arkansas, men and women participated in the political meetings. See, for example, Vincent Harding, *There Is a River: The Black Struggle for Freedom in America* (New York: Harcourt Brace Jovanovich, 1981), 294–97; Laura M. Towne, *Letters and Diary of Laura M. Towne Written from the Sea Islands of South Carolina, 1862–1884*, ed. Rupert sargent Holland New York: Negro Universities Press, 1969 [1912]), 183; testimony of John H. Burch given before a female committee appointed to investigate the exodus of black men and women from Louisiana, 46th Cong., 2d Sess., S. Rept. 693, pt. 2, 232–33, reprinted in Herbert Aptheker, ed., *A Documentary History of the Negro People in the United States* (New York: Citadel Press, 1951), 2:721–22; Thomas Holt, *Black over White: Negro Political Leadership in South Carolina during Reconstruction* (Urbana: University of Illinois Press, 1977), 34–35; Randy Finley, "Freedperson's Identities and the Freedmen's Bureau in Arkansas, 1865–1869," paper presented at the annual meeting of the Southern Historical Association, Orlando, Florida, 11 November 1993 (cited with permission of Finley). Graphic artists recognized the participation of women as a regular feature of parades, mass meetings, and conventions, as evidenced by their illustrations; see "The Celebration of Emancipation Day in Charleston" from *Leslie's Illustrated Newspaper*, reprinted in Francis Butler Simkins and Robert Hilliard Woody, *South Carolina During Reconstruction* (Gloucester, Mass.: Peter Smith, 1966 [1932]), facing 364; "Electioneering at the South," *Harper's Weekly*, 25 July 1868, reprinted in Foner, *Reconstruction*, fol. 386; "Colored People's Convention in Session," reprinted in Sterling, *The Trouble They Seen*, 65.

29. *New York Times*, 11 January 1868; *The Debates and Proceedings of the Constitutional Convention of the State of Virginia, Assembled at the City of Richmond* (Richmond, 1868), 524–27.

30. *New York Times*, 11, 22 January 1868; *Debates and Proceedings, Virginia*, 505–7.

31. Estimates of the number of black people who migrated into Richmond in the immediate postemancipation period run as high as fifteen thousand. Rachleff, *Black Labor in the South*, 14; Virginius Dabney, *Richmond: The Story of a City* (Garden City, N.Y.: Doubleday, 1976), 208; Randolph, *From Slave Cabin to Pulpit*, 59.

32. My discussion of liberal democratic political ideology draws on Macpherson, *Political Theory of Possessive Individualism*; C. B. Macpherson, *Democratic Theory: Essays in Retrieval* (Oxford: Oxford University Press, 1973), and *The Life and Times of Liberal Democracy* (Oxford: Oxford University Press, 1977).

33. For a similar and extended discussion focused on Jamaica and Britain, see Thomas C. Holt, *The Problem of Freedom: Race, Labor, and Politics in Jamaica and Britain, 1832–1938* (Baltimore: Johns Hopkins University Press, 1992); also Thomas C. Holt, " 'The Essence of the Contract': The Articulation of Race, Gender, and Political Economy in British Emancipation Policy, 1838–1866," paper presented at "Seminar on Racism and Race Relations in the Countries of the African Diaspora," Rio de Janeiro, Brazil, 6 April 1992 (cited with permission of Holt).

34. Elizabeth Hyde Botume, *First Days amongst the Contrabands* (New York: Arno Press and New York Times, 1968 [1893]), 273. See also Jones, *Labor of Love*, 66–67; Margaret Washington Creel, "Female Slaves in South Carolina," *TRUTH: Newsletter of the Association of Black Women Historians*, summer 1985.

35. For a discussion of the idea of emancipated slaves earning freedom and political liberties through proper orientation to a market economy, see Holt, " 'An Empire over the Mind.' " An explicit statement of that assumption was given by white Republicans during the Virginia constitutional convention debates. Disagreeing with Bayne's argument regarding the inherent right of suffrage, Judge John

Underwood contended, "I hold that the colored men . . . ought to have the right of suffrage. . . . [T]hey have shown themselves competent . . . they have shown their industry and their effort and desire to elevate themselves. . . . I do not think that the Indians, wandering upon the plains,. . . having no fixed homes, no habits of industry—I do not think that such a class of people should be entitled to vote. . . . Just so soon as they become settled and industrious in their habits like the colored men of this State, then I will go for giving the Indians the right to vote." Bayne, on the other hand, supported suffrage for Indians. *Debates and Proceedings, Virginia*, 527.

36. Percentages computed from figures given by Holt, *Black over White*, 35, 97. *Proceedings of the Constitutional Convention of South Carolina, held at Charleston, South Carolina, beginning January 14 and ending March 17, 1868* (Charleston: Denny and Perry, 1868), 836–38; *New York Times*, 3 April 1869; Terborg-Penn, "Afro-Americans in the Struggle for Woman Suffrage," 52–54; Rosalyn Terborg-Penn, "The Rollin Sisters," in Darlene Clark Hine, Elsa Barkley Brown, and Rosalyn Terborg-Penn, eds., *Black Women in America: An Historical Encyclopedia* (Brooklyn, N.Y.: Carlson Publishing, 1993), 990–91. There are some reports that black women actually voted in Reconstruction-era South Carolina. Benjamin Quarles states that in some "districts in the South Carolina elections of 1870 colored women under the encouragement of Negro election officials, exercised the privilege of voting. By this act the Negro became the first practical vindicator of woman's right to the ballot" ("Frederick Douglass and the Woman's Rights Movement," *Journal of Negro History* 25 [January 1940]: 35). Others have suggested that whenever black men were ill and unable to come to the polls to cast their ballot, their wives or other female relatives were allowed to vote in their place.

37. *Debates and Proceedings, Virginia*, 254.

38. Eric Foner sees Bayne as a primary example of the "distinction between the public sphere of men and the private world of women" that developed with freedom. Quoting only Bayne's comment "It is woman's right to raise and bear children, and to train them for their future duties in life," Foner sees this "militant Virginia political leader" as having a "severely restricted definition of women's rights" (*Reconstruction*, 87). This may be true, but such a conclusion is not necessarily the meaning of Bayne's statement when taken in its full context; only further research on Bayne and his colleagues will clarify these issues. But Bayne's self-conscious explication of his own terminology further reinforces my reading of his discussion of domestic roles of women as in addition to, not instead of, political roles. (Hucles, having pointed out Bayne's terminology, still accepts Foner's reading of Bayne's statement about domestic roles and thus accepts Foner's conclusions regarding Bayne's sexism and exclusion of women from political rights; Michael Hucles, "Many Voices, Similar Concerns: Traditional Methods of African-American Political Activity in Norfolk, Virginia, 1865–1875," *Virginia Magazine of History and Biography* 100 [October 1992]: 543–66.)

I am not ignoring the importance of language but emphasizing the importance of historicizing and investigating language. Bayne, like other Afro-Virginians, used a conventional political language, just as they used conventional political forms, but gave each larger meaning than conventionally intended. A recent literary study that takes these questions of language, gender, citizenship, and freedom as its core is Claudia Tate, *Domestic Allegories of Political Desire: The Black Heroine's Text at the Turn of the Century* (New York: Oxford University Press, 1992). Like most studies, however, its concentration on northern middle-class black women and its reading of the postemancipation period through late-nineteenth-century eyes and texts ignore the different language and meanings of the immediate postemancipation era among ex-slaves in the South. Tate thus assumes that "discourses of citizenship . . . were *inherently* gendered until the ratification of the Twenty second [*sic*] Amendment in 1920" (21, 243 n; emphasis mine). My effort is to understand how an explicitly gendered discourse on citizenship and rights *developed* within late-nineteenth-century black communities, rather than assuming it was either inherently there at emancipation or immediately and uncontestedly assumed thereupon. For a fuller explication of this, see Elsa Barkley Brown, "Negotiating and Transforming the Public Sphere: African American Political Life in the Transition from Slavery to Freedom," *Public Culture* 7 (fall 1994): 107–46.

39. *Richmond Dispatch*, 18 June 1867; Rachleff, *Black Labor in the South*, 48.

40. First African Baptist Church, Richmond, Virginia, Minutes, Books II and III, Virginia State Library Archives, Richmond. These developments are explored in Barkley Brown, "Negotiating and Transforming the Public Sphere." The whole question of the operating procedures of internal community institutions such as churches and mutual benefit and fraternal societies needs investigation; surviving church minute books and denominational minutes offer a promising source for future analyses. In any case, the question of women's participation in the external political arena should be analyzed in the context of developments within internal community institutions. These debates over gender roles within black churches occurred at congregational and denominational levels. For studies that examine these debates at the state and/or national level in the late nineteenth and early twentieth centuries, see

Evelyn Brooks Higginbotham, *Righteous Discontent: The Women's Movement in the Black Baptist Church* (Cambridge, Mass.: Harvard University Press, 1993); Glenda Gilmore, "Gender and Jim Crow: Women and the Politics of White Supremacy in North Carolina, 1896–1920" (Ph.D. diss., University of North Carolina, Chapel Hill, 1992); Cheryl Townsend Gilkes, " 'Together and in Harness': Women's Traditions in the Sanctified Church," *Signs: Journal of Women in Culture and Society* 10 (summer 1985); 678–99.

41. Rachleff, *Black Labor in the South*, 31–32; A. T. Morgan, *Yazoo; or, On the Picket Line of Freedom in the South: A Personal Narrative* (New York: Russell and Russell, 1884), 231–33; W. L. Fleming, *The Civil War and Reconstruction in Alabama* (New York: Peter Smith, 1905), 777.

42. This censuring of women's political participation was part of a larger pattern whereby northern white men attempted to teach southern black men and women "proper" relations. Towne noted that "several speakers have been here who have advised the people to get the women into their proper place" (Towne, *Letters and Diary of Laura M. Towne*, 183–84). It was the participation, not merely the presence, of black women at political meetings that was the issue elsewhere as well. In Richmond, for example, white women certainly on occasion sat in the convention's gallery as visitors, merely watching the proceedings. The problem with the black women and men, as many white observers saw it, was that they participated from the gallery. Avary, *Dixie after the War*, 254–57.

43. Towne, *Letters and Diary of Laura M. Towne*, 183. Despite this example, the various continued activities of women, often with the approval of men, makes clear that ex-slaves' compliance with these norms of "proper" relations was not immediately forthcoming. However, more detailed investigations of the ways in which freedmen and freedwomen came to work out family and community relationships—political, economic, and social—in various areas of the South are needed. Until then, the various formulations that lay out a well-developed public/private dichotomy and patriarchal construction of black family and community life as a fairly immediate occurrence after emancipation amount to nothing more than a presentist reading of an as yet not fully explored past.

44. Holt, *Black over White*, 34–35. A witness before the Senate investigating committee testified in 1872 that the women "have been very active since 1868 in all the political movements, they form a large number in all the political assemblages" in Louisiana. Testimony of John H. Burch in Aptheker, *Documentary History*, 2:721.

45. Lucy McMillan testimony taken at Spartanburg, South Carolina, 10 July 1871, in U.S. Congress, *Testimony Taken by the Joint Select Committee to Inquire into the Condition of Affairs in the Late Insurrectionary States*, 42d Cong., 2d sess., S. Rept. v. 2, n. 11, pt 4. *South Carolina* (Washington, D.C.: Government Printing Office, 1872), 2:605 (hereafter cited as *Ku Klux Klan Testimony*).

46. Holt, *Black over White*, 35; Avary, *Dixie after the War*, 362; Towne, *Letters and Diary of Laura M. Towne*, 284–91.

47. Fleming, *Civil War and Reconstruction in Alabama*; Joel Williamson, *After Slavery: The Negro in South Carolina during Reconstruction, 1861–1877* (Chapel Hill: University of North Carolina Press, 1965), 344; Holt, *Black over White*, 35.

48. U.S. Congress, *Smalls v. Tillman*, 45th Cong., 1st sess., H. Misc. Doc. no. 11 (1877), quoted in Dorothy Sterling, ed., *We Are Your Sisters: Black Women in the Nineteenth Century* (New York: W. W. Norton, 1984), 370; Towne, *Letters and Diary of Laura M. Towne*, 284.

49. *Smalls v. Tillman*, in Sterling, *We Are Your Sisters*, 370; Fleming, *Civil War and Reconstruction in Alabama*, 564–65, 776.

50. Violet Keeling's testimony before the Senate investigating committee, 18 February 1884, 48th Cong., 1st sess., S. Rept. no. 579, reprinted in Aptheker, *Documentary History*, 2:739–41.

51. Avary, *Dixie after the War*, 285–86, 347; Fleming, *Civil War and Reconstruction in Alabama*, 564–65, 776–78; *Ku Klux Klan Testimony: North Carolina*, 9, 289, *Georgia*, 236, 248, 290, 1184, *Alabama*, 684, 878, 1072–73, 1078–80, *Mississippi*, 725, *Florida and Miscellaneous*, 50; Thomas I. Evans, Alexander H. Sands, N. A. Sturdivant, et al., Richmond, to Major General Schofield, 31 October 1867, reprinted in *Documents of the Constitutional Convention of the State of Virginia* (Richmond: Office of the New Nation, 1867), 22–23; John H. Gilmer to Schofield, reprinted in the *New York Times*, 30 October 1867; Joe M. Richardson, *The Negro in the Reconstruction of Florida, 1865–1877* (Tallahassee: Florida State University, 1965), 237–38; Lerome Bennett Jr., *Black Power U.S.A.: The Human Side of Reconstruction, 1867–1877* (Chicago: Johnson Publishing, 1967), 359; Frenise A. Logan, *The Negro in North Carolina, 1876–1894* (Chapel Hill: University of North Carolina Press, 1964), 22–23; Henderson Hamilton Donald, *The Negro Freedman: Life Conditions of the American Negro in the Early Years after Emancipation* (New York: Cooper Square Publishers, 1971 [1952]), 203–5; Charles Nordhoff, *The Cotton States in the Spring and Summer of 1875* (New York: Burt Franklin, 1876), 11, 22; Simkins and Woody, *South Carolina during Reconstruction*, 512; Sir George Campbell, *White and Black: The Outcome of a Visit to the United States* (New York: Negro Universities Press, 1969 [1879]), 181, 317; *New York Times*, 3

November 1867; Proceedings before Military Commissioner, City of Richmond, 26 October 1867, in the case of Winston Jackson, filed as G–423 1867, Letters Received, ser. 5068, 1st Reconstruction Military District, Records of the U.S. Army Continental Commands, Record Group 393, pt. 1, National Archives [SS–1049].

52. Fleming, *Civil War and Reconstruction in Alabama,* 776.

53. Quote is from James E. Sefton, "A Note on the Political Intimidation of Black Men by Other Black Men," *Georgia Historical Quarterly* 52 (December 1968): 448. My analysis here leans heavily on an unpublished essay by Joseph Reidy on Reconstruction-era politics.

54. Robert Gleed testimony before Mississippi Subcommittee, 10 November 1871, *Ku Klux Klan Testimony: Mississippi,* 725. Gleed's statement also challenges feminist theory that attempts to dichotomize men and women's ideas of justice by arguing that men accept a more abstract equal application of the law as justice, whereas women insist upon a notion of justice more closely tied to issues of morality and outcome. See Carol Gilligan, *In a Different Voice* (Cambridge, Mass.: Harvard University Press, 1982). This is, of course, a problematic argument, as it assumes gender to be an analytical category removable from the context of race and class. For a critique of Gilligan that emphasizes the degree to which the elements she sees as female might also be seen as African American, common to both males and females in black communities, see Carol Stack, "The Culture of Gender: Women and Men of Color," *Signs: Journal of Women in Culture and Society* 11 (winter 1986): 321–24. See also Carol B. Stack, "Different Voices, Different Visions: Gender, Culture, and Moral Reasoning," in Maxine Boca Zinn and Bonnie Thornton Dill, eds., *Women of Color in U.S. Society* (Philadelphia: Temple University Press, 1994), 291–301.

55. The larger society reinforced this sense of collective ownership of the vote. Black women (and children) were included in the retribution black men faced when they cast a Republican vote. Harriet Hernandes, a South Carolina woman, testified that her entire community lay out at night to avoid whippings or murder. "Mighty near" everyone in her neighborhood had been whipped "because [when] men . . . voted radical tickets they [the Ku Klux Klan] took the spite out on the women when they could get at them. . . . Ben Phillips and his wife and daughter; Sam Foster; and Moses Eaves, they killed him—I could not begin to tell all—Ann Bonner and her daughter, Manza Surratt and his wife and whole family, even the least child in the family, they took it out of bed and whipped it. They told them if they did that they would remember it." Violet Keeling reported that on election day she carried a knife with her as she walked to and from work for fear that if the Republicans were victorious, black women as well as black men would be held responsible. Harriet Hernandes' testimony taken at Spartanburg, South Carolina, 10 July 1871, in *Ku Klux Klan Testimony: South Carolina,* 586; Keeling testimony in Aptheker, *Documentary History,* 2:739.

56. Petition from Nancy Hodges and other hucksters filed as Geo. Teamoh to Gen. O. O. Howard, 21 May 1866, T–173 1866, Letters Received, ser. 15, Washington Headquarters, Records of the Bureau of Refugees, Freedmen, and Abandoned Lands, Record Group 105, National Archives [A–7619].

57. Avary, *Dixie after the War,* 282–83; Donald, *Negro Freedman,* 207 (emphasis mine).

58. Jones, *Labor of Love,* 66. Jones is not alone in her assessment. In his generally rigorous analysis, Eric Foner, apparently adopting Jones's analysis, also suggests the public/private dichotomy between black men and women, based in part on men's participation in the formal political process; Nell Irvin Painter assumes that since black women were unenfranchised in the Reconstruction era, "they could not act politically as men could." Foner, *Reconstruction,* 87; Nell Irvin Painter, "Comment," in Darlene Clark Hine, ed., *The State of Afro-American History: Past, Present, and Future,* (Baton Rouge: Louisiana State University Press, 1986), 82.

59. My work here and elsewhere questions the usefulness of the public/private dichotomy for understanding African American women's history. Others have also raised questions in relation to the larger fields of women's history and women's studies. Linda Kerber, acknowledging the degree to which conceptualizing this dichotomy opened up many avenues of women's lives to historical investigation, also suggests that such a dichotomy has probably outlived its usefulness. Elsa Barkley Brown, "Womanist Consciousness: Maggie Lena Walker and the Independent Order of Saint Luke," *Signs: Journal of Women in Culture and Society* 14 (spring 1989): 610–33; Linda K. Kerber, "Separate Spheres, Female Worlds, Woman's Place: The Rhetoric of Women's History," *Journal of American History* 75 (June 1989): 9–39. See also Alice Kessler-Harris, "Gender Ideology in Historical Reconstruction: A Case Study from the 1930s," *Gender and History* 1 (spring 1989): 31–49. Kerber echoes Michele Rosaldo's critique of oppositional modes of thought in general and transhistoric conceptions of home versus public life in particular. Linda Nicholson provides a basis for understanding the reification of these categories as a product of Western liberalism. She argues that liberalism as a political theory rests on the assumption that the family, as the sphere of the private, and the political, as the sphere of the public, are "inherently demarcatable." M. Z. Rosaldo, "The Use and Abuse of Anthropology:

Reflections on Feminism and Cross-Cultural Understanding," *Signs: Journal of Women in Culture and Society* 5 (spring 1980): 389–417; Linda Nicholson, *Gender and History: The Limits of Social Theory in the Age of the Family* (New York: Columbia University Press, 1986). For an example of the ways in which those challenging public/private dichotomies often reinvent the same dichotomy, see Elsa Barkley Brown, "Imaging Lynching: African American Women, Communities of Struggle, and Collective Memory," in Geneva Smitherman, ed., *African American Women Speak Out: Responses to Anita Hill-Clarence Thomas* (Detroit: Wayne State University Press, 1995).

60. Even a cursory reading of Reconstruction-era documents makes this clear. The thirteen volumes of *Ku Klux Klan Testimony,* for example, are filled with reports of whipping and/or raping of black women—for their refusal to work in the fields or in white men's and women's homes, for their husbands' political activities, or for their families' efforts to acquire land. One North Carolina man, Essic Harris, reported that the rape of black women by the Ku Klux Klan was so common in his community that "[i]t has got to be an old saying." Some women, such as Lucy McMillan, reported violent attacks as a direct result of their own political activities. McMillan's house was burned after she attended a political meeting and reported back to her community. She was accused of being a "d——d radical," "making laws" and "bragging and boasting that I wanted the land." Essic Harris testimony, 1 July 1871, *Ku Klux Klan Testimony: North Carolina*, 100; McMillan testimony, ibid., 604–11.

61. Harding, *There Is a River,* 296.

62. The point, of course, is that the meaning cannot be presumed merely from the act. The implications of this are far-reaching, for it recalls to our attention the fact, as stated by Michele Rosaldo, "[t]hat woman's place in human social life is not in any direct sense a product of the things she does . . . but of the meaning her activities acquire through concrete social interactions. And the significances women assign to the activities of their lives are things that we can only grasp through an analysis of the relationships that women forge, the social contexts they (along with men) create—and within which they are defined. Gender in all human groups must . . . be understood in political and social terms, with reference . . . to local and specific forms of social relationship" (Rosaldo, "Use and Abuse of Anthropology," 400). Ignoring this is analytically problematic. See, for example, Susan Mann's explication of black women's status under the sharecropping system. Mann, by design, lifts her exploration of economic roles out of the context of political and cultural roles and ideology and thus explores the meaning of labor removed from its social context. More important, her exploration of economic roles assumes that the distinctions between women laboring in the home and men laboring in the field have inherent universal implications rather than ones embedded in a particular historical context. See Susan A. Mann, "Slavery, Sharecropping, and Sexual Inequality," *Signs: Journal of Women in Culture and Society* 14 (summer 1989): 774–98. One point of my essay is to demonstrate that variables such as enfranchisement/disfranchisement (or work in the fields/work in the home) mean different things in different social and historical contexts. Our tendency to attribute inherent meaning to certain activities obscures rather than explains historically specific developments of social relations between black men and black women.

11

"Too Dark to Be Angels"
The Class System among the Cherokees at the Female Seminary

Devon A. Mihesuah

The Cherokee Female Seminary was a nondenominational boarding school established by the Cherokee Nation at Park Hill, Indian Territory, in order to provide high-quality education for the young women of its tribe. The curriculum was based on that of Mount Holyoke Seminary in South Hadley, Massachusetts, and it offered no courses focusing on Cherokee culture. The seminary first opened in 1851, but in 1887 it was destroyed by fire. Two years later a larger, three-story seminary building was erected on the outskirts of the Cherokee Nation's capital, Tahlequah. By 1909, when the building was converted into Northeastern State Normal School by the new state of Oklahoma, approximately three thousand Cherokee girls had attended the seminary. A male seminary was built at the same time, three miles from the female seminary; it educated Cherokee youth until it burned in 1910.[1]

While the female seminary was indeed a positive influence on many of its pupils, there is much evidence to suggest that the social atmosphere at the seminary contributed to the rift between Cherokee girls from progressive, mixed-blood families and those from more traditional, uneducated backgrounds. Although many of the girls hailed from traditional families, the seminary did nothing to preserve or reinforce Cherokee customs among its students. But retention of ancestral Cherokee values was not the purpose of the school's establishment.

The Cherokee National Council was controlled by progressive, educated, mixed-blood tribesmen, many of whom subscribed to the value system of the upper-class antebellum South. Their decisions regarding the seminary were supported by most of the mixed-bloods of the tribe—white men and their Cherokee spouses (for the most part mixed-bloods)—and, to a lesser extent, by the progressive full-bloods. The prime interest of these progressive tribal members was indeed education, but also the proper "refinement" of their daughters so that they could serve as knowledgeable, but dutiful, wives in the Cherokee Nation. Another reason for the seminary was the acculturation of the poor full-blood girls, but apparently this idea did not come about until 1871, after the council was pressured by disgruntled tribesmen to establish a "primary department" to provide education free of charge to poorer full-blood children who could not afford the five-dollar-per-semester tuition charged beginning in 1872.[2]

The social aspects of the seminary are intriguing. Regardless of social, economic, and ancestral backgrounds, all the girls (with the exception of a few white pupils and girls of other tribes) identified themselves as Cherokees. Because of these socioeconomic differences, within the seminary walls a definite class system evolved, creating tension much like that which existed

Figure 11.1. The second Cherokee Female Seminary Building (circa 1902) was closer to Tahlequah with a better water supply. It measured 246′ × 69′, with an eastern wing measuring 70′ × 100′, and it cost $78,000 to build. (All photos in this article courtesy of the University Archives, John Vaughan Library, Northeastern State University, Tahlequah, Oklahoma.)

throughout the Cherokee Nation between the mixed-bloods and the full-bloods, between the traditionalists and the progressives, and between those tribal members who were proslavery and those who were not.[3]

During the seminary's early years (1851–56) there was no tuition fee, but money undoubtedly determined who entered the seminary. In the 1850s, according to the laws of the Cherokee Nation, the only prerequisite for admittance was an acceptable score on the entrance examination (except during the summer sessions, when all students paid), combined, perhaps, with a first-come-first-served priority. But daughters of politically prominent and affluent families (Adair, Bushyhead, Hicks, McNair, Ross, and Thompson, to name a few) were always enrolled.[4] These girls were from acculturated, educated households, had already attended good public schools, and had no difficulty passing the written examination. Most full-bloods who wanted to enroll did not have the educational background that enabled them to pass the test. The schools they attended in the distant reaches of the Cherokee Nation were not as well equipped as those closer to the capital, Tahlequah, nor were there enough Cherokee-speaking teachers to help them learn English.

In 1856 the seminary closed because of financial difficulties. After it reopened in 1872, the enrollment situation changed somewhat, but money still gave students an advantage. Some students who failed courses semester after semester were repeatedly granted readmittance—as long as they could pay the tuition.[5] Indicative of the lenient standards of English for tuition payers is an excerpt from a student's letter to her sister in 1889:

> I seat myself this evening to right you a few lines to let you know that I am well at the present and hope this to find you the same I was glad to hear frome you this evening I haven't got but 2 letters frome home and one frome you and I have writen 6 letters since I have been here and this is the 7 I aint rooming with no body yet here is the picture of the jail house.[6]

Although many students were indeed from affluent families, wealthy students were in the minority.[7] It is true that the majority of the students came from families who could manage to pay the tuition, but they were not necessarily from the monied class. In fact, daughters of the wealthier families were sent to schools outside the Cherokee Nation and never attended the female seminary.[8] And each year dozens of primary-school students went to the school free of charge. The class system at the seminary, then, was based on money from 1851 to 1856, but from 1872 until 1910 was apparently based more on race (Cherokee and white blood quantums), appearance (Indian or Caucasian), and degree of acculturation.

Acculturated students and teachers took tremendous pride in their education and appearance. Mixed-blood students frequently scorned those girls who had less white blood and darker skin. A few progressive full-bloods also belittled those who had limited understanding of white ways. It was the general consensus among the mixed-blood students that the full-blood girls were "a little bit backward," and the full-bloods were well aware of their inferior status at the seminary.[9]

Many factors contributed to the feelings of inferiority and alienation experienced by the full-bloods and "unenlightened" mixed-bloods at the school. Since most full-bloods and some poor mixed-bloods worked for their room and board, they were assigned to the third floor with the primary-school students. Because they were often lagging academically, many were placed in classes with the younger girls. They were left behind on social excursions, because only those in the high-school grades were allowed to attend events in Tahlequah and the male seminarians' ball games. Unlike the pupils whose parents sent them spending money, the poorer students were unable to afford party clothes, nor could they buy after-dinner snacks from the local vendors—also a social occasion.

The attitudes of some of the teachers also led to resentment among many of the full-bloods. The National Council employed many qualified mixed-blood instructors, but there were no traditional Cherokee teachers. Despite the instructors' sympathies for the traditional girls, they rarely understood the problems the full-bloods faced. In 1908, for example, mixed-blood seminary superintendent Albert Sydney Wyly (an 1890 graduate of the male seminary) expressed his impatience with the full-blood girls by referring to the mixed-bloods as "whiter" and therefore "more intellectual." He criticized the full-bloods for their "pathetic attachment to home" and remarked patronizingly that at least they "possess a great deal of artistic ability."[10]

Another example of insensitivity is cited by teacher Dora Wilson Hearon, who in 1895 noted that she and her aunt, principal Ann Florence Wilson, took the third-floor inspection duty because the other teachers were repelled by the students' head lice.[11] In 1907, prior to the school's first rehearsal of the annual Shakespeare production (A Midsummer Night's Dream), a mixed-blood senior responded to the administration's concerned query, "Full-blood girls to do Shakespeare? Impossible!" by saying, "You don't know [teachers] Miss Allen and Miss Minta Foreman!" implying that these instructors were indeed miracle workers.[12]

The teachers also relentlessly reinforced the importance of learning and retaining the values of white society. At the same time they repressed Cherokee values, thereby causing confusion among the more traditional students. One instructor, Kate O'Donald Ringland, later recalled that in regard to seminary philosophy, "anything 'white' was ideal";[13] an alumna remembers learning in the primary grades that the "white way was the only acceptable way."[14] DeWitt Clinton Duncan spoke for his fellow National Council members in a lengthy Cherokee Advocate (the Cherokee Nation newspaper) diatribe when he asked, "Can the mental wants of an Indian youth be satisfied . . . by resources less fruitful than that which caters to the Anglo-Saxon mind? The Cherokee language, at the present advanced period of their [Cherokees'] civilization, cannot meet the exigencies of our people."[15] With the National Council advocating white education, the traditionalists were continually pressured to adopt a different culture if they wanted to attend the seminary.

But not all seminary full-bloods felt ostracized. At least 165 full-bloods enrolled in the seminary (about 11 percent of the fifteen hundred students whose blood quantums can be ascertained), and they stayed enrolled an average of four semesters, two semesters longer than the mixed-bloods, but five semesters less than the graduates.[16] This was probably because girls of one family frequently attended school together, which helped to alleviate homesickness. Some were even adopted into the "big happy seminary family," a phrase used by a mixed-blood (1/32 Cherokee blood) to refer to the upper echelons of the student hierarchy.[17] Because of interruptions such as the Civil War, the destruction of the school by fire, smallpox epidemics, and alternative educational opportunities, not one student, not even a graduate (many of whom enrolled for more than ten semesters), remained in the seminary from first grade through graduation.[18]

Full-bloods who enrolled in the common schools usually learned to speak and read Cherokee, but many were not particularly happy about it and wanted the type of education offered at the seminary. A student at the Cave Springs common school who desired to attend the seminary stated that the common schools could not compete with the female seminary because "we can only interpret Sequoyah's alphabet."[19] After the 1870s many of the neighborhood common schools taught in the Cherokee language for the benefit of the full-bloods; therefore, high-school-age children who could not afford the seminary tuition were limited in their educational choices.

Some full-bloods who wanted a seminary education were willing to work for their tuition, but only a limited number of workers were allowed each semester. Some of the more acculturated full-blood girls at the seminary were from families that could afford the tuition. Thus these students were able to live with the mixed-bloods on the second floor and enjoyed an elevated status. Many of them did not speak Cherokee, nor did they have any interest in traditional

Cherokee customs. As seminary alumna Charlotte Mayes Sanders recalls, the "full-bloods went to Tahlequah to become like the white folk."[20] Indeed, many of their families had already succeeded, and the children came to the seminary armed with the knowledge of white society necessary to function among their acculturated peers.

Especially in the early years, citizens of the Cherokee Nation charged that elitism and prejudice against the full-bloods existed at the seminary. But in 1854 progressive full-blood student Na-Li eloquently defended her seminary by stating in *The Cherokee Rose Buds* (the newspaper of the seminary in the 1850s) that "it is sometimes said that our Seminaries were made only for the rich and those who were not full Cherokee; but it is a mistake. . . . Our Chief and directors would like very much that they [full Cherokees] should come and enjoy these same privileges as those that are here present."[21] Na-Li, however, had been adopted by a mission at an early age, had had a thorough primary education, and easily passed the admittance examination.

In further defense of her heritage and skin color, Na-Li asserted that although her parents were "full Cherokees . . . belonging to the common class," she felt it "no disgrace to be a full Cherokee. My complexion does not prevent me from acquiring knowledge and being useful hereafter. . . . [I will] endeavor to be useful, although I sometimes think that I cannot be."[22] It appears that the more Cherokee blood a girl had, or the more Indian she looked, the more she felt she had to prove herself as a scholar and as a useful member of a society that (she believed) valued only those women who were white in appearance and in attitude.

Na-Li probably was not entirely incorrect in her interpretation of the values of the mixed-bloods. Even progressive mixed-blood girls who were dark-skinned faced prejudice. Florence Waters (5/16 Cherokee) was told by a lighter-skinned classmate that she could not participate in the elocution class production of *The Peri* because "angels are fair-haired and you are too dark for an angel."[23] When the full-blood girls did go to Tahlequah, and especially outside the Cherokee Nation, they had more difficulty adapting to society's "whiteness." In 1899 the preponderance of mixed-blood Cherokees in Tahlequah was illustrated by *Twin Territories* writer Ora Eddleman, who expressed dismay over the wealthy Cherokees and the "blond Cherokee women."[24]

The seminarians were indeed defensive about their hair and skin coloring. In an 1855 issue of *A Wreath of Cherokee Rose Buds*, girls complained in an editorial about the Townsend, Massachusetts, female seminary's paper, *The Lesbian Wreath*, which referred to the Cherokee girls as their "dusky sisters."[25] A popular practice of the Cherokee seminary's paper was to tell anecdotes and stories in which appearance was a prominent factor, particularly blue eyes. For example, one story tells of the consequences that young "Kate M." faced after plagiarizing a poem for literature class. "Fun and abundance," student Lusette writes, "peeped from her blue eyes . . . and the crimson blush stole upon her cheeks." In the same issue, author Inez writes about what her schoolmates might be doing in four years. One student is described as a "fair, gay, blue-eyed girl," and another is a "fairy-like creature with auburn hair." Still another story by student Icy, entitled "Two Companions," pairs Hope ("the very personification of loveliness") with a "tiny, blue-eyed child" named Faith.[26] Evidently, to the seminary students, blue eyes were the epitome of enlightenment and civilization.

Unquestionably ethnocentric, the seminarians were convinced of their superiority over individuals of other tribes. After a group of Osage men visited the seminary in 1855, student Irene wrote a romantic essay—not unlike those of white authors of the day—about the "lofty, symmetrical forms, and proud, free step, of these sons of nature just from their wild hunting ground." She found their war dance amusing ("those tall, dusky forms stomping and stooping around . . . making a wailing sound"). In comparing her tribe and theirs, she pointed out that the Osages listened attentively to the seminarians sing "Over There," because, she figured, at least the "wild and untutored Savage has an ear for music as well as the cultivated and refined."[27]

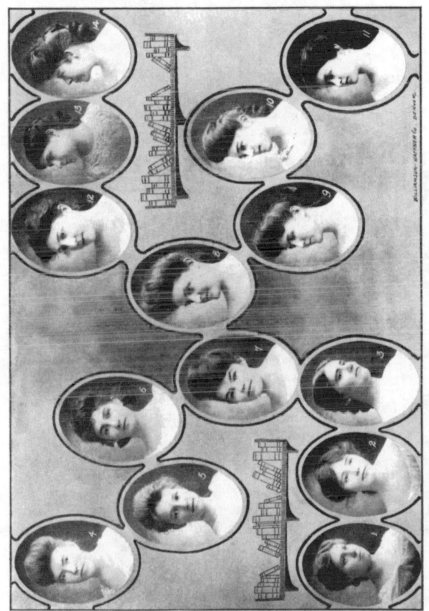

Figure 11.2. The fourteen members of the Cherokee Female Seminary class of 1905.

Figure 11.3. Female seminarians on the school's front porch, 1897.

Other essays in *Rose Buds* include anecdotes about "hostile Indians" attacking peaceful Cherokees in the "wild and unknown regions" on the way to the California gold fields, and about "barbarous Camanches *[sic]*" living in their "wild wilderness." A student named Cherokee described a Seneca Dog Dance in which the drum "made a very disagreeable noise. . . . What there was in such music to excite the Senecas' belles is more than I can imagine." Although she judged the dancers to be graceful, she believed they "ought to have been at something better."[28]

Many of the girls came from slaveholding families, yet the issue of slavery was not mentioned in any issues of the *Rose Buds*, nor in any of the female students' or teachers' memoirs. (A male seminarian later referred to a black man as a "nigger.") Separation of the Cherokee and black races was a fact, however, and the children of the black freedmen could only attend the "Negro High School."[29]

Yet at the same time that the "upper-class" Cherokees believed themselves to be elevated above the unenlightened members of their tribe and above other tribes as a whole, these same girls and teachers felt inferior to the whites, despite the fact that many of them had more "white blood" than Cherokee.[30] So they took every opportunity to flaunt their white ancestry. Female seminary superintendent and male seminary graduate Spencer Seago Stephens, for example, proclaimed in 1889 that "it is the white blood that has made us what we are. . . . If missionaries wish to lift up Indian tribes . . . let them encourage intermarriage with whites." Unsure that the Cherokees could obtain a high level of civilization by themselves, he asserted that "intermarriage will accomplish the purpose quickly."[31]

Commentary from Cherokee citizens who shared Stephens's belief in the productive influence of association with whites appeared in the *Cherokee Advocate*. Writer "Cherokee" observed that "the gloom that pervades the red man's mind is fast disappearing: instead of darkness and doubt, his countenance is being lit up with intelligence." To indicate that the traditionalists of the tribe were perhaps heathenistic compared to their progressive peers, he further asserted that "those who cling with death-like tenacity to our old rites and ceremonies do not consider that a moral change is taking place in the Cherokee world."[32]

The attitude that the Cherokees needed a moral change was also illustrated in *The Sequoyah Memorial*, the newspaper of the Cherokee Male Seminary. One student wrote that "the bow and arrow have been laid aside," and that until the Cherokees reached the "summit of civilization and refinement," they could never be happy and contented." Female seminary student Estelle stated, "O! that all, especially among the Cherokees could but learn the vast importance of a good education. This and this only will place us on equality with other enlightened and cultivated nations."[34]

Students were profoundly influenced by the comments of their chiefs. At the annual May picnic in 1877 celebrating the opening of the seminaries, acculturation advocate William Potter Ross expressed his fears that his tribe would be outdone by other tribes in Indian Territory: "While our neighboring Tribes and Nations are pressing forward in the pursuit of knowledge, let not the Cherokee . . . be second in the race." The last thing his tribe needed, he warned the seminarians, was "lazy and useless men" and "slouchy and slip-shod women."[35] And to make it clear that the Cherokees still had not reached that summit of equality with whites by 1884, Chief Dennis Bushyhead earnestly spoke of the importance of praying at the same altar with "our whiter and stronger brothers [giving] our common thanks to God . . . [that they] will show magnanimity and justice to their weaker brethren."[36]

Students also took pleasure in comparing the old Cherokee ways with the new and improved lifestyles of the tribe to show that many tribal members had progressed past savagery and were on their way to equality with whites. In an 1854 issue of the *Cherokee Rose Buds*, student Edith championed the virtues of nineteenth-century white society and boasted the progress the Cherokees had made: "Instead of the rudely constructed wigwams of our forefathers which stood there [the Park Hill area] not more than half-a-century ago," she wrote, "elegant white buildings are seen. Everything around denotes taste, refinement, and progress of civilization among our people."[37]

The prolific Na-Li collaborated with another student in 1855 to illustrate their uneducated ancestors' backwardness and, more important, to emphasize the vast improvements the tribe had made. In scene one of the essay "Two Scenes in Indian Land," Na-Li describes a "wild and desolate" estate of a Cherokee family composed of "whooping, swarthy-looking boys" and plaited-haired women, all of whom "bear a striking resemblance to their rude and uncivilized hut." She concludes that the poor imbeciles "pass the days of their wild, passive, uninteresting life without any intellectual pleasure or enjoyment," except, she adds, to attend the Green Corn Dance, a "kind of religious festival."[38]

Scene two, by author Fanny, paints a completely different picture of Cherokee life. In her commentary, even the environment around the family's home has magically blossomed from the influence of the missionaries. "Civilization and nature are here united," she expounds. "Flowers, music, and even better, the *Holy Word of God* is here to study, showing that religion has shed its pure light over all." The Indian lad, "in place of his bow and arrow, is now taught to use the pen and wield the powers of eloquence." The girl, "instead of keeping time with the rattling of the terrapin shells [around her ankles], now keeps time with the chalk as her fingers fly nimbly over the blackboard." Fanny then professes her hope that "we may advance, never faltering until all the clouds of ignorance and superstition, and wickedness flee from before the rays of the Suns of Knowledge and Righteousness."[39] In these tales, then, there was the possibility that the "wild Cherokee Indian" could be changed and become a new person. The seminarians were not shy in vocalizing their hope that their unsophisticated peers would do the same.

Other passages reflect the students' feelings of inferiority to whites. The same *Rose Buds* issue that discusses "elegance and civilization" of the Cherokee Nation also compares the tribe unfavorably with the eastern United States by stating that the new bride of Chief John Ross, Mary Stapler, admirably left her more civilized surroundings in Philadelphia in order to "dwell with him in his *wild* prairie home."[40] Another editorial, commenting on the completed 1855 spring term, declares, "We present you again with a collection of Rosebuds, gathered from our Seminary garden. If, on examining them, you chance to find a withered or dwarfish bud, please pass it by. . . . We hope for lenient judgement, when our efforts are compared with those of our white sisters."[41] Another editorial, "Exchanges," acknowledges the newspapers received from other girls' schools in New England. But the Cherokee seminarians did not send copies of *Rose Buds* in return, because, as an editor explains, "we feel ourselves entirely too feeble to make any adequate recompense. . . . We are simply Cherokee school girls."[42]

In light of the reverence held for the Cherokee Female Seminary by the progressive tribal members, and considering the reason for its establishment, it is little wonder that the 212 girls who graduated from the seminary and, to a lesser extent, those who did not graduate but used their seminary education to obtain degrees from other institutions were considered the crème de la crème of the Cherokee Nation.[43] But that narrow-minded attitude ignores the more than 2,770 girls who did not graduate from the female seminary or from any other school.[44] Granted, many girls left the seminary before they had completed their first semester, and some left after only one week. But their early departures do not necessarily indicate an inability to handle the workload or the social atmosphere of the school.

Some dropouts had had problems with the course of study, but not all of them had been unable to master the difficult subjects. According to the student grade lists from 1876 to 1903, most were able to cope with the Mount Holyoke-style curriculum.[45] Prior to their enrollment in the female seminary, many of the pupils had attended the Cherokee common schools, the Cherokee Orphan Asylum, or one of the missionary schools or other high schools outside the Cherokee Nation, and had reasonably good educational backgrounds.[46] In addition, many

Figure 11.4. Female and male seminary drama club members performing in blackface, 1896. This skit was entitled "De Debatin' Club."

mixed-blood parents hired private tutors if their daughters had difficulty with their studies or if the common-school teachers were incompetent.

The graduates, of course, made high grades (80s to 90s) throughout their careers at the seminary. Most of those who graduated were from comparatively affluent families, which enabled them to visit their homes more often than students from remote areas.[47] Many of the graduates were related and attended the school at the same time as their relatives, which helped to alleviate homesickness.[48] And, like successful students today, the girls who performed best received encouragement from their parents. Of the parents whose records could be examined, graduates' fathers had a 98 percent literacy rate and their mothers 100 percent, compared to the 82 percent and 86 percent literacy rate of the nongraduates' fathers and mothers, respectively. Most of the full-bloods' parents could not write in English, and just 69 percent of their fathers and 55 percent of their mothers could read.[49] Only two of the graduates were full-bloods, and they had been adopted by white and mixed-blood parents and were educated in mission schools prior to seminary enrollment.[50]

Most of those who dropped out after one semester still made medium to high grades (70s to 90s). These dropouts usually left because of personal or family illness, an impending marriage, or homesickness. Other factors, such as the seminary's closure in 1856, the destructive fire in 1887, the departure of Principal Wilson in 1901, and the creation of Northeastern State Normal School in 1909, caused students to enroll in other schools. In 1893 several girls voluntarily went home because of the crowded living conditions. In 1902, because of the increased prosperity of the nation's farmers and the need for a "large force" to harvest crops, many students returned to the farm to do "home work."[51] A large number of these dropouts (except those who married immediately) enrolled in and graduated from other institutions.

Dropouts who had made low grades (50 or below) were in the minority. These students often left soon after enrolling (within the first day or month). Most were traditional full-bloods, or mixed-bloods of one-half to three-quarters Cherokee, who had attended distant Cherokee-language common schools and were not prepared for the difficult curriculum or the oppressive white atmosphere of the school.

Figure 11.5 Members of the class of 1903, left to right: Leola "Lee" Ward Newton, Grace Wallace Richards, Caroline "Carri" Freeman Baird, and Laura Effie Duchworth Boatright. All four were 1/32 Cherokee blood.

Indeed, while some Cherokees did want to send their children to the school but could not afford to, some full-bloods opposed the seminaries and did not send their children to them even if they had the money. Prejudice against traditional Cherokees was the parents' main argument, but they also had doubts about the practicality of the school's curriculum. The seminary met the expectations of the National Council, the teachers, and most of the nation's citizens, but some Cherokees protested that the academic curriculum was not applicable to the needs of the students.

This attitude was expressed in a letter to the *Cherokee Advocate* in 1881 signed "Bond Guy." The writer stated, "What our youngsters ought to be . . . are farmers and stock raisers." He doubted that the students heard "the words 'farm' or 'farming' during the entire three or four years' course of instruction." Preferring practical training over academic courses, the writer asked, "What sense or good is there in preparing our youth for their [white] business?" He concluded that both seminaries were merely "pieces of imitation, with the high schools of the United States for models," and therefore served no practical purpose in a nation composed mainly of farmers. The education that the students received, he believed, "ought to conform to, and fit them for, what they expect to become."[52] In 1880— out of a population of approximately 25,438—3,550 Cherokees were farmers, 135 were mechanics, and 82 were teachers.[53]

The debate over educational priorities had begun as early as 1823, when Chief John Ross and Second Principal Chief Charles Hicks disagreed over the type of "national academy" the tribe should establish. Ross advocated the traditional, New England-style school, while Hicks championed what he believed was the most practical education for the tribe, a vocational school.[54] The council disregarded Hicks's suggestion, and thirty-three years later Indian agent W. A. Duncan reported that the seminaries still "were only producing intellectuals . . . but not everyone can become a professional . . . [or] live here without manual labor."[55] Because of pressure from tribal members who wanted vocational training to be available, the National Council gave the board of education permission to declare the boarding schools "industrial or manual labor boarding schools."[56]

Within the next few years, principal chiefs Dennis Bushyhead and Joel B. Mayes took a strong interest in the accomplishments of the seminaries. Bushyhead acknowledged the "gratifying results" of the seminaries' curriculum, but in 1881 he advocated using more of the tax revenue for a mandatory "system of manual labor" for the primary-grade students (who were usually from poor, farming families) that would be "optionary" for the upper grades. In the 1890s Chief Mayes tried to persuade the National Council to purchase Fort Gibson for use as an industrial school, but the council was not receptive to the idea, presumably because most of the councilmen's children attended the seminaries and had no intention of becoming farmers or laborers.[57]

The Department of the Interior's annual report for 1899 stated that instead of "being taught the domestic arts [girls] are given . . . Latin and mathematics while branches of domestic economy are neglected. The dignity of work receives no attention at their hands."[58] The seminary administrators yielded to the pressure, and by 1905 the school's "domestic science" department included lessons in cooking, cleaning (dusting and making their beds; a laundress washed their clothes), sewing (usually to mend torn clothes; only a few girls became skilled seamstresses), and a modest agricultural program that featured botany, gardening, and flower arrangement.[59]

Many alumnae did become agriculturalists, but others had a profound interest in the whites' more lucrative businesses. Because many of their parents and siblings owned and operated stores in Tahlequah or other parts of the Cherokee Nation, the girls already had developed the confidence to pursue careers in the business world and were not afraid to interact with whites. In addition, many of the more progressive girls came from families who had hired help to perform domestic chores.

The girls who graduated were, as a whole, the most acculturated and affluent students at the seminary. After graduation, they became, among other things, educators, businesswomen, physicians, stock raisers, and prominent social workers.[60] They also followed their mothers' examples and "married well." Of the 212 graduates, at least 189 eventually married. Most of them married white men or men who had a smaller amount of Cherokee blood than they had. In a few cases, the husbands had a greater degree of Indian blood, but in every such instance they were either physicians, politicians, or members of prominent (usually wealthy) Cherokee families.[61] Clearly, the more white blood the woman had, the more apt she was to marry a non-Cherokee, a tribal member with high social status, or a man who had at least the same degree of white blood that she possessed. Indicative of the latter were the fifteen women who married graduates of the male seminary.[62]

Another interesting aspect was (and is) the value placed upon blood quantums as a source of identity. Many of the girls who went to the seminaries often had brothers and sisters who did not attend. In a comparison of the quantums of entire families, it is apparent that the women who married white men, or men with a lesser degree of Cherokee blood than they had, had tended during enrollment to claim a lesser degree of Cherokee blood than their siblings—perhaps in an attempt to appear "whiter," while at the same time retaining their Cherokee identity. In contrast to the value systems of the seminarians, many of their descendants today claim a Dawes Roll error and argue that their ancestors were much more Cherokee than they said they were. It appears that there is now a movement among many Americans to find or inflate their Cherokee roots, a distinct contrast to many of the seminarians, who were more interested in their non-Indian backgrounds.[63]

Despite the differences of opinion between the traditional and the progressive Cherokees over education, and despite the school's class system, the Cherokee Female Seminary survived as a tribal institution for over five decades.[64] The hundreds of Cherokee girls who passed through its halls were profoundly influenced—both positively and negatively—by their experiences at the school.

The girls' seminary experiences helped to strengthen their identities as Cherokees, although there were differences in opinion as to what a Cherokee really was. At least 30 percent were of one-sixteenth degree or less Cherokee blood, yet they still considered themselves to be Cherokees.[65] Many girls had never even heard the Cherokee language. One student admitted years later, "I did not realize what my Indian heritage meant to me when I attended the Cherokee Female Seminary."[66] All she heard was the word *Cherokee*, and she assumed that all tribal members lived like the seminarians. But the full-bloods who were fluent in their native language and who participated in tribal ceremonies also saw themselves as Cherokees, and their tenure at what they regarded as an oppressive school only strengthened their ties to their traditional families.

Both the progressive and the traditional tribal members considered themselves to be more Cherokee than the other group. The progressives believed that because of their enlightening educational and religious experiences, their intermarriage with whites, and their successful reestablishment in Indian Territory after their removal from the East, they were the new and improved Cherokees. The traditionalists, on the other hand, viewed the mixed-bloods not as Cherokees but as non-Indian "sellouts" or, at best, "white Cherokees." Interestingly, just like many mixed-bloods today, the Cherokee women who looked Caucasian found that their appearance, in combination with their educational backgrounds, gave them an advantage: They were able to slip back and forth between the white and Cherokee cultures (or at least the Cherokee culture they were used to), depending on their needs.

Not all tribal members subscribed to the school's philosophy, but a large portion of them did. Although there undoubtedly was prejudice against the traditional girls—and these students were often devastated by their seminary experiences—full-bloods were at least exposed to the ways of white society, and the mixed-blood girls had the opportunity to interact for a short time with less acculturated tribal members.

The female seminary is remembered for what it stood for: acculturation, assimilation, enlightenment, or survival, depending on the needs and values of the alumnae. The school was not meant for every female Cherokee; the seminary's atmosphere and attitude were white, and the progressive Cherokees were attempting to acculturate their peers. While the school contributed to a detrimental class system, the education it offered gave a strong educational background to those who went on to colleges and universities and was invaluable to the acculturated girls' success in business and in social circles within and outside of the Cherokee Nation.

Despite its shortcomings, the Cherokee Female Seminary was unquestionably the catalyst for the prosperity of many Cherokee women and their families. To many Cherokees, the old female seminary building, which now stands on the campus of Northeastern State University in Tahlequah, remains a symbol of adaptation and progress in a changing, and often inhospitable, world.

Notes

1. See Devon I. Abbott, "The History of the Cherokee Female Seminary: 1851–1910" (Ph.D. dissertation, Texas Christian University, 1989) and " 'Commendable Progress': Acculturation at the Cherokee Female Seminary," *American Indian Quarterly* 11 (summer 1987): 187–201. The total enrollment is estimated, because ten years of seminary rolls are missing. Although thirty years of rolls are available, my estimate of the enrollment is lower than the apparent totals on the rolls, because many girls attended the seminary for more than one year. For this study, their names were recorded only once—for a total of almost three thousand different names.
2. "An Act in Relation to the Male and Female Seminaries, and Establishing Primary Departments Therein for the Education of Indigent Children," 28 November 1873, in *Constitutions and Laws of the Cherokee Nation* (St. Louis: R. and T. A. Ennis Stationers, Printers and Book Binders, 1975), reprinted as vol. 7 of *Constitutions and Laws of the American Indian Tribes* (Wilmington, Del.: Scholarly Resources, Inc., 1973), 267–69.
3. Not all full-bloods were traditional and/or poor, nor were all mixed-bloods progressive and/or wealthy.
4. Thomas Lee Ballenger, *Names of Students of Cherokee Male and Female Seminaries, Tahlequah, Oklahoma, from 1876 to 1904*, in Special Collections, Northeastern State University (NSU), Tahlequah, Oklahoma.
5. "Ann Florence Wilson's Grade Book" or "Cherokee Female Seminary Records of Grades, 1876–1909," in NSU's Office of Admissions and Records, Administration Building, Tahlequah.
6. Letter dated 10 September 1889, in Cherokee Female Seminary Miscellaneous Box, archives, NSU.
7. The students' socioeconomic backgrounds were compiled by the author, using the Index to the Five Civilized Tribes, the Final Dawes Roll, M1186, roll 1, and the Enrollment Cards for the Five Civilized Tribes, 1898–1914, rolls 2–15, cards 1–11,132, at the Federal Archives in Fort Worth, Texas.
8. Ibid., in combination with Emmett Starr, *History of the Cherokee Indians, Their Legends and Folklore* (Muskogee: Hoffman Printing, Inc., 1984), 489–680.
9. Personal interview with Pearl Mayes Langston, 6 June 1989, Fort Gibson, Oklahoma.
10. Albert Sydney Wyly to John D. Benedict (1908), letter in Miscellaneous Female Seminary Box, archives, NSU.
11. For information on Ann Florence Wilson, see Devon I. Abbott, "Ann Florence Wilson, Matriarch of the Cherokee Seminary," *Chronicles of Oklahoma* 67 (winter 1989–90): 426–37.
12. Maggie Culver Fry, comp., *Cherokee Female Seminary Years: A Cherokee National Anthology by Many Tribal Authors* (Claremore, Okla.: Rogers State College Press, 1988), 83.
13. Kate O'Ringland to Abraham Knepler, 21 April 1938 (Knepler, Ph.D. dissertation, "Digest of the Education of the Cherokee Indians," Yale University, 1939, 323).
14. Personal interview with Rick Corley, 27 December 1988, Arlington, Texas.
15. *Cherokee Advocate*, 23 August 1873, 2.
16. "Wilson's Grade Book."
17. Personal interview with Charlotte Mayes Sanders, 20 October 1988, Tahlequah, Oklahoma.
18. "Wilson's Grade Book."
19. *Cherokee Advocate*, 2 May 1884.
20. Interview with Sanders.
21. *The Cherokee Rose Buds*, 2 August 1854, 2.
22. Ibid.

23. Fry, *Cherokee Female Seminary Years*, 104–5.

24. *Twin Territories*, June 1899.

25. *Wreath of Cherokee Rose Buds*, 14 February 1855, 2, at Anthropological Archives, Smithsonian Institution, Washington, D.C.

26. Ibid., 5; *Cherokee Rose Buds*, 2 August 1854, 6, at archives, NSU.

27. *Wreath of Cherokee Rose Buds*, 14 February 1855, 5.

28. Ibid., 4, 6.

29. Thomas L. Ballenger, "The Colored High School of the Cherokee Nation," *Chronicles of Oklahoma* 30 (winter 1952–53): 454–62.

30. The students' blood quantums were derived by the author from the census records and the Index to the Five Civilized Tribes, the Final Dawes Roll, M1186, roll 1, and the Enrollment Cards for the Five Civilized Tribes, 1898–1914, M1186, rolls 2–15, cards 1–11, 132, at the Federal Archives. The Final Dawes Roll has many errors in regard to the Cherokees' blood quantums, so cross-references of other family members were used. If the student died prior to the opening of the rolls, the quantum was found via either siblings, children, or parents. Married names were located on the census records, in newspapers, and in Emmett Starr, *History of the Cherokees*. A few of the early students, graduates, and husbands had died, leaving no progeny and thus no clue as to their degree of Cherokee blood, but only two were reported to be full-bloods. Some of the students during the later years (1903–9) were not enrolled, because they were recent arrivals to Indian Territory.

31. *Kansas City Times*, 29 July 1889, 2. Stephens's comment almost echoes Thomas Jefferson's speech to Indians visiting Washington, D.C., in 1808, when he said, "You will unite yourselves with us, join in our great councils and form one people with us, and we shall all be Americans; you will mix with us by marriage, your blood will run in our veins, and will spread with us over this great continent." In Saul K. Padover, *Thomas Jefferson on Damocracy* (New York: Mentor, New American Library, Appleton-Century Co., 1939), 106–7, quoted in William G. McLoughlin, *Cherokee Renascence in the New Republic* (Princeton: Princeton University Press, 1986), 37.

32. *Cherokee Advocate*, 4 February 1851, 2.

33. *The Sequoyah Memorial*, 2 August 1855, in archives, NSU.

34. *Wreath of Cherokee Rose Buds*, 14 February 1855, 3.

35. *The Journal*, 17 May 1877, 1.

36. Cited in V.A. Travis, "Life in the Cherokee Nation a Decade after the Civil War," *Chronicles of Oklahoma* 4 (March 1926), 30.

37. *Cherokee Rose Buds*, 2 August 1854, 3.

38. *Wreath of Cherokee Rose Buds*, 1 August 1855, 1–2.

39. Ibid.

40. *Cherokee Rose Buds*, 2 August 1854, 3.

41. *Wreath of Cherokee Rose Buds*, 1 August 1855, 4.

42. Ibid.

43. Statement by Professor Rudi Halliburton at the Seventeenth Annual Symposium on the American Indian, 3–8 April 1989, at NSU.

44. See Abbott, "History of the Cherokee Female Seminary," Appendix A, for some of the nonseminary graduates and the colleges and universities they enrolled in.

45. "Wilson's Grade Book."

46. See N. B. Johnson, "The Cherokee Orphan Asylum," *Chronicles of Oklahoma* 34 (summer 1956): 159–82.

47. The students' home districts were compiled from the 1880 Cherokee Census and Index, schedules 1–6, 7RA–07, rolls 1–4, and the 1890 Cherokee Census (no index), schedules 1–4, 7RA–08, rolls 1–4, at the Federal Archives; "Wilson's Grade Book"; "Mary Stapler's Class Book" at archives, NSU; *Catalog of the C.N.F.S., 1896 and Announcements for 1897 and 1898*, 3–6, at archives, NSU; *Souvenir Catalog: 1850–1905*, at archives, NSU; "Register and Accounts of Female Seminary Primary and Boarding School Students," bound ledger in archives, NSU.

48. At least one hundred families sent three or more children—including sisters and cousins—to attend the seminary at the same time.

49. The parents' literacy rates were compiled from the 1880 Cherokee Census and Index, schedules 1–6, 7RA–07, rolls 1–4, and the 1890 Cherokee Census (no index), schedules 1–4, 7RA–08, rolls 1–4, at the Federal Archives.

50. Catherine Hastings Maxfield, 1855, and Martha Whiting Fox, 1856. The 1880 Cherokee Census and Index, schedules 1–6, 7RA–07, rolls 1–4.

51. *Cherokee Advocate*, 9 September 1893, 2; ibid., 16 September 1893, 2; Ibid., 30 September 1893, 2; Ibid., 7 October 1893, 2; ibid., 14 October 1893, 2, Cop pock to Benedict, 11 July 1901, *Report of the*

Commissioner of Indian Affairs (RCIA), 57th Cong., 1st sess., H. Doc. 5 (serial 4291), 318–19; CHN 97, Cherokee Schools: *Female Seminary, Documents 2735–2777*, 11 May 1887-December 1902, at the Oklahoma Historical Society, Oklahoma City.

52. *Cherokee Advocate*, 31 August 1881, 1.

53. Leslie Hewes, *Occupying the Cherokee Country of Oklahoma* (Lincoln: University of Nebraska, 1978), 39.

54. Ard Hoyt to Jeremiah Evarts, 14 August 1823, American Board Commissioners Foreign Missions, letter 104, ABC, 18.3.1, vol. 3, quoted in William McLoughlin's *The Cherokee Ghost Dance* (Macon, Ga.: Mercer University Press, 1984), 494.

55. Report of W. A. Duncan, 25 September 1856, *RCIA for 1853*, 34th Cong., 3rd sess., H. Exec. Doc. 1 (serial 893), 692.

56. Sec. 20 of "An Act Relating to Education," in *Compiled Laws of the Cherokee Nation* (Tahlequah, I.T.: National Advocate Print, 1881), reprinted as vol. 9 of *Constitutions and Laws of the American Indian Tribes* (Wilmington, Del.: Scholarly Resources, Inc., 1973), 236.

57. "Fourth Annual Message of Chief Dennis W. Bushyhead," in *Annual Messages of Hon. Chief D. W. Bushyhead*, 33, Special Collections, NSU; *Cherokee Advocate*, 17 November 1889, 1; message of Chief Joel B. Mayes to National Council, 17 November 1889, in *Cherokee Letter Book*, vol. 14, p. 4, and J. B. Mayes to T. J. Morgan, 18 October 1890, in *Cherokee Letter Book*, vol. 3, p. 11, Phillips Collection, Western History Collection, University of Oklahoma, Norman.

58. *RCIA for 1899*, 56th Cong., 2d sess., H. Doc. 5 (serial 3915), 92.

59. *Cherokee Female Seminary Souvenir Catalog: 1850–1906*, at archives, NSU.

60. See Abbott, "History of the Cherokee Female Seminary," 181–89, and Appendices B–E.

61. See ibid., 212–13, for the girls' husbands.

62. See ibid., Appendix G for seminarians who married each other.

63. These assertions are based on findings in the 1880 and 1890 Cherokee Census Records, and the Dawes Rolls and Enrollment Cards. Additionally, in almost every interview I conducted during my study of the history of the female seminary, the subjects asserted that they were indeed more Cherokee than they appeared, because, "the Dawes Roll is wrong." My comment regarding Americans' affinity towards the Cherokee tribe is based on the startling numbers of students, colleagues, and acquaintances who have told me that they have a "full-blood Cherokee" mother or grandmother. Unfortunately, few of these individuals can substantiate their claims, since their ancestors were invariably "out of town" during the enrollment.

64. The female seminary was open for business for forty academic years.

65. Statistics compiled from the 1880 Cherokee Census and Index, schedules 1–6, 7RA–07, rolls 1–4, and the 1890 Cherokee Census (no index), schedules 1–4, 7RA–08, rolls 1–4, at Federal Archives.

66. M. Fry, *Cherokee Female Seminary Years*, 157.

12

The Practice of Everyday Colonialism
Indigenous Women at Work in the Hop Fields and Tourist Industry of Puget Sound

Paige Raibmon

In the late nineteenth century, thousands of Indigenous women journeyed hundreds of miles annually along the Pacific Northwest coast and converged around Puget Sound. They came to pick hops in the fields of farmers who occupied lands in western Washington (Figure 12.1). These migrants did not look like modern factory workers, yet they were laborers in a late-nineteenth-century incarnation of industrial agriculture. They came en masse to harvest a cash crop destined for sale on the global market, a crop internationally sought as a preservative and flavoring for beer, a crop that could provide no sustenance to them or their families. Field workers were paid in cash wages, not in kind. This was no shop floor, but a labor hierarchy (both racialized and gendered) structured the conditions of their work all the same. From sunup to sundown, pickers performed specialized labor consisting of repetitive hand motions. They would often mind their children while they did so. No union represented them, but they were known to strike for wages. These women were also independent vendors and craft workers. On their way to and from the harvest, they sold baskets and mats, beadwork and carvings, clams, game, and skins and pelts. A tourist boom grew up around the Puget Sound hop harvest, and these Indigenous women were at the center of it.

Such women do not fit easily into the conventional categories of the labor movement or labor history, but they were workers in more than one sense of the word. Despite, or in some ways because of, the heterogeneous nature of their work, observers have often failed to recognize these women as workers. Nineteenth-century observers did not see wage earners in an industrial economy. They saw romantic characters in a highly gendered colonial script about "vanishing Indians" and "squaw drudges." For a long time, North American labor historians unwittingly followed suit, mirroring the exclusions of nineteenth-century vanishing Indian ideology. Labor historians may or may not have consciously eschewed the insidious gendered pairing of "lazy bucks" with "squaw drudges" that was widespread throughout the nineteenth-century colonial world. But they inherited the powerful colonial binary of "traditional" and "modern" and accepted the mindset that Indians belonged to the former category, workers to the latter.[1] Earlier scholars who did write about Indian workers rejected the notion that there might be something culturally specific about them as *workers*.[2] The term *Indian worker* became an oxymoron.

It is long past time to recouple these words. If we fail to do so, we continue to mimic the gaze of nineteenth-century colonizers. Several scholars have already begun this important work. But, as they have shown, it is not enough simply to throw open the doors of labor history's union halls to Indian workers. Claims that these workers do not fit conventional categories of class and labor analysis are true.[3] Divesting ourselves of our inherited colonial blinders requires more

Figure 12.1. Hop pickers on the Snoqualmie hop ranch, 1895. Women constituted the majority of the workforce. Image SHS 1052, Museum of History and Industry, Seattle.

than a belated invitation to join the club. Thinking of Indian workers as a useful analytical category means rethinking many of the assumptions that previous labor historians took for granted.

This means, first of all, consciously rethinking, and in fact rejecting, the old binary of "traditional culture" and "modern labor." Indigenous workers across North America commonly engaged in so-called traditional and modern economies simultaneously. Participation in wage labor did not entail an end to patterns of resource harvesting that had defined these communities for countless generations, nor did Indigenous workers simply participate in parallel but unconnected economies. Hop pickers who wove baskets to sell to tourists were not unique. Many Indigenous workers took historically entrenched skills and adapted them for introduction into new capitalist markets. This "doorstep economy" helped Indigenous families survive under enormously difficult circumstances; at the same time, the commercialization of Indigenous products helped enable the survival of craft-based, and many women's, knowledge. When Indians traveled to work, they commonly did so in extended family groupings. Wage migrations facilitated visits between family members divided from each other by reserve/reservation and international boundaries. Migratory labor cycles could also offer relief from the intrusive interference of missionaries and Indian agents. To the frustration of officials, wages in their pockets did not turn Indian workers into assimilated subjects. Instead, workers frequently used income from "modern" wage labor to meet "traditional" obligations to kin and community and to invest in

Indigenous economies. In short, Indigenous workers assigned their own meanings to wage work.[4]

In addition to developing our understanding of Indigenous meanings of work, it is also crucial to pay careful attention to the specificity of the colonial context in which Indigenous people labored. Having elsewhere explored the former, it is to this latter task that I turn in the pages that follow. Treating the postrevolutionary United States as a colonial setting is perhaps unusual but certainly not unprecedented.[5] Claimed by two imperial powers—Britain and the United States— until 1846, Washington Territory was carved out of the previously existing Oregon Territory in 1853. Not incidentally, the growth of the hop industry around Puget Sound occurred during the years of Washington's bid for statehood. Hops were among the resources that attracted settlement, investment, and eventually, in 1889, the favor of Congress. Much like British Columbia, its neighbor to the north, late-nineteenth-century and early-twentieth-century Washington was in the throes of the most colonial of processes: the appropriation of land and resources and the dispossession of Indigenous peoples. This was nothing new. Settler societies relied upon turning Indigenous properties into capital through alienating Indigenous people from the means of production. Marx termed this process "primitive accumulation."[6] Extraction of Indigenous labor was thus central to colonialism.[7] Indigenous wage labor played an important role in the development of frontier, national, and global economies.[8] Moreover, the massive transfer of wealth away from Indigenous communities was ever-present in economic exchanges between Indian wage-earners and their bosses. To be sure, Indigenous people often entered the wage economy for their own reasons and of their own volition. At the same time, however, it is undeniable that colonial usurpation of hereditary lands and resources steadily narrowed the range of Indigenous economic choices. It is thus, as one scholar argues, impossible to discuss Aboriginal labor *without* taking land claims into consideration.[9] The histories of Indigenous labor under capitalism have everything to do with questions of capital, land, resources, and colonialism.

Primitive accumulation was not simply the "base" from which subsequent economic transactions proceeded in a linear manner. It was instead an ongoing colonial process that informed the meanings of a multitude of daily practices, simultaneously acquiring meaning from those practices in return. Resisting the dichotomy between "material" labor and "ideological" images, I want to suggest an expanded conception of work, one that investigates the interpenetration of consumption and production. Such a perspective helps make visible what Michel de Certeau calls "errant trajectories," the secondary levels of production embedded in consumption.[10] By broadening our analysis to include the meanings and ramifications attached to all forms and traces of Indigenous labor within their colonial context, we can begin to grasp the incredible power of colonial discourse to enlist the work of unlikely laborers. This enlistment had little to do with individual intentions, nor was it the result of manipulation by some "invisible hand." An innumerable cast of characters did the work of colonialism—often unwittingly—through the mundane practice of everyday life.[11] Personal acts of identity formation and breadwinning were incorporated within a double helix of consumption and production through which colonial modernity was constituted. Only by starting with this picture of colonialism from the ground up—with the minutia of daily acts—can we gain an understanding of colonialism as it appears from above.

I am interested in exploring the particular configurations of work, production, and consumption that accompanied the multiple manifestations of Indian women's work in the hop fields surrounding Puget Sound. Indigenous hop pickers labored in multiple ways; colonizers reaped a multiple yield. The benefits to farmers who paid out wages to workers who brought in the harvest are the most obvious. But as pioneer agriculturalists whose efforts constituted a foundational moment of primitive accumulation upon which future generations of non-Indigenous society would build, theirs was a colonial project, one that, in a strange twist of irony, representations of Indigenous workers helped authorize. Long after hops were picked or a basket was woven, the labor of Indian women continued to do work in the world. Labor upon which workers relied to feed themselves and their families was reappropriated to do the work of bourgeois identity formation, wealth creation, and colonial legitimation. With respect to the fruits of Indigenous women's labor, there were many stakeholders.[12] As I follow this labor through a variety of stages of consumption and production, I aim to suggest the remarkable range of possible stakes and meanings produced through Indigenous women's work in this colonial setting. I begin with the direct sale of Indian labor in the hop fields and in the tourist economy. I then consider how that labor worked to produce race, class, and gender identities of those who consumed its products. In the final section, I sketch the manner in which representations of Indian laborers worked to narrate the overarching project of colonialism.

Hop Pickers: Migrant Workers in a Global Market

Pioneer settler Jacob Meeker cultivated the first hop vine in western Washington in 1865. It was his son, Ezra Meeker, however, who, over the next forty years, developed a small cutting from his father into a multi-million-dollar industry and a major selling point for regional boosters.[13] Hop farming was a capital-intensive endeavor; in the 1870s, the cost of turning a single acre over to hops was close to $200.[14] Hop farming was also labor intensive. Hops required a small but constant amount of labor during the growing season, when they needed to be trained to tall poles between eight and sixteen feet high. But come late summer, each farmer urgently needed hundreds of workers to harvest the feather-light, sticky, yellow cones as soon as they ripened. A crop harvested quickly would be more uniform in color and flavor and thus more valuable. Just as important, mature hops left on the vine were vulnerable to overripening, frost, or mildew. Finding the necessary labor during harvest posed a problem for all farmers, even those with small farms. A single acre planted in hops averaged 1,600 pounds and in some years could yield as much as 3,000 pounds.[15] No farmer could hope to bring in the crop without a large number of hired hands.

It was not just the threat of labor shortages that made hop farming risky. Even in years when the weather was kind, the crop bountiful, and the workers available, farmers were not guaranteed a profitable return. Hops grown in western Washington were a cash crop destined for breweries around the world. Like hop growers from New York, California, and abroad, local farmers sold their crop on a global market. International demand was inelastic, and another region's bumper crop could drive down prices so far that Washington farmers were better off leaving hops to rot on the vine rather than pay workers to harvest them. Such strategies helped farmers cut their losses during desperate times, but they spelled disaster for migrant hop pickers, who, after having traveled from afar, could find themselves stranded and scrambling to pay their passage home.[16]

Yet as with most risky capitalist endeavors, the threat of business losses was—at least for growers—balanced against the promise of potentially enormous returns. Just as growers suffered from gluts caused by bumper crops, they profited enormously when crops elsewhere failed and global supplies ran low.[17] Knowing when to sell was another part of the business. In a given season, prices could fluctuate from eighteen cents to more than a dollar a pound.[18] Once he earned back his initial capital investment, the farmer's cost per pound raised was between seven and eleven cents.[19] A modest profit thus seemed almost certain, and the possibility of tremendous profit was intoxicating. Not unlike gold prospectors, hop farmers hoped to get lucky and strike it rich.

Fortunes stood to be made, and they were. Despite pioneer hop farmer Ezra Meeker's admission that "none of us knew anything about the hop business," over the next forty years, hop farmers added more than $20 million to Washington's economy.[20] Then, in the early twentieth century, tiny aphids devastated crops, effectively eliminating hop farms in western Washington.

During the 1880s, however, Meeker's exports to England alone reached 11,000 bales and total sales of more than $500,000.[21] Successful farmers-turned-philanthropists helped to build some of Washington's early community infrastructure in the 1880s and 1890s: they funded the construction of churches, fraternal lodges, and orphanages.[22]

Indigenous land and labor directly underwrote this remarkable prosperity in several ways. Most straightforward is the fact that the soil in which the hops grew was Indigenous territory. The "Steven's Treaties" signed in the 1850s with Indigenous peoples made it possible for settler-farmers to acquire free land in western Washington. In exchange for their land, Indigenous peoples received numerous promises, including uninterrupted rights to important resources both on and off reservation lands; for many tribes, the question of whether these promises were met is a matter before the courts today.[23] This original subsidy of free land was crucial to the hop industry's success. As Meeker noted, not only did western Washington hop farmers compete successfully in terms of quality (an essential factor, no doubt), they were able to do so "at a cost of production far below that of the older districts of the Atlantic States or of Europe."[24] Although he would not have put it in such terms, Meeker understood Marx's concept of "primitive accumulation." Meeker certainly realized that the cost of production would have increased dramatically had farmers been required to pay for the land. At the same time, this subsidy of free land was so thoroughly naturalized in Meeker's psyche as to not bear mentioning. It was practically invisible, simultaneously colonialism's best-kept and most public secret.

Like land, Indigenous labor enabled the hop industry's prosperity in some hidden ways. Many generations before the arrival of settlers, the Lushootseed created open "prairie" landscapes through careful and long-term fire ecology management.[25] The investors in the Snoqualmie Hop Ranch selected one such "natural prairie," as they mistakenly thought of it, for their hop farm, the largest in Washington and, according to some, the largest in the world.[26] Long before Indigenous women from diverse Pacific Northwest nations came to harvest hops, Lushootseed women had cultivated and harvested camas bulbs on that same land.[27] A crucial change overlaid this degree of continuity: camas cultivators had owned the means of production; hop pickers were in the process of being alienated from it. Oblivious to the land's history, the Snoqualmie investors nonetheless chose their site wisely. Clearing land was no easy task, especially for pioneers without experience in the Pacific coast rainforest.[28] Even after the trees were felled, one man with a horse and dynamite could take four hundred hours per acre to remove the stumps.[29] Would-be farmers selected the lands that could be most easily cleared for obvious reasons.[30]

Wage labor, the most visible Indigenous contribution to the hop industry, followed in the wake of these hidden subsidies to colonial capitalism. Since the 1850s, Indigenous people from as far north as Alaska had traveled south to Puget Sound for a number of reasons, including the search for wages. Throughout the 1850s and 1860s, men found work in sawmills or on farms, and women worked as domestic help or in the sex trade.[31] As the hop industry grew, it became an annual mainstay for thousands of these migrants. One estimate suggests that close to a quarter of all Indigenous people in British Columbia traveled to Puget Sound for the harvest season.[32] Indigenous workers constituted the vast majority of the harvest season labor force, and of these, women outnumbered men. Depending on their age, children worked or played alongside their mothers, grandmothers, and aunts in the fields. Some men also picked hops, while others took work elsewhere on the farm or hunted and fished in the vicinity.[33] Whites and Chinese picked hops too, but there were never enough of them to do the job. Settlers also expressed, sometimes violently, a preference for Indigenous workers over Chinese ones; this preference sometimes held even when Indigenous workers demanded a much higher rate of pay.[34]

Popular accounts often commented on the large numbers of women workers, commonly claiming that Indigenous women were harder, and thus more productive, workers than Indigenous men. As one local historian noted, "the Indian brave and his squaw—particularly the squaw—are the industrious and well paid pickers."[35] Reportedly, even pregnancy did not slow them down. According to Ezra Meeker, who paid a dollar to employees who gave birth while working on his farm, new mothers were back in the fields within two days, babies at their sides.[36] Writers similarly stressed the fortitude of elderly women. According to one, "even old Indian women in their dotage and almost blind" picked 50 percent more per day than any white picker, man or woman.[37] Such simultaneously derisive and romantic characterizations were typical of how various agents of colonization—farmers, tourists, and writers alike—cast Indigenous women. Drinking from the deep well of the squaw drudge stereotype, they valued the work of Indigenous women and, in same moment, with the same rhetorical gesture, identified that work as synecdochic for everything that was wrong with Indigenous societies. Both parts of their contradictory utterances were necessary elements of this colonial discourse. They valorized Indigenous women because without them early capitalism in western Washington could not have prospered as it did. They enfeebled Indigenous women because without assurances of white racial and cultural supremacy, the moral authority and future success of the entire colonial enterprise was suspect.

Invocations of the squaw drudge often implied the image of the lazy buck. As one writer put it: "Indians make the best pickers, and among the Indians the klootchman ranks supreme. She picks hops while the lazy, indolent brave plays cards or lounges in the shadow of his rakish tepee. His great delights are in card playing and pony racing."[38] Such accounts applied the non-Aboriginal categories of "home" and "work" to Indian families. They feminized Indian men by situating them within what white Americans largely assumed to be the Indian approximation of the woman's domestic sphere, the tepee. The image of Indian women working in the hot sun while Indian men lounged in the shade highlighted the dissonance of this gender inversion. This emasculation of Indian men went hand in hand with an emphasis on the morally suspect nature of the activities they did in lieu of work. Missionaries, journalists, and amateur ethnographers alike portrayed hard-working Indian women as enablers of Indian men and their idle natures. Writers in tune with the work ethic of Protestantism suggested that the inactivity of these men rendered them vulnerable to drinking, gambling, and other vices. Squaw drudges who failed to embody the proper gendered division of labor were implicitly to blame for both their own oppression and men's dissolution.[39]

With such invocations, late-nineteenth-century colonizers around Puget Sound revealed the genealogical connections to countless generations of their colonial forebears. Reports of the strength and endurance of colonized women around the world—Africa, Australia, America— had for centuries served the twin purpose of racializing populations and justifying domination of them. The supposed ability to endure childbirth painlessly had featured in European narratives of non-European women since the sixteenth century. These commentaries on women's labor were about economic labor, too. African women's imperviousness to the pain of childbirth, for example, became a racialized marker that excluded them from the Christian genealogy derived from Eve's original sin, placing them beyond the bounds of the European, and in a broader sense human, family. This dehumanization rhetorically justified the forced extraction of their labor.[40]

Perhaps such age-old stereotypes about the strength and fortitude of colonized women influenced hiring practices, or perhaps the sight of Indigenous women in fields ignited them. Regardless, Indigenous women made up the majority of the picking force. They traveled to Puget Sound with their extended families and, in some cases at least, took charge of deciding when and where a family would accept work.[41] This was an important decision because conditions on different farms varied. Some farmers paid pickers' way to the fields from Seattle, a trip that could be quite costly. Access to fresh produce and groceries could not be taken for granted and was another consideration. The quality of living conditions in the hop camps also mattered. With hundreds or sometimes thousands of pickers crowded together in temporary camps, sanitation was always a potential problem.[42] Epidemic diseases spread easily among workers and took a particularly high toll on children and infants who were born in the hop camps.[43] In 1884, for example, a bereaved father stated that his infant son had died of exposure. Some of the other workers, however, were suspicious that the father had murdered the baby and had threatened to kill the mother.[44] Regardless of the truth in this particular case, the incident reminds us that in selecting where to camp and work, women must have also done their best to take the physical safety of themselves and their children into consideration.

In most years pickers could afford to be choosy about where they worked. Demand for labor often exceeded supply. Farmers competed for workers more than workers competed for jobs, often bidding up the price of labor in the process.[45] Migrants located work and obtained knowledge about conditions through word of mouth, kinship networks, and recruitment calls. Farmers sometimes wrote to Indian agents, asking them to send a certain number of workers by a certain date; often they invited the same workers back annually. George and Mary Stiltamult began picking hops for Alderton farmer William Lane sometime before 1888. By 1891, Lane valued their work so much that he wrote offering them cash bonuses if they would return.[46] Farmers also hired Indigenous men to recruit workers from their extended circle or kin and community.[47] Given their strength of numbers in the fields, Indigenous women must have also done this work, although I have found no record of them being paid for it in this period.[48] A Haida woman named Emma Levy almost certainly recruited workers. She was sister-in-law to Henry Levy, part owner of the vast Snoqualmie Hop Ranch. It was Henry who claimed responsibility for recruiting the close to fifteen hundred seasonal workers that the ranch needed, but it was Emma who had the necessary kinship network to draw from. It seems unlikely that the Haida workers at the Snoqualmie Hop Ranch arrived without her involvement.[49]

A gendered labor hierarchy structured pickers' work in the fields. Farmers typically hired Indigenous men as managers. These "hop bosses" helped arrange pickers' transportation, supervised pickers in the field, and oversaw conditions in the camps. The work could be extremely lucrative, sometimes bringing a daily salary three times what most pickers would earn and, in addition, a hefty bonus for ensuring that enough pickers arrived on time.[50] Indigenous men also worked in the coveted position of "pole puller." Below the hop boss in rank and salary, pole pullers performed the crucial task of uprooting the towering poles, heavy with ripe hops, and laying them horizontally on the ground so that pickers could set to work. When pickers finished with one pole, they called for the pole puller and waited for him to come select and uproot another pole for them. Pole pullers could play favorites by choosing which picker to help next or by giving the most densely laden vines to certain pickers. Such favoritism sometimes played out along tribal lines. On the Snoqualmie Hop Ranch, the farm in which Emma Levy's brother-in-law had an interest, it was, perhaps not surprisingly, the Haida who seemed to have the upper hand. A Tsimshian man who worked there recorded in his diary his frustration because Haida men had a monopoly on the plum pole-puller positions and consistently favored Haida workers in the field. Competition between Haida and Tsimshian workers in Puget Sound mirrored labor relations in the Skeena River fishing industry hundreds of miles north, where Haida fishers complained that the Tsimshian enjoyed privileged conditions of employment and higher wages.[51] The dynamics of these workplace relationships mattered because pickers were paid a piece rate for their labor. Accordingly, male pole pullers had significant control over the productivity and, by extension, income of female pickers. Indigenous women who picked hops worked at the bottom of a multilayered, male hierarchy that subordinated them not only to white farmers and white farm hands, but also to Indian hop bosses and pole pullers.

Pickers could expect to earn around a dollar for filling a large box with hops, and most pickers, after they grew accustomed to the work and learned a few tricks of the trade, could fill one box a day. The most important trick they learned was to fill a number of smaller baskets first, transferring them only after they had enough small containers to fill the large boxes that were the scale of pay. Workers who made the mistake of picking directly into the large boxes soon learned that the fluffy hops on the bottom compressed beneath the accumulated weight of those on top. This made it nearly impossible to fill a box and could reduce the worker's wage by 50 percent or more. Experienced women knew to bring baskets that they had woven with them for this purpose. In so doing, they combined their craft labor with their wage labor. They were well aware of their value to farmers once the harvest had begun; a work stoppage of even a few hours could cut profits dramatically. If workers felt the farmer was taking advantage of them, by increasing the box size without increasing the piece rate, for example, they would strike, often to good effect.[52] There was no picking and thus no pay on rainy days.

Hop Pickers: Craft Workers and Entrepreneurs in a Tourist Economy

The structure of the late-nineteenth-century Pacific Northwest coast labor market presented Indigenous women with the opportunity to earn money as hop pickers. In parallel fashion, the structure of the colonial imaginary presented them with the opportunity to earn money as vendors, photographic subjects, and craft workers. Where farmers saw field hands when they looked at Indigenous migrants, white sightseers and tourists saw vanishing Indians. These contradictory views did not need to be reconciled with one another; they could "cohere in contradiction," often within a single individual.[53] The romantic imaginings of observers were in sharp contrast to the material reality of wage laborers tied to a global market, but these imaginings were powerful enough to create a market in artifacts related to the Indigenous hop pickers.

A tourist industry shadowed the hop harvest from the early 1870s.[54] By the end of the century, the hop season in Puget Sound had earned a national profile as a tourist attraction through attention received from writers such as John Muir and popular publications like *Harper's Weekly*.[55] As the hop season began with the arrival of Indigenous migrant workers, residents of towns and cities in western Washington embarked on mini migrations of their own to rural areas where they would view the spectacle of "authentic Indians." Other tourists came from farther afield. Hundreds of visitors a day descended upon the hop-growing regions. They traveled by carriage and interurban passenger trains. Entrepreneurs built hotels near the hop fields to accommodate tourists interested in more extended rural retreats.[56] An urban arm of this tourist industry developed as Indigenous women paused in Seattle and Tacoma on their ways to and from the hop fields. Contemporary descriptions treated migrant hop pickers on city streets as picturesque additions to the urban landscape.

Local Indigenous women also populated city streets, of course. But contemporary newspapers devoted inordinate amounts of attention to hop picker vendors. Urban residents' fascination with these migrant Indians arose in the same decades that urban settlers displaced the people who were indigenous to the territory on which the city stood. As residents of Seattle linked the visible presence of Indians with the itinerancy of hop pickers, they imagined the city as a place that Indians moved through rather than as a place where they lived. The visibility of migrant hop pickers and the invisibility of local Indigenous people were mutually constituted.[57]

Migrant hop pickers might have been alternately amused and annoyed at being treated as tourist attractions. Regardless of their personal reaction, most Indigenous women were not in a position to decline the dollars that tourists wanted to spend. Indigenous women who came to pick hops typically brought a winter's worth of skilled, artistic labor: baskets, mats, beadwork, needlework, and carvings. They sold their wares on street corners and doorsteps.[58] As one Seattle pioneer remembered, in late fall, the homeward-bound hop pickers "would line the sidewalks, the women displaying some of the finest needlework and beadwork, blankets and baskets one ever saw."[59] Dismissively dubbed as curios, such objects were widely sought by tourists, who would pay anywhere from 25¢ to $3 for a basket.[60] These prices were poor remuneration for the hours, effort, and expertise invested in a finely woven basket. Yet at a time when settler usurpation of Indigenous land and resources was accelerating, and when standing all day in the fields was valued at one dollar, curio selling was good business.[61]

Late-nineteenth-century tourists wanted to purchase images as well as objects. Photographs, stereographs, and postcards were popular souvenirs. Professional and amateur photographers often paid Indigenous hop pickers for posing—indeed, the "subjects" often insisted on it.[62] Compared to the many hours it took to fill a box with hops, let alone to weave a basket, a dollar for a split-second's pose must have seemed like a boon.

Indigenous women in the hop fields thus sold their labor several times over. As pickers, they sold their summer's labor directly to the farmers. As weavers, they sold their winter's labor to the tourists. And given that photographs provided income and attracted tourists who might eventually purchase curios themselves, the act of posing ought to also be viewed as labor. The money that women earned from the tourist economy was often crucial to their family's well-being. The income from wages was significant, but, given the vicissitudes of weather and global markets, it was probably less reliable than income from the tourist economy. Whenever the hop harvest failed, and particularly when such failure coincided with a poor salmon run, income from the tourist industry could be all that stood between a woman's family and a hungry winter.[63]

Producing Women Producing Identity

The multiplicity of Indigenous women's labor produced more than hops, curios, and photographs. Women's labor was enlisted in the ongoing production of the class, race, and gender identities of those who consumed its products. Production and consumption are thus inextricably connected: through the act of consumption, products in turn became productive. When labor history focuses exclusively on production, it artificially severs the two categories and obscures the dynamic and mutually constitutive relationship between them. In the simplest sense, the labor of workers produces products—hops or baskets, for example—and the consumption of products, in turn, produces a need for labor. But there is more to it. Products carry, transform, and multiply meanings as they circulate through different contexts. Products do work in the world. Often, they do the work of colonialism. They do so not as pure abstractions but as the material traces of workers' effort. The physical labor—picking or weaving for example—is thus drawn out over space and time into additional cycles of continuous production. "Everyday life invents itself," notes de Certeau, "by *poaching* in countless ways on the property of others."[64] With each additional "product"—difference, politics, or power, for example—the original act of labor is reappropriated and grows increasingly alienated. Following the "social life of things," as Arjun Appadurai neatly put it, unravels the trajectories of Indigenous women's work that produced not only commodities, but also imperial meanings and collective identities.[65]

For example, Indigenous women's labor helped transform hops from plant on the vine to internationally circulating commodity. As commodity, hops were destined for brewers around the world. At the point of consumption, whether in the United States, Britain, or Canada, drinking beer, particularly in pubs, had long been a reference point for class, gender, and racial identities. Various configurations were contradictory and changed over time. As historians have shown, male drinking was a "potent badge of masculine identity" at the same time as it destabilized the masculinity of men who imbibed to an extent that undermined their ability to fulfill the breadwinner role. As working-class women in the early twentieth century increasingly claimed public spaces for themselves, they used the grammar of male drinking as they began to frequent beer parlors, reconstituting those spaces in the process. Women in the temperance movement deployed drinking as a foil for enacting identity in a different fashion. In each instance, however, the supposed maleness of public beer consumption remained an important point of reference.[66] Hops themselves had a more specific meaning within the imperial context. As historians of

British brewing note, "wherever British settlers colonised land, in the East and West Indies, in America, in Ireland and eventually in Australasia, a demand for the native drink of their home-land was established."[67] British brewers thus wanted a beer that would not spoil on long journeys to tropical colonies. The creation of India pale ale, a brew in which a high hop and alcohol content act as preservatives, met this need and enabled English sailors and colonists the world over to sip a piece of home.[68] As they imbibed this safe alternative to local water supplies, they affirmed their Englishness, their loyalty to Empire, and their "clubbability." When natives drank beer, they staked a claim to respect, civilization, and the privileges embodied by English masculinity. Still other narratives surrounded moments when beer was served across the divides of race and class: by servant to master, by Englishman to native chief, by native man to English official. Regardless, drinking beer in the English colonies was a performance of English identity.[69] Consumption of hoppy beer was a small, seemingly innocuous activity, but the accumulation of such activities constituted the practice of everyday life. Indigenous women's fieldwork thus contributed to the production of disperse and disparate identities. Traces of their labor were extended across North America, Britain, and the globe, where they became productive of colonial identities.

Whereas hops as product circulated within masculine spaces of public alcohol consumption, the curios produced by migrant women acquired meaning within the feminized spaces of domestic life. Because hops were a raw ingredient in a complex brew, Indigenous women's labor was invisible to those who consumed the final product. The opposite was true, however, with products of the tourist trade: It was the visibility of Indian women's work that gave the objects value and, in turn, enabled the work they did in the world. Women were the main consumers of the tourist economy's wares, including curios, photographs, cabinet cards, postcards, and stereographs. As commodities, these objects carried a host of meanings as they circulated within and helped produce discourses of domesticity, taste, and distinction. Simultaneously, they produced discourses of colonialism. As with hop pickers, craft workers labored on as the products of their work moved through space and time.

Collecting was a respectable pastime for white, middle-class, Victorian women, and the collection of Indian curios was particularly popular in the late nineteenth century. As one promotional brochure from 1906 succinctly put it: "No home is complete now-a-days without a neat and artistically arranged Indian basket corner."[70] Curiosities, bric-a-brac, and knickknacks from subject peoples were more than simple markers of white, middle-class domesticity; they were constitutive elements of it. The gendering of this domestic sphere as female dated to the so-called separate spheres ideology of the early nineteenth century, which located its notion of "true" womanhood within the private space of the home. Bourgeois respectability and true womanhood were mutually constituted through domesticity.[71] But, as numerous historians have demonstrated, the boundaries of the supposedly separate spheres were notoriously unstable. The "cult of true womanhood" privileged women's moral authority, and although rhetorically confined to the private sphere, in practice, it observed no such bounds. Middle-class women transformed normative ideals about true womanhood and separate spheres by using them to enter public arenas. Such actualizations of middle-class womanhood were simultaneously constituted through class and race. As Christine Stansell has shown, when bourgeois life flourished, "it was the ladies who expanded on its possibilities and the working women who bore the brunt of its oppressions."[72] This was doubly so. Needleworkers, domestic servants, and Indigenous craft workers—frequently racialized, as Irish biddy or squaw drudge, for example—all labored to enable the "physical basis of gentility."[73] Moreover, the public arenas that middle-class women entered were often the private homes of these working women.[74]

The hop field tourist economy put the domestic spaces of migrant workers on display. Viewing and assessing migrant Indian women's labor and lives became one of the pleasurable acts of public consumption through which women constituted themselves as modern. When women purchased items from Indian vendors, they expanded the public spaces of women's consumption from department stores to street corners and field sides.[75] Figure 12.2, taken outside a Seattle department store, captures the vibrant and dynamic public culture of female consumers. The tourist experience and its souvenirs were testimonials to the increasing visibility and respectability afforded to certain forms of certain women's mobility. In juxtaposition to the perceived itinerancy of migrant Indian workers, tourist travel was a marker of taste and privilege.

The freedom, adventure, and mobility of tourism could be celebrated and enshrined back home in the respectable woman's parlor. In Europe and North America, collecting has a long history as part of what James Clifford glosses as "the deployment of a possessive self."[76] In late-nineteenth-century America specifically, home decoration was one of the many mundane domestic practices through which women articulated their identities and by which others judged them.[77] Photos, postcards, and stereographs graphically illustrated the ground that women covered in their travels. Exotic curios displayed the worldly sophistication, civilizational privilege, and good taste of those who owned and arranged them. Indian labor—live in the fields or by proxy in the home—was constitutive of bourgeois identities.[78] Collecting Indian objects could put women in the company of anthropologists, elevating them from the oft-derided status as shoppers.[79] As with imported household goods, Indian curios could also fit within cosmopolitan constructions of self and nation.[80] Or, when cast as the products of "native-born, true Americans," Indian baskets could become reference points within an alternate and more parochial articulation of national style and nationhood.[81] Regardless, the products of Indian women's labor were terrain for other women's self-expression.

This terrain was accessible to women with a wide range of economic means. The tourist economy attendant to the hop harvest was part of the broader postbellum expansion of tourism in the United States that made travel accessible beyond the upper echelons of the very rich.

Figure 12.2. Vendor selling handmade items on Seattle street corner. Purchasing Indigenous artifacts was part of the public culture of non-Indigenous women's consumption. Image 83.10.7.929, Museum of History and Industry, Seattle.

Although the wealthy still rode out to the hop fields in private carriages, for example, less affluent sightseers partook in the spectacle by riding the inexpensive interurban electric cars that connected the city with the rural hinterland.[82] Souvenirs such as baskets, postcards, and photographs were similarly available at a wide range of prices and qualities. Whether they were subject to race, class, and/or gender subordinations in other contexts, the owners of such objects could find common affiliation, through consumption, with a dominant nation.[83]

With the help of Kodak cameras, female tourists not only consumed souvenirs, they produced them. Kodak marketed its product to the increasing numbers of women travelers through its spokesperson, "the Kodak girl," who urged women to "take a Kodak with you" or to "Kodak, as you go."[84] The "Kodak girl" was emblematic of the "New Woman," independent and on the move.[85] That so many female "Kodak fiends," as they were called, shot photographs of Indians was no accident. In so doing, they literally framed their own privileged status in relation to the women on display. In opposition to the squaw drudge who was forced to labor, women behind the camera were united as consumers of leisure; ethnic and class differences among Kodak girls were momentarily excluded from the shot. Indian women's work could reflect and enable the self-actualizations of bourgeois women and women with bourgeois ambitions alike.[86]

Female consumers in the hop-picking tourist economy incorporated Indian women and their commodities into broader patterns of mobility and consumption—a mutual dialectics of moving out and drawing in—through which they fashioned themselves. Using the idiom of taste, they articulated communities of consumers that were as likely to cross as to constitute class, race, and gender divisions. As scholars have shown, such communities could mobilize along conservative or progressive lines.[87] Regardless of whether social distinctions were shored up or papered over, it was Indian women's labor—as materialized in the tourist economy and in souvenirs—that did the work.

Consuming Women

Contemporary viewers ascribed meaning to the consumption patterns of non-Indigenous women; they did the same for the consumption habits of Indigenous women. As Leah Dilworth has noted for the American Southwest, tourists enjoyed the freedom to fashion any number of roles for themselves, whereas Indians were "always caught in the trap of visibility."[88] The rationale that transformed Indigenous laborers into spectacles recognized no distinction between public and private acts or space. It swept the personal consumer choices of Indigenous women into the whirlwind of colonial spectacle. Although female tourists' consumption consecrated bourgeois womanhood, Indigenous women's personal habits were judged in journalistic and tourist accounts to be sorely lacking. Viewers read Indian women's consumer choices as markers of immutable difference. Indigenous women were depicted as so different as to be barely women at all.

Homeward-bound hop pickers purchased a vast array of items, including ploughs, sewing machines, stoves, and furniture. But no category of goods earned as much attention in newspapers and magazines as female fashion. Accounts stressed the impulsiveness of Indigenous consumers, clearly portraying Indian women as lacking in self-control: "On their return from the hop fields . . . money is plenty with them, and they do not scruple to spend it for anything which may attract their attention in the store windows."[89] Indigenous women were said to be easy prey for "unscrupulous" salesmen who attracted their eye and their money by displaying "left-over hats trimmed gaudily with left-over ribbons" in shop windows.[90] In such accounts, ribbons in particular were positioned as sirens for migrant women. The supposedly irresistible draw of such a frivolous, almost childish, product told readers that these women were slaves to their passions. Reportedly there was little check on these whims because contemporary portrayals held that Indigenous women controlled their own earnings.[91] This may or may not have been so in any given situation, and there is no evidence that Indigenous women squandered their hard-earned money. Regardless, the assumption facilitated a contrast with accounts of white families' shopping habits, which portrayed white women consulting and deferring to their husband's judgment.[92]

Not only were the goods that migrant women purchased frivolous, they were, according to accounts, invariably "colorful." Writers thus implicitly reminded readers of the racialized identity of these consumers. The *Seattle Mail and Herald* was typical in its claim that the "Siwash has many weaknesses. The one particular and noticeable among the females is the love of bright ribbons. The old women go barefoot, but the younger generation wear shoes—but they must be yellow shoes. Ordinary black shoes are not bright enough for a Siwash."[93] Some writers singled out the red tones of the Indian fashion palette. A journalist for *Harper's Weekly* fashioned a literary parallel between the hop season's "ruddy-faced invaders" and the "gaudy bits of raiments on the old, flaming red blankets on the young maids, and strange misfits on the children."[94] Self-styled amateur ethnographer J. A. Costello claimed that "on her [labelle klootchman] is lavished all the fashion and vermillion of the sweet society of the natives."[95]

A writer for the California-based magazine the *Overland Monthly* inscribed race and erased womanhood in a slightly different manner when she likened Indigenous women to trees in the forest that changed colors with the seasons:

> A one-color toilet never satisfied the taste of the dusky daughter of the forest. A blue skirt, green waist, brightly striped shawl, and a red handkerchief on the head comprise a stylish outfit for winter. Summer may see a pink or blue print, scant of measure both as to length and width, a hat trimmed expressly to suit Siwash taste, and ribbons of contrasting colors about the neck, waist, and wiry hair.[96]

She thus excluded Indian women from membership in a number of communities at once. Whatever their pretensions to womanhood, their garish taste excluded them from the bourgeois community of female consumers. Their conspicuously "wiry hair" shut them out of any community with whiteness or Anglo-Saxon privilege. And their kinship with nature even questioned their membership in the human community.[97] These exclusions were not so much linear as overlapping. The dehumanizing naturalization of Indians was also about class and race, for example. Other working-class and nonwhite groups also had a long history of being seen as close to nature. Bourgeois women, typically were seen as more natural than their bourgeois male counterparts, but their refined taste distinguished them from these "colorful" shoppers.

These naturalized representations of Indian consumers circled easily back upon other racialized stereotypes. One local historian, for example, reflected on the postharvest shopping habits of an Indigenous family in order to resurrect the time-worn image of the squaw drudge in need of salvation from her state of uncivilized oppression.

> It is a sight worth pausing to contemplate on the streets of Tacoma or Seattle to watch the Indian with his family—squaw, papoose, and minor bare-footed responsibilities—as they plod the streets "doing their trading" on their return from the hop-picking. The buck loads the squaw with their purchases until she resembles an overweighted express wagon rather than a female. She is simply extinguished with his selections, while he in all the dignity of forest manhood leads the little procession gallantly carrying a blanket if there is no place left to hang it in the submissive concentration of ugliness who plods patiently in his rear.[98]

In service of the squaw-drudge image, this writer made the uncommon rhetorical move of turning Indian men into the shoppers.

Contemporary accounts spent considerably less time scrutinizing Indigenous men's identities as consumers than they did women's. Indigenous men did not entirely escape ridicule for how they dressed, but the tone was decidedly different. As one account held, although "the tawny brave . . . himself is no more discriminating in his taste than his half-civilized sister . . . in the nature of men's clothing, he cannot help looking better dressed than she."[99] Even as this writer directed a forgiving condescension toward Indigenous men, he captured the misogyny that characterized descriptions of women's consumption.

These representations cruelly mocked Indigenous women for being, in the eyes of settlers, poor mimics of white, middle-class womanhood. They constituted a form of discursive violence, and enduring their blows was the price Indigenous women paid for accessing the lucrative tourist dollars.[100] There is much here that we might recognize as the colonial ambivalence discussed at length by Homi Bhabha. Viewers derided Indigenous women for being "almost the same but not quite."[101] Viewers invariably treated the Indigenous women as mimics of whiteness, despite the fact that there is nothing inherently "white" about ribbons or hats of any sort. Viewers also treated these women as mimics of womanhood. They were not quite white, nor were they quite women. Accounts often omitted the term *woman* altogether, falling back instead on the Chinook jargon term *klootchman* or the more wide-spread epithet *squaw*. Writers characterized Indian women as "stolid," "stoic," "sluggish," and nearly inanimate "ornaments," barely capable of displaying human emotion or attending to the "papoose" in the crooks of their arms.[102] In denying the existence of these women's emotional lives, accounts situated them in opposition to the emotionality of so-called real women, like those who tastefully consumed the products that they produced. Moreover, by transforming Indigenous domestic practices (including shopping) into public spectacles, viewers denied Indigenous women the privilege of another key marker of respectable womanhood: the right to inhabit a private sphere. Unlike white women's identities, which were produced and performed through the consumption of "Indian" objects, Indigenous womanhood was itself consumed by cross-racial consumption. This simultaneous production and consumption of differentiated womanhood worked in the service of inscribing racial hierarchy.[103]

This discourse of ridicule situated Indigenous women who wore "white" clothes as racial and gender cross-dressers. In terms of both race and gender, colonial viewers believed Indigenous women were attempting to be something they were not. When performed intentionally, cross-dressing can provide access to empowerment and social approval, but even then does not guarantee it.[104] In this case, cross-dressing was not a defiant assertion of agency, ambivalence, or resistance. Instead, it was a label projected onto Indigenous women by those who denied the possibility that Indigenous women could shop and dress *without* reference to colonial taste and desire. This implied assignation of cross-dresser limited Indigenous women's actions to the narrow frame of mimicry. It relegated Indigenous women to the realm of reaction and denied them the possibility of action. If Victorian dress signified modern whiteness, then Indian women who adopted it were, by definition, mimics. But this reading only works if we accept that Indians were, again by definition, traditional and not modern. In fact, Indigenous women migrants lived lives that gave the lie to colonial binaries every day. They integrated traditional prerogatives and priorities into their hop field migrations; they participated simultaneously in the potlatch economy, the curio business, and the global market.[105] They did so not out of strategic defiance of colonial categories, but, more straightforwardly, because their lived experience defied those categories.

Producing Colonialism

The social life of things is political, Appadurai insists.[106] For the products of hop pickers' labor, this was true on at least two levels. For one, they were articulated to and through the personal politics of privilege, identity, and self-differentiation discussed previously. At the same time, they were constitutive of a broader politics of colonial hegemony. The inordinate amount of attention paid to Indigenous hop pickers and curio producers was part of a much broader nineteenth-century culture of spectacle that privileged "seeing as believing." The advent of mass tourism, the popularity of world's fairs and expositions, and the growth of department stores offered spectators cum consumers the privileged opportunity to participate in racialized discourses of modernity and progress.[107] This culture of spectacle acquired particular meaning within the context of nascent capitalist development and Indigenous dispossession occurring throughout western Washington. When trained on Indigenous women—whether as producers or consumers—this invasive ethnographic view reproduced boundaries between colonizer and colonized, legitimized colonial structures of authority, and attracted economic investment. Questions of propriety were intimately linked to questions of property.[108]

The racist and misogynistic accounts of Indian women—the squaw drudge, the undiscerning consumer, the emotionless mother—constituted colonial evaluations of Indigenous domesticity. Narratives of domesticity were crucial signifiers throughout much of the colonial world, and so too around Puget Sound.[109] Long conceptualized in opposition to the notion of the public or political, the domestic, as Amy Kaplan importantly notes, is also a category that must be examined in relation to the foreign. "Manifest Domesticity" and Manifest Destiny were contemporaneous phenomena, and both were implicated in the racialized processes of national expansion and demarcation of the foreign.[110] As U.S. national borders encircled them, American Indians had been made foreigners in their own homelands. Federal law had ascribed to Indian tribes the ambiguous status of "domestic dependent nations."[111] The so-called "Northern Indians" from British Columbia who migrated to the Washington hop fields were doubly foreign.[112] It was, after all, partly the foreignness of their producers that transformed handmade Indian objects into collectibles. Diverted into women's homes, tastefully displayed traces of foreign savagery functioned within what Appadurai calls an "aesthetics of decontextualization."[113] There, they helped establish the home as a civilized refuge at the same time as they spoke to the domestication of their makers. Curios were miniaturized markers of the shift in American consciousness that increasingly saw Indians as pacified rather than threatening.[114] As one advocate of "Indian basketry in house decoration" noted, "it is no fad that makes us seek to know something of the art-life and expression of the people whom we are thrusting to the wall after dispossessing them of the home of their forefathers." Indians were the "native-born, true Americans," but they were not the Americans of the future.[115] The displacement of the objects thus mirrored the displacement of their producers. At the same time, curio displays also aestheticized the domination that underwrote colonialism. As romanticized products of handwork, seen in juxtaposition to the products of industrialism, they facilitated an image of benign or even beneficent imperialism.[116] Domesticity's economy of taste effectively enlisted female consumers and tourists into the work of empire.[117] As Kaplan provocatively puts it, "domesticity makes manifest the destiny of the Anglo-Saxon race, while Manifest Destiny becomes in turn a condition for Anglo-Saxon domesticity."[118] The example of Indian women's craft work in the tourist market is a powerful illustration of Appadurai's point that "diversions" of things, such as baskets, for example, are always morally ambiguous and sometimes morally shocking.[119] The suspect in this case, however, is not any individual consumer. Manifest domesticity was not, as Kaplan rightly argues, a question of individual morality.[120] Nor, I would add, was it particularly a matter of individual intention. Instead, it had much more to do with the centripetal, transformative power of colonialism to incorporate the chaos of everyday practices and marshal the social life of things into doing its work.

Like curios, domestic scenes of migrant hop pickers functioned as part of broader colonial narratives about race, labor, and capital. An article from the *Seattle Mail and Herald* is exemplary. It presented migrant Indian workers as an obvious tourist attraction: "What phases of local color are to be found on Seattle's water front! The return of the Siwashes from the hop fields furnishes a pathetic as well as picturesque etching of life." Any group of Indians might have presented a colorful sight, but significantly, and, as in many other accounts, these Indians were hop pickers. The draw for tourists, settlers, and investors was thus one and the same. The article went on to wax in familiar fashion on the "colorful" character of the workers' domestic scene: "All ages and conditions of the tribes are in evidence, from the dusky baby to the wrinkled old dame who had imbibed too freely of 'fire water,' and who jabbered in Siwash dialect to the crone beside her. . . . Men women and children were huddled in groups of wild confusion of color and attitude."[121] Crucially, and not unlike the world's fairs to which such scenes bore uncanny resemblance, this was a spectacle with a pedagogical point. This self-styled social commentator insinuated that these women and their families could never measure up to bourgeois standards of respectability and civilization. The "wild confusion" of this domestic scene may have been picturesque, but it was not what middle-class viewers recognized as a proper family home. Transformed into a public display, viewers found this domestic scene rife with what Anne McClintock calls the "iconography of domestic degeneracy."[122] What looked picturesque from afar turned ugly as the distance between viewer and viewed lessened:

> It was a gay, pretty picture until one drew near, then the dirty unsanitary condition of these human beings and their surroundings grew revolting. Many of the younger members of these tribes have been partially educated, and their attire modernized—yet the question comes: "What has higher education accomplished for these children of the wild, and were they not better as a class in primitive days?"[123]

Those cast as actors in this scene lived their domestic lives outside the proper bounds of home and thus were cast as homeless. Their private possessions on public view manifested their dispossession. Such accounts positioned Indigenous people as eternally distant from modernity and underscored their inevitable difference as "colorful Indians." As the viewer drew physically closer, the cultural and racial distance increased.

Emphasis on clear boundaries is particularly important when difference cannot be reliably discerned. Elsewhere, representations of domestic inferiority functioned to mark the Irish and other subordinate groups whose difference was hard to spot with the casual eye as "white negroes."[124] A similar process was under way here too. The high numbers of white men who married and had children with Indigenous women in the Northwest meant that, although settlers felt sure that Indians were not white, they could not be sure that they would know one when they saw one.[125]

The significant role played by Indigenous workers in the settler economy further threatened to undermine easy distinctions between Indian and white workers. If Indigenous people labored just like white settlers, wherein lay the justification for denying them equal rights? The rhetoric of difference inscribed in accounts of "colorful" human spectacle preempted such questions by denying that Indigenous migrants were workers at all and insisting that they were, above all, "Indians." Mirroring the specialization of Indigenous field labor, this rhetoric defined a highly specialized and segmented role for Indigenous people in modern capitalist society. They could engage modern capitalism, but they could not be *of* modern capitalism.

McClintock's notion of "white negroes" is doubly useful in this context, because the specter of slavery lurked in the background of more than one account of labor on the western frontier. J. A. Costello, for example, linked an almost excruciatingly picturesque description of Indian hop pickers to a revealing nostalgia for the antebellum South. He began by describing the harvest scene: the "hop field is redolent of perfume and melody. The fields are alive with pickers; the air is joyous with sound. There is a richness and coloring in the surrounding which form a perpetual delight. There is a novelty to the beholder and a rurality of scene so peculiar, that makes one feel as if they were in some enchanted country." As he continued, he starkly revealed the interpenetrations of leisure-time viewing, racial domination, and labor market concerns: "If you have never witnessed a season of hop picking you have missed a rare old time-treat which has its equal only in the maple woods of the East during sugar making time, or in the co'n shuckin' days of old Kentuck, 'when the mast am fallin' and the darkies am a singin' and racoon and possum am simmerin' in the pot.' "[126] Hop pickers were not slaves, and most tourists probably did not make a conscious comparison to the plantation South. But nostalgia for simpler, easier times was in the air in the final quarter of the nineteenth century. And visitors inhaled a healthy lungful of that nostalgia when they breathed the country air of the hop fields. There, amid the towering vines, they could imagine that they saw a laboring population grateful for the work that they had, one that would neither rise up in civil war nor join in the labor revolts of the 1890s.[127]

In a different context, the sight of hundreds or thousands of amassed Indians or workers, let alone both, could easily strike fear into potential settlers and investors. But here, domestic scenes of happy families reassuringly blended the safety of home into the potential hotbed of the racialized workplace. When the *Washington Standard* depicted a familial scene of pickers, the absence of a young and vital male figure—father, brother, uncle, or son—was noticeable:

> There was noticed in many instances an entire Indian family gathered around a box hard at it [picking hops]. There would be the old bent and aged patriarch who had seen the snows of many winters and along side of him the child, and variously disposed, children of larger growth, all picking hops. Some squaws worked with their papooses strapped to their backs, while others let the little urchins play around them.[128]

The implications of domestication in this scene are unmistakable. Many photographers framed their work in similar terms.[129] The prominence of children and women (see Figure 12.1) suggested a docile and compliant workforce. Women workers posed without the company of young men evoked the squaw drudge; children hard at work indicated that they had inherited their mothers' work ethic and would enable a stable labor supply of labor into the future. Images of aged workers (such as the postcard in Figure 12.3) were likewise suggestive of weak and pliant natures. Too old and frail to put the land to what settlers recognized as "proper," "civilized" use themselves, they could nonetheless labor and thus consolidate primitive accumulation. These accounts and images took the labor of hop pickers and turned it toward the work of colonialism. Needless to say, such domesticated representations had little if anything to do with Indigenous realities. One example, perhaps, will suffice. The man on the right in Figure 12.3 is Pliday or "Friday" Consauk from the Upper Skagit. Pliday is remembered in the oral history for his legendary ability to haul enormously heavy loads—not of hops, but of fish. More than a simple sign of physical strength, this was a signifier of power in a much broader sense. It evidenced his masculinity, his care for his family, and his ability to provide. His willingness to establish relationships with settlers was no marker of subjection or submission.[130] Yet domesticated representations of Indigenous hop pickers suggested that, rather than active (and potentially trouble-making) subjects, these workers were passive (and spectacular) objects. Too young, old, frail, or maternal to resist the sweep of capitalist development, they were, remarkably, strong enough to work long days. They were the ideal labor force.

An important trait of this "domesticated" Indian labor force was its willingness to move on after the harvest.[131] Settlers and investors wanted a flexible labor force that was there when they needed it, and one that made no demands on the employer once the work was done. Costello offered his reassurance on this matter in verse: "There's dusky maids / In pinks and plaids," he began, before continuing with predictably derogatory descriptions of Indigenous

Figure 12.3. Postcard of hop pickers, 1906. Such images suggested that the Indigenous workforce was compliant and docile. Negative NA4093, Special Collections, University of Washington Libraries, Seattle.

domesticity, and then, referring to Ballast Island, where many Indigenous migrant workers camped, he concluded in the following way:

> When picking's o'er
> We'll have no more
> The smell that comes from Ballast Isle;
>   Glad then my eyes
>   My spirits rise,
> For they've gone back to their paradise.[132]

Other writers used less poetic forms to express similar messages about the flexible nature of the Indigenous labor force. When *Harper's Weekly* ran a piece that attempted to lure hop farmers to the Puyallup valley, it did so with promises of great wealth, picturesque scenery, and a ready supply of Indian labor that "melted away" at season's end, not unlike the snow on the Northwest's famous mountains. The illustration that accompanied the article superimposed a domestic scene of the hop pickers' camp—filled with women and children—on top of an image of workers picking in the fields. In the upper-right-hand corner of the image, canoes paddled off peacefully into the distance, just as the article promised.[133] Boosters for the Seattle, Lake Shore, and Eastern Railway sent a similar message when they chose a drawing of children picking hops as an illustration for the prospectus they published to attract financial backing (Figure 12.4). The image, simply captioned "Indians gathering hops, Washington Territory, On line of Seattle, Lake Shore and Eastern Railway," assured potential investors that the line would be well positioned to make money on a number of levels at once. Farmers would use the line to get their crop to market. Tourists would travel the line to watch the pickers. Pickers themselves would move on when the harvest was done.[134] A healthy return on investment seemed overdetermined.

A dizzying array of "errant trajectories" spun out from the original production of hops and tourist goods. These products carried the labor of Indigenous women with them as they went on to produce and transform meaning. Non-Indigenous people reaped a multiple yield from Indigenous workers: directly from those who sold their labor and indirectly from the images of

INDIANS GATHERING HOPS, WASHINGTON TERRITORY,
ON LINE OF SEATTLE, LAKE SHORE AND EASTERN RAILWAY.

Figure 12.4. Illustration of hop pickers from promotional material for the Seattle, Lake Shore and Eastern Railway. Such images helped in the industrial development of western Washington state. From R.H. Ruffner, *A Report on Washington Territory* (New York: Seattle, Lake Short and Eastern Railway, 1889), plate facing p. 74.

those same workers. Indigenous women's labor was multiply appropriated. There is no doubt that many Indigenous women sustained themselves and their families with the resulting income, income that was much needed at a time when their lands, resources, and cultures were under threat. In exchange for the opportunity to work in the industrial and craft economies, colonial society extracted a high price from Indigenous women. Hops and tourist goods, in turn, became raw materials for the production of numerous manifestations of bourgeois identity. Such processes of identity formation were political as well as personal. Settlers, tourists, photographers, boosters, investors, and farmers alike circulated images of domesticated Indigenous workers, many of them women, most of them feminized. They enlisted these images to advertise the availability of cheap capital and docile labor, to undermine Indigenous people's hold on land and resources, and to promote the industrial capitalist development of Puget Sound. Consumers of Indian images cast the Indian hop picker as the poster child for the industrial development of the region. And for her work in this role she certainly never was paid.

Notes

An earlier version of this essay was presented at "Labouring Feminism and Feminist Working-Class History in North America and Beyond: An International Conference at the University of Toronto" on September 29, 2005. Thanks to Franca Iacovetta, who extended the invitation to participate, and to conference delegates who offered their commentaries. In addition, I extend my appreciation for the valuable support, assistance, and suggestions of Courtney Booker, Alejandra Bronfman, Hart Caplan, Leon Fink, Joan Sangster, Dick Unger, and Dan Levinson Wilk. Research for this project was conducted with a grant from the Social Sciences and Humanities Research Council of Canada.

1. Colleen O'Neill, "Rethinking Modernity and the Discourse of Development in American Indian History: An Introduction," in *Native Pathways: American Indian Culture and Economic Development in the Twentieth Century*, ed. Brian Hosmer and Colleen O'Neill (Boulder: University Press of Colorado, 2004), 2–24.
2. Rolf Knight, *Indians at Work: An Informal History of Native Labour in British Columbia*, 2nd rev. ed. (Vancouver: New Star Books, 1996), 20.
3. Stephen High, "Native Wage Labour and Independent Production during the 'Era of Irrelevance,' " *Labour/Le Travail* 37 (1996): 247; Hosmer and O'Neill, eds., *Native Pathways*, 16–17.
4. John Lutz, "After the Fur Trade: The Aboriginal Labouring Classes of British Columbia, 1849–1890," *Journal of the Canadian Historical Association*, n.s., 3 (1992): 69–93; High, "Native Wage Labour," 243–64; Alice Littlefield and Martha C. Knack, eds., *Native Americans and Wage Labor: Ethno-historical Perspectives* (Norman: University of Oklahoma Press, 1996); Brian C. Hosmer, *American Indians in the Marketplace: Persistence and Innovation among the Menominees and Metlakatlans, 1870–1920* (Lawrence: University of Kansas Press, 1999); John Lutz, "Work, Sex, and Death on the Great Thoroughfare: Annual Migrations of 'Canadian Indians,' " in *Parallel Destinies: Canadian-American Relations West of the Rockies*, ed. John M. Findlay and Ken S. Coates (Seattle: University of Washington Press, 2002), 80–103; Hosmer and O'Neill, eds., *Native Pathways*; Colleen O'Neill, *Working the Navajo Way: Labor and Culture in the Twentieth Century* (Lawrence: University Press of Kansas, 2005); Paige Raibmon, *Authentic Indians: Episodes of Encounter from the Late-Nineteenth-Century Northwest Coast* (Durham, NC: Duke University Press, 2005); Carol Williams, "Between Doorstep Barter Economy and Industrial Wages: Mobility and Adaptability of Coast Salish Female Laborers in Coastal British Columbia, 1858–1890," in *Native Being, Being Native. Identity and Difference; Proceedings of the Fifth Native American Symposium*, ed. Mark B. Spencer and Lucretia Scoufos (Durant: Southeastern Oklahoma State University, 2005).
5. Amy Kaplan and Donald Pease, eds., *Cultures of United States Imperialism* (Durham, NC: Duke University Press, 1993); Antoinette Burton, ed., *Gender, Sexuality, and Colonial Modernities* (New York: Routledge, 1999), 3 and chap. 1.
6. Karl Marx, *Capital: A Critique of Political Economy*, vol. 1 (New York: Vintage Books, 1977), pt. 8.
7. Adele Perry uses the extraction of labor and the appropriation of land to differentiate between different kinds of colonial enterprises. Adele Perry, "Reproducing Colonialism in British Columbia, 1849–1871," in *Bodies in Contact: Rethinking Colonial Encounters in World History*, ed. Tony Ballantyne and Antoinette Burton (Durham, NC: Duke University Press, 2005), 144.
8. Littlefield and Knack, eds., *Native Americans and Wage Labor*; O'Neill, *Working the Navajo Way*; Knight, *Indians at Work*.
9. Dianne Newell, review of "Aboriginal Workers," *BC Studies*, no. 117 (1998): 78. Some scholars go so far as to claim that "wage employment is a historical measure of the degree of resource loss and dependency." Martha C. Knack and Alice Littlefield, "Native American Labor: Retrieving History, Rethinking Theory," in Littlefield and Knack, *Native Americans and Wage Labor*, 42. See also Cole Harris, *Making Native Space: Colonialism, Resistance, and Reserves in British Columbia* (Vancouver: University of British Columbia Press, 2002).
10. Michel de Certeau, *The Practice of Everyday Life*, trans. Steven Rendall (Berkeley: University of California Press, 1984), xiii, xviii.
11. de Certeau, *The Practice of Everyday Life*, xi.
12. See also Jean Barman, "Aboriginal Women on the Streets of Victoria: Rethinking Transgressive Sexuality during the Colonial Encounter," in *Contact Zones: Aboriginal and Settler Women in Canada's Colonial Past*, ed. Katie Pickles and Myra Rutherdale (Vancouver: UBC Press, 2005), 205–27.
13. Ezra Meeker, *Seventy Years of Progress in Washington* (Tacoma, WA: Allstrum, 1921), 183.
14. "A Puyallup Hop Farm," *Daily Pacific Tribune*, August 30, 1877.
15. Julian Hawthorne, *History of Washington: The Evergreen State, from Early Dawn to Daylight; With Portraits and Biographies*, vol. 2 (n.p.: American Historical Publishing, 1893). 470; Clinton A. Snowden,

History of Washington: The Rise and Progress of an American State, vol. 4 (n.p.: Century History Co., 1909), 304.

16. This occurred, for example, in 1885. *Washington Standard*, August 7, 1885; Charles Moser, *Reminiscences of the West Coast of Vancouver Island* (Victoria, BC: Acme, 1926), 143–45.

17. *Washington Standard*, September 9, 1877.

18. Clarence B. Bagley, *History of King County Washington*, vol. 1 (Chicago: S. J. Clarke, 1929), 408; Snowden, *History of Washington*, 4:203; Hawthorne, *History of Washington*, 2:469; *Washington Standard*, September 19, 1890.

19. Hawthorne, *History of Washington*, 2:470.

20. Ezra Meeker, *The Busy Life of Eighty-five Years of Ezra Meeker* (Seattle: Ezra Meeker, 1916), 227.

21. Meeker, *The Busy Life*, 226.

22. Greg Watson, curator, " 'The Hops Craze': Western Washington's First Big Business," 1996, exhibition labels, Snoqualmie Valley Historical Society, North Bend, Washington.

23. On treaties in western Washington, see Alexandra Harmon, *Indians in the Making: Ethnic Relations and Indian Identities around Puget Sound* (Berkeley: University of California Press, 1998), chaps. 3 and 8.

24. Meeker, *Seventy Years*, 183.

25. On fire ecology in the Pacific Northwest, see Robert Boyd, ed., *Indians, Fire, and the Land in the Pacific Northwest* (Corvallis: Oregon State University Press, 1999).

26. "Hops in Washington," *Pacific Rural Press*, January 3, 1891; Henry Emanuel Levy, "Reminiscences," 1843–1929, British Columbia Archives, Victoria, British Columbia; Ada S. Hill, *A History of the Snoqualmie Valley* (n.p., 1970), 59.

27. Coll-Peter Thrush, "The Lushootseed Peoples of Puget Sound County," American Indians of the Pacific Northwest Collection, University of Washington Digital Collections, content.lib.washington.edu/aipnw/thrush.html (accessed December 31, 2005).

28. Meeker, *Seventy Years*, 253.

29. Richard White, *Land Use, Environment, and Social Change: The Shaping of Island County* (Seattle: University of Washington Press, 1980), 56.

30. John Muir, *Steep Trails*, ed. William Frederic Badè (Boston: Houghton Mifflin, 1918), 183; White, *Land Use*, 37–38.

31. Lutz, "Work, Sex, and Death," 81, 84, 86–87.

32. "Annual report of W. H. Lomas to Superintendent General of Indian Affairs," August 7, 1885, vol. 1353, record group (hereinafter RG) 10, Department of Indian Affairs (hereinafter DIA), National Archives of Canada (hereinafter NAC), Ottawa; Jean Barman, *The West beyond the West: A History of British Columbia* (Toronto: University of Toronto Press, 1991), 363.

33. Harriet U. Fish, "Andy Wold's Tales of Early Issaquah," *Puget Soundings* (1983): 7, 11.

34. "Good for 'Lo,' " *Washington Standard*, September 11, 1875, 2; *Washington Standard*, September 9, 1877, 4; *Report of the Governor of Washington Territory, 1888* (Washington, DC: U.S. Government Printing Office, 1888), 48–53; *Seattle Mail and Herald*, September 21, 1901; Kenneth Tollefson, "The Snoqualmie Indians as Hop Pickers," *Columbia* 8 (1994–95): 39–44.

35. Hawthorne, *History of Washington*, 2:228.

36. Ezra Meeker quoted in Bagley, *History of King County Washington*, 135. For another example of settlers expecting childbirth to be easy for Indigenous women and for an example of women who traveled to the hop fields with their families but did not work in the fields while pregnant, see Williams, "Between Doorstep Barter Economy," 21, 25.

37. Susan Lord Currier, "Some Aspects of Washington Hop Fields," *Overland Monthly*, 2nd ser., 32 (1898), 543.

38. J. A. Costello, *The Siwash: Their Life, Legends, and Tales: Puget Sound and Pacific Northwest* (Seattle: The Calvert Co., 1895), 164.

39. "Siwashes Again Seek the Street," *Seattle Post-intelligencer*, May 31, 1904; Myron Eells, *Ten Years of Missionary Work among the Indians at Skokomish, Washington Territory, 1874–1884* (Boston: Congregational Sunday-School and Publishing Society, 1886), 53–54; Costello, *The Siwash*, 62.

40. Jennifer Morgan, " 'Some Could Suckle over Their Shoulder': Male Travelers, Female Bodies, and the Gendering of Racial Ideology, 1500–1700," *William and Mary Quarterly*, 3rd ser., 54, no. 1 (1997): 167–92. On other invocations of the squaw drudge stereotype, see David D. Smits, "The 'Squaw Drudge': A Prime Index of Savagism," *Ethnohistory* 29, no. 4 (1982): 281; Rayna Green, "The Pocahontas Perplex: The Image of Indian Women in American Culture," *Massachusetts Review* 16 (1975): 698–714; Patricia Grimshaw, "Maori Agriculturalists and Aboriginal Hunter-Gatherers: Women and Colonial Displacement in Nineteenth-Century Aotearoa/New Zealand and Southeastern Australia," in *Nation, Empire, Colony: Historicizing Gender and Rule*, ed. Ruth Roach Pierson and Nupur Chaudhuri

(Indianapolis: Indiana University Press, 1998), 32–38; Margaret D. Jacobs, *Engendered Encounters: Feminism and Pueblo Cultures, 1879–1934* (Lincoln: University of Nebraska Press, 1999), 34–35; Paige Raibmon, "Naturalizing Power: Land and Sexual Violence along William Byrd's Dividing Line," in *Seeing Nature through Gender*, ed. Virginia J. Scharff (Lawrence: University Press of Kansas, 2003), 20–39. The notion that white men needed to "save brown women from brown men" was a common colonial trope. Gayatri Spivak, "Can the Subaltern Speak?" in *Marxism and the Interpretation of Culture*, ed. Cary Nelson and Lawrence Grossberg (Urbana: University of Illinois, 1988), 297.

41. Canada, DIA, Annual Report (hereinafter AR) 1886, *Sessional Papers*, 1887, no. 6, 92; Edward Sapir and Morris Swadesh, *Nootka Texts: Tales and Ethnological Narratives* (Philadelphia: Linguistic Society of America, University of Pennsylvania, 1939; New York: AMS, 1978), 151.

42. Myron Eells, *Indians of Puget Sound: The Notebooks of Myron Eells*, ed. George Pierre Castile (Seattle: University of Washington Press, 1985), 270; Thomas Leadman, "Ledger," 1904, White River Valley Historical Society, Auburn, WA; Arthur Wellington Clah, "Journals," September 6,1899, reel A–1707, NAC; Canada, DIA, AR 1890, *Sessional Papers*, 1891, no. 18, 105; "Great Influx of Indians," *Seattle Post-Intelligencer*, September 10, 1899.

43. Canada, DIA, AR 1888, *Sessional Papers*, 1889, no. 16, 100; E. Meliss, "Siwash," *Overland Monthly*, 2nd ser., 20 (1892): 502; Bagley, *History of King County Washington*, 135; Jack R. Evans, *Little History of North Bend–Snoqualmie, Washington* (Seattle: SCW Publications, 1990), 2; [Charlie Meshel] to W. H. Lomas, October 31, 1889, vol. 1336, DIA, RG 10, NAC; Charlie Meshel to W. H. Lomas [ca. November 1889], vol. 1336, DIA, RG 10, NAC.

44. Father L. Eusfen to W. H. Lomas, November 6, 1884, vol. 1331, DIA, RG 10, NAC; W. H. Lomas to Father L. Eusfen, December 3, 1884, vol. 1353, DIA, RG 10, NAC.

45. "Hop Fields of the Puyallup and White River," *West Shore* 10, no. 11 (1884): 345.

46. C. O. Bean to W. H. Lomas, July 17, 1889, vol. 1336, DIA, RG 10, NAC; C. O. Bean to W. H. Lomas, August 17, 1889, vol. 1336, DIA, RG 10, NAC; W. Lane to W. H. Lomas, August 21, 1888, vol. 1335, DIA, RG 10, NAC; W. Lane to W. H. Lomas, July 26, 1891, vol. 1337, DIA, RG 10, NAC.

47. June Collins, "John Fornsby: The Personal Document of a Coast Salish Indian," in *Indians of the Urban Northwest*, ed. Marian W. Smith (New York: AMS, 1949), 330.

48. In later decades, some Makah women worked as labor contractors. Elizabeth Colson, *The Makah Indians: A Study of an Indian Tribe in Modern American Society* (Manchester: Manchester University Press, 1953), 165.

49. Levy, "Reminiscences," 13; Arthur Wellington Clah, "Journals," August 31, 1897, reel A–1713, N AC; Joyce Walton Shales, personal communication.

50. Collins, "John Fornsby," 330; Leadman, "Ledger."

51. Dianne Newell, *The Tangled Webs of History: Indians and the Law in Canada's Pacific Coast Fisheries* (Toronto: University of Toronto Press, 1997), 81.

52. *Washington Standard*, September 15, 1877; "Hops Steady and Firm," *Puyallup Valley Tribune*, September 26, 1903.

53. Dick Hebdige, "The Function of Subculture," in *The Cultural Studies Reader*, ed. Simon During (New York: Routledge, 1999), 441–50.

54. *Pacific Tribune*, September 18, 1874.

55. Muir, *Steep Trails*, 256; "Hop-Picking in Puyallup," *Harper's Weekly* 32 (1888), 795, 801; W. H. Bull, "Indian Hop Pickers on Puget Sound," *Harper's Weekly* 36 (1892), 545–46.

56. "A Western Hop Center," *West Shore* 16, no. 9 (1890): 137–38; "Hops in Washington," *Pacific Rural Press*, January 3, 1891; *Pacific Tribune*, September 18, 1874; "Hop Picking, "*Washington Standard*, September 24, 1886.

57. "Great Influx of Indians," 6; "Indians Returning from Hop Fields," 16; Bull, "Indian Hop Pickers," 546. On the persistence of Indian residents in Seattle, see Coll-Peter Thrush, "The Crossing-Over Place: Urban and Indian Histories in Seattle" (PhD diss., University of Washington, 2002).

58. Mamie Ray Upton, "Indian Hop-Pickers," *Overland Monthly*, 2nd ser., 17 (1891): 164; Hill, *A History of the Snoqualmie Valley*, 161; Williams, "Between Doorstep Barter Economy," offers further details about the broader entrepreneurial economy of Indigenous women.

59. *Told by the Pioneers: Reminiscences of Pioneer Life in Washington*, vol. 3 (Olympia: Washington Pioneer Project, 1937), 59; Costello, *The Siwash*, 165; "Indian Life on Seattle Streets," *Seattle Post Intelligencer*, December 10, 1905.

60. "Hurrah for Puyallup," flyer, 1901, negative 1903.1.60, Washington State Historical Society, Tacoma; "At the Indian Village," *Puyallup Valley Tribune*, September 19, 1903. For an etymological analysis of the term "curiosity" in the imperial context of the Pacific, see Nicholas Thomas, *Entangled Objects: Exchange, Material Culture, and Colonialism in the Pacific* (Cambridge, MA: Harvard University Press, 1991), 126–51.

61. This was likewise true elsewhere. See, for example, Williams, "Between Doorstep Barter Economy," 17; Patricia Jasen, *Wild Things: Nature, Culture, and Tourism in Ontario, 1790–1914* (Toronto: University of Toronto Press, 1995), 97; Livingston F. Jones, *A Study of the Thlingets of Alaska* (New York: Fleming H. Revell Co., 1914), 85.

62. Carolyn J. Marr, "Taken Pictures: On Interpreting Native American Photographs of the Southern Northwest Coast," *Pacific Northwest Quarterly* 80 (1989): 61; Margaret B. Blackman, " 'Copying People': Northwest Coast Native Response to Early Photography," *BC Studies*, no. 52 (Winter 1981–82): e 88, 107. See also Carolyn J. Marr, "Photographers and Their Subjects on the Southern Northwest Coast: Motivations and Responses," *Arctic Anthropology* 27, no. 2 (1990); Lindsay Batterman, "Kwelth-Elite, the Proud Slave," *Overland Monthly*, 2nd ser., 33, no. 198 (1899): 536.

63. Moser, *Reminiscences*, 143–45. On the importance to Aboriginal women of income from selling curios, see Williams, "Between Doorstep Barter Economy."

64. de Certeau, *The Practice of Everyday Life*, xii; emphasis in original.

65. Arjun Appadurai, "Introduction: Commodities and the Politics of Value," in *The Social Life of Things*, ed. Arjun Appadurai (New York: Cambridge University Press, 1986), 3–63. Fred R. Myers, "Introduction: The Empire of Things," in *The Empire of Things: Regimes of Value and Material Culture*, ed. Fred R. Myers (Santa Fe, NM: School of American Research Press, 2001), 3–64.

66. Catherine Gilbert Murdock, *Domesticating Drink; Women, Men, and Alcohol in America, 1870–1940* (Baltimore: Johns Hopkins University Press, 1998), 4; Elaine Frantz Parsons, *Manhood Lost: Fallen Drunkards and Redeeming Women in the Nineteenth Century* (Baltimore: Johns Hopkins University Press, 2003); Kathy Lee Peiss, *Cheap Amusements: Working Women and Leisure in Turn-of-the-Century New York* (Philadelphia: Temple University Press, 1986); Roy Rosenzweig, *Eight Hours for What We Will: Workers and Leisure in an Industrial City, 1870–1920* (New York: Cambridge University Press, 1983); Craig Heron, *Booze: A Distilled History* (Toronto: Between the Lines, 2003); Valerie Hey, *Patriarchy and Pub Culture* (London: Tavistock, 1986); Robert Campbell, *Sit Down and Drink Your Beer: Regulating Vancouver's Beer Parlours, 1925–1954* (Toronto: University of Toronto Press, 2001); Mark Edward Lender and James Kirby Martin. *Drinking in America: A History* (London: Macmillan, 1982); Perry R. Duis, *The Saloon: Public Drinking Culture in Chicago and Boston, 1880–1920* (Urbana: University of Illinois Press, 1983).

67. T. R. Gourvish and R. G. Wilson, *The British Brewing Industry, 1830–1980* (New York: Cambridge University Press, 1994), 169.

68. The East India Company began exporting heavily hopped India ale to the colonies in the 1780s. The brew became popular overseas and in Britain between 1840 and 1900, the "golden age of British beer drinking." R. G. Wilson, "The Changing Taste for Beer in Victorian Britain," in *Dynamics of the International Brewing Industry since 1800*, ed. R. G. Wilson and T. R. Gourvish (New York: Routledge, 1998), 97, 99. Late-nineteenth-century British brewers often used imported hops in making India pale ale, which required higher-quality hops than other, less heavily hopped beers. Thus, it is quite likely that hops from Washington made their way through Britain to the tropics. Margaret Lawrence, *The Encircling Hop: A History of Hops and Brewing* (Sittingbourne, Kent: SAWD, 1990), 21.

69. See, for example, George Orwell, *Burmese Days* (1934; repr., New York: Harcourt Brace, 1962); Mrinalini Sinha, "Britishness, Clubbability, and the Colonial Public Sphere," in Ballentyne and Burton, *Bodies in Contact*, 183–200.

70. Lloyd W. MacDowell, *Alaska Indian Basketry* (Seattle: Alaska Steamship Company, 1906). See also George Wharton James, "Indian Basketry in Home Decoration," *Chautauquan* (1901): 619–24. On tourist art, see Ruth B. Phillips, *Trading Identities: The Souvenir in Native North American Art from the Northeast, 1700–1900* (Montreal: McGill-Queen's University Press, 1998); Molly Lee, "Tourist and Taste Cultures: Collecting Native Art in Alaska at the Turn of the Twentieth Century," in *Unpacking Culture: Art and Commodity in Colonial and Postcolonial Worlds*, ed. Ruth B. Phillips and Christopher B. Steiner (Berkeley: University of California Press, 1999), 269–73; Jonathan Batkin, "Tourism Is Overrated: Pueblo Pottery and the Early Curio Trade, 1880–1910," in Phillips and Steiner, *Unpacking Culture*, 282–97; Molly H. Mullin, *Culture in the Marketplace: Gender, Art, and Value in the American Southwest* (Durham, NC: Duke University Press, 2001). Collecting could be identified as a male or a female activity. The professional or connoisseur collector was often assumed to be male. In contrast, women who collected were cast as hobbyists, amateurs, or tourists. Women's taste in such matters was characterized as less discerning than that of the male expert, whose guidance women required. Leah Dilworth, *Imagining Indians in the Southwest: Persistent Visions of a Primitive Past* (Washington, DC: Smithsonian Institution Press, 1996), chap. 3; Raibmon, *Authentic Indians*, 151.

71. Christine Stansell, *City of Women: Sex and Class in New York, 1789–1860* (New York: Knopf, 1986), xii.

72. Stansell, *City of Women*, xii.

73. Stansell, *City of Women*, xiii. On labor, women, race, and ethnicity, see also David M. Katzman, *Seven*

Days a Week: Women and Domestic Service in Industrializing America (New York: Oxford University Press, 1978); Alice Kessler-Harris, *Out to Work: A History of Wage-earning Women in the United States* (New York: Oxford University Press, 1982); Susan Anita Glenn, *Daughters of the Shtetl: Life and Labor in the Immigrant Generation* (Ithaca, NY: Cornell University Press, 1990); Nancy Green, *Ready-to-wear and Ready-to-work: A Century of Industry and Immigrants in Paris and New York* (Durham, NC: Duke University Press, 1997); Tera Hunter, *To "Joy My Freedom": Southern Black Women's Lives and Labors after the Civil War* (Cambridge, MA: Harvard University Press, 1997); A. K. Sandoval-Strausz and Daniel Levinson Wilk, "Princes and Maids of the City Hotel: The Cultural Politics of Commercial Hospitality in America," *Journal of Decorative and Propaganda Arts* 25 (2005): 160–85.

74. Stansell, *City of Women*; Peggy Pascoe, *Relations of Rescue: The Search for Female Moral Authority in the American West, 1874–1939* (New York: Oxford University Press, 1990); Sarah Deutsch, *No Separate Refuge: Culture, Class, and Gender on an Anglo-Hispanic Frontier in the American Southwest, 1880–1940* (New York: Oxford University Press, 1987); Jacobs, *Engendered Encounters*; Myra Rutherdale, *Women and the White Man's God: Gender and Race in the Canadian Mission Field* (Vancouver: University of British Columbia Press, 2002). On the public display of Indigenous home life see Paige Raibmon, "Living on Display: Colonial Visions of Aboriginal Domestic Spaces," *BC Studies*, no. 140 (2003–4): 69–89.

75. An impressive literature exists on women, gender, and the consumer economy. See, for example, Susan Porter Benson, *Counter Cultures: Saleswomen, Managers, and Customers in American Department Stores* (Urbana: University of Illinois Press, 1986); Rudi Laermans, "Learning to Consume: Early Department Stores and the Shaping of Modern Consumer Culture (1860–1914)," *Theory, Culture and Society* 10 (1993): 79–102; Elaine S. Abelson, *When Ladies Go A-Thieving: Middle-Class Shoplifters in the Victorian Department Store* (New York: Oxford University Press, 1989); Peiss. *Cheap Amusements*; Kathy Peiss, *Hope in a Jar: The Making of America's Beauty Culture* (New York: Metropolitan Books, 1998); Nan Enstad, *Ladies of Labor, Girls of Adventure: Working Women, Popular Culture, and Labor Politics at the Turn of the Twentieth Century* (New York: Columbia University Press, 1999); Catherine Cocks, *Doing the Town: The Rise of Urban Tourism in the United States* (Berkeley: University of California Press, 2001); Kristin Hoganson, "Cosmopolitan Domesticity: Importing the American Dream, 1865–1920,".*American Historical Review* 107 (February 2002): 55–83, www.historycooperative.org/journals/ahr/107.1/ah0102000055.html (accessed January 16, 2006); Nancy Martha West, *Kodak and the Lens of Nostalgia* (Charlottesville: University Press of Virginia, 2000), chap. 4. On women"s transformations of public space in another context, see Sarah Deutsch, *Women and the City: Gender, Space, and Power in Boston, 1870–1940* (New York: Oxford University Press, 2000).

76. James Clifford, "Objects and Selves—An Afterword," in *Objects and Others: Essays on Museums and Material Culture*, ed. George W. Stocking Jr. (Madison: University of Wisconsin Press, 1985), 238. See also Susan Stewart, *On Longing: Narratives of the Miniature, the Gigantic, the Souvenir, the Collection* (Baltimore: Johns Hopkins University Press, 1984).

77. Hoganson, "Cosmopolitan Domesticity," par. 5. See also Rutherdale, *Women and the White Man's God*, 88–96.

78. Dilworth, *Imagining Indians in the Southwest*, 126.

79. Mullin, *Culture in the Marketplace*, 30–31.

80. Hoganson, "Cosmopolitan Domesticity," pars. 36, 41–47.

81. James, "Indian Basketry in Home Decoration," 619; Hoganson discusses oppositional trends to cosmopolitanism but does not consider the role that Indian arts might have played therein in "Cosmopolitan Domesticity," pars. 51–54.

82. Earl Spencer Pomeroy, *In Search of the Golden West: The Tourist in Western America* (New York: Knopf, 1957), 123. See also Carlos A. Schwantes, "Tourists in Wonderland: Early Railroad Tourism in the Pacific Northwest," *Columbia* 7, no. 4 (1993–94): 28. The round-trip fare from the city of Tacoma to the hop-growing region of Puyallup, for example, was 25¢. "Flyer, 1901," negative 1903.1.60, Washington State Historical Society, Tacoma.

83. I expand here upon Hoganson's point made in specific relation to the subordination of women. Hoganson, "Cosmopolitan Domesticity," par. 36.

84. West, *Kodak and the Lens of Nostalgia*, 23, fig. 29, pls.1 and 2.

85. West, *Kodak and the Lens of Nostalgia*, chaps. 2 and 4.

86. In the Southwest context, Margaret Jacobs has shown how Indian domesticity served as a foil for white feminist self-expressions and explorations that ranged from the assimilationist to the cultural relativist. Jacobs, *Engendered Encounters*.

87. Hoganson, "Cosmopolitan Domesticity," par. 47; Enstad, *Ladies of Labor*; Dana Frank, *Purchasing Power: Consumer Organizing, Gender, and the Seattle Labor Movement, 1919–1929* (New York: Cambridge University Press, 1994); Peiss, *Hope in a Jar*.

88. Leah Dilworth, "Tourists and Indians in Fred Harvey's Southwest," in *Seeing and Being Seen: Tourism in the American West*, ed. David M. Wrobel and Patrick T. Long (Lawrence: University Press of Kansas, 2001), 158.

89. Bull, "Indian Hop Pickers," 546.

90. Meliss, "Siwash," 503.

91. Canada, DIA, AR 1886, *Sessional Papers*, 1887, no. 6, 92; El Comancho, "The Story of the Hop Vine," *Westerner* 16 (1914): 4.

92. *Told by the Pioneers*, 3:59. Even as they stood for modern consumers, white women could also be represented as impulsive. Laermans, "Learning to Consume," 94–96.

93. *Seattle Mail and Herald*, November 29, 1902. See also "Siwash Village on Tacoma Tide Flats," April 15, 1907, *C. B. Bagley Scrapbooks*, vol. 9, p. 26, Special Collections, University of Washington, Seattle.

94. Bull, "Indian Hop Pickers," 546.

95. Costello, *The Siwash*, 66. Bridget Heneghan claims that the colors of commodities were more broadly recognized as markers of race, class, and gender identities and exclusions. Bridget T. Heneghan, *Whitewashing America: Material Culture and Race in the Antebellum Imagination* (Jackson: University Press of Mississippi, 2003).

96. Meliss, "Siwash," 503.

97. In the late nineteenth century, Western conceptions of nature had come to be seen largely in opposition to the human. Indians remained situated as "natural" beings in the Western imagination, however. For a discussion of the implications of this phenomenon in relation to hop pickers in the Puget Sound region see Raibmon, *Authentic Indians*, 124–29.

98. Hawthorne, *History of Washington*, 2:228.

99. Meliss, "Siwash," 503.

100. Andrea Smith argues for an extended conceptualization of violence as the overarching trope of American Indian women's experience with colonization. Andrea Smith, *Conquest: Sexual Violence and American Indian Genocide* (Cambridge, MA: South End, 2005). For similar examples of ridicule directed at supposed "mimicry," see Karen Dubinsky, "Local Colour: The Spectacle of Race at Niagara Falls," in Ballantyne and Burton, *Bodies in Contact*, 72; Barman, "Aboriginal Women on the Streets of Victoria," 220. On the civilizational valence of Indigenous women's dress in the North see Myra Rutherdale, "She Was a Ragged Little Thing': Missionaries. Embodiment. and Refashioning Aboriginal Womanhood in Northern Canada," in Pickles and Rutherdale, *Contact Zones*, 228, 230, 239.

101. Homi K. Bhabha. *The Location of Culture* (New York: Routledge, 1994), 86. Indigenous men were also labeled mimics: "The son dresses in Hashy cloches, smokes a cheap cigar, wears the white man's shoes and apes his manners." "Siwash Village on Tacoma Tide Flats," 9:16. Bhabha's work refers explicitly to "mimic men." For commentary on the racial exclusivity of Bhabha's perspective and an elaboration of it, see Anne McClintock, *Imperial Leather: Race, Gender, and Sexuality in the Colonial Contest* (New York: Routledge, 1995).

102. "Indians Returning from Hop Fields," October 1, 1906, *Seattle Post Intelligencer;* "Siwashes Again Seek the Street." *Seattle Post Intelligencer*, May 13, 1904: *Seattle Mail and Herald*, November 29, 1902.

103. On mimicry and racial hierarchy see Dubinsky, "Local Colour," 69, 72; and Sarah Carter, "Two Acres and a Cow." *Canadian Historical Review* 70, no. 1 (1989): 34–35.

104. On cross-dressing, see McClintock, *Imperial Leather*, 65–69, and chap. 3; Judith Halberstam, "Mackdaddy, Superfly, Rapper: Gender, Race, and Masculinity in the Drag King Scene," *Social Text* 52/53 (1997): 104–31. Racial cross-dressing had long been a component of the construction of American identity. See Eric Lott, *Love and Theft: Blackface Minstrelsy and the American Working Class* (New York: Oxford University Press, 1995); Eric Lott, "White Like Me: Racial Cross-dressing and the Construction of American Whiteness," in Kaplan and Pease, *Cultures of United States Imperialism*, 474–98; Phillip J. Deloria, *Playing Indian* (New Haven, CT: Yale University Press, 1998); Alan Trachtenberg, *Shades of Hiawatha: Staging Indians, Making Americans, 1880–1930* (New York: Hill and Wang, 2004). For a powerfully intentional decision by an Indigenous woman to dress with and against dominant raciahzations of particular forms of dress see Carole Gerson and Veronica Strong-Boag, "Championing the Native: E. Pauline Johnson Rejects the Squaw," in Pickles and Rutherdale, *Contact Zones*, 49–50, 52, 55. For an interesting discussion of British women's adoption of fashion and food from India see Nupur Chaudhuri, "Shawls, Jewelry, Curry, and Rice in Victorian Britain," in *Western Women and Imperialism: Complicity and Resistance*, ed. Nupur Chaudhuri and Margaret Strobel (Bloomington: Indiana University Press, 1992), 231–46.

105. For an elaboration of how hop pickers incorporated Indigenous priorities into their seasonal migrations see Raibmon, *Authentic Indians*, chap. 5.

106. Appadurai, "Introduction: Commodities and the Politics of Value," 57. See also de Certeau, *The Practice of Everyday Life*, xvii.

107. Tony Bennett. "The Exhibitionary Complex," in *Representing the Nation: A Reader*, ed. David Boswell and Jessica Evans (London: Routledge, 1999), 332–61; Raibmon, *Authentic Indians*, chap. 2; Dubinsky, "Local Colour," 67–79; Laermans, "Learning to Consume," 89–98; William R. Leach, *Land of Desire: Merchants, Power, and the Rise of a New American Culture* (New York: Pantheon, 1993); Trachtenberg, *Shades of Hiawatha*, chap. 5.

108. Himani Bannerji, Shahrzad Mojab, and Judith Whitehead, eds., *Of Property and Propriety: The Role of Gender and Class in Imperialism and Nationalism* (Toronto: University of Toronto Press, 2001), 4.

109. John Comaroff and Jean Comaroff, *Ethnography and the Historical Imagination* (Boulder, CO: Westview, 1992), chap. 10.

110. Amy Kaplan, "Manifest Domesticity," *American Literature* 70 (1998): 581–606.

111. David E. Wilkins, *American Indian Sovereignty and the U.S. Supreme Court: The Masking of Justice* (Austin: University of Texas Press, 1997).

112. *Washington Standard*, August 15, 1879: "The Letter of the Law," *Victoria Daily Colonist*, August 25, 1892: *Told by the Pioneers*, 2:116, 133.

113. Appadurai, "Introduction: Commodities and the Politics of Value." 28.

114. Philip Deloria dates this shift to the 1890 massacre at Wounded Knee. Philip J. Deloria, *Indians in Unexpected Places* (Lawrence: University of Kansas Press, 2004), 15–51. See also Dilworth, "Tourists and Indians in Fred Harvey's Southwest," 192. and *Imagining Indians in the Southwest*, 163.

115. James, "Indian Basketry in Home Decoration," 619.

116. Hoganson. "Cosmopolitan Domesticity," par. 28. See also Phillips, *Trading Identities*, 198–212; Dilworth, *Imagining Indians in the Southwest*, 126, 144–45; Leah Dilworth, " 'Handmade by an American Indian': Souvenirs and the Cultural Economy of Southwestern Tourism," in *The Culture of Tourism, the Tourism of Culture: Selling the Past to the Present in the American Southwest*, ed. Hal K. Rothman (Albuquerque: University of New Mexico Press, 2003), 105.

117. Hoganson. "Cosmopolitan Domesticity," pars. 26 and 35; Jacobs, *Engendered Encounters*, 35; McClintock, *Imperial Leather*, 34; Phillips, *Trading Identities*, 198–212.

118. Kaplan, "Manifest Domesticity," 597.

119. Appadurai, "Introduction: Commodities and the Politics of Value," 27, 28.

120. Kaplan, "Manifest Domesticity," 583. Jane Haggis, "Gendering Colonialism or Colonising Gender? Recent Women's Studies Approaches to White Women and the History of British Colonialism," *Women's Studies International Forum* 13, nos. 1/2 (1990): 105–15. A rich literature exists on women's relationship to imperialism and colonialism. See, for example, Chaudhuri and Strobel, eds., *Western Women and Imperialism*; Vron Ware, *Beyond the Pale: White Women, Racism, and History* (New York: Verso, 1992), Antoinette M. Burton, *Burdens of History: British Feminists, Indian Women, and Imperial Culture, 1865–1915* (Chapel Hill: University of North Carolina Press, 1994); Clare Midgley, ed., *Gender and Imperialism* (New York: St. Martin's, 1995); Pierson and Chaudhuri, eds., *Nation, Empire, Colony*; Burton, *Gender, Sexuality, and Colonial Modernities*; Bannerji, Mojab, and Whitehead, eds., *Of Property and Propriety*; Philippa Levine, ed., *Gender and Empire* (New York: Oxford University Press, 2004); Pickles and Rutherdale, eds., *Contact Zones*; Ballantyne and Burton, eds., *Bodies in Contact*.

121. *Seattle Mail and Herald*, October 6, 1906.

122. McClintock, *Imperial Leather*, 53.

123. *Seattle Mail and Herald*, October 6. 1906.

124. McClintock, *Imperial Leather*, 53. See also Arjun Appadurai, "Dead Certainty: Ethnic Violence in the Era of Globalization." *Public Culture* 10 (1998): 225–47.

125. Jean Barman, "What a Difference a Border Makes: Aboriginal Racial Intermixture in the Pacific Northwest," *Journal of the West* 38 (1999): 14–20; Alexandra Harmon, "Lines in the Sand: Shifting Boundaries between Indians and Non-Indians in the Puget Sound Region," *Western Historical Quarterly* 26 (1995): 429–53; Harmon. *Indians in the Making*, chap. 2.

126. Costello, *The Siwash*, 163. On Indian hop pickers as picturesque see also Joe Smith, "The West's Great Harvest," *Seattle Mail and Herald*, October 21, 1905; "Picturesque Hop Pickers," *Puyallup Valley Tribune*, September 10, 1904, 1; "At the Indian Village."

127. This phenomenon was more broadly apparent across the American west. See Dilworth, *Imagining Indians in the Southwest*, 148–49.

128. "Hop Picking," *Washington Standard*, September 24, 1886.

129. See, for example, negatives NA661, NA4093, and NA758. Special Collections, University of Washington, Seattle; negatives SHS 1,052 and 90.45.11, Museum of History and Industry, Seattle, WA.

130. Bruce Miller, personal communication via e-mail, January 25, 2006.

131. Alicja Muszynski argues that industrial wages paid to Indigenous workers were inversely correlated to the strength of Indigenous economies. If she is correct, low wages rather than a simple marker of the superexploitation of Indigenous workers ought to be read, instead, partly as an indicator of

Indigenous economic persistence and independence. Alicja Muszynski, *Cheap Wage Labour: Race and Gender in the Fisheries of British Columbia* (Montreal: McGill-Queen's University Press, 1996), chap. 3.

132. Costello, *The Siwash*, 162.

133. *Harper's Weekly*, October 20, 1888; negative NA 4015, Special Collections, University of Washington, Seattle.

134. R. H. Ruffner, *A Report on Washington Territory* (New York: Seattle, Lake Shore and Eastern Railway, 1889), plate facing p. 74. Trains both enabled and mediated tourist experiences. Dilworth, "Tourists and Indians in Fred Harvey's Southwest," 156–57; Carlos Schwantes, "No Aid and No Comfort: Early Transportation and the Origins of Tourism in the Northern West," in Wrobel and Long, *Seeing and Being Seen*, 135–40; Carlos Schwantes, "Tourists in Wonderland," 30; Edwin L. Wade, "The Ethnic Art Market in the American Southwest, 1880–1980," in Stocking, *Objects and Others*, 167–91. On the streets of Victoria, British Columbia, the sexual labor of Indigenous women similarly generated economic profits for white businessmen. Barman, "Aboriginal Women on the Streets of Victoria," 214–15.

13

Black and White Visions of Welfare
Women's Welfare Activism, 1890–1945

Linda Gordon

One of the pleasures of historical scholarship is that it may lead into unexpected paths, and what begins as a frustration—say, from an apparent shortage of sources—may end as a new opening. This essay began as an attempt to examine gender differences in visions of public welfare among reformers. Having compiled material about women welfare activists who were mainly white, I found I could not distinguish the influence of gender from that of race in their perspectives. (Indeed, to many white historians, the racial characteristics of the white people we studied were invisible until we began to learn from minority historians to ask the right questions.) So I set up a comparison between black and white women welfare activists, with results that were illuminating about both groups. Three major areas of difference between black and white women's ideas emerged: first, about the nature of entitlement, between a black orientation toward universal programs and a white orientation toward supervised, means-tested ones; second, in the attitude toward mothers' employment; third, in strategies for protecting women from sexual exploitation. In what follows I want both to show how those differences were manifest and to suggest their roots in historical experience.[1]

Several historians have recently studied black women's civic contributions, but black women's reform campaigns have not usually been seen as part of welfare history. How many discussions of settlement houses include Victoria Earle Matthews's White Rose Mission of New York City, Margaret Murray Washington's Elizabeth Russell Settlement at Tuskegee, Alabama, Janie Porter Barrett's Locust Street Social Settlement in Hampton, Virginia, or Eugenia Burns Hope's Neighborhood Union in Atlanta, Georgia, among many others? In examining this activism from a welfare history perspective, I came to understand how the standard welfare histories had been by definition white-centered. It was possible to make the widespread welfare reform activity of minority women visible only by changing the definition of the topic and its periodization.[2]

The white experience has defined the very boundaries of what we mean by welfare. Whites were by 1890 campaigning for government programs of cash relief and for regulations such as the Pure Food and Drug Act and anti-child-labor laws. These welfare programs had racial content not only in the perspectives of the reformers (white), but also in the identification of their objects (largely the immigrant working class, which, although white, was perceived as racially different by turn-of-the-century reformers). The programs also had class content, visible, for example, in their rejection of traditional working-class cooperative benevolent societies. Moreover, because of these orientations, welfare in the late nineteenth century was increasingly conceived as an *urban* reform activity.[3]

By contrast, African Americans, still concentrated in the South and in rural communities, had been largely disfranchised by this time, and even in the North had much less power than whites, certainly less than elite whites, to influence government. Southern states had smaller administrative capacities and were paltrier in their provision of public services, even to whites. African Americans did campaign for governmental programs and had some success; at the federal level, they had won an Office of Negro Health Work in the United States Public Health Service, and they had gotten some resources from the extension programs of the United States Department of Agriculture. Nevertheless, black welfare activity, especially before the New Deal, consisted to a great extent of building private institutions. Black women welfare reformers created schools, old people's homes, medical services, and community centers. Attempting to provide for their people what the white state would not, they even raised private money for public institutions. For example, an Atlanta University study of 1901 found that in at least three southern states (Virginia, North Carolina, and Georgia) the private contribution to Negro public schools was greater than that from tax monies.[4] For example, a teacher in Lowndes County, Alabama, appealed for funds in 1912:

> Where I am now working there are 27,000 colored people. . . . In my school district there are nearly 400 children. I carry on this work eight months in the year and receive for it $290, out of which I pay three teachers and two extra teachers. The State provides for three months' schooling. . . . I have been trying desperately to put up an adequate school building for the hundreds of children clamoring to get an education. To complete it . . . I need about $800.[5]

Thus a large proportion of their political energy went to raising money, and under the most difficult circumstances—trying to collect from the poor and the limited middle class to help the poor. White women raised money, of course, but they also lobbied aldermen and congressmen, attended White House conferences, and corresponded with Supreme Court justices; black women had less access to such powerful men and spent proportionally more of their time organizing bake sales, rummage sales, and church dinners. The detailed example of the Gate City Kindergartens, established in Atlanta in 1905, may illustrate this:

> Another method of raising funds was through working circles throughout the city. . . . From Bazaars held at Thanksgiving time, lasting as long as a week, when every circle was responsible for a day, one day of which a turkey dinner was served. Money was made by sales in items of fancy work, aprons, etc., canned fruit, cakes and whatever could be begged. The association realized as much as $250.00 at a Bazaar. From track meets sponsored by colleges, and participated in by the children of the public school, $100.00 gate receipts were cleared. Food and cake sales brought at times $50.00. April sales brought $50.00, and one time the women realized as much as $100.00 from the sale of aprons. Sales of papers, magazines and tin foil brought as much as $50.00. A baby contest brought $50.00. Intercollegiate contest brought $100. Post-season baseball games realized as much as $25.00. Sales of soap wrappers, soap powder wrappers, saved and collected from housewives, and baking powder coupons brought $25.00. . . . [The list goes on.]

It cost twelve hundred dollars in cash to maintain the kindergartens each year. In addition, donations in kind were vital—all five kindergartens were housed in donated locations, clothes were constantly solicited for the needy children, and for several years Procter & Gamble gave five boxes of Ivory soap annually.[6] Some black welfare activists were adept at raising white money but had to accept sometimes galling strings, and even the most successful tried to shift their economic dependence to their own people.[7] No doubt some of these money-raising activities were also pleasurable and community-building social occasions, but often they were just drudgery, and those doing the work hated it. Jane Hunter, a Cleveland black activist, wrote that "this money getting business destroys so much of ones real self, that we cannot do our best."[8]

This essay uses a limited comparison—between black and white women reformers—to alter somewhat our understanding of what welfare is and to bring into better visibility gender and race (and class) influences on welfare thinking. The essay uses two kinds of data: written and oral-history records of the thoughts of these activists, and a rudimentary collective biography of 145 black and white women who were national leaders in campaigns for public welfare between 1890 and 1945.[9] This method emerges from the premise expressed by the feminist slogan "The personal is political": that political views and activities are related not only to macroeconomic and social conditions but also to personal circumstances such as family experiences and occupational histories.

My approach uses a broad definition of welfare. I include reformers who sought regulatory laws, such as the Pure Food and Drug Act, compulsory education, and anti-child-labor regulations. I do not include reformers who worked mainly on labor relations, civil rights, women's rights, or a myriad of other reform issues not centrally related to welfare.[10] In categorizing many different activists, I had to ignore many differences in order to make broad generalization possible. This method inevitably obscures context and some fascinating personalities. Many more monographs are necessary, but I notice that historical thinking develops through a constant interplay between monographs and syntheses, I hope that this essay, because of its very breadth, will stimulate more monographs.

I did not form this sample according to a random or other formal selection principle. Instead I identified members of my sample gradually, during several years of research on welfare campaigns, and then tracked down biographical information. The process is a historian's form of snowball sampling, because often tracking down one activist produces references to another. Naturally, there are many bits of missing information because biographical facts are difficult to find for many women, especially minority women. I make no claim to having created a representative sample or an exhaustive list. But, on the methodological principle of saturation, I doubt that my generalizations would be much altered by the addition of more individuals.

To bound my sample, I included only those who were national leaders—officers of national organizations campaigning for welfare provision or builders of nationally important institutions, such as hospitals, schools, or asylums. (For more on the sample, see the Appendix.) These leaders were not typical welfare activists; more typical were those who worked exclusively locally, and their personal profiles might be quite different. But the national leaders had a great deal of influence on the thinking of other women. I included only activists prominent chiefly after 1890 because it was in the 1890s that such key national organizations as the National Association of Colored Women (NACW) began and that white women welfare activists began a marked emphasis on public provision. I followed welfare activism until 1945 because I wanted to look at broad patterns of ideas across a long period of policy debate; I ended in 1945 because among white women there was a marked decline in such agitation after that date, and among blacks there was a shift in emphasis to civil rights.

My approach sacrifices, of course, change over time. Substantial generational as well as individual differences among women had to be put aside. For example, the early black activists were, on average, more focused on race uplift and the later ones more on integration; during this period the mass northward migration of blacks shifted reformers' concerns not only away from the South but also increasingly toward urban problems. The white women welfare activists of the 1890s tended to divide between Charity Organization Society devotees and settlement advocates; by the 1930s, they were more united in promoting professionalism in public assistance. Nevertheless, I am convinced that there are enough continuities to justify this periodization, continuities that will emerge in the discussion below.

The two groups thus formed were in many ways not parallel. For example, the white women were mainly from the Northeast or Midwest, and there were few southern white women—only 16 percent of the group were either born or active in the South, whereas a majority of the black women were born in the South. For another example, many of the black women were educators by occupation, while white women who were educators were few. But these divergences are part of what I am trying to identify, part of the differences in black and white women's perspectives. Among whites, northerners contributed more to national welfare models than did southerners. And education had particular meanings for African Americans and was integrated into campaigns for the welfare of the race in a distinctive way. Generalizing among a variety of women of several generations, the comparison naturally eclipses some important distinctions, but it does so to illuminate others that are also important.[11]

I identified sixty-nine black women as national leaders in welfare reform. Separating the white from the black women was not my decision: The networks were almost completely segregated. First, the national women's organizations were segregated; those that included blacks, such as the Young Women's Christian Association (YWCA), had separate white and black locals. Second, since black women rarely held government positions, they rarely interacted with white women officially. Third, the national network of white women reformers usually excluded black women even when they could have been included.[12] The exclusion of black women from the white women's clubs and the ignoring or trivializing of life-and-death black issues, such as lynching, have been amply documented.[13] To cite but one example, one of the most important women in the New Deal—Mary McLeod Bethune—was not a part of the tight, if informal, caucus that the white New Deal women formed.[14] There were important counterexamples, interracial efforts of significant impact, particularly local ones: In Chicago, for instance, white settlement and charity workers joined black reformers in campaigning for public services for dependent children, establishing the Chicago Urban League, and responding to the 1919 race riot. In the South interracial efforts arose from evangelical religious activity. Some white members of this sample group worked with the Commission of Interracial Cooperation, forming its Women's Council, which had 805 county-level groups by 1929.[15] The national YWCA became a forum for communication between black and white women. But these efforts were marked by serious and sometimes crippling white prejudice, and the core networks of women remained segregated.

While the black group was created in part by white racism, it was also created from the inside, so to speak, by personal friendships. Often these relationships were born in schools and colleges and continued thereafter, strengthened by the development of black sororities after 1908. The creation of national organizations and networks extended relationships and ideas among these black women leaders across regional boundaries. For example, the Phillis Wheatley Home for the protection of single black urban women, established by Jane Hunter in Cleveland in 1911, spurred the opening of similar homes in Denver, Atlanta, Seattle, Boston, Detroit, Chicago, Greenville, Winston-Salem, Toledo, and Minneapolis by 1934. When Fannie Barrier Williams spoke in Memphis in 1896, she had never been in the South before, having grown up in upstate New York and settled in Chicago.[16] More and more the women began to travel widely, despite the difficult and humiliating conditions of travel for black women. Friendships could be intense, despite distance; black women early in the twentieth century, like white women, sometimes spoke openly of their strong emotional bonds. Darlene Clark Hine quotes Jane Hunter writing Nannie Burroughs, "It was so nice to see you and to know your real sweet self. Surely we will . . . cultivate a lasting friendship. I want to be your devoted sister in kindred thought and love." At other times Hunter wrote to Burroughs of her loneliness "for want of a friend."[17] Mutual support was strong. When in the 1930s the president and trustees of Howard University, led by Abraham Flexner, tried to force Howard's dean of women, Lucy D. Slowe, to live on campus with her girls (something the dean of men was not, of course, required to do) and she refused to comply, a whole network of women interceded on her behalf. A group of five asked for a meeting with Flexner, which he refused. Another group of women interviewed trustees in New York and reported to Slowe their perceptions of the situation. Mary McLeod Bethune urged her to be "steadfast" and campaigned for her among sympathetic Howard faculty.[18] The network was divided by cliques and encompassed conflicts and even feuds. Yet it had a bottom line of loyalty. Even those who criticized Bethune for insufficient militance understood her to be absolutely committed to the network of black women.[19]

The black women's network was made more coherent by its members' common experience as educators and builders of educational institutions. Education was the single most important area of activism for black women. The majority of women in this sample taught at one time or another, and 38 percent were educators by profession. For many, reform activism centered around establishing schools, from kindergartens through colleges, such as Nannie Burroughs's National Training School for Women and Girls in Washington, D.C., Lucy Laney's Haines Institute in Augusta, Georgia, or Arenia Mallory's Saints' Industrial and Literary Training School in Mississippi. In his 1907 report on economic cooperation among Negro Americans, for example, W. E. B. Du Bois counted 151 church-connected and 161 nonsectarian private Negro schools. Although he did not discuss the labor of founding and maintaining these institutions, we can guess that women contributed disproportionately.[20]

Another black welfare priority was the establishment of old people's homes, considered by Du Bois the "most characteristic Negro charity." These too, according to the early findings of Du Bois, were predominantly organized by women.[21] But if we were to take the period 1890 to 1945 as a whole, the cause second to education was health. Black hospitals, while primarily initiated by black and white men, depended on crucial support from black women. Between 1890 and 1930 African Americans created approximately two hundred hospitals and nurse-training schools, and women often took charge of the community organizing and fund-raising labor. Over time black women's health work changed its emphasis, from providing for the sick in the 1890s to preventive health projects after about 1910. Yet even in the first decade of the century, Du Bois found that most locations with considerable black populations had beneficial and insurance societies that paid sickness as well as burial benefits; these can be traced back a century before Du Bois studied them. In several cities the societies also paid for medicines and actually created their own health maintenance organizations (HMOs). With the dues of their members they hired physicians, annually or on a quarterly basis, to provide health care for the entire group.[22]

Many women's clubs made health work their priority. The Washington, D.C., Colored YWCA built a program around visiting the sick. The Indianapolis Woman's Improvement Club focused on tuberculosis, attempting to make up for the denial of service to blacks by the Indianapolis board of health, the city hospital, and the Marion County tuberculosis society. The preventive health emphasis was stimulated in part by educational work. For example, Atlanta's Neighborhood Union did a survey of conditions in the black schools in 1912 to 1913 that revealed major health problems; in 1916 this led the Neighborhood Union to establish a clinic that offered both health education and free medical treatment. Possibly the most extraordinary individual in black women's public health work was Modjeska Simkins, who used her position as director of Negro work for the antituberculosis association of South Carolina to inaugurate a program dealing with the entire range of black health problems, including maternal and infant mortality, venereal disease (VD), and malnutrition as well as tuberculosis. Perhaps the most ingenious women's program was Alpha Kappa Alpha's Mississippi Health Project. These black sorority women brought health care to sharecroppers in Holmes County, Mississippi, for several weeks every summer from 1935 to 1942. Unable to rent space for a clinic because of plantation owners' opposition, they turned cars into mobile health vans, immunizing over fifteen thousand children and providing services such as dentistry and treatment for malaria and VD for between twenty-five hundred and four thousand people each summer.[23]

These reformers were united also through their churches, which were centers of networking and of activism, in the North as well as the South. Indeed, more locally active, less elite black women reformers were probably even more connected to churches; the national leadership was moving toward more secular organization, while remaining more church-centered than white women welfare leaders. Black churches played a large role in raising money, serving in particular as a conduit for appeals for white money, through missionary projects.[24]

The YWCA also drew many of these women together. Victoria Matthews's White Rose Mission influenced the YWCA, through its leader Grace Dodge, to bring black women onto its staff, which experience groomed many black women leaders.[25]

And despite the fact that these were national leaders, they shared a regional experience. At least 57 percent were born in the South. More important, perhaps, two-thirds of these migrated to the Northeast, Midwest, and mid-Atlantic regions, thus literally spreading their network as they fled Jim Crow and sought wider opportunity.[26]

Most members of this network were married—85 percent. More than half of the married women had prominent men as spouses, and their marriages sometimes promoted their leadership positions.[27] Lugenia Burns Hope was the wife of John Hope, first black president of Atlanta University; Irene Gaines was the wife of an Illinois state legislator. Ida Wells-Barnett's husband published Chicago's leading black newspaper. George Edmund Haynes, husband of Elizabeth, was a Columbia Ph.D., a professor at Fisk, an assistant to the secretary of labor from 1918 to 1921, and a founder of the Urban League. George Ruffin, husband of Josephine, was a Harvard Law graduate, a member of the Boston City Council, and Boston's first black judge. Most of the women, however, had been activists before marriage, and many led lives quite independent of their husbands. (Of these married women, 20 percent were widowed, divorced, or separated.)

Their fertility pattern was probably related to their independence. Of the whole group, 43 percent had no children; and of the married women, 34 percent had no children (there were no unmarried mothers).[28] (In comparison, 31 percent of the white married women in this sample were childless.) It thus seems likely that these women welfare activists used birth control, although long physical separations from their husbands may have contributed to their low fertility.[29] In their contraceptive practices these women may have been as modern as contemporary white women of comparable class position.

For most African American women a major reason for being in the public sphere after marriage was employment, due to economic necessity; but for this group of women, economic need was not a driving pressure. A remarkable number had prosperous parents.[30] Crystal Fauset's father, although born a slave, was principal of a black academy in Maryland. Elizabeth Ross Haynes's father went from slavery to ownership of a fifteen-hundred-acre plantation. Addie Hunton's father was a substantial businessman and founder of the Negro Elks. Mary Church Terrell's mother *and* father were successful in business. Most black women in the sample had husbands who could support them; 51 percent of the married women had high-professional husbands—lawyers, physicians, ministers, educators.[31] The women of this network were also often very class-conscious, and many of the clubs that built their collective identity were exclusive, such as the sororities, the Chautauqua Circle, and the Twelve in Atlanta. The fact that about 40 percent were born outside the South provides further evidence of their high status, since the evidence suggests that the earlier northward migrants were the more upwardly mobile.[32] In all these respects, this group probably differed from typical local activists, who were less privileged. Yet even among this elite group only a tiny minority—12 percent—were not employed.[33] To be sure, this economic privilege was only relative to the whole black population; on average, the black women's network was less wealthy than the white women's. Even those who were born to middle-class status were usually newly middle-class, perhaps a generation away from slavery and without much cushion against economic misfortune. Still, among many whites the first and most important emblem of middle-class status was a woman's domesticity.

One can safely conclude that one meaning of these women's combining of public and family lives was the greater acceptance among African Americans, for many historical reasons, of the public life of married women.

The black women's national network was made more homogeneous by educational attainment, high social status, and a sense of superiority to the masses that brought with it obligations of service. Of the black women, 83 percent had a higher education, comparable to the proportion of white women, and 35 percent had attended graduate school. These figures may surprise those unfamiliar with the high professional achievement patterns of black women between 1890 and 1945. The full meaning of the statistics emerges when one compares them with the average educational opportunities for blacks in the United States at this time. In the earliest year for which we have figures, 1940, only 1 percent of African Americans, male and female, had four or more years of college. Moreover, only 41 percent of the women in this sample attended black colleges, whereas those colleges conferred 86 percent of all black undergraduate degrees in the period from 1914 to 1936.[34] Several women in this sample who were born into the middle class described learning for the first time in adulthood of the conditions of poverty in which most African Americans lived—an ignorance characteristic of prosperous whites but rarer among blacks. As Alfreda Duster, Ida Wells-Barnett's daughter, recalled, "It was difficult for me to really empathize with people who had come from nothing, where they had lived in cottages, huts in the South, with no floor and no windows and had suffered the consequences of the discrimination and the hardships of the South."[35] Many black women joined Du Bois in emphasizing the importance of building an intellectual and professional elite, calling upon the "leading" or "intelligent" or "better class of" Negroes to take initiatives for their people. Class and status inequalities, measured by such markers as money, occupation, and skin color, created tensions in this network, as comparable inequalities did in the white network.[36] Some thought of their obligations in the eugenic terms that were so fashionable in the first three decades covered by this study. "I was going to multiply my ability and my husband's by six," Alfreda Duster said in describing her decision to have six children.[37] Such thinking had somewhat different meanings for blacks than for whites, however, reflecting their awareness that race prejudice made it difficult for educated, prosperous blacks to escape the discrimination and pejorative stereotyping that held back all African Americans. As Ferdinand Barnett, later to become the husband of Ida B. Wells, put it in 1879, "One vicious, ignorant Negro is readily conceded to be a type of all the rest, but a Negro educated and refined is said to be an exception. We must labor to reverse this rule; education and moral excellence must become general and characteristic, with ignorance and depravity the exception."[38]

Indeed, the high social status and prosperity common in this group should not lead us to forget the discrimination and humiliation that they faced. Their high levels of skills and education were frustrated by lack of career opportunity. Sadie Alexander, from one of the most prominent black families in the United States, was the first black woman Ph.D., with a degree from the University of Pennsylvania. But she could not get an appropriate job because of her color, and was forced to work as an assistant actuary for a black insurance company. Anna Arnold Hedgeman, one of the youngest women in this sample, from a small Minnesota town where she had attended integrated schools and churches, graduated from Hamline University in St. Paul and then discovered that she could not get a teaching job in any white institution. Instead she went to work in Holly Springs, Mississippi, until she found the Jim Crow laws intolerable. Despite the relatively large black middle class in Washington, D.C., African American women there could not generally get clerical jobs in the federal government until the 1940s.[39]

Moreover, this black activism was born in an era of radically worsening conditions for most African American women, in contrast to the improving conditions for white women. The older women in this network had felt segregation intensify in their adult lifetimes; there was widespread immiseration and denial of what political power they had accumulated after the emancipation.

In the 1920s the second Ku Klux Klan attracted as many as six million members. These experiences, so rarely understood by whites, further reinforced the bonds uniting black women and influenced their welfare visions.[40]

The seventy-six white women, like the blacks, constituted a coherent network. Most of them knew each other, and their compatibility was cemented by a homogeneous class, religious, and ethnic base. Most had prosperous, many even prominent parents; virtually all were of north European, Protestant backgrounds, from the Northeast or Midwest. The nine Jewish members were hardly representative of Jewish immigrants: Five had wealthy German-Jewish parents (Elizabeth Brandeis Raushenbush, Hannah Einstein, Josephine and Pauline Goldmark, and Lillian Wald). There were three Catholics (Josephine Brown, Jane Hoey, and Agnes Regan), but they were hardly typical of Catholics in the United States in the period: They were all native-born of prosperous parents. The shared Protestantism of the others was more a sign of similar ethnic background than of avid religious commitment, for few were churchgoers or intense believers, and churches did not organize their welfare activities.

The great majority (86 percent) were college-educated, and 66 percent attended graduate school. By contrast, in 1920 fewer than 1 percent of all American women held college degrees. It is worth recalling, however, that 83 percent of the black women were college-educated, and their disproportion to the black population as a whole was even greater. The white women had attended more expensive, elite schools; 37 percent had graduated from one of the New England women's colleges.

The white women had even more occupational commonality than the blacks. The great majority were social workers.[41] To understand this correctly we must appreciate the changing historical meanings of social work. Prior to the Progressive Era, the term referred not to a profession but to a range of helping and reform activity; the word *social* originally emphasized the reform, rather than the charity, component. Here it is relevant that many had mothers active in social reform.[42] The early-twentieth-century professionalization of social work has often been conceptualized as creating a rather sharp break both with amateur friendly visiting and with political activism. The experience of the women I am studying suggests otherwise: Well into the 1930s they considered casework, charity, and reform politics as "social work." By contrast to the African American women, very few were educators, a pattern that suggests that creating new educational institutions was no longer a reform priority for white women and that other professional jobs, especially governmental ones, were open to them.[43]

The whites had at least as much geographical togetherness as the black women. Sixty-eight percent worked primarily in the New England and mid-Atlantic states—hardly surprising since the national headquarters of the organizations they worked for were usually located there. Moreover, 57 percent had worked in New York City during the Progressive Era or the 1920s. New York City played a vanguard role in the development of public services and regulation in the public interest, and women in the network were influential in that city's welfare programs. New York City settlement houses specialized in demonstration projects, beginning programs on a small, private scale and then getting them publicly funded. The settlements initiated vocational guidance programs, later adopted by the public schools; they initiated use of public schools for after-hours recreation programs and public health nursing. Lillian Wald, head of the Henry Street Settlement, coordinated the city's response to the 1919 influenza epidemic. The settlements lobbied for municipal legislation regulating tenements and landlord-tenant relations, and milk purity and prices. In 1917 the Women's City Club of New York City opened a Maternity Center in Hell's Kitchen, where they provided prenatal nursing care and education and housekeeping services for new mothers. Expanded to ten locations in Manhattan, this effort served as a model for the bill that eventually became the Sheppard-Towner Act. The Women's City Club provided an important meeting place for many of these women, and it can serve as an indicator of their prosperity: Members had to pay substantial dues and an initiation fee, and the club purchased a mansion on Thirty-fifth Street and Park Avenue for $160,000 in 1917.[44]

Some of these white women had been active in party politics even before they had the vote. Some had been in the Socialist Party, and many were active in the 1912 Progressive Party campaign. Most, however, preferred nonpartisan public activism. During the late 1920s and 1930s they became more active in political parties, and transferred their allegiance to the Democratic Party. Here too New York was important, because the political figure who most attracted these women to the Democrats was Franklin D. Roosevelt, in his governorship and then his presidency. Several women who had been active in reform in the city, notably Belle Moskowitz, Rosa Schneiderman, and Eleanor Roosevelt, took on statewide roles. The Al Smith campaign of 1928 promoted more division than unity, however, because most women social workers were critical of his "wet" positions and his association with machine politics. The reassuring presence of his aide Moskowitz and Franklin Roosevelt's "aide" Eleanor Roosevelt was critical in bringing their network into the Democratic Party.[45]

The black network also underwent a political realignment from Republican to Democratic, but with different meanings, largely associated with migration northward, because the southern Democratic Party was essentially closed to blacks. Ironically, this transition was also in part effectuated by Eleanor Roosevelt, who became the symbol of those few white political leaders willing to take stands on racial equality.[46] Nevertheless Eleanor Roosevelt did not create an integrated network, nor was she able to swing the white network to support the leading black demand during the Roosevelt administration: a federal antilynching law.

Women in both networks taught, mentored, even self-consciously trained each other. Among blacks this occurred in colleges, in white-run organizations such as the YWCAs, and in black organizations such as sororities, the National Association of Colored Women, and many local groups. A higher proportion of the white women than of the black women worked in settlement houses—probably partly because so many of the white women were single. That experience strongly encouraged intergenerational connections and intimacy, because the younger or newer volunteers actually lived with their elders, seeing them in action. In the civic organizations, leaders groomed, protected, and promoted their protégées: Jane Addams did this with Alice Hamilton, Lillian Wald, and Florence Kelley; Sophonisba Breckinridge launched her student Grace Abbott's career by placing her at the head of the newly formed Immigrants' Protective League; the whole network campaigned for Abbott and then for Frances Perkins to become secretary of labor.[47] Such involvements continued when network members became federal or state officials, with other members as their employees. The chiefs of the Children's and Women's Bureaus—the two key federal agencies run by women—exercised extraordinary involvement in the personal lives of their employees. Mary Anderson, for example, head of the Women's Bureau, corresponded frequently with her employees in other parts of the country about their family lives, advising them about the care of aging parents, among other things.[48]

It is quite possible that black women's personal and professional support networks were just as strong; there is less evidence because, as several historians of African American women have suggested, black women left fewer private papers than did white women.[49] Given this caveat, the white women's network does appear to differ in one measure of mutual dependence. The great majority of the white women were single—only 34 percent had ever been married, and only 18 percent remained married during their peak political activity (42 percent of those who ever married were divorced, separated, or widowed). Only 28 percent had children. In this respect they are probably quite different from many local welfare activists, a group that included fewer elite women and more who were married. Moreover, 28 percent were in relationships with other women that might have been called "Boston marriages" a few decades before.[50] (My figure is a conservative one since I counted only those women for whom I could identify a specific partner.

It does not include such women as Edith Rockwood, who lived until her death in 1953 with Marjorie Heseltine of the Children's Bureau and Louise Griffith of the Social Security Agency and who built and owned a summer house jointly with Marion Crane of the Children's Bureau.)[51] At the time these relationships were mainly not named at all, although Mary ("Molly") Dewson referred to her mate as "partner." Contemporaries usually perceived them as celibate.[52] Today some of these women might be called lesbian, but there is much controversy among historians as to whether it is ahistorical to apply the word to that generation, a controversy I wish to avoid here since it is not relevant to my argument. What is relevant is not their sexual activity but their dependence on other women economically, for jobs; for care in grief, illness, and old age; for vacation companionship; for every conceivable kind of help. Despite their singleness, their efforts were very much directed to family and child welfare. It is remarkable to contemplate that so many women who became symbols of matronly respectability and asexual "social motherhood" led such unconventional private lives.

Moreover, they turned this mutual dependency into a political caucus. When lesbian history was first being written, these relationships between women were seen, first, in exclusively private and individual terms, and, second, as a lifestyle that isolated them from the heterosexual social and cultural mainstream. Recently, Estelle Freedman and Blanche Wiesen Cook have helped change that paradigm.[53] The women's female bonding did not disadvantage them but brought them political power, and they got it without making the sacrifices of personal intimacy that men so often did. Privileged women that they were, several of them had country homes, and groups would often weekend together; we can be sure that their conversation erased distinctions between the personal and the political, between gossip and tactics.

In truth, we do not know how different these white women's relationships were from black women's. Many black married women, such as Bethune and Charlotte Hawkins Brown, lived apart from their husbands (but so did several white women counted here as married, such as Perkins); and a few back women, such as Dean Lucy Slowe of Howard, lived in Boston marriages. Many blacks in this sample spoke critically not only of men but of marriage, and feared its potential to demobilize women. Dorothy Height lamented that the "over-emphasis on marriage has destroyed so many people."[54]

Both white and black women, if single, experienced a sense of betrayal when a friend married; and both, if about to marry, feared telling their single comrades.[55] In time, particularly from the 1930s on, the white women's sense that marriage and activity in the public sphere were incompatible choices diminished, and more married activists appeared.[56] This change, however, only makes it the more evident that throughout the period, black women had greater willingness, necessity, or ability to combine marriage and public activism, through coping strategies that may have included informal marital separations.

The white women's friendship network was particularly visible among the most prominent women because they took it with them to their prominent and well-documented jobs. Their friendships transcended boundaries between the public and private sectors, between government and civic organization. In this way they created what several historians have begun calling a "women's political culture"—but again we must remember that this concept has referred primarily to white women. The powerful settlement houses, Hull House and the Henry Street Settlement, for example, became virtually a part of municipal government and were able to command the use of tax money when necessary. When women gained governmental positions, there was as much extra-agency as intra-agency consultation and direction. In its first project, collecting data on infant mortality, the Children's Bureau used hundreds of volunteers from this organizational network to help. In 1920 Florence Kelley of the National Consumers' League (NCL) listed investigations the Women's Bureau should undertake, and these were done. Mary Anderson of the Women's Bureau arranged for the NCL to draft a bill for protection of female employees for the state of Indiana, and Anderson herself wrote comments on the draft. In 1922

Anderson wrote Mary Dewson of the NCL asking her to tone down her critical language about the National Woman's Party, and Dewson complied; in 1923 Dewson asked Anderson to help her draft a response to the National Woman's Party that was to appear in *The Nation* under Dewson's name.

Such cooperation continued throughout the New Deal. A good example was the Women's Charter, an attempt made in 1936, in response to the increased intensity of the campaign for the Equal Rights Amendment (ERA), to negotiate a settlement between the two sides of the women's movement. An initial meeting was attended by representatives of the usual white women's network civic organizations—YWCA, League of Women Voters, Women's Trade Union League, American Association of University Women (AAUW), Federation of Business and Professional Women—as well as several state and federal government women. The first draft of the charter was written by Anderson, still head of the Women's Bureau; Frieda Miller, then head of the women's section of the New York State Department of Labor; Rose Schneiderman, formerly of the National Recovery Administration (until the Supreme Court overruled it) and soon to become head of the New York State Department of Labor; and Mary Van Kleeck. The drafting of the charter exemplifies two of the findings regarding this network: the importance of New York and the predominance of single women.[57]

Singleness did not keep these women from useful connections with men, however. These connections came with kinship and class, if not with marriage. Clara Beyer got her "in" to the network because Felix Frankfurter recommended her to administer the 1918 District of Columbia minimum wage law. She then brought in Elizabeth Brandeis, the daughter of Louis Brandeis, to share the job with her. Brandeis's two sisters-in-law, Josephine and Pauline Goldmark, were also active in this network. Sophonisba Breckinridge, Florence Kelley, Julia Lathrop, and Katherine Lenroot were daughters of senators or congressmen. Loula Dunn's father and two grandfathers had been in the Alabama legislature. Susan Ware computed, about a different but overlapping group of New Deal women, that almost 50 percent (thirteen of twenty-eight) were from political families.[58] These women often learned politics in their households, and knew where to get introductions and referrals to politically influential people when they needed them. When Beyer said, "It was my contacts that made [me] so valuable, that I could go to these people," she was speaking about both her women's network and her male connections.[59]

With these group characteristics in mind, I want to examine the welfare ideas of these two networks.

One major difference in the orientation of the two groups was that the whites, well into the Great Depression, more strongly saw themselves as helping others—people who were "other" not only socially but often also ethnically and religiously. The perspective of the white network had been affected particularly by large-scale immigration, the reconstitution of the urban working class by people of non-WASP origin, and residential segregation, which grouped the immigrants in ghettos not often seen by the white middle class. Much has been written about the arrogance and condescension these privileged social workers showed their immigrant clients. Little has been done to discover the impact of the immigrant population on the reformers' own ideas. The black/white comparison suggests that ethnic difference between the white poor and white reformers not only discouraged identification but also slowed the reformers' development of a structural understanding of the origins of poverty, as opposed to one that blamed individual character defects, however environmentally caused. Thus into the 1940s, the great majority of the white women in this sample supported welfare programs that were not only means-tested but also "morals-tested," continuing a distinction between the worthy and the unworthy poor. They believed that aid should always be accompanied by expert supervision and rehabilitation so as to inculcate into the poor work habits and morals that they so often lacked, or so the reformers believed. (And, one might add, they did not mind the fact that this set up a sexual double standard in which women aid recipients would be treated differently and more severely than men recipients.)[60]

In comparison, black women were more focused on their own kind. Despite the relative privilege of most of them—and there was criticism from blacks of the snobbery of some of these network members—there was less distance between helper and helped than among white reformers. There was less chronological distance, for all their privileges were so recent and so tenuous. There was less geographical distance, for residential segregation did not allow the black middle class much insulation from the black poor. Concentrating their efforts more on education and health, and proportionally less on charity or relief, meant that they dealt more often with universal needs than with those of the particularly unfortunate, and sought to provide universal, not means-tested, services.

These were differences of degree and should not be overstated. Most of the white women in this sample favored environmental analyses of the sources of poverty. Many black women's groups engaged in classic charity activity. In the 1890s Washington, D.C., black women volunteered to work with the Associated Charities in its "stamp work," a program designed to inculcate thrift and saving among the poor. In the depression of 1893 these relatively prosperous black "friendly visitors" donated supplies of coal and food staples. The Kansas Federation of Women's Clubs, Marilyn Brady found, clung to all the tenets of the "cult of true womanhood" except, perhaps, for fragility. As Ena Farley wrote of the Boston League of Women for Community Service, "Their patronage roles toward others less fortunate than themselves not only dramatized their relative superiority within the minority structure, but also gave them the claim to leadership and power positions." But these programs must be understood in a context in which the needy were far more numerous, and the prosperous far fewer, than among whites.[61]

This does not mean that there was no condescension among black women. Black leaders shared with white ones the conviction that the poor needed training, to develop not only skills but also moral and spiritual capacities. Mary Church Terrell could sound remarkably like a white clubwoman:

> To our poor, benighted sisters in the Black Belt of Alabama we have gone and we have been both a comfort and a help to these women, through the darkness of whose ignorance of everything that makes life sweet or worth the living, no ray of light would have penetrated but for us. We have taught them the ABC of living by showing them how to make their huts more habitable and decent with the small means at their command and how to care for themselves and their families.[62]

Like the Progressive Era white female reformers, the blacks emphasized the need to improve the sexual morals of their people.[63] Fannie Barrier Williams declared that the colored people's greatest need was a better and purer home life—that slavery had destroyed home ties, the sanctity of marriage, and the instincts of motherhood.[64]

Concern for sexual respectability by no means represented one class or stratum imposing its values on another; for black women as for white women, it grew also from a feminist, or womanist, desire to protect women from exploitation, a desire shared across class lines. But this priority had profoundly different meanings for black women reformers. Not only were black women more severely sexually victimized, but combating sexual exploitation was for blacks inseparable from race uplift in general, as white sexual assaults against black women had long been a fundamental part of slavery and racial oppression. Indeed, black activists were far in advance of white feminists in their campaigns against rape and their identification of that crime as part of a system of power relations, and they did not assume that only *white* men were sexual aggressors. The historian Darlene Clark Hine suggests that efforts to build recreational programs for boys also reflected women's strategies for protecting girls from assault. Nevertheless, given the difficulties of effecting change in the aggressors, many black welfare reformers focused on protecting potential victims. Many of the earliest black urban institutions were homes designed to protect working women. Black women's considerable contribution to the founding and development of the Urban League had such motives. Just as the efforts by white welfare reformers to protect girls and women contained condescending and victim-blaming aspects, particularly inasmuch as they were directed at different social groups (immigrants, the poor), so victim-blaming was present among black reformers, too. The problem of sex exploitation could not be removed from intrarace class differences that left some black women much more vulnerable than others, not only to assault but also to having their reputations smeared; black women, like white women, defined their middle-class status in part by their sexual respectability. But their sexual protection efforts were so connected to uplift for the whole race, without which the reformers could not enjoy any class privileges, that the victim blaming was a smaller part of their message than among whites.[65]

Moreover, despite the sense of superiority among some, the black women reformers could not easily separate their welfare-related activities from their civil rights agitation.[66] As Deborah White puts it, "The race problem . . . inherently included the problems of poverty."[67] Race uplift work was usually welfare work by definition, and it was always conceived as a path to racial equality. And black poverty could not be ameliorated without challenges to white domination. A nice example: In 1894 Gertrude Mossell, in a tribute to black women's uplift activity, referred to Ida Wells's antilynching campaign as "philanthropy." Several of these women, notably Terrell and Anna J. Cooper, were among the first rebels against Booker T. Washington's domination because of their attraction both to academic educational goals for their people and to challenges to segregation.[68] Those who considered themselves women's rights activists, such as Burroughs, Terrell, and Cooper, particularly protested the hypocrisy in the white feminists' coupling of the language of sisterhood with the practice of black exclusion—as in Terrell's principled struggle, as an elderly woman, to gain admission to the District of Columbia chapter of the American Association of University Women.

To be sure, there was a shift in emphasis from race uplift and thus institution building in the first part of this long period under study to the struggle against segregation in the second. But the shift was visible only in overview, because many women activists had been challenging racism from early in their careers. Williams, for example, as early as 1896 insisted that white women needed to learn from blacks.[69] YWCA women such as Eva Bowles, Lugenia Burns Hope, and Addie Hunton struggled against discrimination in the YWCA soon after the first colored branch opened in 1911. Charlotte Hawkins Brown, who was noted and sometimes criticized for her snobbery and insistence on "respectability," nevertheless "made it a practice, whenever insulted in a train or forced to leave a pull-man coach and enter the Jim Crow car, to bring suit." At least one lawyer, in 1921, tried to get her to accept a small settlement, but she made it clear that her purpose was not financial compensation but justice.[70] Cooper, whose flowery and sentimental prose style might lead one to mistake her for a "soft," accommodating spirit, rarely let a slur against Negroes go unprotested. She wrote to the Oberlin Committee against Al Smith in 1928 that she could not "warm up very enthusiastically with religious fervor for Bible 'fundamentalists' who have nothing to say about lynching Negroes or reducing whole sections of them to a state of peonage."[71]

The many women who had always challenged racism made a relatively smooth transition to a civil rights emphasis in their welfare work. There were conflicts about separatist versus integrationist strategies from the beginning of this period, not only in women's participation in leading black discourse but also in women's own projects. For example, Jane Hunter's establishment of a black YWCA in Cleveland evoked much black criticism, especially from those who thought her success in raising white money sprang from her decision not to challenge the white YWCA. Yet most black women in this network used separate institution-building and antisegregation tactics at the same time. Nannie Burroughs, noted for her work as an educator promoting black Christian and vocational education, urged a boycott of the segregated public transportation system of Washington, D.C., in 1915.[72] (Burroughs was Hunter's model.) In the 1930s Burroughs denounced the Baptist leadership and resisted its control so strongly that that church almost cut off financial support for the National Training School for Girls that she had worked so hard and long to build. " 'Don't wait for deliverers,' she admonished her Listeners. . . . 'There are no deliverers. They're all dead. . . . The Negro must serve notice . . . that he is ready to die for justice.' " The Baptists relented, but Burroughs was still provoking white churchmen a decade later. In 1941 she canceled an engagement to speak for the National Christian Mission because the hierarchy insisted on precensoring her speech.[73] "The Negro is oppressed not because he is a Negro—but because he'll take it."[74] Bethune, who began her career as founder of a black college and was criticized by some for her apologias for segregated New Deal programs, was walking a picket line in front of Peoples Drugs in the District of Columbia, demanding jobs for colored youth, in 1939 even while still at the National Youth Administration.[75]

Moreover, the greater emphasis on civil rights never eclipsed uplift strategies. From the New Deal on, black government leaders were simultaneously trying to get more black women hired, protesting the passing over of qualified black applicants, and working to improve the qualifications and performance of black individuals. In 1943 Corinne Robinson of the Federal Public Housing Authority organized a skit, entitled *Lazy Daisy*, that called upon black government workers to shed slothful habits.[76] Nannie Burroughs in 1950 complained that the average Negro "gets up on the installment plan—never gets dressed fully until night, and by then he is completely disorganized." But that is because, she explained, "He really has nothing to get up to." To repeat: There was for these women no inherent contradiction between race uplift and antidiscrimination thinking.[77]

These black welfare activists were also militant in their critique of male supremacy, that militance, too, arising from their work for the welfare of the race. Deborah White has argued that the black women's clubs, more than the white ones, claimed leadership of the race for women. Charlotte Hawkins Brown declared her own work and thoughts were just as important as Booker T. Washington's.[78] Moreover, their ambitions were just as great as those of the white women: African Americans spoke of uplifting their race; white women described themselves as promoting the general welfare, but only because their focus on their own race was silent and understood. Whether or not these women should be called feminists (and they certainly did not call themselves that), they shared characteristics of the white group that has been called "social feminists"; their activism arose from efforts to advance the welfare of the whole public, not just women, in a context where, they believed, men did not or could not adequately meet the needs.[79]

Black and white women welfare reformers also differed in their thinking about women's economic role. The white women, with few exceptions, tended to view married women's economic dependence on men as desirable, and their employment as a misfortune; they accepted the family wage system and rarely expressed doubts about its effectiveness, let alone its justice. There was substantial variation within this network and change over time in its members' view of the family wage. There was also substantial contradiction. Beginning in the 1890s, women social investigators repeatedly demonstrated that the family wage did not work, because most men did not earn enough, because some men became disabled, and because others were irresponsible toward their families. Sybil Lipschultz has shown that between two key Supreme Court briefs written by women in the white network—for *Muller v. Oregon* in 1908, and for *Adkins v. Children's Hospital* in 1923—the grounds for protective legislation changed considerably. The brief for *Muller* privileged sacred motherhood and treated women's wage labor as an anomaly that should be prevented; the brief for *Adkins* argued from women's weaker position in the labor market and the need for government to intervene because it was not an anomaly.[80] Yet when the women's welfare network moved away from protective labor legislation toward public assistance or family policy, its recommendations presupposed that the desirable position for women was as domestic wives and mothers dependent on male earnings. The many unmarried women in the network viewed their own singleness as a class privilege and a natural condition for women active in the public sphere, and felt that remaining childless was an acceptable price for it. They were convinced that single motherhood and employment among mothers meant danger. They feared other than temporary relief to single mothers if no counseling or employment was offered, because they resisted establishing single-mother families as durable institutions.[81]

This is where the social work legacy is felt. The white reformers were accustomed to, and felt comfortable with, supervising. Long after Jane Addams with her environmentalist, democratic orientation became their hero, they continued to identify with the Charity Organization Society fear of "pauperizing" aid recipients by making it too easy for them and destroying their work incentive— and they feared that too much help to deserted women, for example, would do just this, let men off the hook. They did not share the belief of many contemporary European socialists that aid to single mothers should be a matter of right, of entitlement. Even Florence Kelley, herself a product of a European socialist education, defended the family wage as the appropriate goal of reform legislation. A divorced mother herself, she nevertheless lauded "the American tradition that men support their families, the wives throughout life," and lamented the "retrograde movement" that made the man no longer the breadwinner. The U.S. supporters of mothers' pensions envisioned aid as a gift to the deserving, and felt an unshakable responsibility to supervise single mothers and restore marriages and wives' dependency on husbands whenever possible. This "white" view was clearly a class perspective as well. A troubling question is unavoidable: Did these elite white women believe that independence was a privilege of wealth to which poor women ought not aspire?[82]

The black women reformers also held up breadwinner husbands and nonemployed wives as an ideal; black and white women spoke very similarly about the appropriate "spheres" of the two sexes, equally emphasizing motherhood.[83] The difference I am describing here is not diametric. Lucy D. Slowe, dean of women at Howard, believed that working mothers caused urban juvenile delinquency, and she called for campaigns to "build up public sentiment for paying heads of families wages sufficient to reduce the number of Negro women who must be employed away from home to the detriment of their children and of the community in general."[84] Personally, many of the married black activists had trouble prevailing upon their husbands to accept their activities, and some were persuaded to stay home. Ardie Halyard, recollecting the year 1920, described the process:

> Interviewer: How did your husband feel about your working?
> Halyard: At first, he thought it was very necessary. But afterwards, when he became able to support us, it was day in and day out, "When are you going to quit?"[85]

Dorothy Ferebee's husband could not tolerate her higher professional status. Inabel Lindsay promised her husband not to work for a year and then slid into a lifelong career by taking a job that she promised was only temporary.[86]

Mixed as it was, acceptance of married women's employment as a long-term and widespread necessity was much greater among blacks than among whites. Fanny Jackson Coppin had argued in the 1860s for women's economic independence from men, and women were active in creating employment bureaus. We see the greater black acknowledgment of single mothers in the high priority black women reformers gave to organizing kindergartens, then usually called day nurseries. In Chicago, Cleveland, Atlanta, Washington, and many other locations, daytime child-care facilities were among the earliest projects of women's groups. Terrell called establishing them her first goal, and her first publication was the printed version of a speech she had delivered at a

National American Woman Suffrage Association convention, which she sold for twenty-five cents a copy to help fund a kindergarten.[87] In poor urban white neighborhoods the need for child care may have been nearly as great, and some white activists created kindergartens, but proportionally far fewer. Virtually no northern white welfare reformers endorsed such programs as long-term or permanent services until the 1930s and 1940s; until then even the most progressive, such as Kelley, opposed them even as temporary solutions, fearing they would encourage the exploitation of women through low-wage labor.[88]

Black women decried the effects of the "double day" on poor women as much as did white reformers. They were outspoken in their criticism of men who failed to support families. Burroughs wrote, "Black men sing too much 'I Can't Give You Anything But Love, Baby.' "[89] But their solutions were different. From the beginning of her career, Burroughs understood that the great majority of black women would work all their lives, and she had to struggle against continuing resistance to accepting that fact to get her National Training School funded. And most black women activists projected a favorable view of working women and women's professional aspirations. Elizabeth Ross Haynes wrote with praise in 1922 of "the hope of an economic independence that will some day enable them [Negro women] to take their places in the ranks with other working women."[90] Sadie Alexander directly attacked the view that a married woman's ideal should be domesticity. She saw that in an industrial society the work of the housewife would be increasingly seen as "valueless consumption" and that women should "place themselves again among the producers of the world."[91]

This high regard for women's economic independence is also reflected in the important and prestigious role played by businesswomen in black welfare activity. One of the best-known and most revered women of this network was Maggie Lena Walker, the first woman bank president in the United States. Beginning work at the age of fourteen in the Independent Order of St. Luke, a mutual benefit society in Richmond, Virginia, that provided illness and burial insurance as well as social activity for blacks, in 1903 she established the St. Luke Penny Savings Bank. Walker became a very wealthy woman. She devoted a great deal of her money and her energy to welfare activity, working in the National Association for the Advancement of Colored People (NAACP), the National Association of Wage Earners, and local Richmond groups. In the context of African American experience, Walker's business was itself a civil rights and community welfare activity; many reformers, including prominently Bethune and Du Bois, believed that economic power was a key to black progress. The St. Luke enterprise stimulated black ownership and employment. They opened a black-owned department store in Richmond, thus threatening white economic power, and met intense opposition from white businessmen; indeed, a white Retail Dealers' Association was formed to crush the store. Several noteworthy businesswomen-activists got rich manufacturing cosmetics for blacks: the mother-daughter team of C. J. Walker and A'Lelia Walker (not related to Maggie Walker) of Pittsburgh and Indianapolis, and Annie Turnbo Malone of St. Louis. Reformer Jane Hunter was respected not only because of her welfare contributions but also because, though once penniless, she left an estate of over four hundred thousand dollars at her death; as was Sallie Wyatt Stewart, who left over one hundred thousand dollars in real estate.[92]

These factors suggest considerable differences in orientations (among the numerous similarities) between white and black women activists, although the preliminary stage of research on this topic requires us to consider the differences more as hypotheses than as conclusions. First, black women claimed leadership in looking after the welfare of their whole people more than did comparable whites. Because of this assumption of race responsibility, and because for blacks welfare was so indistinguishable from equal rights, black women emphasized programs for the unusually needy less, and universal provision more, than did white women. Perhaps in part because education was so important a part of the black women's program, and because education developed for whites in the United States as a universal public service, blacks' vision of welfare provision followed that model. Among whites, a relatively large middle class encouraged reformers to focus their helping efforts on others, and kept alive and relatively uncriticized the use of means and morals testing as a way of distributing help, continuing the division of the "deserving" from the "undeserving" poor. Among the black reformers, despite their relatively elite position, welfare appeared more closely connected with legal entitlements, not so different from the right to vote or to ride the public transportation system.[93] Had their ideas been integrated into the white women's thinking, one might ask, would means testing and humiliating invasions of privacy have been so uniformly accepted in programs such as Aid to Families with Dependent Children (AFDC), over which the white women's network had substantial influence?

Another difference is the black women's different attitude toward married women's employment. Most of the white women welfare reformers retained, until World War II, a distinctly head-in-the-sand and even somewhat contradictory attitude toward it: It was a misfortune, not good for women, children, or men; helping working mothers too much would tend to encourage it. Thus they were more concerned to help—sometimes to force—single mothers to stay home than to provide services that would help working mothers, such as child care or maternity leave. Black women were much more positive about women's employment. Despite their agreement that a male family wage was the most desirable arrangement, they doubted that married women's employment would soon disappear, or that it could be discouraged by making women and children suffer for it. In relation to this race difference, it is hard to ignore the different marital status of the majority of the women in the two groups: Most of the black women had themselves had the experience of combining public-sphere activism with marriage, if less often with children.[94] Perhaps the fact that most of the white women had dispensed with marriage and family, probably largely by choice, made them see the choice between family and work as an acceptable one, oblivious to the different conditions of such "choice" among poorer women.

Third, black and white welfare reformers differed considerably about how to protect women from sexual exploitation. Black welfare reformers were more concerned to combine the development of protective institutions for women with an antirape discourse. Among whites, rape was not an important topic of discussion during this period, and in protective work for women and girls, male sexuality was treated as natural and irrepressible. It is not clear how the black activists would have translated antirape consciousness into welfare policy had they had the power to do so, but it seems likely that they would have tried.

There were also substantial areas of shared emphases between white and black women. Both groups oriented much of their welfarist thinking to children, rarely questioning the unique responsibility of women for children's welfare. Neither group questioned sexual "purity" as an appropriate goal for unmarried women. Both groups used women's organizations as their main political and social channels. Both emphasized the promotion of other women into positions of leadership and jobs, confident that increasing the numbers of women at the "top" would benefit the public welfare. Both believed that improving the status of women was essential to advancing the community as a whole. Yet in the 1920s both groups were moving away from explicitly feminist discourse and muting their public criticisms of what we would today call sexism. Moreover, they shared many personal characteristics: low fertility, relatively high economic and social status, very high educational attainment.

These impressions raise more questions than they answer. I wonder, for example, what the relation was between the national leaders and local rank-and-file activists: Were the leaders "representative" of "constituencies"? One might hypothesize that local activists were more often married and less elite, since singleness and prosperity were probably among the factors that allowed women to travel and to function nationally. To what extent were the black/white differences functions of chronology? White reformers were, for instance, active in building educational institutions in the nineteenth century; by the early twentieth century the institutions they needed were in place. Further research might also make it possible to identify historical circumstances that contributed to these race differences, circumstances such as migration, changing demand for labor, and immigration and its closure.

I approached this evidence as part of a general inquiry into welfare thinking in the United States in this century. In this project I found, as have several other historians, that the white women's reform network—but not the black women's—had some influence on welfare policy, particularly in public assistance programs. I have tried to show here that this influence was as much colored by race as by gender. The white women's influence supported the legacies in our welfare programs of means testing, distinguishing the deserving from the undeserving, moral supervision of female welfare recipients, failing to criticize men's sexual behavior, and discouraging women' s employment. Black women's influence on federal welfare programs was negligible in this period; indeed, the leading federal programs—old-age insurance, unemployment compensation, workmen's compensation, and the various forms of public assistance such as AFDC—were expressly constructed to exclude blacks. It is not too late now, however, to benefit from a review of black women's welfare thought as we reconsider the kind of welfare state we want.[95]

Appendix

The women in these samples were selected because they were the leaders of national organizations that lobbied for welfare programs (such as the National Consumers' League, the National Child Labor Committee, the National Association of Colored Women, or the National Council of Negro Women), or government officials responsible for welfare programs who were also important advocates of such programs, or builders of private welfare institutions. Women who were simply employees of welfare programs or institutions were not included; for example, educators were included only when they were builders of educational institutions. For the blacks, this sample of welfare activists overlaps extensively with a sample one might construct of clubwomen and political activists, but not exactly; for example, Ida Wells-Barnett is not here because she must be categorized as primarily a civil rights, not a welfare, campaigner. Among the whites this sample overlaps somewhat with "social feminists," but those who were primarily labor organizers, for example, are not included.

Some of what appear to be race differences are differences of historical time and circumstance. Thus a study of women between, say, 1840 and 1890 would have included more white women educators (because white women were then working to build educational institutions, as black women were later) and more white married women (because the dip in the marriage rate among college-educated white women occurred later). Regional differences are also produced by this definition of the samples: a focus on local or state, as opposed to national, activity would have led to the inclusion of more western and southern women, for example; women in the Northeast and mid-Atlantic were more likely to be important in national politics because New York and Washington, D.C., were so often the headquarters of national activities

In order to simplify this list, only a single, general, major area of welfare activism is given for each woman. Because many women were active in several areas, the identifications given here do not necessarily conform to some figures in the text, for example, how many women were social workers or educators. The categories for the white and black women are not the same. Among the whites I gave more specific identifications to indicate the importance of several key arenas, such as the National Consumers' League and the United States Children's Bureau. To use such specific identifications among the black women would have been uninformative, since virtually all were, for example, active in the NACW. Furthermore, a few black women participated in such a variety of welfarist activity organized through the NACW, sororities, or other women's organizations that I could define their major sphere as simply club work

Table 13.1 Selected Black Women Welfare Activists

Name	Main Reform	Name	Main Reform
Alexander, Sadie Tanner Mossell	Civil rights	Jones, Verina Morton	Social work
Anthony, Lucille	Health	Laney, Lucy Craft	Education
Ayer, G. Elsie	Education	Lawton, Maria Coles Perkins	Education
Barnes, Margaret E.	Education	Lindsay, Inabel Burns	Education
Barrett, Janie Porter	Education	Lyle, Ethel Hedgeman	Club
Bearden, Bessye	Civil rights	Mallory, Arenia Cornelia	Education
Bethune, Mary McLeod	Education	Malone, Annie M. Turnbo	Education
Bowles, Eva Del Vakia	Social work	Marsh, Vivian Osborne	Club
Brawley, Ruth Merrill	Social work	Matthews, Victoria Earle	Social work
Brown, Charlotte Hawkins	Education	Mays, Sadie Gray	Social work
Brown, Sue M.	Education	McCrorey, Mary Jackson	Social work
Burroughs, Nannie Helen	Education	McDougald, G. Elsie Johnson	Education
Callis, Myra Colson	Employment	McKane, Alice Woodby	Health
Carter, Ezella	Education	Merritt, Emma Frances Grayson	Education
Gary, Alice Dugged	Child welfare	Nelson, Alice Ruth Dunbar	Social work
Cook, Coralie Franklin	Education	Pickens, Minnie McAlpin	Civil rights
Cooper, Anna Julia Haywood	Education	Randolph, Florence	Club
Davis, Belle	Health	Ridley, Florida Ruffin	Club
Davis, Elizabeth Lindsey	Club	Ruffin, Josephine St. Pierre	Club
Dickerson, Addie W.	Club	Rush, Gertrude E.	Social work
Faulkner, Georgia M. DeBaptiste	Social work	Saddler, Juanita Jane	Civil rights
Fauset, Crystal Bird	Civil rights	Snowden, Joanna Cecilia	Social work
Ferebee, Dorothy Boulding	Health	Stewart, Sallie Wyatt	Social work
Gaines, Irene McCoy	Civil rights	Talbert, Mary Barnett	Civil rights
Harris, Judia C. Jackson	Social work	Taylor, Isabelle Rachel	Social work
Haynes, Elizabeth Ross	Civil rights	Terrell, Mary Eliza Church	Civil rights
Hedgeman, Anna Arnold	Civil rights	Walker, A'Lelia	Social work
Height, Dorothy I.	Civil rights	Walker, Maggie Lena	Social work
Hope, Lugenia Burns	Social work	Warren, Sadie	Social work
Hunter, Jane Edna Harris	Social work	Washington, Margaret Murray	Education
Hunton, Addie D. Waites	Civil rights	Wells, Eva Thornton	Social work
Jackson, Juanita Elizabeth	Civil rights	Wheatley, Laura Frances	Education
Jeffries, Christina Armistead	Civil rights	Williams, Fannie Barrier	Social work
Johnson, Bertha La Branche	Education	Young, Mattie Dover	Social work
Johnson, Kathryn Magnolia	Civil rights		

Table 13.2 Selected White Women Welfare Activists

Name	Main Reform	Name	Main Reform
Abbott, Edith	Social work	Kelley, Florence Molthrop	Consumers' League
Abbott, Grace	Children's Bureau	Kellor' Frances(Alice)	Immigrant welfare
Addams, Jane	Settlement	Lathrop, Julia Clifford	Childrens' Bureau
Amidon, Beulah Elizabeth	Social work	Lenroot, Katherine Frederica	Children's Bureau
Anderson Mary	Women's Bureau	Loeb, Sophie Irene Simon	Mothers' pensions
Armstrong, Barbara Nachtrieb	Social Security	Lundberg, Emma Octavia	Children's Bureau
		Maher, Amy	Social Security
Armstrong, Florence Arzelia	Social Security	Mason, Lucy Randolph	Consumers'League
Beyer, Clara Mortenson	Children's Bureau	McDowell, Mary Eliza	Settlement
Blair, Emily Newell	Democratic Party	McMain, Eleanor Laura	Settlement
Bradford, Cornelia Foster	Settlement	Miller, Frieda Segelke	Women's Bureau
Breckinridge, Sophonisba Preston	Social work	Moskowitz, Belle Israels	Democratic Party
		Newman, Pauline	Women's Bureau
Brown, Josephine Chapin	Social work	Perkins, Frances	Social Security
Burns, Eveline Mabel	Social Security	Peterson, Agnes L.	Women's Bureau
Cannon, Ida Maud	Medical social work	Pidgeon, Mary Elizabeth	Women's Bureau
Colcord, Joanna	Social work	Rankin, Jeannette Pickering	Congresswoman
Coyle, Grace Longwood	Social work	Raushenbush, Elizabeth Brandeis	Unemployment
Crane, Caroline Bartlett	Sanitation reform		
Deardorff, Neva Ruth	Social work	Regan, Agnes Gertrude	Social work
Dewson, Mary W.(Molly)	Democratic Party	Richmond, Mary Ellen	Social work
Dinwiddie, Emily Wayland	Housing reform	Roche, Josephine Aspinall	Consumers' League
Dudley, Helena Stuart	Settlement	Roosevelt,(Anna) Eleanor	Social work
Dunn, Loula Friend	Social work	Schneiderman, Rose	Labor
Eastman, Crystal (Catherine),	Industrial health	Sherwin, Belle	Club
Einstein, Hannah Bachman	Mothers' pensions	Simkhovitch, Mary Kingsbury	Settlement
Eliot Martha May	Children's Bureau	Springer, Gertrude Hill	Social work
Ellickson, Katherine Pollak	Social Security	Switzer, Mary Elizabeth	Social work
Elliott, Harriet Wiseman	Democratic Party	Taft, (Julia) Jessie	Social work
Engle, Lavinia Margaret	Social Security	Thomas, M. Carey	Education
Evans, Elizabeth Glendower	Consumers' League	Towle, Charlotte Helen	Social work (academic)
Fuller, Minnie Ursula	Child welfare		
Goldmark, Josephine Clara	Consumers' League	Ville, Gertrude	Social work
Goldmark, Pauline Dorothea	Consumers' League	Van Kleeck, Mary Abby	Women's Bureau
Gordon, Jean Margaret	Consumers' League	Wald, Lillian D.	Settlement
Hall, Helen	Settlement	White, Sue Shelton	Democratic Party
Hamilton, (Amy) Gordon	Social work	Wood, Edith Elmer	Housing reform
Hamilton, Alice	Industrial health	Woodbury, Helen Laura Sumner	Children's Bureau
Hoey, Jane Margueretta	Social Security		
Iams, Lucy Virginia Dorsey	Housing reform	Woodward, Ellen Sullivan	Social work
Keller, Helen	Health reform		

Notes

For critical readings of this article in draft I am indebted to Lisa D. Brush, Nancy Cott, Elizabeth Higginbotham, Evelyn Brooks Higginbotham, Jacquelyn D. Hall, Stanlie James, Judith Walzer Leavitt, Gerda Lerner, Adolph Reed Jr., Anne Firor Scott, Kathryn Kish Sklar, Susan Smith, David Thelen, Susan Traverso, Bill Van Deburg, Deborah Gray White, and anonymous readers for *The Journal of American History.* I could not meet all the high standards of these scholars, many of whom took a great deal of time and care with this sprawling essay, but several of them not only offered valuable insights but also saved me from some errors resulting from my venture into a new field, and I am extremely grateful.

1. For a critique of gender bias in existing welfare scholarship and an explanation of the need for further research about the influence of gender, see the introduction to Linda Gordon, ed., *Women, the State, and Welfare* (Madison, 1990), 9–35.
2. One of the subjects of this study, Inabel Burns Lindsay, former dean of the Howard University School of Social Work, wrote a dissertation on this topic at the University of Pittsburgh in 1952, and published it as "Some Contributions of Negroes to Welfare Services, 1865–1900," *Journal of Negro Education* 25 (winter 1956): 15–24. Her publication did not spark others, however. A valuable collection of documents is Edyth L. Ross, ed., *Black Heritage in Social Welfare, 1860–1930* (Metuchen, 1978). Neither publication considers the particular role of women. For suggestions that black women participated more in organized activity than did white women, see Anne Firor Scott, "Most Invisible of All: Black Women's Voluntary Associations," *Journal of Southern History* 56 (February 1990): 5; and Ena L. Farley, "Caring and Sharing since World War I: The League of Women for Community Service—A Black Volunteer Organization in Boston," *Umoja* 1 (summer 1977): 1–12. Victoria Earle Matthews's surname is sometimes spelled "Matthews." Ralph E. Luker, "Missions, Institutional Churches, and Settlement Houses: The Black Experience, 1885–1910," *Journal of Negro History* 69 (summer/fall 1984): 101–13; Dorothy C. Salem, *To Better Our World: Black Women in Organized Reform, 1890–1920* (Brooklyn, 1990), 44–45; Sharon Harley, "Beyond the Classroom: The Organizational Lives of Black Female Educators in the District of Columbia, 1890–1930," *Journal of Negro Education* 51 (summer 1982): 262; Jacqueline Anne Rouse, *Lugenia Burns Hope. Black Southern Reformer* (Athens, Ga., 1989); Elizabeth Lasch, "Female Vanguard in Race Relations: 'Mother Power' and Blacks in the American Settlement House Movement," paper delivered at the Berkshire Conference on the History of Women, Rutgers University, June 1990 (in Linda Gordon's possession). Since the black settlements were often called missions and were often more religious than typical white settlements, historians have not clearly recognized the broad range of services they provided and the organizational/agitational centers they became.
3. On public social welfare programs attacking working-class self-help programs in England, see Stephen Yeo, "Working-Class Association, Private Capital, Welfare, and the State in the Late Nineteenth and Twentieth Centuries," in Noel Parry et al., eds., *Social Work, Welfare, and the State* (London, 1979). Self-help associations of the poor were probably as common in the United States as in England.
4. Charles L. Coon, "Public Taxation and Negro Schools," quoted in W. E. B. Du Bois, ed., *Efforts for Social Betterment among Negro Americans* (Atlanta, 1909), 29. The tax money spent on black schools was, of course, proportionally and absolutely far less than that spent on white.
5. Cynthia Neverdon-Morton, *Afro-American Women of the South and the Advancement of the Race, 1895–1925* (Knoxville, 1989), 79.
6. Louie D. Shivery, "The History of the Gate City Free Kindergarten Association" (from a 1936 Atlanta University M.A. thesis), in Ross, ed., *Black Heritage in Social Welfare,* 261–62.
7. Tera Hunter, " 'The Correct Thing': Charlotte Hawkins Brown and the Palmer Institute," *Southern Exposure* 11 (Sept./Oct. 1983): 37–43; Sandra N. Smith and Earle H. West, "Charlotte Hawkins Brown," *Journal of Negro Education* 51 (summer 1982): 191–206.
8. Darlene Clark Hine, " 'We Specialize in the Wholly Impossible': The Philanthropic Work of Black Women," in Kathleen D. McCarthy, ed., *Lady Bountiful Revisited: Women, Philanthropy, and Power* (New Brunswick, 1990), 84.
9. For help in gathering and analyzing biographical data, I am indebted to Lisa Brush, Bob Buchanan, Nancy Isenberg, Nancy MacLean, and Susan Traverso.
10. For a discussion of the definition of welfare, see Gordon, ed., *Women, the State, and Welfare,* 19–35; and Linda Gordon, "What Does Welfare Regulate?" *Social Research* 55 (winter 1988): 609–30. Child labor is an issue of both welfare and labor reform. I have included it here because, for so many women active in this cause, it seemed a logical, even inevitable, continuation of other child welfare activity; opposition to child labor was a much-used argument for mothers' pensions and Aid to Families with Dependent Children.

11. Although my focus is on welfare, a similar predominance of northern whites and southern blacks occurred among the national women's organizations. For example, Margaret (Mrs. Booker T.) Washington was the first southerner to be head of any national secular women's group—in her case, the National Association of Colored Women (NACW). See Darlene Rebecca Roth, "Matronage: Patterns in Women's Organizations, Atlanta, Georgia, 1890–1940" (Ph.D. diss., George Washington University, 1978), 81. On the integration of education into campaigns for welfare by African Americans, see, for example, Elizabeth Higginbotham, "Too Much to Ask: The Costs of Black Female Success," ch. 3, "Socialized for Survival" (in Elizabeth Higginbotham's possession).

12. Of the sixty-nine black women, five held governmental positions: Mary McLeod Bethune was director of the Division of Negro Affairs at the National Youth Administration under Franklin D. Roosevelt; Alice Cary was a traveling advisor to the Department of Labor during World War I; Crystal Fauset was a state legislator from Philadelphia and race relations advisor to the Works Progress Administration during the New Deal; Anna Hedgeman was assistant to the New York City commissioner of welfare in 1934. By contrast, 53 percent of the white women held federal government positions, and 58 percent held state positions.

13. Neverdon-Morton, *Afro-American Women of the South*, 191–236; Rosalyn Terborg-Penn, "Discrimination against Afro-American Women in the Woman's Movement, 1830–1920," in Sharon Harley and Rosalyn Terborg-Penn, eds., *The Afro-American Woman: Struggles and Images* (Port Washington, 1978), 17–27.

14. These white reformers were not more racist than the men engaged in similar activity and often less so. Eight white women from this sample were among the founding members of the National Association for the Advancement of Colored People (NAACP): Jane Addams, Florence Kelley, Julia Lathrop, Sophonisba Breckinridge, Mary McDowell, Lillian Wald, and Edith and Grace Abbott.

15. Steven J. Diner, "Chicago Social Workers and Blacks in the Progressive Era," *Social Service Review* 44 (December 1970): 393–410; Sandra M. Stehno, "Public Responsibility for Dependent Black Children: The Advocacy of Edith Abbott and Sophonisba Breckinridge," *Social Service Review* 62 (September 1988): 485–503; Gerda Lerner, *Black Women in White America: A Documentary History* (New York, 1972), 459; Salem, *To Better Our World*, 248–50; Jacquelyn Dowd Hall, *Revolt against Chivalry: Jessie Daniel Ames and the Women's Campaign against Lynching* (New York, 1979), 66.

16. Jacqueline Rouse, biographer of Lugenia Burns Hope of Atlanta, lists ten other black activists who, with Hope, formed a close southern network by about 1910—Bethune in Florida, Nettie Napier and M. L. Crosthwait in Tennessee, Jennie Moton and Margaret Washington in Alabama, Maggie Lena Walker in Virginia, Charlotte Hawkins Brown and Mary Jackson McCrorey in North Carolina, and Lucy Laney and Florence Hunt, also in Georgia. Rouse, *Lugenia Burns Hope*, 5. Rouse also identifies an overlapping group of black southern women educators—Hope, Hunt, McCrorey, Washington, Moton, and Bethune, with the addition of Marion B. Wilkinson of South Carolina State College; Julia A. Fountain of Morris Brown College in Atlanta; and A. Vera Davage of Clark College in Atlanta; ibid., 55. Paula Giddings, *In Search of Sisterhood: Delta Sigma Theta and the Challenge of the Black Sorority Movement* (New York, 1988). Darlene Rebecca Roth found that black clubwomen retained closer ties with their schools than did white clubwomen; Roth, "Matronage," 183. Hine, " 'We Specialize in the Wholly Impossible,' " 70–93; Fannie Barrier Williams, "Opportunities and Responsibilities of Colored Women," in James T. Haley, ed., *Afro-American Encyclopaedia; or, the Thoughts, Doings, and Sayings of the Race* (Nashville, 1896), 146–61.

17. Hine, " 'We Specialize in the Wholly Impossible,' " 83.

18. On the attempt to force Lucy D. Slowe to live in the women's dormitory, see the letters in folder 59, box 90–3, and folder 100, box 90–4, Lucy D. Slowe Papers (Moorland-Spingarn Research Center, Howard University, Washington, D.C.), esp. Coralie Franklin Cook et al. to Lucy D. Slowe, 9 June 1933, folder 9, box 90–2; Clayda J. Williams to Slowe, 23 August 1993; and Mary McLeod Bethune to Slowe, 23 November 1933, folder 28. Howard University was notorious for its discriminatory treatment of women, backward even in relation to other colleges at the time. On Howard, see Giddings, *In Search of Sisterhood*, 43.

19. For remarks made about Bethune at the 1938 National Conference of Negro Women White House Conference, praising her for not being satisfied to be the token black but struggling to increase black representation in the New Deal, see folder 4, box 1, series 4, 27–28, National Council of Negro Women Papers (Mary McLeod Bethune Museum and Archives, Washington, D.C.).

20. Tullia Brown Hamilton also found this focus on education predominant among the black women reformers she studied. Tullia Brown Hamilton, "The National Association of Colored Women, 1896–1920" (Ph.D. diss., Emory University, 1978), 45–46. Similarly Roth found that even among Atlanta's most elite organization of black women, the Chautauqua Circle, all had been employed as teachers; Roth, "Matronage," 181. Melinda Chateauvert found that women graduates of Washington, D.C.'s elite black Dunbar High School (who outnumbered males two to one around 1910) were overwhelmingly

likely to go on to the district's free Miner Teacher's College to become teachers; Melinda Chateauvert, "The Third Step: Anna Julia Cooper and Black Education in the District of Columbia," *Sage* 5, student supplement (1988): 7–13. For the same conclusion, see Carol O. Perkins, "The Pragmatic Idealism of Mary McLeod Bethune," *Sage* 5, student supplement (fall 1988): 30–36. W. E. B. Du Bois, ed., *Economic Cooperation among Negro Americans* (Atlanta, 1907), 80–88.

21. Du Bois, ed., *Efforts for Social Betterment among Negro Americans*, 65–77. For a northern local example, see Russell H. Davis, *Black Americans in Cleveland: From George Peake to Carl B. Stokes, 1796–1969* (Cleveland, 1972), 192.

22. Darlene Clark Hine, *Black Women in White: Racial Conflict and Cooperation in the Nursing Profession, 1890–1950* (Bloomington, 1989), xvii; Edward H. Beardsley, *A History of Neglect: Health Care for Blacks and Mill Workers in the Twentieth-Century South* (Knoxville, 1987), 101; Susan L. Smith, "The Black Women's Club Movement: Self-Improvement and Sisterhood, 1890–1915" (M.A. thesis, University of Wisconsin, Madison, 1986); Susan L. Smith, "Black Activism in Health Care, 1890–1950," paper delivered at the conference "Black Health: Historical Perspectives and Current Issues," University of Wisconsin, Madison, April 1990 (in Gordon's possession); Salem, *To Better Our World*, 74; Du Bois, *Economic Cooperation among Negro Americans*, 92–103; Du Bois, *Efforts for Social Betterment among Negro Americans*, 17–22; Scott, "Most Invisible of All," 6; Claude F. Jacobs, "Benevolent Societies of New Orleans Blacks during the Late Nineteenth and Early Twentieth Centuries," *Louisiana History* 29 (winter 1988): 21–33; Kathleen C. Berkeley, " 'Colored Ladies Also Contributed': Black Women's Activities from Benevolence to Social Welfare, 1866–1896," in Walter J. Fraser Jr., R. Frank Saunders Jr., and Jon L. Wakelyn, eds., *The Web of Southern Social Relations: Women, Family, and Education* (Athens, Ga., 1985), 181–203.

23. Colored YWCA, *Fifth and Sixth Years Report, May 1909–May 1911* (Washington, D.C., n.d.), 10–11 (Library, State Historical Society of Wisconsin, Madison); I am indebted to Bob Buchanan for this reference. Earline Rae Ferguson, "The Woman's Improvement Club of Indianapolis: Black Women Pioneers in Tuberculosis Work, 1903–1938," *Indiana Magazine of History* 84 (September 1988): 237–61; Darlene Clark Hine, *When the Truth Is Told: A History of Black Women's Culture and Community in Indiana, 1875–1950* (Indianapolis, 1981). The Atlanta Neighborhood Union also worked against tuberculosis. Cynthia Neverdon-Morton, "Self-Help Programs as Educative Activities of Black Women in the South, 1895–1925: Focus on Four Key Areas," *Journal of Negro Education* 51 (summer 1982): 207–21; Walter R. Chivers, "Neighborhood Union: An Effort of Community Organization," *Opportunity* 3 (June 1925): 178–79; Modjeska Simkins's work is briefly summarized in Beardsley, *History of Neglect*, 108–12. Smith, "Black Women's Club Movement"; Smith, "Black Activism in Health Care."

24. Fannie Barrier Williams, "Social Bonds in the 'Black Belt' of Chicago: Negro Organizations and the New Spirit Pervading Them," *Charities*, October 7, 1905: 40–44; Scott, "Most Invisible of All," 8.

25. The Young Women's Christian Association (YWCA) was segregated, and these activists fought that segregation. Nevertheless, as Dorothy Height points out forcefully in her interview, "It was unmatched by any other major group drawn from the major white population" in the opportunities it offered to black women; Dorothy Height interview by Polly Cowan, 11 February 1974–6 November 1976, 173, Black Women Oral History Project (Schlesinger Library, Radcliffe College, Cambridge, Mass.). See also descriptions of YWCA opportunities in Frankie V. Adams interview by Gay Francine Banks, 26 and 28 April 1977, 9, (Schlesinger Library); Salem, *To Better Our World*, 46.

26. I could not identify birthplaces for all the women, and those with missing information include some likely to have been southern-born.

27. Others have reached similar conclusions. See Marilyn Dell Brady, "Kansas Federation of Colored Women's Clubs, 1900–1930," *Kansas History* 9 (spring 1986): 19–30; Linda Marie Perkins, *Black Feminism and "Race Uplift," 1890–1900* (Cambridge, Mass., 1981), Bunting Institute Working Paper (ERIC microfiche ED 221445), 4; Salem, *To Better Our World*, 67.

28. In the black population in general, 7 percent of all married women born between 1840 and 1859 were childless, and 28 percent of those born between 1900 and 1919 were childless. U.S. Department of Commerce, Bureau of the Census, *Historical Statistics of the United States: Colonial Times to 1970* (Washington, 1975), 1:53.

29. Black women's overall fertility was declining rapidly in this period, falling by one-third between 1880 and 1910, and southern black women had fewer children than southern white women. Some of this low fertility was attributable to poor health and nutrition. Moreover, the women in this network were virtually all urban, and the fertility of urban black woman was only half that of rural black women. See Jacqueline Jones, *Labor of Love, Labor of Sorrow: Black Women, Work, and the Family from Slavery to the Present* (New York, 1985), 122–23. Supporting my view of black women's use of birth control, see Jessie M. Rodrique, "The Black Community and the Birth-Control Movement," in Christina Simmons, eds., *Passion and Power: Sexuality in History* (Philadelphia, 1989), 138–54. This article offers a convincing criticism of my own earlier work, which overstated black hostility to birth control campaigns because

of their genocidal implications. I also learned from Elizabeth Lasch's unpublished paper that Margaret Murray Washington's settlement at Tuskegee offered a course of study on sex hygiene that included birth control; this suggests the need for further research on black women's advocacy of birth control. Lasch, "Female Vanguard in Race Relations," 4.

30. I was able to identify 25 percent (seventeen) with prosperous parents.

31. Marilyn Dell Brady found the same marital patterns for black women reformers in her study of Kansas. Brady, "Kansas Federation of Colored Women's Clubs, 1900–1930," 19–30. The major figures she studied were married and supported by their husbands.

32. Anna Arnold Hedgeman, *The Trumpet Sounds: A Memoir of Negro Leadership* (New York, 1964), 25, 74; Farley, "Caring and Sharing since World War I," 317–37. Hamilton, "National Association of Colored Women," 41; Paula Giddings, *When and Where I Enter: The Impact of Black Women on Race and Sex in America* (New York, 1984), 108; Berkeley, " 'Colored Ladies Also Contributed,' " 185–86.

33. For corroboration on the employment of well-to-do black women, see Roth, "Matronage," 180–81. On black women's socialization toward employment, see Inabel Burns Lindsay interview by Marcia Greenlee, 20 May–7 June 1977, 4, 40, Black Women Oral History Project.

34. Charles S. Johnson, *The Negro College Graduate* (Chapel Hill, 1938), 18–20; U.S. Department of Commerce, Bureau of the Census, *The Social and Economic Status of the Black Population in the United States: An Historical View, 1790–1978* (Washington, 1979), 93.

35. Alfreda Duster interview by Greenlee, 8–9 March 1978, 9, Black Women Oral History Project; Hedgeman, *Trumpet Sounds*, 3–28.

36. In my comments on the class attitudes of black women welfare reformers, I am mainly indebted to the interpretations of Deborah Gray White, especially in Deborah Gray White, "Fettered Sisterhood; Class and Classism in Early Twentieth Century Black Women's History," paper delivered at the annual meeting of the American Studies Association, Toronto, November 1989 (in Gordon's possession). See also Williams, "Social Bonds in the 'Black Belt' of Chicago." On black discrimination against relatively dark-skinned women, see, for example, Nannie Burroughs, "Not Color but Character," *Voice of the Negro* 1 (July 1904): 277–79; Duster interview, 52; Giddings, *In Search of Sisterhood*, 105; Perkins, *Black Feminism and "Race Uplift,"* 4; and Nancy Weiss, *Farewell to the Party of Lincoln: Black Politics in the Age of FDR* (Princeton, 1983), 139. Berkeley argues against the importance of class differences in the NACW, but I found them substantial. See Berkeley, " 'Colored Ladies Also Contributed.' " On class development among blacks, see August Meier and David Lewis, "History of the Negro Upper Class in Atlanta, Georgia, 1890–1958," *Journal of Negro Education* 28 (spring 1959): 128–39.

37. Duster interview, 37.

38. Philip S. Foner, ed., *The Voice of Black America: Major Speeches by Negroes in the United States, 1797–1971* (New York, 1972), 462.

39. Hedgeman, *Trumpet Sounds*, 1–28; Chateauvert, "The Third Step"; Height interview, 40; Caroline Ware interview by Susan Ware, 27–29 January 1982, 94, Women in Federal Government Oral Histories (Schlesinger Library).

40. Robert Alan Goldberg, *Hooded Empire: The Ku Klux Klan in Colorado* (Urbana, 1981), vii.

41. Of the white women reformers, 78 percent had been social workers at some rime; 68 percent had social work as their major reform area. I checked to see if the social work background could have been a characteristic of the less prominent women, but this was not the case. The most prominent two-thirds of the group were even more frequently social workers (84 percent).

42. Stanley Wenocur and Michael Reisch, *From Charity to Enterprise: The Development of American Social Work in a Market Economy* (Urbana, 1989), p. 33.

43. Of the white women, 18 percent had held academic jobs at one time; 9 percent were mainly employed as educators. For only 1 percent was education their major reform area.

44. Lillian Wald, *Windows on Henry Street* (Boston, 1934); Mary Kingsbury Simkhovitch, *Neighborhood: Story of Greenwich House* (New York, 1938); William W. Bremer, *Depression Winters: New York Social Workers and the New Deal* (Philadelphia, 1984); George Martin, *Madame Secretary: Frances Perkins* (Boston, 1976), 134–35; Elisabeth Israels Perry, "Training for Public Life: ER and Women's Political Networks in the 1920s," in Joan Hoff-Wilson and Marjorie Lightman, eds., *Without Precedent: The Life and Career of Eleanor Roosevelt* (Bloomington, 1984), 30.

45. Elisabeth Israels Perry, *Belle Moskowitz: Feminine Politics and the Exercise of Power in the Age of Alfred E. Smith* (New York, 1987), 76–77; Walter Trattner, "Theodore Roosevelt, Social Workers, and the Election of 1912: A Note," *Mid-America* 50 (January 1968): 64–69. On pre-woman-suffrage women's electoral participation, see, for example, S. Sara Monoson, "The Lady and the Tiger: Women's Electoral Activism in New York City before Suffrage," *Journal of Women's History* 2 (fall 1990): 100–135.

46. I thank Anne Firor Scott for pointing out this similarity to me.

47. On settlement house relationships, see Virginia Kemp Fish, "The Hull House Circle: Women's

Friendships and Achievements," in Janet Sharistanian, ed., *Gender, Ideology, and Action: Historical Perspectives on Women's Public Lives* (Westport, Conn., 1986); and Kathryn Kish Sklar, "Hull House in the 1890s: A Community of Women Reformers," *Signs* 10 (summer 1985): 658–77. Lela B. Costin, *Two Sisters for Social Justice: A Biography of Grace and Edith Abbott* (Urbana, 1983), 38–40; Martin, *Madame Secretary*, 233.

48. See, for example, Ethel Erickson to Mary Anderson, 14 July 1938; Anderson to Erickson, 4 August 1938; Erickson to Anderson, 29 July 1942; Anderson to Erickson, 1 August 1942, box 1263, Women's Bureau Papers, RG 86 (National Archives).

49. Darlene Clark Hine, "Rape and the Inner Lives of Black Women in the Middle West: Preliminary Thoughts on the Culture of Dissemblance," in Vicki L. Ruiz and Ellen Carol DuBois, eds., *Unequal Sisters: A Multicultural Reader in U.S. Women's History*, 2nd ed. (New York: Routledge, 1994), 342–47; Deborah Gray White, "Mining the Forgotten: Manuscript Sources for Black Women's History," *Journal of American History* 74 (June 1987): 237–42; Elsa Barkley Brown, comment at Berkshire Conference on the History of Women, 1990.

50. The singleness of the white women reformers was characteristic of other women of their race, class, and education in this period. In 1890, for example, over half of all women doctors were single. Of women earning Ph.D.'s between 1877 and 1924, three-fourths remained single. As late as 1920, only 12 percent of all professional women were married. See, for example, Carl N. Degler, *At Odds: Women and the Family in America from the Revolution to the Present* (New York, 1980), 385. Roth corroborates the significance of marital breaks in the lives of activists, finding that civically active white women in Atlanta in this period were more likely to be widows. Roth, "Matronage," 182. On Boston marriages, see Micaela di Leonardo, "Warrior Virgins and Boston Marriages: Spinsterhood in History and Culture," *Feminist Issues* 5 (fall 1985): 47–68.

51. Mrs. Tilden Frank Phillips, memoir, 22 February, 26 February 1933, folder 22, Edith Rockwood Papers (Schlesinger Library); will of Edith Rockwood, folder 20, ibid.

52. Blanche Wiesen Cook, "The Historical Denial of Lesbianism," *Radical History Review* 20 (spring/summer 1979): 60–65. For quotations from a (hostile) contemporary source, see James Johnson, "The Role of Women in the Founding of the United States Children's Bureau," in Carol V. R. George, ed., *"Remember the Ladies": New Perspectives on Women in American History: Essays in Honor of Nelson Manfred Blake* (Syracuse, 1975), 191.

53. Cook, "Historical Denial of Lesbianism"; Blanche Wiesen Cook, "Female Support Networks and Political Activism: Lillian Wald, Crystal Eastman, Emma Goldman," in Nancy F. Cott and Elizabeth H. Pleck, eds., *A Heritage of Her Own* (New York, 1979), 412–44; Estelle B. Freedman, "Separatism as Strategy," *Feminist Studies* 5 (fall 1979): 512–29.

54. Slowe lived with Mary Burrill, who is treated as a partner in letters to and from Slowe and in letters of condolence to Burrill after Slowe's death in 1937. See letters in box 90–1, Slowe Papers. Height interview, 52.

55. Duster interview, 11; Wendy Beth Posner, "Charlotte Towle: A Biography" (Ph.D. diss., University of Chicago School of Social Service Administration, 1986), 47, 77–78.

56. Mary Dewson to Clara Beyer, 12 October 1931, folder 40, box 2, Clara Beyer Papers (Schlesinger Library); Ware interview, 40–42; Janice Andrews, "Role of Female Social Workers in the Second Generation: Leaders or Followers," 1989 (in Gordon's possession). The possibility of combining marriage and career had been debated intensely starting in the 1920s, but it was in the 1930s that the change began to be evident. See Lois Scharf, *To Work and to Wed: Female Employment, Feminism, and the Great Depression* (Westport, 1980).

57. Florence Kelley to Anderson, 28 June 1920; Anderson to Dewson, 23 August 1920; Anderson to Dewson, 23 October 1922; Dewson to Anderson, 1 June 1923; all box 843, Women's Bureau Papers. Anderson to Mary Van Kleeck, 8 January 1937, folder 22, box 1, Mary Anderson Papers (Schlesinger Library); Judith Scalander, "Feminist against Feminist: The First Phase of the Equal Rights Amendment Debate, 1923–1963," *South Atlantic Quarterly* 81 (spring 1982): 154–56. Mary R. Beard participated in the early meeting to draft the charter but ultimately did not sign it. I thank Nancy Cott for clarification on this point.

58. Susan Ware, *Beyond Suffrage: Woman in the New Deal* (Cambridge, Mass., 1981), 156–57.

59. Vivien Hart, "Watch What We Do: Women Administrators and the Implementation of Minimum Wage Policy, Washington, D.C., 1918–1923," paper delivered at the Berkshire Conference on the History of Women, 1990, 31 (in Gordon's possession).

60. Gordon, "What Does Welfare Regulate?"; Barbara Nelson, "The Origins of the Two-Channel Welfare State: Workmen's Compensation and Mothers' Aid," in Gordon, ed., *Women, the State, and Welfare*, 123–57.

61. Brady, "Kansas Federation of Colored Women's Clubs"; Lindsay, "Some Contributions of Negroes to

Welfare Services," 15–24; Constance Greene, *The Secret City: A History of Race Relations in the Nation's Capital* (Princeton, 1967), 144–46; Neverdon-Morton, *Afro-American Women of the South*; Neverdon-Morton, "Self-Help Programs as Educative Activities of Black Women in the South"; Farley, "Caring and Sharing since World War I," esp. 4.

62. Mary Church Terrell, "Club Work among Women," *New York Age*, January 4, 1900, p. 1. Although this speech was given in 1900, another given in 1928 uses virtually the same rhetoric. See Mary Church Terrell, "Progress and Problems of Colored Women," *Boston Evening Transcript*, December 15, 1928, folder 132, box 102–4, Mary Church Terrell Papers (Moorland-Spingarn Research Collection).

63. For just a few examples, see Elise Johnson McDougald, "The Task of Negro Womanhood," in *The New Negro: An Interpretation*, ed. Alain Locke (New York, 1925), pp. 369–84; Mary Church Terrell, "Up-To-Date," *Norfolk Journal and Guide*, November 3, 1927, folder W, box 102–2, Terrell Papers; Williams, "Opportunities and Responsibilities of Colored Women"; and many speeches by Slowe, box 90–6, Slowe Papers. See also Perkins, *Black Feminism and "Race Uplift."*

64. Williams, "Opportunities and Responsibilities of Colored Women," p. 150.

65. White, "Fettered Sisterhood"; Hine, "Rape and the Inner Lives of Black Women in the Middle West." White reformers rhetoric about protecting women named prostitution, not rape, as the problem. See Ellen DuBois and Linda Gordon, "Seeking Ecstasy on the Battlefield: Nineteenth-Century Feminist Views of Sexuality," *Feminist Studies* 9 (spring 1983): 7–25; Lillian Wald, "The Immigrant Young Girl," in *Proceedings of the National Conference of Charities and Correction at the Thirty-sixth Annual Session Held in the City of Buffalo, N.Y., June 9th to 16th, 1909* (Fort Wayne, n.d.), 264. Jane Edna Hunter, *A Nickel and a Prayer* (Cleveland, 1940); Marilyn Dell Brady, "Organizing Afro-American Girls' Clubs in Kansas in the 1920s," *Frontiers* 9, 2 (1987): 69–73; Greene, *Secret City*, 144–46; Salem, *To Better Our World*, 44–46; Scott, "Most Invisible of All," 15; Monroe N. Work, "Problems of Negro Urban Welfare" (from *Southern Workman*, January 1924) in Ross, ed., *Black Heritage in Social Welfare*, 383–84; "Foreword" (from *Bulletin of National League on Urban Conditions among Negroes*, Report 1912–13), ibid., 241; Guichard Parris and Lester Brooks, *Blacks in the City: A History of the National Urban League* (Boston, 1971), 3–10; Hine, " 'We Specialize in the Wholly Impossible,' " 73.

66. Evelyn Brooks, "Religion, Politics, and Gender: The Leadership of Nannie Helen Burroughs," *Journal of Religious Thought* 44 (winter/spring 1988): 7–22; Cheryl Townsend Gilkes, "Building in Many Places: Multiple Commitments and Ideologies in Black Women's Community Work," in Ann Bookman and Sandra Morgen, eds., *Women and the Politics of Empowerment* (Philadelphia, 1988), 53–76.

67. White, "Fettered Sisterhood," 5.

68. Mrs. N. F. Mossell, *The Work of the Afro-American Woman* (Sharon Harley Freeport, 1971 [1894]), 32. Ida Wells-Barnett is the woman most associated with this challenge to Booker T. Washington, but she was not included in this sample because she was primarily a civil rights, rather than a welfare, activist. On Anna J. Cooper, see Sharon Harley, "Anna J. Cooper: A Voice for Black Women," in Sharon Harley and Rosalyn Terborg-Penn, eds., *Afro-American Woman*, 87–96; and Louise Daniel Hutchinson, *Anna J. Cooper: A Voice from the South* (Washington, 1981). On Mary Church Terrell, see Dorothy Sterling, *Black Foremothers* (New York, 1979); and Elliott Rudwick, *W.E.B. Du Bois: Voice of the Black Protest Movement* (Urbana, 1982), 129–30.

69. Williams, "Opportunities and Responsibilities of Colored Women," 157.

70. Story told in Lerner, *Black Women*, 375–76. On the complexity of Brown's attitudes, see Tera Hunter, " 'The Correct Thing' "; and Smith and West, "Charlotte Hawkins Brown."

71. Anna J. Cooper to A. G. Comings. 1 October Rosalyn Terborg-Penn, 1928, folder 5, box 32–1, Anna J. Cooper Papers (Moorland-Spingarn Research Collection). Cooper was another one of those figures who tirelessly challenged racism even in its apparently small or accidental varieties. For example, she wrote to the *Atlantic Monthly* complaining about an article mentioning a poor Negro with lice. *Atlantic Monthly* editors to Cooper, 31 January 1935, folder 5, box 23–1, ibid.

72. Hine, " 'We Specialize in the Wholly Impossible' "; Evelyn Brooks Barnett, "Nannie Burroughs and the Education of Black Women," in Sharon Harley and Rosalyn Terborg-Penn, eds., *Afro-American Woman*, 97–108; Brooks, "Religion, Politics, and Gender," 12.

73. Burroughs, speech at Bethel AME Church in Baltimore, reported in "Baptists May Oust Nannie H. Burroughs," *Chicago Defender*, 9 September 1939; "Nannie Burroughs Refuses to Speak on National Christian Mission," *Pittsburgh Courier*, 1 February 1941, Burroughs Vertical File (Moorland-Spingarn Research Collection).

74. Burroughs's 1943 remark is quoted in Lerner, *Black Women*, 552.

75. On criticism of Bethune, see B. Joyce Ross, "Mary McLeod Bethune and the National Youth Administration: A Case Study of Power Relationships in the Black Cabinet of Franklin D. Roosevelt," *Journal of Negro History* 60 (January 1975): 1–28. On her defense of the New Deal, see Mary McLeod Bethune, "I'll Never Turn Back No More!' " *Opportunity* 16 (November 1938): 324–26; "Mrs Bethune Praises NYA Courses as 'Bright Ray of Hope for Rural Negroes,' " *Black Dispatch*, 1 May 1937; Bethune,

Vertical File (Moorland-Spingarn Research Collection); "Mrs Bethune Hails Achievements of the New Deal," *Washington Tribune*, 12 November 1935, ibid.; "55,000 Aided by the NYA Program, Says Dr. Bethune," *Washington Tribune*, 23 April 1938, ibid. On her picketing, see photo and caption, "Give US More Jobs," *Washington Afro-American*, 12 August 1939, ibid.

76. Corinne Robinson to Jeanetta Welch Brown, with script of *Lazy Daisy* enclosed, 22 September 1943, folder 274, box 17, series 5, National Council of Negro Women Papers.

77. Era Bell Thompson, "A Message from a Mahogany Blond," *Negro Digest* 9 (July 1950): 31.

78. White, "Fettered Sisterhood"; Smith and West, "Charlotte Hawkins Brown," 199.

79. I am in sympathy with Cott's critique of the use of the concept "social feminism," but it remains descriptive of a widely understood phenomenon, and we have as yet no terms to substitute. Nancy F. Cott, "What's in a Name? The Limits of 'Social Feminism'; or, Expanding the Vocabulary of Women's History," *Journal of American History* 76 (December 1989): 809–29.

80. Sybil Lipschultz, "Social Feminism and Legal Discourse: 1908–1923," *Yale Journal of Law and Feminism* 2 (Fall 1989): 131–60.

81. Linda Gordon, *Heroes of Their Own Lives: The Politics and History of Family Violence, Boston, 1880–1960* (New York, 1988), 82–115.

82. Florence Kelley, "Minimum-Wage Laws," *Journal of Political Economy* 20 (December 1912): 1003.

83. See, for examples, Roth, "Matronage," 87; Brady, "Kansas Federation of Colored Women's Clubs," 19–31; and Marilyn Dell Brady, "Organizing Afro-American Girls' Clubs in Kansas in the 1920s."

84. Lucy D. Slowe, "Some Problems of Colored Women and Girls in the Urban Process" [probably 1930s], folder 143, box 90–6, Slowe Papers.

85. Ardie Clark Halyard interview by Greenlee, 24, 25 August 1978, transcript, p. 15, Black Women Oral History Project.

86. Dorothy Boulding Ferebee interview by Merze Tate, 28–31 December 1979, transcript, p. 9, ibid.; Lindsay interview, 4–5.

87. Sharon Harley, "For the Good of Family and Race: Gender, Work, and Domestic Roles in the Black Community, 1880–1930," *Signs* 15 (winter 1990): 336–49; Helen A. Cook, "The Work of the Woman's League, Washington, D.C.," in W. E. B. Du Bois, ed., *Some Efforts of American Negroes for Their Own Social Betterment*, (Atlanta, 1898), 57; Du Bois, ed., *Efforts for Social Betterment among Negro Americans*, 119–20, 126–27; Giddings, *When and Where I Enter*, 100–101; Hine, *When the Truth Is Told*, 52–54; Ross, ed. *Black Heritage in Social Welfare*, 233–34; Perkins, *Black Feminism and "Race Uplift"*, 7–8; Allan Spear, *Black Chicago: The Making of a Ghetto, 1890–1920* (Chicago, 1967), 102; Stehno, "Public Responsibility for Dependent Black Children"; Harley, "Beyond the Classroom," 254–65; Rouse, *Lugenia Burns Hope*, 28; Davis, *Black Americans in Cleveland*, 195; Stetson, "Black Feminism in Indiana"; Greene, *Secret City*, 144–46; Mary Church Terrell, *A Colored Woman in a White World* (Washington, 1940), 153.

88. The white reformers in the first decades of the twentieth century were campaigning hard for mothers' pensions and feared that daytime child care would be used as an alternative, forcing mothers into poor jobs. But they continued to see mothers' employment as a misfortune. For example, Florence Kelley in 1909 argued that day nurseries should be acceptable only for temporary emergencies and that the social cost of mothers' employment was always too high. "A friend of mine has conceived the monstrous idea of having a night nursery to which women so employed might send their children. And this idea was seriously described in so modern a publication as Charities and the Commons . . . without a word of editorial denunciation." Florence Kelley, "The Family and the Woman's Wage," *Proceedings of the National Conference of Charities and Correction . . .* 1909, 118–21.

89. Giddings, *When and Where I Enter*, 205.

90. Barnett, "Nannie Burroughs and the Education of Black Women." For Elizabeth Ross Haynes's statement of 1922, see Lerner, *Black Women*, 260.

91. Giddings, *When and Where I Enter*, 196.

92. My discussion of Walker is based on Elsa Barkley Brown, "Womanist Consciousness: Maggie Lena Walker and the Independent Order of Saint Luke," *Signs* 14 (spring 1989): 610–33. On the significance of black banks and other businesses, see also Du Bois, *Economic Cooperation Among Negro Americans*, 103–81. Hedgeman, *Trumpet Sounds*, 47–48; *Who's Who in Colored America* (New York, 1927), 209; Hine, " 'We Specialize in the Wholly Impossible,' " 86; Hine, *When the Truth Is Told*, 51.

93. This orientation toward entitlement was evident *despite* the southern state governments' relatively smaller size, and it casts doubt on state capacity explanations for reformers' strategies.

94. Although many of the African American women leaders were legally married, it does not necessarily follow that they lived their daily lives in close partnerships with their husbands or carried much domestic labor responsibility.

95. Gordon, "What Does Welfare Regulate?"

14

Migrations and Destinations

Reflections on the Histories of U.S. Immigrant Women

Donna R. Gabaccia and Vicki L. Ruiz

In the 1975 motion picture *Hester Street*, Carol Kane earned an Oscar nomination for her role as Gitl, a young Eastern European Jewish matron who struggled to make a place for herself in New York's Lower East Side and in the process win back the affections of her thoroughly Americanized husband, Jake. Based on a story by Abraham Cahan, the founder of *The Jewish Daily Forward*, the film captured everyday life and tensions over acculturation and gendered expectations set against the backdrop of a gritty, turn-of-the-twentieth-century New York neighborhood.[1] Feature films that portray immigration through women's eyes are few, yet even the critically-acclaimed *Hester Street* was shown primarily at art house venues. At the time of its opening, *Hester Street's* main themes—accommodation, Americanization, wage work, commercialized leisure, and family—were becoming the focus of study for an emerging new generation of feminist historians. But like the motion picture itself, this scholarship on gender and migration seemed to attract limited notice.

In 1991, co-author Donna Gabaccia asked readers of the *Journal of American Ethnic History* to ponder why the by-then large and still growing literature on immigrant women in the United States had had such limited recognition and impact on both immigration and women's history. She argued that studies of immigrant women, like many immigrant women themselves, seemed "nowhere at home."[2] In this essay, we re-visit that question, offering both a more positive assessment of the continued vigor of scholarship on immigrant women in the United States and a preliminary assessment of the research that has appeared in the intervening fifteen years. Rather than attempt to summarize both gendered and women-centered studies, we focus on studies on immigrant women in the United States written by historians (and a few historically minded social scientists). We acknowledge the transnational approaches that have sought to "internationalize" U.S. history while also identifying four themes that we believe best characterize recent historical work on immigrant women in the United States—making home, community building, memory, and citizenship. These themes that have emerged in studies of women across many different backgrounds might in the near future provide a firm basis for satisfying works of synthesis.

Transnational Analysis

The movie *Hester Street* begins with Gitl's arrival in Ellis Island. Most U.S. historians, too, have concentrated on immigrants once they land on American soil—their focus is decidedly on the peopling of America, not on human mobility. During the early 1990s, scholars began to assert that such narratives failed to capture the experiences of contemporary immigrants whose lives could not be articulated solely within national boundaries. Feminist anthropologists interested in migration to the United States from the Caribbean were among the first to theorize transnationalism as both a new methodology for the study of immigration and as an apt descriptor for migrants who maintained as a matter of course communication, social ties, and identities between more than one nation.[3]

Of course, even before theories of transnationalism were elaborated, some historians of immigration had voiced incisive critiques of assimilationist paradigms. Indeed, historians of immigration from Theodore Blegen in the 1920s to Frank Thistlethwaite in the 1960s had argued for analysis of migration as a form of lived connection between nations. In his benchmark 1964 essay in *The Journal of American History*, Rudolph Vecoli soundly rejected Oscar Handlin's portraits of immigrants as uprooted.[4] High rates of return and of transience among earlier migrants had become well known already by the 1980s.

Nevertheless, analysis of migrants' transnational lives definitely increased during the 1990s as discussions of globalization became ever more heated. Some of the most extensive work on immigrant women from a transnational gaze has focused on Italians, a group that scattered widely around the world for over a century; studies of "Italians everywhere" helped create models for scholars to problematize, to refine, and to place in comparative perspective the growing numbers of studies on U.S. immigrant women. Italianists, for example, studied women who did not become subjects of scrutiny by traditional immigration historians either because the women had remained in Italy while the men migrated or because they had journeyed to other European or Latin American nations as single parents, or in the company of other women, or as family members. Many of the essays in Donna Gabaccia's and Franca Iacovetta's *Women, Gender and Transnational Lives* also trace the movement of ideas of female emancipation and revolutionary activism through anarchist and anarcho-syndicalist migratory networks, linking women's activism in cities as scattered as Buenos Aires, New York, and the mining towns of Illinois.[5]

Transnational analysis reveals how migration transforms as well as connects the United States and other countries around the world. Much scholarship has focused on the recruitment abroad of men's labor for heavy industry, transportation, and agriculture—from forging steel in Pittsburgh to repairing railroad tracks near Topeka to picking cotton outside of Fresno.[6] But under what conditions have women been recruited transnationally for their labor? Catherine Ceniza Choy's study of nurses, *Empire of Care*, elucidates how women's migration has had long-term consequences in both sending and receiving societies. Although Filipina nurses were recruited to alleviate an American "shortage" of nurses, in fact the ratios of nurses per residents in the United States were already six to seven times higher than they were in the Philippines.[7]

In short, transnational lives and consequences were scarcely new in the 1990s, even though new forms of communications and transportation technologies have made connections easier and more widespread than in the past. It seems unlikely, however, that many U.S. immigration historians will choose to explore world history, to expand their geographies of research, to master new languages, and to delve into archives beyond the United States. Throughout the 1990s, the majority of scholars preferred to remain closer to their training and teaching in American history and often turned their attention to micro-level studies (e.g., of specific neighborhoods and/or work spaces). An awareness of the transnational frame around such local places, however, forced historians of immigrant women to problematize even the meaning of home among mobile people who arrive as immigrants in the United States.

Where Is Home?

The task for a woman, like Gitl in *Hester Street*, was as much to make a home as to find one. This theme is cogently captured in Yen Le Espiritu's seminal book, *Home Bound: Filipino American*

Lives Across Cultures, Communities, and Countries. In analyzing the diachronous images of home among Filipino immigrants and their families, she describes home making as "the processes by which diverse subjects imagine and make themselves at home in various geographic locations." Similarly, Donna Gabaccia notes elements of both permanence and transience within Italian communities over a century ago as individuals and households engaged in shifting transnational journeys.[8] More than a metaphor, making home also required enormous investments of women's physical and emotional labor, as Suzanne Sinke's study of nineteenth-century Dutch immigrant women confirms.[9]

Building homes could require rather than negate transnational connections. Lili M. Kim's study of Korean picture brides to Hawaii makes clear the transnational bonds women cherished, especially in their fund-raising efforts for the cause of Korean independence. Some immigrant women reached beyond their racial/ethnic communities. Rumi Yasutake's *Transnational Women's Activism* recounts how women in Japan formed their own chapters of the Women's Christian Temperance Union. When some of these club women journeyed east, they joined their Euro-American allies in proselytizing for the cause of temperance in addition to offering social services for their compatriots in California.[10]

Sorting through these varied narrative threads about home and place has invigorated the field of gender and migration studies in part by turning it toward cultural history. Into her study of working-class Mexican women in Chicago during the 1920s and 1930s, Gabriela Arredondo introduces the concept of "lived regionalities" in which women's past experiences and knowledge "shape the lens through which they live and understand their lives." Through the use of demography, archival research, and oral interviews, Carmen Teresa Whalen deftly connects Philadelphia and Puerto Rico through individual stories of migration, community histories of organizations, and the impact of global assembly lines. Her monograph *From Puerto Rico to Philadelphia* provides an astute gendered exploration of transnationalism as lived experience with women's wage and civic labor at the forefront of creating communities and making home.[11]

For many second-generation teenagers, popular culture also looms large in defining their own social locations as comfortable and home-like. Though she elides ethnicity, Nan Enstad, in *Ladies of Labor, Girls of Adventure*, imaginatively interprets the power of mass fiction, fashion, and film in the lives of Jewish and Italian dressmakers. She examines the contradictions and possibilities inherent in the everyday life of a typical garment worker in New York City at the turn of the century, a young woman who could hold a picket sign in one hand while adjusting her feathered hat with the other.[12] Race and ethnicity, however, were hardly silent partners in this dance of cultural negotiations and formations.[13] Taking the conversation over racial/ethnic women's consumer consciousness into the Cold War, Shirley Jennifer Lim, in *A Feeling of Belonging: Asian American Women's Public Culture, 1930–1960*, contends that young women "claimed a place in the nation" through participation in beauty contests, sororities, and other mainstream heteronormative pursuits typical of 1950s adolescents.[14]

While a "feeling of belonging" can be performed through consumer culture, this sense of affiliation also can be discerned through moments of political activism, creative expression, and paid employment. For example, chronicling Chicana participation in the 1975 International Women's Year Conference in Mexico City. Marisela R. Chávez elaborates on the development of a global consciousness among these young feminists, but a consciousness tempered for them at the time by the disconcerting realization that they were, in fact, Americans. Rather than being accepted as sisters in the struggle by Third World participants, they found themselves unflatteringly lumped together with the majority of the U.S. delegation who ignored them. Seeking to fuse sexual and cultural identities within her avant-garde work that combined photography, drama, and raw natural materials, Cuban American performance artist Ana Mendieta enacted a feminist consciousness that incorporated indigenous and Afro-Cuban beliefs.[15]

Elaborating on the elasticity of identity, class, and employment, Yen Le Espiritu emphasizes the impact of differential inclusion that leaves even affluent Filipinos subject to nativism and uncertain about where they belong. Indeed, the immigrant woman as a middle-class professional or entrepreneur complicates traditional male-centered ethnic migration narratives of upward mobility that provided direct entry into mainstream America. As Diane Vecchio notes in her study of Italians in Milwaukee, Wisconsin and Endicott, New York, women instead created niches for themselves within ethnic communities through their gendered roles as midwives and merchants.[16] In contrast, Mary Ann Villarreal explores the lives of Mexican American women in Texas who operated local cantinas and dance halls, appropriating for profit a very male-identified public space, albeit one still within the ethnic group itself. The preservation of reputation emerges as a salient theme even for women with prestigious professions; they were never above community scrutiny. Dr. Margaret Chung, the first Chinese American woman physician, was not welcomed by the club women profiled in Judy Yung's *Unbound Feet*. As Judy Wu reveals in her fascinating biography of Chung, the good doctor, as a single female with no local family connections, found a chilly reception in San Francisco; however, undaunted she built a lucrative practice by catering to Euro-Americans who ventured into Chinatown as medical tourists.[17] This sampling of recent scholarship on immigrant ethnic women as entrepreneurs and professionals offers fresh direction by imbricating gender and migration within the new business history. The most recent studies of immigrant women have been particularly effective in demonstrating how communities of mobile people meld interior, exterior, and imagined spaces into homes where work, family, business, and identity formation intersect.

Communities In Motion

In a sense, the marriage of *Hester Street*'s Gitl and her husband, Jake, foundered on their differing definitions and expectations of themselves in relation to their compatriots. In exploring the creation of communities (whether rooted in place, culture, religion, a shared past, or contemporary interests) social historians of immigrant women for the past fifteen years have continued to rely on the building blocks of race, class, and gender. Within immigrant communities, scholars now seek clues to the construction of ethnic understandings of manhood and womanhood that supplement or even sometimes undermine gendered notions of American individualism. Immigrant communities inevitably link private and public worlds, making them ideal sites for exploring how men and women negotiate and evaluate the connections and cross-currents of sexuality, family, and work in communal ways across generations.

Two monographs debuted during the early 1980s that foreshadowed many of the new directions in gender and American migration studies. Virginia Sánchez Korrol's *From Colonia to Community* and Judith Smith's *Family Connections* illuminated the ways in which women, in partnership and conflict with men, built local institutions in immigrant neighborhoods, engaged in politics, and worked in the formal and informal economies while simultaneously seemingly adhering to traditional familial roles.[18] Other studies focused primarily on women's experiences, turning the tables on earlier works in ethnic and immigration studies where women appeared only as domestic scenery. Vicki L. Ruiz's *Cannery Women, Cannery Lives* tells the story of how Mexican women in East Los Angeles made common cause with their Euro-American (predominantly Jewish) co-workers and neighbors to nurture a grassroots union that substantively improved their wages and working conditions. Also from a community studies perspective rich in oral history, Judy Yung's *Unbound Feet* provides an engaging gendered generational history demonstrating how Chinese American women in San Francisco during the early decades of the twentieth century created their own personal spaces and how they forged with one another a network of clubs and associations that contributed to a cohesive ethos predicated on family, culture, and social location.[19]

Most immigrant women and their daughters, while visible within their own neighborhoods, received scant public notice. In *Common Sense and a Little Fire*, Annelise Orleck offers rich biographical portraits of Jewish labor activists Clara Lemlich, Rosa Schneiderman, Pauline Newman, and Fannia Cohn, who captured the public imagination during the New York City Shirtwaist Strike of 1909 and two years later the Triangle Fire. In concert with Alice Wexler's path-breaking biography of Emma Goldman, *Common Sense and a Little Fire* brings out women's political consciousness attributed, in part, to the lessons they learned in their villages in Eastern Europe and in New York's Lower East Side.[20] Of course, women's leadership extended beyond the shop-floor, local clubs, and noted individuals. Joyce Antler's *The Journey Home: How Jewish Women Shaped Modern America* encompasses a sweeping survey of political activism among Jewish women during the twentieth century, couching struggles for social justice within a Jewish American domestic sensibility. Social justice as intertwined with feminism, Chicano nationalism, and liberation theology emerges in Lara Medina's *Las Hermanas*. This innovative national group of nuns and laywomen strive to meet the spiritual and material needs of their neighbors though Alinsky-style political mobilization.[21]

Whether understood as physical locale, organizational space, or transnational imaginary, community as it appears in these works is never static but instead constantly fluid, dynamic, and shifting in unanticipated directions. In *Farming the Home Place*, Valerie J. Matsumoto underscores the calibrations of change among Japanese Americans within Cortez, a tightly-knit community in rural California. From the years of initial settlement to the tragedy of internment to the suburbanization of the San Joaquin Valley, Matsumoto offers an intricately detailed study of economic and cultural adaptations by four generations of women and men who have called Cortez home.[22]

For well over half a century, scholars of U.S. immigration also have interrogated generational cleavages within communities, and particularly the tensions that arose between parents and children. In *Southern Discomfort*, Nancy A. Hewitt explains how constructions of race influenced ethnic identification among the children of Cuban immigrants. While these Spanish-speaking immigrants of varying complexions built ethnic community networks, trade unions, and political associations, their children's sense of themselves became predicated on their own racial location in the Jim Crow South where, not surprisingly, Afro-Cubans developed a greater affiliation and kinship with African Americans. Generational conflicts extend beyond individual families. Matt García, in *A World of Its Own*, reveals the fault lines of generation, gender, and citizenship in the suburbs of southern California, especially tensions between Mexican *braceros* and Mexican American men. Conversely, García smartly delineates a Mexican American youth culture of the 1940s and 1950s where Mexican American teenagers mixed and mingled with their Euro-American and African Americans peers through popular music.[23]

Envisioning migration, settlement, and generational change through the prism of gender, Carol McKibben in *Beyond Cannery Row* demonstrates that women determined the direction of migration, built ethnic communities institutions, and in the second and third generation, emerged as the entrepreneurs who enabled families to stay in Monterey, California after the collapse of the fishing industry. Her thick descriptions of cannery work are so vivid that the reader almost can smell the fish and shiver in the foggy dampness of the open-air plant. In elaborating on the intertwined nature of public and private obligations, McKibben teases out the ways in which perception and reputation influence the community standing of women as much as occupation and family background.[24]

Recent studies of community-building and activism, much like recent studies of home-building and transnationalism, have continued to draw on the methods and insights of earlier social histories, while also adding insights from cultural studies and biography. The cultural turn, in particular, also has introduced a new dimension to discussions of the immigrant experience, notably the way in which immigrants have remembered and attempted to preserve their own histories, both in the United States and abroad.

Memory

Hester Street not only obliterates Gitl's and Jake's pre-migration lives in Russia, but leaves us without a clear sense of how they will remember their conflicted marriage once they have spent a life-time in America. In interrogating the multivalent strands of making community, home, and a living, memory must also be taken into account as an increasingly central element in our understanding of the impact of mobility on human lives. Many of the books mentioned in this essay imbricate oral narratives in ways that provide prescient, intimate descriptions of gender in the every day as well as insight into how individuals create meaning in their own lives and shape the lives of others. In linking intertexuality and mobility, historians often rely on memory, personal and collective, as conveyed through speech and written texts or as embedded in buildings and landmarks. Public historian Lydia Otero chronicles the efforts to salvage from urban redevelopment *La Placita* (a historic plaza) in Tucson, Arizona, by Mexican American preservationists for, as local leader Alva Torres explained, "the buildings are not the people but they are part of the story that you try to save."[25]

Physical spaces, when layered with personal, cultural, or religious associations, loom large in the memories and experiences of immigrant women. In *Mapping Memories and Migrations*, a group of Latina historians, including Otero, examines the reciprocal relationships between memory and place, the ways in which region itself and memories of region mold individual and collective identities. The relationship between physical place and memory lends to a fuller recounting of the lives of immigrant women, one that ventures beyond the level of observed experience.

While often personal and culturally specific, the making of communities, homes, and memories also shapes conceptions and practices of citizenship. Social historians have tended to privilege the agency of individuals, but other scholars, influenced by law and political science, emphasize the critical point that foreigners, while diverse among themselves, are also a distinctive group within American law. Providing a path toward synthesis, histories that tackle legislation, public policy, and the law provide a powerful conceptual counterweight to micro-level community studies, especially around issues of citizenship.

Citizenship

The development of whiteness studies and critical race studies in the 1990s alerted scholars to the fundamental ways in which the American nation has been racialized since its origins.[26] This observation in turn has encouraged scholars to recognize women newcomers as a distinctive group of aliens and thus as a logical choice for analyzing citizenship, borders, and U.S. policies such as admission and naturalization. Studies of citizenship, naturalization, and immigration policies helped to reveal what the foreign and female of diverse backgrounds shared, as well as pointing to the ways in which race and class complicated the gendering of American law and the implementation of law as policy both at the boundaries of the United States and in the regulation of everyday immigrant life within the United States.

Studies of immigrant populations have made special contributions to our changing understandings of American citizenship as a mode of incorporation or assimilation. No longer do scholars treat citizenship as a timeless legal and juridical concept based on a sense and obligation of civic culture and enfranchisement. With case studies set in the South, Southwest, California and Hawaii during the Gilded Age and Progressive eras, Evelyn Nakano Glenn's *Unequal Freedom* has demonstrated how gender, race, and class constructed boundaries around American citizenship, creating fundamentally different routes to the privileges of citizenship for immigrant men and women from differing parts of the world.[27] Still, the promise of full citizenship also has provided the grounds for immigrant women, like other disenfranchised groups, to mobilize for civil rights and social justice.

Much like Glenn, Candace Bredbenner, Alexandra Stern, and Natalia Molina in their recent books have focused on issues of citizenship and belonging in the American nation as they have affected the foreign-born and especially female minorities racialized as non-white. In *A Nationality of Her Own*, Bredbenner contrasts how changing notions of the attainment of citizenship through marriage affected foreign-born and native-born women.[28] The former sometimes became American citizens without wanting to do so while the latter on occasion could even lose their status as birthright citizens and become stateless. For example, a woman born on U.S. soil could lose her citizenship if she married a man ineligible for naturalization and citizenship, as were all men from Asia before 1943. Bredbenner traces women's mobilization against these inequities, putting into comparative and global perspective U.S. policies. She provides ample evidence of the complicated ways that the laws of citizenship, the practices of both American and immigrant patriarchy, and the low wages paid women could render foreign-born women vulnerable to deportation.

Alexandra Stern's *Eugenic Nation* and Natalia Molina's *Fit to Be Citizens* are more interested in nation and nation-building and in cultural and social location than in juridical status or citizenship per se. Building on Gary Gerstle's distinction between "racial" and civic nationalism, *Eugenic Nation* deepens our knowledge of eugenics in the day-to-day as Stern narrates how immigrants, especially Mexican immigrants, are framed within a discourse of disease and intellectual dimness. From the disinfecting stations at the border (that sprayed *braceros* with DDT during World War II) to the massive repatriations and deportations of the 1930s to the sterilization cases in Los Angeles during the 1970s and beyond, Mexicans have borne the brunt of eugenics-infused public health, education, and social welfare policies. Similarly, Natalia Molina examines not only the ways in which racial ideologies become wrapped in the language of scientific objectivity of public health but also the impact of these ideologies as public health praxis. She creatively uncovers how Mexican, Chinese, and Japanese immigrants both utilized and avoided public health services, historicizing their individual agency within a larger framework of social and economic stratification in Los Angeles.[29]

Equally innovative work has explored the gendering of U.S. borders, with some of the most prescient studies focusing on the exclusion of people from Asia. Erika Lee interrogates meanings of manhood among the Chinese, including both the perspectives of the immigrants themselves and of U.S. policymakers and politicians. She is especially mindful of the power of the state in shaping the contours of entry. At the gates, so to speak, in the naturalization and regulation of citizenship, women's sexuality, morality, and reproductive capacity have also been central concerns of immigration officials. Sensitive to the moral discourses evoked in the name of border security, Eithne Luibhéid argues that immigration control has been even more important in actively reproducing heterosexual identities as normative and in reinforcing the gendered consequences of class and race for immigrant women who are not married. She seems especially concerned with how immigration policy helped to make hetero-sexuality "official" and in the ways that border agents maintain considerable discretion on whom to exclude.[30]

Martha Gardner's *The Qualities of a Citizen* digs deep into U.S. law and the case files of the Immigration and Naturalization Service, extending and enriching Luibhéid's observations about how immigration and naturalization laws create racial and gender categories. But while Luibhéid focuses mainly on sexuality, Gardner traces linkages among work, morality, marriage, and childbearing. The book is especially helpful in understanding the ambiguities surrounding immigration restriction and provisions for family reunification. It provides readers with detailed case studies on the complex relationship among fears of women becoming "public charges," their high rates of detention and exclusion, and the enforcement of heterosexuality and marriage through restrictive immigration policies.[31]

By focusing attention on the borders needed to define nations, scholarship on women immigrants as aliens and potential citizens reminds readers that the long-standing issue of the relationship between pluralism and unity persists down to the present as a major theme in American nation-building. While historians of immigrant women have continued to emphasize diversity among the many groups of immigrants in the United States, the new scholarship on citizenship also can be juxtaposed with commonalities emerging from studies of home, community, and memory across race and ethnicity to suggest not one but many new paths toward synthesis.

The One and the Many

Most specialists in immigration history have emphasized how ethnic pluralism in American history was rooted in the legacy of diversity among immigrants. For much of the 1970s and 1980s, immigration historians seemed interested mainly in documenting and explaining the proliferation of and distinctions among ethnic groups and identities among European immigrants of differing backgrounds. By contrast, during the 1970s many cultural feminists assumed that women shared a number of key experiences across cultures, regardless of race, class, or ethnicity. By the 1990s, such assumptions had fallen to critiques undertaken by specialists on race and racialization. Increasingly historians of women became interested in how ethnicity, along with race, nationality, and gender, had been constructed and how they changed over time.[32]

Not surprisingly then, a larger synthesis remains elusive. Studies of particular groups of immigrant women, often in particular places, have burgeoned but few scholars have attempted to pull these studies together into a national narrative. After a flurry of interdisciplinary anthologies and review essays in the late 1980s and early 1990s, few scholars have even bothered to review the newest historical research.[33] The few books on immigrant women that have drawn on women of many origins most often have collected primary sources and oral histories. Such approaches, popular in U.S. women's history since the 1970s, offer vibrant but at times poorly contextualized portraits of individual women. Only Maxine Seller's second edition of *Immigrant Women* (that added sources and narratives by newer immigrants) was organized around broad themes.[34]

One study that did attempt synthesis was Donna Gabaccia's *From the Other Side*. Breaking with the then-current models of immigration history (studies of immigrant life in East Coast cities or encyclopedic accounts of individual ethnic groups), this book compared the lives of all immigrant women, past and present. It showed how global economic change and nation-and empire-building sparked a transition from male- to female-majority migrations and called attention to the gendered impacts of U.S. migration policies on immigrant women. Furthermore, Gabaccia challenged readers to consider women's adjustment to life in the United States not as a form of "emancipation" but rather as "domestication" and highlighted the points of contact among foreign-born women and between immigrants and native-born black and white women. *From the Other Side* also devoted an entire chapter to middle-class immigrants, a group that grew proportionately across the twentieth century. But at a time when most historians and social scientists believed that contemporary immigrations diverged sharply from past patterns, *From the Other Side* seemed well outside the mainstream.[35]

Still, other recent studies have suggested ways to generate useful generalizations on a smaller scale. Studies of East-Coast working-class women focused on immigrant women of various backgrounds. A collaborative research project by historians from Europe, led by Christiane Harzig, examined four groups of immigrant women in Chicago—a method Nancy Green has labeled "convergent comparison."[36] Increasingly, too, the burgeoning field of whiteness studies, which focused on how European immigrants acquired white identities, offered an interpretively powerful opportunity to draw together histories of many groups. Unfortunately, among the proliferating studies of Italians, Irish, and Jewish whiteness, only a handful tackled systematically the gendering of racialization itself.[37] In a recent essay, Vicki L. Ruiz traced the racialized yet gendered contours of Chicana/o history over the last twenty years, problematizing notions of *mestizaje* (*morena/o*), whiteness (*blanca/o*), and cultural coalescence (*café con leche*), teasing out the situational nature of racial constructs in the historical (and the historians') moment.[38]

The reclamation in recent scholarship of belonging—whether in community networks or transnational imaginaries—also has addressed a fundamental and persisting concern in historical discourse about immigration—the tension between structure and agency. Richard Ivan Jobs and Patrick McDevitt posit that the "agency/structure divide is not really a dichotomy . . . but an ongoing process of negotiation. Instead of looking away, this Janus confronts itself in conversation, argument, and dialogue." They continue, "We as historians have the challenge of accounting for the manner in which individuals acted within the constraints and possibilities of their broader social world to fashion their own sense of place and community through interpersonal relationships."[39] That challenge has remained at the heart of U.S. immigrant and ethnic women's history over the last two decades.

With increasingly diverse student populations in our classrooms, the field of immigration history remains more salient than ever. Whether in Berlin, New York, North Carolina, Pennsylvania, Minnesota, Texas, Arizona, or California (the places where the two of us have taught over the course of the past twenty-five years), our undergraduates embody both the journeys of transnational migration and an enduring belief in American opportunities. Even when contemporary structures—of economic inequality, immigration policy, or crowded universities—sharply constrain their choices (as they often do), our students' desires for home and for belonging remain strong. They continually generate new experiences that redefine them as "Americans."

Works of synthesis could, it seems, draw on many of these common themes. While daunted by the task of actually co-authoring a big book on immigrant women, we might point at least to a collection of essays that we, ourselves, recently edited (with the evocative title *American Dreaming, Global Realities: Re-Thinking U.S. Immigration History*) as one possible route forward. Placing gender at its center, *American Dreaming, Global Realities* explores the ways in which immigrants and their children are shaped simultaneously by transnational bonds, globalization, family loyalties, and personal choices. In shifting the debate away from models of linear assimilation, we consider how the many pluralities—the very specific historical, economic, regional, familial, and cultural contexts of immigrant lives—encourage interaction, connection, and a sense of belonging. In laying a foundation for a future synthesis, we must interrogate the many individual and collective journeys that cross the boundaries of national states, while recognizing the shared yearnings that motivate human mobility.[40]

Notes

1. *Hester Street* (1975), produced by Raphael D. Silver, 90 minutes, videocassette.
2. Donna R. Gabaccia, "Immigrant Women: Nowhere at Home?" *Journal of American Ethnic History* 10, no. 4 (Summer 1991): 61–87.
3. Most historians who have adopted the transnational paradigm cite as inspiration two collected volumes co-edited by anthropologists of the Caribbean. Nina Glick Schiller, Linda Basch, and Cristina Szanton Blach. See Nina Glick Schiller, et al., eds., *Towards a Transnational Perspective on Migration: Race, Class, Ethnicity, and Nationalism Reconsidered* (New York, 1992); and Nina Glick Schiller, et al., eds., *Nations Unbound: Transnational Projects, Postcolonial Predicaments, and Deterritorialized Nation-States* (Langhorne, PA. 1994). Other path-breaking references would include Eugenia Georges, *The Making of a Transnational Community: Migration, Development and Cultural Change in the Dominican Republic* (New York, 1990); and Patricia R. Pessar and Sherri Grasmuck, *Between Two Islands: Dominican International Migration* (Berkeley, CA, 1991).

4. Theodore C. Blegen, *Norwegian Migration to America* (Northfield, MN, 1931–1940); Frank Thistleth-waite, "Migration from Europe Overseas in the Nineteenth and Twentieth Centuries", XIe Congrès International des Sciences Historiques, *Rapports*, vol. 5 (Uppsala, 1960), 32–60; Rudolph Vecoli, "*Contadini* in Chicago: A Critique of *The Uprooted*," *Journal of American History* 1, no. 3 (December 1964): 404–17.

5. Donna R. Gabaccia and Franca Iacovetta, eds., *Women, Gender, and Transnational Lives: Italian Workers of the World* (Toronto, 2002); Linda Reeder, *Widows in White: Migration and the Transformation of Rural Italian Women, Sicily, 1880–1920* (Toronto, 2003).

6. Recent examples of this literature include Gunther Peck, *Reinventing Free Labor: Padrones and Immigrant Workers in the North American West, 1880–1930* (New York, 2000); and Gilbert G. González, *Culture of Empire: American Writers, Mexico, and Mexican Immigrants, 1880–1930* (Austin, TX, 2004).

7. Catherine Ceniza Choy, *Empire of Care: Nursing and Migration in Filipino American History* (Durham, NC, 2003).

8. Yen Le Espiritu, *Home Bound: Filipino American Lives Across Cultures, Communities, and Countries* (Berkeley, CA, 2003); Donna Gabaccia, "When the Migrants are Men: Italy's Women and Transnationalism as a Working-class Way of Life," in *Women, Gender and Labour Migration: Historical and Global Perspectives*, ed. Pamela Sharpe (London and New York, 2001), 190–208. Quote is from Espiritu, *Homeward Bound*, 2.

9. Suzanne M. Sinke, *Dutch Immigrant Women in the United States, 1880–1920* (Urbana, IL, 2002).

10. Lili M. Kim, "Redefining the Boundaries of Traditional Roles: Korean Picture Brides, Pioneer Immigrant Women, and Their Benevolent Nationalism in Hawai'i," in *Asian/Pacific Islander American Women: A Historical Anthology*, ed. Shirley Hune and Gail M. Nomura (New York, 2003), 106–119; Rumi Yasutake, *Transnational Women's Activism: The United States, Japan, and Japanese Immigrant Communities in California, 1859–1920* (New York, 2004).

11. Gabriela F. Arredondo, "Lived Regionalities: Mujeridad in Chicago, 1920–1940," in *Mapping Memories and Migrations: Locating Boricua and Chicana Histories*, ed. Vicki L. Ruiz and John R. Chavez (Urbana, IL, forthcoming); Carmen Teresa Whalen, *From Puerto Rico to Philadelphia: Puerto Rican Workers and Postwar Economies* (Philadelphia, 2001).

12. Nan Enstad, *Ladies of Labor, Girls of Adventure: Working Women, Popular Culture, and Labor Politics at the Turn of the Twentieth Century* (New York, 1999).

13. A plethora of literature addresses the tensions and transformations in racially diverse communities over "American" cultural norms and consumer pursuits, especially among young women. As an example, see Chapter 5, "The Flapper and The Chaperone," in Vicki L. Ruiz, *From Out of the Shadows: Mexican Women in Twentieth-Century America* (New York, 1998).

14. Shirley Jennifer Lim, *A Feeling of Belonging: Asian American Women's Public Culture, 1930–1960* (New York, 2006).

15. Marisela R. Chávez, "Pilgrimage to the Homeland: California Chicanas and International Women's Year, Mexico City, 1975," in *Mapping Memories and Migrations*. ed. Ruiz and Chávez; Carlos A. Cruz, "Ana Mendieta's Art: A Journey Through Her Life," in *Latina Legacies: Identity, Biography, and Community*, ed. Vicki L. Ruiz and Virginia Sánchez Korrol (New York, 2005), 225–39.

16. Espiritu, *Homeward Bound*; Diane C. Vecchio, *Merchants, Midwives and Laboring Women: Italian Migrant Women in Urban America* (Urbana, IL, 2006).

17. Mary Ann Villarreal, "*Cantantes y Cantineras*: Mexican American Communities and the Mapping of Public Space" (Ph.D. diss., Arizona State University, 2003); Judy Tzu-Chun Wu, *Doctor Mom Chung of the Fair-Haired Bastards: The Life of a Wartime Celebrity* (Berkeley, CA, 2005).

18. Virginia Sánchez Korrol, *From Colonia to Community: The History of Puerto Ricans in New York City, 1917–1948* (Westport, CT, 1983); Judith E. Smith, *Family Connections: A History of Italian and Jewish Immigrant Lives in Providence, Rhode Island, 1900–1940* (Albany, NY, 1985).

19. Vicki L. Ruiz *Cannery Women, Cannery Lives: Mexican Women, Unionization, and the California Food Processing Industry, 1930–1950* (Albuquerque, NM, 1987); Judy Yung, *Unbound Feet: A Social History of Chinese Women in San Francisco* (Berkeley. CA, 1995).

20. Annelise Orleck, *Common Sense and a Little Fire: Women and Working Class Politics in the United States, 1900–1965* (Chapel Hill, NC, 1995); Alice Wexler, *Emma Goldman: An Intimate Life* (New York, 1984).

21. Joyce Antler, *The Journey Home: How Jewish Women Shaped Modern America* (New York, 1997); Lara Medina, *Las Hermanas: Chicana/Latina Religious-Political Activism in the U.S. Catholic Church* (Philadelphia. PA, 2004).

22. Valerie J. Matsumoto, *Farming The Home Place: A Japanese American Community in California, 1919–1982* (Ithaca, NY, 1993).

23. Nancy A. Hewitt, *Southern Discomfort: Women's Activism in Tampa Florida, 1880s to 1920s* (Urbana, IL,

2001); Matt García, *A World of Its Own: Race, Labor, and Class in the Making of Greater Los Angeles, 1900–1970* (Chapel Hill, NC, 2002).

24. Carol McKibben, *Beyond Cannery Row: Sicilian Women, Immigration, and Community in Monterey, California. 1915–1999* (Urbana, IL. 2006).

25. Lydia R. Otero, "La Placita Committee: Claiming Place and History," in *Mapping Memories and Migrations*, ed. Ruiz and Chávez, forthcoming.

26. Gary Gerstle, *American Crucible: Race and Nation in the Twentieth Century* (Princeton, N.J., 2001).

27. Evelyn Nakano Glenn, *Unequal Freedom; How Race and Gender Shaped American Citizenship and Labor* (Cambridge. MA, 2002).

28. Candice Lewis Bredbenner, *A Nationality of Her Own: Women, Marriage and the Law of Citizenship* (Berkeley, CA, 1998).

29. Alexandra Stern, *Eugenic Nation: Faults and Frontiers of Better Breeding in Modern America* (Berkeley, CA, 2005); Natalia Molina, *Fit to Be Citizens?: Public Health and Race in Los Angeles, 1879–1939* (Berkeley, CA, 2006).

30. As examples of this rich literature, see George Anthony Peffer, *If They Don't Bring Their Women Here: Chinese Female Immigration before Exclusion* (Urbana, IL, 1999); Erika Lee, *At America's Gates: Chinese Immigration during the Exclusion Era. 1882–1943* (Chapel Hill, NC, 2003); and Eithne Luibhéid, *Entry Denied: Controlling Sexuality at the Border* (Minneapolis, 2002). See also *Queer Migrations: Sexuality, U.S. Citizenship, and Border Crossings*, ed. Eithne Luibhéid and Lionel Cantú, Jr. (Minneapolis, MN, 2005).

31. Martha Mabie Gardner, *The Qualities of a Citizen: Women, Immigration, and Citizenship, 1870–1975* (Princeton, NJ, 2005).

32. Werner Sollors, ed., *The Invention of Ethnicity* (New York, 1991); Kathleen Neils Conzen, et al., "The Invention of Ethnicity; A Perspective from the USA," *Journal of American Ethnic History* 12, no. 1 (Fall 1992): 3–43. For a prescient critique of cultural feminism, see Peggy Pascoe, *Relations of Rescue: The Search for Female Moral Authority in the American West, 1874–1939* (New York, 1990). xiii–xxiii.

33. For an early effort, see Doris Weatherford, *Foreign and Female: Immigrant Women in America, 1840–1930* (New York, 1986). An exception is *Crafting U.S. Women's History*, a collection of historiographical essays in U.S. women's history co-edited by Susan Jay Kleinberg, Eileen Boris, and Vicki L. Ruiz (in press, Rutgers University Press).

34. Maxine Schwartz Seller, ed., *Immigrant Women*, 2d ed. (Albany, NY, 1994). Kristine Leach, *In Search of a Common Ground: Nineteenth and Twentieth Century Immigrant Women in America* (San Francisco. CA, 1995) is an exceptionally short work based almost exclusively on oral histories and the author's interviews. An innovative if largely policy-oriented work that compares resiliency and duality of identity and orientation in immigrant women's narratives is Roni Berger, *Immigrant Women Tell Their Stories* (New York, 2004).

35. Donna Gabaccia, *From the Other Side: Women, Gender and Immigrant Life in the United States* (Bloomington, IN, 1994). Social scientists who bother to read the work of historians more recently have reached different conclusions. See Nancy Foner, *In a New Land: A Comparative View of Immigration* (New York. 2005).

36. Randy D. McBee, *Dance Hall Days: Intimacy and Leisure among Working-Class Immigrants in the United States* (New York, 2000); Daniel Soyer, ed., *A Coat of Many Colors: Immigration, Globalism, and Reform in the New York City Garment Industry* (New York. 2005); Robyn Burnett and Ken Luebbering, *Immigrant Women in the Settlement of Missouri* (Columbia, MO, 2005); Christiane Harzig. ed., *Peasant Maids, City Women: From the European Countryside to Urban America* (Ithaca, NY, 1997); Nancy Green, "The Comparative Method and Post-structural Structuralism: New Perspectives for Migration Studies," *Journal of American Ethnic History* 13, no. 4 (Summer 1994): 3–22.

37. Here the starting place remains Ruth Frankenberg, *White Women, Race Matters: The Social Construction of Whiteness* (Minneapolis, MN, 1993). See also Karen Brodkin, *How Jews Became White and What that Says about Race in America* (New Brunswick, NJ, 1998).

38. Vicki L. Ruiz, "*Morena/o, Blanca/o y Café con Leche:* Racial Constructions in Chicana/o Historiography," *Estudios Mexicanos/Mexican Studies* 20, no. 2 (Summer 2004): 343–59.

39. Richard Ivan Jobs and Patrick McDevitt, "Introduction: Where The Hell Are The People?," *Journal of Social History* 39, no. 2 (Winter 2005): 309–14. Quotes are on pp. 310, 311, respectively.

40. Donna R. Gabaccia and Vicki L. Ruiz, eds., *American Dreaming, Global Realities: Re-Thinking U.S. Immigration History* (Urbana, IL, 2006).

15

The Social Awakening of Chinese American Women as Reported in *Chung Sai Yat Po*, 1900–1911

Judy Yung

The first decade of the twentieth century saw the advancement of women's emancipation in both China and the United States.[1] In China the women's cause was furthered by the 1898 Reform Movement, which advocated that China emulate the West and modernize in order to throw off the yoke of foreign domination. Modernization included elevating the status of women in Chinese society. As a result anti-footbinding societies, schools for girls, women's rights organizations and magazines, and the increased participation of women in public affairs became evident, particularly in the cities. Soon after the 1911 Revolution, in which women played limited but conspicuous roles—conveying messages, smuggling arms and ammunition, and serving as nurses and soldiers at the war front—Chinese women in Guangdong Province were among the first to be granted suffrage.[2] Meanwhile in the United States women were becoming more educated, independent of men, and visible in the public sphere. Some actively participated in social reform, in the temperance, peace, and labor movements. At the same time the women's suffrage movement was gaining momentum, with the final push beginning in the 1910s, when eight states, including California, passed a women's suffrage amendment.[3]

What was the response of Chinese American women to the changes taking place in China and the United States? Before we attempt to answer this question, we need to gauge their response by comparing the role and status of Chinese American women in the nineteenth century with that of the early twentieth century.

The first wave of Chinese immigrants to California during the Gold Rush included very few women. Early Chinese sojourners, who intended to strike it rich and return home, did not bring their wives or families with them. Cultural restrictions at home, the lack of funds for traveling, and anti-Chinese sentiment in the West further discouraged the early emigration of Chinese women. As a result, the Chinese male/female ratio in America was as high as 19 to 1 in 1860; 13 to 1 in 1870; 21 to 1 in 1880; and 27 to 1 in 1890.[4] The sexual imbalance, combined with anti-miscegenation laws that prohibited marriages between Chinese and whites, created a need for Chinese prostitution. Given this situation, the prostitution trade thrived, proving immensely profitable for the tongs, or secret societies, in Chinatowns.

The majority of Chinese women in nineteenth-century California were indentured prostitutes, kidnapped, lured, or purchased from poor parents in China and resold in America for high profits. Approximately 85 percent of Chinese women in San Francisco were prostitutes in 1860 and 71 percent in 1870. Treated as chattel and subjected to constant physical and mental abuse, the average prostitute did not outlive her contract terms of four to five years.[5] Those who survived the trade either ran away with the help of lovers, were redeemed by wealthy clients, or sought protection from the police or the missionary homes. In the 1880s while prostitution began to decline due to anti-prostitution laws and the successful rescue raids by Protestant missionaries, the number of Chinese wives began to increase due to the arrival of the merchant class and the marriages of former prostitutes to Chinese men here. Although some women did emigrate alone or came as *mui tsai* or domestic servants, most other Chinese women then were wives who lived either in urban Chinatowns or in remote rural areas. Following Chinese tradition, Chinatown wives seldom left their homes, where in addition to their own housework, they often worked for low wages—sewing, washing, rolling cigars, and making slippers and brooms while caring for their children. In rural areas Chinese wives tended livestock and vegetable gardens, hauled in the catch and dried seafood for export, or took in boarders. Regardless of their residence or their husbands' social status, immigrant wives led hardworking lives and were excluded from participation in almost all public affairs.

The restrictive lives of Chinese American women began to change in the twentieth century. A growing number of Chinese women began to free themselves of social restrictions—working outside the home, appearing in public places, educating their daughters, starting and joining Chinese women's organizations, and participating in community affairs.[6] How and why did this change occur? Were Chinese American women socially awakened by the emancipation of women occurring in China or in the United States?

Unfortunately there is no known body of writings by Chinese American women that can help answer these questions. But one valuable source that has remained relatively untapped until recently is the Chinese American press.[7] Among the most successful and long-lasting Chinese language newspapers of the early twentieth century is *Chung Sai Yat Po* (*CSYP*). Started by Presbyterian minister Ng Poon Chew in 1900, *CSYP* was heavily influenced by both Chinese nationalism and Western middle-class ideology. It favored reform in China and advocated equal rights for Chinese Americans, including women. As *CSYP* enjoyed wide circulation among Chinese Americans until its decline in the 1930s, it played an important advocatory and informational role in the Chinese American community.[8]

A close reading of *CSYP* from 1900 to 1911 supports the contention that the role and status of Chinese American women were indeed beginning to change and that women, especially among the literate, were being influenced more by women's issues and events in China than by developments in the United States.[9] This orientation was due as much to the newspaper's reform platform as to strong feelings of Chinese nationalism in the Chinatown community. Excluded from meaningful participation in American society[10] and aware of the adverse impact of China's weak international status upon their lives in America, Chinese Americans concentrated their attention and energies more on politics in China than in the United States. But as *CSYP* advocated as well as reported, Chinese American leaders were adept at using the American courts and diplomatic channels to fight discrimination.

The need to elevate the status of Chinese women was evidently a concern of *CSYP*. Between 1900 and 1911 approximately 550 articles and 66 editorials on women (2 percent of the newspaper's pages), 26 of which reflected the voices of Chinese women themselves, appeared in *CSYP*.[11] Almost all addressed the same women's issues that were being raised in China: (1) the elimination of "barbaric" practices harmful to women, such as polygamy, slavery, arranged marriages, and especially footbinding; (2) education for women; (3) women's rights; and (4) women's role in national salvation. What follows is a summary and analysis of these articles and editorials as they relate to the social awakening of Chinese American women.

The Campaign Against Footbinding and Other Sexist Practices

Begun in the tenth century as an innovation of palace dancers, footbinding remained a popular practice in China until it was denounced by reformers and outlawed after the 1911 Revolution.[12] A symbol of gentility, bound feet was considered an asset in the marriage market. In practice footbinding prevented women from "wandering," as women with bound feet generally found it difficult to walk unassisted. At the same time it reinforced women's cloistered existence, as Chinese etiquette dictated that a Chinese lady should not appear in public or be seen in the company of men. Bound feet came to symbolize the oppressed state of Chinese women and the decadence of old China. Thus, the eradication of bound feet became one of the rallying points in the Reform Movement in China as well as of reformers in the United States, where women with bound feet could still be found.[13]

The earliest reference to footbinding in *CSYP* appeared in 1902 when the Chinese ambassador's wife, Mme. Wu Tingfang, was quoted as saying that it was "quite unthinkable that footbinding, long considered an evil practice in China, is still in vogue in the United States" (*CSYP*, February 19, 1902).[14] In 1904 a Chinese entrepreneur was openly condemned for putting a Chinese woman with bound feet on display at the St. Louis World's Fair (*CSYP*, June 6, 1904). Front-page editorials argued for an end to foot binding for the following reasons: It was detrimental to a woman's health, was unnatural, caused unnecessary pain and suffering for women, and was a barbaric custom.[15] One editorial specifically urged Chinese American women to discontinue the practice. "How can men treat their wives with such contempt? How can women treat their bodies with such contempt?" the editorial asked. Three reasons were given as to why women overseas would choose to have bound feet: The parents were obstinant and at fault; husbands prized and encouraged its practice; and women in general were still uneducated and unenlightened. Its eradication, the editorial concluded, depended on family upbringing and formal schooling for all girls (*CSYP*, December 9, 1907).

In another article, "Corsets Can Harm Your Health," Dr. Tielun reportedly gave a public speech comparing the harmful effects of wearing corsets with footbinding. "Deforming a natural foot [whereby] Chinese women lose their freedom of movement and endure a life of pain and suffering . . . is just as abusive as that of binding the waist—a most barbaric practice," he said. In an editorial note at the end of the article, the reporter commented as follows: "Wearing corsets, although a vile practice, still gives one more freedom of movement than bound feet. Once the Natural Feet Society advocates our women be released from suffering, I suspect the practice of wearing corsets will also decline" (*CSYP*, August 13, 1909).

In a satire, "Ten Good Points About Footbinding," that appeared in the literature section[16] of *CSYP* on May 24, 1910, the "positive" effects of footbinding included the following: One could always use bound feet as an excuse to escape work; bound feet were an especially important asset for a good marriage if one had an ugly face; and a woman with bound feet could always appear helpless and frail to escape the wrath of an abusive mother-in-law.

Equally creative was a poem of twenty-four stanzas, "An Exhortation Against Footbinding," that appeared in the September 16, 1909 issue:

> A daughter's feet,
> A daughter's feet,
> By nature flesh and blood.
> Whether boy,
> Whether girl,
> Both are born of mother.
>
> Ten fine toes,
> Just like siblings,
> Harmonious, from same womb.
> They want to grow,
> Perfect and whole,
> To enjoy their natural due.

Why on earth
Are women folk
Infected by strange ways?
Young or old,
Rich or poor,
All desire the three-inch lotus.

In strict confinement,
Inner apartments,
A virtual living hell.
Beneath hemlines,
Bound like dumplings,
Swathed in restraining layers.

Halting steps,
Walking slow,
Ever fearful toppling over.
Circulation impeded,
Blocked and unmoving,
Painful pecks of birds.

And that is why
Among the girls
Few enjoy long life.
Within their chambers,
For what crime,
Are they so tortured? . . .

Imperial orders against footbinding, printed prominently in *CSYP*, gave the campaign against the practice an aura of official sanction. According to a series of Qing edicts, men whose wives had bound feet could not qualify for civil service; girls with bound feet could not attend government-sponsored schools; women with bound feet would be considered of the "mean" or "common" class; and no court honors could be conferred on women with bound feet.[17]

Similar diatribes were aimed at the "barbaric" practices of polygamy, arranged marriages, and keeping slave girls. In an editorial, "Reflections on the Selection of Courtesans by the Qing Court," the emperor was blamed for promoting polygamy and prostitution by setting a poor example. Whereas polygamy was practiced in most undeveloped countries in Asia, monogamy was the general practice in developed countries, according to the article. In conclusion, "If we wish to correct China's morals in order to have a stronger country, we must establish the law of monogamy. If we wish to develop the character of our women . . . we must promote schools for girls" (*CSYP*, March 28, 1906).

Free marriage and divorce as practiced in America were evidently controversial issues among Chinese Americans during this period. On the one hand, *CSYP* warned against the pitfalls of free marriage, stressing the need for women to maintain traditional morals.[18] On the other hand, an editorial that appeared on April 26, 1907 advocated the American custom of free marriage, defining a good marriage as one between two persons with compatible interests and personalities. Although divorce was still not socially acceptable, *CSYP* reported with sympathy three cases of divorce among Chinese Americans—two involving wives who claimed they were being forced into prostitution and one involving a wife who claimed her husband had taken a concubine.[19]

Of the two editorials that attacked the custom of keeping slave girls, one pointed out that compared with other countries, China was most guilty of the oppression of women. "For centuries we have erred in teaching our women to be obedient . . . to not even step out into the courtyard but remain in their lonely quarters as captive prisoners. . . . Women with bound feet, weakened bodies, and undeveloped intelligence cannot attain equality with men." Such treatment, the editorial continued, was not only detrimental to the interests of women, but since women made up half of the country's population, detrimental to the interests of China (*CSYP*, April 2, 1907). The second editorial exhorted women to learn from Abraham Lincoln's emancipation of black slavery and organize to liberate the slave girls. "If we want to be free, we must first make everyone else free" (*CSYP*, March 16, 1906). In support of the newspaper's reformist platform, both editorials also stressed that keeping slave girls was a sign of China's decadence in the eyes of Western countries and therefore should be eradicated.

Chinese prostitution in the United States was also discussed in *CSYP* editorials. Once a heated topic of debate in the late nineteenth century, Chinese prostitution was on the decline in the early 1900s. However, cases of prostitution were still reported in the newspaper.[20] One case, well covered in *CSYP* for three consecutive months, involved a prostitute by the name of Jingui, who had sought asylum at the Presbyterian mission. She was later arrested on trumped-up charges of grand larceny, and abducted by two Chinese men from a jail near Stanford University. Angered by Jingui's plight and suspecting corruption on the part of local officials, a group of private citizens and university students raised funds, passed resolutions, and held a protest rally on her behalf. In the process of her trial, Jingui revealed that she was born in China and became a prostitute through abduction. The court finally ordered her deported and a full investigation made of alleged corruption on the part of law-enforcement officers.[21]

In another editorial, those involved in the prostitution trade were asked to search their consciences and to mend their ways. With the establishment of shelters for rescued prostitutes by the Presbyterian and Methodist missions, and with a move by both the American government and the imperial government in China to investigate the matter, "your profits will suffer if not your reputation," admonished the editorial (*CSYP*, August 8, 1907).

Although the campaign against footbinding and other sexist practices began in China as part of the 1898 Reform Movement, it soon spread to American Chinatowns, where the same practices were still being followed, although to a lesser degree. Exposed to Western culture and Christianity, constantly criticized and ridiculed for their "heathen" ways by Anglo-Americans, and moved by nationalism to join their compatriots' efforts to reform China, progressive Chinese Americans such as Ng Poon Chew understood well the need to eradicate Chinese practices such as footbinding, polygamy, arranged marriages, and keeping slave girls. Educated Chinese women also rallied behind the campaign, encouraging women in China as well as in America to oppose and free themselves of these sexist practices.

Education for Women

> Two hundred million women—all are naturally endowed with intelligence, mental vigor, and talent. But because they are not educated, they are discarded as useless. A living dream dies under the oppression of husbands. It is greatly lamented (*CSYP*, August 30, 1909).

These feminist sentiments, as expressed in a three-part editorial, "On the Establishment of Independence for Chinese American Women," show *CSYP's* progressive point of view on women's education. Most editorials on the same subject, however, were more conservative and tended to use the following reformist line of reasoning to argue for women's education: Educated women make better wives and mothers; better wives and mothers make better families and citizens; better families and citizens make a stronger China.[22] Another recurring argument stressed that women made up half of China's population. If educated, they would be better able to contribute to their country's prosperity, as did women in Western countries. According to one editorial written by Pan Xuezhen, a female schoolteacher in China:

> Countries in Europe and America are rich and powerful because fundamentally, their women are educated. As to why they are educated, it is because men and women are equal in Europe and America. . . . In France and America, there are women in high offices. In England and America, there are women in astronomy, clerical work, communications, documentation and record keeping, medicine, law, as professors and educators, no different than men. This is because women in these countries are organized to encourage one another to pursue education (*CSYP*, March 4, 1902).

Numerous articles in *CSYP* reported on the establishment of elementary schools, trade schools, medical schools, and teacher-training schools for girls and women in China, especially in the Guangdong Province, from which most Chinese immigrants in American originated.[23] This news not only indicated that reform in the area of education for women was taking place at home but also encouraged overseas Chinese to continue sending remittances home to support schools for girls. Three editorials specifically asked for such support: "An Appeal to Overseas Chinese for Funds to Establish Schools" (*CSYP*, December 14, 1908), "On the Need for Overseas Chinese to Promote Girl Schools" (*CSYP*, December 20, 1909), and "Strengthening Ourselves Through Educating Women" (*CSYP*, April 4, 1910). The last editorial appealed directly to Chinese American women to support schools for girls in China. A number of articles also beseeched Chinese female students studying abroad and Chinese American women to "return home" to teach.[24]

Like their counterparts in China, who were among the earliest advocates of education for girls and women, Protestant missionaries evidently played a similar role in Chinatowns.[25] According to an article in *CSYP* on March 6, 1904, a school to teach Chinese girls Chinese, English, and the fine arts opened at 2 Clay Street under the auspices of the Baptist mission. On January 25, 1911, *CSYP* ran an advertisement announcing a new school established by the Presbyterian mission at 925 Stockton Street to teach girls and women Chinese in the evenings. The newspaper also reported in detail talks given by Chinese Christians encouraging women's education. In a three-part commentary on two speeches delivered at the Baptist and Presbyterian missions by Liu Fengxian, a woman missionary visiting from China, *CSYP* apparently agreed with Liu that women must become educated if they hoped to achieve equality: "Education leads to self-reliance and independence—the essence of freedom and equality . . . the fortuitous future of women for which this reporter truly anticipates" (*CSYP*, September 3, 1909). Earlier this same writer had encouraged Chinese American parents to "breathe in the Western air and bask in the thoughts and ideas of the enlightened. There is no one who does not want women to become educated and useful people in this world" (*CSYP*, September 1, 1909). The second speech was delivered by Mr. Zhong Yongguang at the Presbyterian church on May 25, 1911. According to the newspaper article that appeared the next day, Zhong attributed the devaluation of women to their lack of education and preached that freedom and equality for women could be won through Christianity and education.

Another indication of *CSYP's* support for women's education can be found in the newspaper's coverage of female scholastic achievements, which ranged from short acknowledgments of women graduating from college or professional schools in the United States to an editorial praising outstanding female students.[26] Graduates who expressed interest in returning to China to work, teach, or advocate women's education received special commendation in the newspaper.[27] One editorial, which noted the many female students who were receiving honors in public schools, denounced the Chinese proverb, "Ignorance in a woman is a virtue," and concluded, "We should be grateful that America offers our women education and congratulate the parents and girls on their scholastic achievements" (*CSYP*, June 6, 1904).

As they had in the campaign against footbinding, Protestant missionaries and nationalist reformers took the lead in advocating women's education in China. While Christians believed that educating Chinese women would help to civilize and convert China to Christianity, reformers believed that educating half of the country's population not only would show the rest of the world that China was not decadent but, more importantly, would strengthen the country by encouraging the contributions of all able-minded citizens. Although the latter message was carried in *CSYP*, the issue of women's education took on an added dimension in American Chinatowns. In addition to the nationalist reasons offered, parents were encouraged to educate their daughters because of the American, particularly Christian, emphasis on education for both boys and girls. Yet their children were excluded from attending integrated public schools until the 1920s.[28] Chinese Americans were also led to believe that education would facilitate assimilation into American society and provide improved job opportunities in the future. Yet most Chinese American college graduates could not find jobs in their chosen fields until after World War II. These discriminatory conditions for Chinese Americans only added fuel to the traditional Chinese belief that girls did not need an education. But nonetheless, *CSYP* continued to argue that educating women would help China's cause and lead to equality for women.

Women's Rights

More than any other issue of concern to Chinese American women, the issue of women's rights as covered by *CSYP* indicates clearly the detachment Chinese women felt toward the women's suffrage movement in America and their identification with women's emancipation in China. Although short articles reporting on the struggle to achieve women's rights and suffrage in America as well as in England, Russia, Finland, and Denmark appeared in the newspaper, no mention was made of the involvement of Chinese American women in this struggle.[29] At times *CSYP* even asked why women should be given the right to vote when Chinese men were denied naturalization rights and thus the right to vote.[30]

The names of American feminist leaders during this period—Alice Paul, Carrie Chapman Catt, Elizabeth Gurley Flynn, Crystal Eastman, and Emma Goldman—did not appear in *CSYP*. Instead the newspaper extolled Chinese feminist leaders such as Zhang Zhujun and Xue Jinqin (Sieh King King in the English-language press). Both women were educated in China, Christians, recognized feminist leaders in China, and acclaimed role models for Chinese American women.

According to *CSYP*, Zhang Zhujun came from a well-to-do family in the Cantonese region of China. Taken ill as a child, she stayed in a Western hospital, where she first heard the gospel, chose to be baptized, unbound her feet, and vowed never to marry. After studying Western medicine for three years, Zhang became a doctor and was instrumental in establishing hospitals and vocational schools for girls. At the same time she preached the gospel and advocated women's education, "touring other countries in order to find ways to liberate two million women still in darkness" (*CSYP*, January 21, 1903).

Although there were indications in the newspaper that Zhang intended to visit the United States to seek support for women's education in China, because of illness, she never made the trip.[31] However, two of her articles on education and footbinding were reprinted and featured in *CSYP*. In "The Announcement of the Women's Association for Security Through Learning," which appeared June 9, 10, 11, and 12, 1904, she lamented the miserable conditions for women in China and appealed to Chinese women overseas to support her newly formed Women's Association. According to its bylaws, printed in their entirety, the organization would maintain four schools for girls in China through membership dues and special fund-raising projects. It would also sponsor monthly meetings for members to exchange information and offer mutual support and make an effort to help widows, orphans, and the handicapped. "We must cultivate our intellect in order to be self-reliant, learn skills in order to make our own living, and unite with our comrades for mutual support," she wrote (*CSYP*, June 9, 1904). A commentary in a later issue called Zhang a heroine: By starting the four schools for girls, Zhang was advancing the future of Chinese women and "shaming all those who believe in the absurd idea that ignorance in a woman is a virtue" (*CSYP*, June 16, 1904).

The second article, which appeared July 27, 1904, was the text of a speech Zhang reportedly delivered at the commencement of her practice in Shanghai. In this piece she condemned both the practice of footbinding and the use of cosmetics, emphasizing their harmful effects on women's health. "I beseech women everywhere to practice hygiene and to pursue careers in order to achieve strength and independence. . . . In the future those who support women's rights will not look to Europe but to China," she said (*CSYP*, July 27, 1904).

Acclaimed as a heroine and as the first of Chinese woman orators, Xue Jinqin reportedly delivered her first speech to 500 people in Shanghai in 1901, protesting the Chinese government's intention to grant Russia special rights in Manchuria after the Boxer Rebellion failed.[32] In 1902, at the age of sixteen, Xue registered as a student at a school in Berkeley, having studied earlier in a missionary school in China. "She is petite but ambitious," commented the newspaper reporter. "Her goal, upon completion of her studies, is to return to China to advocate women's education and to free Chinese women of thousand-year-old traditional bindings" (*CSYP*, October 23, 1902).

Xue reportedly made two speeches in San Francisco Chinatown. On November 3, 1902, at the invitation of the Baohuanghui (Society to Protect the Emperor),[33] she spoke at the Danqui Theatre to an audience of 1,000, arguing against footbinding and for women's education (*CSYP*, November 4, 1902). A year later Xue gave another "eloquent and inspiring speech" which again "expounded her views on the role of Chinese women and the need to abolish outdated Chinese customs and emulate the West," this time to an exclusively female audience of 200. She was filling in for reformist leader Lian Qichao, who was unable to attend (*CSYP*, October 12, 1903). *CSYP*, in its New Year issue of 1903, praised her as "an extraordinary woman who brings honor to China" (*CSYP*, January 21, 1903).

CSYP also provided a platform for other feminists who advocated women's rights. A speech delivered in Canton, China, by feminist leader Du Qingqi blamed both men and women for China's state of decline. Men were guilty of oppressing women by denying them education, independence, and nondomestic work, and women were equally guilty for allowing the abridgement of their rights. In order to break the traditional bonds that restrict women's movement and confine them to domestic duties, "women must develop character that can bear the responsibilities of education, reason, judgment, and saving others. This they must do with the mutual love and assistance of their husbands" (*CSYP*, October 25, 1902).

Similar sentiments were echoed in an open letter by the Women's Rights Organization (of China) and in a poem written by Bai Gui, a female scholar. Both drew on classical sayings to illustrate the oppression of women. The letter ended by crying out, "Those who are with us, who are so angry that their hairs stand on end, must raise an army of women to punish the guilty and strip them of their will" (*CSYP*, May 12, 1904). The last refrain of the poem, "Song of Women's Hell," reads:

> I want to arouse women with a rising roar.
> With rage and martial spirit we must unite to set things right.
> Rescuing our sisters out of hell,
> In this will we women be brilliant.
> Though we may die in battle, yet will we be elated
> (*CSYP*, April 8, 1908).

In support of women's emancipation in China, *CSYP* helped to advertise a new women's journal that was to be published weekly in Canton, China. According to the announcement that appeared April 24, 1910, the goals of the journal were to maintain women's morals, advance women's knowledge, promote women's skills, and recover women's rights. *CSYP* encouraged Chinese women overseas to subscribe to it. "The journal can serve as a compass and warning against abuse, thus proving beneficial to all" (*CSYP*, April 24, 1910).

Reports by visitors and by other newspapers on the status of women in China also appeared in *CSYP*. A Baptist minister, recently returned from a conference in Shanghai, commented on the change in women's roles that he witnessed there. "Men and women now have equal rights. Both boys and girls must attend school. Moreover, women recognize the need to learn a skill by which they can firmly establish their independence. Several hundred businesses and factories now employ women workers" (*CSYP*, July 1, 1907). And according to news articles from London and Hong Kong reprinted in *CSYP*, women in China were becoming educated, working in journalism, the military, and commerce, and leading an active public life in the cities.[34]

Such coverage on the issue of women's rights in China encouraged Chinese American women to support women's emancipation in China as well as to examine and challenge their own subordinate role in America. Although the underlying argument for sex equality in China was national salvation, its advocacy in America was also influenced by Protestant values. In either case there were limits to the extent of equality for women. As Ng Poon Chew himself espoused on his lecture tours, women should have the rights of education, livelihood, and free choice of marriage, but "the status of the woman is the home, and there is no excuse for her not being there and rearing a family."[35]

National Salvation

National salvation served as a further impetus to engage Chinese American women in China's politics and to strengthen their identification with their counterparts in China. According to *CSYP*, women on both sides of the ocean expressed their patriotism or nationalism by raising funds for victims of floods and famines and later by supporting the 1911 Revolution. Indeed, it was national crises, such as war and natural disasters in China, that repeatedly called forth a united front among all Chinese and new activism on the part of women in China as well as in America.

When floods and famine occurred in the lower Yangtze River area in 1907 and 1908, *CSYP* reported that female students and women in Guangdong Province donated money and jewelry and raised funds by holding bazaars, giving performances, and selling embroidery and poems.[36] Chinese American women were also moved to action when floods and famines occurred in Jiangbei and Jianquan provinces in 1907 and 1911. In an editorial, "Chinese American Women's Views on Relief Work," women were urged not only to donate their jewelry and their husband's spending money for famine relief, but to encourage others to do likewise. "Things are slowly changing for those here in America. There are now women who are literate and can spread the word" (*CSYP*, May 4, 1907). In 1911 *CSYP* reported a number of fund-raising efforts on behalf of famine relief by Chinese women in Seattle, Portland, Boston, San Francisco, and Oakland.[37] The benefit performance in Seattle was particularly noteworthy, as it was an event marked by interracial harmony. Many Westerners attended, as well as 175 Chinese women out of a total of 400 persons (*CSYP*, February 20, 1911).

As the 1898 Reform Movement waned, failing in its efforts to modernize China and liberate it from foreign domination, popular support turned to Sun Yat-sen's Tongmenghui or Revolutionary Party, which advocated the overthrow of the Qing dynasty and the establishment of a republic. With the support of overseas Chinese money, underground rebels at home attempted eight armed rebellions between 1907 and 1911 in the southern provinces of Guangdong and Guangxi. Victory was not won until the Wuchang uprising of October 10, 1911.[38]

The participation of women in this revolutionary movement in both China and the United States is well documented in *CSYP*. Revolutionary activities on the part of women in China ranged from organizing benefit performances to enlisting in the army.[39] There was reportedly a revolutionary unit in Shanghai consisting of 500 patriotic women, armed and ready to do battle under the leadership of a female commander (*CSYP*, December 9, 1911). Stories of women engaged in dangerous undercover work also appeared in the newspaper—for example, the assassination of Anhui's provincial governor by a female student and the Revolutionary Party's use of women as ammunition smugglers and spies.[40] In another article the patriotism of a female student who tattooed *ai quo* ("love my country") on her right wrist out of frustration was cause for praise. As she told her classmates, she regretted that, being female, she could not challenge a particular traitor to a duel (*CSYP*, October 16, 1911).

Meanwhile Chinese American women were doing their part in support of the revolutionary cause. According to *CSYP*, female orators of the Young China Society were speaking up for the revolution as well as for women's rights. They had also made a two-sided flag—one side bearing the Chinese flag and the other, the flag of the Revolutionary Army (*CSYP*, May 25, 1911). When Dr. Sun Yat-sen, leader of the revolution, spoke to over 600 people in Chinatown, the newspaper noted that there were at least fifty women in attendance.[41] Chinese American women also donated money and jewelry and helped with Red Cross work—fund-raising, preparing bandages and medicines, and sewing garments for the war effort.[42]

In 1907, when the revolutionary heroine Qiu Jin was executed, she was equally mourned and exalted by both Chinese and Chinese American women. Born into the gentry class, Qiu Jin was an accomplished poet, horseback rider, and swordswoman. In response to the failure of the 1898 Reform Movement and the Allied sacking of Peking following the Boxer Rebellion, she resolved to help save China and to fight for women's rights. In 1903 when her arranged marriage proved a failure, she deserted her conservative husband and went to study in Japan. There she became involved in radical politics, participating in the Humanitarian Society, which promoted women's rights and education, and becoming a member of the Tongmenghui. While organizing for the revolution in Zhejiang, she was arrested and executed at the young age of thirty-one. Newspapers in China raged over her unjust execution. So did *CSYP*, which published her biography, accounts of her arrest and death, and poems eulogizing her.[43] One of her followers, Wu Zhiying, wrote a moving account of how hard Giu Jin struggled to get an education in Japan because she believed that only through education could women hope to attain independence (*CSYP*, September 11, 1907). Here again was a Chinese role model and national heroine by which Chinese American women could reaffirm their nationalist and feminist ties with their compatriots in China.

National disasters and the 1911 Revolution gave Chinese and Chinese American women the opportunity to express their patriotism, develop leadership skills, and participate in the public sphere of life. The leaders of the 1911 Revolution, continuing where the 1898 Reform Movement left off in the cause of national salvation, especially encouraged the participation of women because of its strong democratic tenets, thereby helping to groom women for their new roles in public life in the decades to follow.

By examining *CSYP's* coverage of women's issues from 1900 to 1911, we can see the attention that was given to women's emancipation in China in preference to the women's suffrage movement in America. The newspaper's support of women's emancipation was in keeping with its interest in promoting two key concerns: strengthening China through modernization and advocating equal rights for Chinese Americans. By contrasting the restrictive lives of Chinese immigrant women in the nineteenth century with the changing role of Chinese American women in the early years of the twentieth century, we can begin to gauge the influence of these ideas upon the lives of Chinese American women. Although most Chinese American women probably did not read *CSYP*, they were most likely affected by the public opinion it espoused through their husbands, neighbors, and missionary workers looking after their interest. After the 1911 Revolution, it was no longer considered "fashionable" to have bound feet, concubines, and slave girls. The "new woman" not only sought education for herself and her daughters, but began to take advantage of resources in America, to work outside the home, and to participate in community affairs. Certainly other influences, such as the changing composition of the Chinese American population, the efforts of Protestant missionaries to help Chinese American women, and the opening of job opportunities outside the home for women, also affected the role and status of Chinese American women during the period under study. But as a progressive record of the views and activities of Chinese American women as well as an influential molder of public opinion, *CSYP* is an important and helpful source for shedding light on the social awakening of Chinese American women at the turn of the century.

Notes

1. An earlier version of this article was published in *Chinese America: History and Perspectives 1988* (San Francisco: Chinese Historical Society of America), 80–102. "Chinese American women" is used in this paper to include all Chinese women in America, foreign born as well as American born.
2. Suffrage for all women in China was not granted until 1931. For a general history of women in China, including a discussion of women's emancipation, see Elizabeth Croll, *Feminism and Socialism in China* (New York: Schocken Books, 1980); Ono Kazuko, *Chinese Women in a Century of Revolution, 1850–1950* (Stanford: Stanford University Press, 1989); and Esther S. Lee Yao, *Chinese Women: Past and Present* (Mesquite, Texas: Ide House, 1983).
3. Suffrage for all women in the United States was not won until 1920. For a general history of women in America, including a discussion of women's emancipation, see Mary P. Ryan, *Womanhood in America* (New York: Franklin Watts, 1983) and June Sochen, *Her Story: A Record of the American Woman's Past* (Sherman Oaks, CA: Alfred Publishing Co., 1981).
4. U.S. Bureau of Census, *Sixteenth Census of the United States: Population, 1940* (Washington, D. C: Government Printing Office, 1942), vol. 2, 19.
5. For a fuller examination of the lives of Chinese women and prostitutes in nineteenth-century California, see Lucie Cheng Hirata, "Chinese Immigrant Women in Nineteenth-Century California," in *Women in America*, eds. C. R. Berkin and M. B. Norton (Boston: Houghton Mifflin Company, 1979), 224–44; and Lucie Cheng Hirata, "Free, Indentured, Enslaved: Chinese Prostitution in Nineteenth-Century California," *Signs: Journal of Women in Culture and Society* 5:1 (Autumn 1979), 3–29.
6. On the changing role of Chinese American women, see Judy Yung, *Chinese Women of America: A Pictorial History* (Seattle: University of Washington Press, 1986).
7. For a fuller discussion and list of Chinese American newspapers, see Him Mark Lai, "The Chinese-American Press," in *The Ethnic Press in the United States: A Historical Analysis and Handbook*, ed. Sally M. Miller (New York: Greenwood Press, 1987), 27–43; and Karl Lo and Him Mark Lai, *Chinese Newspapers Published in North America, 1854–1975* (Washington, D. C.: Center for Chinese Research Materials, 1977).
8. *CSYP* is available on microfilm at the Asian American Studies Library and East Asiatic Library, University of California, Berkeley. For a fuller discussion of Ng Poon Chew and *CSYP* see Corinne K. Hoexter, *From Canton to California: The Epic of Chinese Immigration* (New York: Four Winds Press, 1976).
9. According to my computation from U. S. National Archives, "U. S. Census of Population" (manuscript schedules), for San Francisco, California, 1900 and 1910, 17 percent of Chinese American women were literate in 1900 and 43 percent in 1910.
10. For example, Chinese could not become naturalized citizens, intermarry, join white labor unions, attend integrated public schools, or own land.
11. Because so many of the articles and editorials in *CSYP* were either unsigned or signed with pen names, it is difficult to determine how many of the pieces on women were written by women themselves. But twenty-six articles and editorials either carried the bylines of women or quoted from speeches delivered by female orators.
12. For a history of footbinding, see Howard S. Levy, *Chinese Footbinding: The History of a Curious Erotic Custom* (New York: Walton Rawls, 1966).
13. Although a smaller percentage of women had bound feet in America than in China (thirty-six

were reported in the 1887 "Annual Report of the Foreign Mission Board of the Presbyterian Church" of San Francisco, 56), the practice was still continued by the merchant class here until the 1911 Revolution.

14. The translations in this paper are by the author, with the assistance of Anne Tsong, Linette Lee, and Ellen Yeung.
15. *CSYP*, July 27, 1904; February 13, 1906; January 2, December 9, 1907.
16. A literature section, consisting of poetry, essays, historical biographies and legends, short stories, songs, and anecdotes, was added to *CSYP* in 1907.
17. *CSYP*, September 5, 26, 1906; October 2, 1907; January 1, 1908.
18. *CSYP*, February 10, 1907; December 10, 1908; March 4, 1910.
19. *CSYP*, July 26, 1902; March 7, 1909; August 27, 1910.
20. *CSYP*, July 20, 1901; May 27, June 28, September 25, October 7, December 16, 1902; December 1, 1903.
21. *CSYP*, March 24, April 2, 3, 5, 13, 14, 16, 25, 28, 30, May 7, 8, 14, 1900.
22. *CSYP*, March 4, 1902; July 14, 1904; April 21, 1905; January 31, 1906; July 8, 1908; October 15, 1909; July 5, 1910.
23. *CSYP*, April 11, 1906; June 28, July 30, August 4, 1908; August 10, 1910.
24. *CSYP*, March 2, June 3, 1907; June 28, 1910. The exclusion of Chinese from mainstream American life heightened nationalist feelings, among them the assumption that regardless of place of birth there was but one motherland for all Chinese living in America–China.
25. On the promotion of education for women in China by Protestant missionaries, see Margaret Burton, *The Education of Women in China* (New York: Fleming H. Revell Company, 1911); and Mary Raleigh Anderson, *Protestant Mission Schools for Girls in South China* (Mobile, Alabama: Hester-Starke Printing Company, 1943).
26. *CSYP*, January 22, 1904; July 8, July 28, August 28, 1908; December 25, 1909; June 7, December 25, 1911.
27. *CSYP*, May 9, 1909; July 12, 1909; September 2, 1909; March 10, 1910; February 6, 1911.
28. On the history of educational discrimination against Chinese Americans, see Victor Low, *The Unimpressible Race: A Century of Educational Struggle by the Chinese in San Francisco* (San Francisco: East/West Publishing; Company, 1982).
29. On women's suffrage in America: *CSYP*, August 5, 1904; January 5, 1909; January 10, 1910; February 16, March 23, March 24, April 5, May 12, August 23, September 26, December 6, 1911. England: *CSYP*, August 5, 1908; April 19, September 22, 1909; July 8, November 20, 1910; May 14, November 23, 1911. Russia: June 19, 1911. Finland: April 9, 1907. Denmark: March 25, 1909.
30. *CSYP*, August 31, 1901; October 23, 1902; January 21, 1903.
31. *CSYP*, October 26, 1902; October 8, 1904.
32. *CSYP*, August 31, 1901; October 23, 1902; January 21, 1903.
33. The Baohuanghui supported the creation of a constitutional monarchy in China, in contrast to the Zhigongtang, which wanted to overthrow the Qing dynasty and restore the Ming, and the Tongmenghui, which wanted to establish a republican government.
34. *CSYP*, October 22, 1907; February 5, 1909.
35. See "Dr. Ng Poon Chew's Views on Love and Marriage" in the Ng Poon Chew manuscript collection, Asian American Studies Library, University of California, Berkeley.
36. *CSYP*, May 1, 1907; August 21, September 30, December 21, 1908.
37. *CSYP*, February 20, March 21, April 19, 21, 23, June 2, 1911.
38. On the history of the reform and revolutionary movements in China, see Jean Chesneaux, Marianne Bastid, and Marie-Claire Bergere, *China: From the Opium Wars to the 1911 Revolution* (New York: Pantheon Books, 1976).
39. *CSYP*, June 11, 1908; November 22, 1911.
40. *CSYP*, July 18, 1907; July 20, 1911. See also Croll, 60–79; and Kazuko, chap. 4.
41. *CSYP*, July 14, 1911. At least a dozen Chinese women were known to have been active members of the San Francisco Branch of the Tongmenghui. See Zeng Bugui, "Sun Zhongshan Yu Jiujinshan Nu Tongmenghui Tuan" (Sun Yat-sen and the women members of San Francisco's Tongmenghui), *Zhongshan Xiansheng Yishi* (Anecdotes of Sun Yat-sen), (Beijing: Zhongguo Wen-shi Chubanshe, 1986), 141–42.
42. *CSYP*, February 21, November 13, 19, 21, 27, December 25, 1911.
43. Her biography is given in *CSYP*, September 9, 11, 13, 1907. The accounts of her arrest and death are recorded in *CSYP*, August 22, 31, September 13, 16, 17, 1907. The poems appear in *CSYP*, August 31, September 12, 1907.

16

Working Women, Class Relations, and Suffrage Militance

Harriot Stanton Blatch and the New York Woman Suffrage Movement, 1894–1909

Ellen Carol DuBois

More than any other period in American reform history, the Progressive Era eludes interpretation. It seems marked by widespread concern for social justice and by extraordinary elitism, by democratization and by increasing social control. The challenge posed to historians is to understand how Progressivism could simultaneously represent gains for the masses and more power for the classes. The traditional way to approach the period has been to study the discrete social programs reformers so energetically pushed in those years, from the abolition of child labor to the Americanization of the immigrants. Recently, historians' emphasis has shifted to politics, where it will probably remain for a time. Historians have begun to recognize that the rules of political life, the nature of American "democracy," were fundamentally reformulated beginning in the Progressive Era, and that such political change shaped the ultimate impact of particular social reforms.

Where were women in all this? The new focus on politics requires a reinterpretation of women's role in Progressivism. As the field of women's history has grown, the importance of women in the Progressive Era has gained notice, but there remains a tendency to concentrate on their roles with respect to social reform. Modern scholarship on the Progressive Era thus retains a separate spheres flavor; women are concerned with social and moral issues, but the world of politics is male. Nowhere is this clearer than in the tendency to minimize, even to omit, the woman suffrage movement from the general literature on the Progressive Era.[1]

Scholarship on woman suffrage is beginning to grow in detail and analytic sophistication, but it has yet to be fully integrated into overviews of the period.[2] Histories that include woman suffrage usually do so in passing, listing it with other constitutional alterations in the electoral process such as the popular election of senators, the initiative, and the referendum. But woman suffrage was a mass movement, and that fact is rarely noticed. Precisely because it was a mass political movement—perhaps the first modern one—woman suffrage may well illuminate Progressive-Era politics, especially the class dynamics underlying their reformulation. When the woman suffrage movement is given its due, we may begin to understand the process by which democratic hope turned into mass political alienation, which is the history of modern American politics.

To illuminate the origin and nature of the woman suffrage movement in the Progressive Era I will examine the politics of Harriot Stanton Blatch. Blatch was the daughter of Elizabeth Cady Stanton, the founding mother of political feminism. Beginning in the early twentieth century, she was a leader in her own right, initially in New York, later nationally. As early as 1903, when politics was still considered something that disreputable men did, like smoking tobacco, Blatch proclaimed: "There are born politicians just as there are born artists, writers, painters. I confess that I should be a politician, that I am not interested in machine politics, but that the devotion to the public cause . . . rather than the individual, appeals to me."[3]

Just as her zest for politics marked Blatch as a new kind of suffragist, so did her efforts to fuse women of different classes into a revitalized suffrage movement. Blatch's emphasis on class was by no means unique; she shared it with other women reformers of her generation. Many historians have treated the theme of class by labeling the organized women's reform movement in the early twentieth century "middle class." By contrast, I have tried to keep open the question of the class character of women's reform in the Progressive Era by rigorously avoiding the term. Characterizing the early twentieth-century suffrage movement as "middle class" obscures its most striking element, the new interest in the vote among women at both ends of the class structure. Furthermore, it tends to homogenize the movement. The very term "middle class" is contradictory, alternatively characterized as people who are not poor, and people who work for a living. By contrast, I have emphasized distinctions between classes and organized my analysis around the relations between them.

No doubt there is some distortion in this framework, particularly for suffragists who worked in occupations like teaching. But there is far greater distortion in using the term "middle class" to describe women like Blatch or Carrie Chapman Catt or Jane Addams. For example, it makes more sense to characterize an unmarried woman with an independent income who was not under financial compulsion to work for her living as "elite," rather than "middle class." The question is not just one of social stratification, but of the place of women in a whole system of class relations. For these new style suffragettes, as for contemporary feminists who write about them, the complex relationship between paid labor, marital status, and women's place in the class structure was a fundamental puzzle. The concept of "middle class" emerged among early twentieth-century reformers, but may ultimately prove more useful in describing a set of relations *between* classes that was coming into being in those years, than in designating a segment of the social structure.

Blatch, examined as a political strategist and a critic of class relations, is important less as a unique figure than as a representative leader, through whose career the historical forces transforming twentieth-century suffragism can be traced. The scope of her leadership offers clues to the larger movement: She was one of the first to open up suffrage campaigns to working-class women, even as she worked closely with wealthy and influential upper-class women; she pioneered militant street tactics and backroom political lobbying at the same time. Blatch's political evolution reveals close ties between other stirrings among American women in the Progressive Era and the rejuvenated suffrage movement. Many of her ideas paralleled Charlotte Perkins Gilman's influential reformulation of women's emancipation in economic terms. Many of Blatch's innovations as a suffragist drew on her prior experience in the Women's Trade Union League. Overall, Blatch's activities suggest that early twentieth-century changes in the American suffrage movement, often traced to the example of militant British suffragettes, had deep, indigenous roots. Among them were the growth of trade unionism among working-class women and professionalism among the elite, changing relations between these classes, and the growing involvement of women of all sorts in political reform.

The suffrage revival began in New York in 1893–1894, as part of a general political reform movement. In the 1890s New York's political reformers were largely upper-class men concerned about political "corruption," which they blamed partly on city Democratic machines and the bosses who ran them, partly on the masses of voting men, ignorant, immigrant, and ripe for political manipulation. Their concern about political corruption and about the consequences of uncontrolled political democracy became the focus of New York's 1894 constitutional convention, which addressed itself largely to "governmental procedures: the rules for filling offices, locating authority and organizing the different branches."[4]

The New York woman suffrage movement, led by Susan B. Anthony, recognized a great opportunity in the constitutional convention of 1894. Focusing on political corruption, Anthony and her allies argued that women were the political reformers' best allies. For while men were already voters and vulnerable to the ethic of partisan loyalty—indeed a man without a party affiliation in the 1890s was damned closed to unsexed—everyone knew that women were naturally nonpartisan. Enfranchising women was therefore the solution to the power of party bosses. Suffragists began by trying to get women elected to the constitutional convention itself. Failing this, they worked to convince the convention delegates to include woman suffrage among the proposed amendments.[5]

Anthony planned a house-to-house canvass to collect signatures on a mammoth woman suffrage petition. For the $50,000 she wanted to fund this effort, she approached wealthy women in New York City, including physician Mary Putnam Jacobi, society leader Catherine Palmer (Mrs. Robert) Abbe, social reformer Josephine Shaw Lowell, and philanthropist Olivia (Mrs. Russell) Sage. Several of them were already associated with efforts for the amelioration of working-class women, notably in the recently formed Consumers' League, and Anthony had reason to think they might be ready to advocate woman suffrage.[6]

The elite women were interested in woman suffrage, but they had their own ideas about how to work for it. Instead of funding Anthony's campaign, they formed their own organization. At parlor meetings in the homes of wealthy women, they tried to strike a genteel note, emphasizing that enfranchisement would *not* take women out of their proper sphere and would *not* increase the political power of the lower classes. Eighty-year-old Elizabeth Stanton, observing the campaign from her armchair, thought that "men and women of the conservative stamp of the Sages can aid us greatly at this stage of our movement."[7]

Why did wealthy women first take an active and prominent part in the suffrage movement in the 1890s? In part they shared the perspective of men of their class that the influence of the wealthy in government had to be strengthened; they believed that with the vote they could increase the political power of their class. In a representative argument before the constitutional convention, Jacobi proposed woman suffrage as a response to "the shifting of political power from privileged classes to the masses of men." The disfranchisement of women contributed to this shift because it made all women, "no matter how well born, how well educated, how intelligent, how rich, how serviceable to the State," the political inferiors of all men, "no matter how base-born, how poverty stricken, how ignorant, how vicious, how brutal." Olivia Sage presented woman suffrage as an antidote to the growing and dangerous "idleness" of elite women, who had forgotten their responsibility to set the moral tone for society.[8]

Yet, the new elite converts also supported woman suffrage on the grounds of changes taking place in women's status, especially within their own class. Jacobi argued that the educational advancement of elite women "and the new activities into which they have been led by it—in the work of charities, in the professions, and in the direction of public education—naturally and logically tend toward the same result, their political equality." She argued that elite women, who had aided the community through organized charity and benevolent activities, should have the same "opportunity to serve the State nobly." Sage was willing to advocate woman suffrage because of women's recent "strides . . . in the acquirement of business methods, in the management of their affairs, in the effective interest they have evinced in civic affairs."[9]

Suffragists like Jacobi and Sage characteristically conflated their class perspective with the role they saw for themselves as women, contending for political leadership not so much on the grounds of their wealth, as of their womanliness. Women, they argued, had the characteristics needed in politics—benevolence, morality, selflessness, and industry; conveniently, they believed that elite women most fully embodied these virtues. Indeed, they liked to believe that women like themselves were elite *because* they were virtuous, not because they were wealthy. The confusion of class and gender coincided with a more general elite ideology that identified the fundamental division in American society not between rich and poor, but between industrious and idle, virtuous and vicious, community-minded and selfish. On these grounds Sage found the purposeless leisure of wealthy women dangerous to the body politic. She believed firmly that the elite, women included, should provide moral—and ultimately political—leadership, but it was important to her that they earn the right to lead.[10]

The problem for elite suffragists was that woman suffrage meant the enfranchisement of working-class, as well as elite, women. Jacobi described a prominent woman who "had interested herself nobly and effectively in public affairs, . . . but preferred not to claim the right [of suffrage] for herself, lest its concession entail the enfranchisement of ignorant and irresponsible women." An elite antisuffrage organization committed to such views was active in the 1894 campaign as well, led by women of the same class, with many of the same beliefs, as the prosuffrage movement. As Stanton wrote, "The fashionable women are about equally divided between two camps." The antis included prominent society figures Abby Hamlin (Mrs. Lyman) Abbott and Josephine Jewell (Mrs. Arthur) Dodge, as well as Annie Nathan Meyer, founder of Barnard College and member of the Consumers' League. Like the elite suffragists, upper-class antis wanted to insure greater elite influence in politics; but they argued that woman suffrage would decrease elite influence, rather than enhance it.[11]

Elite suffragists' willingness to support woman suffrage rested on their confidence that their class would provide political leadership for all women once they had the vote. Because they expected working-class women to defer to them, they believed that class relations among women would be more cooperative and less antagonistic than among men. Elite women, Jacobi argued before the 1894 convention, would "so guide ignorant women voters that they could be made to counterbalance, when necessary, the votes of ignorant and interested men." Such suffragists assumed that working-class women were too weak, timid, and disorganized to make their own demands. Since early in the nineteenth century, elite women had claimed social and religious authority on the grounds of their responsibility for the women and children of the poor. They had begun to adapt this tradition to the new conditions of an industrial age, notably in the Consumers' League, formed in response to the pleas of women wage earners for improvement in their working conditions. In fact, elite antis also asserted that they spoke for working-class women, but they contended that working-class women neither needed nor wanted to vote.[12]

From an exclusively elite perspective, the antisuffrage argument was more consistent than the prosuffrage one; woman suffrage undoubtedly meant greater political democracy, which the political reform movement of the 1890s most fundamentally feared. Elite suffragists found themselves organizing their own arguments around weak refutations of the antis' objections.[13] The ideological weakness had political implications. Woman suffrage got no serious hearing in the constitutional convention, and the 1894 constitutional revisions designed to "clean up government" ignored women's plea for political equality.

The episode revealed dilemmas, especially with respect to class relations among women, that a successful suffrage movement would have to address. Elite women had begun to aspire to political roles that led them to support woman suffrage, and the resources they commanded would be crucial to the future success of suffrage efforts. But their attraction to woman suffrage rested on a portrait of working-class women and a system of class relations that had become problematic to a modern industrial society. Could elite women sponsor the entrance of working-class women into politics without risking their influence over them, and perhaps their position of leadership? Might not working-class women assume a newly active, politically autonomous role? The tradition of class relations among women had to be transformed before a thriving and modern woman suffrage movement could be built. Harriot Stanton Blatch had the combination of suffrage convictions and class awareness to lead New York suffragists through that transition.

The 1894 campaign, which confronted suffragists with the issue of class, also drew Blatch actively into the American woman suffrage movement. She had come back from England, where she had lived for many years, to receive a master's degree from Vassar College for her study of the English rural poor. A powerful orator, she was "immediately pressed into service . . . speaking every day," at parlor suffrage meetings, often to replace her aged mother.[14] Like her mother, Blatch was comfortable in upper-class circles; she had married into a wealthy British family. She generally shared the elite perspective of the campaign, assuming that "educated women" would lead their sex. But she disliked the implication that politics could ever become too democratic and, virtually alone among the suffragists, criticized all "those little anti-republican things I hear so often here in America, this talk of the quality of votes." And while other elite suffragists discussed working-class women as domestic servants and shop clerks, Blatch understood the centrality of industrial workers, although her knowledge of them was still primarily academic.[15]

Blatch's disagreements with the elite suffrage framework were highlighted a few months after the constitutional convention in an extraordinary public debate with her mother. In the *Woman's Journal,* Stanton urged that the suffrage movement incorporate an educational restriction into its demand, to respond to "the greatest block in the way of woman's enfranchisement . . . the fear of the 'ignorant vote' being doubled." Her justification for this position, so at odds with the principles of a lifetime, was that the enfranchisement of "educated women" best supplied "the imperative need at the time . . . woman's influence in public life." From England, Blatch wrote a powerful dissent. Challenging the authority of her venerated mother was a dramatic act that—perhaps deliberately—marked the end of her political daughterhood. She defended both the need and the capacity of the working class to engage in democratic politics. On important questions, "for example . . . the housing of the poor," their opinion was more informed than that of the elite. She also argued that since "the conditions of the poor are so much harder . . . every working man needs the suffrage more that I do." And finally, she insisted on the claims of a group her mother had ignored, working women.[16]

The debate between mother and daughter elegantly symbolizes the degree to which class threatened the continued vitality of the republican tradition of suffragism. Blatch was able to adapt the republican faith to modern class relations, while Stanton was not, partly because of her participation in the British Fabian movement. As a Fabian, Blatch had gained an appreciation for the political intelligence and power of the working class very rare among elite reformers in the U.S. When she insisted that the spirit of democracy was more alive in England than in the U.S., she was undoubtedly thinking of the development of a working-class political movement there.[17]

Over the next few years, Blatch explored basic assumptions of the woman suffrage faith she had inherited in the context of modern class relations. In the process, like other women reformers of her era, such as Charlotte Perkins Gilman, Florence Kelley, Jane Addams, and numerous settlement house residents and supporters of organized labor, she focused on the relation of women and work. She emphasized the productive labor that women performed, both as it contributed to the larger social good and as it created the conditions of freedom and equality for women themselves. Women had always worked, she insisted. The new factor was the shift of women's work from the home to the factory and the office, and from the status of unpaid to paid labor. Sometimes she stressed that women's unpaid domestic labor made an important contribution to society; at other times she stressed that such unpaid work was not valued, but always she emphasized the historical development that was taking women's labor out of the home and into the commercial economy. The question for modern society was not whether women should work, but under what conditions, and with what consequences for their own lives.[18]

Although Blatch was troubled by the wages and working conditions of the laboring poor, her emphasis on work as a means to emancipation led her to regard wage-earning women less as victims to be succored, than as exemplars to their sex. She vigorously denied that women ideally hovered somewhere above the world of work. She had no respect for the "handful of rich women who have no employment other than organizing servants, social functions and charities." Upper-class women, she believed, should also "work," should make an individualized contribution to the public good, and where possible should have the value of their labor recognized by being paid for it.[19] As a member of the first generation of college-educated women, she believed that education and professional achievement, rather than wealth and refinement, fitted a woman for social leadership.

Turning away from nineteenth-century definitions of the unity of women that emphasized their place in the home, their motherhood, and their exclusion from the economy, and emphasizing instead the unity that productive work provided for all women, Blatch rewrote feminism in its essentially modern form, around work. She tended to see women's work, including homemaking and child rearing, as a mammoth portion of the world's productive labor, which women collectively accomplished. Thus she retained the concept of "women's work" for the sex as a whole, while vigorously discarding it on the individual level, explicitly challenging the notion that all women had the same tastes and talents.[20]

Her approach to "women's work" led Blatch to believe that the interconnection of women's labor fundamentally shaped relations among them. Here were the most critical aspects of her thought. Much as she admired professional women, she insisted that they recognize the degree to which their success rested on the labor of other women, who cared for their homes and their children. "Whatever merit [their homes] possess," Blatch wrote, "is largely due to the fact that the actress when on the stage, the doctor when by her patient's side, the writer when at her desk, has a Bridget to do the homebuilding for her." The problem was that the professional woman's labor brought her so much more freedom than the housemaid's labor brought her. "Side by side with the marked improvement in the condition of the well-to-do or educated woman," Blatch observed, "our century shows little or no progress in the condition of the woman of the people." Like her friend Gilman, Blatch urged that professional standards of work—good pay, an emphasis on expertise, the assumption of a lifelong career—be extended to the nurserymaid and the dressmaker, as well as to the lawyer and the journalist. Until such time, the "movement for the emancipation of women [would] remain . . . a well-dressed movement."[21]

But professional training and better wages alone would not give labor an emancipatory power in the lives of working-class women. Blatch recognized the core of the problem of women's work, especially for working-class women: "How can the duties of mother and wage earner be reconciled?" She believed that wage-earning women had the same desire as professional women to continue to enjoy careers and independence after marriage. "It may be perverse in lowly wage earners to show individuality as if they were rich," Blatch wrote, "but apparently we shall have to accept the fact that all women do not prefer domestic work to all other kinds." But the problem of balancing a career and a homelife was "insoluble—under present conditions—for the women of the people." "The pivotal question for women," she wrote, "is how to organize their work as home-builders and race-builders, how to get that work paid for not in so called protection, but in the currency of the state."[22]

As the female labor force grew in the late nineteenth century, so did the number of married women workers and demands that they be driven from the labor force. The suffrage movement had traditionally avoided the conflict between work and motherhood by pinning the demand for economic equality on the existence of unmarried women, who had no men to support them.[23] Blatch confronted the problem of work and motherhood more directly. In a 1905 article, she drew from the Utopian ideas of William Morris to recommend that married women work in small, worker-owned manufacturing shops where they could have more control over their hours and could bring their children with them. Elsewhere, she argued that the workplace should be reorganized around women's needs, rather than assume the male worker's standards, but she did not specify what that would mean. She never solved the riddle of work and children for women—nor have we—but she knew that the solution could not be to force women to choose between the two nor to banish mothers from the labor force.[24]

Blatch's vision of women in industrial society was democratic—all must work and all must be recognized and rewarded for their work—but it was not an egalitarian approach nor one that recognized most working women's material concerns. According to Blatch, women worked for psychological and ethical reasons, as much as for monetary ones. "As human beings we must have work," she wrote; "we rust out if we have not an opportunity to function on something." She emphasized the common promises and problems work raised in women's lives, not the differences in how they worked, how much individual choice they had, and especially in how much they were paid. She was relatively unconcerned with the way work enabled women to earn their livings. No doubt, her own experience partially explains this. As a young woman fresh out of college in the 1870s, she had dared to imagine that her desire for meaningful work and a role in the world need not deprive her of marriage and motherhood, and it did not. Despite her marriage, the birth of two children, and the death of one, she never interrupted her political and intellectual labors. But she also never earned her own living, depending instead on the income from her husband's family's business. In later years, she joked about the fact that she was the only "parasite" in the organization of self-supporting women she headed.[25]

But the contradictions in her analysis of the problem of work and women reflected more than her personal situation. There were two problems of work and women: the longstanding exploitation of laboring women of the working classes and the newly expanding place of paid labor in the lives of all women in bourgeois society. While the two processes were not the same, they were related, and women thinkers and activists of the Progressive period struggled to understand how. As more women worked for pay and outside of the home, how would the meaning of "womanhood" change? What would be the difference between "woman" and "man" when as many women as men were paid workers? And what would be the class difference between women if all of them worked? Indeed, would there be any difference between the classes at all, once the woman of leisure no longer existed? Virtually all the efforts to link the gender and class problems of work for woman were incomplete. If Blatch's analysis of work, like Gilman's, shorted the role of class, others' analyses, for instance Florence Kelley's, underplayed what work meant for women as a sex.

Blatch rethought the principles of political equality in the light of her emphasis on women's work. At an 1898 congressional hearing, Blatch hailed "the most convincing argument upon which our future claims must rest—the growing recognition of the economic value of the work of women."[26] Whereas her mother had based her suffragism on the nineteenth-century argument for natural rights and on the individual, Blatch based hers on women's economic contribution and their significance as a group.

The contradictions in Blatch's approach to women and work also emerged in her attempts to link work and the vote. On the one hand, she approached women's political rights as she did their economic emancipation, democratically: Just as all sorts of women must work, all needed the vote. Wealthy women needed the vote because they were taxpayers and had the right to see that their money was not squandered; women industrial workers needed it because their jobs and factories were subject to laws, which they had the right to shape. On the other hand, she recognized the strategic centrality of the enormous class of industrial workers, whose economic role was so important and whose political power was potentially so great. "It is the women of the industrial class," she explained, "the wage-earners, reckoned by the hundred of thousands, . . . the women whose work has been submitted to a money test, who have been the means of bringing about the altered attitude of public opinion toward woman's work in every sphere of life."[27]

Blatch returned to New York for several extended visits after 1894, and she moved back for good in 1902. She had two purposes. Elizabeth Stanton was dying, and Blatch had come to be with her.

Blatch also intended to take a leading role in the New York City suffrage movement. On her deathbed in 1902, Stanton asked Anthony to aid Blatch. However, hampered by Anthony's determination to keep control of the movement, Blatch was not able to make her bid for suffrage leadership until Anthony died, four years later.[28]

Meanwhile, Blatch was excited by other reform efforts, which were beginning to provide the resources for a new kind of suffrage movement. During the first years of the twentieth century two movements contributed to Blatch's political education—a broadened, less socially exclusive campaign against political corruption and a democratized movement for the welfare of working women. By 1907, her combined experience in these two movements enabled her to put her ideas about women and work into practice within the suffrage movement itself.

Women had become more active in the campaign against political corruption after 1894. In New York City, Josephine Shaw Lowell and Mary Putnam Jacobi formed the Woman's Municipal League, which concentrated on educating the public about corruption, in particular the links between the police and organized prostitution. Women were conspicuous in the reform campaigns of Seth Low, who was elected mayor in 1901.[29]

By the early 1900s, moreover, the spirit of political reform in New York City had spread beyond the elite. A left wing of the political reform movement had developed that charged that "Wall Street" was more responsible for political corruption than "the Bowery." Women were active in this wing, and there were women's political organizations with links to the Democratic party and the labor movement, a Women's Henry George Society, and a female wing of William Randolph Hearst's Independence League. The nonelite women in these groups were as politically enthusiastic as the members of the Woman's Municipal League, and considerably less ambivalent about enlarging the electorate. Many of them strongly supported woman suffrage. Beginning in 1905, a group of them organized an Equal Rights League to sponsor mock polling places for women to register their political opinions on election day.[30]

Through the 1900s Blatch dutifully attended suffrage meetings, and without much excitement advocated the municipal suffrage for propertied women, favored by the New York movement's leaders after their 1894 defeat. Like many other politically minded women, however, she found her enthusiasm caught by the movement for municipal political reform. She supported Low for mayor in 1901 and believed that his victory demonstrated "how strong woman's power really was when it was aroused." By 1903 she suggested to the National American Woman Suffrage Association (NAWSA) that it set aside agitation for the vote, so that "the women of the organization should use it for one year, nationally and locally, to pursue and punish corruption in politics." She supported the increasing attention given to "the laboring man" in reform political coalitions, but she pointedly observed that "the working woman was never considered."[31]

However, working-class women were emerging as active factors in other women's reform organizations. The crucial arena for this development was the Women's Trade Union League (WTUL), formed in 1902 by a coalition of working-class and elite women to draw wage-earning women into trade unions. The New York chapter was formed in 1905, and Blatch was one of the first elite women to join. The WTUL represented a significant move away from the tradition of elite, ameliorative sisterhood at work in the 1894 campaign for woman suffrage. Like the Consumers' League, it had been formed in response to the request of women wage earners for aid from elite women, but it was an organization of both classes working together. Blatch had never been attracted to the strictly ameliorative tradition of women's reform, and the shift toward a partnership of upper-class and working-class women paralleled her own thinking about the relation between the classes and the role of work in women's lives. She and other elite women in the WTUL found themselves laboring not for working-class women, but with them, and toward a goal of forming unions that did not merely "uplift" working-class women, but empowered them. Instead of being working-class women's protectors, they were their "allies." Instead of speaking on behalf of poor women, they began to hear them speak for themselves. Within the organization wage earners were frequently in conflict with allies. Nonetheless, the league provided them an arena to articulate a working-class feminism related to, but distinct from, that of elite women.[32]

Although prominent as a suffragist, Blatch participated in the WTUL on its own terms, rather than as a colonizer for suffrage. She and two other members assigned to the millinery trade conducted investigations into conditions and organized mass meetings to interest women workers in unions. She sat on the Executive Council from 1906 through 1909 and was often called on to stand in for President Mary Dreier. Her academic knowledge of "the industrial woman" was replaced by direct knowledge of wage-earning women and their working conditions. She was impressed with what she saw of trade unionism, especially its unrelenting "militance." Perhaps most important, she developed working relations with politically sophisticated working-class women, notably Leonora O'Reilly and Rose Schneiderman. Increasingly she believed that the organized power of labor and the enfranchisement of women were closely allied.[33]

Working-class feminists in the league were drawn to ideas like Blatch's—to conceptions of dignity and equality for women in the workplace and to the ethic of self-support and lifelong independence; they wanted to upgrade the condition of wage-earning women so that they, too, could enjoy personal independence on the basis of their labor. On the one hand, they understood why most working-class women would want to leave their hateful jobs upon marriage; on the other, they knew that women as a group, if not the individual worker, were a permanent factor in the modern labor force. Mary Kenney O'Sullivan of Boston, one of the league's founders, believed that "self support" was a goal for working-class women, but that only trade unions would give the masses of working women the "courage, independence, and self respect" they needed to improve their conditions. She expected "women of opportunity" to help in organizing women workers, because they "owed much to workers who give them a large part of what they have and enjoy," and because "the time has passed when women of opportunity can be self respecting and work for others."[34]

Initially, the demand for the vote was less important to such working-class feminists than to the allies. Still, as they began to participate in the organized women's movement on a more equal basis, wage-earning women began to receive serious attention within the woman suffrage movement as well. Beginning about 1905, advocates of trade unionism and the vote for women linked the demands. At the 1906 suffrage convention WTUL member Gertrude Barnum pointed out that "our hope as suffragists lies with these strong working women." Kelley and Addams wrote about the working woman's need for the vote to improve her own conditions. In New York, Blatch called on the established suffrage societies to recognize the importance of the vote to wage-earning women and the importance of wage-earning women to winning the vote. When she realized that existing groups could not adapt to the new challenges, she moved to form her own society.[35]

In January 1907, Blatch declared the formation of a new suffrage organization, the Equality League of Self-Supporting Women. The *New York Times* reported that the two hundred women present at the first meeting included "doctors, lawyers, milliners and shirtmakers."[36] Blatch's decision to establish a suffrage organization that emphasized female "self-support"—lifelong economic independence— grew out of her ideas about work as the basis of women's claim on the state, the leadership role she envisioned for educated professionals, and her discovery of the power and political capacity of trade-union women. The Equality League provided the medium for introducing a new and aggressive style of activism into the suffrage movement—a version of the "militance" Blatch admired among trade unionists.

Initially, Blatch envisioned the Equality League of Self-Supporting Women as the political wing of the Women's Trade Union League. All the industrial workers she recruited were WTUL activists, including O'Reilly, the Equality League's first vice-president, and Schneiderman, its most popular speaker. To welcome working-class women, the Equality League virtually abolished membership fees; the policy had the added advantage of allowing Blatch to claim every woman who ever attended a league meeting in her estimate of its membership. She also claimed the members of the several trade unions affiliated with the Equality League, such as the bookbinders, overall makers, and cap makers, so that when she went before the New York legislature to demand the vote, she could say that the Equality League represented thousands of wage-earning women.[37]

Blatch wanted the Equality League to connect industrial workers, not with "club women" (her phrase), but with educated, professional workers, who should, she thought, replace benevolent ladies as the leaders of their sex. Such professionals—college educated and often women pioneers in their professions—formed the bulk of the Equality League's active membership. Many were lawyers, for instance, Ida Rauh, Helen Hoy, Madeleine Doty, Jessie Ashley, Adelma Burd, and Bertha Rembaugh. Others were social welfare workers, for instance the Equality League's treasurer, Kate Claghorn, a tenement housing inspector and the highest paid female employee of the New York City government. Blatch's own daughter, Nora, the first woman graduate civil engineer in the United States, worked in the New York City Department of Public Works. Many of these women had inherited incomes and did not work out of economic need, but out of a desire to give serious, public substance to their lives and to make an impact on society. Many of them expressed the determination to maintain economic independence after they married.[38]

Although Blatch brought together trade-union women and college-educated professionals in the Equality League, there were tensions between the classes. The first correspondence between O'Reilly and Barnard graduate Caroline Lexow was full of class suspicion and mutual recrimination. More generally, there were real differences in how and why the two classes of working women demanded the vote. Trade-union feminists wanted the vote so that women industrial workers would have power over the labor laws that directly affected their working lives. Many of the college-educated self-supporters were the designers and administrators of this labor legislation. Several of them were, or aspired to be, government employees, and political power affected their jobs through party patronage. The occupation that might have bridged the differences was teaching. As in other cities, women teachers in New York organized for greater power and equal pay. The Equality League frequently offered aid, but the New York teachers' leaders were relatively conservative and kept their distance from the suffrage movement.[39]

Blatch's special contribution was her understanding of the bonds and common interests uniting industrial and professional women workers. The industrial women admired the professional ethic, if not the striving careerism, of the educated working women, and the professionals admired the matter-of-fact way wage-earning women went out to work. The fate of the professional woman was closely tied to that of the industrial worker; the cultural regard in which all working women were held affected both. Blatch dramatized that tie when she was refused service at a restaurant because she was unescorted by a man (that is, because she was eating with a woman). The management claimed that its policy aimed to protect "respectable" women, like Blatch, from "objectionable" women, like the common woman worker who went about on her own, whose morals were therefore questionable. Blatch rejected the division between respectable women and working women, pointing out that "there are five million women earning their livelihood in this country, and it seems strange that feudal customs should still exist here."[40]

The dilemma of economically dependent married women was crucial to the future of both classes of working women. Blatch believed that if work was to free women, they could not leave it for dependence on men in marriage. The professional and working-class members of the Equality League shared this belief, one of the distinguishing convictions of their new approach to suffragism. In 1908, Blatch and Mary Dreier chaired a debate about the housewife, sponsored by the WTUL and attended by many Equality League members. Charlotte Perkins Gilman took the Equality League position, that the unemployed wife was a "parasite" on her husband, and that all women, married as well as unmarried, should work, "like every other self-respecting being." Anna Howard Shaw argued that women's domestic labor was valuable, even if unpaid, and that the husband was dependent on his wife. A large audience attended, and although they "warmly applauded" Gilman, they preferred Shaw's sentimental construction of the economics of marriage.[41]

A month after the Equality League was formed, Blatch arranged for trade-union women to testify before the New York legislature on behalf of woman suffrage, the first working-class women ever to do so. The New York Woman Suffrage Association was still concentrating on the limited, property-based form of municipal suffrage; in lethargic testimony its leaders admitted that they had "no new arguments to present." Everyone at the hearing agreed that the antis had the better of the argument. The Equality League testimony the next day was in sharp contrast. Clara Silver and Mary Duffy, WTUL activists and organizers in the garment industry, supported full suffrage for all New York women. The very presence of these women before the legislature, and their dignity and intelligence, countered the antis' dire predictions about enfranchising the unfit. Both linked suffrage to their trade-union efforts: While they struggled for equality in unions and in industry, "the state" undermined them, by teaching the lesson of female inferiority to male unionists and bosses. "To be left out by the State just sets up a prejudice against us," Silver explained. "Bosses think and women come to think themselves that they don't count for so much as men."[42]

The formation of the Equality League and its appearance before the New York legislature awakened enthusiasm. Lillie Devereux Blake, whose own suffrage group had tried "one whole Winter . . . to [interest] the working women" but found that they were "so overworked and so poor that they can do little for us," congratulated Blatch on here apparent success. Helen Marot, organizing secretary for the New York WTUL, praised the Equality League for "realizing the increasing necessity of including working women in the suffrage movement." Blatch, O'Reilly, and Schneiderman were the star speakers at the 1907 New York suffrage convention. "We realize that probably it will not be the educated workers, the college women, the men's association for equal suffrage, but the people who are fighting for industrial freedom who will be our vital force at the finish," proclaimed the newsletter of the NAWSA.[43]

The unique class character of the Equality League encouraged the development of a new style of agitation, more radical than anything practiced in the suffrage movement since . . . since Elizabeth Stanton's prime. The immediate source of the change was the Women's Social and Political Union of England (WSPU), led by Blatch's comrade from her Fabian days, Emmeline Pankhurst. Members of the WSPU were just beginning to be arrested for their suffrage protests. At the end of the Equality League's first year, Blatch invited one of the first WSPU prisoners, Anne Cobden-Sanderson, daughter of Richard Cobden, to the U.S. to tell about her experiences, scoring a coup for the Equality League. By emphasizing Cobden-Sanderson's connection with the British Labour party and distributing free platform tickets to trade-union leaders, Blatch was able to get an overflow crowd at Cooper Union, Manhattan's labor temple, two-thirds of them men, many of them trade unionists.[44]

The Equality League's meeting for Cobden-Sanderson offered American audiences their first account of the new radicalism of English suffragists, or as they were beginning to be called, suffragettes. Cobden-Sanderson emphasized the suffragettes' working-class origins. She attributed the revival of the British suffrage movement to Lancashire factory workers; the heroic figure in her account was the working-class suffragette, Annie Kenney, while Christabel Pankhurst, later canonized as the Joan of Arc of British militance, went unnamed. After women factory workers were arrested for trying to see the prime minister, Cobden-Sanderson and other privileged women, who felt they "had not so much to lose as [the workers] had," decided to join them and get arrested. She spent almost two months in jail, living the life of a common prisoner and coming to a new awareness of the poor and suffering women she saw there. Her simple but moving account conveyed the transcendent impact of the experience.[45]

Cobden-Sanderson's visit to New York catalyzed a great outburst of suffrage energy; in its wake, Blatch and a handful of other new leaders introduced the WSPU tactics into the American movement, and the word *suffragette* became as common in New York as in London. The "militants" became an increasingly distinct wing of the movement in New York and other American cities. But it would be too simple to say that the British example caused the new, more militant phase in the American movement. The developments that were broadening the class basis and the oudook of American suffragism had prepared American women to respond to the heroism of the British militants.[46]

The development of militance in the American suffrage movement was marked by new aggressive tactics practiced by the WSPU, especially open-air meetings and outdoor parades. At this stage in the development of British militance, American suffragists generally admired the heroism of the WSPU martyrs. Therefore, although the press emphasized dissent within the suffrage movement—it always organized its coverage of suffrage around female rivalries of some sort—the new militant activities were well received throughout the movement. And, conversely, even the most daring American suffragettes believed in an American exceptionalism that made it unnecessary to contemplate going to prison, to suffer as did the British militants.[47]

Despite Blatch's later claims, she did not actually introduce the new tactics in New York City. The first open-air meetings were organized immediately after the Cobden-Sanderson visit by a group called the American Suffragettes. Initiated by Bettina Borrman Wells, a visiting member of the WSPU, most of the American Suffragettes' membership came from the Equal Rights League, the left-wing municipal reform group that had organized mock polling places in New York since 1905. Feminist egalitarians with radical cultural leanings, its members were actresses, artists, writers, teachers, and social welfare workers—less wealthy versions of the professional self-supporters in the Equality League. Their local leader was a librarian, Maud Malone, whose role in encouraging new suffrage tactics was almost as important as, although less recognized than, Blatch's own.[48]

The American Suffragettes held their first open-air meeting in Madison Square on New Year's Eve, 1907. After that they met in the open at least once a week. Six weeks later, they announced they would hold New York's first all-woman parade. Denied a police permit, they determined to march anyway. The twenty-three women in the "parade" were many times outnumbered by the onlookers, mostly working-class men. In a public school to which they adjourned to make speeches, the American Suffragettes told a sympathetic audience that "the woman who works is the underdog of the world"; thus she needed the vote to defend herself. Socialists and working women rose from the floor to support them. Two years later the Equality League organized a much more successful suffrage parade in New York. Several hundred suffragettes, organized by occupation, marched from Fifty-ninth Street to Union Square. O'Reilly, the featured speaker, made "a tearful plea on behalf of the working girl that drew the first big demonstration of applause from the street crowd."[49]

Perhaps because the American Suffragettes were so active in New York City, Blatch held the Equality League's first open-air meetings in May 1908 upstate. Accompanied by Maud Malone, she organized an inventive "trolley car campaign" between Syracuse and Albany, using the interurban trolleys to go from town to town. The audiences expressed the complex class character of the suffrage movement at that moment. In Syracuse Blatch had her wealthy friend Dora Hazard arrange a meeting among the workers at her husband's factory. She also held a successful outdoor meeting in Troy, home of the Laundry Workers' Union, one of the oldest and most militant independent women's trade unions in the country. Albany was an antisuffrage stronghold, and its mayor tried to prevent the meeting, but Blatch outwitted him. The highlight of the tour was in Poughkeepsie, where Blatch and Inez Milholland, then a student at Vassar College, organized a legendary meeting. Since Vassar's male president forbade any woman suffrage activities on college grounds, Blatch and Milholland defiantly announced they would meet students in a cemetery. Gilman, who was extremely popular among college women, spoke, but it was the passionate trade-union feminist, Schneiderman, who was the star.[50]

Blatch believed that the first function of militant tactics was to gain much-needed publicity for the movement. The mainstream press had long ignored suffrage activities. If an occasional meeting was reported, it was usually buried in a small backpage article, focusing on the absurdity and incompetence of women's efforts to organize a political campaign. Gilded Age suffragists themselves accepted the Victorian convention that respectable women did not court public ... on the importance of paid labor for women of all ...n. Blatch understood "the value of publicity or rather open-air meetings and trolley car campaigns because ...nger held the conventional horror for her followers.[51] ...ess boycott" by violating standards of respectable ...nd embracing the subsequent ridicule and attention. ...rs and fighting our way to recognition, forcing the ...*agette* manifesto proclaimed. "We glory . . . that we ...blicity was an instant success: Newspaper coverage ...ering *New York Times* reported regularly on suffrage. ...vent, the more prominent the coverage. Blatch was

...they intensified women's commitment to the move ...the boundary of respectability would etch suffrage ...i or modification. Blatch caught the psychology of ...-sacrifice and now this force is to be drawn upon in ...pation," she wrote. "The new methods of agitation, ...y hold of the imagination and devotion of women, wherein lies the strength of the new appeal, the certainty of victory." Borrman Wells spoke of the "divine spirit of self-sacrifice," which underlay the suffragette's transgressions against respectability and was the source of the "true inwardness of the movement."[53]

If suffrage militants had a general goal beyond getting the vote, it was to challenge existing standards of femininity. "We must eliminate that abominable word ladylike from our vocabularies," Borrman Wells proclaimed. "We must get out and fight." The new definition of femininity the militants were evolving drew, on the one hand, on traditionally male behaviors, like aggression, fighting, provocation, and rebelliousness. Blatch was particularly drawn to the "virile" world of politics, which she characterized as a male "sport" she was sure she could master. On the other hand, they undertook a spirited defense of female sexuality, denying that it need be forfeited by women who participated vigorously in public life. "Women are no longer to be considered little tootsey wootseys who have nothing to do but look pretty," suffragette Lydia Commander declared. "They are determined to take an active part in the community and look pretty too." A member of a slightly older generation, Blatch never adopted the modern sexual ethic of the new woman, but she constantly emphasized the fact that women had distinct concerns that had to be accommodated in politics and industry. These two notes— the difference of the sexes and the repressed ability of women for manly activities—existed side by side in the thought of all the suffrage insurgents.[54]

The militant methods, taking suffrage out of the parlors and into the streets, indicated the new significance of working-class women in several ways. Blatch pointed out that the new methods—open-air meetings, newspaper publicity—suited a movement whose members had little money and therefore could not afford to rent halls or publish a newspaper. As a style of protest, "militance" was an import from the labor movement; WTUL organizers had been speaking from street corners for several years. And disrespect for the standards of ladylike respectability showed at least an impatience with rigid standards of class distinction, at most the influence of class-conscious wage-earning women.[55]

Working-class feminists were eager to speak from the militants' platform, as were many Socialists. A Socialist cadre, Dr. Anna Mercy, organized a branch of the American Suffragettes on the Lower East Side, which issued the first suffrage leaflets ever published in Yiddish. Militants also prepared propaganda in German and Italian and, in general, pursued working-class audiences. "Our relation to the State will be determined by the vote of the average man," Blatch asserted. "None but the converted . . . will come to us. We must seek on the highways the unconverted."[56]

However, it would be a mistake to confuse the suffragettes' radicalism with the radicalism of a working-class movement. The ultimate goal of the suffragettes was not a single-class movement, but a universal one, "the union of women of all shades of political thought and of all ranks of society on the single issue of their political enfranchisement." While the Equality League's 1907 hearing before the state legislature highlighted trade-union suffragists, at the 1908 hearing the league also featured elite speakers, in effect deemphasizing the working-class perspective.[57] Militants could neither repudiate the Socialist support they were attracting, and alienate working-class women, nor associate too closely with Socialists and lose access to the wealthy. Blatch—who actually became a Socialist after the suffrage was won—would not arrange for the Socialist party leader Morris Hillquit to join other prosuffrage speakers at the 1908 legislative hearing. Similarly, the American Suffragettes allowed individual Socialists on their platform but barred Socialist propaganda. Speaking for Socialist women who found the "idea of a 'radical' suffrage movement . . . very alluring," Josephine Conger Kaneko admitted that the suffragettes left her confused.[58]

Moreover, the militant challenge to femininity and the emphasis on publicity introduced a distinctly elite bias; a society matron on an open-air platform made page one while a working girl did not, because society women were obliged by conventions and could outrage by flouting them. In their very desire to redefine femininity, the militants were anxious to stake their claim to it, and it was upper-class women who determined femininity. In Elizabeth Robin's drama about the rise of militance in the British suffrage movement, *The Convert*, the heroine of the title was a beautiful aristocratic woman who became radical when she realized the emptiness of her ladylike existence and the contempt for women obscured by gentlemen's chivalrous gestures. The Equality League brought *The Convert* to New York in 1908 as its first large fund-raising effort; working-class women, as well as elite women, made up the audience. Malone was one of the few militants to recognize and to protest against excessive solicitousness for the elite convert. She resigned from the American Suffragettes when she concluded that they had become interested in attracting "a well-dressed crowd, not the rabble."[59]

Blatch's perspective and associations had always been fundamentally elite. The most well connected of the new militant leaders, she played a major role in bringing the new suffrage propaganda to the attention of upper-class women. She presided over street meetings in fashionable neighborhoods, where reporters commented on the "smart" crowds and described the speakers' outfits in society-page detail. Blatch's first important ally from the Four Hundred was Katherine Duer Mackay, wife of the founder of the International Telephone and Telegraph Company and a famous society beauty. Mackay's suffragism was very ladylike, but other members of her set who followed her into the movement were more drawn to militance: Alva Belmont, a veritable mistress of flamboyance, began her suffrage career as Mackay's protégé. The elitist subtext of militance was a minor theme in 1908 and 1909. But by 1910 becoming a suffragette was proving "fashionable," and upper-class women began to identify with the new suffrage style in significant numbers. By the time suffragette militance became a national movement, its working-class origins and trade-union associations had been submerged, and it was in the hands of women of wealth.[60]

From the beginning, though, class was the contradiction at the suffrage movement's heart. In the campaign of 1894, elite women began to pursue more power for themselves by advocating the suffrage in the name of all women. When Cobden-Sanderson spoke for the Equality League at Cooper Union in 1907, she criticized "idle women of wealth" as the enemies of woman suffrage, and she was wildly applauded. But what did her charge mean? Were all rich women under indictment, or only those who stayed aloof from social responsibility and political activism? Were the militants calling for working-class leadership of the suffrage movement or for cultural changes in bourgeois definitions of womanhood? This ambiguity paralleled the mixed meanings in Blatch's emphasis on working women; it coincided with an implicit tension between the older, elite women's reform traditions and the newer trade-union politics they had helped to usher in; and it was related to a lurking confusion about whether feminism's object was the superfluity of wealthy women or the exploitation of the poor. It would continue to plague suffragism in its final decade, and feminism afterwards, into our own time.

Notes

The author wishes to thank Nancy Cott, Elizabeth L. Kennedy, Anne F. Scott, David Thelen, and Eli Zaretsky for their thoughtful reading and challenging comments on earlier drafts. In addition, the Papers of Elizabeth Cady Stanton and Susan B. Anthony, University of Massachusetts, Amherst, provided generous research assistance.

1. A good overview of political history in the Progressive Era can be found in Arthur S Link and Richard L. McCormick, *Progressivism* (Arlington Heights, Ill., 1983), 26–66. The "separate spheres" framework of Progressive-Era historiography has been identified and challenged by Paula Baker, "The Domestication of Politics: Women and American Political Society, 1780–1920," *American Historical Review*, 89 (June 1984), esp. 639–47; and by Kathryn Kish Sklar, "Hull House in the 1890s: A Community of Women Reformers," *Signs*, 10 (Summer 1985),, 658–77; and Kathryn Kish Sklar, "Florence Kelley and the Integration of 'Women's Sphere' into American Politics, 1890–1921," paper delivered at the annual meeting of the Organization of American Historians, New York, April 1986 (in Sklar's possession).

2. Steven M. Buechler, *The Transformation of the Woman Suffrage Movement: The Case of Illinois, 1850–1920* (New-Brunswick, 1986); Mari Jo Buhle and Paul Buhle, eds., *The Concise History of Woman Suffrage: Selections from the Classic Work of Stanton, Anthony, Gage and Harper* (Urbana, 1978); Carole Nichols, *Votes and More for Women: Suffrage and After in Connecticut* (New York, 1983); Anne F. Scott and Andrew Scott, eds., *One Half the People* (Philadelphia, 1975); and Sharon Strom, "Leadership and Tactics in the American Woman Suffrage Movement: A New Perspective from Massachusetts," *Journal of American History*, 52 (Sept. 1975), 296–315.

3. "Mrs. Blatch's Address," clipping, 1903, Women's Club of Orange, N.J., Scrapbooks, IV (New Jersey Historical Society, Trenton). Thanks to Gail Malmgreen for this citation.

4. Richard L. McCormick, *From Realignment to Reform: Political Change in New York State, 1893–1910* (Ithaca, 1979), 53. An excellent account of the political reform movement in the 1890s in New York City can be found in David C. Hammack, *Power and Society: Greater New York at the Turn of the Century* (New York, 1982).

5. Susan B. Anthony and Ida Husted Harper, eds., *The History of Woman Suffrage*, vol. IV: *1883–1900* (Rochester, 1902), 847–52; New York State Woman Suffrage Party, *Record of the New York Campaign of 1894* (New York, 1895); Ida Husted Harper, *The Life and Work of Susan B. Anthony* (3 vols., Indianapolis, 1898–1908), II, 758–76, esp. 759.

6. Mary Putnam Jacobi, "Report of the 'Volunteer Committee' in New York City," in *Record of the New York Campaign*, 217–20; Maud Nathan, *The Story of an Epoch-making Movement* (Garden City, 1926); William Rhinelander Steward, ed., *The Philanthropic Work of Josephine Shaw Lowell* (New York, 1926), 334–56.

7. *New York Times*, April 14, 1894, 2; *ibid.*, April 15, 1894, 5. Mrs. Robert (Catherine) Abbe's suffrage scrapbooks provide extensive documentation of the New York suffrage movement, beginning with this campaign. Mrs. Robert Abbe Collection (Manuscript Division, New York Public Library). Theodore Stanton and Harriot Stanton Blatch, eds., *Elizabeth Cady Stanton As Revealed in Her Letters, Diary and Reminiscences* (2 vols. New York, 1922), II. 299.

8. Mary Putnam Jacobi, "Address Delivered at the New York City Hearing," in *Record of the New York*

Campaign, 17–26; Olivia Slocum Sage, "Opportunities and Responsibilities of Leisured Women," *North American Review*, 181 (Nov. 1905), 712–21.

9. *Ibid.*

10. *Ibid.*

11. Jacobi, "Report of the 'Volunteer Committee,' " 217; Stanton and Blatch, eds., *Elizabeth Cady Stanton*, II, 305; *New York Times*, May 3, 1894, 9 Abby Hamlin Abbott and Josephine Jewel Dodge were both Brooklyn residents; the division between suffragists and antis reflected a conflict between the elites of Manhattan and Brooklyn over the 1894 referendum to consolidate the two cities into Greater New York. See Hammack, *Power and Society*, 209.

12. Jacobi, "Address Delivered at the New York City Hearing," 22; *New York Times*, April 12, 1894, 5. "The woman in charge of the [anti] protest . . . told a reporter . . . that her own dressmaker has secured about forty signatories to the protest among working women," *Ibid.*, May 8, 1894, 1.

13. *Woman's Journal*, May 12, 1894, 147.

14. *Ibid.*, May 1894. The study, patterned after Charles Booth and Mary Booth's investigation of the London poor, on which Blatch worked, was published as Harriot Stanton Blatch, "Another View of Village Life," *Westminster Review*, 140 (Sept. 1893), 318–24.

15. Stanton and Blatch, *Elizabeth Cady Stanton*, II, 304; unidentified clipping, April 25, 1894, Scrapbook XX; Susan B. Anthony Collection (Manuscript Division, Library of Congress); *New York Times*, April 25, 1894, *Ibid.*, May 3, 1894, 9; *New York Sun*, April 15, 1894, n.p.

16. *Woman's Journal*, Nov. 3, 1894, 348–49; *Ibid.*, Dec. 22, 1894, 402; *Ibid.*, Jan. 5, 1895, 1. Blatch wrote that her mother's position "pained" her but there is no evidence of any personal conflict between them at this time. *Ibid.*, Dec. 22, 1894, 402.

17. Harriot Stanton Blatch and Alma Lutz, *Challenging Years: The Memoirs of Harriot Stanton Blatch* (New York 1940), 77. *Woman's Journal*, Jan. 18, 1896, 18.

18. *Woman's Journal*, May 12, 1900, 146–47. Along with Blatch and Charlotte Perkins Gilman, Florence Kelley and Jane Addams were the most important figures to focus on women and class. See Charlotte Perkins Gilman, *Women and Economics: A Study of the Economic Relation between Men and Women as a Factor in Social Evolution* (Boston, 1898); Florence Kelley, *Woman Suffrage: Its Relation to Working Women and Children* (Warren, Ohio, 1906); Florence Kelley, "Women and Social Legislation in the United States," *Annals of the American Academy of Political and Social Science*, 56 (Nov. 1914), 62–71; Jane Addams, *Newer Ideals of Peace* (New York, 1907); and Jane Addams, *Twenty Years at Hull House* (New York, 1910). Some of the other women reformers who wrote on women and work early in the century were: Rheta Childe Dorr, *What Eight Million Women Want* (Boston, 1910); Lillian Wald, "Organization among Working Women," *Annals of the American Academy of Political and Social Science*, 27 (May 1906), 638–45; and Anna Garlin Spencer, *Woman's Share in Social Culture* (New York, 1913).

19. Harriot Stanton Blatch, "Specialization of Function in Women," *Gunton's Magazine*, 10 (May 1896), 349–56, esp. 350.

20. *Ibid.*

21. *Ibid.*, 354–55; see also Blatch's comments at a 1904 suffrage meeting in New York, *Woman's Journal*, Dec. 31, 1904, 423.

22. Blatch, "Specialization of Function in Women," 350, 353.

23. See, for example, the response of the New York City Woman Suffrage League to a proposal before the American Federation of Labor to ban women from all nondomestic employment, *New York Times*, Dec. 23, 1898, 7.

24. Harriot Stanton Blatch, "Weaving in a Westchester Farmhouse," *International Studio*, 26 (Oct. 1905), 102–05; *Woman's Journal*, Jan. 21, 1905; *Ibid.*, Dec. 31, 1904, 423.

25. Blatch, "Weaving in a Westchester Farmhouse," 104; Blatch and Lutz, *Challenging Years*, 70–86; Rhoda Barney Jenkins interview by Ellen Carol DuBois, June 10, 1982 (in Ellen Carol DuBois's possession); Ellen DuBois, " 'Spanning Two Centuries': The Autobiography of Nora Stanton Barney," *History Workshop*, no. 22 (Fall 1986), 131–52. esp. 149.

26. Anthony and Harper, eds., *History of Woman Suffrage*, IV, 311.

27. "Mrs. Blatch's Address," Women's Club of Orange, N. J., Scrapbooks; Anthony and Harper, eds., *History of Woman Suffrage*, IV, 311.

28. Harriot Stanton Blatch to Susan B. Anthony, Sept. 26, 1902, in *Epistolary Autobiography*, Theodore Stanton Collection (Douglass College Library, Rutgers University, New Brunswick, N. J.).

29. Oswald Garrison Villard, "Women in New York Municipal Campaign," *Woman's Journal*, March 8, 1902.

30. *New York Times*, Jan. 14, 1901, 7. The Gertrude Colles Collection (New York State Library, Albany) is particularly rich in evidence of the less elite, more radical side of female political reform in these years.

On the mock voting organized by the Equal Rights League, see *Woman's Journal* Dec. 28, 1905, and *New York Times*, Nov. 7, 1906, 9.

31. Anthony and Harper, eds., *History of Woman Suffrage*, IV, 861; Ida Husted Harper, ed., *History of Woman Suffrage*, vol. VI: *1900–1920* (New York, 1922), 454; *New York Times*, March 2, 1902, 8; *Woman's Tribune*, April 25, 1903, 49. After Blatch had become an acknowledged leader of the New York suffrage movement, the co-worker who, she felt, most shared her political perspective was Caroline Lexow, daughter of the man who had conducted the original investigation of police corruption in New York in 1894. See Blatch and Lutz, *Challenging Years*, 120–21; and Isabelle K. Savell, *Ladies' Lib: How Rockland Women Got the Vote* (New York, 1979).

32. Minutes, March 29, 1906, reel 1, New York Women's Trade Union League Papers (New York State Labor Library, New York). On the WTUL, see Nancy Schrom Dye, *As Equals and As Sisters: Feminism, the Labor Movement, and the Women's Trade Union League of New York* (Columbia, 1980); and Meredith Tax, *The Rising of the Women: Feminist Solidarity and Class Conflict, 1880–1917* (New York, 1980), 95–124.

33. Dye, *As Equals and As Sisters*, 63; Minutes, April 26, Aug. 23, 1906, New York Women's Trade Union League Papers; *New York Times*, April 11, 1907, 8.

34. Mary Kenney O'Sullivan, "The Need of Organization among Working Women (1905)," Margaret Dreier Robins Papers (University of Florida Library, Gainesville); Sarah Eisenstein, *Give Us Bread but Give Us Roses: Working Women's Consciousness in the United States, 1890 to the First World War* (London, 1983), 146–50.

35. *Woman's Journal*, March 17, 1906, 43; Kelley, *Woman Suffrage*; Jane Addams, *Utilization of Women in Government*, in *Jane Addams: A Centennial Reader* (New York, 1960), 117–18; *Woman's Journal*, Dec. 31, 1904, 423; "Mrs. Blatch's Address," Women's Club of Orange, N.J., Scrapbooks. There was a lengthy discussion of working women's need for the vote, including a speech by Rose Schneiderman, at the 1907 New York State Woman Suffrage Association convention. See Minute Book, 1907–10, New York State Woman Suffrage Association (Butler Library, Columbia University, New York). The WTUL identified woman suffrage as one of its goals by 1907. Dye, *As Equals and As Sisters*, 123.

36. *New York Times*, Jan. 3, 1907, 6; *Woman's Journal*, Jan. 12, 1907, 8.

37. *Progress*, June 1907, Carrie Chapman Catt to Millicent Garrett Fawcett, Oct. 19, 1909, container 5, Papers of Carrie Chapman Catt (Manuscript Division, Library of Congress)

38. *Woman's Journal*, Aug. 17, 1907, 129. On Nora Blatch (who later called herself Nora Stanton Barney), see DuBois, " 'Spanning Two Centuries,' " 131–52. Those self-supporters who, I believe, had independent incomes include Nora Blatch, Caroline Lexow, Lavinia Dock, Ida Rauh, Gertrude Barnum, Elizabeth Flinnegan, and Alice Clark. See, for example, on Nora Blatch, *ibid.*, and on Dock, *Notable American Women: The Modern Period*, s.v. "Dock, Lavinia Lloyd."

39. Caroline Lexow to Leonora O'Reilly, Jan. 3, 1908, reel 4, Leonora O'Reilly Papers (Schlesinger Library, Radcliffe College, Cambridge, Mass.); O'Reilly to Trow, Jan. 5, 1908, *Ibid.*; Robert Doherty, "Tempest on the Hudson: The Struggle for Equal Pay for Equal Work in the New York City Public Schools, 1907–1911," *Harvard Educational Quarterly*, 19 (Winter 1979), 413–39. The role of teachers in the twentieth-century suffrage movement is a promising area for research. For information on teachers' organizations in the Buffalo, New York, suffrage movement, I am indebted to Eve S. Faber, Swarthmore College, "Suffrage in Buffalo, 1898–1913" (unpublished paper, in DuBois's possession).

40. *New York Times*, June 6, 1907, 1.

41. On self-support for women after marriage, see *New York World*, July 26, 1908, 3; and Lydia Kingsmill Commander, "The Self Supporting Woman and the Family," *American Journal of Sociology*, 14 (March 1909), 752–57. On the debate, see *New York Times*, Jan. 7, 1909, 9.

42. *New York Times*, Feb. 6, 1907, 6. Harriot Stanton Blatch, ed., *Two Speeches by Industrial Women* (New York, 1907), esp. 8. The Equality League's bill authorized a voters' referendum on an amendment to the New York constitution, to remove the word "male" from the state's suffrage provisions, thus enfranchising New York women. Since the U. S. Constitution vests power to determine the electorate with the states, the aim was to win full suffrage in federal, as well as state, elections for New York women. With minor alterations, the measure finally passed, but in 1915 New York voters refused to enfranchise the women of their state; a second referendum in 1917 was successful. See Blatch and Lutz, *Challenging Years*, 156–238.

43. *Woman's Tribune*, Feb. 9, 1907, 12; Minutes, April 27, 1909, New York Women's Trade Union League Papers; *Progress*, Nov. 1907.

44. Blatch and Lutz, *Challenging Years*, 100–101; *Progress*, Jan. 1908.

45. *Woman's Journal*, Dec. 28, 1907, 205, 206–7.

46. By 1908, there was a racehorse named "suffragette." *New York Evening Telegram*, Sept. 16, 1908. Blatch noted that once she left England in the late 1890s, she and Emmeline Pankhurst did not communicate

until 1907, after they had both taken their respective countries' suffrage movements in newly militant directions. Blatch to Christabel Pankhurst, in Christabel Pankhurst, *Unshackled: How We Won the Vote* (London, 1959), 30.

47. The first American arrests were not until 1917. For American suffragists' early response to the WSPU, see the *Woman's Journal*, May 30, 1908, 87. Even Carrie Chapman Cart praised the British militants at first. *Woman's Journal*, Dec. 12, 1908, 199. For an example of divisive coverage by the mainstream press, see "Suffragist or Suffragette," *New York Times*, Feb. 29, 1908, 6.

48. On Bettina Borrman Wells, see A. J. R., ed., *Suffrage Annual and Women's Who's Who* (London, 1913), 390. Thanks to David Doughan of the Fawcett Library for this reference. The best sources on the Equal Rights League are the Gertrude Colles Collection and *The American Suffragette*, which the group published from 1909 through 1911. See also Winifred Harper Cooley, "Suffragists and 'Suffragettes.'" *World To Day*, 15 (Oct. 1908), 1066–71; and Elinor Lerner, "Jewish Involvement in the New York City Woman Suffrage Movement," *American Jewish History*, 70 (June 1981), 444–45. The American suffragettes found a predecessor and benefactor in seventy-five-year-old Lady Cook, formerly Tennessee Claflin, in 1909 the wife of a titled Englishman. "Our Cook Day," *American Suffragette*, 1 (Nov. 1909). 1.

49. On the first open-air meeting, see *New York Times*, Jan. 1, 1908, 16. On the parade, see *Ibid.*, Feb. 17, 1908, 7; there is also an account in Dort, *What Eight Million Women Want*, 298–99; *New York Evening Journal*, May 21, 1910.

50. Equality League of Self-Supporting Women, *Report for Year 1908–1909* (New York, 1909), 2; Blatch and Lutz, *Challenging Years*, 107–09. On Vassar, see also *New York American*, June 10, 1908.

51. Harriot Stanton Blatch, "Radical Move in Two Years," clipping, Nov. 8, 1908, suffrage scrapbooks, Abbe Collection. Blatch "starred" in a prosuffrage movie, *What Eight Million Women Want*, produced in 1912. Kay Sloan, "Sexual Warfare in the Silent Cinema: Comedies and Melodramas of Woman Suffragism," *American Quarterly*, 33 (Fall 1981), 412–36. She was also very interested in the propaganda possibilities of commercial radio, according to Lee de Forest, a pioneer of the industry, who was briefly married to her daughter. Lee de Forest, *Father of Radio: The Autobiography of Lee de Forest* (Chicago, 1950), 248–49.

52. Many Tyng, "Self Denial Week," *American Suffragette*, 1 (Aug. 1909); *New York Herald*, Dec. 19, 1908.

53. Blatch, "Radical Move in Two Years"; Mrs. B. Borrman Wells, "The Militant Movement for Woman Suffrage," *Independent*, April 23, 1908, 901–3.

54. "Suffragettes Bar Word Ladylike," clipping, Jan. 13, 1909, Suffrage scrapbooks, abbe Collection; Blatch and Lutz, *Challenging Years*, 91–242; *New York Herald*, March 8, 1908. On militants' views of femininity and sexuality, see also "National Suffrage Convention," *American Suffragette*, 2 (March 1910), 3.

55. Blatch and Lutz, *Challenging Years*, 107; Dye, *As Equals and As Sisters*, 47.

56. *Woman's Journal*, May 30, 1908, 87; Blatch, "Radical Move in Two Years."

57. Borrman Wells, "Militant Movement for Woman Suffrage," 901; *Woman's Journal*, Feb. 29, 1908, 34.

58. *New York Times*, Feb. 11, 1908, 6; [Josephine C. Kaneko], "To Join, or Not to Join," *Socialist Woman*, 1 (May 1908). 6.

59. On *The Convert*, see Equality League, *Report for 1908–1909*, 4; Jane Marcus, "Introduction," in *The Convert* (London, 1980), v–xvi; *New York Call*, Dec. 9, 1908, 6; and Minutes, Dec. 22, 1908, New York Women's Trade Union League Papers. Maud Malone also charged the American Suffragettes with discrimination against Socialists and Bettina Borrman Wells with personal ambition. For her letter of resignation, see *New York Times*, March 27, 1908, 4.

60. *New York Times*, May 14, 1909, 5. On Mackay and her Equal Franchise Society, see *New York Times*, Feb. 21, 1909, part 5, 2. On Blatch's relation to Mackay, see Blatch and Lutz, *Challenging Years*, 118. "As for the suffrage movement, it is actually fashionable now," wrote militant Inez Haynes, who very much approved of the development. "All kinds of society people are taking it up." Inez Haynes to Maud Wood Park, Dec. 2, 1910, reel 11, National American Woman Suffrage Association Papers (Manuscript Division, Library of Congress). Gertrude Foster Brown, another wealthy woman recruited by Blatch, wrote her own history of the New York suffrage movement in which she virtually ignored the role of working-class women. Gertrude Foster Brown, "On Account of Sex," Gertrude Foster Brown Papers, Sophia Smith Collection (Smith College, Northampton, Mass.).

17

In Politics to Stay
Black Women Leaders and Party Politics in the 1920s

Evelyn Brooks Higginbotham

Between 1900 and 1930 more than 1.5 million black men and women migrated from the South to the urban North. The massive trek, actually begun in the last decade of the nineteenth century, shifted into high gear during World War I, when wartime demands from northern industry promised employment and, most of all, escape from the southern way of life—from its boll-weevil-ravaged sharecrop farming and from its segregation, disfranchisement, and lynching. In the decade between 1910 and 1920 the black population soared in such cities as Chicago (from 44,103 to 109,458), Detroit (from 5,741 to 40,878), Cleveland (from 8,448 to 34,451), New York (from 91,709 to 152,467), and Philadelphia (from 84,459 to 134,229).[1] Concentrated in the ghettos of urban centers, the migrants soon transformed their restricted residential opportunities into political opportunity.

With migration stepped up to even higher levels between 1920 and 1930, the growing significance of the black vote did not escape the attention of machine politicians. Blacks played an especially influential role in Chicago's machine politics. For instance, in the city's closely contested mayoral race in 1915, the black vote was critical to the victory of Republican William Hale Thompson. Moreover, growing black populations in the northern cities and border states precipitated the rise of black officeholders. In the first three decades of the twentieth century blacks increasingly sent their own to state legislatures, city councils, judgeships, and clerkships. In 1928 the political clout of Illinois blacks carried Oscar DePriest, the first northern black congressman, to the House of Representatives.[2]

Invisible Politics

Black women played an active and valuable role in the electoral politics of the 1920s, but their role is, too often, overlooked as if an unimportant, even impotent factor in the profound political changes under way. Black political behavior during the early decades of the twentieth century has certainly been analyzed in a number of excellent studies. Unfortunately, the overwhelming majority treat black women as invisible participants, silent members of the black electorate. The literature, much of which was written between the 1930s and 1970s, fails to investigate, to any meaningful extent, either the black female vote or the role of black women leaders in getting out the vote.[3]

While the significance of the female vote has not received serious attention from the traditional literature on black politics, it also has been too easily dismissed by the recent scholarship in women's history. And though a growing body of research has appeared on the suffragist activities among black women leaders, very little is known about their political participation in the decade after the ratification of the Nineteenth Amendment.[4] Feminist scholarship has placed black women's club work firmly within the context of the organizational history of suffragism and has identified such individual leaders as Mary Church Terrell, Ida B. Wells Barnett, and Nannie Helen Burroughs as outspoken champions of women's suffrage in the first two decades of the twentieth century, but this scholarship fails to recognize their continuing political activism after 1920. The passage of the Nineteenth Amendment, according to this research, appears to portend the end rather than the starting point of black women's involvement in electoral politics for the next decade. This assumption is based on the following realities.

On the eve of ratification, the handwriting on the wall boldly read, "The full meaning of the Nineteenth Amendment would be denied to black women." Historians of the woman's suffrage movement have exposed the racist and class biases of white women suffragists.[5] In a deliberate effort to win southern white support, they disassociated their cause from black voting rights issues. The white women's movement abandoned its earlier nineteenth century ties with the black freedom struggle in favor of an alliance with white supremacy. The reversal reflected a fundamental shift not only in strategy, but also in the rationale upon which suffragism had rested. By the late nineteenth and early twentieth centuries, white suffragists argued from the position of expediency rather than justice. The National American Woman Suffrage Association, having adopted a states' rights policy toward its member organizations in 1903, paved the way for its southern wing to argue the expediency of woman's suffrage in nullifying the intent of the Fifteenth Amendment and buttressing the cause of white supremacy in general. An assent, if not a direct contributor to the disfranchisement and segregation of southern blacks of both sexes, the strategy assured the denial of black women's ballots. Carrie Chapman Catt, Alice Paul, Ida Husted Harper, and other luminaries of the women's movement added insult to injury by expressing their racist sensibilities in correspondence, segregated marches, and various public statements. The press reported the hard facts once ratification became reality. In state after state in the South, large numbers of black women turned out to register only to be turned back.[6]

Historian Rosalyn Terborg-Penn draws attention to the suffrage clubs of black women in the states that ratified the woman's vote prior to 1920, but she concludes that the postscript to the passage of the Nineteenth Amendment was one of frustration and disillusionment. By the mid-1920s discontented black feminists, Terborg-Penn posits, turned their eyes away from mainstream electoral politics to the renewed antilynching crusade, social service efforts, and separatist or Third World causes such as the International Council of Women of the Darker Races, Pan-Africanism, and the Marcus Garvey movement.[7] Although her assessment correctly emphasizes the hostile, racially charged environment that black women faced, it underestimates the continuing interest of black women leaders in the electoral process.

The work of Ida Wells Barnett, the great black feminist and antilynching crusader, illustrates the potential of black women leaders in mobilizing voters. Her autobiography tells of her activities with the Alpha Suffrage Club for black women soon after Illinois adopted woman's suffrage in 1913. She credited her club with the election of Oscar DePriest in 1915 as Chicago's first black alderman. The large black turnout also played the decisive role in the victory of William Hale Thompson.[8]

Migration and Woman Suffrage

When America returned to normalcy after World War I, the combined realities of Jim Crow and southern disfranchisement, of northern discrimination in housing and jobs, and of pervasive racism both customary and institutionalized created a set of social conditions as inimical to black progress as had existed in previous generations. Although their grievances were just as pronounced, black women, like their men, did not greet these objective conditions with the same degree of resignation and accommodation that had characterized the era of Booker T. Washington. Rather, their response was one of optimism, reflecting a reevaluation of their circumstances and a transformed subjective perception of their own power to bring about change. This subjective transformation was conditioned by new forces at work—namely, migration and the woman's vote. Both appeared to signal a break with the past.

Thousands upon thousands of migrants of voting age annually left states in the Deep South, where voting restrictions had been most repressive. That these states simultaneously imposed the greatest economic and social restrictions upon blacks accounts for the eagerness of so many to uproot themselves and search for greater economic and political freedom. Unskilled and semiskilled jobs in the northern cities offered wage rates considerably higher than the southern agricultural work in which most of the migrants previously had been engaged. Florette Henri's study of the Great Migration observes that "to farm workers in the South who made perhaps $.75 a day, to urban female domestics who might earn from $1.50 to $3.00 a week, the North during the war years beckoned with factory wages as high as $3.00 to $4.00 a day, and domestic pay of $2.50 a day." Despite the higher cost of living and the drastic reduction of factory employment for blacks after the war ended, the urban North's higher wages and greater economic opportunity relative to the South continued to lure hundreds of thousands of black migrants throughout the 1920s. For black southern migrants, the ballot box, no less than heightened employment opportunity and greater social mobility, served as a badge of freedom from the Jim Crow world they fled.[9]

When viewed as an indicator of voting behavior, employment suggests its positive role within the critical mix of urban opportunities that encouraged black women's political integration. Women constituted a sizable proportion of the northern black labor force. In 1920 the black married women's employment rate stood at five times that of white married women. In the largest northern cities in 1930 between 34 and 44 percent of black households had two or more members employed. Moreover, successive waves of migrants contributed to the growth of economic and social differentiation within the black urban community. The appearance of a black male and female elite composed of lawyers, educators, physicians, ministers, and entrepreneurs reflected a leadership ever mindful of black political interests and the importance of voter mobilization for the realization of those interests.[10]

Harold Gosnell indicates the political consciousness of black women in his classic *Negro Politicians* (1935), the earliest systematic study of urban black political behavior. More attentive to women than subsequent works by social scientists, Gosnell's several studies on Chicago politics were written in the 1920s and 1930s, when the implications of woman's recently acquired right to vote were more consciously observed. Gosnell notes that black women "shared with their men folks an intense interest in politics." He reveals that in the 1923 local election relatively fewer black women than white used the antisuffragist argument as an excuse for not voting. While Gosnell does not dwell on the political mobilization of black women, he clearly acknowledges their importance in augmenting the black vote: "The huge increment in the absolute number of the estimated eligible colored voters between 1910 and 1920 was due largely to the adoption of woman suffrage in 1913 and to the flood of newcomers after 1914."[11] The conflation of woman's suffrage and black urban migration made possible greater political opportunity and leverage for blacks as a group. It also served to broaden black women's perceptions of their own influence and activism. Throughout the 1920s black women leaders, far from abandoning the electoral process, envisioned themselves in politics to stay.

The Black Press and Women's Political Consciousness

The black press served as an important vehicle for promoting the political concerns of black women. Varying in form from lengthy informative articles to mere blurbs, its news announced and promoted organizational activities and noteworthy persons and events rarely covered by the white press. Its pages featured the election or appointment of blacks to prominent and, just as often, quite obscure positions across the nation. Papers such as the *Chicago Defender, New York Age, Pittsburgh Courier, Norfolk Journal and Guide*, and *Baltimore Afro-American* served not only their local markets, but a national one hungry for "race news." The *Chicago Defender*, which had the largest readership of all, is often cited for its influential role in the Great Migration out of the South during World War I. The importance of the black press did not go unrecognized by campaigning politicians. Robert L. Vann, editor of the *Pittsburgh Courier*, was appointed chairman of the publicity committee of the Colored Voters' Division of the Republican National Committee during the 1928 presidential race. Claude A. Barnett, of the Associated Negro Press, was secretary. In fact, the Hoover forces enlisted practically every black news editor on this committee.[12]

Black newspapers frequently reprinted or cited each other's stories along with those from such national magazines as the National Association for the Advancement of Colored People's *Crisis*, the National Urban League's *Opportunity*, and the National Association of Colored Women's *National Notes*. Through the Associated Negro Press important news releases were syndicated in the different papers. Hanes Walton draws attention to the historical role of the black press as a transmitter of political culture—as an agent of political socialization. Its role combated the negative black images presented in the white newspapers. The black press provided the counterorientation to forces affirming black inferiority. In its coverage of women's political activities during the 1920s, it also reinforced the idea of a prominent place for women within black political culture.[13]

The *Baltimore Afro-American*, a weekly during the twenties, concisely illustrates the way black women's political activities were portrayed. In the four issues appearing between 17 September and 16 October 1920, twenty-two articles covered one or another aspect of women's newly acquired right to vote. Three articles presented congratulatory responses by various black and white notables to the ratification of the Nineteenth Amendment. One noted the appointment of Lethia Fleming as head of the black woman's advisory committee to the national Republican Party during the 1920 presidential campaign, while another covered Daneva Donnell's appointment as the only black on the first all-woman jury in an Indianapolis court. Five articles exposed the thwarted attempts of black women to register in the southern states. Nine reported political activities among women in Baltimore. Most of these activities took the form of meetings and rallies. One of the local stories featured the results of the first two days of registration in the city's predominantly black wards and concluded that "where the colored women are organized as in the 14th and 17th wards their registration nearly equals that of the men."[14]

The final three articles on black women and politics were represented in the column "A Primer for Women Voters," written by Augusta T. Chissell. Chissell, a member of the Colored Women's Suffrage Club of Maryland, designed the weekly column as a tool for political education. Readers were invited to write in questions, which she in turn answered.

Question—There are some men who will be up for election in this state in November who have bitterly opposed woman suffrage. What do you think of supporting them?

Answer—Women should weigh this question very carefully, not from the standpoint of resentment but from the standpoint of justice.[15]

Question—What is meant by party platform? And where may I go to be taught how to vote?

Answer—Party platform simply means what either candidate promises to do after he is elected. The Just Government League is conducting a polling booth at its head quarters. . . . You may go there and become acquainted with the whole order of things. You will also do well to attend the Thursday night meetings of the YWCA under the auspices of the Colored Women's Suffrage Club.[16]

Black women leaders used the press to voice their political concerns and programs throughout the 1920s.

Clubwomen and Politics

Even more important to the political activism of black women leaders was the organizational network already in place on the eve of the ratification of the Nineteenth Amendment. The National Association of Colored Women (NACW) had stood at the forefront of the suffragist cause among black women and became the logical springboard for future political work. By the 1920s the NACW came to represent the organizational hub of the women's club movement. It was the linchpin that united hundreds of women's clubs throughout the nation in shared goals and strategies of social service and racial uplift. Divided into districts, under which fell regional and state federations, the elaborate infra structure established linkages and opened channels of communication between women's organizations in every black community in America. Through its national leaders and committees, plans were centralized and tasks divided. Through its biennial meetings and national magazine, *National Notes*, the NACW functioned as a clearinghouse, providing a communications network for the dissemination of information and the promotion of collective action.[17]

NACW members, largely of middle-class status, received wide coverage in the black press, and the leaders at the state and national levels were, more often than not, prominent in other progressive groups with respect to racial advancement, such as the National Association for the Advancement of Colored People (NAACP), the National Urban League, and the Commission on Interracial Cooperation. Some of these same leaders also occupied high places of influence within major religious organizations.[18] Tullia Hamilton's study of the first generation of NACW leaders reveals their privileged status vis-à-vis the great majority of black women. Most of the 108 leaders identified by Hamilton had been born in the South between 1860 and 1885 but had settled in the North a decade or two prior to the onslaught of migrants during the World War I period. Unlike the masses of uneducated and unskilled black women who were restricted to domestic service and other menial employment, NACW leaders enjoyed the benefits of education and greater employment opportunities. Approximately three-quarters of them were married. Most of the club-women were career oriented, about two-thirds were teachers and a small proportion were clerical workers and entrepreneurs.[19]

In 1926 the NACW boasted affiliated clubs in forty-one states. Its vast scope and influence prompted Mary McLeod Bethune, national president between 1924 and 1928, to remark: "Every organization is looking to the National Association of Colored Women for assistance in some line of advancement."[20] One organization that looked to the NACW for assistance was the Republican National Committee, which had enlisted outgoing president Hallie Q. Brown to direct its voters' drive among black women in 1924.[21] During the presidential race, the NACW's usual social service activities took a backseat to intense parisan politics. Its magazine, *National Notes*, encouraged political consciousness, shared ideas and strategies, and followed the progress of the campaign in the various states. The selection of Brown, NACW president between 1920 and 1924, reflected the Coolidge forces' recognition of her command over hundreds of thousands of black women.

As director of the Colored Women's Department of the Republican National Committee, Brown built her campaign network on the foundation of the existing regional, state, and local structures of her organization. She recruited her army of workers from the NACW's leadership—from women who had already proved their organizing abilities. Brown appointed Maria C. Lawton of Brooklyn to head the eastern division of the Republican campaign and Myrtle Foster Cook of Kansas to head the western division. At the time, Lawton held the presidency of the Empire State Federation, the association of clubwomen at the New York state level. Her mobilizing ability had been responsible for the tremendous growth in affiliated clubs since 1912. As organizer of the Empire State Federation in 1912 and president from 1916 to 1926, Lawton had expanded the number of clubs from a small concentration mostly in New York City and Buffalo to 103 in all parts of the state. Cook afforded the Republican Party another strong mobilizing resource. As editor-manager of *National Notes*, she transformed the nationally read magazine into a political organ for the Republican Party.[22]

Black women's Republican clubs sprang up everywhere—led by clubwomen already in the vanguard of the civic and political affairs of their communities. The overall operation included precinct captains; ward chairmen; city, county, and district chairmen; state chairmen; and national organizers and speakers. Each state chairman developed circulars and bulletins for her own territory and sent reports to the black press "with accurate and encouraging accounts of women's campaign activities." Their reports highlighted their cooperation in a cause that "has added to our lives a rich chapter of wider friendships with the mutual confidence born of close acquaintance and hard work." The campaign had a tremendous psychological effect on these workers, who described it as rewarding and personally enriching. Lawton referred to the campaign's emotionally fulfilling impact on black women workers. It became an "outlet for their pent up aspirations and ambitions to be counted as integral parts of the body politic."[23]

Reports from state chairmen and organizers revealed optimism in politics and a belief that their efforts were decisive to the electoral outcome. Although the Republican Party had utilized black women leaders in the past, the election in 1924 involved their participation in more extensive, visible, and official ways. The state organizer from Rhode Island typified this attitude in her reflections on Coolidge's victory: "I am sure the work our colored women did during the last campaign helped materially to give the National ticket the large plurality it had in the Nation." Campaign reports indicate that there were hundreds of Coolidge-Dawes clubs and meetings in halls, churches, fraternal lodges, schools, homes, and on the streets. House-to-house canvassing appeared to be their most effective strategy, but bringing in speakers of national reputation also received a good response. Other interesting techniques were employed. The organizer for upstate New York outlined the following activities based on her tour of Elmira, Rochester, Auburn, Buffalo, and Niagara Falls:

> We found the forming of Coolidge-Dawes Clubs using pledge cards an excellent method for tabulating new voters and bringing in old voters who were in the class of stay-at-homes. Another method found very effective was Block Captains in every district. These, with their assistants, kept a list of new voters and registrants of old, in turn. These were given to the chairman of our Get-Out-The-Vote Committee. This committee of twenty women did Yeoman work on election day; no voter of their district was omitted.[24]

Organizers in West Virginia noted the role of special circular letters—one with an appeal to the ministry and another to women directly. West Virginia women also found the question box helpful in identifying issues of concern to voters. The report from Minnesota relied heavily on mass distributions—pamphlets entitled "Important Information for All Legal Voters," "Register Today" cards, and sample ballots. Iowa was the only state to cite telephone canvassing among its techniques. Kentucky reported its least successful technique—getting women to answer mailed questionnaires.[25]

Florie Pugh of Oklahoma City held instructional meetings in the evenings and lectured on how to organize a precinct and district, the duty of a precinct committeewoman, how to poll, how to get the voters registered, new voters, the necessity of voting by 10:00 A.M. on election day, and why black people should be Republicans. Lillian Browder, a precinct captain in Chicago, stressed the need to discuss gender politics in house-to-house canvassing. She found that women exhibited greater responsiveness and interest when told of legislation and political affairs vital to home life. Thus Browder talked to women about laws that touched upon their lives—for example, the Child Labor Law, the Pure Food Act, and the law regulating working hours for women, and she associated passage of this legislation with the Republican Party.[26]

The presidential race of 1924 and Coolidge's ultimate victory reinforced a growing sense of political efficacy among black clubwomen. They interpreted their role as crucial to the Republican victory, and they expected a continued relationship with the party and with political organizations among white women. Estele R. Davis, who served on the Speakers' Bureau during the Coolidge campaign, captured the perceived interconnection between their club movement and political participation:

> How little have we realized in our club work for the last twenty-five years that it was God's way of preparing us to assume this greater task of citizenship. I often wonder what would have happened without our organized club work which has not only trained us for service, but has created a nation-wide sisterhood through which we know the outstanding women of each state who are able to serve our race in the time of need.[27]

The National League of Republican Colored Women

Throughout the summer of 1924 women came to value the need for permanent organization at the state and national levels. In some states political clubs had operated since the adoption of women's suffrage, but in most the presidential campaign had spurred the desire for continued political work. Mamie Williams (Mrs. George S. Williams) and Mary Booze, both NACW women and also the Republican national committeewomen from Georgia and Mississippi, respectively, urged the practicality of uniting black women's Republican clubs in a national organization.[28] On 7 August 1924, hours after the adjournment of the biennial meeting of the NACW, Williams and Booze reconvened a number of the clubwomen for the purpose of forming the National League of Republican Colored Women (NLRCW). Booze and Williams were named honorary presidents, while the official roster also included Nannie Burroughs of the District of Columbia, president; Sue M. Brown (Mrs. S. Joe Brown) of Iowa, vice president; Daisy Lampkin of Pennsylvania, treasurer and chairman of the executive committee; Mary Church Terrell of the District of Columbia, treasurer; and Mrs. Elizabeth Ross Hanes, parliamentarian. These women were well known for their visibility in political affairs and for their work with the NAACP and the Urban League.[29]

The NLRCW sought to become a permanent political force among black women, adopting the slogan "We are in politics to stay and we shall be a stay in politics." It distinguished its goals from that of the NACW and other groups that adopted partisan political activities on a temporary basis and specifically at election time.[30] While endorsing the Republican National Committee's appointment of Brown as director of colored women for the presidential campaign, the members of the NLRCW criticized the NACW for abandoning its nonpartisan image and expressed disapproval of its heavy coverage of the Republican campaign through the pages of *National Notes*.

There are several explanations for this reaction on the part of women whose roles as leaders overlapped both organizations. First, the NLRCW ensured continuation of a partisan political emphasis by taking it out of the hands of an organization whose intentions and objectives had historically been to unite black women of all affiliations and persuasions in the work of social service. The NACW's Citizenship and Legislative departments constituted integral parts of the organization's "lifting as we climb" philosophy, but they were designed to inspire civic duty and legislative study for race and sex advancement, not to advance specific political parties.[31] Second, rivalries existed between women. Some of the NLRCW women claimed that certain NACW leaders had used their position during the presidential campaign to further their own selfish personal ambitions.[32] On the other hand, individuals in the NLRCW might have perceived the new organization as a stepping-stone to a political appointment that had bypassed them in the last campaign.

The crossover of membership in the two organizations invariably blurred distinctions. Reports of campaign activities during the 1924 election were sent to Nannie Burroughs as well as to the NACW officials working with the Republican National Committee.[33] Members of the NLRCW often quoted the slogan of the NACW when confirming their attendance at an event sponsored by the former. In 1928 Daisy Lampkin wrote to Burroughs about Lethia Fleming, an outstanding Republican organizer in Ohio and leader in both the NLRCW and the NACW: "She seemed to confuse the two National organizations, but I made it clear to her that they are in no way connected." By 1926 the NACW, while continuing to urge women's political participation, had relinquished overt partisanship to the NLRCW.[34]

In 1924 Burroughs sent out a questionnaire to black women leaders throughout the country. The exact number mailed is unknown, and only twenty-three responses appear to exist, representing respondents from eleven states. While this number is too small to be representative of black women in general, the questions themselves reveal the major concerns of the NLRCW in the building of its program. Some of the questions read as follows:

—Did you hear of any vote selling among the women?
—What is being done to educate women as to the value of the ballot?
—Are Negro women taking an active part in local politics?
—Is it true that a number of women failed to register and vote because their husbands are opposed to woman suffrage?
—Did you hear that Whites who hire servants tried to influence their votes?
—What is the general attitude of the White women of your city toward Negro women since they have suffrage?
—Give the names of Congressmen from your State who have poor records on the Negro question.
—What should the Negro demand of the incoming administration?
—Who are the women in your city and State best qualified to organize political clubs to assist in the work?[35]

Meeting in Oakland in August 1926, the executive committee of the NLRCW presented its goals and intentions in the form of a resolution—copies of which were sent to Sallie Hert, a vice chairman of the Republican National Committee and head of its Women's Division, and to the Associated Negro Press for distribution in all the black newspapers. The resolution requested formal and active affiliation with the Women's Division of the Republican National Committee and offered the services and counsel of its state leaders in the upcoming congressional election.[36]

The response by the Women's Division of the Republican National Committee could not have been more promising. Sallie Hert invited Burroughs to represent the NLRCW at its first national conference of women leaders. Eighty-five women from thirty-three states met in Washington between 12 and 14 January 1927 to discuss their role in the Grand Old Party. The group included national committeewomen (Booze of Mississippi and Williams of Georgia being the only other blacks present), state vice chairmen, and Republican women's clubs. The women discussed a variety of issues of direct interest to Burroughs: maintaining a functioning organization throughout the year, women's representation in the party organization, problems of organizing and fund-raising, party integrity and loyalty, and overcoming differences among Republican women.[37]

Burroughs was among seventy-five women from the group who visited the White House and received greetings from President and Mrs. Coolidge. She also heard talks by Secretary of War

Dwight Davis and secretary of commerce Herbert Hoover. The high point for Burroughs was the opportunity to address the gathering. She began her remarks by stating: "I'm glad to be able to give a touch of color to this meeting. No political party in America is 100 percent American without this touch of color." She proceeded to inform her seemingly quite receptive audience of the work of her own organization.[38]

In May 1927 the NLRCW called its own three-day conference in Washington, D.C. Leaders from twenty-three states came together to discuss their concerns and to hear high-ranking officials in the GOP discuss issues and policies. Included among the array of speakers were Sallie Hert of the Women's Division, Virginia White Speel of the Republican Central Committee for the District of Columbia, Secretary of Labor James Davis, and Secretary of the Interior Hubert Work. Feelings of efficacy continued to run high among black women.[39]

The presidential election in 1928 witnessed NLRCW leaders in prominent campaign positions. Lampkin, chairman of its executive committee, was appointed by the Republican high command to direct the mobilization of black women voters in the East. Burroughs had deeply wanted the position, but her nonvoting status as a District of Columbia resident operated to her disadvantage. An eloquent orator, Burroughs was appointed to the National Speakers' Bureau and became one of the most highly sought-after speakers on the campaign trail.[40] Many NLRCW members journeyed to Washington for the inauguration of Hoover. They rejoiced in his victory. It seemed just as much their own.

By 1932 the honeymoon had ended between the black women and the Republican Party. The Depression focused the attention of black leaders, male and female, on questions of economic survival. The Hoover administration had little to say to most Americans, least of all to blacks, on economic relief. Burroughs, like most blacks, continued to support Hoover in that year, but with increasing criticism of his policies toward the black poor. Nor had the party of Lincoln fared well in its civil rights record during Hoover's term. In the throes of unprecedented economic suffering, blacks came to challenge their traditional loyalty to the party responsible for their emancipation from slavery.[41]

Black leaders denounced the various racist actions of the Hoover administration. His efforts to render the Republican Party in the South "lily-white," his segregation of the Gold Star Mothers, and his nomination of an avowed advocate of black disfranchisement to the Supreme Court incurred the wrath of black leaders throughout the nation.[42] However, for members of the NLRCW, the unhappy alliance between blacks and the administration was foreshadowed as early as Hoover's inauguration. In March 1929 the chairman of the Inaugural Charity Ball requested that Burroughs retrieve tickets "accidentally" sent to black women workers in the Hoover campaign. Burroughs acquiesced to Republican wishes for a segregated ball, but not without registering the protest of her coworkers: "It is not easy for me to get the others reconciled to embarrassments for which they are not responsible. One has said already, 'They use us in the crisis and humiliate us at will.' " In 1932 Sallie Hert's replacement by Lena Yost as head of the Republican Women's Division further alienated the black women. Yost lacked the sincerity and interest that had characterized Hert's relationship with the NLRCW. Burroughs's correspondence discloses increasing frustration with the party's solicitation of her support at election time, while at all other times treating her suggestions with "silent contempt."[43]

The League of Women Voters

Another organization that captured the interest of black clubwomen during the 1920s was the League of Women Voters (LWV). Lines of communication remained open between the NACW and black units of the LWV. While individual blacks held membership in some of the predominantly white state leagues, separate black leagues operated in Oakland, San Francisco, Los Angeles, Chicago, and St. Louis. Delegates from the Oakland, Chicago, and St. Louis groups were represented at the league's national conferences in the 1920s. They were also represented on the state boards of the California and Illinois leagues. Leaders of the black leagues were, at the same time, leaders of their state federated clubs—the constituent members of the NACW.

Hettie Tilghman, leader among black California women in the LWV, referred to the overlap in membership for the NACW and two black leagues, the Alameda County League of Colored Women Voters and the San Francisco Colored League. She cited their political activities from the dual role of federated women and League of Women Voters. Delilah Beasley, an active member of the NACW and the Alameda County League of Colored Women Voters, devoted press coverage to both in her column, "Activities among Negroes," which ran in the white daily, the *Oakland Tribune.* On 25 November 1925 she announced the interest of the Alameda County League of Colored Women Voters in the observance of World Court Day, scheduled for 17 December. Her column also cited an article written by the president of the Alameda County League for the magazine of the NACW. The article, which had appeared a few weeks earlier in *National Notes,* praised the California State League and National League of Women Voters for their efforts in securing the passage of specific legislation affecting women and children.[44]

On 6 October 1920 the St. Louis League of Women Voters organized a "Colored Committee" to bring before the larger body racial concerns related to education, health, child welfare, and citizenship. Nine years later, B. F. Bowles headed the committee, which functioned as an important liaison between the league and the large black female population in St. Louis. Under Bowles's leadership, the committee assumed a number of projects: gathering data on southern election laws and policies, offering lectures on pending legislation, holding citizenship schools, providing scholarships to black students, entertaining national league officers at gatherings in the black community, forming junior leagues among black girls, and contributing financially to the budget of the St. Louis league. In an editorial in the *St. Louis American,* Carrie Bowles, another black league member and member of the NACW, praised the St. Louis league for being "one of the very few leagues in the U.S. in which the colored members enjoy every privilege of the organization on terms of absolute equality." Writing in the national magazine of the NACW in 1928, Bowles again praised her city league for sending a black delegate to the eighth annual conference.[45]

Illinois black clubwomen also contributed to the work of the league. In 1926 the Illinois State League of Women Voters elected a black woman, Margaret Gainer, to membership on its board of directors. Gainer, also a member of the Illinois State Federation of Colored Women's Clubs, directed the latter's citizenship department, which included the program of the Illinois League of Women Voters. The Illinois State Federation constituted an extensive network of black clubwomen. It organized in 1899 and by 1926 comprised ninety two clubs with 2,074 members divided into three districts: the Chicago and Northern, the Central, and the Southern.[46]

Several clubwomen in the Chicago area were league members. The Douglass League of Women Voters, the black unit of the league in the city, was headed by Irene Goins, a leader of the Illinois State Federation as well. On 18 June 1924 Florence Harrison of the national league met with the black members to discuss their plans for the development of citizenship schools. Attached to Harrison's report were the black women's plans for the national "Get-Out-the-Vote Campaign." In addition to incorporating the campaign into the citizenship program of the Illinois State Federation of Colored Women's Clubs, the Douglass League proposed:

1. Frequent meetings open and advertised, to be held in the Community Center . . . to which the League hopes to rally colored women from a large surrounding territory. At its meetings there will be from time to time (a) Ballot demonstrations (repeated); (b) Importance of registration (repeated); (c) Issues of the Campaign; (d) Candidates' meetings.
2. A system of home teaching for the colored women who cannot come to the Community Center . . . will be carried into the homes by members of the Douglass League.

3. "Excursion tickets" indicating a trip to the polls and asking "have you voted?" will be hung on tags on the doors in the neighborhood.[47]

News of league activities encouraged politically minded black women to seek membership in either separate or integrated units. However, they were usually discouraged. Delilah Beasley of Oakland expressed her frustration in establishing a black league in Los Angeles. Her efforts encountered prejudice throughout the state and especially in Los Angeles itself. Urging the formation of "full Colored Leagues" and auxiliaries to the white leagues, she stressed the need for black women to develop their own leadership, separate from whites so that "they do not antagonize the members of the White league by their presence." Yet Beasley did not demur from strongly recommending black representation on the general state board.[48]

On the other hand, Ohio black women opposed racial separatism in league work. Members of the Ohio Federation of Colored Women's Clubs had hoped to integrate various local leagues, after Sybil Burton, president of the state league, addressed their meeting and solicited their cooperation in mobilizing the vote. Ohio black women were ripe for participation. Burton admitted that the Ohio league found it unnecessary to sponsor educational classes for black women in the state because J. Estelle Barnett, a league member and black woman editor of the newspaper *In the Queen's Garden*, had used her paper to disseminate information on ballot marking and the necessity for voting.[49]

With no uniform guidelines, Burton preferred to leave the decision of accepting blacks to the individual leagues, whose racial policies varied by community. Oberlin accepted blacks freely and equally. Zanesville received black members but made them unwelcome at their luncheons and other social gatherings. The Toledo league sought advice from the national league when black women desired membership. The general consensus of the Toledo league was against integration, but they encouraged black women to form their own separate units. The Cincinnati league likewise contemplated the formation of an all-black unit. The reply from the national league tended to be discouraging in every way. While acknowledging that a few of the states had black leagues and a few others actually integrated individual black women into their ranks, Anne Williams Wheaton, press secretary, asserted: "Those who have expertise in this matter think it is far better not to encourage organizations of colored Leagues."[50] Rather than formal organization, the national league sought to address black issues through its Committee on Negro Problems—the name later being changed, at the request of black members, to the Committee on Interracial Problems.

In 1921 the committee formed in response to a petition by southern black women whose suffrage rights were denied. Interracial in composition, the committee included representatives from states where "the colored vote is a material and accepted fact." Its purpose was to implement educational and citizenship training programs, not augment black league membership. Although plans were devised by its three successive chairmen, Julia Lathrop (1921), Minnie Fisher Cunningham (1921–25), and Adele Clark (after 1925), the small committee left little in the way of accomplishment. A questionnaire was sent out to the states in 1927, but most did not reply, nor did the states that responded always do so thoughtfully and accurately. The ineffectiveness of the committee was evidenced in the infrequency of its meetings, all of which occurred informally at the national conventions and did not carry over into the interim period.[51] By the end of the decade the League of Women Voters had lost, largely by its own choice, the potential for being an important mobilizing force among black women.[52]

Conclusion

At the dawning of the 1930s, blacks found themselves on the brink of a political transition that would greatly accelerate in the next five years. The more dramatic collective action of blacks during the Depression and their strategic placement in the New Deal hierarchy have over-shadowed the contribution of the previous decade to their political mobilization and increased political leverage. The ratification of the Nineteenth Amendment in 1920 lent significant impetus to black women's interest in the American political process, although the continuing legacy of racism conditioned the nature and extent of their participation. The racist policies of the National American Woman Suffrage Association continued in the 1920s with its successor organization, the League of Women Voters, to discourage black participation. Black women leaders, while organizing their own separate organizations, encountered racism from the very elected officials for whom they campaigned. Yet black women's discontent and frustration with white women's organizations, with the Republican Party, and with a racist society in general during the 1920s translated not into an abandonment of politics but into the emergence of new leaders, alliances, and strategies.

In 1936, when the majority of black voters shifted to the Democratic Party, the unswerving Republican allegiance of such leaders as Nannie Burroughs and Mary Church Terrell no longer won the applause of the black electorate. The Democratic Party had shed its long-worn garb of white supremacy, its image as the party of the "solid South," segregation, and black disfranchisement. Under Franklin Roosevelt's New Deal, the Democrats came to be perceived as the party most receptive to black opportunity. Mary McLeod Bethune's visibility in the Roosevelt administration and Crystal Bird Fauset's membership on the Democratic National Committee expressed both the continuation of women's political activism and shifting opportunities for black women leaders. In 1932 Bethune sat on the board of counselors of the Women's Division of the Republican National Committee with such notable Republican stalwarts as Mrs. Theodore Roosevelt and Mrs. William Howard Taft. In 1936 she presided over Roosevelt's Black Cabinet.[53] Bethune 's shifting allegiance symbolized the changed mood of the black electorate and, certainly not least of all, woman's prerogative to change her mind.

Notes

1. Florette Henri, *Black Migration* (Garden City, N.Y.: Anchor/Doubleday, 1975), 50–59, 68–69; Martin Kilson, "Political Change in the Negro Ghetto, 1900–1940," in Nathan I. Huggins, Martin Kilson, and Daniel M. Fox, eds., *Key Issues in the Afro-American Experience* (New York: Harcourt Brace Jovanovich, 1971), 2:175; Jacqueline Jones, *Labor of Love, Labor of Sorrow. Black Women, Work, and the Family from Slavery to the Present* (New York: Basic Books, 1985), 152–60.

2. Harold F. Gosnell, *Negro Politicians* (Chicago: University of Chicago Press, 1935), 13–92, 180–90.

3. Paul Lewinson, *Race, Class, and Party: A History of Negro Suffrage and White Politics in the South* (New York: Oxford University Press, 1932); Harold F. Gosnell, "The Negro Vote in Northern Cities," *National Municipal Review* 30 (1941): 264–67, 268; St. Clair Drake and Horace R. Cayton, *Black Metropolis* (New York: Harper and Row, 1945); James Q. Wilson, *Negro Politics: The Search for Leadership* (New York: Free Press, 1960); Kilson, "Political Change in the Negro Ghetto"; Ira Katznelson, *Black Men, White Cities* (Chicago: University of Chicago Press, 1976).

4. See, for example, Rosalyn Terborg-Penn, "Discontented Black Feminists: Prelude and Postscript to the Passage of the Nineteenth Amendment," in Lois Scharf and Joan M. Jensen, eds., *Decades of Discontent: The Women's Movement, 1920–1940* (Westport, Conn.: Greenwood Press, 1983), 261–78.

5. Aileen S. Kraditor, *The Ideas of the Woman Suffrage Movement, 1890–1920* (Garden City, N.Y.: Anchor/Doubleday, 1971), 138–71; Rosalyn Terborg-Penn, "Discrimination against Afro-American Women in the Woman's Movement, 1830–1920," in Sharon Harley and Rosalyn Terborg-Penn, eds., *The Afro-American Woman: Struggles and Images* (Port Washington, N.Y.: Kennikat Press, 1978), 17–27; Paula Giddings, *When and Where I Enter: The Impact of Black Women on Race and Sex in America* (New York: William Morrow, 1984), 129–30, 165–69, 177, 218–20.

6. "The Woman Voter Hits the Color Line," *Nation*, 6 October 1920.

7. Terborg-Penn, "Discontented Black Feminists."

8. Ida B. Wells-Barnett, *Crusade for Justice: The Autobiography of Ida B. Wells*, ed. Alfreda M. Duster (Chicago: University of Chicago Press, 1970), 345–53.

9. Henri, *Black Migration*, 52–80; Doug McAdam, *Political Process and the Development of Black Insurgency, 1930–1910* (Chicago: University of Chicago Press, 1982), 77–81; Gosnell, *Negro Politicians*, 16–19.

10. Henri, *Black Migration*, 54–55; Kilson, "Political Change in the Negro Ghetto," 170–82; Jones, *Labor of Love*, 162–80, 190, 193–94.

11. Interview with Harold F. Gosnell, 17 March 1986, Bethesda, Maryland; also see Gosnell, *Negro Politicians*, 15, 19, 374; Gosnell, *Machine Politics: Chicago Model* (Chicago: University of Chicago Press, 1968).

12. "Negro Republican Campaign Division," *Norfolk Journal and Guide*, 11 August 1928; also see press release, "Republican National Committee, for Release Thursday, 2 August 1928," Nannie Helen Burroughs Papers, Library of Congress.

13. Hanes Walton, *Invisible Politics: Black Political Behavior* (Albany: State University of New York Press, 1985), 51.

14. See the *Baltimore Afro-American* for "Equal Rights League Sends Congratulations to Women"; "Colored Woman Sits on Jury," and "Committee of Women Named—Mrs. Lethia G. Fleming of Cleveland Is Approved Chairman," 17 September 1920; "Women Hit Color Line," 8 October 1920; "Vital Meeting—Come and Hear Why We Should Stand by Our Race Candidate," 1 October 1920; "Women Spring Big Surprise," 24 September 1920; "Women Make Good," 16 October 1920.

15. Augusta T. Chissell, "A Primer for Women Voters," *Baltimore Afro-American*, 24 September 1920.

16. *Baltimore Afro-American*, 1 October 1920.

17. National Association of Colored Women, *National Notes*, April 1923, 18; Charles H. Wesley, *The History of the National Association of Colored Women's Clubs, Inc.: A Legacy of Service* (Washington, D.C.: National Association of Colored Women's Clubs, 1984), 55–100.

18. Giddings, *When and Where I Enter*, 107–9, 135–36; Evelyn Brooks, "Religion, Politics, and Gender: The Leadership of Nannie Helen Burroughs," *Journal of Religious Thought* 44 (1988): 7–22.

19. Tullia Kay Brown Hamilton, "The National Association of Colored Women" (Ph.D. diss., Emory University, 1978), 53.

20. Mary McLeod Bethune, "Biennial Report of the National Association of Colored Women, 1924–1926," *National Notes*, July and August 1926, 3–4.

21. Hallie Q. Brown, "Republican Colored Women of America," *National Notes*, December 1924, 1.

22. "Report from the Western Division and the Eastern Division," *National Notes*, December 1924, 2–3; Wesley, *History of the National Association*, 91, 201–2.

23. "Report," *National Notes*, December 1924, 2–3.

24. Ibid., 4.

25. Ibid.

26. Gosnell notes a higher percentage of women precinct captains in the black wards. His roster showed as much as one-fourth of the captains to be women in the black Third Ward in Chicago. See Gosnell, *Machine Politics*, 61–63; "Campaign Experiences," *National Notes*, January 1925, 13–14.

27. "Campaign Experiences," *National Notes*, January 1925, 13.

28. In the southern states black disfranchisement and Democratic hegemony combined to effectively nullify any hope of amassing votes for state and local office, but posts within the Republican party as well as federal patronage positions were still available to southern Republicans by virtue of the votes they delivered at the national conventions. The influence of black Republicans and their female officeholders such as Mary Booze of Mississippi and Mamie Williams of Georgia lay largely with the ability of the black Republican organization in each southern state to achieve recognition at the Republican national convention. Termed "black and tans," these organizations distinguished themselves from the Republican organizations with overwhelmingly white membership—"lily-whites." The influence of the black and tans was keenly felt in the presidential nominations of McKinley in 1896, Taft in 1908 and 1912, and Hoover in 1928. See Lewinson, *Race, Class, and Party*, 170–76; V. O. Key, *Southern Politics in State and Nation* (New York: Vintage Books, 1949), 286–89; and Hanes Walton, *Black Republicans: The Politics of the Black and Tans* (Metuchen, N. J.: Scarecrow Press, 1975), 133–35.

29. "Minutes of the Temporary Organization of the National League of Republican Colored Women, 7 August 1924," and "Minutes of the Subsequent Meeting of the NLRCW, 11 August 1924," Burroughs Papers.

30. "The National League of Republican Colored Women," *National Notes*, July 1928, 10.

31. Mary Church Terrell, "An Appeal to Colored Women to Vote and Do Their Duty in Politics," *National Notes*, November 1925, 1; Mary Church Terrell, "What Colored Women Can and Should Do at the Polls," *National Notes*, March 1926, 3.

32. Mazie Griffin to Burroughs, n.d.; Mamie Williams to Burroughs, 5 January 1925, Burroughs Papers; also see "Departments and Their Functions," *National Notes*, January 1925, 2.

33. See, for example, Frannie Givens, of the East-End Colored Women's Political Clubs, to Burroughs,

20 October 1924; Mary E. Gardiner, of the Women's Republican Club of Cambridge, to Burroughs, 21 October 1924; Susan B. Evans, state director of colored women's activities of the St. Paul, Minn., Republican State Central Committee, 22 October 1924; Elizabeth L. Gulley, of the Colored Division, Wayne County Coolidge—Groesbeck Club, Republican State Central Committee of Michigan, 29 October 1924; and Mrs. Charles W. French, Parliamentarian, Kansas State Federation of Colored Women, to Burroughs, 30 October 1924, Burroughs Papers.

34. However, the NACW's *National Notes* carried articles promoting the National League of Republican Colored Women. See "Republican Call," April 1927, 6; "The National League of Republican Colored Women," July 1928, 10.

35. "Colored Women in Politics Questionnaire," Burroughs Papers.

36. "Meeting of the Executive Committee of the National League of Republican Colored Women, Oakland, Calif., 6 August 1926"; and Burroughs to Mrs. Alvin Hert, 11 August 1926, Burroughs Papers.

37. "Summarized Report of the Conference of the Republican National Committeewomen, State Vice-Chairmen, and State Club Presidents, January 12, 13, 14, 1927," Burroughs Papers.

38. Ibid.

39. "G.O.P. Women from Twenty-three States in Session," *Afro-American* (Washington ed.), 21 May 1927.

40. Daisy Lampkin to Burroughs, 2 and 17 July, 8 October 1928, Lampkin to Mrs. Paul FitzSimmons, 8 October 1928; Lampkin to Fellow Republican, 17 July 1928, Burroughs Papers.

41. Nancy J. Weiss, *Farewell to the Party of Lincoln: Black Politics in the Age of FDR* (Princeton: Princeton University Press, 1983), 3–33.

42. Gold Star Mothers were the mothers and widows of men buried in Europe who had died in active service during World War I. The U.S. government sponsored the women's passage to Europe in order to place wreaths on the graves. Black Gold Star Mothers were sent over in separate and blatantly inferior ships; ibid., 16–17.

43. Burroughs to Mrs. John Allen Dougherty, Chairman, Inaugural Charity Ball, 2 March 1929; Burroughs to Sallie Hert, 19 August 1929, 14 April 1930; Susie M. Myers to Burroughs, 3 May 1932; Burroughs to Mrs. Ellis Yost, 27 September 1932, 30 June 1934; Burroughs to Maude B. Coleman, 8 September 1936, Burroughs Papers.

44. Delilah L. Beasley, "Activities among Negroes," *Oakland Tribune*, 22 November 1925; Hettie Tilghman, "What the Study of Legislative Work Has Meant to Our Group," *National Notes*, November 1925, 3; "Miss Delilah L. Beasley," *National Notes*, March 1928, 8; Beasley, "California Women Preparing for Biennial Convention," *National Notes*, April 1926; Belle Sherwin to Sybil R. Burton, 31 March 1925, League of Women Voters Papers, Library of Congress (hereafter cited as LWV Papers).

45. Mrs. B. F. Bowles and Mrs. E. C. Grady, "The Colored Committee of the League of Women Voters of St. Louis: The First Nine Years"; Gladys Harrison to Ruth Siemer, 14 October 1929; Siemer to Beatrice Marsh, 30 June 1930; and Marsh to Adele Clark, 2 July 1930; also written sometime in the late 1920s but undated is Carrie Bowles, "Defends League of Women Voters," *St. Louis American*; clipping and aforementioned letters in LWV Papers; Carrie Bowles, "Women Voters' National League," *National Notes*, May 1928, 15.

46. "Mrs. Elizabeth Lindsay Davis . . . ," *National Notes*, April 1926, 1; "Illinois Federation of Colored Women's Clubs," *National Notes*, July 1926, 24.

47. "Excerpt from letter from Florence Harrison to Miss Sherwin dated 18 June 1924" and attached page, "Sent by Mrs. Rich to B.S. 1924," LWV Papers.

48. Delilah L. Beasley to Mrs. Warren Wheaton, 23 March 1926; Wheaton to Beasley, 25 March 1926, LWV Papers.

49. Sybil R. Burton to Belle Sherwin, 27 March 1925, LWV Papers.

50. Agnes Hilton to Gladys Harrison, 9 August 1928; Anne Williams Wheaton to Hilton, 17 August 1928, LWV Papers.

51. "Special Committee on Inter-Racial Problems, 17 April 1934"; "Report of the Special Committee on Interracial Problems to the Board of Directors, December 1927"; "National League of Women Voters—Report for the Committee on Negro Problems, April 1924–April 1925"; and "Committee on Negro Problems—Chairman Mrs. Minnie Fisher Cunningham, 11 July 1924," LWV Papers.

52. See, for example, a letter written by a black woman, Eva Nichols Wright, of Washington, D.C., to Belle Sherwin: "In reply to the question 'Are colored women of your city interested as members, in the League of Women Voters or the National Woman's Party? If not, why not?' The replies with two exceptions were negative. To the question, 'To what extent do white women and colored women work together politically?' The same negative reply was received with three or four exceptions, and many expressed themselves as being discouraged." Wright to Sherwin, 25 April 1927, LWV Papers.

53. Republican National Committee, Women's Division, *Organization News*, 22 October 1932, 2, in Burroughs Papers; Weiss, *Farewell to the Party of Lincoln*, 137–48, 180–84.

18

Miscegenation Law, Court Cases, and Ideologies of "Race" in Twentieth-Century America

Peggy Pascoe

On 21 March 1921 Joe Kirby took his wife, Mayellen, to court. The Kirbys had been married for seven years, and Joe wanted out. Ignoring the usual option of divorce, he asked for an annulment, charging that his marriage had been invalid from its very beginning because Arizona law prohibited marriages between "persons of Caucasian blood, or their descendants" and "negroes, Mongolians or Indians, and their descendants." Joe Kirby claimed that while he was "a person of the Caucasian blood," his wife, Mayellen, was "a person of negro blood."[1]

Although Joe Kirby's charges were rooted in a well-established and tragic—tradition of American miscegenation law, his court case quickly disintegrated into a definitional dispute that bordered on the ridiculous. The first witness in the case was Joe's mother, Tula Kirby, who gave her testimony in Spanish through an interpreter. Joe's lawyer laid out the case by asking Tula Kirby a few seemingly simple questions:

Joe's lawyer:	To what race do you belong?
Tula Kirby:	Mexican.
Joe's lawyer:	Are you white or have you Indian blood?
Tula Kirby:	I have no Indian blood.
Joe's lawyer:	Do you know the defendant [Mayellen] Kirby?
Tula Kirby:	Yes.
Joe's lawyer:	To what race does she belong?
Tula Kirby:	Negro.

Then the cross-examination began.

Mayellen's lawyer:	Who was your father?
Tula Kirby:	Jose Romero.
Mayellen's lawyer:	Was he a Spaniard?
Tula Kirby:	Yes, a Mexican.
Mayellen's lawyer:	Was he born in Spain?
Tula Kirby:	No, he was born in Sonora.
Mayellen's lawyer:	And who was your mother?
Tula Kirby:	Also in Sonora.
Mayellen's lawyer:	Was she a Spaniard?
Tula Kirby:	She was on her father's side.

Mayellen's lawyer:	And what on her mother's side?
Tula Kirby:	Mexican.
Mayellen's lawyer:	What do you mean by Mexican, Indian, a native [?]
Tula Kirby:	I don't know what is meant by Mexican.
Mayellen's lawyer:	A native of Mexico?
Tula Kirby:	Yes, Sonora, all of us.
Mayellen's lawyer:	Who was your grandfather on your father's side?
Tula Kirby:	He was a Spaniard.
Mayellen's lawyer:	Who was he?
Tula Kirby:	His name was Ignacio Quevas.
Mayellen's lawyer:	Where was he born?
Tula Kirby:	That I don't know. He was my grandfather.
Mayellen's lawyer:	How do you know he was a [S]paniard then?
Tula Kirby:	Because he told me ever since I had knowledge that he was a Spaniard.

Next the questioning turned to Tula's opinion about Mayellen Kirby's racial identity.

Mayellen's lawyer:	You said Mrs. Mayellen Kirby was a negress. What do you know about Mrs. Kirby's family?
Tula Kirby:	I distinguish her by her color and the hair; that is all I do know.[2]

The second witness in the trial was Joe Kirby, and by the time he took the stand, the people in the courtroom knew they were in murky waters. When Joe's lawyer opened with the question "What race do *you* belong to?" Joe answered, "Well . . .," and paused, while Mayellen's lawyer objected to the question on the ground that it called for a conclusion by the witness. "Oh, no," said the judge, "it is a matter of pedigree." Eventually allowed to answer the question, Joe said, "I belong to the white race I suppose." Under cross-examination, he described his father as having been of the "Irish race," although he admitted, "I never knew any one of his people."[3]

Stopping at the brink of this morass, Joe's lawyer rested his case. He told the judge he had established that Joe was "Caucasian." Mayellen's lawyer scoffed, claiming that Joe had "failed utterly to prove his case" and arguing that "[Joe's] mother has admitted that. She has [testified] that she only claims a quarter Spanish blood; the rest of it is native blood." At this point the court intervened. "I know," said the judge, "but that does not signify anything."[4]

From the Decline and Fall of Scientific Racism to an Understanding of Modernist Racial Ideology

The Kirbys' case offers a fine illustration of Evelyn Brooks Higginbotham's observation that although most Americans are sure they know "race" when they see it, very few can offer a definition of the term. Partly for this reason, the questions of what "race" signifies and what signifies "race" are as important for scholars today as they were for the participants in *Kirby v. Kirby* seventy-five years ago.[5] Historians have a long—and recently a distinguished—record of exploring this question.[6] Beginning in the 1960s, one notable group charted the rise and fall of scientific racism among American intellectuals. Today their successors, more likely to be schooled in social than intellectual history, trace the social construction of racial ideologies, including the idea of "whiteness," in a steadily expanding range of contexts.[7]

Their work has taught us a great deal about racial thinking in American history. We can trace the growth of racism among antebellum immigrant workers and free-soil northern Republicans; we can measure its breadth in late-nineteenth-century segregation and the immigration policies of the 1920s. We can follow the rise of Anglo-Saxonism from Manifest Destiny through the Spanish-American War and expose the appeals to white supremacy in woman suffrage speeches. We can relate all these developments (and more) to the growth and elaboration of scientific racist attempts to use biological characteristics to scout for racial hierarchies in social life, levels of civilization, even language.

Yet the range and richness of these studies all but end with the 1920s. In contrast to historians of the nineteenth- and early-twentieth-century United States, historians of the nation in the mid- to late twentieth century seem to focus on racial ideologies only when they are advanced by the far Right (as in the Ku Klux Klan) or by racialized groups themselves (as in the Harlem Renaissance or black nationalist movements). To the extent that there is a framework for surveying mainstream twentieth-century American racial ideologies, it is inherited from the classic histories that tell of the post-1920s decline and fall of scientific racism. Their final pages link the demise of scientific racism to the rise of a vanguard of social scientists led by the cultural anthropologist Franz Boas: When modern social science emerges, racism runs out of intellectual steam. In the absence of any other narrative, this forms the basis for a commonly held but rarely examined intellectual trickle-down theory in which the attack on scientific racism emerges in universities in the 1920s and eventually, if belatedly, spreads to courts in the 1940s and 1950s and to government policy in the 1960s and 1970s.

A close look at such incidents as the *Kirby* case, however, suggests a rather different historical trajectory, one that recognizes that the legal system does more than just reflect social or scientific ideas about race; it also produces and reproduces them.[8] By following a trail marked by four miscegenation cases—the seemingly ordinary *Kirby v. Kirby* (1922) and *Estate of Monks* (1941) and the pathbreaking *Pérez v. Lippold* (1948) and *Loving v. Virginia* (1967)—this article will examine the relation between modern social science, miscegenation law, and twentieth-century American racial ideologies, focusing less on the decline of scientific racism and more on the emergence of new racial ideologies.

In exploring these issues, it helps to understand that the range of nineteenth-century racial ideologies was much broader than scientific racism. Accordingly, I have chosen to use the term *racialism* to designate an ideological complex that other historians often describe with the terms *race* or *racist*. I intend the term *racialism* to be broad enough to cover a wide range of nineteenth-century ideas, from the biologically marked categories scientific racists employed to the more amorphous ideas George M. Fredrickson has so aptly called "romantic racialism."[9] Used in this way, the notion of racialism helps counter the tendency of twentieth-century observers to perceive nineteenth-century ideas as biologically "determinist" in some simple sense. To racialists (including scientific racists), the important point was not that biology determined culture (indeed, the split between the two was only dimly perceived), but that race, understood as an indivisible essence that included not only biology but also culture, morality, and intelligence, was a compellingly significant factor in history and society.

My argument is this: During the 1920s, American racialism was challenged by several emerging ideologies, all of which depended on a modern split between biology and culture. Between the 1920s and the 1960s, those competing ideologies were winnowed down to the single, powerfully persuasive belief that the eradication of racism depends on the deliberate nonrecognition of race. I will call that belief *modernist racial ideology* to echo the self-conscious "modernism" of social scientists, writers, artists, and cultural rebels of the early twentieth century. When historians mention this phenomenon, they usually label it "antiracist" or "egalitarian" and describe it as in stark contrast to the "racism" of its predecessors. But in the new legal scholarship called critical race theory, this same ideology, usually referred to as "color blindness," is criticized by those who recognize that it, like other racial ideologies, can be turned to the service of oppression.[10]

Modernist racial ideology has been widely accepted; indeed, it compels nearly as much adherence in the late-twentieth-century United States as racialism did in the late nineteenth century. It is therefore important to see it not as what it claims to be—the nonideological end of racism—but as a racial ideology of its own, whose history shapes many of today's arguments about the meaning of race in American society.

The Legacy of Racialism and the *Kirby* Case

Although it is probably less familiar to historians than, say, school segregation law, miscegenation law is an ideal place to study both the legacy of nineteenth-century racialism and the emergence of modern racial ideologies.[11] Miscegenation laws, in force from the 1660s through the 1960s, were among the longest-lasting of American racial restrictions. They both reflected and produced significant shifts in American racial thinking. Although the first miscegenation laws had been passed in the colonial period, it was not until after the demise of slavery that they began to function as the ultimate sanction of the American system of white supremacy. They burgeoned along with the rise of segregation and the early-twentieth-century devotion to "white purity." At one time or another, forty-one American colonies and states enacted them; they blanketed western as well as southern states.[12]

By the early twentieth century, miscegenation laws were so widespread that they formed a virtual road map to American legal conceptions of race. Laws that had originally prohibited marriages between whites and African Americans (and, very occasionally, American Indians) were extended to cover a much wider range of groups. Eventually, twelve states targeted American Indians, fourteen Asian Americans (Chinese, Japanese, and Koreans), and nine "Malays" (or Filipinos). In Arizona, the *Kirby* case was decided under categories first adopted in a 1901 law that prohibited whites from marrying "negroes, Mongolians or Indians"; in 1931, "Malays" and "Hindus" were added to this list.[13]

Although many historians assume that miscegenation laws enforced American taboos against interracial sex, marriage, more than sex, was the legal focus.[14] Some states did forbid both interracial sex and interracial marriage, but nearly twice as many targeted only marriage. Because marriage carried with it social respectability and economic benefits that were routinely denied to couples engaged in illicit sex, appeals courts adjudicated the legal issue of miscegenation at least as frequently in civil cases about marriage and divorce, inheritance, or child legitimacy as in criminal cases about sexual misconduct.[15]

By the time the *Kirby* case was heard, lawyers and judges approached miscegenation cases with working assumptions built on decades of experience. There had been a flurry of challenges to the laws during Reconstruction, but courts quickly fended off arguments that miscegenation laws violated the Fourteenth Amendment guarantee of "equal protection." Beginning in the late 1870s, judges declared that the laws were constitutional because they covered all racial groups "equally."[16] Judicial justifications reflected the momentum toward racial categorization built into the nineteenth-century legal system and buttressed by the racialist conviction that everything from culture, morality, and intelligence to heredity could be understood in terms of race.

From the 1880s until the 1920s, lawyers whose clients had been caught in the snare of miscegenation laws knew better than to challenge the constitutionality of the laws or to dispute the perceived necessity for racial categorization; these were all but guaranteed to be losing arguments. A defender's best bet was to do what Mayellen Kirby's lawyer tried to do: to persuade a judge (or jury) that one particular individual's racial classification was in error. Lawyers who defined their task in these limited terms occasionally succeeded, but even then the deck was stacked against them. Wielded by judges and juries who believed that setting racial boundaries was crucial to the maintenance of ordered society, the criteria used to determine who fit in which category were more notable for their malleability than for their logical consistency. Genealogy, appearance, claims to identity, or that mystical quality "blood"—any of these would do.[17]

In Arizona, Judge Samuel L. Pattee demonstrated that malleability in deciding the *Kirby* case. Although Mayellen Kirby's lawyer maintained that Joe Kirby "appeared" to be an Indian, the judge insisted that parentage, not appearance, was the key to Joe's racial classification:

> Mexicans are classed as of the Caucasian Race. They are descendants, supposed to be, at least of the Spanish conquerors of that country, and unless it can be shown that they are mixed up with some other races, why the presumption is that they are descendants of the Caucasian race.[18]

While the judge decided that ancestry determined that Joe Kirby was "Caucasian," he simply assumed that Mayellen Kirby was "Negro." Mayellen Kirby sat silent through the entire trial; she was spoken about and spoken for but never allowed to speak herself. There was no testimony about her ancestry; her race was assumed to rest in her visible physical characteristics. Neither of the lawyers bothered to argue over Mayellen's racial designation. As Joe's lawyer later explained,

> The learned and discriminating judge ... had the opportunity to gaze upon the dusky countenance of the appellant [Mayellen Kirby] and could not and did not fail to observe the distinguishing characteristics of the African race and blood.[19]

In the end, the judge accepted the claim that Joe Kirby was "Caucasian" and Mayellen Kirby "Negro" and held that the marriage violated Arizona miscegenation law; he granted Joe Kirby his annulment. In so doing, the judge resolved the miscegenation drama by adding a patriarchal moral to the white supremacist plot. As long as miscegenation laws regulated marriage more than sex, it proved easy for white men involved with women of color to avoid the social and economic responsibilities they would have carried in legally sanctioned marriages with white women. By granting Joe Kirby an annulment rather than a divorce, the judge not only denied the validity of the marriage while it had lasted but also in effect excused Joe Kirby from his obligation to provide economic support to a divorced wife.[20]

For her part, Mayellen Kirby had nothing left to lose. She and her lawyer appealed to the Arizona Supreme Court. This time they threw caution to the winds. Taking a first step toward the development of modern racial ideologies, they moved beyond their carefully limited argument about Joe's individual racial classification to challenge the entire racial logic of miscegenation law. The Arizona statute provided a tempting target for their attack, for under its "descendants" provision, a person of "mixed blood" could not legally marry anyone. Pointing this out, Mayellen Kirby's lawyer argued that the law must therefore be unconstitutional. He failed to convince the court. The appeals court judge brushed aside such objections. The argument that the law was unconstitutional, the judge held,

> is an attack ... [Mayellen Kirby] is not entitled to make for the reason that there is no evidence that she is other than of the black race. ... It will be time enough to pass on the question she raises ... when it is presented by some one whose rights are involved or affected.[21]

The Culturalist Challenge to Racialism

By the 1920s, refusals to recognize the rights of African American women had become conventional in American law. So had refusals to recognize obvious inconsistencies in legal racial classification schemes. Minions of racialism, judges, juries, and experts sometimes quarreled over specifics, but they agreed on the overriding importance of making and enforcing racial classifications.

Lawyers in miscegenation cases therefore neither needed nor received much courtroom assistance from experts. In another legal arena, citizenship and naturalization law, the use of experts, nearly all of whom advocated some version of scientific racism, was much more common. Ever since the 1870s, naturalization lawyers had relied on scientific racists to help them decide which racial and ethnic groups met the United States naturalization requirement of being "white" persons. But in a series of cases heard in the first two decades of the twentieth century, this strategy backfired. When judges found themselves drawn into a heated scientific debate on the question of whether "Caucasian" was the same as "white," the United States Supreme Court settled the question by discarding the experts and reverting to what the justices called the opinion of the "common man."[22]

In both naturalization and miscegenation cases, judges relied on the basic agreement between popular and expert (scientific racist) versions of the racialism that permeated turn-of-the-century American society. But even as judges promulgated the common sense of racialism, the ground was shifting beneath their feet. By the 1920s, lawyers in miscegenation cases were beginning to glimpse the courtroom potential of arguments put forth by a pioneering group of self-consciously "modern" social scientists willing to challenge racialism head on.

Led by cultural anthropologist Franz Boas, these emerging experts have long stood as the heroes of histories of the decline of scientific racism (which is often taken to stand for racism as a whole). But for modern social scientists, the attack on racialism was not so much an end in itself as a function of the larger goal of establishing "culture" as a central social science paradigm. Intellectually and institutionally, Boas and his followers staked their claim to academic authority on their conviction that human difference and human history were best explained by culture. Because they interpreted character, morality, and social organization as cultural rather than racial phenomena and because they were determined to explore, name, and claim the field of cultural analysis for social scientists, particularly cultural anthropologists, sociologists, and social psychologists, they are perhaps best described as culturalists.[23]

To consolidate their power, culturalists had to challenge the scientific racist paradigms they hoped to displace. Two of the arguments they made were of particular significance for the emergence of modern racial ideologies. The first was the argument that the key notion of racialism—race—made no biological sense.

This argument allowed culturalists to take aim at a very vulnerable target. For most of the nineteenth century, scientific racists had solved disputes about who fit into which racial categories by subdividing the categories. As a result, the number of scientifically recognized races had increased so steadily that by 1911, when the anthropologist Daniel Folkmar compiled the intentionally definitive *Dictionary of Races and Peoples*, he recognized "45 races or peoples among immigrants coming to the United States." Folkmar's was only one of several competing schemes, and culturalists delighted in pointing out the discrepancies between them, showing that scientific racists could not agree on such seemingly simple matters as how many races there were or what criteria—blood, skin color, hair type—best indicated race.[24]

In their most dramatic mode, culturalists went so far as to insist that physical characteristics were completely unreliable indicators of race; in biological terms, they insisted, race must be considered indeterminable. Thus, in an influential encyclopedia article on "race" published in the early thirties, Boas insisted that "it is not possible to assign with certainty any one individual to a definite group." Perhaps the strongest statement of this kind came from Julian Huxley and A. C. Haddon, British scientists who maintained that "the term *race* as applied to human groups should be dropped from the vocabulary of science." Since Huxley was one of the first culturalists trained as a biologist, his credentials added luster to his opinion. In this and other forms, the culturalist argument that race was biologically indeterminable captured the attention of both contemporaries and later historians.[25]

Historians have paid much less attention to a second and apparently incompatible argument put forth by culturalists. It started from the other end of the spectrum, maintaining not that there was no such thing as biological race but that race was nothing more than biology. Since culturalists considered biology of remarkably little importance, consigning race to the realm of biology pushed it out of the picture. Thus Boas ended his article on race by concluding that although it remained "likely" enough that scientific study of the "anatomical differences between the races" might reveal biological influences on the formation of personality, "the study of cultural forms shows that such differences are altogether irrelevant as compared with the powerful influence of the cultural environment in which the group lives."[26]

Following this logic, the contrast between important and wide-reaching culture and unimportant (but biological) race stood as the cornerstone of many culturalist arguments. Thus the cultural anthropologist Ruth Benedict began her influential 1940 book *Race: Science and Politics with* an analysis of "what race is *not*," including language, customs, intelligence, character, and civilization. In a 1943 pamphlet coauthored with Gene Weltfish and addressed to the general public, she explained that real "racial differences" occurred only in "nonessentials such as texture of head hair, amount of body hair, shape of the nose or head, or color of the eyes and the skin." Drawing on these distinctions, Benedict argued that race was a scientific "fact," but that racism, which she defined as "the dogma that the hope of civilization depends upon eliminating some races and keeping others pure," was no more than a "modern superstition."[27]

Culturalists set these two seemingly contradictory depictions of race—the argument that biological race was nonsense and the argument that race was merely biology—right beside each other. The contradiction mattered little to them. Both arguments effectively contracted the range of racialist thinking, and both helped break conceptual links between race and character, morality, psychology, and language. By showing that one after another of these phenomena depended more on environment and training than on biology, culturalists moved each one out of the realm of race and into the province of culture, widening the modern split between culture and biology. Boas opened his article on race by staking out this position. "The term race is often used loosely to indicate groups of men differing in appearance, language, or culture," he wrote, but in his analysis, it would apply "solely to the biological grouping of human types."[28]

In adopting this position, culturalist intellectuals took a giant step away from popular common sense on the issue of race. Recognizing—even at times celebrating—this gap between themselves and the public, they devoted much of their work to dislodging popular racial assumptions. They saw the public as lamentably behind the times and sadly prone to race "prejudice," and they used their academic credentials to insist that racial categories not only did not rest on common sense, but made little sense at all.[29]

The *Monks* Case and the Making of Modern Racial Ideologies

This, of course, was just what lawyers challenging miscegenation laws wanted to hear. Because culturalist social scientists could offer their arguments with an air of scientific and academic authority that might persuade judges, attorneys began to invite them to appear as expert witnesses. But when culturalists appeared in court, they entered an arena where their argument for the biological indeterminacy of race was shaped in ways neither they nor the lawyers who recruited them could control.

Take, for example, the seemingly curious trial of Marie Antoinette Monks of San Diego, California, decided in the Superior Court of San Diego County in 1939. By all accounts, Marie Antoinette Monks was a woman with a clear eye for her main chance. In the early 1930s she had entranced and married a man named Allan Monks, potential heir to a Boston fortune. Shortly after the marriage, which took place in Arizona, Allan Monks declined into insanity. Whether his mental condition resulted from injuries he had suffered in a motorcycle crash or from drugs administered under the undue influence of Marie Antoinette, the court would debate at great length. When Allan Monks died, he left two wills: an old one in favor of a friend named Ida Lee and a newer one in favor of his wife, Marie Antoinette. Ida Lee submitted her version of the will for probate, Marie Antoinette challenged her claim, and Lee fought back. Lee's lawyers contended that the Monks marriage was illegal. They charged that Marie Antoinette Monks, who had told her husband she was a "French" countess, was actually "a Negro" and therefore prohibited by Arizona law from marrying Allan Monks, whom the court presumed to be Caucasian.[30]

Much of the ensuing six-week-long trial was devoted to determining the "race" of Marie Antoinette Monks. To prove that she was "a Negro," her opponents called five people to the witness stand: a disgruntled friend of her husband, a local labor commissioner, and three expert witnesses, all of whom offered arguments that emphasized biological indicators of race. The first so-called expert, Monks's hairdresser, claimed that she could tell that Monks was of mixed blood from looking at the size of the moons of her fingernails, the color of the "ring" around the palms of her hands, and the "kink" in her hair. The second, a physical anthropologist from the nearby San Diego Museum, claimed to be able to tell that Monks was "at least one-eighth negroid" from the shape of her face, the color of her hands, and her "protruding heels," all of which he had observed casually while a spectator in the courtroom. The third expert witness, a surgeon, had grown up and practiced medicine in the South and later served at a Southern Baptist mission in Africa. Having once walked alongside Monks when entering the courthouse (at which time he tried, he said, to make a close observation of her), he testified that he could tell that she was of "one-eighth negro blood" from the contour of her calves and heels, from the "peculiar pallor" on the back of her neck, from the shape of her face, and from the wave of her hair.[31]

To defend Monks, her lawyers called a friend, a relative, and two expert witnesses of their own, an anthropologist and a biologist. The experts both started out by testifying to the culturalist position that it was impossible to tell a person's race from physical characteristics, especially if that person was, as they put it, "of mixed blood." This was the argument culturalists used whenever they were cornered into talking about biology, a phenomenon they tended to regard as so insignificant a factor in social life that they preferred to avoid talking about it at all.

But because this argument replaced certainty with uncertainty, it did not play very well in the *Monks* courtroom. Seeking to find the definitiveness they needed to offset the experts who had already testified, the lawyers for Monks paraded their own client in front of the witness stand, asking her to show the anthropologist her fingernails and to remove her shoes so that he could see her heels. They lingered over the biologist's testimony that Monks's physical features resembled those of the people of southern France. In the end, Monks's lawyers backed both experts into a corner; when pressed repeatedly for a definite answer, both reluctantly admitted that it was their opinion that Monks was a "white" woman.[32]

The experts' dilemma reveals the limitations of the argument for racial indeterminacy in the courtroom. Faced with a conflict between culturalist experts, who offered uncertainty and indeterminacy, and their opponents, who offered concrete biological answers to racial questions, judges were predisposed to favor the latter. To judges, culturalists appeared frustratingly vague and uncooperative (in other words, lousy witnesses), while their opponents seemed to be good witnesses willing to answer direct questions.

In the *Monks* case, the judge admitted that his own "inexpert" opinion—that Marie Antoinette "did have many characteristics that I would say . . . [showed] mixed negro and some other blood"—was not enough to justify a ruling. Turning to the experts before him, he dismissed the hairdresser (whose experience he was willing to grant, but whose scientific credentials he considered dubious); he passed over the biologist (whose testimony, he thought, could go either way); and he dismissed the two anthropologists, whose testimonies, he said, more or less canceled each other out. The only expert the judge was willing to rely on was the surgeon, because the surgeon "seemed ... to hold a very unique and peculiar position as an expert on the question involved from his work in life."[33]

Relying on the surgeon's testimony, the judge declared that Marie Antoinette Monks was "the descendant of a negro" who had "one-eighth negro blood . . . and 7/8 caucasian blood"; he said that her "race" prohibited her from marrying Allan Monks and from inheriting his estate. The racial categorization served to invalidate the marriage in two overlapping ways. First, as a "negro," Marie Antoinette could not marry a white under Arizona miscegenation law; and second, by telling her husband-to-be that she was "French," Marie Antoinette had committed a "fraud" serious enough to render the marriage legally void. The court's decision that she had also exerted "undue influence" over Monks was hardly necessary to the outcome.[34]

As the *Monks* case suggests, we should be careful not to overestimate the influence culturalists had on the legal system. And, while in courtrooms culturalist experts were trying—and failing—to convince judges that biological racial questions were unanswerable, outside the courts their contention that biological racial answers were insignificant was faring little better. During the first three decades of the twentieth century, scientists on the "racial" side of the split between race and culture reconstituted themselves into a rough alliance of their own. Mirroring the modern dividing line between biology and culture, its ranks swelled with those who claimed special expertise on biological questions. There were biologists and physicians; leftover racialists such as physical anthropologists, increasingly shorn of their claims to expertise in every arena *except* that of physical characteristics; and, finally, the newly emerging eugenicists.[35]

Eugenicists provided the glue that held this coalition together. Narrowing the sweep of nineteenth-century racialist thought to focus on biology, these modern biological experts then expanded their range by offering physical characteristics, heredity, and reproductive imperatives as variations on the biological theme. They were particularly drawn to arenas in which all these biological motifs came into play; accordingly, they placed special emphasis on reforming marriage laws. Perhaps the best-known American eugenicist, Charles B. Davenport of the Eugenics Record Office, financed by the Carnegie Institution, outlined their position in a 1913 pamphlet, *State Laws Limiting Marriage Selection Examined in the Light of Eugenics,* which proposed strengthening state control over the marriages of the physically and racially unfit. Davenport's plan was no mere pipe dream. According to the historian Michael Grossberg, by the 1930s, forty-one states used eugenic categories to restrict the marriage of "lunatics," "imbeciles," "idiots," and the "feebleminded"; twenty-six states restricted the marriages of those infected with syphilis and gonorrhea; and twenty-seven states passed sterilization laws. By midcentury, blood tests had become a standard legal prerequisite for marriage.[36]

Historians have rather quickly passed over the racial aspects of American eugenics, seeing its proponents as advocates of outmoded ideas soon to be beached by the culturalist sea change. Yet until at least World War II, eugenicists reproduced a modern racism that was biological in a particularly virulent sense. For them, unlike their racialist predecessors (who tended to regard biology as an indicator of a much more expansive racial phenomenon), biology really was the essence of race. And unlike nineteenth-century scientific racists (whose belief in discrete racial dividing lines was rarely shaken by evidence of racial intermixture), twentieth-century eugenicists and culturalists alike seemed obsessed with the subject of mixed-race individuals.[37]

In their determination to protect "white purity," eugenicists believed that even the tightest definitions of race by blood proportion were too loose. Setting their sights on Virginia, in 1924 they secured passage of the most draconian miscegenation law in American history. The act, entitled "an Act to preserve racial integrity," replaced the legal provision that a person must have one-sixteenth "negro blood" to fall within the state's definition of "colored" with this provision:

> It shall hereafter be unlawful for any white person in this State to marry any save a white person, or a person with no other admixture of blood than white and American Indian.

For the purpose of this act, the term "white person" shall apply only to the person who has no trace whatsoever of any blood other than Caucasian; but persons who have one-sixteenth or less of the blood of the American Indian and have no other non-Caucasic blood shall be deemed to be white persons.

Another section of the Virginia law (which provided for the issuance of supposedly voluntary racial registration certificates for Virginia citizens) spelled out the "races" the legislature had in mind. The list, which specified "Caucasian, Negro, Mongolian, American Indian, Asiatic Indian, Malay, or any mixture thereof, or any other non-Caucasic strains," showed the lengths to which lawmakers would go to pin down racial categories. Within the decade, the Virginia law was copied by Georgia and echoed in Alabama. Thereafter, while supporters worked without much success to extend such laws to other states, defenders of miscegenation statutes added eugenic arguments to their rhetorical arsenal.[38]

Having been pinned to the modern biological wall and labeled as "mixed-race," Marie Antoinette Monks would seem to have been in the perfect position to challenge the constitutionality of the widely drawn Arizona miscegenation law. She took her case to the California Court of Appeals, Fourth District, where she made an argument that echoed that of Mayellen Kirby two decades earlier. Reminding the court of the wording of the Arizona statute, her lawyers pointed out that "on the set of facts found by the trial judge, [Marie Antoinette Monks] is concededly of Caucasian blood as well as negro blood, and therefore a descendant of a Caucasian." Spelling it out, they explained:

As such, she is prohibited from marrying a negro or any descendant of a negro, a Mongolian or an Indian, a Malay or a Hindu, or any of the descendants of any of them. Likewise . . . as a descendant of a negro she is prohibited from marrying a Caucasian or descendant of a Caucasian, which of course would include any person who had any degree of Caucasian blood in them.

Because this meant that she was "absolutely prohibited from contracting valid marriages in Arizona," her lawyers argued that the Arizona law was an unconstitutional constraint on her liberty.[39]

The court, however, dismissed this argument as "interesting but in our opinion not tenable." In a choice that speaks volumes about the depth of attachment to racial categories, the court narrowed the force of the argument by asserting that "the constitutional problem would be squarely presented" only if one mixed-race person were seeking to marry another mixed-race person, then used this constructed hypothetical to dodge the issue:

While it is true that there was evidence that appellant [Marie Antoinette Monks] is a descendant of the Caucasian race, as well as of the Negro race, the other contracting party [Allan Monks] was of unmixed blood and therefore the hypothetical situation involving an attempted alliance between two persons of mixed blood is no more present in the instant case than in the Kirby case. . . . The situations conjured up by respondent are not here involved. . . . Under the facts presented the appellant does not have the benefit of assailing the validity of the statute.

This decision was taken as authoritative. Both the United States Supreme Court and the Supreme Judicial Court of Massachusetts (in which Monks had also filed suit) refused to reopen the issue.[40]

Perhaps the most interesting thing about the Monks case is that there is no reason to believe that the public found it either remarkable or objectionable. Local reporters who covered the trial in 1939 played up the themes of forgery, drugs, and insanity; their summaries of the racial categories of the Arizona law and the opinions of the expert witnesses were largely matter-of-fact.[41]

In this seeming acceptability to the public lies a clue to the development of modern racial ideologies. Even as judges narrowed their conception of race, transforming an all-encompassing phenomenon into a simple fact to be determined, they remained bound by the provisions of miscegenation law to determine who fit in which racial categories. For this purpose, the second culturalist argument, that race was merely biology, had far more to offer than the first, that race was biologically indeterminable. The conception of race as merely biological seemed consonant with the racial categories built into the laws, seemed supportable by clear and unequivocal expert testimony, and fit comfortably within popular notions of race.

The Distillation of Modernist Racial Ideology: from *Pérez* to *Loving*

In the *Monks* case we can see several modern racial ideologies—ranging from the argument that race was biological nonsense to the reply that race was essentially biological to the possibility that race was merely biology—all grounded in the split between culture and biology. To distill these variants into a unified modernist racial ideology, another element had to be added to the mix, the remarkable (in American law, nearly unprecedented) proposal that the legal system abandon its traditional responsibility for determining and defining racial categories. In miscegenation law, this possibility emerged in a case that also, and not coincidentally, featured the culturalist argument for biological racial indeterminacy.

The case was *Pérez v. Lippold*. It involved a young Los Angeles couple, Andrea Pérez and Sylvester Davis, who sought a marriage license. Turned down by the Los Angeles County clerk, they challenged the constitutionality of the California miscegenation law directly to the California Supreme Court, which heard their case in October 1947.[42]

It was not immediately apparent that the *Pérez* case would play a role in the development of modernist racial ideology. Perhaps because both sides agreed that Pérez was "a white female" and Davis "a Negro male," the lawyer who defended the couple, Daniel Marshall, did not initially see the case as turning on race categorization. In 1947 Marshall had few civil rights decisions to build on, so he tried an end run strategy. He based his challenge to miscegenation laws on the argument that because both Pérez and Davis were Catholics and the Catholic Church did not prohibit interracial marriage, California miscegenation law was an arbitrary and unreasonable restraint on their freedom of religion.

The freedom-of-religion argument made some strategic sense, since several courts had held that states had to meet a high standard to justify restrictions on religious expression. Accordingly, Marshall laid out the religion argument in a lengthy petition to the California Supreme Court. In response, the state offered an even lengthier defense of miscegenation laws. The state's lawyers had at their fingertips a long list of precedents upholding such laws, including the *Kirby* and *Monks* cases. They added eugenic arguments about racial biology, including evidence of declining birth rates among "hybrids" and statistics that showed high mortality, short life expectancies, and particular diseases among African Americans. They polished off their case with the comments of a seemingly sympathetic Roman Catholic priest.[43]

Here the matter stood until the California Supreme Court heard oral arguments in the case. At that session, the court listened in silence to Marshall's opening sally that miscegenation laws were based on prejudice and to his argument that they violated constitutional guarantees of freedom of religion. But as soon as the state's lawyer began to challenge the religious-freedom argument, one of the court's associate justices, Roger Traynor, impatiently interrupted the proceedings. "What," he asked, "about equal protection of the law?"

Mr. Justice Traynor: . . . it might help to explain the statute, what it means. What is a negro?

Mr. Stanley: We have not the benefit of any judicial interpretation. The statute states that a negro [Stanley evidently meant to say, as the law did, "a white"] cannot marry a negro, which can be construed to mean a full-blooded negro, since the statute also says mulatto, Mongolian, or Malay.

Mr. Justice Traynor: What is a mulatto? One-sixteenth blood?

Mr. Stanley: Certainly certain states have seen fit to state what a mulatto is.

Mr. Justice Traynor: If there is 1/8 blood, can they marry? If you can marry with 1/8, why not with 1/16, 1/32, 1/64? And then don't you get in the ridiculous position where a negro cannot marry anybody? If he is white, he cannot marry black, or if he is black, he cannot marry white.

Mr. Stanley: I agree that it would be better for the Legislature to lay down an exact amount of blood, but I do not think that the statute should be declared unconstitutional as indefinite on this ground.

Mr. Justice Traynor: That is something anthropologists have not been able to furnish, although they say generally that there is no such thing as race.

Mr. Stanley: I would not say that anthropologists have said that generally, except such statements for sensational purposes.

Mr. Justice Traynor: Would you say that Professor Wooten of Harvard was a sensationalist? The crucial question is how can a county clerk determine who are negroes and who are whites.[44]

Although he addressed his questions to the lawyers for the state, Justice Traynor had given Marshall a gift no lawyer had ever before received in a miscegenation case: judicial willingness to believe in the biological indeterminacy of race. It was no accident that this argument came from Roger Traynor. A former professor at Boalt Hall, the law school of the University of California, Berkeley, Traynor had been appointed to the court for his academic expertise rather than his legal experience; unlike his more pragmatic colleagues, he kept up with developments in modern social science.[45]

Marshall responded to the opening Traynor had provided by making sure that his next brief included the culturalist argument that race was biological nonsense. In it, he asserted that experts had determined that "race, as popularly understood, is a myth"; he played on the gap between expert opinion and laws based on irrational "prejudice" rooted in "myth, folk belief, and superstition"; and he dismissed his opponents' reliance on the "grotesque reasoning of eugenicists" by comparing their statements to excerpts from Adolf Hitler's *Mein Kampf*.[46]

Marshall won his case. The 1948 decision in the *Pérez* case was remarkable for many reasons. It marked the first time since Reconstruction that a state court had declared a state miscegenation law unconstitutional. It went far beyond existing appeals cases in that the California Supreme Court had taken the very step the judges in the *Kirby* and *Monks* cases had avoided— going beyond the issue of the race of an individual to consider the issue of racial classification in general. Even more remarkable, the court did so in a case in which neither side had challenged the racial classification of the parties. But despite these accomplishments, the *Pérez* case was no victory for the culturalist argument about the biological indeterminacy of race. Only the outcome of the case—that California's miscegenation law was unconstitutional—was clear. The rationale for this outcome was a matter of considerable dispute.

Four justices condemned the law and three supported it; altogether, they issued four separate opinions. A four-justice majority agreed that the law should be declared unconstitutional but disagreed about why. Two justices, led by Traynor, issued a lengthy opinion that pointed out the irrationality of racial categories, citing as authorities a virtual who's who of culturalist social scientists, from Boas, Huxley, and Haddon to Gunnar Myrdal. A third justice issued a concurring opinion that pointedly ignored the rationality or irrationality of race classifications to criticize miscegenation laws on equality grounds, contending that laws based on "race, color, or creed" were—and always had been—contrary to the Declaration of Independence, the Constitution, and the Fourteenth Amendment; as this justice saw it, the Constitution was color-blind. A fourth justice, who reported that he wanted his decision to "rest upon a broader ground than that the challenged statutes are discriminatory and irrational," based his decision solely on the religious-freedom issue that had been the basis of Marshall's original argument.[47]

In contrast, a three-justice minority argued that the law should be upheld. They cited legal precedent, offered biological arguments about racial categories, and mentioned a handful of social policy considerations. Although the decision went against them, their agreement with each other ironically formed the closest thing to a majority in the case. In sum, although the *Perez* decision foreshadowed the day when American courts would abandon their defense of racial categories, its variety of judicial rationales tells us more about the range of modern racial ideologies than it does about the power of any one of them.[48]

Between the *Perez* case in 1948 and the next milestone miscegenation case, *Loving v. Virginia*, decided in 1967, judges would search for a common denominator among this contentious variety, trying to find a position of principled decisiveness persuasive enough to mold both public and expert opinion. One way to do this was to back away from the culturalist argument that race made no biological sense, adopting the other culturalist argument that race was biological fact and thus shifting the debate to the question of how much biological race should matter in determining social and legal policy.

In such a debate, white supremacists tried to extend the reach of biological race as far as possible. Thus one scientist bolstered his devotion to white supremacy by calling Boas "that appalling disaster to American social anthropology whose influence in the end has divorced the social studies of man from their scientific base in physical biology."[49] Following the lead of eugenicists, he and his sympathizers tried to place every social and legal superstructure on a biological racial base.

In contrast, their egalitarian opponents set limits. In their minds, biological race (or "skin color," as they often called it), was significant only because its visibility made it easy for racists to identify those they subjected to racial oppression. As Myrdal, the best-known of the mid-twentieth-century culturalist social scientists, noted in 1944 in his monumental work, *An American Dilemma*:

> In spite of all heterogeneity, the average white man's unmistakable observation is that *most Negroes in America have dark skin and woolly hair*, and he is, of course, right. . . . [The African American's] African ancestry and physical characteristics are fixed to his person much more ineffaceably than the yellow star is fixed to the Jew during the Nazi regime in Germany.[50]

To Myrdal's generation of egalitarians, the translation of visible physical characteristics into social hierarchies formed the tragic foundation of American racism.

The egalitarians won this debate, and their victory paved the way for the emergence of a modernist racial ideology persuasive enough to command the kind of widespread adherence once commanded by late-nineteenth-century racialism. Such a position was formulated by the United States Supreme Court in 1967 in *Loving v. Virginia*, the most important miscegenation case ever heard and the only one now widely remembered.

The *Loving* case involved what was, even for miscegenation law, an extreme example. Richard Perry Loving and Mildred Delores Jeter were residents of the small town of Central Point,

Virginia, and family friends who had dated each other since he was seventeen and she was eleven. When they learned that their plans to marry were illegal in Virginia, they traveled to Washington, D.C., which did not have a miscegenation law, for the ceremony, returning in June 1958 with a marriage license, which they framed and placed proudly on their wall. In July 1958 they were awakened in the middle of the night by the county sheriff and two deputies, who had walked through their unlocked front door and right into their bedroom to arrest them for violating Virginia's miscegenation law. Under that law, an amalgam of criminal provisions enacted in 1878 and Virginia's 1924 "Act to preserve racial integrity," the Lovings, who were identified in court records as a "white" man and a "colored" woman, pleaded guilty and were promptly convicted and sentenced to a year in jail. The judge suspended their sentence on the condition that "both accused leave . . . the state of Virginia at once and do not return together or at the same time to said county and state for a period of twenty-five years."[51]

In 1963 the Lovings, then the parents of three children, grew tired of living with relatives in Washington, D.C., and decided to appeal this judgment. Their first attempts ended in defeat. In 1965 the judge who heard their original case not only refused to reconsider his decision but raised the rhetorical stakes by opining:

> Almighty God created the races white, black, yellow, malay and red, and he placed them on separate continents. And but for the interference with his arrangement there would be no cause for such marriages. The fact that he separated the races shows that he did not intend for the races to mix.

But by the time their argument had been processed by the Supreme Court of Appeals of Virginia (which invalidated the original sentence but upheld the miscegenation law), the case had attracted enough attention that the United States Supreme Court, which had previously avoided taking miscegenation cases, agreed to hear an appeal.[52]

On the side of the Lovings stood not only their own attorneys, but also the National Association for the Advancement of Colored People (NAACP), the NAACP Legal Defense and Education Fund, the Japanese American Citizens League (JACL), and a coalition of Catholic bishops. The briefs they submitted offered the whole arsenal of arguments developed in previous miscegenation cases. The bishops offered the religious-freedom argument that had been the original basis of the *Pérez* case. The NAACP and the JACL stood on the opinions of culturalist experts, whose numbers now reached beyond social scientists well into the ranks of biologists. Offering both versions of the culturalist line on race, NAACP lawyers argued on one page, "The idea of 'pure' racial groups, either past or present, has long been abandoned by modern biological and social sciences," and on another, "Race, in its scientific dimension, refers only to the biogenetic and physical attributes manifest by a specified population. It does not, under any circumstances, refer to culture (learned behavior), language, nationality, or religion." The Lovings' lawyers emphasized two central points: Miscegenation laws violated both the constitutional guarantee of equal protection under the laws and the constitutional protection of the fundamental right to marry.[53]

In response, the lawyers for the state of Virginia tried hard to find some ground on which to stand. Their string of court precedents upholding miscegenation laws had been broken by the *Perez* decision. Their argument that Congress never intended the Fourteenth Amendment to apply to interracial marriage was offset by the Supreme Court's stated position that congressional intentions were inconclusive. In an attempt to distance the state from the "white purity" aspects of Virginia's 1924 law, Virginia's lawyers argued that since the Lovings admitted that they were a "white" person and "colored" person and had been tried under a section of the law that mentioned only those categories, the elaborate definition of "white" offered in other sections of Virginia law was irrelevant.[54]

On only one point did the lawyers for both parties and the Court seem to agree: None of them wanted to let expert opinion determine the outcome. The lawyers for Virginia knew only too well that during the twentieth century the scientific foundations of the eugenic biological argument in favor of miscegenation laws had crumbled, so they tried to warn the Court away by predicting that experts would mire the Court in "a veritable Serbonian bog of conflicting scientific opinion." Yet the Lovings' lawyers, who seemed to have the experts on their side, agreed that "the Court should not go into the morass of sociological evidence that is available on both sides of the question." "We strongly urge," they told the justices, "that it is not necessary." And the Court, still reeling from widespread criticism that its decision in the famous 1954 case *Brown v. Board of Education* was illegitimate "sociological jurisprudence," was not about to offer its opponents any more of such ammunition.[55]

The decision the Court issued was, in fact, carefully shorn of all reference to expert opinion; it spoke in language that both reflected and contributed to a new popular common sense on the issue of race. Recycling earlier pronouncements that "distinctions between citizens solely because of their ancestry" were "odious to a free people whose institutions are founded upon the doctrine of equality" and that the Court "cannot conceive of a valid legislative purpose . . . which makes the color of a person's skin the test of whether his conduct is a criminal offense," the justices reached a new and broader conclusion. Claiming (quite inaccurately) that "[w]e have consistently denied the constitutionality of measures which restrict the rights of citizens on account of race," the Court concluded that the racial classifications embedded in Virginia miscegenation laws were "so directly subversive of the principle of equality at the heart of the Fourteenth Amendment" that they were "unsupportable." Proclaiming that it violated both the equal protection and the due process clauses of the Fourteenth Amendment, the Court declared the Virginia miscegenation law unconstitutional.[56]

Legacies of Modernist Racial Ideology

The decision in the *Loving* case shows the distance twentieth-century American courts had traveled. The accumulated effect of several decades of culturalist attacks on racialism certainly shaped their thinking. The justices were no longer willing to accept the notion that race was the all-encompassing phenomenon nineteenth-century racialist thinkers had assumed it to be; they accepted the divisions between culture and biology and culture and race established by modern social scientists. But neither were they willing to declare popular identification of race with physical characteristics (like "the color of a person's skin") a figment of the imagination. In their minds, the scope of the term *race* had shrunk to a point where biology was all that was left; *race* referred to visible physical characteristics significant only because racists used them to erect spurious racial hierarchies. The Virginia miscegenation law was a case in point; the Court recognized and condemned it as a statute clearly "designed to maintain White Supremacy."[57]

Given the dependence of miscegenation laws on legal categories of race, the Court concluded that ending white supremacy required abandoning the categories. In deemphasizing racial categories, they joined mainstream mid-twentieth-century social scientists, who argued that because culture, rather than race, shaped meaningful human difference, race was nothing more than a subdivision of the broader phenomenon of ethnicity. In a society newly determined to be "color-blind," granting public recognition to racial categories seemed to be synonymous with racism itself.[58]

And so the Supreme Court promulgated a modernist racial ideology that maintained that the best way to eradicate racism was the deliberate nonrecognition of race. Its effects reached well beyond miscegenation law. Elements of modernist racial ideology marked many of the major mid-twentieth-century Supreme Court decisions, including *Brown v. Board of Education*. Its effects on state law codes were equally substantial; during the 1960s and 1970s, most American states repealed statutes that had defined "race" (usually by blood proportion) and set out to erase racial terminology from their laws.[59]

Perhaps the best indication of the pervasiveness of modernist racial ideology is how quickly late-twentieth-century conservatives learned to shape their arguments to fit its contours. Attaching themselves to the modernist narrowing of the definition of race to biology and biology alone, conservative thinkers began to contend that unless their ideas rested solely and explicitly on a belief in biological inferiority, they should not be considered racist. They began to advance "cultural" arguments of their very own, insisting that their proposals were based on factors such as social analysis, business practicality, or merit—on anything, in other words, except biological race. In their hands, modernist racial ideology supports an Alice-in-Wonderland interpretation of racism in which even those who argue for racially oppressive policies can adamantly deny being racists.

This conservative turnabout is perhaps the most striking indication of the contradictions inherent in modernist racial ideology, but it is not the only one. Others run the gamut from administrative law to popular culture. So while the U.S. Supreme Court tries to hold to its twentieth-century legacy of limiting racial categories when it cannot eradicate them, U.S. government policies remain deeply dependent on them. In the absence of statutory definitions of race, racial categories are now set by the U.S. Office of Management and Budget, which in 1977 issued a "Statistical Directive" that divided Americans into five major groups—American Indian or Alaskan Native, Asian or Pacific Islander, black, white, and Hispanic. The statistics derived from these categories help determine everything from census counts to eligibility for inclusion in affirmative action programs to the drawing of voting districts.[60] Meanwhile, in one popular culture flashpoint after another—from the Anita Hill/Clarence Thomas hearings to the O. J. Simpson case, mainstream commentators insist that "race" should not be a consideration even as they explore detail after detail that reveals its social pervasiveness.[61]

These gaps between the (very narrow) modernist conception of race and the (very wide) range of racial identities and racial oppressions bedevil today's egalitarians. In the political arena, some radicals have begun to argue that the legal system's deliberate nonrecognition of race erodes the ability to recognize and name racism and to argue for such policies as affirmative action, which rely on racial categories to overturn rather than to enforce oppression. Meanwhile, in the universities, a growing chorus of scholars is revitalizing the argument for the biological indeterminacy of race and using that argument to explore the myriad of ways in which socially constructed notions of race remain powerfully salient. Both groups hope to do better than their culturalist predecessors at eradicating racism.[62]

Attaining that goal may depend on how well we understand the tortured history of mid-twentieth-century American ideologies of race.

Notes

This article was originally presented at the 1992 annual meeting of the Organization of American Historians, and it has benefited considerably from the responses of audiences there and at half a dozen universities. For especially helpful readings, suggestions, and assistance, I would like to thank Nancy Cott, Karen Engle, Estelle Freedman, Jeff Garcilazo, Dave Gutierrez, Ramon Gutiérrez, Eric Hinderaker, Marcia Klotz, Dorothee Kocks, Waverly Lowell, Valerie Matsumoto, Robyn Muncy, David Roediger, Richard White, the Brown University women's history reading group, and the editors and anonymous reviewers of the *Journal of American History*.

1. Ariz. Rev. Stat. Ann. sec. 3837 (1913); "Appellant's Abstract of Record," 8 Aug. 1921, pp. 1–2, *Kirby v. Kirby*, docket 1970 (microfilm: file 36.1.134), Arizona Supreme Court Civil Cases (Arizona State Law Library, Phoenix).
2. "Appellant's Abstract of Record," 12–13, 13–15, 15, *Kirby v. Kirby*.

3. Ibid., 16–18.

4. Ibid., 19.

5. Evelyn Brooks Higginbotham, "African-American Women's History and the Metalanguage of Race," *Signs* 17 (winter 1992): 253. See Michael Omi and Howard Winant, *Racial Formation in the United States: From the 1960s to the 1990s* (New York, 1994); David Theo Goldberg, ed., *Anatomy of Racism* (Minneapolis, 1990); Henry Louis Gates Jr., ed., *"Race," Writing, and Difference* (Chicago, 1986); Dominick LaCapra, ed., *The Bounds of Race: Perspectives on Hegemony and Resistance* (Ithaca, 1991); F. James Davis, *Who Is Black? One Nation's Definition* (University Park, 1991); Sandra Harding, ed., *The "Racial" Economy of Science: Toward a Democratic Future* (Bloomington, 1993); Maria P. P. Root, ed., *Racially Mixed People in America* (Newbury Park, 1992); and Ruth Frankenberg, *White Women, Race Matters: The Social Construction of Whiteness* (Minneapolis, 1993).

6. Among the most provocative recent works are Higginbotham, "African-American Women's History"; Barbara J. Fields, "Ideology and Race in American History," in J. Morgan Kousser and James M. McPherson, eds., *Region, Race, and Reconstruction: Essays in Honor of C. Vann Woodward* (New York, 1982), 143–78; Thomas C. Holt, "Marking: Race, Race-Making, and the Writing of History," *American Historical Review* 100 (February 1995): 1–20; and David R. Roediger, *Towards the Abolition of Whiteness: Essays on Race, Politics, and Working Class History* (London, 1994).

7. On scientific racism, see Thomas F. Gossett, *Race: The History of an Idea in America* (Dallas, 1963); George W. Stocking Jr., *Race, Culture, and Evolution: Essays in the History of Anthropology* (Chicago, 1982 [1968]); John S. Haller Jr., *Outcasts from Evolution: Scientific Attitudes to Racial Inferiority, 1859–1900* (Urbana, 1971); George M. Fredrickson, *The Black Image in the White Mind: The Debate on Afro-American Character and Destiny, 1817–1914* (New York, 1971); Thomas G. Dyer, *Theodore Roosevelt and the Idea of Race* (Baton Rouge, 1980); Carl N. Degler, *In Search of Human Nature: The Decline and Revival of Darwinism in American Social Thought* (New York, 1991); and Elazar Barkan, *Retreat of Scientific Racism: Changing Concepts of Race in Britain and the United States between the World Wars* (Cambridge, Eng., 1992). On the social construction of racial ideologies, see the works cited in note 6, above, and Ronald T. Takaki, *Iron Cages: Race and Culture in Nineteenth-Century America* (New York, 1979); Reginald Horsman, *Race and Manifest Destiny: The Origins of American Racial Anglo-Saxonism* (Cambridge, Mass., 1981); Alexander Saxton, *The Rise and Fall of the White Republic: Class Politics and Mass Culture in Nineteenth-Century America* (London, 1990); David R. Roediger, *The Wages of Whiteness: Race and the Making of the American Working Class* (London, 1991); Audrey Smedley, *Race in North America: Origin and Evolution of a Worldview* (Boulder, 1993); and Tomás Almaguer, *Racial Fault Lines: The Historical Origins of White Supremacy in California* (Berkeley, 1994).

8. On law as a producer of racial ideologies, see Barbara J. Fields, "Slavery, Race, and Ideology in the United States of America," *New Left Review* 181 (May–June 1990): 7; Eva Saks, "Representing Miscegenation Law," *Raritan* 8 (fall 1988): 56–60; and Collette Guillaumin, "Race and Nature: The System of Marks," *Feminist Issues* 8 (fall 1988): 25–44.

9. See especially Fredrickson, *Black Image in the White Mind*.

10. For intriguing attempts to define American modernism, see Daniel J. Singal, ed., *Modernist Culture in America* (Belmont, 1991); and Dorothy Ross, ed., *Modernist Impulses in the Human Sciences, 1870–1930* (Baltimore, 1994). For the view from critical race theory, see Brian K. Fair, "Foreword: Rethinking the Colorblindness Model," *National Black Law Journal* 13 (spring 1993): 1–82; Neil Gotanda, "A Critique of 'Our Constitution Is Color-Blind,'" *Stanford Law Review* 44 (November 1991): 1–68; Gary Peller, "Race Consciousness," *Duke Law Journal* (September 1990): 758–847; and Peter Fitzpatrick, "Racism and the Innocence of Law," in Goldberg, ed., *Anatomy of Racism*, 247–62.

11. Many scholars avoid using the word *miscegenation*, which dates to the 1860s, means "race mixing," and has, to twentieth-century minds, embarrassingly biological connotations; they speak of laws against "interracial" or "cross-cultural" relationships. Contemporaries usually referred to "anti-miscegenation" laws. Neither alternative seems satisfactory, since the first avoids naming the ugliness that was so much a part of the laws and the second implies that "miscegenation" was a distinct racial phenomenon rather than a categorization imposed on certain relationships. I retain the term *miscegenation* when speaking of the laws and court cases that relied on the concept, but not when speaking of people or particular relationships. On the emergence of the term, see Sidney Kaplan, "The Miscegenation Issue in the Election of 1864," *Journal of Negro History* 24 (July 1949): 274–343.

12. Most histories of interracial sex and marriage in America focus on demographic patterns rather than legal constraints. See, for example, Joel Williamson, *New People: Miscegenation and Mulattoes in the United States* (New York, 1980); Paul R. Spickard, *Mixed Blood: Intermarriage and Ethnic Identity in Twentieth-Century America* (Madison, 1989); and Deborah Lynn Kitchen, "Interracial Marriage in the United States, 1900–1980" (Ph.D. diss., University of Minnesota, 1993). The only historical overview is Byron Curti Martyn, "Racism in the United States: A History of the Anti-Miscegenation Legislation

and Litigation" (Ph.D. diss., University of Southern California, 1979). On the colonial period, see A. Leon Higginbotham Jr. and Barbara K. Kopytoff, "Racial Purity and Interracial Sex in the Law of Colonial and Antebellum Virginia," *Georgetown Law Journal* 77 (August 1989): 1967–2029; George M. Fredrickson, *White Supremacy: A Comparative Study in American and South African History* (New York, 1981): 99–108; and James Hugo Johnston, *Race Relations in Virginia & Miscegenation in the South, 1776–1860* (Amherst, 1970), 165–90. For later periods, see Peter Bardaglio, "Families, Sex, and the Law: The Legal Transformation of the Nineteenth-Century Southern Household" (Ph.D. diss., Stanford University, 1987), 37–106, 345–49; Peter Wallenstein, "Race, Marriage, and the Law of Freedom: Alabama and Virginia, 1860s–1960s," *Chicago-Kent Law Review* 70, 2 (1994): 371–437; David H. Fowler, *Northern Attitudes towards Interracial Marriage: Legislation and Public Opinion in the Middle Atlantic and the States of the Old Northwest, 1780–1930* (New York, 1987); Megumi Dick Osumi, "Asians and California's Anti-Miscegenation Laws," in Nobuya Tsuchida, ed., *Asian and Pacific American Experiences: Women's Perspectives* (Minneapolis, 1982), 2–8; and Peggy Pascoe, "Race, Gender, and Intercultural Relations: The Case of Interracial Marriage," *Frontiers* 12, 1 (1991): 5–18. The count of states is from the most complete list in Fowler, *Northern Attitudes,* 336–439.

13. Ariz. Rev. Stat. Ann. sec. 3092 (1901); 1931 Ariz. Sess. Laws ch. 17. Arizona, Idaho, Maine, Massachusetts, Nevada, North Carolina, Oregon, Rhode Island, South Carolina, Tennessee, Virginia, and Washington passed laws that mentioned American Indians. Arizona, California, Georgia, Idaho, Mississippi, Missouri, Montana, Nebraska, Nevada, Oregon, South Dakota, Utah, Virginia, and Wyoming passed laws that mentioned Asian Americans. Arizona, California, Georgia, Maryland, Nevada, South Dakota, Utah, Virginia, and Wyoming passed laws that mentioned "Malays." In addition, Oregon law targeted "Kanakas" (native Hawaiians), Virginia "Asiatic Indians," and Georgia both "Asiatic Indians" and "West Indians." See Fowler, *Northern Attitudes,* 336–439; 1924 Va. Acts ch. 371; 1927 Ga. Laws no. 317; 1931 Ariz. Sess. Laws ch. 17; 1933 Cal. Stat. ch. 104; 1935 Md. Laws ch. 60; and 1939 Utah Laws ch. 50.

14. The most insightful social and legal histories have focused on sexual relations rather than marriage. See, for example, Higginbotham and Kopytoff, "Racial Purity and Interracial Sex"; Karen German, "Sexual Control in the Slaveholding South: The Implementation and Maintenance of a Racial Caste System," *Harvard Women's Law Journal* 7 (spring 1984): 125–34; Martha Hodes, "Sex across the Color Line: White Women and Black Men in the Nineteenth-Century American South" (Ph.D. diss., Princeton University, 1991); and Martha Hodes, "The Sexualization of Reconstruction Politics: White Women and Black Men in the South after the Civil War," in John C. Fout and Maura Shaw Tantillo, eds., *American Sexual Politics: Sex, Gender, and Race since the Civil War* (Chicago, 1993), 59–74; Robyn Weigman, "The Anatomy of Lynching," in Fout and Tantillo, eds., *American Sexual Politics,* 223–45; Jacquelyn Dowd Hall, " 'The Mind that Burns in Each Body': Women, Rape, and Racial Violence," in Ann Snitow, Christine Stansell, and Sharon Thompson, eds., *Powers of Desire: The Politics of Sexuality* (New York, 1983), 328–49; Kenneth James Lay, "Sexual Racism: A Legacy of Slavery," *National Black Law Journal* 13 (spring 1993): 165–83; and Kevin J. Mumford, "From Vice to Vogue: Black/White Sexuality and the 1920s" (Ph.D. diss., Stanford University, 1993). One of the first works to note the predominance of marriage in miscegenation laws was Mary Frances Berry, "Judging Morality: Sexual Behavior and Legal Consequences in the Late Nineteenth-Century South," *Journal of American History* 78 (December 1991): 838–39. On the historical connections among race, marriage, property, and the state, see Saks, "Representing Miscegenation Law," 39–69; Nancy F. Cott, "Giving Character to Our Whole Civil Polity: Marriage and the Public Order in the Late Nineteenth Century," in Linda K. Kerber, Alice Kessler-Harris, and Kathryn Kish Sklar, eds., *U.S. History as Women's History: New Feminist Essays* (Chapel Hill, 1995), 107–21; Ramon A. Gutierrez, *When Jesus Came, the Corn Mothers Went Away: Marriage, Sexuality, and Power in New Mexico, 1500–1846* (Stanford, 1991); Verena Martinez-Alier, *Marriage, Class, and Colour in Nineteenth-Century Cuba: A Study of Racial Attitudes and Sexual Values in a Slave Society* (Ann Arbor, 1989); Patricia J. Williams, "Fetal Fictions: An Exploration of Property Archetypes in Racial and Gendered Contexts," in Herbert Hill and James E. Jones Jr., eds., *Race in America: The Struggle for Equality* (Madison, 1993): 425–37; and Virginia R. Dominguez, *White by Definition: Social Classification in Creole Louisiana* (New Brunswick, 1986).

15. Of the forty-one colonies and states that prohibited interracial marriage, twenty-two also prohibited some form of interracial sex. One additional jurisdiction (New York) prohibited interracial sex but not interracial marriage; it is not clear how long this 1638 statute was in effect. See Fowler, *Northern Attitudes,* 336–439. My database consists of every appeals court case I could identify in which miscegenation law played a role: 227 cases heard between 1850 and 1970, 132 civil and 95 criminal. Although cases that reach appeals courts are by definition atypical, they are significant because the decisions reached in them set policies later followed in more routine cases and because the texts of

the decisions hint at how judges conceptualized particular legal problems. I have relied on them because of these interpretive advantages and for two more practical reasons. First, because appeals court decisions are published and indexed, it is possible to compile a comprehensive list of them. Second, because making an appeal requires the preservation of documents that might otherwise be discarded (such as legal briefs and court reporters' trial notes), they permit the historian to go beyond the judge's decision.

16. Decisions striking down the laws include *Burns v. State*, 48 Ala. 195 (1872); *Bonds v. Foster*, 36 Tex. 68 (1871–72); *Honey v. Clark*, 37 Tex. 686 (1873); *Hart v. Hoss*, 26 La. Ann. 90 (1874); *State v. Webb*, 4 Cent. L. J. 588 (1877); and *Ex parte Brown*, 5 Cent. L. J. 149 (1877). Decisions upholding the laws include *Scott v. State*, 39 Ga. 321 (1869); *State v. Hairston*, 63 N.C. 451 (1869); *State v. Reinhardt*, 63 N.C. 547 (1869): *In re Hobbs*, 12 F. Cas. 262 (1871) (No. 6550); *Lonas v. State*, 50 Tenn. 287 (1871); *State v. Gibson*, 36 Ind. 389 (1871); *Ford v. State*, 53 Ala. 150 (1875); *Green v. State*, 58 Ala. 190 (1877); *Frasher v. State*, 3 Tex. Ct. App. R. 263 (1877); *Ex Parte Kinney*, 14 F. Cas. 602 (1879) (No. 7825); *Ex parte Francois*, 9 F. Cas. 699 (1879) (No. 5047); *Francois v. State*, 9 Tex. Ct. App. R. 144 (1880); *Pace v. State*, 69 Ala. 231 (1881); *Pace v. Alabama*, 106 U.S. 583 (1882); *State v. Jackson*, 80 Mo. 175 (1883); *State v. Tutty*, 41 F. 753 (1890); *Dodson v. State*, 31 S.W. 977 (1895); *Strauss v. State*, 173 S.W. 663 (1915); *State v. Daniel*, 75 So. 836 (1917); *Succession of Mingo*, 78 So. 565 (1917–18); and *In re Paquet's Estate*, 200 P. 911 (1921).

17. Individual racial classifications were successfully challenged in *Moore v. State*, 7 Tex. Ct. App. R. 608 (1880); *Jones v. Commonwealth*, 80 Va. 213 (1884); *Jones v. Commonwealth*, 80 Va. 538 (1885); *State v. Treadaway*, 52 So. 500 (1910); *Flores v. State*, 129 S.W. 1111 (1910); *Ferrall v. Ferrall*, 69 S.E. 60 (1910); *Marre v. Marre*, 168 S.W. 636 (1914); *Neuberger v. Gueldner*, 72 So. 220 (1916); and *Reed v. State*, 92 So. 511 (1922).

18. "Appellant's Abstract of Record," 19, *Kirby v. Kirby*.

19. "Appellee's Brief," 3 Oct. 1921, p. 6, *Kirby v. Kirby*.

20. On the theoretical problems involved in exploring how miscegenation laws were gendered, see Pascoe, "Race, Gender, and Intercultural Relations"; and Peggy Pascoe, "Race, Gender, and the Privileges of Property: On the Significance of Miscegenation Law in United States History," in Susan Ware, ed., *New Viewpoints in Women's History: Working Papers from the Schlesinger Library 50th Anniversary Conference, March 4–5, 1994* (Cambridge, Mass., 1994), 99–122. For an excellent account of the gendering of early miscegenation laws, see Kathleen M. Brown, *Good Wives and Nasty Wenches: Gender, Race, and Power in Colonial Virginia* (Chapel Hill, 1996).

21. "Appellant's Brief," 8 Sept. 1921, *Kirby v. Kirby*; *Kirby v. Kirby*, 206 P. 405, 406 (1922). On *Kirby*, see Roger Hardaway, "Unlawful Love: A History of Arizona's Miscegenation Law," *Journal of Arizona History* 27 (winter 1986): 377–90.

22. For examples of reliance on experts, see *In re Ah Yup*, 1 F. Cas. 223 (1878) (No. 104); *In re Kanaka Nian*, 21 P. 993 (1889); *In re Saito*, 62 F. 126 (1894). On these cases, see Ian F. Haney Lopez, *White by Law: The Legal Construction of Race* (New York, New York University Press, 1996). For reliance on the "common man," see *U.S. v. Bhagat Singh Thind*, 261 U.S. 204 (1923). On *Thind*, see Sucheta Mazumdar, "Racist Responses to Racism: The Aryan Myth and South Asians in the United States," *South Asia Bulletin* 9, 1 (1989): 47–55; Joan M. Jensen, *Passage from India: Asian Indian Immigrants in North America* (New Haven, 1988), 247–69; and Roediger, *Towards the Abolition of Whiteness*, 181–84.

23. The rise of Boasian anthropology has attracted much attention among intellectual historians, most of whom seem to agree with the 1963 comment that "it is possible that Boas did more to combat race prejudice than any other person in history"; see Gossett, *Race*, 418. In addition to the works cited in note 7, see I. A. Newby, *Jim Crow's Defense: Ante-Negro Thought in America, 1900–1930* (Baton Rouge, 1965), 21; and John S. Gilkeson Jr., "The Domestication of 'Culture' in Interwar America, 1919–1941," in JoAnne Brown and David K. van Keuren, eds., *The Estate of Social Knowledge* (Baltimore, 1991), 153–74. For more critical appraisals, see Robert Proctor, "Eugenics among the Social Sciences: Hereditarian Thought in Germany and the United States," in Brown and van Keuren, eds., *The Estate of Social Knowledge*, 175–208; Hamilton Cravens, *The Triumph of Evolution: The Heredity-Environment Controversy, 1900–1941* (Baltimore, 1988); and Donna Haraway, *Primate Visions: Gender, Race, and Nature in the World of Modern Science* (New York, 1989), 127–203. The classic—and still the best—account of the rise of cultural anthropology is Stocking, *Race, Culture, and Evolution*. See also George W. Stocking Jr., *Victorian Anthropology* (New York, 1987), 284–329.

24. U.S. Immigration Commission, *Dictionary of Races or Peoples* (Washington, D.C., 1911), 2. For other scientific racist classification schemes, see *Encyclopaedia Britannica*, 11th ed., s.v. "Anthropology"; and *Encyclopedia Americana: A Library of Universal Knowledge* (New York, 1923), s.v. "Ethnography" and "Ethnology."

25. Franz Boas, "Race," in *Encyclopaedia of the Social Sciences*, ed. Edwin R. A. Seligman (New York,

1930–35), 13:27; Julian S. Huxley and A. C. Haddon, *We Europeans: A Survey of "Racial" Problems* (London, 1935), 107.

26. Boas, "Race," 34. For one of the few instances when a historian has noted this argument, see Smedley, *Race in North America*, 275–82.

27. Ruth Benedict, *Race: Science and Politics* (New York, 1940), 12; Ruth Benedict and Gene Weltfish, *The Races of Mankind* (Washington, D.C., 1943), 5.

28. Boas, "Race," 25–26.

29. See, for example, Huxley and Haddon, *We Europeans*, 107, 269–73; Benedict and Weltfish, *Races of Mankind*; Benedict, *Race*; and Gunnar Myrdal, *An American Dilemma: The Negro Problem and Modern Democracy* (New York, 1944), 91–115.

30. The Monks trial can be followed in *Estate of Monks*, 4 Civ. 2835, Records of California Court of Appeals, Fourth District (California State Archives, Roseville); and *Gunn v. Giraudo*, 4 Civ. 2832, ibid. (Gunn represented another claimant to the estate). The two cases were tried together. For the seven-volume "Reporter's Transcript," see *Estate of Monks*, 4 Civ. 2835, ibid.

31. "Reporter's Transcript," 2:660–67, 3:965–76, 976–98, *Estate of Monks*.

32. Ibid., 5:1501–49, 6:1889–1923.

33. Ibid., 7:2543, 2548.

34. "Findings of Fact and Conclusions of Law," in "Clerk's Transcript," 2 Dec. 1940, *Gunn v. Giraudo*, 4 Civ. 2832, p. 81. One intriguing aspect of the *Monks* case is that the seeming exactness was unnecessary. The status of the marriage hinged on the Arizona miscegenation law, which would have denied validity to the marriage whether the proportion of "blood" in question was "one-eighth" or "one drop."

35. For descriptions of those interested in biological aspects of race, see Stocking, *Race, Culture, and Evolution*, 271–3 07; I. A Newby, *Challenge to the Court: Social Scientists and the Defense of Segregation, 1954–1966* (Baton Rouge, 1969); and Cravens, *Triumph of Evolution*, 15–55. On eugenics, see Proctor, "Eugenics among the Social Sciences," 175–208; Daniel J. Kevles, *In the Name of Eugenics: Genetics and the Uses of Human Heredity* (New York, 1985): Mark H. Haller, *Eugenics: Hereditarian Attitudes in American Thought* (New Brunswick, 1963); and William H. Tucker, *The Science and Politics of Racial Research* (Urbana, 1994), 54–137.

36. Charles B. Davenport, *Eugenics Record Office Bulletin No. 9: State Laws Limiting Marriage Selection Examined in the Light of Eugenics* (Cold Spring Harbor, 1913); Michael Grossberg, "Guarding the Altar: Physiological Restrictions and the Rise of State Intervention in Matrimony," *American Journal of Legal History* 26 (July 1982): 221–24.

37. See, for example, C[harles] B[enedict] Davenport and Morris Steggerda, *Race Crossing in Jamaica* (Westport, Conn., 1970 [1929]); Edward Byron Reuter, *Race Mixture: Studies in Intermarriage and Miscegenation* (New York, 1931); and Emory S. Bogardus, "What Race Are Filipinos?" *Sociology and Social Research* 16 (1931–32), 274–79.

38. 1924 Va. Acts ch. 371; 1927 Ga. Laws no. 317; 1927 Ala. Acts no. 626. The 1924 Virginia act replaced 1910 Va. Acts ch. 357, which classified as "colored" persons with one-sixteenth or more "negro blood." The retention of an allowance for American Indian "blood" in persons classed as white was forced on the bill's sponsors by Virginia aristocrats who traced their ancestry to Pocahontas and John Rolfe. See Paul A. Lombardo, "Miscegenation, Eugenics, and Racism: Historical Footnotes to *Loving v. Virginia*," *U. C. Davis Law Review* 21 (winter 1988): 431–52; and Richard B. Sherman, " 'The Last Stand': The Fight for Racial Integrity in Virginia in the 1920s," *Journal of Southern History* 54 (February 1988): 69–92.

39. "Appellant's Opening Brief," *Gunn v. Giraudo*, 12–13. This brief appears to have been prepared for the California Supreme Court but used in the California Court of Appeals, Fourth District. On 14 February 1942 the California Supreme Court refused to review the Court of Appeals decision. See *Estate of Monks*, 48 C. A. 2d 603, 621 (1941).

40. *Estate of Monks*, 48 C. A. 2d 603, 612–15 (1941); *Monks v. Lee*, 317 U.S. 590 (*appeal dismissed*, 1942), 711 (*reh'g denied*, 1942); *Lee v. Monks*, 62 N.E. 2d 657 (1945); *Lee v. Monks*, 326 U.S. 696 (*cert, denied*, 1946).

41. On the case, see *San Diego Union*, 21 July 1939–6 Jan. 1940. On the testimony of expert witnesses on race, see ibid., 21 Sept. 1939, 4A; 29 Sept. 1939, 10A; and 5 Oct. 1939, 8A.

42. *Pérez v. Lippold*, L.A. 20305, Supreme Court Case Files (California State Archives). The case was also known as *Pérez v. Moroney* and *Perez v. Sharp* (the names reflect changes of personnel in the Los Angeles County clerk's office). I have used the title given in the *Pacific Law Reporter*, the most easily available version of the final decision: *Pérez v. Lippold*, 198 P. 2d 17 (1948).

43. "Petition for Writ of Mandamus, Memorandum of Points and Authorities and Proof of Service," 8 Aug. 1947, *Pérez v. Lippold*; "Points and Authorities in Opposition to Issuance of Alternative Writ of Mandate," 13 Aug. 1947, ibid.; "Return by Way of Demurrer," 6 Oct. 1947, ibid.; "Return by

Way of Answer," 6 Oct. 1947, ibid.; "Respondent's Brief in Opposition to Writ of Mandate," 6 Oct. 1947, ibid.

44. "[Oral Argument] on Behalf of Respondent," 6 Oct. 1947, pp. 3–4, ibid.

45. Stanley Mosk, "A Retrospective," *California Law Review* 71 (July 1983): 1045; Peter Anderson, "A Remembrance," California Law Review 71 (July 1983): 1066–71.

46. "Petitioners' Reply Brief," 8 Nov. 1947, pp. 4, 44, 23–24, *Perez v. Lippold*.

47. *Perez v. Lippold*, 198 P. 2d at 17–35, esp. 29, 34.

48. Ibid., 35–47.

49. For the characterization of Franz Boas by Robert Gayres, editor of the Scottish journal *Mankind Quarterly*, see Newby, *Challenge to the Court*, 323. On *Mankind Quarterly* and on mid-twentieth-century white supremacist scientists, see Tucker, *Science and Politics of Racial Research*.

50. Myrdal, *American Dilemma*, 116–17.

51. *Loving v. Commonwealth*, 147 S.E. 2d 78, 79 (1966). For the *Loving* briefs and oral arguments, see Philip B. Kurland and Gerhard Casper, eds., *Landmark Briefs and Arguments of the Supreme Court of the United States: Constitutional Law* (Arlington, 1975), 64:687–1007. Edited cassette tapes of the oral argument are included with Peter Irons and Stephanie Guitton, eds., *May It Please the Court: The Most Significant Oral Arguments Made before the Supreme Court since 1955* (New York, 1993). For scholarly assessments, see Wallenstein, "Race, Marriage, and the Law of Freedom"; Walter Wadlington, "The Loving Case: Virginia's Antimiscegenation Statute in Historical Perspective," in Kermit L. Hall, ed., *Race Relations and the Law in American History: Major Historical Interpretations*, (New York, 1987), 600–634; and Robert J. Sickels, *Race, Marriage, and the Law* (Albuquerque, 1972).

52. *Loving v. Virginia*, 388 U.S. 1, 3 (1967); Wallenstein, "Race, Marriage, and the Law of Freedom," 423–25, esp. 424; *New York Times*, 12 June 1992, B7. By the mid-1960s, some legal scholars had questioned the constitutionality of miscegenation laws, including C. D. Shokes, "The Serbonian Bog of Miscegenation," *Rocky Mountain Law Review* 21 (1948–49): 425–33; Wayne A. Melton, "Constitutionality of State Anti-Miscegenation Statutes," *Southwestern Law Journal* 5 (1951): 451–61; Andrew D. Weinberger, "A Reappraisal of the Constitutionality of Miscegenation Statutes," *Cornell Law Quarterly* 42 (winter 1957): 208–22; Jerold D. Cummins and John L. Kane Jr., "Miscegenation, the Constitution, and Science," *Dicta* 38 (January–February 1961): 24–54; William D. Zabel, "Interracial Marriage and the Law," *Atlantic Monthly* 216 (October 1965): 75–79; and Cyrus E. Phillips IV, "Miscegenation: The Courts and the Constitution," *William and Mary Law Review* 8 (fall 1966): 133–42.

53. Kurland and Casper, eds., *Landmark Briefs*, 741–88, 847–950, 960–72, esp. 898–99, 901.

54. Ibid., 789–845, 976–1003.

55. Ibid., 834, 1007.

56. *Loving v. Virginia*, 388 U.S. at 12.

57. Ibid., 11.

58. The notion that American courts should be "color blind" is usually traced to Supreme Court Justice John Harlan. Dissenting from the Court's endorsement of the principle of "separate but equal" in *Plessy v. Ferguson*, Harlan insisted that "[o]ur Constitution is color-blind, and neither knows nor tolerates classes among citizens." *Plessy v. Ferguson*, 163 U.S. 537, 559 (1896). But only after *Brown v. Board of Education*, widely interpreted as a belated endorsement of Harlan's position, did courts begin to adopt color blindness as a goal. *Brown v. Board of Education*, 347 U.S. 483 (1954). On the history of the color-blindness ideal, see Andrew Kull, *The Color-Blind Constitution* (Cambridge, Mass., 1992). On developments in social science, see Omi and Winant, *Racial Formation in the United States*, 14–23.

59. *Brown v. Board of Education*, 347 U.S. 483 (1954). The Court declared distinctions based "solely on ancestry" "odious" even while upholding curfews imposed on Japanese Americans during World War II; see *Hirabayashi v. United States*, 320 U.S. 81 (1943). It declared race a "suspect" legal category while upholding the internment of Japanese Americans; see *Korematsu v. United States*, 323 U.S. 214 (1944). By 1983, no American state had a formal race-definition statute still on its books. See Chris Ballentine, "'Who Is a Negro?' Revisited: Determining Individual Racial Status for Purposes of Affirmative Action," *University of Florida Law Review* 35 (fall 1983): 692. The repeal of state race-definition statutes often accompanied repeal of miscegenation laws. See, for example, 1953 Mont. Laws ch. 4; 1959 Or. Laws ch. 531; 1965 Ind. Acts ch. 15; 1969 Fla. Laws 69–195; and 1979 Ga. Laws no. 543.

60. The fifth of these categories, "Hispanic," is sometimes described as "ethnic" rather than "racial." For very different views of the current debates, see Lawrence Wright, "One Drop of Blood," *New Yorker*, 25 July 1994, 46–55; and Michael Lind, *The Next American Nation: The New Nationalism and the Fourth American Revolution* (New York, 1995), 97–137.

61. *People v. O. J. Simpson*, Case no. BA 097211, California Superior Court, L.A. County (1994).

62. See, for example, Kimberle Williams Crenshaw, "Race, Reform, and Retrenchment: Transformation and Legitimation in Antidiscrimination Law," *Harvard Law Review* 101 (May 1988): 1331–87; Dana Y.

Takagi, *The Retreat from Race: Asian-American Admissions and Racial Politics* (New Brunswick, 1992), 181–94; and Girardeau A. Spann, *Race against the Court: The Supreme Court and Minorities in Contemporary America* (New York, 1993), 119–49. See note 5, above. On recent work in the humanities, see Tessie Liu, "Race," in Wightman Fox and James T. Kloppenberg, eds., *A Companion to American Thought* (Cambridge, Mass., 1995), 564–67. On legal studies, see Richard Delgado and Jean Stefancic, "Critical Race Theory: An Annotated Bibliography," *Virginia Law Review* 79 (March 1993): 461–516.

19

Sexual Geography and Gender Economy
The Furnished-Room Districts of Chicago, 1890–1930

Joanne Meyerowitz

The broad outlines of the early twentieth-century sexual revolution in the United States are now well known.[1] From roughly 1890 to 1930 public discussions and displays of sexuality multiplied in popular magazines, newspapers, and entertainments. At the same time, women began to adopt more sexual, or at least less modest, styles; shorter skirts, cosmetics, bobbed hair, and cigarettes, once the styles of prostitutes, all seemed evidence of a larger change in mores when adopted by "respectable" working- and middle-class women. Men and women mingled freely in new commercialized recreation industries and in workplaces. And surveys of the middle class revealed increases in premarital intercourse.

Historians have now written at least three versions of this sexual revolution. In the oldest and now standard account, young, middle-class "flappers" rebelled against the repressive standards of their parents by engaging in shocking behavior, such as petting in automobiles, dancing to jazz music, and using bawdy language.[2] A second version of the sexual revolution developed with the growth of the field of U.S. women's history. In this rendition, young feminist bohemians, or independent "new women," influenced by the writings of Freud and other sexologists, experimented sexually and rejected the homosocial sisterhood of earlier women's rights activists.[3] A third variation points to a working-class component. Urban, working-class "rowdy girls" appear as early as the 1830s but seem to enter historical center stage in precisely the same years that the middle-class "new women" and "flappers" self-consciously rejected Victorian mores. In the workplace and in dance halls, theaters, and amusement parks, young, working-class women adopted an overtly sexual style that dismayed both their parents and middle-class reformers.[4]

This article is a case study of working-class women's sexuality in the furnished-room districts of turn-of-the-century Chicago. In a particular setting, how did women participate in the sexual revolution, and how was their behavior interpreted and publicized? This approach modifies the various versions of the sexual revolution. For one, it locates neglected geographical centers of urban sexual activity—the furnished-room districts—and early active participants in the sexual revolution, the women lodgers. Second, it highlights economic imperatives that motivated and shaped at least part of the sexual revolution. And, finally, it shows how middle-class observers reshaped the experiences of sexually active working-class women and broadcast them to a larger national audience.

Recently U.S. feminists have engaged in heated debates over the meaning of twentieth-century sexual expression. The debates are polarized between those who emphasize the sexual dangers, such as rape, that oppress women and those who focus on the sensual pleasures that await women.[5] While this article does not enter these debates directly, it suggests the importance of studying sexuality in context. Sexual behavior, of course, is neither inherently dangerous for women nor inherently pleasurable. Like other socially constructed behaviors, its meanings derive from the specific contexts in which it is enacted. This study examines how and why a particular group of women adopted the freer modes of sexual expression that characterized the early-twentieth-century sexual revolution. It finds that neither sexual danger nor sensual pleasure provides adequate explanation.

Most major American cities today have a distinct geography of sexuality. That is, one could locate districts and neighborhoods known as the institutional and social centers of various sexual subcultures. Take San Francisco, for example, a city known for its celebration of sexual variety. Upscale heterosexual singles live in apartments and frequent bars in the Marina district. Downscale heterosexual men go to porn shops and massage parlors in the Tenderloin. Female prostitutes sell their services at the corner of Eighteenth and Mission Streets; male prostitutes sell their services on Polk Street. Gay men congregate in the Castro district, and lesbians meet in the bars and coffeehouses in the vicinity of Valencia Street.

A lesser-known geography of sexuality also existed in early-twentieth-century American cities. In 1916 sociologist Robert Park identified what he called "moral regions" of the city, "detached milieus in which vagrant and suppressed impulses, passions, and ideals emancipate themselves from the dominant moral order."[6] Park was not the first to define neighborhoods by sexual behavior. At the end of the nineteenth century, a few urban investigators identified the furnished-room districts, or areas where rooming houses abounded, as "moral regions" of sorts, distinct neighborhoods where unconventional sexual behavior flourished.[7] By the early twentieth century, reformers defined a "furnished-room problem" more precisely. In 1906, for example, in a study of Boston's furnished-room district, Albert Benedict Wolfe lamented the "contamination of young men, the deterioration in the modesty and morality of young women, the existence of actual houses of prostitution in the guise of lodging-houses, the laxity of landladies, the large number of informal unions, the general loosening of moral texture."[8] By the late 1910s and 1920s, more dispassionate sociologists explored "a new code of sex relationships" in the furnished-room districts of Chicago.[9] Evidence from newspapers, autobiographies, vice reports, and social surveys also suggests that the furnished-room districts were indeed the centers of sexually unconventional subcultures.[10]

By the end of the nineteenth century, most major American cities had furnished-room districts. These often first appeared in the city center and later, as business displaced downtown housing, moved out farther along major transportation lines. The large proportion of adult residents and the small proportion of children distinguished these districts demographically from other neighborhoods of the city. A residential street in a furnished-room district usually resembled others in the city: A typical block would consist of single-family homes, buildings of flats, large tenements, or older mansions. The owners of the buildings, however, converted the interiors into one- or two-room dwellings. They might divide a flat into two or three smaller units or divide a large tenement into an "apartment hotel" with as many as a hundred furnished rooms.

In Chicago three such districts emerged in the late nineteenth century. On the South Side, the furnished-room district included major portions of the Chicago black community and also what was, before the 1912 raids, the segregated vice district of the city. On the West Side, the district housed a population of predominantly white service and factory workers. A transient male hobo population congregated on the inner boundaries. On the North Side, where rents were slightly higher, clerical and sales workers lived in rooming houses alongside white service and manufacturing workers, artists, bohemians, and radicals of all stripes. In the early twentieth century, the North Side district included substantial numbers of Irish and Swedish roomers.[11]

These districts burgeoned in the early 1890s, when migrants and visitors streamed to Chicago for the World's Columbian Exposition. They continued to grow in the first decades of the twentieth century. By 1923 the Illinois Lodging House Register reported over eighty-five thousand lodgers in about five thousand rooming houses in the three major furnished-room districts. By 1930 residents of the new small unit apartments (with private bathrooms and kitchenettes) joined lodgers in these neighborhoods.[12]

Several distinctive features of the furnished-room districts fostered the development of extra-marital sexual relationships. Most obviously, women and men lived together in houses where most people did not live in families. In these neighborhoods, lodgers found numerous opportunities to create social and sexual ties with their peers. Further, the high geographic mobility in the furnished-room districts made informal, transient relationships the norm. One writer went so far as to claim that the entire population of Chicago's North Side furnished-room district changed every four months.[13] This high turnover rate created an atmosphere of anonymity in which lodgers rarely knew their neighbors well. Community pressures to conform to conventional familial roles were weaker than in more settled neighborhoods, and parental authorities were absent. Many rooming-house keepers, eager to keep their tenants, refrained from criticizing or interfering with roomers' sexual behavior.[14] In addition, the predominance of men in the North and West Side districts may have encouraged women to participate in extramarital heterosexual relationships: It would have been easy to meet men and difficult to avoid them.[15]

In any case, the prevalence of prostitution in the furnished-room districts created a climate where open expressions of sexuality were common. In the first decade of the twentieth century, the most prominent vice district of Chicago lay in the South Side furnished-room district. Brothels were tolerated in sections of the West and North Side districts as well.[16] In addition, on the South, West, and North Sides, some keepers of rooming houses and hotels rented rooms by the hour or night to prostitutes and their customers.[17] After the municipal government closed the brothels in the 1910s, social investigators repeatedly found rooming houses and hotels used for prostitution.[18]

In addition to hotels and rooming houses, the "bright-light" centers of the furnished-room districts provided settings in which men and women could socialize. Investors who hoped to profit from the demand by lodgers opened cafeterias, cheap restaurants, tearooms, soft-drink parlors, saloons, dance halls, cabarets, and movie theaters. Residents of the districts turned these institutions into social centers. As one observer noted: "Considerable companionship grows up around these resorts. One is struck by the fact that the same people visit and re-visit the same cabaret time and again."[19]

On the North Side, Clark Street and, on the West Side, Halsted Street were well known for their nightlife. In 1918 Clark Street alone housed fifty-seven saloons, thirty-six restaurants, and twenty cabarets.[20] On the South Side, the State Street "Stroll" and Thirty-fifth Street emerged as the "bright-light" centers of the black community. Dance halls, restaurants, movies, and saloons for black customers coexisted with "black and tan" cabarets, which offered racially integrated recreation.[21] When young men and women who lived with their parents were out for a night on the town, and when wealthier people went "slumming," they often went to the furnished-room districts of the city.

These areas, it seems, were geographic settings where behavior considered unacceptable elsewhere was accepted matter-of-factly and even encouraged. In residential communities of Chicago, neighbors often stigmatized sexually active unmarried women. For example, Mamie, a young woman who lived with her parents in a working-class neighborhood of Chicago, first encountered problems in 1918 when a policewoman reported her for "unbecoming conduct with sailors." Later, rumor had it that her neighbors talked of signing a petition to expel her from the neighborhood.[22] Contrast Mamie's brief case history with the comment of a student of Chicago's South Side furnished-room district: "It is said that an attractive woman who does not 'cash in' is likely to be considered a fool by her neighbors, instead of any stigma being attached to a woman who 'hustles' in this neighborhood."[23]

By the early twentieth century the furnished-room districts of Chicago and other large cities were known as havens for women and men who chose to defy conventions.[24] In addition to migrants and transients, they attracted women and men seeking adventure and a chance to break taboos in a community without parental supervision.[25] Here interested lodgers could enter peer-oriented subcultures that sanctioned extramarital sexual behavior. A 1918 account of Chicago's North Side shows the complex and casual nature of social and sexual relationships:

[J. and V.] went to the North Clark Street section where they posed as man and wife. They took a couple of furnished rooms, . . . and remained there for two years. Both of them worked, often bringing in as much as $30.00 a week together. They took their meals out and got along very well.

Then two of the girl's sisters came to Chicago to find work and rented rooms next to them. These girls had good intentions but not securing very lucrative positions, they soon learned how to supplement their wages by allowing young men to stay with them.

These girls struck up an acquaintanceship with another girl who used to remain overnight with them now and again when they had been out to a dance or cabaret. J. liked this new girl and as he put it could not "help monkeying with her" and when V. found it out she became extremely jealous and shortly afterwards left him. Her sisters and the other girl followed her.[26]

Other accounts provide additional glimpses of how women formed social networks in the furnished-room districts. In 1911 two women, seventeen and twenty years old, met at a South Side dance hall. The older woman persuaded the younger to room with her on Chicago's North Side. After they moved in together, they made "pick up acquaintances" with men at dance halls and on the street.[27] Around 1913 Myrtle S., who roomed on the North Side, made friends with a woman at the restaurant where she ate her meals. This woman introduced her to a man, Lew W., with whom she spent several evenings drinking beer. Myrtle testified that she lost her virginity when Lew took advantage of her: "[O]ne night she lost consciousness after her drink of beer and awoke next morning in the Superior Hotel." Despite this betrayal, she returned to the hotel with Lew on two other occasions. Later, Myrtle met another man at a "chop suey" restaurant.[28]

Some of the social circles that developed in the furnished-room districts were distinguished by unconventional lifestyles, sexual preferences, or political leanings. In the North Side district, for example, a subculture of hoboes congregated in and around Washington, or Bughouse, Square. In her autobiography, hobo "Box-Car Bertha" wrote, "Girls and women . . . seemed to keep Chicago as their hobo center. . . . They are centered about the Near North Side, in Bughouse Square, in the cheap roominghouses and light housekeeping establishments, or begged or accepted sleeping space from men or other women there before them." The women hoboes whom Bertha described engaged casually in sexual relationships. One woman, she wrote, had "a group of sweethearts," others lived and traveled with men "to whom by chance or feeling they had attached themselves," and still others engaged in "careless sex relations."[29]

By the 1920s lesbian communities were also visible.[30] According to blues singer Ma Rainey, a black bisexual, lesbians frequented State Street, in the South Side rooming-house area. A song she recorded in 1924 included the following among other more sexually suggestive verses:

Goin' down to spread the news
State Street women wearing brogan shoes
Hey, hey, daddy let me shave'em dry. . . .
There's one thing I don't understand
Some women walkin' State Street like a man,
 Eeh, hey, hey, daddy let me shave 'em dry.[31]

According to Box-Car Bertha, "several tea shops and bootleg joints on the near-north side . . . catered to lesbians," including many among the Chicago hobo population.[32] Another observer found lesbians in the somewhat less transient population of the North Side furnished-room district's bohemian circles. He, too, noted that homosexual women and men frequented the tearooms of the area and held parties in their rented rooms.[33]

The best-known subcultures of the furnished-room districts were undoubtedly the bohemian circles of artists, intellectuals, and political radicals. In Chicago, black bohemians congregated in the South Side furnished-room district, and some white socialists and anarchists lived in the West Side district.[34] But the heart of Chicago's bohemia was on the North Side, where one study found that "[m]ost of the experimenters are young women."[35] In most respects, Chicago's bohemians resembled those of New York's Greenwich Village. Chicago, though, had its own distinctive institutions. The informal Dill Pickle Club provided a setting for lectures, plays, and jazz performances.[36] And the anarchist tradition of soapbox oratory in Washington Square provided a public forum for unconventional speakers.[37]

As in the other subcultures of the furnished-room districts, women who joined bohemian circles expected and often wanted to participate in extramarital sexual activities. For example, Natalie Feinberg, the daughter of working-class Jewish immigrants from Russia, expressed an interest in "free love" before she moved away from her family in Chicago, changed her name to Jean Farway, and "frequented the various gathering places" of the bohemians. According to the sociologist who described her, "She won the reputation of wishing to become a great courtesan."[38]

Historians remember the furnished-room districts primarily for the articulate, "emancipated" middle- and upper-class members of bohemian communities. Such people are often seen as vanguards of modern sexuality, women and men who experimented freely with new sexual possibilities learned from Sigmund Freud, Havelock Ellis, and other sexologists.[39] The geography of sexuality helps place the bohemians in context, as only one subculture among several. The furnished-room districts housed working-class women and men as well as middle- and upper-class bohemians. There is no evidence that the "revolution" of a bohemian and middle-class vanguard trickled down to the working class. In fact, it seems more likely that bohemians learned of new sexual possibilities not only from the "highbrow" writings of the sexologists but also from the "lowbrow" behavior of their less intellectual neighbors.[40]

Furnished-room districts not only provide a setting for observing various participants in the sexual revolution, they also reveal the social and economic context that shaped changing sexual mores. Heterosexual relationships in the furnished-room districts included "dating," "pickups," "occasional prostitution," and "temporary alliances." Like professional prostitution and marriage, these were economic as well as sexual and social relationships. Because employers paid self-supporting women wages intended for dependent daughters and wives, many women lodgers worked in low-paying jobs that barely covered subsistence.[41] In an era of rapidly expanding urban consumerism, these women were forced into scrimping and self-denial. By entering sexual relationships, however, they could supplement their wages with free evenings on the town, free meals in restaurants, and sometimes gifts and money. In many cases, the new sexual expression allowed women to participate in the urban consumer economy.

Even in the most innocent dating, men customarily paid for the evening's entertainment. Women, in return, gave limited sexual favors, ranging from charming companionship to sexual intercourse. A 1910 federal report on self-supporting working women stressed the economic value of dating:

> Even if most of the girls do not spend money for amusements, it is no proof that they go without them. Many of the girls have "gentlemen friends" who take them out. "Sure I go out all the time, but it doesn't cost me anything; my gentleman friend takes me," was the type of remark again and again. . . . Girls who have "steadies" are regarded as fortunate indeed.[42]

A woman need not have a "steady," however, to benefit from dating. In "pickups," "women met male strangers casually on street corners or in dance halls, restaurants, and saloons. They then spent the evening and sometimes the night with them." In Chicago women attempted to pick men up in dance halls and on the streets. In 1911, for example, a vice investigator in a North Side dance hall encountered several women who asked him "to take them to shows or dances."[43] Ten years later, in the heart of the South Side furnished-room district, Gladys B., an eighteen-year-old black woman, "went cabareting" with James P. after she picked him up at the corner of Thirty-fifth and State Streets. They ended the evening in a hotel room.[44] Presumably James paid for the cabarets, the room, and perhaps Gladys's sexual services. (In this case, he paid more than he bargained for: This mundane pickup became newsworthy only when Gladys escaped in the night with James's wad of money.)

In the early twentieth century, young working-class women who lived in their parents' homes also participated avidly in the new urban dating patterns promoted by commercialized recreation facilities.[45] For many women lodgers in the furnished-room districts, though, the necessity of supporting themselves on low wages added a special imperative. Lodgers themselves were highly aware of the economic benefits of dating. A waitress said bluntly, "If I did not have a man, I could not get along on my wages."[46] And a taxi dancer stated, "It's a shame a girl can't go straight and have a good time but I've got to get what I get by 'Sex Appeal.' "[47] One male resident of the North Side furnished-room district concluded: "[Women] draw on their sex as I would on my bank account to pay for the kind of clothes they want to wear, the kind of shows they want to see."[48]

"Occasional prostitution" resembled dates and pickups, but here the economic benefits were even clearer. Women asked men explicitly to pay for the sexual services provided them. These women worked in stores, offices, factories, and restaurants by day and sold their sexual services on occasional nights for extra money. While many women who dated probably exchanged only companionship, flirtation, and petting for evenings on the town, the smaller group of occasional prostitutes stepped up the barter, exchanging sexual intercourse for gifts or money. These women did not necessarily see themselves as prostitutes; they simply played the "sex game" for somewhat higher stakes.[49]

Without watchful relatives nearby, women lodgers could engage in occasional prostitution more easily than working women who lived in their parents' homes. Accordingly, vice investigators in search of occasional prostitutes went to the furnished-room districts to find them. In a North Clark Street saloon, for example, a vice investigator met two women who lived in the North Side district. They worked in a department store for $5.50 per week. "They can't live on this," he reported, "so they 'hustle' on the side." In another case, the investigator reported on a nineteen-year-old migrant from Indiana who worked in a South Side restaurant: "Is not a regular prostitute, goes with men for presents or money. Is poorly paid at restaurant."[50]

With pickups and occasional prostitution, the relationships usually lasted for one night only. In a "temporary alliance," a woman maintained a sexual relationship with one or more "steady" boyfriends, or lived with a man as if she were married. Amy, a twenty-year-old woman who lived on the South Side, worked as a cashier in a downtown restaurant until she met a streetcar conductor who agreed to "keep" her. He had given her a new fall hat and promised to buy her a new winter coat. Amy occasionally went out with other men "to get a little more spending money."[51] Another account of temporary alliances in furnished rooms stated tersely, "For ten months, Marion lived a hand-to-mouth existence, dependent upon the bounty of several men with whom she became intimate."[52] Such alliances were motivated in some cases by "genuine and lasting regard," but in others, "the motive of the girl is simply to find support, and that of the man gratification."[53]

From the limited evidence available, it seems that economic concerns also shaped sexual relationships in the lesbian subculture. Some lesbians depended on men, earning money as prostitutes. Others found higher-paid or wealthier women to support them. For example, in the North Side district in the late 1890s, one lesbian, Beatrice, was supported by her lover Peggy, who earned money as a prostitute. Peggy had "had a dozen sweethearts, all lesbian" and had "always supported them." On at least one occasion, some lesbians also adopted a form of gold digging or, more precisely, veiled blackmail. After a North Side party, some lesbians persuaded the wealthier women attending to pay for their companionship: "The lesbians would get their names and addresses and borrow money by saying, 'I met you at . . . [the] [party]?' " Some lesbians also prostituted themselves to other women.[54]

This emphasis on the economics of sexual relationships should not obscure the sexual dangers or the sensual pleasures that many women experienced. On one hand, some women lodgers encountered undeniable sexual violence, including rape, and others found themselves betrayed by false promises of marriage.[55] On the other hand, many women clearly enjoyed real relationships in which they found physical pleasure, excitement, and companionship. As one woman stated bluntly, "Frankly, I like intercourse!"[56] Further, the economic dependency in these relationships was not necessarily more exploitative or more oppressive than wives' traditional dependence on husbands or daughters' traditional dependence on fathers.

The financial imperatives are important, though, for they point to a neglected economics of the early-twentieth-century sexual revolution. The exchange of sexual services for monetary support moved beyond the marital bedroom and the brothel and into a variety of intermediate forms including dating, pickups, temporary alliances, and occasional prostitution. The sexual revolution was not simply, as one historian has written, "prosperity's child."[57] In the furnished-room districts, economic need shaped sexual experimentation. "What I get is mine. And what they have is mine, too, if I am smart enough to get it," said one self-avowed gold digger. "I'll show you how to take their socks away."[58] "Modern" sexual expression, then, not only threatened women with danger and promised women pleasure; in a variety of forms, it also offered financial reward.

Contemporary feminists who debate the meanings of sexual expression are not the first to define sexuality in terms of danger and pleasure. In the past century and a half, middle-class American commentators, including feminists, have often invested sexual expression with one of two opposing meanings. On one side, many observers, especially in the nineteenth century, have described nonmarital sexual expression with various stories of danger, disease, decay, and disorder. On the other side, some observers, primarily in the twentieth century, have represented nonmarital sexuality with stories of pleasure, vitality, adventure, and freedom.[59] In both constructions, sexuality was stripped of its everyday contexts and inflated with symbolic meaning. In the early twentieth century, the bourgeois attack on Victorian "sexual repression" marked a self-conscious shift in the dominant discourse from sex as danger to sex as pleasure.[60] As this conception of sexuality changed, the woman lodger played a central symbolic role. Through local and national media, a variety of commentators constructed conflicting interpretations of her unconventional sexual behavior. Reformers, manufacturers of popular culture, and sociologists dominated these debates.[61]

At the turn of the century, reformers presented the woman lodger as a symbol of endangered womanhood. In the organized boarding-home movement, the antiprostitution crusade, and the campaign to improve women's wages, reformers wrote with genuine concern for poorly paid, self-supporting women. With a sense of female solidarity, they deplored the economic hardships faced by the wage-earning woman, but they reserved their greatest distress for her sexual vulnerability.[62] Like most middle-class Americans of their day, they lamented female sexual expression outside marriage, but, unlike many, they rarely blamed the women involved."[63] Following earlier female moral reformers, they read sexual expression as a symbol of female victimization in an increasingly ruthless urban world.[64] These writers portrayed sexually active women lodgers as passive, pure, and impoverished orphans duped, forced, or unduly tempted by scheming men. While they occasionally criticized women lodgers for their "tendency ... to drift away from sweet and tender home influences," most often they condemned the "vampires" who trapped "poor, innocent little girls."[65] The reformers acknowledged that a woman lodger might enjoy the companionship she found in the furnished-room districts, but "the glare of cheap entertainments and the dangers of the street," they feared, would overpower her.[66] In short, they adopted a stereotype of female weakness and innocence that absolved the woman lodger of responsibility for her own sexual behavior.

The reformers appointed themselves as maternal protectors. In Chicago and other cities, they opened subsidized boarding homes—"veritable virtue-saving stations"—to lure women from commercial rooming houses.[67] By the 1920s Chicago had over sixty organized homes managed by Protestant, Catholic, Jewish, African American, German, Swedish, Polish, and Norwegian-Danish middle-class women for working women of their own religious, racial, and ethnic background.[68] They established room registries that placed women lodgers with private families in residential neighborhoods. They campaigned for minimum-wage laws because they saw the low pay of women lodgers as a major cause of "immorality." To "outwit evil agents, who would deceive the innocent," they placed charity workers in train stations and police matrons in public dance halls.[69] While they helped women in need of support, they obscured the actions that women lodgers took on their own behalf, and elaborated instead an image of weak-willed women in sexual danger. In fact, well after most reformers had acknowledged the competence of working women living with parents, the "woman adrift," who lodged on her own, bereft of protectors, remained a symbol of endangered womanhood.

A variant of the reformers' discourse reached into popular culture. In the late nineteenth and early twentieth centuries, popular "working-girl" romance novels, printed as cheap books or story-paper serials, adopted the image of orphaned, innocent, and imperiled "women adrift."[70] In these melodramatic stories, young, virtuous, native-born, white women endured countless agonies when alone in the city, and eventually married wealthy men. Here the language of female victimization reached its most sensational. Listen to Charlotte M. Stanley, the author of "Violet, the Beautiful Street Singer; or, an Ill-Starred Betrothal": "Oh, what cruel fate was it that had so suddenly altered the safe, smooth current of her young existence and cast her adrift in this frightful seething whirlpool of vice and crime?"[71] In romance novels, the gravest dangers a woman faced were threats to her sexual purity, generally seduction, abduction, procurement, and forced marriage. The queen of romance was probably Laura Jean Libbey, the author of over sixty novels in the late nineteenth century. Libbey created especially naive heroines who endured unusually frequent and frightening perils. In the opening chapters of one Libbey novel, beautiful Junie, an "artless little country lass" alone in the city, spurns the advances of a cad, follows a seemingly kind male stranger "without the least thought of her danger," and falls into the clutches of the cruel Squire Granger, who abducts her.[72] Like the reformers, Libbey publicized the perils of life in the city and sympathized with the lone woman, whom she portrayed as passive, innocent, and endangered.

The reformers and romance novelists, though, were fighting a losing battle, in part because the women they hoped to help belied the image of helpless victim. In fact, some women lodgers themselves directly attacked the reformers who treated them as pathetic orphans. In 1890, several "self-respecting and self-supporting" residents of the Chicago YWCA home wrote a blistering letter to a local newspaper:

> The idea seems to be in circulation that we who are unfortunate enough to be independent, are a collection of ignorant, weak-minded young persons, who have never had any advantages, educational or otherwise, and that we are brought here where we will be philanthropically cared for, and the cold winds tempered for us. A matron is provided, and

a committee of women who happen to be blessed with a few thousand dollars worth of aristocracy, has charge of the matron.

The women also complained of the furniture and food, and referred to themselves as the "victims of the home."[73]

By the early twentieth century, some reformers began to reassess their outlook. Managers of organized homes and other astute observers could not help note that many women lodgers were competent, assertive, and sexual by choice. Using the fact-gathering methods of the new social science, social investigators met face-to-face with women who pursued sexual companionship actively.[74] While reformers' concern for the woman lodger continued, they dropped their earlier emphasis on her passivity. Some also began to recognize that wage-earning women had sexual feelings. In 1910 one Chicago antivice crusader, who described self-supporting women as innocent, naive, and unprotected, admitted that "every normal girl or woman has primal instincts just as strong as her brother's."[75] Jane Addams, Louise DeKoven Bowen, and other Chicago reformers rejected earlier images of female passionlessness, and instead blamed overwork, commercialized recreation, and alcohol for bringing out natural yearnings and instincts that they preferred to see repressed.

As reformers observed women lodgers, their fears about sexual danger diminished. They saw that women in the furnished-room districts lived in a world that attached less stigma to female sexual activity. Reformers interviewed women who had given up their chastity without an inkling that they had chosen "a fate worse than death," and they saw that a wage-earning woman might choose to sell or exchange sexual services without ruining her life. "The fact that she has earned money in this way does not stamp her as 'lost,'" a 1911 federal report stated. "And the ease with which, in a large city, a woman may conceal a fall of this kind, if she desires to do so, also helps make a return to virtuous ways easy. . . . [O]ccasional prostitution holds its place in their minds as a possible resource, extreme, to be sure, but not in the least unthinkable."[76]

By the mid-1910s the observations of reformers coincided with broader changes in middle-class thought and behavior. In the years before World War I, increasing numbers of middle-class urban women adopted the more open sexual behavior of women in the furnished room districts. This change in middle-class morals further undermined the older image of female innocence and passionlessness, and challenged reformers' fear that female sexual behavior denoted female victimization. After World War I, in a conservative political climate, reformers suffered further from declining public interest and from government repression and indifference.[77]

Ultimately reformers' views on sexuality could not compete with a newer discourse emerging in popular culture. In the early twentieth century, cabaret reviews and movies attracted audiences by using the woman lodger as an appealing symbol of urban vitality, allure, and adventure. In these newer texts, the woman lodger, headstrong and openly sexual, lived freely in a fast-paced urban environment. In the earlier romance novels, unfortunate circumstance—poverty or death in the family—forced timid young women, soon to be victims, from happy parental homes. Or foolish young women left home and soon regretted it. In the newer scenarios, opportunistic women, such as Theodore Dreiser's Sister Carrie, chafed at the restriction of domesticity and the dullness of the small town. As one writer concluded, "[The city] is her frontier and in it she is the pioneer."[78] In the earlier discourse, the woman victim's suffering signified the high cost of urban living; in the newer, the woman pioneer's pleasure pointed to its rewards."[79]

By the first decade of the twentieth century, the new image reached national audiences in stories of chorus girls who achieved stardom and married wealth.[80] These women strutted boldly across the stage, displaying their bodies and commanding attention through their sexual appeal. They won wide publicity in 1908 when the trial of Henry Thaw made sensational headlines and reached larger audiences still in a movie, *The Great Trial*. Thaw had murdered architect Stanford White in a jealous rage over White's affair with Thaw's wife, Evelyn Nesbit. During the trial,

Nesbit, a former chorus girl, told how wealthy men entertained, courted, and, in her case, married the sexually attractive dancers in cabarets and theaters. As she recounted her rise from the life of a hardworking chorus girl to a life of luxury and extravagance, she announced the material and romantic pleasures available to the sexual, independent wage-earning woman.[81]

In the following years, as the number of movie theaters expanded rapidly and the size of audiences grew, the woman lodger emerged as a central character in the new feature films. At first, in early "white slavery" films, the heroines faced threats to their virtue and sometimes eventual victimization. At the same time, though, in early serials—*The Perils of Pauline* and *The Hazards of Helen*—the heroines, independent from family, were "healthy, robust, and self-reliant." They met available and often monied men whom they attracted with their native allure. While they encountered dangers and difficulties, they also enjoyed a daring nightlife in cabarets and dance halls, as well as the high life in opulent villas.[82] By 1915 Mary Pickford, the first major movie queen, was portraying women lodgers who flirted, danced, wore revealing clothing, and enjoyed energetic activities. Always chaste, she combined the purity of the Victorian orphan with the healthy sexuality of the chorus girl. Her exuberance and spunk attracted male suitors, leading to upwardly mobile marriages.[83]

By the 1920s, the movies drew clear connections between independence from family, on one side, and female sexuality and material gain, on the other. In some movies, the woman lodger was the stock heroine in rags-to-riches stories. *At the Stage Door* typifies the formula: "Mary leaves home to become a chorus girl in New York, and soon she achieves stardom. Philip Pierce, a young millionaire, is attracted to her."[84] As the heterosexual activities and assertive behavior of the independent working woman became more explicit in movies, so did the threat she posed to men.[85] The woman lodger as "gold digger" appeared at least as early as 1915. In *The Model: Or, Women and Wine*, wealthy young Dick Seymour pursues an independent working woman, Marcelle Rigadont, an artist's model. Marcelle, as one character advises her, wants to "play him for a sucker . . . and bleed him for every cent he's got." She finally confesses, "I never loved you— It was only your money I was after."[86] In the 1920s at least thirty-four films included the "gold digger" with her "aggressive use of sexual attraction."[87]

Although unrecorded forms of entertainment are harder to document, it seems that similar themes appeared in chorus revues at cabarets and theaters. In the opening number of the Midnight Frolic's *Just Girls*, staged in 1915, "girls from 24 cities and one small home town came to New York for adventure, men, and a new life." *Sally*, a Ziegfield revue staged in 1920, told the story of a working-class orphan who climbed from "the chorus to theatrical fame, wealthy admirers, and riches."[88] By the 1920s, variations on these plot lines appeared repeatedly in new monthly pulp romance magazines such as *True Story* and *True Romances*.

In the late 1910s and 1920s the new image of women lodgers achieved academic legitimacy in writings by urban sociologists at the University of Chicago. Inaugurated in the 1890s, the academic discipline of sociology moved quickly from an antiurban moralism to more rarefied theoretical questions. In Chicago, sociologists, predominantly male, undertook intensive investigations of urban life, using census data, interviews, and observation. They showed little interest in women or in sexuality per se; rather, they used sexual behavior in the furnished-room districts to bolster their theories of "urban evolution." Sociologist Robert Park wrote, "Everywhere the old order is passing, but the new has not arrived. . . . This is particularly true of the so-called rooming-house area."[89] In this view, the furnished-room districts became the vanguard of urban change, characterized by "disorganization" and "individuation." As these terms suggest, some sociologists saw the furnished-room districts as disturbed, soulless, and lonely.[90] For the most part, though, sociologists had a stronger faith in progress. As the vanguard of urban evolution, the furnished-room districts were, in a sense, the most advanced development of urban life. With a marked ambivalence, sociologists described the residents of furnished-room districts as "emancipated" as frequently as they called them "disorganized."[91]

For sociologists, the woman of the furnished-room districts represented the freedom of urban life. As in movies, the urban woman was seen as released from the "monotony of settled family life" in the small town.[92] From a barren, restricted existence, she moved to "a section of the old frontier transplanted to the heart of the modern city" where, competent and self-seeking, she could pursue her individual desires and ambitions.[93] One particularly blunt sociology student stated, "The homeless woman of modern cities is the emancipated woman."[94] In areas where earlier reformers had discovered sexual exploitation of unprotected women, sociologists now found willing participation. Of dating for money, Frances Donovan wrote, "She is not . . . exploited nor driven into it, but goes with her eyes wide open."[95] Another sociologist asserted, more dubiously, that prostitutes were no longer exploited by procurers or pimps.[96] And, as in the movies, some sociologists depicted the sexually "emancipated" woman as a potential threat to men: "In the quest after the material equipment of life . . . the girl becomes not only an individualist but also—frankly—an opportunist."[97] In earlier reformers' portrayals, men exploited naive women; in sociologists' constructions, women lodgers, like Hollywood "gold diggers," took advantage of men.

No less than earlier images of the innocent victim, new images of the urban pioneer reduced women in furnished-room districts to stereotypes, exaggerating certain features of their lives and neglecting others. Sociologists used self-supporting women as examples of uniquely urban personalities, emphasizing those traits that supported their theories of urban evolution: individualism, unconventional sexual behavior, transient personal relationships, and freedom from social control. Their commitment to the idea of evolutionary progress encouraged them to view these urban features as at least somewhat positive and liberating. At the same time, sociologists undermined reform efforts to alleviate female poverty. They downplayed the negative constraints of low wages, sexual harassment, and economic dependence, and thus suggested that reformers were superfluous, even meddling.

Reformers and romance novelists portrayed women lodgers as passive, passionless, and imperiled, while sociologists, moviemakers, and pulp magazine writers depicted them as active, pleasure-seeking, and opportunistic. The changing discourse marks the waning influence of moral reformers and the rise to cultural power of manufacturers of mass entertainment and academic social scientists. It also highlights a larger change in the portrayal of women in America, from the Victorian angel to the sexy starlet. In the late nineteenth century women lodgers, alone in the city, epitomized the purity of endangered womanhood; in the early twentieth century the same women were among the first "respectable" women broadcast as happy sexual objects.

The sexual behavior of women in turn-of-the-century furnished-room districts is not an isolated episode in women's history. Other U.S. historians also describe sexual expression among women lodgers. From at least the 1830s to at least the 1960s, women who supported themselves in the cities sometimes explored the boundaries of sexual convention.[98] In other societies as well, "modern" sexual behavior has reflected in part the changing social and economic relations wrought by wage work and urbanization. The migration of labor to cities has removed some women workers from traditional forms of community or family control and protection, thus opening possibilities for both sexual experimentation and sexual coercion. At the same time, the worldwide gender gap in wages has sustained women's dependence on others, especially on men. In new urban, industrial settings, the traditional exchange of services for support has taken on extrafamilial, sexual forms, including temporary alliances and occasional prostitution.[99]

In turn-of-the-century Chicago, the volume of migrants led entrepreneurs to invest in restaurants, furnished-rooming houses, theaters, cabarets, and dance halls. Women and men flocked to and shaped these institutions, creating new peer-oriented subcultures in specific urban districts. In these districts, most women could not afford to view sex solely in terms of sexual danger or sensual pleasure, for sexual expression was also tied inextricably to various forms of economic reward. In this context, the sexual revolution was, most likely, sometimes oppressive, sometimes exciting, and often an exchange.

The history of women lodgers in the furnished-room districts is important, for these women helped shape the modern sexual expression that other women later adopted. In the furnished-room districts themselves, middle- and upper-class bohemian "new women" observed the unconventional behavior of working-class women who were their neighbors. Middle-class pleasure-seekers and "flappers" may have copied the blueprints of "sexy" behavior they observed while slumming in the districts' cabarets and dance halls. And moviegoers and magazine readers learned from the portrayals of women lodgers, as films, cabarets, and romance magazines used the sexuality of independent wage-earning women to attract and titillate viewers and readers. In these ways, turn-of-the-century women lodgers helped chart the modern American sexual terrain.

Notes

1. This article is reprinted in slightly revised form from Nancy Hewitt, ed., *Women, Families, and Communities: Readings in American History* (New York: Scott Foresman, 1990). It draws on material in Joanne Meyerowitz, *Women Adrift: Independent Wage-Earners in Chicago, 1880–1930* (Chicago: University of Chicago Press, 1988). Thanks to Estelle Freedman, Zane Miller, Leila Rupp, Christina Simmons, and Bruce Tucker for their helpful comments. And special thanks to Nancy Hewitt, who helped sustain this article through its strange publication history.

2. Frederick Lewis Allen, *Only Yesterday* (New York: Harper and Brothers, 1931); William Leuchtenburg, *The Perils of Prosperity, 1914–1932* (Chicago: University of Chicago Press, 1958); James McGovern, "The American Woman's Pre-World War I Freedom in Manners and Morals," *Journal of American History* (September 1968); Gerald F. Critoph, "The Flapper and Her Critics," in Carol V. R. George, ed., *"Remember the Ladies": New Perspectives on Women in American History* (Syracuse: Syracuse University Press, 1975). See also Paula S. Fass, *The Damned and the Beautiful: American Youth in the 1920s* (New York: Oxford University Press, 1977); John Modell, "Dating Becomes the Way of American Youth," in Leslie Page Moch and Gary Stark, eds., *Essays on the Family and Historical Change* (College Station: Texas A & M University Press, 1983).

3. June Sochen, *The New Woman: Feminism in Greenwich Village, 1910–1920* (New York: Quadrangle Books, 1972); Elaine Showalter, ed., *These Modern Women: Autobiographical Essays from the Twenties* (Old Westbury, N.Y.: Feminist Press, 1978); Carroll Smith-Rosenberg, "The New Woman as Androgyne: Social Disorder and Gender Crisis, 1870–1936," in Smith-Rosenberg, ed., *Disorderly Conduct: Visions of Gender in Victorian, America* (New York: Alfred A. Knopf, 1985); Esther Newton, "The Mythic Mannish Lesbian: Radclyffe Hall and the New Woman," *Signs: Journal of Women in Culture and Society* (summer 1984); Ellen Carol DuBois and Linda Gordon, "Seeking Ecstasy on the Battlefield: Danger and Pleasure in Nineteenth-Century Feminist Sexual Thought," in Carole S. Vance, ed., *Pleasure and Danger: Exploring Female Sexuality* (Boston: Routledge and Kegan Paul, 1984); Leila J. Rupp, "Feminism and the Sexual Revolution in the Early Twentieth Century: The Case of Doris Stevens," *Feminist Studies* (summer 1989). For an earlier account, see Henry F. May, *The End of American Innocence: A Study of the First Years of Our Own Time, 1912–1917* (New York: Alfred A. Knopf, 1986).

4. Kathy Peiss, *Cheap Amusements: Working Women and Leisure in Turn-of-the-Century New York* (Philadelphia: Temple University Press, 1986); for the nineteenth century, see Christine Stansell, *City of Women: Sex and Class in New York, 1789–1860* (New York: Alfred A. Knopf, 1986).

5. For a summary of these debates, see "Forum: The Feminist Sexuality Debates," *Signs: Journal of Woman in Culture and Society* (autumn 1984); Carole S. Vance, "Pleasure and Danger: Toward a Politics of Sexuality," in Vance, ed., *Pleasure and Danger*.

6. Robert Park, "The City: Suggestions for the Investigation of Human Behavior in Urban Environment," in Richard Sennett, ed., *Classic Essays on the Culture of Cities* (New York: Meredith Corporation, 1969), 128–29.

7. Robert Woods, ed., *The City Wilderness: A Settlement Study* (Boston: Houghton Mifflin, 1898); see especially William I. Cole's article, "Criminal Tendencies," 166–69.

8. Albert Benedict Wolfe, *The Lodging House Problem in Boston* (Boston: Houghton Mifflin, 1906), 171. See also Franklin Kline Fretz, *The Furnished Room Problem in Philadelphia* (Ph.D. diss., University of Pennsylvania, 1912); S. P. Breckinridge and Edith Abbott, "Chicago's Housing Problems: Families in Furnished Rooms," *American Journal of Sociology* (November 1910): 289–308.

9. Harvey Warren Zorbaugh, *Gold Coast and Slum: A Sociological Study of Chicago's Near North Side* (Chicago: University of Chicago Press, 1929), 153.

10. To avoid being unduly influenced by the sociologists' discourse, I have accepted the sociologists' conclusions only when I could corroborate them with evidence from other sources, such as newspapers accounts, reports of reformers, and memoirs.

11. In the 1910s the South Side district ran from Sixteenth to Thirty-third Streets and from Clark Street to Prairie Avenue; the West Side district ran from Washington to Harrison Streets and from Ashland Boulevard to Halsted Street; the North Side district went from Division Street to the Chicago River and from Wells to Rush Streets. Edith Abbott, *The Tenements of Chicago, 1908–1935 (Chicago:* University of Chicago Press, 1936). Information on the population of the furnished room districts was derived from sociological studies and from the Federal Manuscript Census, Meyerowitz's samples of Chicago "women adrift," 1880 and 1910, and the tract-by-tract census data found in Ernest W. Burgess and Charles Newcomb, eds., *Census Data of the City of Chicago, 1920* (Chicago: University of Chicago Press, 1931), and Ernest W. Burgess and Charles Newcomb, eds. *Census Data of the City of Chicago, 1930* (Chicago: University of Chicago Press, 1933).

12. On growth of districts, see Abbott, *Tenements of Chicago*, ch. 10; also Kimball Young, "Sociological Study of a Disintegrated Neighborhood" (M.A. thesis, University of Chicago, 1918). On the number of lodgers, see T.W. Allison, "Population Movement in Chicago," *Journal of Social Forces* (May 1924): 529–33. The lodging houses included in the 1923 register were only those with more than ten roomers.

13. Zorbaugh, *Gold Coast and Slum*, 72.

14. See Wolfe, *The Lodging Problem in Boston;* for examples of permissive landladies in Chicago, see Louise DeKoven Bowen, *The Straight Girl on the Crooked Path: A True Story* (Chicago: Juvenile Protective Association of Chicago, 1916).

15. In 1920 the sex ratio in the North Side district was 1.4 and in the West Side district 1.6. In 1930 the ratio in the North Side district was 1.3 and in the West Side district 2.0. In both years, the South Side district, which was more dispersed over a larger area, had a sex ratio of 1.0. These sex ratios were derived from tract-by-tract census data found in Burgess and Newcomb, eds., *Census Data of the City of Chicago, 1920* and *Census Data of the City of Chicago, 1930.*

16. Vice Commission of Chicago, *The Social Evil in Chicago: A Study of Existing Conditions with Recommendations by the Vice Commission of Chicago* (Chicago: Vice Commission of Chicago, 1911), 87–91.

17. *The Social Evil in Chicago*, 73, 74, 92–94.

18. "Investigation of Commercialized Prostitution," December 1922, Juvenile Protective Association of Chicago Papers 5:92, University of Illinois at Chicago Manuscript Collections.

19. Young, "Sociological Study of a Disintegrated Neighborhood," 52.

20. Ibid., 42; Abbott, *The Tenements of Chicago*, 322.

21. James R. Grossman, *Land of Hope: Chicago, Black Southerners, and the Great Migration* (Chicago: University of Chicago Press, 1989), 117, E. Franklin Frazier, *The Negro Family in Chicago* (Chicago: University of Chicago Press, 1932), 103. See also Carroll Binder, "Negro Active in Business World," *Chicago Daily News*, 5 August 1927; Junius B. Wood, *The Negro in Chicago* (reprint of articles in *Chicago Daily News*, 11–27 December 1916), 25.

22. Reckless, "The Natural History of Vice Areas," 381.

23. E. H. Wilson, "Chicago Families in Furnished Rooms" (M.A. thesis, University of Chicago, 1929), 100.

24. See Young, "Sociological Study of a Disintegrated Neighborhood," 54; also Zorbaugh, *Gold Coast and Slum:* As early as 1898, Frederick Bushee suggested that "The lodging houses themselves [in Boston's South End district] are the homes of the queer and questionable of every shade," in Woods, ed., *The City Wilderness*, 50.

25. See, for example, Walter C. Reckless, *Vice in Chicago* (Chicago: University of Chicago Press, 1933), 53–54. I use Claude Fischer's definition of subcultures: "social worlds . . . inhabited by persons who share relatively distinctive traits (like ethnicity or occupation), who tend to interact especially with one another, and who manifest a relatively distinct set of beliefs and behaviors." Claude S. Fischer, *The Urban Experience* (New York: Harcourt, Brace, Jovanovich, 1976), 36.

26. Young, "Sociological Study of a Disintegrated Neighborhood," 79.

27. Case record from Chicago Vice Study File, cited in Walter C. Reckless, *Vice in Chicago*, 53, 54.

28. *Chicago Examiner*, 12 April 1913.

29. Box-Car Bertha as told to Dr. Ben L. Reitman, *Sister of the Road: The Autobiography of Box-Car Bertha* (New York: Macauley, 1937), 68, 70, 62, 29.

30. There is some evidence of a lesbian community among prostitutes in Paris as early as the 1880s, and also evidence suggesting that some lesbians in New York participated in the male homosexual subculture there by the 1890s. In general, though, American lesbian communities were not visible until the

1920s, perhaps because the majority of women had fewer opportunities than men to leave family life. Moreover, romantic attachments between women were not usually labeled deviant in America until the early twentieth century. Middle- and upper-class women who lived together as couples in "Boston marriages," for example, were not segregated as outcasts from heterosexual family and friends. On early male homosexual subcultures in American cities, see Jonathan Katz, ed., *Gay American History: Lesbians and Gay Men in the U.S.A.* (New York: Avon Books, 1976), 61–81; John D'Emilio, "Capitalism and Gay Identity," in Ann Snitow, Christine Stansell, and Sharon Thompson, eds., *Powers of Desire: The Politics of Sexuality* (New York: Monthly Review Press, 1983), and George Chauncey Jr., "Christian Brotherhood or Sexual Perversion? Sexual Boundaries in the World War One Era," *Journal of Social History* (winter 1985). On lesbian prostitutes in Paris and on turn-of-the-century tolerance for lesbianism, see Lillian Faderman, *Surpassing the Love of Men: Romantic Friendship and Love Between from the Renaissance to the Present* (New York: William Morrow and Co., 1981), 282, 298.

31. Paul Oliver, *Screening the Blues: Aspects of the Blues Tradition* (London: Cassell and Co., 1968), 225, 226.
32. Box-Car Bertha, *Sister of the Road*, p. 65.
33. "A nurse told me of being called on night duty in an apartment in the 'village' and of being entertained every night by the girls in the apartment across the well, some of whom would put on men's evening clothes, make love to the others, and eventually carry them off in their arms into the bedrooms." Zorbaugh, *Gold Coast and Slum*, 100.
34. Frazier, *The Negro Family in Chicago*, 103; interview with Eulalia B., conducted by author, 16 October 1980.
35. Zorbaugh, *Gold Coast and Slum*, 91.
36. "Dill Pickle Club," in Vivien Palmer, "Documents of History of the Lower North Side," vol. 3, pt. 2, doc. 52, Chicago Historical Society.
37. Zorbaugh, *Gold Coast and Slum*, 114–15.
38. Walter Reckless, "The Natural History of Vice Areas in Chicago" (Ph.D. diss., University of Chicago, 1925), 374, 375. For a similar rejection of social background, see the story of Christina Stranski (aka DeLoris Glenn) in Paul G. Cressey, *The Taxi-Dance Hall: A Sociological Study in Commercialized Recreation and City Life* (Chicago: University of Chicago Press, 1932), 56.
39. On bohemians as a vanguard of sex radicalism, see May, *The End of American Innocence*.
40. A few other historians have suggested that working-class women were pioneers in changing sexual mores. See, for example, Nathan G. Hale Jr., *Freud and the Americans: The Beginnings of Psychoanalysis in the United States, 1876–1917* (New York: Oxford University Press, 1971), 477; Lewis A. Erenberg, *Steppin' Out: New York Nightlife and the Transformation of American Culture, 1890–1930* (Westport, Conn.: Greenwood Press, 1981); Daniel Scott Smith, "The Dating of the American Sexual Revolution: Evidence and Interpretation," in Michael Gordon, ed., *The American Family in Social-Historical Perspective* (New York: St. Martin's Press, 1973).
41. On women's wages, see Leslie Woodcock Tender, *Wage-Earning Women: Industrial Work and Family Life in the United States, 1900–1930* (New York: Oxford University Press, 1979).
42. Charles P. Neill, *Wage-Earning Women in Stores and Factories*, vol. 5, *Report on Condition of Woman and Child Wage-Earners in the United States* (Washington, D.C.: Government Printing Office, 1910), 75.
43. *The Social Evil in Chicago*, 186.
44. *Chicago Defender*, 20 August 1921.
45. See Kathy Peiss, " 'Charity Girls' and City Pleasures: Historical Notes on Working-Class Sexuality, 1880–1920," in Stansell, and Thompson, eds., *Powers of Desire.*
46. Louise DeKoven Bowen, *The Girl Employed in Hotels and Restaurants* (Chicago: Juvenile Protective Association of Chicago, 1912).
47. "Alma N. Z——r," Paul Cressey notes, c. 1926, 5, Ernest Burgess Papers 129:6, University of Chicago Manuscript Collections.
48. Zorbaugh, *Gold Coast and Slum*, 86.
49. Frances Donovan, *The Woman Who Waits* (New York: Arno Press 1974, [1920]), 211–20.
50. *The Social Evil in Chicago*, 133,95.
51. Ibid., 188.
52. Ruth Shonle Cavan, *Suicide* (Chicago: University of Chicago Press, 1928), 206.
53. Wolfe, *The Lodging House Problem in Boston*, 142. In these accounts of heterosexual relationships, most of the women lodgers seem to be under thirty years of age. Older women lodgers were probably somewhat less attractive to the predominantly young male suitors. They also seemed to tire of the nightlife, preferring the more stable support and companionship sometimes provided in marriage. In fact, most women lodgers in Chicago did eventually marry. For a revealing interview with an older woman, see Anderson, "Life History of a Rooming House Keeper," c. 1925, Ernest Burgess Papers 127:2, University of Chicago Manuscript Collections.

54. Box-Car Bertha, *Sister of the Road*, 223, 66, 69, 288. This limited evidence of dependent relationships is corroborated by other evidence that early twentieth-century working-class lesbians often adopted somewhat traditional gender roles, with one partner assuming a masculine role. See Katz, *Gay American History*, 383–90. See also Joan Nestle, "The Fem Question," in Vance, ed., *Pleasure and Danger*, and Elizabeth Lapovsky Kennedy and Madeline Davis, "The Reproduction of Butch-Fem Roles: A Social Constructionist Approach," in Kathy Peiss and Christina Simmons, eds., *Passion and Power: Sexuality in History* (Philadelphia: Temple University Press, 1989).

55. See, for example, Louise DeKoven Bowen, *A Study of Bastardy Cases* (Chicago: Juvenile Protective Association, 1914).

56. Lillian S. W—n," Paul Cressey Notes, 18, Ernest Burgess Papers 129:6, University of Chicago Manuscript Collections.

57. Kenneth Yellis, "Prosperity's Child: Some Thoughts on the Flapper," *American Quarterly* (spring 1969).

58. *Chicago Daily Times*, 31 January 1930.

59. I'm not suggesting that the contemporary feminist sexuality debates replicate the earlier discourse, only that contemporary debates are a new, different, and interesting variant of older associations. On sex as danger, see Caroll Smith-Rosenberg, "Sex as Symbol in Victorian Purity: An Ethnohistorical Analysis of Jacksonian America," in John Demos and Sarane Spence Boocock, eds., *Turning Points: Historical and Sociological Essays on the Family* (Chicago: University of Chicago Press, 1978); Paul Boyer, *Urban Masses and Moral Order in America, 1820–1920* (Cambridge, Mass.: Harvard University Press, 1978); on sex as pleasure, see Paul Robinson, *The Modernization of Sex: Havelock Ellis, Alfred Kinsey, William Masters and Virginia Johnson* (New York: Harper and Row, 1976). For a general history of the changing dominant discourses on sexuality, see John D'Emilio and Estelle Freedman, *Intimate Matters: A History of Sexuality in America* (New York: Harper and Row, 1988). On late-nineteenth-and early-twentieth-century feminist variants of the shift from sex as danger to sex as pleasure, see DuBois and Gordon, "Seeking Ecstasy on the Battlefield," in Vance, ed., *Pleasure and Danger*. For formulations in Britain, see Judith Walkowitz, *Prostitution and Victorian Society: Women, Class, and the State* (Cambridge: Cambridge University Press, 1980); Susan Kingsley Kent, *Sex and Suffrage in Britain, 1860–1914* (Princeton: Princeton University Press, 1987); Frank Mort, *Dangerous Sexualities: Medico-Moral Politics in England Since 1830* (London: Routledge and Kegan Paul, 1987). In general, representations of sex as vitality, pleasure, adventure, and freedom have not been studied as closely by historians as representations of sex as danger, disease, decay, and disorder.

60. On the attack on Victorian "sexual repression," see Christina Simmons, "Modern Sexuality and the Myth of Victorian Repression," in Peiss and Simmons, eds., *Passion and Power*. See also Michel Foucault, *The History of Sexuality*, vol. 1 (New York: Vintage Books, 1980).

61. For psychiatrists' contribution to these public discussions, see Elizabeth Lunbeck, " 'A New Generation of Women': Progressive Psychiatrists and the Hypersexual Woman," *Feminist Studies* (fall 1987).

62. On late-nineteenth-century reformers' interest in working women, see Mari Jo Buhle, "The Nineteenth-Century Woman's Movement: Perspectives on Women's Labor in Industrializing America," Bunting Institute of Radcliffe College, 1979.

63. For a more detailed discussion of the reformers' position, see Meyerowitz, *Women Adrift*, ch. 3. For a similar combination of feminist sympathy and middle-class moralism in the early to mid-nineteenth century, see Stansell, *City of Women*, 70–74.

64. On earlier reformers, see especially Mary P. Ryan, "The Power of Women's Networks: A Case Study of Female Moral Reform in Antebellum America," *Feminist Studies* (spring 1979); Carroll Smith-Rosenberg, "Beauty, the Beast, and the Militant Woman: A Case Study of Sex Roles and Social Stress in Jacksonian America," in Nancy F. Cott and Elizabeth H. Pleck, eds., *A Heritage of Her Own: Toward a New Social History of American Women* (New York: Simon and Schuster, 1979).

65. Women's Christian Association of Chicago, *Fifth Annual Report* (1881), 12; Charles Bryon Chrysler, *White Slavery* (Chicago: n.p., 1909), 13.

66. Annie Marion MacLean, "Homes for Working Women in Large Cities," *Charities Review*, July 1899, 228.

67. MacLean, "Homes for Working Women," 228.

68. Josephine J. Taylor, "Study of YWCA Room Registry," 1928, Ernest Burgess Papers 138:9, University of Chicago Manuscript Collections: Essie Mae Davidson, "Organized Boarding Homes for Self-Supporting Women in the City of Chicago" (M.A. thesis, University of Chicago, 1914); Ann Elizabeth Trotter, *Housing Non-Family Women in Chicago: A Survey* (Chicago: Chicago Community Trust, c. 1921).

69. YWCA of Chicago, *18th Annual Report* (1894), 33. On the national Travelers' Aid movement, see Lynn Y. Weiner, *From Working Girl to Working Mother: The Female Labor Force in the United States, 1820 1980* (Chapel Hill: University of North Carolina Press, 1985). On reforming the dance halls, see Elisabeth I. Perry, " 'The General Motherhood of the Commonwealth': Dance Hall Reform in the Progressive Era," *American Quarterly* (winter 1985).

70. For a brief description of the "working-girl" novel, see Cathy N. Davidson and Arnold E. Davidson, "Carrie's Sisters: The Popular Prototypes for Dreiser's Heroine," *Modern Fiction Studies* (autumn 1977).

71. Charlotte M. Stanley, "Violet, the Beautiful Street Singer; or An Ill-Starred Betrothal," *New York Family Story Paper*, 5 September 1908. See also T.W. Hanshew, "Alone in New York: A Thrilling Portrayal of the Dangers and Pitfalls of the Metropolis," *New York Family Story Paper*, 30 April 1887.

72. Laura Jean *Libbey, Junie's Love Test* (New York: George Munro, 1883), 66.

73. *Sunday Inter Ocean*, 16 November 1890. The women who lived in this YWCA home tended to be white, native-born women who held more middle-class jobs in offices and stores. Black women and immigrant women also expressed displeasure with forms of housing that invaded their privacy and reduced their initiative. See Meyerowitz, *Women Adrift*, ch. 4.

74. See, for example, Louise DeKoven Bowen, *Safeguards of City Youth at Work and at Play* (New York: Macmillan, 1914), 23; Clara E. Laughlin, *The Work-a-Day Girl* (New York: Arno Press, 1974 [1913]), 51.

75. Leona Prall Groetzinger, *The City's Perils* (n.p., c. 1910), 110.

76. Mary Conyngton, *Relation between Occupation and Criminality of Women*, vol. 15, *Report on Condition of Woman and Child Wage-Earners in the United States* (Washington, D.C.: Government Printing Office, 1911), 102–3.

77. Other factors undermining the reformers' image of passive, endangered women included the WWI venereal disease campaign, the decline in the number of women immigrants arriving from Europe, and a slight rise in women's real wages in the 1920s. As these changes occurred, most reformers lost interest in women lodgers; those who maintained their interest lost the power to shape cultural images.

78. Donovan, *The Woman Who Waits*, 9.

79. For a more detailed discussion of this newer image, see Meyerowitz, *Women Adrift*, ch. 6.

80. Lois Banner, American Beauty (Chicago: University of Chicago Press, 1983), 180–84.

81. On the Thaw trial, see Lewis Erenberg, *Steppin' Out*, 53; Lary May, *Screening Out the Past: The Birth of Mass Culture and the Motion Picture Industry* (New York: Oxford University Press, 1980), 34, 43.

82. May, *Screening Out the Past*, 108.

83. Ibid., 119, 142, 143. For a discussion of "heterosocial culture" in earlier films, see Peiss, *Cheap Amusements*, 153–58.

84. Kenneth Munden, ed., *The American Film Institute Catalog, Feature Films, 1921–1929* (New York: R. R. Bowker Co., 1971), 29.

85. The 1920s stories that represented sexual expression as pleasurable and adventurous often had a subtext of potential danger (especially to men), as the "gold digger" movies attest.

86. "The Model; or, Women and Wine," *Picture-Play Weekly*, 12 June 1915, 12–16.

87. Mary P. Ryan, "The Projection of a New Womanhood: The Movie Moderns in the 1920s," in Jean E. Friedman and William G. Shade, eds., *Our American Sisters: Women in American Life and Thought*, 2nd ed. (Boston: Allyn and Bacon, 1976), 376.

88. Erenberg, *Steppin' Out*, 210, 223.

89. Robert E. Park, "Introduction," in Zorbaugh, *Gold Coast and Slum*, viii.

90. Cavan, *Suicide*, 81; Robert E. L. Faris, *Chicago Sociology, 1920–1932* (Chicago: University of Chicago Press, Midway Reprint, 1979 [1967]), 35.

91. See, for examples, Ernest Mowrer, *Family Disorganization: An Introduction to Sociological Analysis* (Chicago: University of Chicago Press, 1927), 111; Faris, *Chicago Sociology*, 79.

92. Walter C. Reckless, "The Natural History of Vice Areas in Chicago," 211.

93. Zorbaugh, *The Gold Coast and the Slum*, 199.

94. Reckless, "The Natural History of Vice Areas," 209.

95. Donovan, *The Woman Who Waits*, 220.

96. W. I. Thomas, *The Unadjusted Girl, with Cases and Standpoint for Behavioral Analysis* (Boston: Little, Brown, and Co., 1923), 150.

97. Cressey, *The Taxi-Dance Hall*, 47.

98. Stansell, *City of Women*, 83–101, 171–192; Linda Gordon, *Woman's Body, Woman's Right: A Social History of Birth Control in America* (New York: Penguin Books, 1977), 203–4; Barbara Ehrenreich, Elizabeth Hess, and Gloria Jacobs, *Re-Making Love: The Feminization of Sex* (Garden City, N.Y.: Anchor Press/Doubleday, 1986), 39–42, 54–62.

99. There is a recent and growing literature on contemporary women migrants in Third World nations. For a good introduction, see the special issue of *International Migration Review* (winter 1984), and Annette Fuentes and Barbara Ehrenreich, *Women in the Global Factory* (Boston: South End Press, 1983). For additional references to sexuality, see also Ilsa Schuster, "Marginal Lives: Conflict and Contradiction in the Position of Female Traders in Lusaka, Zambia," in Edna G. Bay, ed., *Women and*

Work in Africa (Boulder: Westview Press, 1982), and Sharon Stichter, *Migrant Laborers* (Cambridge: Cambridge University Press, 1985). On capitalism, urbanization., migration, and sexuality in Europe, see the now-classic accounts of the eighteenth century in Edward Shorter, "Illegitimacy, Sexual Revolution and Social Change in Modem Europe," *Journal of Interdisciplinary History* (autumn 1971), and Louise A. Tilly, Joan W. Scott, and Miriam Cohen, "Women's Work and Fertility Patterns," *Journal of Interdisciplinary History* (winter 1976). Shorter emphasizes the sexual pleasure pursued by women, while Tilly, Scott, and Cohen underscore women's sexual vulnerability. For a more recent account, see Nicholas Rogers, "Carnal Knowledge: Illegitimacy in Eighteenth-Century Westminster," *Journal of Social History* (winter 1989).

20

Making Faces

The Cosmetics Industry and the Cultural Construction of Gender, 1890–1930

Kathy Peiss

In the late nineteenth and early twentieth centuries, American women began to purchase and wear face powder, rouge, lipstick, and other kinds of visible cosmetics. A society that had scorned Victorian women's makeup as a mark of disrepute and illegitimacy had, by the early decades of the twentieth century, embraced powder and paint as essential signs of femininity. Once marking the prostitute and the aristocratic lady as symbols of rampant sexuality and materialistic excess, cosmetics became understood as respectable and indeed necessary for women's success and fulfillment.

Cosmetics, of course, are nothing new. Throughout history and in many cultures, women and men have colored, distorted, and exaggerated their physical features. In the early twentieth century, however, cosmetics took on new meaning in American culture. They became part of an ongoing discourse on femininity that made problematic women's identity in an increasingly commercial, industrial, and urban world. Women linked cosmetics use to an emergent notion of their own modernity, which included wage-work, athleticism, leisure, freer sexual expressiveness, and greater individual consumption. At the same time, new forms of mass culture shaped this discourse, as women began to see their faces differently in a number of novel cultural mirrors: in motion pictures, in mass-market women's magazines and advertising, in shop windows, on fashion runways, and across the counters of department stores.[1]

This essay focuses, however, on the crucial role of the cosmetics and beauty business in popularizing cosmetics and shaping gender definitions. In this century, cosmetics use has been inextricably tied to the emergence of a mass consumer industry. From the 1870s onward, American business has aggressively developed consumer markets, utilizing new techniques of mass production and distribution. In search of expanded and predictable profits, capitalism has promoted the redefinition and commodification of everyday social needs. The cosmetics business, whose financial success lay in defining the outward appearance of femininity, exemplifies this history. In the cosmetics industry, we can see how specific processes of mass production, distribution, marketing, and advertising rendered new social meanings about female identity and made them compelling to women consumers.

Complicating this story, however, is the segmentation of the industry from its inception into three distinct lines of trade. In modern marketing parlance, the industry has long been divided into the "class," "mass," and "ethnic" markets. The "class market" represents high-priced cosmetic lines, both domestic and imported, whose aura is one of exclusivity and social status. Sold in department stores and exclusive salons, these products are marketed to wealthy and upwardly mobile middle-class women. "Mass" cosmetic products, the low-priced lines available in drugstores, variety stores, and discount beauty outlets, are marketed to a wide range of consumers, but particularly targeted toward working-class and lower-middle-class women, as well as teenagers. The ethnic market is a contemporary euphemism for the African American beauty industry, although this market includes Hispanic Americans, Asian Americans, and other women of color.

Historically the class, mass, and African American segments of the industry shared certain problems in fostering the popular use of cosmetics, especially in their need to convince women that being "painted" was not only respectable but a requirement of womanhood. In some respects they came up with similar solutions, which they projected through techniques of mass marketing and advertising. Each appropriated and manipulated a complex set of images about womanhood during a historic period that witnessed major changes in women's experience and status. However, they represented gender in different and contradictory ways that bespeak the divisions of class and race within the industry and, more broadly, within American society. Thus in this essay I first trace the commercialization of cosmetics and their popularization in each segment of the industry. I then turn to the ideological definition of womanhood, focusing on the ways that class and race were inextricably implicated in the cosmetics industry's projections of gendered appearance.

The Commercialization of Cosmetics

Women's cosmetics use in the nineteenth-century United States is difficult to determine with any exactness. Creams, lotions, and tonics—that is, external cosmetic applications involving skin care or therapeutic treatment—were widespread. From the 1840s, family keepsakes and formularies offered recipes to soften and whiten skin, cure freckles, and remove unwanted hair, and were distributed to a wide range of Americans, from middle-class ladies and gentlemen to farmers and mechanics. Many advice books also instructed women in the simple home manufacture of "make-up," that is, cosmetics involving the application of color to the face: pulverized chalk for face powder, beet root for rouge, burnt cloves or green walnut juice for eyebrow and lash coloring. As was the case with medicinal remedies, an oral tradition concerning hair and skin care probably comprised an aspect of women's culture.[2]

Yet the use of makeup was problematic for many nineteenth-century women. Among fashionable middle- and upper-class women, the obvious use of powder and paint came into vogue in the 1850s and 1860s, only to decline in the late nineteenth century. For the vast majority of middle-class women, however, enameling the face with a white liquid or visibly tinting it with rouge were objectionable practices. By 1900 the use of face powder seems to have become more common among urban middle-class women, judging from advice books and commentators; even the subtle application of rouge and eyebrow pencil, if concealed, was deemed acceptable.[3]

The use of cosmetics by white working-class and black women in the latter half of the nineteenth century is even more difficult to determine. Many working-class women refrained from makeup use, given religious beliefs, ethnic cultural traditions, concepts of respectability, and the cost of the products. Probably the most frequent working-class consumers of cosmetics were prostitutes, who signaled their trade to potential customers through the visible use of face powder and rouge. But other working women used these products as well, particularly the subculture of "disorderly" women oriented toward urban nightlife and sexual pleasure. Their use of cosmetics, as well as fancy dress and hairpieces, marked a distinctive and provocative cultural style, if not an oppositional aesthetics. For example, a ruddy complexion, either naturally or artificially induced, seems to have been an ideal among some working women. Reddish cheeks accompanied their boisterous, high-spirited behavior, and offered a sharp contrast to the pale faces of middle-class women. Other working women, who played with the ideal of being "ladies," powdered themselves so much that various employers, from department store managers to household mistresses, barred the use of face powders.[4] While there is even less evidence concerning cosmetics use among black women, stylishness and adornment were ideals cultivated by postbellum African Americans, signifying freedom and respectability. Although the issue of personal grooming for black women centered more around hair care, some use of cosmetics, particularly homemade products, is probable.[5]

Whatever the patterns of cosmetic use, consumer resistance to commercially manufactured cosmetics was very high in the nineteenth century. One fear concerned the potential health hazards of so-called patent cosmetics, a term that associated cosmetics with the extravagant claims and often ruinous results of patent medicines. American consumers were increasingly sensitive to the dangers of adulterated products and the substitutions of unscrupulous dealers; in the case of cosmetics, such fears were heightened by the centuries-old tradition of using arsenic, white lead, and other toxic substances in powders and enamels. Advice books often cautioned women, in the words of one, to become their "*own manufacturer*—not only as a matter of *economy*, but of *safety*." Indeed, cosmetics were ideologically linked to a larger critique of commerce and its practice of artifice and deception.[6]

The critique of cosmetics on grounds of health and safety was linked to another powerful, if less specific, set of concerns about what it meant to be "painted." On the one hand, for many Americans, cosmetics were associated with aristocratic excess, undemocratic luxury, and female self-indulgence. Artifice was the mode of parasitical ladies of fashion, who sacrificed health and familial duty in frivolous, self-centered pursuits. On the other hand, the "painted woman" most powerfully signified the prostitute, the immoral, public woman who lived outside the sanction of a middle-class society that valorized women's purity and the home. "Paint" demarcated the boundary between respectability and promiscuity, bourgeois gentility and lower-class vulgarity. If cultural definitions of gender were shaped and bounded by the cultural construction of class and race, then cosmetics contributed significantly to the external marking of those boundaries. Thus, handling social divisions and their cultural markers proved a special problem for the nascent cosmetics industry.[7]

The production of commercial cosmetics remained quite limited in the late nineteenth century. The census of manufactures of 1889 lists only 157 companies whose primary business was perfume and cosmetics. In a period when many consumer goods found a national market, the cosmetics industry was slow to take off. A comparison might be made with patent medicines and soaps, two products that, like cosmetics, were related to physical care and appearance. Sale of these goods gave rise to large corporations that had developed mass production, national distribution, and national advertising by the 1880s. Cosmetics, however, remained a small-scale business, highly entrepreneurial and without a distinctive identity. It was not until the years immediately before and after World War I that the industry experienced substantial growth. In 1914 there were 496 companies manufacturing perfume and cosmetics, and the value of their products was nearly $17 million; by 1919, although the number of companies had risen only to 569, the value of products climbed dramatically, to almost $60 million.[8]

The Segmentation of the Industry

Commercial manufacture of cosmetics emerged from several distinct lines of trade in the mid-nineteenth century: the manufacture of pharmaceuticals and drugstore supplies, the local business activity of druggists, and commercial beauty culture. Patent medicine makers produced some cosmetic products, particularly those with therapeutic claims. In addition, companies manufacturing perfumery, flavoring extracts, essential oils, and druggists' sundries also included a few cosmetics in their product lines. These were placed before the public through traditional routes of distribution, including drugstores, general stores, and peddlers. Relatively few of them—such as Pond's Extract and Hagan's Magnolia Balm—achieved national distribution or brand name recognition.

More commonplace were the hundreds of local druggists and hairdressers who compounded their own powders and creams, purchasing raw ingredients through wholesalers and jobbers. The catalogs of leading wholesale druggists, for example, contained only a few commercially made preparations but carried a full line of oils, waxes, powders, chemicals, dyes, and perfumes required in cosmetic formulas. In the late nineteenth century, cosmetics manufactured solely for a local or regional market far outnumbered those that achieved national distribution.[9]

Although drugstores were the primary purveyors of commercial cosmetics to the public, it was "beauty culture"—and its commercial exploitation by beauty parlor owners, cosmetic manufacturers, women's magazines, advertisers, and retailers—that fundamentally altered the market for cosmetics. Beauty culture became the crucial intermediary between a women's culture suspicious of powder and paint to one that delighted in them. Beginning in the 1880s, beauty culturists popularized the notion of ritualizing beautification for women. Beauty salons were initially places for the dressing and ornamentation of hair, but by the 1890s they had expanded their services to include facial treatments, manicures, and massage. At their most grand, these salons were service stations for elite and middle-class women's enhancement and relaxation.[10] But on a more modest scale, beauty culture was also available to women of lesser means, and was particularly important to African American women; indeed, the latter pioneered in the development of hair and skin treatments and products, creating one of the leading black-owned businesses in the United States.

The origins of the "class" segment of the cosmetics industry lie in the development of beauty culture for elite and upwardly mobile white women. In salons located on prestigious commercial streets and at expensive resorts, beauty culturists consciously created a paradoxical world of discipline and indulgence, therapy and luxury.[11] For women who had long been enjoined to sacrifice their own desires on behalf of husband and family, the message was irresistible: Women could fulfill the old prescription of "beauty a duty" while at the same time giving in to the siren call of a newer consumerist message. In the words of cosmetologist Susanna Cocroft, "Don' be ashamed of your desire for beauty."[12]

Ironically, beauty culturists generally did not approve of makeup, stressing breathing, exercise, diet, and bathing as the route to natural beauty. Madame Yale, a typical popularizer, warned women to avoid "fashion's glamor and the artificer's whims." For beauty culturists, as for many nineteenth-century Americans, the face was a window into the soul, and complexion problems were indicative of a life that was disordered, out of balance. Thus Susanna Cocroft asked women: "Is your complexion *clear?* Does it express the clearness of your life? Are there discolorations or blemishes in the skin—which symbolize imperfections within?" Beauty culture promised self-transformation that was both internal and external, an idea that resonated powerfully in American middle-class culture (Fig. 20.1).[13]

Beauty culturists initially offered face powder, rouge, and other makeup somewhat apologetically, or even with a tone of exasperation: "Outward applications only have the office of assisting in, and completing, the process which must begin *within*." Madame Yale in the 1890s sold a liquid powder, rouge, and lip tint that she termed "Temporary Beautifiers." She rather grudgingly noted their purchase by "many ladies . . . too indolent to cultivate natural beauty by the Yale System of Beauty Culture" or by "actresses and all whose inclinations or pursuits render 'makeup' necessary."[14]

Nevertheless, the dynamics of beauty culture led to the greater acceptance of cosmetics. By making the complexion, rather than bone structure or physical features, more central to popular definitions of beauty, it popularized the democratic idea that beauty could be achieved by all women if only they used the correct products and treatment. This logic led to the assertion that every woman *should* be beautiful—as a duty to her husband and children, in order to achieve

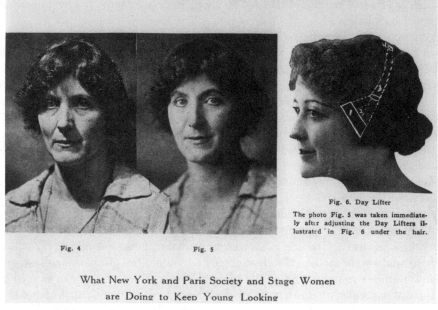

Fig. 6. Day Lifter

The photo Fig. 5 was taken immediately after adjusting the Day Lifters illustrated in Fig. 6 under the hair.

Fig. 4   Fig. 5

What New York and Paris Society and Stage Women
are Doing to Keep Young Looking

Figure 20.1. Detail from Susanna Cocroft's "Success Face Lifters" pamphlet. Warshaw Collection of Business Americana, Archives Center, National Museum of American History, Smithsonian Institution. Photo No. 89-14354.

business success, or to find romance—and those who were not beautiful had only themselves to blame.

Beauty culturists also foregrounded the *process* of achieving beauty, not just the end product, and moved that process into popular discourse—in the semipublic environment of beauty salons and in the widely read pages of women's magazines and newspapers. The development of beauty "systems" or "methods" was particularly important. Such "systems" replaced apprenticeship and oral tradition with formal instruction in beauty culture and cosmetology, and proved quite profitable for a number of entrepreneurs who developed beauty schools and correspondence courses. But the notion of a beauty "system" or "method" also changed the consumer's relationship to cosmetics by encouraging the systematic, step-by-step process of beauty application. Beauty culturists, that is, replaced all-purpose creams and lotions with a series of specialized products, each designed to perform a single function. The more entrepreneurial of them not only manufactured these products for the home use of their clients but also began to market them to women who did not have direct access to exclusive urban salons, largely through department stores, drugstores, and mail order. By the early twentieth century, beauty culturists' ambivalence toward powder and paint diminished as they saw the possibilities for profit in makeup product lines.[15]

The career of Elizabeth Arden, born Florence Nightingale Graham, illustrates a dominant pattern of entrepreneurship in beauty culture that led to the development of the "class market." She began her career in Eleanor Adair's beauty salon in New York City, first as a receptionist and then as a beauty operator specializing in facials. Soon she became partners with cosmetologist Elizabeth Hubbard, opening a Fifth Avenue salon in 1909 on the strength of Hubbard's products and her own treatment techniques. When their partnership dissolved, Graham took over the salon, lavishly decorated it for an elite clientele, and began to improve on Hubbard's formulas. It was at this time that she transformed herself into Miss Elizabeth Arden, a name she perceived to be romantic and high class. After the first salon was successful, she opened others in a number of cities. Initially the salons offered the usual complexion cures, facials, massage, and hairdressing, but by 1915 Arden had begun to make up her customers, although she did not advertise this service. In 1918 Arden decided to expand sales by going after store orders in fancy retail shops and department stores, often giving them exclusive rights to sell her line in a particular locality. She sent trained representatives or "demonstrators" to teach saleswomen how to sell her products. By 1920 she had developed an extensive product line that included skin care treatments and a full line of face makeup, using Ardena and Venetian as tradenames. According to her biographer, by 1925 Arden's domestic wholesale division was grossing two million dollars each year, from sales to women whose families had incomes in the top 3 percent in the United States.[16]

Other beauty culture entrepreneurs, such as Helena Rubinstein and Dorothy Gray, followed the same route to success: first establishing salons for society women, then developing nationally distributed product lines that conveyed a sense of exclusivity and richness to their clientele. At this time, importers also increased the number and variety of products they offered to wholesalers and retailers. Fine-quality imported goods from France and England had long been available to elite women, but by the 1910s firms (such as Coty) from these countries had begun to open branches and offices in the United States to exploit the growing demand for cosmetics. Department store buyers also were increasingly important in providing high-priced goods to the public. Along with beauty culturists, these were critical figures in expanding the class market for cosmetics, countering the image of the painted woman with connotations of gentility, refinement, and social status.

In contrast, the "mass" segment of the cosmetics industry grew out of the pharmaceutical and drugstore trade after 1900, when a few products broke out of their local market and secured national distribution and brand name recognition. Usually these were creams and lotions, often used by both women and men. Hinds' Honey and Almond Cream, for example, was formulated in 1872 by a Portland, Maine, drugstore owner who gradually went into manufacturing full time and entered the Boston and New York City markets. In 1905 Aurelius S. Hinds conducted his first nationwide advertising campaign, and five years later added vanishing cream and other products to his line.[17] While Hinds and other skin care products achieved success in the national market, visible makeup such as rouge and lipstick had more limited distribution before World War I.

The outlets for mass market cosmetics were varied. Independent drugstores and general stores remained important, especially in small towns, but sales of cosmetics were boosted by emergent forms of national distribution: chain drugstores and variety stores, department stores, and large mail-order outfits, as well as systematized house-to-house selling.[18] The new chain stores aggressively pushed a full range of inexpensive brand name products, as well as private label cosmetics. Both independent and chain merchandisers sought to base drugstore profits not only on the dispensing of medicines and drugs but on the sale of goods consumers needed on an everyday basis, including toiletries. Department store merchandisers similarly found that toiletries and sundries, including soaps, brushes, and rubber goods as well as cosmetics and perfumes, could draw women into the stores; some carried both class and mass products, displaying them in eye-catching cases on the main selling floor.[19]

Mail-order houses were initially conservative in the lines they carried, reflecting their small-town and rural clientele of housewives and older women. Catalogs of the late nineteenth century tended to group cosmetics inconsequentially with food, patent medicines, and soaps. Yet as early as 1897 Sears offered its own line of toilet preparations, including rouge, eyebrow pencil, and face powder in three colors, as well as such brand names as Ayer's, Pozzoni's, and Tetlow's. The Larkin Company, which began as a soap manufacturer and expanded into general catalog sales, buried cosmetics in the back pages of the 1907 catalog, but by the early 1920s had begun to feature them in the opening pages, accompanied by flowery descriptions and color illustrations.[20]

The advertising of mass-market cosmetics also underwent important changes in this period. Since few companies in the nineteenth century saw cosmetics as their primary product, relatively little money was spent on developing marketing or advertising strategies. Cosmetics were advertised mainly on trade cards, displays, and posters, as well as almanacs, sample envelopes, sheet music, and broadsides. Some firms advertised at expositions and world's fairs; Lundborg's perfume fountain, for example, was a popular attraction at the 1893 Columbian Exposition in Chicago.[21]

Magazine advertising, however, was quite limited before 1900: Only a few firms advertised in women's magazines, and their advertisements (usually for creams and powders, rarely rouge) were set in small type in the back pages—in contrast, for example, to soap advertisements, which often appeared on full pages or magazine covers. In the 1910s, however, large-scale national advertising of cosmetics began in earnest, and by the early 1920s it had become a dominant force in women's magazines.[22]

In the late nineteenth century manufacturers and advertisers of mass-market cosmetics responded to widespread consumer resistance in several ways. They took pains to stress the safety of their products, seeking to identify them with the widespread cult of health and cleanliness. Some made therapeutic claims for face powders and liquid tints; Stoddart's Peerless Face Powder, for example, was touted as "approved by the medical Profession." The invisibility of the products, moreover, guaranteed that a woman would not be perceived as painted and immoral. Ricksecker's powder, for example, was "*modestly invisible* when used with discrimination." Manufacturers such as Pozzoni's stressed the naturalness and purity of their preparations by using angelic children in their advertising (Fig. 20.2). Even a tag like "Just a Kiss," featured on Tetlow's packaging, played coquetry off against innocence (Fig. 20.3).[23]

While a logical response to consumers' fears, this advertising tactic was ultimately a self-defeating one. The industry's growth depended on its ability to convince women not only to use cosmetics but to buy as many different products as possible. Making appeals to the naturalness and invisibility of cosmetics could not accomplish this; rather, manufacturers needed to convince women of the acceptability of artifice and visible color.

Many companies in the early twentieth century found this a difficult idea to promote; like the beauty culturists, most of them argued that their products merely "improved on nature." Yet the growing importance of color can be seen in the expansion of product lines. Some manufacturers who had succeeded in marketing a cream or lotion began to create coordinated sets of products, somewhat akin to the beauty culturists' notion of "system." Propounding a domino theory of cosmetics use, they argued that once a woman started using face powder, she would inevitably be drawn to complementary, although more daring, products such as rouge and lipstick. Increasingly they appealed to artifice in the pursuit of "natural beauty." Women were urged to buy several face powders and blend them for a natural look; or buy specialized powders, such as a violet tint to wear under artificial light; or wear matching lip tints and rouge to achieve the "bloom of youth."[24]

At this time, a number of entrepreneurs began to produce and market new cosmetic products that asserted and even celebrated artifice. Lipsticks and eyeshadows in colorful shades, for example, made their appearance on the market after World War I. "Mascaro," which in the nineteenth century had been a general-purpose touch-up for light or graying hair used by both men and women, became specialized as "mascara," a woman's cosmetic for eyelashes. Manufacturers sold cosmetics in luxurious sets to be seen on dressing tables, but even more popular were goods packaged in portable containers. Compacts for face powder and rouge and the lipstick cylinder were marketed in the 1910s, suggesting the increasingly public place of cosmetics.

Manufacturers of mass-market goods often developed a single product, one that was socially unacceptable or controversial, and aggressively promoted it in the trade press and in national advertising. In so doing, they turned to sources of cultural legitimation other than that of middle-class and elite beauty culture.

Figure 20.2. Pozzoni's Face Powder advertising card. Warshaw Collection of Business Americana, Archives Center, National Museum of American History, Smithsonian Institution.

Social definitions of womanhood were strongly contested from the late nineteenth century onward. The ideal of the "New Woman" represented a departure from concepts of female identity constituted solely in domestic pursuits, sexual purity, and moral motherhood. Yet this new ideal was an unstable one. For some, the New Woman was a mannish, political, and professional woman who had entered the public sphere on her own terms. For others, the New Woman was a sensual, free-spirited girl—in the 1880s a "Daisy," by the 1910s and 1920s a flapper. The latter figure embodied another set of contradictions: She was at once an independent wage earner, making own way in the world, and a beautiful, romantic girl, seeking marital fulfillment. This image became increasingly important in the selling of mass-market cosmetics, as manufacturers and advertisers sought to appeal particularly to the rising number of young working women of both middle-class and working-class origins.[25]

An important tactic of the industry was to link cosmetics to emergent forms of popular entertainment and leisure, especially the motion pictures. Mary Pickford's screen image of youthful innocence sold such mass-market creams and lotions as Pompeian in general-circulation periodicals and traditional women's magazines (Fig. 20.4). The cosmetics of arti-fice, in contrast, were heavily advertised in the new confession magazines and "fanzines," such as *True Story* and *Photoplay*, directed at young working-class and middle-class women. Drug-store promotions and display windows also capitalized on the movie craze. Maybelline, for example, marketed its sole product, mascara, by using close-up photographs of movie stars

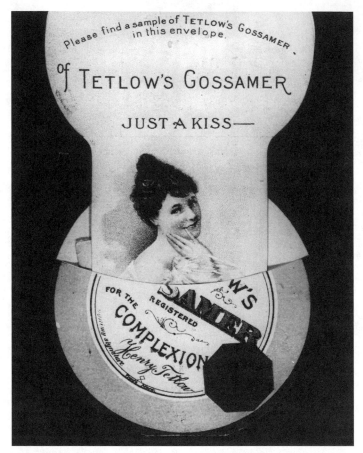

Figure 20.3. Tetlow's Gossamer "Just a Kiss" powder sample envelope. Warshaw Collection of Business Americana, Archives Center, National Museum of American History, Smithsonian Institution. Photo No. 88–1157.

with heavily painted eyes and eyelashes in its magazine advertising and on display cards (Fig. 20.5).[26]

The connection between motion pictures and cosmetics was in some cases quite direct: The movie industry's makeup experts often made technological breakthroughs in products that were then applied to everyday cosmetics. Max Factor, a Russian immigrant, is the most prominent example of a "makeup artist to the stars" who went into cosmetics manufacturing for the mass market. But as important to the cosmetics industry were the "look" and style of female screen stars who promoted the use of color and artifice. Although the theater may have affected everyday makeup practices, the movies were far more influential because of their enormous popularity, and because close-up cinematography could magnify heavily painted lips, eyes, and cheeks. Certainly the cultural style of many working women and early flappers who wore provocative makeup, hair styles, and fashionable clothing was legitimized and reinforced by what they saw on the screen. By the late 1920s, as the Payne Fund studies indicate, young women from a range of socioeconomic backgrounds modeled their cosmetics use, and manners generally, on the movie images they saw. Exploiting the movie industry tie-in, mass-market manufacturers promoted glamor as an integral part of women's identity.[27]

The African American segment of the industry emerged in the late nineteenth century, part of the more general development of an African American consumer market. Constrained even

Figure 20.4. Mary Pickford, 1917, Pompeian Beauty Panel. Warshaw Collection of Business Americana, Archives Center, National Museum of American History, Smithsonian Institution.

more than white working people by poverty, most blacks had little spending money for anything beyond the goods essential for survival. Yet a nascent middle class, black migration, and the growing racial segregation of cities spurred some entrepreneurs to develop businesses serving black consumers.[28] Some white-owned firms cultivated this market for cosmetics in the black community as early as the 1890s. The Lyon Manufacturing Company, for example, a Brooklyn-based firm that sold patent medicines, advertised its Kaitharon hair tonic to blacks through

Figure 20.5. Maybelline advertisement, *Photoplay* (1920). *Courtesy Maybelline, Inc.*

almanacs and ad cards. The product was touted as a straightener for kinky hair, with testimonials from African American ministers, political leaders, and schoolteachers.[29]

Far more important at this time, however, was the development of African American beauty culture and a hair and skin care industry owned by blacks. Such figures as Anthony Overton, Annie Turnbo Malone, and Madame C. J. Walker were among the most successful African American entrepreneurs to market face creams, hair oils, and other products. Several black-owned firms developed out of the drugstore supplies trade or began as small cosmetics companies. Anthony Overton, who by 1916 had built up one of the largest black-owned businesses in the United States, began his career as a peddler and baking powder manufacturer. He shifted into cosmetics when his daughter's formula for a face powder proved popular in their community. Using networks of distribution he had already established, Overton sold his High Brown Face Powder through an army of door-to-door agents.[30]

Even more significant, however, were the women entrepreneurs who developed African American beauty culture. Beauty culture offered black women good employment opportunities in the sex- and race-segregated labor market: It required low capitalization, was an easy trade to learn, and was much in demand. Beauty parlors could be operated cheaply in homes, apartments, and small shops, and hair and skin care products could be mixed in one's kitchen to be sold locally. Since drugstores, chain stores, and department stores often refused to locate in the black community, door-to-door and salon sales were the dominant forms of distribution. Advertising was generally limited to black-owned newspapers, although large companies such as Poro purchased space in many of them throughout the country, achieving a kind of "national" advertising.[31]

Annie Turnbo Malone (the founder of Poro), Madame C. J. Walker, and others pioneered in the development of beauty systems that would ensure black women smooth, manageable hair. White racism had symbolically linked the supposedly "natural" inferiority of blacks to an appearance marked by unruly, "kinky" hair and slovenliness in dress. As Gwendolyn Robinson has argued in her study of the African American cosmetics industry, the dominant culture's ascription of promiscuity to black women led them to stress the importance of looking respectable. For black women, hair care, including straightening, was one external marker of personal success and racial progress, signifying a response to the white denigration of black womanhood. The beauty culturists asserted and exploited this view in their advertising. Madame Walker, for example, ran a full-page newspaper ad in 1928 whose headline announced "Amazing Progress of Colored Race—Improved Appearance Responsible."[32]

Like the white beauty culturists, the leading black entrepreneurs had developed extensive product lines in skin care and cosmetics by World War I, including face creams, bleaches, and powders. Some of these products and beauty systems, especially hair straightening and skin bleaching, were highly controversial in the black community. They sparked debate over black emulation of dominant white aesthetics, and over the issue of color differences among African Americans. The use of cosmetics not only rendered gender definitions (that is, what constituted female respectability) problematic but tied those definitions to "race consciousness" and black resistance to white domination as well.

The response of African American beauty culturists was complex, adhering to the dominant aesthetic while asserting the centrality of the industry to collective black advancement. Unlike the white industry, African American beauty culturists evidenced a genuine commitment to work on behalf of their community. Walker and Malone trained thousands of black women in their methods to become sales agents, salon owners, and beauty operatives; their promotional literature and handbooks continually emphasized their commitment to black women's employment and the economic progress of African Americans. In the absence of many commercial outlets, Walker sought a relationship with women's clubs and churches, offering promotions, beauty shows, and product sales to help raise funds for these organizations. Moreover, the sales methods—salon operatives and door-to-door agents selling to friends and neighbors—probably enhanced the web of mutual support and assistance integral to black women's culture. The integration of this industry with aspects of black community life and politics sets it apart from the white industry.[33]

Cultural Constructions of Gender, Class, and Race

Despite the difference in their origins, patterns of distribution, and markets, the three segments of the cosmetics industry developed a number of similar products and encountered many of the same issues. The industry converged in certain ways in its handling of gender, responding to social and cultural changes affecting women's attitudes toward appearance, redefining popular notions of female sexual and social respectability to include cosmetics use, and then revising definitions of female beauty into ideals that could be achieved only through cosmetics. Whatever the class and race of cosmetics consumers, all segments of the industry in their advertising and marketing reshaped the relationship between appearance and feminine identity by promoting the externalization of the gendered self, a process much in tune with the tendencies of mass culture.[34]

What to beauty culturists had been a simultaneous process of transforming the interior self and external appearance became in the hands of the twentieth-century cosmetics industry the "makeover." Makeup promised each woman the tools to express her "true" self, indeed, to experiment until she found it. Cosmetics communicated the self to others and infused the self with a sense of esteem and legitimacy. In this new attention to personality and novelty, being able to find yourself and change yourself, cosmetics manufacturers began to reorient their industry away from beauty culture and toward "fashion," allowing for an endless number of "looks" and an endless proliferation of products.[35]

But the linkage of female individuality, self-expression, and respectability held different meanings in the different contexts under which cosmetics were sold. While a full-scale analysis of the divisions of class and race embedded in the industry's cultural messages cannot be attempted here, I will suggest one route such an analysis might take: the tension between the appearance of Anglo-Saxon gentility and the exploitation of "foreign" exoticism.

While invoking ideas of female self-expression through the use of makeup, the cosmetics industry in the 1910s and 1920s never transcended the problem of class that had been raised in the nineteenth-century identification of "paint" with immorality. The "class" end of the industry had long stressed the gentility and refinement possible through skin care regimens; they now applied this argument to the use of makeup and artifice. The French cachet of imported goods was especially important in conveying status and "chic." Until the 1906 Food and Drug Act prohibited misbranding and false labeling, U.S. companies frequently identified their products as made in Paris.[36] After 1906 they used foreign-sounding, aristocratic trade names, such as Rubinstein's Valaze line and Arden's Ardena, or they claimed the use of French formulas. Although manufacturing their products in the United States, Arden and Rubinstein commonly made reference to the cosmetic practices of Parisian women as examples American women should emulate. By 1919 national advertisers of cosmetics, particularly of imported brands, had adopted "atmosphere advertisements" depicting the lifestyles of the rich and famous. Dorin face powders and compacts, for example, were associated with Saratoga Springs, the Paris Opera, and the races at Ascot: "Not all the users of La Dorine can be members of smart clubs but they are all eager to enjoy as much of the dainty refinement of the fashionable world as they can."[37]

Companies selling cosmetics to blacks also used images of refinement and social improvement to sell their products, but this strategy must be placed in the overall context of racial stereotyping and black aspirations. The advertising for the highly successful Overton Hygienic Manufacturing Company, for example, featured light-skinned, refined-looking women and appealed more to respectability and gentility than elitism (Fig. 20.6). In contrast, Kashmir

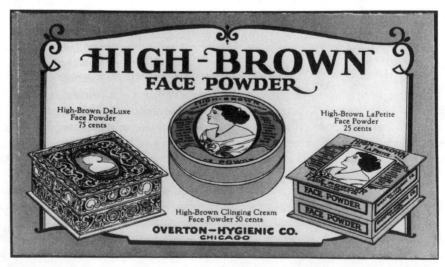

Figure 20.6. Overton-Hygienic High Brown Face Powder packet. Curt Teich Postcard Archives, Lake County Museum, Wauconda, Illionois.

Chemical Company, a black-owned firm with a brief life in the late 1910s and early 1920s, frequently used advertising with very fashionably dressed women sitting at dressing tables or in automobiles—ads that emulated the elite images common in main stream magazines.[38]

Mass-market manufacturers stressed the makeover as a route to upward mobility, arguing that a woman's personal success relied on her appearance. As one manufacturer's pamphlet observed, "You can select ten ordinary girls from a factory and by the skillful use of such preparations as Kijja and proper toilet articles . . . you can in a short time make them as attractive and good-looking as most any ten wealthy society girls . . . [I]t is not so much a matter of beauty with different classes of girls as it is how they are fixed up." A similar story is told in a 1924 trade advertisement for Zip depilatory: A dark-skinned woman, her appearance suggesting an eastern or southern European immigrant, is able to achieve social acceptance, implicitly among her Americanized friends, by ridding herself of superfluous hair (Fig. 20.7).[39]

Some manufacturers, particularly at the class end of the industry, sought to dissociate themselves from any cosmetic practices that might be understood as working-class and "vulgar." The trade press, for example, editorialized against putting on makeup in public places, that is, *showing* the artifice; one writer even wanted to start a campaign among sales personnel to advise

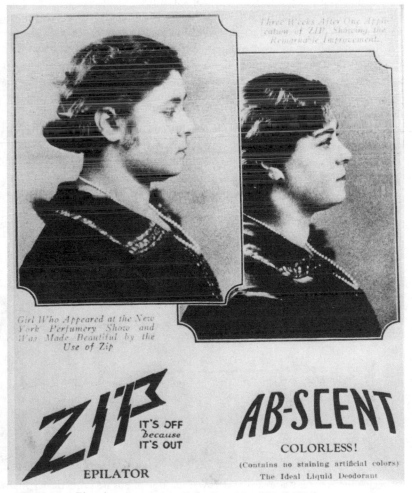

Figure 20.7. Detail from Zip advertisement, in *Toilet Requisites* (April 1924).

their customers against the use of too much face powder. Advice books and women's magazines were particularly directive about extreme cosmetic use: Powdering one's nose in restaurants or shops "stamps you as having poor breeding," noted one; another condemned "girls on the streets everyday with their faces daubed like uncivilized Indians." Of vivid red lips, yet another observed, "You cannot afford to make yourself ridiculous if you have started for success, or you want to attract a REAL man."[40] Much of this was a response to young women's cosmetic practices, particularly the "made-up" look of working-class women.

As the reference above to "uncivilized Indians" suggests, manufacturers not only dealt with the cultural identification of "paint" and artifice with class but also with a deeply embedded set of resonances concerning race, ethnicity, and color in American society. Mass-market manufacturers, for example, often employed exotic images of foreign peoples to advertise products that did not have a distinct place in white bourgeois culture. An instructive comparison might be made with the soap industry, which created advertisements associating cleanliness with colonization and Anglo American supremacy (Fig. 20.8). Cosmetics manufacturers, in contrast, used images of American Indian, Egyptian, Turkish, and Japanese women as well as European women to link reluctant Americans to a global cosmetic culture (Fig. 20.9). Versions of "Little Egypt," who caused a furor at the 1893 Columbian Exposition, sold rouge and other cosmetics of artifice. This fascination with the foreign and exotic, fueled by Western imperialism, can be seen throughout American culture in the late nineteenth century.[41]

In the hands of cosmetics manufacturers, exoticism continued to be powerful long into the twentieth century. Advertisers created narratives about beauty culture through the ages, bypassing the Greco-Roman tradition in favor of Egypt and Persia. Cleopatra was virtually a cult figure, displayed in advertising to all segments of the market. Kashmir's Nile Queen line, for example, juxtaposed images of genteel black womanhood with frankly sensual representations of naked and semiclothed women. Promotions of lower-priced makeup, particularly rouge, eye shadow, and mascara, frequently used exotic "vamp" images.[42]

Advertisers also linked "foreign types" to the realization of women's identity through cosmetics. The Armand complexion powder campaign of 1928–29 instructed women to "find yourself," using a question-and-answer book written by a "famous psychologist and a noted

Figure 20.8. Higgins and Foweler trade card. Warshaw Collection of Business Americana, Archives Center, National Museum of American History, Smithsonian Institution. Photo No. 89–143 52.

Figure 20.9. Murray and Lanham's Florida Water advertising card. Warshaw Collection of Business Americana, Archives Center, National Museum American History, Smithsonian Institution.

beauty expert"; however, individuality was submerged into a typology that coded appearance and personality together according to ethnic euphemisms—Godiva, Colleen, Mona Lisa, Sheba, Sonya, Cheric, Lorelei, and, of course, Cleopatra (Fig. 20.10).[43]

At the same time, the cosmetics industry at all levels projected contradictory cultural messages linking whiteness with social success and refinement. With the sale of bleach cream and light-colored face powders, this issue became a particularly controversial one within the black community. Products with names like Black-No-More and Tan Off, many of which were manufactured by white-owned companies as well as black-owned ones, baldly appealed to European aesthetic standards and the belief that light-skinned African Americans were more successful and, if women, more desirable as wives. Others struck a more ambivalent tone: Golden Brown Ointment, for example, instructed consumers, "Don't be fooled by so-called 'Skin Whiteners.'" The company admonished that its product "won't whiten your skin—as that can't be done," yet claimed that the ointment produced a "soft, light, bright, smooth complexion" that would "help in business or social life."[44]

It is crucial to note, however, that bleach creams, produced by class and mass manufacturers, were also widely advertised to white women. Until the mid-1920s, when the sun-tanning craze swept the United States, bleach creams were touted as a means of acquiring a whiteness that connoted gentility, female domesticity, "protection" from labor, the exacting standards of the elite, and Anglo-Saxon superiority. Most of the time advertisers treated such issues obliquely, but

Cleopatra Type
Masculine hearts pound when she goes by

Godiva Type
Anglo-Saxon, blond, winsome, and how!

Sonya Type
Dark and mysterious, she has a way with her

Cherie Type
She brings the boulevards of Paris to America

Sheba Type
Dark-brown hair and a queenly air

Lorelei Type
Blond and aggressive, she "gets her man"

Mona Lisa Type
Light-brown hair and a devastating smile

Colleen Type
She has more pep than a jazz band

Figure 20.10. "Which of These Alluring Types Are You?" Detail from the Armand Complexion Powder as proof, 1929 N. W. Ayer Collection, Archives Center, National Museum of American History, Smithsonian Institution. Photo No. 89–143 53.

they could be quite direct. One series of silhouettes, appearing in a late-nineteenth-century advertisement for Hagan's Magnolia Balm, a skin bleach sold to white women, used physiognomic signifiers to convey that light skin meant Anglo-Saxon gentility. In these images, not only does the woman's skin color lighten upon using the product, but her features undergo a transformation from a stereotyped rural black woman to a genteel lady (Fig. 20.11). Several

BEFORE USING.   USING.   AFTER USING.

Figure 20.11. Detail from Lyon's Manufacturing Company, "The Secret of Health and Beauty" pamphlet. Warshaw Collection of Business Americana, Archives Center, National Museum of American History, Smithsonian Institution. Photo No. 89–143 51.

decades later, manufacturer Albert F. Wood could declare quite openly; "A white person objects to a swarthy brown-hued or mulatto-like skin, therefore if staying much out of doors use regularly Satin Skin Varnishing Greaseless Cream to keep the skin normally white."[45]

Such explicit and covert attention to race and ethnicity in a business devoted in large part to coloration should not be surprising if we recall the history of this period: the extensive immigration of peoples who looked "different" from earlier Western European immigrants and threatened to be unassimilable; intensified consciousness about "race" spurred by legal segregation, heightened violence against blacks, and northern migration; and the growing acceptance of scientific racism, which ordered human progress, including the attainment of physical beauty, according to racial-ethnic types, with white Anglo-Saxons at the top of that hierarchy. What I would suggest is that the cosmetics industry has historically taken discourses of class, ethnicity, race, and gender—discourses that generate deeply held conscious and unconscious feelings of fear, anxiety, and even self-hatred—and displaced them onto safe rhetorical fields, in this case, a language of "color" and "type," a rhetoric of "naturalness," "expressiveness," and "individuality."[46]

The cosmetics industry played a crucial role in defining the appearance of femininity in the early twentieth century, but it was not the only player. How women consumers of different social groups shaped those definitions remains an open question for historical research. The profound changes in women's lives in this period may well have spurred women to indulge new fantasies of beauty and calculate differently its material and psychological benefits. Undoubtedly many women did not receive the intended messages of manufacturers and advertisers passively, but how they used cosmetics and understood their meaning must, at this point, be left to speculation.[47]

Clearly the cosmetics industry responded to a larger cultural field of established and emergent images and definitions of femininity, crosscut by class and race. In various ways the industry worked with those images, reshaping them in response to its perceptions of women's fears and desires. If, in the early twentieth century, some Americans sought to define female selfhood in meaningful ways (through the act of thinking or through productive labor, for example), the cosmetics industry foregrounded the notion that one's "look" was not only the expression of female identity but its essence as well. In this, the mass, class, and African American ends of the industry converged. Although the cosmetics industry may not have controlled the discourse over femininity, the multibillion-dollar industry that exists today is testimony to its ability to convince women to purchase, as Charles Revson cynically put it, "hope in a jar."

Notes

1. See, e.g., Lary May, *Screening Out the Past: The Birth of Mass Culture and the Motion Picture Industry* (New York: Oxford University Press, 1980); Roland Marchand, *Advertising the American Dream: Making Way for Modernity* (Berkeley: University of California Press, 1985), 176–88; Lewis A. Erenberg, *Steppin'Out: New York Nightlife and the Transformation of American Culture, 1890–1930* (Westport, Conn: Greenwood Press, 1981); Martha Banta, *Imaging American Women: Idea and Ideals in Cultural History* (New York: Columbia University Press, 1987); William R. Leach, "Transformations in a Culture of Consumption: Women and Department Stores, 1890–1925," *Journal of American History* 71 (September 1984): 319–42.
2. Lois Banner, *American Beauty* (Chicago: University of Chicago Press, 1983). Among the many advice books and formularies, see, e.g., *The American Family Keepsake of People's Practical Cyclopedia* (Boston, 1849); Smith and Swinney, *The House-Keeper's Guide and Everybody's Hand-Book* (Cincinnati, 1868); *The American Ladies' Memorial: An Indispensable Home Book for the Wife, Mother, Daughter* (Boston, 1850); Emily Thornwell, *The Lady's Guide to Perfect Gentility* (New York: Derby and Jackson, 1857). See also Cosmetics files in the Warshaw Collection of Business Americana, Archives Center, National Museum of American History, Smithsonian Institution (hereafter cited as Warshaw), a rich collection of advertising graphics, posters, pamphlets, and ephemera.
3. Banner, *American Beauty*, 42–44, 119; Arnold James Cooley, *Instructions and Cautions Respecting the Selection and Use of Perfumes, Cosmetics and Other Toilet Articles* (Philadelphia: J. B. Lippincott and Company, 1873), 428.
4. On working women's subculture, see Christine Stansell, *City of Women: Sex and Class in New York, 1789–1860* (New York: Knopf, 1986); and Kathy Peiss, *Cheap Amusements: Working Women and Leisure in Turn-of-the-Century New York* (Philadelphia: Temple University Press, 1986).
5. Gwendolyn Robinson, "Class, Race and Gender: A Transcultural, Theoretical and Sociohistorical Analysis of Cosmetic Institutions and Practices to 1920" (Ph.D. diss., University of Illinois at Chicago, 1984), ch. 2.
6. Lola Montez, *The Art of Beauty: or Secrets of a Lady's Toilet* (New York: Dick and Fitzgerald, 1853), xii–xiii, 47; Cooley, *Instructions and Cautions;* Karen Haltunen, *Confidence Men and Painted Women: A Study of Middle-Class Culture in America, 1830–1870* (New Haven: Yale University Press, 1982).
7. For analyses that speak to the intersection of class and gender in the nineteenth century, see Stansell, *City of Women*, and Nancy Hewitt, "Beyond the Search for Sisterhood: American Women's History in the 1980s," *Social History* 10 (1985): 299–321.
8. For statistics on the cosmetics industry, see U.S. Bureau of the Census, *Census of Manufactures: Patent & Proprietary Medicines and Compounds & Druggists' Preparations* (Washington, D.C.: U.S. Government Printing Office, 1919); and *Toilet Requisites* 6 (June 1921): 26. On the patent medicine industry, see James Harvey Young, *The Toadstool Millionaires: A Social History of Patent Medicines in America before Federal Regulation* (Princeton: Princeton University Press, 1961); and Sarah Stage, *Female Complaints: Lydia Pinkham and the Business of Women's Medicine* (New York: Norton, 1979). On soap, see Richard L. Bushman and Claudia L. Bushman, "The Early History of Cleanliness in America," *Journal of American History* 74 (1988): 1213–38.
9. For druggists' formularies, see John H. Nelson, *Druggists' Hand-Book of Private Formulas*, 3rd ed. (Cleveland, 1879); Charles E. Hamlin, *Hamlin's Formulae, or Every Druggist His Own Perfumer* (Baltimore: Edward B. Read and Son, 1885). Trade catalogs document wholesale druggists' goods: see, e.g., W.H. Schieffelin and Company, *General Prices Current of Foreign and Domestic Drugs, Medicines, Chemicals . . .* (New York, March 1881); and Bolton Drug Company, *Illustrated Price List* (ca. 1890), both in Archives Center, National Museum of American History; Brown, Durrell and Company, *The Trade Monthly* (Boston, January 1895) and others in *Trade Catalogues at Winterthur, 1750–1980* (Clearwater Publishing Company microfilm collection). For a general history, see Edward Kremers and George Urdang, *Kremer's and Urdang's History of Pharmacy*, 4th ed. (Philadelphia: J. B. Lippincott Company, 1976).
10. Banner, *American Beauty*, 28–44, 202–25. See also Anne Hard, "The Beauty Business," *American Magazine* 69 (November 1909): 79–90.
11. For general background on female cosmetics entrepreneurs, see Margaret Allen, *Selling Dreams: Inside the Beauty Business* (New York: Simon and Schuster, 1981); Maxene Fabe, *Beauty Millionaire: The Life of Helena Rubinstein* (New York: Thomas Y. Crowell, 1972); Patrick O'Higgins, *Madame: An Intimate*

Biography of Helena Rubinstein (New York: Viking Press, 1971); Alfred Allan Lewis and Constance Woodworth, *Miss Elizabeth Arden* (New York: Coward, McCann, and Geoghegan, 1972). The latter two biographies, written in breathless prose, include fascinating gossip but are questionable histories.

12. Susanna Cocroft, *How to Secure a Beatiful Complexion and Beautiful Eyes: A Practical Course in Beauty Culture* (Chicago: James J. Clarke and Company, 1911) in Cosmetics, Warshaw. See also her *Beauty a Duty: The Art of Keeping Young* (Chicago: Rand McNally, 1915).

13. Madame Yale, *The Science of Health and Beauty* (n.p., 1893), 6, in Cosmetics, Warshaw; Cocroft, *Beautiful Complexion.*

14. Yale, *Science of Health and Beauty*, 26.

15. See n. 11, and also Paulette School, *Beauty Culture at Home* (Washington, D.C.: n.p., 1914); E. Burnham, *The Coiffure*, catalog no. 37 (Chicago, 1908), in Hair files, Warshaw.

16. Lewis and Woodworth, *Elizabeth Arden.*

17. *Toilet Requisites* 10 (October 1925): 64. *Toilet Requisites*, later *Beauty Fashion*, was the trade journal for buyers and retailers of cosmetics, toiletries, and druggists' sundries; founded in 1916, it is an excellent source for developments in the industry.

18. Alfred D. Chandler Jr., *The Visible Hand: The Managerial Revolution in American Business* (Cambridge: Harvard University Press, 1977), ch. 7. See also Susan Strasser, " 'Refuse All Substitutes': Branded Products and the Relationships of Distribution, 1885–1920" (paper presented at the annual meeting of the American Studies Association, New York, November 1987).

19. See *Fancy Goods Graphics*, 1879–1890; and catalogs from B. Altman and Company, John Wanamaker, Siegel-Cooper, Simpson Crawford Company, and R. H. Macy and Company, ranging in date from 1880 to 1920, all in Dry Goods files, Warshaw. *Toilet Requisites* carried extensive coverage of department store counter and window displays. For a general discussion, see William R. Leach, "Transformations in a Culture of Consumption," and Susan Porter Benson, *Counter Cultures: Saleswomen, Managers and Customers in American Department Stores, 1890–1940* (Urbana: University Illinois Press, 1986).

20. *Sears General Catalogue*, no. 105 (fall 1897); Larkin Company Catalogues, no. 55 (1907) and no. 86 (fall and winter 1921), in Soap files, Warshaw.

21. For late-nineteenth-century advertising, see the material culture sources in Cosmetics, Patent Medicines, and Hair files, in Warshaw. For discussions of the changes in advertising, see Daniel Pope, *The Making of Modern Advertising* (New York: Basic Books, 1983); Robert Jay, *The Trade Card in Nineteenth-Century America* (Columbia: University of Missouri Press, 1987); and for a later period, Marchand, *Advertising the American Dream.*

22. See such mass circulation women's magazines as *Ladies Home Journal and Delineator*, 1890–1920.

23. Ricksecker's Products brochure; Stoddart's Peerless Liquid and Stoddart's Peerless Face Powder trade cards; Harriet Hubbard Ayer, Recamier Cream, and Recamier Balm advertising cards, all in Cosmetics files, Warshaw.

24. For these trends, and those stated in the following paragraph, see *Toilet Requisites*, 1916–25.

25. For discussions of this new cultural ideal among middle-class women, see Banta, *Imaging American Women*; Carroll Smith-Rosenberg, "New Woman as Androgyne," in *Disorderly Conduct: Visions of Gender in Victorian America* (New York: Oxford University Press, 1985); Sheila Rothman, *Women's Proper Place: A History of Changing Ideals and Practices* (New York: Basic Books, 1979). On working-class women, see Peiss, *Cheap Amusements*; and Elizabeth Ewen, *Immigrant Women in the Land of Dollars* (New York: Monthly Review Press, 1985).

26. See *Photoplay and True Story*, 1920–25. Also Photoplay Magazine, *The Age Factor in Selling and Advertising: A Study in a New Phase of Advertising* (Chicago and New York: Photoplay, 1922).

27. See, for example, *Toilet Requisites* 9 (March 1925): 46, on using a scene from the film *Male and Female* in a window display. On women's response to the movies, see Herbert Blumer, *Movies and Conduct* (New York: Macmillan, 1933), 30–58; and Peiss, *Cheap Amusements.*

28. Vanessa Broussard, "Afro-American Images in Advertising, 1880–1920" (M.A. thesis, George Washington University, 1987).

29. Lyon Manufacturing Company, *What Colored People Say* (n.p., n.d.) and *Afro-American Almanac 1897* (n.p.), Patent Medicine files, Warshaw.

30. For the most extensive discussion of the black cosmetics industry, see Robinson, "Class, Race and Gender"; for her treatment of Overton, see 313–39.

31. For insights into cosmetics advertising in black newspapers, see Claude A. Barnett Papers, Archives and Manuscripts Department, Chicago Historical Society, esp. box 262.

32. Robinson, "Class, Race and Gender," 280–82, 347–411, 515. The Walker advertisement appeared in the *Oklahoma Eagle*, 3 March 1928, rotogravure section, in Barnett Papers, box 262, f4. See also Black Cosmetics Industry File, Division of Community Life, National Museum of American History; "Poro Hair & Beauty Culture" handbook (St. Louis, 1922), Barnett Papers. There were many other African

American beauty culturists: see, e.g., Mrs. Mattie E. Hockenhull, *Imported Method in Beauty Culture. First Lessons* (Pine Bluff, Ark.: Gudger Printing Company, 1917); and W. T. McKissick and Company, *McKissick's Famous Universal Agency or System* (Wilmington, Del.: n.p., n.d.), in Hair files, Warshaw.

33. Robinson, "Class, Race and Gender," 449–551.

34. See Warren I. Susman, *Culture as History: The Transformation of American Society in the Twentieth Century* (New York: Pantheon, 1984), especially "'Personality' and the Making of Twentieth-Century Culture," 271–85.

35. For an example of this reorientation, see the Armand complexion powder and proofs, 1916–32, in Armand Co., N. W. Ayer Collection, Archives Center, National Museum of American History, Smithsonian Institution.

36. See *American Perfumer*, 1906–8, for detailed reporting on the effects of the Food and Drug Act, also Bureau of Chemistry, General Correspondence, Record Group 97, Entry 8, National Archives. For a general discussion, see James Harvey Young, *The Medical Messiahs: A Social History of Health Quackery in Twentieth-Century America* (Princeton: Princeton University Press, 1967), chs. 1–3.

37. *Toilet Requisites* 4 (August 1919): 10, and 4 (April 1919): 3.

38. Overton-Hygienic Manufacturing Company, High Brown Face Powder sample envelope, in Curt Teich Postcard Collection, Lake County Museum, Wauconda, Illinois; Kashmir Chemical Company, Nile Queen Cosmetics advertising, box 4, f1 and f2, in Claude A. Barnett Collection, Prima and Photographs Department, Chicago Historical Society.

39. Countess Ceccaldi (Tokolon Company), *Secrets and Arts of Fascination Employed by Cleopatra, the Greatest Enchantress of All Time* (ca. 1920s), in Cosmetics file, Warshaw; Zip advertisement, *Toilet Requisites* 9, 1 (April 1924).

40. *The Secret of Charm and Beauty* (New York: Independent Corporation, 1923), 19, 22–23; Nell Vinick, *Lessons in Loveliness: A Practical Guide to Beauty Secrets* (New York: Longmans, Green and Company, 1930), 46; *Toilet Requisites* 5 (April 1920): 21, and 6 (June 1921): 30–31.

41. Cf. trade cards for Hoyt's German Soap and Murray and Lanham's Florida Water, in Soap and Cosmetics files, respectively, Warshaw. John Kasson in *Amusing the Millions: Coney Island at the Turn of the Century* (New York: Hill and Wang, 1978) discusses middle-class interest in exoticism; thanks also to James Gilbert for his helpful insights on this subject.

42. See e.g., Ceccaldi, *Secrets and Arts of Fascination*; Kashmir Chemical Company, Nile Queen Cosmetics, Barnett Papers. The King Tut craze in 1923 proved profitable to the cosmetics industry: see *Toilet Requisites* 12 (March 1923): 25, and unnumbered page following 32.

43. Armand ad proofs Ayer Book 382, especially Advt. No. 10039, 1929. N. W. Ayer Collection.

44. Golden Brown Ointment advertisement, *New York Age*, 7 February 1920, 5. These advertisements abound in the African American press; see e.g., Crane and Company, *New York Age*, 5 January 1905, 4; M. B. Berger and Company, *New York Age*, 14 January 1909, 3; Black-No-More, *New York Age*, 16 July 1914.

45. Lyon's Manufacturing Company, *The Secret of Health and Beauty* (n.p, n.d.) in Patent Medicines file, Warshaw; Albert F. Wood, *The Way to a Satin Skin* (Detroit, 1923), 8–9, in Archives Center, National Museum of American History.

46. Cf. Frederic Jameson, "Reification and Utopia in Mass Culture," *Social Text* 1 (1979): 130–48.

47. Reception analysis is fraught with difficulties for the historian, but for a theoretical model, see Janice A. Radway, *Reading the Romance: Women, Patriarchy and Popular Literature* (Chapel Hill: University of North Carolina Press, 1984); and Michael Denning, *Mechanic Accents: Dime Novels and Working Class Culture in America* (New York Meuthuen, 1987).

21

"Star Struck"

Acculturation, Adolescence, and Mexican American Women, 1920–1950

Vicki L. Ruiz

Siga las estrellas

[Follow the stars]
—Max Factor cosmetic ad in *La Opinión*, 1927

Ethnic identity, Americanization, and generational tension first captured the historical imagination during the 1950s with the publication of Oscar Handlin's *The Uprooted* and Alfred Kazin's *A Walker in the City*.[1] These issues continue to provoke discussion among both humanists and social scientists. Within the last decade, feminist scholars have expanded and enriched our knowledge of acculturation through the study of immigrant daughters. Cross-class analysis of adolescent culture provides another window into the world of ethnic youth.[2] This vibrant discourse on generation, gender, and U.S. popular culture has a decidedly East Coast orientation. Are patterns typical of working-class immigrants in New York City applicable to those in Los Angeles?

This essay discusses the forces of Americanization and the extent to which they influenced a generation of Mexican American women coming of age during the 1920s and 1930s. The adoption of new cultural forms, however, did not take place in a vacuum. The political and economic environment surrounding Mexican immigrants and their children would color their responses to mainstream U.S. society. The Spanish-speaking population in the United States soared between 1910 and 1930 as over a million mexicanos* migrated northward. Pushed by the economic and political chaos generated by the Mexican Revolution and lured by jobs in U.S. agribusiness and industry, they settled into the existing barrios and forged new communities in both the Southwest and the Midwest, in small towns and cities. For example, in 1900 only 3,000 to 5,000 Mexicans lived in Los Angeles, but by 1930 approximately 150,000 persons of Mexican birth or heritage had settled into the city's expanding barrios. On a national level, by 1930 Mexicans formed the "third largest 'racial' group," outnumbered only by Anglos and blacks.[3]

---

* *Mexicano(-a)* designates someone of Mexican birth residing in the United States. *Mexican American* denotes a person born in the United States with at least second-generation status. *Mexican* is an umbrella term for both groups. I use the term *Chicano(-a)* only for the contemporary period, as most of the older women whose oral interviews contributed to this study did not identify as Chicanas. *Latino(-a)* indicates someone of Latin American birth or heritage. I refer to "Americanization" within the context of immigration history, that is, as an idealized set of assumptions pushed by state agencies and religious groups to "transform" or "anglicize" newcomers. Bureaucrats and missionaries narrowly defined "America" as signifying only the United States.

Figure 21.1. My mother as a young woman, Erminia Ruiz, ca. 1941. *Collection of the author.*

Pioneering social scientists, particularly Manuel Gamio, Paul Taylor, and Emory Bogardus, examined the lives of these Mexican immigrants, but their materials on women are sprinkled here and there, at times hidden in unpublished field notes. Among Chicano historians and writers there appears a fascination with second-generation Mexican American men, especially as *pachucos*.[4] The lifestyles and attitudes of their female counterparts have gone largely unnoticed, even though women may have experienced deeper generational tensions.[5] "Walking in two worlds," they blended elements of Americanization with Mexican expectations and values.[6] To set the context, I will look at education, employment, and media as agents of Americanization and assess the ways in which Mexican American women incorporated their messages. Drawing on social science fieldwork and oral interviews, I will discuss also the sources of conflict between adolescent women and their parents as well as the contradictions between the promise of the American dream and the reality of restricted mobility and ethnic prejudice.

This study relies extensively on oral history. The memories of thirteen women serve as the basis for my reconstruction of adolescent aspirations and experiences (or dreams and routines). Of the thirteen full-blown life histories, ten are housed in university archives, eight as part of the Rosie the Riveter collection at California State University, Long Beach. I became familiar with most of these interviews during the course of my research for *Cannery Women, Cannery Lives*, and two surfaced as student oral-history projects. I personally interviewed three of the narrators.

The women themselves are fairly homogeneous by nativity, class, residence, and family structure. With one exception, all are U.S. citizens by birth and attended southwestern schools. Ten of the interviewees were born between 1913 and 1929.[7] Although two came from families once considered middle-class in Mexico, all can be considered working-class in the United States. Their fathers' typical occupations included farm work, day labor, and busing tables. Two women had fathers with skilled blue-collar jobs (a butcher and a surveyor), and two were the daughters of small family farmers. The informants usually characterized their mothers as homemakers, although several remembered that their mothers took seasonal jobs in area factories and fields. The mother of the youngest interviewee (Rosa Guerrero) supported her family through domestic labor and fortune-telling. Eleven grew up in urban barrios, ten in Los Angeles. Most families were nuclear rather than extended, although kin usually (but not always) resided nearby. Rich in detail, these interviews reveal the complex negotiations across generations and across cultures.

Education and employment were the most significant agents of Americanization. Educators generally relied on an immersion method in teaching the English language to their Mexican pupils. In other words, Spanish-speaking children had to sink or swim in an English-only environment. Even on the playground, students were enjoined from conversing in their native Spanish. Admonishments such as "Don't speak that ugly language, you are an American now" not only reflected a strong belief in Anglo conformity but also denigrated the self-esteem of Mexican American children and dampened their enthusiasm for education.[8] Ruby Estrada remembered that corporal punishment was a popular method for teaching English: "The teacher was mean and the kids got mean."[9] At times children internalized these lessons, as Mary Luna reflected: "It was rough because I didn't know English. The teacher wouldn't let us talk Spanish. How can you talk to anybody? If you can't talk Spanish and you can't talk English, what are you going to do? . . . It wasn't until maybe the fourth or fifth grade that I started catching up. And all along that time I just felt I was stupid."[10]

Students also became familiar with U.S. history and holidays (e.g., Thanksgiving). In recounting her childhood, Rosa Guerrero elaborated on how in her own mind she reconciled the history lessons at school with her own heritage. "The school system would teach everything about American history, the colonists and all of that," she explained, "then I would do a comparison in my mind of where my grandparents came from, what they did, and wonder how I was to be evolved and educated."[11]

Schools, in some instances, raised expectations. Imbued with the American dream, young women (and men) believed that hard work would bring material rewards and social acceptance. In fact, a California grower disdained education for Mexicans because it would give them "tastes for things they can't acquire."[12] Some teenage women aspired to college; others planned careers as secretaries. "I want to study science or be a stenographer," one Colorado adolescent informed Paul Taylor. "I thinned beets this spring, but I believe it is the last time. The girls who don't go to school will continue to top beets the rest of their lives."[13]

Courses in typing and shorthand were popular among Mexican American women even though few southwestern businesses hired Spanish-surnamed office workers. In 1930 only 2.6 percent of all Mexican women wage earners held clerical jobs. Anthropologist Ruth Tuck noted the contradiction between training and placement. When she asked one teacher why Mexican women were being trained for clerical positions largely closed to them, the educator replied, "To teach them respect for the white collar job." Skin color also played a role in obtaining office work. As one typing teacher pointed out to young Julia Luna, "Who's going to hire you? You're so dark."[14]

Many young Mexican women never attended high school but took industrial or service-sector jobs directly after the completion of the eighth grade. Like the Eastern European and French Canadian workers studied by John Bodnar and Tamara Hareven, they gave family needs priority over individual goals. Family obligations and economic necessity propelled Mexican women into the labor force. One government study appearing in a 1931 issue of *Monthly Labor Review* revealed that in Los Angeles over 35 percent of the Mexican families surveyed had wage-earning children.[15] By 1930 approximately one-quarter of Mexicana and Mexican American female wage earners in the Southwest obtained employment as industrial workers. In California, they labored principally in canneries and garment firms.[16] Like many female factory workers in the United States, most Mexican operatives were young, unmarried daughters whose wage labor was essential to the economic survival of their families. As members of a "family wage economy," they relinquished all or part of their wages to their elders. According to a 1933 University of California study, of the Mexican families surveyed with working children, the children's monetary contributions comprised 35 percent of the total household income.[17]

At times working for wages gave women a feeling of independence. Historian Douglas Monroy asserted that outside employment "facilitated greater freedom of activity and more assertiveness in the family for Mexicanas." Some young women went a step farther and used their earnings to leave the family home. Facing family disapproval, even ostracism, they defied parental authority by sharing an apartment with female friends.[18] Conversely, kin networks, particularly in canneries and packing houses, reinforced a sense of family. Working alongside female kin, adolescents found employment less than liberating. At the same time the work environment afforded women the opportunity to develop friendships with other Spanish-surnamed operatives and occasionally with their ethnic immigrant peers. They began to discuss with one another their problems and concerns, finding common ground both as factory workers and as second-generation ethnic women. Teenagers chatted about fads, fashions, and celebrities.[19]

Along with outside employment, the media also influenced the acculturation of Mexican women. Movie and romance magazines enabled adolescents (and older women as well) to experience vicariously the middle-class and affluent lifestyles heralded in these publications, and thus to nurture a desire for consumer goods. Radios, motion pictures, and Madison Avenue advertising had a profound impact on America's cultural landscape. According to historians John D'Emilio and Estelle Freedman, "Corporate leaders needed consumers . . . who were ready to spend their earnings to purchase a growing array of goods designed for personal use. . . . Americans did not automatically respond to factory output by multiplying their desire for material goods; an ethic of consumption had to be sold."[20] The Mexican community was not immune to this orchestration of desire, and there appeared a propensity toward consumerism among second-generation women. In his 1928 study of Mexican women in Los Angeles industry, Paul Taylor contended that second to economic need, the prevalent motive for employment among single women was a desire to buy the "extras"—a radio, a phonograph, jazz records, fashionable clothes. As Carmen Bernal Escobar revealed, "After I started working, I liked the money. I love clothes—I used to buy myself beautiful clothes."[21] As members of a "consumer wage economy," daughters also worked in order to purchase items for their families' comfort, such as furniture, draperies, and area rugs.[22] Other teenagers had more modest goals. After giving most of her wages to her mother, Rosa Guerrero reserved a portion to buy peanut butter and shampoo. "Shampoo to me was a luxury. I had to buy shampoo so I wouldn't have to wash my hair with the dirty old Oxydol. I used to wash my hair with the soap for the clothes."[23]

The American cinema also made an impression. Although times were lean, many southern California women had dreams of fame and fortune, nurtured in part by the proximity to Hollywood. Movies, both Mexican and American, provided a popular form of entertainment for barrio residents. It was common on Saturday mornings to see children and young adults combing the streets for bottles so that they could afford the price of admission—ten cents for the afternoon matinee. Preteens would frequently come home and act out what they had seen on the screen. "I was going to be Clara Bow," remembered Adele Hernández Mulligan. Another woman recounted that she had definitely been "star struck" as a youngster and attempted to fulfill her fantasy in junior high by "acting in plays galore." The handful of Latina actresses appearing in Hollywood films, such as Dolores Del Rio and Lupe Vélez, also whetted these aspirations. Older star-struck adolescents enjoyed afternoon outings to Hollywood, filled with the hope of being discovered as they strolled along Hollywood and Vine with their friends.[24]

The influential Spanish-language newspaper *La Opinión* encouraged these fantasies in part, by publishing gossipy stories about movie stars such as Charlie Chaplin and Norma Shearer as well as up-to-the-minute reports on the private lives and careers of Latino celebrities. It also carried reviews of Spanish-language films, concerts, and plays.[25] Although promoting pride in Latino cultural events, the society pages reflected the public fascination with Hollywood. One week after its first issue, *La Opinión* featured a Spanish translation of Louella Parsons's nationally syndicated gossip column. Furthermore, the Los Angeles-based newspaper directly capitalized on the dreams of youth by sponsoring a contest with Metro-Goldwyn-Mayer. "Day by day we see how a young man or woman, winner of some contest, becomes famous overnight," reminded *La Opinión* as it publicized its efforts to offer its readers a similar chance. Touted as "the unique opportunity for all young men and women who aspire to movie stardom," this promotion held out the promise of a screen test to one lucky contestant.[26]

For many, show business had obvious appeal; it was perceived as a glamorous avenue for mobility. One could overcome poverty and prejudice as a successful entertainer. As an article on Lupe Vélez optimistically claimed, "Art has neither nationalities nor borders."[27]

Americanization seemed to seep into the barrios from all directions—from schools, factories, and even from the ethnic press. Parental responses to the Americanization of their children can be classified into two distinct categories—accommodation and resistance. These responses seem rooted more in class than in gender. In the sample of thirteen interviews and in my survey of early ethnographies, I can find no indication that intergenerational tension occurred more frequently among fathers and daughters than among mothers and daughters. Although parents cannot be viewed as a monolithic group, certainly both took an active interest in the socialization of their children. While resistance was the norm, some parents encouraged attempts at acculturation, and at times entire families took adult-education courses in a concerted effort to become "good Americans." Paul Taylor argues that middle-class Mexicans desiring to dissociate themselves from their working-class neighbors had the most fervent aspirations for assimilation. Once in the United States, middle-class mexicanos found themselves subject to ethnic prejudice that did not discriminate by class. Because of restrictive real estate covenants and segregated schools, these immigrants had lived in the barrios with people they considered their inferiors.[28] By passing as "Spanish," they cherished hopes of melting into the American social landscape. Sometimes mobility minded parents sought to regulate their children's choice of friends and later their marriage partners. "My folks never allowed us to go around with Mexicans," remembered Alicia Mendeola Shelit, "We went sneaking around, but my Dad wouldn't allow it. We'd always be with white." Interestingly, Shelit was married twice, both times to Anglos. As anthropologist Margarita Melville has concluded in her contemporary study of Mexican women immigrants, "aspirations for upward mobility" emerged as the most distinguishing factor in the process of acculturation.[29] Of course, it would be unfair to characterize all middle-class Mexican immigrants as repudiating their *mestizo* identity. Or as one young woman cleverly remarked, "Listen, I may be a Mexican in a fur coat, but I'm still a Mexican."[30]

Although enjoying the creature comforts afforded by life in the United States, Mexican immigrants retained their cultural traditions, and parents developed strategies to counteract the alarming acculturation of their young. Required to speak only English at school, Mexican youngsters were then instructed to speak only Spanish at home. Even in families that permitted the use of English, parents took steps to ensure the retention of Spanish among their children. Rosa Guerrero fondly remembered sitting with her father and conjugating verbs in Spanish "just for the love of it."[31] Proximity to Mexico also played an important role in maintaining cultural ties. Growing up in El Paso, Texas, Guerrero crossed the border into Ciudad Juárez every weekend with her family in order to partake of traditional recreational events, such as bullfights. Her family, moreover, made yearly treks to visit relatives in central Mexico. Those who lived substantial distances from the border, resisted assimilation by building ethnic pride through nostalgic stories of life in Mexico.[32] As one San José woman related:

> My mother never . . . tired of telling us stories of her native village in Guanajuato; she never let us children forget the things that her village was noted for, its handicrafts and arts, its songs and its stories. . . . She made it all sound so beautiful with her descriptions of the mountains and the lakes, the old traditions, the happy people, and the dances and weddings and fiestas. From the time I was a small child I always wanted to go back to Mexico and see the village where my mother was born.[33]

Though many youngsters relished the folk and family lore told by their parents or grandparents, others failed to appreciate their elders' efforts: "Grandmother Pérez's stories about the witches and ghosts of Los Conejos get scant audience, in competition with Dick Tracy and Buck Rogers."[34]

In bolstering cultural consciousness, parents found help through youth-oriented community organizations. Church, service, and political clubs reinforced ethnic awareness. Examples included the Logia "Juventud Latina" of the Alianza Hispano Americana, the Mexican American Movement initially sponsored by the YMCA, and the youth division of El Congreso de Pueblos de Hablan Española. Bert Corona, a leading California civil rights advocate for over four decades, began his career of activism as a leader in both the Mexican American Movement and the youth auxiliary of the Spanish-speaking Peoples Congress.[35]

Interestingly, only two of the thirteen women mentioned Catholicism as an important early influence. The Catholic church played more of a social role; it organized youth clubs and dances and it was the place for baptisms, marriages, and funerals.[36] For others, Protestant churches offered a similar sense of community. Establishing small niches in Mexican barrios, Protestant missionaries envisioned themselves as the harbingers of salvation and Americanization. Yet some converts saw their churches as reaffirming traditional Mexican values. "I was beginning to think that the Baptist church was a little too Mexican. Too much restriction," remembered Rose Escheverría Mulligan. Indeed, this woman longed to join her Catholic peers, who regularly attended church-sponsored dances: "I noticed they were having a good time."[37] Whether gathering for a Baptist picnic or a Catholic dance, teenagers seemed more attracted to the social rather than the spiritual side of their religion. Certainly more research is needed to assess the impact of Protestant social workers and missionaries on the attitudes of adolescent women. Mary Luna, for example, credited her love of reading to an Anglo educator who converted a small house in the barrio into a makeshift community center and library. The dual thrust of Americanization, education, and consumerism, can be discerned in the following excerpt from Luna's oral history. "To this day I just love going to libraries. . . . There are two places that I can go in and get a real warm, happy feeling; that is, the library and Bullock's in the perfume and make-up department."[38]

Blending new behavior with traditional ideals, young women also had to balance family expectations with their own need for individual expression. Within families, young women, perhaps more than their brothers, were expected to uphold certain standards. Indeed, Chicano social scientists have generally portrayed women as "the 'glue' that keeps the Chicano family together" as well as the guardians of "traditional culture."[39] Parents therefore often assumed what they perceived as their unquestionable prerogative to regulate the actions and attitudes of their adolescent daughters. Teenagers, on the other hand, did not always acquiesce in the boundaries set down for them by their elders. Intergenerational tension flared along several fronts.

Generally, the first area of disagreement between a teenager and her family would be over her personal appearance. During the 1920s a woman's decision to bob or not bob her hair assumed classic proportions within Mexican families. After considerable pleading, Belen Martínez Mason was permitted to cut her hair, though she soon regretted her decision: "Oh, I cried for a month."[40] Differing opinions over fashions often caused ill feelings. One Mexican American woman recalled that when she was a young girl, her mother dressed her "like a nun," and she could wear "no make-up, no cream, no nothing" on her face. Swimwear, bloomers, and short skirts also became sources of controversy. Some teenagers left home in one outfit and changed into another at school. Once María Fierro arrived home in her bloomers. Her father asked, "Where have you been dressed like that, like a clown?" "I told him the truth," Fierro explained. "He whipped me anyway. . . . So from then on whenever I went to the track meet, I used to change my bloomers so that he wouldn't see that I had gone again."[41] The impact of flapper styles on the Mexican community was clearly expressed in the following verse taken from a *corrido* (ballad) appropriately entitled "Las Pelonas [The Bobbed-Haired Girls]":

> Red Bandannas
> I detest,
> And now the flappers
> Use them for their dress.
> The girls of San Antonio
> Are lazy at the *metate*.
> They want to walk out bobbed-haired,
> With straw hats on.
> The harvesting is finished,
> So is the cotton;
> The flappers stroll out now
> For a good time.[42]

With similar sarcasm, another popular ballad chastised Mexican women for applying makeup so heavily as to resemble a piñata.[43]

Once again bearing the banner of glamour and consumption, *La Opinión* featured sketches of the latest flapper fashions as well as cosmetic ads from both Latino and Anglo manufacturers. The most elaborate layouts were those of Max Factor. Using celebrity testimonials, one advertisement encouraged women to "follow the stars" and purchase "Max Factor's Society Make-up." Factor, through an exclusive arrangement with *La Opinión*, went even further in courting the Mexican market by answering beauty questions from readers in a special column—"Secretos de Belleza [Beauty Secrets]."[44]

The use of cosmetics, however, cannot be blamed entirely on Madison Avenue ad campaigns. The innumerable barrio beauty pageants, sponsored by *mutualistas*, patriotic societies, churches, the Mexican Chamber of Commerce, newspapers, and even progressive labor unions encouraged young women to accentuate their physical attributes. Carefully chaperoned, many teenagers did participate in community contests, from La Reina de Cinco de Mayo to Orange Queen. They modeled evening gowns, rode on parade floats, and sold raffle tickets.[45] Carmen Bernal Escobar remembered one incident when, as a contestant, she had to sell raffle tickets. Every ticket she sold counted as a vote for her in the pageant. Naturally the winner would be the woman who had accumulated the most votes. When her brother offered to buy twenty-five dollars' worth of votes (her mother would not think of letting her peddle the tickets at work or in the neighborhood), Escobar, on a pragmatic note, asked him to give her the money so that she could buy a coat she had spotted while window-shopping.[46]

The commercialization of personal grooming made additional inroads into the Mexican community with the appearance of barrio beauty parlors. Working as a beautician conferred a certain degree of status, "a nice, clean job," in comparison with factory or domestic work. As one woman related:

> I always wanted to be a beauty operator. I loved makeup; I loved to dress up and fix up. I
> used to set my sisters' hair. So I had that in the back of my mind for a long time, and my

mom pushed the fact that she wanted me to have a profession—seeing that I wasn't thinking of getting married.[47]

Although further research is needed, one can speculate that neighborhood beauty shops reinforced women's networks and became places where they could relax, exchange *chisme*, and enjoy the company of other women.[48]

Conforming to popular fashions and fads cannot be construed as a lack of ethnic or political consciousness. In 1937 Carey McWilliams spoke before an assembly of fifteen hundred walnut workers in Los Angeles and was "profoundly stirred" by this display of grassroots labor militancy by Eastern European and Mexican women. Describing the meeting, he wrote, "And such extraordinary faces—particularly the old women. Some of the girls had been too frequently to the beauty shop, and were too gotten up—rather amusingly dressy."[49] I would argue that dressing up for a union meeting could be interpreted as an affirmation of individual integrity. Although they worked under horrendous conditions (actually cracking walnuts with their fists), their collective action and personal appearance give evidence that they did not surrender their self-esteem.

The most serious point of contention between an adolescent daughter and her parents, however, centered on her behavior toward young men. In both cities and rural towns, girls had to be closely chaperoned by a family member every time they attended a movie, dance, or even church-related events. Recalling the supervisory role played by her "old-maid" aunt, María Fierro laughingly explained, "She'd check on us all the time. I used to get so mad at her." Ruby Estrada recalled that in a small southern Arizona community, "all the mothers" escorted their daughters to the local dances. Even talking to male peers in broad daylight could be grounds for discipline.[50] Adele Hernández Milligan, a resident of Los Angeles for over fifty years, elaborated, "I remember the first time that I walked home with a boy from school. Anyway, my mother saw me and she was mad. I must have been sixteen or seventeen. She slapped my face because I was walking home with a boy."[51] Describing this familial protectiveness, one social scientist aptly remarked that the "supervision of the Mexican parent is so strict as to be obnoxious."[52]

Faced with this type of situation, young women had three options: They could accept the rules set down for them, they could rebel, or they could find ways to compromise or circumvent traditional standards. "I was *never* allowed to go out by myself in the evening; it just was not done." In rural communities where restrictions were perhaps even more stringent, "nice" teenagers could not even swim with their male peers: "We were ladies and wouldn't go swimming out there with a bunch of boys." Yet many seemed to accept these limits with equanimity. "It wasn't devastating at all," reflected Ruby Estrada. "We took it in stride. We never thought of it as cruel or mean. . . . It was taken for granted that that's the way it was."[53] In Sonora, Arizona, as in other small towns, relatives and neighbors kept close watch over adolescent women and quickly reported any suspected indiscretions. "They were always spying on you," Estrada remarked. Women in cities had a distinct advantage over their rural peers in that they could venture miles from their neighborhood into the anonymity of dance halls, amusement parks, and other places of commercialized leisure. With carnival rides and the Cinderella Ballroom, the Nu-Pike Amusement Park of Long Beach proved a popular hangout for Mexican youth in Los Angeles.[54] It was more difficult to abide by traditional norms when excitement beckoned just on the other side of the streetcar line.

Some women openly rebelled. They moved out of their family homes and into apartments. Considering themselves freewheeling single women, they could go out with men unsupervised, as was the practice among their Anglo peers. "This terrible freedom in the United States," one Mexicana lamented. "I do not have to worry because I have no daughters, but the poor *señoras* with many girls, they worry."[55] Those Mexican American adolescents who did not wish to defy their parents openly would sneak out of the house in order to meet their dates or to attend dances with female friends. A more subtle form of rebellion was early marriage. By marrying at fifteen or sixteen, these women sought to escape parental supervision; yet it could be argued that many of these child brides exchanged one form of supervision for another in addition to the responsibilities of child rearing.[56]

The third alternative sometimes involved quite a bit of creativity as these young women sought to circumvent traditional chaperonage. Alicia Mendeola Shelit recalled that one of her older brothers would always accompany her to dances, ostensibly as a chaperone. "But then my oldest brother would always have a blind date for me." Carmen Bernal Escobar was permitted to entertain her boyfriends at home, but only under the supervision of her brother or mother. The practice of "going out with the girls," though not accepted until the 1940s, was fairly common. Several Mexican American women, often related, would escort one another to an event (such as a dance), socialize with the men in attendance, and then walk home together. In the sample of thirteen interviews, daughters negotiated their activities with their parents. Older siblings and extended kin appeared in the background either as chaperones or as accomplices. Although unwed teenage mothers were not unknown in the Los Angeles barrios, families expected adolescent women to conform to strict standards of behavior.[57] As one might expect, many teenage women knew little about sex other than what they picked up from friends, romance magazines, and the local theater. As Mary Luna remembered, "I thought that if somebody kissed you you could get pregnant." In *Singing for My Echo*, New Mexico native Gregorita Rodríguez confided that on her wedding night, she knelt down and said her rosary until her husband gently asked, "Gregorita, *mi esposa*, are you afraid of me?" At times this naïveté persisted beyond the wedding. "It took four days for my husband to touch me," one woman revealed. "I slept with dress and all. We were both greenhorns, I guess."[58]

Of course, some young women did lead more adventurous lives. A male interviewer employed by Mexican anthropologist Manuel Gamio recalled his "relations" with a woman he met in a Los Angeles dance hall. Though born in Hermosillo, Elisa "Elsie" Morales considered herself Spanish. She helped support her family by dancing with strangers. Although she lived at home and her mother and brother attempted to monitor her actions, she managed to meet the interviewer at a "hot-pillow" hotel. To prevent pregnancy, she relied on contraceptive douches provided by "an American doctor." Although Morales realized her mother would not approve of her behavior, she noted that "she [her mother] is from Mexico. . . . I am from there also but I was brought up in the United States, we think about things differently." Just as Morales rationalized her actions as "American," the interviewer perceived her within a similar though certainly less favorable definition of Americanization. "She seemed very coarse to me. That is she dealt with one in the American way."[59] In his field notes, Paul Taylor recorded an incident in which a young woman had moved in with her Anglo boyfriend after he had convinced her that such living arrangements were common among Americans. Popular *corridos*, such as "El Enganchado" and "Las Pelonas," also touched on the theme of the corrupting influence of U.S. ways on Mexican women.[60]

Interestingly, both Anglo and Mexican communities held almost identical preconceptions of each other's young female population. While Mexicanos viewed Anglo women as morally loose, Latina actresses in Hollywood found themselves typecast as hot-blooded women of low repute. For example, Lupe Vélez starred in such films as *Hot Pepper*, *Strictly Dynamite*, and *The Mexican Spitfire*.[61] The image of loose sexual mores as distinctly American probably reinforced parental fears as they watched their daughters apply cosmetics and adopt the apparel advertised in fashion magazines. In other words, "If she dresses like a flapper, will she then act like one?" Seeds of suspicion reaffirmed the penchant for traditional supervision.

Tension between parents and daughters, however, did not always revolve around adolescent behavior. At times teenagers questioned the lifestyles of their parents. "I used to tell my mother she was a regular maid," Alicia Shelit recalled. "They [the women] never had a voice. They had to have the house clean, the food ready for the men . . . and everything just so."[62] As anthropologist Tuck observed, "Romantic literature, still more romantic movies, and the attitudes of

American teachers and social workers have confirmed the Pérez children in a belief that their parents do not 'love' each other; that, in particular, Lola Pérez is a drudge and a slave for her husband."[63]

However I would argue that the impact of Americanization was most keenly felt at the level of personal aspiration. "We felt if we worked hard, proved ourselves, we could become professional people," asserted Rose Escheverría Mulligan.[64] Braced with such idealism, Mexican Americans faced prejudice, segregation, and economic segmentation. Though they considered themselves Americans, others perceived them as less than desirable foreigners. During the late 1920s the *Saturday Evening Post*, exemplifying the nativist spirit of the times, featured inflammatory characterizations of Mexicans in the United States. For instance, one article portrayed Mexican immigrants as an "illiterate, diseased, pauperized" people who bear children "with the reckless prodigality of rabbits."[65] Racism was not limited to rhetoric; between 1931 and 1934 an estimated one-third of the Mexican population in the United States (over five hundred thousand people) were either deported or repatriated to Mexico even though many were native U.S. citizens. Mexicans were the only immigrants targeted for removal. Proximity to the Mexican border, the physical distinctiveness of *mestizos*, and easily identifiable barrios influenced immigration and social-welfare officials to focus their efforts solely on the Mexican people, people whom they viewed as both foreign usurpers of American jobs and unworthy burdens on relief rolls. From Los Angeles, California, to Gary, Indiana, Mexicans were either summarily deported by immigration agencies or persuaded to depart voluntarily by duplicitous social workers who greatly exaggerated the opportunities awaiting them south of the border.[66] According to historian George Sánchez:

> As many as seventy-five thousand Mexicans from southern California returned to Mexico by 1932. . . . The enormity of these figures, given the fact that California's Mexican population was in 1930 slightly over three hundred and sixty thousand . . ., indicates that almost every Mexican family in southern California confronted in one way or another the decision of returning or staying.[67]

By 1935 the deportation and repatriation campaigns had diminished, but prejudice and segregation remained. Historian Albert Camarillo has demonstrated that in Los Angeles restrictive real estate covenants and segregated schools increased dramatically between 1920 and 1950. The proportion of Los Angeles area municipalities with covenants prohibiting Mexicans and other minorities from purchasing residences in certain neighborhoods climbed from 20 percent in 1920 to 80 percent in 1946. Many restaurants, theaters, and public swimming pools discriminated against their Spanish-surnamed clientele. In southern California, for example, Mexicans could swim at the public plunges only one day out of the week (just before they drained the pool).[68] Small-town merchants frequently refused to admit Spanish-speaking people into their places of business. "White Trade Only" signs served as bitter reminders of their second-class citizenship.[69]

In 1933 a University of California study noted that Mexicans in southern California were among the most impoverished groups in the United States. Regardless of nativity, they were often dismissed as cheap, temporary labor and were paid "from 20 to 50 percent less per day for . . . performing the same jobs as other workers."[70] This economic segmentation did not diminish by generation. Writing about San Bernardino, California, in the 1940s, Ruth Tuck offered the following illustration:

> There is a street . . . on which three families live side by side. The head of one family is a naturalized citizen, who arrived here eighteen years ago; the head of the second is an alien who came . . . in 1905; the head of the third is the descendant of people who came . . . in

1843. All of them, with their families, live in poor housing; earn approximately $150 a month as unskilled laborers; send their children to "Mexican" schools; and encounter the same sort of discriminatory practices.[71]

Until World War II Mexicans experienced restricted occupational mobility, as few rose above the ranks of blue-collar labor. Scholars Mario García and Gilbert González have convincingly argued that the curricula in Mexican schools helped to perpetuate this trend. Emphasis on vocational education served to funnel Mexican youth into the factories and building trades.[72] In the abstract, education raised people's expectations, but in practice, particularly for men, it trained them for low-status, low-paying jobs. Employment choices were even more limited in rural areas. As miners or farm workers, Mexicans usually resided in company settlements where almost every aspect of their lives was regulated, from work schedules to wage rates to credit with local merchants. In 1925 a newspaper editor in Greeley, Colorado, bluntly advocated "a caste system," even though he alleged such a system "will be worse upon us, the aristocracy, than upon the Mexicans in their serfdom."[73] In both urban and rural areas, ethnicity became not only a matter of personal choice and heritage but also an ascribed status imposed by external sources.[74]

Considering these circumstances, it is not surprising that many teenagers developed a shining idealism as a type of psychological ballast. Some adolescents, like the members of the Mexican American Movement, believed that education was the key to mobility; while others placed their faith in the application of Max Factor's bleaching cream.[75] Whether they struggled to further their education or tried to lighten their skin color, Mexican Americans sought to protect themselves from the damaging effects of prejudice.

Despite economic and social stratification, many Mexicanas believed that life in the United States offered hope and opportunity. "Here woman has come to have place like a human being," reflected Señora____.[76] More common, perhaps, was the impact of material assimilation: the purchase of an automobile, a sewing machine, and other accoutrements of the U.S. consumer society. The accumulation of these goods signaled the realization of (or the potential for realizing) the American dream. As Margaret Clark eloquently commented:

> In Sal si Puedes [a San José barrio] where so many people are struggling to escape poverty and want, a "luxury item" like a shiny new refrigerator may be the source of hope and encouragement—it may symbolize the first step toward the achievement of a better way of life.

One of Clark's informants aired a more direct statement: "Nobody likes to be poor."[77]

The era of World War II ushered in a set of new options for Mexican women. In southern California some joined unions in food-processing plants and negotiated higher wages and benefits. Still others obtained more lucrative employment in defense plants. As "Rosie the Riveters," they gained self-confidence and the requisite earning power to improve their standard of living. A single parent, Alicia Mendeola Shelit, purchased her first home as the result of her employment with Douglas Aircraft.[78] The expansion of clerical jobs also provided Mexican American women with additional opportunities. By 1950, 23.9 percent of Mexican women workers in the Southwest held lower white-collar positions as secretaries or salesclerks.[79] They could finally apply the office skills they had acquired in high school or at storefront business colleges. Although beyond the scope of this study, intermarriage with Anglos may have been perceived as a potential avenue for mobility.[80]

Most of the thirteen interviewees continued in the labor force, combining wage work with household responsibilities. Only the oldest (Ruby Estrada, of Arizona) and the youngest (Rosa Guerrero, of Texas) achieved a solid, middle-class standard of living. Though one cannot make facile correlations, both women are the only narrators who attained a college education. Six of the eleven California women took their places on the shop floor in the aerospace, electronics, apparel, and food-processing industries. Two became secretaries and one a salesclerk at Kmart. The remaining two were full-time homemakers. Seven of these eleven informants married Anglo or Jewish men, yet their economic status did not differ substantially from those who chose Mexican spouses.[81] With varying degrees of financial security, the California women are now working-class retirees. Their lives do not exemplify rags-to-riches mobility but rather upward movement within the working class. Though painfully aware of prejudice and discrimination, people of their generation placed faith in themselves and faith in the system. In 1959 Margaret Clark asserted that the second-generation residents of Sal si Puedes "dream and work toward the day when Mexican Americans will become fully integrated into American society at large."[82] The desire to prove oneself appears as a running theme in twentieth-century Mexican American history. I should hasten to add that in the process, most people refused to shed their cultural heritage: "Fusion is what we want—the best of both ways."[83]

In this essay I have attempted to reconstruct the world of adolescent women, taking into account the broader cultural, political, and economic environment. I have given a sense of the contradictions in their lives—the lure of Hollywood and the threat of deportation. The discussion gives rise to an intriguing question. Can one equate the desire for material goods with the abandonment of Mexican values? I would argue that the ideological impact of material acculturation has been overrated. For example, a young Mexican woman may have looked like a flapper as she boarded a streetcar on her way to work at a cannery, yet she went to work (at least in part) to help support her family, as one of her obligations as a daughter. The adoption of new cultural forms certainly frightened parents but did not of itself undermine Mexican identity. The experiences of Mexican American women coming of age between 1920 and 1950 reveal the blending of the old and the new: fashioning new expectations, making choices, and learning to live with those choices.

Notes

I gratefully acknowledge the research assistance of Amagda Pérez and Christine Mann. I appreciate the generosity and long-standing support of Sherna Gluck, who has given me permission to quote from eight volumes of the Rosie the Riveter Revisited Oral History Collection housed at California State University, Long Beach. I also wish to thank the American Council of Learned Societies and the Committee on Research, University of California, Davis, for financial support of this project. Roland Marchand, Ramón Gutiérrez, and Howard Shorr provided incisive comments on earlier drafts, and I appreciate their interest in my work.

1. Oscar Handlin, *The Uprooted* (New York: Grosset and Dunlap, 1951); Alfred Kazin, *A Walker in the City* (New York: Harcourt Brace Jovanovich, 1951).

2. Examples of this rich literature include John Bodnar, *The Transplanted* (Bloomington: Indiana University Press, 1985); Kathy Peiss, *Cheap Amusements: Working Women and Leisure in Turn-of-the-Century New York* (Philadelphia: Temple University Press, 1986); Paula S. Fass, *The Damned and the Beautiful: American Youth in the 1920s* (New York: Oxford University Press, 1977), and John D'Emilio and Estelle B. Freedman, *Intimate Matters* (New York: Harper and Row, 1988).

3. Albert Camarillo, *Chicanos in a Changing Society: From Mexican Pueblos to American Barrios in Santa Barbara and Southern California, 1848–1930* (Cambridge, Mass.: Harvard University Press, 1979), 200–1; Ricardo Romo, *East Los Angeles: History of a Barrio* (Austin: University of Texas Press, 1983), 61; T. Wilson Long-more and Homer L. Hitt, "A Demographic Analysis of First and Second Generation Mexican Population of the United States: 1930," *Southwestern Social Science Quarterly* 24 (September 1943): 140.

4. Manuel Gamio, *Mexican Immigration to the United States. A Study of Human Migration and Adjustment* (New York: Arno Press, 1969 [1930]) Paul S. Taylor, *Mexican Labor in the United States*, 2 vols. (Berkeley: University of California Press, 1928, 1932); Emory S. Bogardus, *The Mexican in the United States* (Los Angeles: University of Southern California Press, 1934). Pachucos were young men who adopted the zoot suit, a badge of adolescent rebellion in Mexican and African American communities

during World War II. Because of their dress and demeanor, they were subject to verbal and physical abuse by law enforcement officials and servicemen. Mauricio Mazón, *The Zoot Suit Riots: The Psychology of Symbolic Annihilation* (Austin: University of Texas Press, 1984) and the Luis Valdez play and feature film *Zoot Suit* provide examples of the literature on *pachucos*.

5. Works that focus on Mexican women during this period include Rosalinda M. González, "Chicanas and Mexican Immigrant Families 1920–1940: Women's Subordination and Family Exploitation," in Lois Scharf and Joan Jensen, eds., *Decades of Discontent: The Women's Movement, 1920–1940* (Westport, Conn.: Greenwood Press, 1983), 59–83, and Vicki L. Ruiz, *Cannery Women, Cannery Lives: Mexican Women, Unionization, and the California Food Processing Industry, 1930–1950* (Albuquerque: University of New Mexico Press, 1987).

6. Ruth Zambrana, "A Walk in Two Worlds," *Social Welfare* 1 (spring 1986): 12.

7. The age breakdown for the thirteen interviewees is as follows: Two women were born between 1910 and 1912; six between 1913 and 1919; four between 1920 and 1929; and one after 1930.

8. Adelina Otero, "My People" [1931] in Carlos Cortés, ed., *Aspects of the Mexican American Experience* (New York: Arno Press, 1976), 150; Ruth Tuck, *Not with the Fist* (New York: Arno Press, 1974 [1946]), 185–88; Vicki L. Ruiz, "Oral History and La Mujer: The Rosa Guerrero Story," in Vicki L. Ruiz and Susan Tiano, eds., *Women on the United States–Mexico Border: Responses to Change* (Boston: Allen and Unwin, 1987), 226–27; interview with Belen Martínez Mason, in Sherna Berger Gluck, ed., *Rosie the Riveter Revisited: Women and the World War II Work Experience* (Long Beach, Calif.: CSULB Foundation, 1983), 23:24–25.

9. Interview with Ruby Estrada conducted by María Hernández, 4 August 1981, The Lives of Arizona Women, Oral History Project, Special Collections, Hayden Library, Arizona State University, Tempe, 6.

10. Mary Luna interview, *Rosie the Riveter* 20:10. During the 1940s, bilingual education appeared as an exciting experiment in curriculum reform. See George I. Sánchez, eds., "First Regional Conference on the Education of Spanish-Speaking People in the Southwest" [1945], in Cortés, ed., *Aspects of the Mexican American Experience*.

11. Margarita B. Melville, "Selective Acculturation of Female Mexican Migrants," in Margarita B. Melville, ed., *Twice a Minority: Mexican American Women* (St. Louis: C. V. Mosby, 1980), 161; Ruiz, "Oral History and La Mujer," 222.

12. Rose Escheverría Mulligan interview, *Rosie the Riveter*, 27:16–17, 24; Ruiz, "Oral History and La Mujer," 227–28; Taylor, *Mexican Labor*, 1:79, 205–6.

13. Tuck, *Not with the Fist*, 162–63, 190–91; Paul S. Taylor, "Women in Industry" field notes for *Mexican Labor*, Bancroft Library, University of California, 1 box; Estrada interview, 10–15; Escheverría Mulligan interview, 40; Taylor, *Mexican Labor*, 1:205. A synthesis of the Taylor study has been published. See Paul S. Taylor, "Mexican Women in Los Angeles Industry in 1928," *Aztlán* 11 (spring 1980): 99–131.

14. Lois Rita Helmbold, "The Work of Chicanas in the United States: Wage Labor and Work in the Home, 1930 to the Present" (seminar paper, Stanford University, 1977), 53; Taylor, field notes; Tuck, *Not with the Fist*, 190–91; interview with Julia Luna Mount, 17 November 1983, conducted by the authors.

15. John Bodnar, "Immigration, Kinship and the Rise of Working-Class Realism in Industrial America," *Journal of Social History* 14 (fall 1980): 53–55; Tamara K Hareven, "Family Time and Industrial Time: Family and Work in a Planned Corporation Town, 1900–1924," in Tamara K. Hareven, ed., *Family and Kin in Urban Communities* (New York: New Viewpoints, 1977), 202; Taylor, notes; U.S. Department of Labor, Bureau of Labor Statistics, "Labor and Social Conditions of Mexicans in California," *Monthly Labor Review* 32 (January–June 1931): 89.

16. Mario Barrera, *Race and Class in the Southwest* (Notre Dame, Ind.: University of Notre Dame Press, 1979), 131; Taylor, notes. The percentage of Mexican women workers employed in industry was comparable to the participation of European immigrant women in eastern industry, where one-third of ethnic women who worked outside the home labored as blue-collar employees (Alice Kessler-Harris, *Out to Work: A History of Wage Earning Women in the United States* [New York: Oxford University Press, 1982], 127).

17. Heller Committee for Research in Social Economics of the University of California and Constantine Panuzio, *How Mexicans Earn and Live*, University of California Publications in Economics 13, 1, Cost of Living Studies (Berkeley University of California, 1933), 5:11, 14–17; Taylor, notes; Luna Mount interview; Alicia Shelit interview, *Rosie the Riveter*, 37:9. For further delineation of the family wage and the consumer wage economy, see Louise A. Tilly and Joan W. Scott, *Women, Work and Family* (New York: Holt, Rinehart, and Winston, 1978).

18. Taylor, notes; Helmbold, "Work of Chicanas," 15, 30–31, 36; Douglas Monroy, "An Essay on Understanding the Work Experience of Mexicans in Southern California, 1900–1939," *Aztlán* 12 (spring 1981): 70; González, "Chicanas and Mexican Immigrant Families," 72.

19. Discussing popular magazines and movies helped build important cross-cultural bridges—bridges

that would facilitate union-organizing drives among southern California food-processing workers during the late 1930s and early 1940s. See Ruiz, *Cannery Women, Cannery Lives*.

20. Roland Marchand, *Advertising the American Dream: Making Way for Modernity, 1920–1940* (Berkeley: University of California Press, 1985), 197–99, 219; D'Emilio and Freedman, *Intimate Matters*, 278.

21. Taylor, notes; Richard G. Thurston, "Urbanization and Sociocultural Change in a Mexican-American Enclave" (Ph.D. diss., University of California, Los Angeles, 1957; reprint, San Francisco: R and E Research Associates, 1974), 128; Helmbold, "Work of Chicanas," 42–44; interview with Carmen Bernal Escobar, 15 June 1986, conducted by the author.

22. Elizabeth Fuller, *The Mexican Housing Problem in Los Angeles*, Studies in Sociology, Sociological Monograph 5, 17 (New York: Arno Press, 1974 [1920]), 4–5.

23. Ruiz, "Oral History and La Mujer," 226.

24. Shelit interview, 4; Adele Hernández Milligan interview, *Rosie the Riveter*, 26:14; Martínez Mason interview, 59–60; Luna interview, 18, 26; Clint C. Wilson II and Felix Gutiérrez, *Minorities and Media* (Beverly Hills: Sage Publications, 1985), 85–86.

25. For examples, see *La Opinión*, 16 and 18 September 1926, 13 and 15 May 1927, 3 and 4 June 1927.

26. Ibid., 23, 24, 27, and 30 September, 1926.

27. Ibid., 2 March 1927.

28. Taylor, notes. Referring to Los Angeles, two historians have argued that "Mexicans experienced segregation in housing in nearly every section of the city and its outlying areas" (Antonio Ríos-Bustamante and Pedro Castillo, *An Illustrated History of Mexican Los Angeles 1781–1985* [Los Angeles: Chicano Studies Research Center/University of California, 1986], 135). Ruth Tuck noted that Anglo Americans also employed the term *Spanish* in order to distinguish individuals "of superior background or achievement" (Tuck, *Not with the Fist*, 142–43).

29. Shelit interview, 32; Mulligan interview, 14; Melville, "Selective Acculturation," 155, 162.

30. Tuck, *Not with the Fist*, 133.

31. Gamio, *Mexican Immigration*, 172–73; Bogardus, *The Mexican in the United States*, 75; Romo, *East Los Angeles*, 142; Ruiz, "Oral History and La Mujer," 224. "Some adolescents are stimulated to play the dual roles of being good Mexicans at home and good 'Americans' at school" (Bogardus, 75).

32. Ruiz, "Oral History and La Mujer," 221, 224–25; Margaret Clark, *Health in the Mexican American Culture* (Berkeley: University of California Press, 1959), 21.

33. Clark, *Health*, 21.

34. Tuck, *Not with the Fist*, 108.

35. Ríos-Bustamante and Castillo, *Illustrated History*, 139; George Sánchez, "The Rise of the Second Generation: The Mexican American Movement" (unpublished paper, courtesy of the author), 26–27; interview with Luisa Moreno, 12–13 August 1977, conducted by Albert Camarillo.

36. Sociologist Norma Williams contends that contemporary Mexican Americans view the Catholic Church almost solely in terms of social, life-cycle functions, such as baptisms and funerals. See Norma Williams, *The Mexican American Family: Tradition and Change* (New York: G. K. Hall, 1990).

37. Vicki L. Ruiz, "Dead Ends or Gold Mines? Using Missionary Records in Mexican American Women's History," *Frontiers* 12 (June 1991): 33–56; Mulligan interview, 24. For an interesting collection of Protestant missionary reports for this period, see Carlos Cortés, ed., *Church Views of the Mexican American* (New York: Arno Press, 1974).

38. Luna interview, 9.

39. George Sánchez, " 'Go after the Women': Americanization and the Mexican Immigrant Woman 1915–1929," Stanford Center for Chicano Research, working paper no. 6, 2.

40. Bogardus, *The Mexican in the United States*, 74; Martínez Mason interview, 44. During the 1920s, Mexican parents were not atypical in voicing their concerns over the attitudes and appearance of their "flapper adolescents." A general atmosphere of tension between youth and their elders existed—a generation gap that cut across class, race, ethnicity, and region. See Fass, *Damned and Beautiful*.

41. Shelit interview, 18; Taylor, *Mexican Labor*, 2:199–200; María Fierro interview, *Rosie the Riveter*, 12:10.

42. Gamio, *Mexican Immigration*, 89; the verse is taken from "Las Pelonas" in the original Spanish:
Los paños colorados
Los tengo aborrecidos
Ya hora las pelonas
Los usan de vestidos.
Las muchachas de S. Antonio
Son flojas pa'l metate
Quieren andar pelonas
Con sombreros de petate.
Se acabaron las pizcas,

Se acabó el algodón
Ya andan las pelonas
De puro vacilón.

43. Taylor, *Mexican Labor*, 2:vi–vii.

44. *La Opinión*, 18 September 1926, 3 May 1927, 5 June 1927. Using endorsements from famous people was a common advertising technique. See Marchand, *Advertising the American Dream*, 96–102.

45. Rodolfo F. Acuña, *A Community under Siege: A Chronicle of Chicanos East of the Los Angeles River 1945–1975* (Los Angeles: UCLA Chicano Studies Research Center Publications, 1984), 278, 407–8, 413–14, 418, 422; *FTA News*, 1 May 1945; Escobar interview. For an example of the promotion of a beauty pageant, see issues of *La Opinión*, June and July 1927.

46. Escobar interview.

47. Sherna B. Gluck, *Rosie the Riveter Revisited: Women, the War and Social Change* (Boston: Twayne, 1987), 81, 85.

48. *Chisme* means "gossip."

49. Letter from Carey McWilliams dated 3 October 1937, to Louis Adamic, Adamic File, carton 1, Carey McWilliams Collection, Special Collections, University of California, Los Angeles.

50. Martínez Mason interview, 29–30; Escobar interview; Fierro interview, 15; Estrada interview, 11–12. Chaperonage was also common in Italian immigrant communities. Indeed, many of the same conflicts between parents and daughters had surfaced a generation earlier among Italian families on the East Coast (Peiss, *Cheap Amusements*, 69–70, 152).

51. Hernández Milligan interview, 17.

52. Evangeline Hymer, "A Study of the Social Attitudes of Adult Mexican Immigrants in Los Angeles and Vicinity: 1923" (M.A. thesis, University of Southern California, 1924; reprint, San Francisco: R and E Research Associates, 1971), 24–25.

53. Escobar interview; Estrada interview, 11, 13.

54. Estrada interview, 12; Shelit interview, 9; Ríos-Bustamante and Castillo, *Illustrated History*, 153.

55. Taylor, notes; Thurston, "Urbanization," 118; Bogardus, *The Mexican in the United States*, 28–29, 57 58.

56. Martínez Mason interview, 30; Beatrice Morales Clifton interview, *Rosie the Riveter*, 8:14–15.

57. Shelit interview, 9, 24, 30; Escobar interview; Martínez Mason interview, 30; Hernández Milligan interview, 27–28; Taylor, notes.

58. Luna Mount interview; Fierro interview, 18; Luna interview, 29; Gregorita Rodríguez, *Singing for My Echo* (Santa Fe, N.M.: Cota Editions, 1987), 52; Martínez Mason interview, 62.

59. "Elisa Morales," Manuel Gamio field notes, Bancroft Library, University of California, 1 box.

60. Taylor, notes; Taylor, *Mexican Labor*, 2:vi–vii; Gamio, *Mexican Immigration*, 89. The *corrido* "El Enganchado" in vol.2 offers an intriguing glimpse into attitudes toward women and Americanization.

61. Wilson and Gutiérrez, *Minorities and Media*, 86.

62. Tuck, *Not with the Fist*, 115; Shelit interview, 26.

63. Tuck, *Not with the Fist*, 115.

64. Taylor, *Mexican Labor*, 1:205–6; Ruiz, "Oral History and La Mujer," 227–28; Sanchez, "Mexican American Movement," 7–10, 12; Escheverría Mulligan interview, 17.

65. Kenneth L. Roberts, "The Docile Mexican," *Saturday Evening Post*, 10 March 1928, as quoted in Sánchez, " 'Go After the Women,' " 8.

66. Rodolfo F. Acuña *Occupied America: A History of Chicanos*, 2nd ed. (New York: Harper and Row, 1981), 138, 140–41; Albert Camarillo, *Chicanos in California* (San Francisco: Boyd and Fraser, 1984), 48–49; Abraham Hoffman, *Unwanted Mexican Americans in the Great Depression* (Tucson: University of Arizona Press, 1974), 43–66; Francisco E. Balderrama, *In Defense of La Raza: The Los Angeles Mexican Consulate and the Mexican Community, 1929–1936* (Tucson: University of Arizona Press, 1982), 16–20; Neil Betten and Raymond A. Mohl, "From Discrimination to Repatriation: Mexican Life in Gary, Indiana, during the Great Depression," in Norris Hundley, ed., *The Chicano* (Santa Barbara: ABC-Clio Press, 1975), 132, 138–39.

67. Sánchez, "Mexican American Movement," 10.

68. Albert Camarillo, "Mexican American Urban History in Comparative Ethnic Perspective" (Distinguished Speakers Series, University of California, Davis, 26 January 1987); Acuña, *Occupied America*, 310, 318, 323, 330–31; Romo, *East Los Angeles*, 139; Tuck, *Not with the Fist*, 51, 53; Shelit interview, 15.

69. Taylor, *Mexican Labor*, 1:221–24; interview with María Arredondo, 19 March 1986, conducted by Carolyn Arredondo.

70. Heller Committee Study, *How Mexicans Earn and Live*, 68–69, 72; Camarillo, *Chicanos in a Changing Society*, 215.

71. Tuck, *Not with the Fist*, 209–10.

72. Barrera, *Race and Class*, 82–91; Mario T. García, *Desert immigrants: The Mexicans of El Paso, 1880–1920* (New Haven, Conn.: Yale University Press, 1981), 110–26; Gilbert González, "Racism, Education, and the Mexican Community in Los Angeles, 1920–30," *Societas* 4 (autumn 1974): 287–300.

73. González, "Chicanas and Mexican Immigrant Families," 63–66; Taylor, *Mexican Labor*, 1:162–66, 176–79, 190–91, 217, 220, 227–28 (quote from 220).

74. Melville, "Selective Acculturation," 159–60; John García, "Ethnicity and Chicanos," *Hispanic Journal of Behavioral Sciences* 4 (1982): 310–11.

75. Sánchez, "Mexican American Movement," 7–9; Guadalupe San Miguel Jr., "Culture and Education in the American Southwest: Towards an Explanation of Chicano School Attendance," *Journal of American Ethnic History* 7 (spring 1988): 15, 17; *La Opinión*, 5 June 1927.

76. "Sra____," Manuel Gamio, field notes.

77. Clark, *Health*, 92.

78. Ruiz, *Cannery Women, Cannery Lives*; Shelit interview, 52–55; Sherna Berger Gluck, "Interlude or Change: Women and the World War II Work Experience," 14, 32–34 (rev. version, courtesy of author; originally published in *International Journal of Oral History* 3 [1982]); see also Gluck, *Rosie the Riveter Revisited*.

79. William H. Chafe, *The American Woman: Her Changing Social, Economic, and Political Roles, 1920–1970* (New York: Oxford University Press, 1972), 137–43, 146; Barrera, *Race and Class*, 131, 140–45.

80. Shelit interview, 32; Escheverría Mulligan interview, 14; Richard Griswold del Castillo, *La Familia: Chicano Families in the Urban Southwest, 1848 to the Present* (Notre Dame, Ind.: University of Notre Dame Press, 1984), 120–22.

81. Many of the husbands were skilled workers in the aerospace industry. The most prestigious occupation for a spouse was firefighter.

82. Clark, *Health*, 20.

83. Tuck, *Not with the Fist*, 134. According to historian Richard Griswold del Castillo, "[P]resent-day Chicano families are a bridge between the social and cultural heritages of Anglo and Latin America" (*La Familia*, 126).

22

Japanese American Women and the Creation of Urban Nisei Culture in the 1930s

Valerie J. Matsumoto

Poring over pictures of Shirley Temple and Marlene Dietrich in the newspapers, listening to Cab Calloway, and dreaming of dashing suitors and romantic evenings, young urban Nisei women of the 1930s were enthusiastic participants in popular youth culture, ingeniously coping with the limitations imposed by depression-era economics and West Coast racial barriers. They formed Girl Scout troops and baseball teams; they sent their poems to the ethnic newspapers and waltzed at Nisei club dances. For most of the twentieth century, historians and social scientists would have interpreted this behavior as part of a debate about whether or not ethnic Americans wanted to "assimilate" into the dominant society. More recently, scholars such as Vicki Ruiz and Judy Yung have reinterpreted the activities of second-generation women as a process of drawing from many possible models in creating their own cultural forms; Ruiz has termed the process "cultural coalescence." This essay examines the ways in which Japanese American women in 1930s Los Angeles engaged in cultural coalescence, giving rise to a vibrant urban, generational culture. To understand girls' and women's engagement in the creation of an urban Nisei world, it is necessary to study their impressive array of peer networks. The importance of such peer support emerges in sharp relief from young women's negotiation of the multiple pressures and influences they faced in the arenas of work, recreation, courtship, and ethnic cultural activities.

Women played energetic roles in pre–World War II Japanese American communities of the West Coast, where the majority of Issei immigrants had settled. The largest of these enclaves was Little Tokyo in Los Angeles, the focus of my research. The English-language sections of the Los Angeles Japanese American newspapers vividly reveal the variety of Nisei women's involvement in urban ethnic culture. The *Kashu Mainichi* (Japan-California Daily News), one of the two largest Japanese American newspapers in southern California, was particularly noted for its extensive literary section, in which the Nisei found a welcoming forum for their poetry, fiction, and essays. Edited by Nisei, the English-language section itself constituted a kind of peer network, announcing milestones and club meetings, and facilitating discourse on a range of topics relevant to the second generation. The ongoing discussion of women's roles generated particularly lively, sometimes heated, reader response.

In the early twentieth century, gender role shifts stirred debate within ethnic communities as well as in the larger society over appropriate female activities. Vigorous club movements proliferated among black and white women, as middle-class matrons moved assertively into the public sphere, taking leading roles in Progressive reform. The "New Woman" emerged, hailed with pride and hope by feminists and viewed with alarm by conservatives who predicted the disintegration of the family and the American character. Yet both feminists and conservatives were disconcerted by the most flamboyant and youthful embodiment of the New Woman, the flapper, who seemed to combine personal independence and income with consumerism, lack of social responsibility, and overt sexuality. While probably only a fraction of middle-class European American women truly matched public expectations or fears about the "Jazz Baby," some of the attributes of the New Woman filtered across class and racial lines.

My research on Japanese American women, like Yung's and Ruiz's findings about Chinese American women and Mexican American women, reveals that a considerable number bobbed their hair and rebelled against parentally proscribed gender-role strictures. While remaining steadfast contributors to the family economy, they also hoped to choose their own spouses, enjoyed mainstream entertainment, and organized a variety of Nisei girls' and women's clubs. Their synthesis of interwar notions of "modern" femininity was, of course, complicated by racial discrimination in the larger society and by their ethnic community's own views with regard to female behavior. Nowhere did their efforts to come to terms with differing sets of expectations become more evident than in the urban setting of Little Tokyo.

Little Tokyo in Los Angeles served as a major cultural hub for the Issei and Nisei in southern California, growing rapidly in the two decades before World War II. Japantowns emerged in San Francisco, Seattle, Sacramento, Tacoma, and Salt Lake City, but Los Angeles boasted the largest. In 1910 the Census Bureau recorded 8,641 Japanese Americans living in Los Angeles County. By 1930 the number had swelled to 35,000, of whom half were American-born Nisei. The majority of these Nikkei (or persons of Japanese descent) resided in the area known as "Lil' Tokio," clustered around First and San Pedro Streets not far from City Hall. They ran shops and restaurants, and worked at the heart of the produce business, the City Market at Ninth and San Pedro. The prospect of living in this bustling, vigorous community thrilled Nisei newcomer Mary Korenaga, who initially viewed California—and Los Angeles more specifically—as "the land of opportunity and fortune, the land of eternal sunshine and flower, and the land where the eyes of the Nisei are focused."[2]

To Korenaga and many of her peers, city life glittered with the allure of modernity and excitement. Indeed, Nisei Ellen Tanna revealed in a prose-poem her identification with the urban ethnic enclave, likening it to a young woman, perhaps the sort of woman she envisioned herself to be: "Little Tokio stands poised, a modern maid . . . her arms flung wide to life and the world . . . eager, facing the sun . . . alive to the encompassing occidental sophistication . . . aware and youthfully impatient of aged traditions and hovering elders. . . ."[3] In personifying Little Tokyo as a feminine gypsy, jeweled with light, serenaded, "the happiness of her own pulsing and sensuous . . .," Tanna also wove a lively and romantic image of urban Nisei womanhood.

In contrast to Japanese American farm women, whose lives Evelyn Nakano Glenn characterizes as having retained "traditional peasant values," urban Nisei daughters had more comfortable, less arduous childhoods.[4] Like their rural counterparts, they helped out in the home and family business, but they were more likely to have free time and, like the urban Mexican American women Ruiz has studied, greater access to commercialized leisure.[5] As Mei Nakano suggests, the prewar period could be "a heady time for urban Nisei females, filled with the scent of gardenias, and the excitement of romance and dating."[6] Certainly the packed social calendar of the Los Angeles *Kashu Mainichi* reflected their opportunities to engage in a range of cultural, recreational, athletic, and social service activities within the ethnic community.

By and large, the Nisei were a very young group. In 1930, the bulk of the second generation in Los Angeles County were under twenty-one years old. In 1934, a journalist reported that the majority of the Nisei in the United States were between the ages of fifteen and eighteen.[7] Regardless of their youth, most Nisei did not lack responsibilities.

The labor of second-generation girls and adolescents proved essential to the support of the family wage economy and the ethnic community. City girls often helped clean and operate family businesses within the Japanese American enclave, sweeping a tofu shop, waiting on restaurant customers, or stocking the shelves of a grocery store. Girls' chores also included housework, from which their brothers were exempt, in addition to the supervision of younger siblings.

As adults, many Nisei women—like other racial-ethnic and working-class women—faced limited job prospects made grimmer by the fact that work outside the home was rarely a choice and more often a necessity. In the prewar period, three narrow paths led urban Japanese American women to jobs inside the ethnic community, work outside the enclave, or—for a small minority—the pursuit of opportunities in Japan. One writer termed them, "Three Roads and None Easy."[8]

Because of racial barriers and the Great Depression, full-time employment opportunities were limited, both within and outside Little Tokyo. Like their Chinese American peers, most Nisei found that in the larger job market, factors of race (and in the case of women, gender) outweighed their education and English proficiency.[9] Educated women and men alike faced a discouraging paucity of jobs. "The chief problem of every nisei grad is that of vocation," asserted T. Roku Sugahara in a 1935 article. Although he believed it was not impossible to "find an opening in the greater community," he aimed to persuade the second generation to consider the "wonderful opportunities" in agriculture and fishing, or in revitalizing the flower markets and other businesses of Little Tokyo.[10] The dearth of options led to a competitive scramble for the more desirable positions in the ethnic enclave.

A small number of Nisei women filled the needs of ethnic professionals and merchants for secretaries and clerks. Women coveted such positions, as Monica Sone recalled from her youth in Seattle. "I knew that the Nisei girls competed fiercely among themselves for white-collar jobs in the Mitsui and Mitsubishi branch firms downtown, local newspaper establishments, Japanese banks, shipping offices and small export and import firms."[11] Some women, like Yoshiko Hosoi Sakurai, channeled their skills into a family business: after graduation from high school, she worked with her parents to operate Mansei An, a popular Little Tokyo udon (noodles) and sushi shop.[12] Others worked as teachers, nurses, seamstresses, and beauticians within the ethnic community.

Domestic work proved the most readily available work outside the urban Japanese American enclave. As Evelyn Nakano Glenn found, domestic work constituted the primary area of non-agricultural wage-paid labor for Issei and Nisei women. In 1941, the Japanese YWCA in San Francisco estimated that two out of every five young women worked in domestic service.[13] This pattern persisted: during the war, the greatest number of jobs advertised in the internment camps were domestic positions recently vacated by black and white women flocking to better-paid defense and industrial work.

It is difficult to estimate how many Nisei women and men decided to seek their fortunes in Japan. Judy Yung notes that more second-generation Chinese Americans than Mexican Americans or Japanese Americans set their sights on working in their parents' homeland.[14] The ongoing discussion of opportunities abroad in the Japanese American newspapers of Los Angeles and San Francisco suggests that at least some gave it serious consideration. A 1926 interview with a Nisei collegian specializing in secretarial work underscores the limitations of the U.S. job market. She said, "After I graduate, what can I do here? No American firm will employ me. All I can hope to become here is a bookkeeper in one of the little Japanese dry goods stores in the Little Tokyo section of Los Angeles, or else become a stenographer to the Japanese lawyer here."[15] Instead she planned to go to Japan where a job in a large shipping company awaited her. Two of her Nisei women friends also intended to journey to Japan to teach English.

The smallest, yet most visible group of Nisei to turn their ambitions toward Japan were those pursuing careers in entertainment and the performing arts. Thwarted by racial barriers in the United States, some found a warm reception abroad. In 1932 the *Kashu Mainichi* reported that singer Agnes Miyakawa, violinist Alice Katayama and pianist Lillian Katayama were "creating a sensational hit in the winter musical debut," and that Kyoko Inoue had gotten a role in a Japanese movie. Concluded the editor, "Japan is indeed the land of opportunity for the second generation who are talented in some special line of endeavor."[16] The large majority of Nisei women and men, however, cast their economic lot with the land of their birth.

Because Nisei women not only brought wages into the family but also notions of how they might be spent, consumerism constituted a second expression of their significance in creating urban ethnic culture. Since the rise of advertising and mass media in the early twentieth century, women have been targeted for the sale of appliances, cosmetics, movies, clothing, home furnishings, and food. The reach of mainstream newspapers, magazines, radio, and film in the 1920s and 1930s made the latest consumer goods and popular icons appealing and familiar to a national audience, including Nisei girls like the protagonist of a Hisaye Yamamoto short story, "A Day in Little Tokyo." When a family beach outing is preempted by a sumo tournament thirteen-year-old Chisato Kushida kills time in Little Tokyo by buying a newspaper, reading the "funnies," and poring over pictures of Marion Davies and Jeannette McDonald. Chisato wishes she had stayed home to listen to "the weekly fairy tale from New York City [on the radio], with kids like Billy and Florence Halop and Albert Alley always perfect in every story."[17] Finally she begins to sing the Cream of Wheat advertising jingle, which she knows by heart.

Urban Nisei women, within their means, tried to keep abreast of current fashions in clothing and cosmetics. In Little Tokyo, a number of beauty salons competed for their patronage. In 1934, the Ginza Beauty Salon lured customers with "specials on shampoo and finger waves every Wednesday" and proudly announced, "The salon, to assure perfect service, now has with them another Nisei operator Miss Marion Miyamoto, who has attended the Paramount Beauty College."[18] In addition, for those desiring instruction, a Miss Brain (who appears to have been a European American consultant) would demonstrate "fine cosmetics" and give makeup analyses.

Nisei discussions about cosmetics, as well as fads like gum chewing and cigarette smoking, reflect more than the second-generation women's participation in popular trends; they also show their staging of the debate over the boundaries of sanctioned female behavior and appearance among their peers. For example, in a newspaper column on lipstick, Alice Suzuki invoked and poked fun at romantic imagery: "In olden times ladies used their ring for the seal of true love, but modern women leave their red lip-prints on the cheeks of the gallant knights—which have caused many heartbreaks and trips to Reno." Although she warned against the excessive use of "loud" red, she concluded by asserting women's right to employ cosmetic enhancement: "it is imperative that ladies must have lip-sticks and indulge in them."[19]

Suzuki's writing reveals some ambivalence, even as she stakes claims to broader parameters of acceptable behavior for "modern women," including practices considered the purview of men. Utilizing and dismissing imagery often applied stereotypically to Asian and Asian American women, she notes, "In this day and age when women are no longer the dainty little creatures that used to flutter about like butterflies, it is not surprising to see them acquiring the habits of the male in landslide fashion. Take smoking, for example. . . . What is good for the men should be good for the women." She concludes, however, by declaring, "And now that we have granted the point that it is all right for women to smoke, may we suggest that they try smoking Havana cigars and be real, real men, or try a pipe—and smell like one."[20] Her words convey the sense of smoking as unfeminine, a prevailing sentiment within the prewar Japanese American community. Another Nisei columnist commented that a "[m]ajority of the [Japanese American] homes have a 'tabu' on women smoking."[21] Playwright Wakako Yamauchi has remarked that smoking was one of the things that "nice girls" didn't do.[22] Perhaps because of this, fewer Nisei women than men became regular smokers.

As Vicki Ruiz has skillfully delineated, female participation in popular culture was complicated for non-white women by the multiple pressures they faced within the family, the ethnic community, and the larger society.[23] At times, Nisei daughters, like their Mexican American sisters, felt torn between powerful mainstream notions of modernity and romance on one hand, and the feminine ideals inculcated by strict parents reared in another country (in this case, Meiji-Era Japan) on the other. As they struggled to integrate popular and parental values, they introduced a range of gender-role issues into the Japanese American community.

The tensions between competing notions of womanhood emerged most clearly in the discourse over romance and marriage—a discourse in which Nisei women took a vocal role. Like their mothers and most U.S. women then, they expected a future centering around marriage and family. In contrast to Issei women, they expected their marital relations to be based on romantic attraction and individual choice—the hallmarks of mainstream ideals—as well as duty. Their preoccupation with "love" reflected the influence of popular literature, songs, and movies. As Lucille Morimoto wrote:

> To-night
> I want to feel your nearness,
> To hear your husky voice fade into a whisper,
> To me they will be like the sweetness of honey,
> The cool breeze on my feverish face.[24]

Margaret Uchiyamada likewise yearned and burned in cinematic style, as she lamented in a 1933 verse:

> There's a reason why I cry at night
> And writhe with pain in my heart,
> While I curse the intervening miles
> That relentlessly keep us apart.
> I know that it's foolish to lie here and dream.
> And wipe eyes that will not be dry,
> But memories are all that I have left
> Since the night we kissed good-bye.[25]

Yet even while testifying to the popularity of heterosexual romantic ideals, one Los Angeles columnist, "Mme. Yamato Nadeshiko," deplored their impact. Her diatribe also underscored the effectiveness of mainstream media as a vehicle for these rosy notions. She felt that "seeing too many movies" and "reading too many novels" had caused Nisei women to harbor unrealistic dreams of "tall stalwart sons of men, bronzed by desert's noonday heat and whipped by bitter rain and hail. Hearts of gold, strength of steel, romantic Romeos." She warned women not to wait for a "Sir Galahad" but to recognize the "everyday heroes [who] exist all about us."[26] Another columnist who identified herself as "a deb" similarly mused, "The trouble with us is— we build too many air castles. And we pick on a man, the dream of our teens as the 'one and only'—who not only seems sincere, but can do no wrong. But that's being over romantic and over idealized. Sort of dangerous, don't you think?" She advised her peers "to be hardboiled towards love" because "we're just bound to undergo some of its misfortunes."[27] Her admonition transmitted not only caution about, but also an expectation of, romantic love.

Given these aims, it is not surprising that second-generation women increasingly challenged the practice of arranged marriage in favor of "love marriage." As Nakano Glenn states, "With the loosening of traditional family controls, the urban nisei had moved toward the ideal of 'free marriage' by the mid 1930s."[28] Nisei women, who had far less veto power over the choice of marital partners than Nisei men, wrote frequently to Nisei advice columnist "Deirdre" to rail against arranged matches.[29] Extensive and heated dialogues among readers often raged for weeks in the popular San Francisco newspaper column. In a 1934 article in the Los Angeles *Kashu*

Mainichi, Mary Korenaga passionately decried such unions, asking rhetorically if Nisei should allow themselves to "become a breeding machine to which we are forced by the third party merely for the purpose of keeping the world populated? Are we to lose emotions which we have harbored merely to become a human mechanism on the order of the common ant?" "No!" she declared. "A thousand times, No!"[30] The priority Korenaga placed on individual choice and romantic love mirrors the Nisei's embrace of mainstream ideals of companionate marriage.

Wedding announcements also revealed the adoption of mainstream female rituals: The *Kashu Mainichi* reported in 1932 that Masao Oshima, who would soon "middle-aisle it with Mr. Eddie Izumi . . . was honored at a linen shower" hosted by her friends.[31] In the same year, Yaeno Sakai was feted with a china shower given by "her feminine acquaintances."[32] The ethnic newspapers also began to take note of honeymoons, as in the case of newlyweds Shigeo and Florence Kato who planned to go to the Grand Canyon.[33] By the 1930s, the honeymoon was another mainstream middle-class practice followed by the second generation, or at least by those who were affluent enough.

Ironically, the dominant society not only broadened but also constrained Nisei marital choices, which were made within the framework established by state codification of racial discrimination, strikingly embodied in the anti-miscegenation laws that Peggy Pascoe examines. Like their mothers, Nisei women retained values of duty and obligation and expected to marry men of their own racial-ethnic group. This stemmed not only from the strong preference of the Japanese American community, but also from the even stronger opposition of the dominant society. In 1880 California's anti-miscegenation law was amended to include Asians. The marriage of a white person to a "Negro, mulatto, Mongolian or Malay" was illegal until the overturn of the law in 1948. By the 1930s, fourteen states—including Arizona, California, Idaho, Montana, Nebraska, Nevada, Oregon, Utah, and Wyoming—had anti-miscegenation laws aimed at Asian immigrants and their children.[34] In the arena of marital choice, as in other social and economic arenas, the Nisei remained highly conscious of the boundaries of race and gender.

Nisei women played a significant if sometimes stereotypical role as representatives of ethnic culture, both within and outside the Japanese American community. Kimono-clad young women and girls became a vivid image to other Nisei as well as to non-Japanese American schoolmates. As war-time events would subsequently show, European Americans on the whole viewed the Nisei as foreigners garbed in exotic robes. Ironically, unless they were learning traditional dance, most Nisei were unaccustomed to wearing kimonos, pulled out on rare occasions from mothball-filled trunks. Novelist Yoshiko Uchida wove this situation into a scene in which an Issei mother helps her daughter and two other Nisei girls dress in kimonos for an International Club program at the daughter's high school:

> The girls gasped for breath as Hana tightened the *obi* around their chests and tried to ease the pressure with their fingers. They stumbled clumsily about the room as the thongs of the *zori* dug at the flesh between their toes. Hana smiled at their awkwardness Although wrapped in silken grace, their unaccustomed bodies resisted, and at least in Hana's eyes, they did not look like anything other than foreigners in Japanese dress.[35]

To Hana, an Issei, the Japanese kimono in fact reveals the Nisei's "Americanness."

The teenaged Nisei protagonist of Yamamoto's story also retains a striking image of girls in kimono. Remembering a program of traditional Japanese dance performed in Little Tokyo, Chisato feels envious of "the child dancers with their faces painted dead white, their blackened eyebrows and bright red bee-stung lips. They seemed a world apart in their brilliant silken kimonos, in their gliding movements to the plucked music and wailing song, in their convoluted wigs adangle with chains of cherry blossoms."[36] While Chisato considers them "privileged" to take odori lessons, it is also clear that she regards them as inhabiting "a world apart" from her in their elaborate costumes and makeup, as they dance to a "wailing" music quite different in rhythm and key from the Cream of Wheat song that she had memorized. From Chisato's point of view, becoming a performer of traditional dance seems glamorous and means receiving approving applause from the ethnic community; but it also appears somewhat alien.

To some Issei parents, the proper wearing of a kimono and the study of traditional dance became intertwined with socializing their daughters to behave with modest feminine grace. Ko Wakatsuki, the father of Jeanne Wakatsuki Houston, co-author of *Farewell to Manzanar*, fell into this camp. He became furious when he learned that Jeanne, dressed in a Dorothy Lamour-style sarong, had been voted the high school carnival queen of 1947. In desperation he tried to bargain with her, saying, "You want to be a carnival queen? I tell you what. I'll make a deal with you. You can be the queen if you start odori lessons at the Buddhist Church as soon as school is out."[37] Both Jeanne and her father knew, however, that it was too late for these classes to have the effect on her that her father desired.

Issei parents like Ko Wakatsuki worried about the impression their daughters would make not only on European American society but also within the ethnic enclave. In addition to being viewed by non-Japanese Americans as representatives of their ethnic group,[38] Nisei women met the scrutiny of sharp-eyed Issei elders as representatives of their families. Community surveillance exerted great pressure on some young women, as reflected by the case of one Nisei who suffered from uterine hemorrhaging. As Dana Takagi has related, the woman's mother waited for months to seek medical treatment for her, fearing that the family would be stigmatized if the Japanese American community found out about her disease.[39] Ironically, because the mother insisted that the daughter's radiation treatment be kept secret, the ethnic community gossiped about the possible reasons for her regular trips to the hospital. Later she discovered that people believed she was sexually promiscuous and routinely going for abortions. While this may be an extreme example, it provides an illustration of the kinds of familial and community pressure with which single young Nisei women lived.

Less dramatic, more mundane pressures were familiar to most second-generation girls. Like Monica Sone, they found that Issei teachers and community leaders wished to mold them into "an ideal Japanese o-joh san, a refined young maiden who is quiet, pure in thought, polite, serene, and self-controlled."[40] As Sone remembered, this meant that children "must not laugh out loud and show our teeth, or chatter in front of guests, or interrupt adult conversation, or cross our knees while seated, or ask for a piece of candy, or squirm in our seats."[41]

Adolescents and young women felt even more keenly the weight of expectations of proper female behavior. In 1934, one rebellious high school student in San Francisco bemoaned the limitations of "Girls who walk the usual tread of life all planned by society and family" and described a dreary round of domesticity, concluding that for women, "Life is a matter of surpressing [sic]."[42] She made it clear that fear of community scrutiny enforced compliance: "We do our darnest [sic] to keep our self free from gossip. Anything different even in a form of an experiment will cause a riot among the sneeking [sic], whispering gossip-front."[43] Although her outspoken defiance may have been unusual, her awareness of social pressure was not.

Once she reached her twenties, a second-generation woman faced increasing pressure to marry. Parental expectations were reinforced by those of the other Issei elders. A writer for the San Francisco *Hokubei Asahi* related the "typical case" of a twenty-four-year-old college-educated Nisei woman who had "staved off four proposals to her father by 'friends' of comparatively unknown or personally repulsive men." According to the author, "The matter becomes worse because of the girl's age, which is a terrible age for an unmarried Japanese daughter to be still on her father's hand—people are already beginning to ask what is the matter with her that she cannot secure a husband." He added, "She is not alone—there are hundreds like her in the same situation."[44]

Given such pressures, Nisei girls and single women found much-needed camaraderie and peer-group understanding in a wide array of urban Japanese American organizations. As Harry H. L. Kitano states, "It would be difficult to overlook the vast network of services and opportunities available to the Japanese youth."[45] There they also gained leadership training and built networks that would aid them in the trying years of wartime incarceration and postwar resettlement. Indeed, as Nakano Glenn suggests, women have "emerged over time as prime movers in the life" of the ethnic community.[46]

Southern California was rich in Nisei organizations; Mei Nakano has reported that more than four hundred could be counted in Los Angeles by 1938.[47] Throughout the decade before World War II, the Nisei social calendars of the *Kashu Mainichi* and other newspapers bristled with meetings and events hosted by a burgeoning array of young women's clubs. In May of 1932, an annual Junior Girl Reserves conference drew members of at least seventeen clubs, ranging from Buddhist and Christian church-sponsored groups, YWCA affiliates and Girl Scouts.[48] Although clubs abounded for every age cohort, adolescents and college-age single women constituted the majority of those involved in Nisei female organizations. Full-time jobs and marriage no doubt cut into the leisure time of older Nisei women in addition to drawing them into different social arenas.

The youth groups served a variety of functions. According to Kitano, they were a means of social control and socialization: "During early and late adolescence, Nisei generally were controlled by organizations within the community. These often took the form of leagues and clubs . . ." Control of these organizations was often exercised by peers rather than parents; Kitano notes that "although the Issei periodically attempted to control them," the groups were "usually guided by the Nisei themselves. The youngsters were left pretty much alone, to make mistakes, to try new things, and to translate their understanding of large community models in ways that could be of use to them."[49] For young Nisei women, who, like their Mexican American sisters "sought to reconcile parental expectations with the excitement of experimentation,"[50] youth clubs afforded a heady opportunity.

These groups provided an important alternative for Japanese American children excluded from European American clubs or unable to assume leading positions in them. "If we hadn't had these ethnic organizations to join," Yoshiko Uchida writes, "I think few Nisei would have had the opportunity to hold positions of leadership or responsibility. At one time I was president of the campus Japanese Women's Student Club, a post I know I would not have held in a non-Japanese campus organization."[51] Within their own organizations, Nisei members received reinforcement of generational and ethnic identification, often finding role models in more senior Nisei advisers. Both Christian and Buddhist churches fostered girls' and boys' clubs, although YWCA-sponsored activities were particularly extensive. The Nisei women who attended college established another tier of organizations, such as the Blue Triangles and the Chi Alpha Delta sorority in Los Angeles. Women forged lifetime friendships in these clubs. The continued meetings of some groups, fifty years later, underscore their significance for the Nisei.

Women's organizations provided socialization in both mainstream and ethnic culture. Some, like the Sumire Kai, a junior women's club, met to learn about the history of Japan and the intricacies of Japanese etiquette.[52] A similar group, the Shira-yuri (white lily) club formed in Long Beach, vowing to speak only Japanese at their meetings.[53] Other organizations provided a forum in which to explore peer-group and intergenerational issues, as well as to participate in a range of activities common to groups like the Girl Scouts of America. For example, the Junior Girl Reserves conference in 1932 included in its schedule swimming, hiking, handicrafts, nature study, music, and outdoor sports. The featured topics of discussion reflected the influence of popular culture: "What the Boy Friend Thinks?" "What is 'It'?" and "What We All Think of Dancing?"[54] The leaders also hoped to facilitate intergenerational understanding by offering discussions of mother-daughter relations.

The reportage of club events reveals how such organizations established and sometimes gently pushed the boundaries of socially sanctioned activities for Japanese American girls, from charitable endeavors to recreation. The growing popularity of dances throughout the prewar years provides an example of changing cultural mores. In this respect, generally speaking, city youth had greater latitude than their rural peers, women as well as men. Indeed, women took the initiative in planning, regulating, and maybe even attending dances, as a stern admonition to southern California gate-crashers indicated in 1931: "Men and women who walked in without invites at the last Blue Triangle dance are getting into hot water and the sooner their crusts melt away the better."[55]

Leap Year dances planned by the Blue Triangles and Chi Alpha Delta received special notice from the *Kashu Mainichi* in January 1932: "Already two dances are scheduled in February for the benefit of the supposed-to-be stronger sex by the weaker sex."[56] The Cherry Blossom and Nadeshiko Clubs of nearby Gardena, California, also planned to sponsor jointly a Leap Year dance. The repeated mention that dances would be "strictly invitational" suggests their success in attracting Nisei youth eager to "glide to the strains of Jack Gary's 8-piece Masonic orchestra" and other ensembles.[57] Such heterosexual couples-dancing would have been unheard-of for the Nisei's immigrant parents and still incurred the disapproval of rural Issei.

Many of the clubs had a social-service component. The first act of the newly formed girls' Calrose Club was to make a gift of a box of apples to a children's organization.[58] Even recreational activities like dances provide opportunities for community service. Of the five spring dances announced in the *Kashu Mainichi* in 1932, three were "benefit dances." Admission to the Savings Association Dance required "the presentation of the invitation cards and three large cans of food, preferably Japanese."[59] Later in May, the Blue Triangles lured the light of foot to their "cabaret style" benefit dance with the promise of waltz and fox-trot contests and live music to be furnished by Dave Sato's Wanderer Orchestra.[60] Through such measures, the Nisei responded to community needs while enjoying "the excitement of experimentation." As they maintained peer-regulated activities and developed their own forums for entertainment, exercise, creative expression, and leadership training, a rich Nisei social world coalesced.

In the decade before the Second World War, young Nisei women played important roles in shaping and sustaining urban ethnic culture, while developing a strong generational consciousness that still continues to permeate Japanese American organizations. Participation in a range of youth groups gave urban Nisei girls and single women high visibility in the ethnic community, which reinforced their position as cultural negotiators. Through service projects, social occasions, athletic events, and a range of cultural arts performances, second-generation women interacted with both the Issei generation and Nisei men, as well as with members of surrounding communities. And, as their poems, short stories, essays, and letters in the Japanese American newspapers testify, the process of defining a position in society engaged and challenged them from early adolescence. In this process they remained mindful of family responsibilities and cultivated ethnic pride, while striving to piece together a kind of modern womanhood appropriate to their dreams and circumstances.

World War II internment not only dashed many Nisei dreams and shattered Japanese American communities; it has, in the historical literature, overshadowed the vibrancy of Little Tokyo and other prewar ethnic enclaves. Researching Nisei women's writings and organizations in the 1930s reveals the complexity of the second generation's negotiation of roles within the urban ethnic community. Their labor materially supported their families through the Great Depression, during World War II, and in the critical period of postwar rebuilding. They have acted as primary conduits of gender-role debate into Japanese American enclaves. And they have earned reputations within the ethnic group for being its premier grassroots organizers.[61] In the process of integrating the worlds of their parents and peers since the prewar period, urban

Nisei women have created networks that continue to shape and sustain Japanese American communities today.

Notes

A version of this paper was presented at the 50th Anniversary Conference of the Arthur and Elizabeth Schlesinger Library on the History of Women in America and published in pamphlet form in Susan Ware, ed., *New Viewpoints in Women's History: Working Papers from the Schlesinger Library 50th Anniversary Conference, March 4–5, 1994* (Cambridge: Schlesinger Library, 1994).

  For their insightful comments on this paper I thank Blake Allmendinger, Estelle Freedman, Peggy Pascoe, Vicki Ruiz, and Judy Yung.

1. Vicki L. Ruiz, "The Flapper and the Chaperone: Historical Memory among Mexican-American Women," *Seeking Common Ground: Multidisciplinary Studies of Immigrant Women in the United States*, ed. Donna Gabaccia (Westport, CT: Greenwood Press, 1992), p.151; see also her article "'La Malinche Tortilla Factory': Negotiating the Iconography of Americanization, 1920–1950," *Privileging Positions: The Sites of Asian American Studies*, ed. Gary Y. Okihiro et al. (Pullman: Washington State University Press, 1995), pp. 201–15. See also Judy Yung, *Unbound Feet: A Social History of Chinese Women in San Francisco* (Berkeley: University of California Press, 1995); George Sanchez, *Becoming Mexican American: Ethnicity, Culture and Identity in Chicano Los Angeles, 1900–1945* (New York: Oxford University Press, 1993); Mei Nakano, *Japanese American Women: Three Generations, 1890–1990* (Berkeley: Mina Press Publishing/San Francisco: National Japanese American Historical Society, 1990). Eileen Tamura's study *Americanization, Acculturation and Ethnic Identity: The Nisei Generation in Hawaii* (Urbana: University of Illinois Press, 1994) provides a richly detailed examination of the Nisei's education, work, and cultural shifts in Hawaii. Dissertations by David K. Yoo and Lon Y. Kurashige provide valuable windows into the history of second-generation Japanese Americans on the U.S. mainland: see Yoo, "Growing Up Nisei: Second Generation Japanese-Americans of California, 1921–1945," Yale University, Ph.D., 1994; and Kurashige, "Made in Little Tokyo: Politics of Ethnic Identity and Festival in Southern California, 1934–1994," University of Wisconsin, Ph.D., 1994.
2. *Kashu Mainichi*, January 5, 1936.
3. *Kashu Mainichi*, October 2, 1932. This excerpt contains no deletions; the ellipses are Tanna's own punctuation.
4. Evelyn Nakano Glenn, *Issei, Nisei, War Bride: Three Generations of Japanese American Women in Domestic Service* (Philadelphia: Temple University Press, 1986), p. 55.
5. Ruiz, "The Flapper and the Chaperone," p. 146.
6. Mei Nakano, p. 120.
7. *Kashu Mainichi*, May 20, 1934.
8. Kazuo Kawai, "Three Roads and None Easy," *Survey Graphic* 9, no. 2 (May 1926), p. 165.
9. Yung, p. 134.
10. *Kashu Mainichi*, June 23, 1935.
11. Monica Sone, *Nisei Daughter* (Seattle: University of Washington Press, 1953), p. 133.
12. Yoshiko Hosoi Sakurai interview, Los Angeles, California, August 28–29, 1996.
13. Gene Gohara, "Domestic Employment," *Current Life* (June 1941): 6.
14. Yung, p. 157.
15. Kawai, p. 165.
16. *Kashu Mainichi*, January 20, 1932.
17. Hisaye Yamamoto, "A Day in Little Tokyo," in *Seventeen Syllables and Other Stories* (Latham, NY: Kitchen Table: Women of Color Press, 1988), p. 119.
18. *Kashu Mainichi*, September 16, 1934.
19. *Kashu Mainichi*, October 30, 1932.
20. Ibid.
21. *Hokubei Asahi*, October 12, 1934.
22. Wakako Yamauchi interview, Gardena, California, October 3, 1995.
23. Ruiz, "The Flapper and the Chaperone," pp. 141–58.
24. From "Three Thoughts," *Kashu Mainichi*, May 22, 1932.
25. From "heartache," *Kashu Mainichi*, August 26, 1933.
26. *Kashu Mainichi*, July 10, 1932.
27. From "Feminine Interest," *Kashu Mainichi*, October 6, 1935.

28. Nakano Glenn, p. 57.
29. I discuss Nisei women's views of love and marriage, and focus on the "I'm Telling You Deirdre" column, in "Redefining Expectations: Nisei Women in the 1930s," *California History* (Spring 1994): 44–53, 88. For more information on "Deirdre"—Mary Oyama Mittwer—see my article, "Desperately Seeking 'Deirdre': Gender Roles, Multicultural Relations, and Nisei Women Writers of the 1930s," *Frontiers* 12, no. 1 (1991): 19–32.
30. *Kashu Mainichi*, March 4, 1934.
31. *Kashu Mainichi*, January 8, 1932.
32. *Kashu Mainichi*, June 4, 1932.
33. *Kashu Mainichi*, December 2, 1931.
34. Peggy Pascoe's work on anti-miscegenation law is especially useful; see her articles: "Race, Gender, and the Privileges of Property: On the Significance of Miscegenation Law in the U.S. West," in this volume; "Miscegenation Law, Court Cases, and Ideologies of 'Race' in Twentieth-Century America," *Journal of American History* 83, no. 1 (June 1996): 44–69; and "Race, Gender, and Intercultural Relations: The Case of Interracial Marriage," *Frontiers* 12, no. 1 (1991): 5–18. For a detailed discussion of anti-miscegenation laws and their application to Asian Americans, see Megumi Dick Osumi, "Asians and California's Anti-Miscegenation Laws," in *Asian and Pacific American Experiences: Women's Perspectives*, ed. Nobuya Tsuchida (Minneapolis: Asian/Pacific American Learning Resource Center and General College, University of Minnesota, 1982), pp. 1–37.
35. Yoshiko Uchida, *Picture Bride* (New York: Simon and Schuster, Inc., 1987), p. 134.
36. Yamamoto, p. 116.
37. Jeanne Wakatsuki Houston and James D. Houston, *Farewell to Manzanar* (New York: Bantam Books, Inc., 1974), p. 127.
38. The Japanese American community was highly conscious of outside scrutiny and responded, in Harry H. L. Kitano's words, with "appeals to all individuals to behave in a manner that would reflect to the benefit of all Japanese." Kitano, *Japanese Americans: The Evolution of a Subculture*, 2nd ed. (Englewood Cliffs, NJ: Prentice-Hall, Inc., 1976), p. 36.
39. Dana Y. Takagi, "Personality and History: Hostile Nisei Women," *Reflections on Shattered Windows: Promises and Prospects for Asian American Studies*, ed. Gary Y. Okihiro et al. (Pullman: Washington State University Press, 1988), p. 187.
40. Sone, p. 28.
41. Sone, p. 27.
42. *Hokubei Asahi*, October 11, 1934.
43. Ibid.
44. *Hokubei Asahi*, November 5, 1934.
45. Kitano, p. 60.
46. Nakano Glenn, p. 38.
47. Mei Nakano, p. 120.
48. *Kashu Mainichi*, May 22, 1932.
49. Kitano, *Japanese Americans*, p. 50.
50. Ruiz, "The Flapper and the Chaperone," p. 151.
51. Yoshiko Uchida, *Desert Exile, The Uprooting of a Japanese American Family* (Seattle: University of Washington Press, 1982), p. 44.
52. *Kashu Mainichi*, April 16, 1932.
53. *Kashu Mainichi*, June 9 and 17, 1932.
54. *Kashu Mainichi*, April 15 and May 22, 1932. The Junior Girl Reserves discussion of "It" was doubtless a legacy of Clara Bow, the "It Girl," and the promotion of "sex appeal" in the 1920s.
55. *Kashu Mainichi*, November 17, 1931.
56. *Kashu Mainichi*, January 5, 1932.
57. *Kashu Mainichi*, November 28, 1931.
58. *Kashu Mainichi*, November 19, 1931.
59. *Kashu Mainichi*, March 29, 1932.
60. *Kashu Mainichi*, May 6, 1932.
61. A good illustration of Nisei women's roles as community organizers can be found in the successful political movement to seek redress and reparations for World War II internment. See Alice Yang Murray's dissertation, "'Silence, No More': The Japanese American Redress Movement, 1942–1992," Stanford University, Ph.D., 1995.

23

In Search of Unconventional Women
Histories of Puerto Rican Women in Religious Vocations Before Mid-Century

Virginia Sánchez Korrol

Oral history is frequently used to document the lives of people deemed typical or representative of their group or community. The three women whose stories form the core of this essay, however, can help us understand a broader history precisely because they are unconventional: at a historical juncture in the development of Puerto Rican *barrios*, when women's roles were circumscribed by social custom and occupation, they chose to break new ground. Each followed a personal calling for spiritual and humanitarian reasons, and came to play an important pastoral and religious role. Though unknown outside of their respective religious communities, their important role in the history of the Puerto Rican community is just beginning to be understood.

The life histories of these unconventional women, as recorded through oral history, illuminate the professional and to a lesser extent, the personal life experiences of each individual, while also documenting their contributions at specific historical points in Puerto Rican community development. In this sense, the oral histories do more than add to our growing knowledge of individual Puerto Rican lives: they are especially valuable in enabling historians to begin to construct an inter-generational view of the Puerto Rican experience.[1]

Two of the women, Sister Carmelita and Reverend Leoncia Rosado, began their careers in the 1920s and 1930s, respectively. A vulnerable period in the development of the young community, it was also a time when women were expected to follow traditional roles and remain in the home as wives and mothers. The third woman, the Reverend Aimee García Cortese, is representative of the transitional second generation of Puerto Ricans, born in the U.S.A., which internalized many of the old customs while accommodating to a mainland reality.

The period between 1917 and 1950 was highly significant for Puerto Ricans in New York City. Under the leadership and influence of the earliest substantial migration from the island's rural and urban sectors, the community in New York City began to take shape as identifiably Puerto Rican. As early as 1910, over a thousand Puerto Ricans were said to reside in the United States. American citizenship, conferred in 1917, stimulated and facilitated migration, and within a decade all of the forty-eight states reported the presence of Puerto Rican-born individuals. Estimates indicate substantial population gains throughout the 1930s and 1940s, culminating in a total population of some 425,000 by mid-century, 80 percent of whom lived in New York City.[2]

Women formed an integral part of the migration experience, comprising over half the migrant flow in some decades. A partial tabulation of representative Hispanic districts in the New York State Manuscript Census of 1925, provides some insights into the earlier migrant population. Of 3,496 women listed in the census, the majority were young housewives, under thirty-five years of age, who had resided in the city for less than six years. For the most part, Puerto Rican family traditions defined women's place in the early New York community. Expected to fulfill traditional roles as wives and mothers, women were conditioned to accept these roles as their primary life functions, regardless of their degree of involvement in community, career, or work-related activities.[3]

However, when confronted with the economic realities of an overwhelmingly poor community, close to 25 percent of the migrant women went to work outside the home in factories, laundries, and restaurants. This figure would rise in the coming decades, and parallel the demand for workers in the garment and other industries. Many women worked as seamstresses and domestics; others found ways to combine homemaking with gainful employment by taking in lodgers, caring for the children of working mothers and doing piecework at home.

While the majority of the migrant women fit into the above categories, a handful—less than 4 percent—established a foothold in other areas. These were the women who were either formally educated, skilled or bilingual, or who, by virtue of their community involvement, exercised leadership roles. Some sought and secured white-collar, office employment upon their arrival in the city; the status inherent in that work was sufficient to raise them above the ordinary. Others proceeded to launch supportive community enterprises, or to form volunteer organizations in response to the special needs of the community, as they had previously done in Puerto Rico. Still others, writers, poets, essayists and journalists, expressed themselves through their creative and artistic talents,[4] Finally, there were the women who chose the church, and in their own way contributed towards—and help us understand—Puerto Rican community development.

Carmela Zapata Bonilla Marrerro was born in Cabo Rojo, Puerto Rico in 1907. Raised in a rural atmosphere on the western coast of the Island, she belonged to a family composed predominantly of middle-class farmers and property owners. After the premature death of her mother in 1918, a move to Mayaguez, the island's third largest city, enabled her to receive a Catholic school education. During this tender period in her life Carmelita first articulated the desire to enter a convent. At sixteen, she made the decision to become a missionary nun in the Roman Catholic Church. Leaving her home and family for Georgia, the conventual center of the Trinitarian Order, in 1923, she hardly imagined that this would be the first of many trips between Puerto Rico and the U.S.

What impressions and images must have crossed the girl's mind as she made the five-day journey alone from San Juan to Brooklyn, where the ship was due to make port! She believes she left on a Thursday because the steamship lines always sailed from Thursdays to Mondays; she remembers traveling second class which offered the same menu as first, but without the dancing; and she recalls that the nuns met her ship at the Columbia Heights Promenade at Fulton Street. Carmelita spent her first night at the Brooklyn convent painfully aware that she was in strange surroundings, and anxiously anticipating her trip to Georgia, where she would enter the Convent of the Holy Trinity to begin her novitiate. Two years later, she was given her first assignment and sent to her order's Court Street Center, in Brooklyn, the first Puerto Rican nun in their community. As a young nun, she had little choice in the matter, but the assignment proved to be propitious for the Brooklyn Puerto Rican community. As she recalled, her first impressions were:

> that center was two old houses and they were put together for the purpose of having clubs—we had boy scouts, girl scouts, brownies, sewing clubs, manual work for the children, mother's clubs, library, arts, crafts, all that. We had hundreds of children. We had no Puerto Ricans in this neighborhood then. We had lots of Polish, Irish. It was called Irishtown . . . (There were) Polish, Lithuanian, Chinese, Filipino.[5]

Although her earliest missionary work was carried out among the poor multi-ethnic children of Brooklyn, it was the plight of the Puerto Rican migrants that sparked Sister Carmelita's imagination and dedication:

> During those years it was when they use to put them, you know, out—dispossess them—and it was very hard. And I thought that it was my duty to save every Puerto Rican that I found—from anything. I felt that terrible, you know, so I remember seeing them on the sidewalk, with all their children, and their beds, and all their things—dispossessed. Then we had no welfare. So then I remember a friend of mine—in 176 Sand Street—she owned that building and one day I met her. And I use to visit Puerto Ricans there. "Sister," she said, "I have this building and nobody pays rent so I'm gonna give you the key to this building. When you see a family dispossessed, you bring them to this building." That's what I did. I had that building filled with people—no heat, but anyway, they had a house for a while.[6]

Sister Carmelita remained in Brooklyn until 1949, active in numerous social welfare programs. A familiar sight in the local precincts and hospitals, she was frequently called upon to intercede on behalf of the Puerto Rican community, to translate for them and guide their general welfare. But her return to her native Puerto Rico allowed Sister Carmelita the opportunity to teach and pursue her own academic interests within the structure of her convent. She earned a Bachelor's degree as well as a Master's from the University of Puerto Rico, concentrating on the study of social work, an area in which she was experienced. In time, a personal desire to return to the Brooklyn community and the families she had left behind motivated Carmelita to request a transfer to the mission center where she had initiated her career.

During the fourteen years that Carmelita spent in New York, a diverse Puerto Rican community—the *Barrio Hispano*—developed. It straddled the East River with *colonias*, or neighborhoods, on both sides. Puerto Ricans predominated among the city's Spanish-speaking population. As American citizens, they were unaffected by the immigration barriers that restricted aliens from coming to the U.S. In terms of actual numbers, however, census figures varied depending on who was taking the count. Puerto Ricans could easily fit into several groupings. They could be counted as blacks or whites or racially mixed, as citizens or immigrants. To further complicate matters, as residents of a U.S. possession, Puerto Ricans did not figure into immigration counts.

A report issued by the New York Mission Society in 1927 estimated a total of between 100,000 and 150,000 Spanish-speaking inhabitants of whom approximately 85,000 were Puerto Ricans engaged in the cigar-making industry.[7] Overwhelmingly working class, theirs was a tightly knit, introspective community whose neighborhood organizations boasted substantial audiences of one or two hundred persons at any given function, and where Spanish-language newspapers and magazines found an appreciative reading public.[8] Culturally, the Puerto Rican community identified strongly with Spanish America. The Spanish language and the Roman Catholic faith served to weld close bonds. The institutionalization of common customs and tradition insured both the insulation and isolation of the nascent *colonias*. Advocacy in their interest frequently rested with the organizations that structured the community.

The work of Sister Carmelita and her Trinitarian Sisters notwithstanding, the Catholic Church was slow to respond to the needs of the growing Puerto Rican settlements, most of which were nominally Catholic. The first church to offer masses in Spanish was Nuestra Señora de la Medalla Milagrosa, founded in East Harlem in the 1920s. La Milagrosa was followed by Santa Agonia and St. Cecilia, both of which were established during the 1930s.[9]

By 1939, the Catholic Diocese initiated reforms based on the premise that all parish churches should become integrated or multinational. Previously, the Diocese had favored ethnic or nationality-oriented churches, and these had adequately provided guidance, pastoral services and a sense of cultural identity for earlier Polish, Irish, and Italian immigrant groups. Influential and respected institutions, the nationality churches cushioned the immigration experience of their congregation by fostering ties with the native land, language, and customs. Moreover, the churches functioned as brokers or mediators between the immigrant and the dominant society. However, in the case of the Puerto Ricans, the new policies that argued against differential treatment were rationalized on several counts. First, unlike other immigrant groups before them, Puerto Ricans did not bring clergy with them to the New York settlements. Indeed, the Church failed to understand the point that in the island there had never been sufficient numbers of native-born Puerto Rican priests. Non-native, Spanish-speaking clergy had been imported to Puerto Rico for decades. Second, and more significant, the Catholic Diocese in New York had weathered a decline in third-generation national church membership. It argued that the already existing clergy, as well as schools and churches, could simply be retrained and restructured to accommodate the Puerto Ricans.[10] Partly because of the failure of this policy, many of the spiritual and social-welfare needs of the Puerto Ricans defaulted to numerous community organizations. These included charitable groups such as the Catholic Settlement Association, the New York City Mission Society, Casita Maria, and the Protestant churches.

Throughout the years, Sister Carmelita utilized the organizations, as well as the church, in her work. She was one of the founders of the settlement house Casita Maria, and she is directly credited with influencing and motivating the academic growth and aspirations of numerous youngsters of that period.[11] Her recollections evoke images of a dismally poor and needy community. She was frequently called upon to advocate for the non-English speaker; to mediate between migrant parents, intent on maintaining island customs, and their rebellious U.S.-born children; and to confront the authorities on behalf of the community. Her vocation dictated expertise in teaching, counseling, and religion, and her dedication to the people she served sharpened her knowledge of the law, public health, the penal system and housing. Her office in St. Joseph's on Pacific Street was open to everyone and she developed a resource network rooted as much in the leadership of the Puerto Rican *barrios* as in the church. She states:

> I was a friend of the politicians. I must admit I used to ask the politicians for help, you know, especially those that sold *bolita* (numbers racket)—the bankers—and they used to help me a lot for the poor people. And then the politicians that didn't belong to the *bolita* were right there in Borough Hall so they were good to the Puerto Ricans. I use to visit everybody who was Spanish-speaking, no matter what it was or when it was and that's how I met all those people. I use to ask them to please help me out, like when Thanksgiving came—*el dia del pavo* – [the day of the Turkey] they used to give me two or three hundred dollars. I used to spend that in food and for Christmas. It was the same for *Reyes* [Three Kings' Day.][12]

Until poor health forced her retirement in the early 1970s, Sister Carmelita continued to do what she could to influence the social, cultural, and educational development of the Brooklyn Puerto Rican community. The number of Catholic institutions providing spiritual and material resources specifically for Puerto Ricans throughout the 1930s and 1940s was clearly limited.

By contrast, there were some twenty-five Puerto Rican Protestant churches, most of them Pentecostal. These were fundamentalist sects which adhered strictly to a literal interpretation of the Bible and encouraged rejection of worldly concerns among the members. The American invasion had facilitated the Protestantization of the island, accelerating a process already evident in the late nineteenth century. By the mid-1930s one observer noted that some of the Protestant churches in New York were located on the second floor of various types of buildings, and that as one approached Upper Harlem, these became more numerous. Some religious congregations met in private homes, while others rented storefronts for prayer and worship. Although the origin of the Pentecostal movement in New York remains unclear, an estimated five percent of the Puerto Ricans living in the city during this period were Protestant.[13] And within a decade, the Pentecostals had become the fastest-growing Protestant group among Puerto Ricans.

Dependent on a grass-roots tradition for their leadership, ministers often came from the ranks of the congregants. Sects were frequently self-starting and self-sustaining, supervised by ministers who were working class themselves. Small and intimate, many Pentecostal or evangelical churches provided a sense of community not found in the more traditional denominations.[14] Women played a pivotal role in this phase of church and community development, as they did within the structure of the Catholic Church. However, if conventual roles were limited under the strict, formal policies of that complex institutional structure, they were also restricted by gender. As a nun, subordinate to a male hierarchy, Sister Carmelita's professional and private life was circumscribed. By contrast, the Pentecostal faith permitted the ascendancy of a few women to the pulpit. Among these was the Reverend Leoncia Rosado Rosseau.

Born on April 11, 1912 in Toa Alta, Puerto Rico, Leoncia Rosado Rosseau believes that she was destined for the ministry from birth. The second of five children born to Señora Gumersinda Santiago Ferrer and don Manuel Rivera Marrerro, Leoncia received her religious calling in 1932 at the age of twenty. Then followed a period of evangelism in the poorest *barrios* of Puerto Rico. A small and slender young woman, she was not afraid to enter the most alien and hostile environments because she was convinced that it was all part of God's mission. Foretold in a vision that she was destined to carry God's word across the ocean, in 1935 she left the island for New York to continue her work as a missionary and evangelist. By 1937 she had received her first certificate in Divinity.[15]

In New York City, life was firmly anchored in church and community. Reverend Leoncia preached on street corners and delighted in debating scripture with nonbelievers. She offered testimony to the glory of God, visited the sick, and assisted in the general organization of her church. She traveled to the Dominican Republic and other Latin countries in the service of her church. There too she continued in her dual roles as missionary and evangelist. But while her spiritual gifts and fervent dedication were acknowledged by her fellow congregants, she was limited by tradition to addressing the congregation from the floor, and not the pulpit. On the eve of the Second World War she married a church elder, Roberto Rosado, and added to her life the dimensions of wife and homemaker.

About this time, the Puerto Rican community in New York City witnessed a decline in the numbers of individuals coming from the island and a rapid dispersement of those already residing in the city into all five boroughs. Puerto Ricans continued to fill the ranks of the working class and competed for the meager unskilled employment of the Depression period. But this situation changed radically in the 1940s, when women, minorities, and foreign nationals from bordering countries were vigorously recruited for factory and farm work. The labor shortages of the Second World War precipitated the large-scale Puerto Rican migration of the period just before and after the war. But this was only part of a broader expansion: close to 400,000 foreign contract workers entered the country in response to the demands of the labor market between 1942 and the end of the war, very few of whom were Puerto Rican. Some scholars argue that despite the general postwar contraction, the departure of many of those workers after the war created a vacuum in particular sectors of the labor market to which Puerto Rican workers responded. Between 1947 and 1949, a yearly net average of 32,000 individuals migrated from Puerto Rico, many destined to work in the garment and needle-trade industries.[16] They continued to be concentrated in blue-collar, low-paying sectors, especially in light industry. By 1948, the Migration Division of the island's Department of Labor established programs to aid potential migrants and to inform them about New York City. And by the start of mid-century, the great migration from Puerto Rico was well under way.[17]

For the charismatic Reverend Leoncia, this period represented a turning point in her life. It signaled the beginning of her ministry as Pastor of the Damascus Christian Church and it brought the church directly into the social service of the community through the creation of the Christian Youth Crusade.

According to the Reverend Leoncia, both events were foretold in a vision in which the Lord took her to the edge of a river where He indicated that she was to retrieve enormous quantities of carrots from the waters. She agonized over her task and exclaimed that she could not do it but He replied "Yes, you can. Continue. Take them out."[18]

Finally, I got them all out of the river and when I turned around I saw that all the carrots had become people and most were young. Then we walked in front of the multitudes which were uncountable and we were going to find Damascus. I don't know what had happened to them, but they had a small congregation. We had loudspeakers to take the message to the entire world. That's how far I went with the Lord and I wondered what this all meant.

Within a short time my husband was drafted. He was already an ordained minister. My husband at that time weighed 105 pounds because he was sick with a heart condition. And he did everything possible, even writing to the President of the United States, not to go into the army. I prayed that he wouldn't have to go but the Lord responded, "Do not pray for this—it is my will that he go, but he will return." He [Rosado] was sure that the army would not take him. When he went for his induction, weighing 105 pounds more infirmed than ever, he was accepted. It never crossed my mind to take over for him because I had forgotten my dream, and I could not seriously think or suggest this to him, and so we spoke of Brothers Fernando Noriega and Belén Camacho as possible substitutes. And I would assist them as I had helped (my husband). And so we went to meet with them to discuss this but they said, "No, not us. The one who should remain here is Sister Léo," and that's how I came to be pastor of the Damascus Christian Church.[19]

Even though precedents for women to act as missionaries and evangelists existed in Puerto Rico and in the New York Puerto Rican *barrios*, it was extremely rare for women to become ministers. In Puerto Rico, Juanita Garcia Peraza, or "Mita" as she was known to her followers, epitomized the role of women as evangelists and ministers.[20] There are few objective accounts of Mita's life and work, but her achievements were known on both sides of the ocean. In the early 1940s she inaugurated her own sect and Pentecostal church, which engaged in the operation of cooperatives and provided social services for its congregants. Her disciples believed she was God's incarnation on earth and referred to her as the "Goddess."

In the daily operations of Pentecostal churches in New York women were also indispensable. They supervised Bible study classes, succored the sick, comforted families in distress and performed countless acts of charity. Missionaries participated in street ministries and proselytized aggressively from door to door. Yet, despite the high degree of visibility and responsibility that women undertook in church matters, their involvement, by tradition, seldom extended to the pulpit.[21]

Although the Reverend Leoncia encountered resistance and discrimination toward her calling because of her gender, it was nothing compared to the obstacles she faced in orienting her church to the social/economic problems of the community. Until that point, pentecostalism among the Puerto Ricans in New York had served as a sanctuary from the cultural and social malaise inherent in the migration experience; it basically shielded the congregants from spiritual contamination by the outside world. Leoncia Rosado's ministry opened the way for new definitions.

When the Christian Youth Crusade was initiated in 1957, Damascus Christian church had expanded to include branches in other boroughs. One of the earliest grass-roots programs to fight drug abuse, it was sustained by funding from within the church. It provided a refuge for gangs, addicts, alcoholics and ex-convicts, and its philosophical base was strictly religious. The addict was viewed as a sinner and only repentance and acceptance of the Lord would bring about a cure. The major center for treatment was in the Damascus Christian Church in the Bronx but there was also an upstate site, Mountaindale, to which recovering addicts would go. In spite of its success, however, the church was most reluctant to engage in such community-oriented tasks. Reverend Leoncia recalled the confrontation with the church leaders on this matter:

> Our church was a church like any other. It did not work with alcoholics, etc. Sophisticated, illuminated with the Holy Spirit, yes, but it did not work with alcoholics. I came and told them of my vision. I understand these are alcoholics and lost souls, and the lowest people in society. But God wants us to do this work and they said, "Not here, no, no, not here," and I said to them, "Yes here! Because God mandates it of us." The church which closes its being and heart to the clamor of lost souls does not have a right to a place in the community. What do you think you're here for? Here is where the work is to be done and if you don't do it, I'll present my resignation. I was the pastor there then. My husband had returned from the army, and he was a bishop with the church council. Then they (the congregation) gave me a place that we call the Tower of Prayer, which was a long room and there I placed beds and cots which I found.
>
> Imagine a person like me, who had never even smoked a cigarette, unworldly, working with addicts, breaking their habits cold turkey, without aspirin or anything. My husband Roberto and I and the brothers and sisters of the church who helped us there . . . legs full of sores, and then when an addict is breaking the habit, their stinking sweat, that fever, the cold, the trembling, the heat, their screams . . . it was a tremendous thing!
>
> And that bunch of kids—about fifteen, sometimes twenty or twenty-five, and their crying Mama—that's where I got the name, Mama Léo—Mama, it hurts here, rub there, or there, and when I would treat there legs and feet, oozing full of sores, I would think, I held the feet of Our Lord.
>
> I would make them a banquet for Thanksgiving and they would come dirty, strung-out, sick, anyway at all but before feeding them I would provide a religious service with the other youths already saved. The kids would say, "Mama, we came for the bird and you gave us the Word!"[22]

An estimated two hundred and fifty to three hundred young people, mostly Hispanic, who were rehabilitated through that program went into the ministry. Many of them are active today in youth-oriented programs. Close to eighteen programs or schools have been established by them worldwide. Reverend Leoncia considers this her greatest and most rewarding mission.

If the community-service programs begun by Mama Léo served to initiate the church's role in the streets, her example as a pastor and as a woman illustrated new directions for some of the young Puerto Rican women growing up in New York during this period. One of these was the Reverend Aimee García Cortese. Aimee García Cortese was born in 1929, raised and educated in the New York Puerto Rican *barrio* of the South Bronx. Her close-knit and religious family offered Aimee and her two brothers and sister a stable and loving environment in which to grow. At thirteen, Aimee encountered Pentecostal outreach efforts for the first time when local church members offered prayers and services for her ailing mother. Soon afterwards, the family became active in church affairs. As New York teenagers, steeped in the world of movies and other social activities, the Garcías at first resisted the rigor, discipline, and sacrifice expected of Pentecostal youth. However, by the time Aimee was fifteen, she confided her intention to become a minister to her pastor, the Reverend Manuel López. He replied, "*las mujeres no predican*"—women do not preach! His pronouncement notwithstanding, and fortified by her personal belief that she was named after the American preacher Aimee Semple McPherson, she returned to him and proceeded to systematically badger him into letting her preach. She received permission to do so before her sixteenth birthday.[23]

> He told me that the next Sunday I would be preaching. Well I was so proud that I was going to preach, I never thought that I had nothing to say, I never thought that I wasn't prepared to face a crowd but I was so proud of the fact that I was going to preach that I got down on my knees and said Lord, you know you've got to bless me. Well next Sunday came and he told me to be at church at 5:30 a.m. I said that's a little early. When I got there, there were four other young people. One had a flag, one had a tambourine, one had a license in his hand and he (the pastor) said to me "Now you go out to Brook Avenue and 134th Street, and you preach." Oh, I thought it was going to be in church. "Oh no, mi hija, ahi es donde se aprende" [no, my daughter, that is where you'll learn] and it was there on that corner that I realized the strangest thing in the world: what do I say? I only knew two verses. All my friends were coming out of the holes, like cockroaches out of a wall. All of a sudden I'm surrounded by eighty, ninety kids of the neighborhood that had never seen me in this posture, and there was the crowd! I recited John 3:16, and then I went on to this other verse about God gives peace. I said this is very important that you know it. So then I went back to John 3:16, and then I went back to God is going to give you peace. I did that about five times and then I realized I had nothing to say. And I looked at the people and said, "Something great's happened in my life but I don't know how to say it. One of these days I'm gonna come back and tell you," and I started to cry. One young man tapped me on the shoulder and said, "vámonos" [Let's go]. And they took me back to the church. When I arrived, I was still crying and the pastor said, "te li'te gusto nena?" [Did you enjoy yourself?] I had nothing to tell them. "Well, he replied, "get ready to tell them something." And that was it. And he taught me my first year, 365 Bible verses.[24]

Aimee García Cortese went on to tell the people something. She was ordained by the Wesleyan Methodist Church in Puerto Rico in 1964, became a missionary evangelist for the Spanish Assemblies of God, Associated Minister of Thessalonica Christian Church in the South Bronx, and the first female chaplain for the New York State Department of Corrections. Reflecting on her past experience, Reverend García Cortese credits Reverend Leoncia Rosado Rosseau, as well as other ministers and missionaries, with opening the way for women in religious life and providing experiences from which to learn.

> There were women in ministry, but different types of ministry. Like, take la hermana Cartegena. She was the missionary of our church. She will be eighty years old, come 1986. Now there was a woman, deep in the Word, a woman dedicated to visitation, and dedicated to doing God's work. To watch her, to be with her . . . and as I grew in the Lord, I grew out of proportion, in terms that I did not go with the young people. They didn't satisfy me. What they were doing didn't satisfy me. What satisfied me was what la hermana Cartegena was doing. She would visit the sick, knock on doors, give out tracts, and I thought to myself, this is God's work! I was kind of ahead of my day. I was a young girl with a "little old lady" mentality. Now I realize it wasn't a "little old lady" mentality, it was "kingdom" mentality, but I didn't know what it was then. I didn't know I wanted to reach the world for Christ. I didn't know the extent of my drive. But now as I look back, I realize.

Elisa (Alicéa) was also a tremendous role model in the sense of daring to be innovative, in music, in leadership. [She] would pick up a trumpet and wake up a whole Puerto Rican town, in Ciales, and she did with music, you know, what, later on, I did with the Word. Just stirred people, woke them up, brought them into a "Hey, here's young people and we're doing something for God."

And there was Mama Léo. I don't ever think there was a moment I wanted to be [exactly] like her. I just loved her for what she was, but, it looked like her walk was a much more difficult walk than what I could do. In other words, to me, Léo was somebody to learn from, but never to want to be. Maybe because Léo was one hundred years ahead of her time. On a one-woman scale, she did what, later on, organizations like Teen Challenge did, or an organization like Odyssey House did in the secular [world]. You're talking about a little lady, all by herself taking on the world.[25]

The congregations directed by Reverend García Cortese, from the 1960s to the present, have incorporated many of the outreach programs that were considered radical in Reverend Leoncia Rosado's period. Today, youth and community programs are naturally included in church planning. Contemporary urban music plays a major role in attracting, and encouraging, religious expression among the youth. In Spanish or English, music has become an integral part of street ministries. If Reverend García Cortese's role as minister is no longer questioned because she is a woman, neither is the direction that she foresees for her congregation challenged. She envisions her church of the future to be a religious complex, including a community center with a swimming pool, gymnasium, physical fitness space, and Bible and Sunday schools. The building of the sanctuary would come last because a congregation's priority should be its youth and community. All of this she believes to be a legitimate part of worship.

From Sister Carmelita's period to Reverend García Cortese's, attitudinal changes toward church and community are apparent. They resulted from a combination of the external transformations of the 1960s, the maturation of the Puerto Rican community, and differing perspectives regarding women's roles. At the same time, similarities abound in the experiences of all three women. The utilization of these oral histories, in conjunction with an analysis of specific historical periods, offers a unique intergenerational perspective. They provide a significant variant on the history of Puerto Ricans in New York City, and more importantly they allow us to understand the continuity of our experience.

The task of recovering and defining women's histories in the New York Puerto Rican community before mid-century is clearly underway. From the 1920s to just after the Second World War, Puerto Ricans struggled to lay the foundations of a distinctive community with formal and informal coping structures, internal leadership, businesses, professions, common cultural interests and modes of behavior. The population movements alone, punctuated by the unique circular nature of the Puerto Rican migration, brought repeated ruptures and renewals of ties, dismantling and reconstructions of familial, individual, and communal networks. We have identified a small segment of the population that contributed to the process of community development, assumed the reins of leadership, and embraced demanding social commitments. Through their ministries and work with young people, women like Aimee García Cortese, Leoncia Rosado Rousseau, and Sister Carmelita aided in the stabilization of the Puerto Rican community at significant points in its historical development.

Notes

1. Oral histories with the Reverends Leoncia Rosado and Aimee García Cortese were taped during the winter of 1985 by the author and Dr. Benjamin Alicéa, New Brunswick Theological Seminary, with the purpose of elucidating a little-known period in the history of the Puerto Rican community in New

York City. The interview with Reverend Rosado was conducted in Spanish and translated by the author for this essay. The interview with Sister Carmelita was conducted and taped, by Professor John Vazquez, New York City Technical College, when he directed one of the earliest oral history projects on the Brooklyn Puerto Rican community in conjunction with the Brooklyn Historical Society.

2. Joseph P. Fitzpatrick, *Puerto Rican Americans: The Meaning of Migration to the Mainland*, Second Edition. (Englewood Cliffs, New Jersey: Prentice-Hall, Inc., 1987), 135.

3. Virginia Sánchez Korrol. From *Colonia to Community: The History of Puerto Ricans in New York City, 1917–1948*. (Westport, Connecticut: Greenwood Press, 1983.) ch. 4. See also: "On the Other Side of the Ocean: Work Experiences of Early Puerto Rican Migrant Women in New York," in *Caribbean Review* (January 1979), 23–30. Altagracia Ortiz explores the role of women in the garment industry from the 1940s to the fifties in "Puerto Rican Women in the ILGWU, 1940–1950." Paper presented at the Women's Studies Conference, Brooklyn College, April, 1984. For a broader and comparative analysis see Palmira Ríos, "Puerto Rican Women in the United States Labor Market," *Line of March* no. 18 (Fall 1985).

4. Numerous articles have appeared on notable women in Puerto Rican society. Among the most substantive are Isabel Picó de Hernández, "The History of Women's Struggle for Equality in Puerto Rico," and Norma Valle, "Feminism and its Influence on Women's Organizations in Puerto Rico," In Edna Acosta-Belén, *The Puerto Rican Women: Perspectives on Culture, History and Society* (New York: Praeger Press, 1986.) For an overview of exceptional women in New York, see: Virginia Sánchez Korrol, "The Forgotten Migrant: Educated Puerto Rican Women in New York City, 1920–1940," in *The Puerto Rican Woman*, 1986.

5. Interview with Sister Carmelita Bonilla, Puerto Rican Oral History Project, Brooklyn Historical Society, Brooklyn, New York, 1977. See also: Anthony Stevens-Arroyo, "Puerto Rican Struggles in the Catholic Church," in Clara E. Rodríguez et al, *The Puerto Rican Struggle: Essays on Survival in the U.S.* (Maplewood, New Jersey: Waterfront Press, 1984).

6. Interview with Sister Carmelita Bonilla.

7. One of the best sources for the Puerto Rican experience in the U.S. during this early period is Cesar Andreu Iglesias (ed.) *Memorias de Bernardo Vega* (Rio Piedras, Puerto Rico: Ediciones Huracán, 1977). English translation, *Memoirs of Bernardo Vega*, by Juan Flores, Monthly Review Press, 1984. See also History Task Force, Centro de Estudios Puertorriqueños, *Labor Migration Under Capitalism: The Puerto Rican Experience* (New York. Monthly Review Press, 1979), and Sánchez Korrol, *From Colonia to Community*, ch. 2.

8. Sánchez Korrol, *From Colonia to Community*, ch. 3. Another account of the community from the twenties to the forties is Jesús Colón's *A Puerto Rican in New York and Other Sketches* (New York: International Publishers, 1982). The Federal Writers Project, *The WPA Guide to New York* (New York: Pantheon Books, 1982) offers interesting observations regarding the Manhattan Puerto Rican community.

9. Fitzpatrick, *Puerto Rican Americans*, ch. 8.

10. Ann María Diaz Ramírez, The Roman Catholic Archdiocese of New York and the Puerto Rican Migration, 1950–1973: A Sociological and Historical Analysis." Ph.D. Dissertation, Fordham University, 1983. See also Anthony Stevens-Arroyo. "Puerto Rican Struggles in the Catholic Church," in Rodríguez et al, *The Puerto Rican Struggle*, and Fitzpatrick, *Puerto Rican Americans*, ch. 8.

11. Interview with Sister Carmelita Bonilla. A number of individuals interviewed in my research, including Elizabeth Guanill, former Commissioner of Human Rights, Suffolk County, New York, credit Sister Carmelita for guiding and encouraging them.

12. The Puerto Rican Oral History Project yielded other life experiences which supported Sister Carmelita's perspective. Among these was the interview with doña Honorina Weber Irizarry.

13. Lawrence R. Chenault. *The Puerto Rican Migrant in New York City* (New York: Russell and Russell, 1970), 129. Refer also to the dissertation in progress of Reverend Benjamin Alicéa, "The Puerto Rican Protestant Churches in East Harlem: 1912–1980," Union Theological Seminary, Columbia University, New York City.

14. Fitzpatrick, *Puerto Rican Americans*, 135–36.

15. Interview with Reverend Leoncia Rosado Rousseau. First Reformed Church, Queens, New York, November, 1985.

16. Sánchez Korrol, *From Colonia to Community*, ch. 2. See also: History Task Force, Centro de Estudios Puertorriqueños, 1979, ch. 2.

17. Numerous studies have appeared on the migration experience of Puerto Ricans during the fifties and sixties. Among these are C. Wright Mills, Clarence Senior and Rose Goldsen, *The Puerto Rican Journey: New York's Newest Migrants* (New York: Harper & Bros., 1950). Also, Elena Padilla, *Up From Puerto Rico* (New York: Columbia University Press, 1958), and Dan Wakefield, *Island in the City: The World of*

Spanish Harlem (Boston: Houghton Mifflin, 1959). Personal narratives include Piri Thomas's *Down These Mean Streets* (New York: Alfred Knopf, 1967), Nicholasa Mohr, *Nilda* (New York: Bantam, 1973), and Edward Rivera, *Family Installments* (New York: William Morrow & Co., 1982).

18. Interview with Reverend Leoncia Rosado Rousseau.

19. *Ibid.*

20. Anthony Stevens-Arroyo, "Religion and the Puerto Ricans in New York," in Edward Mapp (ed.) *Puerto Rican Perspectives* (Metuchen, New Jersey: The Scarecrow Press, Inc., 1974), 119–31.

21. Interviews with missionaries doña Virginia Martínez, New York City, doña Celina Díaz, Brooklyn, New York, and the Reverend Aimee García Cortese; Cross Roads Tabernacle Church, Bronx, New York, December, 1985.

22. Interview with Reverend Leoncia Rosado Rousseau. Reverend Rosado Rousseau's achievements, particularly with the Christian Youth Crusade, were highlighted in an article by Howard Broady, "The Power of Faith," Associated Press, 1959.

23. Interview with Reverend Aimee García Cortese, December, 1985.

24. *Ibid.*

25. *Ibid.*

"We Are that Mythical Thing Called the Public"

Militant Housewives during the Great Depression

Annelise Orleck

⚫

"We are that mythical thing called the public and so we shall demand a hearing."

—Jean Stovel, organizer of a housewives' flour boycott, Seattle, 1936

The last fifteen years have seen a growing literature on women in the 1930s. These new histories have examined organizing among working women of various ethnicities, illuminated women's political networks in the New Deal, and assessed the relationship of women to New Deal social welfare programs. But we still know next to nothing about how poor and working-class housewives fared during the Great Depression. To a large extent our view is shaped by popular imagery of the time, which glorified the self-sacrificing wife and mother. Black-and-white documentary photographs such as Dorothea Lange's portrait of a gaunt migrant woman sheltering her frightened children, novels such as Sholem Asch's *The Mother*, and films such as *The Grapes of Wrath* reinforced the popular view of poor mothers as the last traditionalists, guardians of the beleaguered home. In many ways this idealization of motherhood placed on poor women's shoulders the responsibility for easing the hardships of hunger and joblessness.[1]

In her 1933 book *It's Up to the Women*, Eleanor Roosevelt argued that mothers, through self-sacrifice and creativity, would save their families from the worst ravages of the Depression. There is abundant evidence to show that poor wives and mothers did approach their traditional responsibilities with heightened urgency during the Depression. They did not, however, suffer alone their inability to provide food or shelter for their families; nor did they sacrifice silently for the sake of their husbands and children. Quite the contrary. From the late 1920s through the 1940s, there was a remarkable surge of activism by working-class American housewives.[2]

From New York City to Seattle, from Richmond, Virginia, to Los Angeles, and in hundreds of small towns and farm villages in between, poor wives and mothers staged food boycotts and antieviction demonstrations, created large-scale barter networks, and lobbied for food and rent price controls. Militant and angry, they demanded a better quality of life for themselves and their children. Echoing the language of trade unionism, they asserted that housing and food, like wages and hours, could be regulated by organizing and applying economic pressure.

This was not the first time Americans were treated to the spectacle of housewives demanding food for their families. Since the early nineteenth century, hard times in New York, Philadelphia, and other major cities had moved housewives in immigrant neighborhoods to demonstrate for lower food prices. But never before had Americans seen anything this widespread or persistent. The crisis conditions created by the Depression of the 1930s moved working-class wives and mothers across the United States to organize on a scale unprecedented in U.S. history. By organizing themselves as class-conscious mothers and consumers, they stretched the limits of both working-class and women's organizing in the United States.

Housewives' activism, like that of every other group of Americans during the Depression era, was profoundly influenced by Franklin Roosevelt's New Deal. During the early years of the Depression, prior to the 1932 presidential election, housewives organized to stave off imminent disaster. Their focus was on self-help—setting up barter networks, gardening cooperatives, and neighborhood councils. After 1933 the tactics and arguments used by militant housewives reflected their acceptance of Roosevelt's corporatist vision. By the mid-1930s poor and working-class housewives, like farmers and factory workers, had begun to see themselves as a group that could, by organizing and lobbying, force the New Deal state to respond to their needs.

Press coverage reflected the ambivalence with which many Americans greeted the idea of politically organized housewives. Both mainstream and radical editors took their movement seriously. Housewives' strikes and demonstrations were featured in major newspapers and national magazines. Still, these publications could not resist poking fun at the very idea of a housewives' movement. Writers never tired of suggesting that, by its very existence, the housewives' movement emasculated male adversaries. A typical headline ran in the *New York Times* in the summer of 1935 at the height of housewives' activism nationwide. "Women Picket Butcher Shops in Detroit Suburb," it blared. "Slap. Scratch. Pull Hair. Men Are Chief Victims." A more pointed headline, about Secretary of Agriculture Henry Wallace, ran a few weeks later in the *Chicago Daily Tribune:* "Secretary Wallace Beats Retreat from Five Housewives." Underlying this tone of ridicule was a growing tension over the fact that housewife activists were politicizing the traditional roles of wives and mothers.[3]

In New York City neighborhoods, organized bands of Jewish housewives fiercely resisted eviction, arguing that they were merely doing their jobs by defending their homes and those of their neighbors. Barricading themselves in apartments, they made speeches from tenement windows, wielded kettles of boiling water, and threatened to scald anyone who attempted to move furniture out onto the street. Black mothers in Cleveland, unable to convince a local power company to delay shutting off electricity in the homes of families who had not paid their bills, won restoration of power after they hung wet laundry over every utility line in the neighborhood. They also left crying babies on the desks of caseworkers at the Cleveland Emergency Relief Association, refusing to retrieve them until free milk had been provided for each child. These actions reflected a sense of humor, but sometimes housewife rage exploded. In Chicago, angry Polish housewives doused thousands of pounds of meat with kerosene and set it on fire at the warehouses of the Armour Company to dramatize their belief that high prices were not the result of shortages.[4]

This activity was not simply a reaction to the economic crisis gripping the nation. It was a conscious attempt on the part of many housewives to change the system that they blamed for the Depression. In Seattle in 1931 urban and farm wives orchestrated a massive exchange of timber and fish from western Washington for grain, fruits, and vegetables from eastern Washington. As a result, tens of thousands of families had enough food and fuel to survive the difficult winter of 1931–32. Similar barter networks were established in California, Colorado, Ohio, and Virginia in which housewives gathered and distributed food, clothing, fuel, and building materials.[5]

Understanding their power as a voting bloc, housewives lobbied in state capitals and in Washington, D.C. They also ran for electoral office in numerous locales across the country. In Washington state and in Michigan, housewife activists were elected in 1934 and 1936 on platforms that called for government regulation of food prices, housing, and utility costs. And in Minnesota in 1936, farm wives were key players in the creation of a national Farmer-Labor Party.[6]

These actions were not motivated by desire on the part of poor wives and mothers to be relieved of their responsibilities in the home—although certainly many were attracted by the excitement and camaraderie of activism. These were the actions of women who accepted the traditional sex-based division of labor but who found that the Depression had made it impossible for them to fulfill their responsibilities to the home without leaving it.

Housewife activists argued that the homes in which they worked were intimately linked to the fields and shops where their husbands, sons, and daughters labored; to the national economy; and to the fast-growing state and federal bureaucracies. Mrs. Charles Lundquist, a farmer's wife and president of the Farmer-Labor Women's Federation of Minnesota, summed up this view in a 1936 speech before a gathering of farmers and labor activists.

> Woman's place may be in the home but the home is no longer the isolated, complete unit it was. To serve her home best, the woman of today must understand the political and economic foundation on which that home rests and then do something about it.[7]

The extent and variety of housewives' activism during the Depression suggests that this view of the home was widely accepted by black as well as white women, farm as well as urban women. The housewives' rebellions that swept the country during the 1930s cannot be seen as only spontaneous outcries for a "just price." Like so many others during the Depression, working-class housewives were offering their own solutions to the failure of the U.S. economic system.[8]

Roots of a Housewives' Uprising

This essay focuses primarily on urban housewives' organizing, but it should be noted that farm women played an essential role in Depression-era housewives' activism. Apart from organizing on their own behalf—establishing farmer-labor women's committees and food-goods exchanges with urban women—farm women provided urban women with information about the gap between what farmers were paid and what wholesalers charged. This profit taking formed the basis for activists' critique of what they called "food trusts." Farm wives' activism during the 1920s and 1930s must be studied before a full assessment of this phenomenon is possible. However, because of space limitations, this essay focuses on three of the most active and successful urban housewives' groups: the New York-based United Council of Working-Class Women, the Seattle-based Women's Committee of the Washington Commonwealth Federation, and the Detroit-based Women's Committee against the High Cost of Living.

Greater availability of sources on New York housewives' activism has made possible a deeper analysis of New York than of Detroit or Seattle, both of which merit further study. Still, there is sufficient evidence on the latter two cities to make for a fruitful comparison and to discern some key patterns in working-class housewives' organizing during the Depression.

An examination of these three groups illustrates that although there were some important regional differences in housewives' political style and focus, there were also commonalities. Most significantly, each had a strong labor movement affiliation. Housewives' activism developed in union strongholds, flourishing in the Bronx and Brooklyn among the wives and mothers of unionized garment workers, in Detroit among the wives and mothers of United Auto Workers (UAW) members, and in Seattle among the wives of unionized workers who had begun to argue the importance of consumer organizing during the 1920s.[9]

This union link is important for several reasons. Union husbands' fights for higher wages during the 1910s had resulted in a fairly comfortable standard of living for many families by World War I. But spiraling inflation and the near-destruction of many trade unions during the 1920s eroded the working-class quality of life. By 1929 it had become increasingly difficult, even for families of employed union workers, to make ends meet.[10]

The militance of the Depression-era housewives' movement was an outgrowth of this sudden and rapid decline in working-class families' standard of living. But it was also rooted in women organizers' own experiences in trade unions. There are no statistics detailing exactly how many housewife activists were formerly union members. However, in all the areas where housewives' organizations took hold, it was common for women to work for wages before marriage. And given the age of most leading activists in New York, Seattle, and Detroit, their working years would have coincided with the years of women's labor militance between 1909 and 1920.[11]

Certainly the key organizers of the housewives' movement were all labor leaders before the Depression. In Seattle, Jean Stovel and Mary Farquharson were active in the American Federation of Labor (AFL) before they became leaders of the Women's Committee of the Washington Commonwealth Federation. Detroit's Mary Zuk was the daughter of a United Mine Workers member and was raised on the violent mine strikes of the 1920s. As a young woman, she migrated to Detroit to work on an automobile assembly line and was fired for UAW organizing before founding the Detroit Women's Committee against the High Cost of Living. In New York, Rose Nelson was an organizer for the International Ladies' Garment Workers' Union (ILGWU) before she became codirector of the United Council of Working-Class Women (UCWCW). And the career of the best-known housewife organizer of the 1930s, Clara Lemlich Shavelson, illustrates the importance of both labor movement and Communist Party links. (Only the New York organizers had explicit ties to the Communist Party, although charges of Communist Party involvement were leveled against nearly all the housewife leaders.)[12]

Shavelson's career also roots the housewives' rebellions of the 1930s in a long tradition of Jewish immigrant women's agitation around subsistence issues. Because few immigrant or working-class families in the early twentieth century could afford to live on the salary of a single wage earner, wives, sons, and daughters contributed to the family economy. Clara Lemlich Shavelson's mother ran a small grocery store. Other immigrant women took in boarders, ran restaurants, peddled piece goods, and took in washing or sewing. Their experience with small-scale entrepreneurship gave them a basic understanding of the marketplace that carried over to their management of the home. This economic understanding was deepened by their exposure to unionist principles through their husbands, sons, and daughters and sometimes through their own experience as wage workers.[13]

These experiences nourished a belief among working-class women that the home was inextricably bound in a web of social and economic relationships to labor unions, the marketplace, and government. That view of the home was expressed in a series of food boycotts and rent strikes that erupted in New York; Philadelphia; Paterson, New Jersey and other East Coast cities between the turn of the century and World War I. Clara Lemlich came of age on Manhattan's Lower East Side, where married women led frequent food boycotts and rent strikes during the first decade of the twentieth century. Long before she made the famous speech that set off the massive 1909 shirtwaist makers' strike—"I am tired of the talking; I move that we go on a general strike!"—Lemlich was aware that the principles of unionism could be applied to community activism.[14]

Blacklisted by garment manufacturers after the 1909 strike, fired from her new career as a paid woman's suffrage advocate after conflicts with upper-class suffragists, Lemlich married printer Arthur Shavelson in 1913 and immediately began looking for ways to channel spontaneous outbursts of housewives' anger into an organizational structure. During World War I the U.S. government made her task easier by mobilizing housewives in many city neighborhoods into Community Councils for National Defense. Now, when housewives decided to protest rapidly increasing food prices, they had an organizational structure to build on and a hall in which to meet. In 1917 and 1919 Shavelson and other community organizers were able to spread meat boycotts and rent strikes throughout New York City by winning support from the community councils as well as synagogue groups and women's trade union auxiliaries.[15]

By 1926, when Shavelson established the United Council of Working-Class Housewives (UCWCH), she was working under the auspices of the Communist Party. However, Shavelson's insistence on organizing women made her a maverick within the party, as she had been in the labor and suffrage movements. The male leadership of the Communist Party expressed little interest in efforts to win working-class wives to the party. And the women who ran the UCWCH put no pressure on women who joined the housewives' councils to also join the party.[16]

Around the same time that the united councils were founded, non-Communist organizers such as Rosa Schneiderman of the Women's Trade Union League (WTUL) and Pauline Newman and Fannia Cohn of the ILGWU were also trying to bring housewives into the working-class movement. In the twenty years since the 1909 shirtwaist strike—the largest strike by U.S. women workers to that time—these labor organizers had run up against the incontrovertible fact that working-class women lacked the economic power to achieve their social and political aims unless they allied themselves with more powerful groups such as middle-class women or working-class men.[17]

Seeking a way to maximize working-class women's economic power, they decided to organize women both as consumers and as workers. As workers, women were segregated into the lowest-paid, least-skilled sectors of the labor force. Economic deprivation and discrimination in male-dominated labor unions limited their power, even when they organized. But as consumers, U.S. working-class women spent billions of dollars annually. Organized as consumers, even poor women could wield real economic power. By the late 1920s women organizers were ready to try to link the home to labor unions and government in a dynamic partnership—with wage-earning women and housewives as full partners.[18]

That goal brought women organizers into direct conflict with male leaders in the trade union movement and in the Communist Party, who were unwilling to accept the home as a center of production or the housewife as a productive laborer. Nor did they see a relationship between production and consumption. Poor housewives, whatever their political stripe, understood that relationship implicitly. They responded to the neighborhood organizing strategy because they saw in it a chance to improve day-to-day living conditions for themselves and their families.[19] Jean Stovel explained the surge of militance among Seattle housewives this way: "Women," she said, "have sold the idea of organization—their own vast power—to themselves, the result of bitter experience. We are that mythical thing called the public and so we shall demand a hearing."[20]

It is important to distinguish the aims of veteran women's organizers from the aims of the majority of women who participated in housewives' protests. For the most part, these house-wives had no intention of challenging the traditional sex-based division of labor. Nor were they interested in alternative political philosophies such as socialism or communism. But, desperate to feed, clothe, and shelter their families, poor women challenged traditional limits on acceptable behavior for mothers and wives. In so doing, they became political actors.[21]

From Self-Help to Lobbying the Government

Between 1926 and 1933 housewives' self-help groups sprang up across the United States. In cities surrounded by accessible growing areas (such as Dayton, Ohio, Richmond, Virginia, and Seattle, Washington), housewives and their husbands created highly developed barter networks. Unemployed workers, mostly male, exchanged skills such as carpentry, plumbing, barbering, and electrical wiring. Women—some workers' wives, others unemployed workers themselves—organized exchanges of clothing and food. These organizations grew out of small-scale gardening collectives created by housewives during the late 1920s to feed their communities.[22]

In Seattle, unemployed families organized quickly in the aftermath of the 1929 stock market crash; but then this was an unusually organized city, described by a local paper in 1937 as "the most unionized city in the country." In 1919 Seattle had been the first city in the United States to hold a general strike. During the 1920s Seattle's labor unions again broke new ground by calling on working-class women and men to organize as consumers. When the Depression hit, Seattle's vast subsistence network was described in the national press as a model of self-sufficiency, "a republic of the penniless," in the words of the *Atlantic*. By 1931–32, forty thousand Seattle women and men had joined an exchange in which the men farmed, fished, and cut leftover timber from cleared land, while the women gathered food, fuel, and clothing. The women also ran commissaries where members could shop with scrip for household essentials. By 1934 an estimated eighty thousand people statewide belonged to exchanges that allowed them to acquire food, clothing, and shelter without any money changing hands.[23]

In larger cities such as New York, Chicago, Philadelphia, and Detroit, self-help groups also sprang up during the early years of the Depression, but housewives there had little chance of making direct contact with farmers. Rather than establishing food exchanges, they created neighborhood councils that used boycotts and demonstrations to combat rising food prices. And, rather than rehabilitating abandoned buildings for occupation by the homeless, as the unemployed did in Seattle, housewives in larger cities battled with police to prevent eviction of families unable to pay their rents.[24]

Tenant and consumer councils in those cities took hold in neighborhoods where housewives had orchestrated rent strikes and meat boycotts in 1902, 1904, 1907, 1908, and 1917.[25] They organized in the same way as earlier housewife activists had done—primarily through door-to-door canvassing. Boycotts were sustained in the latter period, as in the earlier one, with picket lines and street-corner meetings. Even their angry outbursts echoed the earlier housewives' uprisings: Meat was destroyed with kerosene or taken off trucks and thrown to the ground. Flour was spilled in the streets, and milk ran in the gutters.[26]

But although its links to earlier housewives' and labor union struggles are important, the 1930s housewives' revolt was far more widespread and sustained, encompassing a far wider range of ethnic and racial groups than any tenant or consumer uprising before it. The earlier outbursts were limited to East Coast Jewish immigrant communities, but the housewives' uprising of the 1930s was nationwide and involved rural as well as urban women. It drew Polish and native-born housewives in Detroit, Finnish and Scandinavian women in Washington state, and Scandinavian farm wives in Minnesota. Jewish and black housewives were particularly militant in New York, Cleveland, Chicago, Los Angeles, and San Francisco.[27]

The 1930s housewives' movement can also be distinguished from earlier housewives' actions by the sophistication and longevity of the organizations it generated. Depression-era housewives moved quickly from self-help to lobbying in state capitals and Washington, D.C., leaders such as the "diminutive but fiery" Mary Zuk of Detroit displayed considerable skill in their use of radio and print media. Their demands of government—regulation of staple food prices, establishment of publicly owned farmer-consumer cooperatives—reflected a complex understanding of the marketplace and the potential uses of the growing government bureaucracy.

Leaders of these groups also demonstrated considerable sophistication about forming alliances. Shortly after Roosevelt was elected president, hostilities between Communist and non-Communist women in the labor movement were temporarily set aside. AFL-affiliated women's auxiliaries and Communist Party-affiliated women's neighborhood councils worked together to organize consumer protests and lobby for regulation of food and housing costs. This happened in 1933, well before the party initiated its Popular Front policy urging members to join with "progressive" non-Communist groups and well before the Congress of Industrial Organizations extended its hand to Communists to rejoin the labor movement.[28]

This rapprochement highlighted the desperation that gripped so many working-class communities during the Depression. Although charges of being Communists were leveled against housewife organizers throughout the Depression, such accusations did not dampen the enthusiasm of rank-and-file council members. To many non-Communists in the movement, the question of who was Communist and who wasn't did not seem terribly relevant at a time when millions faced hunger and homelessness. Detroit housewife leader Catherine Mudra responded this way to charges of Communist involvement in the Detroit meat strike of 1935: "There may be some Communists among us. There are a lot of Republicans and Democrats too. We do not ask the politics of those who join. . . . All we want is to get prices down to where we can feed our families."[29]

Despite this tolerance of Communist leadership, housewife organizers affiliated with the Communist Party were careful not to push too hard. Party regulars such as Clara Lemlich Shavelson were open about their political beliefs, but they did not push members of the housewives' councils to toe the party line. And they organized as mothers, not as Communists. Shavelson did not use the name Lemlich, which still reverberated among New York City garment workers who remembered her fiery speech in 1909. Instead, she organized under her married name and made sure to point out her children whenever they passed by a street corner where she was speaking.[30]

Seasoned organizers such as Shavelson sought to build bonds between women in the name of motherhood. They understood that when appealed to as mothers, apolitical women lost their fears about being associated with radicalism in general and the Communist Party in particular. Meeting women organizers day after day, in the local parks with their babies, in food markets, and on street corners, shy housewives gained the confidence to express their anger. The deepening Depression hastened such personal transformations. Once all sense of economic security had dissolved, temperamentally conservative women became more open to radical solutions. Sophia Ocher, who was a member of a Mother and Child Unit of Communist organizers in the Bronx, wrote that "work among these women was not difficult for there was the baby, the greatest of all issues, and there were the women, all working-class mothers who would fight for their very lives to obtain a better life for their babies."[31]

In New York, ethnic bonding between women facilitated the growth of housewives' councils. Although many community organizers, including Shavelson, Rose Nelson Raynes, Sonya Sanders, and Sophia Ocher, were Communist Party members, they were also genuine members of the communities they sought to organize, familiar with local customs, needs, and fears. They addressed crowds of housewives in Yiddish as well as English. And, steering clear of Marxist doctrine, they emphasized ethnic and community ties in their speeches, likening housewives' councils to the women's charitable associations traditional in East European Jewish culture.[32]

Conscious of the hardship of poor women's lives, the organizers never hesitated to roll up their sleeves and help out. In one Bronx neighborhood, Sonya Sanders created an entire neighborhood council by winning over one resistant housebound woman. After Sanders came into the woman's house when she was sick, cleaned it, bathed the children, and prepared a kosher dinner for the family, the woman gave up her suspicion of Sanders and became an enthusiastic supporter. She invited all her friends to come to her home and listen to Sanders discuss ways to fight evictions and high prices. Before long a new neighborhood council was born. Of course, successes such as these were predicated on the shared ethnicity of organizer and organized. The ploy would not have worked as well if Sanders had not understood the laws of *kashrut* or known how to cook Jewish-style food.[33]

This strength was also a weakness. As a result of New York's ethnic balkanization, the city's neighborhood councils were not ethnically diverse. Organizers tended to have most success organizing women of their own ethnic group. The UCWCW, founded and run by Jewish immigrant women, was primarily composed of Jewish immigrant housewives; owing to the Communist Party's strength in Harlem, black women were the second largest group; small numbers of Irish and Italian housewives also joined.

"We never intended to be exclusively a Jewish organization," Rose Nelson Raynes recalls.

But we built in areas where we had strength. Maybe it was because of the background of so many Jewish women in the needle trades, maybe it was because of the concentration of immigrants from the other side, I don't know. But there was a feeling in the Jewish working class that we had to express ourselves in protest of the rising prices.[34]

As in New York, the Detroit and Seattle housewives' actions were initiated by immigrant women of a particular ethnic group—Polish Catholics in Detroit and Scandinavian Protestants in Seattle. Because those cities were less ghettoized than New York, organizers were more successful in creating coalitions that involved black as well as white women, Protestants as well as Jews and Catholics, immigrants and the native-born. However, ethnic differences were not unimportant, even outside New York. For example, American-born Protestants in the Detroit housewives' councils were far less confrontational in their tactics than their Polish, Jewish, or black counterparts. They signed no-meat pledges rather than picketing butcher shops and handed in petitions rather than marching on city hall.[35]

Women had different reasons for joining housewives' councils in the 1930s, but those who stayed did so because they enjoyed the camaraderie, the enhanced self-esteem, and the shared sense of fighting for a larger cause. During an interview in her Brighton Beach apartment, eighty-eight-year-old Rose Nelson Raynes offered this analysis of why the councils inspired such loyalty:

Women were discriminated against in all organizations in those years and the progressive organizations were no exception. When women joined progressive organizations with men they were relegated to the kitchen. There was a need on the part of the mother, the woman in the house. She wanted to get out. There were so many things taking place that she wanted to learn more about. So women came to our organization where they got culture, lectures. Some developed to a point where they could really get up and make a speech that would meet any politician's speech today. It came from the need, from the heart. We felt we wanted to express ourselves, to learn to speak and act and the only way was through a women's council.[36]

The Meatless Summer of 1935

Depression-era organizing against high food prices reached its peak during the summer of 1935. Working-class women activists from Communist and non-Communist organizations convened two regional conferences the previous winter, one for the East Coast, another for the Midwest, to coordinate protests against the sales tax and high cost of living. Representatives from AFL women's union auxiliaries, parents' associations, church groups, farm women's groups, and black women's groups attended. By that summer, they had laid plans for the most ambitious women's consumer protest to that time.[37]

It began when the Chicago Committee against the High Cost of Living, headed by Dina Ginsberg, organized massive street meetings near the stockyards to let the meat packers know how unhappy they were with rising meat prices. New York housewives in the UCWCW quickly raised the ante by organizing a citywide strike against butcher shops.[38]

On 22 May women in Jewish and black neighborhoods around New York City formed picket lines. In Harlem, according to historian Mark Naison, the meat strike "produced an unprecedented display of coordinated protest by black working-class women."[39] The strike lasted four weeks. More than forty-five hundred butcher shops were closed down by housewives' picket lines. Scores of women and men around the city were arrested. The New York State Retail Meat

Dealers Association threatened to hold Mayor Fiorello LaGuardia responsible for damage to their businesses as a result of the strike. The mayor, in an attempt to resolve the strike, asked federal officials to study the possibilities for reducing retail meat prices.[40]

Raynes, citywide coordinator of the meat strike, describes what happened next.

> It was successful to a point where we were warned that the gangsters were going to get us. . . . We decided to call the whole thing off but first we organized a mass picket line in front of the wholesale meat distributors. . . . About three, four hundred women came out on the picket line. It was supposed to be a final action. But . . . instead of being the wind-up it became a beginning.[41]

Housewives across the United States promptly joined in. Ten thousand Los Angeles housewives, members of the joint Council of Women's Auxiliaries, declared a meat strike on 8 June that so completely shut down retail meat sales in the city that butchers cut prices by the next day. In Philadelphia, Chicago, Boston, Paterson, St. Louis, and Kansas City, newly formed housewives' councils echoed the cry of the New York strike: "Stop Buying Meat until Prices Come Down!"[42]

On 15 June a delegation of housewives from across the country descended on Washington, D.C., demanding that the Department of Agriculture enforce lower meat prices. Clara Lemlich Shavelson described the delegation's meeting with Secretary of Agriculture Henry Wallace: "The meat packers and the Department of Agriculture in Washington tried to make the strikers' delegation . . . believe that the farmer and the drought are to blame for the high price of food. But the delegation would not fall for this. They knew the truth."[43]

The Polish housewives of Hamtramck, Michigan, a suburb of Detroit, did not believe Wallace's explanation, either. A month after the end of the New York strike, thirty-two-year-old Mary Zuk addressed a mass demonstration of housewives gathered on the streets of Hamtramck to demand an immediate reduction in meat prices. When the reduction did not come by that evening, Zuk announced a meat boycott to begin the following day.[44]

On 27 July 1935 Polish and black housewives began to picket Hamtramck butcher shops, carrying signs demanding a 20 percent price cut throughout the city and an end to price gouging in black neighborhoods. When men, taunted by onlookers who accused them of being "scared of a few women," attempted to cross the lines, they were "seized by the pickets . . . their faces slapped, their hair pulled and their packages confiscated. . . . A few were knocked down and trampled." That night Hamtramck butchers reported unhappily that the boycott had been 95 percent effective.[45]

Within a matter of days the meat boycott spread to other parts of Detroit, as housewives in several different ethnic communities hailed the onset of "a general strike against the high cost of living." Jewish women picketed kosher butcher shops in downtown Detroit neighborhoods. Protestant women in outlying regions such as Lincoln Park and River Rouge declined to picket or march but instead set up card tables on streetcorners to solicit no-meat pledges from passing housewives.[46]

Housewives also sought government intervention. Detroit housewives stormed the city council demanding that it set a ceiling on meat prices in the metropolitan area. "What we can afford to buy isn't fit for a human to eat," Joanna Dinkfeld told the council. "And we can't afford very much of that." Warning the council and the state government that they had better act, Myrtle Hoaglund announced that she was forming a statewide housewives' organization. "We feel that we should have united action," she said. "We think the movement of protest against present meat prices can be spread throughout the state and . . . the nation." As evidence, she showed the city council bags of letters she had received from housewives around the country, asking her how to go about organizing consumer boycotts.[47]

Throughout August the meat strikers made front-page news in Detroit and received close attention in major New York and Chicago dailies. The women staged mass marches through the streets of Detroit, stormed meat-packing plants, overturned and emptied meat trucks, and poured kerosene on thousands of pounds of meat stored in warehouses. When these actions resulted in the arrest of several Detroit women, hundreds of boy cotters marched on the city jails, demanding the release of their friends. Two hours after her arrest, Hattie Krewik, forty-five years old and a mother of five, emerged from her cell unrepentant. A roar went up from the crowd as she immediately began to tell, in Polish, her tale of mistreatment at the hands of the police. By the end of the first week in August, retail butchers in Detroit were pleading with the governor to send in state troops to protect their meat.[48]

Although without a doubt the butchers suffered as a result of this boycott, the strikers in Detroit, like the strikers in New York, frequently reiterated that the strike was not aimed at retail butchers or at farmers. It was targeted, in Clara Shavelson's words, at the "meat packer millionaires." To prove that, in the second week of August a delegation of Detroit housewives traveled to Chicago, where they hooked up with their Chicago counterparts for a march on the Union stockyards.

Meeting them at the gates, Armour & Company president R. H. Cabell attempted to mollify the women. "Meat packers," he told them, "are not the arbiters of prices, merely the agencies through which economic laws operate." The sudden rise in prices, he explained, was the fault of the Agricultural Adjustment Administration, which had recently imposed a processing tax on pork.[49]

"Fine," Mary Zuk responded. The housewives would return to Washington for another meeting with agriculture secretary Wallace. On 19 August 1935 Zuk and her committee of five housewives marched into Wallace's office and demanded that he end the processing tax, impose a 20 percent cut on meat prices, and order prompt prosecution of profiteering meat packers.[50] Wallace, perhaps sensing how this would be played in the press, tried to evict reporters from the room, warning that he would not speak to the women if they remained. Zuk did not blink. She replied: "Our people want to know what we say and they want to know what *you* say so the press people are going to stay." The reporters stayed and had a grand tune the next day reporting on Wallace's unexplained departure from the room in the middle of the meeting.[51] "Secretary Wallace Beats Retreat from Five Housewives," the *Chicago Daily Tribune* blared. *Newsweek* reported it this way:

> The lanky Iowan looked down into Mrs. Zuk's deep-sunken brown eyes and gulped his Adam's apple.
> Mrs. Zuk: Doesn't the government want us to live? Everything in Detroit has gone up except wages.
> Wallace fled.[52]

In the aftermath of Zuk's visit to Washington, *Newsweek* reported housewives' demonstrations against the high price of meat in Indianapolis, Denver, and Miami. The *New York Times* reported violent housewives' attacks on meat warehouses in Chicago and in the Pennsylvania towns of Shenandoah and Frackville. And Mary Zuk the "strong-jawed 100 lb. mother of the meat strike," became a national figure. The Detroit post office announced that it was receiving letters from all over the country addressed only to "Mrs. Zuk—Detroit."[53]

Although boycotts and strikes continued to be used as a tool in the housewives' struggle for lower prices, the movement became more focused on electoral politics as the decade wore on. Both Shavelson and Zuk used the prominence they'd gained through housewife activism to run for elected office. Shavelson ran for the New York State Assembly in 1933 and 1938 as a "real . . . mother fighting to maintain an American standard of living for her own family as well as for other families." She did not win, but she fared far better than the rest of the Communist Party ticket.[54]

Zuk ran a successful campaign for the Hamtramck city council in April of 1936. Although the local Hearst-owned paper warned that her election would be a victory for those who advocate "the break-up of the family," Zuk was swept into office by her fellow housewives. She won on a platform calling for the city council to reduce rents, food prices, and utility costs in Hamtramck. After her election she told reporters that she was proof that "a mother can organize and still take care of her family."[55]

In some ways what the Hearst papers sensed was really happening. Zuk's campaign represented an express politicization of motherhood and the family. On Mother's Day 1936 seven hundred Zuk supporters rallied outside the city council to demand public funding for a women's health-care clinic, child care centers, playgrounds, and teen centers in Hamtramck. They also called for an end to evictions and construction of more public housing in their city. The government owed this to mothers, the demonstrators told reporters.[56]

Two years earlier, in Washington state, the Women's Committee of the Washington Commonwealth Federation (WCF) had successfully elected three of its members to the state senate—Mary Farquharson, a professor's wife, and Marie Keene and Katherine Malström, the wives of loggers. Their campaign had been built around a Production-for-Use initiative to prohibit the destruction of food as a way of propping up prices. Such waste, they said, was an outrage to poor mothers in the state, who had been fighting the practice since the beginning of the Depression. The ballot measure also proposed a state distribution system for produce so that farmers could get a fair price and workers' families could buy food directly from farmers. Led by Katherine Smith and Elizabeth Harper, committee members collected seventy thousand signatures to put the measure on the 1936 ballot.[57]

The Production-for-Use initiative failed by a narrow margin, but it made national news as columnists across the country speculated on the impact it might have had on the U.S. economic system. Other WCF campaigns were more successful, however. The most important of these was the campaign to create publicly owned utilities in Washington state. Washington voters were the only ones to approve state ownership of utilities, but voters in localities across the country endorsed the creation of city and county utility companies during the 1930s.[58]

Housewife activists also kept their sights on the federal government during this period. From 1935 to 1941 housewives' delegations from major cities made annual trips to Washington, D.C., to lobby for lower food prices. These trips stopped during World War II but resumed afterward with a concerted campaign to save the Office of Price Administration and to win federal funds for construction of public housing in poor neighborhoods.[59]

The alliance of housewives' councils and women's union auxiliaries continued to grow through the late 1930s, laying the groundwork for two more nationwide meat strikes in 1948 and 1951. These strikes affected even more women than the 1935 action because housewives now had an organizing tool that enabled them to mobilize across thousands of miles: the telephone. "We have assigned fifty-eight women ten pages each of the telephone directory," said one strike leader in Cincinnati. In August 1948 housewives in Texas, Ohio, Colorado, Florida, Michigan, and New York boycotted meat. And during the winter of 1951 a housewives' meat boycott across the country forced wholesalers dealing in the New York, Philadelphia, and Chicago markets to lower their prices. In New York City alone, newspapers estimated, one million pounds of meat a week went begging. Fearing for their own jobs, unionized butchers, then retailers, and finally even local wholesalers called on the federal government to institute price controls on meat.[60]

But even as these actions made front-page news across the country, the housewives' alliance was breaking apart over the issue of Communist involvement. As early as 1933 the Washington state legislature had passed a bill requiring that Seattle take over the commissaries created by the unemployed two years earlier. Conservative politicians claimed that Communists had taken control of the relief machinery in the city and were seeking to indoctrinate the hungry. In 1939 Hearst newspapers charged that the housewives' movement nationwide was little more than a Communist plot to sow seeds of discord in the American home. The Dies Committee of the U.S. Congress took these charges seriously and began an investigation. U.S. entry into World War II temporarily ended the investigation but also quelled consumer protest, because the government instituted rationing and price controls.[61]

Investigations of the consumer movement began again soon after the war ended. During the 1948 boycott housewife leaders were charged by some with being too friendly to Progressive Party presidential candidate Henry Wallace. In 1949 the House Committee on Un-American Activities began investigating the organizers of a 1947 housewives' march on Washington, and in 1950 they were ordered to register with the Justice Department as foreign agents. By the early 1950s national and local Communist-hunting committees had torn apart the movement, creating dissension and mistrust among the activists.[62]

The unique alliance that created a nationwide housewives' uprising during the 1930s and 1940s would not reemerge, but it laid the groundwork for later consumer and tenant organizing. Housewives' militance politicized consumer issues nationwide. "Never has there been such a wave of enthusiasm to do something for the consumer," *The Nation* wrote in 1937. Americans have gained "a consumer consciousness," the magazine concluded, as a direct result of the housewives' strikes in New York, Detroit, and other cities. The uprising of working-class housewives also broadened the terms of the class struggle, forcing male union leaders to admit that "the roles of producer and consumer are intimately related."[63]

Housewives' groups alleviated the worst effects of the Depression in many working-class communities by bringing down food prices, cutting rent and utility costs, preventing evictions, and spurring the construction of more public housing, schools, and parks. By the end of World War II housewives' activism had forced the government to play a regulatory role in food and housing costs. Militant direct action and sustained lobbying put pressure on local and federal politicians to investigate profiteering on staple goods. The meat strikes of 1935 and of 1948 through 1951 resulted in congressional hearings on the structure of the meat industry and in nationwide reductions in prices. The intense antieviction struggles led by urban housewives and their years of lobbying for public housing helped to convince New York City and other localities to pass rent-control laws. They also increased support in Congress for federally funded public housing.[64]

Perhaps an equally important legacy of housewives' activism was its impact on the consciousness of the women who participated. "It was an education for the women," Brooklyn activist Dorothy Moser recalls, "that they could not have gotten any other way." Immigrant women, poor native white women, and black women learned to write and speak effectively, to lobby in state capitals and in Washington, D.C., to challenge men in positions of power, and sometimes to question the power relations in their own homes.[65]

By organizing as consumers, working-class housewives not only demonstrated a keen understanding of their place in local and national economic structures; they also shattered the notion that because homemakers consume rather than produce, they are inherently more passive than their wage-earning husbands. The very act of organizing defied traditional notions of proper behavior for wives and mothers—and organizers were often called upon to explain their actions.

Union husbands supported and sometimes, as Dana Frank argues in her study of Seattle, even instigated their wives' community organizing. However, that organizing created logistical problems, namely, who was going to watch the children and who was going to cook dinner? Some women managed to do it all. Others could not. Complaining of anarchy in the home, some union husbands ordered their wives to stop marching and return to the kitchen. In November 1934 *Working Woman* magazine offered a hamper of canned goods to any woman who could answer the plaint of a housewife whose husband had ordered her to quit her women's council.

First prize went to a Bronx housewife who called on husbands and wives to share child care as "they share their bread. Perhaps two evenings a week father should go, and two evenings, mother." The same woman noted that struggle keeps a woman "young physically and mentally" and that she shouldn't give it up for anything. Second prize went to a Pennsylvania miner's wife who agreed with that sentiment. "There can't be a revolution without women. . . . No one could convince me to drop out. Rather than leave the Party I would leave him." And an honorable mention went to a Texas farm woman who warned, "If we allow men to tell us what we can and cannot do we will never get our freedom."[66] The prize-winning essays suggest that, like many women reformers before them, Depression-era housewife activists became interested in knocking down the walls that defined behavioral norms for women only after they had personally run up against them.[67]

In defending their right to participate in a struggle that did not ideologically challenge the traditional sexual division of labor, many working-class housewives developed a new sense of pride in their abilities and a taste for political involvement. These women never came to think of themselves as feminists. They did, however, begin to see themselves as legitimate political and economic actors. During this period, poor wives and mothers left their homes in order to preserve them. In so doing, whether they intended to or not, they politicized the home, the family, and motherhood in important and unprecedented ways.

Notes

1. For an analysis of the impact of one school of documentary photography on our impressions of poor mothers during the Depression, see Wendy Kozol, "Madonnas of the Field: Photography, Gender, and Thirties' Farm Relief," *Genders* 2 (summer 1988): 1–23.

2. Eleanor Roosevelt, *It's up to the Women* (New York: Frederick A. Stokes, 1933). A less friendly version of this argument can be found in Norman Cousins's 1939 article skewering those who suggested that women who left the home to work were somehow responsible for the ongoing unemployment crisis. See Norman Cousins, "Will Women Lose Their Jobs?" *Current History and Forum*, September 1939, 14–18, 62–63.

3. The *New York Times, Newsweek, The Nation, The New Republic*, the *Saturday Evening Post, Harper's*, the *Christian Century, Business Week*, and *American Mercury* all covered and commented on housewife organizing. The *Chicago Daily Tribune* and the *Detroit Free Press* also provided detailed coverage of housewives' activism in their cities. *Working Woman*, the monthly publication of the Women's Commission of the Communist Party, was invaluable. Although extremely dogmatic in its early years, the magazine is one of the most complete sources available on working-class women during the Depression. The two main archives consulted for this paper were the Tamiment Library in New York City and the Robert Burke Collection in the Manuscripts Division of the University of Washington Library, Seattle. See *New York Times*, "Buyers Trampled by Meat Strikers," 28 July 1935; "Secretary Wallace Beats Retreat from Five Housewives," *Chicago Daily Tribune*, 20 August 1935.

4. See *Working Woman*, April 1931, June 1931, April 1933, June 1935; *New York Times*. 30 January–28 February 1932; *Detroit Free Press*, 6–9 August 1935; *Chicago Daily Tribune*, 18 August 1935.

5. See *The Atlantic*, October 1932; *Collier's* 31 December 1932; *Literary Digest*, 11 February 1933; *The Nation*, 1 March 1933 and 19 April 1933; *Survey*, 15 December 1932 and July 1933; *Saturday Evening Post*, 25 February 1933; *Commonweal*, 8 March 1933, *Good Housekeeping*, March 1933.

6. *Working Woman*, June 1935; *The Woman Today*, April 1936; *New York Times*, 10 April 1936; *Party Organizer*, September 1935. Meridel Le Sueur describes the radicalization of one of those farm women, Mary Cotter, in her 1940 short story "Salute to Spring," in Meridel Le Sueur, *Salute to Spring* (New York: International Publishers, 1940).

7. *The Woman Today*, April 1936.

8. For selected sources on housewife activism early in the Depression, see *Working Woman*, 1931–35. See also *New York Times*, 23, 30 January; February; 22 March; 22 May; 7 June; 7, 11 July; 13–26 September; 9 October; 7, 21 December 1932; January–February; 23, 30 March; 13, 24 May; 1, 2, 8 June; 2, 31 August; 7, 9, 26 September; 9 December 1933. See also *The Atlantic*, October 1932; *The Nation*, 1 March 1933; 19 April 1933; 14, 18 March 1934; *The New Republic*, 15 November 1933; *Ladies' Home Journal* October 1934.

9. For information on the links between union activity and community organizing in New York City neighborhoods between 1902 and 1945, see Annelise Orleck, "Common Sense and a Little Fire: Working-Class Women's Activism in the Twentieth-Century United States" (Ph.D. diss., New York University, 1989); on Seattle politics in the post–World War I period, see Albert Acena, "The Washington Commonwealth Federation: Reform Politics and the Popular Front" (Ph.D. diss., University of Washington, 1975); and Dana Frank, "At the Point of Consumption: Seattle Labor and the Politics of Consumption, 1919–1927" (Ph.D. diss., Yale University, 1988).

10. A leaflet distributed by the UCWCW in 1929 noted that "the prices of most essential foodstuffs are still very high, while . . . the wages of those workers still employed, and part time workers, have been cut more and more." See "Working-Class Women, Let Us Organize and Fight" (leaflet, n.d., Tamiment Library).

    A *Working Woman* study in the winter of 1931 reported that even among those workers still employed in the big cities of the United States, income had declined 33 percent, but food prices had decreased only 7 percent. See *Working Woman* 3 (March 1931).

11. Rose Nelson Raynes, one of the chief organizers of the UCWCW, recalls that in 1931, when she first became involved with the organization, most of the women were older than thirty-five. Interview with Rose Nelson Raynes, New York City, 8 October 1987. *New York Times* reports of arrests in antieviction actions and consumer boycotts between 1931 and 1935 show that all the women were married and the vast majority were between the ages of thirty and forty-two. *Detroit Free Press* accounts of arrests in the 1935 meat strike list the majority as having been between the ages of twenty-eight and forty-eight. In 1932 T. J. Party (*The Atlantic*, October 1932), writing about members of the food exchanges in Seattle, commented that most of them were "near life's half-way mark or beyond."

12. See *The Woman Today*, July 1936; Mary Farquharson Papers, Burke Collection, boxes 12–14, and folders 30 and 94; and Frank, "At the Point of Consumption."

13. In *The Jewish Woman in America* (New York: New American Library, 1976), 99–114, Charlotte Baum, Paula Hyman, and Sonya Michel review some of the voluminous immigrant literature highlighting the entrepreneurship of Jewish immigrant mothers. See Orleck, "Common Sense and a Little Fire," ch. 1, for a fuller analysis of the literature on working-class women's entrepreneurship, their conception of home, and their involvement in activism around tenant and consumer issues in the first decade of the twentieth century.

14. Paula Hyman makes this point in her essay "Immigrant Women and Consumer Protest: The New York City Kosher Meat Boycott of 1902," *American Jewish History* 70 (September 1980): 91–105. See also *New York Times* for May–June 1902; 13 July–2 September 1904; 30 November–9 December 1906; 26 December 1907–27 Jan. 1908. These sources indicate that many of the women involved were the wives and mothers of garment workers.

15. See *New York Times*, 3, 4, 7–10, 12–15 May; 17 June; 4–6 September 1919. Also see "Women's Councils in the 1930s," a paper presented by Meredith Tax at the June 1984 Berkshire Conference on the History of Women, Smith College, Northampton, Mass. Also see *The Daily Worker*, 23 May 1927.

16. Communist Party women complained consistently in the *Party Organizer* during the 1930s that party men were hindering or ignoring their efforts at organizing women in urban neighborhoods. See particularly the August 1937 issue in which Anna Damon, head of the Communist Party Women's Commission, lashes out at party leaders for undercutting her efforts with black women in St. Louis.

17. See New York Women's Trade Union League, *Annual Reports*, 1922, 1926, 1928; and Summary of Speeches, Women's Auxiliary Conference, Unity House, Forest Park, Penn., 30 June–1 July 1928, New York WTUL Papers, Tamiment Library. See also Mary Van Kleeck Papers, Sophia Smith Collection, Smith College, Northampton, Mass. See also correspondence between Fania M. Cohn and women's auxiliary leaders, Grace Klueg and Mary Peake: Cohn to Klueg, 27 August 1926; 15 January 1927; 3 March 1927; Cohn to Peake, 20 April 1927; Klueg to Cohn, 7 April 1927, in Fania Cohn Papers, New York Public Library.

18. A study by the American Federation of Women's Auxiliaries of Labor estimated in 1937 that U.S. women in union households spent $6 billion annually. See *Working Woman*, March 1937.

19. Robert Shaffer notes that the national Communist Party leadership condemned party feminist theorist Mary Inman particularly for her assertion that the home was a center of production and that housewives did productive labor. See his "Women and the Communist Party, USA, 1930–1940," *Socialist Review* 45 (May–June 1979): 73–118. See also Mary Inman, *Thirteen Years of CPUSA Misleadership on the Women Question* (published by the author, Los Angeles, 1949).

20. *The Woman Today*, July 1936.

21. See Temma Kaplan, "Female Consciousness and Collective Action: The Case of Barcelona, 1910–1918," *Signs* 7 (spring 1982): 545–66.

22. See *The Atlantic*, October 1932; *Collier's*, 31 December 1932; *Literary Digest*, 11 February 1933; *The*

Nation, 1 March 1933, 19 April 1933; *Survey*, 15 December 1932, July 1933; *Saturday Evening Post*, 25 February 1933; *Commonweal*, 8 March 1933; *Good Housekeeping*, March 1933.

23. See Parry (note 11); *New York Times*, 7 June, 3 September 1936; *The Woman Today*, July 1936; *Ladies' Home Journal* October 1934; *Seattle Post-Intelligencer*, 11 January 1937; *American Mercury*, February 1937.

24. *Working Woman*, June–September 1931. For antieviction activity, see *New York Times* almost daily in February, as well as 1, 2, 13 March; 28 May; 7 June; 7 July; 13, 15–18, 20, 26 September; 7, 21 December 1932; 6, 12, 17, 28 January; 1, 22 February; 8, 23, 30 March; 13, 24 May; 1, 2, 8 June; 2, 3 August; 7, 9, 26 September; 9 December 1933.

25. Identifiable links to these earlier events, in addition to Clara Lemlich Shavelson, include Dorothy Moser, another New York activist of the 1930s, who remembers her mother's involvement in the 1917 boycotts. Moser, interview with the author, New York City, 8 October 1987. Judging from the age of the women arrested in New York and Detroit actions (see *New York Times* and *Detroit Free Press*, 1931–35), mostly in their forties, most of the 1930s activists were old enough to remember earlier actions.

26. See Hyman, "Immigrant Women and Consumer Protest," 91–105; and Dana Frank, "Housewives, Socialists, and the Politics of Food: The 1917 New York Cost-of-Living Protests," *Feminist Studies* 11 (summer 1985): 255–85. See also Kaplan, "Female Consciousness and Collective Action."

27. Rose Nelson Raynes, interviews with author, 8 October 1987 and 17 February 1989. *Working Woman*, June, July, and August 1935; *The Woman Today*, July 1936; *New York Times*, *Chicago Daily Tribune*, *Detroit Free Press*, *Newsweek*, and the *Saturday Evening Post* also provided coverage of housewife actions. See particularly *New York Times*, 28 July; 4, 6, 11, 18, 24, 25 August 1935; *Saturday Evening Post*, 2 November 1935; *Chicago Daily Tribune*, 18, 20, 21 August 1935; *Newsweek*, 17, 31 August 1935.

28. In 1933, pleased with the success of their neighborhood organizing strategy, the UCWCW, the umbrella organization for New York housewives' councils, began working to build a coalition with other New York women's organizations, many of which had previously been quite hostile to anyone with Communist Party affiliations. This was an important turning point in the housewives' movement. (See *Working Woman*, October 1933, December 1933.)

29. *New York Times*, 6 August 1935.

30. "Who Is Clara Shavelson?" (leaflet from her 1933 campaign for New York State Assembly in the 2d Assembly District, courtesy of her daughter, Rita Margulies); interview with daughter Martha Shaffer, 11 March 1989.

31. *Party Organizer* 10 (July 1937): 36.

32. Brighton Beach, Brooklyn, where Clara Shavelson organized, is a perfect example of this strategy. Shavelson built on a highly developed network of Jewish women's religious and cultural associations to create the effective Emma Lazarus Tenants' Council during the 1930s. See Orleck, "Common Sense and a Little Fire," ch 8.

33. *Party Organizer* 11 (March 1938): 39–40.

34. Raynes interview, 8 October 1987.

35. Information on the New York UCWCW comes from interviews with Raynes, 8 October 1987 and 17 February 1989. Also, both *New York Times* and *Working Woman* coverage of New York City housewives' actions from 1932 to 1937 show that the most consistently militant sections of the city were Jewish immigrant communities. Information on the composition of the Seattle housewives' groups was drawn from membership lists of the Renters' Protection, Cost of Living, and Public Ownership committees of the Women's League of the Washington Commonwealth Federation, Burke Collection, folders 30, 94, 182, 183, 188. Information on the composition of the Detroit housewives' movement comes from the *Detroit Free Press*, 26 July–25 August 1935 when housewife activists made the paper, quite often the front page, almost every day.

36. Raynes interview, 8 October 1987.

37. *Working Woman*, March 1935.

38. *Chicago Daily Tribune*, 18 August 1935; *Working Woman*, August 1935.

39. Mark Naison, *Communists in Harlem during the Depression* (New York: Grove Press, 1983), 149.

40. See *New York Times*, 27–31 May; 1, 2, 6, 10–12, 14–16 June 1935.

41. Raynes interview, 8 October 1987

42. *Working Woman*, June 1935; *New York Times*, 15, 16 June 1935.

43. *Working Woman*, August 1935.

44. *Detroit Free Press*, 27 July 1935; *New York Times*, 28 July 1935.

45. *Detroit Free Press* and *New York Times*, both for 28 July 1935.

46. *Detroit Free Press*, 29–31 July 1935; *New York Times*, 30 July 1935.

47. *Detroit Free Press*, 1 August 1935; *New York Times*, 4 August 1935.

48. *Detroit Free Press*, 3–5 August 1935.

49. *Chicago Daily Tribune,* 18 August 1935; *Newsweek,* 17 August 1935; *Saturday Evening Post,* 2 November 1935.
50. *New York Times,* 20 August 1935.
51. Ibid.
52. *Newsweek,* 31 August 1935.
53. *Detroit Free Press,* 6–7, 9 August 1935; *Newsweek,* 31 August 1935; *New York Times,* 19 August 1, 5 September 1935.
54. "Who Is Clara Shavelson?" (see note 30 Martha Shaffer, interview with the author, 11 March 1989; and Sophie Melvin Gerson, interview with the author, 17 February 1989.
55. *Detroit Free Press* and *New York Times,* both for 10 April 1936; *The Woman Today,* July 1936.
56. *The Woman Today,* July 1936.
57. Ibid.; *New York Times,* 7, 13 June; 5, 26 July; 3, 9, 10, 13 September; 1, 9 November 1936; "A Few Honest Questions and Answers about Initiative 119" (handbill, n.d., Burke Collection).
58. "A Few Honest Questions and Answers" (leaflet of the Washington Commonwealth Federation, n.d., Burke Collection). See *The Nation,* 28 November 1934; 19 August 1939.
59. *The Woman Today,* March 1937; *New York Times,* 4 December 1947; 20 May; 20 July; 3–31 August 1948; 24, 26–28 February; 25, 26 May; 14 June; 18 August 1951.
60. Raynes interview, 17 February 1989: *New York Times,* 3, 5, 8–11, 19, 28, 31 August 1948; 24, 26–28 Feb.; 14 June 1951.
61. *New York Times,* 26 February 1933; *The Woman Today,* March 1937; *The Notion,* 5, 12 June 1937; 18 February 1939; *Business Week,* 11 November 1939; *Forum,* October 1939; *The New Republic,* 1 January 1940.
62. *New York Times,* 23 October 1949; 7 January 1950.
63. *The Nation,* 5, 12 June 1937; *The New Republic,* 8 April 1936.
64. *New York Times,* 20, 24, 25 August 1935; 20 May; 20 July; 3–31 August 1948; 24, 26–28 February; 25, 26 May; 14 June; 18 August 1951.
65. Moser interview.
66. *Working Woman,* March 1935.
67. Frank argues that during the 1920s working-class women in Seattle resisted their husbands' and brothers' calls to consumer action, because they resented their exclusion from meaningful participation in governance and policy making of the labor unions. See Frank, "At the Point of Consumption"; Schaffer interview.

25

Raiz Fuerte
Oral History and Mexicana Farmworkers

Devra Anne Weber

Mexicana field workers, as agricultural laborers, have been remarkable for their absence in written agricultural history. Most studies have focused on the growth of capitalist agriculture and the related decline of the family farm. Concern about the implications of these changes for American culture, political economy, and the agrarian dream has generally shaped the questions asked about capitalist agriculture. If freeholding family farmers were the basis of a democratic society, capitalist and/or slave agriculture was its antitheses. Studies of capitalist agriculture have thus become enclosed within broader questions about American democracy, measuring change against a mythologized past of conflict-free small farming on a classless frontier.

When considered at all, agricultural wage workers have usually been examined in terms of questions framed by these assumptions. Rather than being seen in their own right, they have usually been depicted as the degraded result of the family farm's demise. The most thoughtful studies have been exposés, written to sway public opinion, that revealed the complex arrangement of social, economic, and political power perpetuating the brutal conditions under which farmworkers lived and toiled. As was the case with the history of unskilled workers in industry, the written history of farmworkers became molded by the pressing conditions of their lives. The wretchedness of conditions became confused with the social worlds of the workers. Pictured as victims of a brutal system, they emerged as faceless, powerless, passive, and ultimately outside the flow of history. Lurking racial, cultural, ethnic, and gender stereotypes reinforced this image. This was especially true for Mexican women.[1]

These considerations make oral sources especially crucial for exploring the history of Mexican women.[2] Oral histories enable us to challenge the common confusion between the dismal conditions of the agricultural labor system and the internal life of workers. They enable us to understand the relationship for Mexicanas between the economic system of agriculture and community, politics, and familial and cultural life. Oral histories help answer (and reconceptualize) fundamental questions about class, gender, life and work, cultural change, values, and perceptions neglected in traditional, sources. They also provide an insight into consciousness.

In conducting a series of oral histories with men and women involved in a critical farmworker strike in the 1930s, I began to think about the nature of gender consciousness. How does it intersect with a sense of class? How does it intersect with national and ethnic identity? In the oral histories of Mexican women, their sense of themselves as workers and Mexicans frequently coincided with that of the men, and drew upon similar bonds of history, community, and commonality. Yet the women's perceptions of what it meant to be a Mexican or a worker were shaped by gender roles and consciousness that frequently differed from that of the men. This seemed to correspond to what Temma Kaplan has defined as "female consciousness." According to Kaplan,

> Female consciousness, recognition of what a particular class, culture and historical period expect from women, creates a sense of rights and obligations that provides motive force for actions different from those Marxist or feminist theory generally try to explain. Female consciousness centers upon the rights of gender on social concerns, on survival. Those with female consciousness accept the gender system of their society; indeed such consciousness emerges from the division of labor by sex, which assigns women the responsibility of preserving life. But, accepting that task, women with female consciousness demand the rights that their obligations entail. The collective drive to secure those rights that result from the division of labor sometimes has revolutionary consequences insofar as it politicizes the networks of everyday life.[3]

This essay will explore how oral histories can help us understand the consciousness of a group of Mexican women cotton workers (or *compañeras* of cotton workers) who participated in the 1933 cotton strike in California's San Joaquin Valley. One was a woman I will call Mrs. Valdez.

Mrs. Valdez and the 1933 Cotton Strike

Mrs. Valdez came from Mexico, where her father had been a *sembrador*, a small farmer or sharecropper, eking out a livable but bleak existence. She had barely reached adolescence when the Mexican Revolution broke out in 1910. With the exception of a sister-in-law, neither she nor her immediate family participated in the revolution.[4] As is the case with many noncombatants, her memories of the revolution were not of the opposing ideologies nor of the issues, but of hunger, fear, and death.[5] Fleeing the revolution, the family crossed the border into the United States. By 1933 she was twenty-four, married with two children, and living in a small San Joaquin Valley town.

The agricultural industry in which she worked was, by 1933, California's major industry. Cotton, the most rapidly expanding crop, depended on Mexican workers who migrated annually to the valley to work.[6] Larger cotton ranches of over three hundred acres dominated the industry. Here workers lived in private labor camps, the largest of which were rural versions of industrial company towns: Workers lived in company housing, bought from (and remained in debt to) company stores, and sent their children to company schools. Work and daily lives were supervised by a racially structured hierarchy dominated by Anglo managers and foremen; below them were Mexican contractors who recruited the workers, supervised work, and acted as intermediaries between workers and their English-speaking employers.

With the Depression, growers slashed wages. In response, farmworkers went on strike in crop after crop in California. The wave of strikes began in southern California and spread north into the San Joaquin Valley. While conducted under the banner of the Cannery and Agricultural Workers Industrial Union (CAWIU), the strikes were sustained largely by Mexican workers and Mexican organizers. The spread and success of the strikes depended on the familial and social networks of Mexican workers as much as, if nor more than, the small but effective and ambitious union. The strike wave crested in the cotton fields of the San Joaquin Valley when eighteen thousand strikers brought picking to a standstill. Growers evicted strikers, who established ad hoc camps on empty land. The largest was near the town of Corcoran, where thirty-five hundred workers congregated. The strikers formed mobile picket lines, to which growers retaliated by organizing armed vigilantes. The strikers held out for over a month before a negotiated settlement was reached with the growers and the California, United States, and Mexican governments.

Mexicanas were a vital part of the strike, and about half of the strikers at Corcoran were women. They ran the camp kitchen, cared for children, and marched on picket lines. They distributed food and clothing. Some attended strike meetings, and a few spoke at the meetings. And it was the women who confronted Mexican strikebreakers. In short, women were essential to this strike, though they have been largely obscured in accounts of its history. Mrs. Valdez went on strike and was on the picket lines. She was not a leader, but she was one of the many women who made the strike possible.

Voice and Community

Before examining her testimony, a word is in order about voice and tone as a dimension of oral histories. How information is conveyed is as important as what is said and can emphasize or contradict the verbal message. Conversation and social interaction are a major part of women's lives, and gesture and voice are thus particularly crucial to their communications. The verbal message, the "song" of a story, is especially important for people with a strong oral tradition, which, as Jan Vansina has pointed out, has meaning as art form, drama, and literature. Oral histories or stories are often dramatic, moving with a grace and continuity that embody analytical reflections and communicate an understanding of social relations and the complexities of human existence.

Mrs. Valdez structured the telling of her oral history in stories or vignettes. Most sections of her oral history had distinct beginnings and endings, interrupted only if I interjected a question. She developed characters, villains and heroes, and hardship and tragedy (but little comedy). How this story was constructed and its characters developed embodied her assessment of the conflict.

As she told her story, the characters emerged with voices of their own, each with separate and distinct tones and cadence, perhaps reflecting their personalities to an extent, but more generally expressing Mrs. Valdez's assessment of them and their role in the drama. Strikebreakers, for example, spoke in high-pitched and pleading voices, and the listener understood them immediately as measly cowards. Her rendition of the strikers' voices, offered a clear contrast: Their words were given in sonorous, deep, and steady tones, in a voice of authority that seemed to represent a communal voice verbalizing what Mrs. Valdez considered to be community values.

Mrs. Valdez's sense of collective values, later embodied in collective action either by the strikers as a group or by women, was expressed in what I would call a collective voice. At times individuals spoke in her stories: the grower, Mr. Peterson; her contractor, "Chicho" Viduarri; and the woman leader "la Lourdes," but more often people spoke in one collective voice that transcended individuality. This sense of community as embodied in a collective voice became a central feature of her narrative and permeated everything she said about the strike. This manner of telling underscored the sense of unanimity explicit in her analysis of solidarity and clear-cut divisions.[7] How she told the story underlined, accentuated, and modified the meaning of the story itself.

Beyond her use of different voices, Mrs. Valdez's narrative contains substantial non verbal analysis of the "facts" as she remembered them. Her voice, gestures, and inflections conveyed both implications and meanings. She gestured with her arms and hands—a flat palm down hard on the table to make a point, both hands held up as she began again. Her stories had clear beginnings and often ended with verbal punctuations such as "and that's the way it was." She switched tenses around as, in the heat of the story, the past became the present and then receded again into the past. Vocal inflections jumped, vibrated, climbed, and then descended, playing a tonal counterpoint to her words.

Mrs. Valdez's memories of the 1933 strike focused on two major concerns: providing and caring for her family, and her role as a striker. How she structured these memories says much about her perceptions and her consciousness as a woman, a Mexican, and a worker. It is striking to what extent her memories of the strike focused on the collectivity of Mexicans and, within this, the collectivity of Mexican women.

Mrs. Valdez's sense of national identity, an important underpinning to her narrative, reflects the importance of national cohesion against a historic background of Anglo-Mexican hostility.[8] Mrs. Valdez vividly recounted the United States' appropriation of Mexican land in 1848 and the Treaty of Guadalupe Hidalgo, which ceded the area to the United States. She drew from stories of Mexican rebellion against U.S. rule in California and the nineteenth-century California guerrillas Tiburcio Vásquez and Joaquin Murieta; the knowledge that Mexicans were working on land that had once belonged to Mexico increased her antagonism toward Anglo bosses. Mrs. Valdez may well have felt the same way as another interviewee, Mrs. Martinez, who, upon arriving at the valley, pointed out to her son and told him, "Mira lo que nos arrebataron los bárbaros."[9]

Most of these workers had lived through the Mexican Revolution of 1910–20, and they utilized both the experience and legacy within the new context of a strike-torn California. The military experience was crucial in protecting the camp: Often led by former military officers, Mexican veterans at the Corcoran camp constituted a formidable armed security system. Mrs. Valdez remembers that during the strike stories of the revolution were told, retold, and debated. The extent to which Mexicans employed the images and slogans of the revolution helped solidify a sense of community. Workers named the rough roads in the camp after revolutionary heroes and Mexican towns. Even Mrs. Valdez, whose individual memories of the revolution were primarily of the terror it held for her, shared in a collective memory of a national struggle and its symbols: She disdainfully compared strikebreakers with traitors who had "sold the head of Pancho Villa."[10]

Mrs. Valdez expressed a sense of collectivity among Mexicans. There were, in fact, many divisions—between strikers and strikebreakers, contractors and workers, people from different areas of Mexico, and people who had fought with different factions of the revolution or Cristero movement. Yet conflict with Anglo bosses on what had been Mexican land emphasized an identification as Mexicans (as well as workers) that overshadowed other divisions.

The Community of Mexican Women

Mrs. Valdez remembered a collectivity of Mexican women. By 1933 Mexican women were working alongside men in the fields. Like the men, they were paid piece rates and picked an average of two hundred pounds per ten-hour day. Picking required strength, skill, and stamina. As one woman recalled:

> But let me describe to you what we had to go through. I'd have a twelve-foot sack. . . . I'd tie the sack around my waist and the sack would go between my legs and I'd go on the cotton row, picking cotton and just putting it in there. . . . So when we finally got it filled real good then we would pick up the hundred-pound sack, toss it up on our shoulders, and then I would walk, put it up there on the scale and have it weighed, put it back on my shoulder, climb up on a wagon and empty that sack in.[11]

As Mrs. Valdez recounted, women faced hardships in caring for their families: houses without heat (which contributed to disease), preparing food without stoves, and cooking over fires in oil barrels. Food was central to her memory, reflecting a gender-based division of labor. Getting enough food, a problem at any time, was exacerbated by the Depression, which forced some women to forage for berries or feed their families flour and water. Food was an issue of survival. As in almost all societies, women were in charge of preparing the food, and Mrs. Valdez's concern about food was repeated in interviews with other women. Men remembered the strike in terms of wages and conditions; women remembered these events in terms of food. Men were not oblivious or unconcerned, but women's role in preparing food made this a central aspect of their consciousness and shaped the way they perceived, remembered, and articulated the events of the strike.

Mrs. Valdez's memory of leadership reflects this sense of female community. After initially replying that there were no leaders (a significant comment in itself), she named her labor contractor and then focused on a woman named Lourdes Castillo, an interesting choice for several reasons. Lourdes Castillo was an attractive, single woman who lived in Corcoran. She used makeup, bobbed her hair, and wore stylish dresses. Financially independent, she owned and ran the local bar. Lourdes became involved with the strike when union organizers asked her to store food for strikers in her cantina.

In some respects Lourdes represented a transition many Mexican women were undergoing in response to capitalist expansion, revolution, and migration. When the revolution convulsively disrupted Mexican families, women left alone took over the work in rural areas, migrated, and sometimes became involved in the revolution. *Soldaderas*, camp followers in the revolution, cooked, nursed, and provided sexual and emotional comfort. Some fought and were even executed in the course of battle. This image of *la soldadera*, the woman fighting on behalf of the Mexican community, was praised as a national symbol of strength and resistance. Yet it was an ambivalent image: Praised within the context of an often mythified revolution, the *soldaderas* were criticized for their relative sexual freedom and independence. The term *soldadera* became double-edged. When used to describe an individual woman, it could be synonymous with *whore*.

Gender mores in the United States differed from those in rural Mexico. Some changes were cosmetic manifestations of deeper alterations: Women bobbed their hair, adopted new styles of dress, and wore makeup. But these changes reflected shifts in a gender-based division of labor. Women, usually younger and unmarried, began to work for wages in canneries or garment factories, unobserved by watchful male relatives. Some women became financially independent, as Lourdes did, and ran bars and cantinas. Financial independence and a changing gender-based division of labor outside the house altered expectations of women's responsibilities and obligations. Yet these women still risked the approbation of segments of the community, male and female.

According to Mrs. Valdez, during the strike Lourdes was in charge of keeping the log of who entered and left the camp and who spoke at meetings. She was also in charge of distributing food.[12] Lourdes thus reflects women's traditional concern about food, while at the same time she epitomized the cultural transition of Mexican women and the changing gender roles from pre-revolutionary Mexico to the more fluid wage society of California. It was precisely her financial independence that enabled her to store and distribute the food. Perhaps Mrs. Valdez's enthusiastic memories of Lourdes suggests Mrs. Valdez's changing values concerning women, even if these were not directly expressed in her own life.

While Mrs. Valdez described the abysmal conditions under which women labored, the women were active, not passive, participants in the strike. Women's networks, which formed the lattice of mutual assistance in the workers' community, were transformed during the strike. The networks helped organize daily picket lines in front of the cotton fields. Older women still sporting the long hair and rebozos of rural Mexico, younger women who had adapted the flapper styles of the United States, and young girls barely into their teens rode together in trucks to the picket lines. They set up makeshift child-care centers and established a camp kitchen.

With the spread of the conflict, these networks expanded and the women's involvement escalated from verbal assaults on the strikebreakers to outright physical conflict. When, after three weeks, growers refused to settle, women organized and led confrontations with Mexican strikebreakers. According to Mrs. Valdez, the women decided that they, not the men, would enter the fields to confront the strikebreakers.[13] They reasoned that strikebreakers would be less likely to physically hurt the women.

In organized groups, the women entered the field, appealing to strikebreakers on class and national grounds—as "poor people" and "Mexicanos"—to join the strike. Those from the same regions or villages in Mexico appealed to compatriots on the basis of local loyalties, denouncing as traitors those who refused.

Exhortations turned to threats and conflict. The women threatened to poison one man who had eaten at the camp kitchen—an indication again of the centrality of (and their power over) food. But women had also come prepared. Those armed with lead pipes and knives went after the strikebreakers. One ripped a cotton sack with a knife. Others hit strikebreakers with pipes, fists, or whatever was handy. Although strikers had felt that the women would not be hurt, the male strikebreakers retaliated, and at least one woman was brutally beaten:

> Las mismas mujeres que iban en los troques . . . que iban en el picoteo. Adentro, les pegaron. Les rompieron su ropa. Les partieron los sombreros y los sacos y se los hicieron asina y todo. Y malos! Ohh! Se mira feo! Feo se miraba. Y nomas miraba y decia "no, no." Yo miraba la sangre que les escurria. [She imitates the strikebreakers in high-pitched, pleading tones:] "No les peguen, déjenlos, no les peguen." [Her voice drops as the voice of the strikers speaks:] "Que se los lleve el esto. . . . Si a nosotros nos esta llevando de frio y de hambre pos que a ellos también. No tienen, vendidos, muertos de hambre!" [Her voice rises as the strikebreakers continue their plea:] "Pos nosotros vivemos muy lejos, venimos de Los Angeles . . . tienes que saber de donde, que tenemos que tener dinero pa' irnos." [Her voice lowers and slows as it again becomes the voice of the strikers:] "Si . . . nosotros también tenemos que comer y también tenemos familia. *Pero no somos vendidos!*"[14]

This passage underlines the importance of the female collectivity. The women went in because it was women's business, and they acted on behalf of the community. Mrs. Valdez implied that the men had little to do with the decision or even opposed it: "Porque las mujeres tenemos más chanza. Siempre los hombres se detenian más porque son hombres y todo. Y las mujeres no. Los hombres no nos pueden hacer nada. No nos podian hacer nada pos ahi vamos en zumba."[15]

The issues of confrontation focused around food. This underlines a harsh reality: Strikebreakers worked to feed their families, and without food strikers would be forced back to work. Her memory reflects the reality of the confrontation but also her understanding of the central issue of the strike. Mrs. Valdez recalls the strikebreakers justifying themselves to the women in terms of the need to feed their families. But the striking women's ultimate rebuke was also expressed in terms of this need: "Si. . . . nosotros también tenemos que comer y también tenemos familia. *Pero no somos vendidos!*"[16] Food remained central in her memories. Discussions about the strike and strike negotiations were all couched in relation to food. Her interests as a Mexican worker were considered, weighed, and expressed within the context of her interests as a woman, mother, and wife.

As the strike wore on, conditions grew harsher in the Corcoran camp. Growers lobbed incendiaries over the fence at night. Food became hard to get, and at least one child died of malnutrition.[17] In response to public concern following the murder of two strikers, California's governor overrode federal regulations withholding relief from strikers under arbitration and, over the protestations of local boards of supervisors, sent in truckloads of milk and food to the embattled camp. Mrs. Valdez remembers nothing of federal, state, or local government or agencies, but she remembered the food: "rice, beans, milk, everything they sent in."

At a meeting where Lourdes addressed strikers, food, or lack of food, was juxtaposed against their stance in the strike:

Pa' [Lourdes] decirles que pasaran hambre.

"Mira," dice ... "aunque alcanzemos poquito pero no nos estamos muriendo de hambre," dice. "Pero no salsa. Pero *ninguno* a trabajar ... aunque venga el ranchero y les diga que, que vamos y que pa'ca. *No* vaya ninguno!" dice.

"Miren, aunque sea poquito estamos comiendo ... pero no nos hemos muerto de hambre. Ta viniendo comida ... nos estan trayendo comida."

[Mrs Valdez interjected:] Leche y todo nos daban.... Si. Y a todos ahi los que trabajában diciendo que no fueran con ningún ranchero. Que no se creeran de ningúin ranchero. Que todos se agarraban de un solo modo que nadien, todos parejos tuvieran su voto, parejos.[18]

Mrs. Valdez was clear about the effects of a united front on both sides—that if one grower broke with the others, the rest would follow. [The collective voice speaks:] "No. Y no que no. No. Si nos paga tanto vamos, Y al pagar un ranchero tenían que pagar todos los mismo. Tenían, ves."[19]

Unity and the centrality of women carried over into her recollection of the final negotiations:

El portuguese [a growers' representative] ... le dijera que ahí iban los rancheros ... a tener un mitin en el campo donde estaban todos ahí campados con la Lourdes Castillo y todo

"Sí," dice. "Ahí vamos a juntarnos todos los rancheros. Y vamos a firmai. Les vamos a pagai tanto. Y vamos a firmar todos para que entonces, sí, ya vayan cada quien a sus campos a trabajar."

"Sí," dice [the strikers' representative], "pero no menos de un centavo. No. No salimos hasta que tengan un ... sueldo fijo. Todos vamos. Pero de ahí en más ni uno vamos. *Ni uno* salimos del camps." Y todo.[20]

The strike was settled, the ranchers had been beaten, and wages went up.

The Structure of Memory

Mrs. Valdez's account of the strike and women— how she structured her memories—tells us more about why Mexicanas supported the strike than interviews with leaders might have. Without the perceptions of women such as Mrs. Valdez it would be more difficult to understand strike dynamics.

Of particular interest is the fact that she remembers (or recounts) a collectivity among Mexican strikers. In her telling, workers speak in a collective voice and act as a united group. She remembers little or no dissent. In her account, *all* the workers on the Peterson ranch walked out together to join the strike, *all* the women were on the picket lines, and *all* the strikers voted unanimously to stay on strike. Growers, also a united group, spoke with one voice as a collective opposition. The lines between worker and grower were clearly drawn. According to Mrs. Valdez, it was this unity that accounted for the strike's success.

But within this collectivity of Mexicans was the collectivity of women. Mrs. Valdez focused on female themes and concerns about food, caring for their families and, by extension, the greater community. Women were the actors on the picket line, made decisions about the strike, and acted as a unit. It is perhaps this sense of female collectivity and the concern around the issue of food that accounts for why Lourdes was considered a leader, though she is never mentioned by men in their accounts. Men played little part in Mrs. Valdez's narrative; she stated flatly that the women were braver. She remembered female leadership, female participation, female concerns, and a largely female victory. While other interviews and sources may disagree (even among women), it does suggest Mrs. Valdez's reality of the strike of 1933.

What Mrs. Valdez did not say suggests the limitations of oral narratives. She either did not know, could not recall, or chose not to recount several crucial aspects of the story: Like many other strikers, she remembered nothing of the CAWIU, nor of Anglo strike leaders mentioned in other accounts. This was not uncommon, and I discuss elsewhere the implications of this and the nature of Mexican leadership within the strike.[21] The role of the New Deal and the negotiations of the governments—Mexican, United States, and California—play no part in her narrative. The visit by the Mexican consul to the camp, visits by government officials, threats to deport strikers—she recounted nothing about the negotiations that led to the settlement of the strike.

Her memory of the strike thus is limited. But the fact that Mrs. Valdez's memories were so similar to those of other women indicates that hers is not an isolated perception. There are also many points at which the women's memories intersect with the men's. We thus may be dealing with a community memory made up of two intersecting collective memories: the collective memory (history) of the group as a whole, and a collective memory of women as a part of this.

Conclusion

Oral narratives reflect people's memory of the past: they can be inaccurate, contradictory, altered by the passage of time and the effects of alienation. In terms of historical analysis, Mrs. Valdez's oral history, used alone, raises questions. Was there really such unity in the face of such an intense conflict? There were, obviously, strikebreakers. Were there no doubts, arguments? In part she may have been making a point to me. But it may be also indicative of her consciousness, of the things important to her in the event. Mrs. Valdez also remembers a largely female collectivity. Certainly it is clear from other sources that men played a crucial role as well. Yet her focus on women provides information unavailable in other sources, and provides a woman's point of view. It suggests which issues were important to the female collectivity, how and why women rallied to the strike, and how they used their networks within the strike.

So how may an oral history be used? Seen on its own, it remains a fragment of the larger story. Oral narratives must also be read critically as texts in light of the problem of alienation, especially in the United States, where various forms of cultural and historical amnesia seem so advanced. Used uncritically, oral histories are open to misinterpretation and may reinforce rather than reduce the separation from a meaningful past. This is especially true of the narratives of those people usually ignored by written history. Readers may lack a historical framework within which to situate and understand such narratives. The filters of cultural and class differences and chauvinism may also be obstacles. Some may embrace these narratives as colorful and emotional personal statements, while ignoring the subjects as reflective and conscious participants in history.

In the case of the Mexican women farm laborers considered in this essay, oral testimonies are not a complete history, nor can they, by themselves, address the problems of historical amnesia. Used with other material and read carefully and critically, however, such narratives prove crucial to a reanalysis of the strike. They need to be interpreted and placed within a historical framework encompassing institutional and social relations, struggle, and change. But when this is done, testimonies such as that of Mrs. Valdez become a uniquely invaluable source. Used critically, they reveal transformations in consciousness and culture; they suggest the place of self-conscious and reflective Mexican women—and farm-laboring women in general—in the broader history of rural women in the United States.

Notes

1. Portions of this essay appear in Devra A. Weber, "Mexican Women on Strike: Memory, History and Oral Narrative," in Adelida Del Castillo, ed., *Between Borders: Essays on Mexicana/Chicana History* (Encino, Calif.: Floricanto Press, 1990), 161–74.

2. I use the term used by the women themselves. They called themselves Mexicans. Although all had lived in the United States over fifty years, all but one identified themselves as Mexicanas by birth, culture, and ethnicity. The one woman born and raised in the United States, and a generation younger, referred to herself interchangeably as Mexicana and Chicana.

3. Temma Kaplan, "Female Consciousness and Collective Action: The Case of Barcelona, 1910–1918," *Signs* (spring 1982): 545.

4. The sister-in-law is an interesting, if fragmentary, figure in Mrs. Valdez's memory. From Mrs. Valdez's account, the sister-in-law left her husband (Mrs. Valdez's brother) to join a group of revolutionaries, as a *companera* of one of them. When she returned to see her children, she threatened to have the entire family killed by her new lover. It was in the wake of this threat that the family fled to the United States.

5. That these were the main concerns of many Mexicans does not undermine the importance of the revolution in their lives, nor the extent to which the images and symbols of the revolution *later* became symbols of collective resistance, on both class and national scales.

6. By 1933 the overwhelming majority of Mexican workers migrated not from Mexico but from settled communities around Los Angeles or the Imperial Valley, adjacent to the Mexican border. Some came from Texas. The point is that they were not the "homing pigeons" described by growers —people who descended on the fields at harvest and cheerfully departed for Mexico. They were residents, and some of the younger pickers were United States citizens.

7. I want to emphasize that this is *her* analysis. I would disagree with the picture of solidarity; disputes among strikers would, I think, bear this out. Nevertheless, the point is that Mrs. Valdez's historical analysis tells us a great deal about her conception of the strike—and perhaps her conception of what I should be told about it.

8. In Mexico, Mexicans tended to have a greater sense of identity with the town or state they came from than with the country as a whole. These identities were still strong in the 1980s, as were the rivalries that existed between them. It has been argued that the Mexican revolution helped create a sense of national consciousness. One of the primary reasons was its opposition to foreign interests. For those who migrated north, across the Rio Bravo, the sense of opposition to Anglo-Americans was even greater. It was on the border areas, after all, where the corridors of resistance developed, and where many have argued the sense of Mexican nationalism was strongest.

9. "Look at what the barbarians have stolen from us." Interview by author with Guillermo Martinez, Los Angeles, April 1982.

   Note: Having encountered strong objections to using the original Spanish in such a text, a word of explanation is in order. Translating another language—especially if the language is colloquial and therefore less directly translatable—robs the subjects of their voices, diminishing the article as a consequence. This is especially true if, as in this case, the language is colloquial and, to those who know Spanish, manifestly rural and working-class. The original text gives such readers an indication of class and meaning unavailable in a translation. It also underscores the value of bridging monolingual parochialism in a multilingual and multicultural society. In any event, full English translations for all quotations will be provided in the Notes.

10. After his death, Villa's corpse was disinterred and decapitated. His head was stolen in the 1920s, and the incident became a legend.

11. Interview by author with Lydia Ramos. All names used here are pseudonyms.

12. It is unclear whether Lourdes did keep the log. In a brief interview, Lourdes confirmed that she spoke at meetings and distributed food.

13. It is unclear exactly who made this decision. Roberto Castro, a member of the central strike committee, said the strike committee decided that women should enter the fields to confront strikebreakers because the women would be less likely to be hurt. The women remembered no such decision, and said that they made the decision themselves. It is hard to fix definitively the origins of the idea, but this may not matter very much: even if the strike committee made the decision, the action was consistent with spontaneous decisions by women that both antedated and followed this strike. Mexican women in Mexico City and other parts of the republic had taken part in bread riots in the colonial period. They had fought in the revolution. And in California, later strikes, in the 1930s but also as recently as the 1980s, were punctuated by groups of Mexican women invading the fields to confront strikebreakers both verbally and physically. In short, it was a female form of protest women had used both before and after the strike.

14. "The same women who were in the trucks, who were in the . . . picket line . . . these women went in and beat up all those that were inside the fields picking cotton.. . . They tore their clothes. They ripped their hats and the [picking] sacks. . . . And bad. Ohhh! It was ugly! It was an ugly sight. I was just looking and said 'No. No.' I watched the blood flowing from them.

     [she imitates the strikebreakers voice in high-pitched, pleading tones:] 'Don't hit us. Leave them [other strikebreakers] alone. Don't hit them.'

     [Her voice drops as the collective voice of the strikers speaks:] 'Let them be set upon. . . . If we are going cold and hungry then they should too. They're cowards . . . sellouts. Scum.'

     [Her voice rises as the strikebreakers continue their plea:] 'Because we live far away, we come from Los Angeles. . . . We need to have money to leave. . . .'

     'Yes,' she says [her voice lowers and slows as it again becomes the voice of the strikers]. 'We also have to eat and we also have family,' she says. *But we are not sellouts!*"

15. "Because women take more chances. The men always hold back because they are men and all. But the women, no. The men couldn't make us do anything. They couldn't make us do anything [to prevent us from going] and so we all went off in a flash."

16. "Yes . . . we also have to eat and we also have family. *But we are not sellouts!*"

17. As the local district attorney admitted after the strike, conditions in the strikers' camp were no worse than those of the cotton labor camps. Growers did use the bad conditions, however, to pressure the health department to close the strikers' camp as a menace to public health.

18. "She [Lourdes] was telling them that they might have to go hungry for awhile.

     " 'But look,' she said . . . 'they are bringing us food. We'll each get just a little, but we're not going to starve,' she says. 'But don't leave. But don't *anybody* go to work. Even if a rancher comes and tells you 'come on, lets go,' don't anybody go," she says.

     " 'Look, even if its a little bit, we're eating. But we aren't starving. They're bringing us food.' "

     [Mrs. Valdez interjected:] They brought us milk and everything. Yes, everybody that was working [in the strikers' camp] was told not to go with any rancher. They were told not to believe any rancher. But everyone had to stand together as one. Everyone had an equal vote [in what was decided] . . . equal."

19. " 'No. And no [they said]. No. No. If you pay us this much, then we go. And if one [rancher] pays [the demand] then all the ranchers have to pay the same.' They had to, you see."

20. "The Portuguese [a growers' representative] told [the strikers' representative] that the ranchers . . . were going to have a meeting at [the strikers' camp] with 'la Lourdes.'

     ' "Yes," he says. "We're going to pay you so much. All of us are going to sign so that then all of you can return to your camps to work.'

     " 'Yes,' said [the strikers' representative]. 'But not a cent less. No. We won't go until we have a set wage. Then all of us go. But if there is something more [if there is more trouble] *none* of us go. Not even *one* of us leaves the camp.' "

21. Devra Weber, *Dark Sweat, White Gold: California Farm Worker, Cotton, and the New Deal* (Berkeley: University of California Press, 1994).

26

From Servitude to Service Work
Historical Continuities in the Racial Division of Paid Reproductive Labor

Evelyn Nakano Glenn

Recent scholarship on African American, Latina, Asian American, and Native American women reveals the complex interaction of race and gender oppression in their lives. These studies expose the inadequacy of additive models that treat gender and race as discrete systems of hierarchy.[1] In an additive model, white women are viewed solely in terms of gender, while women of color are thought to be "doubly" subordinated by the cumulative effects of gender plus race. Yet achieving a more adequate framework, one that captures the interlocking, interactive nature of these systems, as been extraordinarily difficult. Historically, race and gender have developed as separate topics of inquiry, each with its own literature and concepts. Thus features of social life considered central in understanding one system have been overlooked in analyses of the other.

One domain that has been explored extensively in analyses of gender but ignored in studies of race is social reproduction. The term *social reproduction* is used by feminist scholars to refer to the array of activities and relationships involved in maintaining people both on a daily basis and intergenerationally. Reproductive labor includes activities such as purchasing household goods, preparing and serving food, laundering and repairing clothing, maintaining furnishings and appliances, socializing children, providing care and emotional support for adults, and maintaining kin and community ties.

Marxist feminists place the gendered construction of reproductive labor at the center of women's oppression. They point out that this labor is performed disproportionately by women, and is essential to the industrial economy. Yet because it takes place mostly outside the market, it is invisible, not recognized as real work. Men benefit directly and indirectly from this arrangement—directly in that they contribute less labor in the home while enjoying the services women provide as wives and mothers, and indirectly in that, freed of domestic labor, they can concentrate their efforts in paid employment and attain primacy in that area. Thus the sexual division of reproductive labor in the home interacts with and reinforces sexual division in the labor market.[2] These analyses draw attention to the dialectics of production and reproduction, and to male privilege in both realms. When they represent gender as the sole basis for assigning reproductive labor, however, they imply that all women have the same relationship to it, and that it is therefore a universal female experience.[3]

In the meantime, theories of racial hierarchy do not include any analysis of reproductive labor. Perhaps because, consciously or unconsciously, they are male-centered, they focus exclusively on the paid labor market, and especially on male-dominated areas of production. In the 1970s several writers seeking to explain the historical subordination of peoples of color pointed to dualism in the labor market—its division into distinct markets for white workers and for racial-ethnic workers—as a major vehicle for maintaining white domination.[4] According to these formulations, the labor system has been organized to ensure that racial-ethnic workers are relegated to a lower tier of low-wage, dead-end, marginal jobs; institutional barriers, including restrictions on legal and political rights, prevent their moving out of that tier and competing with European American workers for better jobs. These theories draw attention to the material advantages whites gain from the racial division of labor. However, they either take for granted or ignore women's unpaid household labor and fail to consider whether this work might also be "racially divided."

In short, the racial division of reproductive labor has been a missing piece of the picture in both literatures. This piece, I would contend, is key to the distinct exploitation of women of color, and is a source of both hierarchy and interdependence among white women and women of color. It is thus essential to the development of an integrated model of race and gender, one that treats them as interlocking, rather than additive, systems.

In this article I present a historical analysis of the simultaneous race and gender construction of reproductive labor in the United States, based on comparative study of women's work in the South, the Southwest, and the far West. I argue that reproductive labor has divided along racial as well as gender lines, and that the specific characteristics of the division have varied regionally and changed over time as capitalism has reorganized reproductive labor, shifting parts of it from the household to the market. In the first half of the century, racial-ethnic women were employed as servants to perform reproductive labor in white households, relieving white middle-class women of onerous aspects of that work; in the second half of the century, with the expansion of commodified services (services turned into commercial products or activities), racial-ethnic women are disproportionately employed as service workers in institutional settings to carry out lower-level "public" reproductive labor, while cleaner, white-collar, supervisory and lower professional positions are filled by white women.

I will examine the ways race and gender were constructed around the division of labor by sketching changes in the organization of reproductive labor since the early nineteenth century, presenting a case study of domestic service among African American women in the South, Mexican American women in the Southwest, and Japanese American women in California and Hawaii, and finally examining the shift to institutional service work, focusing on race and gender stratification in health care and the racial division of labor within the nursing labor force. Race and gender emerge as socially constructed, interlocking systems that shape the material conditions, identities, and consciousnesses of all women.

Historical Changes in the Organization of Reproduction

The concept of reproductive labor originated in Karl Marx's remark that every system of production involves both the production of the necessities of life and the reproduction of the tools and labor-power necessary for production.[5] Recent elaborations of the concept grow out of Engels's dictum that the "determining force in history is, in the last resort, the production and reproduction of immediate life." This has, he noted, "a two-fold character, on the one hand the production of subsistence and on the other the production of human beings themselves."[6] Although often equated with domestic labor, or defined narrowly as referring to the renewal of labor power, the term *social reproduction* has come to be more broadly conceived, particularly by social historians, to refer to the creation and re-creation of people as cultural and social, as well as physical, beings.[7] Thus it involves mental, emotional, and manual labor.[8] This labor can be organized in myriad ways—in and out of the household, as paid or unpaid work, creating exchange value or only use value—and these ways are not mutually exclusive. An example is the preparation of food, which can be done by a family member as unwaged work in the household, by a servant as waged work in the household, or by a short-order cook in a fast-food restaurant as waged work that generates profit for the employer. These forms exist contemporaneously.

Prior to industrialization, however, both production and reproduction were organized almost exclusively at the household level. Women were responsible for most of what might be designated as reproduction, but they were simultaneously engaged in the production of foodstuffs, clothing, shoes, candles, soap, and other goods consumed by the household. With industrialization, production of these basic goods was gradually taken over by capitalist industry. Reproduction, however, remained largely the responsibility of individual households. The ideological separation between men's "productive" labor and women's nonmarket-based activity that had evolved at the end of the eighteenth century was elaborated in the early decades of the nineteenth. An idealized division of labor arose, in which men's work was to follow production outside the home, while women's work was to remain centered in the household.[9] Household work continued to include the production of many goods consumed by members, but as an expanding range of outside-manufactured goods became available, household work became increasingly focused on reproduction.[10] This idealized division of labor was largely illusory for working-class households, including immigrant and racial-ethnic families, in which men seldom earned a family wage; in these households women and children were forced into income-earning activities in and out of the home.[11]

In the second half of the twentieth century, with goods production almost completely incorporated into the market, reproduction has become the next major target for commodification. Aside from the tendency of capital to expand into new areas for profit-making, the very conditions of life brought about by large-scale commodity production have increased the need for commercial services. As household members spend more of their waking hours employed outside the home, they have less time and inclination to provide for one another's social and emotional needs. With the growth of a more geographically mobile and urbanized society, individuals and households have become increasingly cut off from larger kinship circles, neighbors, and traditional communities. Thus, as Harry Braverman notes:

> The population no longer relies upon social organization in the form of family, friends, neighbors, community, elders, children, but with few exceptions must go to the market and only to the market, not only for food, clothing, and shelter, but also for recreation, amusement, security, for the care of the young, the old, the sick, the handicapped. In time not only the material and service needs but even the emotional patterns of life are channeled through the market.[12]

Conditions of capitalist urbanism also have enlarged the population of those requiring daily care and support: elderly and very young people, mentally and physically disabled people, criminals, and other people incapable of fending for themselves. Because the care of such dependents becomes difficult for the "stripped-down" nuclear family or the atomized community to bear, more of it becomes relegated to institutions outside the family.[13]

The final phase in this process is what Braverman calls the "product cycle," which "invents new products and services, some of which become indispensable as the conditions of modern life change and destroy alternatives."[14] In many areas (for example, health care) we no longer have choices outside the market. New services and products also alter the definition of an acceptable standard of living. Dependence on the market is further reinforced by what happened earlier with goods production, namely, an "atrophy of competence," so that individuals no longer know how to do what they formerly did for themselves.

As a result of these tendencies, an increasing range of services has been removed wholly or partially from the household and converted into paid services yielding profits. Today activities such as preparing and serving food (in restaurants and fast-food establishments), caring for handicapped and elderly people (in nursing homes), caring for children (in child-care centers), and providing emotional support, amusement, and companionship (in counseling offices, recreation centers, and health clubs) have become part of the cash nexus. In addition, whether impelled by a need to maintain social control or in response to pressure exerted by worker and community organizations, the state has stepped in to assume minimal responsibility for some reproductive tasks, such as child protection and welfare programs.[15] Whether supplied by corporations or the state, these services are labor-intensive. Thus, a large army of low-wage workers, mostly women and disproportionately women of color, must be recruited to supply the labor.

Still, despite vastly expanded commodification and institutionalization, much reproduction remains organized at the household level. Sometimes an activity is too labor-intensive to be very profitable. Sometimes households or individuals in them have resisted commodification. The limited commodification of child care, for example, involves both elements. The extent of commercialization in different areas of life is uneven, and the variation in its extent is the outcome of political and economic struggles.[16] What is consistent across forms, whether commodified or not, is that reproductive labor is constructed as "female." The gendered organization of reproduction is widely recognized. Less obvious, but equally characteristic, is its racial construction: Historically, racial-ethnic women have been assigned a distinct place in the organization of reproductive labor.

Elsewhere I have talked about the reproductive labor racial-ethnic women have carried out for their own families; this labor was intensified as the women struggled to maintain family life and indigenous cultures in the face of cultural assaults, ghettoization, and a labor system that relegated men and women to low-wage, seasonal, and hazardous employment.[17] Here I want to talk about two forms of waged reproductive work that racial-ethnic women have performed disproportionately: domestic service in private households, and institutional service work.

Domestic Service as the Racial Division of Reproductive Labor

Both the demand for household help and the number of women employed as servants expanded rapidly in the latter half of the nineteenth century.[18] This expansion paralleled the rise of industrial capital and the elaboration of middle-class women's reproductive responsibilities. Rising standards of cleanliness, larger and more ornately furnished homes, the sentimentalization of the home as a "haven in a heartless world," and the new emphasis on childhood and the mother's role in nurturing children all served to enlarge middle-class women's responsibilities for reproduction, at a time when technology had done little to reduce the sheer physical drudgery of housework.[19]

By all accounts, middle-class women did not challenge the gender-based division of labor or the enlargement of their reproductive responsibilities. Indeed, middle-class women—as readers and writers of literature; as members and leaders of clubs, charitable organizations, associations, reform movements, and religious revivals; and as supporters of the cause of abolition—helped to elaborate the domestic code.[20] Feminists seeking an expanded public role for women argued that the same nurturant and moral qualities that made women centers of the home should be brought to bear in public service, in the domestic sphere, instead of questioning the inequitable gender division of labor, they sought to slough off the more burdensome tasks onto more oppressed groups of women.[21]

Phyllis Palmer observes that, at least through the first half of the twentieth century, "most white middle-class women could hire another woman—a recent immigrant, a working class woman, a woman of color, or all three—to perform much of the hard labor of household tasks."[22] Domestics were employed to clean house, launder and iron clothes, scrub floors, and care for infants and children. They relieved their mistresses of the heavier and dirtier domestic chores.[23] White middle-class women were thereby freed for supervisory tasks and for cultural, leisure, and volunteer activity or, more rarely during this period, for a career.[24]

Palmer suggests that the use of domestic servants also helped resolve certain contradictions created by the domestic code. She notes that the early-twentieth-century housewife confronted inconsistent expectations of middle-class womanhood: domesticity and "feminine virtue." Domesticity—defined as creating a warm, clean, and attractive home for husband and children—required hard physical labor and meant contending with dirt. The virtuous woman, however, was defined in terms of spirituality, refinement, and the denial of the physical body. Additionally, in the 1920s and 1930s there emerged a new ideal of the modern wife as an intelligent and attractive companion. If the heavy parts of household work could be transferred to paid help, the middle-class housewife could fulfill her domestic duties, yet distance herself from the physical labor and dirt, and also have time for personal development.[25]

Who was to perform the "dirty work" varied by region. In the Northeast, European immigrant women, particularly those who were Irish and German, constituted the majority of domestic servants from the mid-nineteenth century until World War I.[26] In regions where there was a large concentration of people of color, subordinate-race women formed a more or less permanent servant stratum. Despite differences in the composition of the populations and the mix of industries in the regions, there were important similarities in the situation of Mexicans in the Southwest, African Americans in the South, and Japanese people in northern California and Hawaii. Each of these groups was placed in a separate legal category from whites, excluded from rights and protections accorded full citizens. This severely limited their ability to organize, compete for jobs, and acquire capital.[27] The racial division of private reproductive work mirrored this racial dualism in the legal, political, and economic systems.

In the South, African American women constituted the main and almost exclusive servant caste. Except in times of extreme economic crisis, whites and Blacks did not compete for domestic jobs. Until World War I, 90 percent of all nonagriculturally employed Black women in the South were employed as domestics. Even at the national level, servants and laundresses accounted for close to half (48.4 percent) of nonagriculturally employed Black women in 1930.[28]

In the Southwest, especially in the states with the highest proportions of Mexicans in the population—Texas, Colorado, and New Mexico—Chicanas were disproportionately concentrated in domestic service.[29] In El Paso nearly half of all Chicanas in the labor market were employed as servants or laundresses in the early decades of the century.[30] In Denver, according to Sarah Deutsch, perhaps half of all Chicano/a households had at least one female member employed as a domestic at some time, and if a woman became a widow, she was almost certain to take in laundry.[31] Nationally, 39.1 percent of nonagriculturally employed Chicanas were servants or laundresses in 1930.[32]

In the far West—especially in California and Hawaii, with their large populations of Asian immigrants—an unfavorable sex ratio made female labor scarce in the late nineteenth and early twentieth centuries. In contrast to the rest of the nation, the majority of domestic servants in California and Hawaii were men: in California until 1890 and in Hawaii as late as 1920.[33] The men were Asian—Chinese and later Japanese. Chinese houseboys and cooks were familiar figures in late-nineteenth-century San Francisco; so too were Japanese male retainers in early-twentieth-century Honolulu. After 1907 Japanese women began to immigrate in substantial numbers, and they inherited the mantle of service in both California and Hawaii. In the pre-World War II years, close to half of all immigrant and native-born Japanese American women in the San Francisco Bay area and in Honolulu were employed as servants or laundresses.[34] Nationally, excluding Hawaii, 25.4 percent of nonagricultural Japanese American women workers were listed as servants in 1930.[35]

In areas where racial dualism prevailed, being served by members of the subordinate group was a perquisite of membership in the dominant group. According to Elizabeth Rae Tyson, an Anglo woman who grew up in El Paso in the early years of the century:

> [A]lmost every Anglo-American family had at least one, sometimes two or three servants: a maid and laundress, and perhaps a nursemaid or yardman. The maid came in after breakfast and cleaned up the breakfast dishes, and very likely last night's supper dishes as well; did the routine cleaning, washing and ironing, and after the family dinner in the middle of the day, washed dishes again, and then went home to perform similar services in her own home.[36]

In southwestern cities, Mexican American girls were trained at an early age to do domestic work and girls as young as nine or ten were hired to clean house.[37]

In Hawaii, where the major social division was between the haole (Caucasian) planter class and the largely Asian plantation-worker class, haole residents were required to employ one or more Chinese or Japanese servants to demonstrate their status and their social distance from those less privileged. Andrew Lind notes that "the literature on Hawaii, especially during the second half of the nineteenth century, is full of references to the open-handed hospitality of Island residents, dispensed by the ever-present maids and houseboys."[38] A public-school teacher who arrived in Honolulu in 1925 was placed in a teacher's cottage with four other mainland teachers. She discovered a maid had already been hired by the principal.

> A maid! None of us had ever had a maid. We were all used to doing our own work. Furthermore, we were all in debt and did not feel that we wanted to spend even four dollars a month on a maid. Our principal was quite insistent. Everyone on the plantation had a maid. It was, therefore, the thing to do.[39]

In the South, virtually every middle-class housewife employed at least one African American woman to do cleaning and child care in her home. Southern household workers told one writer that in the old days, "if you worked for a family, your daughter was expected to, too."[40] Daughters of Black domestics were sometimes inducted as children into service to baby-sit, wash diapers, and help clean.[41] White-skin privilege transcended class lines, and it was not uncommon for working-class whites to hire Black women to do housework.[42] In the 1930s white women tobacco workers in Durham, North Carolina, could mitigate the effects of the "double day"—household labor on top of paid labor—by employing Black women to work in their homes for about one-third of their own wages.[43] Black women tobacco workers were too poorly paid to have this option, and had to rely on the help of overworked husbands, older children, Black women too old to be employed, neighbors, or kin.

Where more than one group was available for service, a differentiated hierarchy of race, color, and culture emerged. White and racial-ethnic domestics were hired for different tasks. In her study of women workers in Atlanta, New Orleans, and San Antonio during the 1920s and 1930s, Julia Kirk Blackwelder reported that "Anglo women in the employ of private households were nearly always reported as housekeepers, while Blacks and Chicanas were reported as laundresses, cooks or servants."[44]

In the Southwest, where Anglos considered Mexican or "Spanish" culture inferior, Anglos displayed considerable ambivalence about employing Mexicans for child care. Although a modern-day example, this statement by an El Paso businessman illustrates the contradictions in Anglo attitudes. The man told an interviewer that he and his wife were putting off parenthood because the major dilemma would be what to do with the child. We don't really like the idea of leaving the baby at home with a maid . . . for the simple reason if the maid is Mexican, the child may assume that the other person is its mother. Nothing wrong with Mexicans, they'd just assume that this other person is its mother. There have been all sorts of cases where the infants learned Spanish before they learned English. There've been incidents of the Mexican maid stealing the child and taking it over to Mexico and selling it.[45]

In border towns, the Mexican group was further stratified by English-speaking ability, place of nativity, and immigrant status, with non-English-speaking women residing south of the border occupying the lowest rung. In Laredo and El Paso, Mexican American factory operatives often employed Mexican women who crossed the border daily or weekly to do domestic work for a fraction of a U.S. operative's wages.[46]

The Race and Gender Construction of Domestic Service

Despite their preference for European immigrant domestics, employers could not easily retain their services. Most European immigrant women left service upon marriage, and their daughters moved into the expanding manufacturing, clerical, and sales occupations during the 1910s and 1920s.[47] With the flow of immigration slowing to a trickle during World War I, there were few new recruits from Europe. In the 1920s domestic service became increasingly the specialty of minority-race women.[48] Women of color were advantageous employees in one respect: They could be compelled more easily to remain in service. There is considerable evidence that middle-class whites acted to ensure the domestic labor supply by tracking racial-ethnic women into domestic service and blocking their entry into other fields. Urban school systems in the Southwest tracked Chicana students into homemaking courses designed to prepare them for domestic service. The El Paso school board established a segregated school system in the 1880s that remained in place for the next thirty years; education for Mexican children emphasized manual and domestic skills that would prepare them to work at an early age. In 1909 the Women's Civic Improvement League, an Anglo organization, advocated domestic training for older Mexican girls. Their rationale is explained by Mario García:

> According to the league the housegirls for the entire city came from the Mexican settle-
> ment and if they could *be* taught housekeeping, cooking and sewing, every American
> family would benefit. The Mexican girls would likewise profit since their services would
> improve and hence be in greater demand.[49]

The education of Chicanas in the Denver school system was similarly directed toward preparing students for domestic service and handicrafts. Sarah Deutsch found that Anglo women there persisted in viewing Chicanas and other "inferior-race" women as dependent, slovenly, and ignorant. Thus, they argued, training Mexican girls for domestic service not only would solve "one phase of women's work we seem to be incapable of handling" but would simultaneously help raise the (Mexican) community by improving women's standard of living, elevating their morals, and facilitating Americanization.[50] One Anglo writer, in an article published in 1917 titled "Problems and Progress among Mexicans in Our Own Southwest," claimed, "When trained there is no better servant than the gentle, quiet Mexicana girl."[51]

In Hawaii, with its plantation economy, Japanese and Chinese women were coerced into service for their husbands' or fathers' employers. Prior to World War II:

> It has been a usual practice for a department head or a member of the managerial staff of
> the plantation to indicate to members of his work group that his household is in need of
> domestic help and to expect them to provide a wife or daughter to fill the need. Under the

conditions which have prevailed in the past, the worker has felt obligated to make a member of his own family available for such service, if required, since his own position and advancement depend upon keeping the goodwill of his boss. Not infrequently, girls have been prevented from pursuing a high school or college education because someone on the supervisory staff has needed a servant and it has seemed inadvisable for the family in disregard the claim.[52]

Economic coercion also could take bureaucratic forms, especially for women in desperate straits. During the Depression, local officials of the federal Works Project Administration (WPA) and the National Youth Administration (NYA), programs set up by the Roosevelt administration to help the unemployed find work, tried to direct Chicanas and Blacks to domestic service jobs exclusively.[53] In Colorado, local officials of the WPA and NYA advocated household training projects for Chicanas. George Bickel, assistant state director of the WPA for Colorado, wrote: "The average Spanish-American girl on the NYA program looks forward to little save a life devoted to motherhood often under the most miserable circumstances."[54] Given such an outlook, it made sense to provide training in domestic skills.

Young Chicanas disliked domestic service so much that slots in the programs went begging. Older women, especially single mothers struggling to support their families, could not afford to refuse what was offered. The cruel dilemma that such women faced was poignantly expressed in one woman's letter to President Roosevelt:

My name is Lula Gordon. I am a Negro woman. I am on the relief. I have three children. I have no husband and no job. I have worked hard ever since I was old enough. I am willing to do any kind of work because I have to support myself and my children. I was under the impression that the government or the W.P.A. would give the Physical [sic] fit relief clients work. I have been praying for that time to come. A lady, Elizabeth Ramsie, almost in my condition, told me she was going to try to get some work. I went with her. We went to the Court House here in San Antonio, we talked to a Mrs. Beckmon. Mrs. Beckmon told me to phone a Mrs. Coyle because she wanted some one to clean house and cook for ($5) five dollars a week. Mrs. Beckmon said if I did not take the job in the Private home I would be cut off from everything all together. I told her I was afraid to accept the job in the private home because I have registered for a government job and when it opens up I want to take it. She said that she was taking people off of the relief and I have to take the job in the private home or none. . . . I need work and I will do anything the government gives me to do. . . . Will you please give me some work.[55]

Japanese American women were similarly compelled to accept domestic service jobs when they left the internment camps in which they were imprisoned during World War II. To leave the camps they had to have a job and a residence, and many women were forced to take positions as live-in servants in various parts of the country. When women from the San Francisco Bay area returned there after the camps were closed, agencies setup to assist the returnees directed them to domestic service jobs. Because they had lost their homes and possessions and had no savings, returnees had to take whatever jobs were offered them. Some became live-in servants to secure housing, which was in short supply after the war. In many cases domestic employment became a lifelong career.[56]

In Hawaii the Japanese were not interned, but there nonetheless developed a "maid shortage" as war-related employment expanded. Accustomed to cheap and abundant household help, haole employers became increasingly agitated about being deprived of the services of their "mamasans." The suspicion that many able-bodied former maids were staying at home idle because their husbands or fathers had lucrative defense jobs was taken seriously enough to prompt an investigation by a university researcher.[57]

Housewives told their nisei maids it was the maids' patriotic duty to remain on the job. A student working as a live-in domestic during the war was dumbfounded by her mistress's response when she notified her she was leaving to take a room in the dormitory at the university. Her cultured and educated mistress, whom the student had heretofore admired, exclaimed with annoyance: " 'I think especially in war time, the University should close down the dormitory.' Although she didn't say it in words, I sensed the implication that she believed all the [Japanese] girls should be placed in different homes, making it easier for the haole woman."[58] The student noted with some bitterness that although her employer told her that working as a maid was the way for her to do "your bit for the war effort," she and other haole women did not, in turn, consider giving up the "conveniences and luxuries of prewar Hawaii" as their bit for the war.[59]

The dominant group ideology in all these cases was that women of color—African American women, Chicanas, and Japanese American women—were particularly suited for service. These racial justifications ranged from the argument that Black and Mexican women were incapable of governing their own lives and thus were dependent on whites—making white employment of them an act of benevolence—to the argument that Asian servants were naturally quiet, subordinate, and accustomed to a lower standard of living. Whatever the specific content of the racial characterizations, it defined the proper place of these groups as in service: They belonged there, just as it was the dominant group's place to be served.

David Katzman notes that "ethnic stereotyping was the stock in trade of all employers of servants, and it is difficult at times to figure out whether blacks and immigrants were held in contempt because they were servants or whether urban servants were denigrated because most of the servants were blacks and immigrants."[60] Even though racial stereotypes undoubtedly preceded their entry into domestic work, it is also the case that domestics were forced to enact the role of the inferior. Judith Rollins and Mary Romero describe a variety of rituals that affirmed the subordination and dependence of the domestic; for example, employers addressed household workers by their first names and required them to enter by the back door, eat in the kitchen, and wear uniforms. Domestics understood they were not to initiate conversation but were to remain standing or visibly engaged in work whenever the employer was in the room. They also had to accept with gratitude "gifts" of discarded clothing and leftover food.[61]

For their part, racial-ethnic women were acutely aware that they were trapped in domestic service by racism, and not by lack of skills or intelligence. In their study of Black life in prewar Chicago, St. Clair Drake and Horace Cayton found that education did not provide African Americans with an entree into white-collar work. They noted, "Colored girls are often bitter in their comments about a society which condemns them to the 'white folks' kitchen.' "[62] Thirty-five years later, Anna May Madison minced no words when she declared to anthropologist John Gwaltney:

Now, I don't do nothing for white women or men that they couldn't do for themselves. They don't do anything I couldn't learn to do every bit as well as they do it. But, you see, that goes right back to the life that you have to live. If that was the life I had been raised up in, I could be President or any other thing I got a chance to be.[63]

Chicana domestics interviewed by Mary Romero in Colorado seemed at one level to accept the dominant culture's evaluation of their capabilities. Several said their options were limited by lack of education and training. However, they also realized they were restricted just because they were Mexican. Sixty-eight-year-old Mrs. Portillo told Romero, "There was a lot of discrimination, and Spanish people got just regular housework or laundry work. There was so much discrimination that Spanish people couldn't get jobs outside of washing dishes—things like that."[64]

Similarly, many Japanese domestics reported that their choices were constrained because of language difficulties and lack of education, but they, too, recognized that color was decisive. Some nisei domestics had taken typing and business courses and some had college degrees, yet they had to settle for "schoolgirl" jobs after completing their schooling. Mrs. Morita, who grew up in San Francisco and graduated from high school in the 1930s, bluntly summarized her options: "In those days there was no two ways about it. If you were Japanese, you either worked in an art store ['oriental curios' shop] where they sell those little junks, or you worked as a domestic. . . . There was no Japanese girl working in an American firm."[65]

Hanna Nelson, another of Gwaltney's informants, took the analysis one step further, recognizing the coercion that kept African American women in domestic service. She saw this arrangement as one that allowed white women to exploit Black women economically and emotionally and exposed Black women to sexual assaults by white men, often with white women's complicity. She says:

> I am a woman sixty-one years old and I was born into this world with some talent. But I have done the work that my grandmother's mother did. It is not through any failing of mine that this is so. The whites took my mother's milk by force, and I have lived to hear a human creature of my sex try to force me by threat of hunger to give my milk to an able man. I have grown to womanhood in a world where the saner you are, the madder you are made to appear.[66]

Race and Gender Consciousness

Hanna Nelson displayed a consciousness of the politics of race and gender not found among white employers. Employers' and employees' fundamentally different positions within the division of reproductive labor gave them different interests and perspectives. Phyllis Palmer describes the problems the YWCA and other reform groups encountered when they attempted to establish voluntary standards and working hours for live-in domestics in the 1930s. White housewives invariably argued against any "rigid" limitation of hours; they insisted on provisions for emergencies that would override any hour limits. Housewives saw their own responsibilities as limitless, and apparently felt there was no justification for boundaries on domestics' responsibilities. They did not acknowledge the fundamental difference in their positions; they themselves gained status and privileges from their relationships with their husbands—relationships that depended on the performance of wifely duties. They expected domestics to devote long hours and hard work to help them succeed as wives, without, however, commensurate privileges and status. To challenge the inequitable gender division of labor was too difficult and threatening, so white housewives pushed the dilemma onto other women, holding them to the same high standards by which they themselves were imprisoned.[67]

Some domestic workers were highly conscious of their mistresses' subordination to their husbands, and condemned their unwillingness to challenge their husbands' authority. Mabel Johns, a sixty-four-year-old widow, told Gwaltney:

> I work for a woman who has a good husband; the devil is good to her, anyway. Now that woman could be a good person if she didn't think she could just do everything and have everything. In this world whatsoever you get you will pay for. Now she is a grown woman, but she won't know that simple thing. I don't think there's anything wrong with her mind, but she is greedy and she don't believe in admitting that she is greedy. Now you may say what you willormay [sic] about people being good to you, but there just ain' a living soul in this world that thinks more of you than you do of yourself. . . . She's a grown woman, but she have to keep accounts and her husband tells her whether or not he will let her do thus-and-so or buy this or that.[68]

Black domestics are also conscious that a white woman's status comes from her relationship to a white man, that she gains privileges from the relationship that blinds her to her own oppression, and that she therefore willingly participates in and gains advantages from the oppression of racial-ethnic women. Nancy White puts the matter powerfully when she says:

My mother used to say that the black woman is the white man's mule and the white woman is his dog. Now, she said that to say this: we do the heavy work and get beat whether we do it well or not. But the white woman is closer to the master and he pats them on the head and lets them sleep in the house, but he ain' gon' treat neither one like he was dealing with a person. Now, if I was to tell a white woman that, the first thing she would do is to call you a nigger and then she'd be real nice to her husband so he would come out here and beat you for telling his wife the truth.[69]

Rather than challenge the inequity in the relationship with their husbands, white women pushed the burden onto women with even less power. They could justify this only by denying the domestic worker's womanhood, by ignoring the employee's family ties and responsibilities. Susan Tucker found that southern white women talked about their servants with affection and expressed gratitude that they shared work with the servant that they would otherwise have to do alone. Yet the sense of commonality based on gender that the women expressed turned out to be one way. Domestic workers knew that employers did not want to know much about their home situations.[70] Mostly the employers did not want domestics' personal needs to interfere with serving them. One domestic wrote that her employer berated her when she asked for a few hours off to pay her bills and take care of pressing business.[71] Of relations between white mistresses and Black domestics in the period from 1870 to 1920, Katzman says that in extreme cases "even the shared roles of motherhood could be denied." A Black child nurse reported in 1912 that she worked fourteen to sixteen hours a day caring for her mistress's four children. Describing her existence as a "treadmill life," she reported that she was allowed to go home "only once in every two weeks, every other Sunday afternoon—even then I'm not permitted to stay all night. I see my own children only when they happen to see me on the streets when I am out with the children [of her mistress], or when my children come to the yard to see me, which isn't often, because my white folks don't like to see their servants' children hanging around their premises."[72]

While this case may be extreme, Tucker reports, on the basis of extensive interviews with southern African American domestics, that even among live-out workers in the 1960s,

[w]hite women were also not noted for asking about childcare arrangements. All whites, said one Black woman, "assume you have a mother, or an older daughter to keep your child, so it's all right to leave your kids." Stories of white employers not believing the children of domestics were sick, but hearing this as an excuse not to work, were also common. Stories, too, of white women who did not inquire of a domestic's family—even when that domestic went on extended trips with the family—were not uncommon. And work on Christmas morning and other holidays for black mothers was not considered by white employers as unfair. Indeed, work on these days was seen as particularly important to the job.[73]

The irony is, of course, that domestics saw their responsibilities as mothers as the central core of their identity. The Japanese American women I interviewed, the Chicana day workers Romero interviewed, and the African American domestics Bonnie Thornton Dill interviewed all emphasized the primacy of their role as mothers.[74] As a Japanese immigrant single parent expressed it, "My children come first. I'm working to upgrade my children." Another domestic,

Mrs. Hiraoka, confided she hated household work but would keep working until her daughter graduated from optometry school.[75] Romero's day workers arranged their work hours to fit around their children's school hours so that they could be there when needed. For domestics, then, working had meaning precisely because it enabled them to provide for their children.

Perhaps the most universal theme in domestic workers' statements is that they are working so their own daughters will not have to go into domestic service and confront the same dilemmas of leaving their babies to work. A Japanese American domestic noted, "I tell my daughters all the time, 'As long as you get a steady job, stay in school. I want you to get a good job, not like me.' That's what I always tell my daughters: Make sure you're not stuck."[76]

In a similar vein, Pearl Runner told Dill, "My main goal was I didn't want them to follow in my footsteps as far as working."[77] Domestic workers wanted to protect their daughters from both the hardships and the dangers that working in white homes posed. A Black domestic told Drake and Cayton of her hopes for her daughters: "I hope they may be able to escape a life as a domestic worker, for I know too well the things that make a girl desperate on these jobs."[78]

When they succeed in helping their children do better than they themselves did, domestics may consider that the hardships were worthwhile. Looking back, Mrs. Runner is able to say,

> I really feel that with all the struggling that I went through, I feel happy and proud that I was able to keep helping my children, that they listened and that they all went to high school. So when I look back, I really feel proud, even though at times the work was very hard and I came home very tired. But now, I feel proud about it. They all got their education.[79]

Domestics thus have to grapple with yet another contradiction. They must confront, acknowledge, and convey the undesirable nature of the work they do to their children, as an object lesson and an admonition, and at the same time maintain their children's respect and their own sense of personal worth and dignity.[80] When they successfully manage that contradiction, they refute their white employers' belief that "you are your work."[81]

The Racial Division of Public Reproductive Labor

As noted earlier, the increasing commodification of social reproduction since World War II has led to a dramatic growth in employment by women in such areas as food preparation and service, health care services, child care, and recreational services. The division of labor in public settings mirrors the division of labor in the household. Racial-ethnic women are employed to do the heavy, dirty, "back-room" chores of cooking and serving food in restaurants and cafeterias, cleaning rooms in hotels and office buildings, and caring for the elderly and ill in hospitals and nursing homes, including cleaning rooms, making beds, changing bedpans, and preparing food. In these same settings white women are disproportionately employed as lower-level professionals (for example, nurses and social workers), technicians, and administrative support workers to carry out the more skilled and supervisory tasks.

The U.S. Census category of "service occupations except private household and protective services" roughly approximates what I mean by "institutional service work." It includes food preparation and service, health care service, cleaning and building services, and personal services.[82] In the United States as a whole, Black and Spanish-origin women are overrepresented in this set of occupations: in 1980 they made up 13.7 percent of all workers in the field, nearly double their proportion (7 percent) in the workforce. White women (some of whom were of Spanish origin) were also overrepresented, but not to the same extent, making up 50.1 percent of all "service" workers, compared with their 36 percent share in the overall workforce. (Black and

Spanish-origin men made up 9.6 percent, and white men, who were 50 percent of the workforce, made up the remaining 27.5 percent.)[83]

Because white women constitute the majority, institutional service work may not at first glance appear to be racialized. However, if we look more closely at the composition of specific jobs within the larger category, we find clear patterns of racial specialization. White women are preferred in positions requiring physical and social contact with the public, that is, waiters/waitresses, transportation attendants, hairdressers/cosmetologists, and dental assistants, while racial-ethnic women are preferred in dirty, back-room jobs as maids, janitors/cleaners, kitchen workers, and nurse's aides.[84]

As in the case of domestic service, who does what varies regionally, following racial-ethnic caste lines in local economies. Racialization is clearest in local economies where a subordinate racial-ethnic group is sizable enough to fill a substantial portion of jobs. In southern cities, Black women are twice as likely to be employed in service occupations as white women. For example, in Atlanta in 1980, 20.8 percent of African American women were so employed, compared with 10.4 percent of white women. While they were less than one-quarter (23.9 percent) of all women workers, they were nearly two-fifths (38.3 percent) of women service workers. In Memphis 25.9 percent of African American women, compared with 10.2 percent of white women, were in services; though they made up only a third (34.5 percent) of the female workforce, African American women were nearly three-fifths (57.2 percent) of women employed in this field. In southwestern cities Spanish-origin women specialized in service work. In San Antonio 21.9 percent of Spanish-origin women were so employed, compared with 11.6 percent of non-Spanish-origin white women; in that city half (49.8 percent) of all women service workers were Spanish-origin, while Anglos, who made up two-thirds (64.0 percent) of the female workforce, were a little over a third (36.4 percent) of those in the service category. In El Paso, 16.9 percent of Spanish-origin women were service workers, compared with 10.8 percent of Anglo women, and they made up two-thirds (66.1 percent) of those in service. Finally, in Honolulu, Asian and Pacific Islanders constituted 68.6 percent of the female workforce, but 74.8 percent of those were in service jobs. Overall, these jobs employed 21.6 percent of all Asian and Pacific Islander women, compared with 13.7 percent of white non-Spanish-origin women.[85]

Particularly striking is the case of cleaning and building services. This category—which includes maids, housemen, janitors, and cleaners—is prototypically "dirty work." In Memphis one out of every twelve Black women (8.2 percent) was in cleaning and building services, and Blacks were 88.1 percent of the women in this occupation. In contrast, only one out of every two hundred white women (0.5 percent) was so employed. In Atlanta, 6.6 percent of Black women were in this field—constituting 74.6 percent of the women in these jobs—compared with only 0.7 percent of white women. Similarly, in El Paso, 4.2 percent of Spanish-origin women (versus 0.6 percent of Anglo women) were in cleaning and building services—making up 90 percent of the women in this field. And in San Antonio the Spanish and Anglo percentages were 5.3 percent versus 1.1 percent, respectively, with Spanish-origin women 73.5 percent of women in these occupations. Finally, in Honolulu, 4.7 percent of Asian and Pacific Islander women were in these occupations, making up 86.6 percent of the total. Only 1.3 percent of white women were so employed.[86]

From Personal to Structural Hierarchy

Does a shift from domestic service to low-level service occupations represent progress for racial-ethnic women? At first glance it appears not to bring much improvement. After domestic service, these are the lowest-paid of all occupational groupings. In 1986 service workers were nearly two-thirds (62 percent) of the workers in the United States earning minimum wage or less.[87] As in domestic service, the jobs are often part-time and seasonal, offer few or no medical and other benefits, have low rates of unionization, and subject workers to arbitrary supervision. The service worker also often performs in a public setting the same sorts of tasks that servants did in a private setting. Furthermore, established patterns of race-gender domination-subordination are often incorporated into the authority structure of organizations. Traditional race-gender etiquette shapes face-to-face interaction in the workplace. Duke University Hospital in North Carolina from its founding in 1929 adopted paternalistic policies toward its Black employees. Black workers were highly conscious of this, as evidenced by their references to "the plantation system" at Duke.[88]

Still, service workers, especially those who have worked as domestics, are convinced that "public jobs" are preferable to domestic service. They appreciate not being personally subordinate to an individual employer and not having to do "their" dirty work on "their" property. Relations with supervisors and clients are hierarchical, but they are embedded in an impersonal structure governed by more explicit contractual obligations and limits. Also important is the presence of a work group for sociability and support. Workplace culture offers an alternative system of values to that imposed by managers.[89] Experienced workers socialize newcomers, teaching them how to respond to pressures to speed up work, to negotiate workloads, and to demand respect from superiors. While the isolated domestic finds it difficult to resist demeaning treatment, the peer group in public settings provides backing for individuals to stand up to the boss.

That subordination is usually not as direct and personal in public settings as in the private household does not mean, however, that race and gender hierarchy is diminished in importance. Rather, it changes form, becoming institutionalized within organizational structures. Hierarchy is elaborated through a detailed division of labor that separates conception from execution, and allows those at the top to control the work process. Ranking is based ostensibly on expertise, education, and formal credentials.

The elaboration is especially marked in technologically oriented organizations that employ large numbers of professionals, as is the case with health care institutions. Visual observation of any hospital reveals the hierarchical race and gender division of labor. At the top are the physicians, setting policy and initiating work for others; they are disproportionately white and male. Directly below, performing medical tasks and patient care as delegated by physicians and enforcing hospital rules, are the registered nurses (RNs), who are overwhelmingly female and disproportionately white. Under the registered nurses and often supervised by them are the licensed practical nurses (LPNs), also female but disproportionately women of color. At about the same level are the technologists and technicians who carry out various tests and procedures and the "administrative service" staff in the offices; these categories tend to be female and white. Finally, at the bottom of the pyramid are the nurses's aides, predominantly women of color; housekeepers and kitchen workers, overwhelmingly women of color; and orderlies and cleaners, primarily men of color. They constitute the "hands" that perform routine work directed by others.

The Racial Division of Labor in Nursing

A study of stratification in the nursing labor force illustrates the race and gender construction of public reproductive labor. At the top in terms of status, authority, and pay are the RNs, graduates of two-, three-, or four-year hospital- or college-based programs. Unlike the lower ranks, registered nursing offers a career ladder. Starting as a staff nurse, a hospital RN can rise to head nurse, nursing supervisor, and finally director of nursing. In 1980 whites were 86.7 percent of RNs, even though they were only 76.7 percent of the population. The LPNs, who make up the second grade of nursing, generally have had twelve months' training in a technical institute or community college. The LPNs are supervised by RNs and may oversee the work of aides. Racial-ethnic workers constituted 23.4 percent of LPNs, with Blacks, who were 11.7 percent of the population, making up fully 17.9 percent. Below the LPNs in the hierarchy are the nurse's aides (NAs), who typically have on-the-job training of four to six weeks. Orderlies, attendants, home health aides, and patient care assistants also fall into this category. These workers perform housekeeping and routine caregiving tasks "delegated by an RN and performed under the direction of an RN or LPN." Among nurse's aides, 34.6 percent were minorities, with Blacks making up 27.0 percent of all aides.[90]

Nationally, Latinas were underrepresented in health care services but were found in nurse's aide positions in proportion to their numbers—making up 5.2 percent of the total. The lower two grades of nursing labor thus appear to be Black specialties. However, in some localities other women of color are concentrated in these jobs. In San Antonio 48 percent of aides were Spanish-origin, while only 15.1 percent of the RNs were. Similarly, in El Paso, 61.5 percent of aides were Spanish-origin, compared with 22.8 percent of RNs. In Honolulu, Asian and Pacific Islanders, who were 68.6 percent of the female labor force, made up 72.3 percent of the NAs but only 45.7 percent of the RNs.[91]

Familial Symbolism and the Race and Gender Construction of Nursing

How did the present ranking system and sorting by racial-ethnic category in nursing come about? How did the activities of white nurses contribute to the structuring? And how did racial-ethnic women respond to constraints?

The stratification of nursing labor can be traced to the beginnings of organized nursing in the 1870s. However, until the 1930s grading was loose. A broad distinction was made between so-called trained nurses, who were graduates of hospital schools or collegiate programs, and untrained nurses, referred to—often interchangeably—as "practical nurses," "hospital helpers," "nursing assistants," "nursing aides," or simply as "aides."[92]

During this period health work in hospitals was divided between male physicians (patient diagnosis and curing) and female nursing staff (patient care) in a fashion analogous to the separate spheres prescribed for middle-class households. Nurses and physicians each had primary responsibility for and authority within their own spheres, but nurses were subject to the ultimate authority of physicians. The separation gave women power in a way that did not challenge male domination. Eva Gamarinikow likens the position of the British nursing matron to that of an upper-class woman in a Victorian household who supervised a large household staff but was subordinate to her husband.[93] Taking the analogy a step further, Ann Game and Rosemary Pringle describe the pre-World War II hospital as operating under a system of controls based on familial symbolism. Physicians were the authoritative father figures, while trained nurses were the mothers overseeing the care of patients, who were viewed as dependent children. Student nurses and practical nurses were, in this scheme, in the position of servants, expected to follow orders and subject to strict discipline.[94]

Like the middle-class white housewives who accepted the domestic ideology, white nursing leaders rarely challenged the familial symbolism supporting the gender division of labor in health care. The boldest advocated, at most, a dual-headed family.[95] They acceded to the racial implications of the family metaphor as well. If nurses were mothers in a family headed by white men, they had to be white. And, indeed, trained nursing was an almost exclusively white preserve. As Susan Reverby notes, "In 1910 and 1920, for example, less than 3% of the trained nurses in the United States were black, whereas black women made up 17.6% and 24.0% respectively of the female working population"[96]

The scarcity of Black women is hardly surprising. Nursing schools in the South excluded Blacks altogether, while northern schools maintained strict quotas. Typical was the policy of the New England Hospital for Women and Children which by charter could only admit "one Negro and one Jewish student" a year.[97] Black women who managed to become trained nurses did so through separate Black training schools and were usually restricted to serving Black patients, whether in "integrated" hospitals in the North or segregated Black hospitals in the South.[98]

White nursing leaders and administrators justified exclusion by appeals to racist ideology. Anne Bess Feeback, the superintendent of nurses for Henry Grady Hospital in Atlanta declared that Negro women under her supervision had no morals: "They are such liars. . . . They shift responsibility whenever they can. . . . They quarrel constantly among themselves and will cut up each other's clothes for spite. . . . Unless they are constantly watched they will steal anything in sight."[99] Perhaps the most consistent refrain was that Black women were deficient in the qualities needed to be good nurses: They lacked executive skills, intelligence strength of character, and the ability to withstand pressure. Thus Margaret Butler chief nurse in the Chicago City Health Department, contended that Black nurses' techniques were "inferior to that of the white nurses they are not punctual and are incapable of analyzing a social situation." Apparently Black nurses did not accept white notions of racial inferiority for Butler also complains about their tendency "to organize against authority" and "to engage in political intrigue."[100] Another White nursing educator, Margaret Bruesche, suggested that although Black women lacked the ability to become trained nurses, they "could fill a great need in the South as a trained attendant who would work for a lower wage than a fully trained woman."[101] Even those white nursing leaders sympathetic to Black aspirations agreed that Black nurses should not be put in supervisory positions, because white nurses would never submit to their authority.

Similar ideas about the proper place of "orientals" in nursing were held by haole nursing leaders in pre-World War II Hawaii. White-run hospitals and clinics recruited haoles from the mainland, especially for senior nurse positions, rather than hiring or promoting locally trained Asian American nurses. This pattern was well known enough for a University of Hawaii researcher to ask a haole health administrator whether it was true that "oriental nurses do not reach the higher positions of the profession." The administrator confirmed this: "Well, there again it is a matter of qualification. There is a limit to the number of nurses we can produce here. For that reason we have to hire from the mainland. Local girls cannot compete with the experience of mainland haole girls. In order to induce haole nurses here we could not possibly put them under an oriental nurse because that would make them race conscious right at the start. And as I said before, Japanese don't make good executives."[102] Because of the racial caste system in Hawaii, Japanese American women who managed to get into nursing were not seen as qualified or competent to do professional work. The chairman of the Territorial Nurses Association noted that

> before the war [started], our local nurses were looked down [upon] because they were mostly Japanese. . . . The Japanese nurses feel they can get along better with Mainland nurses than local haole nurses. That is true even outside of the profession. I remember hearing a Hawaiian-born haole dentist say, "I was never so shocked as when I saw a white man shine shoes when I first went to the Mainland." Haoles here feel only orientals and other non-haoles should do menial work.[103]

The systematic grading of nursing labor into three ranks was accomplished in the 1930s and 1940s, as physician-controlled hospital administrations moved to establish "sound business" practices to contain costs and consolidate physician control of health care.[104] Hightech medical and diagnostic procedures provided an impetus for ever-greater specialization. Hospitals adopted Taylorist principles of "scientific management," separating planning and technical tasks from execution and manual labor. They began to hire thousands of subsidiary workers, and created the licensed practical nurse (LPN), a position for a graduate of a one-year technical program, to perform routine housekeeping and patient care. With fewer discriminatory barriers and shorter training requirements, LPN positions were accessible to women of color who wanted to become nurses.

The lowest level of nursing workers, nurse's aides, was also defined in the 1930s, when the American Red Cross started offering ten-week courses to train aides for hospitals. This category expanded rapidly in the 1940s, doubling from 102,000 workers in 1940 to 212,000 in 1950.[105] This occupation seems to have been designed deliberately to make use of African American labor in the wake of labor shortages during and after World War II. A 1948 report on nursing told the story of how nurse's aides replaced the heretofore volunteer corps of ward attendants: "In response to this request for persons designated as nursing aides, the hospital discovered among the large Negro community a hitherto untapped reservoir of personnel, well above the ward attendant group in intelligence and personality."[106] One reason for their superiority can be deduced: They often were overqualified. Barred from entry into better occupations, capable, well-educated Black women turned to nurse's aide work as an alternative to domestic service.

In the meantime, RNs continued their struggle to achieve professional status by claiming exclusive rights over "skilled" nursing work. Some nurses, especially rank-and-file general duty nurses, called for an outright ban on employing untrained nurses. Many leaders of nursing organizations, however, favored accepting subsidiary workers to perform housekeeping and other routine chores so that graduate nurses would be free for more professional work. Hospital administrators assured RNs that aides would be paid less and assigned nonnursing functions and that only trained nurses would be allowed supervisory roles. One administrator claimed that aide trainees were told repeatedly that "they are not and will not be nurses."[107]

In the end, the leaders of organized nursing accepted the formal stratification of nursing, and turned their attention to circumscribing the education and duties of the lower grades to ensure their differentiation from "professional" nurses. Indeed, an RN arguing for the need to train and license practical nurses, and laying out a model curriculum for LPNs, warned: "Overtraining can be a serious danger. The practical nurse who has a course of over fifteen months (theory and practice) gets a false impression of her abilities and builds up the unwarranted belief that she can practice as a professional nurse."[108] Hospital administrators took advantage of race and class divisions and RNs' anxieties about their status to further their own agenda. Their strategy of co-opting part of the workforce (RNs) and restricting the mobility and wages of another part (LPNs and NAs) undermined solidarity among groups that might otherwise have united around common interests.

Nursing Aides: Consciousness of Race and Gender

The hierarchy in health care has come to be justified less in terms of family symbolism and more in terms of bureaucratic efficiency. Within the new bureaucratic structures, race and gender ordering is inherent in the job definitions. The nurse's aide job is defined as unskilled and menial; hence, the women who do it are too. Nurse's aides frequently confront a discrepancy, however, between how their jobs are defined (as unskilled and subordinate) and what they actually are allowed or expected to do (exercise skill and judgment). Lillian Roberts's experiences illustrate the disjunction. Assigned to the nursery, she was fortunate to work with a white southern RN who was willing to teach her:

> I would ask her about all kinds of deformities that we would see in the nursery, the color of a baby, and why this was happening and why the other was happening. And then I explored with her using my own analysis of things. Sometimes I'd be right just in observing and putting some common sense into it. Before long, when the interns would come in to examine the babies, I could tell them what was wrong with every baby. I'd have them lined up for them.[109]

The expertise Roberts developed through observation, questioning, and deduction was not recognized, however. Thirty years later Roberts still smarts from the injustice of not being allowed to sit in on the shift reports: "They never dignify you with that. Even though it would help you give better care. There were limitations on what I could do."[110]

She had to assume a deferential manner when dealing with white medical students and personnel, even those who had much less experience than she had. Sometimes she would be left in charge of the nursery and "I'd get a whole mess of new students in there who didn't know what to do. I would very diplomatically have to direct them, although they resented to hell that I was both black and a nurse's aide. But I had to do it in such a way that they didn't feel I was claiming to know more than they did."[111] One of her biggest frustrations was not being allowed to get on-the-job training to advance. Roberts describes the "box" she was in:

> I couldn't have afforded to go to nursing school. I needed the income, and you can't just quit a job and go to school. I was caught in a box, and the salary wasn't big enough to save to go to school. And getting into the nursing schools was a real racist problem as well. So there was a combination of many things. And I used to say, "Why does this country have to go elsewhere and get people when people like myself want to do something?"[112]

When she became a union organizer, her proudest accomplishment was to set up a program in New York that allowed aides to be trained on the job to become LPNs.

While Roberts's experience working in a hospital was typical in the 1940s and 1950s, today the typical aide is employed in a nursing home, in a convalescent home, or in home health care. In these settings, aides are the primary caregivers.[113] The demand for their services continues to grow as treatment increasingly shifts out of hospitals and into such settings. Thus, even though aides have lost ground to RNs in hospitals, which have reorganized nursing services to re-create RNs as generalists, aides are expected to remain among the fastest-growing occupations through the end of the century.[114]

Whatever the setting, aide work continues to be a specialty of racial-ethnic women. The work is seen as unskilled and subordinate, and thus appropriate to their qualifications and status. This point was brought home to Timothy Diamond during the training course he attended as the sole white male in a mostly Black female group of trainees: "We learned elementary biology and how we were never to do health care without first consulting someone in authority; and we learned not to ask questions but to do as we were told. As one of the students, a black woman from Jamaica used to joke, 'I can't figure out whether they're trying to teach us to be nurse's aides or black women.' "[115]

What exactly is the nature of the reproductive labor that these largely minority and supposedly unskilled aides and assistants perform? They do most of the day-to-day, face-to-face work of caring for the ill and disabled: helping patients dress or change gowns, taking vital signs (temperature, blood pressure, pulse), assisting patients to shower or giving bed baths, emptying bedpans or assisting patients to the toilet, changing sheets and keeping the area tidy, and feeding patients who cannot feed themselves. There is much "dirty" work, such as cleaning up incontinent patients. Yet there is another, unacknowledged, mental and emotional dimension to the work: listening to the reminiscences of elderly patients to help them hold on to their memory, comforting frightened patients about to undergo surgery, and providing the only human contact some patients get. This caring work is largely invisible, and the skills required to do it are not recognized as real skills.[116]

That these nurse's aides are performing reproductive labor on behalf of other women (and ultimately for the benefit of households, industry, and the state) becomes clear when one considers who would do it if paid workers did not. Indeed, we confront that situation frequently today, as hospitals reduce the length of patient stays to cut costs. Patients are released "quicker and sicker."[117] This policy makes sense only if it is assumed that patients have someone to provide interim care, administer medication, prepare meals, and clean for them until they can care for themselves. If such a person exists, most likely it is a woman—a daughter, wife, mother, or sister. She may have to take time off from her job or quit. Her unpaid labor takes the place of the paid work of a nurse's aide or assistant and saves the hospital labor costs. Her labor is thereby appropriated to ensure profit."[118] Thus, the situation of women as unpaid reproductive workers at home is inextricably bound to that of women as paid reproductive workers.

Conclusions and Implications

This article began with the observation that the racial division of reproductive labor has been overlooked in the separate literatures on race and gender. The distinct exploitation of women of color and an important source of difference among women have thereby been ignored. How, though, does a historical analysis of the racial division of reproductive labor illuminate the lives of women of color and white women? What are its implications for concerted political action? In order to tackle these questions, we need to address a broader question, namely, how does the analysis advance our understanding of race and gender? Does it take us beyond the additive models I have criticized?

The Social Construction of Race and Gender

Tracing how race and gender have been fashioned in one area of women's work helps us understand them as socially constructed systems of relationships—including symbols, normative beliefs, and practices—organized around perceived differences. This understanding is an important counter to the universalizing tendencies in feminist thought. When feminists perceive reproductive labor only as gendered, they imply that domestic labor is identical for all women and that it therefore can be the basis of a common identity of womanhood. By not recognizing the different relationships women have had to such supposedly universal female experiences as motherhood and domesticity, they risk essentializing gender—treating it as static, fixed, eternal, and natural. They fail to take seriously a basic premise of feminist thought, that gender is a social construct.

If race and gender are socially constructed systems, then they must arise at specific moments in particular circumstances and change as these circumstances change. We can study their appearance, variation, and modification over time. I have suggested that one vantage point for looking at their development in the United States is in the changing division of labor in local economies. A key site for the emergence of concepts of gendered and racialized labor has been in regions characterized by dual labor systems.

As subordinate-race women within dual labor systems, African American, Mexican American, and Japanese American women were drawn into domestic service by a combination of economic need, restricted opportunities, and educational and employment tracking mechanisms. Once they were in service, their association with "degraded" labor affirmed their supposed natural inferiority. Although ideologies of "race" and "racial difference" justifying the dual labor system already were in place, specific ideas about racial-ethnic womanhood were invented and enacted in everyday interactions between mistresses and workers. Thus ideologies of race and gender were created and verified in daily life.[119]

Two fundamental elements in the construction of racial-ethnic womanhood were the notion of inherent traits that suited the women for service and the denial of the women's identities as wives and mothers in their own right. Employers accepted a cult of domesticity that purported to elevate the status of women as mothers and homemakers, yet they made demands on domestics that hampered them from carrying out these responsibilities in their own households. How could employers maintain such seemingly inconsistent orientations? Racial ideology was critical in resolving the contradiction: it explained why women of color were suited for degrading work. Racial characterizations effectively neutralized the racial-ethnic woman's womanhood, allowing the mistress to be "unaware" of the domestic's relationship to her own children and household. The exploitation of racial-ethnic women's physical, emotional, and mental work for the benefit of white households thus could be rendered invisible in consciousness if not in reality.

With the shift of reproductive labor from household to market, face-to-face hierarchy has been replaced by structural hierarchy. In institutional settings, stratification is built into organizational structures, including lines of authority, job descriptions, rules, and spatial and temporal segregation. Distance between higher and lower orders is ensured by structural segregation. Indeed, much routine service work is organized to be out of sight: It takes place behind institutional walls where outsiders rarely penetrate (for example, nursing homes, chronic care facilities), in back rooms (for example, restaurant kitchens), or at night or other times when occupants are gone (for example, in office buildings and hotels). Workers may appreciate this segregation in time and space because it allows them some autonomy and freedom from demeaning interactions. It also makes them and their work invisible, however. In this situation, more-privileged women do not have to acknowledge the workers or to confront the contradiction between shared womanhood and inequality by race and class. Racial ideology is not necessary to explain or justify exploitation, not for lack of racism, but because the justification for inequality does not have to be elaborated in specifically racial terms; instead it can be cast in terms of differences in training, skill, or education.[120]

Because they are socially constructed, race and gender systems are subject to contestation and struggle. Racial-ethnic women continually have challenged the devaluation of their womanhood. Domestics often did so covertly. They learned to dissemble, consciously "putting on an act" while inwardly rejecting their employers' premises and maintaining a separate identity rooted in their families and communities. As noted earlier, institutional service workers can resist demeaning treatment more openly because they have the support of peers. Minority-race women hospital workers have been in the forefront of labor militancy, staging walkouts and strikes and organizing workplaces. In both domestic service and institutional service work, women have transcended the limitations of their work by focusing on longer-term goals, such as their children's future.

Beyond Additive Models: Race and Gender as Interlocking Systems

As the foregoing examples show, race and gender constructs are inextricably intertwined. Each develops in the context of the other; they cannot be separated. This is important because when we see reproductive labor only as gendered, we extract gender from its context, which includes other interacting systems of power. If we begin with gender separated out, then we have to put race and class back in when we consider women of color and working-class women. We thus end up with an additive model in which white women have only gender and women of color have gender plus race.

The interlock is evident in the case studies of domestic workers and nurses's aides. In the traditional middle-class household, the availability of cheap female domestic labor buttressed white male privilege by perpetuating the concept of reproductive labor as women's work, sustaining the illusion of a protected private sphere for women, and displacing conflict away from husband and wife to struggles between housewife and domestic.

The racial division of labor also bolstered the gender division of labor indirectly, by offering white women a slightly more privileged position in exchange for accepting domesticity. Expanding on Judith Rollins's notion that white housewives gained an elevated self-identity by casting Black domestics as inferior contrast figures, Phyllis Palmer suggests the dependent position of the middle-class housewife made a contrasting figure necessary. A dualistic conception of women as "good" and "bad," long a part of Western cultural tradition, provided ready-made categories for casting white and racial-ethnic women as oppositional figures.[121] The racial division of reproductive labor served to channel and recast these dualistic conceptions into racialized gender constructs. By providing them an acceptable self-image, racial constructs gave white housewives a stake in a system that ultimately oppressed them.

The racial division of labor similarly protects white male privilege in institutional settings. White men, after all, still dominate in professional and higher-management positions, where they benefit from the paid and unpaid services of women. And as in domestic service, conflict between men and women is redirected into clashes among women. This displacement is evident in health care organizations. Because physicians and administrators control the work of other health workers, we would expect the main conflict to be between doctors and nurses over workload, allocation of tasks, wages, and working conditions. The racial division of nursing labor allows some of the tension to be redirected so that friction arises between registered nurses and aides over work assignments and supervision.

In both household and institutional settings, white professional and managerial men are the group most insulated from dirty work and contact with those who do it. White women are frequently the mediators who have to negotiate between white male superiors and racial-ethnic subordinates. Thus race and gender dynamics are played out in a three way relationship involving white men, white women, and women of color.

Beyond Difference: Race and Gender as Relational Constructs

Focusing on the racial division of reproductive labor also uncovers the relational nature of race and gender. By "relational" I mean that each is made up of categories (for example, male/female, Anglo/Latino) that are positioned, and therefore gain meaning, in relation to each other.[122] Power, status, and privilege are axes along which categories are positioned. Thus, to represent race and gender as relationally constructed is to assert that the experiences of white women and women of color are not just different but connected in systematic ways.

The interdependence is easier to see in the domestic work setting, because the two groups of women confront each other face-to-face. That the higher standard of living of one woman is made possible by, and also helps to perpetuate, the other's lower standard of living is clearly evident. In institutional service work the relationship between those who do the dirty work and those who benefit from it is mediated and buffered by institutional structures, so the dependence of one group on the other for its standard of living is not apparent. Nonetheless, interdependence exists, even if white women do not come into actual contact with women of color.[123]

The notion of relationality also recognizes that white and racial-ethnic women have different standpoints by virtue of their divergent positions. This is an important corrective to feminist theories of gendered thought that posit universal female modes of thinking growing out of common experiences such as domesticity and motherhood. When they portray reproductive labor only as gendered, they assume there is only one standpoint—that of white women. Hence, the activities and experiences of middle-class women become generic "female" experiences and activities, and those of other groups become variant, deviant, or specialized.

In line with recent works on African American, Asian American, and Latina feminist thought, we see that taking the standpoint of women of color gives us a different and more critical perspective on race and gender systems.[124] Domestic workers in particular—because they directly confront the contradictions in their lives and those of their mistresses—develop an acute consciousness of the interlocking nature of race and gender oppression.

Perhaps a less obvious point is that understanding race and gender as relational systems also illuminates the lives of white American women. White womanhood has been constructed not in isolation but in relation to that of women of color. Therefore, race is integral to white women's gender identities. In addition, seeing variation in racial division of labor across time in different regions gives us a more variegated picture of white middle-class womanhood. White women's lives have been lived in many circumstances; their "gender" has been constructed in relation to varying others, not just to Black women. Conceptualizing white womanhood as monolithically defined in opposition to men or to Black women ignores complexity and variation in the experiences of white women.

Implications for Feminist Politics

Understanding race and gender as relational, interlocking, socially constructed systems affects how we strategize for change. If race and gender are socially constructed rather than being "real" referents in the material world, then they can be deconstructed and challenged. Feminists have made considerable strides in deconstructing gender; we now need to focus on deconstructing gender and race simultaneously. An initial step in this process is to expose the structures that support the present division of labor and the constructions of race and gender around it.

Seeing race and gender as interlocking systems, however, alerts us to sources of inertia and resistance to change. The discussion of how the racial division of labor reinforced the gender division of labor makes clear that tackling gender hierarchy requires simultaneously addressing race hierarchy. As long as the gender division of labor remains intact, it will be in the short-term interest of white women to support or at least overlook the racial division of labor, because it ensures that the very worst labor is performed by someone else. Yet as long as white women support the racial division of labor, they will have less impetus to struggle to change the gender division of labor. This quandary is apparent in cities such as Los Angeles, which have witnessed a large influx of immigrant women fleeing violence and poverty in Latin America, Southeast Asia, and the Caribbean. These women form a large reserve army of low-wage labor for both domestic service and institutional service work. Anglo women who ordinarily would not be able to afford servants are employing illegal immigrants as maids at below minimum wage.[125] Not only does this practice diffuse pressure for a more equitable sharing of household work, but it also recreates race and gender ideologies that justify the subordination of women of color. Having a Latino or Black maid picking up after them teaches Anglo children that some people exist primarily to do work that Anglos do not want to do for themselves.

Acknowledging the relational nature of race and gender and therefore the interdependence between groups means that we recognize conflicting interests among women. Two examples illustrate the divergence. With the move into the labor force of all races and classes of women, it is tempting to think that we can find unity around the common problems of "working women." With that in mind, feminist policy makers have called for expanding services to assist employed mothers in such areas as child care and elderly care. We need to ask, Who is going to do the work? Who will benefit from increased services? The historical record suggests that it will be women of color, many of them new immigrants, who will do the work and that it will be middle-class women who will receive the services. Not so coincidentally, public officials seeking to reduce welfare costs are promulgating regulations requiring women on public assistance to work. The needs of employed middle-class women and women on welfare might thus be thought to coincide: The needs of the former for services might be met by employing the latter to provide the services. The divergence in interest becomes apparent, however, when we consider that employment in service jobs at current wage levels guarantees that their occupants will remain poor. However, raising their wages so that they can actually support themselves and their children at a decent level would mean many middle-class women could not afford these services.

A second example of an issue that at first blush appears to bridge race and ethnic lines is the continuing earnings disparity between men and women. Because occupational segregation, the concentration of women in low-paying, female-dominated occupations, stands as the major obstacle to wage equity, some feminist policy makers have embraced the concept of comparable worth.[126] This strategy calls for equalizing pay for "male" and "female" jobs requiring similar levels of skill and responsibility, even if differing in content. Comparable worth accepts the validity of a job hierarchy and differential pay based on "real" differences in skills and responsibility. Thus, for example, it attacks the differential between nurses and pharmacists but leaves intact the differential between nurses and nurses's aides. Yet the division between "skilled" and "unskilled" jobs is exactly where the racial division typically falls. To address the problems of women service workers of color would require a fundamental attack on the concept of a hierarchy of worth; it would call for flattening the wage differentials between the highest- and lowest-paid ranks. A claim would have to be made for the right of all workers to a living wage, regardless of skill or responsibility.

These examples suggest that forging a political agenda that addresses the universal needs of women is highly problematic, not just because women's priorities differ but because gains for some groups may require a corresponding loss of advantage and privilege for others. As the history of the racial division of reproductive labor reveals, conflict and contestation among women over definitions of womanhood, over work, and over the conditions of family life are part of our legacy as well as the current reality. This does not mean we give up the goal of concerted struggle. It means we give up trying falsely to harmonize women's interests. Appreciating the ways race- and gender-based divisions of labor create both hierarchy and interdependence may be a better way to reach an understanding of the interconnectedness of women's lives.

Notes

Work on this project was made possible by a Title F leave from the State University of New York at Binghamton and a visiting scholar appointment at the Murray Research Center at Radcliffe College. Discussions with Elsa Barkley Brown, Gary Glenn, Carole Turbin, and Barrie Thorne contributed immeasurably to the ideas developed here. My thanks to Joyce Chinen for directing me to archival materials in Hawaii. I am also grateful to members of the Women and Work Group and to Norma Alarcón, Gary Dymski, Antonia Glenn, Margaret Guilette, Terence Hopkins, Eileen McDonagh, JoAnne Preston, Mary Ryan, and four anonymous *Signs* reviewers for their suggestions.

1. Patricia Hill Collins, "Learning from the Outsider Within: The Sociological Significance of Black Feminist Thought," *Social Problems* 33, 6 (1986): 14–32; Deborah K. King, "Multiple Jeopardy, Multiple Consciousness: The Context of a Black Feminist Ideology," *Signs: Journal of Women in Culture and Society* 14, 1 (1988): 42–72; Elsa Barkley Brown, "Womanist Consciousness: Maggie Lena Walker and the Independent Order of Saint Luke," *Signs: Journal of Women in Culture and Society* 14, 3 (1989): 610–33.

2. For various formulations, see Margaret Benston, "The Political Economy of Women's Liberation," *Monthly Review* 21 (September 1969): 13–27; Wally Secombe, "The Housewife and Her Labour under Capitalism," *New Left Review* 83 (January–February 1974): 3–24; Michèle Barrett, *Women's Oppression Today: Problems in Marxist Feminist Thought* (London: Verso, 1980); Bonnie Fox, ed., *Hidden in the Household: Women's Domestic Labour under Capitalism* (Toronto: Women's Press, 1980); and Natalie J. Sokoloff, *Between Money and Love: The Dialectics of Women's Home and, Market Work* (New York: Praeger, 1980).

3. Recently, white feminists have begun to pay attention to scholarship by and about racial-ethnic women, and to recognize racial stratification in the labor market and other public arenas. My point here is that they still assume that women's relationship to domestic labor is universal; thus they have not been concerned with explicating differences across race, ethnic, and class groups in women's relationship to that labor.

4. Robert Blauner, *Racial Oppression in America* (Berkeley: University of California Press, 1972); Mario Barrera, *Race and Class in the Southwest: A Theory of Racial Inequality* (Notre Dame, Ind.: University of

Notre Dame Press, 1979). See also Mark Reisler, *By the Sweat of Their Brow: Mexican Immigrant Labor in the United States, 1900–1940* (Westport, Conn.: Greenwood, 1976), which, despite its title, is exclusively about male Mexican labor. I use the term *racial-ethnic* to refer collectively to groups that have been socially constructed and constituted as racially as well as culturally distinct from European Americans, and placed in separate legal statuses from "free whites" (cf. Michael Omi and Howard Winant, *Racial Formation in the United States* [New York: Routledge, 1986]). Historically, African Americans, Latinos, Asian Americans, and Native Americans were so constructed. Similarly, I have capitalized the word *Black* throughout this article to signify the racial-ethnic construction of that category.

5. Karl Marx and Friedrich Engels, *Selected Works*, vol. 1 (Moscow: Progress, 1969), 31.

6. Friedrich Engels, *The Origins of the Family, Private Property, and the State* (New York: International Publishers, 1972), 71.

7. Mary P. Ryan, *Cradle of the Middle Class: The Family in Oneida County, New York, 1790–1865* (New York: Cambridge University Press, 1981), 15.

8. Johanna Brenner and Barbara Laslett, "Social Reproduction and the Family," in Ulf Himmelstrand, ed., *Sociology, from Crisis to Science?* vol. 2, *The Social Reproduction of Organization and Culture* (London: Sage, 1986), 117.

9. Jeanne Boydston, *Home and Work: Housework, Wages, and the Ideology of Labor in the Early Republic* (New York: Oxford University Press, 1990), esp. 46–48.

10. Robert W. Smuts, *Women and Work in America* (New York: Schocken, 1959), 11–13; Alice Kessler-Harris, *Women Have Always Worked: A Historical Overview* (Old Westbury, N.Y.: Feminist Press, 1981). Capitalism, however, changed the nature of reproductive labor, which became more and more devoted to consumption activities, i.e., using wages to acquire necessities in the market and then processing these commodities to make them usable (see Batya Weinbaum and Amy Bridges, "The Other Side of the Paycheck," *Monthly Review* 28 [1976]: 88–103; and Meg Luxton, *More than a Labour of Love: Three Generations of Women's Work in the Home* [Toronto: Women's Press, 1980]).

11. Alice Kessler-Harris, *Out to Work: A History of Wage-Earning Women in the United States* (New York: Oxford University Press, 1982).

12. Harry Braverman, *Labor and Monopoly Capital: The Degradation of Labor in the Twentieth Century* (New York: Monthly Review Press, 1974), 276.

13. This is not to deny that family members, especially women, still provide the bulk of care of dependants, but to point out that there has been a marked increase in institutionalized care in the second half of the twentieth century.

14. Braverman, *Labor and Monopoly Capital*, 281. For a discussion of varying views on the relative importance of control versus agency in shaping state welfare policy, see Linda Gordon, "The New Feminist Scholarship on the Welfare State," in Linda Gordon, ed., *Women, the State, and Welfare* (Madison: University of Wisconsin Press, 1990). Frances Fox Piven and Richard A. Cloward note that programs have been created only when poor people have mobilized, and are intended to defuse pressure for more radical change (*Regulating the Poor: The Functions of Public Welfare* [New York: Pantheon, 1971], 66). In their *Poor People's Movements: Why They Succeed, How They Fail* (New York: Pantheon, 1979), Piven and Cloward document the role of working-class struggles to win concessions from the state. For a feminist social control perspective, see Mimi Abramovitz, *Regulating the Lives of Women: Social Welfare Policy from Colonial Times to the Present* (Boston: South End Press, 1988).

15. Abramovitz, *Regulating the Lives of Women*.

16. Brenner and Laslett, "Social Reproduction and the Family," 121; Barbara Laslett and Johanna Brenner, "Gender and Social Reproduction: Historical Perspectives," *Annual Review of Sociology* 15(1989): 384.

17. Evelyn Nakano Glenn, "Racial Ethnic Women's Labor: The Intersection of Race, Gender, and Class Oppression," *Review of Radical Political Economy* 17, 3 (1985): 86–108; Evelyn Nakano Glenn, *Issei, Nisei, Warbride: Three Generations of Japanese American Women in Domestic Service* (Philadelphia: Temple University Press, 1986), 86–108; Bonnie Thornton Dill, "Our Mothers' Grief: Racial Ethnic Women and the Maintenance of Families," *Journal of Family History* 12, 4 (1988): 415–31.

18. David Chaplin, "Domestic Service and Industrialization," *Comparative Studies in Sociology* 1 (1978): 97–127.

19. These developments are discussed in Carl Degler, *At Odds: Women and the Family in America from the Revolution to the Present* (New York: Oxford University Press, 1980); Susan Strasser, *Never Done: A History of American Housework* (New York: Pantheon, 1982); Ruth Schwartz Cowan, *More Work for Mother: The Ironies of Household Technology from the Open Hearth to the Microwave* (New York: Basic Books, 1983); and Faye Dudden, *Serving Women: Household Service in Nineteenth-Century America* (Middletown, Conn.: Wesleyan University Press, 1983), esp. 240–42. Quoted phrase is from Christopher Lasch, *Haven in a Heartless World: The Family Besieged* (New York: Basic Books, 1977).

20. Brenner and Laslett, "Social Reproduction and the Family." See also Karen Blair, *The Clubwoman as Feminist: True Womanhood Redefined, 1868–1914* (New York: Holmes & Meier, 1980); Barbara Epstein, *The Politics of Domesticity: Women, Evangelism, and Temperance in Nineteenth Century America* (Middletown, Conn.: Wesleyan University Press, 1981); Ryan, *Cradle of the Middle Class; and* Dudden, *Serving Women.*

21. See, e.g., Elaine Bell Kaplan, " 'I Don't Do No Windows': Competition between the Domestic Worker and the Housewife," in Valerie Miner and Helen E. Longino, eds., *Competition: A Feminist Taboo?* (New York: Feminist Press at the City University of New York, 1987).

22. Phyllis Palmer, "Housewife and Household Worker: Employer–Employee Relations in the Home, 1928–1941," in Carole Groneman and Mary Beth Norton, eds., *"To Toil the Livelong Day": America's Women at Work, 1790–1980* (Ithaca, N.Y.: Cornell University Press, 1987), 182–83.

23. Phyllis Palmer, in *Domesticity and Dirt: Housewives and Domestic Servants in the United States, 1920–1945* (Philadelphia: Temple University Press, 1990), 70, found evidence that mistresses and servants agreed on what were the least desirable tasks—washing clothes, washing dishes, and taking care of children on evenings and weekends—and that domestics were more likely to perform the least desirable tasks.

24. It may be worth mentioning the importance of unpaid cultural and charitable activities in perpetuating middle-class privilege and power. Middle-class reformers often aimed to mold the poor in ways that mirrored middle-class values, but without actually altering their subordinate position. See, e.g., George J. Sanchez, " 'Go after the Women': Americanization and the Mexican Immigrant Woman, 1915–1929," in Ellen Carol DuBois and Vicki L. Ruiz, eds., *Unequal Sisters: A Multicultural Reader in Women's History* (New York: Routledge, 2nd ed., 1990), for discussion of efforts of Anglo reformers to train Chicanas in domestic skills.

25. Palmer, *Domesticity and Dirt,* 127–51.

26. David M. Katzman, *Seven Days a Week: Women and Domestic Service in Industrializing America* (New York: Oxford University Press, 1978), 65–70.

27. Glenn, "Racial Ethnic Women's Labor."

28. U.S. Bureau of the Census, *Fifteenth Census of the United States: 1930, Population, vol. 5, General Report on Occupations* (Washington, D.C.: Government Printing Office, 1933), ch. 3, "Color and Nativity of Gainful Workers," tables 2, 4, 6. For discussion of the concentration of African American women in domestic service, see Glenn, "Racial Ethnic Women's Labor."

29. I use the terms *Chicano, Chicana,* and *Mexican American* to refer to both native born and immigrant Mexican people in the United States.

30. Mario T. Garcia, *Desert Immigrants: The Mexicans of El Paso, 1880–1920* (New Haven: Yale University Press, 1981), 76.

31. Sarah Deutsch, *No Separate Refuge: Culture, Class, and Gender on an Anglo–Hispanic Frontier in the American Southwest, 1880–1940* (New York: Oxford University Press, 1987), 147.

32. U.S. Bureau of the Census, *Fifteenth Census of the United States: 1930, Population, vol. 5, General Report on Occupations* (Washington, D.C.: Government Printing Office, 1933).

33. Katzman, *Seven Days a Week,* 55; Andrew Lind, "The Changing Position of Domestic Service in Hawaii," *Social Process in Hawaii* 15 (1951), table 1.

34. U.S. Bureau of the Census, *Fifteenth Census of the United States: 1930, Outlying Territories and Possessions* (Washington, D.C.: Government Printing Office, 1932), table 8; Glenn, *Issei, Nisei, Warbride,* 76–79.

35. U.S. Bureau of the Census, *Fifteenth Census of the United States: 1930, Population, vol. 5, General Report on Occupations.*

36. Mario T. García, "The Chicana in American History: The Mexican Women of El Paso, 1880–1920: A Case Study," *Pacific Historical Review* 49, 2 (1980): 327.

37. For personal accounts of Chicano children being inducted into domestic service, see Vicki L. Ruiz, "By the Day or the Week: Mexican Domestic Workers in El Paso," in Vicki L. Ruiz and Susan Tiano, eds., *Women on the U.S.–Mexico Border: Responses to Change* (Boston: Allen and Unwin, 1987); and interview of Josephine Turietta in Nan Elsasser, Kyle MacKenzie, and Yvonne Tixier y Vigil, *Las Mujeres: Conversations from a Hispanic Community* (Old Westbury, N.Y.: Feminist Press, 1980), 28–35.

38. Lind, "The Changing Position of Domestic Service in Hawaii," 73.

39. Ibid., 76.

40. Tucker, "The Black Domestic in the South," 98.

41. Elizabeth Clark Lewis, "This Work Had an End: African American Domestic Workers in Washington, D.C., 1910–1940," in Carole Groneman and Mary Beth Norton, eds., *"To Toil the Livelong Day": America's Women at Work, 1780–1980* (Ithaca, N.Y.: Cornell University Press, 1987), 200–1. See also

life–history accounts of Black domestics, such as Dorothy Bolden, "Forty-two Years a Maid: Starting at Nine in Atlanta," in Nancy Seifer, ed., *Nobody Speaks for Me! Self-Portraits of American Working Class Women* (New York: Simon and Schuster, 1976), and that of Anna Mae Dickson in Wendy Watriss, "It's Something Inside You," in Maxine Alexander, ed., *Speaking for Ourselves: Women of the South* (New York: Pantheon, 1984).

42. C. Arnold Anderson and Mary Jean Bowman, "The Vanishing Servant and the Contemporary Status System of the American South," *American Journal of Sociology* 59 (1953): 215–30.

43. Dolores Janiewski, "Flawed Victories: The Experiences of Black and White Women Workers in Durham during the 1930s," in Lois Scharf and Joan M. Jensen, eds., *Decades of Discontent: The Women's Movement, 1920–1940* (Westport, Conn.: Greenwood, 1983), 93.

44. Julia Kirk Blackwelder, "Women in the Work Force: Atlanta, New Orleans, and San Antonio, 1930 to 1940," *Journal of Urban History* 4, 3 (1978): 349. Blackwelder also found that domestics themselves were attuned to the racial-ethnic hierarchy among them. When advertising for jobs, women who did not identify themselves as Black overwhelmingly requested "housekeeping" or "governess" positions, whereas Blacks advertised for "cooking," "laundering," or just plain "domestic work."

45. Vicki L. Ruiz, "Oral History and La Mujer: The Rosa Guerrero Story," in Vicki L. Ruiz and Susan Tiano, *Women on the U.S.-Mexico Border*, 71.

46. Melissa Hield, "Women in the Texas ILGWU, 1933–50," in Alexander, *Speaking for Ourselve*, 64.

47. This is not to say that daughters of European immigrants experienced great social mobility and soon attained affluence. The nondomestic jobs they took were usually low-paying and the conditions of work often deplorable. Nonetheless, white, native-born, and immigrant women clearly preferred the relative freedom of industrial, office, or shop employment to the constraints of domestic service (see Katzman, *Seven Days a Week*, 71–72).

48. Phyllis Palmer, *Domesticity and Dirt*, 12.

49. Garcia, *Desert Immigrants*, 113.

50. Sarah Deutsch, "Women and Intercultural Relations: The Case of Hispanic New Mexico and Colorado," *Signs: Journal of Women in Culture and Society* 12, 4 (1987): 736.

51. Mary Romero, "Day Work in the Suburbs: The Work Experience of Chicana Private Housekeepers," in Anne Statham, Eleanor M. Miller, and Hans O. Mauksch, eds., *The Worth of Women's Work: A Qualitative Synthesis* (Albany: State University of New York Press, 1988), 16.

52. Lind, "The Changing Position of Domestic Service in Hawaii," 77.

53. Julia Kirk Blackwelder, *Women of the Depression: Caste and Culture in San Antonio, 1929–1939* (College Station: Texas A&M University Press, 1984), 120–22; Deutsch, *No Separate Refuge*, 182–83.

54. Deutsch, *No Separate Refuge*, 183.

55. Blackwelder, *Women of the Depression*, 68–69

56. Glenn, *Issei, Nisei, Warbride*.

57. Document Ma 24, Romanzo Adams Social Research Laboratory papers, University of Hawaii Archives, Manoa. I used these records when they were lodged in the sociology department; they are currently being cataloged by the university archives and a finding aid is in process.

58. Document Ma 15, Romanzo Adams Social Research Laboratory papers, 5.

59. Ibid.

60. Katzman, *Seven Days a Week*, 221.

61. Judith Rollins, *Between Women: Domestics and Their Employers* (Philadelphia: Temple University Press, 1985), ch. 5; Mary Romero, "Chicanas Modernize Domestic Service" (manuscript, 1987).

62. St. Clair Drake and Horace Cayton, *Black Metropolis: A Study of Negro Life in a Northern City*, vol. 1 (New York: Harper Torchbooks, 1962 [1945], 246.

63. John Gwaltney, ed., *Drylongso: A Self-Portrait of Black America* (New York: Random House, 1980), 173.

64. Mary Romero, "Renegotiating Race, Class, and Gender Hierarchies in the Everyday Interactions between Chicana Private Household Workers and Employers" (paper presented at the 1988 meeting of the Society for the Study of Social Problems, Atlanta), 86.

65. Glenn, *Issei, Nisei, Warbride*, 122.

66. Gwaltney, *Drylongso*, 7.

67. Kaplan, "I Don't Do No Windows'"; Palmer, *Domesticity and Dirt*.

68. Gwaltney, *Drylongso*, 167.

69. Ibid., 148.

70. Kaplan, " 'I Don't Do No Windows,' " 96; Susan Tucker, "The Black Domestic in the South: Her Legacy as Mother and Mother Surrogate," in Carolyn Matheny Dillman, ed., *Southern Women* (New York: Hemisphere, 1988).

71. Palmer, *Domesticity and Dirt*, 74.

72. "More Slavery at the South: A Negro Nurse," from the *Independent* (1912), in David M. Katzman and

William M. Tuttle Jr., eds., Plain Folk: *The Life Stories of Undistinguished Americans* (Urbana: University of Illinois Press, 1982), 176–85, 179.

73. Tucker, "The Black Domestic in the South," 99.

74. Dill, "Our Mothers' Grief"; Glenn, *Issei, Nisei, Warbride*; Romero, "Renegotiating Race, Class, and Gender Hierarchies."

75. From an interview conducted by the author in the San Francisco Bay area in 1977.

76. Ibid.

77. Bonnie Thornton Dill, "The Means to Put My Children Through: Childrearing Goals and Strategies among Black Female Domestic Servants," in La Frances Rodgers-Rose, ed., *The Black Woman* (Beverly Hills: Sage, 1980), 109.

78. Drake and Cayton, Black Metropolis, 246.

79. Dill, "The Means to Put My Children Through," 113.

80. Ibid., 110.

81. Gwalteny, *Drylongso* 174.

82. The U.S. Labor Department and the U.S. Bureau of the Census divide service occupations into three major categories: "private household," "protective service," and "service occupations except private household and protective services." In this discussion, "service work" refers only to the latter. I omit private household workers, who have been discussed previously, and protective service workers, who include firefighters and police, as these jobs, in addition to being male-dominated and relatively well-paid carry some degree of authority, including the right to use force.

83. Computed from U.S Bureau of the Census, *Census of the Population, 1980*, vol. 1, *Characteristics of the Population* (Washington D.C.: Government Printing Office, 1984) chap. D, "Detailed Population Characteristics," pt. 1 "United States Summary," table 278: "Detailed Occupation of Employed Persons by Sex Race and Spanish Origin 1980."

84. Ibid.

85. Figures computed from table 279 in each of the state chapters of the following: U.S. Bureau of the Census, *Census of the Population, 1980*, vol. 1, *Characteristics of the Population*, chap. D, "Detailed Population Characteristics," pt. 6: "California"; pt. 12: "Georgia"; pt. 13: "Hawaii"; pt. 15: "Illinois"; pt. 44: "Tennessee"; and pt. 45: "Texas." The figures for Anglos in the Southwest are estimates, based on the assumption that most "Spanish-origin" people are Mexican, and that Mexicans, when given a racial designation are counted as whites. Specifically the excess left after the "total" is subtracted from the "sum" of white, Black, American Indian/Eskimo/Aleut, Asian and Pacific Islander, and Spanish-origin" is subtracted from the white figure. The remainder is counted as "Anglo." Because of the way "Spanish-origin" crosscuts race (Spanish-origin individuals can be counted as white Black or any other race), I did not attempt to compute figures for Latinos or Anglos in cities where Spanish-origin individuals are likely to be more distributed in some unknown proportion between Black and white. This would be the case, e.g., with the large Puerto Rican population in New York City. Thus I have not attempted to compute Latino versus Anglo data for New York and Chicago. Note also that the meaning of *white* differs by locale, and that the local terms *Anglo* and *haole* are not synonymous with *white*. The "white" category in Hawaii includes Portuguese who because of their history as plantation labor are distinguished from haoles in the local ethnic ranking systems. The U.S. Census category system does not capture the local construction of race and ethnicity.

86. Computed from tables specified in ibid.

87. The federal minimum wage was $3.35 in 1986. Over a quarter (26.0 percent) of all workers in these service occupations worked at or below this wage level. See Earl F. Mellor, "Workers at the Minimum Wage or Less: Who They Are and the jobs They Hold," *Monthly Labor Review,* July 1987, esp. 37.

88. Karen Brodkin Sacks, *Caring by the Hour: Women, Work, and Organizing at Duke Medical Center* (Urbana: University of Illinois Press, 1988), 46. Paternalism is not limited to southern hospitals; similar policies were in place at Montefiore Hospital in New York City. See Leon Fink and Brian Greenberg, "Organizing Montefiore: Labor Militancy Meets a Progressive Health Care Empire," in Susan Reverby and David Rosner, eds., *Health Care in America: Essays in Social History* (Philadelphia: Temple University Press, 1979).

89. Susan Porter Benson, *Counter Cultures: Saleswomen, Customers, and Managers in American Department Stores, 1890–1940* (Urbana: University of Illinois Press, 1986). See also the many examples of workplace cultures supporting resistance cited in Karen Brodkin Sacks and Dorothy Remy, eds., *My Troubles Are Going to Have Trouble with Me: Everyday Trials and Triumphs of Women Workers* (New Brunswick, NJ.: Rutgers University Press, 1984); and Louise Lamphere, *From Working Daughters to Working Mothers: Immigrant Women in a New England Industrial Community* (Ithaca, N.Y.: Cornell University Press, 1987).

90. American Nurses' Association, *Health Occupations Supportive to Nursing* (New York: American Nurses' Association, 1965), 6. Reflecting differences in status and authority, RNs earn 20–40 percent more than LPNs and 60–150 percent more than NAs (U.S. Department of Labor, *Industry Wage Survey: Hospitals, August 1985*, Bureau of Labor Statistics Bulletin 2273 [Washington D.C.: Government Printing Office, 1987]; and U.S. Department of Labor, *Industry Wage Survey: Nursing and Personal Care Facilities, September 1985*, Bureau of Labor Statistics Bulletin 2275 [Washington, D.C.: Government Printing Office, 1987]).

91. For the national level, see U.S. Bureau of the Census, *Census of the Population, 1980*, vol. 1, *Characteristics of the Population*, ch. D, "Detailed Population Characteristics," pt. 1: "United States Summary," table 278. For statistics on RNs and aides in San Antonio, El Paso, and Honolulu, see U.S. Bureau of the Census, *Census of the Population, 1980*, vol. 1, *Characteristics of the Population*, ch. D, "Detailed Population Characteristics," pt. 13: "Hawaii"; and pt. 45: "Texas," table 279.

92. Kathleen Cannings and William Lazonik, "The Development of the Nursing Labor Force in the United States: A Basic Analysis," *International Journal of Health Sciences* 5, 2 (1975): 185–216; Susan M. Reverby, Ordered to Care: *The Dilemma of American Nursing, 1850–1945* (New York: Cambridge University Press, 1987).

93. Eva Gamarinikow, "Sexual Division of Labour: The Case of Nursing," in Annette Kuhn and Ann-Marie Wolpe, eds., *Feminism and Materialism: Women and Modes of Production* (London: Routledge and Kegan Paul, 1978).

94. Ann Game and Rosemary Pringle, *Gender at Work* (Sydney: Allen and Unwin, 1983), 99–100.

95. Reverby, *Ordered to Care*, 71–75.

96. Ibid.

97. Darlene Clark Hine, *Black Women in White: Racial Conflict and Cooperation in the Nursing Profession, 1890–1950* (Bloomington: Indiana University Press, 1989), 6.

98. For accounts of Black women in nursing, see Darlene Clark Hine, ed., *Black Women in the Nursing Profession: A Documentary History* (New York: Pathfinder, 1985); and Mary Elizabeth Carnegie, *The Path We Tread: Blacks in Nursing, 1854–1954* (Philadelphia: Lippincott, 1986). Hine (*Black Women in White*, ch. 7) makes it clear that Black nurses served Black patients not just because they were restricted but because they wanted to meet Black health care needs. Blacks were excluded from membership in two of the main national organizations for nurses, the National League of Nursing Education and the American Nurses' Association. And although they formed their own organizations, such as the National Association of Colored Graduate Nurses, and enjoyed the respect of the Black community, Black nurses remained subordinated within the white-dominated nursing profession.

99. Hine, *Black Women in the Nursing Profession*, 101.

100. Hine, *Black Women in White*, 99.

101. Ibid., 101.

102. Document Nu21–I, p. 2, Romanzo Adams Research Laboratory papers A1989–006, box 17, folder 1.

103. Document Nu10–I, p. 3, Romanzo Adams Research Laboratory papers, A1989–006, box 17, folder 4.

104. This was one outcome of the protracted and eventually successful struggle waged by physicians to gain control over all health care. For an account of how physicians established hospitals as the main site for medical treatment, and gained authority over "subsidiary" health occupations, see Paul Starr, *The Social Transformation of American Medicine* (New York: Basic Books, 1982). For accounts of nurses' struggle for autonomy and their incorporations into hospitals, see Reverby, *Ordered to Care*, and also David Wagner, "The Proletarianization of Nursing in the United States, 1932–1945," *International Journal of Health Services* 10, 2 (1980): 271–89.

105. Cannings and Lazonik, "The Development of the Nursing Labor Force in the United States," 201.

106. Ibid.

107. Reverby, *Ordered to Care*, 194.

108. Dorothy Deming, *The Practical Nurse* (New York: Commonwealth Fund, 1947), 26.

109. Susan M. Reverby, "From Aide to Organizer: The Oral History of Lillian Roberts," in Carol Ruth Berkin and Mary Beth Norton, eds., *Women of America: A History* (Boston: Houghton Mifflin, 1979), 297–98.

110. Ibid., 298–99.

111. Ibid., 298.

112. Ibid., 299.

113. For example, it has been estimated that 80 percent of all patient care in nursing homes is provided by nurse's aides (see Barbara Coleman, "States Grapple with New Law," *AARP News Bulletin* 30, 2 [1989]: 5). In 1988, 1,559,000 persons were employed as RNs, 423,000 as LPNs, 1,404,000 as nurses's aides, orderlies, and attendants, and 407,000 as health aides (U.S. Department of Labor, *Employment*

and Earnings, January 1989 [Washington D.C.: Government Printing Office, 1989], table 22). Nurses's aides and home health care aides are expected to be the fastest-growing occupations through the 1990s, according to George T. Silvestri and John M. Lukasiewicz, "A Look at Occupational Employment Trends to the Year 2000," *Monthly Labor Review*, September 1987, 59.

114. Edward S. Sekcenski, "The Health Services Industry: A Decade of Expansion," *Monthly Labor Review*, May 1981, 10–16. For a description of trends and projections to the year 2000, see Silvestri and Lukasiewicz, "A Look at Occupational Employment Trends to the Year 2000."

115. Timothy Diamond, "Social Policy and Everyday Life in Nursing Homes: A Critical Ethnography," in Anne Statham, Eleanor M. Miller, and Hans O. Mauksch, eds., *The Worth of Women's Work: A Qualitative Synthesis* (Albany: State University of New York Press, 1988), 40.

116. Feminists have pointed to the undervaluing of female-typed skills, especially those involved in "caring" work (see Hilary Rose, "Women's Work: Women's Knowledge," in Juliet Mitchell and Ann Oakley, eds., *What Is Feminism?* [Oxford: Basil Blackwell, 1986]).

117. Sacks, *Caring by the Hour*, 165.

118. Nona Glazer, "Overlooked, Overworked: Women's Unpaid and Paid Work in the Health Services' 'Cost Crisis.' " *International Journal of Health Services* 18, 2 (1988): 119–37.

119. Barbara Fields, "Ideology and Race in American History," in J. Morgan Kousser and James M. McPherson, eds., *Region, Race, and Reconstruction: Essays in Honor of C. Vann Woodward* (New York: Oxford University Press, 1982).

120. That is, the concentration of minority workers in lower-level jobs can be attributed to their lack of "human capital"—qualifications—needed for certain jobs.

121. Lenore Davidoff, "Class and Gender in Victorian England: The Diaries of Arthur J. Munby and Hannah Cullwick," *Feminist Studies* 5 (spring 1979): 86–114; Palmer, *Domesticity and Dirt*, 11, 137–39.

122. Michèle Barrett, "The Concept of 'Difference,' " *Feminist Review* 26 (July 1987): 29–41.

123. Elsa Barkley Brown pointed this out to me in a personal communication.

124. Alma Garcia, "The Development of Chicana Feminist Discourse, 1970–1980," *Gender and Society* 3, 2 (1989): 217–38; Gloria Anzaldúa *Making Face, Making Soul—Haciendo Caras: Creative Critical Perspectives by Women of Color* (San Francisco: Aunt Lute Foundation, 1990); Patricia Hill Collins, *Black Feminist Thought: Knowledge, Consciousness, and the Politics of Empowerment* (New York: Allen and Unwin, 1990).

125. Mary Jo McConoway, "The Intimate Experiment," *Los Angeles Times Magazine*, 19 February 1987, 18–23, 37–38.

126. Heidi I. Hartmann, ed., *Comparable Worth: New Directions for Research* (Washington, D.C.: National Academy Press, 1985); Joan Acker, *Doing Comparable Worth: Gender, Class, and Pay Equity* (Philadelphia: Temple University Press, 1989).

27

Open Secrets

Memory, Imagination, and the Refashioning of Southern Identity

Jacquelyn Dowd Hall

Some stories simply come and take you, occupy you, make you work out again and again what it is they mean, and the meaning of your own obsession with them.

—Carolyn Steedman, *Past Tense*

The purpose of all interpretation is to conquer a remoteness, a distance between the past cultural epoch and the interpreter himself. By overcoming this distance . . . the exegete can appropriate its meaning to himself; foreign, he makes it familiar, that is, he makes it his own. It is thus the growth of his own understanding of himself that he pursues through his understanding of others.

—Paul Ricoeur, *The Conflict of Interpretations*

Me and you, we got more yesterdays than anybody. We need some kind of tomorrow.

—Toni Morrison, *Beloved*

For most of the twentieth century black Americans abandoned the southern countryside in a steady, ever-widening stream. In the 1970s this exodus suddenly turned back upon itself. By 1990 the South had regained a half million black citizens from the cities of the North and West. Many came home not to the booming cities of the Sunbelt, but to the stripped and devastated counties of the rural South.

In *Call to Home*, an uplifting, heartbreaking book about this startling reversal, the anthropologist Carol Stack offers a meditation on the power of place and the gallantry of people who—under the most crushing circumstances—are struggling to remake the South in their own images. Pushed from the Rust Belt that used to be the Promised Land, pulled by the dread and longing with which the South has always filled its daughters and sons, these women and men find themselves on a "redemptive mission"—a mission that confronts them both with the ghosts of a palpable past and with their own emerging sense of who they are and want to be. Earl Hydrick, one of the storytellers in Stack's book, put it this way: When you go home, "you go back to your proving ground, the place where you had that first cry, gave that first punch you had to throw in order to survive." Eula Grant, a day care crusader in eastern North Carolina, says, "You definitely can go home again. You can go back. But you don't start from where you left. To fit in, you have to create another place in that place you left behind."[1]

Call to Home takes seriously the imaginative, performative, and political aspects of a process that social scientists usually see as a one-dimensional response to economic push and pull. The stories told by these return migrants contribute to a powerful literary tradition, a tradition of writing about the South as a longed-for—yet vexed and dangerous—home. Such stories are actions. They send people moving across the country, confounding our expectations about migration and modernity. They influence not just individual lives but the unfolding of entire communities.

This essay is about an earlier turn to home. It is a story within a story: first, the story of Katharine Du Pre Lumpkin (see Figure 27.1), a white southerner who, as a sociologist, historian, and autobiographer, allied herself with the cause of racial justice and spent a lifetime trying to reconfigure the South as a place she could call home; second, the story of my entanglement with Katharine and her sisters. At both levels, what interests me is the power of "open secrets" as strategies of cultural amnesia—but also of reticence and love.

Born in Georgia in 1897, Katharine was the youngest of seven children in a dispossessed planter family, a family haunted by defeat, obsessed with race, and determined to win back the pride and power lost in the Civil War. Her father, William, fought with the Confederacy and then rode with the Ku Klux Klan. Reduced to working for the railroad, he moved his family to South Carolina, where he spent his life romanticizing slavery and promulgating the cult of the Lost Cause.[2]

Figure 27.1. Katharine Du Pre Lumpkin. *Courtesy of the Southern Historical Collection, University of North Carolina.*

Katharine's childhood was bathed in her father's memories; bittersweet, self-serving, and beguiling, they surrounded human bondage with a noxious golden glow. But memories are stories of experience, not experience itself, and his were shot through with the disquiet caused by Reconstruction, populism, and turn-of-the-century white supremacy campaigns. It took tremendous effort for men such as William Lumpkin to reconcile an early-twentieth-century present of intense racial and class alienation with a "dream replica" of a paternalistic past.[3] Katharine sensed that effort, those rifts and contradictions—and through them she would eventually slip into critical consciousness. She would have her own stories to tell.

It was, moreover, Katharine's mother and her older sister Elizabeth, a popular speaker on the Lost Cause circuit, who effectively carried forward the battle for public memory. William, in the end, became a pathetic figure, a relic of another age. His sons, embarrassed by their father's failure, chased after money. It fell to elite white women gathered in massive voluntary organizations, the most powerful of which was the United Daughters of the Confederacy, to assert their cultural authority over virtually every public representation of the southern past.[4] In their hands, the performance of southern identity secured the identification of southernness with whiteness. But it also carved out for white women a new public space.

Katharine and her sister Grace jettisoned the ideology of white supremacy and expanded that public space. Graduating from college at the end of World War I, each found her way to New York, where Katharine studied sociology at Columbia University and Grace wrote proletarian novels in which she reworked Lumpkin family history to attack every shibboleth that her parents defended. While Grace stayed on in Greenwich Village, weaving new identities from a swirl of sex, art, and revolution, Katharine returned home to lead the Young Women's Christian Association's (YWCA) unprecedented effort to build an interracial student movement in the South.

Eventually Katharine left the South again, first to complete a doctorate at the University of Wisconsin and then to settle in Northampton, Massachusetts. She entered the job market in the late 1920s, just as professionalization, discrimination, and depression combined to push women to the margins of the academy and stamp sociology as a masculine domain. Unable to secure a teaching position, she helped to found alternative institutions: first a Council of Industrial Studies at Smith College whose focus on women, family, and community foreshadowed the new labor history that would emerge in the 1970s; then an independent Institute of Labor Studies that tracked World War II developments in labor relations. The left-wing ferment of the 1930s inspired her to return to intellectual home ground—to the issues of race and region that had animated her work for the YWCA. Writing from the fringes of a New England college community that, as Katharine put it, still imagined southerners "with horns and forked tails," she "came out" as a southerner, first in a book called *The South in Progress* and then, in 1946, in *The Making of a Southerner*, the autobiography that became her major work.[5]

The South has always elicited from its writers and intellectuals what Fred Hobson aptly terms a "rage to explain."[6] Whether they looked back in pride, anger, or sorrow, most white southerners who committed themselves to print shared a belief in the region's categorical *difference* from the rest of the country. Katharine, by contrast, grew up in a family in which a static, unified, iconic South was an article of faith, and she understood all too well that idea's invidious ideological uses. The burden of her work is the essential Americanness of a large, diverse, and conflicted region, a region enmeshed in modernity and shaped by change.

Katharine's project, her lifelong endeavor, was to convince southerners and northerners alike to tell a new story, a story in which the South ceased to figure either as the not-modern—a landscape of nostalgia, a touchstone of yearning and loss—or as the nation's collective unconscious, the repository of American nightmares that America could not face. Both were dream states, and against them she deployed what she called the "plain . . . truths" of revisionism, a new southern history that turned the old tales upside down.[7] She took her cues from a small group of dissenters—men such as W. E. B. Du Bois and C. Vann Woodward—who were on the cusp of overturning the work of U. B. Phillips and William Dunning, towering figures who had forged a North-South consensus around a story of paternalistic slaveholders and the criminal outrages of Reconstruction. But unlike the revisionists—indeed, unlike most historians of the South to the present day—she placed a woman at the center of southern history. Taking herself as her subject, she sought to problematize "whiteness," to denaturalize racism, and to show how race is grounded in the child. Above all, she sought to trace the messy process by which consciousness changes, with all its backward and forward movements, its ground gained and then lost, its beachheads rarely secured once and for all.

Race, writes Dominick LaCapra, is "a feeble mystification with formidable effects." Those effects arise, Tessie P. Liu argues, in part from the historical association between race and kinship, one of the fundamental organizing principles of human societies. Before contact with non-Western peoples, Europeans arranged themselves hierarchically along kinship lines. Power flowed from lineage. A child was marked indelibly by the privileges, entitlements, and stigmas of birth. As Europeans came to define themselves as "white" in contrast to subjugated others, skin color superseded bloodlines as the marker that drew diverse peoples together in a privileged community. Yet the older formulation lived on; assimilated and transformed, it gave emotional power to the metaphor of race as a substance passed on by fathers in legitimate line.[8] It was this potent association between race, home, family, and kindred, this deep structure of racial reasoning, that Katharine used autobiography both to represent and to undo.

When *The Making of a Southerner* appeared in paperback, Katharine chose for the cover a turn-of-the-century image of herself as a child (Fig. 27.2). The girl in the photograph seems incandescent, from her cloud of blond hair to her long lacy dress. Yet there is no remnant here of a treasured plantation past, not a jasmine or a magnolia in sight. A tree splits the scene; the border is patrolled by a dark spiky fence. Weeds brush the child's feet, her hand rests on the edge of a huge wooden barrel half filled with dead leaves. Swaddled in whiteness yet confined by fences and dwarfed by obelisks, she is a daughter not of the Old South but of the New, now living in rented houses and playing on sad, sparse lawns. She glances to her right with a doubtful, questioning expression. She is poised to step forward, out of the frame.[9]

Katharine's protagonist is this vulnerable, watchful girl, at the mercy of good people who create monstrous systems, drilled in a racism, as she put it, that "takes hold of us . . . through our loyalties, affections . . . [and] ideals." But she is also the writer who claims the authority to tell this tale. Taught to believe that the plantation South was the real South, haunted by the dogma "that but one way was Southern, and hence there could be but one kind of Southerner," Katharine could not, it seemed to her, turn against her "old heritage of racial beliefs" without turning against her own people. In the end, she writes, it was the discovery of a different heritage—that of the "white millions whose forbears had never owned slaves," and the "Negro millions whose people had been held in slavery"—"that drew me to my refashioning."[10]

As Katharine tells it, there were two moments in particular on which her refashioning turned. The first shocked her into color consciousness; the second confronted her with the injuries of class. Together they helped to create a structure of feeling in which new, emancipatory stories could take root and grow.

The first moment occurred when she was six years old. Playing in the yard one summer morning, she suddenly heard a terrible noise. "Sounds," she remembered, "to make my heart pound and my hair prickle at the roots. Calls and screams were interspersed with blow upon blow. Soon enough I knew someone was getting a fearful beating." Peeking in the kitchen window, Katharine saw the family's black cook

Figure 27.2. Katharine Du Pre Lumpkin. *Courtesy of the Southern Historical Collection, University of North Carolina.*

writhing under the blows of a descending stick wielded by the white master of the house. I could see her face distorted with fear and agony and his with stern rage. I could see her twisting and turning as she tried to free herself from his firm grasp.[11]

That "white master," whom Katharine leaves unnamed in her account of this incident, was, of course, her father. The beating was an open secret, omnipresent but never spoken of in the family. There were no repercussions from the outside world.

Eventually, this scene—a tiny woman, a furious man, the thud of a stick on flesh and bone— would reverberate backward, causing Katharine to revise her inherited views of slavery and of the heroism of the Klan. At the time, however, it had a more convoluted result. It made her anxious to distance herself from people to whom such things could be done. To a girl who was herself subject to the disciplinary power of adults, the spectacle of the whipped black woman was horrifying in part because of the dangerous possibilities it represented. Her father, a man for whom chivalry toward women was an article of faith, could do this: He could beat a woman because she was black.[12] "Thereafter," she recalled, "I began to be self-conscious about the . . . signs and symbols of my race position," signs and symbols that policed the line between black and white.[13]

Longing, as all children do, to feel at one with her surroundings, Katharine tried to forget the dissonant image of violence in the kitchen, at the center of family life. But never again could she enfold herself quite so securely in her family's assumptions about the benevolence of patriarchy and the righteous superiority of their race. Never again could her home of origin be so simply a safe, sheltering place. Her confidence had been fissured as if by an earthquake, leaving on one side innocence and trust and on the other mixed feelings, and, faintly at first, the hairline cracks of doubt.[14]

Those doubts were widened in a most unlikely place—on a farm in the poverty-stricken Sand Hills of South Carolina, to which Katharine's family moved in 1909, when she was eleven years old. This sojourn represented William's last desperate attempt to recapture the glories of the plantation past. But three months later he died of throat cancer, leaving his wife and children to make a living on two hundred acres of God-forsaken land.

In the Sand Hills Katharine found herself, for the first time, in close proximity to the black and white rural poor. Freed of her father's influence just as she reached adolescence, she saw things around her that she might not otherwise have seen. She watched the black washerwomen and field hands come and go as strangers—a far cry from the cheerful, devoted slaves that her father's nostalgic stories had conjured up. To be sure, she was used to black poverty, but in the Sand Hills her white playmates were also hobbled by destitution—a destitution that the logic of racial thinking could not excuse or explain.[15]

Katharine had learned the meaning of whiteness—as a metaphor for family, a mark of privilege, and a boundary between herself and others that must, at all cost, be maintained—when she saw her father beat the cook. Now, to that secret imprint of racial violence, she added a perception of grinding *class* inequity—a perception that would, as it grew, denaturalize black poverty. For if white skin was no defense against immiseration, then the poverty of black people could not be blamed on the *racial* inferiority of the poor.

All of these doubts about the rightness of her world, however, might have come to nothing had Katharine chanced to be a student in less dynamic times. In college in north Georgia during World War I, she found herself swept up in the interracial student movement led by the YWCA. In the 1920s, traveling through the Jim Crow South with her black coworkers, she glimpsed the indignities of segregation from their point of view. She also glimpsed a new kind of solidarity, the solidarity that results from political effort, not from an affinity that is supposed to reside naturally in the members of a privileged group. Guided toward a leftist literature in sociology and economics by the YWCA's industrial secretaries, she learned to think of the South not as an icon but as a social system and to apply to it a critique of racism and capitalism that would grow more radical as time wore on.

I first stumbled upon *The Making of a Southerner* in the early 1970s. I was drawn to its mix of empathy and irony, to its gentle tone and elliptical style. Plainness, I thought, has its advantages, especially in a literature of regional self-discovery so given to mournful apologia and Gothic excess. But I was puzzled by the book's obscurity and its silences. It ended abruptly in the 1920s. Who and where was its author, I wondered, by the mid-1940s, when she turned to auto-biography as social critique? And what were the lines of interinfluence among these fascinating sisters, each vying with the other to speak for her family and her region's past?

I met Grace before Katharine. I found her in a ramshackle farmhouse near King and Queen Courthouse, Virginia, a crossroads that could barely be called a town. It was early August, the paint was peeling, and the garden behind the house had gone to seed. A bright-eyed woman with wild yellow hair opened the ragged screen door when I knocked. She led me to what seemed less like a living room than a shrine, dominated by a portrait of Jacob Lumpkin, who had settled on crown lands in Virginia early in the eighteenth century. It was Jacob's grave that had drawn her to this place. I learned later that this was the house-with-a-garden of Grace's dreams, the old-fashioned cottage she had tried to conjure up when she lived with her lover (later her husband), Michael Intrator, in a brick walk-up in New York City on East Eleventh Street near Tompkins Square. But to me the house seemed decrepit and lonely drab browns and faded greens, bric-a-brac every-where, an atmosphere of mildew and must. On the coffee table lay an inscribed copy of *Witness*, the story of her idol Whittaker Chambers, his sojourn in and out of the Communist Party, and his famous accusations against Alger Hiss. With Chambers as her mentor, Grace had joined in the orgy of confession through which former radicals purged themselves of their Communist pasts.[16]

Our conversation was as disconcerting as it was mesmerizing. Grace described her younger self as an innocent abroad, led astray not so much by the engaging young Communists she met in Greenwich Village as by Katharine—who was, she said, "always the radical one." Over and over, Grace had cut herself off from the past—when she left home in the 1920s, when she left the Party in the 1940s, when she moved to the Virginia countryside in the 1950s. Each move deepened her isolation, each required new layers of secrecy and rationalization. By the time I met her, she was so snarled in a web of deception that she had "forgotten" the barest outline of her life.[17]

I could hear the echo of the left-wing passions of the 1920s and 1930s in the voice of this isolated woman who still took herself seriously as a writer and who was absolutely certain of her ideas, however much those ideas now contradicted, even canceled out, the values that had produced her best work. Yet she struck me as an orphaned spirit, sustained, paradoxically, by the thin gruel of a past she had so willfully discarded.

She had always been a storyteller. Once she began to write, she spun her fiction out of autobiographical elements and patched together a personal history from half-truths and suggestions. The details were malleable; what mattered to Grace was artistic control. When I met her she was eighty-three years old. She could no longer drive, she was virtually penniless, and she was in the throes of a reluctant move to a retirement home in South Carolina, where most of her nieces and nephews still lived. The time was long past when she might have been willing or able to peel away the encrusted layers of memory, fantasy, and reality that had settled over what she had to tell. Looking back, I see the impossibility, even treachery, of basing my vision of Grace Lumpkin's life on this encounter in her later years. Still, I am grateful to have met her, twisted as she was by querulousness and resentment, yet clinging valiantly to the rural idyll she had salvaged from the wreck of her marriage, her politics, and her writing career.

Two hours away in Charlottesville, Katharine lived with her companion, Elizabeth Bennett, in a tiny house that they had furnished meticulously. There were books and magazines and polished antiques—all the trappings of a well-educated retired couple eager to stay current in a stimulating college town. No sign of ancestor worship, no atmosphere of mildew and must.

The years that Grace could—or would—only fleetingly conjure up Katharine willingly and vividly recalled. But when I shifted from the 1920s to questions about her relationship to her family and about her own activities after she left the South, she resisted, politely but firmly, with a fixed and practiced resolve.[18] Her reticence went further: Not only were there large areas about which she would not speak, but before she died she purged those same subjects from her papers, destroying not only much of her private correspondence but Grace's diary as well.

In the process, Katharine erased from the narrative of her life her relationship with Dorothy Douglas, a radical economist with whom she had shared her life in Northampton for almost thirty years. Gone were the years when she was cut off from her family, who felt betrayed by her revelations and refused to acknowledge her book. Gone also was what Lillian Hellman called "Scoundrel Time"—the 1950s, when Grace, called before the House Committee on Un-American Activities, had named names, apparently going so far as to finger Dorothy Douglas, thus colluding in a storm of red-baiting that silenced Katharine and shattered the life that she and Dorothy had so carefully built.[19]

Generation, profession, sexuality, and politics—all contributed to Katharine's reserve. She grew up in an era when telling secrets to strangers was not the pastime it has become today. She was trained in an objectivist sociology that denied emotion a role in the public self.[20] She lived her adult life in committed partnerships with women, over a period in which such relationships were medicalized, morbidized, sexualized, and finally celebrated—none of which was commensurate with how she saw herself. She was, moreover, protective of fragile ties to her family in South Carolina, fetters and lifelines that, especially in old age, she had labored to mend. No wonder she had been so ambivalent about being "discovered" by me. Word about my project had gone out on the grapevine. She had talked to old friends on the left about my motives: Was I really interested in them as "southern women activists," an identity they were eager to claim, or did I want to dredge up the charges of Communism that had wrecked their later lives? As with Grace, though for different reasons, the anti-Communism and homophobia of the 1950s had dropped a curtain between then and now. I kept up with Katharine in the years that followed, but our relationship never escaped that legacy: a habit of secrecy, a shadow of fear.

I never lost interest in the Lumpkin sisters, especially in Katharine, who had spent her life in a quest to understand, explain, and change a place that she always saw as home. But I found myself caught in the eddies of what seemed to be irreconcilable desires. I wanted to write about her; I also wanted to befriend her. The very reserve that stymied one desire evoked the other. You could say that I loved her for the secrets she did not want to tell. In the end, I was not courageous—or bloody-minded—enough to write about her while she was alive. And even now, as I take up the dropped threads of that project, my memory of our conversations confronts me with what is so tantalizing and poignant about biography: the feelings of loyalty and responsibility it generates, the intimacy it simultaneously frustrates and invites, the tension it produces between respect for privacy and lust for knowledge, the way it can position even the most respectful author as an intruder, a thief in the houses of the living and the dead.[21]

These dilemmas, moreover, are not limited to biography. They lie at the heart of scholarly procedures. We inherit an idea of truth as a buried secret, always out of reach. Scientists, psychoanalysts, historians—all rely on metaphors of interrogation. Truth lies outside of us, in the other—Mother Nature, the unconscious, the relics of another place and time. We wrest it from them violently.[22]

We can, however, draw on more democratic traditions. We can, for instance, conceive of truth not as a secret to be extracted but as understanding forged in dialogue. Such a conception situates our scholarship "in the realm of symbolic exchange"—exchange between the present and the past, between the scholar and the women about whom and to whom she talks and writes.[23]

As Katharine wrote, she could hear the hurt, disapproving voices of people she loved humming in her ears. For her, those voices personified the resistance that keeps a writer from writing: the withering voice that contests one's authority to interpret the past.[24] As for me, I never sit down to work on this project without feeling the power of open secrets as sites of not knowing as well as knowing and trying to situate myself in the productive, imaginative space between the two.

Katharine ended her autobiography in the mid-1920s in part to avoid calling attention to her sexuality and her politics—each of which would have undercut the moral and political authority of the autobiographical persona she sought to create. Lesbianism and Communism were, for Katharine, "open secrets": prevailing, omnipresent, but unspoken dimensions of her life that for me, writing women's history in the 1990s, it is unthinkable to ignore. There is, however, a big difference between reburying family secrets and perpetuating a tabloid culture of exposé that depends on fixed identities, on a series of either/ors. We *know* that the nuances of sexual difference go well beyond the polarities of gay and straight, well beyond the "was she or wasn't she" in which we have learned to think. But that does not make it any easier to honor silence as a speech act as eloquent as any other or to understand sexuality as an axis of difference in which "difference" encompasses the infinite varieties of desire.[25]

In *Epistemology of the Closet*, Eve Kosofsky Sedgwick argues that since the late nineteenth century same-sex desire has been *the* "open secret" of Western culture. The will to classify and regulate along the axes of homosexual/heterosexual has assumed primary importance—not just for a homosexual minority but for everyone—precisely because of the ways in which it has marked the categories of secrecy and disclosure, knowledge and ignorance. In Katharine's case, I cannot know in advance, perhaps can never know, how sexuality figured in her identity; nor can I ever know the full meaning to her of that other, related "open secret"—Dorothy's (and Katharine's, at least by association) involvement with the Communist Party. What I can do, however, is confront both questions directly. I can also admit the sound of doubt, the crack in the author's self-assurance that breaks the spell of biography—the spell that lies in its promise to reveal whole and hidden truths.[26] Finally, I can suggest that whatever we can or cannot know about these particular women, we do know that southern history, like all modern history, has been crosscut by valiant radicalisms and transgressive identities and desires.

Since *The Making of a Southerner* appeared in 1947, the American South has changed dramatically. Yet the *historiography* of the South remains a story of limits—a story of racism, of white male demagoguery, and of ugly electoral politics. This view of the South and of southern history has served a useful, perhaps invaluable purpose. It has allowed us to externalize and thus to expunge conditions that were American in scope without forfeiting our belief in America as a land of equality, innocence, and success.[27] That strategy, however, has grown tattered, irrelevant, and self-defeating. The last thirty years have exposed the national dimensions of racism, the roots of poverty in the nation's political economy, and the pervasiveness of what W. J. Cash termed the South's "savage ideal"—the mix of individualism, machismo, and violence that drew southern white men together, trumping any possibility of class action or cross-race solidarity.[28] We can no longer muster the political will to address our failings by projecting them onto a distinctive and "unAmerican" region. What we need is what Katharine tried, so long ago, to provide: a history of imagination, of possibility, of people—women and men, black and white—who never quit believing they could create a new place in the place they left behind.

The discipline of history is defined by prohibitions—against doubt, against dialogue, against excess, against utopianism, against self-revelation. As we go about the business of rewriting history, I hope that we will find ways to burst those boundaries, to give those disciplines the slip. To do that, as many have argued, we need new categories and more sensitive analytic tools. But we also need new forms of writing. Writing that exceeds the norms of scholarly representations, writing that speaks, writing that stands its ground, writing that throws and keeps on throwing that punch, writing that seeks not only to represent what was but to bring into being "what has never been."[29]

As for me, this project has become a journey back to the site of my first excursions into oral history, southern history, women's history. It has also allowed me to tack back and forth between memory and imagination, the fragile materiality of the past (the present that is always absent, no matter how anxiously we seek it out) and the exigencies of political resolve.[30] A bricolage? A proving ground? A redemptive mission? Certainly, a return. Not to a place I left behind but to a female antiracist tradition that is still in the making and to a way of writing that is beginning to feel like home.

Notes

This essay is drawn from a book-in-progress tentatively titled *Writing Memory: Katharine Du Pre Lumpkin and the Refashioning of Southern Identity*. An earlier version was delivered at a plenary Session on "Gendering Historiography" at the Berkshire Conference of Women Historians, Chapel Hill, N.C., 7 June 1996. I am deeply indebted to a circle of ideal readers and friends: Glenda Gilmore, Nancy Hewitt, Robert Korstad, and the members of my writing group, Joy Kasson, Carol Mayor, and Della Pollock.

1. Carol Stack, *Call to Home: African Americans Reclaim the Rural South* (New York, 1996), xvi, 199.

2. *Charles Reagon Wilson, Baptized in Blood: The Religion of the Lost Cause, 1865–1920* (Athens, Ga., 1980), and Gaines M. Foster, *Ghosts of the Confederacy: Defeat, The Lost Cause, and the Emergence of the New South, 1865 to 1913* (New York, 1987).

3. Katherine Du Pre Lumpkin, *The Making of a Southerner* (New York, 1946), 130.

4. Fitzhugh Brundage, "White Women and the Creation of Southern Public Memory, 1865–1950" (unpublished paper in Brundage's possession) 7; and Anastatia Sims, *The Power of Femininity in the New South: Women's Organizations and Politics in North Carolina, 1880–1930* (Columbia, S.C.), 128–54. For African American counter-memories and histories, see David W. Blight, "For Something Beyond the Battlefield': Frederick Douglass and the Memory of the Civil War," *Journal of American History* 75 (March 1989): 1156–78, and Genevieve Fabre and Robert O'Meally, eds., *History and Memory in African-American Culture* (New York, 1994).

5. Katharine Du Pre Lumpkin, Lecture to a General Audience, 1947, p. 1, Katharine Du Pre Lumpkin Papers, Southern Historical Collection, University of North Carolina at Chapel Hill (hereinafter KDL Papers) (quote); Katharine Du Pre Lumpkin, *The South in Progress* (New York, 1940), and *The Making of a Southerner* (New York, 1946); all subsequent page references are to this edition.

6. Fred Hobson, *Tell about the South: The Southern Rage to Explain* (Boston Rouge, La., 1983), 4.

7. Lumpkin, *The Making of a Southerner*, 206.

8. Dominick LaCapra, ed., *The Bounds of Race: Perspectives on Hegemony and Resistance* (Ithaca, N.Y., 1991), 1; Tessie P. Liu, "Race," in Richard Wightman Fox and James T. Kloppenberg, eds., *Companion to American Thought* (Cambridge, 1995), 564–67. See also Barbara Fields, "Ideology and Race in America," in J. Morgan Kousser and James M. McPherson, eds., *Region, Race, and Reconstruction: Essays in Honor of C. Vann Woodward* (New York, 1982), 143–77.

9. Katharine Du Pre Lumpkin, *The Making of a Southerner, with an Afterword by the author* (Athens, Ga., 1981).

10. Katharine Du Pre Lumpkin, Lecture to Prof. Harlow's Class, spring 1947, p. 8. KDL Papers; Lumpkin, *The Making of a Southerner*, 235–36, 239.

11. Lumpkin, *The Making of a Southerner*, 131–32.

12. For the abuse of black women under slavery, and how its crippling effects were carried forward by blacks and whites alike, see Deborah E. McDowell, "In the First Place" Making Frederick Douglass and the Afro-American Narrative Tradition," in William L. Andrews, eds., *Critical Essays on Frederick Douglass* (Boston, 1991), 192–214; Nell Irvin Painter, "Soul Murder and Slavery: Toward a Fully Loaded Cost Accounting," in Linda K. Kerber, Alice Kessler-Harris, and Kathryn Kish Sklar, eds., *U.S. History as Women's History: New Feminist Essays* (Chapel Hill, NC., 1995), 125–46; and Jennifer Fleischner, *Mastering Slavery: Memory, Family, and Identity in Women's Slave Narratives* (New York, 1996).

13. Lumpkin, *The Making of a Southerner*, 133.

14. This metaphor is drawn from Susan Cheever, *Home before Dark: A Biographical Memoir of John Cheever by His Daughter* (Boston, 1984), 4.

15. Lumpkin, *The Making of a Southerner*, 151–73.

16. Whittaker Chambers, *Witness* (New York, 1952).

17. Grace Lumpkin interview by Jacquelyn Hall, King and Queen Courthouse, Virginia, 6 August 1974, in interviewer's possession.

18. Katharine Du Pre Lumpkin interview by Jacquelyn Hall, Charlottesville, Virginia, 4 August 1974, Southern Oral History Program Collection, Southern Historical Collection, University of North Carolina at Chapel Hill.

19. Lillian Hellman, *Scoundrel Time* (Boston, 1976).

20. Robert C. Bannister, *Sociology and Scientism: The American Quest for Objectivity, 1880–1940* (Chapel Hill, N.C., 1987), 10.

21. The metaphor of the biographer as burglar was suggested to me by Janet Malcolm, "The Silent Woman I," *The New Yorker*, 23–30 August 1993, 86.

22. Page duBois's *Torture and Truth* (New York, 1991) argues that the idea of truth embedded in our philosophical tradition is intimately bound up with the deliberate infliction of human suffering. The ancient Greeks and Romans routinely tortured slaves as a means of forcing them to speak truly, thus reinforcing the nation that truth was a buried secret and that the body of the "other" was the site from which truth could be produced.

23. Tania Modleski, *Feminism without Women: Culture and Criticism in a "Postfeminist" Age* (New York, 1991), 46.

24. Malcolm, "The Silent Woman I," 124.

25. Eve Kosofsky Sedgwick, *Epistemology of the Closet* (Berkeley, Calif., 1990), 22–29 and passim.

26. Malcolm, "The Silent Woman I," 87.

27. Lari J. Griffin, "Why Was the South a Problem to America?" in Larry J. Griffin and Don H. Doyle, eds., *The South as an American Problem* (Athens, Ga., 1995), 10–32.

28. W. J. Cash, *The Mind of the South* (New York, 1941), 137.

29. Della Pollock, "Performing Writing," in Peggy Phelan and Jill Lane, eds., *Ends of Performance* (New York, 1998); Hayden White, "The Politics of Historical Interpretation: Discipline and De-Sublimation," in *The Content of the Form: Narrative Discourse and Historical Representation* (Baltimore, 1987), 58–82; and Modleski, *Feminism without Women*, 46 (quote).

30. Shannon Jackson, "Performances at Hull-House: Museum, Micro-fiche, Historiography," in Della Pollock, ed., *Exceptional Spaces: Essays on Performance and History*, (Chapel Hill, N.C., 1997).

28

Was Mom Chung a "Sister Lesbian"?
Asian American Gender Experimentation and Interracial Homoeroticism

Judy Tzu-Chun Wu

Margaret Chung (1889–1959), reputedly the first American-born woman of Chinese descent to become a physician, achieved recognition during the 1930s and 1940s for her patriotic activities on behalf of China and the United States. As part of her efforts to support the Allied cause, she "adopted" over one thousand "sons," most of whom were white American military men. Known as "Mom Chung," she entertained, corresponded with, and inspired her sons to fight against the Japanese invasion of China. Newspaper articles consistently noted two seemingly contradictory aspects of her character: First, Chung, then in her forties and fifties, was a successful doctor who never married or bore children. Second, she was a devoted mother to her adopted sons, who called themselves "Fair-Haired Bastards," because of their racial background and her status as an unmarried woman. Her respectability, premised on her professional success and asexuality, allowed her to be identified, in a humorous fashion, with such sexual improprieties as childbirth outside wedlock and miscegenation. Chung's unpublished autobiography and papers, which contain scant evidence of her romantic desires, behavior, or attitudes, help maintain this image of asexuality.

Chung cultivated this asexual persona to protect her public image. In a letter to singer and actress Sophie Tucker about Tucker's autobiography, Chung expressed the belief that certain experiences should not be discussed publicly: "What a good girl you are! You *did* take my advice after all, you *did* delete the paragraph about 'doubling' up with [Frank] Westphal, and I appreciate the love and the friendship that prompted you to take that advice! As the book now stands, it is a terrific inspiration which any youth may read and emulate your life–you see, Boss–I love you deeply–I care very much what people say about you! I can't bear it if people criticize you–and that one little paragraph which is *not* essential to the interest of the book draws the censure of the blue noses and the ignorant."[1] Although Chung is discussing Tucker's autobiography, the opinions expressed in the letter most likely reflected Chung's strategy toward her own autobiography, which she began writing during this period. Her concern about self-image is understandable, considering that both her professional and political success depended on public trust in her character. Being a single, professional woman in San Francisco's Chinatown, and one of the few widely recognized Chinese American spokespersons for the war, placed her under heavy scrutiny. To attract patients and serve as a role model, she needed to exemplify and follow high moral standards.

Recognizing Chung's desire for privacy reinforces the need to explore carefully her personal relationships and attitudes toward sexuality. Her significance as a historical figure stems not only from her accomplishments in the public realm of work and politics but also from her choices in the private realm. She chose not to marry or have children during a time when the social pressure for Chinese American women to do both was considerable. Due to immigration exclusion acts, the number of Chinese American men outnumbered women by an average of eight to one from the years 1910 to 1930.[2] During this same period, antimiscegenation laws in California forbade interracial marriages between people of color and white Americans. Instead of marrying, Chung developed erotic relationships with other women, especially white women, thereby transgressing heterosexual norms and racial boundaries. She also experimented with gender presentation throughout her life, adopting a masculine or androgynous persona during the early part of her professional career and then a glamorous, feminine identity beginning in the 1930s.

Chung's transgressiveness encouraged writer Elsa Gidlow, a self-identified lesbian, to regard her as a "sister lesbian."[3] However, describing Chung as a lesbian, a woman who constructed her identity based on a desire to seek romantic and sexual relationships with other women, is inadequate for two reasons. First, the designation ignores Chung's efforts to define her own identity. Second, the concept of lesbianism, which developed during the turn of the century, does not embody the historical variety of gender identifications and expressions of homoeroticism.[4] Analyzing the evolution of Chung's gender personas and interracial relationships from the late Victorian era to the modern era provides an opportunity to explore the ways in which Asian American women negotiated shifting gender, sexual, and racial norms of both mainstream American society and their own ethnic communities. Chung was a liminal figure who not only transcended social barriers but also lived through a historical period in which these boundaries were destabilized and reformulated. Because norms were in flux, she developed strategies that challenged restrictive roles for women of color yet also deflected social criticism of her behavior.

Chung's life provides an opportunity to complicate the existing understanding of Asian American sexuality.[5] Most studies in Asian American history have focused on racial, economic, and, more recently, gender oppression and resistance. Discussions of sexuality provide incidental examples in these studies of inequality and cultural conflict. For example, the gender imbalance among Chinese immigrants and the prevalence of prostitution in these "bachelor societies" have been viewed as indicators of the detrimental impact of immigration exclusion and antimiscegenation laws on family formation. Conversely, the entry of women and the creation of conjugal families, two indicators of the "settlement" phase of community development, have demonstrated the resilience of an oppressed minority in overcoming racial discrimination.[6] These discussions of sexuality in relation to structural inequalities are important for understanding how social values and institutions influence private attitudes and behavior. However, lack of critical analysis of the category of sexuality leads scholars to make assumptions concerning the nature of sexual behavior and attitudes among Asian Americans. The condemnation of bachelor societies, combined with the celebration of conjugal family formation, naturalizes intra-racial heterosexuality.

To illustrate the complexities of Chung's gender personas and interracial homoerotic desires, this article will focus on her relationships with two women, writer Elsa Gidlow and singer/actress Sophie Tucker. These two relationships, one in the late 1920s and early 1930s and the other in the 1940s and 1950s, reveal Chung's willingness to experiment with modern gender identities as well as her unwillingness to accept a modern lesbian sexual identity. Furthermore, her preference for white women as potential romantic partners demonstrates how evolving notions of race and ethnicity shaped definitions of desirability.

Masculine dress, "mannish" desires, and oriental eroticism

Elsa Gidlow's relationship with Margaret Chung, told from Gidlow's perspective, was one of unconsummated but not unrequited love. When they first met in the late 1920s, Chung was a recently established physician in her late thirties, and Gidlow was a struggling writer in her late twenties. Born in Santa Barbara, California, in 1889, Chung was raised and educated in agricultural areas and small towns in southern California, "where there were hardly any other Chinese people."[7] Influenced by her family's Presbyterian background, she chose to become a medical missionary among the Chinese. After graduating from the University of Southern California in 1916 and completing her internship and residency in Illinois, she established one of the first Western medical clinics in San Francisco's Chinatown in the early 1920s. During the early years of her medical career, Chung adopted a Western masculine persona, an identity that symbolized her efforts to transcend traditional racial and gender barriers. Her liminal cultural and gender identity attracted the interest of Gidlow, a British-Canadian who moved to San Francisco in 1926.[8] Because no cohesive, visible lesbian community existed at the time, she and her female lover, Tommy, relied on personal networks to identify and socialize with other lesbians. Gidlow interpreted Chung's gender persona as an indication of her sexuality. Furthermore, Gidlow's orientalist fascination with Chinese culture fueled her interest in the Chinese American doctor.[9] The relationship between the writer and physician reveals Chung's disobedience to gender and racial restrictions in the social and professional realms. At the same time, she distanced herself from the modern sexual identity of lesbianism; she also upheld more traditional notions of Chinese culture as mysterious and exotic. This mixture of transgressiveness and traditionalism in Chung's strategies reflects the opportunities as well as the constraints that women of color faced during the early twentieth century.

When they first met, Gidlow recalled that she was immediately attracted to Chung's androgyny and liminal cultural background: "By this time, Margaret Chung became Tommy's and my doctor and our friend. She was Chinese, but American-born and educated, western in her general medical practice and in surgery at which she excelled. . . . Her office was a couple of blocks down the steep Sacramento Street hill where we lived. As I walked home from work, I would see her sleek blue sports car. She was a striking woman in her late thirties, smartly dressed in a dark tailored suit with felt hat and flat-heeled shoes. . . . With my increasing interest in Chinese people, their philosophy and literature (and suspecting she might be a sister lesbian) I was immediately attracted."[10] Gidlow's fascination with Chung's intermediate status between Asian and Western cultures as well as between male and female genders resonates with feminist scholar Marjorie Garber's analysis of transgenderism: "The blurring of gender binaries evoked desire through its association with transcendence of other forms of racial, class, and cultural dualisms."[11]

At the time, Chung practiced partial cross-dressing.[12] While her female identity was publicly known, she adopted Western masculine clothing and a male persona. One of her professional mentors, physician Bertha Van Hoosen, recalled that Chung "never wore Chinese clothes, but on all occasions appeared in a thin black tailored suit, a white silk shirtwaist, and when on the street, a black sailor hat. This costume would have been very inconspicuous had she not always carried a short sport cane."[13] Chung's choice of dress could be understood partly as a uniform for the medical profession. Photographs from her medical school annuals make it difficult to determine her sex on the basis of her attire.[14] Her hair is either short or pulled back, and she wears a dark suit with a tie. While some women dressed in male clothing as a protective measure that allowed them to assimilate into the existing professional culture, Chung apparently enjoyed adopting a masculine persona.[15] Van Hoosen's comment about the ostentatious sport cane suggests that Chung did not mind attracting attention to her appearance. One of Chung's favorite photographs during her early professional career featured her with slicked-back hair, dark-rimmed glasses, and a dark suit. She sent autographed versions of the photo to friends and chose to identify herself as "Mike."

The choice of Western masculine attire and nickname symbolized Chung's desire to enter the professional and social world on an equal basis with white men. In her autobiography, she noted that members of the opposite sex rarely treated her with gallantry. As a young girl working on a farm pitting apricots, she noticed that attractive girls received favored treatment from boys: "I was a homely little child, and there were always some pretty teenage girls around whom the boys liked. The boys would give them the large ripe apricots which they could simply run a knife through and slip the pit out; whereas they would give me the small green ones. . . . Needless to say, I did not make very much money pitting apricots."[16] Instead of emphasizing her femininity to gain favors from men, Chung participated in traditionally masculine activities as an equal companion. While she was in medical school, she used various strategies to finance her education: "When I was too broke to pay the carfare to and from the County Hospital and the Medical School I would borrow a penny or two from some of the boys, shoot craps with them until I won about thirty-five or forty cents which would be enough to buy a half a pie, a sandwich, and assure me of carfare for the next day."[17] In addition to gambling, Chung was also fond of drinking and swearing. As many of her surrogate sons attested, "Mom, she's a great guy!"[18] By dressing like a man, Chung claimed opportunities traditionally denied to women.

Chung's efforts to transcend social and professional barriers, visually represented by her Western masculine dress, took on additional significance because of her racial status. Chinese American women during the early twentieth century were popularly viewed as either exploited prostitutes or secluded wives with bound feet.[19] The former's access to the public arena was associated with heterosexual deviance, while the latter's respectability was associated with crippled confinement to the private realm.[20] Chung's adoption of Western masculine clothing symbolized her efforts to claim social freedom and professional opportunities for Chinese American women.[21]

Chung's attempts to transcend gender and racial boundaries resonated with the goals of other second-generation Chinese Americans. For example, Bessie Jeong, a physician who began practicing in the 1930s, echoed Chung's desire to participate as an equal in a white, masculine world. Born in San Francisco Chinatown, across from the Chinese Hospital, Jeong ran away to the Presbyterian Mission Home, when she feared that her father might arrange a marriage for her. Instead of returning to China as her father intended, Jeong sought the assistance of the Mission Home to gain an education. She became the first Chinese American woman to graduate from Stanford University and eventually attended the Women's Medical College in Philadelphia. Jeong explained that her desire to study biology and medicine stemmed from an early childhood interest in "boys' games," which were much more challenging to her than "girls' games." Medicine, to her, was a "man's game," and she believed she had a "man's mind."[22] Similar to Chung, Jeong accepted existing gender divisions, which associated certain abilities and privileges with male identity, even as she sought to transcend those boundaries.

Jeong distinguished between women, like herself, who sought opportunities in traditionally male professions, and women, like Chung, who extended their challenge to include dress and behavior. While in medical school, Jeong observed that two sororities existed: "[In] one of them, the girls smoked and drank a little. They wore those gloves and wore suits and acted mannish. They'd sit down and put their legs this way. They were the mannish type. The men don't like them and the girls don't like them. The other group was more socially acceptable–real girls."[23] Jeong's comments suggest that while Chung was certainly not alone in her practice of cross-dressing, "mannish" women faced social censure for their choice in dress and mannerism.

During the late nineteenth and early twentieth centuries, medical and social attention increasingly focused on the topic of "gender inversion," linking cross-dressing with mental and sexual degeneracy.[24] While scholars have debated the social significance of these medical theories, Chung's adoption of partial cross-dressing was interpreted as an indication of her sexuality. Not only did Gidlow think of Chung as a "sister lesbian," but members of the Chinese American community also questioned her sexual orientation. When Jeong was asked whether she and Chung shared a sense of camaraderie, she exclaimed defensively: "Oh, no! Margaret and I were as different as [pause] She was a homo, a lesbian."[25] One Federal Bureau of Investigation agent also reported that within the Chinese American community "there were rumors that she was a Lesbian."[26] Such comments suggest that Chung's sexuality, signified by her masculine dress, was socially unacceptable.

Although prevailing social attitudes and medical literature equated Chung's gender identity with her sexual orientation, the connections between the two were more complicated.[27] Evidence suggests that she participated in physical, possibly sexual, relationships with women early in her professional career. When Chung served as an intern at the Mary Thompson Hospital in Chicago in 1916 and 1917, she was banned from sharing a bed with other women. Van Hoosen, her supervisor there, commented that Chung "was a favorite with nurses and interns to the degree that the hospital, for the first time, made a ruling that two people must not sleep in a single bed."[28] The regulation of sleeping arrangements and omission of this passage in the final version of Van Hoosen's autobiography suggest that Chung's interactions with women were viewed by others as socially suspect. The hospital's censure most likely encouraged Chung to be more circumspect in her relationships with women. While her emotions are difficult to gauge given the lack of sources from her perspective, Gidlow's accounts of their flirtatious friendship suggest that Chung reciprocated emotionally but had greater reserve about expressing her desires publicly or acting upon them.

Gidlow, who had a nonmonogamous relationship with Tommy, courted Chung. Gidlow invited the doctor to her apartment for dinner and regularly visited Chung in her office, sometimes bringing her flowers. Gidlow even wrote poetry about Chung and gave her a copy of "Teasedale's Anthology of Women's Love Lyrics."[29] According to Gidlow, Chung understood the nature of these advances. Gidlow recalled one particular house call that Chung made: "Observing Tommy's and my domestic scene, [she] smiled a knowing smile."[30] A turning point in their relationship occurred when Gidlow departed for Europe to attempt a writing career. Chung invited Gidlow to a speakeasy in North Beach, the Italian community bordering Chinatown, for a farewell luncheon. Drinking bootleg liquor helped Chung reveal more about herself.[31] The growing intimacy of their relationship was sealed two days later by an exchange of good-bye presents and a kiss. Gidlow wrote: "I believe she was really sorry to see me go and heaven knows she is one of the few I part from with a pang. She gave me a pint bottle of bourbon, Government sealed, 160 proof and—what I value many times more, a spontaneous kiss on the mouth. I had never dared to hope she would kiss me."[32]

Chung made no apparent attempts to contact Gidlow while the writer lived in Europe. However, when Gidlow returned to San Francisco the following year and became dangerously ill, Chung finally expressed her growing feelings. Gidlow composed poems about Chung while under her care at the Chinese Hospital. After reading one of the poems, Chung was moved to kiss Gidlow again.[33] In and out of consciousness following an operation, Gidlow recalled two conversations she had with Chung: "I took her hand and would not let it go. How long she stayed I do not know, nor whether it was there or while still on the operating table that I heard myself say: 'Do you love me?' Her answer seemed to come after a long time: 'yes—if it will make you feel better."[34] Hours later, Gidlow and Chung conversed again: "The door opened and M[argaret]. came in 'I have been thinking about you all afternoon,' I heard myself say. Then I begged her to stay with me for a little while and she said she would. . . . Was it then that M said: 'You gave me hell this morning for operating on you; and then you asked me if I loved you. There were people around too,' I felt a vague concern for her. Had I put her in an awkward position? 'Was I very indescrete?' [sic] I asked her? 'No, no,' she assured me. . . . For a while—I remember it as a long while—my mind was a blank, yet I was aware, with the curious comfort, of Ms presence and thought of her constantly. Suddenly I asked: '*Do* you love me?' This time she said 'Yes' immediately and quietly."[35] Chung apparently never acted on her declaration of love. After Gidlow's recovery, Chung avoided contact with her. Gidlow wrote, "M. denies herself to me almost completely."[36] A few months after the operation, Gidlow's journal reported Chung's engagement to a wealthy man: "M is going to get married. It is bald, but it is a man and it has half a million—another sacrifice to the twin gods, manners and respectability."[37] Although Chung did not marry her fiancé, she and Gidlow never resumed the intimacy of their former relationship.

The interactions between the two women revealed that Chung felt romantic attraction toward Gidlow but also ambivalence about lesbian sexuality. The meals, gifts, and kisses that they exchanged demonstrated the eroticism underlying their professional relationship as doctor and patient. Despite this attraction, Chung's reluctance to express her feelings initially, her refusal to act upon them, and then her engagement to a man, soon after her declaration of love to a woman, confirmed that she was retreating from her homoerotic desires.

Chung's decision to distance herself from a lesbian relationship reflected her efforts to negotiate not only sexual norms but also cultural and racial boundaries in mainstream society as well as her own ethnic community. Gidlow's orientalist fascination with Chinese culture fueled her attraction to Chung. Although Chung embraced Western science and culture, she also evoked the mysteriousness and exoticness of Asian culture for Gidlow. In her journal, Gidlow reflected, "One of her fascinations for me is perhaps the ambiguity of this blend in her of East and West."[38] She viewed Chung as someone wise, who could perhaps explain life's mysteries: "There is no one to whom I can talk. . . . I want someone neutral, and someone with a special sort of maturity and wisdom. M seems to me the one person. . . . More, far more than I want to possess M physically, I want to understand her; but she eludes me continually."[39] Gidlow's poems about Chung also demonstrate how Western perceptions of Chinese culture as exotic and mysterious could be transferred to people of Chinese descent. In "For a Gifted Lady, Often Masked," the author claimed to see past the professional persona of the physician: "Matter-of-fact manner,/ Brusque speech,/Expert hands—These are not *you*." Instead, Gidlow posited the doctor's real identity as evocative of lush, tropical lands. "Your soul is a cool tuberose/Drowsy with perfume,/ Languorous, dreaming. . . . Its fragrance wafts me/To far-off times and lands."[40] Chung's liminal status between Western and Chinese cultures allowed Gidlow access to the mysteries of a foreign civilization.

Gidlow's fascination with cultural difference and her perception of Chinese culture as exotic resonated with emerging liberal notions regarding race. As historian Henry Yu has pointed out in his study of interracial sexuality, cultural pluralists of the 1910s and 1920s argued "for an inclusive vision of America that maintained the stark differences of various immigrant communities" and propagated "theories of culture that stressed understanding different communities from the inside or 'native' perspective."[41] Cultural pluralist views both reinforced and challenged more conservative racial thinking, which emphasized the biological and cultural inferiority of "Mongolians." Both ideologies assumed fixed cultural differences. However, conservatives denigrated these differences as inherently inferior, while cultural pluralists "placed a value on the exotic."[42]

Chung understood the attention that her liminal cultural status granted her. In some ways, she resisted Gidlow's orientalist image of her. Chung described Gidlow as an "old soul," therefore having a greater affinity with the "Orient." In contrast, she positioned herself as a Westerner: "I am Chinese, yes, but I am a new soul."[43] On the one hand, Chung suggested that Gidlow's fascination with her and Asian culture originated less from her actual identity and more from the writer's interest in orientalist difference. On the other hand, Chung accepted the dichotomous perception of Eastern and Western culture and used this juxtaposition to gain opportunities for herself. The physician who never wore Chinese clothing decorated her medical office in Chinatown with "furnishings in Oriental artistry."[44] Her choice in furniture reflected a pride in her ancestral culture. At the same time, the use of "oriental" decorations suggested that she staged her office as a tourist site for her increasing white clientele. Other Asian American women used this strategy of using their "otherness" to gain economic opportunities. Historian Judy Yung notes that few second-generation Chinese American women during the early twentieth century found positions outside Chinatown. The few openings used these women as "exotic showpieces," requiring them to "wear oriental costumes" to add "atmosphere" for "teahouses, restaurants, stores, and nightclubs."[45]

Although Chung cultivated an orientalist image to attract interest from mainstream Americans, she was reluctant to pursue an explicitly lesbian relationship with a white woman. Her vigilance regarding her personal reputation dovetailed with her efforts to gain professional recognition in Chinatown. That the intimate conversations between Gidlow and Chung took place at the Chinese Hospital is significant. As a relative newcomer to the community, she had to guard her personal image carefully to protect her professional reputation, especially because her initial efforts to establish herself had met with mixed results. In her autobiography, Chung cited her limited Chinese language skills as the main reason for her sense of isolation. However, her status as a single, professional woman who adopted masculine dress also contributed to her marginalization. Questions concerning her sexual orientation created an additional social barrier. While homophobia existed within broader American society as well, Chung very likely felt more vulnerable about her status in the close-knit Chinatown community.

Chung's engagement and subsequent rejection of marriage also reflected her concerns regarding respectability and social status. Her intended marriage partner was probably white. Her sister-in-law, Lucile, remembered that Margaret was engaged to an "American" doctor.[46] Chung's Chinese American friends and family expected her to marry someone of her own class status, and few eligible candidates existed within the Chinatown community because of the scarcity of educated professionals. Although her fiancé's racial background could have contributed to Chung's marginalization in Chinatown, his class status would have assisted her efforts to gain social acceptance and recognition from both the Chinese American and white American communities.[47] According to Lucile, Chung sought her fiancé's assistance in financing her sisters' education and eventually declined to marry him because he refused to provide the economic support she requested. If this interpretation of Chung's decision not to marry was correct, marriage without a corresponding increase in social status held few attractions.

Chung's experimentation with racial groomings, gender identities, and homoeroticism during her early medical career reflected her efforts both to challenge restrictions placed upon Chinese American women and deflect criticisms directed toward marginalized individuals. Her adoption of a Western masculine persona symbolized her efforts to gain social and professional opportunities traditionally denied to women and Chinese Americans. At the same time, her incorporation of "orientalist" forms of identification reflected an interest in capitalizing on mainstream fascination with Asian culture. Just as Chung negotiated cultural expectations, she also navigated conflicting sexual norms. The decisions in her personal life reflected both romantic interest in other women and a desire for respectability. Her retreat from Gidlow suggests Chung's inability to reconcile a lesbian identity with her professional and social goals. Her simultaneous rejection of marriage, however, also indicates her desire to seek an alternative to heterosexuality.

Maternal homoeroticism and interethnic alliances

Chung's relationship with Sophie Tucker, which occurred more than a decade after her relationship with Gidlow, demonstrated another approach to negotiating her private desires and public image. During the intervening years, Chung had crafted a new gender persona. Instead of dressing and behaving as a man, she embraced a glamorous maternal identity. Her new public image assisted her efforts to affiliate with the white upper middle class. Following Japan's invasion of Manchuria in 1931 Chung began to socialize with and adopt white men in the military, entertainment industry, and political arena as an expression of her patriotism for China. Her new persona also provided her with a language to express her feelings for Tucker and allowed their relationship to be perceived as co-mothering the war effort. Their ages—both women were in their fifties—contributed to their maternal image. Instead of the more explicit lesbian relationship that Gidlow offered, Chung's relationship with Tucker could be characterized as a romantic friendship. Chung expressed sensual desire for Tucker, yet their relationship could have been perceived by others, and possibly Chung herself, as nonsexual. Although her interest in Tucker might have been viewed as part of her effort to assimilate into the white social elite, the strength of their relationship also stemmed from a mutual recognition and appreciation of ethnic differences.

Tucker first met Chung in 1913 on a vaudeville tour in the West.[48] Always a self-publicist, the singer kept lists of people she met in various cities and sent postcards to remind them of her return performances. Their relationship did not become more personal until World War II. Just as Chung adopted aviators into her organization of "Fair-Haired Bastards," she also adopted musicians and actors, whom she frequently called "Kiwis" for the bird that does not fly. By January 1943, Tucker had become Kiwi number 107.

Chung's increasing fascination with entertainers and celebrities during the 1930s and 1940s undoubtedly spurred her interest in Tucker and inspired her own adoption of a more glamorous, feminine image. Chung's sisters recalled that her "clothing changed from almost mannish suits to more frivolous attire under the influence of 'stars.' "[49] Her favorite photograph during this time period featured her in an evening gown and white ermine cape, with coiffed hair and makeup. Apparently, the image accurately represented Chung's attire, as Bessie Jeong recalled that "Margaret used to drape herself in ermine and jewelry."[50] Chung's growing identification with female roles was not just inspired by her adoption of a public maternal persona but also by commercialized images of women from movies and theater. Beginning in the 1930s, Hollywood increasingly focused on the lives of "strong, autonomous, competent, and career oriented" women.[51] Even the physical appearance of female movie stars changed. Instead of the waif-like look of Mary Pickford, the movie industry favored such larger women with "more flesh and physical strength" as Mae West.[52] It must have been gratifying for Chung to emulate the desirable image of these celebrities, considering her memories of herself as a "homely little child."

The transformation of Chung's gender identity paralleled the evolution of Tucker's stage persona. When Tucker began performing in vaudeville, she was billed as a "world-renowned coon shouter" and performed in blackface. A large woman, she was viewed as lacking the sex appeal to perform in whiteface. Similar to Chung, Tucker was treated by men as a friend, not a potential love interest. In her autobiography, she recalled, "I wasn't the type of girl the boys like to play around with on tour. But they liked me as a pal, a good egg."[53] Tucker struggled to gain the opportunity to perform in whiteface and eventually became known for her sexually charged stage persona. The experiences of Chung and Tucker suggest that the ability to assume or perform a feminine role represented a privilege that not all woman could attain. A woman's racial identity, economic resources, and physical characteristics shaped her ability to assume a feminized gender image.

Chung's adoption of a glamorous identity held racial, class, and gender implications. Her new persona both resonated with and departed from the experiences of other Chinese American women. As Yung has argued, the Great Depression ironically created new economic and social opportunities for the Chinatown community. The expanding entertainment industry during the 1930s encouraged Chinese American women to find work as performers in Hollywood and in newly established Chinatown nightclubs.[54] Individuals who associated with this glamorous industry, however, continued to be somewhat marginal to the Chinese American community. Chung's ability to purchase expensive clothing and patronize these clubs, often in the company of white Americans, separated her from both the working class and respectable merchant families of San Francisco's Chinatown. The possession of glamorous clothing, necessary for attending operas, elegant restaurants, and other forums of urban sociability, demonstrated her entry into mainstream middle-class realms of leisure.

Chung's new maternal identity both deflected criticisms regarding gender-appropriate attire and allowed her to maintain social freedoms previously associated with masculine dress.[55] Her new persona did not signal growing dependence on men, but rather symbolized her status as an independent woman. In contrast to marriage, in which a woman expressed love and commitment to one man, her voluntary maternal status allowed her to select as many sons as she desired to befriend. Instead of being a helpmate, she became the center of the network. In contrast to the pattern of attractive women receiving favors from men, Chung was often in the superior economic position, hosting parties and mailing care packages to her sons.

The asexual quality of Chung's feminine persona reinforced her autonomy. In contrast to the heterosexual image of celebrities, her age, physical presence, and maternal identity projected a predominantly nonsexual quality. Letters from her sons, many of whom were half her age, demonstrate that they did not view her as a potential romantic partner. She also took great care to protect her reputation. Although she entertained extensively in her home, only female or married friends were allowed to spend the night. The mixture of femininity without heterosexual allure perfectly suited Chung's lifestyle. She could enjoy the excitement of nightclubs and late-night card games with her sons with minimal damage to her reputation as a single woman.

Ironically, as Chung's gender image became more modern and commercialized, her erotic desires were expressed in traditional and circumspect language. She and Tucker became close companions when the singer returned to San Francisco for nightclub appearances in 1943. Chung regularly drove Tucker to her evening performances, attended shows in company with large groups of her sons, and then stayed up late into the night playing cards with Tucker.[56] During the performer's stay in San Francisco, the two spent so much time together that a local gossip columnist referred to them as "me and my shadow."[57] Their relationship continued in intensity, even after Tucker left San Francisco. Chung traveled to attend Tucker's performances. They also telephoned one another and corresponded regularly.

Chung's letters and actions revealed the depth of her feelings. While she expressed love for all her adopted children, her relationship with Tucker was laced with romantic undertones. When Tucker returned to San Francisco in January 1945, she became a regular houseguest of Chung. Mutual friends recalled that the doctor reserved for Tucker a special bedroom with a large, pink, satin bed.[58] During her stay, Chung wrote affectionate notes, using romantic and comical endearments to Tucker, known by her nickname "Boss":

Ah Boss—I surely do love you—and I'm so happy you are with me (13 January 1945);
Goodnight Sweet Heart (14 January 1945);
Peek-a-boo—I love you (14 January 1945);
Hi, Angel! Love You (14 January 1945);
Hi—Stinky—Love You! (14 January 1945);
Love & Kisses Nightie Night (17 January 1945);
You are the most wonderful Pal in the whole world—and I adore you (19 January 1945).[59]

The content and frequency of these notes suggest an infatuation on Chung's part that blurred the boundary between platonic and romantic friendship.

While Chung's correspondence tended to express emotional intimacy with Tucker, a desire for physical intimacy occasionally emerged. Unable to spend Christmas together in 1947, Chung sent Tucker a series of presents and commented on the meaning of the gifts: "The silver shell, I want you to keep with you always—on your desk to keep your little candle in—and to remind you of my shining love—Please wear the blue nightgown—Christmas night because it will be *close* to you—as I will be."[60] By describing her emotional closeness to Tucker as comparable to the physical sensation of wearing a nightgown, Chung revealed the connection between emotional and sensual intimacy.

Chung more commonly expressed her feelings of love through maternal and religious language. In one good-night note, she, as the mother, promised to care for all Tucker's needs: "Angel, it's wonderful having you to come home to! If you'll stay–I'll always draw your bath and cook for you and wait on you forever!"[61] The relationship was sometimes reversed, with Tucker as mother and Chung as child. In addition to describing herself as Tucker's "Baby," Chung also compared herself to the Biblical figure of Ruth, devoted daughter-in-law of Naomi: "Boss, I don't want to be sent home with all the rest of your junk to be put away in storage!! *I want to go with you*–wherever you go–to be *your shadow*–Can't I ride with your music in the music case? 'Cause I want to go where you go–do what you do—then I'll be happy'!–and you want your baby to be happy don't you? Remember what Ruth said to Naomi? 'Whither thou goest, I will go–and thy people shall be my people–and thy god, my god."[62]

Chung's reference to Ruth and Naomi provides insight into her negotiations of sexual, racial, and ethnic boundaries. The Old Testament story demonstrates the love and loyalty between women of different national and religious backgrounds. Ruth, a Moabitess, married into a Hebrew family. When she became a widow, Naomi entreated Ruth to stay in Moab and find another husband for herself. However, Ruth refused to abandon her widowed mother-in-law, choosing instead to follow her into the land of Judah and care for her.[63] The expression of Chung's desires through maternal and religious language both highlighted her passionate commitment to Tucker and masked the eroticism of her feelings. By comparing her love to maternal and religious devotion, Chung emphasized the power of her feelings. At the same time, her expression of a lifelong commitment to Tucker could be interpreted as spiritually and idealistically, not *sexually*, motivated. As scholar Martha Vicinus has argued, this "transference of sexual tensions into the language of the family (and sexual love into the language of religion). . . . [helped] conceal the physical basis of so much. . . . love."[64] The practice of "transference" was more characteristic of female romantic relationships during the Victorian era than the lesbian relationships of the modern era.

Given Chung's ambivalence about pursuing a romantic relationship with Gidlow, her expressions of maternally and religiously inspired love could be interpreted as a conscious attempt to reconcile her homoerotic desires with her rejection of a modern lesbian identity. Her strategy resonated with the experiences of other middle-class women who came of age during the turn of the century. As historian Estelle B. Freedman has suggested, the subjective sexual identities of these women stemmed from their liminal historical positions. They represented "individuals raised with the sexual categories of an earlier culture" who then "partake in the social changes that redefine their behaviors" in a later era.[65] While one should caution against exaggerating the acceptability of romantic friendships during the Victorian era, Chung's choice of erotic expression suggests that the nineteenth-century notion of female "passionlessness," reinforced in this particular case by her class status, maternal persona, and use of religious language, continued to provide some protection from social and perhaps even personal recognition of lesbian sexuality well into the twentieth century.[66]

Chung's religious and maternal language also provides insight into the significance of racial and ethnic identity in her intimate relationships. Ruth's abandonment of her native land of Moab could be interpreted as a rejection of her own culture. Similarly, Chung's preference for white Americans as romantic partners and friends could be explained by internalized racism. Her statements and behavior indicate her idealization of white definitions of beauty. Karen Garling Sickel, whose father was one of Chung's surrogate sons, recalled a startling remark from her adopted grandmother: "She turned to me one time and said, 'I wish I could wake up one morning and be blonde-haired and blue-eyed. All my troubles would go away.' "[67] Chung's apparent desire to alter her physical appearance, based on an awareness of the social advantages of achieving normative ideas of beauty, may have encouraged her enthusiasm for befriending white Americans. In fact, the two groups that she most adored, actresses and military heroes, epitomized mainstream cultural standards of femininity and masculinity.

Chung's attitudes and behavior suggest the power of mainstream racial thinking in shaping definitions of beauty and sexual desire. At the same time, her experiences reveal that conceptions of race, which shifted over the course of her lifetime, represented just one of many factors that shape identity formation and explain attraction.[68] Although Chung's romantic partners may not have shared a common racial background, they did have similar gender, class, and ethnic affinities. Chung, Gidlow, and Tucker were independent women who lived outside traditional family structures. In addition, both Gidlow and Tucker came from working-class, immigrant backgrounds. Like Chung, Gidlow grew up in a poor, large family in a rural community. Tucker, a Russian Jew, spent her childhood years working to contribute to the family income. Like Chung, she expressed a sense of obligation to her ethnic community and contributed time and effort to social causes.

Chung's reference to an Old Testament story to compare her relationship to Tucker suggests that she sought a common cultural reference to bridge their religious and cultural differences. As an American-born Chinese Christian, she tried to identify similarities with Tucker's Jewish immigrant background. While they spent Christmas together, they also celebrated Jewish holidays. Separated during one Passover, Chung sent a telegram to wish: "Happy Holidays to you and your family. Wish I were having matzofry with you in the kitchen. Am nostalgic with many beautiful and happy memories of seder and passover spent with you and yours. I cherish your friendship above all else and love you."[69] Chung's interest in developing personal connections across ethnic and racial lines paralleled the formation of political alliances during World War II. She sought not to erase race and ethnicity entirely but rather to craft possibilities for recognizing and uniting individuals of different backgrounds. Her adoption of a maternal persona and the creation of a surrogate network translated the Allied political agenda into familial language.

Chung's negotiation of racial and ethnic identities reflects broader transformations of social attitudes during the first half of the twentieth century, when the incorporation of European ethnic groups into the racial category of whiteness intensified.[70] Yu noted that "what began in the 1910s and 1920s as a fascination with the exotic became by the 1940s and 1950s a desire to erase the exotic. . . . The 1950s were marked by a belief in America as potentially homogeneous, and . . . the desirability of the 'melting pot.' "[71] As European ethnic groups viewed themselves and became viewed as "white," they also struggled to maintain a sense of ethnic identity. Chung's efforts to assimilate into the white middle class and yet maintain her affiliation with the Chinese community paralleled this transformation. Her relationships with "white" individuals from immigrant, ethnic backgrounds reflected a mutual desire for, as well as sense of anxiety about, incorporation.[72]

Chung's relationship with Tucker reveals her efforts to redefine her gender, class, racial, and sexual identities. Her adoption of a glamorous, maternal persona in the 1930s through 1950s fulfilled multiple functions. She responded to social pressure to adopt appropriate gender attire and behavior by crafting a feminine identity that nevertheless emphasized her financial independence and social autonomy. While her maternal performance indicated her growing identification with the white middle class, she continued to express political commitment to the Chinese in the United States and China. Her preference for white Americans as friends and romantic partners demonstrated her internalization of racial attitudes as well as her desire for companionship from women of similar ethnic and class backgrounds. Finally, her new persona helped redefine her homoerotic longings as maternally and religiously, not sexually, inspired. Chung's new maternal identity expressed her conflicting desire to balance respectability and independence.

Conclusion

Chung's relationships with Gidlow and Tucker offer insight into her attempts to define an acceptable self-identity while negotiating the shifting gender, sexual, racial, and class boundaries of the first half of the twentieth century. Perhaps because Chung felt isolated at times due to her personal choices, she created alternative family and community networks. Among her acquaintances and "sons" were individuals, such as Tallulah Bankhead, Anna May Wong, Tyrone Power, and Liberace, who became known as or were rumored to be homosexual or bisexual.[73] The coexistence or comingling of heterosexuals and nonheterosexuals in Chung's circle of friends shared similarities with middle-class lesbian communities during the middle decades of the twentieth century. During the 1930s, gay bars such as Mona's and the Black Cat Cafe opened in San Francisco, attracting a predominantly young, working-class clientele. Lesbians from middle- and upper-class backgrounds, however, continued to socialize privately in homes with their own networks of homosexual and heterosexual friends. The middle-class lesbian subculture rejected the butch masculine roles that were performed in working-class bar culture. Instead, middle-class lesbians sought integration into the existing heterosexual culture and emphasized dressing "appropriately" and behaving with "sufficient, though never excessive, femininity."[74] This pattern of coexistence, which continued through the war and into the 1950s, provided middle-class women who pursued same-sex relationships with a degree of protection from social persecution.

Although Chung developed her community of friends mainly with white Americans, she was not the only Chinese American living an alternative private life. Author Russell Leong recalled a conversation with his uncle regarding homosexuality in San Francisco's Chinatown: "I ask him about growing up in San Francisco Chinatown in the 1930s and 1940s before World War II. I ask him about gays and lesbians before I was born. He laughs. He says that there were many white homosexuals in North Beach 'who had a thing for Asian and Black boys,' at the time. But that there were also many spinsters and unmarried sisters in the families he knew about."[75] In addition to these "spinsters and unmarried sisters," at least one wife and mother, and probably many more, formed romantic and sexual relationships with other women. In a poem entitled "Chinatown Talking Story," novelist and poet Kitty Tsui described her grandmother, a Chinese opera singer who traveled to the United States in 1922:

> my grandfather had four wives
> and pursued many women
> during his life.
> the chinese press loved
> to write of his affairs.
>
> my grandmother,
> a woman with three daughters,
> left her husband
> to survive on her own.
> she lived with another actress,
> a companion and a friend.[76]

Chung's experimentation with gender identities and her participation in interracial homoerotic relationships provide insight into how other individuals with alternative sexual desires may have negotiated racial, gender, and class boundaries during the first half of the twentieth century. Her decisions to adopt masculine as well as feminine identities, express her erotic feelings through religious and maternal language, and engage in romantic friendships with white women revealed her efforts to contain transgressive behavior and feelings through normative forms of expression. Chung's ability to maneuver within social barriers stemmed from her liminal position between historical eras. During her lifetime, American society witnessed the transformation from the Victorian to the modern world. While her adoption of masculine dress and identity expressed discontent with the separation of gender spheres that characterized the Victorian era, her creation of a glamorous, feminine persona embraced the opportunities available for middle-class women within a commercialized society. While her choices in gender scripts exhibited an enthusiasm for change, her rejection of lesbianism, of same-sex sexuality as the basis of identity, indicated a desire to uphold Victorian notions of homosociality and asexuality as forms of protection. Her desire for companionship with white Americans called upon emerging notions of liberal equality to challenge social beliefs and practices of racial segregation. At the same time, those interracial relationships mirrored the persistence of ethnicity and social hierarchy within modern America. Chung's textured strategies reflected the challenge of crafting identities that foster social acceptance yet allow for transcendence.

Notes

This article has benefited from the comments of my advisors, colleagues, students, and friends. I particularly want to thank Estelle Freedman, Gordon Chang, Mary Louise Roberts, Leila Rupp, Birgitte Søland, Marc Stein, Nan Alamilla Boyd, Henry Yu, Evelyn Nakano Glenn, John Kuo Wei Tchen, Pamela Paxton, Kira Sanbonmatsu, Stephanie Gilmore, Heather Lee Miller, Kristina de los Santos, Jeong-eun Rhee, and Oona Besman. Chung's papers, held at the Asian American Studies Library, University of California, Berkeley, contain little correspondence from Tucker, although they wrote to one another. There is also no reference to Gidlow in Chung's writings or collection. I accidentally discovered their relationship by browsing through Susan Stryker and Jim Van Buskirk, *Gay by the Bay: A History of Queer Culture in the San Francisco Bay Area* (San Francisco: Chronicle Books, 1996), 21–23, which published a photograph of Chung and identified her as Gidlow's friend.

1. Chung to Tucker, 29 March 1945, Sophie Tucker Scrapbook Collection, 10,957, New York Public Library, Performing Arts Branch, New York City. From the passage, it appears that Tucker and Westphal, her second husband, lived together or "doubled" up before they were married.
2. See Judy Yung, *Unbound Feet: A Social History of Chinese Women in San Francisco* (Berkeley: University of California Press, 1995), 293.
3. Elsa Gidlow, *Elsa: I Come with My Songs* (San Francisco: Booklegger, 1986), 207.
4. I situate Chung's sexuality historically by differentiating between the concept of lesbianism that developed during the turn of the century and other forms of homoeroticism. See Leila J. Rupp, " 'Imagine My Surprise': Women's Relationships in Mid-Twentieth Century America," in *Hidden from History: Reclaiming the Gay and Lesbian Past*, ed. Martin Bauml Duberman, Martha Vicinus, and George Chauncey, Jr. (New York: New American Library, 1989): 395–410; and Estelle B. Freedman, " 'The Burning of Letters Continues': Elusive Identities and the Historical Construction of Sexuality," *Journal of Women's History* 9, no. 4 (1998): 181–200
5. See *Amerasia Journal: Dimensions of Desire* 20, no. 1 (1994); David L. Eng and Alice Y. Hom, eds., *Q & A: Queer in Asian America* (Philadelphia: Temple University Press, 1998); Chris Friday, *Organizing Asian American Labor: The Pacific Coast Canned-Salmon Industry, 1870–1942* (Philadelphia: Temple University Press, 1994); Russell Leong, ed., *Asian American Sexualities: Dimensions of the Gay and Lesbian Experience* (New York: Routledge, 1996); Jennifer Ting, "Bachelor Society: Deviant Heterosexuality and Asian American Historiography," in *Privileging Positions: The Sites of Asian American Studies*, ed. Gary Y. Okihiro, Marilyn Alquizola, Dorothy Fujita Rony, and K. Scott Wong (Pullman: Washington State University Press, 1995), 271–80, and Jennifer Ting, "The Power of Sexuality," *Journal of Asian American Studies* 1, no. 1 (1998): 65–82.
6. Brett de Bary and Victor Nee use the phrases "bachelor society" and "family society" to characterize the development of San Francisco's Chinatown community. See Brett de Bray and Victor Nee, *Longtime Californ': A Documentary Study of an American Chinatown* (Stanford, Calif.: Stanford University Press, 1972). For overviews of Asian American history, see Ronald Takaki, *Strangers from a Different Shore: A History of Asian Americans* (Boston: Little, Brown, 1989); and Sucheng Chan, *Asian Americans: An Interpretive History* (Boston: Twayne, 1991).
7. Gidlow, *Elsa*, 207. For more information about Chung, see Judy Tzu-Chun Wu, "Mom Chung of the

Fair-Haired Bastards: A Thematic Biography of Doctor Margaret Chung (1889–1959)" (Ph.D. diss., Stanford University, 1998); and Yung, *Unbound Feet.*

8. In 1923, Gidlow published *On a Grey Thread*, considered the first collection of explicitly lesbian poetry in North America. For more information about her life, see Gidlow, *Elsa*; and Stryker and Van Buskirk, *Gay by the Bay.*

9. In Edward W. Said's study *Orientalism*, he argues that the West historically has imaged the Orient as its "contrasting image." While the West is associated with progress, rationality, science, and normativity, the East represents "a place of romance, exotic beings, haunting memories and landscapes, [and] remarkable experiences." Because of this juxtaposition, the East holds an exotic allure for the West. At the same time, the contrast between the Occident and the Orient situates the West in a superior position in relation to non-European cultures. Orientalism thus represents "a Western style for dominating, restructuring, and having authority over the Orient." Edward W. Said, *Orientalism* (New York: Vintage, 1979), 1–3. For studies of American forms of orientalism, see John Kuo Wei Tchen, *New York before Chinatown: Orientalism and the Shaping of American Culture, 1776–1882* (Baltimore, Md.: Johns Hopkins University Press, 1999); and Robert G. Lee, *Orientals: Asian Americans in Popular Culture* (Philadelphia: Temple University Press, 1999).

10. Gidlow, *Elsa*, 207.

11. Marjorie Garber, *Vested Interests: Cross-Dressing and Cultural Anxiety* (New York: Routledge, 1992).

12. Vern L. Bullough and Bonnie Bullough define cross-dressing as a "symbolic incursion into territory that crosses gender boundaries." Because dress represents a visible marker of gender differences, cross-dressing challenges the naturalness of masculinity and femininity. See Vern L. Bullough and Bonnie Bullough, *Cross Dressing, Sex, and Gender* (Philadelphia: University of Pennsylvania Press, 1993), viii. For discussions of gender and performativity, see Judith Butler, "Performative Acts and Gender Constitution: An Essay in Phenomenology and Feminist Theory," in *Performing Feminisms: Feminist Critical Theory and Theatre*, ed. Sue-Ellen Case (Baltimore, Md.: Johns Hopkins University Press, 1990), 270–82; and Judith Halberstam, *Female Masculinity* (Durham, N.C.: Duke University Press, 1998).

13. Bertha Van Hoosen, *Petticoat Surgeon* (Chicago: Pelligrini & Cudahy, 1947), 219.

14. *El Rodeo* 9 (Los Angeles: University of Southern California, 1915), 221, 233.

15. While some professional women adopted masculine dress to symbolize their entry into traditionally male occupations, others viewed male dress as "protective coloring." See Bullough and Bullough, *Cross Dressing*; and Lillian Faderman, *Odd Girls and Twilight Lovers: A History of Lesbian Life in Twentieth-Century America* (New York: Columbia University Press, 1991), 21.

16. Margaret Chung autobiography, Margaret Chung Collection, Box 1, folder 1, Asian American Studies Library, University of California, Berkeley. The autobiography is not paginated.

17. Ibid.

18. " 'Mom, She's a Great Guy' to Her 465 Flying 'Sons': Dr. Margaret Chung, Chinese American, Keeps Close Watch over Brood: Each Wear Buddha," Chung Scrapbook, Chung Collection, Box 10.

19. Judy Yung provides a richer depiction of Chinese American women's lives in San Francisco during this time period. See Yung, *Unbound Feet*; and Peggy Pascoe, *Relations of Rescue: The Search for Female Moral Authority in the American West, 1874–1939* (New York: Oxford University Press, 1990).

20. Ting, "Bachelor Society."

21. Around the turn of the century, women in China also adopted masculine clothing to challenge the existing gender order and to proclaim their support for the emerging republican nation. For a discussion of the possible sexual connotations of adopting masculine clothing, see Vivien Ng, "Looking for Lesbians in Chinese History," in *The New Lesbian Studies: Into the Twenty-First Century*, ed. Bonnie Zimmerman and Toni A. H. McNaron (New York: Feminist Press, 1996), 160–64.

22. Bessie Jeong, interview by Suellen Cheng and Munson Kwok, 17 December 1981, 17 October 1982, Southern California Chinese American Oral History Project, Special Collections, University of California, Los Angeles. For biographical information about Jeong, see Yung, *Unbound Feet*, 131–33.

23. Jeong, interview.

24. See Garber, *Vested Interests*; San Francisco Lesbian and Gay History Project, " 'She Even Chewed Tobacco': A Pictorial Narrative of Passing Women in America," in *Hidden from History*, 183–94; and Carroll Smith-Rosenberg, "Discourses of Sexuality and Subjectivity: The New Woman, 1870–1936," in ibid., 269–71.

25. Jeong, interview.

26. L B. Nichols to Tolson, memorandum, 9 October 1940, Federal Bureau of Investigation file on "Dr. Margaret Jesse Chung," Department of Justice, Washington, D.C.

27. Given the difficulties of uncovering past sexual lives, scholars have focused on the figure of the "mannish" woman as a signifier of the sexually assertive lesbian. In contrast, romantic friendships,

characterized as erotic but nongenital relationships, are associated with the homosocial world of the Victorian era. Elizabeth Lapovsky Kennedy has noted that this framework tends to portray non-mannish women as lacking sexual initiative and experience. For discussions of the methodological approaches of lesbian/sexuality studies, see Lisa Duggan, "The Trials of Alice Mitchell: Sensationalism, Sexology, and the Lesbian Subject in Turn-of-the-Century America," *Signs* 18, no. 4 (1993): 791–814; Martha Vicinus, ed., *Lesbian Subjects: A Feminist Studies Reader* (Bloomington: Indiana University Press, 1996); and Elizabeth Lapovsky Kennedy, " 'But we would never talk about it': The Structures of Lesbian Discretion in South Dakota, 1928–1933," in *Inventing Lesbian Cultures in America*, ed. Ellen Lewin (Boston: Beacon Press, 1996), 15–39.

28. Bertha Van Hoosen, "Manuscript of Autobiography," 403, Bertha Van Hoosen Papers, Box 3, folder 1, Bentley Historical Library, University of Michigan, Ann Arbor.

29. Gidlow journal, 13, 25 January, 30 August 1928, Elsa Gidlow Collection, Box 1, Gay and Lesbian Historical Society of Northern California, San Francisco. The poems that Gidlow wrote about Chung include "Chinese Lotus," "For a Gifted Lady, Often Masked," "Miracle," and "Surgeon's Hands," Gidlow Collection, Box 11.

30. Gidlow, *Elsa*, 208.

31. Gidlow journal, 28 August 1928.

32. Ibid., 30 August 1928.

33. Ibid., 12 May 1931.

34. Ibid., 28 May 1931.

35. Ibid.

36. Ibid., 4 July 1931.

37. Ibid., 13 August 1931.

38. Ibid., 10 November 1928.

39. Ibid., 4, 13 July 1931.

40. Gidlow wrote and published various versions of this poem. The earliest typed version was entitled, "An Exercise in Free Verse, Dashed off for Doctor Margaret Chung," 22 September 1927, Gidlow Collection, Box 11.

41. Henry Yu, "Mixing Bodies and Cultures: The Meaning of America's Fascination with Sex between 'Orientals' and 'Whites,' " in *Sex, Love, Race: Crossing Boundaries in North American History*, ed. Martha Hodes (New York: New York University Press, 1999), 444–65, quotation on 446–47. Although Yu's article focuses on the racial ideas of social scientists, his findings also reflect changes in popular culture.

42. Ibid., 447.

43. Gidlow journal, 10 November 1928.

44. Shirley Radke, "We Must Be Active Americans," *Christian Science Monitor*, 3 October 1942.

45. Yung, *Unbound Feet*, 136.

46. Lucile Chung, interview by author, Vista, California, 28 January 1996.

47. Although antimiscegenation laws in California forbade interracial marriage, some local officials overlooked the state laws. Some couples also traveled to states that allowed interracial unions. See Karen Isaksen Leonard, *Making Ethnic Choices: California's Punjabi Mexican Americans* (Philadelphia: Temple University Press, 1992).

48. Michael Freedland, *Sophie: The Sophie Tucker Story* (London: Woburn, 1978), 211.

49. Mariko Tse, " 'Made in America': Project for East West Players and CBS," 12 June 1979, Research Project for East West Players on Chinese in Southern California, in possession of author.

50. Jeong, interview.

51. Elaine Tyler May, *Homeward Bound: American Families in the Cold War Era* (New York: Basic, 1988), 42.

52. Ibid.

53. Sophie Tucker, *Some of These Days* (1945), 58.

54. Yung, *Unbound Feet*, 200–201.

55. In her study of female athletes, Susan K. Cahn argues that women who threaten the gender hierarchy by excelling in traditionally masculine activities are pressured to emphasize their femininity. Susan K. Cahn, *Coming on Strong: Gender and Sexuality in Twentieth-Century Women's Sport* (New York: Free Press, 1994).

56. Chung described their daily interaction in a series of letters to Tucker. See Chung to Tucker, 4, 5 January 1944, Tucker Scrapbooks, 10,950.

57. Untitled clipping, *San Francisco Call-Bulletin*, 17 November 1943, Chung Scrapbook.

58. Barbara Bancroft, "Creating Homes for Real Living: Dr. Chung's Decorative Furnishings Express Her," newspaper clipping provided by Betsy Bingham Davis.

59. Chung to Tucker, 13, 14, 17, 19 January 1945, Tucker Scrapbooks, 10,955. These notes were most likely attached to a series of birthday presents.

60. Chung to Tucker, [25 December] 1947, Tucker Scrapbooks, 10,980.

61. Chung to Tucker, 17 January 1945.

62. [Chung] to Tucker, n.d., Tucker Scrapbooks, 10,950.

63. I thank Pamela Paxton for pointing out the ethnic and religious implications of Ruth's decision to follow Naomi.

64. See Martha Vicinus, "Distance and Desire: English Boarding School Friendships, 1870–1920," in *Hidden from History*, 212–29, quotation on 224.

65. Freedman, " 'Burning of Letters Continues,' " 185.

66. The use of religious and maternal language to express romantic longing represents a different strategy than the concept of "private lesbianism" suggested by Kennedy. She has argued for the possibility of women who "considered themselves lesbians but were completely private . . . about their erotic love for women." In contrast, Chung may not have embraced a lesbian identity, even in private, but instead fashioned alternative means to express her romantic desire for women. See Kennedy, " 'But we would never talk about it.' "

67. Karen Garling Sickel, interview by author, Palo Alto, California, 17 September 1996.

68. Yu's study of interracial sexuality ("Mixing Bodies and Cultures") influenced my effort to contextualize historically the conception of race. See also Colleen Fong and Judy Yung, "In Search of the Right Spouse: Interracial Marriage among Chinese and Japanese Americans," *Amerasia Journal* 21, no. 3 (1995): 77–98. For an overview of social science literature on interracial marriage, most of which focused on heterosexual relationships during the post-World War II and post-1965 eras, see Timothy P. Fong, *The Contemporary Asian American Experience: Beyond the Model Minority* (Upper Saddle River, N.J.: Prentice Hall, 1998), 224–33.

69. Chung to Tucker, 10 April 1955, Tucker Scrapbooks, 15,850.

70. Karen Brodkin, *How Jews Became White Folks and What That Says about Race in America* (New Brunswick, N.J.: Rutgers University Press, 1998); and Matthew Frye Jacobson, *Whiteness of a Different Color: European Immigrants and the Alchemy of Race* (Cambridge, Mass.: Harvard University Press, 1998).

71. Yu, "Mixing Bodies and Cultures," 447.

72. Because Chung was of Chinese ancestry, she was less likely to be perceived as "white" compared to individuals of European ancestry.

73. Neil Okrent, "Right Place Wong Time," *Los Angeles Magazine*, May 1990, 84.

74. Faderman, *Odd Girls*, 181. For histories of the San Francisco gay and lesbian communities, see Stryker and Buskirk, *Gay by the Bay*, 22–27; and Faderman, *Odd Girls*, 107, 175–87.

75. Rusell Leong, "Home Bodies and the Body Politic," in *Asian American Sexualities*, 1–20, quotation on 11.

76. Kitty Tsui, "Chinatown Talking Story," in *The Words of a Woman Who Breathes Fire* (Iowa City, Iowa: Spinsters Ink, 1983). Tsui is writing a historical novel based on her grandmother's experiences. Kitty Tsui, "*Bak Sze*, White Snake," in *Asian American Sexualities*, 223–26, quotation on 223.

29

Telling Performances
Jazz History Remembered and Remade by the Women in the Band

Sherrie Tucker

Scholars and writers in the burgeoning field of jazz studies are critically reevaluating some of the timeworn patterns of how mainstream jazz histories have been written. According to writers such as those anthologized in *Jazz among the Discourses*, jazz scholarship is too "devoted to exalting favored artists," too invested in "campaigns for superiority of genres"; jazz history is too neatly constructed into a misleading "coherent whole" of "styles or periods, each with a conveniently distinctive label and time period"; and, finally, the jazz historical record is too reliant on the very small portion of music that gets made into jazz records.[1]

As someone who does research on all-woman bands, I am heartened by these critiques. The conventional standards for what counts as jazz history make it very difficult to construct historical narratives that include all-woman bands. I would also like to suggest that scholars seeking more complex historical frameworks should take a listen to oral histories of women jazz musicians. The kind of listening I am advocating would not be limited to merely skimming jazzwomen's stories for data to add to the existing historical record, nor would it be geared solely toward the creation of separate women-in-jazz histories. Rather, I believe that through serious study of jazzwomen's oral histories, scholars might learn new narrative strategies for imagining and telling jazz histories in which women and men are both present. Because women who played instruments other than piano were seldom the "favored artists" of the "superior genres," and because they were hardly ever recorded, they have had little access to the deceptive "coherence" of mainstream histories. Therefore, they are uniquely positioned to suggest new frameworks for telling and interpreting jazz history.

Listening to narratives of women instrumentalists might also help jazz scholars to engage in more rigorous gender analysis than has been customary. Women musicians do not tend to construct separate "women's jazz" histories when they talk about their careers, nor do they simply "add themselves in" to dominant historical frameworks. Yet historians aiming to include women seem to be stuck at the crossroads of these two narrative options. Instead, women musicians tend to construct narratives in which they dramatize themselves, at various stages of their careers, as negotiating gendered identities (often in creative ways) as jazz musicians. Indeed, these "telling performances"—the narrations themselves—may prove a rich site for learning about the function of oral history-telling in female artists' construction and maintenance of identities as jazz musicians in a discourse that has historically denied them a place.

Engaged listening to oral histories of women jazz musicians might help historians to reframe jazz history so that it is possible to see "gender" not only as a mode of social organization, but, in

Joan Scott's terms, as a "field on which power is articulated."[2] This would involve not only looking at what women did and what men did, but looking at what kinds of masculinities and femininities were performed in specific historical contexts and how they were valued—asking, for instance, which masculinities and femininities were deemed marketable on a national scale and which were relegated to local scenes only. Jazz scholars would do well to examine critically the kinds of gender constructions that have dominated jazz journalism, recording, marketing, and historiography and to ask questions such as: Who is served by the popular construction of the modernist jazz hero as personifying a kind of black masculinity defined (usually by white male writers) as isolated, self-destructive, and childlike?[3] Or by the quintessential jazzwoman as a "girl singer," so often constructed as a bubblehead rather than a knowledgeable professional? Or by the figure of the jazz/blues singer as the embodiment of stereotypes about black femininity,

Figure 29.1. Saxophone section, International Sweethearts of Rhythm, publicity photo, 1994. Grace Bayron, fourth tenor (lower left); Helen Saine, third alto (upper left); Rosalind "Roz" Cron, lead alto (center); Vi Burnside, second/jazz tenor (upper right); Willie Mae Wong, baritone (lower right). *Photo courtesy of Rosalind Cron.*

oversexed and underloved, the musician who is assumed to have no musical knowledge, but is thought to express, naturally, through her pain, an extra-earthy feminine wisdom that may do the singer no good but which nurtures and entertains listeners?

Clearly the persistence of such problematic representations of race and gender in dominant jazz discourse covers up and damages much more than the history of all-woman bands. Rigorous gender analysis is needed, in conjunction with historically specific, critical analyses of race, racialization, and racism. Again, I suggest that the oral histories of black and white women who played in all-woman bands contain narrative strategies useful to jazz studies scholars in general—not only those of us who write about all-woman bands.

Scratching the Historical Record

When women musicians tell their stories, jazz history tends to come out differently from the usual parade of stars and superlative recordings we often get from mainstream jazz historians. Jazzwomen's stories also have a knack for shaking up the assumptions of an idealistic feminist historiographer who comes along expecting to dig up and celebrate a lost or forgotten jazz sisterhood in such a way as to obliterate sexist practices once and for all. As someone who has spent the last seven years interviewing women who played in all-woman jazz and swing bands of the 1940s, I am so overwhelmed with examples of how women's stories have moved me to rethink and complicate my notions of jazz history and women's history, it is hard to figure out where to start. I "drop the needle," so to speak, on a hot day in June 1994. I am in the Burger King at Washington and Grand in Los Angeles, interviewing Vi Wilson about her half-a-century-and-running career as a jazz bassist. I begin here, over fries and coffee, because it is one of the moments in which I have been most struck with the three-way contrast between how jazz history looks in the mainstream books on the subject, how I, as a feminist jazz historian, imagine it will look, and how jazz history looks when women musicians tell about their lives.

Wilson, who played briefly with the International Sweethearts of Rhythm before switching over to the Darlings of Rhythm in the late 1940s, is telling me about the infrequent but exciting occasions when African American all-woman bands, such as these two or Eddie Durham's All-Star Girls Orchestra, bumped into each other on the road.

> Fellas in those days, they had a competition between the Sweethearts and the Darlings. But the Darlings could play. Boy, we would get in jam sessions with them like, whatever town we were in. The fellas, it was a novelty to them to come see these girls play. They said, "Those girls play like men." We'd have a big jam session. Boy, Vi Burnside would really play. And Padjo, we called her Padjo [Margaret Backstrom], she would really play. And, see, the best players, tenor players, were Padjo and Vi Burnside. And Vi Burnside would call Padjo "Lester Young"—I think one was "Lester Young" and the other one was called "Ben Webster." And they'd come shake hands and get on the bandstand. "Let's blow these fellas down!" Oh, we had some good times. . . . And we'd all say, "Let's give them something to talk about!" They'd get up there with the fellas.[4]

Even the most casual reader of jazz history knows that in the mainstream versions women do not tote horns and "blow fellas down" in after-hours jam sessions. Nor are jam sessions coed in dominant versions of history. Jazz is more often portrayed as an exclusive world of male musicians roughing it on the road, tearing it up in legendary jam sessions, waxing creative in clubs, sometimes sharing the spotlight with a lone, begowned female vocalist. Wilson's narrative issues a challenge to the familiar old jazz histories in much the same way that her fondly recalled colleagues gave skeptical male musicians "something to talk about."

Figure 29.2. Violet "Vi" Wilson, publicity photo, circa 1950s. *Photo courtesy of Violet Wilson.*

And this story also gives feminist historiographers "something to talk about." The coed jam sessions were probably at least as unexpected to me as they would have been to someone working on the assumption that men played instruments and women sang. Presuming that women musicians met with nothing but resentment at every turn, I am surprised that Wilson recalls being welcomed at after-hours jam sessions in strange cities. It astonishes me that the burden of proving to men that women musicians can "really play" is presented here as an occasion for fun, rather than as a perpetual nuisance. Wilson's story in which women musicians square off competitively while amazed men look on, where women take nicknames of men musicians before "blowing the fellas away," issues a challenge to my feminist sensibilities, and tells me I have a great deal to learn from jazzwomen's stories.

I drop the needle again. It is another hot day in June, only this time I am partaking of cranberry juice with two trumpet giants, Jane Sager and Clora Bryant, in Sager's Hollywood trumpet studio. I am enjoying their stories immensely, many of which take up the problem of men's expectations that women musicians are "novelties" and end with the women "blowing them away." Suddenly Sager, who played with many of the major white all-woman bands of the 1930s and 1940s, including those led by Rita Rio and Ada Leonard, regales us with a tale about women musicians "blowing away" quite a different set of unbelievers. While working on vaudeville in the early 1930s, a situation arose where the "tall girls" in the chorus line believed themselves superior to the women musicians in the "all-girl" band, a status that entitled them, they felt, to the best seats on the bus.

So these girls, when we would be packing up our instruments, they'd go out on the Greyhound and get the best seats. And we'd have to sit over the wheel and bounce and, you know. In the band, we were getting crap. So we weren't going to take it. So what we did, Alice [Raleigh the drummer] says, "Look, I am going to fix things. You do not have to say a word. Wait till the next show and watch your step because I am going to do something crazy." So she comes to their dance and they're going, "dah, ta-dah, ta-dah, ta-dah," and Alice goes, "one-two-three one-two one-two-three one-two. . . ." Five-four time! And those girls fell on each other, they fell on the stage! I am telling you, after that, they'd say, "Where would you like to sit on the bus?"[5]

While dancers in the chorus line were not exactly the Victorian ideal of traditional womanhood, they were in a more traditional occupation than women drummers or trumpet players in "all-girl" bands. The woman drummer (and Sager in telling this story) proves with humor and panache that women musicians in "all-girl" bands were every bit as important to the success of vaudeville as the glamorous long-legged women of the front line. Indeed, women musicians emerge victorious.[6]

Clora Bryant has an entertaining and amazing story equally unsettling to any remaining feminist assumptions of a "sisterhood" of support for women musicians in a sexist world. While "doing one-nighters up and down the coast" in 1944 with the all-female band from historically black Prairie View College, Bryant found herself playing an army base in Alabama where several male jazz musicians were stationed, including trombonist Jimmy Cheatham and drummer Chico Hamilton. But the competition that ensued was not between male and female musicians, but between women in the audience and women on the bandstand.

Chico Hamilton was a good-looking guy. He was fine! And he's an egotistical little something anyway. He was a big flirt and it was a small town, and these girls were fighting over who was going to go with him. And we were playing this dance and we were on the stage and we'd had intermission and Chico had introduced himself [to the band] and the whole thing. And after intermission, we're up there playing and all of a sudden we heard a loud commotion and then this bottle—this broad threw this Coke bottle, she was throwing it at the girls! Our front line we had saxophone players and most of them were light girls with long, pretty hair. This broad had thrown a Coke bottle at the band! It just so happened it hit the jukebox and made a loud noise. We all hit the floor. It was something else.[7]

Keeping these three stories in the air is no easy matter. Each stands alone as an expertly crafted and delivered anecdote, each tells of experiences jazzwomen had that are unlikely to have been shared by men, and each is completely different. Yet they all took place in a world historicized as a masculine environment. This juggling act of listening to and learning from women musicians also requires a drastic rethinking of jazz history.

Thanks to the meticulous, groundbreaking work of a small number of researchers and writers devoted to uncovering the histories of women in jazz, we now have a number of what feminist historians call "compensatory" histories. I am grateful to authors such as D. Antoinette Handy, Linda Dahl, Sally Placksin, Frank Driggs, and Leslie Gourse; record producer/historian Rosetta Reitz; and filmmakers Greta Schiller and Andrea Weiss for the extant body of histories of women in jazz. Yet the more I interview women jazz musicians, the more I cannot help but feel that the next step is to find ways of imagining jazz history that include both women and men. I say this as someone who is deeply involved with writing a book on all-woman bands of the 1940s—yet another separate history![8] But even my research on all-woman bands tells me that it is high time to crack open the historical narrative of jazz so that it encompasses the profession as experienced by the women who have been there all along. And the best place to go to learn how to imagine a sphere of jazz history that includes women is the stories of women musicians who already imagine themselves, quite correctly, in jazz history.

Jazz as History

When historian Elsa Barkley Brown urged her colleagues to be more like jazz musicians, she was not talking to jazz historians in particular, but she could have been. Basically, she thought this would be a good idea because history, like jazz,

> is everybody talking at once, multiple rhythms being played simultaneously. The events and people we write about did not occur in isolation but dialogue with a myriad of other people and events. In fact, at any given moment, millions of people are talking at once. As historians we try to isolate one conversation and explore it, but the trick is then how to put that conversation in a context which makes evident its dialogue with so many others—how to make this one lyric stand alone and at the same time be in conjunction with all the other lyrics being sung.[9]

One common theme of the three stories I set in motion in the beginning of this paper is that they all present conversations, dialogues, multiple voices. None of them stakes a claim to a single lyric that can be sung alone. Wilson's story animates a conversation between men who think women players are "novelties" and the women who "blow the fellas away." Sager's pits superior attitudes of dancers against the unrecognized powers of the women who play the tunes. Bryant's demonstrates a contest between women in the audience and women on the band stand. All of these stories contain dialogues missing from mainstream accounts of jazz history.

What if jazz historians were more like women jazz musicians? What if jazz history got told in such a way that we could hear dialogues such as "Women musicians are novelties," "Let's blow these fellas down," "Those women play like men," and so forth? What if the tension, omnipresent in these stories, between a public that assumes that women musicians are "novelties" and women musicians who prove they can "really play" was characterized as a conversation within jazz history, rather than as an inconsequential voice from the margins? What if there was room in the mainstream jazz histories for "conversion" stories, such as this one from Vi Wilson?

> We made them respect us because we could blow our instruments. And that was a challenge to them at the same time. Now, with a women's band, it is just a matter of you're all the same sex, and, you know, the best person plays. It doesn't matter. But with men, they always, they have that guard up. "Woman musician, she can't play," you know. Then when we play, that knocks them out. That surprises them. That puts them back in history. Lets them know that women could play just as good as they can. Anytime we walked in, even myself, as a bass player, when I walked in on a set, eyes was raised. When I got through playing, I made a believer out of them.[10]

As Wilson tells it, jazz is a place where women instrumentalists take pride in their work, play just as well as men, and win converts. It is also a world where women are well aware of the powerful belief systems that work against them: the widespread skepticism about their abilities, their reputations as "novelties," and the classic paradoxes of what it means to cross the gender division of labor. In Wilson's history, women know that what they do is considered a "man's job," and when they walk in, men (and sometimes women) will say (or think), "Woman musician, she can't play." And they also know that if they do the job well, they will be said to be good "for girls," or that they "play like men." And they know that even if they "make believers out of them" today, the same battles will have to be fought tomorrow. Her narrative is not one of ultimate triumph over struggle, but one in which struggle is a constant and triumph is cyclical. Wilson's telling of her history, like so many oral narratives of jazzwomen I have interviewed, is a performance that not only renders women visible in a history that erased them, but portrays a savvy understanding of the structures of power that made such erasure possible. Her story also makes what I think is a marvelous intervention into the prevalent notion that women can simply be added into extant versions of jazz history, which are thought to be ungendered. According to Wilson, when men realize that women can play, that puts *the men* back in history.

Jane Sager also told me many stories in which skeptics are convinced, only to be replaced by new skeptics. In one interesting twist on the theme, a skeptic becomes a convert in a most dramatic way, only to be revealed as a perpetual skeptic after all. A white male bandleader hires Sager only after auditioning every male trumpet player in the room first, making her wait in a bar until the wee hours before giving her a chance. Just before the club closes for the night, he calls her to the stand. She outplays the others and gets the job. After playing with the band for a while, however, Sager noticed that the bandleader was watching her closely.

> He would follow me around, you know. And he kept waiting for me to get tired. He said, "Aren't you tired?" I said, "Am I supposed to be?" I am holding down a musician's job, it is a man's job, too. But I said, "Why should I be tired?" He said, "Well, I understand that girls menstruate and they do not play so good!" I said, "Ahhh." I said, "I play twice as good when that happens. Where did you get that crazy propaganda?" He followed me around waiting for me to menstruate to see if I would fall over![11]

Cause for More than Celebration

It is tempting to celebrate such stories as recovered bits of women's history, as evidence of women's activity in realms where they were thought not to exist, as proof that women could "really play" in the 1940s. But even then, what we would end up "celebrating" is not a historical nugget tossed to us from jazzwomen of the past, but one story that one writer has selected from hours of others from taped interviews with living sources at particular moments. Women musicians' stories are already shaped by how they perceive the interviewer, and how that perception has influenced decisions over what stories to contribute and what versions of those stories to tell. Even the contents of that vast pool of possible stories most certainly owe a great deal to how women of the 1990s have come to make sense of their careers in the 1940s—not just what happened, but what they remember and how they remember it. As trombonist Helen (Jones) Woods replied when I told her I wanted to tape-record our interview so I could quote her accurately: "As accurately as possible! Be sure to say that. Say you quoted me 'as accurately as she thought she was.' "[12]

And then there is the complicating detail of the interviewer's role in shaping the text that appears before you. In recent years, feminist oral historians have begun to realize that even "celebration" is an executive decision, yet another clue that the relationship between narrator and researcher is rarely an equal one. Usually, as in this case, while it is the narrator who tells the tales during the interview, it is the historian who decides which segments will serve as "something to talk about," and how and in what context to talk about them. The realization that we are not merely benevolent megaphones for "letting women speak for themselves" has sent many a feminist researcher into crisis. While I have certainly lost sleep over this myself, I am ultimately happy to be rid of the fantasy that it is possible for a person to be a conduit. The conduit model fails to notice differences between women (not to mention differences between women and conduits). The assumption that I can be a conduit, channeling voices of jazzwomen to written history, depends upon an assumption that jazzwomen are merely conduits to lived history. Neither assumption seems suitable (or feminist) to me.[13]

Also, while it might feel good to celebrate the fact that Burnside and Backstrom were out there proving that women could "really play" fifty years ago, what does that do for the everyday fact that many female jazz musicians continue to experience the burden of "proving that women can play" whenever they take the stand?[14] As recently as April 1996 Fostina Dixon told the *Washington Post*, "People still come up to me and say, 'You're the first female saxophone player I have ever heard.' "[15] What does celebration do to the fact that mainstream historical narratives that ignore jazzwomen's lives continue to get written? I would like to suggest other ways in which stories of jazzwomen might be even more useful.

There are those who would argue that oral histories and interviews are not particularly useful in jazz historiography. The main criticism, according to Burton Peretti, "asks how any testimony presented decades after the fact could possibly 'clear up' the historical record." Peretti then points out that in jazz history, there is often a lack of hard evidence from the past; thus oral histories become the only way for finding out histories of particular periods, people, and relationships.[16] I would add that this is especially so in the case of jazzwomen's history. Peretti also argues that perhaps more value can come from taking the folklorists' approach of studying oral history narratives as performances. Making a similar case for the value of looking at "textual strategies" and "performance dynamics" in jazz autobiographies, Kathy Ogren argues that "historians need to recognize the possibilities—not merely the limitations—of self–fashioned personas."[17] My interests in studying the ways women jazz instrumentalists tell their stories include my conviction that (1) the memories of living jazzwomen hold much history that is not to be found elsewhere, (2) there is great value in learning how they interpret their own lives, and (3) the shapes jazz history takes when women musicians tell their stories may prove instructive to anyone interested in expanding our repertoire of this thing we call jazz history.

More than an artifact of history, Wilson's story of the coed jam session is an interpretation of history, one that she contributes knowing full well how different it is from dominant ideas about masculine jam sessions and feminine "novelty" acts.[18] The female saxophonists in Wilson's story are well aware that the men who come to hear them and play with them consider them "a novelty." But that doesn't mean the women musicians see themselves as a "novelty." It also doesn't mean that they are able to get rid of the stigma of "novelty" once and for all. The women nickname each other after favorite male tenor sax players, "Lester Young" and "Ben Webster," before proving to the skeptics that women can "really play." They are portrayed as confident and skilled, yet Wilson's repeated insistence that "they would really play" also conveys a historical relationship between women musicians and their ubiquitous doubting public: "Can they play?"

When mainstream jazz histories omit women musicians, it is like saying, "Women musicians, they can't play." When women-in-jazz researchers celebrate the accomplishments of women musicians, it is like saying, "Yes, they can!" (which has been an important argument to assert, since the other side has received so much press). But what if the frameworks of jazz history were to incorporate both sides of the tension, as women musicians so often do when they interpret their careers? What if the scope of jazz history was made wide enough to recognize all the voices Wilson hears from that perpetual after-hours club of fifty years ago: the male skeptics who come to hear a "novelty," the female tenor sax stars who "blow these fellas away," the converts, the next set of skeptics?

Another reason to do more than "celebrate" the stories of women jazz musicians is that "celebration" assumes a kind of "sisterhood" among women that does not always appear in the historical narratives. Many women musicians did not like to play with women. There was some crossing of race lines when black bands such as the International Sweethearts of Rhythm and the Darlings of Rhythm occasionally hired white members who passed as black onstage. For the most part, however, all-female bands, like male bands, were segregated along a black-white binary and played for segregated audiences in the 1920s, 1930s, and 1940s. Jim Crow constructions of whiteness as a "pure" category meant that mixed-race women and women of color who were not African American were more likely to be included in bands on the more inclusive, yet decidedly less privileged, "black" side of the race division. Chinese American Willie Mae Wong (Scott) recalls that she was never required to pass as black to play in black bands in the South and was never harassed by the police for traveling with a black band.[19] Latinas were sometimes coded "white." Some women who were legally black under laws that defined anyone with any black ancestry as black passed as "Spanish" to play in white bands, though it must be said that this kind of passing, and indeed black-to-white passing in general, was quite different from the passing of white women who played with black bands. White alto saxophonist Roz Cron speculated that her presence in the International Sweethearts of Rhythm endangered the black women in the band more than it did herself. "They were the ones that would have suffered. I would have gotten slapped on the wrist and sent home or something."[20] White women could regain white privilege at any time. In order for black women to get work in the most famous and lucrative all-woman bands, they would have to pass as white offstage as well as on, in many areas of their lives. I know of only one white all-woman band in the 1940s whose leader knowingly hired a black musician—and this musician was very light-skinned and had blue eyes. These histories are too complex and too unbalanced to warrant uncritical celebration.[21] A "celebration" of women's stories might also miss the fact that some male musicians were supportive and encouraging of some female musicians, and that men weren't the only people in jazz history who have sometimes been skeptical of women instrumentalists.

Utopian Spaces and Jazz Futures

I would like to close with Clora Bryant's story of jamming in the clubs on Central Avenue, Los Angeles, in the 1940s. This reverie, which she has related to me many times, is an excellent

Figure 29.3. Sax section, International Sweethearts of Rhythm, After Hours club, Seattle, 1994. *Courtesy of Rosalind Cron.*

example of how history might be opened up to include unrecorded performances, lesser-known jazz practitioners, and local scenes as sites where we might look if we want to account for lives of both male and female musicians. It also brings me to the topic of jazzwomen's nostalgia, which I see as an area that could be productively explored, again not simply for data nor for proof of participation, but for the conceptual and narrative strategies therein.

During the same period in which Bryant was playing trumpet professionally in all-female combos such as the Queens of Swing, touring all-white towns in the western states where they were often thought to be not merely "novelties" but "exotic," Bryant also spent the time she had in her home base of Los Angeles participating in those now-famous jam sessions with artists such as Wardell Gray, Sonny Criss, Teddy Edwards, and Hampton Hawes. While records, radio broadcasts, and "favored artists" all make appearances in her narrative, Bryant's definition of what counts as jazz history is not dependent on industry support. Her vivid telling of her own engagement with bebop is one of participation, not marginalization.

> I would sit and play Dizzy's record. The first thing that I could play by him was a ballad, "I Can't Get Started," because before that, everybody was doing Bunny Berigan's version. Everybody imitated Bunny Berigan playing "I Can't Get Started." Then when I heard Dizzy play it, I said, "Wait a minute!" I bought the record and learned it note for note, it was fun. Those were some fun times. I mean the guys, there was a camaraderie that we do not have now. You always knew where you could go and see the best musicians and your friends and hear the best music and get up there and try to play with those people. And you knew you were going to be bopped to death. You know, you knew it was going to be so great! There would be no doubt about it. And you would come out of there and "whew!" I would come out of there with my little trumpet and go home and get the records and I would be in that record player, boy. At that time we had wire recording. Tape wasn't in, but it was wire recording. I had a wire recorder and, man, I would get that and I would try to be playing and I would listen and say, "What was that I was playing?" It was a learning time, and it was a happy time, it was a friendly time, it was a musical time, and it was, you know, it was just something that if you haven't been at that place at that time, you can't explain it.[22]

In her nostalgic portrait of Central Avenue in the 1940s, Bryant evokes a scene in which jazz practice was as serious a calling for those who played with the records as for those who played on the records, for both the known and unknown artists who encountered each other at jam sessions and got "bopped to death." While Bryant is not alone in identifying playing along with records as an important historical site for jazz education and practice, her story is unique because it reveals the participation of women in this important training ground.[23] She portrays herself as a wide-eyed seventeen-year-old, immersed in music and in the technologies that help her to discover what Gillespie is doing and to hone her own skills. Other portions of her narrative explore the kinds of skepticisms, sexisms, and racisms she experienced both on and off the road in her fifty-year career as a jazz musician, but the private sessions with records and public musical collaborations in jam sessions in the clubs of Central Avenue are recalled again and again as utopian spaces for thinking about jazz. And, according to Paul Gilroy, utopian spaces are not just sites for nostalgia, they are important keys to imagining egalitarian futures.[24] If Bryant's account of her participation on Central Avenue in its prime was included in mainstream histories, how might it break up assumptions that serious jazz involvement was out of reach for women trumpet players in the 1940s?[25] How might Bryant's vision of jazz history as something that happens at home as well as in clubs, to underrecorded artists as well as to oft-recorded ones, and to women as well as men, prepare musicians, historians, scholars, and fans to believe in and care about the women trumpet players who arrived later—who are arriving now?

Anyone interested in a more complete account of jazz history, as well as in a more egalitarian jazz future, would do well to listen to jazzwomen's "telling performances." Such stories should be studied carefully for women musicians' myriad tactics for asserting and maintaining identities as jazz musicians: in the business, on the bandstand, and in their memories. If histories were remade to encompass the stories women jazz musicians tell when they talk about their lives, we would know more about jazz and we would know more about women.

Notes

1. Krin Gabbard, "The Jazz Canon and Its Consequences," in Krin Gabbard, ed., *Jazz among the Discourses* (Durham: Duke University Press, 1995), 8–9, 16; Scott De Veaux, "Constructing the Jazz Tradition: Jazz Historiography," *Black American Literature Forum* 25, 3 (fall 1991): 525; Jed Rasula, "The Media of Memory: The Seductive Menace of Records in Jazz History," in Gabbard, *Jazz among the Discourses*, 136, 144.
2. Joan Wallach Scott, *Gender and the Politics of History* (New York: Columbia University Press, 1988), 42–43.
3. See Ingrid Monson's discussion of the gendered dimensions and prevalence of "primitivist ideas of the African American artist unspoiled by culture or civilization" in fanatically well-intentioned jazz prose penned by white men. Ingrid Monson, "The Problem with White Hipness: Race, Gender, and Cultural Conception in Jazz Historical Discourse," *Journal of the American Musicological Society* 48, 3 (fall 1995): 396–422.
4. Vi Wilson, interview by author, 13 June 1994.
5. Jane Sager, interview by author, 10 June 1994.
6. Many jazzwomen, both black and white, who played in the 1920s, 1930s, and 1940s have told me stories in which they distanced themselves from dancers in chorus lines. One musician informed me that chorines were notoriously underpaid and often supplemented their incomes by practicing the "world's oldest profession." Whether or not this was always the case, the widespread public perception of chorines as musical prostitutes would seem to explain why women musicians, who were already fighting against stereotypes of women on the stage as sexually excessive, might wish to distance themselves from such stigmas.
7. Clora Bryan, interview by author, 5 August 1993.
8. Sherrie Tucker, *Changing the Players, Playing the Changes: "All-Girl" Bands during World War II* (Durham: Duke University Press, forthcoming).
9. Elsa Barkley Brown, "Polyrhythms and Improvisation: Lessons for Women's History," *History Workshop Journal* (spring 1991), 84.
10. Vi Wilson, interview by author, 9 November 1993.
11. Jane Sager, interview by author, 2 April 1994. For expanded accounts of this story, see Sally Placksin *Jazz Women: 1900 to the Present* (London: Pluto Press, 1982), 105–6; and Sherrie Tucker, "Interview with Jane Sager," *Newsletter of the International Women's Brass Conference* 2, 1 (February 1995).
12. Helen (Jones) Woods, interview by author, 20 February 1995.
13. See Sherna Berger Gluck and Daphne Patai, eds., *Women's Words: The Feminist Practice of Oral History* (New York: Routledge, 1991). In her essay "Can There Be a Feminist Ethnography," Judith Stacey worried that if the researcher controls the product, alliance is merely a delusion. And "delusions of alliance" inevitably lead to "betrayal" (113). While I take these concerns to heart, and in fact do often feel closely "allied" with my informants (close enough to worry about "betraying" them), I am also persuaded by Kamala Visweswaran's suggestion that yearning for the lost "innocence" of the conduit is less suitable as a feminist principle than the disappointing specter of betrayal. See Visweswaran, "Betrayal: An Analysis in Three Acts," in Inderpal Grewal and Caren Kaplan, eds., *Scattered Hegemonies: Postmodernity and Transnational Feminist Practices* (Minneapolis: University of Minnesota Press, 1994).
14. See any number of reviews of the contemporary all-woman band Diva, including Zan Stewart, "All-Female Band Diva Breaking Stereotypes," *Los Angeles Times*, 16 June 1995, F12.
15. Richard Harrington, "The Rhythm Queens at the Kennedy Center, a Celebration of Women in Jazz," *Washington Post*, 28 April 1996, G1.
16. Burton Peretti, "Oral Histories of Jazz Musicians: The NEA Transcripts as Text in Context," in Gabbard, ed., *Jazz among the Discourses*, 122.
17. Kathy Ogren, " 'Jazz Isn't Just Me': Jazz Autobiographies as Performances," in Reginald T. Buckner and Steven Weiland, eds., *Jazz in Mind: Essays on the History and Meanings of Jazz* (Detroit: Wayne State University Press, 1991), 112–14.

18. Writes Douglas Henry Daniels, "The musicians' conception of history and desire to make a contribution needs to be rigorously examined." Douglas Henry Daniels, "Oral History, Masks, and Protocol in the Jazz Community," *Oral History Review* 15, 1 (1987): 143–64.

19. Willie Mae Wong (Scott), interview by author, 3 December 1996.

20. Roz Cron, interview by author, 13 August 1990.

21. For more on the "one-drop rule" and the Jim Crow South, see F. James Davis, *Who Is Black? One Nation's Definition* (University Park: Pennsylvania State University Press, 1991), and Michael Omi and Howard Winant, *Racial Formation in the United States: From the 1960s to the 1990s*, 2nd ed. (New York: Routledge, 1994). For more on how the International Sweethearts of Rhythm negotiated these structures with racially diverse personnel, see D. Antoinette Handy, *The International Sweethearts of Rhythm* (Metuchen, N.J.: Scarecrow Press, 1983) and the documentary by Greta Schiller and Andrea Weiss, *International Sweethearts of Rhythm* (Jezebel Productions, 1986).

22. Clora Bryant, interview by author, 7 October 1990.

23. Paul Berliner includes learning from records as part of his study of the "wide compass of practice and thought that improvisers give to music outside formal performance events." Paul Berliner, *Thinking in Jazz: The Infinite Art of Improvisation* (Chicago: University of Chicago Press, 1994), 15. See also Charles Keil and Steven Feld, "Dialogue 1: Getting into the Dialogic Groove," in *Music Grooves* (Chicago: University of Chicago Press, 1994), 1–31.

24. See Paul Gilroy, "Diaspora, Utopia and the Critique of Capitalism," in *There Ain't No Black in the Union Jack: The Cultural Politics of Race and Nation* (Chicago: University of Chicago Press, 1987). In fact, in Bryant's privileging of playing along with records (rather than passively listening to them) and jam sessions over gigs, the utopian spaces of her narrative are similar to some of Gilroy's examples of cultural practices that he sees as critiques of capitalism.

25. It is important to note that this work is increasingly being done in jazz oral history archives, though less so in books and films about jazz history. The inclusion of female jazz musicians' narratives in major repositories presents opportunities for jazz historians interested in multivocal approaches, in frameworks that account for both men and women, and in exploring how gender operated in particular times and places in jazz history. Bryant's oral history has been collected by the Smithsonian Jazz Oral History Program (along with those of many other women musicians), as well as by the Central Avenue Sounds Oral History Project at the University of California, Los Angeles. Steven Isoardi's interviews with Bryant and trombonist Melba Liston appear alongside those of male musicians in Clora Bryant et al., ed., *Central Avenue Sounds: Jazz in Los Angeles* (Berkeley: University of California Press, 1998).

30

Rethinking Betty Friedan and *The Feminine Mystique*
Labor Union Radicalism and Feminism in Cold War America

Daniel Horowitz

> In a certain sense it was almost accidental—coincidental—that I wrote *The Feminine Mystique*, and in another sense my whole life had prepared me to write that book; all the pieces of my own life came together for the first time in the writing of it.
>
> —Betty Friedan, 1976

In 1951 a labor journalist with a decade's experience in protest movements described a trade union meeting where rank-and-file women talked and men listened. Out of these conversations, she reported, emerged the realization that the women were "fighters—that they refuse any longer to be paid or treated as some inferior species by their bosses, or by any male workers who have swallowed the bosses' thinking."[1] The union was the UE, the United Electrical, Radio and Machine Workers of America, the most radical American union in the postwar period and in the 1940s what historian Ronald Schatz, appreciative of the UE's place in history, has called "the largest Communist-led institution of any kind in the United States."[2] In 1952 that same journalist wrote a pamphlet, *UE Fights for Women Workers*, that the historian Lisa Kannenberg, unaware of the identity of its author, has called "a remarkable manual for fighting wage discrimination that is, ironically, as relevant today as it was in 1952." At the time, the pamphlet helped raise the consciousness of Eleanor Flexner, who in 1959 would publish *Century of Struggle*, the first scholarly history of American women. In 1953–54 Flexner relied extensively on the pamphlet when she taught a course at the Jefferson School of Social Science in New York on "The Woman Question." Flexner's participation in courses at the school, she later said, "marked the beginning of my real involvement in the issues of women's rights, my realization that leftist organizations—parties, unions—were also riddled with male supremacist prejudice and discrimination."[3] The labor journalist and pamphlet writer was Betty Friedan.

In 1973 Friedan remarked that until she started writing *The Feminine Mystique* (published in 1963), "I wasn't even conscious of the woman problem." In 1976 she commented that in the early 1950s she was "still in the embrace of the feminine mystique."[4] Although in 1974 she revealed some potentially controversial elements of her past, even then she left the impression that her landmark book emerged only from her own captivity by the very forces she described. Friedan's portrayal of herself as so totally trapped by the feminine mystique was part of a reinvention of herself as she wrote and promoted *The Feminine Mystique*. Her story made it possible for readers to identify with its author and its author to enhance the book's appeal. However, it hid from view the connection between the union activity in which Friedan participated in the 1940s and early 1950s and the feminism she inspired in the 1960s. In the short term, her misery in the suburbs may have prompted her to write *The Feminine Mystique*; a longer-term perspective makes clear that the book's origins lie much earlier—in her college education and in her experiences with labor unions in the 1940s and early 1950s.[5]

The establishment of an accurate narrative of Betty Friedan's life, especially what she wrote in the 1940s and early 1950s, sheds light on the origins of 1960s feminism. Most historians believe that 1960s feminism emerged from events particular to that decade, but some have argued for a connection between the protest movements of the 1940s and the 1960s.[6] Friedan's life provides evidence of such continuity by suggesting a specific and important connection between the struggle for justice for working women in the 1940s and the feminism of the 1960s. This connection gives feminism and Friedan, both long under attack for a lack of interest in working-class and African American women, a past of which they should be proud.

More generally, understanding *The Feminine Mystique* in light of new information illuminates major aspects of American intellectual and political life in the postwar period. Friedan offered a feminist reworking of important themes in a genre of social criticism, including the notion of a faltering masculine identity. The story of Friedan's life provides additional evidence of the artificiality of the separation of a turbulent 1960s from the supposedly complacent preceding years. Recognition of continuity in Friedan's life gives added weight to the picture that is emerging of ways in which World War II, unions, and those influenced by American radicalism of the 1940s provided some of the seeds of protest movements of the 1960s.[7] At the same time, the continuities between Friedan's labor union activity and her feminism underscore the importance of what George Lipsitz has called "collective memory," the way the experiences of the immediate postwar period later reemerged in unexpected places.[8] Moreover, a new reading of *The Feminine Mystique* sheds light on the remaking of progressive forces in America, the process by which a focus on women and the professional middle and uppermiddle classes supplemented, in some ways replaced, a focus on unions. Finally, an examination of *The Feminine Mystique* reminds us of important shifts in the ideology of the left: from an earlier economic analysis based on Marxism to one developed in the 1950s that also rested on humanistic psychology, and from a focus on the impact of conditions of production on the working class to an emphasis on the effect of consumption on the middle class.

Her Story

In print and in interviews, Friedan has offered a narrative of her life that she popularized after she became famous in 1963.[9] A full biography might begin in Peoria, where Bettye Naomi Goldstein was born on 4 February 1921 and grew up with her siblings and their parents: a father who owned a jewelry store and a mother who had given up her position as a society editor of the local paper to raise a family.[10] My analysis of Friedan's political journey starts with her years at Smith College, although it is important to recognize Friedan's earlier sense of herself as someone whose identity as a Jew, a reader, and a brainy girl made her feel freakish and lonely.[11]

As an undergraduate, she has suggested, her lonely life took a turn for the better. "For the first time," she later remarked of her years in college, "I wasn't a freak for having brains." Friedan has acknowledged that she flourished at Smith, with her editorship of the student newspaper, her election to Phi Beta Kappa in her junior year, and her graduation summa cum laude among her most prominent achievements. She has told the story of how Gestalt psychology and Kurt Koffka (one of its three founders) were critical in her intellectual development.[12]

Friedan has described the years between her graduation from Smith in 1942 and the publication of her book twenty-one years later as a time when the feminine mystique increasingly trapped her. In her book and in dozens of speeches, articles, and interviews beginning in 1963, she mentioned a pivotal moment in her life, one that she felt marked the beginning of the process by which she succumbed. She told how, while in graduate school at Berkeley in the year after her graduation from college, the university's offer of a prestigious fellowship forced her to make a painful choice. Her first serious boyfriend, a graduate student who had not earned a similarly generous award, threatened to break off the relationship unless she turned down her fellowship. "I never could explain, hardly knew myself, why" she turned away from a career in psychology, she wrote in 1963. She decided to reject the fellowship because she saw herself ending up as an "old maid college teacher" in part because at Smith, she said, there were so few female professors who had husbands and children.[13] The feminine mystique, she insisted, had claimed one of its first victims.[14]

After leaving Berkeley, the copy on the dust jacket of *The Feminine Mystique* noted Friedan did some "applied social-science research" and freelance writing for magazines. Friedan's biography in a standard reference book quotes her as saying that in the 1940s "for conscious or unconscious reasons," she worked at "the usual kinds of boring jobs that lead nowhere."[15] This story continues in 1947 with her marriage to Carl Friedan, a returning vet who would eventually switch careers from theater to advertising and public relations. She has told of how she gave birth to three children between 1948 and 1956 and the family moved to the suburbs, with these experiences making her feel trapped. Friedan's picture of her years in the suburbs is not one of contentment and conformity.[16] Though she acknowledged her role in creating and directing a program that brought together teenagers and adult professionals, Friedan portrayed herself as someone who felt "freakish having a career, worried that she was neglecting her children."[17] In an oft-repeated story whose punch line varied, Friedan recounted her response to the census form. In the space where it asked for her occupation, she put down "housewife" but remained guilty, hesitant and conflicted about such a designation; sometimes the story has it that she paused and then added "writer."[18]

Friedan laced *The Feminine Mystique* with suggestions of how much she shared with her suburban sisters. In the opening paragraph, she said that she realized something was wrong in women's lives when she "sensed it first as a question mark in my own life, as a wife and mother of three small children, half-guiltily, and therefore half-heartedly, almost in spite of myself, using my abilities and education in work that took me away from home.[18] Toward the end of the paragraph, when she referred to "a strange discrepancy between the reality of our lives as women and the image to which we were trying to conform," she suggested that she experienced the feminine mystique as keenly and in the same way as her readers. Using the first person plural, she wrote that "all of us went back into the warm brightness of home" and "lowered our eyes from the horizon, and steadily contemplated our own navels." Her work on newspapers, she wrote in *The Feminine Mystique*, proceeded "with no particular plan." Indeed, she claimed that she had participated as a writer in the creation of the image of the happy housewife.[19]

Friedan asserted she embarked on a path that would lead to *The Feminine Mystique* only when, as she read over the responses of her college classmates to a questionnaire in anticipation of their fifteenth reunion in 1957, she discovered what she called "the problem that has no name," the dissatisfaction her suburban peers felt but could not fully articulate. When she submitted articles to women's magazines, Friedan said, editors changed the meaning of what she had written or rejected outright her suggestions for pieces on controversial subjects. Then at a meeting of the Society of Magazine Writers, she heard Vance Packard recount how he had written *The Hidden Persuaders* (1957) after *Reader's Digest* turned down an article critical of advertising. Friedan decided to write her book.[20]

In *"It Changed My Life": Writings on the Women's Movement* (1976), a book that included a 1974 autobiographical article, Friedan suggested some of what she had omitted from earlier versions of her life.[21] Perhaps responding to attacks on her for not being sufficiently radical, she acknowledged that before her marriage and for several years after she participated in radical activities and worked for union publications.[22] She and the friends with whom she lived before marrying considered themselves in "the vanguard of the working-class revolution," participating in "Marxist discussion groups," going to political rallies, and having "only contempt for dreary bourgeois capitalists like our fathers." Without getting much more specific, Friedan noted that right after the war she was "very involved, consciously radical. Not about women, for heaven's sake!" but about African Americans, workers, the threat of war, anti-Communism, and "Communist splits and schisms." This was a time, Friedan reported briefly, when, working as a labor journalist, she discovered "the grubby economic underside of American reality."[23]

"I was certainly not a feminist then—none of us," she remarked in the mid-1970s, "were a bit interested in women's rights." She remembered one incident, whose implications she said she only understood much later. Covering a strike, she could not interest anyone in the fact that the company and the union discriminated against women. In 1952, she later claimed, pregnant with her second child, she was fired from her job on a union publication and told that her second pregnancy was her fault. The Newspaper Guild, she asserted, was unwilling to honor its commitment to grant pregnancy leaves. This was, Friedan later remembered as she mentioned her efforts to call a meeting in protest, "the first personal stirring of my own feminism, I guess. But the other women were just embarrassed, and the men uncomprehending. It was my own fault, getting pregnant again, a *personal* matter, not something you should take to the union. There was no word in 1949 for 'sex discrimination.' "[24]

Though in the 1970s Friedan suggested this more interesting version of her life in the 1940s and 1950s, she distracted the reader from what she had said. She began and ended the 1974 piece with images of domestic life. Even as she mentioned participation in Marxist discussion groups, she talked of how she and her friends read fashion magazines and spent much of their earnings on elegant clothes. Describing what she offered as a major turning point in her life, she told of how, after campaigning for Henry Wallace for president in 1948, all of a sudden she lost interest in political activity. The 1940s and 1950s were a period, she later asserted, when she was fully exposed to what she would label the feminine mystique as she learned that motherhood took the place of career and politics. She gave the impression of herself in the late 1940s as a woman who embraced domesticity, motherhood, and housework, even as she admitted that not everything at the time resulted from the feminine mystique.[25]

In her 1974 article Friedan filled her descriptions of the late 1940s and 1950s with a sense of the conflicts she felt over her new roles, as she surrendered to the feminine mystique with mixed emotions. She reported how wonderful was the time in Parkway Village, Queens, a period when she experienced the pleasure of a spacious apartment, edited the community newspaper, and enjoyed the camaraderie of young marrieds. Yet, having read Benjamin Spock's *Child and Baby Care*, she felt guilty when she returned to work after a maternity leave. With her move to a traditional suburb, she said, the conflicts intensified. She spoke of driving her children to school and lessons, participating in the PTA, and then, when neighbors came by, hiding "like secret drinking in the morning" the book on which she was working.[26]

Accomplishing practical, specific tasks around the house and in local politics was "somehow more real and secure than the schizophrenic and even dangerous politics of the world revolution whose vanguard we used to fancy ourselves." Friedan remarked that by 1949 she realized that the revolution was not going to happen in the United States as she anticipated, in part because workers, like others, wanted kitchen gadgets. She reported that she found herself disillusioned with what was happening in unions, in Czechoslovakia, and in the Soviet Union, despite the fact that cries about the spread of Communism merely provided the pretext for attacks on suspected subversives. In those days, she continued, "McCarthyism, the danger of war against Russia and of fascism in America, and the reality of U.S. imperial, corporate wealth and power" combined to make those who once dreamed of "making the whole world over, uncomfortable with the Old Left rhetoric of revolution." Using the first person plural as she referred to Margaret Mead's picture in *Male and Female* of women fulfilled through motherhood and domesticity, Friedan wrote, "we were suckers for that apple." It hardly occurred to any of those in her circle, who themselves now wanted new gadgets, that large corporations profited from marketing household appliances by "overselling us on the bliss of domesticity."[27]

The new information Friedan offered in 1974 did not dislodge the accepted understanding of how she became a feminist. Historians and journalists have repeated Friedan's narrative of her life, though they have occasionally offered evidence for an alternative script.[28] In 1983 Marilyn French wrote of Friedan's decision not to "spend her life sorrowing over a lost career: She would embrace the man, the home, the children, and live in a bath of felicity." In 1991 the historian of feminism Donald Meyer skipped over her years as a labor journalist and wrote that Friedan herself was "the exemplary victim of the feminine mystique." Similarly, in his 1993 book *The Fifties*, David Halberstam covered nine years of Friedan's career as a labor journalist with the sentence "Betty Goldstein worked as a reporter for a left-wing paper."[29] Yet data that could have provided a different interpretation has been available for a number of years: in what she published as a Smith student, as a labor journalist, and later as a freelance author; in what Friedan herself said in 1974; and in what her personal papers, opened since 1986, contained.

An Alternative Story: Betty Goldstein, Class of '42

What the written record reveals of Friedan's life from her arrival at Smith in the fall of 1938 until the publication of *The Feminine Mystique* makes possible a story different from the one she has told. To begin with, usually missing from her narrative is full and specific information about how at college she first developed a sense of herself as a radical.[30] Courses she took, friendships she established with peers and professors, events in the United States and abroad, and her campus leadership all turned Friedan from a provincial outsider into a determined advocate of trade unions as the herald of progressive social change, a healthy skeptic about the authority and rhetorical claims of those in power, a staunch opponent of fascism, a defender of free speech, and a fierce questioner of the social privilege expressed by the conspicuous consumption of some of her peers.[31]

What and with whom she studied points well beyond Gestalt psychology and Koffka.[32] Though Friedan acknowledged the importance of James Gibson, she did not mention his activity as an advocate of trade unions.[33] Moreover, her statement that at Smith there were few role models is hard to reconcile with the fact that the college had a number of them; indeed, she took courses from both James Gibson and Eleanor Gibson, husband and wife and parents of two children, the first of them born in 1940.[34] As a women's college, and especially one with an adversarial tradition, Smith may well have fostered in Friedan a feminism that was at least implicit—by enabling her to assume leadership positions and by encouraging her to take herself seriously as a writer and thinker.

In the fall of her junior year, Friedan took an economics course taught by Dorothy W. Douglas, Theories and Movements for Social Reconstruction. Douglas was well known at the time for her radicalism.[35] In what she wrote for Douglas, and with youthful enthusiasm characteristic of many members of her generation, Friedan sympathetically responded to the Marxist critique of capitalism as a cultural, economic, and political force.[36]

Friedan also gained an education as a radical in the summer of 1941 when, following Douglas's suggestion, she participated in a writers' workshop at the Highlander Folk School in Tennessee, an institution active in helping the Congress of Industrial Organizations (CIO) organize in the South. The school offered a series of summer institutes for fledgling journalists which, for 1939 and 1940 (but not 1941), the Communist-led League of American Writers helped sponsor. For three years beginning in the fall of 1939, opponents of Highlander had sustained a vicious red-baiting attack, but an FBI investigator found no evidence of subversive activity.[37] In good Popular Front language, Friedan praised Highlander as a truly American institution that was attempting to help America to fulfill its democratic ideals. She explored the contradictions of her social position as a Jewish girl from a well-to-do family who had grown up in a class-divided Peoria, gave evidence of her hostility to the way her parents fought over issues of debt and extravagance, and described the baneful influence of the mass media on American life. Though she also acknowledged that her Smith education did "not lead to much action," she portrayed herself as someone whose radical consciousness relied on the American labor movement as the bulwark against fascism.[38]

At Smith, Friedan linked her journalism to political activism. She served as editor-in-chief of the campus newspaper for a year beginning in the spring of 1941. The campaigns she undertook and the editorials she wrote reveal a good deal of her politics. Under Friedan's leadership, the newspaper's reputation for protest was so strong that in a skit a fellow student portrayed an editor, perhaps Friedan herself, as "a strident voice haranguing from a perpetual soap-box."[39] While at Smith, a Peoria paper reported in 1943, Friedan helped organize college building and grounds workers into a union.[40] Under her leadership, the student paper took on the student government for holding closed meetings, fought successfully to challenge the administration's right to control what the newspaper printed, campaigned for the relaxation of restrictions on student social life, censured social clubs for their secrecy, and published critiques of professors' teaching.[41] In response to an article in a campus humor magazine that belittled female employees who cleaned the students' rooms and served them food, an editorial supported the administration's censorship of the publication on the grounds that such action upheld "the liberal democratic tradition of the college."[42]

The editorials written on her watch reveal a young woman who believed that what was involved with almost every issue—at Smith, in the United States, and abroad—was the struggle for democracy, freedom, and social justice. Under Friedan's leadership the editors supported American workers and their labor unions in their struggles to organize and improve their conditions. With an advertisement for a dress in which students could "TWIRL AWAY AT TEA-TIME!" on the same page, one editorial asserted that life, liberty, and the pursuit of happiness meant very different things to employers and employees. The inequality of power in America, the editorial argued in good social democratic terms, "has to be admitted and dealt with if democracy is to have meaning for 95% of the citizens of this country."[43]

Above all, what haunted the editorials was the spread of fascism and questions about America's involvement in a world war. In April of 1941 the editors made it clear that the defeat of fascism was their primary goal and one that determined their position on questions of war or peace. In the fall of 1941, after the German invasion of the Soviet Union during the preceding summer, the editors increasingly accepted the inevitability of war even as they made it clear that they believed "fighting fascists is only one part of fighting fascism."[44] Some Smith students responded with red-baiting to the newspaper's antifascism and reluctance to support intervention whole-heartedly, accusing the editorial board of being dominated by Communists, at a time when the Communist Party reached its greatest membership in the years after Pearl Harbor while the United States and the Soviet Union were allies. Though one editor denied the charge of Communist influence, on the paper's staff were students attracted to the political analysis offered by radical groups; this was true of many newspapers at American colleges in these years. In the fall of 1940 one columnist argued against lumping Communists and Nazis together, remarking that Communism was not a "dark terror" but "a precarious scheme worked out by millions of civilized men and women."[45]

When America entered the war in December 1941, the editors accepted the nation's new role loyally, albeit soberly. The central issue for them was how American students, especially female ones, could "contribute *actively* to the American cause." Those in charge of the newspaper found academic life "detached and fruitless." Lamenting student reluctance to make serious sacrifices, the editorial writers were mindful of their privileged positions and retained their commitment to the well-being of working-class women, even when it meant they might have to clean their own rooms or work in campus kitchens. They insisted that any new arrangement not force into unemployment the hundreds of women whose jobs student sacrifice might threaten. By her senior year, Friedan and her peers conveyed a sense that they were chafing against the isolation of Smith College from the world of action and were eager to find ways to act upon their commitments.[46] When she left Smith, she dropped the final *e* from her first name, perhaps a symbolic statement that she was no longer a girl from Peoria.

Betty Goldstein: Labor Journalist

Friedan's experiences at Smith cast a different light on her decision to leave Berkeley after a year of graduate school. The editorials she and her peers had written immediately after Pearl Harbor revealed an impatience to be near the action. A 1943 article in the Peoria paper reported that Friedan turned down the fellowship because "she decided she wanted to work in the labor movement—on the labor press."[47] Another issue doubtlessly affected her decision to leave Berkeley. When her father accused her of immorality while she was home at Christmas vacation, she was so upset that she returned to Berkeley without saying goodbye to him. A few days later, on 11 January 1943, he died at age sixty-one.[48]

The period that Friedan has treated most summarily in her narrative covers the years from 1943 to 1952, when she worked as a labor journalist. Off and on from October 1943 until July 1946 she was a staff writer for the Federated Press, a left-wing news service that provided stories for newspapers, especially union ones, across the nation.[49] Here Friedan wrote articles that supported the aspirations of African Americans and union members. She also criticized reactionary forces that, she believed, were working secretly to undermine progressive social advances.[50] As early as 1943 she pictured efforts by businesses, coordinated by the National Association of Manufacturers, to develop plans that would enhance profits, diminish the power of unions, reverse the New Deal, and allow businesses to operate as they pleased.[51]

At the Federated Press, Friedan also paid attention to women's problems. Right after she began to work there, she interviewed UE official Ruth Young, one of the clearest voices in the labor movement articulating women's issues. In the resulting article, Friedan noted that the government could not solve the problem of turnover "merely by plthning up thousands of glamorous posters designed to lure more women into industry." Neither women, unions, nor management, she quoted Young as saying, could solve problems of escalating prices or inadequate child care that were made even more difficult by the fact that "women still have two jobs to do." Action by the federal government, Friedan reported was needed to solve the problems working women faced.[52] In the immediate postwar period, she pictured the wife in a union family as more savvy than her husband in figuring out how large corporations took advantage of the consumer.[53] She paid special attention to stories about protecting the jobs and improving the situation of working women, including married ones with children.

For about six years beginning in July 1946, precisely at the moment when the wartime Popular Front came under intense attack, Friedan was a reporter for the union's paper, *UE News*.[54] At least as early as 1943, when she quoted Young, Friedan was well aware of the UE's commitments to equity for women.[55] Friedan's years on *UE News*, which made her familiar with radicalism in the 1940s and early 1950s, provided a seedbed for her feminism. Her writings in the 1940s and early 1950s reveal that although she did not focus on the Soviet Union or on American-Soviet relations, Popular Front ideology shaped the way Friedan viewed American society and politics. As Flexner said of her own work for justice for working-class and African American women from the 1930s to the 1950s, left-wing movements welcomed "an enormous latitude of opinions under a very broad umbrella."[56] Specific political affiliation was not important; what was critical was commitment to a broad range of issues within the framework of a fight for social justice. The end of the cold war makes it possible to look at the left in the 1940s without the baggage of red-baiting. Indeed, the world in which Friedan moved in the 1940s and early 1950s was varied, containing as it did Communist Party members, pacificists, socialists, union activists, fighters for justice for African Americans—and at *UE News*, Katherine Beecher, the grandniece of the nineteenth-century feminist Catharine Beecher.[57]

In the immediate postwar period, the UE fought for justice for African Americans and women.[58] In 1949–50, union activists who followed the recommendations of the Communist Party, torn in the postwar years by bitter internal divisions, advocated the automatic granting of several years of seniority to all African Americans as compensation for their years of exclusion from the electrical industry. If the UE pioneered in articulating what we might call affirmative action for African Americans, then before and during World War II it advocated what a later generation would label comparable worth. Against considerable resistance from within its ranks, the UE also worked to improve the conditions of working-class women, in part by countering a seniority system that gave advantage to men.[59] After 1949, with the UE out of the CIO and many of the more conservative union members out of the UE, women's issues and women's leadership resumed the importance they had had in the UE during World War II, when it had developed, Ruth Milkman has written, a "strong ideological commitment to gender equality."[60]

Beginning in 1946, Friedan witnessed the efforts by federal agencies, congressional committees, major corporations, the Roman Catholic Church, and the CIO to break the hold of what they saw as the domination of the UE by Communists. The inclusion of a clause in the Taft-Hartley Act of 1947, requiring union officers to sign an anti-Communist affidavit if they wished to do business with the National Labor Relations Board, helped encourage other unions to challenge the UE, whose leaders refused to sign.[61] Internecine fights took place within the UE, part of a longer-term fight between radicals and anti-Communists in its ranks. One anti-Communist long active in the union spoke of how a Communist minority "seized control of the national office, the executive board, the paid staff, the union newspaper and some district councils and locals." The division in union ranks had reverberations in national politics as well: In 1948 the anti-Communists supported President Harry S. Truman, while their opponents campaigned for Henry Wallace. In the short term the attack on the UE intensified its commitment to equity for working women, something that grew out of both ideological commitments and practical considerations. Before long, however, the UE was greatly weakened: In 1949 its connection with the CIO was severed and the newly formed and CIO-backed IUE recruited many of its members. Membership in UE, numbering more than 600,000 in 1946, fell to 203,000 in 1953 and to 71,000 four years later.[62]

Reading the pages of *UE News* in the late 1940s and early 1950s opens a world unfamiliar to those who think that in this period Americans heard only hosannas to American exceptionalism. The villains of the publication were Truman, Hubert H. Humphrey, Richard M. Nixon, Walter Reuther, the House Un-American Activities Committee (HUAC), and American capitalists. The heroes included Wallace, Franklin D. Roosevelt, and union leaders who fought to protect the rights and lives of working people. Above all, the paper celebrated ordinary workers, including women and African Americans, who found themselves engaged in a class struggle against greedy corporations and opportunistic politicians.

At *UE News*, from her position as a middle-class woman interested in the lives of the working class, Friedan continued to articulate a progressive position on a wide range of issues. She again pointed to concerted efforts, led by big corporations under the leadership of the NAM, to increase profits, exploit labor, and break labor unions.[63] In 1951 she contrasted the extravagant expenditures of the wealthy with the family of a worker who could afford neither fresh vegetables nor new clothes.[64] Friedan also told the story of how valiant union members helped build political coalitions to fight congressional and corporate efforts to roll back gains workers made during the New Deal and World War II.[65] She drew parallels between the United States in the

1940s and Nazi Germany in the 1930s as she exposed the way HUAC and big business were using every tactic they could to destroy the UE. Friedan hailed the launching of the Progressive Party in 1948.[66] She exposed the existence of racism and discrimination, even when they appeared among union officials and especially when directed against Jews and African Americans. Praising heroic workers who struggled against great odds as they fought monopolies, Friedan, probably expressing her hopes for herself, extolled the skills of a writer "who is able to describe with sincerity and passion the hopes, the struggle and the romance of the working people who make up most of America."[67]

Throughout her years at *UE News*, Friedan participated in discussions on women's issues, including the issue of corporations' systematic discrimination against women. Going to factories to interview those whose stories she was covering, she also wrote about working women, including African Americans and Latinas.[68] In the worlds Friedan inhabited in the decade beginning in 1943, as the historian Kathleen Weigand has shown, people often discussed the cultural and economic sources of women's oppression, the nature of discrimination based on sex, the special difficulties African American women faced, and the dynamics of discrimination against women in a variety of institutions, including the family.[69] Moreover, for the people around Friedan and doubtless for Friedan herself, the fight for justice for women was inseparable from the more general struggle to secure rights for African Americans and workers.[70] As she had done at the Federated Press, at *UE News* in the late 1940s and early 1950s she reported on how working women struggled as producers and consumers to make sure their families had enough on which to live.[71]

Friedan's focus on working women's issues resulted in her writing the pamphlet *UE Fights for Women Workers*, published by the UE in June 1952.[72] She began by suggesting the contradiction in industry's treatment of women as consumers and as producers. "In advertisements across the land," Friedan remarked, "industry glorifies the American woman—in her gleaming GE kitchen, at her Westinghouse laundromat, before her Sylvania television set. Nothing," she announced as she insightfully explored a central contradiction women faced in the postwar world, "is too good for her—unless" she worked for corporations, including GE, or Westinghouse, or Sylvania.[73]

The central theme of the piece was how, in an effort to improve the pay and conditions of working women, the UE fought valiantly against greedy corporations that sought to increase their profits by exploiting women. Friedan discussed a landmark 1945 National War Labor Board decision against sex-based wage discrimination in favor of the UE. Remarking that "*fighting the exploitation of women is men's business too*," she emphasized how the discriminatory practices that corporations used against women hurt men as well by exerting downward pressure on the wages of all workers. To back up the call for equal pay for equal work and to fight against segregation and discrimination of women, she countered stereotypes justifying lower pay for women: They were physically weaker, entered the workforce only temporarily, had no families to support, and worked only for pin money. She highlighted the "even more shocking" situation African American women faced, having to deal as they did with the "double bars" of being female and African American.[74] Friedan set forth a program that was, Lisa Kannenberg has noted, "a prescription for a gender-blind workplace."[75]

Nor did Friedan's interest in working women end with the publication of this pamphlet. For a brief period she worked as a freelance labor journalist. In the winter of 1952–53 she was probably the author of a series of articles for *Jewish Life: Progressive Monthly*. These pieces were somewhat more radical in tone than those Friedan had written for *UE News*, in part because her foil was the International Ladies' Garment Workers' Union, whose commitment to women workers and progressive politics was no match for the UE's. She explored the contradiction of a situation where wealthy women dressed in clothes working-class women labored to produce. She told a story of rising profits and declining wages in a union that had, she argued, taken a conciliatory position with employers.[76] Then, in May 1953, she carefully tracked and probably participated in what a historian has said "appears to be one of the first national women's conferences in the postwar era."[77] There Friedan followed discussions of the importance of sharing household duties. She also heard of the efforts of profit-hungry corporations to divide the working class by emphasizing divisions between whites and African Americans as well as between men and women. She again learned of the union's advocacy of federal legislation to lower military expenditures and support programs for child care, maternity benefits, and equal pay.[78]

Friedan's association with the labor movement gave her a sustained education in issues of sexual discrimination and shaped her emergence as a feminist. However, the precise impact of the influence is not clear. If, as some historians have suggested, the UE remained committed to gender equality, then Friedan's years as a labor journalist may well have provided a positive inspiration.[79] In contrast, the historian Nancy Palmer has argued that women in the UE persistently faced difficulties when they articulated their grievances but, in the name of solidarity, were told not to rock the boat.[80] Such a situation might mean that her experience with radical organizations that could not live up to their vision of a just and egalitarian society served more as a negative spur than a positive inspiration. At both the Federated Press and *UE News*, she lost her jobs to men who had more seniority, a general policy issue that had concerned the UE at least since the early 1940s.

The conditions under which she left the Federated Press and *UE News* are not entirely clear. In May 1946, during her second stint at the Federated Press, she filed a grievance with the Newspaper Guild, saying she had lost her job in June 1945 to a man she had replaced during the war. Later she claimed she was "bumped" from her position "by a returning veteran." There is evidence, however, that Friedan had to give up her position to a man who returned to the paper after two years in prison because he refused to serve in the military during what he considered a capitalists' war.[81] Friedan later claimed that she lost her job at the UE during her second pregnancy because the labor movement failed to honor its commitment to maternity leaves. Yet a knowledgeable observer has written that when the union had to cut the staff because of the dramatic drop in its membership, something that resulted from McCarthyite attacks, Friedan "offered to quit so another reporter," a man with more seniority, could remain at *UE News*.[82] Although her experience with unions may have provided a negative spur to her feminism, it also served as a positive inspiration. Friedan was indebted to the UE for major elements of her education about gender equity, sex discrimination, and women's issues.

The reason Friedan left out these years in her life story is now clear. Her stint at the *UE News* took place at the height of the anti-Communist crusade, which she experienced at close quarters. When she emerged into the limelight in 1963, the issue of affiliation with Communists was wracking the Committee for a Sane Nuclear Policy (SANE), Students for a Democratic Society (SDS), and the civil rights movement. In the same years, HUAC was still holding hearings, the United States was pursuing an anti-Communist war in Vietnam, and J. Edgar Hoover's FBI was wiretapping Martin Luther King Jr., ostensibly to protect the nation against Communist influence. Had Friedan revealed all in the mid-1960s, she would have undercut her book's impact, subjected herself to palpable dangers, and jeopardized the feminist movement, including the National Organization for Women (NOW), an institution she was instrumental in launching. Perhaps instead of emphasizing continuities in her life, she told the story of her conversion in order to heighten the impact of her book and appeal to white middle-class women. Or maybe, having participated in social movements that did not live up to her dreams, in *The Feminine Mystique*, whether consciously or not, she was trying to mobilize middle-class readers and thus prove something to the men on the left. When constructing a narrative, she may have adopted a convention that made it difficult to discuss anger, ambition, excitement, and power.[83] Why she did not tell her full story between the early 1970s and the present raises other issues. Some of the explanation lies with her ongoing commitment to accomplishing urgent tasks as a writer and political figure. Perhaps she hoped to write a memoir that would have the impact of her 1963 book. The way a participant remembers events is bound to differ from the way a historian recovers them, largely from written records. Friedan may have come to believe a narrative that outlived the needs it originally fulfilled.

Betty Friedan: Freelance Writer and Housewife

Until 1952, almost everything Friedan published as a labor journalist appeared under the name Betty Goldstein, though she had married in 1947. When she emerged as a writer for women's magazines in 1955, it was as Betty Friedan. Aside from indicating her marital status, the change in name was significant. It signaled a shift from an employee for a union paper who wrote highly political articles on the working class to a freelance writer for mass-circulation magazines who concentrated on the suburban middle class in more muted tones.

Around 1950 the Friedans moved from the Upper West Side of Manhattan to Parkway Village in Queens.[84] Developed to house United Nations personnel from around the world and the families of returning veterans, this apartment complex contained a cosmopolitan mix of people, including diplomats, American Jews, and African Americans.[85] For two years beginning in February 1952, Friedan edited *The Parkway Villager*, transforming it from a chatty source of community news into an activist publication.[86] Beginning in the spring of 1952, she led an extended protest and rent strike, actions she couched in terms of protecting an authentic community from greedy bankers. Something else enriched Friedan's perspective in the years after she stopped working for the UE. Shortly after its 1953 publication in English, Friedan appreciatively read Simone de Beauvoir's *The Second Sex*. Yet when she mentioned this later, she did not point to the book's Marxism or to the author's politics. Instead in *The Feminine Mystique* she hailed its "insights into French women," and in 1975 she stated that from it she learned "my own existentialism."[87]

In the 1950s the Friedans spent many weekends trying to find another place to live that had an authentic sense of community. With other families they explored the possibility of creating a communal group of homes north of New York City.[88] After the birth of a third child in May 1956, the Friedans accepted a more individualistic solution, moving later that year to a stone barn in Sneden's Landing, on the west side of the Hudson in Rockland County, New York, just above the New Jersey border. A year later they settled in nearby Grandview, in an eleven-room Victorian house, which they bought with the help of the GI Bill and some money Friedan inherited from her father.[89]

What Friedan wrote for mass-circulation women's magazines belies her claim that she had contributed to what she later attacked in *The Feminine Mystique*. Joanne Meyerowitz, relying on a systematic analysis of articles in widely read periodicals, has called into question Friedan's assertion that articles such as the ones she wrote and then later attacked fostered the worst kind of cold war ideology that focused on domesticity and togetherness.[90] Meyerowitz has demonstrated that pieces such as the ones Friedan authored actually "expressed overt admiration for women whose individual striving moved them beyond the home," in the process supporting women's work outside the home and women's activity in politics. As a result, Meyerowitz has enabled us to see that mass-circulation magazines, even as they advocated domesticity and femininity, portrayed women as independent, creative, and nonconformist. Moreover, she has demonstrated that Friedan's work, "remarkably rooted in postwar culture," had resonance for contemporaries because it both relied on and reformulated what others had stated.[91]

An examination of Friedan's articles adds weight to Meyerowitz's conclusions.[92] By the mid-1950s Friedan was achieving success as a writer. Sylvie Murray has demonstrated that Friedan drafted, but was unable to get into print, articles that fully celebrated women's political activism, expressed skepticism about male expertise, and described blue-collar and lower-middle-class families, not generic middle-class ones. Yet Friedan was able to sell articles that went against the grain of the cold war celebration by criticizing middle-class conformity. The pieces she published between 1955 and the early 1960s reveal a woman who was thinking about how to find authentic community life, satisfactory motherhood, and a productive career. Friedan critiqued suburban life by drawing a dismal picture of those who conformed, by offering alternatives to conventional choices, and by exploring the strength of cooperative communities.[93] She drew portraits of American women that opposed the picture of the happy suburban housewife who turned her back on a career in order to find satisfaction at home.[94] Friedan also portrayed women accomplishing important tasks as they took on traditionally feminine civic roles, thus implicitly undercutting the ideal of the apolitical suburban housewife and mother.[95] The theme of independent women also emerged in an unpublished piece that was an illuminating precursor of *The Feminine Mystique*. "Was Their Education UnAmerican?" relied on a questionnaire Friedan's Smith classmates filled out for their tenth reunion. She repudiated McCarthyism and upheld academic freedom by showing that, despite exposure to radicalism in college, many of her peers were conservatives who took seriously their obligations as citizens.[96]

In one particularly revealing piece, Friedan prefigured some of the issues she later claimed she began to discover only when she started to work on *The Feminine Mystique*. In "I Went Back to Work," published in *Charm* in April 1955, she wrote that initially she did not think highly of housework or of housewives and felt guilty about what she was doing. Eventually she decided that her commitment to being a good mother was not "going to interfere with what I regarded as my 'real' life." Finding it necessary to be away from home for nine hours a day in order to work, she solved the problem of child care by hiring "a really good mother-substitute—a housekeeper-nurse." In the end, Friedan had no regrets about her decision or apparently about her privileged position. She believed her work outside the home improved her family's situation and acknowledged that her "whole life had always been geared around creative, intellectual work" and "a professional career."[97] A revealing bridge between Friedan's community activity in the 1940s and *The Feminine Mystique* was a 1957 article in *Parents' Magazine*. Here Friedan told the story of a group of women who lived in a housing project an hour from Manhattan and organized a day camp for their children. In the process, the mothers demonstrated their ability to work cooperatively without replicating hierarchical organizations and developed a model for a cross-class summer camp for urban children.[98]

In what ways, then, was Friedan a captive of the feminine mystique? There is no question but that she was miserable in the suburbs. Her emphasis on her captivity may have expressed one part of her ambivalence. Yet though she claimed that she shared so much with her suburban white middle-class sisters in the postwar world, during much of the two decades beginning in 1943 Friedan was participating in left-wing union activity, writing articles that went against the grain of cold war ideology, and living in a cosmopolitan, racially integrated community. During most of the time between her marriage in 1947 and the publication of *The Feminine Mystique*, Friedan combined career and family life. As a woman who worked with her at the Federated Press later noted, at the time Friedan and her female colleagues expected to have professional careers.[99] Caution about the predominantly suburban origins of her book is also in order because Friedan's move to suburban Rockland County in 1956 preceded by only a few months her initial work on the survey for her reunion that was so critical to *The Feminine Mystique*.[100]

To be sure, in the postwar world Friedan experienced at first hand the trials of a woman who fought against considerable odds to combine marriage, motherhood, and a career.[101] Yet in critical ways her difficulties did not stem from the dilemmas she described in her book: lack of career and ambition, a securely affluent household, and absence of a political sensibility. Friedan experienced psychological conflicts over issues of creativity in writing and motherhood.[102] Researching and writing her freelance articles was a laborious process.[103] She had three young children, hardly felt comfortable in the suburbs, had no local institutions to provide a supportive environment for an aspiring writer, and continually faced financial difficulties. Her income from writing articles was unpredictable, a situation exacerbated by the pressure she was under to help support the household and justify the expenses for child care. Tension persisted between the Friedans over a wide range of issues, including who was responsible for earning and spending the family's income. Moreover, she was in a marriage apparently marked by violence.[104]

Rereading *The Feminine Mystique*

Friedan was largely right when she said "all the pieces of my own life came together for the first time in the writing" of *The Feminine Mystique*. The skills as a journalist she had developed beginning as a teenager stood her in good stead as she worked to make what she had to say accessible to a wide audience. Her identity as a Jew and an outsider gave her a distinctive perspective on American and suburban life. Her years at Smith boosted her confidence and enhanced her political education. Her life as a wife and mother sensitized her to the conflicts millions of others experienced but could not articulate. Her education as a psychologist led her to understand the gestalt, the wholeness of a situation, and to advocate self-fulfillment based on humanistic psychology. Above all, her work as a labor journalist and activist provided her with the intellectual depth, ideological commitments, and practical experiences crucial to her emergence as a leading feminist in the 1960s.

Why did a woman who had spent so much energy advocating political solutions focus in *The Feminine Mystique* largely on adult education and self-realization and turn social problems into psychological ones? How did a woman who had fought to improve the lives of African Americans, Latinas, and working-class women end up writing a book that saw the problems of America in terms of the lives of affluent, suburban white women?[105]

Even at the time, at least one observer, Gerda Lerner, raised questions about what Friedan emphasized and neglected. Active in the trade union movement in the 1940s, present at the founding meeting of NOW, and after the mid 1960s one of the nation's leading historians of women, Lerner wrote Friedan in February 1963. "I have just finished reading your splendid book and want to tell you how excited and delighted I am with it. . . . You have done for women," she remarked, "what Rachel Carson did for birds and trees," referring to the author who had warned about the destruction of the environment. Yet, Lerner continued,

> I have one reservation about your treatment of your subject: you address yourself solely to the problems of middle class, college-educated women. This approach was one of the shortcomings of the suffrage movement for many years and has, I believe, retarded the general advance of women. Working women, especially Negro women, labor not only under the disadvantages imposed by the feminine mystique, but under the more pressing disadvantages of economic discrimination. To leave them out of consideration of the problem or to ignore the contributions they can make toward its solution, is something we simply cannot afford to do. By their desperate need, by their numbers, by their organizational experience (if trade union members), working women are most important in reaching *institutional* solutions to the problems of women.[106]

The dynamics of Friedan's shifts in attention from working-class to middle-class women are not entirely clear. At some point after May 1953, when she followed the proceedings at the UE conference on the problems of women workers, Friedan turned away from working-class and African American women, something that undercut the power of *The Feminine Mystique*. An important question is whether the shift from her UE radicalism and focus on working-class women was a rhetorical strategy designed for the specific situation of *The Feminine Mystique* or part of a longer-term deradicalization. Until her personal papers are fully open and extensive interviewing is carried out, and perhaps not even then, we may not know the dynamics of this change. Among the things that call for examination is what role her distinctive and in some ways privileged social position—Peoria, merchant's daughter, Smith College—played in the change in her stance.[107]

Given what Friedan wrote and observed for the UE as late as 1953, the obliteration from *The Feminine Mystique* of the experiences of a wider range of women is quite striking.[108] After the mid-1950s Friedan never returned to working-class women and labor unions as the primary or even major objects of her attention. In the mid-1950s Friedan may have undergone some deradicalization, although her departure from radical commitments, unlike those of many contemporaries, did not result in her becoming a conservative. Possibly, behind what she wrote in *The Feminine Mystique* was a series of events that burned her out politically and made her skeptical about how seriously American labor unions, even radical ones, took their commitment to advance the cause of women.

Whatever may yet be learned of Friedan's personal life and political journey, along with shifts in her politics and the consequences of McCarthyism, issues of genre, audience, and persona go a long way in explaining why *The Feminine Mystique* did not more accurately reflect her experience. During much of her life, but especially for the ten years beginning in 1953, Friedan thought of herself primarily as a writer, a professional journalist looking for the story that would increase her income and make her career. From her teenage years on, she had developed a keen understanding of her readers and of a variety of genres. Three children and an upper-middle-class life to support, as well as conflicts with her husband over issues of breadwinning, make understandable the change in the focus of her writing that resulted from the necessity to use her skills as a writer to generate income. She cast *The Feminine Mystique*, and her situation in the world it described, as part of an effort to enhance the book's popularity and impact.

With *The Feminine Mystique*, she was writing for a middle-class audience that had certain expectations about social criticism. She and her publishers thought her book might have the same kind of reverberations as William W. Whyte Jr.'s *The Organization Man* (1955) and Vance Packard's *The Status Seekers* (1959).[109] To that list, she might have added David Riesman's *The Lonely Crowd* (1950), on which she drew extensively. What Friedan's book shared with these best-sellers accounts to some extent for her shift in focus from her earlier political positions. Friedan adapted what they had written about suburban, middle-class men to their female counterparts. Like them, Friedan held a mirror up to Americans, both frightening and encouraging them with the shock of recognition. With them, she assumed that the problem resulted from the struggle to enhance identity amid widely experienced affluence, not from the prevalence of poverty or discrimination.[110]

Central to *The Feminine Mystique* was a series of issues about which her male counterparts had also written but on which her history could have given her a different perspective. Like her predecessors, she psychologized social problems and considered identity and mythology but not social structure as the principal impediments to a coherent identity. Friedan followed others with a book that was longer on analysis designed to shock readers than on public policies that provided solutions.[111] Consequently, in her last chapter, she offered "A New Life Plan for Women." Having acknowledged the importance of some policy issues, she ended by emphasizing how women should break the mental chains of the feminine mystique in order to achieve fuller self-realization.[112]

Nonetheless, Friedan's book contained themes that drew on what she had learned in the 1930s, 1940s, and 1950s. *The Feminine Mystique* had two autobiographical narratives. One, which provided its spine and strengthened its appeal, suggested that Friedan herself experienced uncertainty, blocked career mobility, and an identity crisis throughout her adult life.[113] The second, for which Friedan provided the evidence though she kept the plot line and its relevance to her life obscure, involved a concerted effort by men and corporations to suppress the aspirations of women. Throughout her book, although she had the evidence to do so, Friedan drew back from declaring that men—as fathers, husbands, editors, psychologists, social scientists, educators, corporate heads, and advertising executives—had coordinated the postwar counterrevolution against women.[114] Friedan could not highlight this second story for several reasons. As a labor journalist (and later as a nationally known feminist), Friedan argued for building coalitions of men and women to fight for social justice. Any process of deradicalization she had undergone may have impelled her to hedge her discussion of a capitalist conspiracy. More immediately, she may have felt that to have developed the idea of a conspiracy more fully would have undermined the book's impact, given what middle-class women supposedly believed about their situations at the time. Friedan had to hide her own radical past and create a believable persona. Perhaps guessing at how far she might push an audience whose consciousness she wished to raise, she decided that she had to temper her position.

Still, not very hidden in her book was a simplified Marxist view of ideological domination. In the pivotal chapter of her second and more radical narrative, titled "The Sexual Sell," the task she set for herself was to explain the "powerful forces" served by the feminine mystique. What, she asked, undermined the force of feminism and fueled the retreat of women into the privatism of the suburban home? In seeking an answer, Friedan articulated arguments congruent with what she learned from Dorothy W. Douglas and as a labor journalist. Friedan thus provided a bridge between the discussions in radical circles of the 1940s about the problems women faced and the feminism that many women would articulate in the late 1960s. Because of the importance of business in America, she said at the beginning of the chapter, making purchases for the home was the housewives' crucial function. Since women were "the chief customers of American business," she argued, "somehow, somewhere, someone must have figured out that" they would purchase more "if they are kept in the underused, nameless-yearning, energy-to-get-rid-of state of being housewives." Having hinted at the possibility of a conspiracy in which the heads of major corporations decided to mount a campaign to keep women home so they would consume household products, Friedan then ducked the logic of her argument and evidence. "Conspiratorial theories of history," she wrote in a way that differed from her 1940s and early 1950s attacks on the postwar plans of the NAM, were not adequate to explain what she had observed.[115]

Having examined a range of strategies adopted by corporations, Friedan concluded her consideration of the sexual sell by using rhetorical strategies that offered vague hints of larger issues. She suggested that America was a "sick society," not willing to confront its problems or see its purposes in terms commensurate with the ambitions of its citizens, including women.[116] Like the young radicals who wrote the Port Huron Statement for SDS in 1962, Friedan seemed unable to utter the word *capitalism.* Though C. Wright Mills in *The Power Elite* (1956) went farther in exploring how elites operated undemocratically, Friedan provided the evidence for such an analysis and then hinted at what it would mean for a male power elite to suppress women systematically.

This second narrative emerged elsewhere. Without mentioning her version of her own experience, Friedan talked of the transformative power of women's experience in World War II. She wrote at one point that "women were often driven embittered" from their jobs by returning veterans. Ever since the end of World War II, she asserted, "a propaganda campaign, as unanimous in this democratic nation as in the most efficient of dictatorships," had exalted the prestige of housework. Although others would date the counterrevolution against women to the 1920s or 1930s, Friedan focused on the late 1940s, a period linked in her own experience with a time when cold warriors undermined the left and, more specifically, the UE's fight for justice for women. She explored the alienating nature of women's work, not in factories but in suburban homes. She talked about the "devastating" effects of discrimination against women. At one moment, also without mentioning herself, she spoke of women of her generation, who, though not focusing on women's rights, were "still concerned with human rights and freedom—for Negroes, for oppressed workers, for victims of Franco's Spain and Hitler's Germany."[117]

There were other suggestions of a radical analysis. Absent from the book was any hint of a critique of the Soviet Union or a celebration of Cold War America. Indeed, Friedan's phrase "comfortable concentration camp" invoked the antifascism that she had articulated at Smith. In addition, perhaps the call for women to express themselves on public issues was a code for the politics she could not openly express. Rejecting a narcissistic version of self-fulfillment, Friedan instead emphasized that people fulfilled themselves by pursuing "a human purpose larger than themselves." She argued that people developed a healthy identity not through routine work, but by purposeful and committed effort outside the confines of the home. She insisted that it was important to recognize that there were still battles to fight in the United States. Institutions of higher education would have to make provision for people, women especially, whose lives did not fit easily into the pattern of college completion by age twenty-two, followed directly by a career. Drawing on her UE experience, Friedan also briefly mentioned the importance of enabling married women with children to have "the right to honorable competition" by providing maternity leaves, "professionally run nurseries, and the other changes in the rules that may be necessary."[118]

Others will assume the task of rethinking Friedan's post-1963 career in light of new evidence, but several comments are in order. In important ways, *The Feminine Mystique* marked a brief interlude in Friedan's longer-term political commitments. In the early 1950s the UE agenda included many of the commitments that Friedan would return to beginning in the mid-1960s: opposition to government infiltration into social movements, the end of racial and gender segregation and discrimination, commitment to comprehensive social welfare legislation, and opposition to unjust wars.[119] The UE and Friedan (post-1963) shared much that *The Feminine Mystique* lacked, including a commitment to a coalition that included unions, men, and African Americans. To be sure, her aims, language, ideology, and the subjects of her agitation shifted between 1953 and the mid-1960s. Yet in important ways she remained on the left. Full equality for women, she wrote in 1973, "will restructure all our institutions."[120] One further proof of continuity in her ideology came in *The Second Stage* (1981). Though in important ways more conservative than *The Feminine Mystique*, this book nonetheless offered an analysis of the relationship between women and consumer culture that was more radical than her 1963 book and echoed many of the themes in her writings as a labor journalist.[121]

Friedan's experiences in the 1940s and early 1950s help explain but do not excuse her attack in 1973 on "disrupters of the women's movement" who were constantly advocating "lesbianism and hatred of men" and who did so, she claimed, with the encouragement of the FBI and the CIA. Those who were "pushing lesbianism" in NOW, she wrote, "were creating a sexual red herring that would divide the movement and lead ultimately to sexual McCarthyism." At the same time she distanced herself from her past when questioning those who based their feminism "on a false analogy with obsolete or irrelevant ideologies of class warfare or race separatism."[122] Whatever their origins in her personal experiences and in partisan battles, in complicated ways such remarks connect Friedan's later life with her early experiences with red-baiting, government suppression of radicalism, the dangers of factionalism, and class-based coalition politics. To someone rooted in 1940s radicalism, the identity politics of the 1970s were anathema.

Conclusion

A more complete story of Friedan's past illuminates a wide range of issues in recent American history. Moreover, this fuller story reveals information that enhances our sense of the importance of Friedan's contribution to American feminism. Recognizing the origins of Friedan's 1963 book reminds us of the way that journalists of the 1950s emerged as social critics who helped shape the consciousness of the next decade.[123] The recovery of her past suggests the importance of thinking of her in comparison with New York intellectuals who, although they did much to shape postwar ideology, generally neglected issues of gender. *The Feminine Mystique* sheds light on important dimensions of gender issues. If Riesman, Whyte, and Packard suggested the troublesome nature of male identity in the 1950s, then we can understand how Friedan gave this theme a twist. "Male outrage," she remarked as she pointed to "the homosexuality that is spreading like a murky smog over" America, "is the result, surely, of an implacable hatred for the parasitic women who keep their husbands and sons from growing up."[124] The homophobia of such a comment is standard for the period. What is also of note is Friedan's promise that the liberation of women would strengthen a male identity that she and others found fragile. From writers such as Whyte and Riesman, Friedan took an analysis that blamed life in the suburbs, jobs in large organizations, and consumer culture for their inability to promote healthy masculinity and then turned this analysis into an argument for women's liberation.

The Feminine Mystique played a critical role in reshaping the ideology and social composition of the American left. Along with others, such as Herbert Marcuse, Friedan was exploring how to ground a cultural and social critique by rethinking the contributions of Freud and Marx. What Marcuse did in *Eros and Civilization: A Philosophical Inquiry into Freud* (1955) Friedan did almost a decade later: respond to the cold war by attempting to minimize her debt to Marx even as she relied on him. For her solutions, if not her analysis, she relied on psychology. In the process, she recovered the lessons of the discipline in which she majored at college, joining others such as Paul Goodman, David Riesman, Margaret Mead, Erik Erikson, and Erich Fromm in using humanistic psychology and neo-Freudianism to ground a powerful cultural critique at a time when other formulations were politically discredited. In her 1963 book Friedan was reshaping American social criticism by focusing not on the working class and the processes of production but on the way changes in consumer culture were reshaping the lives of the middle class.

Friedan was not alone in experiencing what it meant to have a radical past and eventually end up living in the suburbs, cut off from the realities of urban industrial life that once gave radicalism its palpability.[125] The trajectory of her career provides another example of the transition in the media from working-class, ethnically charged cultural representations to largely suburban, middle-class, and deracinated ones.[126] Moreover, the widening division between the working class and the urban poor brought issues of race to the surface in ways that made some of Friedan's analysis outdated. At a time when unions (although not the UE) accommodated themselves to the cold war consensus and Mills was noting the key role of university students and intellectuals in progressive politics, Friedan was arguing that middle- and upper-middle-class white women would replace workers in the vanguard of American social protest.[127] Her image of herself as the frustrated housewife came from a number of sources, including her recognition that the rhetoric of the Old Left shed little light on the realities of millions of American women. The persona of the suburban house wife enabled her to talk about alienation and discrimination in a new setting and in less radical terms.

A reconsideration of Friedan's career deepens our understanding of the relationship of the 1930s, 1940s, and 1950s to the social protests of the 1960s.[128] Her life underscores the difficulty of separating history into neatly packaged decades. Friedan's experiences in the 1940s and 1950s show us once again that life in the years before the 1960s was hardly calm.[129] It reminds us of how issues of Communism and anti-Communism shaped a generation. Friedan's life suggests discontinuities as well as continuities between the Old Left and the protests of the 1960s.[130] If McCarthyism prompted her to hide elements of her past from view, it also made it difficult for her to directly confront her debt to the Old Left, perhaps out of a sense that she may have betrayed a problematic or martyred cause.

Yet her life makes clear how important were World War II, unions, issues of the 1940s, and the fights by radicals for justice for women and African Americans in setting the stage for the reemergence of protests in the 1960s. Robert Korstad and Nelson Lichtenstein have demonstrated that in the 1940s union members and radicals created what E. P. Thompson called a "window of opportunity" in the struggle for civil rights for African Americans. We may come to see that the 1940s offered a somewhat parallel situation for millions of women. Among the forces at work, the roughly similar consequences of which Korstad and Lichtenstein have explored for African Americans, were the war-induced economic boom that created new types and levels of economic opportunities, the wartime entry of millions of women into the workforce and a smaller but significant number into CIO unions, the commitment of agencies of the federal government to women's advancement, the organizational and ideological leadership of the Communist Party, the generation of a "rights consciousness," and the broadening of public discourse. Following the war, the returning veterans and, more significantly, an employer-led offensive closed that window by isolating Communist-influenced leaders, curbing union ambitions, and undermining the Popular Front coalition. The result, Korstad and Lichtenstein's model suggests, was that when feminism reemerged in the 1960s, "it would have a different social character and an alternative political agenda," transformed by the consequences of the lost opportunities of the 1940s.[131]

This revision of Friedan's past sheds light on the history of women and second-wave feminism by enriching our sense of the origins of what happened in the 1960s. It offers vivid proof of the intertwined processes of containment and resistance of women in the 1940s and 1950s.[132] Moreover, it suggests that we think of Friedan, at some crucial points in her life, as a "left feminist" and a crucial link between generations of advocates for women's advancement.[133] American feminism, most historians agree, emerged in the 1960s from two sources: white, professional, and well-educated liberals, including Friedan and a few acknowledged union activists, who relied on a Washington-based approach as they called for national legislation; and a diverse group of women, shaped by the civil rights movement, who worked from the grassroots to develop a more adversarial insurgency.[134] However, if Rosa Parks refused to take a seat at the back of a segregated bus not simply because her feet hurt, then Friedan did not write *The Feminine Mystique* simply because she was an unhappy housewife. Nor was Friedan alone. Gerda Lerner, Bella Abzug, Eleanor Flexner, and Milton Meltzer are among those active in the labor movement in the 1940s who would emerge in the 1960s as people who helped shape post-1963 feminism.[135] Once we recover the stories of their counterparts among middle-class activists across the nation (perhaps, like those discussed above, predominantly Jews) and among working-class and African American women, the importance of the 1940s in the history of American feminism will be clearer.[136]

Friedan's experiences happened in specific contexts, especially the cauldron of labor union activism and even more particularly that provided by the UE. Whatever the accompanying frustrations and however much her focus shifted, her work for the UE shaped her engagement with the issues women faced. Friedan's story suggests that, at least as far as she and some others are concerned, what we have seen as liberal feminism had radical origins. Consequently, it underscores the importance of a reconsideration of the nature of the breach between the proponents of women's rights in the early 1960s and the late-1960s advocates of women's liberation, especially socialist feminists. For Friedan, labor union activity in the 1940s and early 1950s provided the bridge over which she moved from the working class to women as the repository of her hopes as well as much of the material from which she would fashion her feminism in *The Feminine Mystique*.

Notes

Many friends and colleagues at Smith College and in Northampton helped me think through the issues discussed in this article, and I am especially indebted to those who made extensive comments on various drafts: Travis Crosby, Alice L. Hearst, Helen L. Horowitz, Thomas F. Jackson, Gina Rourke, Donald Weber, and Robert Weir. I am grateful to others whose responses to earlier versions sharpened what I have to say: Robert H. Abzug, Lynn Dumenil, Ronald Schatz, and Judith Smith. I am grateful to Jane S. De Hart and Linda K. Kerber for helping me think through a series of key issues when, in response to an earlier draft, they agreed with me on some issues and disagreed on others. Casey Blake and Howard Brick, readers for *American Quarterly*, provided exceptionally thoughtful critiques that contributed considerably to how I framed my argument. Jennifer L. Hootman carried out research into Peoria materials. At Smith, Rachel Ledford and Gina Rourke helped track down materials. From his position at the UE Archives at the University of Pittsburgh, David L. Rosenberg provided important leads. The librarians at Smith College responded to my questions with thoroughness and alacrity and the staff of the Schlesinger Library facilitated my use of the Friedan and Flexner collections. Throughout, Lucy Maddox ably served as advisor and editor. I am grateful to the National Endowment for the Humanities, which awarded me a Fellowship for College Teachers, under whose auspices I did the initial research and writing of this article.

1. Betty Goldstein, "UE Drive on Wage, Job Discrimination Wins Cheers from Women Members," *UE News*, 16 April 1951, 6. My interview of Friedan in 1987 first brought to my attention the possibility of this alternative story, as did the research my colleague Helen L. Horowitz carried out in the late 1980s. The appearance of the article by Joanne Meyerowitz in 1993, cited below, added an important piece of evidence. Because Friedan has denied me permission to quote from her unpublished papers and has not responded to my request that she grant me an opportunity to interview her again or to have her provide answers to my questions, I have not been able to present as full and perhaps as accurate a story as I wished to do.

2. Ronald W. Schatz, *The Electrical Workers: A History of Labor at General Electric and Westinghouse, 1923–60* (Urbana, Ill., 1983), xiii.

3. Lisa Kannenberg, "The Impact of the Cold War on Women's Trade Union Activism: The UE Experience," *Labor History* 34 (spring–summer 1993): 318; Jacqueline Van Voris, interview with Eleanor Flexner, Northampton, Mass., 16 October 1982, 70–71, Eleanor Flexner Papers, Schlesinger Library, Radcliffe College, Cambridge, Mass. [hereinafter cited as FP-SLRC]; [Eleanor Flexner], "The Woman Question" (syllabus for course at Jefferson School of Social Science, 1953–54) 1, 2, 5. For information on Flexner, I am relying on Ellen C. DuBois, "Eleanor Flexner and the History of American Feminism," *Gender and History* 3 (spring 1991): 81–90. On the Jefferson School, see Annette T. Rubinstein, "David Goldway," *Science and Society* 54 (winter 1990–91): 386–89; Daniel F. Ring, "Two Cultures: Libraries, the Unions, and the 'Case' of the Jefferson School of Social Science," *Journal of Library History* 20 (1985): 287–88.

4. Betty Friedan, "Up from the Kitchen Floor," *New York Times Magazine*, 4 March 1973, 8; Betty Friedan, "*It Changed My Life*". *Writings on the Women's Movement* (New York, 1976), 304.

5. For evidence of the continuing importance of Friedan and her book, see, for example, Elaine T. May, *Homeward Bound: American Families in the Cold War Era* (New York, 1988), 209–17, 219; and Joanne Meyerowitz, "Beyond the Feminine Mystique: A Reassessment of Postwar Mass Culture, 1946–1958," *Journal of American History* 79 (March 1993): 1455–82. For textbooks, see John M. Faragher et al., *Out of Many: A History of the American People* (Englewood Cliffs, N.J., 1994), 2:865, 943; James A. Henretta et al., *America's History*, 2nd ed. (New York, 1993), 2:909, 910, 911, 968; William H. Chafe, *The Unfinished Journey: America since World War II*, 3rd ed. (New York, 1995), 124, 330, 433. A widely used reader in American women's history contains a selection from Friedan's book, introducing its author as "a suburban housewife": Linda K. Kerber and Jane S. De Hart, eds., *Women's America: Refocusing the Past*, 4th ed. (New York, 1995), 512.

6. Kathleen A. Weigand, "Vanguards of Women's Liberation: The Old Left and the Continuity of the Women's Movement in the United States, 1945–1970s" (Ph.D. diss., Ohio State University, 1995) contains the fullest treatment of this continuity, as well as the best bibliography on the issue of women and radicalism in the postwar period. Gerda Lerner, "Midwestern Leaders of the Modern Women's Movement: An Oral History Project," *Wisconsin Academy Review*, Winter 1994–95, 11–15 provides an important corrective to the notion that 1960s feminism emerged spontaneously in that decade and that its leadership was mainly white and middle class. Among the other historians who have suggested such a connection, focusing mostly on women union activists, peace advocates, proponents of civil rights for African Americans, and radicals are Susan Lynn, *Progressive Women in Conservative Times: Racial Justice, Peace and Feminism, 1945 to the 1960s* (New Brunswick, 1992); Michael E. Brown et al., *New Studies in the Politics and Culture of US. Communism* (New York, 1993); Kannenberg, "Impact," 323; Nancy F. Gabin, *Feminism in the Labor Movement: Women and the United Auto Workers, 1935–1975* (Ithaca, 1990); Dorothy Healey and Maurice Isserman, *Dorothy Healey Remembers: A Life in the American Communist Party* (New York, 1990). Many of the contributors to Joanne Meyerowitz, ed., *Not*

June Cleaver: Women and Gender in Postwar America, 1945–1960 (Philadelphia, 1994) emphasize how the persistence of adversarial traditions in the 1940s and 1950s provided important bridges to social movements in the 1960s. The same is true of several articles in Linda K. Kerber, Alice Kessler-Harris, and Kathryn K. Sklar, eds., *U.S. History as Women's History: New Feminist Essays* (Chapel Hill, N.C., 1995), especially Joyce Antler, "Between Culture and Politics: The Emma Lazarus Federation of Jewish Women's Clubs and the Promulgation of Women's History, 1944–1989," 267–95 (also in this volume), and Amy Swerdlow, "The Congress of American Women: Left Feminist Peace Politics in the Cold War," 296–312. For Flexner's location of the origins of 1960s feminism in 1940s and 1950s radicalism, see Eleanor Flexner to Pat King, 13 May 1983, FP-SLRC.

7. See, for example, Robert Korstad and Nelson Lichtenstein, "Opportunities Found and Lost: Labor, Radicals, and the Early Civil Rights Movement," *Journal of American History* 75 (December 1988): 786–811; Maurice Isserman, *If I Had a Hammer: The Death of the Old Left and the Birth of the New Left* (New York, 1987).

8. George Lipsitz, *Time Passages: Collective Memory and American Popular Culture* (Minneapolis, 1990), 42.

9. For biographical information, in addition to what Friedan has said in print, I am relying on Kathleen Wilson, "Betty (Naomi) Friedan," *Contemporary Authors*, New Revision Series (New York, 1995), 45:133–36; David Halberstam, *The Fifties* (New York, 1993), 592–98; Marilyn French, "The Emancipation of Betty Friedan," *Esquire* 100 (December 1983): 510, 512, 514, 516, 517; Jennifer Moses, "She's Changed Our Lives: A Profile of Betty Friedan," *Present Tense* 15 (May–June 1988): 26–31; Lyn Tornabene, "The Liberation of Betty Friedan," *McCall's*, May 1971, 84, 136–40, 142, 146; Paul Wilkes, "Mother Superior to Women's Lib," *New York Times Magazine*, 29 November 1970, 27–29, 140–43, 149–50, 157; Marcia Cohen, *The Sisterhood: The True Story of the Women Who Changed the World* (New York, 1988), 25, 54–71, 83–84, 89–99; Lisa Hammel, "The 'Grandmother' of Women's Lib," *New York Times*, 19 November 1971, 52; Friedan, *Changed My Life* 5–16; Jacqueline Van Voris, interview of Betty Friedan, New York, N.Y., 17 April 1973, College Archives, Smith College, Northampton, Mass. [hereinafter cited as CA-SC]; Daniel Horowitz, interview of Betty Friedan, Santa Monica, Calif., 18 March 1987. As late as 6 November 1995, the date she sent me a letter denying me permission to quote from her unpublished papers, Friedan reiterated key elements of her story. I am grateful to Rachel Ledford for reporting to me on Friedan's 6 November 1995 talk at the Smithsonian Institution, Washington, D.C. Ironically, two biographies aimed at children provide fuller stories than do other treatments (for instance, they are the only published sources I have been able to locate that make clear that Friedan worked for the UE): Sondra Henry and Emily Taitz, *Betty Friedan: Fighter for Women's Rights* (Hillside, N.J., 1990) and Milton Meltzer, *Betty Friedan: A Voice for Women's Rights* (New York, 1985).

10. This article is based on considerable but hardly exhaustive examination of the available written record. When other researchers examine the Friedan papers (including those to which access is still restricted) and are able to carry out extensive interviews, they will be able to offer a fuller exploration of several issues, especially the shifts in Friedan's commitments as a radical at a time of great factionalism, when and how the feminine mystique did or did not trap her, how she interpreted the research on which *The Feminine Mystique* relied, and the pressures Friedan faced from her publisher to shape her 1963 book in certain ways.

11. An examination of what Friedan wrote for her high-school paper reveals someone less lonely than she has often portrayed herself; see articles by Friedan in *Peoria Opinion* from the fall of 1936 until the spring of 1938. For one political piece that reveals an early antifascism, see Bettye Goldstein, "Long, Coughlin, Roosevelt in 'It Can't Happen Here,' " *Peoria Opinion*, 18 September 1936, 8.

12. Friedan, quoted in Wilkes, "Mother Superior," 140; Betty Friedan, *The Feminine Mystique* (New York, 1963), 12.

13. Friedan, *Feminine Mystique*, 70; Friedan, quoted in Wilkes, "Mother Superior," 140. On the paucity of role models at Smith, see Van Voris, Friedan interview.

14. Horowitz, interview.

15. Dust jacket of 1963 copy of *The Feminine Mystique*, author's possession. See also "About Betty Friedan . . . ," biographical note accompanying Betty Friedan, "How to Find and Develop Article Ideas," *The Writer* 75 (March 1962), 13.

16. Friedan, quoted in "Betty Friedan," Charles Moritz, ed, *Current Biography Yearbook 1970* (New York, 1971), 146; Betty Friedan, "New York Women: Beyond the Feminine Mystique," *New York Herald Tribune*, 21 February 1965, 7–15; women's liberation, biographies, individuals, box 4, folder 31, clippings on Betty Friedan, Sophia Smith Collection, Smith College [hereinafter referred to as SSC-SC]; Wilkes, "Mother Superior," 141; Friedan, quoted in Wilkes, "Mother Superior," 141; Tornabene, "Liberation," 138; and Friedan, "Kitchen Floor," 8.

17. Tornabene, "Liberation," 138. See Betty Friedan, "The Intellectual Pied Pipers of Rockland County," (unpublished paper, written in 1960–61, FP-SLRC, carton 9, folder 347, Friedan Collection, Schlesinger

Library, Radcliffe College, Cambridge, Mass. [hereinafter cited as BF-SLRC; unless otherwise noted, the references are to collection 71–62 . . . 81–M23]).

18. Rollene W. Saal, "Author of the Month," *Saturday Review*, 21 March 1964; women's liberation, biographies, individuals, box 4, folder 31, SSC-SC; *Hackensack Record*, 2 May 1963; Class of 1942 folders, Betty Goldstein folder, CA-SC; Friedan, "Kitchen Floor," 8.

19. Friedan, *Feminine Mystique*, 9, 20, 66, 70, 186–87.

20. Horowitz, interview; Betty Friedan, "Introduction to the Tenth Anniversary Edition" of *Feminine Mystique* (New York, 1974), 1–5. For early articles with the themes that would emerge in the book, see Betty Friedan, "I Say: Women Are *People* Too!" *Good Housekeeping*, September 1960, 59–61, 161–62; Betty Goldstein Friedan, "if One Generation Can Ever Tell Another," *Smith Alumnae Quarterly*, February 1961, 68–70.

21. The 1974 article, which in the book was called "The Way We Were—1949," was originally published with some relatively unimportant differences, but with a more revealing title, as Betty Friedan, "In France, de Beauvoir Had just Published 'The Second Sex,' " *New York*, 30 December 1974–6 January 1975, 52–55. In Horowitz, interview, which covered mainly the years up to 1963, Friedan discussed her move to a radical politics even as she emphasized captivity by the feminine mystique beginning in the Berkeley years. Though Friedan has revealed a good deal about her life, to the best of my knowledge she has not acknowledged in print the full range of reasons she left Berkeley, that she worked for the UE, her authorship of the 1952 pamphlet, and her leadership of the rent strike. Moroever, she has insisted that in the late 1940s and early 1950s she had interest neither in a career nor in women's problems.

22. I am grateful to Judith Smith for helping me to think through this and other issues.

23. Friedan, *Changed My Life*, 6, 8–9.

24. Ibid., 6, 9, 16; Halberstam, *Fifties*, 593; French, "Emancipation," 510. Horowitz, interview, dates the firing in 1952. In the immediate postwar years, the term *feminist* often referred to women who were Republicans, independent businesswomen, and professionals.

25. Friedan, *Changed My Life*, 5, 6–7, 8–9, 15, 16. She gave 1949 as the turning point because she had been asked to do a piece in 1974 on what had happened a quarter of a century earlier; Horowitz, interview.

26. Friedan, *Changed My Life*, 14–16.

27. Ibid., 12, 16.

28. An extensive examination of the letters that Friedan received from women may well reveal the success of her strategy of encouraging her readers to identify with her situation: for an astute examination of these letters, carried out in a different context, see May, *Homeward Bound*, 209–17.

29. French, "Emancipation," 510; Donald Meyer, "Betty Friedan," in G. J. Barker-Benield and Catherine Clinton, eds., *Portraits of American Women: From Settlement to the Present* (New York, 1991), 601; Halberstam, *Fifties*, 593–94. For other problematic accounts, see "Friedan," *Current Biography*, 146; Wilson, "Friedan," 134; Donald Meyer, *Sex and Power: The Rise of Women in America, Russia, Sweden, and Italy* (Middletown, Corns., 1987), 389; Rosalind Rosenberg, *Divided Lives: American Women in the Twentieth Century* (New York, 1992), 138–39.

30. Cohen, *Sisterhood*, 63, and Wilkes, "Mother Superior," 140 briefly draw a picture of Friedan as a college rebel, but to the best of my knowledge, the politics of that rebellion have remained largely unknown.

31. This summary relies on unsigned editorials that appeared under Friedan's editorship, which can be found in *SCAN* from 14 March 1941 to 10 March 1942, ? Although members of the editorial board held a wide range of opinions, I am assuming that as editor-in-chief Friedan had a significant role in shaping editorials. Friedan placed four editorials in her papers: "They Believed in Peace," "Years of Change and Unrest," "Behind Closed Doors," and "Answer No Answer": carton 7, folder 310, BF-SLRC.

32. For the article she published on the basis on her honors thesis, see H. Israel and B. Goldstein, "Operationism in Psychology," *Psychological Review* 51 (May1944): 177–88.

33. See James J. Gibson, "Why a Union for Teachers?" *Focus* 2 (November 1939): 3–7.

34. I am grateful to Margery Sly, archivist of Smith College, for providing this information. She has also pointed out that teaching at Smith in Friedan's years were several married female faculty members who had children and that Harold Israel and Elsa Siipola, two of Friedan's mentors, were married but without children.

35. In 1955 Douglas took the Fifth Amendment before HUAC as she was red-baited, and accused of having been a member of a Communist teachers union in the late 1930s. I am grateful to Margery Sly and Jacquelyn D. Hall for providing this information on Douglas. See also Betty Friedan, "Was Their Education UnAmerican?" unpublished article, 1953 or 1954, carton 11, folder 415, BF-SLRC, 3. For Friedan's continued use of Marxist analysis, see Friedan, *Changed My Life*, 110.

36. Bettye Goldstein, "Discussion of Reading Period Material," paper for Economics 319, 18 January 1941,

carton 1, folder 257, BF-SLRC, 1, 2, 4, 8. See also "Questions on *Communist Manifesto*" and "Questions on Imperialism," papers for Economics 319, carton 1, folder 257, BF-SLRC.

37. John M. Glen, *Highlander: No Ordinary School, 1932–1962* (Lexington, Ky., 1988), 47–69. I am grateful to Professor Glen for a letter in which he clarified the timing of the league's sponsorship. Meltzer, *Friedan*, 20, says that Friedan's economics professor pointed her to Highlander but identifies that professor as a male; since the only economics course Friedan took was from Douglas, I am assuming that it was she who urged her student to attend the workshop. Meltzer thinks that is a reasonable assumption: Milton Meltzer, phone conversation with Daniel Horowitz, 24 September 1995.

38. Bettye Goldstein, "Highlander Folk School—American Future," unpublished paper, 1941, carton 6, folder 274, BF-SLRC; Goldstein, "Learning the Score," 22–24.

39. Epilogue of Failure," *SCAN*, 10 March 1942, 2.

40. "Betty Goldstein, Local Girl, Makes Good in New York," clipping from Peoria newspaper, probably 10 December 1943 issue of *Labor Temple News*, carton 1, folder 86, BF-SLRC.

41. "Behind a Closed Door," *SCAN*, 3 October 1941, 2; "Declaration of Student Independence," *SCAN*, 5 December 1941, 1–2; "SCAN Protests Against Censorship," *SCAN*, 5 December 1941, 1; "A Few Hours More," *SCAN*, 10 October 1941, 2; "Review of Philosophy Courses," *SCAN*, 10 March 1942, 2.

42. "The Tatler Suspension," *SCAN*, 7 November 1941, 2; for the article in question see "Maids We Have Known and Loved," *Tatler*, October 1941, 9, 21. When the administration moved against *SCAN*, over a different incident, the editors changed their minds about the earlier suspension of the *Tatler*: *SCAN*, 5 December 1941, 1–2.

43. "Education in Emergency," *SCAN*, 15 April 1941, 2; "The Right to Organize," *SCAN*, 21 October 1941, 2; "Comment," *SCAN*, 14 November 1941, 2; Filene's advertisement, *SCAN*, 21 October 1941, 2. Bettye Goldstein, "For Defense of Democracy," *Smith College Monthly* 1 (October 1940): 11, 12, 28, is a passionate defense of democracy and a warning about the possibility of American fascism.

44. "They Choose Peace," *SCAN*, 22 April 1941, 2; for the minority opinion, see "The Case for Intervention," *SCAN*, 2 May 1941, 2; "War Against Fascism," *SCAN*, 24 October 1941, 2. Placing the editorials written on Friedan's watch in the national context of student politics makes clear that after the Nazi-Soviet pact the student movement was more active and radical at Smith than elsewhere. In addition, the commitment of Friedan and her fellow editors to antifascism and their reluctance to embrace interventionism fully after the German invasion of the Soviet Union suggests that they dissented from the Communist Party position. On the national context see Robert Cohen, *When the Old Left Was Young: Student Radicals and America's First Mass Student Movement, 1929–1941* (New York, 1993), especially 315–37.

45. J. N., "The Red Menace," *SCAN*, 14 October 1941, 2; Neal Gilkyson, "The Gallery," *SCAN*, 21 October 1941, 2.

46. "We Cannot Rejoice," *SCAN*, 9 December 1941, 2; "Our Duty Now," *SCAN*, 12 December 1941, 2; "Campus Cooperatives," *SCAN*, 24 February 1942, 2; "No Change in Emphasis," *SCAN*, 26 September 1941, 2.

47. "Betty Goldstein, Local Girl." Meltzer, *Friedan*, 21, provides explanations for Friedan's decision that do not rely on the standard story.

48. Certificate of Death for Harry M. Goldstein, County of Peoria, State of Illinois, copy in author's possession; Henry and Taitz, *Friedan*, 31. Keeping in mind the problematic nature of such documents, see FBI reports on Betty Goldstein, 1944, carton 1, folder 67, BF-SLRC.

49. To date her work for the Federated Press, see Betty Friedan, job application for Time Inc., 1 July 1951, carton 1, folder 61, BF-SLRC. For information on the Federated Press, see Doug Reynolds, "Federated Press," in Mari Jo Buhle, Paul Buhle, and Dan Georgakas, eds., *Encyclopedia of the American Left* (New York, 1990), 225–27.

50. Betty Goldstein, "Negro Pupils Segregated, Parents Strike; Issue Headed for Courts," Federated Press, 15 September 1943, carton 8, folder 328, BF-SLRC; Betty Goldstein, "Peace Now: Treason in Pious Garb," Federated Press, 16 February 1944, carton 8, folder 328, BF-SLRC; Betty Goldstein, "Well-Heeled 'White Collar League' Seen as Disguised Native Fascist Threat," Federated Press, 16 March 1944, carton 8, folder 328, BF-SLRC.

51. Betty Goldstein, "Big Business Getting Desperate, Promising Postwar Jobs," Federated Press, 19 November 1943, carton 8, folder 328, BF-SLRC; Betty Goldstein, "NAM Convention Pro-War—For War on Labor, New Deal, Roosevelt," Federated Press, 14 December 1943, carton 8, folder 328, BF-SLRC; Betty Goldstein, "Details of Big Business Anti-Labor Conspiracy Uncovered," Federated Press, 11 February 1946, carton 8, folder 328, BF-SLRC. For the larger story, see Elizabeth A. Fones-Wolf, *Selling Free Enterprise: The Business Assault on Labor and Liberalism, 1945–60* (Urbana, 1994).

52. Betty Goldstein, "Pretty Posters Won't Stop Turnover of Women in Industry," Federated Press, 26 October 1943, and Ruth Young quoted in same, carton 8, folder 328, BF-SLRC.

53. Betty Goldstein, "Post War Living: 'Are They Putting Something over on Us?' Mrs. Jones Wonders," Federated Press, 23 January 1946, carton 8, folder 329, BF-SLRC.

54. Job application, 1951.

55. For information on women in the UE see Schatz, *Electrical Workers*; Ruth Milkman, *Gender at Work: The Dynamics of Job Segregation by Sex during World War II* (Urbana, 1987); Kannenberg, "Impact"; Lisa A. Kannenberg, "From World War to Cold War: Women Electrical Workers and Their Union, 1940–1955" (M.A. thesis, University of North Carolina, Charlotte, 1990). Robert H. Zieger, *The CIO, 1935–1955* (Chapel Hill, N.C., 1995), 253–93, assesses the role of Communists in the CIO, including the UE, and discusses the vagueness of the line between sympathy and party membership in unions such as the UE; Ronald L. Filippelli and Mark McCulloch, *Cold War in the Working Class: The Rise and Decline of the United Electrical Workers* (Albany, N.Y., 1994) charts the attack on the UE and discusses the issue of Communist presence in the UE.

56. Van Voris, Flexner interview, 8 January 1977, 16 October 1982, and 11 May 1983, 2, 62, 67, 70–71, 81–82. Helen K. Chinoy, who shared a house with Friedan in the summer of 1944 or 1945, confirmed this judgment that in the 1940s Communist Party membership was not the critical issue among those on the left who identified themselves with a wide range of political positions: Daniel Horowitz, interview with Helen K. Chinoy, Northampton, Mass., 7 October 1995.

57. For Beecher's ancestry, I am relying on James Lerner, interview with Daniel Horowitz, Brooklyn, N.Y., 21 August 1995.

58. For the positive responses of this union and other Communist-led ones to problems of minority and female workers, see Zieger, *CIO*, 87, 255–56.

59. Schatz, *Electrical Workers*, 30, 89, 116–27, 129–30.

60. Milkman, *Gender at Work*, 77–78; see also Kannenberg, "Impact," esp. 311, 315. Nancy B. Palmer, "Gender, Sexuality, and Work: Women and Men in the Electrical Industry, 1940–1955" (Ph.D. diss., Boston College, 1995), more skeptical of women's gains in the UE, focuses on how the construction of gender in labor unions, including the UE, limited women's advances; see esp. ch. 4.

61. Zieger, *CIO*, 251.

62. This summary relies on Schatz, *Electrical Workers*, 167–240. The 1946 quote is from Harry Block in Schatz, *Electrical Workers*, 181. For the impact of the attack on UE on women's issues, see Kannenberg, "From World War to Cold War," 95.

63. Betty Goldstein, "NAM Does Gleeful War Dance to Profits, Wage Cuts, Taft Law," *UE News*, 13 December 1947, 4. What follows relies on the more than three dozen articles signed by Betty Goldstein in the *UE News* from the fall of 1946 until early 1952.

64. Betty Goldstein, "A Tale of 'Sacrifice': A Story of Equality in the United States, 1951," *March of Labor*, May 1951, 16–18, carton 8, folder 334, BF-SLRC. This also appeared in *UE News*, 12 March 1951, 6–7.

65. Betty Goldstein, "It'll Take a Strong Union to End Winchester Tyranny," *UE News*, 7 December 1946, 9; Betty Goldstein, "Fighting Together: We Will Win!" *UE News*, 31 May 1947, 5, 8; Betty Goldstein, "Labor Builds New Political Organization to Fight for a People's Congressman," *UE News*, 23 August 1947, 4.

66. Betty Goldstein, "People's Needs Forgotten: Big Business Runs Govt.," *UE News*, 12 May 1947, 5; Betty Goldstein, "In Defense of Freedom! The People vs. the UnAmerican Committee," *UE News*, 8 November 1947, 6–7; Betty Goldstein, "They Can't Shove the IBEW down Our Throats," *UE News*, 4 September 1948, 6–7; Betty Goldstein, "UnAmerican Hearing Exposed as Plot by Outsiders to Keep Grip on UE Local," *UE News*, 22 August 1949, 4; Betty Goldstein, "New NAM Theme Song: Labor-Management Teamwork," *UE News*, 9 January 1950, 5; Betty Goldstein, "Plain People of America Organize New Political Party of Their Own," *UE News*, 31 July 1948, 6–7.

67. B.G., review of Sinclair Lewis, *Kingsblood Royal*, *UE News*, 6 September 1947, 7; B.G., review of the movie *Gentleman's Agreement*, *UE News*, 22 November 1947, 11; B.G., review of movie *Crossfire*, *UE News*, 9 August 1947, 8–9; Betty Goldstein, "CIO Sold Out Fight for FEPC, T-H Repeal, Rep. Powell Reveals," *UE News*, 17 April 1950, 4; B.G., review of Fielding Burke, *Sons of the Stranger*, *UE News*, 24 January 1948, 7.

68. These two sentences rely on James Lerner, interview. For treatments of the relationship between Communism and women's issues, see Ellen K. Trimberger, "Women in the Old and New Left: The Evolution of a Politics of Personal Life," *Feminist Studies* 5 (fall 1979): 432–61; Van Gosse, " 'To Organize in Every Neighborhood, in Every Home': The Gender Politics of American Communists between the Wars," *Radical History Review* 50 (spring 1991): 109–41; Kannenberg, "From World War to Cold War"; and Weigand, "Vanguards." For her coverage of Latinas, see Betty Goldstein, "It's a Union that Fights for All the Workers," *UE News*, 3 September 1951, 6–7.

69. Though she does not discuss Friedan's situation, the best treatment of the prominent role of women's issues in radical circles in the 1940s and 1950s is Weigand, "Vanguards." In working on *The Feminine*

Mystique, Friedan may have been influenced by writings she may have encountered in the 1940s, such as Mary Inman, *In Women's Defense* (Los Angeles, 1940) and Betty Millard, "Woman Against Myth," *New Masses*, 30 December 1947, 7–10 and 6 January 1948, 7–20. There is evidence that Friedan was well aware of *New Masses*. Under a pseudonym, she published two articles in *New Masses*: Lillian Stone, "Labor and the Community," *New Masses* 57 (23 October 1945): 3–5; Lillian Stone, "New Day in Stamford," *New Masses* 58 (22 January 1946): 3–5. In identifying Friedan as the author, I am relying on a 22 September 1995 conversation with Kathy Kraft, an archivist at the Schlesinger Library and on a letter in carton 49, folder 1783, BF-SLRC.

70. Chinoy, interview.
71. Betty Goldstein, "Price Cuts Promised in Press Invisible to GE Housewives," *UE News*, 1 February 1947, 7; Betty Goldstein, "Union Members Want to Know—WHO Has Too Much Money to Spend," *UE News*, 26 March 1951, 8.
72. [Betty Goldstein], *UE Fights for Women Workers*, UE Publication no. 232, June 1952 (New York, 1952). To authenticate her authorship, I am relying on the following: Horowitz, interview; James Lerner, interview; Betty Friedan, postcard to author, late August 1995; Meltzer, *Friedan*, 25. Meltzer, who knew Friedan in the 1940s, discusses her work on women's issues at the UE. Friedan may also have written *Women Fight for a Better Life!* (New York, 1953): see Friedan, postcard.
73. [Goldstein], *UE Fights*, 5.
74. [Goldstein], *UE Fights*, 9–18, 26–27, 38.
75. Kannenberg, "Impact," 318.
76. See the following articles in *Jewish Life* by Rachel Roth: " 'We're Worse off Every Year,' " 7 (April 1953): 11–14; "A 'Sick' Industry—But the Bosses Don't Suffer," 7 (May 1953): 10–13; "The Price of 'Collaboration,' " 7 (June 1953): 21–24. In identifying Friedan as the author, I am relying on the 22 September 1995 conversation with Kathy Kraft.
77. Kannenberg, "Impact," 318; the conference took place in New York in early May 1953.
78. These issues appear in "Resolution on Job Discrimination," "Resolution on Legislative Action," and "National Conference on the Problems of Working Women," mimeographed documents in carton 8, folder 336, BF-SLRC.
79. Generally speaking, Kannenberg and Schatz emphasize the genuineness of the UE's commitments, despite opposition within the union.
80. Palmer, "Gender, Sexuality, and Work."
81. Betty Goldstein to Grievance Committee of Newspaper Guild of New York, 23 May 194 carton 8, folder 330, BF-SLRC; Friedan, *Changed My Life*, 9; Mim Kelber, phone conversation with Daniel Horowitz, 16 September 1995, identified the man as James Peck, obituary for James Peck, *New York Times*, 13 July 1993, B7.
82. Meltzer, *Friedan*, 29. For additional perspectives on Friedan's departure from the *UE News*, see Kelber, conversation, and James Lerner, interview. Lerner, who had more seniority than Friedan, worked for the UE for more than forty years, eventually becoming managing editor of *UE News*. He shared an office with Friedan during her years at *UE News* and has noted that the union protected Friedan's position during her first pregnancy: James Lerner, interview.
83. Margery Sly pointed me toward discussions of how women write about themselves, especially Carolyn G. Heilbrun, *Writing a Woman's Life* (New York, 1988), 13, 17, 24, 25; Jill K. Conway, "Introduction," in Conway, ed., *Written by Herself Autobiographies of American Women: An Anthology* (New York, 1992), x–xi.
84. The precise dates of Friedan's residence in Parkway Village are difficult to nail down, and I am relying in part on the existence in her papers of copies of the Parkway Village newspaper from April 1949 to January 1956; Friedan, *Changed My Life*, 13; Betty Friedan, "Accomplishments," unpublished manuscript, c. 1959, 1, carton 1, folder 62, BF-SLRC, 2, which dates the departure to 1955; *Smith College Bulletin: Alumnae Register Issue* (Northampton, Mass., November 1949, November 1952, March 1956, and November 1958). From the written record, it is possible to determine little, if anything, of Carl Friedan's politics and of his role in shaping his wife's ideology.
85. Roy Wilkins lived there: see "Village Profile: Roy Wilkins," *Parkway Villager*, February 1954, 2.
86. See, for example, the headlines from the May 1952 issue: carton 10, folders 381–85, BF-SLRC.
87. Friedan, *Feminine Mystique*, 10; Friedan, *Changed My Life*, 304–16; Sandra Dijkstra, "Simone de Beauvoir and Betty Friedan: The Politics of Liberation," *Feminist Studies* 6 (summer 1980): 290–303.
88. Betty Friedan, conversation with Daniel Horowitz, Washington, D.C., 29 March 1995.
89. To date these moves, I am relying on a number of sources, including Betty Friedan to Mrs. Clifford P. Cowen, 5 August 1957, carton 7, folder, 313, BF-SLRC; Friedan, "New York Women"; "About the Author," in "New York Women"; "Friedan," *Current Biography*, 146; *Smith College Bulletin*.
90. Friedan, *Feminine Mystique*, 33–68.

91. Meyerowitz, "Beyond the Feminine Mystique," 1458, 1481.

92. For her claim, made before 1963, for the seriousness of her journalism in these magazines, see Friedan, "Accomplishments," 2.

93. Betty Friedan, "Two Are an Island," *Mademoiselle*, July 1955, 88–89, 100–101; Betty Friedan, "Teenage Girl in Trouble," *Coronet*, March 1958, 163–68; Betty Friedan, "The Happy Families of Hickory Hill," *Redbook*, February 1956, 39, 87–90; Marian Stone and Harold Stone [fictitious names], as told to Betty Friedan, "With Love We Live . . ." *Coronet*, July 1957, 135–44. For another article on a suburban development that relied on cooperation, see Betty Friedan, " 'We Built a Community for Our Children," *Redbook*, March 1955, 42–45, 62–63. Friedan's papers contain information on scores of articles that she was working on; this analysis focuses on those actually published. Sylvie Murray's "Suburban Citizens: Domesticity and Community Politics in Queens, New York, 1945–1960" (Ph.D. diss., Yale University, 1994) ably contrasts the adversarial politics of Friedan's unpublished pieces with the milder tone of her published ones; on the difficulty of getting into print articles on women who were not middle-class, I am relying on Sylvie Murray, phone conversation with Daniel Horowitz, 9 October 1995.

94. Betty Friedan, "The Gal Who Defied Dior," *Town Journal*, October 1955, 33, 97–98; Betty Friedan, "Millionaire's Wife," *Cosmopolitan*, September 1956, 78–87; Betty Friedan, "New Hampshire Love Story," *Family Circle*, June 1958, 40–41, 74–76. An influential book on the origins of 1960s feminism begins with a discussion of Friedan's magazine articles without seeing how they might connect parts of her career: Sara Evans, *Personal Politics: The Roots of Women's Liberation in the Civil Rights Movement and the New Left* (New York, 1979), 3.

95. Betty Friedan, "Now They're Proud of Peoria," *Reader's Digest*, August 1955, 93–97.

96. Friedan, "Was Their Education UnAmerican?" 1–3.

97. Betty Friedan, "I Went Back to Work," *Charm*, April 1955, 145, 200.

98. Betty Friedan, "Day Camp in the Driveways," *Parents' Magazine*, May 1957, 36–37, 131–34.

99. Kelber, conversation.

100. Parkway Village had some suburban characteristics and was marketed on the basis of its suburban qualities: Murray, conversation. Yet Friedan has made it clear that she was happy there: Friedan, *Changed My Life*, 14. Moreover, being in Parkway Village did not involve inhabiting a single-family home or living individualistically among conformists.

101. Especially crucial but nonetheless elusive is the period from May 1953, when she appears to have ended her union work, to 1955, when her first article appeared in a women's magazine.

102. Friedan, "How to Find and Develop Article Ideas," 12–15, has some discussion of these conflicts.

103. This becomes clear through an examination of her files on her freelance work, especially when compared with the files of Vance Packard in the same years.

104. Wilkes, "Mother Superior," 141. On violence in the marriage, see also Tornabene, "Liberation," 138; Cohen, *Sisterhood*, 17–18; Meyer, "Friedan," 608; Myra MacPherson, "The Former Mr. Betty Friedan Has Scars to Prove It," probably 1971, newspaper article from unidentified source, women's liberation, biographies, individuals, box 4, folder 31, clippings on Betty Friedan, SSC-SC.

105. On this problem, see Elizabeth V. Spelman, *Inessential Woman: Problems of Exclusion in Feminist Thought* (Boston, 1988).

106. Gerda Lerner to Betty Friedan, 6 February 1963, box 20a, folder 715, BF-SLRC; quoted with permission of Gerda Lerner. For information on Lerner's participation in the labor movement, the Congress of American Women, and at the founding meeting of NOW, I am relying on Daniel Horowitz, phone conversation with Gerda Lerner, 18 October 1995; Swerdlow, "Congress of American Women," 306.

107. Meltzer, *Friedan*, 23, hints at the limitation that stemmed from her social position.

108. For criticism of Friedan for defining women so narrowly in *The Feminine Mystique*, see, for example, bell hooks, *Feminist Theory: From Margin to Center* (Boston, 1984), 1–15; among the many astute analyses of Friedan's 1963 book, none of which has taken into account accurate information about Friedan's early career, see Rachel Bowlby, " 'The Problem With No Name': Rereading Friedan's *The Feminine Mystique*," *Feminist Review* 27 (September 1987): 61–75.

109. Betty Friedan to Scott Fletcher, 29 September 1959, carton 20a, folder 707, BF-SLRC.

110. For a reference to racial discrimination, see Friedan, *Feminine Mystique*, 180.

111. Friedan to Fletcher makes it clear that the germ of the idea that continuing education was a solution came from Betty Friedan, "Business Problems? Call in Plato," *Rotarian* 97 (August 1960): 19, 55–58.

112. Friedan, *Feminine Mystique*, 370, 378.

113. Ibid., 69, 70, 75, 76, 186, 187.

114. See, for example, the discussion of male editors in Friedan, *Feminine Mystique*, 51–54, which Friedan did not connect to the action of male social and behavioral scientists, college and university educators, and corporate executives.

115. Frieclan, *Feminine Mystique*, 205–7. In Horowitz, interview, Friedan connected what she wrote in this chapter with her work as a labor journalist. Meyer, "Friedan," 206, briefly discussed Friedan's anticipation of socialist feminism.

116. Friedan, *Feminine Mystique*, 232.

117. Ibid., 100, 185–86, 255–57.

118. Ibid., 309, 333–37, 372, 374, 375.

119. Compare "GEB Presents Union Position to Convention," *UE News*, 23 June 1952, 6–7, and many of the documents in Friedan, *Changed My Life*, 87–145; Friedan, "Kitchen Floor," 33–34.

120. Friedan, "Kitchen Floor," 30.

121. Betty Friedan, *The Second Stage* (New York, 1981), 299–307.

122. Friedan, "Kitchen Floor," 33–34.

123. See, for example, Daniel Horowitz, *Vance Packard and American Social Criticism* (Chapel Hill, N.C., 1994).

124. Friedan, *Feminine Mystique*, 274, 276.

125. I am grateful to Robert H. Abzug for helping me to think through this and other issues.

126. Here I am relying on Lipsitz, *Time Passages*, especially 39–75, and on unpublished papers by Donald Weber and Judith Smith.

127. See, for example, C. Wright Mills, "The New Left," in Irving L Horowitz, ed., *Power, Politics and People: The Collected Essays of C. Wright Mills* (New York, 1963), 247–59.

128. See, for example, Todd Gitlin, *The Sixties: Years of Hope, Days of Rage* (New York, 1987), 11–71.

129. For some examples of this reinterpretation of the 1950s, see Wini Breines, *Young, White, and Miserable: Growing up Female in the Fifties* (Boston, 1992); Brett Harvey, *The Fifties Women's Oral History* (New York, 1993); Lary May, ed., *Recasting America: Culture and Politics in the Age of Cold War* (Chicago, 1989).

130. Isserman, *If I Had a Hammer*; Susan Lynn, "Gender and Post World War II Progressive Politics: A Bridge to Social Activism in the 1960s U.S.A.," *Gender and History* 4 (summer 1992): 215–39.

131. Korstad and Lichtenstein, "Opportunities," 787, 800, 811; the Thompson quote appears on 811.

132. May, *Homeward Bound*.

133. I am borrowing the term from DuBois, "Flexner," 84.

134. Jane S. De Hart, "The New Feminism and the Dynamics of Social Change," in Linda K. Kerber and Jane S. De Hart, eds., *Women's America: Refocusing the Past*, 4th ed. (New York, 1995), 539–60. De Hart, 547–48, acknowledges the presence of "a few feminist union activists" but did not so characterize Friedan's earlier career. For the scholarship on the ways women in the 1950s struggled to resist the dominant tendencies of American society in that decade, see Eugenia Kaledin, *Mothers and More: American Women in the 1950s* (Boston 1984); George Lipsitz, *A Life in the Struggle: Ivory Perry and the Culture of Opposition* (Philadelphia, 1988); Susan Ware, "American Women in the 1950s: Nonpartisan Politics and Women's Politicization," in Louise A. Tilly and Patricia Gurin, eds., *Women, Politics, and Change* (New York, 1990), 281–99; Kate Weigand, "The Red Menace, the Feminine Mystique, and the Ohio Un-American Activities Commission: Gender and Anti-Communism in Ohio, 1951–1954," *Journal of Women's History* 3 (winter 1992): 70–94; Amy Swerdlow, *Women Strike for Peace: Traditional Motherhood and Radical Politics in the 1960s* (Chicago, 1993). In their study of the persistence of a women's movement into the 1950s, Leila J. Rupp and Verta Taylor, in *Survival in the Doldrums: The American Women's Rights Movement, 1945 to the 1960s* (New York, 1987), state that in 1955 Friedan was "on the verge of discovering women's inequality in American society for herself" (7).

135. Beginning in the 1940s, Bells Abzug provided legal counsel to workers and African Americans. Milton Meltzer, who knew Friedan when they were both labor journalists, emerged in the 1960s as an author of books on women, African Americans, workers, and dissenters that post-1963 feminists read to their children.

136. On Flexner's work in the labor movement, see DuBois, "Flexner," 84.

31

Nonmothers as Bad Mothers
Infertility and the "Maternal Instinct"

Elaine Tyler May

For conception to take place a woman must be a woman. Not only must she have the physical structure and hormones of a woman but she must feel she is a woman and accept it. A girl child becomes and feels herself a developing woman if she has made a proper identification with her own mother and has also learned to accept her femininity and also masculinity as represented by her father and later, by her husband. Being a woman means acceptance of her primary role, that of conceiving and bearing a child. Every woman has a basic urge and need to produce a child. Being a woman means a complete readiness to look forward to the delivery of that child when it is sufficiently nourished by her to take its place as an infant in the outside world. Being a woman means her feeling of her own readiness and capability to rear that child and aid in its physical, emotional and mental development.[1]

> — Abraham Stone, medical director of the Margaret
> Sanger Research Foundation, 1950

In the years following World War II, as the baby boom exploded and a powerful ideology of domesticity gripped the nation, the definition of womanhood articulated by Dr. Abraham Stone gained widespread acceptance. Some medical experts, particularly specialists in the growing field of infertility, frequently based their diagnoses and treatments on the theory that women often caused their own infertility by a subconscious rejection of their maternal instinct. Unless they could be restored to psychological health—which meant a full and eager acceptance of motherhood—such women were not considered to be good candidates for infertility treatment. According to these neo-Freudian theorists, if such women were helped to conceive, they would become bad mothers. The first step in treating them was to help them become psychologically ready for motherhood.

Margaret Valen encountered this theory when she consulted a physician in 1945 to discover why she was not getting pregnant. She was twenty-five and her husband was twenty-seven, and they had been married only a year, but since they married "late" by 1945 standards, most of her friends no doubt had children already. Medical experts encouraged childless couples to seek help early, warning that "the longer sterility has existed, the harder it is to correct. Only a qualified physician can answer for each man and wife the question of when they should undergo examination." Margaret went through the usual infertility workup and tried "everything kookie," but nothing worked. The physicians could find no physiological cause for the Valens' childlessness.

The Valens were among the 50 percent of infertile couples at the time who could not be diagnosed.[2] But that did not prevent her physician from suggesting treatment. When no physiological cause could be found, some physicians looked for psychological explanations. As a working woman in the postwar era, Margaret was not behaving in an appropriately feminine way. Perhaps, the theory went, she was inhibiting her own fertility because she held a job—an unwomanly thing to do and evidence that maybe she did not *really* want a child. Particular warnings were directed toward employed women, who allegedly put their fertility at risk: "The pressures of modern living and the strains of occupations in which women have been engaging are . . . significant causes" of infertility, cautioned a leading expert. "The same can be said of men, but to a lesser extent."[3] In keeping with such theories, Margaret's physician told her she should quit her job, so she did. Like most infertile women who sought medical advice, she did whatever her physician told her to do, even if she thought it was "kookie." But Margaret never got pregnant. Quitting her job did not do the trick.

Advising a woman to quit her job was not a standard treatment for infertility, but it was one approach to a problem that was still difficult to diagnose and treat. Researchers had found that stress could be a factor in infertility, by causing fallopian tubes to contract or by affecting the motility of sperm. If employment was a cause of stress, it was not entirely "kookie" for physicians to suggest quitting a job to relieve stress. The problem, however, is that there was no way to be certain that job-related stress caused a woman's tubes to contract. It was just as likely that stress at work affected a man's fertility. But it was unthinkable to suggest that a male breadwinner should quit his job. The woman's job during these years appeared to be expendable. Moreover, in most cases it was the woman, not the man, who sought treatment.

Most infertility practitioners were specialists in female reproductive medicine. The vast majority of the members of the American Society for the Study of Sterility, for example, were in the field of obstetrics and gynecology, followed by urology, with a few in related fields, such as internal medicine, endocrinology, general practice, and pathology.[4] At its annual meeting in 1963, Herbert H. Thomas, the president of the society, justified the continued focus on the female patient: "This does not indicate that we are unaware of the responsibility of the male in the problem of infertility, but the incidence of primary male infertility is variable but relatively low and, in our culture, it is usually the women who initiate the request for assistance." Surely, the president of the society knew the widely published statistics by its own members indicating that approximately half the infertility cases involved a problem with the man. Yet he remained focused on the woman as the patient:

> In seeking counsel with us, she . . . admits to frustration and failure . . . as we endeavor to probe and explore the innermost secrets of her life in order to alleviate her barrenness. As she bares her personal life before us and submits to many indignities and both painful and somewhat hazardous diagnostic procedures . . . we must not betray this trust. . . . The responsibility to our frustrated patient and her husband is a great one.[5]

The definition of the patient as female extended into medical language itself, which cast the female body as inherently flawed. Medical texts, as well as physicians and their patients, routinely described infertility in terms of "failure," "blame," and "fault." One woman, for example, who wrote to a noted specialist about her repeated miscarriages, wondered whether he agreed with her local physician that surgery might correct her "defective cervix." The specialist agreed that surgery might solve the difficulty, but referred to the condition not as a "defective cervix," as the woman's letter had, but as an "incompetent cervix."[6] Medical terminology was filled with metaphors of the "incompetent" female body, while presenting the male reproductive system as robust. This cultural casting of biological phenomena not only described women's physiology as weak and flawed, it also disadvantaged men, whose reproductive systems might need attention and repair.

The anthropologist Emily Martin analyzed the language of reproduction in standard twentieth-century medical textbooks that have been used routinely in medical schools. She found such statements as these: Ovaries "shed" eggs but testicles "produce" sperm, unfertilized eggs "degenerate" and are "wasted," and "menstruation is the uterus crying for lack of a baby." In contrast, although millions of sperm that do not fertilize eggs die within a few hours, the textbooks never called them "wasted," "failed," or "degenerating"; rather, they described the male reproductive physiology as a "remarkable cellular transformation . . . amazing characteristic of spermatogenesis is its sheer magnitude." Descriptions of fertilization in these textbooks reflect cultural ideas about male aggressiveness and female passivity. Although research documented the active role of the egg in traveling through the tube and showed that the process of fertilization involves mechanisms in both the sperm and the egg that make them "mutually active partners," the loaded language persisted. As if cast as a villain in a film noir, the advancing egg "captures and tethers" the sperm and "clasps" the sperm to its nucleus. The egg has become the femme fatale or the overbearing Mom, devouring its male victim.[7]

Psychological Diagnoses

Infertility treatment was frequently unsuccessful, because half the cases eluded diagnosis. Clinical research continued to focus on the development of more precise diagnostic methods and more effective treatments. Practitioners did not all agree about the basic underlying causes of infertility. Some staunchly believed that if a physiological cause could not be identified, it simply had not been discovered yet. Most, however, agreed that emotional factors could be involved. Researchers had already established that stress could affect hormonal secretions, tubal contractions, and even sperm motility. But the causes of the emotional stresses that led to these physiological outcomes, as well as the prescriptions for reducing these stresses, were a subject of considerable debate. Some leading physicians downplayed the psychological factor. "It is easy to overestimate its importance," said the medical director of the Planned Parenthood Center of Los Angeles. "Admittedly, emotional disturbances can play a part in infertility, but physical conditions are a more frequent cause.[8] Others, however, emphasized psychological causes.

At the extreme end of this debate in the 1940s and 1950s were the psychoanalytically oriented practitioners. If they could find no physiological cause for a couple's childlessness, they often looked for evidence of their patients' unconscious desires to avoid parenthood. This psychological scrutiny was generally directed toward women. Although men were more likely than women to resist treatment, physicians rarely considered the possibility that reluctant men had a psychological difficulty that contributed to their impaired fertility or that they "subconsciously" did not really want children. Stress caused by pressure at work was the only psychological factor mentioned in the medical literature on the evaluation of male patients. Experts in the field never suggested that men thwarted their own potential for parenthood by "unconscious wishes" or "a rejection of their masculinity." On the contrary, specialists frequently reassured men that infertility did not mean they were lacking in masculinity. Clearly, most physicians believed that masculinity was not something that men were likely to avoid. But psychoanalytically oriented physicians claimed that some women contributed to their own infertility by their reluctance, consciously or unconsciously, to "accept their femininity." According to these practitioners, even the most eager and cooperative female patient might "subconsciously" wish to avoid motherhood.

As infertility continued to gain attention from the popular media, as well as the scientific community, these psychoanalytic perspectives began to infuse the discussion of childlessness. The postwar years witnessed a romance with all forms of psychology, especially Freudian and neo-Freudian theories. Psychoanalytic jargon appeared everywhere, from scientific journals to popular articles, and even in casual conversations. Some neo-Freudian theorists breathed new life into prescriptions that were first voiced by their Victorian forebears about the importance of women attending to their proper role. Old notions that education and careers hindered women's reproductive potential resurfaced, as did exhortations about women's sexual behavior. Although many infertility experts were skeptical of psychoanalytic explanations, neo-Freudian practitioners received a remarkable amount of attention in both the medical and popular literature.[9]

One example of this approach was a 1951 article by a sociologist, a psychologist, and a gynecologist that was published in the *Journal of the American Medical Association*. The authors began with the premise that normal, healthy adults naturally desire children. "Most people who do not truly want them probably have personality defects—for example, infantilism. . . . Women totally lacking the desire for children are so rare that they may be considered as deviants from the normal." Infertile women, they reasoned, might subconsciously thwart their own fertility by rejecting their femininity. They described three "types" of such women:

> The masculine-aggressive woman insists on having a child of her own body, cost what it may. She is a ready, though rarely ideal, candidate for donor insemination, sometimes obtaining her husband's reluctant consent by a species of emotional blackmail. Second, there is the wife who accepts childlessness and lives on good terms with her sterile husband but demands from him constant proofs of his masculinity in the way of achievement and material success. And, third, the truly motherly woman compensates for her lack of children by directing her motherliness toward other persons or objects, real or symbolic.

The three male authors asserted that whatever intrusive procedures were required to enable a woman to get pregnant, including artificial insemination with the sperm of an anonymous donor, the women did not mind. In fact, they argued, the women may even enjoy it.

> The patients are seldom troubled by any notion of violation of their bodies; indeed, some of them derive a peculiar satisfaction from the coldly scientific nature of the operation. Successful results create a feeling of superiority and triumph over the male, as well as a sense of fulfillment.[10]

Some specialists who agreed with these psychological theories warned other practitioners not to treat "neurotic" women for infertility. One advised: "The wise physician will be able to ascertain the psychic health of his patients. He will then be in an enviable position to determine whether or not attempts should be made to relieve sterility." It was important to do so, he argued, for "allowing an emotional [sic] immature woman to become fertile may open up the proverbial hornet's nest. The repercussions may result in neurotic children, broken homes, and divorce."[11] Some gynecologists, as well as psychologists and psychiatrists, pointed to "personality" factors in infertility. "The emotional maturity of the patient, that is, her ability adequately to meet the demands of pregnancy as well as motherhood, should always be considered in the treatment of sterility," argued W. S. Kroger, director of Psychosomatic Gynecology at Mount Sinai Hospital in Chicago and one of the leading voices in the application of psychoanalytic theories to infertility treatment. Kroger urged his fellow practitioners to take note of "those unhealthy attitudes and personality factors likely to complicate or contraindicate pregnancy." To determine if a woman should be treated for infertility, the physician should "seek answers to the following questions":

1) Is the patient a cold, selfish, demanding person, or is she a warm, giving woman?
2) What is her motivation for becoming pregnant?
3) Could the absence of so-called "motherliness" be due to environmental factors, permanent or temporary, and does this account for her sterility?
4) How much does her emotional past . . . influence her attitudes toward motherhood?

5) What are the deeper meanings underlying her surface attitudes toward pregnancy, motherhood, and sterility?

Those who should be rejected for treatment included "the aggressive and masculine women who are competitive, strong, ambitious, and dominating. They 'wear the pants in the family' and are usually successful career women, possessing considerable executive ability." The greatest exemplar of the maladjusted female was the career woman. "We have all seen a long-desired pregnancy follow the renunciation of a career. This may be the result of the development of 'motherliness' and the consequent hormonal changes." Kroger concluded that "it should not be necessary for every physician to have training in psychoanalysis" to understand these basic principles. In other words, physicians who were not trained in psychology should make a psychological diagnosis that would determine whether the personality of the patient disqualified her for motherhood, in which case the physician should refuse treatment.[12] Kroger ended with a word of caution to the physician who might unwittingly treat a woman who was emotionally unqualified to become a mother: "If such a woman finally does conceive, the same psychological difficulties which once prevented conception, may adversely affect the child's psychic development, and . . . another individual is added to an endless procession of neurotics."[13]

Psychoanalytic ideas moved easily from the medical journals to the popular press. An article in *Coronet* magazine in 1953, entitled "Sterility Can Be a State of Mind," asserted that emotional states—hatred, fear, anxiety, poor adjustment to marriage—could inhibit fertility in from one-fourth to one-third of all cases of involuntary childlessness. According to the author, infertility often resulted from "high-strung women"; "strong parental prohibitions against sex"; and other psychological inhibitions, such as unresolved Oedipal conflicts. "Some specialists point out that to many persons, the doctor has become the highest authority in the conduct of their personal lives. . . . [He] has taken the place of the father of their childhood." Sometimes a visit to such a physician "may be reassuring to the wife and lead to a relaxation of her Fallopian tubes." The author also argued for the importance of sexual adjustment " 'The act of love' must, in truth, *be an act of love*, rather than just an act of sex, if fruitful union is to ensue." Repeating a common refrain, the article concluded, "If the wife is working, perhaps she can take a leave of absence for a while, or quit her job and stay at home. Rest and relax, and just forget all about doctors for a while. And see what happens."[14]

Some experts claimed that mere association with children would bring out a woman's "maternal instinct," which could stimulate fertility. *American Magazine* suggested a "plan that sometimes does wonders for childless couples. This is to go out babysitting. . . . [A] woman's maternal instincts are tremendously stimulated when there are children around." This was also the argument frequently given for the alleged "cure" of infertility by adoption. "Sometimes the adoption of a child is the secret," wrote an observer. "In the sunlight of a new happiness, the adoptive mother bears a child of her own." In one case, a psychoanalyst argued that the reason pregnancy followed adoption was because the wife quit her job after adopting a baby.

> Her conflict . . . resolved [sic] around the fact that if she became pregnant, she would have to stop working outside the home and abandon the masculine role. The decision to adopt a baby solved this unconscious conflict by making it absolutely necessary for her to give up her job. This, in some strange way, added to her femininity, and allowed her to conceive. Cases in which pregnancy follows the adoption of a baby are by no means rare. Everyone knows of similar instances.[15]

Some physicians were skeptical of these explanations. One cautioned those who believed that adoption often leads to biological parenting. "This popular belief has no justification. Some couples adopt a child, then subsequently have children of their own, and when this occurs, there's a lot of comment. But we don't hear about the many more couples who do not have children subsequent to adoption." This physician was also cautious about placing too much emphasis on emotional factors in infertility. He noted that emotional tension was as likely to be a *result* of infertility as a cause, since trying to conceive a child and seeking medical help in the effort were stressful activities in themselves: "Many childless couples are emotionally upset because of their failure to have children, but often the tensions have been built up as a result of years of frustration and hence may be an effect rather than a cause of the problem."[16]

This physician had a point. Infertile couples in the postwar years faced tremendous stresses. First, there was the stigma of childlessness at a time when having many children, at a young age, was the norm. Next was the suggestion, reinforced by psychoanalytic theories and echoed in the popular press, that infertile women were to blame for their own condition. Women were labeled abnormal if they were ambivalent about having children, they were suspected of not *really* wanting children even if they truly believed that they did, they were accused of unconscious wishes to remain childless, they were chastised for holding jobs or aspiring to careers, and they were admonished if they were not adequately passive and submissive. They were made to feel guilty if they had an abortion, held a job or pursued a career, or found sexual satisfaction in any way other than through a vaginal orgasm resulting from male penetration.

Since researchers had determined that stress might affect fertility, some of these pressures may have had the ironic effect of contributing to infertility. Women who were accused of being "abnormal," "selfish," "neurotic," or "immature" as a result of normal and healthy ambivalence toward or resistance to the accepted female role of full-time wife and mother may indeed have suffered enough stress to cause their fallopian tubes to contract. Meanwhile, in spite of the efforts of many specialists to improve the treatment of male infertility and the recognition that most infertility cases involved some problem with the male partner, infertility remained defined as a female complaint.

The New Pronatalism

According to feminist author Susan Faludi, the renewed push toward parenthood in the 1980s took the form of a media blitz aimed at educated career women, warning them that if they delayed childbearing, they were likely to find themselves infertile. Few of the alarmists who pointed to a new "infertility epidemic" took note of studies showing a troubling trend in male fertility: the decline in the average sperm count by more than half in the past thirty years. Nor did they mention the fact that less-educated poor women were more likely than professional women to be infertile, as a result of pelvic inflammatory disease, caused frequently by sexually transmitted diseases. Rather, many articles claimed that the alleged increase in infertility resulted from women postponing motherhood until they were in their thirties, when it might be too late to conceive.[17]

In 1987, NBC correspondent Maria Shriver called childlessness "the curse of the career woman." In the same year, *Life* published a special report entitled "Baby Craving." Headlines warned against "Having It All: Postponing Parenthood Exacts a Price" and bemoaned "The Quiet Pain of Infertility: For the Success-Oriented, It's a Bitter Pill." A columnist for the *New York Times* described the infertile woman as "a walking cliché" of the feminist generation, "a woman on the cusp of forty who put work ahead of motherhood." *Newsweek* noted the "trend of childlessness," and *Mademoiselle* warned, "Caution: You Are Now Entering the Age of Infertility."[18] . . .

Many observers assume that infertility is on the rise. But there is no evidence that the proportion of infertile Americans has increased. There is evidence, however, that the number of people who are seeking treatment has risen dramatically The number of visits to physicians for infertility treatment rose from 600,000 in 1968 to 1.6 million in 1984. The increase has been due, in part, to the huge baby-boom generation; the infertile among them are a large and visible group. But there are other reasons as well. Even if the chances for successful treatment are not much better than they were a half-century ago, dramatic new technological interventions are now available. High-tech approaches, such as in-vitro fertilization (IVF, fertilization of the egg in a laboratory petri dish and then its insertion directly into the uterus), first successfully used in the birth of Louise Brown in England in 1978, appear to offer "miracle babies" to the childless. Treatments using assisted reproduction techniques jumped 30 percent from 1990 to 1991, even though the chance of ending up with a "take-home baby" from these procedures was only about 15 percent.[19]

The promise of a technological fix, combined with a faith in medical progress, led many Americans to believe that they could triumph over most physical limitations. Physicians have responded to the demand. Studies have shown that American physicians are more likely than British practitioners to resort to heroic measures for treating infertility, probably because their patients request such intervention.[20] But reproductive medicine, despite its many advances over the past century, remains an imperfect art, available only to those who can afford it. Nor does it guarantee success. Infertility treatment is a high-stakes gamble: It is possible to lose all the money, time, and effort invested and gain nothing in return. If all the efforts of modern science, human struggle, and economic sacrifice do not result in the desired child, the rage, desperation, and anguish can be overwhelming.

Because birth control and reproductive choice are widely taken for granted, the infertile experience extreme frustration. Reproductive choice is much easier to achieve if the goal is to avoid pregnancy. Contraceptive technologies offer a success rate of nearly 100 percent, and legal abortion provides a backup when birth control methods fail. But infertile couples who seek treatment have only a 50 percent chance for success in the 1990s, odds that have not dramatically improved since the 1950s.[21] The inability to "control" one's reproductive fate is among the most exasperating experiences of infertility, especially for those who have put so much effort into the struggle. As the reporter Susan Sward wrote of her struggle with infertility, "As an organized, energetic person, I was used to getting what I wanted in life most of the time. To a major extent, I was also used to feeling in control of my life and knowing what I did would produce results if I tried hard enough. When it came to making babies, I found I had a lot to learn."[22]

Those who become pregnant while using birth control tend to blame the technology. But infertility patients who do not conceive often blame themselves. They feel unable to control their bodies or their destinies, even with medical intervention. For Roberta O'Leary, "It gets more and more difficult to pick up the pieces after each failure. I also don't like the feeling of having no control over what happens." Amanda Talley "felt like a freak of nature . . . embarrassed and shameful. . . . I felt as though my body betrayed me." Dierdre Kearney explained, "My feelings of helplessness have been hard to handle. We humans like to have control over our own lives and the one thing we think we can control is our body." She has done everything to have a baby and

> still my body betrays me and deprives me of one of the things I want most in life. I cannot make my body do what I want . . . I've heard some women say that being infertile makes them feel less like a woman. I've never really felt this. I guess, this has made me feel all too much like a woman because it's what makes me a woman that has caused my problem— PERIODS and HORMONES! I just feel helpless in determining my own future. Sometimes I feel like a ship at sea and just when I am close to land, a huge wave washes me out to sea again.[23]

The inability to control one's reproductive functions often leads to feelings of shame and worthlessness, especially for women. Maureen Wendell explained, "I began to feel defective, ashamed. I can't do a 'normal' biological function that most anyone else could do. I had to reevaluate my life, my hopes, my dreams and my identity as a woman. I am blessed to have a very supportive husband but even with that I felt inadequate as a wife." Feelings of inadequacy were magnified by the association of fertility with sexuality. In a taped message, Patricia Painter used the language of sexual potency when describing her husband's healthy sperm. "My husband has this, you know, magnificent, I guess he's extremely virile. He has like super sperm. . . . Everybody from the lab technicians to the receptionist at the doctor's office was always so amazed at the amount and the virility of this sperm. It's like super-human sperm." When they accidentally spilled some of the semen sample, a physician replied,

> "It doesn't matter. He could impregnate the whole block with what's left in here. It's amazing." Which made me feel absolutely horrible because he couldn't impregnate me. Well, it was real obvious who had the problem in this relationship, as far as who was the one responsible for us not getting pregnant, and that was me. So I felt extremely terrible about that. This resulted in my being very embarrassed around people. I felt very defect- ive. . . . It was just really such a blow. . . . I would get physically ill . . . 'cause I felt so defective and so embarrassed.

Laura Lerner also felt "abnormal," even though she was not infertile. But she was single, and her singleness deprived her of the opportunity to become a mother. "I am a woman. I am supposed to have children, right? What am I if I don't produce children?" She considered adopting as a single parent or trying donor insemination. But she could not bring herself to do it: "Withdrawing some sperm from the sperm bank sounds so cold and mechanical." Without children, she felt "unnatural. . . . I have had these damn menstrual cycles since age 11 and I have nothing to show for it. . . . I get so I hate the cycle when it comes. . . . I have the most trouble trying to determine why I am here. I feel very incomplete, and very abnormal."

Before she discovered she was infertile, Leila Ember felt that "Life was good! Most import- antly I was in control of it!" When she did not get pregnant, however, she began treatment, even though she recoiled at the invasive procedures: "For a person who had never had so much as a band-aid applied to any part of their body I found it quite difficult to endure the poking and prodding and exploratory procedures which were both financially and emotionally expensive." But her body remained uncooperative. Infertility destroyed her peace of mind and self- confidence: "I remember sitting on the floor of my bathroom for what seemed like hours and sobbing. I'd look at my husband and begin to scream how sorry I was that I 'messed up again!' " Blaming herself, she wrote, "My biological clock isn't ticking; it isn't working at all!"

Many childless women who wanted children questioned their own womanhood. Suzanna Drew felt "less of a woman—somehow not complete." Kate Foley felt "barren." Paula Kranz described feelings of "failure . . . it's like an empty space within yourself that you cannot fill." Marie Gutiérrez blamed herself when her husband's semen analysis

> came back ok, then O Boy! All fingers pointed to me, *wow* was I ever so unhappy, people don't know what it is like to try and try and never succeed. . . . I told no one . . . we were both embarrassed, marked, hurt. My husband is a very supportive husband, a good man and tells me that he accepts whatever happens, but . . . I can't accept the fact that I feel like some sort of alien, all women who are "normal" have children.

Along with at least four other women and men who wrote me, Marie offered to release her spouse from the marriage so that he could find a fertile partner and have children.

One reason why infertility is so wrenching is that treatment holds out the possibility of a "miracle cure," making it difficult to give up, grieve, and find acceptance. To pursue medical intervention means to hold out hope and experience disappointment month after month, while the possibility of pregnancy still exists.[24] Many infertility patients described the experience as an "emotional roller coaster." Marie Gutiérrez explained, "After each surgery and taking the fertility drug Clomid still trying and holding onto every good word from the Doctor that it could possibly happen this time, what a real drop in my Soul and a real letdown for my husband's ego, every test, every pill still no hope."

Amelia Monterey described the cycles of hope and disappointment. A thirty-three-year-old medical secretary married fifteen years to a construction worker, she lives in a trailer house in rural Minnesota. Like many others, she and her husband planned, dreamed, worked hard, saved, and assumed that they would achieve their goals. "We're poor," she wrote, but they pursued every possible treatment available before they finally gave up, heartbroken. Amelia wrote: "I've always been a caretaker. . . . I had no plans for college or even a career. . . . My whole childhood was built on the dream of becoming a wife and more—a Mother. I had no other life goals." When she did not become pregnant,

> I tried EVERYTHING! I took Clomid, got [hormone] shots, took my [temperature] every morning for years and even put an experimental drug up my nose. . . . I even had major surgery. They removed part of my ovaries. . . . What I want to get across is the feelings and the heartbreak of all these years of poking and probing that I went through. Looking at that thermometer *every* morning and not seeing it rise. . . . I went through that hurt, ache and devastation EVERY month. . . . [It] was like killing a small part of my womanhood.

In a similar cycle of hope and devastation, Susan Delmont had eight miscarriages and one failed adoption attempt. "I feel like a failure," she wrote. The experience destroyed her self-confidence, she quit her job, because she did not have "time enough to cry." She doubts her ability to raise a child. "I can't seem to apply for adoption. I don't know if I'm fit to be a mother or not, and I can't just say that I am. If God or whoever won't let me have my babies, why should an adoption agency?" Still, depressed as she was, she knew when she was getting the wrong advice from experts. One psychiatrist told her "just having 8 miscarriages couldn't make me as sad as I was. He was sure that my father sexually abused me as a child, and that my subconscious covered it up. Needless to say, I dumped him." But she was still left with her anguish. "I don't feel like I've had miscarriages, I feel like I've lost children. . . . I have 'phantom' children—you know, like an amputee has a phantom limb."

Rage

Along with pain and frustration, many infertile respondents expressed almost bottomless rage—at themselves, their bodies, and the fertile world. Carey Van Camp described feeling "almost hateful" and feeling "a burning rage inside me," especially toward pregnant women or infants. Lydia Sommer said infertility

> came as a shock to us—like being punched in the stomach and not being able to catch your breath. . . . The world turns and we stand still. . . . I detest all pregnant women—whether they are my friends or not. They carry their pregnancy like a badge of honor, when they did nothing special to achieve it. Honestly, they make me sick. Sounds pretty bad, doesn't it? I'm becoming more cynical about it as I get older and my clock ticks away.

For many, the sight of their desired goal did not bring out warm feelings toward children. Rather, they felt hateful—even murderous. As Patricia Painter explained,

> It was *so* painful to see anybody that was pregnant or had a baby. . . . I was the proverbial woman that was leaving the fertility doctor's office and saw the pregnant lady with two

kids, a baby and a, you know, a toddler, in the crosswalks, and wanted to run over them all. God I felt *so* guilty for feeling that way until I got involved with Resolve. I really thought I was a horrible person. I thought God was punishing me or something. . . . I really wanted to run them over very badly with my car. . . . And I knew that every pregnant woman, every woman that had a new baby . . . got pregnant just to hurt my feelings. And God knows they did!

Patricia realized that her initial motivation for pursuing infertility treatment, her "love for children," virtually vanished. "I had a point where I could not see children at all. It was so painful." One friend, to protect her feelings when her toddler ran to the door, "looked around in her house, grabbed a newspaper, and put it in front of his face. Wasn't that nice? So I didn't have to see the kid. I thought that was nice. I'm sure my friends thought I was nuts." She even began to question her own sanity. "My values got real distorted and screwed up. . . . It felt very weird. . . . I had the ability to stand back and say, 'You're getting real strange, Patricia.' . . . And yet I couldn't seem to stop it. Kind of like trying to stop an avalanche, I think. The flood of emotion was so difficult."

Many of the desperately infertile expressed their most intense rage and disdain toward those who they believed neither wanted nor deserved their children, especially the young and the poor. Sonia Everly wrote, "It just doesn't seem fair . . . that young girls are getting pregnant when they have no desire to be parents." Daisy Posner's hatred went in all directions. As a nurse, she worked in labor and delivery. "I hated all the patients, even more so the ones with 3–4 kids who were on cocaine. I was sick with envy and hated God for being so unfair to me." In 1990, after infertility treatment, Daisy had a healthy daughter. "But having one child isn't enough. . . . I still feel like a failure for all the miscarriages. I hate my body—it has felt empty and useless ever since my daughter was born. I hate reading about all the pregnant teenagers in the paper. . . . All my friends here are pregnant with their second child. It is all I can do to stay friendly with them—I hate them so much. . . . I pray all the time for another baby but God must hate me. He gives lots of babies to poor drug addicts and only one to me. . . . And I still hated my labor and delivery patients for having more kids. Needless to say I work elsewhere now. . . . but I am still stuck in anger and despair."

Some infertile women expressed anger at women who had abortions. Paula Kranz felt "anger, bitterness and jealousy. . . . And then there are women out there being blessed with babies, and they are killing them with abortions." Dierdre Kearney wrote, "Each time I read of a child abuse case or of a woman having a third abortion, I cannot help but question, 'Why?' " But many infertile women saw abortion as a choice, much like infertility treatment. Karen Pasmore found it ironic that "so many women become pregnant without even thinking about it, many when they'd rather not," but she was nevertheless "strongly pro-choice. Many of my friends don't understand my position but if another woman becomes pregnant against her wishes, my infertility is not affected. I guess the grass is always greener."

Infertile women who had abortions themselves often felt guilty for years. Sue Kott got pregnant when she was twenty-five. Although she wanted to have the baby, her boyfriend wanted her to have an abortion. Two years later they married, and she has not been able to conceive again. She never forgave herself for the abortion. After years of infertility treatment, she is still childless, and her husband "refuses to adopt." Sonia Everly, on the other hand, has forgiven herself. Between her two marriages, she became pregnant while in graduate school and had an abortion.

The abortion was traumatic, as it always is; never an easy decision, but the right one for me, and my partner, at the time. I obviously did not know that would be my only pregnancy. Would my choice have been different had I known? I think so, but I made my decision based on what I knew at that time. I still assumed I could become pregnant when I wanted to, when I was ready.

If abortion was difficult for some infertile women to accept, others found the fecundity of the poor unbearable. Some who believed that they had earned their right to reproductive self-determination were quick to deny the same right to others. Several shared the sentiments of Lisa Brown, who wrote, "I don't appreciate females having more kids than they can provide for and go on welfare. . . . I think there should be a law of 2 kids on welfare only. I think there should be sterilization inforced after the 2nd child."

Lisa's fury was directed toward the wrong target. Poor women on welfare were not responsible for her infertility, but she blamed them, rather than the real villains. In her case, as in many others, there were real villains. She was one of several respondents whose infertility resulted from severe damage to their bodies caused by sexual abuse when they were children. These respondents well understood the source of their problem, but did not express anger directly toward the men who raped them. None, in fact, mentioned whether their molesters had been apprehended. Thirty-one respondents, including two men, specifically mentioned abuse as a direct cause of their childlessness, ranging from emotional abuse to physical and sexual abuse.[25] The most horrifying were the stories of women like Lisa whose reproductive organs were damaged because they were raped when they were young children.

Lisa did not mention the rapes until the end of her letter. She began without a standard salutation, asking "if your some weirdo, getting off on others pain." She described years of infertility treatment, including several reconstructive surgeries, tubal pregnancies, and miscarriages. She and her husband tried to adopt, but they learned that it would take approximately ten years, because they wanted a child under age two. At age forty-three, Lisa had lost her struggle to have a child and lost her marriage as well. She explained,

> When your husband goes out and gets a bar whore pregnate after 12 years of marriage and 4 miscarriages and 2 tubal pregnancies and the loss of 7 children, your mom says, "what do you expect? He wants kids, you can't give him any." So the marriage is gone and death looks good! What good am I to anyone? . . , Bitter? VERY! Being a female has not been fun for me. . . Why did God see fit to take my kids but lets whores, child beaters and molesters have kids? And hurt or kill them?

Lisa was on the list for IVF when her husband "got a bar whore pregnant" and the marriage ended. "That was the hardest phone call I had to make in my life—calling and cancelling my only sure promise of a child." Although it was certainly far from a "sure promise," she was prepared to pay the $4,500 to try it. It was not until a brief postscript added after she signed her letter that she revealed the source of her difficulty: She was repeatedly raped by her step-grandfather and half-uncle from ages four through seven. "And by the way the rapes were performed (on the top of the bathroom toilet tank lid with my legs drawn up like I was squatting). It tilted my uterus so severely it caused all my future female problems."

Trudy Mayer, a white married factory worker, was also a victim of incest as a child and cannot carry a baby. She wrote three letters explaining her experience and her anguish, expressing anger not toward her molester but toward herself.

> When I first found out that I may never have a child I tried to kill myself because I was raised to believe that women are to reproduce so that made me feel like if I can't do what God intend women to do then I didn't belong. After that I felt very angry I was angry at me, at God at my Mother for having Me I was looking for some one to hate or blame I still have these feelings.

But the true villain remained unnamed.

> Doctors and friends and family say oh just keep trying it will happen even my husband says we will just keep trying. Me I'm tired of it I want a baby but I don't want to keep going throw the hurt I have been pregnant seven times and each one I have lost and everyone says oh I understand but there is no way that they can understand what I go throu. I read the paper and see where some parents kill there kids or leave them in a trash can or something and stop and say to myself why would someone do such a thing to their own child but how can I understand I have never been in there shoes the same as you, you could never understand no matter how much you would like to.

She has seen specialists and had many surgeries, "so many that my stomach looks like a war zone." It was not until the end of her letter that she gave the reason for her misery: "I was molested very young . . . but it did not stop there it continued until I was 10 years old because I did not know that this was wrong."

Trudy did not name her abuser until her second letter: "I was molested when I was five years old by my father and it went on for years and I thought of suicide many of times through the years." She lived with her husband seven years before she finally married him

> because if he can handle all these things we have been throu then I would be dum not to marrie him. . . . he has been at every doctors appointment been write there with every miscarriage he has cryed throu them with me he has been my clown but even with all this he new that he could leave and be with some one who can have children but he wanted to be with me even thou being with me hurts him a little of him dies every day because of are childless problem we have a specialist we go to and even with insurance it hurts the pocket book and we have looked in to adoption but they want you to be millionaire just to adopt a child this is what kills us every day a little to a time but what can you do.

In cases of sexual violence, the cause of infertility was grimly evident. But brutality surfaced in the letters of only a minority of respondents. In other cases, the very technologies that were developed to improve individual control over reproduction led to infertility. Ironically, many infertile individuals turned to medical experts to cure a problem that medical technology had created. Vivian Johnson discovered that her tubes were scarred from her previous use of an intrauterine device (IUD), and surgery did not correct the problem. Ultimately, high-tech reproductive medicine overcame the problem created by high-tech contraception. She had twins from her first IVF attempt. Karen Pasmore had a problem shared by tens of thousands of her peers; she was infertile because her mother was treated with diethylstilbestrol, or DES, during pregnancy. The drug was used widely in the 1940s and 1950s to prevent miscarriages.[26] In college, "DES became the specter in my life that it remains today." She turned to invasive high-tech infertility treatment, with no luck. Lorraine Pascasio was luckier. She, too, was a DES daughter. Initially she felt, "I'm defective' . . . Damaged goods." But she finally had a "miracle baby" and wrote her story for the *Ladies Home Journal*.[27]

It is now nearly fifty years since Dr. Abraham Stone offered his definition of a woman as one who accepts "her primary role, that of conceiving and bearing a child." Today most physicians, as well as most women, know that infertility can result from a wide range of factors, affecting both male and female. But the power of that psychological and behavioral definition of womanhood has persisted long after its scientific validity has been questioned. Articles in the popular press still blame career women for an "infertility epidemic," even though infertility continues to affect poor people to a much greater extent than the affluent. This fact should be obvious, since infertility, like other health problems, is more likely to plague those with fewer resources and less access to good medical care. Nevertheless, in spite of all evidence to the contrary, infertility still carries a stigma suggesting that women are to blame for their own inability to conceive.

Notes

This essay is excerpted from Elaine Tyler May, *Barren in the Promised Land: Childless Americans and the Pursuit of Happiness* (New York: Basic Books, 1995), chaps. 5 and 7.

1. "Psychological Aspects of Fertility," manuscript draft, dated November 8, 1950, *New York Times*, Stone File, Countway Library of Medicine, Rare Books and Manuscripts, Harvard University, Boston (hereafter Stone File, Countway Library).
2. By 1990, only 20 percent of infertility remained unexplained, yet only half of all infertile couples undergoing medical treatment would achieve pregnancies. See Margarete J. Sandelowski, "Failures of Volition: Female Agency and Infertility in Historical Perspective," *Signs: Journal of Women in Culture and Society* 15 (1990): 475–99.
3. I. C. Rubin, M.D., as told to Margaret Albrecht, "Childlessness and What Can Be Done about It," *Parents*, March 1957, 46ff.
4. Herbert H. Thomas, M.D., "Thirty-Two Years of Fertility Progress," Presidential Address, *Fertility and Sterility* 27 (October 1976): 1125–31.
5. Edward T. Tyler, M.D., as told to Roland H. Berg, "Childless Couples Can Have Babies," *Look*, September 17, 1957, 41–50; and Willis E. Brown, M.D., "Privilege and Responsibility: Presidential Address," *Fertility and Sterility* 14 (1963): 475–81.
6. Mrs. Gary B., Hurst, Texas, January 14, 1964, to Dr. Rock; reply from Robert E. Wheatley, M.D., March 23, 1964, Rock Papers, Countway Library.
7. Emily Martin, "The Egg and the Sperm: How Science Has Constructed a Romance Based on Stereotypical Male-Female Roles," *Signs: Journal of Women in Culture and Society* 16 (1991): 485–501; see also Emily Martin, *The Woman in the Body: A Cultural Analysis of Reproduction* (Boston: Beacon Press, 1987), 45–48.
8. Tyler, "Childless Couples Can Have Babies."
9. For an excellent study of the transformation of psychiatry during the early twentieth century and its cultural significance, see Elizabeth Lunbeck, *The Psychiatric Persuasion: Knowledge, Gender, and Power in Modern America* (Princeton: Princeton University Press, 1994).
10. Herbert D. Lamson, Willem J. Pinard, and Samuel R. Meaker, "Sociologic and Psychological Aspects of Artificial Insemination with Donor Semen," *Journal of the American Medical Association* 145 (April 7, 1951): 1062–63.
11. "Program: American Society for the Study of Sterility, Eighth Annual Conference," June 7 and 8, 1952, Chicago, 10 and 11, and descriptions of papers by Therese Benedek, M.D., "Infertility as a Psychosomatic Defense," and W. S. Kroger, M.D., "The Evaluation of Personality Factors in the Treatment of Infertility," in Tyler Clinic Archives, Los Angeles.
12. Sandelowski, "Failures of Volition," 475–99.
13. W. S. Kroger, M.D., "Evaluation of Personality Factors in the Treatment of Infertility," *Fertility and Sterility* 3 (November–December 1952): 542–51.
14. Vera G. Kinsler, "Sterility Can Be a State of Mind," *Coronet*, April 1953, 109–12.
15. "Family Problems," *American Magazine*, August 1951, 108; William Engle, "Maybe You *Can* Have a Baby," *American Weekly*, November 8, 1953, 8; J. D. Ratcliff, "Clinics for the Childless," *Hygeia* 19 (October 1941): 854 Joseph D. Wassersug, "More Help for Childless Couples," *Hygeia* 25 (November 1947); 384–85.
16. Tyler, "Childless Couples Can Have Babies."
17. Susan Faludi, *Backlash: The Undeclared War against American Women* (New York: Crown, 1991), 24–27. On the declining sperm count, see Amy Linn, "Male Infertility: From Taboo to Treatment," *Philadelphia Inquirer*, May 31, 1987, A1, cited in Faludi, *Backlash*, 31–32. On the new pronatalism, see also Margarete J. Sandelowski, *With Child in Mind: Studies of the Personal Encounter with Infertility* (Philadelphia: University of Pennsylvania Press, 1993), 9.
18. Articles cited in Faludi, *Backlash*, 104–10.
19. On the proportion of the infertile, see Arthur L Greil, *Not Yet Pregnant: Infertile Couples in Contemporary America* (New Brunswick, N.J.: Rutgers University Press, 1991), 27–28; data on physicians visits from Office of Technology Assessment, in Philip Elmer-Dewitt, "Making Babies," *Time*, September 30, 1991, 56–63; see also David Perlman, "The Art and Science of Conception: Brave New Babies," *San*

Francisco Chronicle, March 3, 1990, B3; on the success of IVF, see Nancy Wartik, "Making Babies," *Los Angeles Times Magazine*, March 6, 1994, 18ff.

20. Study cited in Greil, *Not Yet Pregnant*, 11.

21. Most estimates gave infertile couples a 50 percent chance, as they did in the 1950s and 1960s, although some physicians were more conservative. One physician in 1962, for example, gave infertile couples a 40 percent chance of a cure, saying that "more could be helped if husbands would cooperate completely with medical examination and treatment." See Grace Naismith, "Good News for Childless Couples," *Today's Health* 40 (January 1962): 24ff. For 1990 data, see Greil, *Not Yet Pregnant*, 11.

22. Susan Sward, "I Thought Having a Baby Would Be Easy," *San Francisco Chronicle*, March 5, 1990, B4. See also Miriam D. Mazor, "Barren Couples," *Psychology Today*, May 1979, 101–12.

23. The quotations from infertile women, unless otherwise indicated, were gathered using an author's query sent to newspapers and journals across the country. The query letter, addressed to the editors, asked individuals who had experienced childlessness at some point in their lives to write to me about their experiences and feelings. We had no way of knowing which journals published the query, but more than five hundred people wrote back from all over the country. None of the respondents is identified by his or her real name. For a more detailed discussion of the sample, see "Appendix: A Note on the Sample Letters," in May, *Barren in the Promised Land*, 261–65.

24. See Greil, *Not Yet Pregnant*, esp. chap. 4.

25. The abuse mentioned included psychological or physical abuse that the respondents did not wish to perpetuate or made them feel they would be bad parents. Some said that they had only recently "discovered their childhood sexual abuse in therapy, by retrieving repressed memories. Although these approaches are highly controversial in the professional therapeutic community, it is noteworthy that several childless people mentioned these "repressed memories" in relation to their childlessness. Other cases, however, like those quoted in this chapter, were not repressed memories. They were well-remembered rapes that continued for years.

26. See Philip Elmer Dewitt "Making Babies," *Time*, September 30, 1991, 56–62. DES Action and other groups have been formed by and on behalf of women who have been harmed by DES, the Dalkon Shield, and other medical products. See Karen M. Hicks, *Surviving the Dalkon Shield IUD: Women v. The Pharmaceutical Industry* (New York: Teachers College Press, 1994).

27. Lorraine Pascasio, "A Christmas Baby," *Ladies Home Journal*, December 1991, 14–17.

32

Polishing Brown Diamonds

African American Women, Popular Magazines, and the Advent of Modeling in Early Postwar America

Laila Haidarali

In 1969, the *New York Times* declared the work of Ophelia DeVore in training hundreds of African American women in the skills of modeling as "Polishing Black Diamonds." Reflecting on her twenty-three years at the DeVore School of Charm, Ophelia DeVore—the first African American professional model by some accounts—described the women attending the school as "rough diamonds," and her mission as "polish[ing] them and show[ing] up their individual lustre." By contemporary standards the "rough diamond" metaphor is somewhat clichéd, but the newspaper article illustrates the late 1960s celebratory view of African American women's beauty as not only obscured and uncultivated, but also as potentially dazzling. "Polishing Black Diamonds" reflected on the growth of African American modeling from its inception in the mid-1940s to its then burgeoning state. Beginning in 1946, the DeVore School of Charm presented skills deemed essential for those in the modeling industry—namely charm, poise, and elegance—as democratic ideals to be purchased and displayed by "ordinary" African American women as both symbols of, and avenues to, success.[1] Although the designation of "Black" reflects the period's usage of the term, this study attends to the early postwar era when it was not the "Black," but rather the "Brown" diamond who was being polished. On the eve of the civil rights movement, this "Brown" diamond emerged in the gendered image of the "Brownskin" who exemplified the dominant ideal of African American womanhood. Far from being presented as an unattainable standard, "Brownskin" womanhood was cast as possible for all "rough diamonds."

In early postwar America, social and economic success seemed to be awaiting "rough diamonds" or "ordinary" African American women who witnessed an increase in employment opportunities and in economic gain. Small in comparison to those experienced by white America, these improvements were largely restricted to those in urban and Northern centers. However limited and limiting, postwar advances brought new opportunities for members of the race, especially for women. Between 1940 and 1950, the number of African American women employed as domestics dropped from 60 percent to 41 percent; by 1960, that number fell even more significantly to 36 percent. Accompanying this decline was the relative growth of African American women in clerical work.[2] Between 1870 and 1930, clerical work became increasingly gendered and racialized as white female labor. Additionally clerical work grew ever more tied to class-bound notions of respectability deemed the sole possession of white women.[3] Not only were African American women viewed as lacking middle-class morals and manners "necessary" for white-collar work, but racist attitudes also kept white employees and customers "safe" from African American workers. When hired, African American women were slotted into clerical positions that restricted interracial contact.[4] Although these prejudices did not disappear after 1945, and African American women did not flood the clerical labor force, there was a modest increase in white-collar workers among African American women; this was largely the combined result of organized urban protest, the rise of liberal consensus, and demographic changes.[5] Whereas in 1940, white women comprised 24 percent of the clerical labor force, African American women represented less than 1 percent of workers in this field. By 1950, those numbers changed to 31 percent and 4 percent respectively; by 1960, statistics showed 33 percent of white and 8 percent of African American women working as "clerical and kindred workers."[6] Small, but perceptible, the movement of some African American women into previously white enclaves enhanced their visibility and tested their viability as middle-class, white-collar workers.[7]

The growth of the African American female clerical workforce augmented the already heavy burden carried by women. While the segregated clerical and sales labor market traditionally employed more African American men than women, the feminization of clerical work and its prescriptions of middle-class respectability translated into greater opportunities for African American women.[8] For example, in 1950, African American women comprised 4 percent of the clerical workforce, with 3 percent of African American men being employed in like positions; by 1960 those numbers changed to 8 percent and 5 percent respectively.[9] As a result, the onus rested on women to prove the race worthy of social integration and white-collar status; this "proof" involved imparting an image of clean, respectable, middle-class femininity. Although good grooming did not constitute a new formula for social advancement, the discourse assumed new relevance in the postwar era.[10] Directed at a generation supposedly on the brink of full civil liberties, prescriptions on middle-class African American femininity were fleshed out in mass-circulated photographic magazines. In the decade immediately following the war, "rough diamonds" or "ordinary" African American women witnessed a series of images and ideas that lauded respectable femininity, consumptive lifestyle, and heterosexual fulfillment as the measure of African American womanhood.

The displays of professional African American models assisted the "rough diamond" in cultivating femininity, poise, and charm. Professional models most often emerged in the body of the "Brownskin"—a heterosexual and feminine creature who was visibly African American and virtuously middle-class. "Brownskin" models permeated the pages of another postwar invention, *Ebony* magazine. Here, the "Brownskin's" stylized display of respectable, feminized heterosexuality embodied the crowning glory of an attendant African American middle class. If that were not enough in the way of popular guidance for the "rough diamond" to learn how to polish her image and to acquire the necessary skills to negotiate her way on the horizon of the promised land, then charm and modeling schools offered further assistance. These schools advanced beauty and poise as necessary commodities to succeed in the expectant postwar climate. These three entities—the "Brownskin" model, the medium of the photographic magazine, and the mentoring of the charm and modeling school—disseminated a new understanding of African American womanhood on the eve of the civil rights era.

Model, medium, and mentor intertwined to form a class-bound discourse on African American women's social and sexual status. The apex of this tripartite transmission was the image of the "Brownskin," whose centrality to the commodification of poise, charm, and femininity is the focus of this article. Ubiquitous in early postwar popular magazines, the gendered image of the "Brownskin" became a signifier of democratic promise by representing economic and social triumph in a period when these goals remained unfulfilled for many African Americans. Grounding the birth of the "Brownskin" in the search for advertising appeals to African American consumers, this article demonstrates how the modeling profession positioned African American women in the concomitant roles of the feminized worker and the domestic, heterosexual homemaker.

The "Brownskin" remained central to the visual discourse that exhibited African Americans as successful, well-dressed, and attractive, but that did not forge a racial identity wholly independent from white America. The "Brownskin" occupied the middle space of being visibly "black," but not too dark-skinned to disrupt dominant aesthetic values. Although the imagery most certainly did not overturn notions of womanhood as heterosexual, feminine, and respectable, it reclaimed these attributes from the sole possession of white women. Conservative elements continued to contour the postwar visual discourse, but this imagery can nonetheless be understood as an important juncture in the formation of racial identity through the eyes of African Americans. Photographic magazines such as *Ebony* attempted to overturn the racist stereotyping of African American women as dark-skinned, unattractive mammies, maids, and laundresses by endowing the "Brownskin" with attributes historically denied African American women—beauty, poise, and success. And while the "Brownskin" exhibited her sexual attractiveness and heterosexual fulfillment, the performance occurred within the parameters of the African American community, simultaneously freeing her from the unwanted advances of white men and confining her identity to the needs of the race. At once libratory in its attempted redress of racist stereotyping and restrictive in its narrow dictates of racialized gender expectations, this postwar visual discourse allows us to glean some understanding of an era when African America began to visualize a different public racial reality with the "Brownskin" woman—the polished "Brown" diamond—at its center.

Advertising the Brownskin

The birth of the "Brownskin" as a particularly gendered and commodified representation emerged from the needs of advertisers to attract a newly important demographic: the African American consumer. In the early 1940s, white businesses recognized that the growing incomes of this demographic equaled enhanced consumer power. This new prosperity among African Americans was relative to advances made by whites in the same period. White racism undoubtedly continued to limit opportunities available to African Americans, but the financial improvements experienced by many, during and after World War II, are well documented by historians. The continuous African American migration to the North between 1941 and 1960 occurred largely for the same reasons as the earlier "Great Migration"—declining agricultural conditions, virulent racism, and the promise of better jobs.[11] The added stimulus in the latter period emerged from wartime economic opportunities that spiked wages to a historic high.[12] Buoyed by new promises of economic opportunity, African American populations in the rural South decreased, transferring themselves mostly to urban centers in the North, the West, and also in the South. The changing demography resulted in an increasing urbanization of the African American population: between 1940 and 1950 African American urban inhabitants increased by 46 percent.[13]

During the war years, David J. Sullivan, an African American market researcher whose study of African American consumers achieved some attention, rose as the expert analyst of the "Negro Market."[14] By 1945, Sullivan provided numbers to underscore the importance of this neglected demographic. Without citing his source, Sullivan approximated that African American incomes amounted to $10.29 billion or $779 per capita.[15] Indeed, median incomes of "Negro and other races" climbed from $489 in 1939 to $1,448 in 1947. While this rise was a far cry from the white median income of $1,325 and $2,999 in the same years, it was still significant.[16] Those who had ignored the African American consumer potential could no longer continue to do so. Indeed, the "Negro Market" did not intrigue all; some businesses made little effort to lure this "new" consumer, but for those who desired to do so, help was available.

Framing the discussion as the "Negro Market," business periodicals explored the most effective ways to secure this demographic. One important article appeared in a 1943 issue of *Sales*

Management; it cautioned, "Don't Do This—If You Want to Sell Your Products to Negroes!" and provided ten examples of negative stereotyping that repelled the race-proud consumer. The article, written by Sullivan, provided ten factors to avoid in such advertising. Ranging from the avoidance of "exaggerated Negro characters, with flat noses, thick lips, kinky hair," to not offending the clergy, Sullivan's fifth point was specific in its address of the representation of African American women. Denouncing the term "Negress"—and its host of meanings—as antiquated, Sullivan pointed to the denigrating images of African American women as "buxom, broad-faced, grinning mammies and Aunt Jemimas." In providing the ameliorative, Sullivan asserted that representations of "laundresses, cooks, and domestic servants" presented a limited vision of African American women's work.[17] Sullivan's assessment confirmed the findings of what historian Robert Weems Jr. considers one of the "first truly systematic studies of African American consumers."[18] Authored by Paul K. Edwards, a white economics professor at Fisk University, this 1932 study assessed consumption patterns among a cross-section of African American Southern urban consumers. *The Southern Urban Negro as Consumer* highlighted negative consumer reactions to advertisements that employed images of African Americans. The study presented advertisements that displayed images of African Americans to urban African American Southerners, and asked for their assessment of its "appeal"; two of these images employed the image of women as laundresses, and one represented the now-notorious Aunt Jemima. Consistently ranked as a reason for disfavor with the images was the demeaning position of African Americans as menial workers, subservient and inferior to whites. Additionally, the representation of the African American female as a "big, fat colored woman"—the mammy image—offended almost all who cited the "red kerchief" and earrings as deterrents to their purchase of the product. Many respondents found these outmoded and inflammatory images restored ideas of slavery. The responses gathered from Edwards's study on "selling appeals" reflected that consumers yearned for new, race-proud representations.[19]

Sullivan's marketers' warning "Don't Do This" reinforced these earlier academic findings. While Edwards made implicit references to skin tone, and the "exaggerated[d] . . . color of the Negro," by 1943, Sullivan made explicit these meanings. He warned white advertisers about the use of skin tone in their advertisements; Sullivan argued: "By no means color them black. Use brown-skinned girls for illustrations; then you satisfy all."[20] The invocation of brownskin as the happy medium appears consistently throughout the period, and it was the period's dominant construction of African American womanhood celebrated in images, texts, and popular understanding. Sullivan's advisement on the use of brownskin models reflects the cultural prevalence of the "Brownskin" as the happiest negotiator of race, class, sex, and gender.

Brandford Models: "Another Step Up"

The need for brown-skinned women to advertise goods to the new "Negro Market" ignited the birth, and growth, of modeling as a profession opened to African American women. Brandford Models, the first African American agency, opened in New York City in July 1946. One caption in an unidentified newspaper heralded the event as "Another Step Up: First Agency for Negro Models Opens," and quoted actor Canada Lee's assessment that this was "an historic moment in our lives, and also . . . a new era in the advertising field."[21] Edward Brandford, a commercial photographer and the agency's founder, emphasized the paucity of attention paid to African American consumers despite their "vast spending power." His particular concern was the plight of African American female consumers who "in their buying have never had proper guidance, [and] have always been neglected."[22] This statement reiterated the findings of market researchers such as Sullivan and economists such as Edwards who underscored the deficient efforts of advertisers to attract an African American clientele. It also positioned the role of women, as both models to advertise products and consumers to purchase these commodities, as central to a middle-class consumptive lifestyle.

When Brandford Models opened in 1946, the availability of cosmetics to African American women was not the primary concern; these products had long been peddled to African American women.[23] According to Mary Louise Yabro, one of Brandford's agency's fashion stylists, the crucial missing component was advice on cosmetic use. Yabro defined one of the agency's roles as ameliorating the paucity of "proper fashion and beauty guidance," and noted that the unique "problems in makeup and clothes" facing African American women were too long overlooked. In the interest of "giving fair play to the Negro," Yabro underscored the need for Brandford Models to provide such guidance.[24] By employing the language of "fair play," Yabro implied that by appropriating the right image African American women could more easily achieve success through the use of the correct cosmetics and clothing. Indeed, this view reflects the more general therapeutic consumerist ethos emitted to American society as a whole,[25] but according to Yabro's assessment, it was the deficiency of advice directed at African American women that hindered social and economic success.

"Another Step Up" was optimistic in its assessment of Brandford Models' ability to overturn the barriers facing African Americans in the early postwar period—the article's reporter cheerfully concluded that "one more barrier to economic freedom for the American Negro was lifted."[26] While the need for African American models to advertise goods played an essential role in the opening of Brandford Models, the vehicle for the display of models was equally important. In an atmosphere of postwar optimism, African American popular magazines emerged as a stage for models to display consumer goods and assisted in constructing a new visual discourse of urban middle-class African America.

The Rise of *Ebony*

Constructed in response to advertisers' needs, the gendered body of the "Brownskin" materialized into a glossy, photographic representation of heterosexually respectable African American womanhood. The expansion of photography and the emergence of *Ebony*, the first popular magazine geared at a specifically African American audience, popularized a new visual discourse on middle class life with the "Brownskin" woman at its center. First appearing in November 1945, *Ebony* presented to its readers a celebratory vision of middle-class African America. Clearly stated in its inaugural issue in November 1945, *Ebony's* editorial stance mirrored the views of its publisher John H. Johnson. The editors declared themselves to be "rather jolly folks" who wished to accent "all the swell things . . . Negroes can do and will accomplish." The editorial pledged: "*Ebony* will try to mirror the happier side of Negro life—the positive, everyday achievements from Harlem to Hollywood. But when we talk about race as the No. 1 problem in America, we'll talk turkey."[27] This significant departure from the long history of the African American press as the voice of protest against racial injustice did not initially curtail the magazine's success. Indeed, *Ebony* flourished as one of the most widely circulated African American popular magazines of the period reaching a circulation of 500,000 by 1954.[28] But after this crescendo, sales plummeted; by 1954 the magazine's formulaic, optimistic depiction of African American life was out of synchronicity with the growing movement for civil rights. Under great social pressure, *Ebony's* post-1954 gaze sharpened into a more politically militant focus.

At the outset, *Ebony* provided a racial corrective to its prototype *Life*; its glossy pages displayed prosperity, consumerism, and "Brownskin" beauties, thereby sustaining dominant ideals and furnishing proof of middle-class African America. While *Ebony* exaggerated the reality of economic attainment, the impact of these images on the African American psyche cannot be overstated. In a country where the mass-produced, public, visual representation of African America—if at all visible—was mostly a disparaging one, *Ebony's* photos of successful, exquisitely groomed and dressed men and women opened a window into a different world. Furthermore, if one flipped through the pages of *Ebony*, these images were in continuous motion rather than in isolated display. The tangibility of the magazine, the movement of the pages, and the persistence of the "Brownskin" photographic image diverged from depictions of successful "Brownskins" in film, most notably Lena Horne and Dorothy Dandridge. No doubt, the film images of these two entertainers—both commonly featured in *Ebony*—profoundly influenced African Americans, but the medium elicited a different sensory perception. Within the magazine—a physical and permanent consumer good—the repetitive and recurrent imagery stressed the reality of economic, social, and sexual well-being. *Ebony* magazine laid before its readers the American dream as a kaleidoscopic racialized spectacle of American achievement.[29]

Through its images and stories of successful women and men, *Ebony* furnished evidence that prosperity and social achievement, unattained by many African Americans in the period, was possible. *Ebony* reaffirmed the liberal ideal of economic opportunity and championed a capitalistic system that ignored the unequal structures maintaining the economic divide. Surely many readers were frustrated by their distance from Ebony's depiction of African American life, but the proof that some members of the race achieved economic well-being and some had indeed obtained a piece of the American pie may have renewed belief in racial progress. *Ebony*'s great success reveals that African Americans either believed, or wanted to believe, or at the very least were entertained by, such displays of middle-class comfort and consumerism.

Ebony, Advertising, and African American Models

Although *Ebony* proved a crucial site for white businesses to sell their goods to the "Negro Market," the use of "Brownskin" models in advertisements was far from automatic. In his autobiography, John H. Johnson recalled the difficulties in attaining advertisers in the first years of the magazine, and his aggressiveness in both the recruitment of advertising accounts and the encouragement of the use of African American models. Despite the research defining the "Negro Market," Johnson demonstrated that many white businesses needed further coaxing to make such investments.[30] "Duplicate advertising"—the practice of substituting African American models for white—allowed companies to keep cost low: while layout and planning remained the same, the only necessary change was the model. These strategic maneuvers on the part of white businesses translated into new revenue, but for *Ebony* readers, the effects were profound; "duplicate advertising" illustrated that African American people could successfully be placed in the same psychic space as whites, thus mediating the racial divide emblematic of the American social order.

Although the marketing space that African American popular magazines provided facilitated the growth of modeling agencies, the direct call for models remained limited and provided mostly part-time work. One model considered herself lucky to secure a thirty-hour-a-week position as a fur model in a Seventh Avenue shop. Noting the precarious nature of the business, Elaine Brooks explained to the *New York Post* that "fashion and commercial modelling just isn't stable enough for a Negro. As far as I know I'm the only Negro model on Seventh Avenue in any kind of wholesale business."[31] Jamaican-born Brooks represented one of the lucky ones who found steady, although not the most prestigious, employment. Another ambivalent success story was that of Bostonian-turned-New Yorker Muriel French who, in 1955, was one of the top African American models in America, earning between $5,000 and $6,000 a year. French also deemed modeling an insecure profession for African American women, and, similar to many others, maintained her position as a receptionist.[32]

Ebony's September 1954 issue questioned, "Can Negro Models Make the Bigtime?" The article pointed to the industry's expansion and the doubling of incomes from the 1949 rate of $5 per hour to the 1954 average of $10 per hour, with a select few models making an hourly wage of $25. One model working in the period noted that African American and white models engaged "the same rates very often," and cited the irregularity of work, rather than the actual pay, as the true hindrance for African American models.[33] *Ebony* concluded that "out of the 200 or more Negro women and men who model regularly or in spare time in New York City, a handful have emerged from the glamor masses."[34] Citing New York City as the base for 80 percent of the modeling industry, the article also pointed to the opportunities for African American models in Los Angeles and Chicago, although these assignments were often less prestigious. Although models in New York City landed positions as photographic models for magazine advertisements and fashion layouts, those in Los Angeles "lead a more precarious existence, depending on fashion shows, demonstration jobs in five & dime stores, combination sales-model work in smaller concerns."[35] One year later, the *New York Post* featured a segment entitled "All About Negro Models," underscoring the continued resistance to African American female representations. The use of Negro models, the *Post* noted, should not be attributed to "a sudden seizure of social consciousness" but rather to "simple economic facts of life" that propelled "one big industry after another into the field of 'duplicate advertising.' "[36]

The demand for African American models was not the only limitation facing those in the industry. When advertisers sought out African American models, they demanded a particular type of woman. Not only did height and weight and curvaceousness count, but so too did color. Working against the popular contemporary conception that fairness of skin was a premium, advertisers heeded Sullivan's advice and relied on brown-skinned models to advertise their products.

Preference for the "Brownskin" did not translate into complete disqualification of dark- or light-skinned models—it simply made their efforts, especially for the former, more difficult. At times, lighter-skinned models were preferred over women with dark skin tones. Indeed, Sylvia Fitt, described by *Ebony* as one of the period's top models, was fairer than the average "Brownskin," occasionally being described as "olive" rather than "brown" skinned.[37] Generally, however, models on either side of the brownskin scale—those who were darker- or lighter-skinned—had greater difficulty negotiating their professional careers. One such model was Lucille Rich, a twenty-three-year-old woman, who the *New York Post* writer designated as "stunningly pretty." Nonetheless, Rich described her fair skin as a "disadvantage." She stated: "I've been told by clients I'm too fair for the typical Negroid type. . . . They'll call the agency and say, 'Send us a girl we know is colored.' "[38] Another model, Marion Baker, confirmed that advertisers sustained a preconception of a "typical Negroid type." Possessing a bone structure and features commonly associated with whites, Baker often lost modeling assignments because she was not "typical enough" as a Negro model. Baker recalled that while posing for an advertisement for a cigarette company, she was photographed "from a different angle just to give [her] nose a broader look." Baker rationalized: "It didn't make me look as good as I can, but that's what they seem to want."[39] Another example emerges in the experiences of Ophelia DeVore. Her 1940s entry into modeling at the age of fifteen presented little difficulty because of her fair skin. Triracial in ancestry—Native American, European, and African—DeVore's fair skin and unusual features made her a desirable model who photographed white.[40] Although DeVore never declared herself to the agency as African American, and never admitted to passing, she stated in a 1969 article in *Sepia*: "I found out later that they basically thought I had a suntan, . . . I had no idea. I just thought they knew what I knew."[41]

Darker-skinned women also faced problems in the industry, although there are few examples of these experiences. These models appeared infrequently in such publications as *Jet* and *Ebony*; throughout the period, the majority of models are described as "tan" or "brown-skinned." One reference to dark-skinned models appears in the September 1954 *Ebony* article "Can Negro Models Make the Bigtime?" and demonstrates the use of African American women as "manikins" for illustrators. Although photography remained the popular medium for magazine advertisements, hand-drawn illustrations persisted throughout the era. When using illustrations in lieu of photographs, African American models possibly presented a cheaper alternative, but as demonstrated earlier, there was no disparity in wages earned by African American and white models.

Mainstream white magazines such as *True Story* and *Redbook*, as well as "pocket books," often employed African American models to pose for illustrators, but as *Ebony* demonstrated, "in the final illustrations, colored models appeared to be white."[42] *Ebony* related the employment of Tina Marshall, "a dark skinned exotic-featured New Yorker," as an artist's model for a Marlboro advertisement. Marshall "was made to appear white in [the] final picture" because "[a]rtists often ignore color, say[ing] they are primarily interested in [the] features of a model."[43] Implicit in this assessment is the use of darker-skinned models to appropriate a certain typology of womanhood without pronouncing racial identification. The example of the Marlboro advertisement is especially telling; it employed the image of a dark-skinned African American woman to render its depiction of a female cigarette smoker. By 1950s standards, this female consumer would be epitomized by sophisticated and mature femininity—the domain of white womanhood.[44] The whitening out of blackness, so easily achieved by the artist's pen, effectively erased the presence of African American women in white mainstream media; such practices reinforced ideas that beauty, sexual attractiveness, and sophistication were the sole possessions of white women. This erasure demonstrates the continued failure to equate beauty with African American women; it also highlights the importance of the new visual discourse of the "Brownskin."

"Is it True What They Say about Models?"

The "Brownskin" model's display of femininity, beauty, and heterosexual appeal asserted her attractiveness and middle-class respectability, but the exhibition of the female body did not escape criticism. As Joanne Meyerowitz has demonstrated, women's responses to *Ebony*'s and *Negro Digest*'s "cheesecake" images were hardly unilateral. In a study of letters to the editor, Meyerowitz shows that reactions ranged from disgust at the "immoral" displays to appreciation of the "racial advancement" of beauty as inclusive of African American women.[45] Capturing this ambivalence about the display of the African American female body, *Ebony* addressed and attempted to overturn the myths surrounding the women who posed for these photographs.

The need to refute the immorality associated with modeling was especially acute for African American women who already battled disparaging, racist sexual stereotyping. Enticing the reader with sensational captions, *Ebony*'s November 1951 issue posed the question "Is It True What They Say about Models?" adjacent to its cover image. Clad in a leopard-skin bikini, the brown-skinned model's head tilts backward, one painted red fingernail tips her jaw upward as if to hint a kiss may be necessary. Her light brown eyes and full red lips seem to hold the answer to the question, and to find the answer, *Ebony* readers needed to purchase the magazine. If the reader made the purchase, the magazine's cover—a bright pink and red backdrop now commonly associated with the romance of Valentine's Day—also promised to reveal the heart-rending story of a Harlem mother who laments "My Children Are Going to Die," in addition to the forwarding of civil liberties as "Negroes Vote in Mississippi." In the table of contents, respectability was instantly restored to the model, Vera Francis, a trained nurse who turned to modeling as an entry into the movie industry. Perhaps, after all, that pointed, painted finger lay along the jaw in thoughtful musing and not coquettish jest. The first page of the article, a double-page spread, refuted the negative associations with modeling, its subtitle reading "Widely-accepted slurs about loose morals [are] resented by glamour queens of profession." In the diligent pursuit of "facts concerning . . . the truth about models," *Ebony* summarized the findings, though not its method, of its "poll[ing] some of the most successful in New York, Chicago and Los Angeles" and concluded that these women are "neither . . . husband snatchers or night club barflies." The reader learned that the majority of

"Estranged from her husband," the sixth woman in the *Our World* article, Mary Cunningham, is described as a mother of a fourteen-year-old who apparently was not in her custody, as Cunningham "lives by herself in the suburbs." Like the other Brandford models, she is represented as a success story—one image displays her astride her "snappy Buick convertible." But of the six women, Cunningham's image is presented in the most sexualized fashion and, as the magazine declared, she "is loaded with what lensmen call 'cheesecake' appeal."[50] While hardly downplaying the sexual attractiveness of the other five women, the subsequent images did not assert such overt sexuality, suggesting that Cunningham (despite her "snappy Buick") needed to compensate for her single status with greater effort. The image closest in "cheesecake" appeal was that of wife, mother, and model Courtenaye Olden. Olden appears seated, legs amply displayed, prettily perusing a book on Matisse. While both images can be described as "cheesecake," the poses and the props expose a divergence between the two. Perhaps the magazine's editors perceived the differences between married and unmarried women as being the harnessing of sexuality in marriage and felt more comfortable in Cunningham's more sexualized "cheesecake" display.

Although four of the five married women intermittently participated in some aspect of modeling—the fifth too busy with young children—Cunningham continued to work "steadily in fashion."[51] Cunningham's tenuous position as a separated African American mother of a fourteen-year-old possibly pressured her to continue posing in "cheesecake" photographs long after she desired to do so. Although the other women may have possessed greater economic security through marital partnership, Cunningham possibly needed to maintain her modeling job; the heightened publicity offered through posing for "cheesecake" photographs in this feature can explain the discrepancy in the images.

The hierarchical structure in the modeling industry is also displayed but not discussed in *Ebony*'s "Is It True What They Say About Models?" Flanking the article are four full body 4 × 6 black and white photos of women in bathing suits; two 4 × 6 images of a model, one emphasizing her face, the other of her preparing dinner at home for her husband; and finally four smaller portrait-type images. Posing for the four large "cheesecake" images were Vera Francis, Dorothy Browne, Gloria Forman, and Daphne Moore, all fairly new or fairly steadily employed models. The smaller portrait images represented a range of women. The only two large portrait-type images were those of Sylvia Fitt, "one of the most photographed models in New York City." Unlike the less successful models, Fitt apparently did not need to pose in a swimsuit; rather, her achievement permitted fully clothed photos, equal in size to the "cheesecake" images. One photograph captured Fitt in the kitchen, frying pan in hand, while she prettily posed for the camera. Fitt, positioned next to the images of bathing beauties, seemingly represented the quintessential African American model—the one who has achieved fame, family, and fortune. Yet by juxtaposing the happy homemaker model adjacent to "cheesecake" images, the reader knew that Fitt once too appeared in such a manner. The images of Fitt did not trivialize the sexual displays of the other four models, but rather worked to support the collage of African American women as heterosexual, middle-class, and respectable homemakers.

Beauty for Sale: "Racket or Business?"

If images of the "Brownskin" acted as both the index of social attainment and the prize of the race, they also endorsed the view that this status was viable for all women. As historian Lois Banner has demonstrated, by the early twentieth century the pursuit and sale of beauty was increasingly presented as a democratic right.[52] By the early postwar period, this democratization of beauty applied to the "Brownskin." Although some African American women moved into white-collar jobs, they did so with the added burden of presenting themselves in the shadow of the "Brownskin" ideal. Lest that shadow become too long or intimidating, the characteristics of

these women were too busy to be engaged in "mischievous leisure," as employment a
nurses, and clerks, as well as studies in law and speech, kept them productive and resp

Ebony explained that advertisers' early use of white chorus girls to sell their produc
be the unfortunate association of loose morality with modeling. By the turn of the tw
century, chorus girls attained new respectability; their working-class backgrounds oper
their favor, contouring them as symbols of self-made success, sexual freedom, glamorou
style, and independent womanhood.[47] But the old correlation between the two occupations
the association of chorus girls with the "gay life," "sugar daddies," and "orchids and champa
persisted. Demonstrating the falsehood of such associations, *Ebony* also pointed to the impi
ticability of a "loose, night-clubbing, home-wrecker" lifestyle. Beauty, the model's premiu
demanded careful attention. In addition to the reputation earned by such actions, long nigh
and alcoholic binges were represented as detrimental to a model's looks and ruinous to he
profession. Far from holding beauty as an ideal unattainable to the average African American
woman, *Ebony* clearly exposed the accessibility of this vision and defined the way in which such
attributes should be experienced. Stressing the ethic of hard work, *Ebony* underscored the value
of labor and the effort that beauty mandated, suggesting that unattractive women did not work
hard enough.

Beautiful models, smart enough to reject a lifestyle of all night parties and heavy drinking,
nevertheless acknowledged the temptation to indulge in such practices; some even stressed
moderation—as opposed to outright rejection—as the key. Many of the women spoke in the
language of sacrifice necessary for thriving careers. Francis noted that keeping busy was "one
sure way of staying out of trouble," while model Daphne Moore confessed that, in her effort to
succeed, she pared back "some dating, night clubbing and partying," and Gloria Forman, who
also held a night job, decided to "forget the play side of life" until she attained her dream of full-
time modeling. Representing somewhat of a balance was twenty-year-old Ellen Holly, who noted
that models are "just like other people—clean living girls, neither sober nor fast." Other models,
such as Sylvia Fitt, one of the most successful models, rejected outright any such lifestyle and
embraced more genteel pursuits such as reading and knitting in her spare time. Finally, *Ebony*
firmly asserted the period's dominant social values of the heterosexual wife, mother, and diligent
homemaker. By representing glamorous models as ordinary women who studied, worked,
married, and tended to homes, children, and husbands, *Ebony* reinforced postwar valuations
of heterosexual marital fulfillment.

Another African American popular magazine, *Our World*, reinforced this celebratory fusion
of middle-class marriage and careers in modeling. "What Happened to the Brandford Models?"
provided an update on six of the agency's earliest African American models, five of whom were
represented as blissfully wed. Despite continuing to model on part-time bases, the article concluded that "in the long run all of these girls will give up modeling to take care of growing
families and to give way to younger models."[48] Accompanying the text were images that demonstrated the full lives of these five women as models, mothers, and wives. Several images represented these women as homemakers fulfilling the period's expected domestic duties such as
cooking and ironing. Sylvia Fitt appears in the more conventional role of housewife as she tends
to her husband. Other images depicted the models, in partnership with their husbands, engaged
in the leisurely and middle-class athleticism of golfing and bowling. The portrayal of happy
marriages, successful careers, dutiful motherhood, and efforts to stay fit—while, of course,
having great fun—rendered these women not merely as commercial models, but also as models
for African American womanhood. Presented to the average woman was the ultimate ideal of
African American middle class womanhood—balancing glamorous work with home and husband and attaching greater status to the husband's job.[49] In the world drawn by *Ebony* and *Our
World*, the African American man's beautiful "Brownskin" wife was a testament to capitalistic
success, democratic triumph, and male dominance.

beauty, poise, and femininity—exemplified in the "Brownskin"—were advertised, packaged, and available for purchase.

Support for the democratization of beauty, heterosexual appeal, and middle-class status appeared in *Jet*, another Johnson publication, in an article that queried, "What Makes a Good Model?" and found that "beauty is an asset but not a necessity."[53] The magazine featured Chicago-based Crest Modeling School that, for $125, offered a six-month course in the rudiments of modeling. Mrs. Lightsey, a "veteran model" and the school's proprietor, overturned the perception that only beautiful women could dream of modeling, and that modeling skills were only useful to the model; apparently all women benefited from such training. Mrs. Lightsey explained: "Most girls come to me . . . because they are 'ugly ducklings' in search of charm and grace to utilize in their respective professions. My most astute pupils become models in their spare time. The only qualification that I have for girls entering my school is that they are clean and have the inclination to learn."[54]

The emphasis on the utilitarian nature of the training, of course, is partially a marketing attempt to represent this education as a great investment. In urban centers, there was no shortage of beauty, modeling, and charm schools throughout the period; their endurance and continued appearance indicates that African American women enrolled in these schools in significant numbers. Modeling school, and its older cousin, the charm school, enjoyed success in African American communities across the country, imparting "important social graces and professional skills" to middleclass youth.[55] Unlike modeling agencies, these schools did not participate in booking and handling models, but attended to the education of "use of make-up, diction, figure control, hair styling, correct posture," among other social graces.[56]

Aware that ignominious schools threatened the good name of many, *Ebony*'s September 1950 article mused "Model Schools: Racket or Business?" Describing the underworld of disreputable schools, *Ebony* forewarned readers of falling prey to charlatans; the article described the peril as "shady operators of schools that bilk ambitious young ladies and their mothers of cash on promises of jobs . . . there have been fly-by-night, untrained teachers, quickie six-week beauty courses and even some slick fringe photographic deals bordering on pornography."[57]

The article declared that the novelty of modeling as a profession for African American women limited the chances for deception, and most schools were reputable ones "that operate with a minimum of job promises but a maximum of excellent training in poise and personality."[58] *Ebony* reinforced that training in beauty and social skills were useful to the average woman, conceding that due to the shortage of jobs for African American models, these schools essentially acted as "charm schools [for] housewives [and] high school students." Age and size seemed no deterrent, as the magazine reported one Chicago school enrolling "at least two fifty-year-old students as well as a third who weighed nearly 300 pounds." At least theoretically, modeling schools presented to all African American women the opportunity to attain femininity grace, and status. Describing the role of charm schools and using the DeVore School of Charm as its prototype, the *New York Times* explored the appeal of such institutions. Established in 1946 by DeVore, the institution's first class graduated only thirteen women; by 1969, the time that the article was written, that number increased to an annual count of two to three hundred. Reflecting on the unchanged role of the charm school, DeVore asserted that only a small percentage of women enrolled for the purpose of modeling as a career; a greater number sought career advancement and the majority "want[ed] confidence in themselves as women." Defining the intangible nature of charm was not difficult for DeVore, who stated: "[I]t's a sort of bloom on a woman. If you have it, you don't need anything else; and if you don't have it, it doesn't much matter what else you have."[59]

Testament to the value of training in charm, poise, and etiquette also came from the correspondence of individual women. Writing from Dayton, Ohio, Phyllis J. Hunt expressed her gratitude to Brandford Model and Charm School. Addressed to Barbara M. Watson,[60] Hunt's

1949 letter is an apparent response to an invitation to attend a model course, but the writer qualified its purpose as "a combination business and personal letter." Regretting that she could not attend, Hunt explained that she had returned to Dayton where, unlike New York, "a Negro girl has a harder time getting a clerical position."[61] However, as the "Home of Aviation," Dayton's three airfields presented opportunities for government employment, enabling Hunt to secure a clerical position. Despite Hunt's good fortune, her letter expressed the isolation and otherness of working in a predominantly white environment; she stated: "I believe I am the only stenographer on this floor who is 'technicolored.' "[62] Hunt's correspondence expressed anxiety in maintaining the new clerical position with assurance and comfort, and credited the charm course in providing her with confidence, poise, and dignity—characteristics she considered essential to her success. As a success story intended to invoke the pride of her mentor, Hunt divulged, "If I hadn't completed my charm course I don't think I could have gone through the first days as there had never been any Negro girls up here with these colonels and generals, etc., and everyone was just a little too nice. I had made a very nice rating on my test, though, and I knew that if I conducted myself as a lady everything would turn out in my favor. At this point my charm course did come in handy."[63]

No other record of Phyllis Hunt is available, and the invitation to attend the model course was more than likely a bulk mailing to past students of the Brandford charm course. Why and for how long Hunt remained in New York is unknown, as are the reasons she initially enrolled in the charm course. Perhaps she received clerical training in the city and found the charm course—through advertising, solicitation, or word of mouth—to be a good complement. In her letter, Hunt expressed uncertainty that Watson would remember her, suggesting that their interludes were entirely professional. Hunt's reference to "the nights you taught us to walk with our hips tucked under" reveals that instruction took place in the evening, indicating that most participants held day jobs or other responsibilities and partook in the course for recreation or for social and professional improvement. It is this anonymity that renders Hunt's letter as significant—it reveals the importance that one African American woman attached to such courses. When furnished with new economic opportunities—displayed as imminent in publications such as *Ebony* which epitomized African America's expectant climate—respectable deportment facilitated successful integration and professional achievement. When it came to integrated professional and social situations, femininity, grace, and manners apparently surpassed the value of aesthetic beauty; good grooming was necessary for professional acceptance, but it was equally important to conduct oneself in a respectable manner. Pondering the remote possibility of future attendance at a model course, Hunt asserted: "not that I could ever be a model, but it does so much for a girl's morale to know that she's doing the correct thing."[64] Such training benefited the individual woman by boosting confidence and allowing successful interplay in professional settings. Accomplished social intercourse in the workplace demonstrated that African American women were diligent and dignified workers—welcome additions to both the integrated and segregated workplace.

Another letter, penned by Barbara M. Watson, revealed the efforts to recruit enrollment in charm and modeling courses; it also offers a blueprint for the unavailable letter that elicited Hunt's response and demonstrates that standards of beauty, deportment, and middle-class femininity were presented as ideals for all working women. Addressed to Miss Leonora Cox, Recreational Director of Lincoln Nursing Home in Bronx, New York, the letter outlined the benefits of a "Charm Clinic"—the language suggesting the treatment of an ailment with both brevity and scientific management. In addition to "provid[ing] a new avenue of activity for those under your supervision," Watson elucidated the growing concern of "business women of today [who] are more aware of the importance of their general appearance than ever before."[65] Including teachers, secretaries, nurses, and executives in this category, Watson pointed to the continual need of these women to "stay on a par with others in their field." Assuming that these women kept abreast of the professional requirements of their positions, Watson's "Charm Clinic" offered assistance in the equally serious work of "counting calories, trying a new make-up and changing hairstyles."[66] Watson's letter; and Cox's brief positive response, reveals the vital role that beauty and grooming played in the working lives of African American women.

Enclosed in the letter to Cox was the brochure "You—All New"; it guaranteed not merely the refinement of beauty but rather a dramatic metamorphosis in appearance and personality. In the dual trope of self-help and success, Brandford Model and Charm School, under Barbara M. Watson's tutelage, articulated the democratic spirit behind the courses; the brochure declared the potential beauty of all women, conditional only on the "earnest desire for personal self-improvement." For $55, the eight-week course, offered one evening a week, promised "A New Figure, A New Face, A New Fashion, A New Poise." The course focused on crucial aspects of femininity and beauty; grooming and deportment; diet and exercise; cosmetic application with special consideration of skin tone; fashion: "what to wear, when [and] how to wear it"; charm; and personality.[67] Such training presented African American women with the additional task of appropriating aesthetic values dominant in the mass media, namely film and magazines such as *Ebony*. An undated lecture by Watson declared that contemporary society placed great demands on both men and women, although the courses that promised to "lea[d] [them] to the ultimate objective—a charming, poised personality" were undoubtedly geared towards women. With clarity, Watson asserted that contemporary society granted "charm and poise" significant weight; it was no longer "enough to have education and knowledge—one must also have a charming and pleasant personality and a good appearance. This is necessary for personal as well as professional relationship."[68]

Postwar employment expansion into clerical positions presented African American women with new anxieties concerning their behavior, actions, and appearance. Charm and modeling schools played important roles in instilling pride and confidence in those seeking the necessary skills to transition smoothly into a world that possessed little knowledge of, or respect for, African American women. Charm and modeling courses facilitated interactions in the workplace and presented a methodology for social mobility within the African American community. Despite the narrow parameters that defined femininity and ideals of female beauty, these courses provided some way for urban African American women to measure their attainment of the middle class standard.

Concerted efforts to address the issues surrounding employment in clerical services are reflected in a 1953 "Secretarial Clinic." Organized by the National Urban League's Administrative and Clerical Council, the clinic focused on the issues surrounding work in the burgeoning profession. In a report on the proceedings, chairman Mary E. Finger deemed the event a success and called for its development into an annual event. Finger explained that future meetings should continue to represent the concerns of the clerical workforce; she stated: "Such meetings could be the clearing house of ideas, hopes and problems for the perspective [sic] worker, the girl about to leave school for the business-world—for the unsatisfied worker, who needs to take a fresh look at herself and her job experience—for the fortunate worker happily established in her job, but must never get too complacent about herself. . . ."[69]

Included in the report was Watson's address, "The Well-Groomed Secretary." Finger indicated that Watson was one of the "two major speakers . . . highlight[ing] the interest-areas touched upon by the clinic participants."[70] Highlighting good grooming and cleanliness, Watson stressed the importance of "neat, clean, and well-pressed" clothes. According to Watson, "the really efficient career girl" considered grooming to be "an intricate part of her life each and every day," and, employing "smartness and chic," relied on "simplicity and subtlety" when constructing her appearance.[71] Invoking the ethics of the skilled worker, Watson supplied the understanding that one's appearance reflected one's ability, and in a period when small numbers of African

American women were entering the clerical workforce, such appearance proved fundamental to one's success.

Efficiency, however, did not occlude femininity. Calling on the judicious application of makeup, Watson counseled women not to forgo its use "because you might frighten people away"; she stressed that one need not look "drab, dull and uninteresting" since a feminine look could be achieved without "being extremely exotic." Referring to the "exotic" appearance, Watson explained that a nightclub look was inappropriate in the office. Never once referring to race or racist attitudes, Watson's allusion to exoticism reveals the need for African American women to maintain a subdued appearance. Although it is unlikely that women would have considered donning evening wear to the office, Watson's citing the matter suggests her belief that some were unable to render such a distinction. Addressing hairstyles, posture, diction, and manicures, Watson provided workers with a blueprint for professional success. Somewhat softening the daunting task of being both immaculately groomed and highly skilled, the clinic's participants were informed that physical beauty was not important. Using Mary McLeod Bethune and Eleanor Roosevelt as examples, Watson argued that their "beauty of personality" was all that mattered.[72] Surely the references were designed to offer comfort, and while it is improbable that this was her intention, Watson's conjuring the mental images of these two highly accomplished women reinforced a standardized ideal of beauty. Neither woman fulfilled the physical ideals of either African American or white womanhood; their success apparently was attained in spite of this deficiency and not regardless of their divergence from prototypical concepts of beauty.

Consistently deploying the image of the "Brownskin," popular magazines in America's early postwar era actively participated in producing new iconographic understandings of African American womanhood. The images simultaneously objectified, and then restored, respectable middleclass status to African American women's bodies. Successful and sexual, these images redressed the denigrating and pervasive stereotypes of African American women as unattractive washerwomen, laundresses, maids, and mammies, but did so without wholly restructuring the dominant understanding of racial and gender identity. The brown-skinned complexion acted as both a badge of race pride and a shield from white disparagement of dark skin tones. The success of brown-skinned models over their lighter- and darker-skinned sisters illustrates that this middling representation exemplified the most suitable public female face for postwar African America.

Predating the late 1960s "Polishing [of] Black Diamonds" was the early postwar display of the "Brownskin"; this feminized, heterosexually appealing, socially mobile, and consumerist image reflected the era's hope for full democratic rights. The opulence of the "Brownskin," like the expectancy of the period, waned by the mid-1950s; the militancy of the later decades generated new challenges for African American women and new commodifications of female beauty. Although the Polished Brown Diamond dazzled for a relatively short period of time—between the end of World War II and the onset of the civil rights movement—the "Brownskin" remains central to understanding the postwar visual discourse of an attendant, middle-class African America and to the reworking of ideals of sex, color, and African American female beauty in later decades.

Notes

1. Ophelia DeVore as quoted in "Her Name is Ophelia DeVore and Her Specialty is Polishing Black Diamonds," *New York Times*, 20 August 1969, 50.
2. Daniel O. Price, *Changing Characteristics of the Negro Population*, U.S. Department of Commerce, Bureau of the Census, 1960 Census Monograph (Washington, DC: Government Printing Office, 1969), 116–18; and Paula Giddings, *When and Where I Enter* (New York: William Morrow, 1984), 231–58.
3. Lisa Fine, *The Souls of the Skyscraper* (Philadelphia: Temple University Press, 1990); and Angel Kwolek-Folland, *Engendering Business* (Baltimore: Johns Hopkins University Press, 1994).

4. Jacqueline Jones, *labor of Love, Labor of Sorrow* (New York: Random House, 1985), 178.

5. Karen Tucker Anderson, "Last Hired, First Fired: Black Women Workers during World War II," *Journal of American History*, 69, no. 1 (June 1982): 90; and Jones, *Labor of Love, Labor of Sorrow*, 266.

6. Price, *Changing Characteristics of the Negro Population*, 116–18.

7. E. Franklin Frazier noted the increase in clerical workers as largely responsible for the growth of the African American middle class. See E. Franklin Frazier, *The Black Bourgeoisie* (New York: Free Press, 1957).

8. Jones, *Labor of Love, Labor of Sorrow*, 181; and Kwolek-Folland, *Engendering Business*.

9. Price, *Changing Characteristics of the Negro Population*, 116–18.

10. The history of good grooming practices as a mode for social advancement and as race-proud representation has been well documented. For example, see Evelyn Brooks Higginbotham, *Righteous Discontent: The Women's Movement in the Black Baptist Church, 1880-1920* (Cambridge, MA: Harvard University Press, 1993); Darlene Clark Hine, "Rape and the Inner Lives of Black Women in the Middle West," *Signs* 14 (summer 1989): 912–20; Kathy Peiss, *Hope in a Jar: The Making of America's Beauty Culture* (New York: Metropolitan, 1998); Bruce Taylor, "Black Hairstyles," *Western Journal of Black Studies* 14, no. 4 (1990): 235–50; and Maxine Craig, *Ain't I a Beauty Queen? Black Women, Beauty and the Politics of Race* (New York: Oxford University Press, 2002).

11. Joe Trotter, *The Great Migration in Historical Perspective* (Bloomington: Indiana University Press, 1991); and Earl Lewis, *In Their Own Interests* (Berkeley: University of California Press, 1991).

12. For discussions on women and wartime opportunities see Anderson, "Last Hired, First Fired," 82 97, Jones, *Labor of Love, Labor of Sorrow*, 232–60; and Susan M. Hartmann, *The Home Front and Beyond* (Boston: Twayne Publishers, 1982).

13. Earl Lewis, *In Their Own Interests;* Rex R. Campbell and Daniel M. Johnson, *African American Migration in America* (Durham, NC: Duke University Press, 1981).

14. See Dwight Brooks, "Consumer Markets and Consumer Magazines" (PhD diss, University of Iowa, 1991); and Robert E. Weems Jr., *Desegregating the Dollar: African American Consumerism in the Twentieth Century* (New York: New York University Press, 1998), 32.

15. David J. Sullivan, "Negro Incomes and How They are Spent," *Sales Management* 54 (14 June 1945): 106.

16. *Historical Statistics of the United States*, Part 1, U.S. Department of Commerce, Bureau of the Census (New York: Kraus International Publications, 1989), 303.

17. David J. Sullivan, "Don't Do This—If You Want to Sell Your Products to Negroes!" *Sales Management* 52 (1 March 1943): 48, 50

18. Weems, *Desegregating the Dollar*, 22.

19. Paul K. Edwards, *The Southern Urban Negro as Consumer* (New York: Negro Universities Press, 1932), 135–46.

20. Sullivan, "Don't Do This," 50.

21. Canada Lee, as quoted in "Another Step Up: First Agency For Negro Models Opens," unidentified newspaper clipping, 31 July 1946, Box 10, Barbara Watson Collection, Schomburg Center for Research in Black Culture, Manuscripts, Archives, and Rare Books Division, New York Public Library, Astor, Lenox, and Tilden Foundations, New York City, New York, hereafter BWC.

22. Edward Brandford as quoted in "Another Step Up."

23. The complex history behind African American women's consumption and use of cosmetics is an important ongoing debate. See Noliwe M. Rooks, *Hair Raising* (New Brunswick, N.J.: Rutgers University Press, 1996); Maxine Craig, "The Decline and Fall of the Conk," *Fashion Theory* 1, no. 4 (1997): 399–420; Robin D. Kelley, "Nap Time," *Fashion Theory* 1, no. 4 (1997): 339–51; Kobena Mercer, "Black Hair/Style," in *Marginalization and Contemporary Cultures*, ed. Russell Ferguson et al. (Cambridge, MA: MIT Press, 1990), 247–64; and Peiss, *Hope in a Jar*, 203–37.

24. Mary Louise Yabro as quoted in "Another Step Up."

25. For example, see T. Jackson Lears, "From Salvation to Self-Realization," in *The Culture of Consumption*, ed. Richard Wrightman Fox and T. Jackson Lears (New York: Pantheon Books, 1983), 3–38; and William R. Leach, "Transformations in a Culture of Consumption," *Journal of American History* 71, no. 2 (1994): 319–42.

26. "Another Step Up."

27. "Backstage," *Ebony* (November 1945), 1.

28. Ronald F. Wolseley, *The Black Press, USA* (Ames: Iowa State University Press, 1971), 142.

29. On the impact of photography on the African American psyche, see bell hooks, " 'In Our Glory,' " in *Picturing Us*, ed. Deborah E. Willis (New York: New Press, 1994), 43–53; and Maren Stange, "Photographs Taken in Everyday Life," in *The Black Press: New Literary and Historical Essays*, ed. Todd Vogel (New Brunswick, NJ: Rutgers University Press, 2001), 207–227.

30. John H. Johnson with Lerone Bennett Jr., *Succeeding Against the Odds* (New York: Amistad Press, 1989), 153–56.
31. Elaine Brooks, "All About the Negro Models," *New York Post*, 16 June 1955, 4.
32. Lucille Rich, "All About the Negro Models," 4.
33. Dolores Jackson, "All About the Negro Models," 30.
34. "Can Negro Models Make the Bigtime?" *Ebony* (September 1954), 100.
35. Ibid., 103–104.
36. "All About the Negro Models," 4.
37. "Is It True What They Say About Models?" *Ebony* (November 1951), 60–61.
38. Lucille Rich, "All About the Negro Models," 30.
39. Marion Baker, "All About the Negro Models," 30.
40. Barbara Summers, *Black and Beautiful* (New York: Amistad Press, 1998), 25–26.
41. Ophelia DeVore as quoted in Summers, *Black and Beautiful*, 26.
42. "Can Negro Models Make the Bigtime?" 103.
43. Ibid.
44. For example, see Giddings, *When and Where I Enter*.
45. Joanne Meyerowitz, "Women, Cheesecake, and Borderline Material," *Journal of Women's History* 8, no. 3 (1996): 18–21.
46. "Is It True What They Say About Models?" 60–61.
47. Lois Banner, *American Beauty* (New York: Knopf, 1983), esp. 181–83.
48. "What Happened to the Brandford Models?" *Our World* (February 1954), 37.
49. Jacqueline Jones describes *Ebony*'s glorified depiction of African American womanhood as "Superwoman" long before this ideology came into popular thought. Jones, *Labor of Love, Labor of Sorrow*, 268–74. Important works on women in mass magazine culture include Joanne Meyerowitz, "Beyond the Feminine Mystique," *The Journal of American History* 79, no. 4 (1993): 1455–82; Jennifer Scanlon, *Inarticulate Longings* (New York: Routledge, 1995); Eva Moskowitz, "It's Good to Blow Your Top," *Journal of Women's History* 8, no. 3 (1996): 66–98; Carolyn Kitch, *Girl on the Magazine Cover* (Chapel Hill: University of North Carolina Press, 2001); and Craig, *Ain't I a Beauty Queen?* For discussions on constructions of masculinity, see Tom Pendergast, *Creating the Modern Man* (Jackson: University of Mississippi Press, 2000).
50. "What Happened to the Brandford Models?" 31–32.
51. Ibid., 31.
52. *Banner, American Beauty*, 205–207.
53. "What Makes a Good Model?" *Jet* (23 April 1955), 38.
54. Mrs. Betty Lightsdey as quoted in "What Makes a Good Model?" 42.
55. Summers, *Black and Beautiful*, 24.
56. "What Makes a Good Model?" 42.
57. "Model Schools: Racket or Business?" *Ebony* (September 1950), 73.
58. Ibid.
59. DeVore as quoted in "Her Name is Ophelia DeVore and Her Specialty is Polishing Black Diamonds," 50.
60. A Brandford Models 1948 brochure lists Barbara M. Watson as "Prominent Lecturer and Fashion Authority." A 1 October 1953 card announces the name change from Brandford Models to Barbara Watson Models, Box 9, folder 3, BWC.
61. Phyllis J. Hunt to Barbara M. Watson, 2 September 1949, Box 9, folder 1, BWC.
62. Ibid.
63. Ibid.
64. Ibid.
65. Barbara M. Watson to Leonora Cox, 26 May 1955, Box 9, folder 1, BWC.
66. Ibid.
67. "You . . . All New" booklet, Box 9, folder 8, BWC.
68. The Barbara Watson Lecture, no date, Box 9, folder 3, BWC.
69. Mary E. Finger, Chairman, Administrative and Clerical Council, "Foreword," included in Barbara M. Watson's speech entitled "The Well-Groomed Secretary," Box.9, folder 8, BWC.
70. Ibid.
71. "The Well-Groomed Secretary," Box 9, folder 8, BWC.
72. Ibid.

33

"More than a Lady"

Ruby Doris Smith Robinson and Black Women's Leadership in the Student Nonviolent Coordinating Committee

Cynthia Griggs Fleming

Throughout the history of this country, countless African American activists have resisted racism and oppression in a wide variety of ways. A number of these activists were women, and a few of them became famous. Most Americans have at least heard of legendary black women such as Harriet Tubman and Sojourner Truth, who were passionately committed to black freedom. There are many, however, who were never recognized for their achievements and their importance. One such woman was Ruby Doris Smith Robinson, who worked with the Student Nonviolent Coordinating Committee from its earliest days in 1960 until her death at age twenty-five in October 1967.

Robinson was born in Atlanta, Georgia, on 25 April 1942 to Alice and J. T. Smith. She was the second of seven children; the oldest was a girl named Mary Ann, and then came Ruby, Catherine, Bobby, John, Willie, and Gregory.[1] The Smith family owned their own home in Summerhill, the oldest black neighborhood in Atlanta. While Summerhill had its share of crime, it also provided positive experiences for its residents. Mary Ann Smith Wilson, Robinson's older sister, described Summerhill as a "mosaic" that included all kinds of people. Middle-class families lived alongside those who were mired in abject poverty. Wilson also remembered that the community provided a network of support for its youngsters. Schools, churches, and other institutions such as the YMCA sponsored activities and provided encouragement to neighborhood youth while they also protected community youngsters from the worst part of segregation.[2]

In such a warm and supportive atmosphere Ruby Doris Smith Robinson developed a keen sense of social and racial justice. She watched the events of the 1950s—the integration of Little Rock's Central High School, the Montgomery bus boycott—with a growing sense of concern. When she entered Spelman College as a freshman in the fall of 1958, Robinson was excited about the prospect of change in the South's system of segregation. But, Robinson remembered, "I wasn't ready to act on my own." By the next academic year other idealistic black college students in the Atlanta University Center, which served Atlanta University, Gammon Theological Seminary, and Spelman, Morehouse, Morris Brown, and Clark colleges, created the Atlanta Committee on Appeal for Human Rights. The group sponsored its first demonstration on 15 March 1960 at the state capital building—a short distance from their campuses. This was just what Robinson had been waiting for. She enthusiastically joined the Atlanta committee and participated in that first demonstration.[3]

At the same time that Ruby Doris Smith Robinson and her colleagues were protesting segregation in Atlanta, black college students all across the South were engaged in similar activities. It soon became obvious to some that all these student movements could benefit by establishing an organization to coordinate their activities. Accordingly, in April 1960 black student leaders from all over the South met and established the Student Nonviolent Coordinating Committee (SNCC). By early 1961, even as Robinson continued her work with the Atlanta committee, she began to work with this new group, serving SNCC as an activist in the field as well as an administrator in the Atlanta central office.

In May 1966 she succeeded Jim Forman as SNCC's executive secretary. She was the only woman ever to serve in this capacity.[4] Robinson was elected during a particularly emotional and difficult staff meeting in Kingston Springs, Tennessee. The heated debates about strategies and goals that occupied the staff at that meeting were complicated by the serious splits that had developed within the ranks of the staff by this time. Divisions based on gender, race, and status in the organization produced a great deal of suspicion and mistrust. Despite these problems, however, Robinson commanded the respect of the majority of her SNCC colleagues. They admired her unshakeable commitment to the cause of civil rights in general and the Student Nonviolent Coordinating Committee in particular.

While Robinson had the practical experience and the firm commitment necessary to administer SNCC, she faced some unique problems and challenges because of her gender. Like some other female leaders in the organization, she found that her femininity was questioned because she exercised power over men. Furthermore, in the midst of her SNCC work Robinson married (1964) and had a child (1965). This added dimension provoked a great deal of tension in her life as she sought to fulfill the traditional roles of wife and mother as well as the unusual role of female civil rights leader.

SNCC colleagues recognized Robinson's importance. One recalled, "You could feel her power in SNCC on a daily basis." Another insisted, "As a female, she was a pretty powerful person."[5] As SNCC's membership enlarged and its character changed over time, it became increasingly difficult to administer. But Robinson tried. SNCC had always had a flexible view of leadership. Most in the group believed that everyone could be a leader. Whereas this belief served to inspire broad participation by the membership, it also caused serious discipline problems. There were times when some members simply refused to follow orders. Regardless of the existence of such attitudes, Robinson demanded hard work and dedication from all those around her. Jack Minnis, a member of SNCC's research staff, insisted that it was almost impossible to fool Robinson; he had no doubt that she had "a 100 percent effective shit detector." Above all, she made sure that nobody abused the organization's limited financial resources. Stanley Wise, who would later succeed Robinson as executive secretary when she became ill, clearly recalled a particularly illustrative incident. It occurred when a group of field workers came to Atlanta for a meeting.

> She absolutely did not tolerate any nonsense. I remember some people came in there [the Atlanta central office] once from Mississippi. They had driven their car over there and they said they needed new tires. And she pulled out [a card] from her little file. She said, "Listen, I've given you sixteen tires in the last four months. . . . I've sent you four batteries, you had two motors in the car. You're not getting another thing. Now take that car out of here and go on back to Mississippi."[6]

Coworker Reginald Robinson remembered that Robinson could be uncompromising about procedure. "When she became in charge of the payroll and you had reports to do—you had expense accounts to turn [in]. Well, if you didn't do what you were supposed to do, Big Mama [Robinson] would cut your money." Movement colleague Charles Jones succinctly summed up her no-nonsense approach. "You didn't run any games on her." As coworker Worth Long declared, "The office would not have run except for her; and then the field would not have survived." Long recalled her as "a cantankerous person. . . . She's set in her ways, and she's mostly right. . . . She would take a principle[d] stand. . . . She'd argue, and she'd huff and puff too." In the freewheeling discussions that SNCC staff members had about organizational policy, Long remembered Robinson as "a formidable opponent. I wouldn't want to play poker with her."[7] There were indeed many sides to Ruby Doris Smith Robinson. Regardless of what colleagues thought of her administrative techniques and her office demeanor, all agreed that Robinson's actions were always guided by her sincere commitment to SNCC.

Despite her importance to SNCC, however, Robinson has received little attention from scholars and others who are now writing the civil rights movement's story. Has her gender consigned her to obscurity? That is part of the answer. Still another part of the answer, however, is rooted in Robinson's personality and her vision of her role in the movement. Even in childhood, Robinson had been an intensely private and independent person. Her older sister remembered that their parents understood this and accepted it. They knew that "whatever she's going to do, she's going to do."[8] They never expected their daughter to consult them or even inform them of her activities, and she never did.

Robinson so guarded her privacy that she actively discouraged those who wanted to extend special recognition to her for her protest activities. While she understood that such activities themselves attracted a good deal of attention, she absolutely did not want any personal notoriety. Her attitude toward personal publicity became quite obvious in early 1961 when she became part of a SNCC delegation that was jailed in Rock Hill, South Carolina. The SNCC action in Rock Hill grew out of a decision that the group made at its February 1961 meeting. During that meeting, staff members expressed concern about the jail-versus-bail question. All over the South, thousands of black college students involved in protest activities were being arrested. In the majority of cases students posted bail and were released. Increasingly, however, some argued that there were compelling reasons why protestors should start refusing to post bail and should serve out their jail sentences instead.

Tactically, some insisted, those who protested segregation could do the movement a great service by remaining in jail. Clogging the jails with increasing numbers of protesters would put additional pressure on segregation by straining local resources. At the same time, others insisted that attempts to bail black students out of jail were placing a terrible financial burden on local black communities— a burden that could eventually interfere with their will and their ability to continue the fight against segregation. Finally, others argued that the protestors' presence in jail would provide powerful moral reinforcement for their position. The SNCC members attending that February meeting were aware that a group of South Carolina students had already taken a public stand on this issue. On 1 February, just prior to the beginning of the meeting, students from Friendship College in Rock Hill, South Carolina, were convicted of trespassing after they had demonstrated in downtown variety stores and drugstores. The students refused to post bail, and they expressed a determination to serve out their full sentences. Participants in that February SNCC meeting unequivocally expressed their view of the stand taken by the Rock Hill students:

> Their sitting-in shows their belief in the immorality of racial segregation and their choice to serve the sentence shows their unwillingness to participate in any part of a system that perpetuates injustice. Since we too share their beliefs and since many times during the past year we too have sat-in at lunch counters, we feel that in good conscience we have no alternative other than to join them.[9]

Robinson and the others who attended SNCC's February meeting were invigorated by their new stand. They excitedly debated the question of which SNCC members should go to Rock Hill to inaugurate this new policy. Finally the decision was made: Charles Jones, Charles Sherrod, Diane Nash, and Mary Ann Smith, Robinson's older sister, were selected. But Smith remembered that after she left the meeting she began to have some serious second thoughts about going to jail in Rock Hill. "I started thinking about all the little things I had in the making for next year, you know. Academically—fellowships and what have you." While Smith became increasingly uncertain, Robinson became increasingly excited. "So what happened eventually is Ruby Doris talked it up, and I just bowed out and let her go."[10]

After they protested segregation at Good's Drug Store in downtown Rock Hill, Robinson and the others were arrested. They served thirty-day sentences in the York County jail. As the end of her jail sentence approached, Robinson began to worry that she would be the target of special recognition. She told her sister: "I think the Rock Hillians are planning something for us when we get out. . . . I don't care for the publicity that they'll probably give us when we come out." Robinson clearly did not want any special recognition from anyone. She did not even want family members and friends to celebrate her achievements. "Please don't plan anything for me," she insisted. "I'm no celebrity and you know it."[11]

Despite Robinson's wishes, the *Atlanta Inquirer* had photographers on hand at the airport when she returned from serving her jail time in South Carolina.[12] After her Rock Hill experience, Robinson participated in a number of protest activities over the next few months in Atlanta and other Georgia cities and other states. Regardless of the media coverage that these protests attracted, Robinson continued to shun personal publicity.

Movement colleagues all agreed that Robinson was a team player. She did not want the movement to be affected by individual attitudes and aspirations. This conviction sometimes prompted Robinson to make pointed comments about civil rights veterans who seemed to enjoy the inevitable publicity and notoriety that accompanied their protest activities. She was particularly concerned that the media attention lavished on some could lead to serious distortions and dangerous misrepresentations. Her views of Stokely Carmichael's relationship to the press clearly indicate the depth of her concern. She charged that because of the media attention Carmichael attracted, he had become "the only consistent spokesman for the organization, and he has had the press not only available but seeking him out for whatever ammunition could be found—FOR OUR DESTRUCTION." Because of Carmichael's penchant for attracting press coverage, Robinson half-jokingly and half-seriously christened him "Stokely Starmichael."[13]

Robinson's attempts to stay in the background even in the face of her growing influence in SNCC clearly illustrate one of the conflicts that complicated her life as an activist. Indeed, her gender, race, personal convictions, personality, and position all meant that she would inevitably face conflicts in the environment of the civil rights movement of the sixties. Among the most painful of those conflicts was the issue of her own femininity—a problem that many of her African American female friends shared. Against the backdrop of the peculiar status of black women in American society, black female activists' efforts have routinely been tied to a de-emphasis of black femininity. Such a linkage is entirely consistent with negative notions of black femininity that are firmly anchored in the nineteenth century and slavery. One scholar has identified the roots of this negative nineteenth-century notion:

> The slave system defined Black people as chattel. Since women, no less than men, were viewed as profitable labor-units, they might as well have been genderless as far as the slaveholders were concerned. . . . Judged by the evolving nineteenth century ideology of femininity, which emphasized women's roles as nurturing mothers and gentle companions and housekeepers for their husbands, Black women were practically anomalies.[14]

In the popular consciousness, notions of accepted female behavior are inconsistent with popularized views of the black female activist persona. Consequently, one does not think of the fierce "General" Tubman primping in front of a mirror, or the legendary Sojourner Truth worrying about which hat to wear. Of course, women in leadership roles, regardless of race, have often been vulnerable to attacks on their femininity. Yet the experience of black women activists is unique, since it is firmly based in the broader context of negative notions of black femininity in general.

Predictably, as Robinson gained power and influence in SNCC, increasing numbers of her movement colleagues came to identify her by her role in the organization, not her gender. Some insist that part of the perception they have of her is rooted in their view of Robinson's physical appearance. Many remember her as a rather plain woman. She was five feet two inches tall with a stocky build. She had large hips, a small waist and bowed legs. Because of her build she had a very distinctive walk. Her older sister, Mary Ann, remembered that this earned her the nickname "Duck." Robinson's skin color was medium, and she had a broad nose, relatively large lips, and kinky hair. Because she possessed these characteristics, Charles Jones described her as "practical and black" in terms of attitude and appearance. Coworker Courtland Cox insisted that people in SNCC "didn't view her as a man or woman, they viewed her as a strength." Her friend and coworker Joanne Grant remembered, "I think that everybody accepted her as one of the boys."[15]

A number of Robinson's colleagues were particularly impressed by her commanding voice. Constancia Romilly vividly recalled the impression Ruby's voice made on her. "Ruby . . . was as tough as the men, and as courageous, and her voice was as strong as any man's voice. . . . Yes, she had a—she had a carrying voice, and a very well defined [voice]. When she spoke, you could definitely hear what she had to say." Curtis Muhammad was also deeply impressed by Robinson's voice. He described it as authoritative, masculine, but not too heavy. In his words, "She didn't have a whiny female thing . . . none of that."[16]

Earlier acquaintances who observed Robinson before she began her movement work recalled a demeanor and behavior that were remarkably similar to those she would display as a mature activist. Fellow Spelman College student Norma June Davis remarked that "she [Robinson] seemed so atypical of Spelman, I mean at that point in time. It was amazing that she was even there. She didn't look like a Spelmanite, she didn't dress like a Spelmanite, she didn't act like one." Another early acquaintance, the Reverend Albert Brinson, explained that students at Spelman "were always taught to be a lady. A lady stood back and waited to be waited upon by a man." Brinson thought that Ruby did not fit too well in this atmosphere, since "she was not the ladylike kind. . . . She was rather aggressive."[17]

Robinson was indeed aggressive whenever issues of racial justice were at stake. It seemed to her that there was always so much to be done. When idealistic and enthusiastic students first organized the Student Nonviolent Coordinating Committee in April 1960, they expected that their new committee would function as a coordinating body linking student protest movements in various communities. They soon recognized, though, that this was only the beginning. By February 1961 the group became involved in plotting movement strategy when they made the decision to send the delegation to Rock Hill, South Carolina.

In May 1961, shortly after Robinson and her colleagues finished serving their sentences in the York County jail, SNCC became involved in the Freedom Rides. Although the Congress of Racial Equality organized the rides, SNCC stepped in and provided the volunteers to continue when white resistance threatened to disrupt them. Robinson was one of those volunteers. She was later arrested and jailed for sixty days along with the other Freedom Riders. The riders served the first part of their sentence in the Hinds County jail in Jackson, Mississippi. They were later transferred to Parchman Penitentiary, a large state facility. Robinson's release came on 11 August 1961. By that time SNCC had decided to organize a voter registration campaign in McComb, Mississippi. Once again Robinson was right there. She went door to door urging people in McComb to register.

It seemed that Robinson was always willing to volunteer for the most hazardous movement duty. Furthermore, in such circumstances colleagues could depend on her to be bold, daring, and frequently outrageous. Because of her attitude and her actions, Ruby Doris Smith Robinson soon became a legend—even among the bold and brave young people of the Student Nonviolent Coordinating Committee. Most people who were with SNCC in the early years could recount at least one Robinson story. For example, Julian Bond remembered that when a delegation of SNCC staff members was preparing to board a plane for Africa in September 1964, an airline representative told them that the plane was full, even though they had tickets for that flight. He wanted to know if they would wait and take a later flight. This angered Robinson so much that, without consulting the rest of the group, she went and sat down in the jetway, preventing passengers from boarding the plane, and refused to move. The group was given seats on that flight.[18]

Coworker Michael Sayer particularly remembered Robinson's actions during an important SNCC staff meeting at Waveland, Mississippi, in November 1964. The group confronted some very difficult and emotional issues at that meeting, but the conferees still managed to find time for recreation. After one especially intense and emotional day, "someone suggested we have a football game. And . . . we played tackle football with no equipment. . . . Ruby was quarterback. We played eleven on a side . . . and I was playing the line and she ran over me." Robinson's intensity generally affected everything she did. James Bond, who worked in the SNCC print shop, witnessed still another Robinson incident, which occurred when a group of SNCC staff members went to the airport to meet some of the organization's celebrity supporters in 1963.

> So we went out there and met the first plane which was coming from California, which had Marlon Brando and Tony Franciosa on it. And then we had to go meet a second plane, which had Paul Newman on it. So we took them down to the other gate. . . . Ruby Doris was with us. And as we stood out at the gate waiting . . . the first person to come off the plane was Governor George Wallace. And Ruby Doris went up to him and said, "How are you, Governor?" and introduced herself and said, "I've spent time in your jails." And he said, "Well, I hope they treated you well, and if you're ever back, look me up."[19]

She never did.

Robinson's assertiveness, brashness, and courage were important, but they were not unique. Rather, her actions and her attitude mirror the boldness displayed by many African American women in the movement, and by many others over time. Consider the example of Annelle Ponder. Ponder, a Southern Christian Leadership Conference voter education teacher, was arrested in Winona, Mississippi, in 1963. Fannie Lou Hamer, who was arrested with her, remembered hearing an exchange between Ponder and her white prison guard. He demanded that she use a title of respect when addressing him: "Cain't you say yessir, bitch?" Ponder answered, "Yes, I can say yessir." The guard then demanded that she say it. Ponder's reply: "I don't know you well enough." The guard was so incensed that he beat her. Hamer remembered, "She kept screamin' and they kept beatin' her . . . and finally she started prayin' for 'em, and she asked God to have mercy on 'em because they didn't know what they was doin'."[20]

Then there was the case of Annie Pearl Avery. During the course of a demonstration in Montgomery, Alabama, in 1965, Avery came face-to-face with a white policeman who had a billy club aimed straight at her head. He had already beaten several others. Avery "reached up, grabbed the club and said, 'Now what you going to do, motherfucker?' " Then she slipped back into the crowd of demonstrators. Another activist, Judy Richardson, had more than a verbal confrontation with a policeman. During the course of a demonstration, she kicked an Atlanta policeman in the groin. Richardson explained what prompted her to take such drastic action. "He was mistreating a Black demonstrator, and it forced me to do something."[21]

In an era when American women were regularly told that a woman's place was in the home, women such as Ruby Doris Smith Robinson, Annie Pearl Avery, Judy Richardson, and Annelle Ponder definitely did not conform to contemporary notions of ladylike behavior. The advice offered by diplomat Adlai Stevenson in his commencement address to the class of 1955 at Smith College clearly illustrates contemporary expectations: "The assignment to you, as wives and mothers, you can do in the living room with a baby in your lap or in the kitchen with a can opener in your hand. If you are clever, maybe you can even practice your saving arts on that unsuspecting man while he's watching television. I think there is much you can do . . . in the humble role of housewife."[22]

Even though the behavior of black women activists did not always fit contemporary notions of proper female behavior, it did fit comfortably into an established tradition of black female assertiveness. Yet because of the predominance of broader notions of a woman's place, the actions of Robinson and some of her African American movement sisters brought them into conflict with many who questioned or ignored their femininity. Many, including Robinson, were troubled by this. Her colleague Cynthia Washington explained the frustration that many felt.

> I remember discussions with various women about our treatment as one of the boys and its impact on us as women. We did the same work as men—organizing around voter registration and community issues in rural areas—usually with men. But when we finally got back to some town where we could relax and go out, the men went out with other women. Our skills and abilities were recognized and respected, but that seemed to place us in some category other than female.[23]

The feminine side of their natures was a vital part of all of these women, including Robinson. Indeed, the feminine side of Robinson's nature dictated many of the choices she had made earlier in her life while she was growing up. A number of her SNCC colleagues who knew her only as a legendary freedom fighter and hard-nosed administrator would have been surprised to know that she was a debutante in 1958. She was also one of the head majorettes with the Price High School marching band. Years later, her younger sister Catherine recalled how much Robinson cared about her appearance when she was in high school. She was very concerned about fashion and she had a keen sense of style. She liked wide skirts, wide belts, and sweaters. "She had very expensive tastes. *Very*. She wore nothing cheap. She couldn't stand cheap clothes, and cheap shoes she would not put on her feet." She was concerned that her clothes should flatter her figure.[24]

Her concern about her appearance did not end once Robinson entered the movement. Although she became less inclined to indulge her expensive tastes, she still took a great deal of care with her appearance, sometimes under very difficult circumstances. Movement colleague Connie Curry remembered one particularly illustrative incident that occurred when the SNCC delegation went to Rock Hill, South Carolina, in 1961.

> They all knew that they were going to be arrested and go to jail. And Rock Hill was a very scary place. We got up real, real early that morning. Everybody was ready to go. And Ruby Doris said, "Well, everybody can just sort of sit down and do whatever because my hair is not right, and I'm rolling it, and I'm not leaving until it's curled." I thought, my God, this woman—she's going to be in jail within two hours. And she had these great big rollers . . . and everybody there just said, "Oh, okay."[25]

Robinson was not really "one of the boys" after all. What is clear is that Ruby Doris Smith Robinson was a woman whose existence called into question a whole range of stereotypes. Because she was an activist, she was not supposed to be "ladylike." Because she was an African American woman, she was not supposed to be feminine.

As she wrestled with the issue of femininity, Robinson was faced with a related problem: relationships between black and white women in SNCC. These relationships were the source of a great deal of tension within the organization at certain times. Part of this tension was rooted in the opposing perspectives of black and white women on some very fundamental issues. Cynthia Washington discussed some of those differences.

> During the fall of 1964, I had a conversation with Casey Hayden about the role of women in SNCC. She complained that all the women got to do was type, that their role was limited to office work no matter where they were. What she said didn't make any particular sense to me because, at the time, I had my own project in Bolivar County, Mississippi. A number of other black women also directed their own projects. What Casey and other white women seemed to want was an opportunity to prove they could do something other than office work. I assumed that if they could do something else, they'd probably be doing that.

Washington recognized how hard the work of a project director was, and besides that, "it wasn't much fun." Because of her insider's view, she was at a loss to understand why white women were complaining about their assignments. Their discontent over such issues only convinced Washington "how crazy they [white women] were."[26]

Even as they were conscious of the opposing perspectives of many of their white female colleagues, African American women in the movement were also painfully aware of the differences in the way society viewed them. One black female civil rights worker frankly discussed the resentment. "We've been getting beaten up for years trying to integrate lunch counters, movies, and so on, and nobody has ever paid us no attention or wrote about us. But these white girls come down here for a few months and get all the publicity. Everybody talks about how brave and courageous *they* are. What about us?" Another black female civil rights worker was both angered and amazed. When she was with a group demonstrating at a bus station, "a cop grabbed me by the arm and slapped my face. I don't know why I was surprised, but I really was." She decided to remind him of a basic tenet of southern etiquette. "I looked at him and I say, 'Listen Man, take another look at me. I'm a woman! You don't hit a woman! Didn't they teach you that?' He look kinda sorry, but he say, 'You're a niggah and that's all you are!' " Such a pervasive and negative view was bound to wound black women's sense of themselves. One black female civil rights worker clearly explained how deep those wounds were. White women, she said, did the less glamorous and domestic jobs "in a feminine kind of way, while [black women] . . . were out in the streets battling the cops. So it did something to what [our] femininity was about. We became amazons, less than and more than women at the same time."[27]

African American women's resentment about society's differential treatment of them was further complicated by the issue of physical appearance. Robinson and her African American colleagues came of age in a society that, from its earliest days, had judged African women by a European standard of beauty. Many women of African descent, including Robinson, had only to look in the mirror to see that they could never measure up physically. But many tried, and it was often quite painful.

Zohara Simmons, one of Robinson's SNCC colleagues and a fellow Spelman student, was keenly aware of the European standard of beauty that was idealized by so many. That awareness was born of Simmons's experience on the Spelman campus, a place famous for the "beauty" of its student body. Translation: A fairly high proportion of the students had light skin, keen features, and straight or nearly straight hair. Simmons explained the prevailing view at Spelman in the early sixties.

> First of all, the best of all possible worlds is that you are light as you can be, you have green eyes, or light brown, and you have long straight hair. They [Morehouse students] would be lined up outside your door, trying to get a date. Then you could be paper bag brown or

above and have long hair that you have to straighten, you know, that's still real cool, right? 'Cause we were all straightening—tough—in those days. Then, of course, you could be darker and have straight hair, long straight hair. . . . Then the last, of the last category was that you were dark-skinned and you had short hair or medium-length hair, you know?[28]

Having physical features that did not measure up to the white standard of beauty could be painful for black women sometimes. Because she was dark-skinned, Simmons learned that the pain was caused less by white reaction than by black rejection. She insisted, "Some of the Morehouse guys were so nasty to a person who looked like myself. *Overt.* I mean, straight up."[29] Appearance was important, but black women were powerless to change their appearance, at least permanently. Feelings of insecurity about their looks were a terrible burden that African American women were forced to bear. Ruby Doris Smith Robinson had to carry her share of this black women's burden because she was not particularly light-skinned, she had broad features, and her hair was not naturally straight. Like so many African American women of her generation, she wrestled with negative views of who and what she was—views that were popularized by white society and then embraced, at least in part, by black society.

Thus the relationship between black female SNCC staffers and their white female activist colleagues was influenced by black female resentment about American society's history of negative perceptions and treatment of them. At the same time, however, the attitudes of white females also contributed to tension between black females and themselves. American white people, even sympathetic female activists, had all been touched to a greater or lesser extent by the negative black stereotypes so popular in their society. Psychiatrist Alvin Poussaint, in his evaluation of the adjustment of white women volunteers to the rigors of Freedom Summer, found that a number of these women were indeed struggling with racist stereotypes. In Poussaint's estimation, some of them lost that struggle. He identified a syndrome he labeled the White African Queen Complex.

> At the center of this "complex" is probably a tabooed and repressed fantasy of the intelligent, brave, and beautiful white woman leading the poor, downtrodden, and oppressed black man to freedom and salvation. One white female worker told me she sometimes felt like "the master's child come to free the slaves." Another confided, "What an electrifying feeling it is to be worshipped by the Negroes."[30]

Black women bitterly resented this attitude and the condescending behavior that accompanied it.

A further complicating factor in this white female–black female conflict was the issue of class. Many of the white women who worked in the civil rights movement were middle-class or even upper-middle-class. On the other hand, many of the African American activists, including Robinson, were from families with middle-class aspirations but only working-class incomes. Some of these black women had faced very difficult economic circumstances during their lives. Consequently, when middle-class white women doing office work began to complain about being oppressed, Robinson and other black women like her simply lost their patience. Joyce Ladner recalled tense times in the office.

> The impression Ruby conveyed was that . . . white women were always at kind of uneasy peace around her. She didn't mistreat them, but they sure didn't pull that . . . on her. She was the last person they would run to with some complaint about, "Oh, we're poor oppressed, we're poor oppressed white women here. . . ." She'd been in jail and was from a poor background herself. So it was hard for her to have sympathy for a girl from Sarah Lawrence who felt put upon.[31]

Some in the movement charged that even though a preponderance of the white women on the permanent staff were limited to office work, they tried to exert too much influence. Regardless of its accuracy, this perception helped to intensify the conflict. Joyce Ladner clearly recalled this notion. "See, a lot of white women who came into SNCC even though they felt they were discriminated against, in quotes, . . . they still tried to dominate the office. I mean it was a matter of [not] being content anywhere—[even] if you put them in the field. They were white women; that's all that was necessary to know about them."[32] Because Robinson was such a critical part of the central office staff, she found herself in the middle of this complex of feelings and resentments plaguing both black and white women. In retrospect, at least one white female staff member in SNCC understood why Robinson and the other black women were so suspicious. "If I were to put myself in Ruby Doris's head, what I would say is, you know, 'Here comes Dinky Romilly, here comes Mary King. Why are they here? They don't have any intrinsic interest in promoting the rights of black people. They're middle-class white women. . . .' And I can understand that . . . she would be very suspect of that."[33]

In such an atmosphere Robinson exerted her increasing authority. She had to cope with a variety of attitudes, resentments, and behaviors exhibited by white women staff members. At the same time, she had to balance these against the resentments and perceptions of the black women on the staff. In the midst of this she was still dragging around her share of the black woman's burden as she sought to cope with the historical and recent negative assessments of black female morality, femininity, physical appearance, and capabilities.

As Robinson wrestled with questions of femininity and black female–white female tensions, her life was complicated by still another factor. In addition to being a full-time freedom fighter, Ruby Doris Smith Robinson was also a wife and a mother. She married Clifford Robinson in 1964 and gave birth to a son, Kenneth Toure, in 1965. Even though she was totally committed to the movement, her family obligations were also important to her. One of her close movement friends, Mildred Forman, remembered that Robinson was "ecstatic over the baby and the husband." Even though Robinson was already extraordinarily busy with her work in SNCC, Forman felt that motherhood further enriched her life: "I think that was the best thing that could have happened to her, because she just . . . beamed and glowed with the baby." Although motherhood added a unique richness, it also added tasks to Robinson's already overburdened schedule. As she juggled motherhood and movement work, at times the frantic pace of her life caught up with her. Movement colleague and friend Freddie Greene Biddle clearly recalled an incident that graphically illustrated how overwhelming things sometimes became.

> I remember once Ruby came out [of her house] with all these bags and her pocketbook and all this stuff, and we're going to the office, and she's going to drop, uh, Toure . . . off. . . . Well she's backing out of the . . . driveway and I'm in the car. . . . She had all these bags and stuff and so then all of a sudden she said, "Oh shit!" [I] said "What's wrong?" She's forgotten the baby![34]

As Robinson settled into motherhood, she was still struggling to find a balance between her marital and movement duties. Her husband, Clifford, was also a SNCC staff member. Despite his membership in the organization, however, Clifford's commitment paled in comparison to Ruby's. He freely admitted that he joined the movement only because of his wife's involvement. This disparity in commitment was sometimes the source of a certain amount of tension. Zohara Simmons recalled:

> I can just remember, you know, you run in the office and he's [Clifford] standing there waiting on her to go. And, you know, everybody's saying, "Ruby Doris, so and so and so." And he's saying, "Look, we got to go." And she's saying, "Cliff, wait a minute. . . . I got to

take care of this." And him stalking off mad. And her saying, "Oh, God . . . later for him, then." I imagine she caught hell when she got home.

But Clifford insisted that the volume of work Ruby did in SNCC did not cause a strain on their relationship, even though "it was going on all the time around the house." Clifford went on to explain, though, that when *he* thought Ruby was doing too much movement work after office hours, "I was there to stop it."[35]

Robinson tried very hard to balance her family relationships and her movement obligations. At the same time, she was confronted by enormous pressures and tensions in SNCC. Her determination and commitment had always given her the strength to cope with all these concerns. As a Freedom Rider, Robinson faced down hostile white mobs. She confronted brutal southern sheriffs and assorted Klan representatives when she canvassed for voter registration. As a powerful leader, Robinson had confronted numerous and strident conflicts in SNCC. But when she was diagnosed with terminal cancer in April 1967, even her strength and determination were not enough. She wanted to continue with the important things in her life: raising her son, caring for her husband, and guiding her beloved Student Nonviolent Coordinating Committee. But the cancer would not let her. Ruby Doris Smith Robinson died on 9 October 1967, at the age of twenty-five.

Many of her SNCC colleagues are convinced that it was not cancer but the frantic pace of her life that killed her. They all remember how Robinson always tried to do everything; her commitment to the civil rights movement did not stop her from trying to be a fulltime wife and mother. Furthermore, according to some, the SNCC conflicts were exacerbated because of her gender. It was simply too much for one woman. Despite the conflicts and difficulties that faced her, however, Robinson would not have lived her life any other way. She was a woman who believed that she could and should do it all.

Notes

1. Mary Ann Smith Wilson, interview by author, Atlanta, Ga., 19 November 1989.
2. Ibid.
3. Howard Zinn, *SNCC: The New Abolitionists* (Boston: Beacon Press, 1964), 17.
4. Clayborne Carson, *In Struggle: SNCC and the Black Awakening of the 1960s* (Cambridge: Harvard University Press, 1981), 203.
5. Matthew Jones, interview by author, Knoxville, Tenn., 24 April 1989; Mildred Forman, interview by author, Chicago, Ill., 6 November 1989.
6. Jack Minnis, interview by author, New Orleans, La., 4 November 1990; Stanley Wise, interview by author, Atlanta, Ga., 11 November 1990.
7. Reginald Robinson and Charles Jones, interview by author, McComb, Miss., 28 June 1991; Worth Long, interview by author, Atlanta, Ga., 8 February 1991.
8. Wilson, interview.
9. *Student Voice* 2, February 1961.
10. Wilson, interview.
11. Ruby Doris Smith to Mary Ann Smith, 25 February 1961, in Mary Ann Smith Wilson's private papers, Atlanta, Ga.
12. *Atlanta Inquirer*, 18 March 1961.
13. Carson, *In Struggle*, 230; Mucasa (Willie Ricks), interview by author, Atlanta, Ga., 8 April 1990.
14. Angela Davis, *Women, Race, and Class* (New York: Random House, 1983), 5.
15. Wilson, interview; Robinson and Jones, interview; Courtland Cox, interview by author, Washington, D.C., 16 December 1988; Joanne Grant, interview by author, New Orleans, La., 4 November 1990.
16. Constancia Romilly, interview by author, Atlanta, Ga., 14 June 1991; Curtis Muhammad (Curtis Hayes), interview by author, McComb, Miss., 29 June 1991.
17. Norma June Davis and Lana Taylor Sims, interview by author, Atlanta, Ga., 11 November 1990; Albert Brinson, interview by author, Atlanta, Ga., 10 November 1990.
18. Julian Bond, interview by author, Washington, D.C., 16 December 1988.

19. Michael Sayer, interview by author, New Market, Tenn., 5 May 1990; James Bond, interview by author, Atlanta, Ga., 8 February 1991.

20. Paula Giddings, *When and Where I Enter: The Impact of Black Women on Race and Sex in America* (New York: Morrow, 1984), 290.

21. Ibid., 292.

22. Ibid., 243.

23. Cynthia Washington, "We Started from Different Ends of the Spectrum," *Southern Exposure* 5 (winter 1977): 14.

24. Catherine Smith Robinson and Ruby O'Neal, interview by author, Atlanta, Ga., 3 March 1990.

25. Connie Curry, interview by author, Atlanta, Ga., 10 November 1990.

26. Washington, "We Started from Different Ends," 14.

27. Alvin Poussaint, "The Stresses of the White Female Worker in the Civil Rights Movement in the South," *Journal of American Psychiatry* 123 (October 1966): 403; Josephine Carson, *Silent Voices* (New York: McGraw Hill, 1969), 60; Sara Evans, *Personal Politics: The Roots of Women's Liberation in the Civil Rights Movement and the New Left* (New York: Random House, 1979), 81.

28. Zohara Simmons, interview by author, Philadelphia, Pa., 17 December 1988.

29. Ibid.

30. Poussaint, "The Stresses of the White Female Worker," 404.

31. Joyce Ladner, interview by the author, Washington, D.C., 18 December 1988.

32. Ibid.

33. Romilly, interview.

34. Forman, interview; Freddie Greene Biddle, interview by author, McComb, Miss., 29 June 1991.

35. Simmons, interview; Clifford Robinson, interview by author, Atlanta, Ga., 17 March 1989.

34

Towards Trans-Pacific Social Justice
Women and Protest in Filipino American History

Catherine Ceniza Choy

In July 1972, Prosy Abarquez-Delacruz arrived in the United States with a recent Bachelor of Science degree in Food Technology from the University of the Philippines. Today, she is the regional administrator of the California State Department of Health Services' Food and Drug branch. While her life history might be read in the context of the rise of Filipino professional immigration to the United States in the post-1965 period, Abarquez-Delacruz tells a different story. While a science student at the University of the Philippines in the 1960s and early 1970s, she had become part of a generation that is now referred to as the "first quarterstorm," a primarily student-led movement for social change in the Philippines that challenged deeply rooted socio-economic inequalities. She later recollected how student activist testimonies about witnessing children dying from lack of nutrition and medical attention had convinced her to become involved in the struggle for social change and to confront the issues of unequal land ownership, exploitive foreign business investors, and local government corruption.

Abarquez-Delacruz's story reveals that immigration was not her individual choice, but rather the result of family dynamics as well as Philippine political forces. Her parents worked on her visa papers because they feared for her life. Stories of student activists being "salvaged," a practice that referred to their disappearances, torture, and executions, had become more widely circulated. Upon her arrival in the United States, Abarquez-Delacruz claimed that she felt "lost." But upon hearing the news that martial law was declared in the Philippines on September 21, 1972, she related, "I found myself suddenly feeling relevant again, no longer lost and having a mission. I needed to find a group to organize with and to help restore civil liberties in the Philippines."[1]

By 1972, there were already in existence several Filipino organizations in the United States that were opposing U.S. imperialism in the Philippines. These activist organizations argued that U.S. imperialism had persisted even after official Philippine independence from U.S. colonial rule on July 4, 1946, through the passage, for example, of the 1947 Military Bases Agreement that enabled the U.S. to maintain military installations in the archipelago. The groups included the *Kalayaan* or the Freedom Collective, the Support Committee for a Democratic Philippines in New York, and the *Samahan ng Makabayang Pilipino* (SAMAPI-Association of Nationalist Filipinos) in Chicago.[2]

In early 1972, the *Kalayaan* proposed bringing together the locally-based Filipino progressive organizations in the United States in order to address the role of Filipino Americans in Philippine political issues as well as to discuss Filipino Americans' shared struggles with other minorities in the United States. The *Kalayaan* was also the only group at that time whose membership included significant numbers of both U.S.-born Filipinos and Filipino immigrants. The national organization they had proposed might have resulted in a trans-Pacific political agenda that advocated for civil rights in the Philippines and the United States. But, Ferdinand Marcos's declaration of martial law in the Philippines in September 1972 changed Filipino American political priorities (especially the priorities of recent immigrants) and prompted a show of unity among anti-imperialist activists to oppose the Marcos regime.

Prosy Abarquez-Delacruz became involved in the National Committee for the Restoration of Civil Liberties in the Philippines, which called for the release of political prisoners and the end of U.S. support of the Marcos regime. Although Abarquez-Delacruz had found a way in the United States to organize against martial law in the Philippines, she reflected upon the multiple political differences during that time that divided Filipinos in America. These differences went beyond pro- and anti-Marcos factions and reflected the tensions resulting from the shift of Filipino immigrant activism during the 1970s and 1980s towards Philippine political issues and away from U.S. race-, gender-, and class-based concerns, such as employment discrimination against Filipino immigrants. The division between Philippine and U.S. issues caused another Filipina immigrant and anti-martial law activist, Carol Ojeda-Kimbrough, to self-reflect: "Am I a Filipino first or a Filipino American? Where do my loyalties reside—in my country of birth or in the country of residence? Intuitively I knew that this was a misdirected question and that my community involvement should not waver."[3]

Although immigrant transnational activism—the endurance of social, political, and economic commitments in their countries of origin—is hardly a new historical topic,[4] it has not been fully explored in the case of Filipino Americans, especially during the 1960s and 1970s, a pivotal time period in Philippine, U.S., and Asian American histories. Furthermore, Filipino American women's activism is a severely understudied topic in Asian American Studies in general. The objective of this essay is threefold: first, to connect the histories of the Asian American Movement and the Anti-Martial Law Movement through the personal narratives of Prosy Abarquez-Delacruz and Carol Ojeda-Kimbrough; second, to illuminate how both U.S. and Philippine nation-based histories marginalize these women's histories and their transnational political commitments; and third, to suggest how a transnational historical perspective can highlight the roles of women and protest in Filipino American history more effectively.

In doing so, this essay suggests that the dichotomous assumption between Philippine issues on the one hand and Filipino American issues on the other needs to be historicized. For in the case of Abarquez-Delacruz and Ojeda-Kimbrough, that dichotomy is a false one. Recent Filipino American Studies feminist scholarship has made similar conclusions. As Asian American Studies scholar Melinda de Jesus self-reflected in her introduction to *Pinay Power: Peminist Critical Theory*: "Initially, I was adamant that the anthology privilege the voices of Filipina *Americans*— as opposed to Filipina *Filipinas*. . . .I began to comprehend how my own identity crisis as an American-born Filipina led me to privilege a split between 'peminists' that does not exist."[5]

This essay was inspired by a teaching moment during the fall 2004 semester, when I was concluding an upper-division undergraduate course on Filipino American History. In that course, students heard lectures about Filipino American participation in the Asian American Movement of the late 1960s, 1970s, and early 1980s, such as their support for the Great Grape Boycott of 1965, which began with 1,300 Filipino farm workers led by Larry Itliong and culminated with the participation of Cesar Chavez's National Farm Work Association and the formation of the United Farm Workers (UFW) union; their participation in the protests against the eviction of *manong*, or Filipino elderly bachelors, from the I-Hotel in San Francisco; and their demand for a relevant ethnic studies curriculum that would foreground the experiences of racialized minorities in the United States.

In that Filipino American history course, students also heard lectures about Filipino American participation in the Anti-Martial Law Movement in the United States that protested the dictatorship and human rights abuses of former Philippine President Ferdinand Marcos, who in 1972 had suspended the Philippine constitution and had violently attempted to stamp out political dissent. Those who went into exile abroad and primarily in the United States organized as groups and individuals under a coalition known as the Anti-Martial Law Alliance.

After these lectures, the teaching assistant posed the question to me in class: Was there a connection between the Asian American Movement and the Anti-Martial Law Movement? And if so, what was it?[6] Her questions illuminated the traditional historiographical treatment of the Asian American Movement as by-and-large a U.S. story, separate and distinct from Philippine political issues. History books, such as William Wei's *The Asian American Movement*, reify this separation by not even mentioning the existence of the Anti-Martial Law Movement.[7] This divide is problematic because it marginalizes the histories of Filipino American women whose lives were profoundly affected by both of these movements and whose activism made the movements possible. It also downplays the important lessons we can glean from these women's stories about the gendered material and psychological difficulties that accompany the pursuit of a truly international vision of civil rights.

Even the anthology *Asian Americans: The Movement and the Moment*, which published the personal narratives of Prosy Abarquez-Delacruz and Carol Ojeda-Kimbrough and which provides an important corrective to William Wei's interpretation of Filipino American activism during the Asian American Movement, downplays their trans-Pacific vision of social justice. In his preface to the anthology, Don Nakanishi claims that the anthology is "truly a book about America" and that it seeks to capture the Movement's significance for an audience of primarily "Asian Pacific Americans in today's multiracial America."[8] And in her introduction to the personal narratives of the Filipina American activists, Cecile Caguingin Ochoa oversimplifies their activism as "one aspiration—to carve an agenda of substance to make the presence of Filipino and Asian Americans in this country valued the way other cultures are held in high esteem."[9]

However, neither U.S.-based issues nor trans-Pacific social justice had animated Prosy Abarquez-Delacruz's and Carol Ojeda-Kimbrough's activism at first. Rather, Philippine state power and foreign domination had played a formative role in the development of their activism. In the early 1970s in the Philippines, Carol Ojeda-Kimbrough was pursuing a medical degree at the University of the Philippines, but after the declaration of martial law she had decided to drop out of school and joined a small collective of community activists engaged in organizing squatters in Quezon City:

> The pejorative "squatter" describes the large number of urban poor who were forced into illegally building shelters on private or public owned land. Squatters lived under constant threat of eviction, often through violent confrontations with the private armies of landowners or the military. With the imposition of Martial Law and the loss of the democratic process, activists could not organize in the open; we did our organizing underground. We met with small groups of squatters and discussed concrete problems they were facing, basic human rights like decent housing and access to water. This served as a prelude to more abstract discussions about the link between Martial Law and foreign domination of the Philippine economy and the need to overthrow both in order to have a truly just and democratic government.[10]

Ojeda-Kimbrough soon fell in love with Lando, another activist, and became pregnant. Birth control in the predominantly Catholic Philippines was forbidden. Carol chose to keep the baby over having an illegal abortion, a decision that alienated her from the revolutionary movement for which she had sacrificed her college education. She recollected that "it was becoming more difficult to outrun the military with a bulging belly."[11] Yet, as she scaled back her activities, her "comrades" interpreted this decision as ideological wavering and, although the child was also Lando's, according to Ojeda-Kimbrough he had made it clear that his life was with the movement. By "choosing" to become a parent, Ojeda-Kimbrough had settled into what her fellow activists' referred to "domesticity."

But, domesticity did not remove her from the life-and-death dangers of the Marcos regime's political repression. The military began to visit her at home frequently to interrogate her about a high school friend who had joined the underground opposition. By this time, her parents had emigrated to the United States. Faced with the threat of arrest, Ojeda-Kimbrough had made the major decision to move to the United States with her son in 1975. Like Prosy Abarquez-Delacruz, her emigration did not weaken her commitment to Philippine revolution. Ojeda-Kimbrough reaffirmed, "Though far from the Philippines, I sought ways to be part of the nationalist movement to overthrow the dictatorship."[12] She participated in meetings of the Los Angeles chapter of the Anti-Martial Law Alliance, a coalition of organizations and individuals who espoused different political ideologies but were united in the vision of an independent Philippines. At these meetings, Ojeda-Kimbrough bonded with activists from the KDP (*Katipunan ng mga Demokratkong Pilipino* or the Union of Democratic Filipinos), an organization that had formed in 1973.[13]

Her decision to work with the KDP reflected how her immigrant experience had begun to inform an increasingly trans-Pacific view of social justice. Like other Philippine-focused national democratic organizations, the KDP opposed martial law in the Philippines and the persistence of U.S. imperialism in the archipelago. What distinguished the KDP, however, from other anti-martial law organizations was its focus on the "dual nature" of the Filipino American community, a community that was at once an overseas community bound to the history and culture of the Philippine nation, but becoming increasingly aware of its position as a racialized minority group in the United States. For example, former KDP member and Filipino immigrant nurse Esther Hipalao Simpson characterized discrimination as a "general Filipino experience" in the United States, but it was also an experience that was not often directly acknowledged or understood by Filipino immigrant professionals: "[Filipinos in the United States] may have experienced discrimination, but they can't understand why they have to work as draftsmen when they were engineers in the Philippines. Why are they working as dental hygienists when they were all dentists in the Philippines?"[14] Anti-martial law activists in the United States became exposed to different literatures, which Simpson referred to as "books you never heard of before," such as Carlos Bulosan's *America Is In The Heart*, and began making connections between racism and economic exploitation experienced by Filipino migrants to the United States before and after 1965.[15] As a result, the KDP advocated for Philippine democracy *and* U.S. socialism, with the question of race as the core issue of its socialist program.

The core issue of race was deeply interwoven with issues of citizenship, class, and gender. Ojeda-Kimbrough recollected her early experiences as an immigrant:

> Life as an immigrant had its own set of contradictions and resolutions. Starting life over as newcomers, my parents found themselves in entry-level jobs. My father had a regular daytime job as a clerk for the phone company. My mother worked full-time for a bank and by day's end would go to her part-time job with an appliance maker. She would leave at 7:30am and not return home until 11:00pm. I remember how my father would walk over to the bus stop every night to meet her and together they walked home. Home was a two-bedroom apartment in East Hollywood. Nine people were crammed into this apartment: my parents had one room, my three sisters, my son and I shared the other room, and my two brothers slept in the living room. As the oldest of six children, I had to get a job to help the family out. The second oldest, a sister, took care of my son while I looked for a job. She had already started college but could not continue her studies in America for our family

had no college funds. The rest of my siblings were either in elementary or in junior high school. I soon found a job as a clerk, earning about $400 a month, and my mother was able to quit her part-time job.[16]

This passage is rich with the intersection of racial, gender, and socioeconomic inequalities that challenge the dominant interpretation of U.S. immigration as emancipatory. Her parents' entry-level jobs speak to the phenomenon of underemployment and to the racialization of Filipino workers as inferior as a result of their Philippine educational training and work experience. Ojeda-Kimbrough's mother's evening employment with an appliance maker hints at the detailed assembly work for which immigrant women of color in the United States as well as Third World women in export processing zones are targeted. The routine of the father escorting the mother from the bus stop after her second job ended at 11:00pm speaks to the gendered violence that women face in the United States and to the absence of safety in their neighborhood. And, finally, the need for Ojeda-Kimbrough to enter the workforce to reduce her mother's economic burden creates what feminist scholars have called a "chain of care" that displaces the burden of the care of her son onto her sister, who is then constrained from socioeconomic mobility because she drops out of college.[17] Although this "chain of care" has been used by feminist scholars to analyze the plight of Filipina overseas contract workers who leave their children in Philippines at displace their children's care onto relatives there, Ojeda-Kimbrough's story illustrates how Filipino immigrant women in the United States experience similar processes.

It was at the intersection of these U.S. immigrant struggles that Ojeda-Kimbrough was drawn to the KDP's socialist vision of what the United States could be, a vision inspired by left-wing Filipino American organizations in the 1920s and 1930s that envisioned an American society governed in the interests of its working classes. In her personal narrative, Ojeda-Kimbrough reflects upon her growing critique of her own Philippine nationalism as narrow: "My own narrow nationalist view was slowly expanded and I embraced my experience in American society. I learned about the general immigrant experience in this country and how this experience was racialized."[18]

As the 1970s progressed, the KDP became more involved in issues that focused on Filipino American struggles as racialized minorities in the United States. These agendas included support for affirmative action; immigration reform legislation; equity in licensure for foreign medical and nursing graduates: support for two immigrant Filipina nurses (Leonora Perez and Filipina Narciso) who were scapegoated by the FBI for murder, poisoning, and conspiracy at the V.A. Hospital in Ann Arbor, Michigan; and international solidarity work with South Africa and Central America political struggles.

Yet this activism did not translate into a shift away from Philippine political issues. Ojeda-Kimbrough received a letter informing her that Lando had disappeared along with two women activists. Only one of the women had survived. Ten years after Lando's disappearance, Adora Faye de Vera, who had been a classmate of Ojeda-Kimbrough's at the University of the Philippines, was able to tell her of their ordeal and Lando's death at the hands of his military torturers. Ojeda-Kimbrough recalled her sorrow after learning her lover's fate:

My sense of loss was compounded by the guilt I felt for having chosen to leave the Philippines when Lando and other activists couldn't. Had I stayed, would he have gone on that trip? My friends wrote that he missed us so much and that to cope with our separation, he took on more and more work just to keep himself occupied. If we hadn't been separated, maybe he would still be alive. Or maybe I would have fallen victim to this military practice as well. There are times when I replay this scene in my mind and there's little comfort in knowing that things turned out the way they did because of the choices we made. But we move on.[19]

However, her physical presence in the United States did not guarantee her safety because she continued to be involved in anti-martial law work. The killing of KDP activists and union leaders Gene Viernes and Silme Domingo in Seattle in June 1981 by the Marcos regime was a shocking reminder of the risks of anti-martial law work even in the United States.[20] According to Ojeda-Kimbrough, anti-martial law activists in the United States also deeply feared deportation for their "subversive activities." The Marcos regime attempted to cull U.S. government support and to stifle political dissent by portraying anti-martial law activists in the United States as well as in the Philippines as communists. Ojeda-Kimbrough's parents pleaded with her to place the interest of her son before her political commitments.

This notion of removing herself from anti-martial law activism for the sake of her son contrasts with a poignant scene in *Spirits Rising*, Ramona Diaz's critically acclaimed 1995 documentary film about People Power, the Philippine pro-democracy movement of 1986 that toppled the Marcos regime and led to Cory Aquino's presidency.[21] In the film, a Filipina anti-martial law activist claims that many mothers participated on the frontlines of People Power protests for their children's sake. While Carol Ojeda-Kimbrough might have felt the same way, her personal narrative also emphasizes with moving honesty the maternal guilt that she experienced about the time her activism took:

> One of the questions [I am] asked by . . . students was how did we manage to remain committed to the "cause." I told them it was not easy. I can't speak for all KDP activists, or for that matter, women activists, but I know that I had moments of uncertainty triggered by guilt for not spending enough time with my son. Guilt is such an unproductive emotion, but it plagued a number of women activists. Recently I spent a weekend with five (women) former KDP activists. Four of us were young mothers at the time of our involvement. We had not seen each other since the late 1980s (the KDP formally disbanded in 1986 after the fall of the Marcos regime), and although the reunion was supposed to be a happy occasion, in the course of the weekend, we found that guilt was a recurring theme. Guilt about abandoning our children to countless child care providers, so that we could go about our organizing work; guilt that our children may have suffered permanent emotional or psychological damage because of that; and, guilt that we were too busy caring about the world when we couldn't even care enough to be with our children. We knew we could have given up political work and stayed home, but we chose to be activists (sic) moms. This was the comforting thought: we had company from each other's lament.[22]

The above passage cries for more empirical and theoretical research on Filipino American motherhood. Did their feelings of guilt stem from Western idealized notions of motherhood that takes place in a heterosexual, nuclear, middle class family, from Western notions popularized by restrictive gendered social norms under Spanish and/or U.S. imperialism? Ramona Diaz's *Spirits Rising* is helpful in beginning to answer this question for it does not document the People Power movement in a linear fashion, but rather weaves that history with Philippine women's history beginning with pre-colonial times. The film highlights the equality of Filipino men and women, based on the creation myth that man and woman sprang together from the same bamboo (thus signifying the equality of men and women) and the power of Filipino women priests known as *babaylan* who healed the sick, foretold the future, and found lost things. Diaz's historical narrative goes on to claim that when Spanish colonizers came, Filipino women's choices became restricted to the convent, spinsterhood, and marriage.[23]

Although U.S. colonial rule brought more educational opportunities for Filipino women under the guise of liberation, in *Spirits Rising* Ramona Diaz claims that this supposedly new freedom meant little more than a costume change for Filipino women. Indeed, one of the major contradictions of U.S. colonial rule reveals that U.S. colonialism was very much a gendered project: to "liberate" Filipino women and prepare Filipinos for self-rule, Filipino men and women had to adopt U.S. gendered social norms about the proper roles of men and women, roles that placed Filipino women in domestic and care work and that placed Filipino men in the public political sphere.[24] Thus, *Spirits Rising* suggests that the role of Filipino women in People Power was not the result of the impact of Western ideologies of freedom and democracy, but rather the result of pre-colonial spirits rising *in spite* of the imposition of Western ideas about women's secondary role in politics.

On one level, this essay contests the marginalization of these Filipino American women's history in Asian American Studies and its related disciplines. But, it also illuminates a different perspective of Philippine history and contemporary society. Like Asian American histories that emphasize the centrality of U.S.-based experiences, Ramona Diaz's history in *Spirits Rising* focuses on Philippine-based experiences and does not mention the role of anti-martial law women activists in the United States. Interestingly, this "invisibility" of the history of Filipino women's activism in the United States contrasts sharply with the almost hyper visibility of Filipina overseas contract workers in today's global economy. The Philippines is the largest labor-exporting nation in the world with seven million Filipinos working in 187 countries. Filipino women are quite visible as "servants of globalization"—to use ethnic studies scholar Rhacel Parrenas's phrase—Filipina overseas contract workers who work primarily as domestic helpers in Italy, Singapore, and Hong Kong, among other places.[25] While the numbers of Filipino anti-martial law activists in the United States pale in comparison to the millions of Filipino overseas contract workers, I would argue that demographics alone do not determine the invisibility of the former and the hyper-visibility of the latter. I believe that this observation reflects how nation-building continues to be a formidable force in Philippine Studies. The global diaspora of Filipino contract workers animates Philippines Studies in large part because since the 1970s the Philippine government has linked overseas labor to the Philippine nation-building project, which continues to honor these workers as the "new national heroes." Furthermore, despite what could be called the recent "transnational turn" in Filipino American Studies,[26] tensions and gaps between what counts as Philippine Studies, on the one hand, and Filipino American Studies, on the other, persist. As writer Luis Francia eloquently mused, "The Filipino-American finds himself or herself in a strange predicament: not quite American, say, in Boston, or Filipino enough in Manila. Where then does he/she belong? Borders are said to be disappearing, and yet I find that certain borders retain their preeminence—not the least of which is the Proprietary attitude towards the Philippines as a concept. Who exactly does it belong to?"[27]

Prosy Abarquez-Delacruz and Carol Ojeda-Kimbrough, however, were not overseas contract workers, although it was Marcos's regime that initiated a labor export-oriented economy. And, they were not among the thousands of Filipino nurses whose immigration had been facilitated by the new occupational preferences of the U.S. Immigration Act of 1965 (although Carol opened her personal narrative by writing, "I can't get over how often I am asked this question all the time": "Are you a nurse?"[28]). But, their trans-Pacific political visions speak to the heart of the transnational intellectual project outlined by historian of international relations Akira Iriye: "If what is at the heart of our historical inquiry is the human condition, then it makes sense to go beyond the nation or the state as the sole framework of analysis and deal with human affairs, human aspirations, human values, and human tragedies. States do play a role, but only a partial role in all of these. The task that challenges historians of international relations is to devise a new transnational perspective that takes into account both states and non-state actors."[29]

After supporting the Marcos regime for over a decade, the U.S. government abandoned its support of Marcos rule in 1986, in large part due to the organizing and publicity work of the People Power Movement and the Anti-Martial Law Movement. And, in 1991, the Anti-Martial Law Movement claimed a victory when the Philippine Senate rejected the renewal of the military bases agreement with the United States. Writing in the new millennium, both

Abarquez-Delacruz and Ojeda-Kimbrough ended their personal narratives with thoughts that speak to "spirits rising" in ways that Ramona Diaz may or may not have intended in her film. Abarquez-Delacruz claimed that "commitment to the struggle does not mean being held in a cage. Commitment is the spirit that you hang on to."[30] And, Ojeda-Kimbrough concluded her final reflections about the years of difficult activist labor by writing that "sometimes, when our bodies or psyches could no longer take the stress of political life, we shut out by 'laying low' or temporarily leaving the organization, not unlike a soldier wounded in war, who retreats from the front lines to heal and fight again another day."[31] Their personal narratives make me believe that spirits do indeed rise in both the Philippines and the United States. Although Philippine and U.S. revolutions did not take place the way these activists had ideally hoped for, their stories provide those of us interested in social justice within *and* across national borders with two things: inspiration and hope.

Notes

This essay is based on the Edith Kreeger-Wolf lecture originally delivered by the author in April 2005 at Northwestern University. The author wishes to acknowledge the generosity of the Edith Kreeger-Wolf endowment. Established in 1973 by Chicago philanthropist Edith Kreeger Wolf, the endowment has had the goal of deepening students' familiarity with fields of study fostered largely by women, and with the insights into many realms of knowledge that emerge when the role and treatment of women is included.

1. Prosy Abarquez-Delacruz, "Holding a Pigeon in My Hand: How Community Organizing Succeeds or Falters," *Asian Americans: The Movement and the Moment*, Steve Louie and Glenn Omatsu, eds. (Los Angeles: UCLA Asian American Studies Center Press, 2001), 61.
2. Barbara S. Gaerlan, "The Movement in the United States to Oppose Martial Law in the Philippines, 1972–1991: An Overview," *Pilipinas* 33 (Fall 1999): 75–98.
3. Carol Ojeda-Kimbrough, "The Chosen Road," *Asian Americans: The Movement and the Moment*, Steve Louie and Glenn Omatsu, eds. (Los Angeles: UCLA Asian American Studies Center Press. 2001) 71.
4. Transnational historical frameworks have animated recent Filipino American Studies scholarship. See Catherine Ceniza Choy, *Empire of Care: Nursing and Migration in Filipino American History* (Durham, NC: Duke University Press, 2003); Yen Le Espiritu, *Home Bound: Filipino American Lives Across Cultures, Communities, and Countries* (Berkeley, CA: University of California Press, 2003); Dorothy Fujita-Rony, *American Workers, Colonial Power* (Berkeley, CA: University of California Press, 2003); and Augusto Fauni Espiritu, *Five Faces of Exile: The Nation and Filipino American Intellectuals* (Stanford, CA: Stanford University Press, 2005).
5. Melinda L. de Jesus, "Introduction: Toward a Peminist Theory, or Theorizing the Filipina/American Experience," *Pinay Power: Peminist Critical Theory Theorizing the Filipina/American Experience*, ed. Melinda L. de Jesus (New York: Routledge 2005), 5–6.
6. I wish to acknowledge Joanne Rondilla for asking such thoughtful and generative questions.
7. William Wei, *The Asian American Movement: A Social History* (Philadelphia: Temple University Press, 1993).
8. Don T. Nakanishi, "Moving the Historical Moment Forward," *Asian Americans: The Movement and the Moment*, Steve Louie and Glenn Omatsu, eds. (Los Angeles: UCLA Asian American Studies Center Press, 2001), viii.
9. Cecile Caguinguin Ochoa, "Touching the Fire: An Introduction to Three Essays from Filipina American Activists," *ibid.*, 53.
10. Carol Ojeda-Kimbrough, "The Chosen Road," 66.
11. *Ibid.*, 67.
12. *Ibid.*, 68.
13. Helen Toribio, "We Are Revolution: A Reflective History of the Union of Democratic Filipinos (KDP)," *Amerasia Journal* 24:2 (Summer 1998): 155–178.
14. Catherine Ceniza Choy, *Empire of Care*, 156.
15. *Ibid.*, 157–158.
16. Carol Ojeda-Kimbrough, "The Chosen Road," 68.
17. Building upon the work of Rhacel Parrenas, Maruja M.B. Asis's report on Asian migrants makes this important observation about the costs of women's migration: "Also hidden from the picture are other costs that are shouldered by families in the countries of origin. Sociologist Rhacel Parreñas has

observed that, as 'servants of globalization,' women migrants, in turn, transfer their caregiving responsibilities to other female family members or other less-privileged women in the countries of origin." Maruja M.B. Asis, "Asian Women Migrants: Going the Distance, But Not Far Enough," Internet on-line, accessed 15 July 2005, available from http://www.migrationinformation.org/Feature/display.cfm?id=103

18. Carol Ojeda-Kimbrough, "The Chosen Road," 71.

19. *Ibid.*, 70.

20. See Madge Bello and Vince Reyes, "Filipino Americans and the Marcos Overthrow," *Amerasia Journal* 13:1 (1987): 73–84 and "The Reform Movement of Local 37: The Work of Silme Domingo and Gene Viernes," Internet On-line, accessed 1 August 2005, available from http://www.bulosan.org/html/local_37.html

21. "Spirits Rising," directed by Ramona S. Diaz, 56 min., National Asian American Telecommunications Association, 1995, videocassette.

22. Carol Ojeda-Kimbrough, "The Chosen Road," 71–72.

23. Diaz cites Carmen Guerrero Nakpil's work in making this point. Carmen Guerrero Nakpil, *Woman Enough and Other Essays* (Quezon City, Philippines: Vibal Publishers, 1963). Several other Philippine women's studies scholars have critiqued the liberatory impact of Spanish colonial rule on Filipino women by highlighting Filipino women's precolonial high status in creation myths, the family unit, and society. See Encarnacion Alzona, *The Filipino Woman: Her Social, Economic, and Political Status, 1565–1937*, rev. ed. (Manila: Benipayo Press, 1938) and Sr. Mary John Mananzan, OSB, "The Filipino Women: Before and After The Spanish Conquest of the Philippines," *Essays on Women*, rev. ed., Sr. Mary John Mananzan, OSB, ed. (Manila, Philippines: Institute of Women's Studies, St. Scholastica's College, 1991), 6–35.

24. Catherine Ceniza Choy, *Empire of Care*, 34.

25. Rhacel Parrenas, *Servants of Globalization: Women, Migration, and Domestic Work* (Stanford, CA: Stanford University Press, 2001).

26. In her 2004 presidential address to the American Studies Association, Shelley Fisher Fishkin cited several Filipino American Studies works to support her analysis on the "transnational turn" in contemporary American Studies. Shelley Fisher Fishkin, "Crossroads of Cultures: The Transnational Turn in American Studies-Presidential Address to the American Studies Association, November 12, 2004," *American Quarterly* 57:1 (2005): 17–57.

27. Luis H. Francia, "The Filipino American Artist: Imagination is Funny," *Philippine Daily Inquirer*, 30 August 2003, Internet On-line, accessed 1 August 2005, available from http://modelminority.com/modules.php?name=News&file=article&sid=516

28. Carol Ojeda-Kimbrough, "The Chosen Road," 65.

29. Akira Iriye, "Internationalizing International History," *Rethinking American History in a Global Age*, Thomas Bender, ed. (Berkeley: University of California Press, 2002), 60

30. Prosy Abarquez-Delacruz, "Holding a Pigeon in My Hand," 62.

31. Carol Ojeda-Kimbrough, "The Chosen Road," 73.

35

Migrant Melancholia

Emergent Discourses of Mexican Migrant Traffic in Transnational Space

Alicia Schmidt Camacho

It is not, then, just a question of mapping social relations (economic, socio-logical, or whatever) *on to* space. The fact that those relations *occur over* space matters. It is not just that "space is socially constructed"—a fact with which geographers have for a while been coming to terms—but that social processes are constructed over space.

—Doreen Massey, *Spatial Divisions of Labor: Social Structures and the Geography of Production*

> It was a Holiday Inn
> downtown El Paso
> where she crossed the line daily
> paso por paso
> mal paso que das
> al cruzar la frontera
>
> There was the work permit
> sealed in plastic
> like the smile
> she flashed every morning
> to the same uniformed eyes
> —Marisela Norte, "Act of the Faithless"

Reports of migrant deaths and disappearances in the transnational circuit linking the United States and Mexico should disturb the fiction of the regulated border. The fate of the undoc-umented reveals the violence with which both states have acted over time to rationalize the boundaries of their territory and citizenship.[1] In recent years, sharp increases in the numbers of undocumented migrants and the concurrent escalation of border militarization have made the journey to the United States more hazardous and the possibilities of return to Mexico more uncertain. Furthermore, as migration increasingly extends outward from the Southwest, it chal-lenges the dominant frameworks for depicting or explaining the Mexican presence in the United States. As the costs of Mexican labor migrations have become more visible, state institutions and communications media in both countries have had to address the hazards, both physical and psychological, of unauthorized entry and settlement in the United States. Disappearances of various sorts are revealed in the growing rosters of missing persons kept by the Mexican Office of Foreign Relations (Secretaría de Relaciones Exteriores) and immigrant organizations; these numbers reveal the instability of those narratives of kinship, class, and nationality that have historically functioned to delimit accounts of migration as loss or rupture for sending communities.

Given the recent developments, the melancholic aspect of the journey north has surfaced with a new urgency, putting the tale of the enterprising migrant "seeking a better life" in crisis. Stories of disappearance and lonely deaths put the flesh back on the bare-bones figure of the "guest worker" at a moment when the Mexican state confers neither a living nor rights to poor citizens and when U.S. officials and civilians alike routinely detain, abuse, and exploit migrants with little regard for international human rights conventions. The two nations collude in producing a class of stateless subjects whose personhood is discursively consigned to mere economic being as disposable labor, or legally reduced to the mere status of criminal trespassers.

In what follows, I examine the discourses that produce what I am calling "migrant melancholia" in order to consider the effects of the decade of Operation Gatekeeper, free trade, and neoliberalism for Mexican migrants and what these changes may signify for current understandings of human mobility and transnational community. Alongside established accounts of transnational labor and remittances, other narratives of loss and wounding have always coexisted in tension with the legitimating discourses of international cooperation, development, and economic opportunity that depict the sojourn in the United States as a matter of elective choice.[2] These narratives can be found across a number of media, including television documentaries on migration, *telenovelas* on Telemundo, Internet photos of missing migrants, and cultural productions by border artists. The narration of migrant sorrows constitutes a political act, cast against the prerogatives of neoliberal development and the global division of labor—in particular, the erosion of substantive citizenship and communal belonging but also the collusion with resurgent forms of racial governance in both countries.

I am especially interested in how women's border literature and testimonials provide a counternarrative to official depictions of migration as temporary economic necessity, just as they disrupt conventional narratives of male migration. In contrast to historic masculinist claims to cross-border unity between Mexico and *México de afuera*, women's testimonies reveal a distinct female imaginary operating in the border space, one that moves with ambivalence and caution through competing claims of family, class, and nation in the transnational arena. Women and children are increasingly protagonists of the border crossing, rather than simply dependents left behind by male breadwinners. Their accounts reveal how social relations structuring kinship and community are not simply reconstructed over transnational space but may also provide insufficient refuge from the perils of the cross border passage.

Lost Citizens

In the days following the destruction of the World Trade Center, members of El Asociación Tepeyac de New York, an advocacy center for Latino immigrants, found themselves inundated with calls from households across Latin America, asking for news of missing relatives believed to be working in the United States. Eventually, El Asociación Tepeyac identified 113 cases of missing people and 857 displaced workers connected to the 9/11 disaster.[3] The organization has been instrumental in documenting these cases and helping survivors obtain relief funds. Just as impressive, however, are the hundreds of petitions for assistance in locating missing family members that may have no direct relationship to the events in New York and that remain unresolved. Esperanza Chacón, Director of Urgent Affairs for Tepeyac, argues that the enforced invisibility of undocumented workers in the United States makes it impossible to clarify the status of these reports of missing persons.[4] Despite the ready availability of cellular phones and electronic communications media for sustaining communal and familial ties among migrants, it was all too clear in 2001 that migration can still threaten sending households with dissolution and loss.

The events of 9/11 foreclosed on the plans of Presidents Bush and Fox for a binational agreement that would facilitate guest worker programs and provide amnesty to thousands of undocumented Mexicans residing in the United States. For Mexico, the losses at the World Trade Center provoked renewed debate about the implications of mass migrations and economic dependency for the exercise of state sovereignty and the coherence of its national community. In 2003, public pressure forced Gerónimo Gutiérrez Fernández, then Subsecretary for North America to the Office of Foreign Relations (SRE), to admit openly that his office received an annual average of five thousand requests for assistance in locating persons presumed missing in the course of emigration to the United States.[5] Mexican officials consider the actual number to be far higher, since the SRE figure only reflects the fraction of incidents where the state becomes involved. Gutiérrez Fernández reported that his office resolves 20 percent of the cases, but he did not elaborate on the specific outcomes of these investigations. The SRE has since outlined a proposal for creating an electronic database for biogenetic data that would assist the state in tracking and identifying the missing, a proposal made urgent by the rising costs of repatriating the remains of Mexicans who die abroad.

Ghosts of Development

As the United States and Mexico pursued policies of accelerated economic integration in the late twentieth century that exacerbated the demand for Mexican labor in the United States, on the one hand, and decimated communal Mexican agriculture, on the other, the U.S.-Mexican border has lost its peripheral status within national processes for either country. The unstoppable movement of people to the border cities and across the international boundary that began before World War I has exerted considerable pressure on the structures of governance, commerce, income generation, and justice for both nations as they have responded to rising levels of undocumented migration since the 1990s (and had to cope with the new exigencies of national security linked to the U.S. war on drugs and the war on terror). Mexican policies for stimulating economic growth and development have effectively redrawn the compact between the state and its poor, its working class, and its rural citizens. The neoliberal programs that culminated in the 1994 North American Free Trade Agreement were heralded by some as "Mexico's second revolution," not so much for their promise of social advancement as for their stark contrast to the revolution of 1910.[6] While nation-building reforms of the "institutionalized" revolution promoted economic restructuring in the name of redistributive reforms, the market-led restructuring of the Mexican economy following the 1980s subordinated social reform to economic growth at enormous cost to the urban and rural poor.

Although Mexican officials and financiers may argue that the first decade of NAFTA brought Mexico new foreign investment and jobs with the unexpected dividend of the democratic transition from PRI dominance, the actual economic and political benefits accruing from neoliberal reforms have largely bypassed the poorer sectors of society. The rapid restructuring of Mexican agriculture has only exacerbated the historical process of out-migration from the countryside and small towns. In this period, changes to the Mexican state have failed to extend democratic inclusion to marginalized populations, just as they have weakened those institutions that provide the substance of citizenship: access to goods and services, justice, security, and political representation. The forms of exchange and consumption that have underwritten neoliberal development depend on the social relations institutionalized in the border region: in particular, an economic caste system that demands workers well versed in both service and low-skilled labor, whose weak social integration assures that they make relatively few demands on either state.

Increased rates of interdiction at the Mexico-U.S. border, along with unprecedented levels of undocumented migration from Mexico and farther south, have added to the perils of the border crossing and settlement in the United States in the last decade.[7] Migrants confront the travails of the desert and anti-immigrant hostilities along the frontier as a passage through a space of death, or what Luis Alberto Urrea calls "the devil's highway."[8] Migrant fatalities have risen 500 percent over the last decade due to stricter U.S. border policing and the expansion of organized crime in the border region.[9] Mexican consuls apportion ever-greater percentages of their budgets to the forensic identification and repatriation of bodies, both of migrants who perish in transit and of those who die in the United States; they also face increased demands for assistance from families searching for missing relatives, now numbering in the thousands.[10] The space of death is not confined to the border, however, but incorporates the limited spheres of agency afforded undocumented people in the United States: Migrants occupy the legal minefield between labor and human rights protections, on the one hand, and U.S. immigration policy, on the other.

As a result, established patterns of seasonal migration for work have given way to higher rates of permanent settlement following the inception of Operation Gatekeeper in 1994.[11] Greater numbers of women and children are migrating from Mexico to the United States, both to obtain work and to unify families, despite conditions of increased risk.[12] Contracting with "coyotes," once simply optional, has become vital for successful crossings; traffickers are likely responsible for many of the recent disappearances of migrants now that the movement of people has become so lucrative for criminal entities in the region.[13]

The border crossing has always threatened migrants with disappearance or death, and certainly with dislocation from kin and community. The 2001 catastrophe in New York brought the fragility of transnational ties into focus once more during the same period that migrant remittances reached their peak share of Mexican GDP.[14] Mexican settlements in New York followed patterns established by earlier labor migrations; new arrivals to Manhattan and Long Island in the 1990s were just as successful in forming mutual aid societies and exerting economic and political force in their Puebla hometowns as their conationals in Los Angeles or Houston.[15] Many perils of recent migration are in fact not *new*, but the diffusion of migrant circuits beyond the southwestern United States does reflect significant changes in traditional forms of transnational settlement, even from older sending regions. Emigration has shifted from being a rural phenomenon to encompassing industrialized towns and cities, and every Mexican state now confronts the vast scale of out-migration to the United States. These demographic shifts correspond to stalled economic and political reforms in Mexico as state failure continues to promote mass emigration. Jorge Durand and Douglas Massey comment that in Mexico, "migrant networks are much stronger in rural than in urban areas because rural social networks are stronger and more dense.[16] If so, it remains to be seen whether newer migrants can mobilize the same forms of social capital as their predecessors.

Such transformations in Mexican political economy and state policy have profound implications for how displaced Mexicans, both internal and transnational migrants, may experience and express their nationality in the migratory circuit. Mexicans living abroad form hometown associations in order to provide resources for sending communities, a process the government seeks to co-opt through a program of matching funds for migrant remittances. Federal, state, and local authorities promise to match migrant donations on a three-to-one ratio, with the hopes of diverting private remittances to state expenditures. In Chicago, for example, a group of migrants from Indaparapeo, Michoacán, have pooled resources to establish a scholarship program for the town's youth, resisting the state government's suggestion that monies be set aside for new roads and drainage.[17] Grupo Indaparapeo chose to develop the town's human capital over state-run projects as a direct rebuke to officials for their failure to meet its most basic obligations to the townspeople. While the private contributions for the scholarship are always on time, Grupo Indaparapeo reports that matching funds are always in short supply. Members of the hometown association may be exercising the forms of *postnational* agency described in current studies of migration, but they do so in a concerted effort to recover and reconstitute *national* citizenship.[18] The Michoacán migrants designed the scholarship program so that townspeople will not have to leave home to seek their livelihood. After a century of out-migration, their initiative represents a purchase against loss and estrangement in the next generation.

Mourning and Migration

U.S. immigration policies and border policing have effectively cancelled the option for circular migration, making Mexicans much more likely to pursue permanent settlement in the United States. The coercive aspect of these developments warrants further inquiry. In fact, studies overwhelmingly show that most migrants do not wish to stay: "Left to their own devices, the vast majority would return to participate in Mexico's growth as an economy and a society."[19] The prevailing metric of immigration studies, centered as it is on the economic and social productivity of the migrant, cannot measure the melancholic aspect of the shift from circular migrations to a "national population of settled dependents scattered throughout the country". A focus on the relative economic integration between migrants and sender communities, measured in remittances, may obscure the social upheaval and deformations of kinship that extended migrations impose on sender households. The unacknowledged costs of Mexican mobility find expression in the rumors of human traffic and bondage that circulate within migrant communities. The spectacular horror of these stories may correspond to actual incidents, but in their elaboration, rumors also project the phantasmagoric aspect of migrant imaginaries.[20] Lists of missing persons obtain symbolic significance as an inchoate form of contestation to the way government policies continue to displace the burden of maintaining transnational labor circuits from the state onto private individuals and households.

In his 1917 essay "Mourning and Melancholia," Sigmund Freud addressed the ways individuals contend with the death or absence of a beloved person, object, or idea. He noted that distress leads the mourner to deny the loss but that the healthy person will eventually relinquish the attachment and recover a capacity for everyday life. The melancholic person, he argued, refuses to "relinquish the lost object" and cannot therefore overcome the psychic burden of loss. For Freud, melancholia arises from a pathological or thwarted process of mourning, in which the absent object becomes constitutive of the melancholic self. Recent scholarship has applied Freudian models of mourning and melancholia to forms of subjection or abjection enacted in the political sphere.[21] Here I want to consider how the border crossing implies a psychic wounding for migrants and invests their nostalgic desires for return with political significance.

If current conditions make the option of circular migration unavailable to many migrants, then the notion of "home" may take on the qualities of the beloved object whose loss threatens the integrity of the border crosser's personhood. In the same way, the migrant's departure may constitute a catastrophic separation for the sending family and community. In a recent television documentary about a family in rural Michoacán that sent three sons to Kentucky for work, the mother of the young men describes a sense of desperation at her economic dependence on her children's remittances: "Yo sé que me va a ayudar, pero para mí cada partida es una muerte" (I know that it will help me, but for me every departure is a death).[22] Marcelo, the last son to leave, describes his trip to the United States through the Sonoran Desert as an indelible trauma:

> Yo no sabía si podía aguantar. Pasé tres días sin alimentos, tomando sólo tragitos de agua. El sol era tan caliente. Tenía tanta sed. Mi mamá estaba llorando. Eso me afectó mucho. Créo que me afectó psicológicamente.

[I was not sure if I would make it. I went three days without food, taking only small sips of water. The sun was so hot. I was so thirsty. My mother was crying. This affected me. I think it affected me psychologically.][23]

This exchange, captured in an episode of *Assignment Discovery*, offers a rare pedagogy for U.S. viewers on migrant subjectivity. Marcelo's reflection on his border passage captures exactly the process of melancholic incorporation that Freud describes: As he recalls the hardships of his desert passage, the son makes no distinction between his mother's grieving and his own. Although his mother remained behind, the son narrates his experience as if his mother traveled alongside him in the desert—as a source not of comfort or protection but of the profound guilt and distress that Freud ascribed to the melancholic person.

By extension, we may consider how undocumented status itself might constitute a melancholic condition for migrants in the United States. In 2004, I participated in a local effort to uncover a confidence scheme to defraud undocumented migrants of thousands of dollars through the sale of false papers. That summer, a friend who migrated to New Haven from Veracruz, Rita (a pseudonym), told me that a woman she worked for had offered to assist her in obtaining legal status for herself and her family. While cleaning the home, Rita had observed her employer operating a business in immigration documents out of her home. This woman, a Latina resident of Hamden, Connecticut, said she was a New York immigration official, offering to process paperwork "under the table" and expedite clients' legalization. Dozens of Latin Americans came from New York, Connecticut, and New Jersey to pay fees of as much as $25,000 for the "green cards" that they thought would permit them to work legally, sponsor family members, and move freely between the United States and their home countries.[24]

Rita paid her employer approximately $2,500 to process paperwork for her husband, herself, and her four-year-old son, who had all entered the United States without authorization a few years earlier. She grew alarmed when I communicated my doubts about the veracity of the woman's promises and my concerns that Rita and her family could get into trouble because of the scam. At the time, Rita was a client of Junta for Progressive Action, an advocacy center that serves the predominantly Latino neighborhood of Fair Haven. Having seen the numbers of migrants falling for her employer's false promises, Rita made the courageous decision to report the criminal operation to the police. Junta's director, the attorney Kica Matos, and I mediated between the migrants and the police so as to secure promises that the police would not pursue the immigration cases of the people caught up in the scam. In January 2006, the alleged perpetrator of the crime, María Agosto, a fifty-five-year-old resident of New York, was arraigned in the Superior Court of Connecticut on charges of first-degree larceny and criminal impersonation. Rita was the chief witness in the proceeding.

As I translated for Rita and other victims during their exchanges with Hamden police, I came to understand how easy it was for the imposter to persuade her clients that she could help them circumvent the most elaborate and impenetrable apparatus of U.S. law enforcement, that of immigration. The people she stole from were hardly naive—they had experienced theft at the hands of coyotes, employers, immigration lawyers, and other migrants—but they were unwilling to relinquish the fantasy of reunion with the lost objects that haunted their residence in the United States—family and citizenship. As a Puerto Rican migrant herself, Agosto must have had intimate knowledge of her clients' melancholic disposition and just how far it would lead her clients into her trap. Even after she was exposed, having abandoned her Hamden residence without delivering the papers, many of her clients remained unwilling to accept the reality of their situation. Rita continued to confide to me after her testimony that she was certain that the police proceeding was a mistake and that perhaps Señora Agosto would return with her documents if she withheld her charges.

Proponents of anti-immigration measures commonly represent the undocumented as people with no respect for the rule of law. This assumption reflects a total misunderstanding of what "law" means for the unauthorized migrant. One could say that the undocumented come from countries where bribes are routinely paid to expedite state services; however, this explanation is, in my opinion, an inadequate answer to the question of how so many migrants came to pay unimaginable sums for the dream of legalization. It is precisely because of their investment in legality, both in practical and moral terms, that the victims of the Hamden scam could invest so heavily in false papers. The migrants did not deliberately seek to circumvent state authority when they paid the imposter to act on their behalf; rather, they sought incorporation into the state through the only means available. Beyond their desire for the goods of citizenship, freedom of movement, better wages, working conditions, and health care, the migrants were gullible because of their profound desire to be recognized as legitimate subjects, to inhabit the status of citizen. Even in simple economic terms, the theft of migrant earnings represents a terrible crime: Consider for a moment how many people were willing to work an inordinate number of hours under difficult conditions to amass $25,000 in the vain hope of bringing children north from Ecuador or Guatemala and making them into U.S. nationals.

The horror of the Hamden incident, then, comes from the reminder that it is so easy to exploit migrant desire. For many, the costs of entering the United States for work preclude the seasonal visits to Mexico that might placate the sense of loss and isolation. In New Haven, far from the ethnic centers of the Southwest, nationality is easily reduced to a consular card and the vague promises of protection it confers. For Mexicans here, U.S. citizenship or legal residence represents the single best option for securing a livelihood and retaining viable connections to family and hometown over time. And yet, the vast majority of the undocumented are unlikely to obtain such a prize.

The material and psychic hungers that propel migrants to abandon, in their quest for wages, the most basic elements of sociality—residence, kinship, language, culture, and landscape: in short, *home*—exert a violence that immigration scholarship and political discourse have yet to fully address. The condition of being "undocumented" does not simply imply a lack of legal protection or status but rather entails the active conversion of the migrant into a distinct category of stateless personhood. This peculiar status emerges with the contradiction between market demands for mobile labor and consumable goods and the immobility of rights beyond the bounds of the nation-state. Mexican migrants, like other displaced peoples, continually invent forms of agency within that space of opposition. It is a melancholy task. Stories of border mortality and disappearance are a means to narrate the other kinds of death that Marcelo's mother describes, the leave-taking that extinguishes one form of connection to make way for another. In this ritual of departure, the family enacts, in intimate form, the migrant's detachment from the state, a severing of citizenship that is also a death, a death that produces.

Disappearing Migrants

Current anxieties about border hazards also appear in popular media, in texts that narrate significant shifts in how migration is managed both at the level of lived experience and at the level of consumer culture. In December 2003, Telemundo aired the Mexican *telenovela El Alma Herida* (*The Wounded Soul*), a serial melodrama devoted to a migrant family shattered at the border crossing.[25] The show earned strong ratings and became known as "una de las novelas más queridas por el público hispano.[26] The storyline followed familiar motifs for reinforcing national identity by depicting the dangers of pursuing material aspirations in the United States:

> Una familia llena de esperanzas toma la difícil decision de cruzar la frontera en busca del sueño Americano, dejándolo todo atrás sin sospechar que el destino les jugará una mala pasada separándolos trágicamente.

[Full of hope, a family makes the difficult decision to cross the border in search of the American Dream. They leave everything behind, not knowing that destiny is about to play them a bad hand, separating them tragically from one another.][27]

The family does not make it across the border intact: The father and two children meet up with abusive police, while the *pollero* forces Catalina, the mother, across to the United States. The sixty-five episodes follow the daughter and mother's efforts at family reunification, allegorizing the broader process of Mexican migration since 1965. The border imposes total familial separation and threatens its annihilation: The plot turns on the family's question of whether the mother has died or abandoned them. The story ultimately ends in a bloodbath, with the daughter electing between two male partners in two countries, a choice which implies that her honor can be safeguarded only in Mexico. However contrived, *El Alma Herida* nevertheless departs from standard nationalist discourse by anchoring its story in a female, rather than a male, migrant. The status of the family depends on the recovery of the missing mother, not its wage-earning father, while her recuperation comes through the agency of the enterprising daughter Eugenia, who first crosses the border at age eleven. *El Alma Herida* thus fulfills the function of melodrama to nourish a female spectatorship; it does so through a migrant imaginary now thoroughly feminized.

For Mexicans living a precarious permanence in the United States, the border operates as a critical juncture for imagining community and exerting claims on either nation. In this context, the crossing *itself*—in its various legal, economic, cultural, and social aspects—shapes the political disposition of the larger transnational community of unauthorized migrants and noncitizens in the United States and their hometowns in Mexico. Here I refer not only to the political apparatus of the border, as it regulates the mobility of peoples or their access to rights and citizenship, but also to the broader binational space that contains the institutions devoted to national security, immigration, and trade at the boundary checkpoints. The trans-border corridor is not only the largest urbanized region in Mexico; it is also one of the fastest-growing settlement sites in the Western Hemisphere.[28] The complex communal ecologies of this space do not simply give the border an internal sense of distinction and shared identity; they also influence the form broader transnational linkages and communities may take. So, too, border cities socialize migrants in their passage from citizenship to noncitizenship, authorized status to unauthorized status. As greater numbers of people find themselves stranded in the border space because of failed crossings or deportation, or the availability of jobs in service work and export manufacturing created by neoliberal development, the normative force of this movement to the transnational corridor increases.[29]

This passage may exact different political costs for the federal government from those facing sender communities: Despite new legislation permitting migrants to cast absentee ballots in the upcoming presidential elections, the expatriate vote is likely to disappoint.[30] The stagnation of democratic reform in Mexico means that migrants may opt to retain home-town connections while resisting their interpellation as national subjects. According to Rodolfo Rubio, a researcher at El Colegio de la Frontera Norte, fewer than 10 percent are likely to register out of an estimated 4 million eligible voters, making it less possible for the migrant vote to sway the presidential election.[31] The cost of absentee voter registration effectively functions as a poll tax, repeating a long-standing process whereby the state discourages poor voters. Daniel Solis, director of the Alliance for Community Development in El Paso, argues that eligible voters, even those residing in the border, are "losing hope of better prospects at home and putting stock in their future as new immigrants."[32] The intense nationalism of migrants, in this context, may not extend to a sense of political obligation to the nation-state.

The new hazards and congestion of the border crossing may thus ultimately alter the social networks observed in studies of migrant communities.[33] The proliferating reports of migrant disappearances reflect the uncertainties of this period for sending communities in Mexico. It is impossible to examine the ephemeral Web sites devoted to the missing without considering the weight of the disappearances on the fragile linkages of kin and conationals in transnational space. Family photographs, passport pictures, and identification cards posted to sites operated by the Mexican consulate adopt both the form of official immigration documents and more personal narrative to describe the disappeared. "Odilon Vera Méndez, 32," listed by height, weight, hair and eye color, complexion, and facial features, appears online in a photograph depicting the young man at a track meet (Figure 35.1). The race tag on his chest, "L959," stands in for the official imprint of the state identification number, the mug shot, passport, or perhaps the Bracero registration number of past migrations. The photo caption reads: "Lugar de Origen: Huauchinango, Puebla. Últimos datos conocidos: Salió de Tetela de Ocampo, Puebla el pasado 13 de noviembre de 2001, con destino a Estados Unidos para trabajar, pero hasta la fecha su familia no tiene noticias de él."[34] Between the precision of Tetela de Ocampo, Puebla (population 25,859, 304.89 square kilometers in area, and 3,000 meters above sea level), and the uncharted route to work in the United States, the vast terrain of transnational space presents its threat to identity, to kinship, to territoriality itself.

The interrupted biographies of the disappeared represent a rupture in time and space for sending families and towns. For the bereft, not knowing whether the missing are alive or dead disrupts the narrative of transnational community, both in its symbolic unity and in the material sense of economic survival and the futurity of family lines. One image in particular, from the Consul General Web site, invites analysis: Azucena Quezada Olea, of Morelos, last seen in 2002 (Figure 35.2).[35] The young woman in the photograph stands in a parking lot that could be anywhere in the north/south circuit of migrant travels. Her shirt bears the tourist logo for Kentucky, perhaps a sign of her connection to this new outpost of Mexican labor, or perhaps a souvenir of her tourist travel. The nondescript background is nonetheless an occasion for a portrait, for memorialization of the moment, of her being there. Azucena Quezada Olea smiles

Figure 35.1. Odilon Vera Méndez, missing since November 13, 2001. Protección a Mexicanos, Consul General de México, online resource for missing persons.

Figure 35.2. Azucena Quezada Olea, missing since 2002. Protección a Mexicanos, Consul General de México, online resource for missing persons.

as she gazes out at the camera, one hand shyly at her face, another hand holding a young child. She occupies the whole of the image: The child next to her is only partly in the picture. The child looks so much like Azucena that the image can only imply their relatedness, yet the border of the photograph splits the child in half. What Roland Barthes would call the *punctum* of the image lies in this bisection of the child's figure.[36]

The photograph of the missing woman captures what seems ineffable in narratives of border crossing: the sense that the migrant occupies a place and no place at once. Disappearance does not only imply the loss of the woman herself, but the destruction her death or departure means for the child. Familial dislocation, occurring across national boundaries, puts children's identities and protection in crisis. Children lose their minimal political status once separated from their parents in the migrant circuit. In a larger sense, the photograph illuminates the profoundly unsettling ways in which transnational migration remakes kinship and reveals how kinship cannot mitigate against loss. In this instance, the vanishing of Azucena makes a ghost of her child.

The formal institutions that enshrine Mexican citizenship seem equally strained by the uncertainties of the border passage: the Office of Foreign Relations (SRE), which oversees Mexican consulates, vacillates between a discourse that interpellates migrants as full nationals and something approaching an official language of mourning. "Tu calidad de indocumentado no te convierte en delincuente," reads a Web site for the Consul General of New York, which goes on to explain the human rights protections that cover migrants in the United States.[37] Within this assertion is a latent recognition of the threat of loss—of personal sovereignty for the migrant, of national sovereignty for the Mexican state—inherent in the unauthorized border crossing. The transit from citizenship to unauthorized status in the United States is, in fact, a process of conversion, effected *through* violence—the sanctioned interdiction of the state, which may seize and remove migrants by its use of force or by the extralegal, informal aggressions of nonstate actors like the Arizona Minutemen.

The Instituto Nacional de Migración (INM/National Institute of Migration) generated controversy in recent years by issuing pamphlets to potential migrants that delineate the hazards of the border crossing. The guides contain emergency telephone numbers, the details of consular services and immigration documents, and information about migrants' protections under international law. With their graphic depictions of migrant deaths, the books become an inventory of *passing* as well as passage in pages devoted to the many ways the border can kill. In a section devoted to the Sonoran Desert, the *Guía del Migrante Yucateco* lists the symptoms of dehydration, only to conclude: "Si tienes estos síntomas, estás en peligro de morir lentamente."[38] The irony is, of course, that the Mexican government cannot do more than forecast this death. Mexican sovereignty does not extend to providing gainful employment to nationals at home, nor does it provide safe passage for those leaving the country.

This point came home to me in an interview with officers from the Grupos Beta de Protección a Migrantes (Beta Group for the Protection of Migrants), the Mexican border patrol in Ciudad Juárez, in 2003. C. Roberto Gaytan Saucedo, the interim director for the INM in Juárez, reported that the scale of migration makes the task of policing the desert region impossible. Officially a humanitarian operation of the INM, Grupos Beta claimed just seven officers for the vast Juárez metropolitan region in 2003. Like generations of border officers before him, Gaytan Saucedo admitted that every seizure of a migrant merely delays the eventual crossing.[39] Grupos Beta has resorted to posting signs in the desert about the perils of migration, advising women to purchase pepper spray as a defense against male aggressors. The empty gesture makes it clear that women alone are responsible for their personal safety. The state functions of security do not extend into this denationalized border zone, nor do they cover the bodies of women moving through this space. Mexican sovereignty and state power are so compromised in the border region that the Grupos Beta does not dare to venture into the path of armed criminal groups operating in the desert; the absurdity of pepper spray here makes a cruel joke of the state's disinterest in women's suffering. In March 2005, Claudia Smith, president of the Coalition in Defense of the Migrant, presented the statistic that one in ten women report being raped in the attempt to cross the border.[40]

In this context, the INM warning "Hay caminos sin regreso" doubles as an admonition and an admission of state complicity in migrant suffering.[41] Neoliberal governance has only exacerbated the government's role as a broker for cheap labor. The failure of market-led development has forced individual states to compete with one another for migrant remittances. Various states now issue their own localized migrant guidebooks, which combine the national discourse on the border crossing with promotions of regional identity and loyalty. The *Guía del Migrante Yucateco* offers information on Yucatecan clubs and mutual aid societies in California, stressing the interest of the state government in helping migrants organize abroad. "Yendo o viniendo Yucateco sigue siendo," it reads, displaying an official regard for how local Mayan ethnicity offers a vital resource for group survival in the United States.[42] Of course, those Yucatecos who perish or vanish do not remain Yucateco. On average, five migrants from southern Mexican states die every month trying to reach the northern border, and many more disappear. The state's invocation of human rights or cultural unity as a supplement to citizenship collapses under the pressure to obtain migrant remittances at any cost. The final assertion, "Cuida tu vida," underlines how life, in this instance, gets reduced to a vehicle for income generation.[43] In their ambivalent discourse of nationalism and mourning, migrant guides articulate contradictions in Mexican development: The links between nation building and migration mark the state's intimacy with death.

Women's Border Imaginaries

On May 10, 1948, "Concepción Zapata" presented her retablo to the Santísima Virgen de San Juan de los Lagos as a testament to the saint's protection during her sojourn in the United States.[44] The retablo, or votive painting, is a popular form of devotion that renders compensation for the miraculous intercession of the patron saint. The votive practice records a private act of supplication and gives witness to the person's deliverance from illness or danger. For Mexican migrants, the retablo combines a holy image with a visual rendition of perils faced in the border crossing, forming a closed narrative of departure and return once the painting is deposited in its shrine. As the patroness of Los Altos de Jalisco, La Virgen de San Juan de los Lagos has heard many stories of emigration and has made many border crossings of her own.[45] Alongside accounts of averted deaths and wondrous cures, this guardian of migrants knows the particular gender terror of the passage northward.

In her account of divine protection, Concepción Zapata relates:

Dedico el presente RETABLO a la Sma. V. de San Juan de los Lagos por aberme salbado de un TEXANO que me liebara, me escodi [sic] debajo de un arbol con mi hermanito ala orilla de la carretera.

[I dedicate the present retablo to the Holiest Virgin of San Juan de los Lagos for having saved me from a Texan who tried to carry me off. I hid under a tree by the side of the road with my little brother.][46]

Unlike conventional votive paintings, this retablo does not depict the traumatic encounter itself, but Concepción's act of devotion after the fact. The image places the kneeling figure of Concepción just beyond a drawn curtain, as if the viewer is looking in on a confessional. Staged this way, this public disclosure of the young woman's experience reinscribes the private, unspeakable nature of sexual aggression. The anonymous artist painted the nationality of the aggressor in capital letters, "TEXANO," as if to locate the threat of gender violence *en el otro lado*, on the other side. The story describes the peril of a young woman traveling alone, her younger brother too small to act as her guardian or chaperone. Concepción's narrative leaves open the question of what might have happened. She describes the male threat in the verb *llevar* (carry off) ("un TEXANO me llebara"), a taking that is both rape and capture. The verb shows how the sexual violation is discursively linked to disappearance, a taking from which there is no return. The story ascribes the agency behind the young woman's evasion of harm to the saint rather than to her own resourcefulness. Concepción's escape under the tree anticipates her enclosure back at home. The narrative figures the border as the open road, "la carretera," in opposition to the protective closeness of the interior space rendered in the painting.

In its reticence toward depicting Concepción as a fully autonomous agent in her border crossing, the retablo presciently anticipates current concerns about Mexican women's mobility through transnational space. Women's perceived sexual availability and vulnerability incite social anxieties about the nation's exposure at the northern frontier. The question of women's autonomy of movement takes on greater urgency at the international boundary, where disappearance can also be a matter of a change in political status altogether. The story of Concepción Zapata's miraculous deliverance speaks to us from midcentury San Luis Potosí as a testament to the ways sex has historically been constructed as a woman's price for a successful border crossing.[47]

Zapata traveled north to Texas at the height of the Bracero Program, a period of mass emigration in which women's mobility remained invisible in public discourse, rendering women migrants doubly undocumented. Some fifty years later, we might inquire into the strategies of rendering visible these journeys—artistic strategies for elucidating the complex relationships linking women's bodies, processes of deterritorialization, and the fabric of social bonds.

I'm just Passing Through Here

By way of conclusion, I want to draw out the possibilities for locating alternate imaginaries of the border space in recent literary productions by women emerging from the transnational migrant circuit. For this, I turn to Los Angeles author Marisela Norte, whose spoken-word composition "Act of the Faithless" narrates the relationship between a young Chicana girl and her uncle's girlfriend, a Juárez woman who crosses the border for daily work in a luxury hotel in El Paso.[48]

> The story would have to begin with her.
> She worked as a maid
> in the El Paso Holiday Inn.
> El Paso
> Mal paso que te das
> al cruzar la frontera
> I mean
> I'm just passing through here.

Chicana poet and performer Marisela Norte is an "Eastside Girl," a voice for urban Los Angeles. Born in 1955 to Mexican parents who immigrated to Southern California in the 1930s and 1940s, Norte grew up in a community with strong kinship and cultural ties to Ciudad Juárez.[49] "Act of the Faithless" first appeared in recorded form in 1991, on the poet's album *Norte/Word*. Rather than publish her compositions in book form, Norte chose to circulate her work in a format that would make it available to a broader audience and would also retain the texture of her voice. Norte's work exploits shifts in narrative time and perspective in order to convey the multiplicity of female subjectivity in the border space; her poem appropriates a working-class, migrant vernacular to delineate the complex alteration of female agency and perspective taking place in the border crossing.

In Norte's poem, the urban environs of Ciudad Juárez and El Paso appear as sites of economic and personal transactions that convert Mexican women into commodified beings. Norte's story of a young Chicana girl's relationship to her uncle's girlfriend, whom she calls her "aunt," embeds the relationship in a longer narrative on family, danger, and desire at the U.S.-Mexican border. But Norte tells us that if she were to tell her story straight, it would begin with the aunt cleaning rooms in the luxury hotel, "twenty stories high" above the squalor of the urban frontier. Their crossing into El Paso, narrated as a momentary departure from the confines of class, is described as "a bad step" or a "wrong move." For the protagonist, the border crossing doubles as a change in cultural identity and a passage from girlhood to maturity. The story links the formation of the girl's critical consciousness to her separation from the maternal figure of her aunt.

Border crossing is doubly hazardous, both because *mexicanas* are pressed into the service of a foreign and punishing racial system in the United States and also, for the young narrator, because it signifies loss:

> El paso con la frontera
> Por vida
> con safos
> mas vale
> as it is written
> up and down that border
> that runs up and down our backs
> like a bad tattoo

The severing of national ties symbolized in the border forces an understanding of migrant identity as a violation, "the bad tattoo" marking emigrants to the United States in difference.

The racial inscription of the migrant's body is analogous to the division of social space by the national boundary. "Por vida / con safos," the tags of graffiti that adorn the crossing, are ironic articulations of presence and ownership written into the interstices of nation and property that exclude migrant subjects. "The acceptance of difference," writes Ramón Saldívar, "does not diminish the pain of separation that difference implies," a loss that resides at the heart of identity.[50] Norte's poem turns on jagged inflections of loss within the gestures of intimacy between family and workers, on the particular forms of nonidentity produced in the border crossing.

"She was an aunt / I would know too briefly," Norte warns us from the beginning. Norte's poem enacts the dialectic of identification and disidentification that Saldívar prescribes, as she continually delivers an affirmative statement, "she cleaned up / decorated their home" only to more effectively communicate its negation, "with objects of rejection." As Norte's narrator visits the Holiday Inn with her aunt, her trip features an ascent "in the hotel elevator / from the basement / to the honeymoon suite," a crossing of class boundaries that far exceeds the physical distance of her journey from home. The young girl quickly perceives that this visit has significance beyond her entertainment, as her aunt shows her the workings of leisure and bourgeois values:

> A slow curtain is pulled
> by the delicate hand
> holding the heavy gold cord.
> Slowly and deliberately
> she will expose, letting out a little sigh.
> She cannot believe it herself.
> This is what it could all look like,
> this view from twenty stories high.

Like a magician, the aunt ceremoniously presents her niece with a glimpse of a world of privilege wholly distinct from life as it is lived on the ground floor. The view signifies not only the romantic temporal disengagement from worldly cares promised by the tourist industry, however; here it is described in spatial terms as the deliberate construction of an insular social landscape. As the "delicate hand" that services this fantasy, the maid experiences the crossing of class boundaries as a kind of cognitive dissonance—even as she reveals it to her niece, "she cannot believe it herself."

The view alternately figures a space of possibility beyond the social restrictions of the border and reinscribes the aunt and niece's outsider status within this cosmopolitan realm. The statement "This is what it could all look like" reminds us that the landscape can only reflect the gazers' own social position. Looking out, the narrator situates herself in relation to the luxury that encloses her by reading the storefronts:

> There was a dance hall
> called El Peor es Nada,
> Better than Nothing,
> and then there was
> that narrow stretch of nothing,
> the remains of a dried-out sewer.
> She told me it was El Río,
> El Grande grande.
> Surely these were the things
> bad dreams were made of.

The place-names signify the absolute negation of the social mobility manifested in the gilded ornaments of the luxury suite. Even the river, made heroic in border legend, betrays its name by serving as the washed-out basin for pollution and waste generated in the tourist trade and the maquiladora industry. The repetition of "nothing" inscribes the landscape with a fatalism sharply divergent from Chicana feminist constructions of the border as a crossroads.[51] This nothingness exerts a material force on its subjects, expressed as the substance of nightmares. Norte's border insistently spatializes the racial and gender formations that make up the neocolonial tourist economy.

At first, the narrator wishes to experience her ascent to the luxury suite as an escape, to close her eyes:

> I only wanted to lay down
> and shut my eyes
> to the annoying Texas sun
> in the sky
> and make these feet
> leave the ground
> for one moment
> and imagine the afterlife,
> eternity at twenty stories high

Abandonment of her place under the "annoying Texas sun" connotes not only relief but also a kind of death. The ability to evacuate her subject position for that of the tourist is figured as immobility and stasis, not mobility or freedom of choice. The girl's lesson continues in a trip to the rooftop swimming pool. "If there's no one up there," the maid tells her, "you can take your shoes off / and put your feet in the water." This episode speaks to the innumerable hidden acts by which migrant women contest the dehumanizing control of their labor in forms of resistance that feminize class struggle. The act of putting her feet in the pool alleviates tiredness from long hours spent standing; it also signifies a transgression of the boundaries between the domestic worker and the customer. For the niece, getting her feet wet is an experience of what it means to be a tourist.

The inscription of race within a class hierarchy serves as the occasion for a struggle over the meanings of the girl's transnational identity:

> You are not from here,
> nor are you from over there,
> you understand m'hija?
> Entiendes?

The aunt understands her niece's identity as a condition of homelessness, of estrangement from both Mexican and U.S. national unities. She ascribes a particular cognitive advantage to the girl's ambivalent national status, but also an utter lack of a coherent identity. The narrator counters with a recitation that reclaims the border as the "sitio y lengua" which both authorize and give form to her utterance.[52]

> Los dos idiomas?
> Claro que sí.
> Que no soy de aquí
> Que no soy de allá

> But I can speak
> the language, I insisted,
> both of them.
> Entiendes?

One important detail of this exchange is the way the aunt distinguishes between her own border identity and her niece's. The niece belongs to both worlds on either side of the border; "she speaks both languages," though her aunt does not. The maid merely travels to render her services at the hotel. The whole of the girl's adventure in the pool is staged as a foreshadowing of her future travels beyond the confines of her border existence. This transient destiny is shaded with both pleasure and danger: "mal paso que das / al cruzar la frontera," she warns, "I mean, I'm just passing through here."

Norte's narrator takes pleasure in transgressing the boundaries of privilege. But as she imagines her immersion in the luxury pool, she is pulled back to the present by the sight of her aunt performing her duties as a maid, wiping down the patio furniture: "I watched her body move inside the uniform / . . . / the sound of her nylon stockings." Immediately she senses her separation from her aunt's status as a worker and wishes to repudiate her fantasy. Her aunt, observing the girl in her dark glasses, laughs at her pantomime of the role of U.S. tourist: "Ahora sí pareces turista americana." Her niece, threatened with the gulf of difference opening between them, hands the sunglasses back:

> She began to laugh, but I shook my head.
> I don't belong here and neither do you.
> I'm just passing through here, remember?
> I'm not from here and neither are you.

The niece recognizes that her play creates a separation between her aunt as a worker and her own mobility of identifications. She refuses to identify as a tourist, seeking instead to make her aunt share in her own position of "passing through." But the aunt knows better.

Rather than assume that kinship unites the girl and her aunt within a shared class position, Norte allows us to see precisely how the labor of the maid figures in the production of her niece's cognitive desire as a writer. In a moment of great poignancy, the maid reveals how the lesson she gives her niece plays a part of her own gendered class struggle:

> She gave me a pair of sunglasses to wear
> "Toma, cuidate los ojos
> take care of your eyes.
> There's so much you should see."

The sunglasses signify both the trappings of class privilege and a shield against the potential harm of exposure that the girl faces in her formation as a writer. The aunt prepares her niece to bear witness and also, in a moment of great generosity, to protect herself. Here the poem contrasts the relative social mobility of the Chicana niece and the Mexican maid.

The poem articulates the divides of class and citizenship instantiated in the border, revealing how the girl's transient status at the border ("passing through") is simultaneously a matter of wounding and of agency. In the final scene of the poem, the narrator relates the conclusion to her poolside fantasy. As the maid pushes her cart toward the door back to the elevator, the voice of a U.S. tourist calls her back:

> Excuse me. Señorita, can you come here, por favor?
> . . . .

> He waves an empty glass at her.
> The wife looks up at him smiling
> The "He's all mine" smile.

The drama of the formation of the girl's critical consciousness thus takes place within an ongoing conflict over the terms of sale for migrant women's labor. Opposed to the maid and her niece are a white tourist and his wife, who play out their heterosexual travel adventure against the neocolonial backdrop of the luxury hotel.

This final scene instructs us in the way the struggle over signification shares space with the class struggle over production:

> I tug at her arm.
> I point at the man now silent.
> "There is too much to see," she said.
> "Too much to remember."

By leaving open the problematic of seeing and narrating, Norte "problematizes women's discursive practices" in the border space: "There is too much to see / too much to remember.[53] The girl's formation as a border subject separates the cognitive agency of "knowing" and "seeing" from the security of kinship and rootedness. Her "passing through" is a process both of personal transformation and of leave-taking, dislocating her from the resourceful aunt she "would know all too briefly."

"Act of the Faithless" narrates the border traffic in Mexican women in terms that banish any fantasy of the border's dissolution or permeability. Through her protagonist's fond recollection of the aunt she has lost, Norte gives voice to the "longing for unity and cohesion" that critic Rolando Romero ascribes to Chicana/Chicano narrative, even as her story of fractured kinship refutes any notion of an organic class or kinship unity among Mexicans, migrants, and Mexican Americans across the boundary.[54] In this piece, Norte details the intimate and often conflicted relationships among women in this clandestine labor economy, relationships complicated by the constant presence of sexual danger, transgressive erotic relations, and personal violence accompanying the binational sale of women's labor.

Norte's work exists alongside the consular lists of the disappeared that preserve accounts of the missing as parents, children, partners, friends—they are a form of desperate contestation to the binational state apparatus that converts the undocumented into people without status, without a place. Yet the disappeared are nonetheless *present*; their stories of loss remake the narratives of kinship, community, and belonging that sustain the transnational circuit.

In closing, I want to consider the significance of other vanishings. Ciudad Juárez is not only the place of arrival and departure for thousands in the migrant circuit; throughout this period of increased migration, the city has been a final terminus of utter brutality for the victims of *feminicidio*.[55] The northern boomtown, whose principal function is to support the mobility of capital, goods, and labor, has been the site of unprecedented killings of girls and women, residents of the Juárez colonias.[56] Many more young women are missing. For more than a decade, state and federal officials have permitted the murders to continue with impunity. The nation that sends thousands of its people into the migrant labor circuit has little to offer as protection for the female citizens whose vitality and labors sustain the fragile social ecology of the border space. Images of the missing girls travel the same networks as the pictures advertising the names of disappeared migrants. Currently, El Paso and Ciudad Juárez are the sites of ardent campaigns against both the *feminicidio* and the death of migrants in the border crossing. The success of these local mobilizations will depend on effective witness to migrants' stories of bereavement and absence. There is much to admire in the melancholic will to deny loss, to refuse to surrender the lost object, to refuse to go quietly. The political forms we devise in this moment of global transformation must partner the melancholic work against the violence that bring the circuits of human mobility into traffic with death, an immovable death, a departure with no return.

Notes

The author thanks Jane Juffer, along with *SAQ* managing editor Christi Stanforth for their contributions to this article. Special acknowledgments are also offered to the staff at Junta, to "Rita," and to Elizabeth Alexander, Jorge Durand, Jonathan Fox, Kellie Jones, Alondra Nelson, Stephen Pitti, Arthur Schmidt, and María Aurora Camacho de Schmidt.

1. I use the term *undocumented* to refer to migrants who either enter the United States without proper documents or overstay their visas. Jeffrey S. Passel offers a useful discussion of the term. See Jeffrey S. Passel, "Estimates of the Size and Characteristics of the Undocumented Population" (Washington: Pew Hispanic Center Project Report, March 21, 2005), www.pewhispanic.org (accessed November 18, 2005).
2. See, for instance, the works of Jorge Durand and Patricia Arias, *Experiencia migrante: iconografía de la migración México-Estados Unidos* (Mexico DF: Altexto, 2000), and María Herrera Sobek, *Northward Bound: The Mexican Immigrant Experience in Ballad and Song* (Bloomington: University of Indiana Press, 1993).
3. Asociación Tepeyac, "Missing But Not Counted," November 2002, compiled in 9/11 digital archive, 911digitalarchive.org/collections/asntepeyac (accessed November 15 2002).
4. Ibid.
5. See press communications of the Secretaría de Relaciones Exteriores –México, sre.gob.mx (accessed January 5, 2006).
6. See Manuel Pastor and Carol Wise, "State Policy, Distribution, and Neoliberal Reform in Mexico," *Journal of Latin American Studies* 29 (1997): 419–56.
7. Passel, "Estimates of the Size and Characteristics of the Undocumented Population."
8. Luis Alberto Urrea, *The Devil's Highway; A True Story* (New York: Little, Brown, 2004).
9. This figure comes from Amnesty International, "United States of America: Human Rights Concerns in the Border Region with Mexico," May 20, 1998. Further details are available in statistics compiled by the Mexican Foreign Relations Office for the past decade. The figure is corroborated by various nongovernmental agencies, including the California Rural Legal Assistance Foundation of El Centro, California (www.crla.org). At the time of this writing, the U.S. Border Patrol has acknowledged the December 30, 2005, shooting of Guillermo Martínez Rodríguez, an eighteen-year-old Mexican national, who met his death just north of the San Ysidro crossing point in San Diego County. President Vicente Fox is under political pressure in Mexico for his weak response to the incident. The killing occurred just days after the U.S. House of Representatives had approved the installation of 700 miles of new walls along the border as part of the punitive immigration reform bill H.R. 4437, which would make undocumented entry into the United States a felony.
10. Miguel Escobar Valdez, consul for Mexico at Douglas, Arizona, interview by the author, Tempe, Arizona, April 9, 2004. For an illustration of consular functions related to the disappearance of Mexican migrants, see the Web site for the Mexican Consulate of New York, www.consulmexny.org/esp/proteccion_tabla_desaparecidos.htm (accessed November 20, 2005).
11. Durand and Massey, *Crossing the Border.*
12. Jeffrey S. Passel, "Unauthorized Migrants: Numbers and Characteristics" (Washington: Pew Hispanic Center Project Report, June 14, 2005), www.pewhispanic.org (accessed November 2, 2005).
13. For data on the migrants' use of coyotes or *polleros*, see Jorge Durand and Douglas S. Massey, "What We Learned from the Mexican Migration Project," in Durand and Massey, *Crossing the Border*, 1–14. On human traffic, see Peter Andreas, "The Transformation of Migrant Smuggling across the U.S.-Mexican Border," in *Global Human Smuggling: Comparative Perspectives*, ed. David Kyle and Rey Koslowski (Baltimore: Johns Hopkins University Press, 2001), 107–28. See also John Bailey and Jorge Chabat, eds., *Transnational Crime and Public Security: Challenges to Mexico and the United States* (La Jolla: Center for U.S.-Mexican Studies, University of California at San Diego, 2002).
14. See Roberto Suro, "Remittance Senders and Receivers: Tracking the Transnational Channels," Pew Hispanic Center Report written in partnership with the Multilateral Investment Fund (Washington: Pew Hispanic Center, November 24, 2003), available at www.pewhispanic.org/page.jsp?page=reports (accessed November 15, 2005).

15. Robert C. Smith, "Los ausentes siempre presentes': The Imagining, Making, and Politics of a Transnational Community between Ticuani, Puebla, and New York City" (Ph.D. diss., Columbia University, 1994).

16. Durand and Massey, "What We Learned," 10.

17. Carrie Kahn and Lourdes García Navarro for National Public Radio, "Immigrants Run Scholarship Program for Mexicans." aired January 6, 2006, on *Morning Edition*. See npr.org.

18. The term *postnational* describes the exercise of political agency outside the migrant's country of origin. The term also references a range of loyalties, social networks, or political claims that extend beyond the boundaries of national citizenship. See Linda Basch, Nina Glick Schiller, and Cristina Szanton Blanc, *Nations Unbound: Transnational Projects, Postcolonial Predicaments, and Deterritorialized Nation-States* (Langhorne: Gordon and Breach, 1994); Linda Bosniak, "The State of Citizenship: Citizenship Denationalized," *Indiana Journal of Legal Studies* 7.2 (2000):447–510; Saskia Sassen, "The Repositioning of Citizenship: Emergent Subjects and Spaces for Politics," *CR: The New Centennial Review* 3.2 (Summer 2003): 41–66; and Yasemin Nuhoólu Soysal, *Limits of Citizenship: Migrants and Postnational Membership in Europe* (Chicago: University of Chicago Press, 1994).

19. Durand and Massey, "What We Learned," 13.

20. Accounts of human traffic, organ trafficking, and slavery are not only limited to the border cities, where narcotrafficking and the *feminicidio* in Ciudad Juárez have raised the specter of other forms of predatory violence. Spanish-language media catering to new immigrants commonly carries stories of superexploitation and crimes against migrants. Both Univisión and Telemundo maintain Web sites devoted to immigration. In addition, Telemundo carries the syndicated program *Sin Fronteras*, which is devoted to immigrant concerns.

21. See Judith Butler, *The Psychic Life of Power: Theories in Subjection* (Palo Alto: Stanford University Press, 1997); David Eng and David Kazanjian, eds., *Loss: The Politics of Mourning* (Berkeley: University of California Press, 2002); and Ann Anlin Cheng, *The Melancholy of Race: Psychoanalysis, Assimilation, and Hidden Grief* (New York: Oxford University Press, 2001).

22. "Battling Beyond U.S. Borders," *Assignment Discovery*, 2005.

23. My translations and transcription.

24. Details of the case appear in Mary E. O'Leary, "Scam Cost Illegal Aliens $150G," *New Haven Register*, January 6, 2006.

25. *El Alma Herida* (The Wounded Soul) was a coproduction of Telemundo and Argos in Mexico. The program completed shooting in 2003 and aired in the United States throughout 2004.

26. "One of the most beloved novelas of the Hispanic public": Organic Broadcast Project, http://broadcast.organicframework.com (accessed November 18, 2005).

27. My translation. Story synopsis and cast information are available at http://tdmnovelas.tripod.com/elalmaherida/ (accessed November 18, 2005).

28. See Daniel D. Arreola and James R. Curtis. "Cultural Landscapes of the Mexican Border Cities," *Aztlán* 21.1–2 (1992–96): 1–48.

29. In fact, many of those stranded or deported are children. María Eugenia Hernández Sánchez, "Deported Children in Ciudad Juárez." paper presented at the Center for Latin American and Iberian Studies, Yale University, New Haven, CT, October 12, 2005.

30. "Mexican Expatriate Voter Registration Falling Flat," *Frontera NorteSur* (online newsgroup circulated by Center for Latin American and Border Studies, New Mexico State University at Las Cruces), November 21, 2005.

31. Ibid.

32. Ibid.

33. See especially Smith, "'Los ausentes siempre presentes'"; Roger Rouse, "Mexican Migration to the U.S.: Family Relations in a Transnational Migrant Circuit" (Ph.D. diss., Stanford University, 1989), and Luin Goldring, "Diversity and Community in Transnational Migration: A Comparative Study of Two Mexican U.S. Migrant Communities" (Ph.D. diss., Cornell University, 1992).

34. "Place of birth: Huauchinango, Puebla. Last known: He departed from Tetela de Ocampo, Puebla, on 13 November, 2001, on route to work in the United States, but to this date, his family has received no news of his whereabouts." Protección a Mexicanos, Consulado General de México, www.consulmexny.org/esp/proteccion_tabla_desaparecidos.htm (accessed November 12, 2005).

35. Protección a Mexicanos, Consulado General de México, www.consulmexny.org/esp/proteccion_tabla_desaparecidos.htm (accessed November 12, 2005).

36. Roland Barthes, *Camera Lucida*, trans. Richard Howard (New York: Hill and Wang, 1981). "The punctum *punctuates* the meaning of the photograph (the studium) and as a result punctures or pierces its viewer" (27).

37. "Your undocumented status does not make you a criminal." Protección a Mexicanos, Consulado

General de México, www.consulmexny.org/esp/proteccion_migratorios.htm (accessed November 12, 2005).

38. "If you have these symptoms, you are in danger of dying slowly." Gobierno del Estado de Yucatán, *Guia del Migrante Yucateco* (Yucatán, 2004), 32.

39. The United States instituted an official border patrol unit in 1924. C. Roberto Gaytan Saucedo, interview by author, Ciudad Juárez, November 13, 2003.

40. Claudia Smith, quoted in "Rapes on the U.S.-Mexico Border Up," United Press International, March 18, 2005, www.feeds.bignewsnetwork.com/?sid=2768526633891249 (accessed March 18, 2005). Smith argues that given the low rates of reporting crime, the actual number of rapes may be much higher.

41. "There are paths of no return."

42. "Going or coming, you remain Yucatecan." *Guía del Migrante Yucateco*, 79.

43. "Protect your life."

44. *Retablo of Concepción Zapata*, in Jorge Durand and Douglas S. Massey, *Miracles on the Border: Retablos of Mexican Migrants to the United States* (Tucson: University of Arizona Press, 1995), 138–39.

45. Ibid.

46. Ibid., 138.

47. See Sylvanna M. Falcón, "Rape as a Weapon of War: Advancing Human Rights for Women at the U.S.-Mexico Border," *Social Justice* 28.2 (2001): 31–50.

48. Marisela Norte, "Act of the Faithless," in *Norte/Word* 062/Cr02 (Lawndale, CA: New Alliance Records, 1991).

49. My discussion of Marisela Norte is informed by Michelle Habell-Pallán's definitive work on the poet, "No Cultural Icon: Marisela Norte and Spoken Word—East L.A. Noir and the U.S./Mexico Border," in *Loca Motion: The Travels of Chicana and Latina Popular Culture* (New York: NYU Press, 2005), 43–80.

50. Ramón Saldívar, *Chicano Narrative: The Dialectics of Difference* (Madison: University of Wisconsin Press, 1990), 190.

51. This concept of the border appears in Gloria Anzaldúa, *Borderlands/La Frontera: The New Mestiza* (San Francisco: Aunt Lute, 1987), and Sonia Saldívar-Hull, *Feminism on the Border: Chicana Gender Politics and Literature* (Berkeley: University of California Press, 2000). See also Norma Alarcón, "The Theoretical Subject(s) of *This Bridge Called My Back* and Anglo-American Feminism," in *Criticism in the Borderlands: Studies in Chicano Literature*, ed. Héctor Calderón and José David Saldívar (Durham, NC: Duke University Press, 1991), 28–39.

52. Emma Pérez, "Sexuality and Discourse: Notes from a Chicana Survivor," in *Chicana Lesbians: The Girls Our Mothers Warned Us About*, ed. Carla Trujillo (Berkeley: Third Woman Press, 1991), 159–84. Pérez's phrase "sitio y lengua" means "place and language/tongue."

53. The phrase comes from María Socorro Tabuenca Córdova and Debra A. Castillo, *Border Women: Writing from La Frontera* (Minneapolis: University of Minnesota Press, 2002), 64.

54. Rolando Romero, "Postdeconstructive Spaces," *Siglo XX/Twentieth Century II* (1993): 225–33, cited in ibid., 15.

55. Since 1993, some 370 women have been murdered in Chihuahua City and Ciudad Juárez; approximately 137 were sexually assaulted before their death. Of these, 100 fit a pattern of serial killings. Some 75 of the bodies have not been identified or claimed. The mothers' organization Nuestras Hijas de Regreso a Casa (Bring Our Daughters Home) estimates that in addition to these documented killings, 600 women have disappeared from the Juárez/Chihuahua metropolitan areas. Amnesty International, "Mexico. Intolerable Killings: Ten Years of Abductions and Murders in Ciudad Juárez and Chihuahua," August 11, 2003, AI index: AMR 41/027/2003.

56. See my discussion of the *feminicidio* in Alicia Schmidt Camacho, "Body Counts on the Mexico-U.S. Border: *Feminicidio*, Reification, and the Theft of Mexicans Subjectivity," *Chicana/Latina Studies* 4.1 (2004): 22–60.

36

Silencing Religiosity
Secularity and Arab American Feminisms

Lara Deeb

Despite recent interest in and awareness of what has often been termed "Islamic feminism" in the Arab world, the potential link between religiosity and feminist activism has not been accepted to the same extent when it comes to Arab American feminisms in the United States. Instead, a secularist silencing of religion, sometimes in the form of disdain or mistrust, pervades many of our discussions and much of our work. Women who may reject feminism semantically, but embrace a notion of gender equity that plays out on the ground in ways that often fit within the rubric of what many feminists would themselves embrace as feminist, are invisible in Arab American feminist circles. In what follows, I want to take a closer look at this secularist silencing. In so doing, I begin in the Arab world and travel transnationally to the U.S., in the hopes that a comparative analysis will provide a useful foil for similar dynamics that emerge here in North America.

A Lebanese Contrast

Between 1999 and 2001, I conducted ethnographic field research in the southern suburbs of Beirut. A mostly Shi'i Muslim area, the neighborhoods in which I worked forms the urban locus of a longstanding Shi'i Islamist mobilization in Lebanon, most prominently represented today by the political party Hizbullah. My interlocutors were mainly devout Shi'i women,[1] some of whom were members of Hizbullah while others followed the religious leadership of Sayyid Muhammad Hussein Fadlallah.[2] During these two years, I participated as a volunteer with an Islamic women's social welfare organization and interviewed women volunteers at this and a number of other Islamic organizations in the area. Everyday I would have long conversations with women who believed that they were inherently different from men, that their strengths and weaknesses were gender bound, and that those "natural" differences made them more suitable to different kinds of work and behavior than men. And everyday these same women discussed politics, economics, religion, and gender relations with far more confidence, openness, and eloquence than many women students and colleagues I knew in the United States. The Lebanese women with whom I worked and who I interviewed spent long hours running, working in, and volunteering with organizations that essentially provided the only available means of support for the poor in their neighborhoods, literally forming the backbone of their community.

Whenever I asked about feminism, they would laugh and say that it was terribly misguided of women in the West to think that it was desirable to be equal to men. They proposed *equity* (*'adala*) instead as an alternative ideal, rejecting equality (*masawa*) because to them equality meant the erasure of differences between men and women—differences which were, in their view, essential to their identities as strong women. Pious Shi'i women I spoke with based a rejection of "feminism" on their definition of the concept as the desire for equality (read: sameness) with men (a definition with which many self-identified feminists might also take issue). Their understanding of equity, as an alternative, was an understanding based on equivalent but not identical rights, and an understanding that promoted interpretations of Islam that emphasized what Leila Ahmed terms its "ethical egalitarianism."[3]

When I pursued my question, defining feminism in terms of social justice and women's rights, many Shi'i women readily accepted that the definition applied to them; their struggles, goals, and methods could be defined as feminist, but they continued to resist the term for reasons having to do with its problematic history and its linkage to colonial and neoimperialist powers. They felt that the term "feminism" was not broad enough to embrace their entire vision, which included working for greater educational and employment opportunities for women, concerns about economic survival, and opposition to Israeli military bombings of villages in south Lebanon.[4]

I offer this example of a typical rejection of "feminism" as a point of departure in order to emphasize how the terms we choose make a big difference not only in communication across languages; more importantly, they speak to the content of what feminism is and to whom it is relevant. Setting aside the term, "feminism," then, I will use a similar argument to discuss how some feminists here in the U.S. as well as in Lebanon respond to "religiosity."

Moving across Beirut to another neighborhood and to a secular feminist organization with whose members I had a number of conversations about my research, I found a curious reaction. When I discussed the work pious Shi'i women were doing, and how outspoken and eloquent they were, I was often met with skepticism and doubt. One woman dismissed my observations by attributing Shi'i women's views to false consciousness. This was not particularly surprising to me, given the Lebanese history of division among people of different religious backgrounds, conflict between the "religious" and the "secular", and a sixteen-year civil war that—though it did not begin as a primarily religious conflict—had the effect of entrenching sectarian divisions in the spaces of Beirut and the nation.[5] In the late 1990s, a long and necessary process of discussion and debate among various feminist groups (whether self-identified as such or not) was only beginning to take place.

Today, Hizbullah's women's committee is one of the 170 groups that make up the Lebanese Women's Council, and the Shi'i party recently had one of its representatives elected to the Council's administrative committee. Women party members with whom I spoke explained that they were able to work with other groups through the Council, including secular groups, provided that everyone focused on discussing only shared issues, usually focusing on Palestine and combating neoimperialism. When the recent headscarf debates exploded in Europe,[6] Hizbullah's women's committee invited the other Council members to discuss the issue and carefully framed the discussion around concepts of religious freedoms, drawing on a shared understanding, rather than engaging in the pros and cons of the headscarf itself. However, such cooperative efforts are recent in Lebanon and remain infused with a secularist disregard for religiosity.

Religiosity and Secularity in the United States

The Lebanese discussions seemed to accompany me as I traveled back to the United States. I have been active in a number of Arab American arenas for over a decade now, most recently in Arab American feminist circles. Throughout, I have noticed an almost clear-cut division between secular and religious activists, particularly among feminists. A disdain for religiosity seems to infect our discussions in ways similar to those I encountered in the Lebanese contexts—ways that reinforce many of the stereotypes and divisions that we often intend to combat. Despite recent Islam-based interventions in struggles for women's and community rights, the moment religion enters the discussion, a number of secularist activists—those who believe that social change necessitates the separation of religion from other aspects of life—respond warily or patronizingly, contemptuously looking at those who identify or are identified as religious as "backward." This view is rooted in an Enlightenment ideal that defines progress, in part, through the separation of religion from politics and other aspects of public life, a legacy most clearly conveyed by the Weberian linking of modernization and secularization, also discussed as "the secularization thesis."[7]

This is most readily apparent in relation to the relatively small numbers of devout Arab American women in our feminist circles. And while many Arab American feminist groups accept women who wear the *hijab*, and indeed actively recruit women "for a religious perspective," there sometimes exists an unstated assumption that such women, who express their religiosity on their bodies in public space, must either "prove" their feminism or accept being reluctantly embraced in feminist circles with the understanding that they are there "to learn." Secularist feminists, on the other hand, are often unwilling to comprehend or allow for a religious perspective. Furthermore, secularist and religious activists alike share an assumption that a person's views on or expressions of religiosity somehow determine their views on other issues. For some secularists, this means that religious expression is incompatible with feminism. The two examples that arise most frequently here are the notion that religiosity implies homophobia and that religiosity implies support for Palestinian rights. With regard to the former, there are numerous ongoing debates *within* faith communities about sexualities that cannot be ignored, and it is crucial within feminist circles to embrace these debates and dialogues as we work against homophobia in our communities. And with regard to the latter, support for Palestinian rights—and equally critically, the specific ideas and views expressed in that support—does not necessarily map onto religiosity. Again, dialogue and debate around the Palestinian-Israeli conflict, as around other political and military conflicts like the current U.S. occupation of Iraq, exists *within* both Arab American secularist and faith-based communities. These examples of complex political dynamics within communities also remind us that the category "Arab American" is also implicated in the erasure of other differences, including those of generation and national origin.

The silencing of, and assumptions about, religiosity in Arab American feminist circles, to a certain extent, mirror particular problematic aspects of certain liberal white feminisms in the United States. Dominant white U.S. feminisms have long been suspicious of religiosities, assuming that all forms of religious commitments are by definition patriarchal and thus bad for women. Of the major world religions, Islam is seen as being especially detrimental for women. Hegemonic feminist interventions and analysis are often filtered through standard assumptions about the oppression of Arab and Muslim women, or more nuanced assumptions about the ways that Arab and Muslim women experience sexism and patriarchal structures and about their limited abilities to act as agents within and against those structures. Arab or Muslim "patriarchy" is assumed to be essentially worse than other patriarchal systems, and Arab and Muslim women are seen as being incapable of their own agentive actions within and against that system.

When Arab American feminists insist on secularism as part of their current agenda, or assume that religious women and women who are visibly pious are somehow less empowered than those who are not, we fall into a pattern of privileging secularity at the expense of other forms of commitments and worldviews. One of the problematics of this slippage lies in its elision of the intimate history that dialectically links secularism and Christianity in Europe.[8] Furthermore, while secularist feminists often see all expressions of religiosity as suspect, Islam is particularly singled out. Wearing a cross is not assumed to be inherently conflictual with feminism as often as wearing the *hijab* is.

Relationships between religious and secularist feminists are further complicated by the intersections of other axes of identity—such as class, nationality, race, and sexuality—with both Arab Americanness and religiosity/secularity. In addition to whether the women in question are practicing Muslims, Christians, or Jews—and Arab Americans are Christians, Muslims, Jews, and atheists, to name a few standpoints vis-à-vis religiosity—aspects such as how long they have lived in the United States, nation of origin, and socio-economic status play into this dynamic as well. A dominant trend among earlier Christian Arab immigrants to the U.S. was assimilation in ways that were not possible or necessarily desirable for newer and/or Muslim Arab immigrants.

Another layer of complexity emerges when the dynamics of religion, politics, and identity come into play, especially, but not exclusively, in the Lebanese case. By this I mean the ways in which persons who are not pious or do not practice the faith into which they were born continue to identify with—or are identified with—a particular religious community. Some secularist Arab Americans consider non-religious Muslim-born activists to have more political credibility than non-religious Christian-born activists. This assumption stems from the homogenization of all Lebanese and "Christians" as one and the same as the right-wing Phalangist political party and militia in Lebanon, which played a role of complicity with Israel during the Lebanese civil-war and, after Israel's invasion of Lebanon, participated in the Sabra and Chatila refugee camp massacres in 1982. Such a conflation problematically assumes that some essentializable religious identity is determinative of a person's political views. While many Arab American feminists would agree that a person's religious background does not determine either her religiosity or her political perspective, these same feminists are less likely to accept that a woman's experiences or expressions of piety do not determine her views on all sorts of social and political issues; as I have noted, a pious woman's sartorial practices do not necessarily indicate that she is homophobic, pro-Palestinian, or, for that matter, anti-feminist.

Moving Past Silence

The dynamics I have described clearly point to the need to treat religious background, religiosity, and political perspective as plurally constructed, experienced, and practiced, and as existing in complex and non-determinative but mutually constituting relationships to one another. Conflating political position with religiosity makes it all too easy to erase or negate what Lila Abu-Lughod has termed "uncomfortable politics" in favor of issues that can be cast as "cultural" and therefore politically "safe" for discussion—thus allowing issues like the "veil" to displace critical questions, such as the effects of Israeli state terrorism on Palestinian women's lives or the effects of years of U.S. imposed sanctions, or its more recent occupation, on Iraqi women's lives.

For Arab American feminist agendas to take shape and be productive, we need to take seriously the attempts of my Hizbullah interlocutors in Lebanon to collaboratively work with secular and other women's groups around shared perspectives and commonalities. Such a step would allow Arab American secular feminists to work with religious Arab American women activists on questions of global politics and political-economy, as well as on domestic violence and civil rights in the U.S. I am convinced that far more social justice struggles are shared between women for whom conversations are derailed as soon as God is invoked and those who insist that no conversation can continue with God's presence than not. Halting our conversations because of the inclusion or exclusion of a deity does not allow for the potential for people's ideas and beliefs to shift with time and experience, in a wide range of directions. Building alliances within our communities sometimes comes down to language, sometimes it amounts to listening to what is being said in the spaces around and between the words; above all, it is about appreciating the complementarity of the various social, political, and economic justice struggles in which we are all engaged on a daily basis.

Notes

I would like to thank Nadine Naber and Rabab Abdulhadi for their comments, as well as all the participants on the Arab American Feminisms panels at the American Studies Association meeting in 2003, and the many inspiring Arab, Arab American, and SWANA activist and feminist women I have had the privilege of working with in both Lebanon and the United States

1. In the interest of space and returning quickly to my main purpose in this reflection, I am glossing shamelessly over variation among my devout Shi'i interlocutors—differences in class, ideology, and politics, among other things. These have been detailed at length in other forums, including in: Lara Deeb, *An Enchanted Modern: Gender and Public Piety in Shi'i Lebanon* (New Jersey: Princeton University Press, 2006).
2. Every practicing Shi'i Muslim looks to a *marji' al-taqlid*—a religious leader who is emulated with regard to his interpretations on all religious matters. Sayyid Fadlallah is an internationally prominent *marji'*. Hizbullah is a Shi'i political party that officially follows Khamenei in Iran as the party's *marji'*. In the southern suburbs of Beirut, it is possible for an individual to be a member or supporter of Hizbullah and a follower of Fadlallah at the same time. Religious emulation and political allegiance are two separate issues that may or may not overlap for an individual.
3. Leila Ahmed, *Women and Gender in Islam: Historical Roots of a Modern Debate* (New Haven: Yale University Press, 1992).
4. During most of my field research, the south of Lebanon was still under Israeli occupation. Israel, and its proxy army in the south, withdrew their forces in May 2000. Women in this community remain concerned about smaller conflicts along the border, as well as about the long process of rebuilding their villages and reconstituting the lives of those who live in or have returned to the recently liberated south.
5. In brief, during the French Mandate, an unwritten national pact between Maronite Christians and Sunni Muslims was instituted, and then later written into the 1943 constitution of Lebanon at independence. This pact left Lebanon with a legacy of religious sectarianism, as it ensured that government and Parliament were divided along strict sectarian lines. For example, the President is always a Maronite Christian, while the Prime Minister is always a Sunni Muslim, and Parliamentary seats are similarly allotted to various communities in the country by sect. Demographic trends have ensured that this system is not representative of the populations of Lebanon's many communities. Sectarian political power translated to selective access to resources for various areas of the country, with the under-represented Shi'i Muslims historically constituting the most marginalized group.
6. In the wake of the French government's banning the wearing of the headscarf in public schools.
7. For discussion and critique of the "secularization thesis," see Jose Casanova, *Public Religions in the Modern World* (Chicago: University of Chicago Press, 1994).
8. I am aware of the religious conflicts that eventually produced the Enlightenment in Europe, but still insist on understanding secularism as drawn from the Christian canon. See Talal Asad, *Formations of the Secular. Christianity, Islam, Modernity,* (California: Stanford University Press, 2003).
9. Lila Abu-Lughod, "Do Muslims Women Really Need Saving? Anthropological Reflections on Cultural Relativism and Its Others" in *American Anthropologist* 104 (2002):783–790.

Selected Bibliographies
African American Women

Compiled by Zakiya R. Adair

Anthologies

Abel, Elizabeth, Barbara Christian, and Helene Moglen, eds. *Women Subjects in Black and White: Race, Psychoanalysis, Feminism*. Berkeley: University of California Press, 1997.

Bell-Scott, Patricia, ed. *Flat-footed Truths: Telling Black Women's Lives*. New York: Henry Holt, 1998.

Bobo, Jacqueline. *Black Women as Cultural Readers*. New York: Columbia University Press, 1995.

Boswell, Angela and Judith N. McArthur, eds. *Women Shaping the South: Creating and Confronting Change*. Columbia: University of Missouri Press, 2006.

Crawford, Vicki L., Jacqueline Anne Rouse, and Barbara Woods, eds. *Women in the Civil Rights Movement: Trailblazers and Torchbearers, 1941–1965*. Bloomington: Indiana University Press, 1993.

Giddings, Paula. *"When and Where I Enter": The Impact of Black Women on Race and Sex in America*. New York: William Morrow, 1984.

Gordon, Ann D. et al. *African American Women and the Vote 1831–1965*. Amherst: University of Massachusetts Press, 1997.

Harley, Sharon. *The Timetables of African-American History; A Chronology of the Most Important People and Events in African-American History*. New York: Simon and Schuster, 1995.

Hine, Darlene Clark, ed. *Black Women in United States Historys: vols. 1–4, From the Colonial Times through the Nineteenth Century; vols. 5–8, The Twentieth Century; vols. 9–10, Theory and Practice*. Brooklyn: Carlson Publishing, 1990.

Hine, Darlene Clark, Elsa Barkley Brown, and Roslyn Terborg-Penn, eds. *Black Women in America: An Historical Encyclopedia*. Bloomington: Indiana University Press, 1993.

Hine, Darlene Clark, Wilma King, and Linda Reed, eds. *"We Specialize in the Wholly Impossible": A Reader in Black Women's History*. New York: Carlson Publishing, 1995.

James, Joy, ed. *The Angela Davis Reader*. Malden, Mass.: Blackwell, 1998.

——, and Ruth Farmer, eds. *Spirit, Space, and Survival: African American Women in (White) Academe*. New York: Routledge, 1993.

Japtok, Martin, ed. *Postcolonial Perspectives on Women Writers from Africa, the Caribbean, and the US*. Trenton, N.J.: African World Press, 2003.

Kaufman, Polly Welts and Katharine T. Corbett, eds. *Her Past Around Us*. Malabar, Fla.: Krieger, 2003.

Lerner, Gerda, ed. *Black Women in White America*. 1972. Reprint, New York: Vintage Books, 1992.

Morrison, Toni, ed. *Race-ing Justice, En-Gendering Power: Essays on Anita Hill, Clarence Thomas and the Construction of Social Reality*. New York: Pantheon Books, 1992.

Smitherman, Geneva, ed. *African American Women Speak out on Anita Hill–Clarence Thomas*. Detroit: Wayne State University Press, 1995.

Steady, Filomina, ed. *The Black Woman Cross-Culturally*. Cambridge, Mass.: Schenkman Publishing Company, 1981.

Sterling, Dorothy, ed. *We Are Your Sisters: Black Women in the Nineteenth Century*. New York: W. W. Norton and Company, 1984.

Vaz, Kim Marie, ed. *Black Women in America*. New York: Sage Publications, 1995.

Books

Aidoo, Ama Ata. *Changes: A Love Story*. New York: The Feminist Press, 1993.

Alexander, Adele Logan. *Ambiguous Lives: Free Women of Color in Rural Georgia, 1798–1879*. Fayetteville: University of Arkansas Press, 1991.

Anderson, Karen. *Changing Woman: A History of Racial Ethnic Women in Modern America*. New York: Oxford University Press, 1996.

Breslaw, Elaine G. *Tituba, Reluctant Witch of Salem: Devilish Indians and Puritan Fantasies*. New York: New York University Press, 1996.

Carby, Hazel. *Reconstructing Womanhood: The Emergence of the Afro-American Woman Novelist*. New York: Oxford University Press, 1987.

Collins, Patricia Hill. *Fighting Words: Black Women and the Search far Justice*. Minneapolis: University of Minnesota Press, 1998.

——. *Black Feminist Thought: Knowledge, Consciousness, and the Politics of Empowerment*. New York: Routledge, 1990.

Davis, Angela Y. *Blues Legacies and Black Feminism*. New York: Vintage Books, 1998.

——. *Women, Race, and Class*. New York: Vintage Books, 1981.

Fox-Genovese, Elizabeth. *Within the Plantation Household: Black and White Women of the Old South*. Chapel Hill: University of North Carolina Press, 1988.

Gaspar, David Barry, and Darlene Clark Hine, eds. *More than Chattel: Black Women and Slavery in the Americas*. Bloomington: Indiana University Press, 1996.

Gordon, Linda. *Pitied but Not Entitled: Single Mothers and the History of Welfare, 1890–1935*. New York: Free Press, 1994.

Gross, Kali N. *Colored Amazons: Crime, Violence, and Black Women in the City of Brotherly Love, 1880–1910*. North Carolina: Duke University Press, 1998.

Hendricks, Wanda. *Gender, Race, and Politics in the Midwest: Black Club Women in Illinois*. Bloomington: Indiana University Press, 1998.

Higginbotham, Evelyn Brooks. *Righteous Discontent: The Women's Movement in the Black Baptist Church, 1880–1920*. Cambridge, Mass.: Harvard University Press, 1993.

Hill, Anita. *Speaking Truth to Power*. New York: Anchor Books, 1998.

Hine, Darlene Clark. *Hine Sight: Black Women and the Re-construction of American History*. Bloomington: Indiana University Press, 1997.

Hine, Darlene Clark, and Kathleen Thompson. *A Shining Thread of Hope: The History of Black Women in America*. New York: Broadway Books, 1998.

Hunter, Tera W. *To 'joy My Freedom: Southern Black Women's Lives and Labors after the Civil War*. Cambridge: Harvard University Press, 1997.

Jones, Jacqueline. *American Work: Black and White Labor since 1600*. New York: W. W. Norton and Company, 1998.

——. *Labor of Love, Labor of Sorrow: Black Women, Work, and the Family, from Slavery to the Present*. New York: Vintage Books, 1985.

King, Wilma. *Stolen Childhood: Slave Youth in Nineteenth-Century America*. Bloomington: Indiana University Press, 1995.

Lee, Chana Kai. *For Freedom's Sake: The Life of Fannie Lou Hamer*. Urbana: University of Illinois Press, 1999.

Lemke-Santangelo, Gretchen. *Abiding Courage: African American Migrant Women and the East Bay Community*. Chapel Hill: University of North Carolina Press, 1996.

Leslie, Kent Anderson. *Woman of Color, Daughter of Privilege: Amanda America Dickson, 1849–1893*. Athens: University of Georgia Press, 1995.

Marable, Manning. *Living Black History: How Re-imagining the African American Past Can Remake America's Racial Future*. New York: Basic Civitas, 2006.

McLaurin, Melton A. *Celia, a Slave*. New York: Avon Books, 1993.

Mink, Gwendolyn. *The Wages of Motherhood: Inequality in the Welfare State, 1917–1942*. Ithaca: Cornell University Press, 1995.

Morton, Patricia, ed. *Discovering the Women in Slavery: Emancipating Perspectives on the American Past*. Athens: University of Georgia Press, 1996.

Neverdon-Morton, Cynthia. *Afro-American Women of the South and the Advancement of the Race, 1895–1925*. Knoxville: University of Tennessee Press, 1989.

Painter, Nell Irvin. *Sojourner Truth: A Life, a Symbol*. New York: W. W. Norton and Company, 1996.

Robinson, Jo Anne. *The Montgomery Bus Boycott and the Women Who Started It: The Memoir of Jo Anne Gibson Robinson*, ed. David Garrow. Knoxville: University of Tennessee Press, 1987.

Robnett, Belinda. *How Long? How Long?: African American Women in the Struggle for Civil Rights.* New York: Oxford University Press, 1997.

Schwalm, Leslie A. *A Hard Fight for We: Women's Transition from Slavery to Freedom in South Carolina.* Urbana: University of Illinois Press, 1997.

Shaw, Stephanie. *What a Woman Ought to Be and to Do: Black Professional Women During the Jim Crow Era.* Chicago: University of Chicago Press, 1996.

Smith, Susan L. *Sick and Tired of Being Sick and Tired: Black Women's Health Activism in America, 1890–1950.* Philadelphia: University of Pennsylvania Press, 1995.

Smith, Valerie. *Not Just Race, Not Just Gender: Black Feminist Readings.* New York: Routledge, 1998.

Stevenson, Brenda. *Life in Black and White: Family and Community in the Slave South.* New York: Oxford University Press, 1996.

Terborg-Penn, Rosalyn. *African American Women in the Struggle for the Vote, 1850–1920.* Bloomington: Indiana University Press, 1998.

Weiner, Marli F. *Mistresses and Slaves: Plantation Women in South Carolina, 1830–80.* Urbana: University of Illinois Press, 1998.

White, Deborah Gray. *Too Heavy a Load: Black Women in Defense of Themselves, 1894–1994.* New York: W. W. Norton and Company, 1999.

———. *Ar'n't I a Woman?: Female Slaves in the Plantation South.* New York: W. W. Norton and Company, 1985.

Williams, Patricia. *The Alchemy of Race and Rights: Diary of a Law Professor.* Cambridge: Harvard University Press, 1991.

Wood, Betty. *Women's Work, Men's Work: The Informal Slave Economies of Lowcountry Georgia.* Athens: University of Georgia Press, 1995.

Wyatt, Gail Elizabeth. *Stolen Women: Reclaiming Our Sexuality, Taking Back Our Lives.* New York: John Wiley and Sons, 1997.

Journal/Anthology Articles

Amott, Teresa. "Black Women and AFDC: Making Entitlement out of Necessity." In Linda Gordon, ed., *Women, the State, and Welfare.* Madison: University of Wisconsin Press, 1990.

Armstrong, Erica R. "A Mental and Moral Feast: Reading, Writing, and Sentimentality in Black Philadelphia." *The Journal of Women's History* 16, 1 (2004): 78–102.

Boris, Eileen. "Mothers and Other Workers: (Re)Conceiving Labor, Materialism, and the State." *Journal of Women's History* 15, 3 (autumn 2003): 90–117.

Bunch-Lyons, Beverly. "A Novel Approach: Using Fiction by African American Women to Teach Black Women's History." *The Journal of American History* 86, 4 (March 2000): 1700–8.

Farnham, Christie. "Sapphire? The Issue of Dominance in the Slave Family, 1830–1865." In Carol Groneman and Mary Beth Norton, eds., *"To Toil the Livelong Day": America's Women at Work, 1780–1980.* Ithaca: Cornell University Press, 1987.

Fehn, Bruce. "African-American Women and the Struggle for Equality in the Meatpacking Industry, 1940–1960." *Journal of Women's History* 10 (spring 1998): 45–69.

Fulton, DoVeanna S. "Speak Sister, Speak: Oral Empowerment in *Louisa Picquet: The Octoroon.*" *Legacy* 15, 1 (1998): 98–103.

Hammonds, Evelyn. "Missing Persons: African American Women, AIDS, and the History of Disease." *Radical America* 24, 2 (1990): 7–23.

Hanger, Kimberly S. " 'Desiring Total Tranquility' and Not Getting It: Conflict Involving Free Black Women in Spanish New Orleans." *Americas* 54 (April 1998): 541–56.

Harris, Paisley Jane. "Gate-keeping and Remaking: The Politics of Respectability in African American Women's History and Black Feminism." *Journal of Women's History* 15, 1 (spring 2003): 212–20.

Higginbotham, Evelyn Brooks. "African American Women's History and the Metalanguage of Race." *Signs* 17 (winter 1992): 251–74.

Hoy, Suellen M. "No Color Line at Loretto Academy: Catholic Sisters and African Americans on Chicago's East Side." *Journal of Women's History* 14, 1 (spring 2002): 8–33.

Johnson, Joan Marie. "Ye Gave Them a Stone: African American Women's Clubs, The Frederick Douglas Home, and The Black Mammy Monument." *Journal of Women's History* 17, 1 (2005): 62–86.

Johnson, Wittington B. "Free African-American Women in Savannah, 1800–1860: Affluence and Autonomy amid Adversity." *Georgia Historical Quarterly* 76, 2 (summer 1992): 260–83.

Jones, Maxine D. "The Rosewood Massacre and the Women Who Survived It." *Florida Historical Quarterly* 76 (fall 1997): 193–208.

Judson, Sarah Mercer. "Leisure is a Foe to Any Man: The Pleasures of Atlanta During World War I." *Journal of Women's History* 15, 1 (spring 2003): 92–115.

Knapper, Karl. "Women and the Black Panther Party: An Interview with Angela Brown." *Socialist Review* 26, 1–2 (1996): 25–67.

Marks, Carole C. "The Bone and Sinew of the Race: Black Women, Domestic Service and Labor Migration." *Marriage and Family Review* 19, 2 (fall 1995): 149–73.

McKnight, Andrew N. "Lydia Broadnax, Slave and Free Woman of Color." *Southern Studies* 5 (spring–summer 1994): 17–30.

Morgan, Jennifer L. " 'Some Could Suckle over Their Shoulder': Male Travelers, Female Bodies, and the Gendering of Racial Ideology, 1500–1700." *William and Mary Quarterly* 54 (January 1997): 167–92.

Phillips, Stephanie L. "Claiming Our Foremothers: The Legend of Sally Hemings and the Tasks of Black Feminist Theory." *Hastings Women's Law Journal* 8 (fall 1997): 401–65.

Ramey, Daina L. " 'She Do a Heap of Work': Female Slavery on Glynn County Rice and Cotton Plantations." *Georgia Historical Quarterly* 82, 4 (winter 1998): 707–34.

Ramey, Felicenne H. "Obstacles Faced by African American Women Administrators in Higher Education: How They Cope." *Western Journal of Black Studies* 19, 2 (summer 1995): 113–19.

Richardson, Mattie Udora. "No More Lies: African American History and Compulsory Heterosexuality." *Journal of Women's History* 15, 3 (autumn 2003): 63–76.

Scott, Anne Firor. "Most Invisible of All: Black Women's Voluntary Associations." *Journal of Southern History* 56 (February 1990): 3–22.

Shaw, Stephanie J. "Black Club Women and the Creation of the National Association of Colored Women." *Journal of Women's History* 3 (fall 1991): 10–25.

Tate, Gayle T. "Free Black Resistance in the Antebellum Era, 1830 to 1860." *Journal of Black Studies* 28 (July 1998): 764–82.

Taylor, Ula Y. "Negro Women Are Great Thinkers as Well as Doers: Amy Jacques-Garvey and Community Feminism, 1924–1927." *Journal of Women's History* 12, 2 (summer 2000): 104–26.

Venkatesh, Sudhir Alladi. "Gender and Outlaw Capitalism: A Historical Account of the Black Sisters United 'Girl Gang.' " *Signs* 23 (spring 1998): 683–709.

Zipf, Karin L. "Reconstructing 'Free Woman': African American Women, Apprenticeship, and Custody Rights during Reconstruction." *Journal of Women's History* 12, 1 (spring 2000): 8–31.

Websites

The African American Mosaic
http://www.loc.gov/exhibits/african/intro.html

African American Women: On-Line Archival Collections
http://odyssey.lib.duke.edu/collections/african-american-women.html

African American Women Writers of the Nineteenth Century
http://digital.nypl.org/schomburg/writers_aa19/

American Slave Narratives: An Online Anthology
http://xroads.virginia.edu/~HYPER/wpa/wpahome.html

Black Past
http://www.blackpast.org

Modern History Sourcebook: Sojourner Truth: "Ain't I A Woman?", December 1851
http://www.fordham.edu/halsall/mod/sojtruth-woman.html

Women of Color Web
http://www.hsph.harvard.edu/grhf/WoC/

Asian and Pacific Islander American Women

Compiled by Shirley Jennifer Lim

Anthologies

Eng, David L., and Alice Y. Hom, eds. *Q & A: Queer in Asian America.* Philadelphia: Temple University Press, 1998.

Gupta, Sangeeta. *Emerging Voices: South Asian American Women Redefine Self, Family, and Community.* Walnut Creek: Alta Mira Press, 1999.

Hune, Shirley, and Gail Nomura, *Asian Pacific American Women: A Historical Anthology.* New York: NYU Press, 2003.

Leong, Russell, ed. *Asian American Sexualities: Dimensions of the Gay and Lesbian Experience.* New York: Routledge, 1996.

Ng, Franklin, ed. *Asian American Women and Gender.* New York: Garland, 1998.

Books

Chan, Sucheng. *Entry Denied: Exclusion and the Chinese Community in America, 1882–1943.* Philadelphia: Temple University Press, 1991.

Chin, Soo-Young, *Doing What Had to Be Done: The Life Narrative of Dora Yum Kim,* 1999.

Choy, Catherine Ceniza, *Empire of Care: Nursing and Migration in Filipino American History.* Durham: Duke University Press, 2003.

Chun, Gloria Heyung. *Of Orphans and Warriors: Inventing Chinese American Culture and Identity.* New Brunswick, N.J.: Rutgers University Press.

Diggs, Nancy Brown. *Steel Butterflies: Japanese Women and the American Experience.* Albany: State University of New York Press, 1998.

Donnelly, Nancy D. *Changing Lives of Refugee Hmong Women.* Seattle: University of Washington Press, 1994.

Espana-Maram, Linda. *Creating Masculinity in Los Angeles's Little Manila: Working-Class Filipinos and Popular Culture, 1920s–1950s.* New York: Columbia University Press, 2006.

Espiritu, Yen Le. *Asian American Women and Men: Labor, Laws and Love.* Thousand Oaks, Calif.: Sage Publications, 1997.

Fujita-Rony, Dorothy. *American Workers, Colonial Power: Philippine Seattle and the Transpacific West, 1919–1941.* Berkeley: University of California Press, 2002.

Glenn, Evelyn Nakano. *Issei, Nisei, Warbride: Three Generations of Japanese American Women in Domestic Service.* Philadelphia: Temple University Press, 1986.

Hsu, Madeline. *Dreaming of Gold, Dreaming of Home: Transnationalism and Migration between the United States and South China, 1882–1943.* Palo Alto: Stanford University Press, 2002.

Kikumura, Akemi. *Issei Pioneers: Hawaii and the Mainland, 1885 to 1924.* Honolulu: University of Hawaii Press, 1993.

Lee, Erika. *At America's Gates: Chinese Immigration during the Exclusion Era, 1882–1943.* Chapel Hill: University of North Carolina Press, 2003.

Lee, Mary Paik, *Quiet Odyssey: A Pioneer Korean Woman in America.* Seattle: University of Washington Press, 1990.

Lee, Rose Hum. *The Chinese in the United States of America.* New York and Oxford: Oxford University Press, 1960.

Leong, Karen, *The China Mystique: Pearl S. Buck, Anna May Wong, Mayling Soong Chiang, and the Transformation of American Orientalism.* Berkeley: University of California Press, 2005.

Lim, Shirley Jennifer. *A Feeling of Belonging: Asian American Women's Public Culture, 1930–1960.* New York: NYU Press, 2005.

Ling, Huping. *Surviving on the Gold Mountain: A History of Chinese American Women and Their Lives.* Albany: State University of New York Press, 1998.

Lui, Mary. *The Chinatown Trunk Mystery: Murder, Miscegenation, and Other Dangerous Encounters in Turn-of-the-Century New York City.* Princeton: Princeton University Press, 2005.

Matsumoto, Valerie. *Farming the Home Place: A Japanese American Community in California, 1919–1982.* Ithaca, New York: Cornell University Press, 1993.

Ngai, Mae. *Impossible Subjects: Illegal Aliens and the Making of Modern America.* Princeton: Princeton Unversity Press, 2004.

Peffer, George Anthony. *If They Don't Bring Women Here: Chinese Female Immigration before Exclusion.* Urbana: University of Illinois Press, 1999.

Sarasohn, Eileen Sunada. *Issei Women: Echoes from Another Frontier.* Palo Alto, Calif.: Pacific Books, 1997.

Trask, Haunani-Kay. *From a Native Daughter: Colonialism and Sovereignty in Hawai'i.* Monroe, Me.: Common Courage Press, 1993.

Wong, K. Scott. *Americans First: Chinese Americans and the Second World War.* Cambridge, Mass.: Harvard University Press, 2005.

Wu, Judy Tzu-Chun, *Dr. Mom Chung of the Fair-Haired Bastards: The Life of a Wartime Celebrity.* Berkeley: University of California Press, 2005.

Yuh, Ji-Yeon, *Beyond the Shadow of Camptown: Korean Military Brides in America.* New York: NYU Press, 2002.

Yung, Judy. *Unbound Feet: A Social History of Chinese Women in San Francisco.* Berkeley: University of California Press, 1995.

Zhao, Xiaojian. *Remaking Chinese America: Immigration, Family, and Community, 1940–1965.* New Brunswick: Rutgers University Press, 2002.

Journal/Anthology Articles

Abraham, Margaret. "Ethnicity, Gender and Marital Violence: South Asian Women's Organizations in the United States." *Gender & Society* 9, 4 (1995): 450–68.

Agbayani-Siewert, Pauline, and Loring Jones. "Filipino American Women, Work and Family: An Examination of Factors Affecting High Labor Force Participation." *International Social Work* 40, 4 (1997): 407–33.

Alquizola, Marilyn. "The Incorporation of Gender in Minority Discourses: Does the Body Play a Part?" In Gary Okihiro et al., eds., *Privileging Positions: The Sites of Asian American Studies.* Pullman: Washington State University Press, 1995.

Bhattacharjee, Anannya. "The Habit of Ex-Nomination: Nation, Woman, and the Indian Immigrant Bourgeoisie." *Public Culture* 5, 1 (1992): 19–44.

Chan, Sucheng. "The Exclusion of Chinese Women, 1870–1943." *Chinese America, History and Perspectives,* 1994: 75–125.

Chow, Esther Ngan-Ling. "Asian American Women at Work." In Maxine Baca Zinn et al., eds., *Through the Prism of Difference: Readings on Sex and Gender.* Boston: Allyn and Bacon, 1997.

De Vera, Arleen G. "Rizal Day Queen Contests, Filipino Nationalism, and Femininity." Chapter 4, in Jennifer Lee and Min Zhou, eds., *Asian American Youth: Culture, Identity and Ethnicity.* New York: Routledge, 2004, pp. 67–81.

Dong, Lorraine. "The Forbidden City Legacy and Its Chinese American Women." *Chinese America, History and Perspectives,* 1992: 125–48.

Duleep, Harriet Orcutt, and Seth Sanders. "The Decision to Work by Married Immigrant Women." *Industrial Labor Relations Review* 46, 4 (1993): 677–90.

Espiritu, Yen Le. "The Intersection of Race, Ethnicity, and Class: The Multiple Identities of Second-Generation Filipinos." *Identities: Global Studies in Culture and Power* 1, 2–3 (1994): 249–73.

Geschwender, James A., and Rita Argiros. "On the Proletarianization of Asian-American Women in Hawaii." *Research in Social Movements, Conflicts and Change* 15 (1993): 29–53.

Hirata, Lucie Cheng. "Free, Indentured, Enslaved: Chinese Prostitutes in Nineteenth-Century America." *Signs: A Journal of Women in Culture and Society*. 5, 1 (autumn 1979): 3–29.

Hune, Shirley. "Higher Education as Gendered Space, Asian American Women and Everyday Inequalities." In Carol Rambo Ronai, Barbara A. Zsembik, and Joe Feagin, eds., *Everyday Sexism in the Third Millennium*. New York: Routledge, 1997.

Imada, Adria. "Hawaiians On Tour: Hula Circuits through the American Empire." *American Quarterly* 56, 1 (2004): 111–49.

Kwong, Peter. "American Sweatshops 1980s Style: Chinese Women Garment Workers." In Cathy J. Cohen, Kathleen B. Jones, and Joan C. Tronto, eds., *Women Transforming Politics*. New York: New York University Press, 1997.

Jun, Helen Heran. "Contingent Nationalisms: Renegotiating Borders in Korean and Korean American Women's Oppositional Struggles." *Positions: East Asia Cultures Critique* 5, 2 (1997): 325–55.

Kim, Lili. "The Limits of Americanism and Democracy: Korean Americans, Transnational Allegiance, and the Question of Loyalty on the Homefront During World War II." *Amerasia Journal* 29, 3 (2004): 79–96.

Lam, Maivan Clech. "Feeling Foreign in Feminism." *Signs* 19, 4 (1994): 865–93.

Lawsin, Emily Pocincula. "Beyond 'Hanggang Pier Only': Filipino American War Brides of Seattle, 1945–1965." *Filipino American National Historical Society Journal* 4 (1996): 50–50G.

Liang, H. "Fighting for a New Life: Social and Patriotic Activism of Chinese American Women in New York City, 1900 to 1945." *Journal of American Ethnic History* 17, 2 (1998): 22–38.

Lieu, Nhi T. "Remembering 'the Nation' through Pagentry: Femininity and the Politics of Vietnamese Womanhood in the Hoa Hua Ao Dai Contest." *Frontiers* 21, 1/2 (2000).

Ling, Huping. "A History of Chinese Female Students in the United States, 1880s–1990s." *Journal of American Ethnic History* 16, 3 (1997): 81–109.

Lowe, Lisa. "Work, Immigration, Gender: New Subjects of Cultural Politics." *Social Justice* 25, 3 (1998): 31–41.

Mabalon, Dawn. "Urban Redevelopment and Little Manila." In Antonio Tiongson and Ed Gutierrez, eds., *Positively No Filipinos Allowed*. Philadelphia: Temple University Press, 2005.

Matsumoto, Valerie. "Desperately Seeking Deirdre': Gender Roles, Multicultural Relations, and Nisei Women Writers in the 1930s." *Frontiers* 12 (1991): 19–32.

Mazumdar, Sucheta. "What Happened to the Women." In Shirley Hune and Gail Nomura eds., *Asian Pacific Islander Women: A Historical Anthology*. New York: NYU Press, 2003.

Min, Pyong Gap. "Korean Immigrant Wives' Labor Force Participation, Marital Power, and Status." In Elizabeth Higginbotham and Mary Romero, eds., *Women and Work: Exploring Race, Ethnicity, and Class*. Women and Work: A Research and Policy Series, vol. 6. Thousand Oaks, Calif.: Sage Publications, 1997.

Nomura, Gail M. "Significant Lives: Asian and Asian Americans in the History of the U.S. West." *Western Historical Quarterly* 25, 1 (1994): 69–88.

Parrenas, Rhacel Salazar. " 'White Trash' Meets the 'Little Brown Monkeys': The Taxi Dance Hall as a Site of Interracial and Gender Alliances Between White Working Class Women and Filipino American Immigrant Men in the 1920s and 1930s." *Amerasia Journal* 24 (1998): 115–34.

Pascoe, Peggy. "Miscegenation Law, Court Cases, and Ideologies of 'Race' in Twentieth-Century America." *Journal of American History*, 1996.

Shukla, Sandyha. "Feminisms of the Diaspora Both Local and Global: The Politics of South Asian Women against Domestic Violence." In Cathy J. Cohen, Kathleen B. Jones, and Joan C. Tronto, eds., *Women Transforming Politics*. New York: University of New York Press, 1997.

Wong, Victoria. "Square and Circle Club: Women in the Public Sphere." *Chinese America, History and Perspectives*, (1994), 127–53.

Yamamoto, Eriko. "Miya Sannomiya Kikuchi: A Pioneer Nisei Woman's Life and Identity." *Amerasia Journal* 23, 3 (1997): 72–101.

Yung, Judy. "It Is Hard to Be Born a Woman but Hopeless to Be Born a Chinese: The Life and Times of Flora Belle Jan." *Frontiers* 18, 3 (1997): 66–91.

Websites

Japanese American National Museum
www.janm.org/nrc/

Filipino American National Historical Society (FANHS)
www.fanhs-national.org/

Museum of Chinese in the Americas
www.moca-nyc.org/

Latinas

Compiled by Mary Ann Villarreal

Anthologies

Acosta-Belen, Edna, ed. *The Puerto Rican Woman.* 2nd ed. New York: Praeger, 1986.

Alarcón, Norma, ed. *Chicana Critical Issues.* Berkeley: Third Woman Press, 1993.

——, Ana Castillo, and Cherríe Moraga, eds. "The Sexuality of Latinas" (special issue). *Third Woman* 4 (1989).

Armitage, Susan, and Elizabeth Jameson, eds. *Writing the Range: Race, Class, and Culture in the Women's West.* Norman: University of Oklahoma Press, 1997.

Browne, Irene, ed. *Latinas and African American Women at Work: Race, Gender, and Economic Inequality.* New York: Russell Sage Foundation, 1999.

De la Torre, Adela, and Beatríz Pesquera, eds. *Building with Our Hands: New Directions in Chicana Studies.* Berkeley: University of California Press, 1993.

Del Castillo, Adelaida, ed. *Between Borders: Essays on Mexicana/Chicana History.* Los Angeles: Floricanto Press, 1989.

—— and Magadelena Mora, eds. *Mexican Women in the U.S.: Struggles Past and Present.* Los Angeles: UCLA Chicano Studies Research Center Publications, 1980.

Flores, William V., and Rina Benmayor, eds. *Latino Cultural Citizenship: Claiming Identity, Space, and Rights.* Boston: Beacon Press, 1997.

Gabaccia, Donna R., and Vicki L. Ruiz, eds. *American Dreaming, Global Realities: Rethinking U.S. Immigration History.* Urbana: University of Illinois Press, 2006.

Galindo, D. Leticia, and Marla D. Gonzales, eds. *Speaking Chicana: Voice, Power, and Identity.* Tucson: University of Arizona Press, 1999.

García, Alma, ed. *Chicana Feminist Thought.* New York: Routledge, 1997.

Habell-Pallán, Michelle, and Mary Romero. *Latino/a Popular Culture.* New York: New York University Press, 2002.

Lopez, Tiffany A., ed. *Growing Up Chicana/o.* New York: William Morrow, 1993.

Matos Rodríguez, Félix V., and Linda C. Delgado, eds. *Puerto Rican Women's History: New Perspectives.* Armonk, N.Y.: M. E. Sharpe, 1998.

Oboler, Suzanne, and Deena J. González, eds. *The Oxford Encyclopedia of Latinos and Latinas in the United States.* New York: Oxford University Press, 2005.

"Oral History and Puerto Rican Women" (special issue). *Oral History Review* 16, 2 (1988).

Ortiz, Altagracia, ed. *Puerto Rican Women and Work: Bridges in Transnational Labor.* Philadelphia: Temple University Press, 1996.

Romero, Mary, Pierrette Hondagneau-Sotelo, and Vilma Ortiz, eds. *Challenging Fronteras: Structuring Latina and Latino Lives in the U.S.: An Anthology of Readings.* New York: Routledge, 1997.

Ruiz, Vicki L., ed. *Las Obreras: The Politics of Work and Family.* Los Angeles: UCLA Chicano Studies Research Center Publications, 1999.

——, and Virginia Sánchez Korrol, eds. *Latina Legacies: Identity, Biography, and Community.* New York: Oxford University Press, 2005.

——, and Virginia Sánchez Korrol, eds. *Latinas in the United States: A Historical Encyclopedia*. Bloomington: Indiana University Press, 2006.

——, and Susan Tiano, eds. *Women on the U.S.-Mexico Border: Responses to Change*. Boston: Allen and Unwin, 1987.

Segura, Denise and Patricia Zavella, eds. *Women and Migration in the U.S.-Mexico Borderlands: A Reader*. Durham: Duke University Press, 2007.

Trujillo, Carla, ed. *Living Chicana Theory*. Berkeley: Third Woman Press, 1998.

Whalen, Carmen Teresa, and Víctor Vázquez-Hernández, eds. *The Puerto Rican Diaspora: Historical Perspectives*. Philadelphia: Temple University Press, 2005.

Books

Acosta, Teresa Palomo, and Ruthe Winegarten. *Las Tejanas: 300 Years of History*. Austin: University of Texas Press, 2003.

Anzaldúa, Gloria, and AnaLouise Keating. *Interviews = Entrevistas*. New York: Routledge, 2000.

Aparicio, Frances R. *Listening to Salsa: Gender, Latin Popular Music, and Puerto Rican Cultures*. Hanover, N.H.: University Press of New England, 1998.

Arrizón, Alicia. *Latina Performance Traversing the Stage*. Bloomington: Indiana University Press, 1999.

Baker, Ellen R. *On Strike and On Film: Mexican American Families and Blacklisted Filmmakers in Cold War America*. Chapel Hill: University of North Carolina Press, 2007.

Blackwelder, Julia. *Women of the Depression: Caste and Culture in San Antonio, 1929–1936*. College Station: Texas A&M University Press, 1984.

Cabeza de Baca, Fabiola. *We Fed Them Cactus*. Albuquerque: University of New Mexico Press, 1954.

Cantú, Norma. *Canícula*. Albuquerque: University of New Mexico Press, 1995.

Castillo, Debra A., and María Socorro Tabuenca Córdoba. *Border Women: Writing from La Frontera*. Minneapolis: University of Minnesota Press, 2002.

Chavez-Garcia, Miroslava. *Negotiating Conquest: Gender and Power in California, 1770s to 1880s*. Tucson: University of Arizona Press, 2004.

Cotera, Marta. *The Chicana Feminist*. Austin: Information Systems Development, 1977.

Deutsch, Sarah. *"No Separate Refuge": Culture, Class and Gender on an Anglo-Hispanic Frontier in the American Southwest, 1880–1940*. New York: Oxford University Press, 1987.

Doran, Terry, Janet Satterfield, and Chris State. *A Road Well-Traveled: Three Generations of Cuban American Women*. Fort Wayne, Ind.: Latin American Educational Center, 1988.

Esquibel, Catrióna Rueda. *With Her Machete in Her Hand: Reading Chicana Lesbians*. Austin: University of Texas Press, 2006.

Facio, Elisa. *Understanding Older Chicanas*. Thousand Oaks, Calif.: Sage Publications, 1995.

García, María Cristina. *Havana, USA: Cuban Exiles and Cuban Americans in South Florida, 1959–1994*. Berkeley: University of California Press, 1996.

Gaspar de Alba, Alicia. *Chicana Art Inside/Outside the Master's House: Cultural Politics and the CARA Exhibition*. Austin: University of Texas Press, 1998.

González, Deena J. *Refusing the Favor: Spanish-Mexican Women of Santa Fe, 1820–1880*. New York: Oxford University Press, 1999.

Gutiérrez, Ramón A. *When Jesus Came, The Corn Mothers Went Away: Power and Sexuality in New Mexico, 1500–1846*. Stanford: Stanford University Press, 1990.

Haas, Lisbeth. *Conquests and Historical Identities in California, 1769–1936*. Berkeley: University of California Press, 1995.

Hardy-Fanta, Carol. *Latina Politics, Latino Politics*. Philadelphia: Temple University Press, 1993.

Henkes, Robert. *Latin American Women Artists of the United States: The Works of 33 Twentieth-Century Women*. Jefferson, N.C.: McFarland, 1999.

Hondagneu-Sotelo, Pierrette. *Dómestica: Immigrant Workers Cleaning and Caring in the Shadows of Affluence*. Berkeley: University of California Press, 2001.

——. *Gendered Transitions: Mexican Experiences of Immigration*. Berkeley: University of California Press, 1994.

Hurtado, Albert L. *Intimate Frontiers: Sex, Gender, and Culture in Old California*. Albuquerque: University of New Mexico Press, 1999.

Lucas, María Elena. *Forged Under the Sun/Forjada Bajo el Sol: The Life of María Elena Lucas*. ed. Fran Leeper Buss. Ann Arbor: University of Michigan Press, 1993.

Martin, Patricia Preciado. *Songs My Mother Sang to Me: An Oral History of Mexican American Women*. Tucson: University of Arizona Press, 1992.

Medina, Lara. *Las Hermanas: Chicana/Latina Religious-Political Activism in the U.S. Catholic Church.* Philadelphia: Temple University Press, 2004.

Menjívar, Cecilia. *Fragmented Ties: Salvadoran Immigrant Networks in America.* Berkeley: University of California Press, 2000.

Oropeza, Lorena. *Raza sí!, guerra no!: Chicano Protest and Patriotism During the Viet Nam War Era.* Berkeley: University of California Press, 2005.

Pardo, Mary S. *Mexican American Women Activists: Identity and Resistance in Two Los Angeles Communities.* Philadelphia: Temple University Press, 1998.

Pedraza-Bailey, Sylvia. *Political and Economic Migrants in America: Cubans and Mexicans.* Austin: University of Texas Press, 1985.

Pérez, Emma. *The Decolonial Imaginary: Writing Chicanas into History.* Bloomington: Indiana University Press, 1999.

Pérez, Gina. *The Near Northwest Side Story: Migration, Displacement, and Puerto Rican Families.* Berkeley: University of California Press, 2004.

Ponce, Mary Helen. *Hoyt Street: An Autobiography.* Albuquerque: University of New Mexico Press, 1993.

Pulido, Laura. *Black, Brown, Yellow, and Left: Radical Activism in Los Angeles.* Berkeley: University of California Press, 2006.

Ramírez, Elizabeth C. *Chicanas/Latinas in American Theatre: A History of Performance.* Bloomington: Indiana University Press, 2000.

Rivas-Rodriguez, Maggie. *A Legacy Greater than Words: Stories of U.S. Latinos & Latinas of the WWII Generation.* Austin: University of Texas Press, 2006.

Rodríguez, Clara. *Latin Looks: Images of Latinas and Latinos in the U.S. Media.* Boulder: Westview Press, 1997.

Roth, Benita. *Separate Roads to Feminism: Black, Chicana, and White Feminist Movements in America's Second Wave.* Cambridge, UK: Cambridge University Press, 2004.

Ruiz, Vicki L. *From Out of the Shadows: Mexican Women in Twentieth-Century America.* New York: Oxford University Press, 1998.

——— . *Cannery Women, Cannery Lives: Mexican Women, Unionization, and the California Food Processing Industry, 1939–1950.* Albuquerque: University of New Mexico Press, 1987.

Saldívar-Hull, Sonia. *Feminism on the Border: Chicana Gender Politics and Literature.* Berkeley: University of California Press, 2000.

Sánchez, George. *Becoming Mexican American: Ethnicity, Culture, and Identity in Chicano Los Angeles, 1900–1965.* New York: Oxford University Press, 1993.

Sánchez, Marta Ester. *"Shakin' up" Race and Gender: Intercultural Connections in Puerto Rican, African American, and Chicano Narratives and Culture (1965–1995).* Austin: University of Texas Press, 2005.

Sánchez Korrol, Virginia. *From Colonia to Community: The History of Puerto Ricans in New York City.* Westport, Conn.: Greenwood Press, 1983.

Strachwitz, Chris, and James Nicolopulos, eds. *Lydia Mendoza: A Family Autobiography.* Houston: Arte Público Press, 1993.

Torres, Andrés. *Latinos in New England.* Philadelphia: Temple University Press, 2006.

Weber, Devra. *Dark Sweat, White Gold: California Farm Workers, Cotton and the New Deal.* Berkeley: University of California Press, 1994.

Whalen, Carmen Teresa. *From Puerto Rico to Philadelphia: Puerto Rican Workers and Postwar Economies.* Philadelphia: Temple University Press, 2001.

Williams, Norma. *The Mexican-American Family Tradition and Change.* Boston: G. K. Hall, 1990.

Yohn, Susan. *A Contest of Faiths: Missionary Women and Pluralism in the American Southwest.* Ithaca: Cornell University Press, 1995.

Zavella, Patricia. *Women's Work and Chicano Families: Cannery Workers of the Santa Clara Valley.* Ithaca: Cornell University Press, 1987.

Journal/anthology articles

Acosta-Belen, Edna, and Christine E. Bose. 2000. "U.S. Latina and Latin American Feminisms: Hemispheric Encounters." *Signs* 25, 4 (2000): 1113–19.

Aranda, Elizabeth M. 2003. "Global Care Work and Gendered Constraints: The Case of Puerto Rican Transmigrants." *Gender and Society* 17, 4: 609–26.

Arrizón, Alicia. "Monica Palacios: 'Latin Lezbo Comic.' " *Crossroads* 31 (May 1993): 25.

Benmayor, Rina. "Testimony, Action Research and Empowerment: Puerto Rican Women and Popular Education." In Sherna Berger Gluck and Daphne Patai, eds., *Women's Words: The Feminist Practice of Oral History.* New York: Routledge, 1991.

Benton-Cohen, Katherine. "Common Purposes, Worlds Apart: Mexican-American, Mormon, and Mid-western Women Homesteaders in Cochise County, Arizona." *Western Historical Quarterly*, 36,4 (winter 2005): 429–52.

Boone, Margaret S. "The Use of Traditional Concepts in the Development of New Urban Roles: Cuban Women in the United States." In Erika Bourguignon, ed., *A World of Women*. New York: Praeger, 1980.

Castañeda, Antonia I. "The Political Economy of Nineteenth Century Stereotypes of Californianas." In Michael R. Orñelas, ed., *Between the Conquests*. Dubuque, Iowa: Kendall Hunt Publishing, 1991.

Córdova, Teresa. "Roots and Resistance: The Emergent Writings of Twenty Years of Chicana Feminist Struggle." In Félix Padilla, ed., *Handbook of Hispanic Cultures in the United States: Sociology*. Houston: Arte Público Press, 1994.

Ellis, M., D. Conway, and A. J. Bailey. "The Circular Migration of Puerto Rican Women: Towards a Gendered Explanation." *International Migration* 34, 1 (1996): 31–64.

García, Mario T. "The Chicana in American History: The Mexican Women of El Paso, 1880–1920," *Pacific Historical Review* 49, 2 (1980): 315–37.

Géliga Vargas, Jocelyn A. "Expanding the Popular Culture Debates: Puertorriqueñas, Hollywood and Cultural Identity." *Studies in Latin American Popular Culture* 15 (1996): 155–73.

Gonzalez, Gabriela. "Carolina Munguia and Emma Tenayuca: The Politics of Benevolence and Radical Reform," *Frontiers: A Journal of Women's Studies* 24, 2 (2004): 200–29.

González, María C. "Cultural Conflict: Introducing the Queer in Mexican–American Literature Classes." In Linda Garber, ed., *Tilting the Tower: Lesbians, Teaching Queer Subjects*. New York: Routledge, 1994.

González, Yolanda Broyles. "Toward a Re–Vision of Chicano Theatre History: The Women of El Teatro Campesino." In Lynda Hart, ed., *Making a Spectacle: Feminist Essays on Contemporary Women's Theatre*. Ann Arbor: University of Michigan Press, 1989.

Hernández, Inés. "Sara Estela Ramírez: Sembradora." *Legacies*, 1989, 13–26.

Jones, Correa Michael. "Different Paths: Gender, Immigration and Political Participation." *International Migration Review* 32, 2 (summer 1998): 326–49.

Ledesma, Irene. "Texas Newspapers and Chicana Workers' Activism, 1919–1974." *Western Historical Quarterly* 26, 3 (autumn 1995): 309–31.

Menjívar, Cecilia. "Immigrant Kinship Networks and the Impact of the Receiving Context: Salvadorans in San Francisco in the Early 1990s." *Social Problems* 44 (1997): 104–23.

Ochoa, Gilda Laura. "Everyday Ways of Resistance and Cooperation: Mexican American Women Building Puentes with Immigrants." *Frontiers: A Journal of Women's Studies* 20, 1 (1999): 1–20.

Pessar, Patricia. "Sweatshop Workers and Domestic Ideologies: Dominican Women in the New York Apparel Industry." *International Journal of Urban and Regional Research* 18, 1 (March 1994): 127–42.

Prieto, Yolanda. "Cuban Women in New Jersey: Gender Relations and Change." In Donna R. Gabaccia, ed., *Seeking Common Ground: Multidisciplinary Studies of Immigrant Women in the United Sates*. Westport, Conn.: Greenwood Press, 1992.

Ramirez, Catherine S. " 'Saying Nothin': Pachucas and the Languages of Resistance," *Frontiers: A Journal of Women's Studies* 27, 3 (2007): 1–33.

Rich, B. Ruby, and Lourdes Arguelles. "Homosexuality, Homophobia, and Revolution: Notes Toward an Understanding of the Cuban Lesbian and Gay Male Experience." *Signs* 9, 4 (summer 1984), 11, 1 (autumn 1985), 683–99, 120–36.

Rose, Margaret. "The Community Service Organization, 1947–1962." In Joanne Meyerowitz, ed., *Not June Cleaver: Women and Gender in Postwar America, 1945–1960*. Philadelphia: Temple University Press, 1994.

Ruiz, Vicki L. "Nuestra América: Latino History as United States History." *Journal of American History* 93, 3 (2006): 655–72.

Salas, Elizabeth. "Ethnicity, Gender and Divorce: Issues in the 1922 Campaign by Adelina Otero-Warren for the U.S. House of Representatives." *New Mexico Historical Review* 70, 4 (1995): 367–82.

Segura, Denise. "Challenging the Chicano Text: Toward a More Inclusive Causa." *Signs* 26, 2 (2001): 541–50.

———. "Chicana and Mexican Immigrant Women at Work." *Gender and Society* 3, 1 (March 1989): 37–52.

Sosa Riddell, Adaljiza. "Chicanas and El Movimiento." *Aztlán* 5, 2 (1974): 155–65.

Warren, Alice E. Colon. "Puerto Rico: Feminism and Feminist Studies." *Gender and Society* 17, 5 (2003): 664–90.

Zavella, Patricia. "Reflections on Diversity among Chicanas." *Frontiers: A Journal of Women's Studies* 12, 2 (1991): 763–85.

Zentgraf, Kristine M. "Immigration and Women's Empowerment: Salvadorans in Los Angeles." *Gender and Society* 16, 5 (2001): 625–46.

Websites

Azúcar: The Life and Music of Celia Cruz
http:/americanhistory.si.edu/exhibitions/exhibition.cfm?key=38&exkey=353

California Cultures
http://www.calisphere.universityofcalifornia.edu/calcultures/

Latino Cultural Heritage Digital Archives.
http://digital-library.csun.edu/LatArch/

Recommended U.S. Latino Websites
http://www.public.iastate.edu/~savega/us_latin.htm

Tejano Voices
http:/libraries.uta.edu/tejanovoices/

U.S, Latinos and Latinas in World War II
http://utopia.utexas.edu/explore/latino/index.html

Native American Women

Compiled by Annette L. Reed

Anthologies

Albers, Patricia, and Beatrice Medicine, eds. *The Hidden Half: Studies of Plains Indian Women.* Washington, D.C.: University Press of America, 1983.

Bataille, Gretchen M., and Kathleen Mullen Sands, eds. *American Indian Women, Telling Their Lives.* Lincoln: University of Nebraska Press, 1984.

Erdrich, Heid E. and Laura Tohe, ed. *Sister Nations: Native American Women Writers on Community.* St. Paul, MN: Minnesota Historical Society Press, 2002.

Floristine, Kiyukanpi Renville. *Shaping Survival: Essays by Four American Indian Tribal Women.* Lanham: The Scarecrow Press, Inc, 2006.

Harlan, Teresa. *Watchful Eyes: Native American Women Artists,* 1994, Heard Museum, Phoenix, AZ. Exhibition catalog.

Hogan, Linda, ed. *Frontiers: Special Issue on Native American Women* 6, 3 (1981).

Shoemaker, Nancy, ed. *Negotiators of Change: Historical Perspectives on Native American Women.* New York: Routledge, 1995.

Books

Allen, Paula Gunn. *Pocahontas: Medicine Woman, Spy, Entrepreneur, Diplomat.* San Francisco: Harper, 2003.

——— . *The Sacred Hoop: Recovering the Feminine in American Indian Traditions.* Boston: Beacon Press, 1986.

Bahr, Diana Meyers. *Viola Martinez, California Paiute: Living in Two Worlds.* Norman: University of Oklahoma Press, 2003.

——— . *From Mission to Metropolis: Cupeno Indian Women in Los Angeles.* Norman: University of Oklahoma Press, 1993.

Bataille, Gretchen M. *American Indian Women: A Guide to Research.* New York: Garland Publishing, 1991.

——— , and Laurie Lisa. *Native American Women : A Biographical Dictionary.* New York: Routledge Press, 2001.

Bettelyoun, Susan Bordeaux, Josephine Waggoner, and Emily Levine. *With My Own Eyes: A Lakota Woman Tells Her People's History.* Lincoln: University of Nebraska Press, 1998.

Canfield, Gae Whitney. *Sarah Winnemucca of the Northern Paiutes.* Norman: University of Oklahoma Press, 1983.

Child, Brenda J. *Boarding School Seasons: American Indian Families, 1900–1940.* Lincoln: University of Nebraska Press, 1998.

Cobb, Amanda J. *Listening To Our Grandmothers' Stories: The Bloomfield Academy for Chickasaw Females, 1852–1949.* Lincoln: University of Nebraska Press, 2000.

Crow Dog, Mary, with Richard Erdoes. *Lakota Woman.* New York: Harper Perennial, 1990.

Cruickshank, Julie. *Life Lived like a Story: Life Stories of Three Yukon Native Elders.* Lincoln: University of Nebraska Press, 1990.

Cuera, Delphina. *The Autobiography of Delphina Cuero*. Ed. Florence Shipek. 1970. Reprint, Menlo Park, Calif.: Ballena Press, 1991.

Deloria, Ella Cara. *Waterlily*. Lincoln: University of Nebraska Press, 1988.

Dunn, Carolyn and Carol Comfort. *Through the Eye of the Deer: An Anthology of Native American Women Writers*. San Francisco: Aunt Lute Books, 1999.

Green, Rayna. *Women in American Indian Society*. Indians of North America. Gen. ed. Frank W. Porter Ill. New York: Chelsea House Publishers, 1992.

——. *Native American Women: A Contextual Bibliography*. Bloomington: Indiana University Press, 1983.

Hopkins, Sarah Winnemucca. *Life among the Piutes: Their Wrongs and Claims*. Ed. Mrs. Horace Mann. 1883. Reprint, Bishop, Calif.: Sierra Media Inc., 1969.

Horne, Esther Burnett, and Sally McBeth. *Essie's Story: The Life and Legacy of a Shoshone Teacher*. Lincoln: University of Nebraska Press, 1998.

Hungry Wolf, Beverly. *The Ways of My Grandmothers*. New York: Morrow, 1980.

Jacobs, Margaret D. *Engendered Encounters: Feminism and Pueblo Cultures, 1879–1934*. Lincoln: University of Nebraska Press, 1999.

Jones, David. *Sanapia: Commanche Medicine Woman*. New York: Holt, Rinehart and Winston, 1972.

Kessler, Donna J. *The Making of Sacagawea: A Euro-American Legend*. Tuscaloosa: University of Alabama Press, 1996.

Linderman, Frank B. *Pretty-Shield: Medicine Woman of the Crows*. 1932. Reprint, New York: John Day Co., 1972.

Lurie, Nancy. *Mountain Wolf Woman, Sister of Crashing Thunder*. Ann Arbor: University of Michigan Press, 1961.

Mankiller, Wilma, and Michael Mankiller. *Mankiller: A Chief and Her People*. New York: St. Martin's Press, 1993.

Marubbio, M. Elise. *The Indian Maiden Images of Native American Women in Film*. Lexington: University Press of Kentucky, 2006.

Mihesuah, Devon A. *Indigenous American Women: Decolonization, Empowerment, Activism*. Lincoln: University of Nebraska Press, 2003.

——. *Cultivating the Rosebuds: The Education of Women at the Cherokee Female Seminary, 1851–1909*. Urbana: University of Illinois Press, 1993.

Modesto, Ruby, and Guy Mount. *Not for Innocent Ears: Spiritual Traditions of a Desert Cahuilla Medicine Woman*. Arcata, Calif.: Sweetlight Books, 1980.

Osburn, Katherine. *Southern Ute Women: Autonomy and Assimilation on the Reservation, 1887–1934*. Albuquerque: University of New Mexico Press, 1998.

Perdue, Theda. *Sifters: Native American Women's Lives*. New York Oxford University Press, 2001.

——. *Cherokee Women: Gender and Culture, 1700–1835*. Lincoln: University of Nebraska Press, 1998.

Pesantubbee, Michelene E. *Choctaw Women in a Chaotic World: The Clash of Cultures in the Colonial Southeast*. Albuquerque: University of New Mexico Press, 2005.

Qoyawayma, Polingaysi Elizabeth White. *No Turning Back: A Hopi Indian Woman's Struggle to Live in Two Worlds*. Ed. Vada F. Carlson. Albuquerque: University of New Mexico Press, 1964.

Ross, Luana. *Inventing the Savage: The Social Construction of Native American Criminality*. Austin: University of Texas Press, 1998.

Sarris, Greg. *Mabel McKay: Weaving the Dream*. Berkeley: University of California Press, 1994.

Senier, Siobhan. *Voices of American Indian Assimilation and Resistance: Helen Hunt Jackson, Sarah Winnemucca, and Victoria Howard*. Norman: University of Oklahoma Press, 2001.

Shepherd, Alice. *In My Own Words: Stories, Songs, and Memories of Grace McKibbin, Wintu*. Berkeley: Heyday Press, 1997.

Smith, Andrea. *Conquest: Sexual Violence and American Indian Genocide*. Cambridge, Mass.: South End Press, 2005.

St. Pierre, Mark. *Madonna Swan: A Lakota Woman's Story*. Norman: University of Oklahoma Press, 1991.

——, and Tilda Long Soldier. *Walking in the Sacred Manner: Healers, Dreamers, and Pipe Carriers—Medicine Women of the Plains Indians*. New York: Simon and Schuster, 1995.

Stockel, H. Henrietta. *Chiricahua Apache Women and Children: Safekeepers of the Heritage, Elma Dill Russell Spencer Series in the West and Southwest, No. 21*. College Station: Texas A&M University Press, 2000.

Talamantez, Ines and Robin May Schott. *Indigenous Women in the Americas: Feminist Philosophy and the Problem of Evil*. Bloomington: Indiana University Press, 2003.

Thompson, Lucy [Che-na wah Weitch-ah-wah]. *To The American Indian: Reminiscences of a Yurok Woman*. 1916. Reprint, Berkeley: Heyday Books, 1991.

Udell, Louise, ed. *Me and Mine: The Life Story of Helen Sekaquaptewa*. Tucson: University of Arizona Press, 1969.

Van Kirk, Sylvia. *Many Tender Ties: Women in Fur-Trade Society, 1670–1870.* Norman: University of Oklahoma Press, 1980.

Voget, Fred W., assisted by Mary K. Mee. *They Call Me Agnes: A Crow Narrative Based on the Life of Agnes Yellowtail Deernose.* Norman: University of Oklahoma Press, 1995.

Wallis, Velma. *Raising Ourselves: A Gwitch'in Coming of Age Story from the Yukon River.* Kenmore: Epicenter Press, 2002.

Youst, Lionel. *She's Tricky like Coyote: Annie Miner Peterson, an Oregon Coast Indian Woman.* Norman: University of Oklahoma Press, 1997

Journal/anthology articles

Almeida, Deirdre A. "The Hidden Half: A History of Native American Women's Education." *Harvard Educational Review* 67, 4 (1997): 757–71.

Begay, R. Cruz. "Changes in Childbirth Knowledge." *American Indian Quarterly* 28, 3–4 (summer–fall 2004): 550–66.

Carpio, Myla Vicenti. "The Lost Generation: American Indian Women and Sterilization Abuse." *Social Justice* 31, 4 (2004): 40–54.

Castle, Elizabeth A. " 'Keeping One Foot in the Community': Intergenerational Indigenous Women's Activism from the Local to the Global (and Back Again)." *American Indian Quarterly* 27, 3–4 (summer 2003): 840–61.

Cotera, Maria Eugenia. " 'All My Relatives Are Noble': Recovering the Feminine in Ella Cara Deloria's *Waterlily.*" *American Indian Quarterly* 28, 1–2 (winter 2004): 523–32.

Denetdale, Jennifer Nez. "Chairmen, President, and Princesses: The Navajo Nation, Gender, and the Politics of Tradition." *Wicazo Sa Review* 21, 1 (spring 2006): 9–29.

——. "Representing Changing Woman: A Review Essay on Navajo Women." *American Indian Culture and Research Journal* 25, 3 (summer 2001): 1–26.

Donaldson, Laura E. "Red Woman, White Dreams: Searching for Sacagawea." *Feminist Studies* 32, 3 (fall 2006): 523–34.

Dunaway, Wilma A. "Rethinking Cherokee Acculturation: Women's Resistance to Agrarian Capitalism and Cultural Change, 1800–1838." *American Indian Culture and Research Journal* 21, 1 (1997): 155–92.

Foster, M. H. "Lost Women of the Matriarchy: Iroquois Women in the Historical Literature." *American Indian Culture and Research Journal* 19 (1995): 121–40.

Gardner, Susan. " 'Though it Broke My Heart to Cut Some Bits I Fancied': Ella Deloria's Original Design for *Waterlily.*" *American Indian Quarterly* 27, 3–4 (summer 2003): 667–96.

Green, Rayna. "The Pocahontas Perplex: The Image of Indian Women In Popular Culture." *Massachusetts Review* 16 (autumn 1975): 678–714.

Jaimes-Guerrero, Annette. "Civil Rights versus Sovereignty: Native American Women Life and Land Struggles." In Chandra and Jacqui Alexander Mohanty, eds., *Feminist Genealogies, Colonial Legacies. Democratic Futures.* New York: Routledge Press, 1997.

——. "American Indian Women: Center of Indigenous Resistance." In Annette Jaimes, ed., *The State of Native America.* Boston: South End Press, 1992.

Kidwell, Clara Sue. "Indian Women as Cultural Mediators." *Ethnohistory* 39, 2 (1992): 97–107.

Krouse, Susan Applegate. "What Came Out of the Takeovers: Women's Activism and the Indian Community School of Milwaukee." *American Indian Quarterly* 27, 3/4 (summer 2003): 533–47.

——, and Heather Howard-Bobiwash. "Keeping the Campfires Going: Urban American Indian Women's Community Work and Activist. (Preface)." *The American Indian Quarterly* 27, 3/4 (summer–fall 2003): 489–91.

Lacourt, Jeanne A. "Descriptions of a Tree Outside the Forest: An Indigenous Woman's Experiences in the Academy." *American Indian Quarterly* 27, 1–2 (winter 2003): 296–307.

Langston, Donna Hightower. "American Indian Women's Activism in the 1960s and 1970s." *Hypatia* 18, 2 (spring 2003): 114–34.

Lawrence, Jane. "The Indian Health Service and the Sterilization of Native American Women." *American Indian Quarterly* 24, 3 (summer 2000): 400–19.

Lobo, Susan. "Urban Clan Mothers: Key Households in Cities. (Case Study of Native American Women in San Francisco, California)." *American Indian Quarterly* 27, 3–4 (summer–fall 2003): 505–23.

Loupe, Leleua. "Cultural and Educational Preservation Among Southern California Native Women." *Journal of the West* 43, 3 (summer 2004): 61–71.

Mann, Barbara A. "The Lynx in Time: Haudenosaunee Women's Traditions and History." *American Indian Quarterly* 21, 3 (1997): 423–49.

Medicine, B. "Native American Indigenous Women and Cultural Domination." *American Indian Culture and Research Journal,* 17, 3 (1993): 722–43.

Mihesuah, Devon A. "A Few Cautions at the Millennium on the Merging of Feminist Studies with American Indian Women's Studies." *Signs* 25, 4 (summer 2000): 1247.

——— . "Commonality of Difference: American Indian Women and History." *American Indian Quarterly* 20, 1 (1996): 15–27.

Murphy, Lucy Eldersveld. "Public Mothers: Native American and Metis Women as Creole Mediators in the Nineteenth-Century Midwest." *Journal of Women's History* 14, 4 (winter 2003): 142–66.

Ogden, Stormy. "Ex-prisoner Pomo Woman Speaks Out. (Kashaya Pomo, Native American Women Social Conditions)." *Social Justice* 31, 4 (winter 2004): 63–70.

Patterson, Victoria D. "Indian Life in the City: A Glimpse of the Urban Experience of Pomo Women in 1930s." *California History* 71 (fall 1992): 402–31.

Pugh, Eneida Sanderson. "Rhoda Strong Lowry: The Swamp Queen of Scuffletown." *American Indian Culture and Research Journal* 26, 1 (winter 2002): 67 82.

Ramirez, Renya. "Julia's Story: An Indigenous Woman Between Nations." *Frontiers: A Journal of Women's Studies* 23, 3 (2002): 65–84.

Round, Phillip H. "There Was More to It, but that Is All I Can Remember: The Persistence of History and the Autobiography of Delfina Cuero." *American Indian Quarterly* 21, 2 (1997): 171–93.

Roundtree, Helen C. "Powhatan Indian Women: The People Captain John Smith Barely Saw." *Ethnohistory* 45, 1 (1998): 1–29.

Shoemaker, Nancy. "The Rise and Fall of Iroquois Women." *Journal of Women's History* 2 (1991): 39–54.

Smith, Andrea and Luana Ross (eds.). "Native Women and State Violence." *Social Justice—Special Edition* 31, 4 (2004).

Torpy, Sally J. "Native American Women and Coerced Sterilization: On the Trail of Tears in the 1970s." *American Indian Culture and Research Journal* 24, 2 (spring 2000): 1–2.

Totten, Gary. "Zitkala-Sa and the Problem of Regionalism: Nations, Narratives, and Critical Traditions." *American Indian Quarterly* 29, 1–2 (winter 2005): 84–123, 355.

Trucks-Bordeaux, Tammy. "Academic Massacres: The Story of Two American Indian Women and Their Struggle to Survive Academia." *American Indian Quarterly* 27, 1–2 (winter 2003): 416–19.

Vernon, Irene S. "Facts and Myths of AIDS and Native American Women." *American Indian Culture and Research Journal* 24, 3 (summer 2000): 93–111.

Waters, Anne. "Introduction: Special Issue on 'Native American Women, Feminism, and Indigenism'." *Hypatia* 18, 2 (spring 2003): 12.

Welch, Deborah. "American Indian Women: Reaching Beyond the Myth." In Colin G. Galloway, ed., *New Directions in American Indian History.* Norman: University of Oklahoma Press, 1988.

Wilson, Angela C. "Grandmother to Granddaughter: Generations of Oral History in a Dakota Family." *American Indian Quarterly* 20, 1 (1996): 7–13.

Wright, Mary C. "The Woman's Lodge: Constructing Gender on the Nineteenth-Century Pacific Northwest Plateau." *Frontiers—A Journal of Women's Studies* 24, 1 (Jan. 2003): 1–20.

Websites

American Women: A Gateway to Library of Congress Resources for the Study of Women's History and Culture in the United States
http://memory.loc.gov/ammem/awhhtml/index.html

American Women's History: A Research Guide
http://frank.mtsu.edu~kmiddlet/history/women/wh-indn.html

Indianz.Com: Your Internet Resource
http://www.indianz.com

Indigenous Women's Network
http://www.indigenouswomen.org

Native American Women Photographers as Storytellers
http://www.cla.purdue.edu/WAAW/Jensen/NAW.html

Native American Women Playwrights Archive
http://staff.lib.muohio.edu/nawpa

Permissions Acknowledgments

Every attempt was made to obtain permission for images and articles used in this book.

Estelle B. Freedman, "Race and the Politics of Identity in U.S. Feminism," Chapter Four of *No Turning Back: The History of Feminism and the Future of Women* (New York: Ballantine Books, 2002): 73–94. *Reprinted with permission of the publisher.*

Nan Alamilla Boyd, "Bodies in Motion: Lesbian and Transsexual Histories," in Duberman, ed., *A Queer World: The Center for Lesbian and Gay Studies Reader* (New York: NYU Press, 1997). Copyright 1997 Nan Alamilla Boyd.

Tessie Liu, "Teaching the Differences among Women from a Historical Perspective: Rethinking Race and Gender as Social Categories," reprinted from *Women's Studies International Forum*, 14, 4: 265–76 (1991). *Reprinted with permission of the publisher.*

James F. Brooks, " 'This Evil Extends Especially to the Feminine Sex': Captivity and Identity in New Mexico, 1700–1846," in Jameson and Armitage, eds., *Writing the Range: Race, Class, and Culture in the Women's West* (Norman: University of Oklahoma Press, 1997): 97–121. © 1997 by the University of Oklahoma Press. *Reprinted with permission.*

Jennifer L. Morgan, " 'Deluders and Seducers of Each Other:' Gender and the Changing Nature of Resistance," Chapter Six of *Laboring Women: Reproduction and Gender in New World Slavery* (Philadelphia: University of Pennsylvania Press, 2004): 166–95. *Reprinted with permission of the publisher.*

Stephanie H. M. Camp, "The Pleasures of Resistance: Enslaved Women and Body Politics in the Plantation South, 1830–1861," *The Journal of Southern History*, 68, 3 (August 2002): 533–72. *Reprinted with permission of the publisher.*

Miroslava Chávez-García, "Guadalupe Trujillo: Race, Culture and Justice in Mexican Los Angeles," in Davis and Igler, eds., *The Human Tradition in California* (Wilmington, DE: Scholarly Resources, 2002): 31–46. *Reprinted with permission of the publisher.*

Jeanne Boydston, "To Earn Her Daily Bread: Housework and Antebellum Working-Class Subsistence," *Radical History Review*, 35 (April 1986): 7–25. Copyright 1986, MARHO: The Radical Historians Organization, Inc. All rights reserved. *Reprinted with permission of the publisher.*

Alice Fahs, "The Feminized Civil War: Gender, Northern Popular Literature, and the Memory of War, 1861–1900," *The Journal of American History*, 85, 4 (March 1999): 1461–94. *Reprinted with permission of the publisher.*

Elsa Barkley Brown, "To Catch the Vision of Freedom: Reconstructing Southern Black Women's Political History, 1865–1880," in Ann D. Gordon et al., eds., *African American Women and the Vote, 1837–1965* (Amherst: University of Massachusetts Press, 1997). *Reprinted with permission of the publisher.*

Devon A. Mihesuah, " 'Too Dark to be Angels': The Class System Among the Cherokees at the Female Seminary," *American Indian Culture and Research Journal*, 15, 1 (1991): 29–52. *Reprinted with permission of the publisher.*

Paige Raibmon, "The Practice of Everyday Colonialism: Indigenous Women at Work in the Hop Fields and Tourist Industry of Puget Sound," *LABOR*, 3, 3 (fall 2006): 23–56. *Reprinted with permission of the publisher.*

Linda Gordon, "Black and White Visions of Women's Welfare Activism, 1890–1945," reprinted with permission of the *Journal of American History* 78 (1991). *Reprinted with permission of the publisher.*

Donna R. Gabaccia and Vicki L. Ruiz, "Migrations and Destinations: Reflections on the Histories of U.S. Immigrant Women," *Journal of American Ethnic History*, 26, 1 (fall 2006): 3–19. *Reprinted with permission of the publisher.*

Judy Yung, "The Social Awakening of Chinese American Women as Reported in *Chung Sai Yat Po*, 1900–1911," *Chinese America: History and Perspectives*, 2 (fall 1988). *Reprinted with permission of the author.* Please see the author's larger work, *Unbound Feet: A Social History of Chinese Women in San Francisco* for additional material.

Ellen Dubois, "Working Women, Class Relations, and Suffrage Militance: Harriot Stanton Blatch and the New York Suffrage Movement, 1894–1909," *Journal of American History*, 74, 1 (June, 1987): 34–58. *Reprinted with permission of the publisher.*

Evelyn Brooks Higginbotham, "In Politics to Stay: Women Leaders and Party Politics in the 1920s," in Tilly and Gurin, eds., *Women, Politics and Change*, Russell Sage Foundation, 1990. © Russell Sage Foundation. *Reprinted with permission of the publisher.*

Peggy Pascoe, "Miscegenation Law, Court Cases, and Ideologies of 'Race' in Twentieth-Century America," *Journal of American History*, 83, 1 (1996). *Reprinted with permission of the publisher.*

Joanne Meyerowitz, "Sexual Geography and Gender Economy: The Furnished-Room Districts of Chicago, 1890–1930," *Gender and History*, 2 (1990): 274–96. *Reprinted with permission of the publisher.*

Kathy Peiss, "Making Faces: The Cosmetics Industry and the Cultural Construction of Gender, 1890–1930," *Genders*, 7: 143–69. *Reprinted by permission of the author.*

Vicki L. Ruiz, " 'Star Struck': Acculturation, Adolescence, and Mexican American Women, 1920–1950," in West and Petrick, eds., *Small Worlds: Children and Adolescents in America* (Lawrence: University of Kansas Press, 1992). *Reprinted with permission of the publisher.*

Valerie J. Matsumoto, "Japanese American Women and the Creation of Urban Nisei Culture in the 1930s," in Blake and Allmendinger, eds., *Over The Edge: Remapping the American West* (Berkeley: University of California Press, 1999): 291–306. *Reprinted with permission of the publisher.*

Virginia Sánchez Korrol, "In Search of Unconventional Women: Histories of Puerto Rican Women in Religious Vocations Before Mid-Century," *Oral History Review*, 16, 2 (1988): 47–64. *Reprinted with permission of the publisher.*

Annelise Orleck, " 'We Are that Mythical Thing Called the Public': Militant Housewives during the Great Depression." This article is a revised version of an article originally published in *Feminist Studies*, 19, 1 (spring 1993): 147–72. *Reprinted with permission of the publisher, Feminist Studies, Inc.*

Devra Anne Weber, "*Raiz Fuerte*: Oral History and Mexican Farmworkers," *Oral History Review*, 17, 2 (1989): 47–62. © 1989, Oral History Association. *Reprinted with permission of Oral History Review.*

Evelyn Nakano Glenn, "From Servitude to Service Work: Historical Continuities in the Racial Division of Paid Reproductive Labor," *Signs*, 18, 1 (1992). *Reprinted by permission of the University of Chicago Press.*

Jacquelyn Dowd Hall, "Open Secrets: Memory, Imagination, and the Refashioning of Southern Identity," *American Quarterly* 50, 1 (1998): 109–24. © 1998, the American Studies Association. *Reprinted by permission of the Johns Hopkins University Press.*

Judy Tzu-Chun Wu, "Was Mom Chung a 'Sister Lesbian'? Asian American Gender Experimentation and Interracial Homoeroticism," *Journal of Women's History* 13, 1 (spring 2001): 58–82. *Reprinted with permission of the publisher.*

Sherrie Tucker, "Telling Performances: Jazz History Remembered and Remade by the Women in the Band," *Women and Music*, vol. 1 (1997): 12–23, reprinted in *Oral History Review*, 26 (1999): 67–84. *Reprinted by permission of Oral History Review.*

Daniel Horowitz, "Rethinking Betty Friedan and *The Feminine Mystique*: Labor Union Radicalism and Feminism in Cold War America," *American Quarterly*, 48 (1996): 1–38. © 1996, the American Studies Association. *Reprinted by permission of the Johns Hopkins University Press.*

Elaine Tyler May, "Non Mothers as Bad Mothers: Infertility and the 'Maternal Instinct,' " in Ladd-Taylor and Lauri Umansky, eds., *"Bad" Mothers: The Politics of Blame in Twentieth-Century America* (New York: New York University Press, 1998): 198–219. *Reprinted with permission of the publisher.*

Laila Haidarali, "Polishing Brown Diamonds: African American Women, Popular Magazines, and the Advent of Modeling in Early Postwar America," in *Journal of Women's History* 17, 1 (spring 2005): 10–37. *Reprinted with permission of the publisher.*

Cynthia Griggs Fleming, " 'More than a Lady': Ruby Doris Smith Robinson and Black Woman's Leadership in the Student Nonviolent Coordinating Committee," *Journal of Women's History* 4, 3: 204–23. *Reprinted by permission of the publisher.*

Catherine Ceniza Choy, "Towards Trans-Pacific Social Justice: Women and Protest in Filipino American

History," *Journal of Asian American Studies,* October 2005: 293–307. *Reprinted with permission of the Johns Hopkins University Press.*

Alicia Camacho Schmidt, "Migrant Melancholia: Emergent Discourses of Mexican Migrant Traffic in Transnational Space," *South Atlantic Quarterly,* 195, 4 (fall 2006): 831–67. Copyright, 2006, Duke University Press. All rights reserved. *Reprinted with permission of the publisher.*

Lara Deeb, "Silencing Religiosity: Secularity and Arab American Feminisms," *The MIT Electronic Journal of Middle East Studies,* 5 (spring 2005): 202–7.

Contributors

Zakiya Adair is a Ph.D. candidate in Women Studies at the University of Washington. Her areas of focus are: late nineteenth-century–early twentieth-century women's cultural and social history and African American history. Zakiya's dissertation project is on representations of modernity, colonial sexualities, and race as represented in Black women's cultural production abroad in France and England during the interwar period. Her dissertation chair is Dr. Shirley Yee.

Nan Alamilla Boyd has a Ph.D. in American Civilization from Brown University. She has published widely in queer studies and is the author of *Wide Open Town: A History of Queer San Francisco to 1965* (2003). She is currently Chair of Women Studies at San Francisco State University.

Jeanne Boydston is Robinson-Edwards Professor of American History at the University of Wisconsin-Madison, where she teaches in the Program on Gender and Women's History. She is the author of *Home and Work: Housework, Wages, and the Ideology of Labor in the Early Republic*, among other books and essays on gender in the early American republic.

James F. Brooks is president and CEO of the School for Advanced Research on the Human Experience (SAR) in Santa Fe, New Mexico. His 2002 monograph *Captives & Cousins: Slavery, Kinship, and Community in the Southwest Borderlands* won eight major awards, including the Turner, Bancroft, and Parkman prizes. He also edited *Confounding the Color Line: the Indian-Black Experience in North America* (2002); co-edited *Women & Gender in the North American West* (2004); and a volume in press, *Small Worlds: Method, Meaning and Narrative in Microhistory*. He is at work on a new book to be published by W. W. Norton entitled *Mesa of Sorrows: Archaeology, Prophecy, and the Ghosts of Awat'ovi Pueblo*.

Elsa Barkley Brown is Associate Professor of History and Women's Studies at the University of Maryland. She is co-editor of the two-volume *Major Problems in African-American History* (2000) and the two-volume *Black Women in America: An Historical Encyclopedia* (1993). Her articles have appeared in *Signs, Feminist Studies, History Workshop, Sage, Public Culture*, and *The Journal of Urban History*. Brown currently serves on the Executive Council of the Southern Historical Association and on the editorial boards of the *Journal of Women's History* and the *Virginia Magazine of History and Biography*.

Stephanie M. H. Camp is Associate Professor of History at the University of Washington. She was co-editor of *New Studies in the History of American Slavery*, and her first book, *Closer to Freedom: Enslaved Women's Everyday Resistance in the Plantation South, 1830–1865*, was published in 2004. Camp is currently at work on a project which will explore the lives, interactions, and representations of black (African and American) and white (English and American) women in Jamaica and Virginia in the eighteenth and nineteenth centuries.

Miroslava Chávez-García is an Associate Professor in the Chicana/o Studies Program at the University of California at Davis. She has published *Negotiating Conquest: Gender and Power in California, 1770s to 1880s* (2004) and articles on gender, patriarchy, and the law in nineteenth-century California. Her current research focuses on youth, juvenile justice, race, and science in early twentieth-century California.

Catherine Ceniza Choy is an Associate Professor of Ethnic Studies at the University of California, Berkeley. She is the author of *Empire of Care: Nursing and Migration in Filipino American History* (2003). She is writing a book on the history of Asian international adoption in the United States.

Lara Deeb is an anthropologist and Assistant Professor of Women's Studies at the University of California at Irvine. She is the author of *An Enchanted Modern: Gender and Public Piety in Shi'i Lebanon* (2006).

Ellen Carol DuBois, who was co-editor of the first three editions of *Unequal Sisters*, is a professor of history at UCLA, where her specialty is U.S. history. She has published extensively on the U.S. woman suffrage movement and is now writing on the history of international feminism between 1920 and 1975. She is also the co-author, with Lynn Dumenil, of *Through Women's Eyes: An American History with Documents*.

Alice Fahs is Associate Professor of History at the University of California, Irvine. Her publications include *The Imagined Civil War: Popular Literature of the North and South, 1861–1865; The Memory of the Civil War in American Culture*, co-edited with Joan Waugh; and an edition of *Hospital Sketches* by Louisa May Alcott. She is also a co-author of the textbook *Liberty, Equality, Power: A History of the American People*. Specializing in cultural history and gender history, she is currently at work on a book titled *Newspaper Women and the Making of the Modern, 1885–1918*.

Cynthia Griggs Fleming is Associate Professor of History at the University of Tennessee, Knoxville. She is the author of *Soon We Will Not Cry: The Liberation of Ruby Doris Smith Robinson*, and co-author of *The Chicago Handbook for College Teachers*. She is currently writing a book that examines the impact of the civil rights movement on an Alabama Black Belt county.

Estelle B. Freedman, the Edgar E. Robinson Professor in U.S. History at Stanford University, is the author of *No Turning Back: The History of Feminism and the Future of Women* (2002) and the co-author (with John D'Emilio) of *Intimate Matters: A History of Sexuality in America* (1988, rev. ed. 1997). She has also written several books on women's prison reform. Her most recent book, *Feminism, Sexuality and Politics* (2006), collects her major essays. She is currently writing about the politics of rape in American history.

Donna R. Gabaccia is Professor of History and Director of the Immigration History Research Center at the University of Minnesota. She is the author of many books and articles on immigrant life in the U.S. and on Italian migration worldwide. She is currently directing a multi-disciplinary research project on gender ratios among global migrants, past and present.

Evelyn Nakano Glenn is Professor of Gender and Women's Studies and of Ethnic Studies and Founding Director of the Center for Race and Gender at the University of California, Berkeley. She received the Jessie Bernard Award from the American Sociological Association for career achievement. Her book, *Unequal Freedom, How Race and Gender Shaped American Citizenship and Labor* won several awards including the Oliver Cromwell Cox Book Award of the American Sociological Association Section on Racial and Ethnic Minorities and Distinguished Contribution to Scholarship Award, Pacific Sociological Association.

Linda Gordon is Professor of History at New York University As a domestic violence expert, she serves on the Departments of Justice/Health and Human Services Advisory Council on Violence Against Women. Her 1999 book, *The Great Arizona Orphan Abduction* was the winner of the Bancroft prize for best book in American history. Gordon's most recent book, *Dear Sisters*, edited with Ros Baxandall (Basic Books, 2000), offers an historical introduction to the women's movement of the 1970s through essays and documents.

Laila Haidarali recently completed her doctoral dissertation entitled, " 'The Vampingest Vamp is a Brownskin': Colour, Sex, Beauty and African American Womanhood, 1920–1954" at York University in Toronto. Her article " 'Is It True What They Say About Models?': Modeling African American Womanhood on the Eve of the Civil Rights Era" is forthcoming in *Atlantis: A Women's Studies Journal*. Laila is also a contributor to a forthcoming edited collection entitled *Fashioning Models: Images, Text and Industry*.

Jacquelyn Dowd Hall is the Julia Cherry Spruill Professor of History and Director of the Southern Oral History Program at the University of North Carolina at Chapel Hill. She is the founding president of the Labor and Working Class History Association (1999–01) and past president of the Southern Historical Association (2001–02) and the Organization of American Historians (2003–04). She is the author of *Revolt Against Chivalry: Jessie Daniel Ames and the Women's Campaign Against Lynching* (1979, 1993) and co-author of *Like a Family: The Making of a Southern Cotton Mill World* (1987, 2000). Her most recent article, "The Long Civil Rights Movement and the Political Uses of the Past," *Journal of American History* (March 2005) was included in *Best Articles in American History*, 2007.

Evelyn Brooks Higginbotham is the Victor S. Thomas Professor of History and of African and African American Studies at Harvard University. She is co-editor of *African American Lives* (2004), as well as *The Harvard Guide to African-American History* (2001). Her 1993 book, *Righteous Discontent: The Women's Movement in the Black Baptist Church: 1880–1920* has won book prizes from the American Historical Association, the American Academy of Religion, the Association of Black Women Historians, and the Association for Research on Non-Profit and Voluntary Organizations. Her article, "African-American Women's History and the Meta-language of Race," *Signs* (Winter 1992) won the Best Article prize of the Berkshire Conference of Women Historians in 1993.

Daniel Horowitz is Mary Huggins Gamble Professor of American Studies at Smith College. He has written extensively on the history of consumer culture and social criticism in the United States. Among his publications are *Betty Friedan and the Making of The Feminine Mystique: The American Left, The Cold War, Modern Feminism* (1998) and *The Anxieties of Affluence: Critiques of American Consumer Culture, 1939–1979* (2003).

Shirley Jennifer Lim is an Associate Professor of history at SUNY Stony Brook. Her book, *A Feeling of Belonging: Asian American Women's Public Culture, 1930–1960* (NYU 2006) examines Chinese American, Japanese American, and Filipina American women's beauty pageants, sororities, film careers, and magazines. She is currently researching the careers of Josephine Baker and Anna May Wong.

Tessie P. Liu is Professor of History at Northwestern University. In 1994 she published *The Weaver's Knot: The Contradictions of Class Struggle and Family Solidarity in Western France, 1750 to 1914*. Her current research focuses on the role of gender in the historical construction of the concept of race during the French Revolution. She also has published articles on race and multiculturalism in women's history, and has recently joined *Feminist Studies* as an editor.

Valerie J. Matsumoto is Associate Professor of History at the University of California Los Angeles. She co-edited *Over the Edge: Remapping The American West*, and served as guest editor of *Amerasia Journal* 26:1 (2000) special issue, "Histories and Historians in the Making." Matsumoto's research interests include Asian American History, U.S. Twentieth Century, Women's History, and Oral History.

Elaine Tyler May is Professor of American Studies and History at the University of Minnesota. Her publications include *Great Expectations: Marriage and Divorce in Post-Victorian America* (1980); *Homeward Bound: American Families in the Cold War Era* (1988 and 1999); *Pushing the Limits: American Women, 1940–1961* (1996); and *Barren in the Promised Land: Childless Americans and the Pursuit of Happiness* (1997). She is also co-author, with Jacqueline Jones, Peter Wood, Thomas Borstelmann, and Vicki Ruiz, of a college-level textbook, *Created Equal: A Social and Political History of the United States*.

Joanne Meyerowitz is Professor of History and American Studies at Yale University, where she teaches courses on the history of gender and sexuality. She is the author of *How Sex Changed: A History of Transsexuality in the United States* and *Women Adrift: Independent Wage Earners in Chicago, 1880 and 1930*, and the editor of *Not June Cleaver: Women and Gender in Postwar America, 1945–1960* and *History and September 11ᵗʰ*. From 1999 to 2004, she served as the editor of the *Journal of American History*.

Devon Mihesuah is a citizen of the Choctaw Nation of Oklahoma and is the Cora Lee Beers Price Professor in the Center for Indigenous Nations Studies at the University of Kansas. An historian by training, she was Editor of the *American Indian Quarterly* from 1998 to 2007 and is the author of a dozen award-winning books on indigenous issues, most recently *Recovering Our Ancestors' Gardens: Indigenous Recipes and Guide to Diet and Fitness; So You Want to Write About American Indians? A Guide for Scholars, Students and Writers;* and *American Indigenous Women: Decolonization, Empowerment, Activism*.

Jennifer L. Morgan is Associate Professor of Social and Cultural Analysis in the American Studies department at New York University. She is the author of *Laboring Women: Gender and Reproduction in New World Slavery* (2004) as well as numerous articles. Her research interests include Early African American History, Comparative Slavery, and Histories of Racial Ideology.

Annelise Orleck is the author of several books and numerous articles on U.S. women's activism including: *Common Sense and a Little Fire: Women and Working Class Politics in the United States* (1995) and *Storming Caesars Palace: How Black Mothers Fought Their Own War on Poverty*

(2005). She is also co-editor of *The Politics of Motherhood: Activist Voices from Left to Right* (1997). She teaches History, Women's and Gender Studies and Jewish Studies at Dartmouth College.

Peggy Pascoe is Associate Professor and Beekman Chair of Northwest and Pacific History at the University of Oregon. Her previous publications include *Relations of Rescue: The Search for Female Moral Authority in the American West, 1874–1939*. She is currently finishing *What Comes Naturally*, a book on miscegenation law in U.S. history.

Kathy Peiss is the Nichols Professor of American History at the University of Pennsylvania. She is the author of *Cheap Amusements: Working Women and Leisure in Turn-of-the-Century New York, Hope in a Jar: The Making of America's Beauty Culture*, and *Major Problems in the History of American Sexuality*.

Paige Raibmon is Associate Professor of History at the University of British Columbia in Vancouver, Canada. She is the author of *Authentic Indians: Episodes of Encounter on the Late-Nineteenth-Century Northwest Coast* (Duke University Press, 2005).

Annette L. Reed is Director of Native American Studies at California State University, Sacramento. Her research interests include Native American History, Women of Color, California History, and Women's History.

Vicki L. Ruiz is Professor of History and Chicano/Latino Studies at the University of California, Irvine and Interim Dean, School of Humanities. She is the author of *Cannery Women, Cannery Lives* (1987) and *From Out of the Shadows: Mexican Women in Twentieth Century America*, (1998). She is the co-editor of *American Dreaming, Global Realities* (with Donna R. Gabaccia). With Virginia Sánchez Korrol, she co-edited *Latina Legacies* (2005) and *Latinas in the United States: A Historical Encyclopedia* (2006). Past president of the Organization of American Historians and the Berkshire Conference of Women's Historians, she is currently president of the American Studies Association.

Virginia Sánchez Korrol is Professor Emerita at Brooklyn College, City University of New York, and directs the Latinas in History digital project. Among her many publications, the most recent are the three volume *Latinas in the United States: A Historical Encyclopedia*, and *Latina Legacies: Identity, Biography and Community*, both co-edited with Vicki L. Ruiz.

Alicia Schmidt Camacho is Assistant Professor of American Studies at Yale University and has served as the Director of Undergraduate Studies for the Program in Ethnicity, Race and Migration. She is the author of the forthcoming book *Migrant Dreams: Development and Subalternity in the U.S.-Mexico Borderlands*. Her current scholarship centers on migration and violence at the U.S.–Mexico border as a departure point for conceptualizing the uneven processes of capitalist development and globalization.

Sherrie Tucker is Associate Professor of American Studies at University of Kansas. In addition to numerous articles, she is the author of *Swing Shift: "All-Girl" Bands of the 1940s* (2000). Tucker is co-editor of *Big Ears: Listening for Gender in Jazz Studies* (forthcoming), and is currently writing her second monograph, an oral history of the dance floor at the Hollywood Canteen during the 1940s, entitled, *Dance Floor Democracy: The Social Geography of Memory at the Hollywood Canteen*. She co-edits, with David Katzman, the journal *American Studies*.

Mary Ann Villarreal is Assistant Professor of History at the University of Utah. She has had articles published in the *Oral History Review*, as well as the *Journal of Women's History*, and is currently writing a new book, entitled, *Con Ganas y Amor: Tejano Family and Women Owned Businesses*.

Devra Anne Weber is Associate Professor of History at the University of California, Riverside. She has published two books: *Dark Sweat, White Gold: California Cotton, Farmworkers and the New Deal, 1919–1939* (1994), and edited *La Historia de Vida del Inmigrante Mexicano por Manuel Gamio* (2002). Weber is also an advisor of the Frente Indigena Oaxquena Binacional (Binational Indigenous Front of Oaxaca).

Judy Tzu-Chun Wu received her Ph.D. from Stanford University in 1998 and is currently an Associate Professor of History at Ohio State University. She is the author of *Dr. Mom Chung of the Fair-Haired Bastards: The Life of a Wartime Celebrity* (2005). Her current project, tentatively entitled *Radicals on the Road: Third World Internationalism and American Orientalism*, examines the travels of American anti-war activists during the U.S. War in Viet Nam and how these experiences abroad shaped their identities and politics.

Judy Yung is Professor Emerita of American Studies at the University of California, Santa Cruz. She is the co-author of *Island: Poetry and History of Chinese Immigrants on Angel Island* (1980) and *Chinese American Voices: From the Gold Rush to the Present* (2006), and the author of *Unbound Feet: A Social History of Chinese Women in San Francisco* (1995), *Unbound Voices: A Documentary History of Chinese Women in San Francisco* (1999), and *The Adventures of Eddie Fung: Chinatown Kid, Texas Cowboy, and Prisoner of War* (2007).

Index

Note: page numbers in *italics* denote illustrations